Directory of
ZOOLOGICAL
TAXONOMISTS
of
THE WORLD

COMPILED BY

RICHARD E. and RUTH M. BLACKWELDER

Directory of

ZOOLOGICAL

TAXONOMISTS

of

THE WORLD

Published for

THE SOCIETY OF SYSTEMATIC ZOOLOGY

by

SOUTHERN ILLINOIS UNIVERSITY PRESS

CARBONDALE, ILLINOIS

1961

TABLE OF CONTENTS

LIST OF ABBREVIATIONS

Abbreviations are used in addresses only where they are a secondary part of the address, as in the case of states or provinces. Two exceptions to this are the consistent use of U.S.A. and U.S.S.R. The names of some governmental organizations which are customarily written as initials (e.g., WVINGI) are written out in full whenever we could learn the full name. The unknown abbreviations are not listed here.

ABBREVIATIONS

Ala., Alabama
Alta., Alberta
Arch., Archipelago
Ariz., Arizona
Ark., Arkansas
B. C., British Columbia
Belg., Belgian
Brit., British
br-w., brackish-water
c., central
Calif., California
Colo., Colorado
Commonw. Terr.,
   Commonwealth Territory
Conn., Connecticut
cst., coast
D. C., District of Columbia
Del., Delaware
devel. st., developmental stages
e., eastern

econ. import., economic importance
espec., especially
excl., excluding
f-l., free-living
Fla., Florida
f-w., fresh-water
Ga., Georgia
I., Island
Ida., Idaho
Ill., Illinois
incl., including
Ind., Indiana
Is., Islands
Kans., Kansas
Ky., Kentucky
L., Lower
La., Louisiana
M., Middle
Md., Maryland
Mass., Massachusetts
med. import., medical importance

Mich., Michigan
Minn., Minnesota
Miss., Mississippi
Mo., Missouri
Mont., Montana
Mts., Mountains
mw., midwestern
myrmecoph., myrmecophilous
Neb., Nebraska
Nev., Nevada
n., northern
N. H., New Hampshire
N. J., New Jersey
N. M., New Mexico
N. Y., New York
N. C., North Carolina
N. D., North Dakota
N. S., Nova Scotia
Okla., Oklahoma
Ont., Ontario
Ore., Oregon
Pa., Pennsylvania
Pen., Peninsula

Penna., Pennsylvania
Prov., Province
Que., Quebec
reg., region
R. I., Rhode Island
s., southern
Sask., Saskatchewan
S. C., South Carolina
S. D., South Dakota
Tenn., Tennessee
termitoph., termitophilous
terr., terrestrial
Up., Upper
U. S. A., United States of America
U. S. S. R., Union of
    Soviet Socialist Republics
Vt., Vermont
Va., Virginia
w., western
Wash., Washington
W. Va., West Virginia
Wis., Wisconsin
Wyo., Wyoming

INTRODUCTION

RESPONSIBILITY

The Directory of Zoological Taxonomists was started in October 1956 at the instigation of the National Science Foundation and with funds provided by the Foundation. The grant was later extended for a third year, but a fourth year was found necessary and was financed by the Society of Systematic Zoology.

All details of coverage, procedure, and style were determined by the compilers. Many situations called for novel solutions, and no model was found which could be followed for the many problems of alphabetization, diacritic marks, arrangement, format, abbreviations, symbols, and so on.

Publication was handled by the Southern Illinois University Press. This did not include composition, as the final typescript prepared by the compilers was used directly to produce the offset-lithography plates for printing.

COVERAGE

At the beginning, the compilers, with approval of the Society of Systematic Zoology, decided that coverage should be world-wide and should include specialties on fossil animals (paleontologists). Although it had originally been suggested to us that inclusion should be limited to "qualified" taxonomists, it was at once evident that there is no way to determine the qualifications of 9000 candidates. It was therefore decided to include all who submitted appropriate data, as well as those recommended to us who failed to respond to our questionnaires. At least two requests were sent to every possible taxonomist known to us.

Obviously the initial coverage was most complete for North America. Western Europe and Japan became reasonably well covered because of ready response from most workers in these areas. The rest of the world was more difficult to reach. Eastern Europe and the U.S.S.R. were unrepresented in early lists, but, during the third and fourth years of compiling, a great many workers in these areas became known to us, and most of these returned data on their specialties. Only the People's Republic of China remains virtually unrepresented in this list.

Early coverage was also inadequate for workers on fossil animals. Paleontologists have often inclined to consider themselves geologists rather than zoologists, and they were slower to co-operate than the neontologists. The very timely help of Mrs. Katherine Van Winkle Palmer of the Paleontological Research Institution, at Ithaca, New York, gave the real start in this field and enabled us to include a substantial number of paleontological taxonomists.

PREPARATION

The manner of preparation of the Directory may be of interest to persons attempting to understand its purposes and limitations. The following major steps were followed: (1) The available lists of specialists and society members produced a list of prospective taxonomists, largely American, with the general field of their specialization. Preliminary lists were made from these for each class, order, or phylum. (2) Each person on this list was then sent a card requesting data about his specialty, his mail address, and his institutional connection, along with a copy of the appropriate preliminary lists. These he was asked to annotate with additions from all parts of the world. (If no reply was received, a second notice was sent.) (3) All persons reported to us in the response to the above were immediately sent invitations to submit data and other names. (4) As soon as the response in a group warranted, a new preliminary list for that group was prepared and included with invitations to those subsequently reported to us. (5) After two years of mailing to all persons suggested to us or listed in any of the numerous specialized directories that became known to us, the personal data received were filed in two ways, alphabetically by taxonomist and systematically by the groups of animals. (6) From this file, augmented daily by late returns, a manuscript was typed using a format designed to save space but present the maximum information. This manuscript was proofread against the original cards. (7) From this typescript was prepared the final pages of the Directory on a special typewriter, for photographic printing. This second typescript (as seen in the printed pages) was proofread against the first. The numerous diacritic marks, the proportional spacing, the variety of languages, and the extreme variety of spellings and capitalization made this final typescript a very tedious job. Corrections were made in this manuscript up to the time of going to press. (8) The data filed by specialties had to be checked in detail against the specialties listed under each name, and they had to be kept up to date to the time of final typing. The filing arrangement had to be such that an adequate subdivision of specialties could be shown, with reasonable uniformity for clarity of use, but without undue waste of space. (9) A preliminary manuscript was then typed and checked back against the cards. (10) From this a final typescript was made on the special typewriter for photographic printing. This was proofread against the previous draft. (11) During the final typings, a considerable number of late replies, corrections, death notices, etc., reached us. Many were incorporated into the final manuscript, but some could not be. These were assembled into a list of Addenda, to be printed as a supplement. Only such persons as could be added to the systematic section were put in this Addenda. A few others will be accumulated for a separate Supplement, which may be published elsewhere at a later date.

ARRANGEMENT

The systematic section is arranged by phyla and classes. The order of these phyla follows closely the recent classification of Hyman (1940–1959), but for convenience of reference a list is given below. The classes are in alphabetical order. The term class is not to be taken strictly, as some groups are admitted as classes here for convenience which might be given higher or lower rank in a formal classification. In a few phyla the classes are omitted, and in certain classes the orders are also used.

ANIMALIA

(Miscellaneous groups)
PROTOZOA
  Ciliata
  Flagellata
  Sarcodina
    Actinopoda
    Amoebida
    Foraminifera
    Heliozoa
    Mycetozoa
    Proteomyxa
    Radiolaria
    Rhizopoda
    Testacea
  Sporozoa
  Suctoria
(Invertebrates)
PORIFERA
MESOZOA
ARCHAEOCYATHA

COELENTERATA
  Anthozoa
  Conularida
  Hydrozoa
  Scyphozoa
  Stromatoporoidea
CTENOPHORA
PLATYHELMINTHES
  Cestoda
  Trematoda
  Turbellaria
(Nemathelminthes)
NEMERTINEA (Rhynchocoela)
ACANTHOCEPHALA
GORDIACEA (Nematomorpha)
PRIAPULIDA
GASTROTRICHA
NEMATODA

KINORHYNCHA (Echinodera)
ROTIFERA (Rotatoria)
ENDOPROCTA
BRYOZOA
PHORONIDA
BRACHIOPODA
MOLLUSCA
  Amphineura
  Cephalopoda
  Gastropoda
  Monoplacophora
  Pelecypoda
  Scaphopoda
  Solenogastres
SIPUNCULOIDEA
ECHIUROIDEA
ANNELIDA
  Archiannelida
  Hirudinea
  Myzostomida
  Oligochaeta
  Polychaeta
PENTASTOMIDA (Linguatulida)
TARDIGRADA
ONYCHOPHORA
ARTHROPODA
  Trilobita
  Merostomata
  Pycnogonida
  Arachnida
    Acarina
    Anthracomarti
    Araneae
    Architarbi
    Haptopoda
    Kustarachne
    Opiliones
    Palpigradi
    Pedipalpi
    Phrynichida
    Pseudoscorpionida
    Ricinulei
    Schizomida
    Schizonotida
    Scorpionida
    Solpugida
    Thelyphonida
    Trigonotarbi

  Crustacea
    Amphipoda
    Branchiopoda
    Cirripedia

Copepoda
Decapoda
Isopoda
Malacostraca
Ostracoda
Stomatopoda
(Myriapoda)
Chilopoda
Diplopoda
Pauropoda
Symphyla
Insecta
  Protura
  Thysanura
  Entotrophi
  Collembola
  Ephemeroptera
  Odonata
  Plecoptera
  Grylloblattoidea
  Protoperlaria
  Orthoptera
  Phasmidia
  Blattariae
  Mantodea
  Glosselytrodea
  Dermaptera
  Embioptera
  Isoptera
  Psocoptera
  Zoraptera
  Mallophaga
  Thysanoptera
  Hemiptera
  Heteroptera
  Homoptera
  Anoplura
  Neuroptera
  Megaloptera
  Rhaphidioptera
  Mecoptera
  Trichoptera
  Lepidoptera
  Diptera
  Hymenoptera
  Coleoptera
  Siphonaptera
CHAETOGNATHA
POGONOPHORA
ECHINODERMATA
  Asteroidea
  Auluroidea
  Blastoidea
  Carpoidea

Crinoidea
Cystoidea
Echinoidea
Edrioasteroidea
Eocrinoidea
Haplozoa
Holothurioidea
Machaeridia
Ophiocystoidea
Ophiuroidea
Paracrinoidea
Somasteroidea

GRAPTOZOA

PTEROBRANCHIA

HEMICHORDATA

ENTEROPNEUSTA

TUNICATA
Copelata
Ascideacea
Thaliacea

CEPHALOCHORDATA

VERTEBRATA
Pisces
(Tetrapoda)
Amphibia
Reptilia
Aves
Mammalia

Under each phylum are listed first the taxonomists who did not specify any specialty within the phylum, and those whose specialties include the entire phylum. These are grouped under side-headings that indicate either geographic restrictions, ecological limitations, or paleontological distribution. Taxonomists are listed under each heading in alphabetical order (all alphabetizing is by the first capital letter), with parenthetical indication of further restriction of specialty, if this is known. Three sets of abbreviations are used: (1) geological time periods, (2) zoogeographical regions, and (3) general ecological habitats. In this way restrictions of the specialties can be shown by the side-headings and the parenthetical notes together. The abbreviations are always in the following order: Under all headings small letters come first and indicate the following:

b, benthic
bw, brackish-water
fw, fresh-water
m, marine

p, parasitic
s, soil-inhabiting
t, terrestrial

Under all headings except "Fossils," the capital letters, alone or following the small letters after a colon (:) show the zoogeographic realm or realms. These are:

A, Australian
AO, Atlantic Ocean
Ant, Antarctic
Arc, Arctic
E, Ethiopian
H, Holarctic
N, Nearctic

Nt, Neotropical
O, Oriental
Oc, Oceania
P, Palearctic
PO, Pacific Ocean
Trop, Tropics of World
W, World

Under the headings "Fossils" the first capital or the first group separated by commas shows the geological period or subdivision, as follows:

C, Cenozoic
M, Mesozoic
P, Paleozoic

Q, Quaternary
R, Recent
T, Tertiary

The second group of capitals (after the colon) shows the zoographic realms as above.

The colon (:) separates either the ecological from the geographical or the paleontological from the geographical. Where the colon is present, it is always followed by the geographical abbreviations (or by a question mark).

Examples: "Fossils: Doe, J. (P:?)" means Paleozoic with geography unspecified. "Fossils: Doe, J. (P-M)" means Paleozoic to Mesozoic. "Fossils: Doe, J. (T:N)" means Tertiary of Nearctic. "Parasites of mammals: Doe, J. (m:W)" means marine (mammals) of World. "Euglenoidina: Doe, J. (N, P, E)" means Nearctic and Palearctic and Ethiopian.

Thus, the small letters always show ecology. The final letter or letters, if there is a colon, always show the geography. The first of two groups of capitals separated by a colon always shows the geological range. A capital or group of capitals (with hyphen or commas) show geography unless the heading is "Fossils," when they show the geologic period.

Inasmuch as the limits of some of the regions and time zones had to be arbitrarily set, the extent of each is given here. (It is not intended to imply that these are the "correct" limitations, — merely that they are the ones used herein.)

WORLD, of course, covers all land areas or all oceans.

NEW WORLD, includes Nearctic, Neotropical, and surrounding seas.

OLD WORLD, includes Palearctic, Ethiopian, Oriental, Australian, and Oceania.

TROPICS, includes all regions except Nearctic, Palearctic, Arctic, and Antarctic.

HOLARCTIC, includes Nearctic, Palearctic, and surrounding seas.

NEARCTIC, includes America north of Mexico, Greenland, and surrounding seas.

NEOTROPICAL, includes Mexico, Central America, South America, and the West Indies, with surrounding seas and islands.

ATLANTIC OCEAN, from European and African western shores to eastern shores of America, from the Arctic to the Antarctic. (Includes oceanic islands therein.)

PALEARCTIC, includes Europe, North Africa to the Tropic of Cancer, Arabia, the Near East, Iran, Afghanistan, Asia north of the Himalayas, China north of the Yangtze, and Japan, with included and surrounding seas and islands.

PALEOTROPICAL, includes Ethiopian, Oriental, Indian Ocean, Australian, Oceania, and Pacific Ocean.

ETHIOPIAN, Africa south of the Sahara Desert, Madagascar, with surrounding seas.

ORIENTAL, includes Pakistan, India, southern China, and south to Singapore, the Malay Archipelago to Wallace's Line, the Philippines, and Taiwan (Formosa).

INDIAN OCEAN, from southern Asia to the Antarctic and from Madagascar to Australia, with included islands.

AUSTRALIAN, includes Australia, Tasmania, New Zealand, and surrounding seas.

OCEANIA, the islands from Wallace's Line east to Easter Island, from New Guinea and the Tuamota Archipelago to the Hawaiian and Mariana Islands.

PACIFIC OCEAN, the entire sea area from Alaska to the Antarctic and from the Asian coast to the west coasts of America. (Terrestrial animals would be cited as Oceania.)

ARCTIC, the circumpolar seas north of the Nearctic and Palearctic, sometimes including Greenland, Iceland, and the northern edges of Asia and America.

ANTARCTIC, the continent of Antarctica and surrounding seas and islands.

PALEOZOIC, includes Cambrian through Permian periods, with some Karroo (Permo-Triassic) included.

MESOZOIC, includes Triassic, Jurassic, and Cretaceous, with some Karroo (Permo-Triassic) included.

CRETACEOUS, occasionally separated from the rest of the Mesozoic for convenience.

CENOZOIC, the Tertiary and Quaternary together.

TERTIARY, the Paleocene, Eocene, Miocene, Oligocene, and Pliocene together.

QUATERNARY, the Pleistocene and Recent together.

RECENT, used only to extend the interest in fossils to include an interest in the forms living at the present time. (After another period and a hyphen, simply extends the range of interest up to the Recent.)

It must always be remembered that the regions cited in this section are often very much larger than the ones cited in the specialty. For example, P (Palearctic) may actually mean only Japan. The groups are also often much larger than those actually studied. And the geological range is very often too great, as most paleontologists specialize more narrowly than could be shown by P (Paleozoic) or M (Mesozoic). **Limitations must always be checked in the Address section.**

There are a few special decisions to be noted in these citations of specialties. (1) The general heading of Invertebrates-Fossils includes fossil Foraminifera and other Protozoa, as it was found to be impossible to separate the two. When a reply was received, the specialist is of course listed only under the group he cited. (2) Many of the geographic areas cited included the note "and surrounding regions." These could not be shown. (3) Localities in Germany (West) and the Deutsche Demokratische Republik (East) are kept distinct whenever possible. In a few cases we were unable to identify the locality and had to leave it as Germany. (4) Nationalist China is listed as Taiwan (Formosa) to keep it distinct from the communist People's Republic of China.

The arrangement of subdivisions under each "class" is in three groups. First come general headings: names for which no further data are available, ecological groups, immature stages, and fossils not specified further. Second come the groups within the "class" but above the rank of family. These are generally in alphabetical order, regardless of rank, and little attention is paid to the form of the name, which varies greatly among taxonomists. Third come all the families of the "class" which were listed by any taxonomists; these are again alphabetical, with ecology or fossil range shown either by sub-headings or by parenthetical codes. To emphasize these three groups, the group names are capitalized, the miscellaneous headings and the families are in small letters.

The alphabetical address section contains the names of all persons who submitted appropriate data and all those others who failed to respond but who were represented to us as being taxonomists. The names of these latter persons are preceded by an asterisk (*). The asterisk thus indicates the persons whose address and specialty were not verified by them. Two requests or more were sent to each of them, so there is a good chance that these addresses are no longer correct.

Two other classes of names are included in this alphabetical listing. Persons whose names were submitted as taxonomists but who replied that they do not have an interest in any group of animals were omitted, but those who reported that they have permanently given up taxonomic studies are listed as "Not now active in taxonomy." This is done for the benefit of persons who might not be aware of this change of activity.

Persons who were suggested to us as taxonomists but who were later found to be deceased were listed in proper order with an indication of address and specialty and the date of death, if known. To have omitted these would simply have been to further obscure the fact of their demise.

A few persons in these last two groups had already been included in the final typescript. The new status was added or placed in the Addenda, with an arrow for cross-reference.

All names of those who replied are written in the exact form which they specified as their preference, including capitalization, diacritic marks, spacing, prepositional prefixes, and titles. All unusual spellings were checked directly with the person involved.

These names are alphabetized according to the only rule which was found to suit the requirements: All names are alphabetized by the first capital letter. Spaces in the name are ignored, as well as apostrophes and hyphens. Where two or more last names of exactly the same spelling occur, they are arranged by the initials only of the first names. Thus, SMITH, John D. comes ahead of SMITH, James P. This is the only way that names can be arranged when either initials or full first names are used indiscriminately. This alphabetical section is designed as a detailed source or cross-reference from the systematic section. There, only the initials are given, so only the initials are used in alphabetizing.

Addresses are given as specified by the taxonomist except for the following considerations: (1) the order of items is always Street-city-country or institution-city-country; (2) cities are always spelled as in the Dictionnaire des Bureaux de Poste of the Union Postale Universelle; (3) countries are listed in the form used in the United States Official Postal Guide, Part II, International Service, as there is no accepted international source. The local spellings are often unsuitable outside of the country.

If the institution with which the taxonomist is connected is not shown in the mail address, it is cited in brackets after the taxonomic specialty.

The taxonomic specialties are listed as nearly as practicable in the manner reported by the taxonomist. Each group of animals is cited by the name which he employed, unless there is a conflict of usage of synonyms, restricted by appropriate adjectives. To these are prefaced the phylum, class, or order, wherever necessary. In a very few cases the taxon cited proved to be unidentifiable by us and is enclosed within quotation marks.

The geographic limits and geologic time spans are indicated with as much detail as we received, with a minimum of standardization and few abbreviations.

Most taxonomists who responded gave an answer to the question whether or not they are willing to make identifications for other people in each of the groups listed. The replies are "Yes," "No," and in a very few cases "Fee" (a fee to be charged for the service) or a statement of dollars per hour as fee. The "Yes" must not be construed as permission to send specimens without prior correspondence. It is often qualified in additional ways which we are unable to record.

A small arrow in the lefthand margin refers to additional listings to be found in the addenda section at the end of the book. If the arrow points between two entries, there will be found a new entry that would be inserted at that point. If the arrow points directly at a name, additional or later information on that name will be found in alphabetical order in the Addenda section.

ACKNOWLEDGMENTS

The number of persons who have substantially helped in the compilation of data is so great that any listing would be impractical. We do acknowledge with gratitude the many lists, corrections, and suggestions sent by many taxonomists. Many institutions, societies, and individuals sent copies of directories or lists of specialists in many fields. These will be acknowledged separately in a list of such directories that we plan to publish elsewhere. We have depended very heavily upon such lists at one stage, and we express our thanks to those whose hard work produced them.

The exacting work of typing the final copy for photographing, and inserting the numerous changes up to the last minute, was ably accomplished through the skill of Mrs. Gloria Stokes of Carbondale. Her continuing efforts have literally made the publication possible.

SYSTEMATIC LIST

ANIMALS

Miscellaneous groups

CALCISPHAERIDA - fossils: Bonet, F. (F:W).
CHITINOZOA - fossils: Campau, D. E. (P:N), Collinson, C. W. (P:W), Deflandre, G.,
    Eisenack, A. (P:P), Lange, F. W. (P:Nt).
COCCOLITHOPHORIDA: Bernard, F. (P), Braarud, T., Kamptner, E., Ringdal-Gaarder, K.
    Fossils: Sullivan, F. E. (T:N), Trexler, D. W. (M:N).
CONODONTS - fossils: Mehl, M. G., Rexroad, C. B., Sannemann, D., Thomas, L. A.
    All ages: Downs, H. R. (N), Fay, R. O. (W), Müller, K. J. (W), Rhodes, F. H. T. (W),
        Schmidt, H., Scott, H. W., Serre, -, Youngquist, W. L., Ziegler, W. (P).
    Paleozoic: Beckman, H. (P), Bischoff, G. (P), Bond, R. H. (N), Bright, R. C. (N),
        Clark, D. L., Cooper, C. L., Dineley, D. L. (P), Elias, M. K. (H), Ellison, S. P., Jr.,
        Ethington, R. L., Furnish, W. M., Gross, W., Helms, J. (P), Lamont, A. (P),
        Lindström, M. (P), Lys, M., McCoy, M. R., McTavish, R. (A), Stanley, E. A.,
        Sweet, W. C., Tasch, P., Turco, C. A. (N), Walliser, O. H. (W), Wilkie, L. C.
    Mesozoic: Beckman, H. (P), Bischoff, G., (P), Clark, D. L., Dede, E. (P),
        Diebel, K. (P, E), Ellison, S. P., Jr., Ethington, R. L., Huckriede, R., Tatge, U. (P).
DISCOASTERIDA: Stradner, H.   FOSSILS: Stradner, H., Sullivan, F. R. (T:N).
HYSTRICOSPHAERIDA - fossils: Deflandre, G., Deunff, J. (P:N,Nt,P), Eisenack, A.(P:P),
    Gocht, H. (M:P), Jeffords, R. M. (P-M:?), Lange, F. W. (P:Nt), Schopf, J. M. (P:?),
    Valensi, L. (M:P), Wetzel, O., Wilson, L. K.
SCOLECODONTS: See Annelida: Polychaeta.
           * * * * *
Cave Faunas: Anciaux de Faveaux, F. (E), Boldori, L., Bureš, I., Cerruti, M. (P),
    Franciscolo, M. E. (P), Lanza, B. (P).
Pluvial faunas: Perkins, E. J. (P).
Ectoparasites: Davis, D. H. S. (E), Fox, I., Gjessing, H. W. (N), Hensens, E. J. (N),
    Khan, M. A. (W), Rapp, W. F., Jr. (N), Whitehead, W. E.
Parasites - unspecified: Bacigalupo, J., Baer, J. G., Bessière, C., Bone, G. V., Bravo-Hollis,
    M., Cameron, T. W. M., Cort, W. W., Davison, M. L., Dehnel, P. D., Dobrovolny, C. G.,
    Dollfus, R. P., Duggan, T. L., El-Gindy, M. S., Esslinger, J. H., Fonseca, O, Filho,
    Jones, M. F., Kuntz, R. E., Lal, M. B., Leiper, R. T., Prado Barrientos, L., Rees, F. G.,
    Ricci, M., Sandground, J. H., Sudarikov, V. E., Talice, R. V.
    World: Antipin, D. N., Chertkova, A. N., Ershov, V. S., Kadenatsii, A. N., Kasimov,
        G. B. S., Krotov, A. I., Kurashvili, B. E., Ljubimov, M. P., Lopez-Neyra, C. L.,
        Macy, R. W., Markevitch, A. P., Mitskevitch, V. Y., Mozgovoy, A. A., Orlov, I. V.,
        Oshmarin, P. G., Otto, G. F., Petrotchenko, V. I., Petrov, A. M., Popov, N. P.,
        Popova, T. I., Potemkina, W. A., Ruchlyadev, D. P., Rygikov, K. M.
    Tropics & subtropics: Martin, W. E.
    Nearctic: Macy, R. W.
    Neotropical: Diaz-Ungria, C., Gutierrez, R. O.
    Palearctic: Bondareva, V. I., Crastin, N. I., Davtjan, E. A., Gagarin, V. G., Gnedina, M. P.,
        Gubanov, N. M., Ivashkin, V. M., Klesov, M. D., Kopyrin, A. V., Markov, G. S.,
        Morozov, F. N., Ozerskaya, V. N., Sultanov, M. A.
    Oriental: Anantaraman, M., Datta, A. K., Dissanaike, A. S., Ramakrishna, G.
    Of marine invertebrates: Montreuil, P. (AO).
    Of mollusks: Uzmann, J. R.
    Of insects: Jolivet, P. (E), Laird, M. (W).
    Of fish: Achmerov, A. H. (P), Chauhan, B. S. (W), Grabda, E., Lyaiman, E. M. (W),
        Mazurmovitch, B. N. (P), Nybelin, O., Uzmann, J. R. (N).
    Of marine fish: Montreuil, P. (AO), Nigrelli, R. F. (N), Reichenbach-Klinke, H. (P).
    Of fresh-water fish: Adams, J. R.(N), Bangham, R. V. (N), Bauer, O. N. (H),
        Bogitsh, B. J. (N), Nigrelli, R. F. (N), Reichenbach-Klinke, H. (P), Venard, C. (N).
    Of amphibians: Bogitsh, B. J. (N), Mazurmovitch, B. N. (P), Parker, M. V. (N).
    Of reptiles: Parker, M. V. (N).
    Of birds: Boyd, E. M. (N), Furmaga, S, Gvozdev, E. V. (P).
    Of mammals: Adams, J. R. (N), Alicata, J. E. (N, Oc), Allen, R. W. (N, Nt), Badanin,
        N. V. (P), Boyer, C. D., Delamure, S. L. (W), Furmaga, S. (P), Gorshkov, I. P. (P),
        Gvozdev, E. V. (P), Hansen, M. F. (N), Honess, R. F. (N), Smith, W. N. (N),
        Tarczyński, S. (P), Todd, A. C., Wolfgang, R. W. (N, Nt).   Dinnik, J. A. (E).

Of man: Alicata, J. E. (N, Oc), Boyer, C. D. , Faust, E. C. , Leon, L. A. (N, Nt),
Plotnikov, N. N. (W), Podyapolskaja, V. P. (W), Summers, W. A. (W),
Swartzwelder, J. C. (N).
Marine benthos: Perkins, E. J. (P).
Marine borers: Kramp, P. L. (W).
Venomous marine animals: Dammann, A. E. (W), Halstead, B. W. (W).
Zooplankton, marine: Aurich, H. J. (AO), Deevey, G. B. (AO, PO), Fraser, J. H. (AO),
Kielhorn, W. V. (AO), Lovegrove, T. (AO), Perkins, E. J. (AO).
* * * * *

Fossils, unspecified: Biernat, G. , Bodmer, W. , Brady, L. F. (N), Brockelmann, S. , Lin, C. C. ,
Öpik, A. , Poulsen, C. , Rao, S. R. N. , Ronai, P. H. , Rothpletz, K. , Singleton, O. P. ,
Smedley, J. E. , Streiff-Becker, R. , Sutter, F. , Tercier, J. , Toerien, M. J. , Toombs,
H. A. , Trikkalinos, J. , Whitcomb, L. , Yang, K. O.
All ages: Barat, C. A. (P), Danner, W. R. (N), Lochman-Balk, C. (N, Nt),
Murray, G. E. (N), de la Torre, A. (Nt).
Paleozoic: Alkins, W. E. , Burk, C. A. (N), Délépine, G. (P), Gortani, M. (P), Harper,
J. C. (P), Krommelbein, K. (Nt, P), Lamont, A. (P), Leutze, W. P. (N), Mellen,
F. F. (N), Waite, R. H. (N).
Mesozoic: Burk, C. A. (N), Mellen, F. F. (N), Müller, A. H. (P), Sanchez Reig, M. (Nt),
Winton, W. M. (N).
Cenozoic: Lewis, E. (N), Sanchez Reig, M. (Nt).
Incertae sedis groups: Ayala C. , A. (F:Nt), Hughes, D. D. (P:?).
Microfossils: Chamney, T. P. (M:N), Cuvillier, J. (?:P), Frizzell, H. E. , de Klasz, J. ,
Maccagno, A. M. (M, T:P), Robinson, J. E. (P:P), Sellier de Civrieux, J. M. (?:Nt),
Setzer, F. M. (T:N), Stauble, A. , Thalmann, H. E. (P-T:W), Wetzel, W. (F:W),
Weynschenk, R. (M:?), Winslow, M. R. R. (P:?).

PROTOZOA

No other data: Balech, E. , Byrd, R. , Cummings, R. H. , Dain, L. G. , Dawson, J. A. ,
Derbyshire, R. C. (N), De Saedeleer, H. , Diller, W. F. , Jr. , Fernandez Martinez, J. ,
Ferreira de Almeida, W. , Fjeld, P. , Garapati, -, von Gelei, G. , Hall, R. P. ,
Hollande, A. , Kaveda, M. , Lee, J. W. , Meier, M. , Messikommer, E. (P), Narain, N. ,
Noble, A. E. , Oxford, A. E. , Perez-Canto, J. R. , Ritter, E. , Roudabush, R. L. ,
Shawhan, F. M. , Stolk, A. , Subbotine, N. N. , Thomsen, R. (Nt), Voloschinora, N. A. ,
Zanyiu, G. H.
Free-living: Cairns, J. , Jr. (H), Hada, Y. (P, O, Oc), Hahnert, W. F. (N), Perkins, E. J. (P),
Savoie, A. (P), Varga, L. (P), Vuxanovici, I. A.
Parasites & commensals: Beltran, E. , Brown, R. L. , Budzier, H. H. ,
Bullock, W. L. (N), Coatney, G. R. (W), Costello, L. C. (Trop), Fallis, A. M. , Faust,
E. C. , da Fonseca, F. (Nt), Herman, C. M. (W), Jepps, M. W. , Laird, M. (O, Oc),
Leon, L. A. (N, Nt), Levine, N. D. (W), Mackin, J. G. (W), Manwell, R. D. , Nigrelli,
R. F. (N), Summers, W. A. (W), Swartzwelder, J. C. (N), Uzmann, J. R. (N),
Westphal, A.
Fossils, unspecified: van der Burg, W. J. (T:P), Cummings, R. H. (P:?), Vašiček, M.

Ciliata

No other data: Balamuth, W. (W), Beers, C. D. , Bick, H. , Canella, M. F. , Czapik, A. ,
Dragesco, J. (W), Dupré, H. M. , Earl, P. (W), Elliott, A. M. , Gellert, J. (P), Klein,
B. M. , Parducz, B. , Poljansky, G. I. , Raikow, I. B. (P), Šrámek-Hušek, R. (P),
Wenrich, D. H. , Wetzel, A. , Wichterman, R. , Yagiu, R. (P).
Marine: Bock, K. J. , Gajewskaja, N. S. , Lackey, J. B. (W), Tuffrau, M. (P), Wichterman, R. ,
Fresh-water: Bock, K. J. , Evans, F. R. (N), Finely, H. E. (N), Gajewskaja, N. S. , Katashima,
R. (P), Lackey, J. B. (W), Noland, L. E. (N), Tuffrau, M. (P), Wichterman, R.
Soil-inhabiting: Biczok, R. (P), Stout, J. D. , Wenzel, F.
Parasites & commensals: Balamuth, W. (W), Burch, J. B. (W), Kazubski, S. L. (P), Lom, J. (P),
Raabe, Z. (P), Ray, H. N. (O), Shigematsu, A. (P), Sudgen, B. (W), Wichterman, R.
Fossils: Duenff, J. (F:E), Zázvorka, V. (M:P).
* * * * *

ASTOMATA: Cheissin, E. M. (P), Katashima, R. (P), de Puytorac, P.
CHONOTRICHIDA: Mohr, J. L. (W).
ENTODINIOMORPHA: Strelkow, A.
EUCILIATA: Lepsi, I. (fw).
HETEROTRICHIDA: Chakravarty, M. (O), Shigematsu, A. (m:P).

2

HOLOTRICHIDA: Corliss, J. O. (W), Furgason, W. H. (fw), Kozloff, E. N. (p:W), Roque, M.,
    Shigematsu, A. (m:P), Thompson, J. C., Jr. (N, Nt, P), Wenzel, F.
HYPOTRICHIDA: Horvath, F. (P).
OLIGOTRICHINA: Chakravarty, M. (O), Sebestyén, O. (fw:P).
PERITRICHIDA: Biegel, M. (fw:P), Finely, H. E. (W), Green, J. (P), Hamilton, J. M. (fw),
    Matthes, D. (W), Precht, H., Stiller, J. (fw, m:P), Vavra, J.
THIGMOTRICHINA: Cheissin, E. M. (P).
TINTINNIA: Campbell, A. S. (W), Duran, M. (P, AO), Komarovsky, B. (m:P), Marshall,
    S. M. (P), Rampi, L. (P, Oc), Schwarz, S. (AO).
    Fossils: Campbell, A. S. (F:W).

* * * * *

Balantidae: Fernandez-Galiano, D.
Bursariidae: Krascheninnikow, S.
Colpodidae: Burch, J. B. (W), Franceschi, T.
Cycloposthiidae: Fernandez-Galiano, D., Noirot-Timothée, C. (W).
Euplotidae: Bovee, E. C. (N, Nt), Katashima, R. (m, fw:P).
Folliculinidae: Hadzi, J. (P).
Frontoniidae: Williams, N. E.
Hysterocinetidae: Cheissin, E. M. (P), de Puytorac, P.
Opalinidae: Chen, T. T., Fernandez-Galiano, D., Mohr, J. L. (W), Sukanowa, K. M.,
    Wessenberg, H. (N).
Ophryoscolecidae: Christle, H., Eadie, J. M., Fernandez-Galiano, D., Krascheninnikow, S.,
    Lubinsky, G. (W), Noiret-Timothée, C. (W).
Parameciidae: Hairston, N. G. (N).
Scyphidiidae: Hirshfield, H. I. (m:N).
Tetrahymenidae: Furgason, W. H., Williams, N. E.
Tintinnidae: Hirshfield, H. I. (Oc).
    Fossils: Bonet, F. (F:W), Colom, G. (F:W).
Urceolariidae: Hirshfield, H. I. (m:N).

Flagellata

No other data: Bielecka, W., Bijvank, G., Droop, M. R., Hollande, A., Jahn, T. L.,
    Joyon, J. (P), Lackey, J. B. (m, fw:W), Pavillard, J., Postuma, T. A.,
    Scorza, J. V. (Nt), Valkanov, A. (P), Wasbuzky, T., Winsnes, T.
Parasites & commensals: Evans, F. R. (N), Ludvik, J., Packard, C. E. (N), Saxe, L. H., Jr.
Soil-inhabiting: Biczok, F. (P).
Fossils: Deflandre, G. (M-R:?).

* * * * *

CHRYSOMONADINA: Joyon, J. (P), Parke, M. (P), Thompson, R. H. (fw:W).
DINOFLAGELLATA: Braarud, T., Bursa, A. S. (Arc), Deflandre, G., Graham, H. W.,
    Hirshfield, H. I. (Oc), Komarovsky, B. (m:P), Marshall, S. M. (m:H),
    Ringdal-Gaarder, K., Thompson, R. H. (fw:W).
    Fossils: Gocht, H. (T:P), Jeffords, R. M. (P, M:?).
EUGLENOIDINA: Earl, P. (W), Gojdics, M., Packard, C. E.
HYPERMASTIGINA: Chakravarty, M. (O).
PERIDININA: Rampi, L. (P, OC).
    Fossils: Gocht, H. (M:P), Valensi, L. (M:P), Wetzel, O.
PHYTOMASTIGINA: Bamforth, S. (N), Bourrelly, P. (W), Hovasse, R. (P).
POLYMASTIGINA: Chakravarty, M. (O).
PROTOMASTIGINA: Hiregaudar, L. S. (O).
RHIZOMASTIGINA: Hiregaudar, L. S. (O).
SILICOFLAGELLATA: Marshall, S. M. (P), Stradner, H.
    Fossils: Jeffords, R. M. (P-M:?), Stradner, H.
ZOOMASTIGINA: Filice, F. P. (Oc), Grassé, P., Honigberg, B. M. (p:W).

* * * * *

Bodonidae: Pittam, M. J. (P).
Cryptobiidae: Kozloff, E. N. (N, P).
Ellobiopsidae: Hoenigman, J. (W).
Euglenidae: Johnson, L. P. (W).
Hexamitidae: Hinchey, M. C.
Opalinidae: See under Ciliata.
Peridinetidae - fossils: Schopf, J. M (P:?).
Phacotidae: Allegre, C. (N).
Tetramitidae: Pittam, M. J. (P).
Trichomonadidae: Buttrey, B. W.
Trypanosomidae: Hoare, C. A. (W), Ketterer, J. J., Reichenow, E., Roskin, G. J.,
    Wallace, F. G. (W).
Volvocidae: Pocock, M. A. (N, Nt, P, E, O, A).

3

Sarcodina

No other data: Biczok, F. (s:P), Deflandre, G., de Graaf, D. F. (P), de Groot, A. A. (fw:W),
Pavillard, J.
Fossils: Deflandre, G.

Actinopoda

(None)

Amoebida

No other data: Hiregaudar, L. S. (O), Pittam, M. J.
Soil inhabiting: Balamuth, W. (W), Ray, D. L., Štěpánek, M. (P, E, O).
Fresh-water: de la Arena y Fernandez, J. (Nt), Balamuth, W. (W), Bovee, E. C. (N),
Jones, D. T. (N), Lepsi, I., Pappas, G. D., Schaeffer, A. A., Štěpánek, M. (P, E, O).
Marine: Balamuth, W. (W), Bovee, E. C. (N), Pappas, G. D., Schaeffer, A. A.
Parasitic: Balamuth, W. (W), Jacobs, L. (W), Noble, G. A., Štěpánek, M. (P, E, O).
* * * * *
Amoebidae: Honegger, C., Kudo, R. R. (W).
Endamoebidae: Kudo, R. R. (W), Noble, G. A., Schneider, C. R.

Foraminifera

No other data: Barker, R. W., Borro, P., Coryell, H. N., Cummings, R. H., Douglass, R. C.,
Dusenbury, A. N., Jr., Echols, D. J., Fernández, R., Grekulinski, E., Grell, K. G.,
Grimsdale, T. F., Hedley, R. H., Hill, B. L., Jr., Jepps, M. W., McCulloch, I.,
Messina, A. R., Phleger, F. B., Jr., Salmon, E. S., Selli, R., Terpstra, G. R. J.
World: Bandy, O. L., Frizzell, D. L., Galloway, J. J,, Henbest, L. G., Keijzer, C. J. (m),
Rainwater, E. H., Rankin, W. D., Shchedrina, Z. G.,
Nearctic: Allison, E. C., Arnal, R. E., Aves, C. A., Church, C. C., Holcomb, L. D.,
Johnston, I. M., Petri, S., Pietschker, H., Schell, W. W., Uchio, T.
Neotropical: Acosta, J. T., Bermudez, P. J., Boltovskoy, E., Hewitt, P. C., Milow, E. D.,
Parker, F. L., Petri, S., Saunders, J. B., Stacy, H.
Atlantic Ocean: Christiansen, B., Le Calvez, Y., Parker, F. L., Tinoco, I. M.
Palearctic: Alfirevic, S., Asano, K., Edgell, H. S., Hoglund, H., Le Calvez, Y.,
Macfadyen, W. A., Morishima, M., Murata, S., Parker, F. L., Uchio, T.,
van Voorthuysen, J. H.
Oriental: Bhatia, S. B., Nagappa, Y., de Nève, G. A.
Australian: Collins, A. C., Hornibrook, N. B., Vella, P.
Oceania: Asano, K., Bhatia, S. B., Enbysk, B. J., Harrington, G. L., Hirshfield, H. I.,
Morishima, M., Saidova, H. M., Stach, L. W.
Arctic & Antarctic: Kierstead, C. E. H. (Ant), Saidova, H. M. (Ant), Stschedrina,
Z. G. (Arc, Ant).
Subfossils: Bartenstein, H., (m:P).
Fossils - no age specified: Acosta, J. T. (Nt), Adams, C. G. (W), Alemany-Proenza, M., Al-
varez A., J., Ayala C., A. (Nt), Bandy, O. L. (N), Bartenstein, H. (W),
Beck, R. S. (N), Bermudez, P. J. (Nt), Bettenstaedt, F., Bower, R. N. C., Buning, W. L.,
Burma, B. (W), Camacho, E. (N, Nt), Camacho, H., Cary, C. W. (N), Chatterji, A. K.,
Ciry, M. (P), Cummings, R. H., Cuvillier, J. (P), Dorman, J. H. (N), Echols, D. J.,
Erk, A. S., Frizzell, D. L. (W), Garmon, G. (N), Graham, J. J. (N, O), Henbest,
L. G. (W), Hewitt, P. C. (N, Nt), Hofker, J., Hutcheson, R. B., Kaever, M. (N, P),
Kessinger, W. P., Jr. (N), Limon-Guttierrez, L., Loeblich, A. R. (W), Loeblich, H. T.,
Luczkowska, E., Mantovani, M. P., Matsunaga, T., Means, J. A. (N), Messina, A. R.,
Munsey, G. C., Jr. (N), Myers, E. H., Petri, S. (N, Nt), Pope, D. E. (N), Pozaryski, W.,
Rankin, W. D. (W), Ritsema, L., Robles-Ramos, M. L., Rolshausen, F. W. (N, Nt),
Ronai, L., Ruscelli, M. A., Salmon, E. S., Siddiqui, I. H. (O), Smith, B. L. (N),
Smout, A. H. (P), Sztejn, J., Tacoli, M. L., Tamajo, E. (m), Tobon, Y. D., Troelsen,
J. C., Wissler, S. G. (N, Nt, Oc), Wood, A., Wootton, C. M. (N).
Paleozoic: Bartenstein, H. (P), Bhatia, S. B. (O), Conkin, J. E. (N, P), Cooper, C. L.,
Coryell, H. N., Duszynska, S. (N), Ellison, S. P., Jr., Fujimoto, H. (P), Galloway,
J. J. (W), Grekulinski, E., Grimsdale, T. F., Keathley, K. S., Loranger, D. M. (N),
Lys, M., Monk, W. J. (N), Nelson, D. O. (Nt, P), Serre, -, St. Jean, J., Jr., (N),
Tasch, P., Toomey, D. F. (W).
Mesozoic: Banner, F. T., Bartenstein, H. (W), Berry, E. W., Bourdon, M., Brand, E.,
Brotzen, F. (W), Chamney, T. P. (N), Cooper, W. C. (N), Coryell, H. N.,
Dede, H. E. (P), Dunnington, H. V. (P), Edgell, H. S. (P), Ellis, B. F., Ellison,
S. P., Jr., Galloway, J. J. (W), Gibson, L. (N, Nt), Glaessner, M. F., Harrell, D. C.,

4

Haynes, J. (N), Heacock, R. L. (N), Higgs, W. R. (N), Howe, H. V. , Kaska, H. V. (Nt),
Lalicker, C. G. , Ludbrook, N. H. (A), Macfadyen, W. A. (P), Nelson, D. O. (Nt, P),
Payne, M. W. , Puri, H. S. (N, O, Oc), Rainwater, E. H. (W), Sartoni, S. (P),
Schell, W. W. (N), Selli, R. , Sigal, J. , Thalmann, H. E. (W), Wall, J. H. (N).
Cretaceous only: Allison, E. C. (N), Amato, F. L. (Nt), Andrews, G. C. (N),
Anisgard, H. W. (N, Nt), Arnal, R. E. (N), Beckmann, J. P. (N, Nt, P), Belford, D. J. (A),
Bergquist, H. R. (N), Braunstein, J. (N), Brown, N. K. , Jr. , Bürgl, H. (Nt),
Carlson, S. A. (N), Čepek, P. (P), Church, C. C. (N), Conkin, J. E. (N), Dusenbury,
A. N. , Jr. , Edgell, H. S. (N, A), Eicher, D. L. (N), Etter, J. (N), Ghorab, M. A. (P),
Griesbach, F. (N), Hay, W. W. , Hedberg, H. D. (Nt), Holcomb, L. D. (N),
Hornibrook, N. B. (A), Hill, B. L. , Jr. , Kingma, J. T. (A), Kirby, L. C. (N, Nt),
Kock, W. (P), Lackman, F. J. B. (N), Lys, M. , Marianos, A. W. (N), McGugan, A. (W),
McLean, J. D. (N, Nt), McNulty, C. L. (N, Nt, P), Middour, E. S. (N, Nt), Milow, E. D. (N),
Morris, C. B. (P), Morris, W. J. (N), Nagappa, Y. (O), Nakkady, S. E. , Olson, R. ,
Phillips, H. H. (N), Pietschker, H. (N), Quigley, C. M. (N), Reiss, Z. (P),
Renz, H. H. (Nt), Sambe Gowda, S. (O, A, Oc), Sandidge, J. R. (N), Skinner, H. C. ,
Spillmann, F. (Nt), Stelck, C. R. (N), Sturz, C. E. (N), Sung, G. C. L. (P), Tasman, M. I. ,
Terpstra, G. R. J. , Tinoco, I. M. (Nt), Uchio, T. (P), Vella, P. (A),
Wickenden, R. T. D. (N).
Cenozoic: Akers, W. (W), Asano, K. (P, Oc), Aves, C. A. (N), Banner, F. T. , Bourdon, M. ,
Bush, J. (N, Nt), Collins, A. C. (A), Cooper, W. C. (N), Coryell, H. N. , Ellis, B. F. ,
Everett, R. W. , Jr. , Galloway, J. J. (W), Higgs, W. R. (N), Hill, B. L. , Jr. , Howe, H. V. ,
Mangin, J. P. , Molander, G. E. (N), Morishima, M. (P, Oc), Murata, S. (P), Parker,
F. L. (AO), Payne, M. W. , Pierce, R. L. (N), Pietschker, H. (N), Puri, H. S. (N, O, Oc),
Rainwater, E. H. (W), Sambe Gowda, S. (O, A, Oc), Saunders, J. B. (Nt), Schell,
W. W. (N), Selli, R. , Sigal, J. , Terpstra, G. R. J. , Uchio, T. (P), Vella, P. (A),
van Voorthuysen, J. H. (P).
Tertiary: Albers, C. C. (N), Allison, E. C. (N), Amato, F. L. (Nt), Andersen, H. V. (N),
Andrews, G. C. (N), Anisgard, H. W. (N, Nt), Arnal, R. E. (N), Ashworth, E. T. (Nt),
Bane, R. (N), Barker, R. W. (Nt), Batjes, D. A. J. (P), Beach, P. R. (N), Beckmann,
J. P. (N, Nt, P), Belford, D. J. (Oc), Berry, E. W. , Bhatia, S. B. (P, O), Bowen, R. N. C. ,
Brown, N. K. , Jr. , Bürgl, H. (Nt), Butler, E. (N), Campbell, A. R. (N), Caralp,
M-H. (P), Carlson, S. A. (N), Carson, C. M. (N), Carter, A. N. (A),
Caudri, C. M. B. (Nt, O, Oc), Christodoulou, G. , Church, C. C. (N), Classen,
W. J. , Jr. (N), Conkin, J. E. (N), Dempsey, J. E. (N), Drooger, C. W. , Dunnington,
H. V. (P), Dusenbury, A. N. , Jr. , Edgell, H. S. (N, A), Ellis, A. D. , Jr. (N), Etter,
J. (N), Fairchild, W. W. , Fournier, G. (Nt), Ghorab, M. A. (P), Gianotti, A. (P),
Gibson, L. (N, Nt), Glaessner, M. F. , Gohrbandt, K. , Grill, R. (P), Grimsale, T. F. ,
Haas, M. W. (N, Nt), Harrell, D. C. , Hay, W. W. , Haynes, J. (P), Hedberg, H. D. (Nt),
Hodson, F. (Nt), Hornaday, G. R. (N), Hussey, K. M. (N), Israelsky, M. C. (N),
Kaska, H. V. (Nt), Keathley, K. S. , Kierstead, F. H. (Nt), Kilgore, J. E. (N), Kingma,
J. T. (A), Kirby, L. C. (N, Nt), Kupper, I. (P), Lackman, F. J. B. (N), Le Calvez, Y. (P),
Levinson, S. A. (N), Luczkowska, E. (P), Ludbrook, N. H. (A), Lumsden, W. (N),
Lys, M. , Martin, G. P. R. (P), McLean, J. D. (N, Nt), McTavish, R. (O, Oc), Middour,
E. S. (N, Nt), Milow, E. D. (N), Morris, C. B. (P), Morris, W. J. (N), Nagappa, Y. (O),
Nakkady, S. E. , Natland, M. L. (N), Neely, R. M. (N), Nelson, D. O. (Nt, P), de Nève,
G. A. (O), Nieves, E. J. (Nt), Olson, R. , Parker, F. L. (P), Parker, W. G. (N),
Petrusek, B. J. (N), Phillips, H. H. (N), Pyeatt, L. M. (N), Quigley, C. M. (N), Rau,
W. W. (N), Reiss, Z. (P), Renz, H. H. (Nt), Rothwell, W. T. , Jr. (N), Rudick, W. (N),
Ruth, J. W. (N), Sandidge, J. R. (N), Skinner, H. C. , Smith, D. J. (N), Socin, C. (P),
Souaya, F. J. (P), Spillmann, F. (Nt), Stach, L. W. (Oc), Stuckey, C. W. (N), Sturz,
C. E. (N), Sullivan, F. R. (N), Sung, G. C. L. (O), Tabbert, R. L. (N), Tasman, M. I. ,
Tatum, E. P. (N), Tewari, B. S. (O, Oc), Thalmann, H. E. (W), Tinoco, I. M. (Nt),
Tipsword, H. L. (N, Nt), Turnovsky, K. , Veillon, M. P. (P), Weaver, D. E. (N), Weiss,
L. (Nt), Wesendunk, P. (N), Westmoreland, F. S. (N).
Quaternary: Enbysk, B. J. (PO), Feyling-Hanssen, R. W. (Arc), Funnel, B. M. (P),
Hussey, K. M. (N), Macfadyen, W. A. (P), de Nève, G. A. (O), Parker, F. L. (AO, P),
Parker, W. G. (N), Selli, R. , van Voorthuysen, J. H. (P).
Planktonic: Bé, A. W. H. (W), Blow, W. H. , Bolli, H. M. (N, Nt, P), Ericson, D. B. (AO),
Grimsdale, T. F. , Hamilton, E. L. (W), di Napoli, E. G. (P), Neely, R. M. (Nt), Ovey,
C. D. , Parker, F. L. (W), Warren, A. D. (Nt).
Fossil: Bé, A. W. H. (F:W), Blow, W. H. , Ericson, D. B. (F:AO), Grimsdale, T. F. (P-R:?),
de Napoli, E. F. (F:P), Stainforth, R. M. (T:?), Warren, A. D. (M:?; C:N, Nt),
Wiles, W. W. (C:W).
Pelagic: Percival, S. F. , Jr. (Nt), Warren, A. D. (Nt), Zÿlmans, A. J. C.
Fossils: Graffham, A. A. (T:N, Nt), Hagn, H. (M-T:P), Martinez, A. (Nt), Percival,
S. F. , Jr. (M-R:Nt), Raffi, G. (M-T:P), Warren, A. D. (T-R:Nt), Zylmans,
A. J. C. (M-R:?).

Benthonic, fossils: Burnaby, T. P. (M:P), Hagn, H. (M-T:P), Hendrix, W. E. (T:N), Warren,
    A. D. (C:N, Nt).
Arenaceous, fossils: Gutschick, R. C. (P:N), Ireland, H. A. (P:W), Moreman, W. L. (P:N),
    Summerson, C. H. (P:?), Van Sant, J. R. (P:N).
Brackish-water: Bartenstein, H. (P).   FOSSILS: Bartenstein, H. (P:P).

* * * * *

Larger: Bursch, J. G. (Oc), Cole, W. S. (N, Nt, O, Oc), Easton, W. H. (Nt, P), Martin, G. B. (N),
    di Napoli, E. F. (P).
    Fossils: Azzaroli, A. (T:P, E), Bishal, Y., Butterlin, J. (P-T:Nt), Carter, D. J. (M-T:P),
        Caudri, C. M. B. (T:Nt, O, Oc), Cole, W. S. (M-R:N, Nt, O, Oc), Douglass, R. C. (M-R:?),
        Gigon, W. (M-T:?), Hanna, M. A. (T:N), Hewitt, P. C. (Nt), Khan, M. H. (M-T:O),
        MacGillavry, H. J. (M-T:?), Martin, G. B. (M-R:N), Moore, W. E. (M-T:N, Nt),
        di Napoli, E. F. (F:P), Sander, N. J. (T:P), Singh, S. N. (T:O), Van der Vlerk,
        I. M. (T:?), Van Raadshooven, B. (T:Nt).
Smaller: Artusy, R. L., Bursch, J. G. (Nt), Carter, D. J. (P), Chang, L-S. (O), Chiji, M.,
    Hosmer, F. (Nt), Hughes, D. D., Magné, J. (P), Marie, F. (O, Oc), Martin, G. B. (N),
    Martinez, R., Ravera, O., Smitter, Y. H. (Nt, E), Todd, R.
    Fossils: Chang, L-S. (F:O), Herrick, S. M. (F:N), Hiltermann, H. (F:W), Jones, B. C. (F:?),
        Khan, M. H. (F:O), Magné, J. (F:P), Marie, F. (F:P), Souaya, F. J. (F:P).
    Paleozoic: Marie, F. (P), Sanderson, G. A. (N).
    Mesozoic: van den Bold, W., Cifelli, R. (P), Cita, M. B. (P), Gallitelli, E. M. (P),
        Hughes, D. D., Linares, A. (P), Martin, L. (N, Nt), Said, R. (P), Stacy, H. (N, Nt),
        Zingula, R. P. (N, Nt).
    Cretaceous: Albritton, C. C., Jr., Applin, E. R. (N), Artusy, R. L., Balseiro, L. M. (Nt),
        Bursch, J. G. (Nt), Carter, D. J. (P), Hanna, M. A. (N), Haque, A. F. M. M. (N, O),
        Laiming, B. (N), Martin, G. B. (N), Martinez, R., Montanaro-Gallitelli, E. (P),
        Petters, V. (Nt, P), Smitter, Y. H. (Nt, E), Young, G. A. (Nt).
    Cenozoic: van den Bold, W., Carter, D. J. (P), Chiji, M., Gallitelli, E. M. (P), Garrett,
        J. B., Jr. (N), Hughes, D. D., Kaasschieter, J. P. H. (P), Kleinpell, R. M. (O, Oc),
        Martinez, R., Nyi, N. (O), Oinomikado, T. (P, O), Said, R. (P), Stacy, H. (N, Nt).
    Tertiary: Applin, E. R. (N), Artusy, R. L., Balseiro, L. M. (Nt), Bursch, J. G. (Nt),
        Carter, D. J. (P), Cifelli, R. (N), Cita, M. B. (P), Colom, G. (P), Haque,
        A. F. M. M. (N, O), Huang, T. Y. (O), Kleinpell, R. M. (N), Laiming, B. (N), Linares,
        A. (P), Magné, J. (E), Mallory, V. S. (N), Martin, L. (N, Nt), Montanaro-Gallitelli,
        E. (P), Petters, V. (Nt, P), Ravera, O., Rogers, K. J. (N), Samaan, S. M. (P), Singh,
        S. N. (O), Smitter, Y. H. (Nt, E), Todd, R., Toulmin, L. D. (N), Upshaw, C. F. (N),
        Wade, M., Wilkins, E. M. (N), Young, G. A. (Nt).
    Quaternary: Montanaro-Gallitelli, E. (P).

* * * * *

ENDOTHYROIDEA - fossils: Zeller, D. (P:N, Nt, P).

* * * * *

Allogromiidae: Arnold, Z. M.   FOSSILS: Arnold, Z. M.
Alveolinidae: Reichel, M.   FOSSILS: Hottinger, L. (T:P, O), Reichel, M. (M-R:?).
Amphisteginidae - fossils: Singh, S. N. (T:O).
Calcarinidae - fossils: Singh, S. N. (T:O).
Camerinidae: See Nummulitidae.
Discocyclinidae - fossils: Hanzawa, S. (T:O, Oc), Sachs, K. N., Jr. (T:N, Nt).
Endothyridae - fossils: Armstrong, A. K. (P:?), Hewitt, P. C. (P:N).
Fusulinidae - fossils, all ages: Downs, H. R. (N), Lokke, D. H. (N), Nygreen, P. W. (N),
    Ruiz de Gaona, M. (P), Scott, H. W., Stewart, W. J. (N, O), Tabbert, R. L. (N),
    Thompson, M. L. (W), Verville, G. J. (N), Waite, R. H. (N).
    Paleozoic: Ashworth, E. T. (N), Campau, D. E. (N), Chronic, J., Coogan, A. H. (N, P),
        Danner, W. R. (P), Dodge, H. W., Jr. (N), Douglass, R. C. (N), Dunbar, C. O., Forbes,
        C. L. (W), Hanzawa, S. (P), Harker, P. (N, Arc), Hewitt, P. C. (N), Hollingsworth,
        R. V., Igo, H. (P), Jarvis, D., Kahler, F. (P), Kahler, G. (P), Lloyd, A. J. (P),
        Morikawa, R. (P), Myers, D. A. (N), de Nève, G. A. (O), Peltier, E. J. (N), Pitrat, C. W.,
        Roberts, T. G., Ross, C. A., Sadlick, W. (N), Sanderson, G. A. (N), Skinner, J. W. (N, P),
        Spivey, R. C., Steele, G. (N), Tasch, P., Thorsteinsson, R., Toriyama, R. (P),
        Van Sant, J. F. (N), Wanless, H. R., Wilde, G. L. (W), Williams, T. E. (N), Zeller,
        D. (N, Nt, P), Zimmermann, D. A.
    Mesozoic: Ciry, M. (P), Turnovsky, K.
    Tertiary: Sachs, K. N., Jr. (N, Nt).
Globigerinidae: Bradshaw, J. S. (W), Percival, S. F., Jr. (Nt).
    Fossils: Ovey, C. D., Percival, S. F., Jr. (M-R:Nt).
Globorotaliidae: Blow, W. H., Bradshaw, J. S. (W), Percival, S. F., Jr. (Nt).
    Fossils: Blow, W. H., Dalbiez, F. (T:?), Ovey, C. D., Percival, S. F., Jr. (M-R:Nt).

Globotruncanidae: Blow, W. H. , Percival, S. F. , Jr. (Nt).
    Fossils: Blow, W. H. , Borsetti, A. M. (F:P), Dalbiez, F. (P, E), Klaus, J. (M:P),
        Koch, W. (M:P), Maslakova, N. I. (M:P), Oberhauser, R. (M:P), Percival,
        S. F. , Jr. (M-R:Nt), Seiglie, G. A. (F:N, Nt).
Heterohelicidae: Blow, W. H.
    Fossils: Blow, W. H. , Koch, W. (M:P), Seiglie, G. A. (M:N, Nt).
Lagenidae: Gullentops, F.
    Fossils: Adams, C. G. (M:P), Albers, J. (M:?), Gullentops, F. (C:?), Lloyd, A. J. (M:P),
        Singh, S. N. (T:O).
Lepidocyclinidae - fossils: Drooger, C. W. (T:W).
Lituolidae - fossils: Cati, F. (M:P), Maync, W. (M:W), Skolnick, H. (M:N), Zeller,
        D. (P:N, Nt, P).
Miliolidae: Le Calvez, Y. (P).   FOSSILS: Singh, S. N. (T:O).
Miogypsinidae - fossils: Drooger, C. W. (T:W), Hanzawa, S. (T:O, Oc), Kupper, I. (F:E),
        Sachs, K. N. , Jr. (T:N, Nt).
Nonionidae - fossils: Singh, S. N. (T:O).
Nummulitidae: Hanzawa, S. (O, Oc), Vialli, V. (P).
    Fossils: Bieda, F. (F:N, Nt, P, E,), Hanzawa, S. (C:O, Oc), Schaub, H. (T:P, E).
Orbitoididae: Grimsdale, T. F.
    Fossils: Grimsdale, T. F. (P-R:?), Hanzawa, S. (M-T:O, Oc), Hewitt, P. C. (F:Nt), Mallory,
        V. S. (T:N), Ruiz de Gaona, M. (F:P), Sachs, K. N. , Jr. (T:N, Nt), Zingula, R. P. (M:Nt).
Orbitolinidae - fossils: Douglass, R. C. (M-T:?), Maync, W. (M:W).
Orbulinidae: Blow, W. H. , Percival, S. F. , Jr. (M-R:Nt).
    Fossils: Blow, W. H. , Percival, S. F. , Jr. (M-R:Nt),
Planorbulinidae - fossils: Singh, S. N. (T:O).
Polymorphinidae - fossils: Lloyd, A. J. (M:P).
Rissoinidae - fossils: Militante, P. (F:O).
Rotaliidae - fossils: Oberhauser, R. (M:P), Singh, S. N. (T:O).

Heliozoa

No other data: Štěpánek, M. (t, fw, p:P, E, O).
                                        * * * * *
Actinophryidae: Barrett, J. M. (W).

Mycetozoa

(None).

Proteomyxa

(None).

Radiolaria

No other data: Campbell, A. S. (W), Hirshfield, H. I. (m:Oc), Hollande, A. , Middour, E. S. (N),
        Riedel, W. R. (W), Strelkow, A. (Oc).
    Fossils: Burma, B. H. (F:W), Campbell, A. S. (F:W), Deflandre, G. (P-Q:?), Foreman, H. ,
        Ichikawa, K. (M:?), Middour, E. S. (M-R:N), Riedel, W. R. (F:W).

Rhizopoda

No other data: Ertl, M. (fw:P), van Oye, P. , Valkanov, A. (P).

Testacea

No other data: Bartoš, E. (P), Chardez, D. (P), Decloitre, L. , (W), Gauthier-Lievre, L. ,
        Grospietsch, T. (W), Janiszewska, J. (W), Nectoux, P, (P), Thomas, R. (W), Warren,
        A. D. (N, Nt).
Fresh-water: Lepsi, I. , Štěpánek, M. (P, E, O).
Soil-inhabiting: Bonnet, L. (P), Štěpánek, M. (P, E, O), Stout, J. D.
Parasitic: Štěpánek, M. (P, E, O).
Marine: Neely, R. M. (Nt).
Fossils: Grospietsch, T. (Q:?), Neely, R. M. (T:N).

Sporozoa

No other data: Barnett, S. F. (E), Ludvík, J. , Scorza, J. V. (Nt).
* * * * *

ACEPHALINA: Dissanaike, A. S. (O).
ACTINOMYXIDA: Janiszewszka, J. (W).
CEPHALINA: Crusz, H. (W).
CNIDOSPORIDIA: Jirovec, O. (W).
COCCIDIA: Becker, E. R. , Bull, P. C. (A), Chakravarty, M. (O), Cheissin, E. M. (P), Farr,
       M. M. (N), Hiregaudar, L. S. (O), Levine, N. D. (W), Pellérdy, L. (P), Ray, H. N. (O),
       Reichenow, E. , Senger, C. M. (N), Tuzet, O. (W).
EUGREGARINIDA: Théodoridès, J. (W).
GREGARINIDA: Ball, G. H. (W), Bush, S. F. (E), Chakravarty, M. (O), Filipponi, A. (P),
       Kozloff, E. N. (N), Ray, H. N. (O), Tuzet, O. (W).
HAEMOSPORIDIA: Chakravarty, M. (O), Hiregaudar, L. S. (O), Jacobs, L. (W), Garnham,
       P. C. C. (W), Jakowska, S. , Jirovec, O. (W), Reichenow, E. , Schneider, C. R.
HAPLOSPORIDIA: Jirovec, O. (W).
MICROSPORIDIA: Dissanaike, A. S. (O), Kudo, R. R. (W), Vavra, J. , Weiser, J. (W).
MYXOSPORIDIA: Chakravarty, M. (O), Jakowska, S. , Kudo, R. R. (W), Matsumoto, K. (P, Oc),
       Meglitsch, P. A. (W), Noble, E. R. (W), Schulmann, S. (W), Weiser, J. (W).
SCHIZOGREGARINIDA: Dissanaike, A. S. (O), Weiser, J. (W).
* * * * *

Eimeriidae: Bovee, E. C. (N), Kruidenier, F. J. (N), Marquardt, W. C.
Gregarinidae: Jolivet, P. (E).
Plasmodiidae: Huff, C. G. (W).
Triactonomyxidae: Naidu, K. V. (P).

Suctoria

No other data: Gajewskaja, N. S. (m, fw), Guilcher-Skreb, Y. , Hamond, R. (P), Hull, R. W. (N),
       Jahn, T. L. , Kormos, J. (P), Matthes, D. (W), Štěpánek, M. (t, fw, p:P, E, O).
* * * * *

Dendrocometidae: Small, E. B. (N, P).
Discophryidae: Small, E. B.

INVERTEBRATES

No other data: Deviney, E. M. (N), Lisenko, I. M. , Picard, J. (P), Untermann, B. R. (N),
       Untermann, G. E. (N).
Marine: Baker, N. W. (N), Bassindale, R. (P), Bennett, I. , Demel, K. (P), Forsman, B. (P),
       Hewatt, W. G. (N, Nt), MacIntyre, J. (A), Voss, G. L. (Nt), Zenkevitch, L. A.
Marine borers: Bernath, R. J.
Estuarine: Harrington, R. W. , Jr. (N), Sacchi, C. (P).
Fresh-water: Carrick, L. , Clegg, J. (P), Cozart, D. E. , Curtin, C. B. (N), Figueroa, M. C. ,
       Fraser, L. A. , Jonasson, P. M. , Jones, B. R. , Mackenthun, K. M. (N), Pennak, R. W. (N).
Fossils, no age: Arnould, M. , Arnould-Saget, -, Azevedo Martins, E. , Bainton, J. D. , Banks,
       M. R. (A), Barnard, T. , Barrios, M. , Bataller, J. R. , Becker, L. E. , Behm, H. ,
       Bennett, A. A. , Blaisdell, R. C. , Boada, L. V. , Bolton, T. E. , Borragan, J. , Bouxin,
       H. L. , Boyd, H. , Brand, J. P. , Broadhurst, F. M. , Brock, J. A. , Brookley, A. , Brown,
       P. M. , Browning, J. L. , Buck, E. , Calabro, F. J. , Calver, M. A. , Cambridge, P. ,
       Caner, A. , Casey, R. , Channon, P. J. , de Cizancourt, M. , Clarke, M. H. , Collins, R. L. ,
       Cook, T. D. , Coombs, B. , Cox, B. B. , Crawford, F. D. , Crespin, I. , Crosbie, J. M. ,
       Crouch, R. W. , Davies, A. M. , Debourle, A. , Dillingham, H. , Doane, G. H. , Edmonds,
       J. M. , Ehlers, G. M. , Eltysheva, R. S. , Emeis, J. D. , Forman, J. , Fox, J. P. ,
       Fox, S. K. , Jr. , Fraunfelter, G. , Fritz, M. A. , Ganger, D. , Hadley, W. H. , Hall, C. ,
       Hallam, A. , Hamill, J. M. , Hamilton, I. B. , Hanna, G. D. (W), Harold, A. , Harrell,
       G. C. , Harrassowitz, O. , Harris, J. Z. , Hawkins, H. L. , Hester, S. W. , Hirayama, K. ,
       Honeyman, A. M. , Ida, K. , Jobe, T. C. , Johnson, G. P. , Jones, D. J. , Kew, W. S. W. ,
       Kirkaldy, J. F. , Kniker, H. T. , Laws, C. R. , Lecompte, M. , Lemon, R. , Lowenstam,
       H. A. , Ludford, A. , Ma, T. Y. H. , Macomber, D. , MacFarquhar, W. K. , Marinos, G. ,
       Marks, E. , Martin, L. T. , McLearn, F. H. , McNair, A. H. , McGuirt, J. H. ,
       de Medina, N. P. , Mehl, M. G. , Mendes, J. C. , Montgomery, J. C. , Moore, W. W. ,
       Müller, A. H. , Neumann, M. , Norris, A. W. , Norton, P. , Ogose, S. , Pacock, A. F. ,
       Patton, J. L. , Polugar, M. , Protic, M. , Rau, J. L. , Rivero, F. C. , Rucker, L. M. ,
       Sandoval, J. , Saxena, I. P. , Schouten, G. B. , Shulga-Nesterenko, M. I. , Simonson, R. R. ,
       Smith, B. L. (N), Sterens, R. , Stewart, R. E. , Stewart, Mrs. R. E. , Subbotina, -,
       Sulek, J. A. , Szenk, B. J. , Temple, J. T. , Termier, G. , Termier, H. , Thorslund, P. ,

Tillman, J. R. , Tischler, H. , Urbanek, A. , Vanasia, S. , Waldron, R. P. , Warthin,
A. S. Jr. , Water, J. A, Weaver, W. R. , Windham, S. , Winslow, A. C. , Wood, L. E.
Paleozoic: Banks, M. R.   (A), Caster, K. E. (W), Clark, T. H. (N), Collinson, C. W. (N),
Conkin, J. E. , Craig, G. Y. , Dickins, J. M. (A), Heller, R. L. (N), Heuer, E. (N),
Higgs, W. R. (N), Jeffords, R. M. , Jewett, J. M. (N), Kent, L. S. (N), Lamont, A. (P),
Langenheim, R. L. , Jr. (N), Lintz, J. , Jr. (N), Richardson, E. S. , Jr. , Rigby, J. K. (N),
Rusconi, C. (Nt), Shaw, A. B. , Smith, J. D. D. (P), Stearn, C. W. (N), Sturgeon,
M. T. (N), Untermann, B. R.   (N), Untermann, G. E. (N), Walmsley, V. G. (P),
Wanless, H. R. , Willard, B. , Wilson, A. E.
Mesozoic: Haas, O. H. , Higgs, W. R. (N), van Hoepen, E. C. N. , Jeffords, R. M. , Kauffman,
E. G. (N), Melville, R. V. , Miller, H. W. , Jr. (N), Silberling, N. J. (W), Untermann,
B. R. (N), Untermann, G. E. (N), Wetzel, W. (P).
Cenozoic: Fulmer, C. V. (N), Higgs, W. R. (N), Kanakoff, G. P. (N), Keen, A. M. (N),
Oleksyshyn, J. (N, P), Picard, J. (P), Untermann, B. R. (N), Untermann, G. E. (N).
Microfossils: Halstead, M. E. , Harris, R. W. (F:N, Nt, P), Macke, W. B. (P:N), Rice,
E. M. (P-M:N), Summerson, C. H. (P:?), Toepelmann, W. C. (M:N).
Tracks, burrows, trails: Seilacher, A. (P-T:?), Simpson, S.

PORIFERA

No other data: Eigenbrodt, H. , Forster, G. R. (P), Given, R. R. (N), Hartman,
W. D. (N, Nt, O, Oc), Hejskova-Červenková, E. (P), Kilian, E. F. (Nt), Rao, S. H. ,
de Ruiz, S. M. , Sara, M. (P), Tanita, S. , Vacelet, J. (P), Wintermann-Kilian, G. (Nt).
Marine: Old, M. C. (W), Resvoy, P. D. (Arc).
Fresh-water: Eshleman, S. K. , III. (N), Sebestyén, O. (P), Soota, T. D. (O), Svilha, A. (W),
Wurtz, C. B. (N).
Fossils: Deflandre-Rigaud, M. (M-T:?), Finks, R. M. (P-M:?), Gutschick, R. C. (P:N), Howell,
B. F. (F:W), Rigby, J. K. (P:N), Ware, S. (P:?).
* * * * *
CALCAREA (Calcispongea): Jones, W. C. (P).
HEXACTINELLIDA (Hyalospongea): Reid, R. E. H.   FOSSILS: Reid, R. E. H. (M-R:?).
SPHINCTOZOA - fossils: Seilacher, A. (P-M:?).
* * * * *
Monaxonidae: de Mello-Leitao, A. (Nt).
Porosphaeridae - fossils: Hampton, J. S. (M:P).
Spongillidae: Ankel, W. E. , Jewell, M. E. (N), Moore, W. G. (N), Old, M. C. (W), Penney,
J. T. (N), Pradhan, K. S. (O), Racek, A. A. (W), Rodewald-Rudescu, L. (P),
Simon, L. K. (P).

MESOZOA

No other data: McConnaughey, B. H. (N).
* * * * *
DICYEMIDA: Nouvel, H. (W).
ORTHONECTIDA: Nouvel, H. (W).

ARCHAEOCYATHA

Fossils: Melendez, B. (P:P), Okulitch, V. J. (P:?), Vologdin, A. G.

COELENTERATA
(Cnidaria)

No other data: Aurich, H. J. (AO), Babnik, P. , Berrill, N. J. , Brønsted, H. V. , Dohrn,
P. F. R. (P), Giles, D. E. , Hamond, R. (P), Illick, J. T. , Kinne, O. , Kramp, P. L. (W),
de Leira, A. (AO, P), Mamman, T. A. , Nyholm, K-G. , Parker, R. H. (Nt), Petersen,
K. W. , Rao, S. H. , Riveros Zuñiga, F. ,   Rossi, L. (P), Sebestyén, O. (fw:P),
Teissier, G. (m).
Fossils: Banks, M. R. (P:A), Flerova, N. A. (P:P), Forbes, C. L. (P:W), Gallitelli,
E. M. (P-T:P), Smith, D. J. (T:N), Yavorsky, V. I. (F:P).

No other data: Amos, W. H. (bw:N), Deichmann, E. (Nt), Eguchi, M., Field, L. R. (N).
Fossils: Crickmay, C. H. (P-M:N), Eguchi, M. (M-R:?), Fritz, M. A. (P:N), Harker, P.
    (P:N, Arc), Montanaro-Gallitelli, E. (P, C:P), Smith, D. J. (T:N), Thomas, H. D. (F:W).
Corals: Chevalier, J. P., Ranson, G. (W).
  Fossils: Chevalier, J. P. (C:?), Easton, W. H. (P:N), Hayasaka, I. (P:?), Hoffmeister, J. E.,
    Holwill, F. J. W. (P:?), Jeffords, R. M. (P:?), Johnson, R. B. (P:N), Lehmann, U. (P:?),
    Le Maitre, D. (P:P), McLaren, D. J. (P:N), Mitchell, M. (P:P), Monk, W. J. (P:N),
    Nelson, S. J. (P:N), Olson, E. P. (P:N), Pinto, I. D. (P:?), Sando, W. J. (P:N), Stelck,
    C. R. (P:N), Stumm, E. C. (P:N), Taylor, P. W. (P:N, P), Tischler, H. (P:?).
* * * * *

ACTINIARIA: Atoda, K. (P), Cutress, C. E. (W), Dave, M. J. (O), Hand, C. (W), Panikkar,
    N. K. (O, Oc), Parry, G., Phillips, J. (N), Stephenson, T. A. (W), Uchida, T. (PO),
    Weill, R. (P).
ALCYONACEA: Broch, H. (Arc, Ant), Tixier-Durivault, A., Verseveldt, J. (O, Oc).
ALCYONARIA (Octocoralla): Bayer, F. M. (W), Madsen, F. J. (AO), Utinomi, H. (W).
CERIANTHARIA: Cutress, C. E. (W), Leloup, E., Panikkar, N. K. (O, Oc).
CORALLIMORPHARIA: Cutress, C. E. (W).
GORGONACEA: Bayer, F. M. (Nt, Oc), Broch, H. (Arc, Ant).
HELIOLITIDA - fossils: Bondarenko, O. B. (P:?), Dzübo, P. S. (P:?), Leleshus, V. L. (F:P).
MADREPORARIA: Kolosváry, G., Rossi, L. (AO, O, Oc), Salter, K. E. W. (A), Stephenson, W.
  Fossils: Alloiteau, J. (M:W), Kolosváry, G., Schindewolf, O. H. (P:?).
PENNATULACEA: Broch, H. (W).
RUGOSA (Tetracoralla) - fossils, Paleozoic: Besprozvannikh, N. I. (P:?), Buehler, E. J.,
    Bulvanker, E. Z., Dobrolubova, T. A., Duncan, H. M., Ermakova, K. A. (P), Fagerstrom,
    J. A., Fomichev, V. D., Fujimoto, H. (P), Gorsky, I. I. (P), Hill, D. (W), Hudson,
    R. G. S., Igo, H. (P), Ivania, V. A., Ivanovsky, A. B., Jackson, J. S. (P), Johnson,
    G. A. L. (N), Kabakovich, N. V., Kaljo, D. L., Merriam, C. W. (N), Minato, M. (P),
    Okulitch, V. J. (N), Oliver, W. A., Jr. (N), Moore, R. C. (W), Nikolaeva, T. V., Parks,
    J. M., Jr., Pitrat, C. W., Porfiriev, G. S., Prantl, F. (P), Reiman, V. M., Sutherland,
    P. K., Sytova, V. A., Taylor, P. W. (W), Thomlinson, A. G. (N), Volkova, M. S.,
    Watkins, J. L., Zhizhina, M. S.
SCLERACTINIA: Nemenzo, F. (O, Oc), Siegel, F. (N), Wells, J. W. (W).
  Fossils: Barnard, J. L. (C:PO), Flugel, E. (M:?), Perkins, B. F. (M:N, Nt), Squires,
    D. F. (F:W), Wells, J. W. (M-C:W).
SCLERAXONIA: Verseveldt, J. (O, Oc).
STOLONIFERA: Gohar, H. A. F. (P), Verseveldt, J. (O, Oc).
TABULATA - fossils, Paleozoic: Bondarenko, O. B., Buehler, E. J., Chekhovich, V. D.,
    Dubatolov, V. N., Duncan, H. M., Dzübo, P. S., Ermakova, K. A. (P), Fujimoto, H. (P),
    Hill, D. (W), Ichoudinova, I. I., Igo, H. (P), Kim, A. A., Koksharskaya, K. B.,
    Kovalevsky, O. P., Leleshus, V. L. (P), Mironova, N. V., Moore, R. C. (W), Okulitch,
    V. J. (N), Prantl, F. (P), Ross, M. H., Smirnova, M. A., Stasińska, A. (P), Swann, D. H.,
    Tesakov, J. I., Thomlinson, A. G. (N), Watkins, J. L., Yanet, F. E., Zhizhina, M. S.
ZOANTHARIA (Hexacoralla): Cutress, C. E. (W), Dollfus, R. P. (P), Durham, J. W. (N),
    Müller, I.
  Fossils: Bendukidse, N. S. (M:?), Durham, J. W. (M-C:N), Kühn, O. (M-T:?), Reiman,
    V. M. (M:?).
ZOANTHIDEA: Ray, D. L., Wood, R. L. (N).
* * * * *

Acervulariidae - fossils: Taylor, F. M. (P:P).
Acroporidae: Siegel, F. (N).
Agariciidae: Siegel, F. (N).
Astrocoeniidae: Siegel, F. (N).
Chaetetidae - fossils: Sokolov, B. S. (P:P).
Faviidae: Siegel, F. (N).
Heliolitidae - fossils: Sokolov, B. S. (P:P).
Lithostrotiontidae - fossils: Taylor, F. M. (P:P).
Lonsdaleiidae - fossils: Taylor, F. M. (P:P).
Meandrinidae: Siegel, F. (N).
Palaeosmiliidae - fossils: Taylor, F. M. (P:P).
Phillipsastraeidae - fossils: Taylor, F. M. (P:P).
Siderastreidae: Siegel, F. (N).
Thamnophilidae - fossils: Rozkowska, M. (P:P).
Xeniidae: Gohar, H. A. F. (P).
Zaphrenthidae - fossils: Sadlick, W. (P:N).

Conularida

Fossils: Bouček, B. (P:P).
Tentaculitidae - fossils: Fisher, D. W. (P:N).

Hydrozoa

No other data: Amos, W. H. (bw:N), Bell, F. H., Eguchi, M., Hadži, J. (P), Millard,
    N. H. (m:E), Russell, F. S. (P), Schulz, E. (W), Uchida, T. (PO).
Fossils: Eguchi, M. (M-C:?), Flugel, E. (M-C:?), Hudson, R. G. S. (P:?), Picard, J. (Q:P),
    St. Jean, J., Jr. (P:W).

* * * * *

ANTHOMEDUSAE: Rees, W. J. (W).
CALYPTOBLASTEA (Leptomedusae, Thecophora): Blackburn, M. (A), Hamond, R. (W).
GYMNOBLASTEA (Anthomedusae, Athecata): Blackburn, M. (A), Hamond, R. (W),
    Rees, W. J. (AO).
HYDROIDEA (Hydromedusae): Leloup, E., Stechow, E.
    World: Deevey, E. S., Jr., Ranson, G.
    Nearctic: Crowell, S., Deevey, E. S., Jr., Foerster, R. E., Hand, C., Jackson, D. F.
    Neotropical: Hummelinck, P. W.
    Palearctic: Christiansen, B., Edwards, C., Itô, T. (fw, bw), Jaschnow, W. A.,
        Yamada, M.
    Paleotropical: Nagabhushanam, R. (O, IO), Ralph, P. M. (A).
    Atlantic Ocean: Picard, J., Vannucci, M.
    Pacific Ocean: Naumov, D. V., Yamada, M.
    Arctic & Antarctic: Broch, H., Naumov, D. V.
MILLEPORIDA (Hydrocorallinae): Broch, H. (Arc, Ant).
NARCOMEDUSAE: Blackburn, M. (A).
SIPHONOPHORIDA: Fraser, J. H. (AO), Gamulin, T. (P), de Leira, A. (AO, P), Le Loup, E.,
    Totton, A. K. (W).
STYLASTERIDA: Boschma, H. (W).
TRACHYLIDA: Jackson, D. F. (N).
TRACHYMEDUSAE: Blackburn, M. (A).

* * * * *

Acaulidae: Brinckmann, A.
Aequoridae: Brinckmann, A.
Bougainvilliidae: Brinckmann, A.
Campanulariidae: Brinckmann, A.
Cladocorynidae: Brinckmann, A.
Cladonemidae: Brinckmann, A.
Clavidae: Brinckmann, A.
Corymorphidae: Brinckmann, A.
Corynidae: Brinckmann, A.
Eirenidae: Brinckmann, A.
Eleutheridae: Brinckmann, A.
Eudendridae: Brinckmann, A.
Eutimidae: Brinckmann, A.
Haleciidae: Brinckmann, A.
Hydractiniidae: Brinckmann, A.
Hydridae: Bryden, R. P. (N), Hadley, C. E.
Laodiceidae: Brinckmann, A.
Lovenellidae: Brinckmann, A.
Mitrocomidae: Brinckmann, A.
Moerisiidae: Valkanov, A. (P).
Olindiidae: Lytle, C. F. (W).
Pandeidae: Brinckmann, A.
Plumulariidae: Brinckmann, A.
Rathkeidae: Brinckmann, A.
Sertulariidae: Brinckmann, A.
Tubulariidae: Brinckmann, A.
Zankleidae: Brinckmann, A.

Scyphozoa

No other data: Foerster, R. E. (N), Gwilliam, G. F. (PO), Naumov, D. V. (PO, Arc, Ant), Ranson, G. (W), Uchida, T. (PO), Vannucci, M. (AO).

* * * * *

CUBOMEDUSAE (Carybdeida): Southcott, R. V. (W).
STAUROMEDUSAE (Lucernariida): Gwilliam, G. F. (Oc).

* * * * *

Cassiopeidae: Hummelinck, P. W. (Nt).

Stromatoporoidea

Fossils: Flerova, N. A. (P:P), Flugel, E. , (P:?), Fritz, M. A. (P:N), Galloway, J. J. (P:W), Gogolczyk, W. (P:P), Hudson, R. G. S. (P-M:?), Khalfina, V. K. (P:?), Le Maitre, D. (P:P), Schnorf, A. (F:P), Špinar, Z. V. (F:P), Stearn, C. W. (P:N), St. Jean, J. , Jr. (P:W).

CTENOPHORA

No other data: Foerster, R. E. (N), Pfitzner, I. (P), Ray, D. L.

PLATYHELMINTHES

No other data: Chardome, M. , Joan, T.
Parasitic: Levine, N. D. (W), Miller, R. B. (N), Semenov, V. D. (P), Shachtachtinskaya, Z. H. (W), Shichobalova, N. P. (W), Shivitskis, P. K. (P), Skrjabin, K. I. (W), Skvortsov, A. A. (P). (See also Parasites, under Animals).

Cestoda

No other data: Heyneman, D. , Jones, A. W. , Lacey, R. J. , Luttermoser, G. W. , Mankau, S. K. , Michajlow, W. , Spassky, A. A. , Stunkard, H. W. , Wardle, R. A. , Yeh, L-S.
World: Baer, J. G. , Bashkirova, E. J. , Bona, F. , Goodman, J.D., Mathevossian, E. M. , Mendivil-Herrera, J. , Myers, B. J. , Ortlepp, R. T. , Prudhoe, S. , Schwartz, B.
New World: Byrd, E. E. , Read, C. P. , Voge, M.
Nearctic: Anderson, M. G. , Bogitsh, B. J. , Derbyshire, R. C. , Hannum, C. A. , Harkema, R. , McLeod, J. A. , Meinkoth, N. A. , Thomas, L. F. , Wagner, E. D.
Neotropical: Madrigal, R. B. , Thomas, L. J.
Palearctic: Della Santa, E. , Guevara Pozo, D. , Iwata, S. , Puchov, W. I. , Spasskaja, L. P. , Wetzel, R. , Yamaguti, S.
Paleotropical: Edwards, E. E. (E), Hannum, C. A. (Oc), Johri, L. N. (O), Koratha, K. J. (O), Lynsdale, J. (O), Ortlepp, R. T. (E), Sandars, D. F. (A), Thapar, G. S. (O), Wetzel, R. (E).
Parasites of fish: Arnold, J. G. , Jr. (N), Curtin, C. B. (fw), Dubinina, M. N. (P), Haderlie, E. C. (fw:N), Hart, J. G. , Hugghins, E. J. (fw:N), Morton, W. M. (N, P), Sandeman, I. (P), Sproston, N. G. (P).
Of amphibians: Dubinina, M. N. (P), Walton, A. C. (W).
Of reptiles: Dubinina, M. N. (P).
Of birds: Abuladze, K. I. (P), Burt, D. R. R. (N, O), Clark, D. T. , Coil, W. H. , Dubinina, M. N. (P), Hugghins, E. J. (N), Jordano, D. (Nt, P), Kerr, K. B. (N), Reid, W. M. , Sprehn, C. (P), Timmermann, G. (W), Webster, J. D. (N, Nt).
Of mammals: Allen, R. W. (N, Nt), Arnold, J. G. , Jr. (N), Coil, W. H. , Dubinina, M. N. (P), Hugghins, E. J. (N), Jordano, D. (Nt, P), Ogren, R. E. (N), Sprehn, C. (P).
Of man: Brown, R. L.
Larvae: Torpy, T. F.

* * * * *

CYCLOPHYLLIDEA: Bona, F. (W), Heck, O. B. (N), Hiregaudar, L. S. (O), Mahon, J. (W), Rausch, R. (Arc, N, P).
PSEUDOPHYLLIDEA: Rausch, R. (Arc, N, P).
TETRAPHYLLIDEA: Alexander, C. G. (N), Euzet, L. (W), Khambata, F. S. (O), Riser, N. W. (W).
TRYPANORHYNCHA (Tetrarhynchoidea): Dollfus, R. P.

* * * * *

Anoplocephalidae: Biguet, J. (P, E), Freeman, R. S. (N), Loewen, S. L. , Porter, D. A. (N).
Dibothriocephalidae: Garoian, G. (N), Mueller, J. F. (W).
Larvae: Wikgren, B-J. (P).

Hymenolepidae: Cheng, T. (N, Nt), Czaplinski, B. (P), Schiller, E. L. (N), Zarnowski, E. (P).
Linstowiidae: Millemann, R. E. (N, Nt, P).
Lytocestidae: Anthony, J. D. (W).
Nematotaeniidae: Douglas, L. T. (W).
Proteocephalidae: La Rue, G. R. (N).
Taeniidae: Crusz, H. (W), Freeman, R. S. (N), Loewen, S. L. , Senger, C. M. (N).

Trematoda

No other data: Annereaux, R. F. , Barroeta, L. F. , Bravo-Hollis, M. , Cercero, M. C. ,
Chavarria y Chavarria, M. , Ciordia, H. , Daugherty, J. , Fallis, A. M. , Heyneman, D. ,
Kotlán, A. , Kuntz, R. E. , Larios, I. , Le Zotte, L. A. , Jr. , Luttermoser, G. W. ,
Nydegger, L. , Odlaug, T. O. , Olivier, L. J. , Olsen, O. W. , Rankin, J. S. , Jr. , Ruiz, J. M. ,
Sokoloff, D. , Stunkard, H. W. , Watson, M. E. , Woodhead, A. E. , Yeh, L-S.
World: Baer, J. G. , Bashkirova, E. J. , Bona, F. , Brinkmann, A. , Coil, W. H. , Gushanskaja,
L. H. , Macy, R. W. , Myers, B. J. , Ortlepp, R. T. , Prudhoe, S. , Shumakovitch, E. E. ,
Spassky, A. A. , Witenberg, G.
Nearctic: Ameel, D. J. , Byrd, E. E. , Caballero y Caballero, E. , Derbyshire, R. C. ,
Dickerman, E. E. , Doran, D. J. , Fischthal, J. H. , Hannum, C. A. , Harkema, R. , Healy,
G. R. , Hunter, W. S. , Leigh, W. H. , Macy, R. W. , McLeod, J. A. , Miller, J. H. , Patten,
J. A. , Thomas, L. J.
Neotropical: Byrd, E. E. , de Freitas, J. F. T. , Grocott, R. G. , Healy, G. R. , Madrigal,
R. B. , Szidat, L. , Thomas, L. J. , Zerecero y Diaz, M. C.
Palearctic: Bondareva, V. I. , Dawes, B. , Fischthal, J. H. , Koval, V. P. , Okabe, K. ,
Petruschewsky, G. K. , Wetzel, R. , Yamaguti, S. , Yamashita, J. , Zdun, V. I.
Ethiopian: Edwards, E. E. , Ortlepp, R. T. , Wetzel, R.
Oriental: Fernando, W. , Koratha, K. J. , Thapar, G. S.
Australian: Sandars, D. F.
Oceania: Hannum, C. A.
Parasites, of fish: Arnold, J. G. , Jr. (N), Bychovskaja-Pavlovskaja, I. E. (P), Chauhan,
B. S. (W), Morton, W. M. (N, P), Tendeiro, J. (P, E).
Of marine fish: Bullock, W. L. (N), Copsey, J. E. (N), Guberlet, J. E. (PO), Zhukov, E. V. (W).
Of fresh-water fish: Allison, R. (N), Curtin, C. B. (N), Haderlie, E. C. (N), Hugghins, E. J. (N).
Of amphibians: Walton, A. C. (W).
Of birds: Bychovskaja-Pavlovskaja, I. E. (P), Ginetzinskaja, T. A. (P), Hugghins, E. J. (N),
Sprehn, C. (P).
Of mammals: Arnold, J. G. , Jr. (N), Babero, B. B. (N), Bychovskaja-Pavlovskaja, I. E. (P),
Crusz, H. (t, m:O), Gjessing, H. W. (N), Grundmann, A. W. (N), Hugghins, E. J. (N),
McIntosh, A. , Sprehn, C. (P).
Of man: Brown, R. L. , Sadun, E. H. (P), Vercammen-Grandjean, P. H. (E).
Larvae: Ginetzinskaja, T. A. (P), Goodman, J. D. (W), Hasegawa, M. (P), Rothschild, M. (P),
Pratt, I. (N).

* * * * *

DISTOMATA: Dollfus, R. P.
GYRODACTYLOIDEA: Berry, J. E. (N).
HETEROCOTYLEA (Monogenea): Brinkmann, A. (Arc, AO), Euzet, L. (P), Gussev, A. V. (W),
Hargis, W. J. , Jr. (W), Koratha, K. J. (W), Meserve, F. G. (W), Mizelle, J. D. , Palombi,
A. (P), Price, E. W. (W), Seamster, A. P. (N), Sproston, N. G. (P), Tripathi, Y. R. (O),
Winter, H. A. (N, Nt. PO), Wood, R. A. (N).
Parasites, of fish: Llewellyn, J. , Manter, H. W. , Prost, M. (P), Ronald, K. (N, Nt).
MALACOCOTYLEA (Digenea): Cable, R. M.
World: Price, E. W. , Kruidenier, F. J. , Hopkins, S. H.
Nearctic: Bogitsh, B. J. , Etges, F. J. , Goodchild, C. G. , La Rue, G. R. , Najarian, H. H. ,
Ulmer, M. J. , Winter, H. A. , Wootton, D.
Neotropical: Winter, H. A.
Palearctic: Najarian, H. H. , Palombi, A. , Sevadjian, B. K. , Timon-David, J.
Paleotropical: Angel, L. M. (A), Hiregaudar, L. S. (O).
Parasites, of marine animals: Arai, H. P. (PO), Sparks, A. K. (W), Winter, H. A. (PO).
Of mollusks: Hopkins, S. H. (W).
Of fish: Bennett, H. J. (N), Hopkins, S. H. (W), Manter, H. W. , Margolis, L. (PO),
Pritchard, C. G. , (AO, PO), Sproston, N. G. (P).
Of amphibians: Bennett, H. J. (N), Senger, C. M. (N).
Of reptiles: Bennett, H. J. (N), Goodman, J. D. (W).
Of mammals: Margolis, L. (PO), Senger, C. M. (N).
Larvae: Ito, J. (P), Palombi, A. (P), Wikgren, B-J. (P).
MONOSTOMATA: Herber, E. C. (W).
STRIGEATA: Bogitsh, B. J. (N), Dubois, G. (W), Hoffman, G. L. (N), Niewiadomska, K. (P),
Pearson, J. C. (N, A).

* * * * *

Allocreadiidae: Cheng, T. (N, Nt), Jaxon-Deelman, J. (N), Ozaki, Y. (P), Schulmann-Albova,
 R. E. (W), Ślusarski, W. (P).
Aspidogastridae: Tandon, R. S. (W).
Azygiidae: Anderson, M. G. (N), Sillman, E. I. (W).
Brachycoeliidae: Cheng, T. (N, Nt).
Brachylaimidae (Harmostomiidae): Kagan, I. G. (W), Robinson, E. J.
Capsalidae: Copsey, J. E. (N).
Cyathocotylidae: Komiya, Y. (P), Myer, D. G. (N).
 Larvae: Myer, D. G. (N).
Dactylogyridae: Berry, J. E. (N), Gussev, A. V. (P), Monaco, L. H. (N).
Diclidophoridae: Frayne, N. Z. (N).
Dicrocoeliidae: Cheng, T. (N, Nt), Denton, J. F. (N), Kingston, N. (N).
 Larvae: Sevadjian, B. K. (P).
Echinostomatidae: Beaver, P. C. (N, Nt).
Eucotylidae: Kingston, N. (N).
Fasciolidae: Boettger, C. R. (E), Komiya, Y. (P), Sarwar, M. M. (W), Ślusarski, W. (W),
 Tandon, R. S. (W).
Gorgoderidae: Loewen, S. L. , Markell, E. K. , Steen, E. B. (N).
Gyrodactylidae: Ikezaki, M. F. (N), Malmberg, G. (W), Turnbull, E. R. (W).
Hemiuridae: McCauley, J. E. (N).
Heterophyidae: Komiya, Y. (P).
Hexostomatidae: Millemann, R. E. (N, Nt, P).
Lecithodendriidae: Cheng, T. (N, Nt).
Microphallidae: Belopolskaia, M. M. (P), Biguet, J. (W).
Opecoelidae: Deelman, J. J. (N), Ozaki, Y. (P), Ślusarski, W. (P).
Opisthorchidae: Hsü, S. Y. L. (W), Sillman, E. I. (W), Wallace, F. G. (W).
Paramphistomidae: Dinnik, J. A. (E), Fukui, T. (P), Tandon, R. S. (W), Willey, C. H. (N).
Plagiorchidae: Cheng, T. (N, Nt), Harwood, P. D. (W), McMullen, D. B. (W).
Polystomidae: Czaki, Y. (P).
Schistosomatidae (Bilharziidae): Boettger, C. R. (E), Buttner, A. (Nt, E, O), Dinnik, J. A. (E),
 Grodhaus, G. (N), Hsü, S. Y. L. (W), Kagan, I. G. (W), Komiya, Y. (P), McMullen,
 D. B. (W), Moore, D. V. (N), Ozaki, Y. (P), Penner, L. R. (W), Sarwar, M. M. (W),
 Short, R. B. , Wright, C. A. (W).
Troglotrematidae (Renicolidae): Miyazaki, I. (N, P), Wallace, F. G. (W), Wright, C. A. (W).

Turbellaria

No other data: Castle, W. A. , Kaburaki, T. , Karling, T. G. , Marcus, Ern. , Marcus, Eve. ,
 Reisinger, E. , Steinbock, O. , Stunkard, H. W. (p).
World: An der Lan, H. (m, fw, t), Ax, P. (m), Ferguson, F. F. , Gieysztor, M. , Hyman, L. H. ,
 Papi, F.
Nearctic: Wurtz, C. B. (fw).
Palearctic: de Beauchamp, P. (m), Riedl, R.
Australian: Stock, A.
* * * * *
ACOELA: Ivanov, A. V. , Kato, K. (O, Oc), Riedl, R. (W), Stirewalt, M. A. (N).
ALLOEOCOELA: Darlington, J. T. (N), Jones, E. R. , Jr. (N), Stirewalt, M. A. (N).
NOTANDROPORA (Catenulida): Nuttycombe, J. W. (N).
POLYCLADIDA: de Beauchamp, P. , Kato, K. (O, Oc), Palombi, A. (P, E), Prudhoe, S. (W),
 Reisinger, E.
POLYCYSTIDEA: Filipponi, A. (P).
RHABDOCOELIDA: de Beauchamp, P. , Darlington, J. T. (N), Hazen, W. E. , Jones,
 E. R. , Jr. (N), Knapp, S. E. , Luther, A. (W), Stirewalt, M. A. (N), Vialli, M. (P).
TEMNOCEPHALIDA: Fernando, W. (O), Sawaya, P. (Nt).
TRICLADIDA: Allison, F. (A), de Beauchamp, P. (N, Nt, P, E, Oc), Benazzi, M. (P), Codreanu,
 R. (W), Darlington, J. T. (N), Dahm, A. (P), Froehlich, C. G. (W), Froehlich,
 E. M. (W), Kenk, R. (fw:W), Livanow, N. (P), Luther, A. (P), Okugawa, K. I. (fw:P, O),
 Pfitzner, I. (P), Reisinger, E. , Reynoldson, T. B. (P), Vialli, M. (P).
Planariidae: Fyfe, M. (A).
Rhynchodemidae: Ogren, R. E. (N).

NEMATHELMINTHES

No other data: Althaus, B. (P), Brown, R. L.
(See also the following three phyla).

NEMERTINEA
(Rhynchocoela)

No other data: Corrêa, D. D. (Nt), Friedrick, H. (W), Müller, G. I. (P), Posner, G.,
    Prudhoe, S. (W).
Marine: Dawson, E. W. (A), Korotkevitsch, V. S. (W), Mulicki, Z. (P), Riser, N. W.,
    Southgate, A. J. (A).
Fresh-water: Sudzuki, M. (P).
Terrestrial: Southgate, A. J. (Oc).

ACANTHOCEPHALA

No other data: Hensley, J. R., Yeh, L-S.
    World: De Giusti, D., Golvan, Y., Inglis, W. G., Lincicome, D. R., Petrotchenko, V. I.,
        Ward, H. L., Witenberg, G.
    Nearctic: Holloway, H. L., Moore, D. V., Thomas, L. J.
    Neotropical: Diaz-Ungria, C., Holloway, H. L., Moore, D. V., Thomas, L. J.
    Palearctic: Fukui, T., Harada, I., Yamaguti, S.
    Oriental: Edmonds, S. J., Harada, I., Koratha, K. J., Soota, T. D., Thapar, G. S.
    Oceania: Edmonds, S. J.
Parasites, of fish: Sproston, N. G. (P), Tripathi, Y. R. (P).
  Of fresh-water fish: Bangham, R. V. (N), Haderlie, E. C. (N).
  Of marine fish: Bullock, W. L. (N), Margolis, L. (PO).
  Of reptiles: Cable, R. M.
  Of birds: Sprehn, C. (P).
  Of mammals: Margolis, L. (PO), Sprehn, C. (P).
               * * * * *
Polymorphidae: Montreuil, P. (W).

GORDIACEA
(Nematomorpha)

No other data: Čanadjija, S. (P), Chitwood, B. G., Dorier, A. H. (W), Feio, J. L. A., Havlik, O.,
    Inglis, W. C. (P), Inoue, I. (P), Johnston, E. B. W. (P), Kirjanova, E. S. (W), Montén, E.,
    Riek, E. F. (A), Sciacchitano, I. (E), Yeh, L-S.
Parasites, of insects: Jolivet, P. (E).

PRIAPULIDA

No other data: Itô, T. (P), Mulicki, Z. (P), Murina, W. W. (PO), Stephen, A. C. (W).

GASTROTRICHA

No other data: Davison, D. B., Goldberg, R. J. (fw), Jakubski, A. W., Remane, A.
    World: Wieser, W. (m:W), Sacks, M. (W), Brunson, R. B. (W), Gerlach, S. (m:W),
        Papi, F. (W).
    Nearctic: Friauf, J. J. (N), Packard, C. E. (N), Roark, T. R. (fw:N).
    Palearctic: Rodewald-Rudescu, L. (P), Varga, L. (P).
               * * * * *
MACRODASYOIDEA: Levi, C., Swedmark, B. (P).

NEMATODA

No other data: Adhami, A. R. , Amrein, Y. U. L. , Annereaux, R. F. , Atkinson, K. M. , Baines,
R. C. , Basir, M. A. , Bevan, W. J. , Blancas, F. , Boardman, E. T. , Brunetti, B. ,
Capstick, C. K. , Calvino, E. M. , Cercero, M. C. , Chapman, S. M. ,
Chavarria y Chavarria, M. , Christie, J. R. , Clapham, P. A. , Colbran, R. C. ,
Cooper, B. A. , Daulton, K. A. C. , De Bona, A. , Dumitrescu, D. , Dunn, E. , Durbin, C. G. ,
Duthoit, C. M. C. , Duthy, B. L. , Gadea, E. , Gallego Berenguer, G. , Gerichter, C. B. ,
Golightly, W. H. , Gorsac, S. A. , Gunhold, P. , Heindl-Mengert, H. , Henderson, V. E. ,
Hoeppli, R. , Johanson, E. , Johnston, T. , Kaktina, D. K. , Kips, R. H. , Krusberg, L. ,
Kung, C. C. , LeRoux, P. L. , Lüling, H. , Lynch, A. , McMahon, E. , Mengert, H. ,
Mirza, M. B. , Morishita, K. , Morgan, D. O. , Murdoch, G. , Noble, A. E. , Olsen, O. W. ,
Peng, O. H. , Prasse, J. , Schmidt, J. , Slootweg, A. F. G. , Sokoloff, D. , Sveshnikova,
H. M. , Thomas, G. E. , Vogel, W. , Volz, P. , Wehunt, E. J. , Weingartner, I. , Wenham,
H. T. , Widdowson, E. , Williams, D. W. , Yeh, L-S. , Zehle, E.
World: Goodman, J. D. , Schwartz, B. , Witenberg, G.
Nearctic: Derbyshire, R. C. , Graham, T. W. , Hannum, C. A. , Thomas, L. J. ,
Williams, A. S.
Neotropical: Caballero y Caballero, E. , Grocott, R. G. , Madrigal, R. B. , Thomas, L. J. ,
Zerecero y Diaz, M. C.
Palearctic: Guevara Pozo, D. , Menzel, R. , Oberthur, K. , Puchov, W. I. , Rogerson, J. P. ,
Støen, M. , Tarczyński, S. , Yamashita, J.
Paleotropical: Hannum, C. A. (Oc), Soota, T. D. (O), Thapar, G. S. (O).
Free-living: Allgen, C. (W), Altherr, E. (P, E), Andrássy, I. (W), Coles, J. W. (P),
Hirschmann, H. (N, P), Kort, J. (P), Kreis, H. A. , Loos, C. (Trop), Noffsinger,
E. M. (N), Paesler, F. (P), Stefanski, W. (P), Twinn, D. C. (P), Weischer, B. (P).
Free-living, marine: Coman, D. (P), De Coninck, L. A. P. (W), Gerlach, S. (W),
Hopper, B. E. (AO), Jensen, H. J. (N), Luc, R. (P), Perkins, E. J. (P), Riser, N. W. ,
Steiner, G. , Thomas-Mawson, P. M. (A, Ant), Timm, R. W. (W), Wieser, W. (W).
Free-living, fresh-water: Allen, M. W. (W), Coman, D. (P), De Coninck, L. A. P. (W),
Hooper, D. J. (W), Hopper, B. E. (N), Jensen, H. J. (W), Krall, E. (P), Loof,
P. A. A. (P), Meyl, A. H. (W), Paetzold, D. (P), Rühm, W. , Schindler, A. F. (W).
Free-living, soil: Bassus, W. (P), Bergeson, G. (N), Brunold, E. (P), Cayeness,
F. E. (N), Clark, W. C. (A), Coman, D. (P), De Coninck, L. A. P. (W), Fielding, M. J. ,
Good, J. M. (N), Hooper, D. J. (W), Hope, D. (N), Hopper, B. E. (N), Jenkins, W. R. (N),
Jensen, H. J. (W), Kirjanova, E. S. (P), Krall, E. (P), Kühn, H. (P), van der Linde,
W. J. (W), Loof, P. A. A. (P), Nielsen, C. O. (P), Oteifa, B. A. (P), Paetzold, D. (P),
Paramonov, A. A. (W), Peters, B. G. , Pologentsev, P. A. (W), Rühm, W. , Sanwal,
K. C. (N), Schindler, A. F. (W), Steiner, G. , Tulaganov, A. T. (P), Twinn, D. C. (P),
Whitlock, L. S. , Winslow, R. D. (P).
Saprophytic: Apt, W. (N), Chitwood, B. J.
Plant-parasitic: Buhrer, E. M. , Chamberlain, R. , Chitwood, B. G. , Dropkin, V. H. , Fielding,
M. J. , Rühm, W. , Taylor, A. L. , Whitlock, L. S.
World: Allen, M. W. , Hannon, C. I. , Hooper, D. J. , Jensen, H. J. , van der Linde, W. J. ,
Meyl, A. H. , Paramonov, A. A. , Schindler, A. F.
Nearctic: Andrássy, I. , Apt, W. , Bergeson, G. , Caveness, F. E. , Ferris, J. , Harrison,
M. B. , Hirschmann, H. , Hollis, J. P. , Hope, D. , Hopper, B. E. , Noffsinger, E. M. ,
Sanwal, K. C. , Wu, L. Y.
Neotropical: Loos, C. , Luc, R. , Moreno, A. F. , Zamith, A. P. L.
Palearctic: Andrássy, I. , van den Brande, J. , Carroll, J. , D'Herde, J. , Duggan, J. J. ,
Gillard, A. , Goffart, H. , Grainger, J. , Hirschmann, H. , Kirjanova, E. S. , Kühn, H. ,
Loof, P. A. A. , Mabbott, T. W. , Oteifa, B. A. , Paesler, F. , Savary, A. , Seinhorst, J. W. ,
Simon, L. K. , Skarbilovich, T. S. , Southey, J. F. , Stefanski, W. , Thomas, P. R. ,
Triantaphyllou, A. C. , Tulaganov, A. T. , Twinn, D. C. , Ustinov, A. A. , Wallace, H. R. ,
Weischer, B. , Winslow, R. D.
Paleotropical: van den Brande, J. (E), Edwards, E. E. (E), Holtzmann, O. (Oc), Loos,
C. (Trop), Luc, R. (Trop), Timm, R. W. (O).
Parasites, of animals: Asadov, S. L. (P), Burdalev, T. E. (P), Chitwood, M. B. (W),
Grundmann, A. W. (N), Koratha, K. J. (O), Kreis, H. A. , Myers, B. J. (W), Ortlepp,
R. T. (W), Paramonov, A. A. (W), Peebles, C. R. (N, Nt), Peters, B. G. , Sobolev,
A. A. (W), Spassky, A. A. (W), Sprehn, C. (P), Threlkeld, W. L. (N), Yamaguti, S. (P).
Of Insects: Allen, M. W. (N), Chitwood, B. J. , Hoy, J. M. (A), Khan, M. A. (W), Rühm, W. ,
Théodoridès, J. (W).
Of vertebrates: Chabaud, A. (W), Crusz, H. (O), Edwards, E. E. (E), de Freitas, J. F. T. (Nt),
Hartwich, G. (P), Hsü, S. Y. L. (W), Inglis, W. G. (W), Lucker, J. T. (N), Ogren,
R. E. (N), Olsen, L. S. , Stefanski, W. (P), Thomas-Mawson, P. M. (A).
Of fish: Campana-Rouget, Y. (W), De Giusti, D. (W), Hugghins, E. J. , Margolis, L. (m:PO),
Morton, W. M. (N, P).

Of amphibians: Walton, A. C. (W).
Of reptiles: Read, C. P. (W), Schad, G. A. (W).
Of birds: Böhm, L. K. (P), Hugghins, E. J. (N), Kerr, K. B. (N), Madsen, H. , Sanwal,
    K. C. (O), Supperer, R. (P).
Of mammals: Biocca, E. (P, E), Böhm, L. K. (P), Bull, P. C. (A), Kruidenier, F. J. (N),
    Lukasiak, J. (P), Margolis, L. (PO), Oldham, J. N. (N, P), Read, C. P. (W),
    Supperer, R. (P), Tiner, J. D. (N).
Of domestic animals: Allen, R. W. (N, Nt), Andrews, J. S. (N, Nt), Becklund, W. W. (N),
    Boev, S. N. (P), Clark, D. T. , Goldberg, A. (N), Hugghins, E. J. (N), Kates, K. C. (N),
    Knight, R. A. (N), Levine, N. D. (W), Lindquist, W. D. (N, E), Mayhew, R. L. ,
    McIntosh, A. (N), Oldham, J. N. (N, P), Sarwar, M. M. (W), Skrjabin, K. I. (W).
Of man: Beaver, P. C. , Skrjabin, K. I. (W).
Of economic importance: John, M. E. , Light, W. I. S. , Moreton, B. D.
Larvae: Myers, B. J. (W).

* * * * *

APHELENCHOIDEA: Baker, A. D. (N), Lordello, L. G. E. (Nt), Nishizawa, T. (P).
ASCAROIDEA: Hartwich, G. (W), Hiregaudar, L. S. (O), Osche, G. (P), Sprent, J. F. A. (W),
    Wetzel, R. (P, E).
DORYLAIMOIDEA: Baker, A. D. (N), Jorgenson, E. C. (N, Nt, P), Lordello, L. G. E. (Nt),
    Lownsbery, B. F. (W), Mai, W. F. (N, Nt), Mankau, R. (N), Perry, V. G. (N), Rau,
    G. J. (N), Tarjan, A. C. (W), Thorne, G. (W).
ENOPLIDA: Mai, W. F. (N, Nt).
FILARIOIDEA: Anderson, R. C. (W), Buckley, J. J. C. (Trop), Highby, P. R. (N), Wehr, E. E. (N)
RHABDITOIDEA: Baker, A. D. (N), Goodey, J. B. (W), Mai, W. F. (N, Nt), Ritter, M. (P),
    Santmyer, P. H. (N).
SPIRUROIDEA: Hiregaudar, L. S. (O), Milleman, R. E. (N, Nt), Santmyer, P. H. (N).
STRONGYLOIDEA: Hiregaudar, L. S. (O), Kassai, T. (P), Schulz, R. S. , Stoll, N. R. , Wetzel,
    R. (P, E), Whitlock, J. H.
TRICHOSTRONGYLOIDEA: Osche, G. (N, P), Schikhobalova, N. P. , Senger, C. M. (N),
    Zarnowski, E. (P).
TRICHUROIDEA (Trichinelloidea): Hiregaudar, L. S. (O), Schikhobalova, N. P.
TYLENCHIDA: Franklin, M. T. , Oostenbrink, I. M.
    World: Golden, A. M. , Goodey, J. B. , Lownsbery, B. F. , Perry, V. G. , Tarjan, A. C. ,
        Welford, N. D. N. , Whitehead, A. G.
    Nearctic: Birchfield, W. , Brown, G. L. , Esser, R. P. , Fassuliotis, G. , Hutchinson,
        M. T. , Jorgenson, E. C. , Mai, W. F. , Mankau, R. , Rau, G. J. , Santmyer, P. H. ,
        Thames, W. H. , Jr. , Van Weerdt, L. G.
    Neotropical: Jorgenson, E. C. , Mai, W. F.
    Palearctic: Boghossian, H. E. , Jorgenson, E. C. , Kuiper, I. K. , Pitcher, R. S. ,
        Ritter, M. , Saigusa, T. , Yokoo, T.
    Paleotropical: Fisher, J. M. (A), Mankau, R. (O), Sauer, M. (A).
TYLENCHOIDEA: Baker, A. D. (N), Garriss, H. R. (N, Nt), Golden, T. S. (W), Lordello,
    L. G. E. (Nt), Thorne, G. (W).

* * * * *

Aphelenchidae: Good, J. M. (N).
Ascaridae: Jaskoski, B. J. (N).
Cephalobidae: Tarjan, A. C. (W), Thorne, G. (W).
Criconematidae: Good, J. M. (N), Nishizawa, T. (P), Raski, D. J. (W).
Cystoopsidae: Schikhobalova, N. P.
Diaphonocephalidae: Schad, G. A. (W).
Diplogasteridae: Tarjan, A. C. (W).
Dorylaimidae: Fennel, W. E. (N), Golden, A. M. (W).
Heteroderidae: MacIntosh, G. , Miller, L. I.
    World: Cobb, G. S. , Sasser, J. N.
    Nearctic: Cairns, E. J. , Mulvey, R. H. , Orchard, W. R.
    Palearctic: Budzier, H. H. , Gillard, A. , Graf, A. , Ichinohe, M. , Kämpfe, L. , Kort, J. ,
        Mulvey, R. H. , Nishizawa, T. , den Ouden, H. , Sandner, H. , Shepherd, A. M. ,
        Stelter, H. , Stenuit, D. F. E.
    Paleotropical: Gillard, A. (E), Martin, G. C. (E). Meagher, J. W. (A).
Mermithidae: Coman, D. (W), Welch, H. E. (W).
Metastrongylidae: Dougherty, E. C. (W), Kassai, T. (P).
Mononchidae: Mulvey, R. H. (N).
Neotylenchidae: Iyatomi, K. (P), Nishizawa, T. (P).
Oxyuridae: Cuckler, A. C. , Feldmesser, J. (N).
Plectidae: Maggenti, A. R. (N, P).
Rhabditidae: Dougherty, E. C. (W), Nigon, V. (P), Osche, G. (W), Tarjan, A. C. (W),
    Wessing, A. , (P).
Setariidae: Bezubik, B. (P), Furmaga, S. (P).

17

NEMATODA (continued)

Strongyloididae: Graham, G. L.
Thelaziidae: Douvres, F. W. (W).
Trichostrongylidae: Herlich, H. (N), Porter, D. A. (N), Rohrbacher, G. H. (N).
Trichuridae: Durbin, C. G. , Sarwar, M. M. (W).
Tylenchidae: Bingefors, S. , Goheen, A. C. , Salentiny, T.
    World: Sher, S. A.
    Nearctic: Courtney, W. D. , Feldmesser, J. , Good, J. M. , Hollis, J. P. , Khan, S. A. ,
      Taylor, D. P. , Waseem, M.
    Palearctic: Decker, H. , Gotoh, A. , Graf, A. , Iyatomi, K. , Nishizawa, T. , Rolfe, S. W. H. ,
      Sandner, H.
    Paleotropical: Holtzmann, O. (Oc), Khan, S. A. (O), Meagher, J. W. (A), Waseem, M. (O).
Tylenchulidae: Nishizawa, T. (P), Raski, D. J. (W).

KINORHYNCHA
(Echinodera)

No other data: Chitwood, B. G. , Higgins, R. P. (N).

ROTIFERA
(Rotatoria)

No other data: Bakr, A. , Barroso, M. S. , Bellido, A. G. , Börje, C. , Burger, A. , Czapik, A. ,
    Damas, H. F. C. , Ferrero, L. , Jakubski, A. W. , Lansing, A. , vay Oye, P. , Remane, A. ,
    Rudescu, R. , Rudlin, C. , Ruttner-Kolisto, A. , Sabaneef, P. , Sato, H. , Velez, M. J. , Jr. ,
    Vorstman, A. G. , Wang, C. C.
    World: Bennetch, L. M. , Bērziņś, B. V. A. , Edmondson, W. T. , Gallagher, J. J. , Galliford,
      A. L. , Hollowday, E. , Pawlowski, L. K. , Wulfert, K.
    New World: Neal, G. M. (N), Thomasson, K. (Nt), Thomsen, R. (Nt).
    Palearctic: Althaus, B. , Bartoš, E. , Bogoslovsky, A. S. , Garner, W. E. , de Graaf, D. F. ,
      Hada, Y. , Kertész, G. , Megyeri, J. , Messikommer, E. , Rodewald-Rudescu, L. ,
      Valkanov, A. , Varga, L.
    Paleotropical: Evans, J. (A), Kertész, G. (E), Russell, C. R. (E, O, A, Oc, Ant),
      Thomasson, K. (E).
Marine: De Ridder, M. (W), Markman, B. (P).
Brackish-water: De Ridder, M. (W).
Fresh-water: Ahlstrom, E. H. (W), Beach, N. W. (N), Gossler, O. (P), Klimowicz, H. (W),
    Pejler, B. (P), Resvoy, (P), Rühmann, D. (P), Sladecek, V. (P).
Soil-inhabiting: Donner, J. , Meyl, A. H. (W).

           * * * * *

COLLOTHECACEA: Pourriot, R. (fw: P), Wright, H. G. S. (P).
FLOSCULARIACEA: Neal, G. M. (W), Pourriot, R. (P), Wright, H. G. S. (P).
MONOGONONTA: Buchholz, H. A. (m, fw: P), Fott, J. (W), Hauer, J. (W), Klement, V. (P).
PLOIMA: de Beauchamp, P. , Pourriot, R. (fw: P), Yamamoto, K. (P).
RHIZOTA: de Beauchamp, P.

           * * * * *

Asplanchnidae: Sudzuki, M. (P).
Brachionidae: Buchner, H. (P), Gillard, A. (W), Schepens, D. (W), Sudzuki, M. (P).
Gastropodidae: Sudzuki, M. (P).
Notommatidae: Sudzuki, M. (P), Wlastov, B. (P).
Synchaetidae: Sudzuki, M. (P).
Testudinellidae: Sudzuki, M. (P).

ENDOPROCTA

No other data: Angel, L. M. (W), Rattenbury, J. C. (N), Yamada, M. (PO).
Marine: Rogick, M. D. (N, Ant), Ryland, J. H. (P), Soule, J. D. (N).
Fresh-water: Rogick, M. D. (N).

           * * * * *

Loxosomatidae: Atkins, D. (P).

BRYOZOA

No other data: Arvy, L. , Astrova, G. G. , Balavoine, P. , Bobin, G. , Cheetham, A. H. , Coryell,
H. N. , Marcus, Ern. , Marcus, Eve. , Nekhoroshev, V. P. , O'Donoghue, C. H. ,
Prenant, M.
New World: Howard, R. S. (N), Martin, G. B. (N), Parker, R. H. (N, Nt).
Palearctic: Bloklander, A. , Hamond, R. , Hejskova-Červenková, E.
Paleotropical: Androssova, H. (PO), Cotton, B. C. (A), Okada, Y. (O, Oc), Uttley,
G. H. (A).
Marine: Hastings, A. B. , Lacourt, A. W. (P), Lagaaij, R. (N, Nt), Macken, J. (A, Oc),
Mawatari, S. (P, O, Oc), Rattenbury, J. C. (N), Rogick, M. D. (N, Ant), Ryland, J. H. (P),
Silén, L. (W), Soule, J. D. (N), Stach, L. W. (PO).
Estuarine: Amos, W. H. (N).
Fresh-water: Abricossov, G. G. (P, E), Hastings, A. B. , Rogick, M. D. (N).
Fossils, no other data: Feofanova, M. , Makowski, H. , Morozova, I. P. , Shulga-Nesterenko, M. I.
Paleozoic: Astrova, G. G. (P), Barbosa, M. M. , Bassler, R. S. , Boardman, R. S. ,
Chronic, J. , Coryell, H. N. , Elias, M. K. (N, P), Ellison, R. L. (N), Fritz, M. A. (N),
Galloway, J. J. (W), Martin, G. B. (N), Monk, W. J. (N), Moore, R. C. (W), Olson,
E. P. (N), Phillips, J. R. P. (N, A), Prantl, F. (P), Shishova, N. A. (P), Spheldnaes, N. ,
Ware, S.
Mesozoic: Buge, E. , Cheetham, A. H. , Coryell, H. N. , Ducasse, J. (P), Illies, G. (P),
Kühn, O. , Lagaaij, R. (N, Nt, P), Thomas, H. D. (W), Voigt, E.
Cenozoic: Barbosa, M. M. , Bloklander, A. (P), Buge, E. , Bush, J. (N, Nt), Cheetham,
A. H. , Coryell, H. N. , Hatai, K. (Oc), Kühn, O. , Larwood, G. P. , Malecki, J. (P),
Martin, G. B. (N), Souaya, F. J. (P), Stach, L. W. (Oc), Thomas, H. D. (W), Uttley,
G. H. (A), Vigneaux, M.

* * * * *

CHEILOSTOMATA: Brown, D. A. (A), Cheetham, A. H. , Gostilovskaia, M. (Arc), Vigeland,
I. (Nt, Arc, Ant).
Fossils: Berthelsen, O. (M-C:P), Brown, D. A. (T:A, Ant), Butler, E. (M:N, Nt).
CRIBRIMORPHA - fossils: Larwood, G. P.
CRYPTOSTOMATA: Kräusel, W. (P).
Fossils: Blake, O. D. (P:?), Duncan, H. M. (P:?), Koenig, J. W. (P:N), Toots, H. A. (P:?).
CYCLOSTOMATA: Brown, D. A. (A, Ant).
Fossils: Brown, D. A. (T:A, Ant), Duncan, H. M. (P:?), Pitt, L. J. (M:P).
GYMNOLAEMATA: Gautier, Y. (P), FOSSILS: Gautier, Y. (F:P).
PHYLACTOLAEMATA: Lacourt, A. W. (W).
TREPOSTOMATA - fossils: Blake, O. D. (P:?), Duncan, H. M. (P:?), Perry, T. G. (P:N),
Toots, H. A. (P:?).

* * * * *

Cristatellidae: Toriumi, M. (W).
Fenestellidae - fossils: Bartlett, H. A. (P:A), Sadlick, W. (P:N).
Fistuliporidae - fossils: Perry, T. G. (P:N).
Fredericellidae: Toriumi, M. (W).
Lophopodidae: Toriumi, M. (W).
Nolellidae: Abricossov, G. G. (W).
Plumatellidae: Toriumi, M. (W).
Victorellidae: Toriumi, M. (W).

PHORONIDA

No other data: Marcus, Ern. , Rattenbury, J. C. (N), Silén, L. (W), Uchida, T. (PO).

BRACHIOPODA

No other data: Berry, S. S. , Cloud, P. E. , Jr. , Percival, E. , Stehli, F. G.
World: Cooper, G. A. , Dutro, J. T. , Jr. , Helmcke, J-G. , Muir-Wood, H. M. , Williams, A.
Palearctic: Atkins, D. , Sebestyén, O. (fw), Uozumi, S.
Paleotropical: Allan, R. S. , Cotton, B. C. (A), Konzhukova, E. D. (Oc).
Fossils: no other data: Makridin, V. P. , Sahni, M. R.
All ages: Cloud, P. E. , Jr. , Cooper, G. A. (W), Dutro, J. T. , Jr. (W), Havliček, V. (P),
Muir-Wood, H. M. (W), Rudwick, M. J. S. (W), Williams, A. (W).
Paleozoic: Allan, R. S. (A), Amsden, T. W. , Armstrong, A. K. , Bell, W. C. , Boucot,
A. J. (W), Brill, K. G. , Jr. , Campbell, K. S. W. , Chronic, J. , Cochran, W. A. (N),
Cowie, J. W. , Crickmay, C. H. (N), Dean, W. T. (P), Dunbar, C. O. , Dutro, J. T. , Jr. (N),
Elias, M. K. (N, P), Ellison, R. L. (N), Fagerstrom, J. A. , Gill, E. D. (O, A, Oc),

Grant, R. E. (N), Gutschick, R. C. (N), Harker, P. (N, Arc), Harlow, F. J., Jr. (N),
Hayasaka, I., Hoare, R. D. (N), Holland, F. D., Jr. (N), Imbrie, J., Johnson, G. A. L. (N),
Johnson, R. B. (N), Jones, D. G. (P), Kent, L. S. (N), Lamont, A. (P), Larson, E. R. (N),
Lawson, J. D. (P), Le Maitre, D. (P), McKee, E. D., McLaren, D. J. (N), Minato, M. (P),
Monk, W. J. (N), Nelson, S. J. (N), Nelson, S. J. (N), Northrop, S. A., Nosow, E., Olson,
E. P. (N), Parkinson, D. (P), Pope, J. K. (N), Prentice, J. E., Ross, R. J., Jr., (N),
Sadlick, W. (N), Sanders, J. E. (N, P), Sando, W. J. (N), Sass, D. B. (N), Scott, W. F. (N),
Shaw, A. B., Simpson, S. (P), Spreng, A. C. (N), Stehli, F. G., Stelck, C. R. (N),
St. Joseph, J. K. S., Stoyanow, A. (N, Nt, P), Struve, W. (P), Sutherland, P. K., Talent,
J. A., Taylor, P. W. (W), Tesmer, I. H. (N), Thomas, G. A. (A), Tillman, C. G. (N),
Ulmer, J. W., Jr. (E), Veevers, J. J. (A), Waterhouse, J. B. (A), Whittard, W. F. (P),
Wilkie, L. C. (N), Wright, J. D. (N), Young, F. P., Jr. (N).
Mesozoic: Ager, D. V. (P), Campbell, J. D. (A, Oc), Crickmay, C. H. (N), Hancock,
M. J. (P), Lieb, F., Owen, E. F. (W), Ramsdell, R. C., Selli, R., Stehli, F. G.,
Sylvester-Bradley, P. C., Tokuyama, A. (P).
Cenozoic: Allan, R. S. (A), Berry, S. S., Elliott, G. F. (P), Uozumi, S. (P).
* * * * *
ACROTRETACEA - fossils: Rowell, A. J. (P:?).
ARTICULATA - fossils: Jaanusson, V. (P:?), Weiss, M. P. (P:N).
ATRYPACEA - fossils: Struve, W. (P:P).
CRANIACEA - fossils: Rowell, A. J. (P-C:?).
INARTICULATA: Chuang, S. H. (W), Rowell, A. J.
　Larvae: Rowell, A. J.
DALMANELLACEA - fossils: Biernat, G. (P:P), Walmsley, V. G. (P:?).
ORTHACEA - fossils: Biernat, G. (P:P), Solle, G. (P:P), Young, R. S. (F:N).
PRODUCTACEA - fossils: Maxwell, W. H. G. (P:A).
RHYNCHONELLACEA - fossils: Schmidt, H. (F:P).
SIPHONOTRETACEA - fossils: Rowell, A. J. (P:?).
SPIRIFERACEA - fossils: Maxwell, W. H. G. (P:A), Solle, G. (P:P), Struve, W. (P:P).
STROPHOMENACEA - fossils: Sokolskaya, A. N. (P:P), Solle, G. (P:P), Spjeldnaes, N. (P:?).
SYNTROPHIOIDEA - fossils: Biernat, G. (P:N, P).
TELOTREMATA - fossils: McKerrow, W. S. (M:P).
TEREBRATULACEA - fossils: Middlemiss, F. A. (M:P), Stehli, F. G. (P:?).
TEREBRATELLACEA: Elliott, G. F.　FOSSILS: Elliott, G. F.
* * * * *
Camarotoechiidae - fossils: Veevers, J. J. (P:A).
Chonetidae - fossils: Sokolskaya, A. N. (P:P).
Lingulidae: Chuang, S. H. (W).
　Larvae: Chuang, S. H. (W).
　Fossils: Cave, R. (P:?), Chuang, S. H. (F:N, P).
Productidae - fossils: Coogan, A. H. (P:N), Goldring, R. (P:P), Sarytcheva, T. G. (P:?).
Rhynchonellidae - fossils: Burri, F. (M:P), Parkinson, D. (P:P), Sartenaer, P. (P:W).
Spiriferidae - fossils: Coogan, A. H. (P:N), Dunlop, G. (P:P), George, T. N. (P:?), Sartenaer,
　P. (P:W), Thomas, G. (P:P), Vandercammen, A. C. A. (P-M:?).
Syringothyridae - fossils: Sokolskaya, A. N. (P:P).
Terebratulidae - fossils: Ochoterena, H. (F:Nt).

MOLLUSCA

No other data: Addicott, W. O., Allabough, E. A., Jr., Allan, J., Allen, C. A., Alves, W.,
Ankel, W. E., Azevedo Martins, E., de Bartolomé, J. F. M., Baughman, J. L., Beets,
C., Bloomer, H. H., Bronson, A. B., Brookes, A. E., Brouwer, J., Brown, D. E.,
Chavan, A., Chestnut, A. F., Crofts, D. R., Dedman, M., De Mesa, P., Deslandes, N.,
Doello-Jurado, M., Draga, K. L., Ellis, A. E., Emura, S., Erickson, C. W., Evans,
A. G. T., Feliksiak, S., Fowler, T. G., Franco, A. B., Fretter, V., Gabriel, C. J.,
Giglioli, M. E. C., Gines, H. C., Graham, A., Haan, C., Harbison, A., Hartley, T.,
Ikebe, N., Iliffe, C., Iredale, T., Jodot, P., Kaas, P., Kellner, S., Kennelly, D. H.,
Kinoshita, T., Knaben, N., Lee, C. B., MacCormick, J. R., MacFarland, O. H.,
Machin, J., Machon, R. P., de Medina, N. P., Mermod, G., Miles, L. O., Morrison,
J. P. E., Oliver, M., Perez Farfante de Canet, I., Petit, G., Prashad, B., Ramsden,
C. T., Rao, S. H., Rasmussen, E., Ray, H. C., Ricketts, H. O., Riveros Zuñiga, F.,
Robertson, J. D., Rombouts, A., Saulgz, P., Servaas, M., Smith, M., Stevenson, A. G.,
Stoltenberg, N. C., Swaneveld, C., Thaanum, D., Thake, C., Tittoni, E., Trechmann,
C. T., Urbański, J., Ureta, E., Verhaeghe, M. A. P., Verhaeghe, R., Warwick, T.,
White, K. M., Wind, J.

World: Boettger, C. R. , van Bruggen, A. C. , Duarte, E. , Hill, H. R. , Horvath, A. ,
Jaeckel, S. G. A. , Jr. , Salisbury, A. E. , Yen, J. T-C.
Nearctic: Allison, E. C. , Andrews, J. D. , Driver, E. C. , Harry, H. W. , McMillin, H. C. ,
Parker, R. H. , Porter, H. J. , Touring, R. M. , Wesendunk, P. , Hanks, R. W.
Neotropical: Aguayo, C. G. , Barker, R. W. , Duarte, E. , Easton, W. H. , Klappenbach,
M. A. , McMillin, H. C. , Olsson, A. A. , Parker, R. H.
Palearctic: Adam, W. , Bloklander, A. , van der Burg, W. J. , Easton, W. H. ,
van der Feen, W. S. S. , Grensted, L. W. , Horvath, A. , Inaba, A. , Jaeckel,
S. G. A. , Jr. , Kaltenbach, H. , Morton, J. E. , Muntaner, A. , Nos, P. , Oyama, K. ,
Rutllant, J. , Settepasgi, F. , Trueman, E. R., Wiktor, W.
Ethiopian: Hemming, C. F. , Pringle, J. A.
Oriental: Oyama, K.
Australian: Buick, W. G. , Cotton, B. C. , Crofts, J. , Dell, R. K. , Laseron, C. F. ,
LeSouef, J. C. , Morton, J. E. , Richardson, E. S. , Smith, E.
Oceania: Boerner, C. , Dell, R. K. , Oyama, K. , Spicer, V. D. P.
Antarctic: Dell, R. K. , Powell, A. W. B.
Fossils, no ages: Allabough, E. A. , Jr. , Chavan, A. , Desio, A. (P), Dusenbury, A. N. , Jr. (Nt),
Olsson, A. A. (N), Oyama, K. (O).
Paleozoic: Caudri, C. M. B. , Chronic, J. , Ellison, R. L. (N), Hayasaka, I. , Nicolaus,
H. (P), Sieber, R. (W), Sloan, R. E. (N), Ware, S.
Mesozoic: Allison, E. C. (N), Botero-Arango, G. (Nt), Hantke, R. , van Hoepen, E. C. N. ,
Kellum, L. B. (N), Leonardi, P. (P), Marwick, J. (A), Murphy, M. A. (N), Olson, R. ,
Rosenkrantz, A. (N, P), Royo y Gomez, J. (Nt, P), Selli, R. , Sieber, R. (W), Trümpy, R.
Cenozoic: Allison, E. C. (N), Bloklander, A. (P), Boettger, C. R. (W), Castell, C. P. (P),
Charig, A. J. , Cooke, C. W. (N), Ferreira, C. S. (Nt), Gale, H. R. (N), Grant,
U. S. , 4th. (N), Itoigawa, J. (P), Kanno, S. (P), Kellum, L. B. (N), Kotaka, T. (P),
Malatesta, A. (P), Mizuno, A. (P), Oleksyshyn, J. (N, P), Ômori, M. (P), Oyama,
K. (P, O), Richardson, E. S. (A), Sieber, R. (W), Touring, R. M. (N).
Tertiary: Addicott, W. O. , Afshar, F. A. (P), Baldwin, E. M. (N), Bartsch, P. (W),
Barwick, A. R. (N), Bloklander, A. (P), van der Burg, W. J. (P), Caudri, C. M. B. (Nt),
Cotton, B. C. (A), Curry, D. (P), Gardner, J. (N, AO), Hodson, F. (Nt), Kent, L. S. (N),
Ladd, H. S. (Oc), Ludbrook, N. H. (A), Makiyama, J. (P), Marks, J. G. (N, Nt),
Montanaro-Gallitelli, E. (P), Olsson, A. A. (Nt), Powell, A. W. B. (A), Pratviel,
A. M. (P), Rosenkrantz, A. (N, P), Royo y Gomez, J. (Nt, P), Russell, L. S. (N),
Seneš, J. (P), Socin, C. (P), Stinton, F. C. (P), Weaver, D. E. W. (N), Wilson, D. ,
Winkler, V. (Nt).
Quaternary: Adam, W. (P), Cuerda Barceló, J. (P), Horvath, A. (W), Jaeckel,
S. G. A. , Jr. (W), Laursen, D. (Arc), Parker, R. H. (Nt, AO), Settepasgi, F. (P).
Marine, no locality: Berry, S. S. , Boerman, D. J. , Franc, A. , Koch, H. J. , Stickney, A. P. ,
Teissier, G.
World: Blok, A. , Clarke, A. H. , Jr. , Dodge, H. , Friedrich, H. , Sanchez, S. F. ,
Schuitema, A. K.
Nearctic: Baker, N. W. , Chace, E. P. , Clarke, A. H. , Jr. , Eyerdam, W. J. , Gregg, W. O. ,
Hanks, R. W. , Hulings, N. , Jacobs, F. E. , Jacobson, M. K. , McGinty, T. L. , Schwengel,
J. S. , Smith, A. G. , Valentine, J. W.
Neotropical: Alayo Dalmau, P. , Contreras, F. , Jaume, M. , McGinty, T. L. , Moore, D. ,
Rios, E. C. , de la Torre, A. , Warmke, G.
Palearctic: Azuma, M. , Cambridge, P. , Coxhead, P. , Cuerda Barceló, J. , Fischer,
P. H. , Kanamaru, T. , Kisch, B. A. , Kono, H. , Mars, P. , Priolo, O. , Purchon, R. D. ,
Ruggieri, G. , Schuitema, A. K. , Stratton, L. W.
Ethiopian: Collignon, J. , van Hoepen, E. C. N. , Knudsen, J. , Le Roux, P. J. , Nickles, M.
Oriental: Abbott, R. T. , van der Feen, W. S. S. , Fischer, P. H. , Horikoshi, M. , Rehder,
H. A.
Australian: Ayres, W. S. , Barker, C. E. , Macpherson, J. H. , Marwick, J. , McMichael,
D. F. , Powell, A. W. B.
Oceania: Abbott, R. T. , Bryan, E. H. , Burch, J. Q. , van der Feen, W. S. S. , Fischer,
P. H. , Horikoshi, M. , McMichael, D. F. , Rehder, H. A. , Richert, T. H.
Atlantic Ocean: Burdon-Jones, C. , Clench, W. J. , Foster, R. W. , Freeman, H. L. ,
Liliefelt, K. G. , Robertson, R. , Turner, R. D. , Weber, J. A.
Arctic: Chamberlin, J. L. , MacGinitie, N.
Fossils, no age: Berry, S. S. , Contreras, F. (Nt).
Mesozoic: Mongin, D. (P), de Oliveiro, P. E. (Nt).
Cenozoic: Cambridge, P. (P), Carcelles, A. R. (Nt), Fischer, P. H. (P), Hertlein,
L. G. (N), Hulings, N. (N), Kanehara, K. (P), Ruggieri, G. (P), van der Slik, L. (P),
Weisbord, N. E. (Nt).
Tertiary: Cunha, O. R. (Nt), Doney, H. H. (N), Mongin, D. (N, P), Trumbull, E. J. (N),
Woodring, W. P. (Nt).
Quaternary: Chace, E. P. (N), Mars, P. (P), Trumbull, E. J. (N), Valentine, J. W. (N).

21

Brackish-water, fossils: Papp, A. (T:?).
Fresh-water, no locality: Alkins, W. E. , Blume, W.
    World: Blok, A. , Friedrich, H. , Haas, F. , Klemm, W. , Sanchez, S. F. , Schuitema, A. K.
    Nearctic: Baily, J. L. , Clarke, A. H. , Jr. , Clench, W. J. , Dawley, C. , Drake, R. J. ,
        Gregg, W. O. , Roscoe, E. J. , Russell, L. S. , Smith, A. G. , Solem, G. A. ,
        Van der Schalie, H. , Walter, W. M. , Webb, G. R. , Wurtz, C. B.
    Neotropical: Contreras, F. , Drake, R. J. , Jaume, M. , Klappenbach, M. A. , Pain, T. ,
        Solem, G. A.
    Palearctic: Akramowski, N. N. , Altimira Aleu, C. , Azuma, M. , Biggs, H. E. J. ,
        Devidts, J. , Grahle, H-O. , Hunter, W. D. R. , Ingram, H. A. P. , Jaeckel, S. H. ,
        Klimowicz, H. , Knipper, H. , Kuroda, T. , Llabador, F. , Mandahl-Barth, G. , Mozley,
        A. , Nilsson, A. , Priolo, O. , Schlesch, H. , Schlickum, W. R. , Schuitema, A. K. ,
        Stratton, L. W. , Verdcourt, B. , Žadin, V. I. , Zeissler, H.
    Ethiopian: Adam, W. , Bequaert, J. C. , Fischer-Piette, E. , Knipper, H. , Mandahl-Barth,
        G. , Mozley, A. , Pain, T. , Verdcourt, B.
    Oriental: van der Feen, W. S. S. , Kuroda, T. , Satyamurti, T. S. , Solem, G. A. ,
        Villadolid, D.
    Australian: McMichael, D. F.
    Oceania: van der Feen, W. S. S. , Franc, A. , McMichael, D. F. , Solem, G. A.
    Arctic: Mozley, A. , Schlesch, H.
  Fossils, no age: Contreras, F. (Nt), Hanna, G. D. (W), Schlickum, W. R. (P).
    Mesozoic: La Rocque, J. A. (N), Zhou, M-Z. (P).
    Cenozoic: Akramowski, N. N. (P), Carcelles, A. R. (Nt), Franzen, D. , La Rocque,
        J. A. (N).
    Tertiary: Papp, A. , Taylor, D. W. (N), Zhou, M-Z. (P).
    Quaternary: Adam, W. (E), Dehm, R. (P, E, O, A, Oc), Drake, R. J. (N, Nt), Grahle,
        H-O. (P), Roscoe, E. J. (N), Zeissler, H. (P).
Terrestrial, no locality: Alkins, W. E. , Blume, W.
    World: Baker, H. B. , Blok, A. , Friedrich, H. , Haas, F. , Jacobson, M. K. , Klemm, W. ,
        Sanchez, S. F. , Schuitema, A. K.
    Nearctic: Alzona, C. , Beetle, D. E. , Chace, E. P. , Dawley, C. , Drake, R. J. , Gregg,
        W. O. , Hinshaw, M. E. , Mead, A. R. , Roscoe, E. J. , Russell, L. S. , Smith, A. G. ,
        Solem, G. A. , Walton, M. L.
    Neotropical: Alayo Dalmau, P. , Clench, W. J. , Drake, R. J. , Eyerdam, W. J. , Hinshaw,
        M. E. , Jaume, M. , Klappenbach, M. A. , Pain, T. , Solem, G. A. , Turner, R. D.
    Palearctic: Akramowski, N. N. , Altimira Aléu, C. , Alzona, C. , Azuma, M. , Biggs,
        H. E. J. , Devidts, J. , Ingram, H. A. P. , Jaeckel, S. H. , Knipper, H. , Kono, H. ,
        Kühnelt, W. , Kuroda, T. , Likharev, I. M. , Llabador, F. , Lohmander, H. ,
        Mandahl-Barth, G. , Nilsson, A. , Ortiz de Zárate, A. , Priolo, O. , Schlesch, H. ,
        Schlickum, W. R. , Schuitema, A. K. , Stratton, L. W. , Verdcourt, B. , Zeissler, H.
    Ethiopian: Adam, W. , Bequaert, J. C. , Fischer-Piette, E. , Knipper, H. ,
        Ortiz de Zárate, A. , Pain, T. , Verdcourt, B.
    Oriental: van der Feen, W. S. S. , Kuroda, T. , Laidlaw, F. F. , Madge, E. H. , Satyamurti,
        T. S. , Solem, G. A.
    Australian: Barker, C. E. , Gardner, N. W. , McMichael, D. F. , Powell, A. W. B.
    Oceania: Clench, W. J. , van der Feen, W. S. S. , Franc, A. , McMichael, D. F. , Solem, G. A.
    Arctic: Schlesch, H.
  Fossils: Adam, W. (Q:E), Akramowski, N. N. (Q:P), Chace, E. P. (Q:N), Dehm,
    R. (Q:P, E, O, A, Oc), Drake, R. J. (Q:N, Nt), Franzen, D. (C:?), La Rocque,
    J. A. (M-C:N), Roscoe, E. J. (Q:N), Schlickum, W. R. (F:P), Taylor, D. W. (T:N),
    Zeissler, H. (Q:P).
Larvae: Carriker, M. R. (N).
Borers: Edmondson, C. H. (PO), Horvath, C. , Turner, R. D. (W).
Prehistoric: Drake, R. J. (N, Nt).

Amphineura
(Polyplacophora)

No other data: Berry, S. S. (W), Hunter, E. B. (N, Nt), Leloup, E. , Lyons, R. B. (N),
    Robertson, R. (AO), Smith, A. G. , Stohler, R. (W), Taki, I. (O, A, Oc),
    Yakovleva, A. M. (P).
Fossils: Berry, S. S. (F:N), Horný, R. (P:P), Smith, A. G.

* * * * *

Chitonidae: Johns, P. M. (A).
Mopaliidae: Lyons, R. B. (N).

Cephalopoda

No other data: Adam, W. (W), Akimuschkin, J. J. (PO), Berry, S. S. (W), Boolootian, R. A. (W), Foster, R. W. (AO), Galbraith, I. C. J., Kumpf, H. E. (Nt), McConnaughey, B. H. (N), Morales, E. (P), Muus, B. (AO), Otterlind, G. (P), Reyment, R., Sacarrão, G. F. (P), Taki, I. (P), Thore, S. (W), Voss, G. L. (W), Wirz, K. (P), Ximenez-Trianon, I.

Fossils, no age: Basse de Ménorval, E., Le Blanc, J., Peck, J. H. (F:N), Teves, J. S., Voglev, E. A.

    Paleozoic: Branson, C. C. (N), Collinson, C. W. (N, Nt, P), Conlin, J. P. (W), Gutschick, R. C. (N), Jones, D. G. (P), Nelson, S. J. (N), Reyment, R., Sturgeon, M. T. (N), Unkelsbay, A. G., Young, F. P., Jr. (N), Youngquist, W. L.

    Mesozoic: Bomford, G. (P), Cobban, W. A. (N), Conlin, J. P. (W), Johnston, F. N. (W), Muller, S. W., Reyment, R., Scott, W. F. (N).

    Cenozoic: Hinsch, W. (P), Malicoat, A. F., Reyment, R.

          * * * * *

AMMONITOIDEA - fossils, no age: Besairie, H. (E), Conlin, J. P. (W), Kasakova, V. P., Moreman, W. L. (N), Renngarten, V. P. (P), Young, K. P.

    Paleozoic: Crickmay, C. H. (N), Furnish, W. M., Harker, P. (N, Arc), House, M. R. (P), Lehmann, U., Miller, A. K., Müller, K. J., Schindewolf, O. H., Stoyanow, A. (N, Nt, P).

    Mesozoic: Barthel, K. W. (P), Basse de Ménorval, E., Brunnschweiler, R. O. (O, A, Oc), Collignon, G. (P, E), Crickmay, C. H. (N), Frebold, H. (N, P, Arc), Furnish, W. M., Howarth, M. K. (P), Imlay, R. W. (N), Jeletzky, J. A. (N), Kühn, O., Leanza, A. F. (W), Mauberge, D. L. (P), Parnes, A. (P), Reyment, R., Shannon, E. C. (Nt).

    Triassic: Kummel, B., Stoyanow, A. (N, Nt, P), Tozer, E. T.

    Jurassic: Arnould-Saget, -, Callomon, J. H., Donovan, D. T., Frebold, H. (W), Hoffman, K. (W), Hölder, H. (P), Krimholz, G. J. (P), Lieb, F., Mouterde, A. R., Tintant, H., Trümpy, R. (P), Westermann, G. A. G. (W), Zeiss, A. (P).

    Cretaceous: Benavides-Caceres, V. E., Breistroffer, M. (W), Bürgl, H. (Nt), Drushits, V. V. (P), Dubourdieu, G. (P), Hancock, M. J. (P), van Hoepen, E. C. N. (E), Humphrey, W. E., Matsumoto, T. (N, P), Murphy, M. A. (N), Nagy, I. Z., Najdin, D. P. (P), O'Gara, W. T. (N, Nt), Packard, E. L. (N), Rodda, P. U. (N, P), Sarkar, S. S. (P, O), Sornay, J. (P), Stelck, C. R. (N), Stoyanow, A. (N, Nt, P), Waage, K. M. (N), Wright, C. W.

    Cenozoic: Rodda, P. U. (N, P).

BACTRITACEA - fossils: Erben, H. K. (P:?).

BELEMNOIDEA - fossils: Besairie, H. (F:E), Hancock, M. J. (M:P), Kongiel, R. (M:P), Krimholz, G. J. (M:P), Pugaczewska, H. (M:P).

COLEOIDEA (Dibranchiata) - fossils: Bairstow, L., Flower, R. H. (P:?), Jeletzky, J. A. (P-Q:?).

DECAPODA: Bidder, A. (Ant.), Fields, G. (PO), Squires, H. J. (N).

GONIATITACEA - fossils: Bisat, W. S. (P:P), Clark, D. L. (P:?), Currie, E. (P:P), Elias, M. K. (P:N, P), Erben, H. K. (P:?), Hodson, F., Nicolaus, H. (P:P), Sadlick, W. (P:N), Taylor, P. W. (P:N, P), Walliser, O. H. (P:W).

HAPLOCERATACEAE - fossils: Ziegler, B. (M:?).

NAUTILOIDEA: Kummel, B., Miller, A. K.

    Fossils, no age: Shimansky, V. N.

    Paleozoic: Cecioni, G. (Nt), Flower, R. H., Hansman, R. H. (N), Holland, C. H. (P), Kobayashi, T. (P), Miller, A. K., Sweet, W. C., Teichert, C., Turner, J. S. (P).

    Mesozoic: Avnimelech, M., Kummel, B., Miller, A. K.

    Cenozoic: Avnimelech, M., Miller, A. K.

OCTOPODA: Kumpf, H. E. (AO), Pickford, G. E. (O), Townsley, S. J. (O, Oc).

PERISPHINCTACEAE - fossils: Ziegler, B. (M:?).

SCAPHITACEAE - fossils: Schmid, F. (M:P).

TEUTHOIDEA - fossils: Muus, B. (F:W).

VAMPYROMORPHA: Pickford, G. E. (O).

          * * * * *

Bactritidae - fossils: Horný, R. (P:P).

Belemnitellidae - fossils: Najdin, D. P. (M:P).

Belemnitidae - fossils: Schmid, F. (M:P), Stevens, G. R. (M:N, Nt, E, O, Oc).

Cardioceratidae - fossils: Zeiss, A. (M:?).

Clymeniidae - fossils: Selwood, E. B. (P:?).

Dactylioceratidae - fossils: Sylvester-Bradley, P. C. (M:?).

Dawsonoceratidae - fossils: Horný, R. (P:P).

Lytoceratidae - fossils: Clark, D. L. (M:?).

Oppeliidae - fossils: Zeiss, A. (F:W).

Sepiidae: Carter, A. N. (A).

No other data: Bartha, F. , Edlauer, A. , Galkin, U. I.
    World: Gavala, J. , Rutllant, J.
    Nearctic: Eggleton, F. E. , Glen, W. , Kanakoff, G. P. , Matteson, M. R. , Mattox, N. T. ,
       Merrill, A. S. , Palmer, K. V. , Stohler, R. , Swan, E. F.
    Neotropical: Figueiras, A. , Palmer, K. V.
    Palearctic: Allen, J. A. , Avnimelech, M. , Bolé, J. , Drozdowski, A. , Grossu, A. ,
       Koyama, T. , Lever, J. , San Nicolas, E.
    Paleotropical: Eyerdam, W. J. (A, Oc), Fleming, C. A. (A), Gardner, N. W. (Oc), Keen,
       A. M. (PO), Koyama, T. (Oc, Ant), Laseron, C. F. (A), Marche-Marchad, I.(E),
       Tinker, S. W. (O, Oc).
Fossils, no age: Alencáster de Cserna, G. (Nt), Bock, W. , Fleming, C. A. (A).
    Paleozoic: Bond, G. (E), Boucot, A. J. (W), Bowsher, A. L. (N), Cox, L. R. (W),
       Dickins, J. M. (W), Fisher, D. W. (N), Jones, D. G. (P), Kent, L. S. (N), Knight, J. B. ,
       Linsley, R. M. (N), Pope, J. K. (N), Rossouw, P. J. (E), Sartenaer, P. , Sturgeon,
       M. T. (N), Talent, J. A. , Waterhouse, J. B. (A), Winters, S. S. (N), Yochelson, E. L.
    Mesozoic: Bond, G. (E), Collignon, G. (P, E), Cox, L. R. (W), King, L. C. (E),
       von der Osten, E. , Pipiringos, G. N. (N), Popenoe, W. P. (N), Ramsdell, R. C. ,
       Richards, E. F. (N), Rocker, A. W. (N), Rodda, P. U. (N, P), Sohl, N. F. (N),
       Yen, J. T-C. (N, P).
    Cenozoic: Bürgl, H. (Nt), Du Bar, J. R. (N), Glen, W. (N), Hatai, K. , (Oc), Hayasaka,
       S. (P), King, L. C. (E), Korobkov, I. A. (P), Nyi, N. (O), Palmer, K. V. (N, Nt),
       Rodda, P. U. (N, P), Švagrovský, J. (P).
    Tertiary: Aoki, S. (P), van der Burg, W. J. (P), Cox, L. R. (W), Durham, J. W. (N, Nt),
       Gallitelli, E. M. (P), Krach, W. (P), Lumsden, W. (N), MacNeil, F. S. (N, P),
       Nuttall, C. P. (W), Ozaki, H. (P), Shuto, T. (P), Smith, D. J. (N), Vella, P. (A),
       Yen, J. T-C. (N, P).
    Quaternary: Avnimelech, M. (P).
Marine, World: Barker, R. W. , Bullis, H. , Fischer, P. H.
    New World: Alexander, R. C. (N), Coomans, H. E. (Nt), Kincaid, T. (N), Rutsch,
       R. F. (N, Nt), Saul, L. R. (N), Smith, A. B. (N).
    Old World: Amio, M. (P), Dance, S. P. (IO), Fujie, T. (P), Grigg, J. A. (A), Merklin,
       R. L. (P), Robertson, R. (Oc), Rutsch, R. F. (P), Satyamurti, T. S. (O), Uozumi,
       S. (P), Weaver, C. S. (Oc).
    Atlantic Ocean: Bullis, H.
    Fossils, Paleozoic: Nelson, L. A.
    Mesozoic: Kamada, Y. (P), Peck, J. H. (N), Richards, H. G. (N), Saul, L. R. (N),
       Van de Poel, L. (W).
    Cenozoic: Fujie, T. (P), Glibert, M. (P), Kamada, Y. (P), Smith, A. B. (N),
       Uozomi, S. (P).
    Tertiary: Peck, J. H. (N), Richards, H. G. (N), Rutsch, R. F. (N, Nt, P), Schenck,
       H. G. (N, P), Susuki, T. (N).
    Quaternary: Merklin, R. L. (P), Richards, H. G. (N), Wagner, F. J. E. (N).
Non-marine, fossils: Hässlein, L. (Q:P), Kerney, M. P. (Q:P), Krolopp, E. (Q:P), Ložek,
       V. (C:P), Moore, R. G. (M-T:N), Taylor, D. W. (Q:N).
Estuarine: Allen, J. F. (N), Amos, W. H. (N).
Fresh-water: Arias C. , S. , DeWitt, R. M. , Matëkin, P. V.
    World: Abbott, R. T. , Venmans, L. A. W. C.
    Nearctic: Branson, B. A. , Cheatum, E. P. , Hahnert, W. F. , Jones, D. T. , Michelson, B. S.
       Miller, R. B. , Parodiz, J. J. , Taylor, D. W. , Waldén, H. , Wayne, W. J.
    Neotropical: Michelson, B. S. , Parodiz, J. J.
    Palearctic: Alvarez Sanchez, J. , Dance, S. P. , Fraga de Azevedo, J. , Hässlein, L. ,
       Kerney, M. P. , Krolopp, E. , Ložek, V. , Meise, W. , Økland, J. , Plate, H-P. , Sparks,
       B. W. , Waldén, H. , Watson, H.
    Ethiopian: Fraga de Azevedo, J. , Watson, H.
    Oriental: Dance, S. P.
    Fossils: Jones, D. T. (Q:N), Parodiz, J. J. (Q:Nt), Sparks, B. W. (Q:P), Wayne, W. J. (Q:N).
Terrestrial: Arias C. , S. , DeWitt, R. M. , Matëkin, P. V.
    World: Venmans, L. A. W. C. , Zilch, A.
    Nearctic: Branson, B. A. , Bushey, C. J. , Cheatum, E. P. , Hahnert, W. F. , Hubricht, L. ,
       Ingram, W. M. , Jones, D. T. , Miller, R. B. , Rawls, H. C. , Waldén, H. , Wayne, W. J. ,
       Wurtz, C. B.
    Neotropical: Parodiz, J. J. , Thomé, J. W. , Thompson, F. G. , Wurtz, C. B.
    Palearctic: Dance, S. P. , Hässlein, L. , Kerney, M. P. , Krolopp, E. , Ložek, V. ,
       Meise, W. , Plate, H-P, , Riedel, A. , Sparks, B. W. , Waldén, H. , Watson, H.
    Paleotropical: Dance, S. P. (O), Watson, H. (E).
    Fossils: Conkin, J. E. (Q:?), Jones, D. T. (Q:N), Papp, A. (T:?), Parodiz, J. J. (Q:Nt),

Sparks, B. W. (Q:P), Waldén, H. (F:P), Wayne, W. J. (Q:N).
Parasitic: Ivanov, A. V. (W).
* * * * *

APLYSIACEA: Macnae, W. (O, Oc).
ASPIDOBRANCHIA: Robertson, R. (N, Nt).
BASOMMATOPHORA: Van Eeden, J. A. (E).
BELLEROPHONTACEA - fossils: Horný, R. (P:P).
HETEROPODA: Forrest, J. E. (AO, P, Ant), Tchindonova, J. G. (IO, PO), Tokioka, T.
LOXONEMATACEA - Fossils: Horný, R. (P:P).
NERITACEA: Ĥunter, W. D. R. (Nt).
NUDIBRANCHIA: Aboul-Ela, I. (P), Agersborg, H. P. K. (W), Engle, H. (P), Gohar, H. A. F. (P),
    Lance, J. R. (N), Macnae, W. (O, Oc), Moore, G. M. (N), Risso-Dominguez, C. J. (W),
    Russell, H. D. (N), Sanchez, S. F. (P), Steinberg, J. (N), Thompson, T. E. (P).
OPISTHOBRANCHIATA, no locality: Baba, K. , Evans, R. G. , Odhner, N. H. , Marcus, Eve. ,
    Pruvot-Fol, A.
  World: Eales, N. B. , Lemche, H. , Marcus, Ern.
  Nearctic: Milburn, W. P.
  Palearctic: Forrest, J. E. , Gantes, H. , Habe, T. , Inaba, A. , Portmann, A. ,
    Starmühlner, F.
  Paleotropical: Burn, R..F. (A, Oc), Forrest, J. E. (Ant), Pilgrim, R. (A), Rao, K. V. (O),
    Starmühlner, F. (E), Steinberg, J. (Oc).
PLEUROTOMARIACEA - fossils: Sadlick, W. (P:N).
PROSOBRANCHIATA: Habe, T. (P), Liliefelt, K. G. (P), Moscalev, L. I. (W).
  Marine: Starmühlner, F. (P).
  Fresh-water: Quick, H. E. (P), Starmühlner, F. (P, E).
  Terrestrial: Licharev, I. M. (P), Quick, H. E. (P).
  Larvae: Laursen, D. (N, AO), Thorson, G. (W).
PTEROPODA: Howard, A. D. (N), Menzies, R. J. , Morton, J. E. (W), Tchindonova,
    J. G. (IO, PO), Tokioka, T.
  Fossils: Avnimelech, M. (T:P), Menzies, R. J. (Q:?).
PULMONATA, World: Baker, N. B.
  Nearctic: Burch, J. B. , MacMillan, G. K. , Myer, D. G. , Oughton, J. , Webb, G. R.
  Palearctic: Alvarez Sanchez, J. , Kaiser, P. , Licharev, I. M. , Paget, O. , Pfitzner, I. ,
    Quick, H. E. , Soós, L. , Waterston, A. R.
  Paleotropical: Buick, W. G. (A), Butot, L. J. M. (O), Cumber, R. A. (A), Kondo, Y. (Oc).
  Fossils: Frankel, L. (Q:N).
SACOGLOSSA: Macnae, W. (O, Oc).
STYLOMMATOPHORA: Karlin, E. J. (N, P), Michelson, B. S. (N).
TECTIBRANCHIA - fossils: Rosenkrantz, A. (M-T:N, P).
TENTACULITIDA - fossils: Bouček, B. (F:P).
* * * * *

Achatinellidae: Welch, A. A. (Oc).
Achatinidae: Mead, A. R. (E).
Acmaeidae: Fritchman, H. (N), Macpherson, J. H. (O, Oc), McKey-Fender, D. (N), Moscalev,
    L. I. (W), Old, W. E. , Jr. (N).
Amphiperatidae: Schilder, F. A. (W).   FOSSILS: Schilder, F. A. (F:W).
Ampullariidae: Arias C. , S. (Nt).
Ancylidae: Basch, P. F. (N).
Aplysiidae: Eales, N. B. (W).
Arionidae: Altena, C. O. R. , Mead, A. R. (N), Wiktor, A. (P).
Buccinidae: Golikov, A. N. (W).
Bulimulidae: Weyrauch, W. (Nt).
Bulinidae: Najarian, H. H. (P).
Calyptraeidae: Taki, I. (O, Oc).
Camaenidae: Archer, A. F. (N, Nt), Arias C. , S. (Nt).
Carinariidae: Okutani, K. (P).
Cepoliidae: Archer, A. F. (N, Nt).
Cerionidae: Hummelinck, P. W. (Nt).
Cerithiidae: Gaillard, J. M. , Old, W. E. , Jr. (N).
Chilinidae: Risso-Dominguez, C. J. (Nt).   FOSSILS: Risso-Dominguez, C. J. (F:Nt).
Clausiliidae: Arias C. , S. (Nt), Gerini, F. (W), Loosjes, F. E. (W), Weyrauch, W. (Nt).
Cochlicopidae: Berger, L. (P).
Conidae: Boswell, H. (W), D'Attilio, A. (O, Oc), Greene, K. W. (Oc), Kohn, A. J. (IO, Oc).
Cyclophoridae: Arias C. , S. (Nt).
Cypraeidae: Boerner, C. (Oc), Burgess, C. M. (W), Cate, C. N. (W), Gavala, J. (W), Griffiths,
    R. J. (W), Ingram, W. M. , Kay, E. A. (Oc), Ostergaard, J. M. (Trop), Schilder,
    F. A. (W), Summers, R. (W), Verdcourt, B. (E).
  Fossils: Ingram, W. M. (M:R:?), Schilder, F. A. (F:W).

25

MOLLUSCA, Gastropoda (continued)

Ellobiidae: · Berger, L. (P), Holle, P. A. (AO), Morton, J. E. (W), Paulson, E. (N, Nt, Oc).
Epitoniidae: Kerslake, J. (A).
Eratoidae: Schilder, F. A. (W). FOSSILS: Schilder, F. A. (F:W).
Haliotidae: Cox, L. R. (N), Ino, T. (PO), Talmadge, R. R. (W).
Helicellidae: Altimira Aléu, C. (P).
Helicidae: Comfort, A. (W), Paulson, E. (N), Sacchi, C. (P).
Helicinidae: Arias C., S. (Nt).
Hyolithidae - fossils: Bouček, B. (P: P), Fisher, D. W. (P:N).
Hydrobiidae (Bythinellidae): Berry, E. G. (N, Nt, E), Bolling, W. (P).
Janthinidae: Laursen, D. (W).
Lacunidae: Rosewater, J. (AO).
Lepetidae: Moscalev, L. I. (W).
Limacidae: Altena, C. O. R., Lupu, D. (P), Mead, A. R. (N), Waldén, H. (N, P), Wiktor, A. (P).
Littorinidae: Golikov, A. N. (AO, PO, Arc).
Lymnaeidae: Arias C., S. (Nt), Hubendick, B. (W), Itagaki, H. (P), Jackiewicz, M. (P),
     McCraw, B. (N), Walter, H. J. (W).
Melaniidae: Bouillon, J. (E).
Melongenidae: Magalhaes, H. (N).
Muricidae: Boswell, H. (W), D'Attilio, A. (O, Oc), Golikov, A. N. (AO, PO, Arc).
Nassidae: Golikov, A. N. (AO, PO, Arc).
Nerineidae - fossils: Karczewski, L. (F:P).
Olividae: Olsson, A. A. (Nt), Zeigler, R. (W).
Orthalicidae: Arias C., S. (Nt).
Patellidae: Macpherson, J. H. (O, Oc), Moscalev, L. I. (W), Old, W. E., Jr. (E).
Physidae: Arias C., S. (Nt).
Planorbidae: Arias C., S. (Nt), Barbose, F. A. S. (Nt, E), Berry, E. G. (N, Nt, E), Clarke,
     V. V. (E), Correa, R. R. (Nt), Hubendick, B., de Lucena, D. T. (Nt), Malek,
     E. T. A. (E), Paraense, W. L. (Nt), Schutte, C. H. J. (E), Starobogatov, Y. I. (W),
     Wright, C. A. (E).
Platyceratidae - fossils: Kopf, R. W. (P:N).
Pleuroceridae: Arias C., S. (Nt), Rosewater, J. (N).
Pleurotomariidae - fossils: Batten, R. L. (P-M:?).
Polygyridae: Archer, A. F. (N, Nt), Pahl, G. (N), Webb, G. R. (N, Nt).
     Fossils: Webb, G. R. (F:N, Nt).
Pomatiasidae: Arias C., S. (Nt), Hummelinck, P. W. (Nt).
Pterotrachaeidae: Okutani, K. (P).
Pupillidae: Altimira Aléu, C. (P), Arias C., S. (Nt).
Rissoidae: Desjardins, M. FOSSILS: Desjardins, M.
Siliguariidae: Morton, J. E. (W).
Stomatellidae: Talmadge, R. R. (W).
Streptaxidae: Arias C., S. (Nt).
Strombidae: Morton, J. E. (W), Old, W. E., Jr. (O, Oc).
Strophocheilidae: Arias C., S. (Nt).
Succineidae: Arias C., S. (Nt), Miles, C. D. (N), Odhner, N. H.
Thaisidae: Old, W. E., Jr. (O, Oc).
Thiaridae: Arias C., S. (Nt), Itagaki, H. (P).
Titiscaniidae: Taki, I. (O, Oc).
Tonnidae: Old, W. E., Jr. (O, Oc).
Trochidae: Clark, W. C. (A), Coats, R. E. (W).
Turridae: Gibson, T. G. (AO). FOSSILS: Gibson, T. G. (F:N, Nt).
Turritellidae: Johnston, I. M. (N). FOSSILS: Kotaka, T. (C:PO), Merriam, C. W. (M-C:N).
Urocoptidae: Arias C., S. (Nt), Hummelinck, P. W. (Nt).
Valvatidae: Lüttig, G. (P).
Vermetidae: Morton, J. E. (W).
Veronicellidae: Arias C., S. (Nt), Colosi, G. (W), Forcart, L. (W).
Vitrinellidae: Moore, D. (Nt).
Vitrinidae: Arias C., S. (Nt), Forcart, L. (P).
Viviparidae: Grahle, H-O. (P). FOSSILS: Grahle, H-O (Q: P).
Volutidae: Boswell, H. (W), Gardner, N. W. (W), Wistar, E. M.
Xenophoridae: Dance, S. P. (W).
Zonitidae: Forcart, L. (P), Riedel, A. (P).

Monoplacophora

No other data: Lemche, H. (W).
Fossils: Knight, J. B. (P:?).

Pelecypoda

No other data: Altena, C. O. R. , Edge, E. R. , Hori, M. , Koejwo, K. , Vokes, H. E.
    World: Gavala, J.
    Nearctic: Allen, J. F. , Glen, W. , Howard, A. D. , Keen, A. M. , Liliefelt, K. G. , Redick,
        T. F. , Swan, E. F.
    Neotropical: Foster, R. W. , Keen, A. M. , Pulley, T. E.
    Palearctic: Allen, J. A. , Andreu, B. , Habe, T. , Malatesta, A. , Okutani, K. , Owen, G. ,
        Tanaka, Y.
    Paleotropical: Fleming, C. A. (A), Liliefelt, K. G. (E, O), Marche-Marchad, I. (E),
        Rao, K. V. (O).
Fossils, no age: Agrawal, S. K. , Akiyama, M. , Alencaster de Cserna, G. (Nt), Fleming,
    C. A. (A), Stewart, R. B. , Walmsley, V. G.
    Paleozoic: Bond, G. (E), Cox, L. R. (W), Dickins, J. M. (W), Doney, H. H. (N), Jones,
        D. G. (P), La Rocque, J. A. (N), Newell, N. D. , Pohl, E. R. , Rossouw, P. J. (E),
        Ružička, B. (P), Sartenaer, P. , Stoyanow, A. (N, Nt, P), Tesmer, I. H. (N),
        Waterhouse, J. B. (A), Winters, S. S. (N), Wright, E. P. (N).
    Mesozoic: Amano, M. (P), Bond, G. (E), Collignon, G. (P, E), Cox, L. R. (W), Dickins,
        J. M. (A), Hayami, I. (P), Ichikawa, K. , King, L. C. (E), Miller, H. W. , Jr. (N),
        Muller, S. W. , Newell, N. D. , von der Osten, E. , Pipiringos, G. N. (N), Popenoe,
        W. P. (N), Pope, J. K. (N), Ramsdell, R. C. , Richards, E. F. (N), Rocker, A. W. (N),
        Rodda, P. U. (N, PO), Stoyanow, A. (N, Nt, P), Tokuyama, A. (P), Tozer, R. T. ,
        Vokes, H. E. , Waterhouse, J. B. (A), Yen, J. T-C. (N, P).
    Cenozoic: Du Bar, J. R. (N), Bürgl, H. (Nt), Glen, W. (N), Hatai, K. (PO), King, L. C. (E),
        Korobkov, I. A. (P), Nyi, N. (O), Palmer, K. V. (N, Nt), Rodda, P. U. (N, PO), Roger,
        J. (P), Švagrovský, J. (P), Vokes, H. E.
    Tertiary: Aoki, S. (P), Connell, J. F. L. (N), Cox, L. R. (W), Durham, J. W. (N, Nt),
        Eberzin, A. G. (W), Hinsch, W. (P), Krach, W. (P), Lumsden, W. (N), MacNeil,
        F. S. (N, PO), Ozaki, H. (P), Shuto, T. (P), Smith, D. J. (N), Vella, P. (A),
        Yen, J. T-C. (N, P).
    Quaternary: Feyling-Hanssen, R. W. (Arc).
Marine: Alexander, R. C. (N), Butot, L. J. M. (P), Coomans, H. E. (Nt), Dance, S. P. (IO),
    Figueras, A. (P), Fujie, T. (P), Keen, A. M. (N, Nt), Kuroda, T. (P, O), Merklin,
    R. L. (P), Nicol, D. , Rutsch, R. F. (N, Nt, P), Saul, L. R. (N), Satyamurti, T. S. (O),
    Scarlato, O. A. (Arc, PO), Smith, A. B. (N), Uozumi, S. (P), Weaver, C. S. (Oc).
    Fossils, no age: Fujie, T. (P), Nicol, D. , Smith, A. B. (N).
    Paleozoic: Nakazawa, K. (P), Wilson, R. B. (P).
    Mesozoic: Kamada, Y. (P), Nakazawa, K. (P), Peck, J. H. (N), Richards, H. G. (N),
        Saul, L. R. (N), Trexler, D. W. (N), Uozumi, S. (P), Van de Poel, L. (W).
    Cenozoic: Glibert, M. (P), Kamada, Y. (P), Merklin, R. L. (P), Uozumi, S. (P).
    Tertiary: Peck, J. H. (N), Richards, H. G. (N), Rutsch, R. F. (N, Nt, P), Schenck,
        H. G. (PO), Susuki, T. (N).
    Quaternary: Merklin, R. L. (P), Richards, H. G. (N), Wagner, F. J. E. (N).
Deep-sea: Filatova, Z. A. , Mulicki, Z.
Non-marine, fossils: Bennison, G. M. (P:P), Hässlein, L. (Q:P), Kerney, M. P. (Q:P), Ložek,
    V. (C:P), Modell, H. (M-C:W), Sparks, B. W. (Q:P), Weir, J. (P:P).
Estuarine: Amos, W. H. (N).
Fresh-water, Nearctic: Eggleston, H. R. , Hahnert, W. F. , Parmalee, P. W.
    Neotropical: Thomé, J. W.
    Palearctic: Butot, L. J. M. , Dance, S. P. , Hässlein, L. , Kerney, M. P. , Krolopp, E. ,
        Ložek, V. , Sparks, B. W.
    Oriental: Dance, S. P.

                      * * * * *

ASTARTACEA: Ockelmann, W. K. (AO).
DYSODONTA - fossils: Branson, C. C. (P:W).
HETERODONTA: Chavan, A.   FOSSILS: Chavan, A.
LUCINACEA: Ockelmann, W. K. (AO).
MYTILACEA: Ockelmann, W. K. (Arc).
NUCULANACEA: Puri, H. S. (W).
PANDORACEA: Ockelmann, W. K. (AO).
PECTINACEA: Ockelmann, W. K. (AO).
RUDISTACEA - fossils: Kühn, O. (F:W), MacGillavry, H. J. (M:?), Renngarten, V. P. (F:P).
POROMYACEA: Ockelmann, W. K. (AO).
TAXODONTA: Merklin, R. L. (AO, PO).
UNIONACEA: Brander, T. (P).

                      * * * * *

Anadaridae: Nicol, D.   FOSSILS: Nicol, D.
Anthracosiidae - fossils: Eager, R. M. C. (P:?).

27

MOLLUSCA, Pelecypoda (continued)

Arcidae: Hiramatsu, T. (P), Nicol, D. , Soot-Ryen, H. (W).
   Fossils: Nicol, D.
Aucellidae: Brunnschweiler, R. O. (A, Oc).   FOSSILS: Jeletzky, J. A. (F:N, P).
Bakevelliidae - fossils: Nakazawa, K. (P-M:P).
Cardiidae: Eberzin, A. G. (P), Keen, A. M. , Marriage, L. D. (m:N, PO).
   Fossils: Eberzin, A. G. (F:P), Keen, A. M. (M-C:?), Tremlett, W. E. (T:P).
Carditidae - fossils: Heaslip, W. G. (C:N).
Chamidae: Nicol, D.   FOSSILS: Nicol, D.
Cucullaeidae: Nicol, D.   FOSSILS: Nicol, D.
Donacidae: Loesch, H. C. (N, Nt).
Fimbriidae: Nicol, D.   FOSSILS: Nicol, D.
Glossidae: Nicol, D.   FOSSILS: Nicol, D.
Glycymeridae: Nicol, D.   FOSSILS: Nicol, D.
Hiatellidae: Hunter, W. D. R. (m:P, AO).
Mactridae: Chamberlin, J. L. (W).
Mutelidae: Modell, H. (fw:W), Van der Schalie, H. (fw:N).
   Fossils: Modell, H. (fw:M-C:W).
Myacidae (Myidae): Glude, J. B. (N), Marriage, L. D. (m:N, PO).
Myalinidae - fossils: Eager, R. M. C. (P:?).
Mytilidae: Marriage, L. D. (m:N, PO), Soot-Ryen, T.
Ostreidae: Glude, J. B. (N), Gunter, G. (N, Nt), Lunz, G. R. (N), Marriage, L. D. (m:N, PO),
      Nelson, T. C. (N, Nt, P), Ranson, G. (W), Stenzel, H. B. , Thomson, J. M. (A),
      Westley, R. E. (N).
   Larvae: Tanaka, Y. (P), Westley, R. E. (N).
   Fossils: Sylvester-Bradley, P. C. (M:?), Stenzel, H. B. (M-C:?).
Parallelodontidae: Nicol, D. ,   FOSSILS: Nicol, D.
Pectinidae: Grau, G. (W), Hiramatsu, T. (P), Johnston, I. M. (N), Marriage, L. D. (m:N, PO),
      Mason, J. (P), Masuda, K. (P, O), Olsen, A. M. (A), Webb, J. H. (W).
   Fossils: Akiyama, M. (C:P), Mongin, D. (T:N, P), Ômori, M. (C:P), Zázvorla, V. (M:P).
Pernidae (Inoceramidae) - fossils: Jeletzky, J. A. (F:N, P), Jones, D. L. (F:N), Renngarten,
      V. P. (M:P), Sornay, J. (M:P, E).
Pholadidae: Marriage, L. D. (m:N, PO), Nagabhushanam, R. (IO).
Pinnidae: Rosewater, J. (AO).
Pteriidae: Okutani, K. (O, Oc).
Solenidae: Marriage, L. D. (m:N, PO).
Sphaeriidae: Berger, L. (P), Dance, S. P. (W), Eggleton, F. E. (N), Heilman, R. A. (N),
      Herrington, H. B. (N), Kuiper, J. G. J. (W), Odhner, N. H.
   Fossils: Herrington, H. B. (C:N).
Tellinidae: Rust, J. D. (N).
Teredinidae: Nagabhushanam, R. (IO), Rajagopalaiengar, A. S. (O), Rancurel, P. (Nt, P, E, O, A, Oc).
Trigoniidae - fossils: Kambe, N. (M:P), Nakano, M. (M:W).
Unionidae: Aldrich, F. A. (N), Athearn, H. D. , Hertel, R. (P), Howard, A. D. (N), Johnson,
      R. I. (N), Matteson, M. R. (N), Modell, H. (W), Pahl, G. (N), Stansbury, D. H. (N),
      Van der Schalie, H. (N).
   Fossils: Modell, H. (fw:M-C:W).
Veneridae: Fischer-Piette, E. , Glude, J. B. (N), Hiramatsu, T. (P), Marriage, L. D. (m:N, PO).
   Fossils: Tremlett, W. E. (T:P).

Scaphopoda

No other data: Emerson, W. K. (PO), Habe, T. (P).
   Fossils: Aoki, S. (T:P), Emerson, W. K. (F:N), Hatai, K. (C:PO), Hayasaka, S. (C:P),
      Smith, D. J. (T:N), Švagrovský, J. (C:P).
                                    * * * * *
Dentaliidae: Eyerdam, W. J. (A, Oc).

Solenogastres
(Aplacophora)

No other data: Gustafson, G. (P), Thompson, T. E. (P).

SIPUNCULOIDEA

No other data: Edmonds, S. J. (O, Oc), Itô, T. (P), Jorge, A. R. (P), Murina, W. W. (PO),
      Ray, D. L. (PO), Stephen, A. C. (W), Wesenberg-Lund, E. (Nt, Ant).

ECHIUROIDEA

No other data: Edmonds, S. J. (O, Oc), Itô, T. (P), Jorge, A. R. (P), Ray, D. L. (PO), Stephen, A. C. (W), Wesenberg-Lund, E. (O, Oc), Zenkevitch, L. A.

ANNELIDA

No other data: Amos, W. H. (br:N), Chamberlin, R. V. (W), Kisselova, M. , Malevich, Y. J. , Moore, J. P. (W), Valente, D. (Nt).

Fossils: Ball, H. W. (P-T:?), Howell, B. F. (F:W), Ware, S. (P:?).

Archiannelida

No other data: Gerlach, S. (W), Jones, E. R. , Jr. (N), Uchida, T. (PO), Wieser, W. (W).

* * * * *

Nerillidae: Ax, P. (W), Swedmark, B. (P), Uéno, S-I. (PO).

Hirudinea

No other data: Autrum, H. , Powell, E. F.

World: Meyer, M. C. , Moore, J. P.

Nearctic: Hahnert, W. F. , Mann, K. H. , Mathers, C. K. , Myers, R. J. , Pawlowski, L. K. , Shuster, C. N. , Jr.

Neotropical: Caballero y Caballero, E. , Ringuelet, R. A.

Palearctic: Dresscher, T. G. N. , Engel, H. , Herter, K. , Livanow, N. , Lukin, E. J. , Mann, K. H. , Pawlowski, L. K. , Sciacchitano, I. ,

Paleotropical: Bhatia, M. L. (O), Pawlowski, L. K. (E), Sciacchitano, I. (E).

* * * * *

ARHYNCHOBDELLIDA: Walton, B. C. (O).

RHYNCHOBDELLIDA: Sanjeeva Raj, P. J. (W).

* * * * *

Piscicolidae: Epstein, W. M. (m, fw:P), Knight-Jones, E. W. (m), Richardson, L. R. (PO), de Silva, P. H. D. (m:W).

Myzostomida

No other data: Fedotov, D. M. , Jägersten, G.

Oligochaeta

No other data: Abbott, B. J. , von Bülow, T. , Dahl, I. , Dahl, S. O. , Gavrilov, K. , Gehweiler, W. J. (fw), Khalaf el-Duweini, A. , Marcus, Ern. , Marcus, Eve. , Pickford, G. E. , Pool, G. , Sokolskaja, N. L. , Turner, C. D. , Tuzelaat, M. A.

World: Omodea, P.

Nearctic: Causey, D. , Gates, G. E. , Goodnight, C. J. (fw), Hahnert, W. F. , Moment, G. B. , Murchie, W. R. , Tomlinson, J. , Wurtz, C. B. (fw).

Neotropical: Jamieson, B.

Atlantic Ocean: Roots, B. I.

Palearctic: Adachi, T. , Čekanovskaja, O. (fw, t), Gates, G. E. , Izosimov, W. , Jamieson, B. , Kunst, M. , Mulicki, Z. , Roots, B. I. , Szczepanski, A. , Timm, T. (t, fw), Wilcke, D. E. , Yamaguchi, H.

Paleotropical Gates, G. E. (O, A, Oc).

* * * * *

MEGADRILI: McKey-Fender, D. (N).

MICRODRILI: Causey, D. (N), McKey-Fender, D. (N), Yamaguchi, H. (P).

* * * * *

Aeolosomatidae: Ercolini, A. (N, Nt), Naidu, K. V. (P).

Branchiobdellidae: Holt, P. C. (N), Pop, V. (P).

Enchytraeidae: Backlund, H. O. (P), Bell, A. W. (W), Christensen, B. (P), Nielsen, C. O. (P), O'Connor, E. B. (P), Peachey, J. (P).

Lumbricidae, World: Pop, V. , Roots, B. I.

Nearctic: Harman, W. J. , Olson, H. W. , Oughton, J.

Palearctic: Backlund, H. O. , Baldasseroni, V. , Doeksen, J. , Graff, O. , Karppinen, E. O. , Moszyńska, M. , Muldal, S. , Saussey, M. , Siivonen, L. , Støp-Bowitz, C. , Svendsen, J. A. , Wilcke, D. E. , Zajonc, I. , Zicsi, A.

Australian: Lee, K. E.

Lumbriculidae: Hrabě, S. (W).

Megascolecidae: Graff, O. (N, Nt, A), Harman, W. J. (N), Lee, K. E. (A), Macnab, J. A. (N),
  Murchie, W. R. (Nt), Ohfuchi, S. (P, Oc).
Naididae: Brinkhurst, R. O. (fw:P), Ercolini, A. (N, Nt), Naidu, K. V. (P), Sperber, C. (W).
Tubificidae: Brinkhurst, R. O. (fw:P), Hrabě, S. (W), Naidu, K. V. (P).

Polychaeta

No other data: Clark, R. B., Eliason, A., Herpin, R., Rankin, J. S., Jr., Rasmussen, E.,
  Stickney, A. P., Winogradov, K., Ziegelmeier, E.
  World: Dales, R. P., Hartman, O., Hartman-Schröder, G., Kirkegard, J. B., Rullier, F.,
  Støp-Bowitz, C., Tebble, N.
  Nearctic: Berkeley, C. J., Grainger, E. H., Hanks, R. W., Sveshnikov, V. A.
  Neotropical: Mendivil-Herrera, J., Sveshnikov, V. A.
  Palearctic: Banse, K., Chlebowitch, V., Gustafson, G., Hamond, R., Jorge, A. R.,
  Lucas, J. A. W., Mulicki, Z., Newell, G. E., Southward, E. C., Takahashi, K.,
  Wilson, D. P., Wu, B-L., Zei, M.
  Paleotropical: Banse, K. (O), Day, J. H. (E), Knox, G. A. (A, Oc), Reish, D. J. (Oc),
  Takahashi, K. (Oc).
  Atlantic Ocean: Pettibone, M. H., Wesenberg-Lund, E.
  Pacific Ocean: Levenstein, R. J., Uschkov, P. V.
  Arctic: Pettibone, M. H., Sveshnikov, V. A., Uschakov, P. V.
  Antarctic: Knox, G. A.
Scolecodonts - fossils: Eller, E. R. (P-C:?), Kielan, Z. (P:P), Lange, F. W. (Nt), Šnajdr,
  M. (F:P), Sylvester, R. K. (P:N).
Tubes - fossils: Schmidt, W. J. (F:W).
 * * * * *

ERRANTIA - fossils: Šnajdr, M. (P:P).
TEREBELLOIDEA: Livanow, N. (P).
 * * * * *

Aphroditidae: Uschakov, P. V. (PO, Arc).
Arenicolidae: Stach, L. W., Wells, G. P. (W).
Chrysopetalidae: Jorge, A. R. (W).
Disomidae: Hannerz, L. (P).
Eunicidae: Kott, P. (A).
Flabelligeridae: Støp-Bowitz, C. (AO, Arc).
Glyceridae: Støp-Bowitz, C. (AO, Arc).
Maldanidae: Moment, G. B. (N).
Nephtyidae: Clark, R. B.
Nereidae· Chlebowitch, V. (PO, Arc), Durchon, M. (P), Kott, P. (A).
Opheliidae: Støp-Bowitz, C. (AO, Arc).
Phyllodocidae: Uschakov, P. V. (PO, Arc).
Pisionidae: Siewing, R. (W).
Poecilochaetidae: Hannerz, L. (P).
Polynoidae: Pettibone, M. H. (AO).
Sabellidae: Banse, K. (W).
Scalibregmidae: Støp-Bowitz, C. (AO, Arc).
Serpulidae: Dew, B. (O, A, Oc), de Silva, P. H. D. (W).
  Fossils: Avnimelech, M. (M-T:?).
Spionidae: Hannerz, L. (P), Woodwick, K. H. (N).
Syllidae: Durchon, M. (P), Okada, Y. K. (W).

PENTASTOMIDA
(Linguatulida)

No other data: Chitwood, M. B. (W), Doucet, J. (W), Hill, H. R. (W), Keegan, H. L., Self, J. T. (W).
Parasites of reptiles: Schad, G. A. (W).
 * * * * *

POROCEPHALIA: da Fonseca, F. (N, Nt).

TARDIGRADA

No other data: Baumann, H. , Bertolani, M. , Chitwood, B. G. , Franceschi, T. , Marcus, Ern. ,
   Marcus, Eve. , Ramazzotti, G. , Riggin, G. W. , Jr.
World: Curtin, C. B. , Petersen, B. , Schulz, E.
Nearctic: Higgins, R. P.
Palearctic: Bartoš, E. , Čanadjija, S. , Iharos, G. , Mihelčič, F. , Morikawa, K. ,
   Rodewald-Rudescu, L. , Rodriquez-Roda, R. J.

ONYCHOPHORA

No other data: Arnett, R. H. , Jr. (W), Lawrence, R. F. (E), Marcus, Ern.
   * * * * *
Peripatopsidae: Alexander, A. J. (E).

ARTHROPODA

No other data: Bianchi, C. , Bo Larsen, E. , Marquardt, W. , Sato, I. , Stickney, A. P. ,
   Turpaeia, E.
Of medical importance: Smith, E. A. (O).
Fossils: Copeland, M. J. (t, fw: P:N).
   * * * * *
CHELICERATA - fossils: Lamont, A. (P:P).

Trilobita
(all fossils)

No other data: Curtis, M. L. K. , Harrington, H. J. , Hupé, P. R. (P, E), Leanza, A. F. (W),
   Lochman-Balk, C. (N, Nt), Přibyl, A. (P), Tripp, R. P. , Vaněk, J. (P).
Paleozoic, no locality: Begg, J. L. , Cowie, J. W. , Endo, R. , Erben, H. K. , Evitt, W. R. ,
   Goldring, R. , Hoppinger, J. J. , Jaanusson, V. , Kindle, C. H. , Osmolska, H. ,
   Prentice, J. E. , Sdzuy, K. , Selwood, E. B. , Shaw, A. B. , Strnad, V. , Tasch, P. ,
   Whittington, H. B.
World: Howell, B. F. , Rasetti, F. , Stubblefield, C. J.
Nearctic: Bright, R. C. , Deiss, C. F. , DeMott, L. L. , Duncan, D. C. , Ellison, R. L. ,
   Fisher, D. W. , Frederickson, E. A. , Grant, R. E. , Hintze, L. F. , Kauffman, E. G. ,
   Kurtz, V. E. , Nelson, C. A. , Palmer, A. R. , Pope, J. K. , Ross, R. J. , Jr. , Stoyanow, A. ,
   Stumm, E. C. , Susuki, T. , Taylor, P. W. , Weller, J. M. , Wilson, J. L. , Young, F. P. , Jr.
Neotropical: Frederickson, E. A. , Stoyanow, A.
Palearctic: Dean, W. T. , Henningsmoen, G. , Kielan, Z. , Kobayashi, T. , Lamont, A. ,
   Prantl, F. , Šnajdr, M. , Størmer, L. , Stoyanow, A. , Tjernvik, T. E. , Whittard, W. F.
Paleotropical: Gill, E. D. (O, A, Oc).
   * * * * *
LICHACEA: Edgell, H. S. (W).
PHACOPACEA: Struve, W.
   * * * * *
Calmoniidae: Struve, W.
Calymenidae: Kauffman, E. G. (P:N).
Dalmanitidae: Struve, W.
Olenellidae: Best, R. V. (F:N).
Phacopidae: Struve, W.
Proetidae: Struve, W. (P:P).

Merostomata

No other data: Størmer, L. (P:W), Van Straelen, V.
   * * * * *
EURYPTERIDA - fossils: Kjellesvig-Waering, E. N. (F:W), Leutze, W. P. (F:N), Přibyl,
   A. (P:P), Waterston, C. D. (F:P).
LIMULACEA: Shuster, C. N. , Jr. (N, P).   FOSSILS: Shuster, C. N. , Jr. (F:N, P).
XIPHOSURIDA: Waterman, T.

Pycnogonida

No other data: Bourdillon, A. (P, AO), Clark, W. C. (A, Oc), Fage, L., Gordon, I. (P, Ant), Hedgpeth, J. W. (W), Mañé-Garsón, F., Marcus, Ern., de Mello-Leitao, A. (Nt), Sanchez, M. S. (P), Sawaya, M. P. (Nt), Stock, J. H. (W), Utinomi, H. (W).
Fossils: Hedgpeth, J. W. (P-C:W).

Arachnida

No other data: Auber, M., Bacelar, A., Balderston, B. C., Biraben, M. (Nt), Bozzini, M., Camargo, H. F. A. (Nt), Chamberlin, R. V. (N, Nt), Cloudsley-Thompson, J. L. (P), Cooke, J. A. (P), Dunn, A. P., Dunn, R. A. (A), Edwards, R. J., Eglitis, V. K., Frade, F., Gabe, M., Jeekel, C. A. W. (P), Kullmann, E. (P), Lawrence, R. F. (E), Szalay, L. (P).
Fossils: Petrunkevitch, A. (P:W).

Acarina

No other data: Aragão, H. B., Austin, M. D., Bal, D. V., Bottazzi, E., Cockings, K. L., Cross, H. F., Ferrer y Galdiano, M., Haramoto, F. H., Heisch, R. B., Ibarra-Grasso, A., Janisch, M., Kishida, K., Kotlán, A., Lange, A. B., Maiello, D. G., Orghidan, T., Patterson, P. M., Piatakov, M. L., Soarec-Tanasachi, J., Solomon, M. E., Starkoff, I., Taberly, G., Turk, F. A., Wallwork, J. A.
World: Cooreman, J., Matthysse, J. G., Newell, I. M., Schuster, R., Wharton, G. W.
Nearctic: Branch, N., Drummond, R. O., Krantz, J. W.
Neotropical: Fox, I.
Palearctic: Morisita, T., Schuster, R., Sheals, J. G., Yunker, C. E.
Paleotropical: Meyer, M. K. P. (E), Womersley, H. (A, Oc).
Marine: Hobart, J. (P), Teissier, G.
Terrestrial: Balogh, J. I. (Nt, P, E,), Hobart, J. (P), Macfayden, A. (P, Arc), Schmölzer, K. (P), Sheals, J. G. (P), Turk, F. A., Willmann, C.
Parasites: Clark, G. M., Davis, D. H. S. (E), Doetschman, W. H. (W), Rao, T. R. (O), Sasa, M. (P).
  Of insects: Samšiñák, K. (W), Treat, A. E. (W), Turk, F. A.
  Of vertebrates: Fain, A. (W), da Fonseca, F. (W), Fuller, H. S. (W), Till, W. M. (E), Wilson, N. (N), Zumpt, F. (E).
  Of birds: Boyd, E. M. (N), Turk, F. A.
  Of mammals: Domrow, R. (A), Eads, R. B. (N, Nt), van Eyndhoven, G. L. (W), Lane, J. E. (N), Willmann, C.
Economically important: Baeta Neves, C. M. L. (P, E), Baker, E. W. (W), Cleveland, M. (N), Collado, J. G. (P), Jeppson, L. R. (N), Krantz, J. W. (W), Micherdzinski, W. (P), Weidhaas, J. A., Jr. (N).

TICKS

IXODOIDEA, no locality: Bequaert, J. C., Bishopp, F. C., Boero, J. J., Vogelsang, E. G.
  World: Anastos, G., Dias, J. A. T. S., Elishewitz, H., Kohls, G. M.
  Nearctic: Brennan, J. M., Brown, N. R., Donoso, R., Gould, D. J., Gregson, J. D., Jorgensen, C. D., Joyce, C. R., Miller, A., Stannard, L. J., Jr., Stone, P. C., Teller, L. W.
  Neotropical: Donoso, R., Floch, H., Gutierrez, R. O., Hoffmann-Sandoval, A., Ortiz Cordero, I.
  Palearctic: Abbassian-Lintzen, R., Balashov, J. S., Burtt, E. T., Černý, V., Drenski, P. S., Feider, Z., Filippova, N. A., Kaiser, M. N., Starkoff, O., Teller, L. W., Tendeiro, J., Toshioka, S., Toumanoff, C.
  Paleotropical: Abdussalam, M. (O), Anantaraman, M. (O), Joyce, C. R. (Oc), Sousa Dias, V. A. (E), Swan, D. C. (A), Tendeiro, J. (E), Theiler, G. (E).
                         * * * * *
Argasidae: Augustson, G. F. (N), Colas-Belcour, J., Hiregaudar, L. S. (O), Hoogstraal, H. (W), Hopla, C. E. (N, Nt), Keh, B. (N), Morel, P. C. (P, E), Pospelova-Shtrom, M. V. (W), Smith, C. N. (N), Theodor, O. (P, E, O, A, Oc), Walker, J. B. (E), Walton, G. A.
Ixodidae, no locality: Dunham, D. W., Pavlovsky, E. N., Rosický, B.
  World: Arthur, D. R., Feldman-Muhsam, B., Hoogstraal, H.
  Nearctic: Augustson, G. F., Bargren, W. C., Blickle, R. L., Clifford, C. M., Hays, K., Hopla, C. E., Keh, B., McIntosh, A., Rogers, A. J., Russell, H. G., Jr., Smith, C. N.
  Neotropical: Diaz-Ungria, C., Hopla, C. E.
  Palearctic: Arthur, D. R., Britz, L., Delpy, L., Feldman-Muhsam, B., Ghaffary, E. N., Kurtpinar, H., Morel, P. C., Nemenz, H., Pospelova-Shtrom, M. V., Ohandjanian, A., de Prada, J., Tambs-Lyche, H., Yajima, A.

Ethiopian: Guggisberg, C. A. W. , Morel, P. C. , Rageau, J. G. F. , Walker, J. B. ,
    Wiley, A. J.
Oriental: Hiregaudar, L. S. , Rao, T. R. , Trapido, H. , Varma, M. G. R.
Australian: Dumbleton, L. J. , Roberts, F. H. S.
Oceania: Rageau, J. G. F. , Roberts, F. H. S.
Arctic & Antarctic: Tambs-Lyche, H.
Larvae: Clifford, C. M. (N).

MITES

No other data: Anantaraman, M. (O), van Eyndhoven, G. L. (W), Macfarlane, D. (P, E, O, A, Oc),
    Rapp, W. F. , Jr. (N).

* * * * *

CUNAXOIDEA: Ehara, S. (P).
GAMASOIDEA: Ohandjanian, A. (P).
HYDRACARINA: Angelier, E. (P, E), Bergstrom, D. W. (N), Boliek, M. I. (N), Cook, D. R. (N),
    Crowell, R. M. (N), Sokolov, I. I. (P), Stout, V. M. (A), Szalay, L. (P), Uchida,
    T. (P, O), Yankowskaja, A. I. (P).
HYDRACHNELLAE: Bader, C. (P, E), Besseling, A. J. (P), Cooreman, J. (P), Georgievski, M. ,
    Habeeb, H. (N), Halik, L. , Imamura, T. (P), Láska, F. (P), Lundblad, O. (W),
    Mitchell, R. D. (W), Münchberg, P. (N, Nt, P, E, A,), Motas, C. (W), Neuman, T. (P),
    Schwoerbel, J. (P), Svenonius, B. , Tanasachi, J. , Viets, K. (W), Viets, K. O. (W),
    Wainstein, B. A. (P).
LIROASPOIDEA: Camin, J. H. (W).
MESOSTIGMATA: Abdussalam, M. (O), Bourdeau, F. G. (W), Camin, J. H. (W), Haarløv,
    N. (P, Arc), Hiregaudar, L. S. (O), Hirschmann, W. , Hull, W. B. (P), Hyatt, K. H. (P, O),
    Kawashima, K. (P), Ryke, P. A. J. (E), Sellnick, M. (W), Stammer, H-J. (P), Woolley,
    T. A. (N).
Parasitic: Furman, D. P. (N, Nt).
Myrmecophilous: Rettenmeyer, C. W. (N, Nt).
ORIBATEI, no locality: Schaller, F. , Stanworth, G. T.
    World: Schuster, R. , Sellnick, M. , Walker, N. A. , Winkler, J. R.
    Nearctic: Bohnsack, K. K. , Higgins, H. , Rohde, C. J. , Sengbusch, H. G. , Woolley, T. A.
    Palearctic: Forsslund, K. H. , Gunhold, P. , Haarløv, N. , Karppinen, E. O. , Kunst, M. ,
    Mihelčič, F. , Murphy, P. , Rajski, A. , Schuster, R. , Strenzke, K. ,Tarras-Wahlberg, N. ,
    von Törne, E. , Travé, J. , Zachvatkina, E. M. , Zivkovic, V.
    Paleotropical: van Pletzen, R. (E), Ramsay, G. W. (A).
PARASITIFORMES: Daniel, M. (P), Evans, G. O. (N, Nt, P, E, O), Holzmann, C. (P),
    Schweizer, J. (P).
PROSTIGMATA: Haarløv, N. (P, Arc), Mihelčič, F. (P), Starkoff, O. (P).
RAPHIGNATHOIDEA: Ehara, S. (P).
SARCOPTIFORMES: Kawashima, K. (P), Rosas Costa, J. A. (W), Schweizer, J. (P), Starkoff,
    O. (P), Woolley, T. A. (N), Yunker, C. E. (W).
TETRANYCHOIDEA: Ehara, S. (P), Reck, H. F. (P), Wainstein, B. A. (P).
TETRAPODILI: Shevtskenko, V. G. (P).
TRACHYTOIDEA: Camin, J. H. (W), Johnston, D. (N, P).
TRIGYNASPIDA: Camin, J. H. (W).
TROMBIDIFORMES: André, M. (P, E), Beer, R. E. (W), Cunliffe, F. (N, Nt), Feider, Z. (P, E),
    Hiregaudar, L. S. (O), Kawashima, K. (P), Mihelčič, F. (P), Schweizer, J. (P),
    Winkler, J. R. (P), Woolley, T. A. (N).
TYDEOIDEA: Ehara, S. (P).
TYROGLYPHOIDEA: Behura, B. K. (O), Klimaszewska, H. (P), Robertson, P. L. (W),
    Volgin, V. I. (P).
UROPODINA: Camin, J. H. (W), Evans, G. O. (N, Nt, P, E, O), Valle, A. (W), Zirngiebl, I. (P).

* * * * *

Acaridae: Nesbitt, H. H. J. (N, P), Samšiňák, K. (W), Woodroffe, G. E. (W).
Aceosejidae: Wainstein, B. A. (P).
Analgesidae: Farner, D. S. , Gaud, J. (W).
Anoetidae: Hughes, R. D. (W), Samšiňák, K. (W).
Ascaidae: Bernhard, F. (P).
Bdellidae: Atyeo, W. T. (W), Mahon, J. A. (A), Wallace, M. M. (A).
Bryobiidae: Bagdasarian, A. T. (P), van Eyndhoven, G. L. (W).
Caeculidae: Enns, W. R. (N), Franz, H. , Higgins, H. (N, P), Mulaik, S. B. (W).
Calyptostomidae: Atyeo, W. T. (W).
Cheyletidae: Volgin, V. I. (P), Woodroffe, G. E. (W).
Demodicidae: Nutting, W. L. (W).
Dermanyssidae: Allred, D. M. (N), Hunt, O. E. (N, Nt), Keegan, H. L. , Mrciak, M. (P).
Diplogyniidae: Hicks, E. A. (N).

33

Entonyssidae: Hunt, O. E. (N, Nt), Radford, C. D. (W), Spangler, P. J. (N), Tibbetts, T. (W).
Epidermoptidae: Micherdzinski, W. (P), Tibbetts, T. (W).
Eriophyidae: Attiah, H. H. (P), Batchelor, G. S. (W), Cromroy, H. L. (Nt), Farkas, H. (W),
 Hall, C. C. , Jr. (N), Keifer, H. H. , Krott, G. (P), Lamb, K. P. (A), Roivainen, H. (W),
 Swan, D. C. (A).
Erythraeidae: Ishii, Y. (P), Newell, I. M. (W), Rosas Costa, J. A. (W), Schluger, E. G. ,
 Southcott, R. V. (W), Vercammen-Grandjean, P. H. (E).
Eupodidae: Narayan, D. S. (W).
Galumnidae: Bregetova, N. G. (P), Gretillat, E. H. S. (E).
Gamasidae: Morlan, H. B. (N), Strandtmann, R. (W).
Glycyphagidae: Woodroffe, G. E. (W).
Gnathostomidae: Miyazaki, I. (N, P).
Haemogamasidae: Micherdzinski, W. (P), Mrciak, M. (P).
Halacaridae: Green, J. (P), Imamura, T. (P), Hull, W. B. (W), Motas, C. (W), Newell, I. M. (W),
 Schulz, E. (W), Viets, K. (W).
Hydracaridae: Petkowski, T. K. (P).
Hydrarachnidae: Åbro, A. (P).
Ixodorhynchidae: Tibbetts, T. (W).
Labidostommatidae: Greenberg, B. (W).
Laelaptidae: Grant, C. D. (N), Hays, K. (N), Hunt, O. E. (W), Jameson, E. W. , Jr. (N, P),
 Keegan, H. L. , Micherdzinski, W. (P), Mrciak, M. (P), Radford, C. D. (W), Sinha,
 T. B. (O), Taufflieb, R. (E), Teller, L. W. (N, P), Thurman, E. B. (W), Tipton,
 V. J. (N, Nt).
Liponyssidae: Micherdzinski, W. (P).
Listrophoridae: Gunther, C. E. M. (Oc), Radford, C. D. (W).
Macronyssidae: Radford, C. D. (W).
Myobiidae: Gjessing, H. W. (N), Jameson, E. W. , Jr. (N, P), Radford, C. D. (W), Tibbetts, T. (W).
Oribatidae: Birch, R. L. , Dalenius, P. (P, Ant), Franke, A. (P), Grandjean, F. (W),
 van der Hammen, L. (P, Oc), Hammer, M. (N, Nt, P), Morikawa, K. (P), Nevin,
 F. R. (N), Piffl, E. (P), Tuxen, S. L. (N, P).
Parasitidae: Lombardini, G. (P).
Penthaleidae: Mahon, J. A. (A), Narayan, D. S. (N, Nt).
Phytoptipalpidae: Dosse, G. (P), Düzgünes, Z (P), Jeppson, L. R. (N), Matthysse, J. G. (N).
Phytoseiidae: Chant, D. A. (W), DeLeon, D. (N), Dosse, G. (P), Ehara, S. (P), Garman, P. (N),
 Hall, J. C. (N), Jeppson, L. R. (N), Lamb, K. P. (A), Matthysse, J. G. (N), Muma,
 M. H. (N), Nesbitt, H. H. J. (N, P), Wainstein, B. A. (P).
Podapolipodidae: Stammer, H-J. (W).
Porohalacaridae: Schwoerbel, J. (P), Viets, K. O. (W).
Pterolichidae: Micherdzinski, W. (P).
Pterygosomidae: Jack, K. M. (W).
Pyemotidae: Krczal, H. (P), Sengbusch, H. G. (N), Stammer, H-J. (P).
Rhinonyssidae: Crossley, D. A. (N), van Eyndhoven, G. L. (W), Hunt, O. E. (N, Nt), Spangler,
 P. J. (N).
Scutacaridae: Cross, E. A. (W), Karafiat, P.
Smaridiidae: Newell, I. M. (W), Rosas Costa, J. A. (W), Southcott, R. V. (W), Vercammen-
 Grandjean, P. H. (E).
Speleognathidae: Crossley, D. A. (N).
Spinturnicidae: Gjessing, H. W. (N), Imamura, T. (P), Rudnick, A. (W), Spangler, P. J. (N),
 White, J. S. (N).
Stigmaeidae: Summers, F. (N, Nt).
Tarsonemidae: Beer, R. E. (W), Cromroy, H. L. (Nt), DeLeon, D. (N), Meserve, F. G. (W),
 Reed, J. P. , Schaarschmidt, L. (P), Stammer, H-J. (P).
Tenuipalpidae: Attiah, H. H. (P), DeLeon, D. (N).
Tetranychidae, no locality: McGregor, E. A. , Sayeh, M. T.
 World: Beer, R. E. , Boudreaux, H. B. , Pritchard, A. E.
 Nearctic: Denmark, H. A. , Farrier, M. H. , Garman, P. , Jeppson, L. R. , Malcom, D. R. ,
 Matthysse, J. G. , Morgan, C. V. G.
 Neotropical: Geijskes, D. C.
 Palearctic: Attiah, H. H. , Bagdasarian, A. T. , Dosse, G. , Düzgünes, Z. , Nishio, Y. ,
 Zacher, F.
 Paleotropical: Lamb, K. P. (A, Oc), Rimando, L. C. (O).
Trombiculidae, no locality: Abonnenc, E. , Fukuzumi, S. , Le Gac, P. , Schluger, E. G.
 World: Huber, I. , Hyland, K. E. , Kepka, O. , Radford, C. D. , Rosas Costa, J. A. ,
 Wharton, G. W.
 New World: Brennan, J. M. , Greenberg, B. , Feider, Z. , Jenkins, D. W.
 Nearctic: Crossley, D. A. , Farrell, C. E. , Gould, D. J. , Jameson, E. W. , Jr. , Kardos, E. H. ,

Loomis, R. B. , Teller, L. W. , Tuxen, S. L.
Neotropical: Floch, H. , Hoffmann-Sandoval, A.
Palearctic: Audy, J. R. , Daniel, M. , Feider, Z. , Gunther, C. E. M. , Hiromatsu, S. ,
    Jameson, E. W. , Jr. , Kamo, H. , Kaneko, K. , Kano, R. , Kardos, E. H. , Kitahara, K. ,
    Kobulej, T. , Kumada, N. , Lipovsky, L. J. , Miyazaki, I. , Obata, Y. , Teller, L. W. ,
    Toshioka, S. , Traub, R. , Tuxen, S. L.
Ethiopian: Audy, J. R. , Vercammen-Grandjean, P. H.
Oriental: Audy, J. R. , Sinha, T. B. , Traub, R.
Australian: Audy, J. R. , Dumbleton, L. J. , Gunther, C. E. M. , Southcott, R. V.
Oceania: Audy, J. R. , Gunther, C. E. M.
Larvae: Kardos, E. H. (N), Lipovsky, L. J. (W), Taufflieb, R. (E).
Trombidiidae: Crossley, D. A. (N), Daniel, M. (P), Franke, A. (P), Kobulej, T. (P), Newell,
    I. M. (W), Rosas Costa, J. A. (W), Southcott, R. V. (W), Vercammen-Grandjean, P. H. (E).
Typhlodromidae: Bernhard, F. (P).
Tyroglyphidae: Attiah, H. H. (P), Gretillat, E. H. S. (E), Hughes, A. M. (W), Türk, F. (P),
    Zyromska-Rudzka, H. (P).
Veigaiidae: Farrier, M. H. (W), Holzmann, C. (P).

Anthracomarti

(None)

Araneae

No other data: Berland, L. , Cohen, A. , Dyal, S. , Hassan, R. I. , Hull, J. E. , Jones, S. E. ,
    Kempel, J. G. , Ketterer, C. M. , Petrunkevitch, A. , Petrusewicz, K. , de Pikelin,
    B. S. G. , Ramont, R. , von Riper, W. , Schiapelli, R. D. E. , Sherriffs, W. R. ,
    Utotschkin, -.
World: Bonnet, P. , Crome, W. , Kraus, O. , Roewer, C-F.
Nearctic: Barnes, R. D. , Branson, B. A. , Drew, L. C. , Exline, H. , Frizzell, H. E. ,
    Gertsch, W. J. , Ivie, W. , Kaston, B. J. , Levi, H. W. , Levi, L. R. , Lowrie, D. C. ,
    Mikulska, I. , Muma, M. H. , Noland, G. B. , Schlinger, E. I. , Seyler, P. J. , Turnbull, A. L.
Neotropical: Buckup, E. H. Chickering, A. M. , Drew, L. C. , Exline, H. , Feio, J. L. A. ,
    Frizzell, H. E. , Hummelinck, P. W. , de Jong, B. , Loksa, I. , Piza, S. T. , Soares, B. ,
    Vellard, J.
Palearctic: Aechter, R. , Böggild, O. , Braendegaard, J. , Braun, R. , Bristow, W. S. ,
    Chrysanthus, -, Denis, J. , Drenski, P. S. , Engelhardt, W. , Hackman, W. L. V. ,
    Hadzissarantos, H. , Holm, Å. , Höregott, H. , Hyatt, K. H. , Jarvi, T. H. , de Jong, B. ,
    Kaestner, A. , Kayashima, I. , Kekenbosch, J. , Kim, K. C. , Komatsu, T. , Kritscher, E. ,
    Locket, G. H. , Loksa, I. , Łuczak, J. , Mikulska, I. , Miller, F. , Millidge, A. F. , Nikolić,
    F. , Oi, R. , Paik, K. Y. , Palmgren, P. , Polenec, A. , Saito, S. , Savory, T. H. , Schmidt,
    G. , Shulov, A. , Šilhavý, V. , Soyer, B. , Spassky, S. , Spoek, G. L. , Tambs-Lyche, H. ,
    Tretzel, E. , Uyemura, T. , Wiehle, H. , Yaginuma, T. , Yoneda, H. , Yoshikura, M.
Ethiopian: Clark, D. J. , Cooke, J. A. , Hewitt, J. , Holm, Å. , Legendre, R. , Loksa, I. ,
    Schmidt, G.
Oriental: Hyatt, K. H. , Kayashima, I. , Millot, J. , Saito, S.
Australian: Butler, L. S. G. , Dunn, R. A. , Forster, R. R. , Jobson, A. E. , Levitt, V. C. ,
    Parrott, A. W.
Oceania: Chrysanthus, -, Kayashima, I. , Marples, B. J. , Parrott, A. W.
Arctic & Antarctic: Braendegaard, J. (Arc), Holm, Å. (Arc), Pruitt, E. N. (Arc),
    Tambs-Lyche, H. (Arc, Ant).
Cavernicolous: Dresco, E. (P), Komatsu, T. (P), Kratochvíl, J. (W), Nikolić, F. (P).
Halophilous: Nemenz, H. (P).
Larvae: Schmidt, G. (P, E).
Fossils: Petrunkevitch, A. (T-C:W).
        * * * * *
APNEUMONOMORPHAE: Hickman, V. V. (A), Machado, A. B. (E).
DIPNEUMONOMORPHAE: Monterosso, B. (P).
MYGALOMORPHAE: Main, B. Y. (A), Todd, V. (A).
        * * * * *
Agelenidae: Gering, R. L. (N), Roth, V. D. (W).
Argiopidae: Archer, A. F. (N, Nt, E, O, Oc), Peters, H. M. , Sekiguchi, K. (P).
Aviculariidae: Hewitt, J. (E).
Clubionidae: Lohmander, H. (P).
Ctenidae: Bücherl, W. (Nt).
Dipluridae: Barnard, R. A. S. (A), McKenzie, R. J. (A).
Epeiridae: Nemenz, H. (P).
Erigonidae: Casemir, H. (N, P), Denis, J. (P), Dondale, C. D. (N).

ARTHROPODA, Araneae (continued)

Gnaphosidae: Lohmander, H. (P).
Hahniidae: Lohmander, H. (P).
Linyphiidae: Blest, A. D. (P), Casemir, H. (N, P), Denis, J. (P).
Lycosidae: Bücherl, W. (Nt), Lohmander, H. (P), Wallace, H. K. (N), Wiebes, J. T. (P).
Mimetidae: Archer, A. F. (N, Nt, E, O, Oc).
Pisauridae: McAlister, W. H. (N).
Salticidae: Clark, D. J. (P, E), Lohmander, H. (P), Wallace, H. K. (N).
Sparassidae: Sekiguchi, K. (P).
Theraphosidae: Schmidt, G. (Nt).
Theridiidae: Levi, H. W. (N, Nt).
Thomisidae: Comellini, A. (P, E), Dondale, C. D. (N), Lohmander, H. (P), Schick, R. X. (N).
Zodariidae: Denis, J. (P).

Architarbi

(None)

Haptopoda

(None)

Kustarachne

(None)

Opiliones

No other data: Heinajoki, M. , de Lerma, D.
    World: Roewer, C-F, Spoek, G. L.
    Nearctic: Davis, N. W. , Goodnight, C. J., Goodnight, M. L.
    Neotropical: Goodnight, C. J. , Goodnight, M. L. , Piza, S. T. , Soares, B. , Turk, F. A.
    Palearctic: Cârdei, F. , Dresco, E. , Hadži, J. , Kauri, H. , Kratochvil, J. , Lohmander, H. ,
       Meinertz, T. , Pfeifer, H. , Rafalski, J. , Rambla, M. , Sankey, J. H. P. , Savory, T. H. ,
       Šilhavý, V. , Suzuki, S. , Tambs-Lyche, H. , Todd, V. , Trossarelli, F. , Turk, F. A.
    Paleotropical: Kauri, H. (E, A), Parthasarathy, M. D. (O), Suzuki, S. (O), Turk, F. A. (O).
    Arctic & Antarctic: Tambs-Lyche, H. (Arc, Ant).
             * * * * *
CYCLOPHTHALMI: Rafalski, J. (W).
             * * * * *
Phalangiidae: Forster, R. R. (A).
Sironidae: Janczyk, F. (P).

Palpigradi

No other data: Condé, B. (W), Remy, P. A. (W).

Pedipalpi

No other data: Dunn, R. A. (A), Hummelinck, P. W. (Nt), Kraus, O. (W), McDonald, W. A. (W),
    Piza, S. T. (Nt), Schaller, F. , Takashima, H. (P, O).
(See also Schizomida, Thelyphonida, and Phrynichida)

Phrynichida

(None)

Pseudoscorpionida
(Chelonethida)

No other data: Schaller, F.
    World: Beier, M. , Chamberlin, J. C. , Verner, P. H.
    Nearctic: Gering, R. L. , Hoff, C. C. , Malcolm, D. R. , Muchmore, W. B.
    Neotropical: Feio, J. L. A. , Hoff, C. C. , Hummelinck, P. W. , Turk, F. A.
    Palearctic: Cârdei, F. , Hadži, J. , Kaestner, A. , Kaisila, J. , Lohmander, H. , Meinertz,
       T. , Morikawa, K. , Rafalski, J. , Turk, F. A. , Vachon, M.
    Paleotropical: Morris, J. C. H. (A), Turk, F. A. (O), Vachon, M. (E).

Ricinulei

No other data: Bolivar y Pieltain, C. (N, Nt), Coronado, L. (N, Nt).

Schizomida

(None)

Schizonotida

(None)

Scorpionida

No other data: Belfield, W. , Boyer, F. D. , Schaller, F.
    World: Kraus, O. , Stahnke, H. L. , Vachon, M.
    Nearctic: Humphrey, F. L. , Owens, V. H. , Peláez Fernández, D. , Stahnke, L.
    Neotropical: Bücherl, W. , Buckup, E. H. , Hummelinck, P. W. , Meise, W. , Moreno, A. ,
        Peláez Fernández, D. , Piza, S. T.
    Palearctic: Hadži, J. , Shulov, A. , Takashima, H.
    Ethiopian: Alexander, A. J. , Hewitt, J.
    Oriental: Meise, W. , Parthasarathy, M. D. , Takashima, H.
    Australian: Dunn, R. A. , Glauert, L. , Southcott, R. V.
              * * * * *
Buthidae: Main, B. Y. (A).
Chactidae: Angermann, H. (P).

Solpugida

No other data: Kraus, O. (W), Muma, M. H. (N), Panouse, J. B. (P, E), Roewer, C-F. (W),
    Turk, F. A. (P, E, O, A, Oc).

Thelyphonida

(None)

Trigonotarbi

(None)

Crustacea

No other data: Alikunhi, K. H. , Amar, R. , Attardo, C. , Baumann, H. , Bazicalova, A. N. , Borza,
    A. , Brodsky, K. A. , Caroli, E. , Caron, J. R. , Chapman, R. F. , Creaser, E. P. , Dahl,
    E. , Delye, G. , Derjavin, A. N. , Dion, Y. , Evans, F. , Gasull, L. , Glassell, S. A. ,
    Gonzalez, J. G. , Haruhiko, T. , Hiraiwa, Y. K. , Johnson, D. S. , Kubicek, F. , Macquart,
    M. , Mestrov, M. , Mogk, H. , Moore, L. B. , Ortiz, E. , Pljakic, M. , Powell, E. F. ,
    Ramadan, M. M. , Rasmussen, E. , Rioja, E. , Sandison, E. , Vaas, K. F.
    Nearctic: Hahnert, W. F. , Jean, Y.
    Neotropical: Reed, C. T. , Ringuelet, R. A. , Valente, D.
    Palearctic: Gruner, H. E. , Hamond, R. , Mulicki, Z.
    Oriental: Biswas, S. , George, R. W.
    Australian: George, R. W. , Shipway, B.
Parasitic: Causey, D. (Nt).
Cavernicolous: Forti, M. A. L. (P).
Fossils: Brooks, H. K. (P:?).
Microcrustacea: Cole, G. A.
Shrimps: Rasmussen, B. (AO), Stevens, B. A. (N).
              * * * * *
CEPHALOCARIDA: Sanders, H. L.
ENTOMOSTRACA: Eberly, W. R. (N), Ekman, S. P. , Fish, C. J. (m:AO), Harding, J. P. (W),
    Margalef, R. (fw:P), Martinez Fontes, E. (Nt), Megyeri, J. (P), Messikommer, E. (P),
    Røen, U. (fw:Arc).
STENOPODIDEA: Thompson, J. R. (Nt, AO).
              * * * * *
Chirostylidae: Thompson, J. R. (Nt, AO).
Microcerberidae: Siewing, R. (W).

Amphipoda

No other data: Bulycheva, A. , Clemens, H. P. , Dahl, E. , Larkin, P. A. , Patton, W. K. ,
Stankovic, S.
    World: Reid, D. M. , Ruffo, S.
    Nearctic: Eberly, W. R. (N), Henson, E. B. , Ide, F. P. , Marchette, N. J. , Rosine, W. N. ,
        Shoemaker, C. R. , Steele, D.
    Neotropical: Shoemaker, C. R.
    Palearctic: Dudich, A. , Gordon, I. , Gottlieb, E. , Jones, N. S. , Ponyi, E.
    Paleotropical: Barnard, K. H. (E), Hurley, D. E. (Oc), Nagappan, N. K. (O),
        Pillay, N. K. (O).
Marine: Birstein, J. A. (PO), Bousfield, E. L. (N), Brunel, P. (AO, Arc), Dunbar, M. J. (Arc),
    Fage, L. , Iwasa, M. (P), Macnae, W. (IO, PO), Shoemaker, C. R. (AO, PO), Vinogradov,
    M. E. (O, PO, Ant).
Estuarine: Amos, W. H. (N).
Fresh-water: Birstein, J. A. (P), Bousfield, E. L. (N), De Costa, J. , Dobreanu, E. (P),
    Hubricht, L. (N), Hynes, H. B. N. (P), Iwasa, M. (P), Rejic, M. (P), Straškraba, M. (P),
    Sturm, C. W. , Wurtz, C. B. (N).
Terrestrial: Iwasa, M. (P), Karaman, S. K. (P).
Cavernicolous: Balazuc, J. (P).

* * * * *

CAPRELLIDEA: Dougherty, E. C. (W), Mokiyevsky, O. B. (P), Utinomi, H. (PO).
GAMMARIDEA: Cărăuşu, S. (P), Gurjanova, E. F. (AO, PO, Arc), Sheard, K. (IO),
    Spooner, G. M. (P).
HYPERIIDEA: Irie, H. (PO), Sheard, K. (IO, PO), Spooner, G. M. (W).

* * * * *

Calliopidae: Wigley, R. L. (N).
Caprellidae: Steinberg, J. (W).
Cyamidae: Bowman, T. E. (W), Margolis, L. (W).
Dairellidae: Yang, W. T. (AO).
Gammaridae: Barnard, J. L. (PO), Edwards, C. (m, bw:AO, P), Forsman, B. (m:P), Ginet,
    R. (P), Kinne, O. (bw:P), MacIntyre, J. (Arc), Matsumoto, K. (P), Segerstråle,
    S. (m:P), Wigley, R. L. (m:N).
Haustoriidae: Watkin, E. E. (P), Wigley, R. L. (m:N).
Hyperiidae: Yang, W. T. (AO).
Oxycephalidae: Hoenigman, J. (P).
Phronimidae: Yang, W. T. (AO).
Phrosinidae: Yang, W. T. (AO).
Pontogeneidae: Wigley, R. L. (m:N).
Stegocephalidae: Wigley, R. L. (m:N).
Talitridae: Bousfield, E. L. (t:W), MacIntyre, J. (m:A), Mokiyevsky, O. B. (PO).

Branchiopoda

No other data: Biraben, M. (Nt), Gauthier, H. , Mattox, N. T. (N, Nt), Tiwari, K. K. (O).
Fossils: Tasch, P.

* * * * *

ANOSTRACA: Akatova, N. A. (P), Brtek, J. (P), Coopey, R. W. (N), Dexter, R. W. (N),
    Kertész, G. (P), Linder, F. , Lynch, J. E. (N), Mackin, J. G. (N), Moore, W. G. (N, Nt),
    Müller, G. I. (P), Wootton, D. (N).
CLADOCERA, no locality: Lieder, U. , Stella, E.
    World: Harrison, A. C. , Johnson, D. S. , Kiser, R. W.
    Nearctic: Boliek, M. K. , Bradshaw, A. S. , Deevey, G. B. , Jackson, D. F. , Jones, W. H.
    Neotropical: Brehm, V. , Deevey, G. B.
    Palearctic: Brzek, G. , Findenegg, I. , Galliford, A. L. , Green, J. , Hoenigman, J. ,
        Messikommer, E. , Ponyi, E. , Šrámek-Hušek, R. , Straškraba, M. , Tonolli, V. ,
        Uéno, M. , Ulomsky, S. N.
    Paleotropical: Brehm, V. (E,O, A, Oc), Deevey, G. B. (PO), Green, J. (E).
Fresh-water: Andrews, T. F. (N), Cannicci, G. (P), Frey, D. G. (N, P), Meshkova, T. (P),
    Patalas, K. (P), Pesta, O. , Poulsen, E. M. (P), Pourriot, R. (P), Purasjoki, K. J. (P),
    Resvoy, P. D. (P), Rzoska, J. (E), Sladecek, V. (P), Tonolli, L. (P), Zinn, D. J. (N).
Brackish-water: Purasjoki, K. J. (P).
Marine: Cannicci, G. (P), Komarovsky, B. (P), Pesta, O.
Fossils: Frey, D. G. (Q:N, P).
CONCHOSTRACA: Kertész, G. (P), Wootton, D. (N).
    Fossils: Talent, J. A. (P-M: ?), Tasch, P.
NOTOSTRACA: Kertész, G. (P), Linder, F. , Longhurst, A. R. (W), Lynch, J. E. (N).
PHYLLOPODA: Barnard, K. H. (E), Botnariuc, N. (P), Røen, U. (P), Uéno, M. (P).
    (See also Anostraca, Notostraca, Conchostraca)

Fossils: Bond, G. (P-M:E), Teixeira, C. (P-M:E).
* * * * *
Chydoridae: Frey, D. G. (N, P).
Daphniidae: Brooks, J. L. (N, Nt), Hrbáček, J. (W).

Cirripedia

No other data: Costlow, J. D., Jr.
    World: Barnes, H., Broch, H., Cornwall, I. E., Southward, A. J., Utinomi, H.
    Nearctic: Bousfield, E. L., Connell, J. H., Hatch, M. H., Marchette, N. J.
    Palearctic: Bassindale, R., Brattström, H. O., Connell, J. H., Crisp, D. J., Read, R.
    Ethiopian: Barnard, K. H.
Epizoic: Connell, J. H. (PO).
Larvae: Lovegrove, T. (P).
Fossils: Kopf, R. W. (P:N).
* * * * *
ACROTHORACICA: Tomlinson, J. (W).   FOSSILS: Tomlinson, J. (P-C:W).
ASCOTHORACICA: Brattström, H. O. (W), Okada, Y. K. (W), Yosii, N.
RHIZOCEPHALA: Bocquet-Vedrine, J. (P), Boschma, H. (W), Reischman, P. (N, Nt),
    Shiino, S. M. (P).
THORACICA: Buchholz, H. A. (P), Cantell, C. A. N. (W), Henry, D., Newman, W. A. (W).
    Larvae: Buchholz, H. A. (P).
* * * * *
Balanidae: Kolosváry, G., Pope, E. (O, A, Oc).
    Fossils: Kolosváry, G.

Copepoda

No other data: Anderson, G. C., Bai, S., Barnett, P., Bauibridge, V., Borutzky, E. B., Bozie,
    B., Burd, A. C., Digby, P. S. B., Dussart, B. H., Francoise, Y., Heberer, G., Heldt,
    J. H., Heller, A. F., Hertzog, L. A., Honjo, K., Hsiao, S. C., Jaczo, I., Kare, E.,
    King, J. E., Kirtisinghe, P., Knapp, S. E., Lüling, H., Mazepova, G. F., Monard, A.,
    Percival, E., Pintea, M., Ranise, S., Remane, A., Rose, M., Schachter, -, Smidt, E.,
    Stella, E., Tërëk, P., Thomas, H. J., Tsuruta, A., Wickstead, P., Yin, W-Y.
    World: Lang, K. G. H., Thomsen, R.
    New World: Boliek, M. I. (N), Bradshaw, A. S. (N), de Oliveira, L. P. H. (Nt).
    Old World: Egami, N. (P), Elster, H. J. (P), Hure, J. (P), Menzel, R. (O), Onabamairo,
      S. D. (E), Plesa, C. (P), Ponyi, E. (P), Ramakrishna, G. (O), Tonolli, V. (P).
    Marine, no locality: Davis, C. C., Motoda, S., Pesta, O.
    Atlantic Ocean: Attridge, M., Aurich, H. J., Brandes, C-H., Candeias, A., Causey, D.,
      Deevey, G. B., Fraser, J. H., Marques, E., Raymont, J. E. G., Sutcliffe, W. H., Jr.,
      Zinn, D. J.
    Palearctic Seas: Brian, A., Cattley, J. G., Gamulin, T., Hoenigman, J., Marcus, A.,
      Petkovski, T. K.
    Indian Ocean: Seymour Sewell, R. B.
    Pacific Ocean: Anraku, M., Attridge, M., Deevey, G. B., Johnson, M. W., Komaki, Y.,
      Nemoto, T., Tanaka, O.
    Arctic Seas: Johnson, M. W., Østvedt, O. J., Wiborg, K. F.
Brackish-water: Ito, T. (P), Purasjoki, K. J. (P).
Fresh-water, no locality: Davis, C. C., Pesta, O.
    World: Gauthier, H., Kiefer, F.
    Nearctic: Andrews, T. F., Causey, D., Comita, G. W., Reed, E. B., Zinn, D. J.
    Palearctic: Brian, A., Buchholz, H. A., Damian, A., Ito, T., Purasjoki, K. J., Rejic, M.,
      Resvoy, P. D., Røen, U., Sladecek, V., Tonolli, L.
    Paleotropical: Harada, I. (O), Rzoska, J. (E).
Parasites: Brian, A. (P), Capart, A., Causey, D. (Nt), Dollfus, R. P., Fryer, G. (W),
    Grainger, J. N. R. (P), Hockley, A. R. (P), Heegaard, P. (W), Illg, P. L., Kurian,
    C. V. (IO), Mason, J. (P), Nunez-Ruivo, L. (AO, P), Rangnekar, M. P. (O),
    Rangnekar, P. G. (O), Rao, T. S. S. (IO), Tidd, W. M. (N, Nt).
    On invertebrates: Bocquet, C. (P), Gray, P., Stock, J. H. (W).
    On fish: Candeias, A. (P), Carvalho, J. P. (Nt), Gussev, A. V., Lewis, A. (fw, m:N, Nt, Oc),
      Morton, W. M. (N, P), Ronald, K. (W), Sproston, N. G. (P), Tripathi, Y. R. (O),
      Yamaguti, S. (P).
Commensals: Hockley, A. R. (P), Illg, , P. L.
Larvae: Hanaoka, T. (P).
Fossils: Berousek, J., Brand, E. (M:?), Campau, D. E. (P:N).
* * * * *
BRANCHIURA: Fryer, G. (fw:W), Tokioka, T. (P).

ARTHROPODA, Copepoda (continued)

CALANOIDA: Brehm, V. (Nt, E, O, A, Oc), Grice, G. D. (N), Noodt, W. (W), Smith, W. A. (P),
 Ulomsky; S. N. (P).
  Marine, World: Bowman, T. E., Jones, E. C., Nicholls, A. G., Vervoort, W.
   Atlantic Ocean: Buchholz, H. A., Duran, M., Fleminger, A., Fontaine, M., Gauld, D. T.,
    Jaschnov, W. A., Krishnaswamy, S., Marshall, S. M., Owre, H. B., St, John, P. A.
   Indian Ocean: Krishnaswamy, S.
   Pacific Ocean: Bary, B. M., Dall, W., Fontaine, M.
  Brackish-water: Wilson, M. S. (N, Nt).
  Fresh-water: Brtek, J. (P), Grainger, J. N. R. (P), Mashiko, K. (P), Wilson, M. S. (N, Nt).
CALIGOIDA: Humes, A. G. (W), Shiino, S. M. (P, PO), Vaissière, R. (P, E).
CYCLOPOIDA: Coker, R. E. (N, Nt), Grice, G. D. (N), Humes, A. G. (W), Nicholls, A. G.,
 Wierzbicka, M.
  Marine: Duran, M. (AO, P), Gotto, R. V. (W), Herbst, H. V., Krishnaswamy, S. (P, O),
   Olson, J. B. (W).
  Fresh-water: Fryer, G. (P, E), Herbst, H. V., Meshkova, T. (P), Pór, F. (P),
   Yeatman, H. C. (N).
EUCOPEPODA: Delamare Deboutteville, C. (W).
GNATHOSTOMA: Lindberg, K. (fw, m), Plesa, C. (W).
GYMNOPLEA: Chiba, T. (IO, Oc), Hansen, V. (AO).
HARPACTICOIDA: Carter, M. E., Coker, R. E. (N, Nt), Humes, A. G. (W), Jakobi, H. (W),
 Nicholls, A. G., Noodt, W. (W), de Oliveira, L. P. H. (Nt), Perkins, E. J. (P), Roe,
 K. (P), Serban, M. (P).
  Marine: Clogston, F. (PO), Fahrenbach, W. H. (N, P), Krishnaswamy, S. (P, O), Kunz,
   H. (W), Lance, J. R. (W), Monk, C. R. (N), Pór, F. (P), Zinn, D. J. (N).
  Fresh-water: Fryer, G. (P, E), Kulhavý, K. (W), Kunz, H. (P), Loffler, H. (W), Pór, F. (P),
   Wilson, M. S. (N, Nt), Yeatman, H. C. (N).
  Brackish-water: Kunz, H. (W), Wilson, M. S. (N, Nt).
  Fossils: Chappuis, P. A. (F:W).
LERNAEOPODOIDA: Humes, A. G. (W), Shiino, S. M. (P, PO).
MYSTACOCARIDA: Delamare Deboutteville, C. (W), Noodt, W. (W).
PODOPLEA: Chiba, T. (Oc, IO).
POECILOSTOMA: Plesa, C. (W), Pór, F. (P).
SIPHONOSTOMA: Eiselt, J., Pór, F. (P).

* * * * *

Ameiridae: Humes, A. G. (W), Serban, M. (W).
Argulidae: Lemos de Castro, A. (Nt), Romanovsky, A. (P).
Ascidicolidae: Montgomery, D. H. (N).
Boeckellidae: Loffler, H. (W).
Botryllophilidae: Dudley, P. L. (W), Montgomery, D. H. (N).
Calanidae: Kincaid, T. (fw:N).
Caligidae: Gnanamuthu, C. P. (O), Humes, A. G. (W).
Clausidiidae: Bolster, G. C. (P), Gooding, R. U. (W), Humes, A. G. (W).
Corycaeidae: Zavodnik, D. (P).
Cyclopidae: Patalas, K. (fw:P), Price, J. L. (N, Nt), Smith, W. A. (P), Šrámek-Hušek, R. (P),
 Štěrba, O. (P), Straškraba, M. (P), Ulomsky, S. N. (P), Vranovský, M. (P).
Diaptomidae: Bănărescu, P. (P), Meshkova, T. (P), Patalas, K. (P), Serban, M. (P),
 Šrámek-Hušek, R. (P).
Dichelesthidae: Gnanamutha, C. P. (O).
Diosaccidae: Humes, A. G. (W).
Doropygidae: Montgomery, D. H. (N).
Enterocolidae: Dudley, P. L. (W), Montgomery, D. H. (N).
Ergasilidae: Gnanamutha, C. P. (O), Humes, A. G. (W), Shiino, S. M. (P, PO).
Harpacticidae: Štěrba, O. (P).
Lamippidae: Humes, A. G. (W).
Laophontidae: Serban, M. (W).
Lernaeidae: Gnanamutha, C. P. (O), Grabda, J. (P), Kabata, Z. (AO).
Lernaeopodidae: Friend, G. F. (W), Gnanamutha, C. P (O), Grabda, J. (P), Kabata, Z. (AO).
Lichomolgidae: Humes, A. G. (W).
Myicolidae: Humes, A. G. (W).
Notodelphyidae: Dudley, P. L. (W), Gotto, R. V. (W), Montgomery, D. H. (N).
Temoridae: Patalas, K. (P).
Tisbidae: Humes, A. G. (W).

No other data: Fize, A. , Francois, D. , Liu, J. Y. , Maccagno, T. P. , Perez Farfante de Canet, I. ,
    Schmitt, W. L. , Shen, C. J. , Stenzel, H. B. , Vernberg, F. J. , Waldron, K. D.
World: Armstrong, J. C. , Chace, F. A. , Jr. , Gordon, I.
Nearctic: Leim, A. H. , Lunz, G. R. , Tomlinson, J. , Wass, M. L.
Neotropical: Bahamonde Navarro, J. N. , Lemos de Castro, A. , Sawaya, M. P.
Palearctic: Allen, J. A. , Băcescu, M. , Figueira, A. J. G. , Gottlieb, E. , Kono, H. (P),
    Miyake, S. , Palau Camps, J. M. , Pike, R. B. , Zariquiey, R.
Paleotropical: Barnard, K. H. (E), Chopra, B. N. (O, Oc), Hale, H. M. (A, Ant), Johnson,
    D. S. (O), Ramakrishna, G. (O), Tiwari, K. K. (O).
Marine: Birstein, J. A. (a:PO), Black, W. F. (AO), Hult, J. (P), Karlovac, O. (P), Kobjakova,
    Z. I. (PO, Arc), Macnae, W. (O, Oc), Maurin, C. M. J. E. (P), McNeill, F. A. (O, Oc),
    Nunez-Ruivo, L. (P), Parker, R. H. (Nt), Pesta, O. , Sivertsen, E. (Arc, Ant), Squires,
    H. J. (AO, Arc), Williams, A. B. (N), Wolff, T. (a), Yaldwyn, J. C. (O, Oc).
Fresh-water: Birstein, J. A. (P), De Costa, J. , Lopez, M. T. (Nt), Pesta, O. , Riek, E. F. (A),
    Stansbury, D. H. (N).
Larvae: Johnson, M. W. (PO), Kurian, C. V. (AO, P), Pike, R. B. (P), Williamson, D. I. (W).
Blood sera: Leone, C. A. (W).
Fossils, no age: Glaessner, M. F. , Holland, F. D. , Jr. (N).
    Mesozoic: Bachmayer, F. (P), Ball, H. W. , Houša, V. (P), Remy, J-M. (W), Roberts,
        H. B. (N, Nt), Stenzel, H. B. , Václav-Houša, -. (P).
    Cenozoic: Bachmayer, F. (P), Ball, H. W. , Houša, V. (P), Menzies, R. J. , Remy,
        J-M. (W), Roberts, H. B. (N, Nt), Stenzel, H. B. , Václav-Houša, -. (P), Via, L. (P).
Crayfish: Brown, P. L. (N), Eberly, W. R. (N), Rhoades, R. , Turner, C. L. (N).
    Fossils: Rhoades, R. (Q:?).

* * * * *

ANOMURA: Forest, J. (AO), Miyake, S. (P, O, PO).
BRACHYURA: Atkins, D. (P), Capart, A. (m:AO;fw:E), Chhapgar, B. F. (m:O), Contreras,
    F. (Nt), Edmondson, C. H. (Oc), Forest, J. (O, Oc), Garth, J. S. (PO), Hiatt, R. W. (PO),
    Hoestlandt, H. (P), Miyake, S. (P, O, PO), Monod, T. (E), Ow-Yang, C. K. (m:O), Sakai,
    T. (P, Oc), Serene, R. (O, Oc), Wolff, T. (P, E).
    Fossils: Imaizumi, R. (F:N, Nt, P), Wright, C. W. (M:P).
CARIDEA: Nouvel, H. (W).   •
MACRURA: Butler, T. H. (N), Forest, J. (AO), Holthuis, L. B. (W), Kobjakova, Z. I. (PO, Arc),
    Kubo, I. (P).
NATANTIA: Figueira, A. J. G. (W), Sollaud, E. (P), Yaldwyn, J. C. (A).
PENAEIDEA: Thompson, J. R. (N, Nt).
REPTANTIA: Hart, J. F. L. (m:N).
    Fossils: Imaizumi, R. (F:N, Nt, P).

* * * * *

Alpheidae: Banner, A. H. (O, Oc).
Astacidae: Bott, R. (W), Crocker, D. W. (N), Francois, D. D. (N, P), Hobbs, H. H. , Jr. (N),
    Penn, G. H. (N), Riegel, J. A. (N), Villalobos, A. (N, Nt), Williams, A. B. (N).
Atyidae: Frey, D. G. (O, Oc), Johnson, D. S. (O), Racek, A. A. (O, A), Villalobos, A. (N, Nt).
Callianasidae: Stevens, B. A. (N).
Cancridae: Marriage, L. D. (N, PO).
Cirolanidae: Băcescu, M. (P).
Coenobitidae: Provenzano, A. J. (N, Nt, Trop).
Eryonidae: Thompson, J. R. (AO).
Galatheidae: Thompson, J. R. (AO).
Gecarcinidae: Archer, A. F. (Nt).
Grapsidae: Archer, A. F. (Nt).
Hapalocarcinidae: Serene, R. (AO, IO, PO).
Nephropsidae: Thompson, J. R. (AO).
Ocypodidae: Archer, A. F. (Nt), Crane, J. (m:W).
Paguridae: Coffin, H. G. (N, Nt), Forest, J. (O, Oc), Provenzano, A. J. (N, Nt, Trop), Stevens,
    B. A. (N), Wass, M. L. (N).
Palaemonidae: Boschi, E. E. (Nt), Frey, D. G. (O, Oc), Johnson, D. S. (O), Villalobos, A. (N, Nt).
    Larvae: Broad, A. C. (m, bw:N).
Palinuridae: George, R. W. (W), Lindberg, R. G. (N, Oc), Racek, A. A. (O, Oc), Sheard, K. (W).
    Larvae: George, R. W. (W).
Pandalidae: Marriage, L. D. (N, PO).
Panuliridae: Olsen, A. M. (A).
Parastacidae: Francois, D. D. (Nt, E, O, A, Oc), Racek, A. A. (O, A).
Penaeidae: Boschi, E. E. (Nt), Broad, C. (N), Burkenroad, M. D. (W), Dall, W. (O, Oc), Hall,
    D. (O), Koratha, K. J. (W), Massuti, M. (P), Núñez, R. , Racek, A. A. (O, Oc).
Porcellanidae: Haig, J. (N), Johnson, D. S. (O).

Portunidae: Leene, J. E. (O, Oc), Ow-Yang, C. K. (O), Porter, H. J. (N), Ryan, E. P. (N, Oc),
    Stephenson, W. (PO, IO), Wallace, S. L. (N).
Potamonidae: Bott, R. (W).
Scyllaridae: Thompson, J. R. (AO).
Xanthidae: Ryan, E. P. (N, Oc).

Isopoda

No other data: Arcangeli, A., Buturović, A., Frankenberger, Z., Herold, W., Mañé-Garzón, F.,
    Searle, H. R., Stankovic, S.
    Nearctic: Eberly, W. R., Henson, E. B., Ide, F. P., Miller, M. A.
    Neotropical: Miller, M. A.
    Palearctic: Bocquet, C., Gordon, I., Hoestlandt, H., Holthuis, L. B., Meinertz, T.,
      Naylor, E.
    Paleotropical: Barnard, K. H. (E), Hale, H. M. (A), Hurley, D. E. (Oc), Miller, M. A. (Oc),
      Omer-Cooper, J. (E), Pillay, N. K. (O), Tiwari, K. K. (O).
 Marine, World: Cattley, J. G., Gruner, H. E., Wolff, T. (a).
    Atlantic Ocean: Black, W. F., Forsman, B., Gurjanova, E. F., Kjennerud, J., Hult, J.,
      Monod, T., Polk, P., Sheppard, E.
    Indian Ocean: Cattley, J. G.
    Pacific Ocean: Birstein, J. A., Gurjanova, E. F., Iwasa, M., Kussakin, O. G.
    Arctic & Antarctic Oceans: Gurjanova, E. F. (Arc), Hale, H. M. (Ant), Kussakin,
      O. G. (Arc), Sheppard, E. (Ant), Sivertsen, E. (Arc, Ant).
Fresh-water: Birstein, J. A. (P), Brtek, J. (P), De Costa, J., Hubricht, L. (N), Iwasa, M. (P),
    Wurtz, C. B. (N).
Terrestrial: Brian, A. (P), Iwasa, M. (P), Karaman, S. K. (P), Lohmander, H. (P), Mulaik,
    S. B. (N, Nt), Radu, V. (P), Schmölzer, K. (P), Strouhal, H. (W), Vandel, A. (N, Nt, P, A).
Parasitic: Dollfus, R. P.
Fossils: Bachmayer, F. (M-Q: P), Chappuis, P. A. (F: W), Wall, J. H. (M: N).
* * * * *

ASELLOTA: Strouhal, H. (P).
EPICARIDEA: Shiino, S. M. (P, PO), Stock, J. H. (W).
ONISCOIDEA: Černý, W. (P), Edney, E. B. (P), Legrand, J. J. (W), Lemos de Castro, A. (Nt),
    Muchmore, W. B. (N), Polk, P. (P).
* * * * *

Asellidae: Braga, J. M. (P, E), Codreanu, R. (W), Mackin, J. G. (N), Matsumoto, K. (P).
Bopyridae: Chopra, B. N. (O, Oc), Pike, R. B. (P).
Cymothoidae: Bowman, T. E. (W), Lemos de Castro, A. (Nt), Szidat, L. (AO).
Limnoriidae: Hockley, A. R. (P), Ray, D. L.

Malacostraca

No other data: Balke, N. P. W., Borghorst, G., Gordon, I. (W).
Marine: Birstein, J. A. (a: PO), Cannicci, G. (P).
Fresh-water: Birstein, J. A. (P), Cannicci, G. (P).
Fossils: Brooks, H. K. (P: ?), Glaessner, M. F., Van Straelen, V.
* * * * *

ANASPIDACEA: Karaman, S. K. (P).
BATHYNELLACEA: Botosăneanu, L. (P), Jakobi, H. (W), Kulhavý, K. (W).
CARIDEA: Thompson, J. R. (AO).
CUMACEA: Băcescu, M. (P), Fage, L., Forsman, B. (P), Hale, H. M. (A, Ant), Harada, I. (PO),
    Hart, J. F. L. (N), Jones, N. S. (W), Kurian, C. V. (IO), Lomakina, N. B. (PO, Arc, Ant).
EUPHAUSIACEA: Banner, A. H. (PO), Bary, B. M. (Oc), Boden, B. P. (W), Brinton, E. (W),
    Dall, W. (Oc), Johnson, M. W. (PO, Arc), Komaki, Y. (PO), Lomakina, N. B. (W),
    Nemoto, T. (PO), Nouvel, H. (W), Sheard, K. (W).
INGOLFIELLIDA: Karaman, S. K. (P).
MYSIDACEA: Clarke, W. D. (W), Holmquist, C., Larkin, P. A., Nouvel, H. (W), Tattersall,
    O. S. (W), Villalobos, A. (N, Nt).
    Marine: Băcescu, M. (P), Banner, A. H. (PO), Bary, B. M. (Oc), Birstein, J. A. (a: PO),
      Black, W. F. (AO), Hoenigman, J. (P), Ii, N. (PO), Lomakina, N. B. (PO, Arc, Ant),
      Tchindonova, J. G. (IO, PO, Ant).
    Fresh-water: Birstein, J. A. (P), Holmquist, C., Stammer, H-J. (W).
SCHIZOPODA: Pillay, N. K. (O).
SYNCARIDA: Delamare Deboutteville, C. (W), Siewing, R. (W).
TANAIDACEA: Brown, A. C. (E), Cattley, J. G. (IO), Jones, N. S. (P), Lang, K. G. H. (W),
    Mañé-Garzón, F., Miller, M. A. (N, Nt, Oc).

42

THERMOSBAENACEA: Barker, D. (P), Delamare Deboutteville, C. (W), Karaman, S. K. (P), Stella, E.

* * * * *

Apseudidae: Băcescu, M. (P).
Bathynellidae: Braga, J. M. (P, E), Ponyi, E. (P), Uéno, M. (W).
Potamonidae: Colosi, G. (W).
Sergestidae: Tchindonova, J. G. (PO).

Ostracoda

No other data: Adamczak, F. , Akatova, N. A. , Apostolescu, V. (P), Coryell, H. N. , Dusenbury, A. N. , Jr. , Gibson, L. (N, Nt, P), Grekoff, N. (P, E), Grekulinski, E. , Hartman, G. (W), Hill, B. L. Jr. , Hoare, R. D. (N), Hornibrook, N. B. (A), Imanishi, S. , Levinson, S. A. (W), Munsey, G. C. , Jr. (N), Petkovski, T. K. (P), Pietschker, F. (N), Sohn, I. G. , Svivastava, V. K. , Sylvester-Bradley, P. C. , Triebel, E.
Fresh-water: Ferguson, E. , Jr. (N), Gutentag, E. D. , Hoff, C. C. (N), Loffler, H. (W), Lüttig, G. (P), van Morkhoven, F. , Pinto, I. D. , Poulsen, E. M. (P), Purasjoki, K. J. (P), Rome, R. (P, E), Schaefer, H. W. (W), Tressler, W. L. , de Vos, A. P. C. (P).
Brackish-water: van Morkhoven, F. , Purasjoki, K. J. (P).
Marine: Elofson, O. (P), Gauthier, H. , Hartman, G. (W), Hulings, N. (N), van Morkhoven, F. , Rothwell, W. T. , Jr. (N, Nt), Ruggieri, G. (P), Schaefer, H. W. (W), Stacy, H. (N, Nt), Tressler, W. L. , de Vos, A. P. C. (P).
Fossils, no age: Echols, D. J. , Foster, G. L. , Grossman, S. , Krömmelbein, K. (Nt), Levinson, S. A. (W), Martin, G. P. R. (P), Salmon, E. S. , Scott, H. W. , Smout, A. H. (P), Swain, F. M. (N, Nt).
   Paleozoic: Anderson, F. W. , Bassler, R. S. , Benson, R. H. , Berdan, J. M. , Bond, G. (E), Bouček, B. (P), Campbell, A. R. , Carter, G. F. E. (N), Cooper, C. L. , Copeland, M. J. (N), Cordell, R. J. , Coryell, H. N. , Grekoff, N. (P, E), Grekulinski, E. , Gutschick, R. C. (N), Hessland, I. , Hoskins, D. M. (N), Jones, P. J. (A), Kay, M. , Kesling, R. V. , Kraft, J. C. (N), Krömmelbein, K. (P), Loranger, D. M. (N), Marple, M. F. , van Morkhoven, F. , Oertli, H. (P), Olson, E. P. (N), Peterson, R. M. , Pinto, I. D. , Pokorný, V. (P), Přibyl, A. (P), Robinson, J. E. (P), Rome, R. (P), Shaver, R. H. , Smith, J. E. I. , Smith, M. L. (N), Šnajdr, M. (P), Sohn, I. G. (P), Stover, L. E. (N), Swartz, F. M. , Sylvester-Bradley, P. C. , Tasch, P. , Taylor, P. W. (N, P), Wilson, C. W. , Jr.
   Mesozoic: Anderson, F. W. , Apostolescu, V. (P), Benson, R. H. , van den Bold, W. , Bond, G. (E), Chamney, T. P. (N), Copeland, M. J. (N), Coryell, H. N. , Deroo, G. (P), Drouant, R. , Dusenbury, A. N. , Jr. , Goerlich, F. , Grekoff, N. (P, E), Grekulinski, E. , Hill, B. L. , Jr. , Hornibrook, N. B. (A), Howe, H. V. , Kingma, J. T. (A), Loranger, D. M. (N), Malz, H. (N, P), McLean, J. D. (N, Nt), Mertens, E. , Moos, B. (P), van Morkhoven, F. , Munsey, G. C. , Jr. (N), Oertli, H. (P), Peck, R. E. (W), Peterson, J. A. (N), Pietschker, H. (N), Pinto, I. D. , Pokorný, V. (P), Puri, H. S. (N, O, Oc), Reyment, R. , Skinner, H. C. , Sohn, I. G. , Stacy, H. (N, Nt), Sung, G. C. L. (P), Sylvester-Bradley, P. C. , Thorsen, C. (N), Triebel, E.
   Cenozoic: Apostolescu, V. (P), Benson, R. H. , van den Bold, W. , Coryell, H. N. , Dusenbury, A. N. , Jr. , Edwards, R. A. , Grekoff, N. (P, E), Grekulinski, E. , Gutentag, E. D. , Hartman, G. (W), Hill, B. L. , Jr. , Hornibrook, N. B. (A), Howe, H. V. , Keij, A. J. (Oc), Moos, B. (P), Munsey, G. C. , Jr. (N), Pietschker, F. (N), Puri, H. S. (N, O, Oc), Sohn, I. G. , Stacy, H. (N, Nt), Sylvester-Bradley, P. C. , Triebel, E.
   Tertiary: Artusy, R. L. Bowen, R. N. C. (P), Butler, E. (N), Goerlich, F. , Hay, W. W. (P), Hulings, N. (N), Keij, A. J. (P), Key, A. J. (P), Kingma, J. T. (A), Kollmann, K. (P), Lumsden, W. (N), McLean, J. D. (N, Nt), Mertens, E. , van Morkhoven, F. , Moyes, J. (P), Nagappa, Y. (O), Neely, R. M. (N), Oertli, H. (P), Peterson, J. A. (N), Pokorný, V. (P), Reyment, R. , Ruggieri, G. (P), Singh, S. N. (O), Smith, D. J. (N), Tewari, B. S. (O, Oc), Turner, K. , Valentine, J. W. (N).
   Quaternary: Anderson, F. W. , Lüttig, G. (P), Mertens, E. , Ruggieri, G. (P), Tressler, W. L. , Wagner, C. W. (P).

* * * * *

CLADOCOPA: Kornicker, L. S.   FOSSILS: Kornicker, L. S.
ENTOMOZOACEA - fossils: Rabien, A. (P:P).
HALOCYPRIFORMES: Poulsen, E. M. (m:W).
MYODOCOPA: Kornicker, L. S.   FOSSILS: Kornicker, L. S.
PALAEOCOPA - fossils: Henningsmoen, G. (P:P), Jaanusson, V. (P:?), Martinsson, A. (F:P), Morris, R. W. (F:N, P).
PODOCOPA: Kornicker, L. S.
   Fossils: Kornicker, L. S. , Morris, R. W. (N, P), Wolburg, J. (M:P).

* * * * *

Beyrichiidae - fossils: Adamczak, F. (F:P), Martinsson, A. (F:W).
Cyprideidae - fossils: Martin, G. P. R. (M:P).

Cytheridae: Hobbs, H. H. , Jr. (N), Stamper, M. N. (N).
  Fossils: Pinto, I. D. (M:W).
Primitiopsidae - fossils: Martinsson, A. (F:W).

Stomatopoda

No other data: Barnard, K. H. (E), Bott, R. (W), Chace, F. A. , Jr. (W), Chopra, B. N. (O, Oc),
    Holthuis, L. B. (W), Lunz, G. R. (N), Manning, R. B. (AO), Serene, R. (O, Oc),
    Stephenson, W. (IO, Oc), Tiwari, K. K. (O), Townsley, S. J. (W), Yaldwyn, J. C. (A).

Myriapoda

No other data: Aleinikova, M. M. , Gyger, H. P. (W), Read, R. (P), Williamson, M. H.
  (See also Chilopoda, Diplopoda, Pauropoda, Symphyla)
        * * * * *
ORTHOGNATHA: Bücherl, W. (Nt).

Chilopoda

No other data: Kacsmarek, J.
    World: Chamberlin, R. V. , Crabill, R. E. , Demange, J. M. , Dobroruka, L. J. , Kraus, O.
    Nearctic: Causey, N. B. , Hefner, R. A. , Ide, F. P. , Johnson, B. M.
    Neotropical: Buckup, E. H. , Turk, F. A.
    Palearctic: Åbro, A. , Blower, J. G. , Brade-Birks, S. G. , Cloudsley-Thompson, J. L. ,
      Eason, E. H. , Folkmanova, B. , Gulička, J. , Jeekel, C. A. W. , Kanellis, A. , Lohmander,
      H. , Loksa, I. , Manfredi, P. , Matic, Z. , Miyosi, Y. , Paik, K. Y. , Palmén, E. ,
      Takakuwa, Y. , Tomanterä, E. A. , Turk, F. A.
    Paleotropical: Lawrence, R. F. (E), Loksa, I. (O), Turk, F. A. (E), Wang,
      Y-H. M. (O, A, Oc).
        * * * * *
ANAMORPHA: Murakami, Y. (P).
GEOPHILOMORPHA: Bücherl, W. (Nt), Shinohara, K. (P, Oc).
LITHOBIOMORPHA: Matic, Z. (P).
SCOLOPENDROMORPHA: Coscarón, S. (Nt).
SCUTIGEROMORPHA: Bücherl, W. (Nt).
        * * * * *
Geophilidae: Auerbach, S. I. (N, P, E).
Henicopidae: Shinohara, K. (P, Oc).
Lithobiidae: Auerbach, S. I. (N, P, E), Shinohara, K. (P, Oc).
Scolopendridae: Auerbach, S. I. (N, P, E), Bücherl, W. (Nt), Jangi, B. S. (W), Shinohara,
    K. (P, Oc).

Diplopoda

No other data, World: Chamberlin, R. V. , Demange, J. M. , Jeekel, C. A. W. , Keeton, W. T. ,
    Kraus, O.
    Nearctic: Causey, N. B. , Hefner, R. A. , Hoffman, R. L. , Ide, F. P. , Johnson, B. M. ,
      Loomis, H. F.
    Neotropical: Hoffman, R. L. , Loomis, H. F. , Schubart, O. , Turk, F. A.
    Palearctic: Blower, J. G. , Brade-Birks, S. G. , Ceuca, T. , Eason, E. H. , Gulička, J. ,
      Homoláč, M. E. , Jawlowski, H. , Lang, J. , Lohmander, H. , Loksa, I. , Manfredi, P. ,
      Miyosi, Y. , Paik, K. Y. , Palmén, E. , Rolfe, S. W. H. , Sahli, F. , Schubart, O. ,
      Stojałowska, W. , Takakuwa, Y. , Takashima, H. , Turk, F. A.
    Ethiopian: Hoffman, R. L. , Lawrence, R. F. , Schubart, O. , Turk, F. A.
    Oriental: Loksa, I. , Wang, Y-H. M.
    Australian: Dawson, E. W. , Wang, Y-H. M.
    Oceania: Dawson, E. W. , Hoffman, R. L. , Wang, Y-H. M.
Fossils: Brade-Birks, S. G. (F:P), Kukalová, J. (P:W).
        * * * * *
POLYDESMIDA: Hoffman, R. L. (N, Nt, E, Oc), Shinohara, K. (P, Oc).
PSELAPHOGNATHA: Condé, B. (W).
SPIROBOLIDA: Hoffman, R. L. (N, Nt, E, Oc).
SPIROSTREPTIDA: Hoffman, R. L. (N, Nt, E, Oc).
        * * * * *
Blaniulidae: Ceuca, T. (P).
Harpagophoridae: Velanker, S. R. (O).

Polydesmidae: Ceuca, T. (P).
Sphaerotheridae: Holloway, B. A. (A).
Sphaerotrichopidae: Johns, P. M. (A).

Pauropoda

No other data: Bonet, F. (W), Lawrence, R. F. (E), Niwa, H. (P), Remy, P. A. (W),
Scheller, U. , Starling, J. H.

Symphyla

No other data: Hartland-Rowe, R. , Ravoux, P. , Scheller, U.
World: Edwards, C. A. T. , Michelbacher, A. E. , Williams, E. C. , Jr.
Neotropical: Juberthie-Jupeau, L.
Palearctic: Dobroruka, L. J. , Imamura, T. , Juberthie-Jupeau, L. , Takashima, H.
Paleotropical: Dobroruka, L. J. (E), Juberthie-Jupeau, L. (E, Oc).

Insecta

No other data: Čekalovic Kuschević, T. (Nt), Clemente, L. S. (O), Cunningham, J. R. (A),
Dale, P. S. , Dreisbach, R. R. (N), Elgee, D. E. (N), Giglioli, M. E. C. , Gonzalez, M. C. ,
Hrisafi, C. , Khatib, S. M. H. , Marquardt, W. , Menon, M. G. R. (O), Morisita, T. (P),
Morrison, L. G. , Noland, G. B. (N), Puls, J. J. , Rios Castaño, D. (Nt), Suehiro, A. (Oc),
Washburn, R. H. (N), de Zayas Muños, F. (Nt).
Aquatic: Fournier, O. , Henson, E. B. (N), Judd, W. W.
Parasite vectors: Fox, R. M. (W).
Leaf miners: Hering, E. M. (P).
Galls: van Leeuwen, W. M. D. (P, O).
Wood-boring: Hickin, N. E. (W), Milligan, R. H. (A).
Myrmecophilous: Wing, M. W. (W).
Of oaks: Sternlicht, M. (P).
Of prairies: Brooks, A. R. (N).
Of stored products: Baeta Neves, C. M. L. (P, E), Barratt, P. R. (P), de Jong, C. (W), Mallis,
A. (N), Papp, C. S. , Williams, D. W. (W).
Of medical interest: Collado, J. G. (P), Forattini, O. P. (Nt), Fox, R. M. (W), Hasegawa, M. (P),
Rageau, J. G. F. (Oc), Vercammen-Grandjean, P. H. (E).
Wings: Jolivet, P. (W).
Larvae: Stammer, H-J. (P).
Fossils: Carpenter, F. M. (P, M:?), Kukalová, J. (P, M:W), Pierce, W. D. (C:N), Richardson,
E. S. , Jr. (P:?), Riek, E. F. (F:A), Teixeira, C. (P:?).
* * * * *
APTERYGOTA: Absolon, S. K. , Chourdhuri, D. K. , Ionescu, M. A. , Quadri, M. A. H. , Selga, D. ,
Stach, J. (W), Tuxen, S. L. (N, P), Womersley, H. (A, Oc).
Fossils: Sharov, A. G. (P, M:?).
EXOPTERYGOTA: Ahmad, T. , Jotwani, M. G. , Patel, G. A. , Spiller, D.
ENDOPTERYGOTA: Gaumont, R. L. , Geyer, J. W.

Protura

No other data: Bonet, F. (W), Condé, B. (W), Copeland, T. P. (N), da Cunha, A. X. (P, E),
Imadaté, G. (P, Oc), Ionescu, M. A. (P), Nosek, J. (P), Paclt, J. , Tuxen, S. L. (W).
Fossils: Paclt, J.

Thysanura

No other data: Delamare Deboutteville, C. (W), Delany, M. J. (P), Nosek, J. (P), Paclt, J. ,
Remington, C. L. (W), Sharov, A. G. (P), Wall, W. J. (N).
Fossils: Paclt, J.
* * * * *
Lepismatidae: Uchida, H. (P, O, Oc), Wygodzinsky, P. (W).
Machilidae: Bitsch, J. (W), Janetschek, H. (P), Riezler, H. (P), Wygodzinsky, P. (W).

Entotrophi
(Diplura)

No other data: Arevad, K. (P), Kosaroff, G. , Nosek, J. (P), von Orelli, M. , Paclt, J. ,
Pagés, J. (W), Remington, C. L. (W).
Fossils: Paclt, J.
* * * * *

Campodeidae: Condé, B. (W).
Japygidae: Gyger, H. P. (P), Smith, L. M. (N, Nt).
Procampodeidae: Condé, B. (W).
Projapygidae: Smith, L. M. (N, Nt).

Collembola

No other data: Agrell, I., Alvarez, C., Bagnall, R. S., van Damme, E. N. G., Durkop, A. H.,
    Lindenmann-Nebiker, W., Macfadyen, A., Massera, M. G., Miles, P., Paclt, J.
    World: Bonet, F., Delamare Deboutteville, C., Goto, H. E., Richards, W. R., Salmon, J. T.,
        Scott, H. G., Yosii, R.
    Nearctic: Copeland, T. P., Haarløv, N., Maynard, E. A., Mills, H. B., Scott, D. B.,
        Scott, H. G., Strenzke, K., Wade, L. E., Wilkey, R. F., Wray, D. L., Jr.
    Neotropical: Mills, H. B., Rapoport, E. H., Wray, D. L., Jr.
    Palearctic: Altner, H., Barratt, P. R., Bödvarsson, H., Brian, M. V., Cassagnau, P.,
        Christiansen, K. A., Gisin, H., Haarløv, N., Jacquemart, S., Jeannenot, F., Kholova,
        H., Murphy, D. H., Nosek, J., Palissa, A., Steiner, W., Strenzke, K., von Törne, E.
    Paleotropical: Baijal, H. N. (O), Green, C. D. (E), Mahon, J. A. (A), Murphy,
        D. H. (E), van Pletzen, R. (E), Scott, H. G. (O).
Fossils: Paclt, J.
                                    * * * * *
Entomobryidae: Baijal, H. N. (O), Christiansen, K. A. (W), Uchida, H. (P, O, Oc).
Isotomidae: Baijal, H. N. (O), Bellinger, P. F. (W), Schmidt, F. (N).
Onychiuridae: Baijal, H. N. (O), Imadaté, G. (P).
Poduridae: Baijal, H. N. (O).
Sminthuridae: Richards, W. R. (W), Uchida, H. (P, O, Oc).

Ephemeroptera

No other data: Balch, R. F., Daggy, R. H., Kimmins, D. E., Lyman, F. E., Štěrba, O.
    World: van Bruggen, A. C., Demoulin, G., Edmunds, G. F., Jr., Thew, T. B.
    Nearctic: Berner, L., Britt, N. W., Day, W. C., Edmunds, G. F., Jr., Ide, F. P.,
        Leonard, J. W., Mikulski, J., Traver, J. R.
    Neotropical: Traver, J. R., Ulmer, G.
    Palearctic: Aubert, J., Biancheri, E., Bogoescu, C., Brekke, R., Degrange, C.,
        Fontaine, J., Grandi, M., Ikinomov, P., Illies, J., Kefermüller, M., Landa, V.,
        Mikulski, J., Müller-Liebenau, J., Pleskot, G., Réal, P., Uéno, M., Ujhelyi, S.,
        Ulmer, G.
    Paleotropical: Chopra, B. N. (O), Crass, R. S. (E), Fontaine, J. (E), Rieg, E. F. (A),
        Ulmer, G. (E, O, A, Oc).
Larvae: Dolan, T. (N), Henson, E. B. (N), Macan, T. T. (P).
Fossils: Demoulin, G. (F:W), Thew, T. B. (F:W).
                                    * * * * *
Caenidae: Thew, T. B. (W).
Leptophlebiidae: Thew, T. B. (W).

Odonata

No other data: Agarwal, J. P., Aguesse, P., Attlee, H. G., Berly, J. A., Bird, R. D., Calvert,
    P. P., Chao, H., Clark, C. A., Corbet, P. S., Cowley, J., Dietrich, A. S., van Eldik,
    H. C., Faris, R. C., Fluno, J. A., French, R. A., Garcia-Diaz, J., Gaunitz, S.,
    Gehweiler, W. J., Gortler, A., Grieve, E. G., Harbison, C. F., Harden, P. C., Harker,
    J., Jones, V. E., Kimmins, D. E., Krieger, F., Lederer, G., Martin, J. E. H., Mayo,
    V. K., Michael, P., Morera, A. B., Müller, O. H., Oksala, T., Pelton, J. Z., Perutik,
    R., Pisano, R. G., Popova, A. N., Prenn, F., Ratcliffe, D. A., Ries, M. D., Schottner,
    A., Seidel, F., Smith, M. E., Tabacaru, Y., Urbański, J., Valle, K. I., Watson, B.,
    Whitehouse, F. C., Willey, R. L., Wolfe, L. S., Yamamoto, Y., Zahner, R.
    World: Beatty, A. F., Beatty, G. H., III, Buchholz, K. F., Cook, C., Donnelly, T. W.,
        Gardner, A. E., Montgomery, B. E., Racenis, J., Schmidt, E., Svihla, A.
    Nearctic: Ahrens, C., Albright, P. N., Bick, G. H., Borror, D. J., Byers, C. F.,
        Cumming, R. B., Cuyler, R. D., Fisher, E., Garman, P., Gibbs, R. H., Jr., Gloyd,
        L. K., Harwood, P. D., Hertel, R., Klots, E., Kormondy, E. J., Leonard, J. W.,
        Morse, W. J., Price, H. F., Pritchard, A. E., Robert, A., Walker, E. M., Westfall, M. J.
    Neotropical: Cumming, R. B., Fraser, F. C., Geijskes, D. C., Gloyd, L. K., Klots, E.,
        Kormondy, E. J., Leonard, J. W., Machado, A. B. M., dos Santos, N. D., St. Quentin, D.,
        Westfall, M. J.

Palearctic: Åbro, A., Adamovic, Z. R., Akramowski, N. N., Ander, K., Andoh, T.,
   Asahina, S., Belyshev, B. F., Bērziņš, B. V. A., Bilek, A., Cârdei, F., Conci, C.,
   Consiglio, C., Degrange, C., Ford, W. K., Fraser, F. C., Hammond, C. O.,
   Klimaszewska, H., Klots, E., Kühlmann, D., Leth, K. O., Lieftinck, M. A., MacNeill,
   N., Moore, B. P., Moore, N. W., Naumann, H., Nielsen, C., O'Farrell, A. F., Okada,
   H., Okumura, T., Pinniger, E. B., Pór, F., Prose, H., Réal, P., Robert, P. A.,
   Rosenbohm, A., Samsonovna-Sengelia, E., Schiemenz, H., Schoffeniels, E., Schumann,
   H., Sømme, S., Spuris, Z., Steinmann, H., St. Quentin, D., Teyrovsky, V., Tomanterä,
   E. A., Ujhelyi, S., Valletta, A., Wenger, O. P.
Ethiopian: Balinsky, B. I., Fraser, F. C., Klots, E., Nielsen, C., Pinhey, E. C. G.,
   Whellan, J. A.
Oriental: Chujo, M., Dasgupta, J., Fraser, F. C., O'Farrell, A. F., Okumura, T.
Australian: Dobson, R., Fraser, F. C., Lieftinck, M. A., Moore, B. P., O'Farrell, A. F.
Oceania: Fraser, F. C., Leonard, J. W., Lieftinck, M. A., O'Farrell, A. F.
Larvae: Akramowski, N. N. (P), Beatty, A. F. (W), Beatty, G. H., III (W), Cumming, R. B. (N, Nt),
   Dolan, T. (N), Gardner, A. E. (P), Kormondy, E. J. (N), Montgomery, B. E. (N),
   Westfall, M. J. (N, Nt).
Fossils: Asahina, S. (F:P), Fraser, F. C. (P-R:Nt, P, E, O, A, Oc).
                               * * * * *
ANISOPTERA: Baijal, H. N. (O), Cross, W. H. (N), Grabau, M. C. (N), Larsen, W. P. (N).
   Larvae: Grabau, M. C. (N).
ARCHODONATA - fossils: Demoulin, G. (W).
                               * * * * *
Agrionidae: Fudakowski, J. (P).   Larvae: Fudakowski, J. (P).
Calopterygidae: Buchholtz, C. (P), Montgomery, B. E. (N, Nt).
   Larvae: Montgomery, B. E. (N, Nt).
Libellulidae: Borror, D. J. (N, Nt), Longfield, C. E. (E), McMahan, E. A. (N).

                               Plecoptera

No other data: Balch, R. F., Kimmins, D. E.
   World: Brinck, P., Hanson, J. F.
   Nearctic: Castle, G. B., Gaufin, A. R., Jewett, S. G., Ricker, W. E.
   Neotropical: Aubert, J., Geijskes, D. C., Illies, J., Jewett, S. G.
   Palearctic: Aubert, J., Bogoescu, C., Brekke, R., Consiglio, C., Degrange, C., Hynes,
      H. B. N., Illies, J., Kawai, T., Kohno, M., Pomeisl, E., Rauser, J., Ujhelyi, S.,
      Winkler, O., Zhiltzova, L.
   Paleotropical: Balinsky, B. I. (E), Hynes, H. B. N. (E), Jewett, S. G. (E, O, A), Neboiss,
      A. (A), Paulian, R. M. A. (E), Perkins, F. A. (A).
Larvae: Dolan, T. (N), Garner, W. V. (N), Henson, E. B. (N).

                               Grylloblattoidea

No other data: Asahina, S. (P), Rehn, J. W. H. (W).

                               Protoperlaria

MIOMOPTERA, fossils: Martynova, O. M.

                               Orthoptera

No other data: Albrecht, F. O., Bozzo, B., Chapman, K. H., Furukawa, H., Jacobs, W., Karny,
   H. H., Kronmark, H., Lux, E., Machado, J. P., Maljkovskij, M. P., Röber, H., Stark,
   E., Teichmann, H., Thomas, J. G., Travassos, L. P., Filho, Wavloff, N., Wiesmeier,
   J., Zeuner, F. E.
   World: Bolivar y Pieltain, C., Gurney, A. B., Rehn, J. A. G., Rehn, J. W. H.
   Nearctic: Bigelow, R. S., Brooks, A. R., Cantrall, I. J., Cross, W. H., Dehner, E. W.,
      Friauf, J. J., Gangwere, S. K., Grant, H. J., Jr., Hubbell, T. H., Strohecker, H. F.,
      Tinkham, E. R., Urquhart, F. A., Wallace, H. S., Wasserman, M.
   Neotropical: Cantrall, I. J., Grant, H. J., Jr., Hubbell, T. H., Marquez, C. M., Saez, F. A.,
      Willemse, C. J. M.
   Palearctic: Baccetti, B., Bazyluk, W., Capra, F., Čejchan, A., Ebner, R., Fischer, H.,
      Galvagni, A., Harz, K., Holzel, E., Kis, B., Knipper, H., La Greca, M., Măndru, C.,
      Maŕan, J., Mishchenko, L., Mistshenko, L. L., Morales Agacino, E., Nadig, A.,
      Popovici Biznosanu, A., Rungs, O., Schiemenz, H., Shiraki, T., Sokołowski, J. B.,
      Soyer, B., Ujhelyi, S., Vichet, G., Weidner, H.
   Ethiopian: Jago, N. D., Knipper, H., Morales Agacino, E.

                               47

    Oriental: Shiraki, T. , Willemse, C. J. M.
    Australian: Giles, E. T. , Ramsay, G. W. , Salmon, J. T.
    Oceania: Willemse, C. J. M.
Cavernicolous: Chopard, L.
Fossils: Sharov, A. G. (P-M:?), Weidner, H. (C:P), Zeuner, F. E.
           * * * * *

ACRIDOIDEA: Bey-Bienko, G. Y. (P), Carbonell, C. S. (Nt), Colombo, G. (P), Dirsh, V. M. (W),
    Fishelson, L. (P), Helwig, E. R. (N), Jannone, G. (P, E), Key, K. H. L. (E, A), Richter,
    P. (P), Roy, R. (E), Steinmann, H. (P), White, M. J. D. (N, A).
GRYLLODEA: Chopard, L. (W), Ohmachi, F. (P).
SALTATORIA (Tettigonioidea): Åbro, A. (P), Bey-Bienko, G. Y. (P), Eades, D. (N), Nagy,
    B. (P), Vasiliu, M. (P), Whellan, J. A. (E).
           * * * * *

Acrididae (Locustidae), World: Kevan, D. K. M. , Rehn, J. W. H. , Uvarov, B. P. , Wallace, H. S.
    Nearctic: Alexander, G. , Barnum, A. H. , Genung, W. , Hilliard, J. R. , King, R. L. ,
    Knutson, H. , Smith, D. S.
    Neotropical: Barnum, A. H. , Liebermann, J.
    Palearctic: Adamovič, Z. R. , Čejchan, A. , Jago, N. D. , Kevan, D. K. M. , Matvejev, S. D. ,
    Nozawa, C. N. Pener, M. P. , Tinkham, E. R. , Wiesend, P.
    Ethiopian: Jago, N. D. , Kevan, D. K. M. , Weidner, H.
    Oriental: Tinkham, E. R.
  Larvae: Handford, R. H. (N).
Conocephalidae: Piza, S. T. (Nt).
Copiphoridae: Piza, S. T. (Nt).
Ephippigeridae: Verdier, M. (P, E).
Eumastacidae: Bolivar y Pieltain, C. (W), Coronado, L. (W).
Gryllidae: Alexander, R. D. (N), Fulton, B. B. (N), Huber, F. (P), Nozawa, C. N. (P),
    Sternlicht, M. (P), Walker, T. J. (N), Wiesend, P. (P).
Gryllacrididae: Ander, K. (W).
Henicidae: Richards, A. (A).
Lathiceridae: Kevan, D. K. M. (N, Nt, E).
Locustidae: See Acrididae.
Phaneropteridae: Verdier, M. (P, E), Piza, S. T. (Nt).
Pyrgomorphidae: Kevan, D. K. M. (W).
Rhaphidophoridae: Eades, D. (W), Hubbell, T. H. (W), Richards, A. (A).
Tetrigidae: Grant, H. J. , Jr. (W), Günther, K. (Nt, E, O, A, Oc), Widdows, R. E. (N).
Tettigoniidae: Alexander, R. D. (N), Ander, K. (P, E, O, A, Oc), Cohn, T. J. (N, Nt), de Jong,
    C. (P), Karabag, T. (P), Nozawa, C. N. (P), Ragge, D. R. (E), Sternlicht, M. (P),
    Tinkham, E. R. (P, O), Wiesend, P. (P).
Trigonopterygidae: Kevan, D. K. M. (O).
Xyronotidae: Kevan, D. K. M. (N, Nt, E).

Phasmidia

No other data: Castellani, O. (P), Günther, K. (W), Key, K. H. L. (A).
           * * * * *

Phasmatidae: Key, K. H. L. (A).
Phasmidae: Vichet, G. (P, E), Wandschneider, W. (W).

Blattariae

No other data: Asahina, S. (P), Bazyluk, W. (P), Bey-Bienko, G. Y. (P), Cameron, H. (A),
    Castellani, O. (P), Čejchan, A. (P), Friauf, J. J. (N, Nt), Harz, K. (P), Jago, N. D. (E),
    Peschev, G. (P), Piza, S. T. (Nt), Princis, K. (W), Rehn, J. W. H. (W).
  Fossils: Rehn, J. W. H. (F:W).
           * * * * *
Blattidae: Bruijning, C. F. A. , Edmunds, L. R. (N).

Mantodea

No other data: Bazyluk, W. (P), Bregante, H. (Nt), Castellani, O. (P), La Greca, M. (W),
    Peschev, G. (P), Roy, R. (E), Wahrman, J. (P).
           * * * * *
Mantidae: Beier, M. , Piza, S. T. (Nt), Wandschneider, W. (W).
  Larvae: Breland, O. P. (N).

Glosselytrodea

Fossils: Martynova, O. M.

Dermaptera

No other data, World: Gurney, A. B. , Hincks, W. D. , Rehn, J. A. G. , Rehn, J. W. H. , Townes, H. K.
    Nearctic: Cantrall, I. J. , Gangwere, S. K. , Howard, R. S. (m), Hubbell, T. H.
    Neotropical: Cantrall, I. J. , Hubbell, T. H.
    Palearctic: Bazyluk, W. , Bey-Bienko, G. Y. , Castellani, O. , Čejchan, A. , Galvagni, A. ,
    Harz, K. , Kis, B. , Shiraki, T. , Weidner, H.
    Paleotropical: Baijal, H. N. (O), Giles, E. T. (A), Jago, N. D. (E), Shiraki, T. (O),
    Whellan, J. A. (E).

* * * * *

EUDERMAPTERA: Sakai, S. (W).
PROTODERMAPTERA: Sage, B. L. (P), Sakai, S. (W).

Embioptera

No other data: Derbeneva, N. N. , Kapur, A. P. (O), Menon, M. G. R. (O), Michieli, Š. (P), Mühn,
    J. B. (Nt), Ross, E. S. (W), Seshadri, A. R. , Stefani, R. (P).

Isoptera

No other data: Webb, G. C.
    World: Emerson, A. E. , Griffin, F. J. , Krishna, K. , Noirot, C.
    New World: Araujo, R. L. (N, Nt), Castle, G. B. (N), Miller, E. M. (N).
    Palearctic: Grassé, P. P. , Harris, W. V. , Yakhontov, V. V.
    Ethiopian: Coaton, W. G. H. , Ernst, E. , Ghidini, G. M. , Grassé, P. P. , Harris, W. V. ,
    Machado, A. B. , Noirot, C. , Schmidt, R.
    Oriental: Ahmad, M. , Harris, W. V. , Mathur, R. N. , Roonwal, M. L.
    Australian: Calaby, J. H. , Gay, F. J. , Greaves, T. , Harris, W. V.
    Oceania: Crook, F. P. , Gay, F. J. , Harris, W. V. , McMahan, E. A.
Fossils: Weidner, H. (C:P).

* * * * *

Termitidae: Kalshoven, L. G. E. (O).

Psocoptera
(Corrodentia)

No other data: Edwards, A. B. , Nyholm, T.
    World: Badonnel, A. , Gurney, A. B. , Mockford, E. L. , Pearman, J. V. , Roesler, R.
    Nearctic: Chapman, P. J. , Sommerman, K. M.
    Neotropical: Nadler, A. M. , Williner, G. J.
    Palearctic: Broadhead, E. , Danks, L. , von Keler, S. , Obr, S. , Vishnjakova, V. N.
    Paleotropical: Cumber, R. A. (A), Menon, M. G. R. (O), Nadeau, A. M. (Oc), Smithers,
    C. N. (E), Soehardjan, -.(O), Thornton, I. W. B. (O).

Zoraptera

No other data: Bolivar y Pieltain, C. (N, Nt), Delamare Deboutteville, C. (W), Gurney, A. B. (W),
    Paulian, R. M. A. (E).

Mallophaga

No other data: Clinton, H. F. , Guimarães, L. R. , Rahman-Ansari, M. A. , Scanlon, J. E. ,
    Stenram, H. , Uchida, S.
    World: Carriker, M. A. , Jr. , Edwards, R. L. , Eichler, W. , Emerson, K. C. , Holloway, B. A. ,
    von Keler, S. , Tandan, B. K. , Thompson, G. B. , Ward, R. A.
    Nearctic: Stafford, E. W. , Ward, R. A. , Wilson, F. H. , Wilson, N.
    Palearctic: Balát, F. , Bechet, I. , Blagoveshtchensky, D. I. , Brelih, S. , Conci, C. , Harant,
    H. , Nakagawa, H. , Negru, S. , Tuleskov, K.
    Paleotropical: Elbel, R. E. (E, O, A, Oc), Ward, R. A. (Oc).
Of birds: Johnson, J. C. , Jr. (N), Tendeiro, J. (P, E), Timmermann, G. (W), Ward, R. A. (N, Nt).
Of mammals: Clay, T. , Joyce, C. R. (N, Oc), Plomley, N. J. B. (A), Senger, C. M. (N), Werneck,
    F. L. (W).

* * * * *

Menoponidae: Kaneko, K. (P).
Trichodectidae: Cook, E. F. (N).

Thysanoptera

No other data: Blanchard, E. E. , Kurosawa, M.
    World: Jacot-Guillarmod, C. F. , Morison, G. D. , O'Neill, K. , Pelikan, J. , Priesner, H.
    Nearctic: Andre, F. , Bailey, S. F. , Bianchi, F. A. , Bigelow, R. S. , Ewart, W. , Gromadska,
      M. , Hood, J. D. , Post, R. L. , Stannard, L. J. , Jr. , Watts, J. G.
    Neotropical: Bahamondes, L. , Bianchi, F. A. , De Santis, L. , Hood, J. D. , Tapia, E. A.
    Palearctic: Ahlberg, O. , Bournier, A. , Doeksen, J. , Franssen, C. J. H. , Gabor, J. ,
      Gromadska, M. , Knechtel, W. , Melis, A. , Skalon, O. I. , zur Strassen, R. , Titschack, E. ,
      Weitmeier, H.
    Ethiopian: Faure, J. C. , Hartwig, E. K. , zur Strassen, R.
    Oriental: Ananthakrishnan, T. N. , Bianchi, F. A. , Doull, K. M.
    Australian: Doull, K. M.
    Oceania: Bianchi, F. A. , Doull, K. M. , Sakimura, K.
                   * * * * *
TEREBRANTIA: Sakimura, K. (O, Oc), Speyer, E. R. (W).
TUBULIFERA: Cott, H. E. (W).
                       * * * * *
Thripidae: Bryan, D. E. (N).

Hemiptera

No other data: Alfonso Ribera, H. (P), Blöte, H. C. , Borcea, P. (P), Brimley, J. F. , Campbell,
    J. (P), Dauguet, P. , Förster, H. (P), Gaun, S. E. (P), Geier, P. , Hacker, H. ,
    Hiregaudar, L. S. (O), Manolache, F. , Marcoci, S. , Moore, G. A. , Muthukrishna, T. S. ,
    Parfentijev, V. J. , Roberti, D. , Salmon, M. A. , Sasaki, K. , Simonet, J. , Strübing, H. ,
    Szienkievicz, I. , Weis, S. , Yosifov, M.
Larvae: DeCoursey, R. M. (N).

Heteroptera

No other data: Abalos, J. W. , Bator, A. , van den Boorn, M. C. J. , Brooks, G. T. , Chapman, H. ,
    Hasegawa, H. , Izzard, R. J. , Remane, R.
    World: China, W. E. , Kelton, L. A. , Kiritshenko, A. N. , Scudder, G. G. E. , Usinger, R. L.
    Nearctic: Ashlock, P. D. , Downes, W. , Froeschner, R. C. , Hussey, R. F. , Lutz, J. C. ,
      Mead, F. W. , Medler, J. T. , Reichart, C. V. , Richards, W. R. , Sailer, R. I.
    Neotropical: Cobben, R. H. , Hussey, R. F. , Lutz, J. C. , Piran, A. A.
    Palearctic: Alfieri, A. , Brakman, P. J. , Buettner, K. , Cobben, R. H. , Dobšik, B. , Dupuis,
      C. , Eckerlein, H. , Emsley, M. G. , Filippi, N. , Gravestein, W. H. , Hoberlandt, L. ,
      Jordan, K. H. C. , Le Quesne, W. J. , Lindberg, H. , Lutz, J. C. , Massee, A. M. , Meurer,
      J. J. , Ossiannilsson, F. , Polentz, G. , Putshkow, W. J. , Roubal, J. , Scudder, G. G. E. ,
      Seidenstücker, G. , Servadei, A. , Sienkiewicz, I. , Southwood, T. R. E. , Stichel, W. ,
      Strawinski, K. , Stusak, J. M. , Štys, P. , Tamanini, L. , Vilbaste, J. , Wagner, E. ,
      Waterston, A. R. , Weber, H. H. , Woodroffe, G. E.
    Paleotropical: Dasgupta, J. (O), Gross, G. F. (A, Oc), Lindberg, H. (Oc), Lutz, J. C. (E, A),
      Musgrave, A. (A), Schouteden, H. (E).
Aquatic, no locality: De Carlo, J. , Hoffmann, W. E. , Menke, A. , Probst, R. T.
    World: Hungerford, H. B. , Jaczewski, T.
    Nearctic: Anderson, J. B. , Ellis, L. L. , Jr. , Porter, T. W. , Reichart, C. V. , Wilson, C. A.
    Neotropical: Herring, J. L.
    Palearctic: Brown, E. S. , Hoberlandt, L. , Josifov, M. , Leth, K. O. , Naumann, H. , Poisson,
      R. , Walton, G. A. , Wróblewski, A.
    Paleotropical: Brown, E. S. (E, O, A, Oc), Herring, J. L. (E, O, A, Oc), Hoberlandt,
      L. (E, O, A, Oc), Kellen, W. R. (Oc), Poisson, R. (E), Pradhan, K. S. (O).
Marine: Herring, J. L. (W).
Terrestrial: Ashlock, P. D. (N), Hidaka, T. (P), Josifov, M. (P).
Larvae: Michalk, O. (P), Sienkiewicz, I. (P), Štys, P. (P).
Fossils: Jordan, K. H. C. (F:P), Leston, D. (M:?).
                     * * * * *
AMPHIBIOCORISAE: Miyamoto, S. (P).
ARADOIDEA: Hoberlandt, L. (P, E, O, A, Oc).
CRYPTOCERATA: Pendergrast, J. G. (A), Popham, E. J. (P).
GEOCORISAE: Sienkiewicz, I. (P).

GERROIDEA: Matsuda, R.
GYMNOCERATA: Bliven, B. P. (N).
HYDROCORISAE: Miyamoto, S. (P), Sienkiewicz, I. (P).
PENTATOMOIDEA: Lattin, J. D. (N), Leston, D. (W), Polivanova, E. N. (P).
  Larvae: Polivanova, E. N. (P).

* * * * *

Anthocoridae: Anderson, N. H. (N), Carayon, J. (W), Harris, H. M. (N), Hill, A. (W), Hiura,
  I. (P, O), Odhiambo, T. R. (E), Schaffner, J. C. (W), Štys, P. (W).
Aradidae: Kormilev, N. A. (W), Matsuda, R. , Pendergrast, J. G. (A).
Belostomatidae: Menke, A. (W).
Berytidae: Stusak, J. M. (W).
Cimicidae: Lee, R. D. (N, Nt).
Colobothristidae: Kormilev, N. A. (W).
Coreidae: Brown, E. S. (W), Deay, H. O. (N, Nt), Halászfy, E. (P), Hsiao, T. Y. (P), Ruckes,
  H. (N, Nt), Schaffner, J. C. (W), Stichel, W. (Nt).
Corixidae: Chen, L. (P), Deay, H. O. (N, Nt), Förster, H. (P), Hutchinson, G. E. (P, E, O, A, Oc),
  Jaczewski, T. (W), Lansbury, I. (P, E), Morgan, H. G. (P), Teyrovsky, V. (P),
  Wróblewski, A. (W).
Cydnidae: Froeschner, R. C. (W), Macek, J. (W).
Dipsocoridae: Štys, P. (W), Wygodzinsky, P. (W).
Enicocephalidae (Henicocephalidae): Woodward, T. E. (A).
Gelastocoridae: Todd, E. L. (W).
Gerridae: Anderson, L. D. (N), Drake, C. J. (N, Nt), Gould, G. E. (N), Harris, H. M. (N, Nt),
  Kuitert, L. C. (N, Nt), Lansbury, I. (P, E).
Hebridae: Drake, C. J. (N, Nt), Porter, T. W. (W).
Hydrometridae: Åbro, A. (P), Drake, C. J. (N, Nt), Jaczewski, T. (W).
Isometopidae: Carvalho, J. C. M. (W).
Largidae: Stehlik, J. L. (W).
Leptopodidae: Darke, C. J. (W).
Lygaeidae: Ashlock, P. D. (W), Bobšik, B. (P), Hidaka, T. (P, O), Pendergrast, J. G. (A),
  Scudder, G. G. E. (W), Slater, J. A. (W), Woodward, T. E. (A).
Mesoveliidae: Drake, C. J. (N, Nt), Jaczewski, T. (W).
Microphysidae: Štys, P. (W).
Miridae: Becker, J. (Nt), Carvalho, J. C. M. (W), Hsiao, T. Y. (P), Kelton, L. A. (W), Knight,
  H. H. (N), Lattin, J. D. (N), Moore, T. E. (N), Odhiambo, T. R. (E), Slater, J. A. (N),
  Southwood, T. R. E. (W), Wagner, E. (W), Watson, S. A. (N), Woodward, T. E. (A).
Nabidae: Carayon, J. (W), Harris, H. M. (W), McDaniel, B. , Jr. (W).
Naucoridae: LaRivers, I. (W).
Nepidae: Drake, C. J. (N, Nt), Kuitert, L. C. (N, Nt).
Notonectidae: Hutchinson, G. E. (P, E, O, A, Oc), Jaczewski, T. (W), Lansbury, I. (N, Nt, P, E,),
  Truxal, F. S. (W).
Ochteridae: Drake, C. J. (W), Jaczewski, T. (W).
Pentatomidae: Bliven, B. P. (O), Buckup, L. (Nt), De La Paz, J. , Halászfy, E. (P), Lattin,
  J. D. (W), Pendergrast, J. G. (A), Rosewall, O. W. , Ruckes, H. (N, Nt), Sailer, R. I. (W),
  Stichel, W. (Nt), Woodward, T. E. (A), Ziarkiewicz, T. (P).
Phymatidae: Kormilev, N. A. (W), Maa, T-C. (P, E, O, A, Oc).
Piesmidae: Ash, C. (N), Drake, C. J. (W).
Pleidae: Drake, C. J. (N, Nt).
Pyrrhocoridae: Odhiambo, T. R. (E), Stehlik, J. L. (W).
Reduviidae: Anduze, P. J. (Nt), Biagi, F. (Nt), Deane, L. (Nt), Dispons, P. (P, E), Elkins,
  J. C. (W), Lent, H. (W), Maldonado-Capriles, J. (Nt), Miller, N. C. E. (P, E, O, A, Oc),
  Ryckman, R. E. (W), Stichel, W. (Nt), Villiers, A. M. (E), Wygodzinsky, P. (W).
Rhopalidae: Harris, H.M. (W).
Saldidae: Cobben, R. H. (W), Drake, C. J. (W), Wróblewski, A. (P).
Tingidae: Ash, C. (N), Bailey, N. S. (N), Drake, C. J. (W), Stusak, J. M. (P), Takeya, C.
  Larvae: Stusak, J. M. (P).
Triatomidae: Correa, R. R. (Nt), Del Ponte, E. (Nt), Hack, W. H. (Nt), de Lucena, D. T. (Nt),
  Martinez, A. (Nt).
Urostylidae: Maa, T-C. (P, E, O, A, Oc).
Veliidae: Banon, J. (N, Nt), Drake, C. J. (N, Nt), Gould, G. E. (N).

No other data: Brooks, A. R. (N), Carey, L. E. , China, W. E. (W), Gravestein, W. H. (P),
Medler, J. T. (N, Nt), Nast, J. , Stearns, L. A. , Zahvatkin, A. A.
Fossils: Evans, J. W. (P-M:W).

* * * * *

ALEYRODOIDEA: Dobreanu, E. (P), Ghesquière, J. (W), Lang, V. (P), Zahradnîk, J. (P).
APHIDOIDEA: Hill, A. R. (P), Pintera, A. (P), Mamontova-Solucha, V. A. (P), Remaudiere,
G. (N, Nt, P), Rusanova, V. N. (P), Swirski, E. (P), Tapia, E. A. (Nt).
AUCHENORHYNCHA, no locality: Mancini, C.
World: Dlabola, J. , Ramos, J. A.
New World: Barattini, L. (Nt), Cobben, R. H. (Nt), Froeschner, R. C. (N).
Palearctic: Borcea, P. , Cobben, R. H. , Holgersen, H. , Ishihara, T. , Lauterer, P. ,
Le Quesne, W. J. , Linnavuori, R. , Müller, H. J. , Nuorteva, P. , Roth, M. ,
Samsonovna-Sengelia, E. , Sáringer, G. , Servadei, A. , Wagner, W. , Waterston, A. R. ,
Zecchini, R.
Ethiopian: Roth, M.
CERCOPOIDEA: Fennah, R. G. (N, Nt).
CICADELLOIDEA (Jassoidea): Evans, J. W. (W), Kontkanen, P. (P), Oman, P. W. (W).
CICADOIDEA: Cantoreanu, M. (P), Lang, V. (P), Logvinenko, V. N. (P), Razviaskina,
G. M. (N, P), Vilbaste, J. (P).
COCCOIDEA, no locality: Goux, L. , Koroneos, J.
World: Hall, W. J. , Morrison, H. , Williams, D. J.
New World: Balachowsky, A. (Nt), Kosztarab, M. (N), McKenzie, H. L. (N), Richards,
W. R. (N), Tapia, E. A. (N, Nt).
Palearctic: Balachowsky, A. , Boratynski, K. L. , Borchsenius, N. S. , Chadzibejli, Z. ,
Gomez-Menor, J. , Kosztarab, M. , Matesova, G. , Sǎvescu, A. , Schmutterer, H. ,
Shiraga, T. , Takagi, S. , Takahashi, R.
Paleotropical: Balachowsky, A. (E), Beardsley, J. W. (Oc), Borchsenius, N. S. (O),
Brimblecombe, A. R. (A), Cohic, F. (Oc), Mamet, J. R. (E, IO), McDaniel, B. , Jr. (Oc),
Takahashi, R. (O).
FULGOROIDEA: Caldwell, J. S. (Nt), Fennah, R. G. (W), Kramer, J. P. (N, Nt), Soós, Á. (P).
Fossils: Fennah, R. G. (F:W).
JASSOIDEA: See Cicadelloidea.
PSYLLOIDEA: Dobreanu, E. (P), Loginova-Dudykina, M. M. (P), Vilbaste, J. (P),
Vondráček, K. (W).

* * * * *

Achilidae: Synave, H. (E).
Adelgidae: Inouye, M. (P).
Aetalionidae: Russell, L. M. (N, Nt, P).
Aleyrodidae: Doncaster, J. P. (W), Dumbleton, L. J. (A, Oc), Eastop, V. F. (W), Gomez-Menor,
J. (P), Manolache, C. (P), Rakshpal, R. (O), Russell, L. M. (W), Sampson,
W. W. (N, Nt), Takahashi, R. (P, Oc), Trehan, K. N. (P, O).
Aphididae, no localtiy: Essig, E. O. , Moritsu, M. , Shaposhnikov, G. , Shibata, B. , Suenaga, H.
World: Aizenberg, E. E. , Dickson, R. C. , Doncaster, J. P. , Eastop, V. F. , Granovsky,
A. A. , Hille Ris Lambers, D. , Laing, F. , Miller, F. W. , Russell, L. M. , Smith, C. F. ,
Stroyan, H. L. G.
Nearctic: Boudreaux, H. B. , Bradley, G. A. , Davis, J. J. , Denmark, H. A. , Harper, A. M. ,
Hottes, F. C. , Ignoffo, C. M. , Johansen, C. , Knowlton, G. F. , Kring, J. B. , Leonard,
M. D. , MacGillivray, M. E. , Miller, F. W. , Müller, F. P. , Olive, A. T. , Palmer, M. A.
Pepper, J. O. , Richards, W. R. , Sampson, W. W. , Smith, C. F. , Tissot, A. N.
Neotropical: Bahamondes, L. , Müller, F. P.
Palearctic: Düzgünes, Z. , Elkady, E. A. , van Heerdt, P. F. , Heinze, K. , Inouye, M. ,
Jacob, F. H. , Kloft, W. , Krzywiec-Rajska, D. , Lindberg, H. , Manolache, C. , Martelli,
M. , Meier, W. , Morgan, H. G. , Müller, F. P. , Ossiannilsson, F. , Ribaut, H. , Rogerson,
J. P. , Szelegiewicz, H. , Takahashi, R. , Tanaka, T. , Tao, C. C. , Taylor, C. E. ,
Wood-Baker, C. S.
Ethiopian: Müller, F. P. , Pinhey, E. C. G. , Taylor, C. E.
Oriental: Behura, B. K. , Chaudhuri, D. N. R. , David, S. K. , Takahashi, R. , Uichanco, L. B.
Australian: Carver, M. , Cottier, W.
Oceania: Chaudhuri, D. N. R. , Lindberg, H. , Tao, C. C.
Asterolecaniidae: Habib, A. (P), Russell, L. M. (W).
Callaphididae: Quednau, W. (W).
Cercopidae: Doering, K. (N), Moore, T. E. (N), Russell, L. M. (N, Nt, P).
Chaitophoridae: Quednau, W. (W).
Chermidae: Moser, J. C. (W), Uichanco, L. B. (O).
Cicadidae: Alexander, R. D. (N), Burns, A. N. (A), Gomez-Menor, J. (P), Kato, M. (W),

Keller, O. P. (W), Moore, T. E. (N, Nt), Russell, L. M. (N, Nt, P), Torres, B. A. (Nt), Uichanco, L. B. (O).

Cicadellidae, no locality: Crowder, H. W. , Cunningham, H. B. , Edwards, J. S.
    World: Maldonado-Capriles, J. , Ross, H. H. , Young, D. A. , Jr.
    Nearctic: Beirne, B. P. , Bliven, B. P. , Brown, H. E. , Christian, P. J. , Davidson, R. H. , DeLong, D. M. , Flock, R. A. , Hepner, L. W. , Hollinsworth, H. R. , Knull, D. J. , Kramer, J. P. , Mead, F. W. , Medler, J. T. , Moore, T. E. , Nielson, M. W. , Schröder, H. , Sinha, R. N.
    Neotropical: DeLong, D. M. , Kramer, J. P. , Linnavuori, R. , Ruppel, R. F. , Schröder, H.
    Palearctic: Chiswell, J. R.
    Paleotropical: Linnavuori, R. (E, Oc), Merino, G. (O), Namba, R. (Oc).
Cixiidae: Synave, H. (E).
Coccidae, no locality: Le Page, H. S. , Le Pelley, R. , Lizer y Trelles, C. , Mahdihassan, S. , Merrill, G. B. , Murillo, L. M. , O'Connor, B. A. , Russo, G. , Vayssière, P. , Zeck, E. H.
    World: Laing, F. , Lindinger, L.
    Palearctic: Bielenin, I. , Düzgünes, Z. , Kawecki, Z. , Lupo, V. , Řeháček, J. , Reyne, A. , Szelényi, G.
    Paleotropical: Cottier, W. (A), De Lotto, G. (E), Rao, V. P. (O), Reyne, A. (O, Oc).
Conchaspididae: Mamet, J. R. (W).
Dactylopiidae: Hoy, J. M. (A).
Delphacidae: DuBose, W. P. , Jr. (N).
Diaspididae: Bachmann, F. (P), Balachowsky, A. (Nt, P, E), Davidson, J. A. (N), Dickson, R. C. (W), Dušková, F. (P), Ezzat, Y. M. (P), McDaniel, B. , Jr. (N), McKenzie, H. L. (W), Zahradník, J. (P).
Dictyopharidae: Synave, H. (E).
Eriosomatidae: Düzgünes, Z. (P), Inouye, M. (P).
Flatidae: Synave, H. (E).
Fulgoridae: Doering, K. (N), Flock, R. A. (N), Lallemond, V. (W), Rosales, C. J. (Nt).
Jassidae: Helson, G. A. H. (A), Maillet, P. (P).
Kermesidae: Sternlicht, M. (P).
Lachnidae: Quednau, W. (W), Wille, H. P. (P).
Lecaniidae: Habib, A. (P).
Lophopidae: Synave, H. (E).
Machaerotidae: Maa, T-C. (P, E, O, A, Oc).
Margarodidae: Jakubski, A. W.
Meenoplidae: Synave, H. (E), Woodward, T. E. (A).
Membracidae: Behura, B. K. (O), Caldwell, J. S. (N, Nt), Capener, A. L. (E), Cook, P. P. , Jr. (W), Flock, R. A. (N), Peláez Fernández, D. (W), Pinto da Fonseca, J. (Nt), Richter, L. (Nt), Russell, L. M. (N, Nt).
Peloridiidae: Woodward, T. E. (A).
Phylloxeridae: Wright, K. H. (N).
Pseudococcidae: Brookes, H. M. (A), Davidson, J. A. (N), Düzgünes, Z. (P), Ezzat, Y. M. (W), Reyne, A. (Oc), Zahradník, J. (P).
Psyllidae: Bliven, B. P. (N), Caldwell, J. S. (Nt), Doncaster, J. P. (W), Eastop, V. F. (W), Heslop-Harrison, C. , Jensen, D. D. (W), Kuwayama, S. (P), Laing, F. (W), Manolache, C. (P), Mathur, R. N. (O), Matsumura, S. , Riemann, J. (N), Russell, L. M. (W), Taylor, K. L. (A), Tuthill, L. D. (N, Nt, Oc), Wagner, W. (P), Wille, H. P. (P), Yu, F-L. (O).
Tettigellidae: Lauterer, P. (W).
Thausmatocoridae: Drake, C. J. (W).
Tropiduchidae: Synave, H. (E).

Anoplura

No other data: Del Ponte, E. , Gerwel, C. , Jobling, B. , Scanlon, J. E.
    World: Brinck, P. , Eichler, W. , Emerson, K. C. , Ignoffo, C. M. , Johnson, P. T. , von Keler, S. , Quay, W. B. , Webb, J. E.
    Nearctic: Bell, I. L. , Branch, N. , Brown, N. R. , Cook, E. F. , Jellison, W. L. , Joyce, C. R. , Pratt, H. D. , Spencer, G. J. , Wilson, N.
    Neotropical: Bell, I. L.
    Palearctic: Blagoveshtchensky, D. I. , Britz, L. , Burtt, E. T. , Conci, C. , Tuleskov, K.
    Paleotropical: Davis, D. H. S. (E), Joyce, C. R. (Oc), Paulian, R. M. A. (E).
Of mammals: Clay, T. , Fiedler, O. G. H. (E), Lane, J. E. (N), Senger, C. M. (N), Werneck, F. L. (W).

* * * * *

Echinophthiriidae: Murray, M. D. (Ant).
Haematopinidae: Kaneko, K. (P),
Hoplopleuridae: Kaneko, K, (P).

Neuroptera

No other data: Burden, J. H. , Harwood, R. D. , Kimmins, D. E.
    World: Handschin, E.
    Nearctic: Froeschner, R. C. , Huber, I. , MacLeod, E. G. , Parfin, S. I. , Rehn, J. W. H. ,
        Spiegler, P. E.
    Palearctic: Asahina, S. , Auber, J. , Bartoš, E. , Fraser, F. C. , Kawashima, K. , Kis, B. ,
        Kuwayama, S. , Michieli, Š. , Principi, M. M. , Réal, P. , Schumann, H. , Tjeder, B. C. H.
    Paleotropical: Auber, J. (E), Fraser, F. C. (E, O, A, Oc), Riek, E. F. (A), Tjeder,
        B. C. H. (E).
Larvae: MacLeod, E. G. (N).
Fossils: Martynova, O. M.
* * * * *
PLANIPENNIA: Jackh, E. (P), Rosenbohm, A. (P), Rousset, A. (P).
* * * * *
Ascalaphidae: Martynova, O. M. (P), Williner, G. J. (Nt).
Chrysopidae: Adams, P. A. (N, Oc), Bickley, W. E. (N).
Coniopterygidae: Carpenter, F. M. (N, Nt), Rousset, A. (W).
Hemerobiidae: Carpenter, F. M. (N), Nakahara, W. (W).
Mantispidae: Williner, G. J. (Nt).
Myrmelionidae: Adams, P. A. (N, Oc), El-Moursy, A. A. (P), Markl, W. (W), Stange, L. A. (N).
Nemopteridae: Cowley, J. (W), El-Moursy, A. A. (P), Martynova, O. M. (P).
Sisyridae: Brown, H. P. (N), Parfin, S. I. (W), Smithers, C. N. (E).

Megaloptera

No other data: Bartoš, E. (P), Handschin, E. (W), MacLeod, E. G. (W), Riek, E. F. (A),
    Schumann, H. (P), Tjeder, B. C. H. (P, E).
Fossils: Martynova, O. M.
* * * * *
RHAPHIDIOPTERA: Bartoš, E. (P), MacLeod, E. G. (N), Martynova, O. M. (P).
    Fossils: Martynova, O. M. (F:P).
Corydalidae: Cuyler, R. D. (W).
Sialidae: Ross, H. H. (W).
* * * * *

Mecoptera

No other data: Bartoš, E. (P), Byers, G. W. (N), Carpenter, F. M. (N), Handschin, E. (W),
    Issiki, S. (P), MacLeod, E. G. (N), Martynova, O. M. , Parfin, S. I. (N), Réal, P. (P),
    Rehn, J. W. H. (N), Riek, E. F. (A), Schumann, H. (P), Tjeder, B. C. H. (P, E).
Fossils: Martynova, O. M.
* * * * *
Bittacidae: Cheng, F-Y. (P).
Panorpidae: Bouseman, J. (W), Cheng, F-Y. (P).

Trichoptera

No other data: Balch, R. F. , Chihara, A. , Corbet, P. S. , Döhler, W. , Merkley, D. R. , Schmid, F.
    World: Fischer, F. C. J. , Ross, H. H.
    Nearctic: Betten, C. Blickle, R. L. , Denning, D. G. , Flint, O. S. , Jr. , Hall, C. C. , Jr. ,
        Hyland, K. E. , Jacquemart, S. , Leonard, J. W. , Morse, W. J. , Robert, A. , Wiggins, G. B.
    Neotropical: Jacquemart, S. , Ulmer, G.
    Palearctic: Botosăneanu, L. , Brekke, R. , Crichton, M. I. , Florin, J. , Forsslund, K. H. ,
        František, K. , Jacquemart, S. , Kimmins, D. E. , Kobayashi, M. , Kuwayama, S. ,
        Moretti, G. P. , Murgoci, A. , Nielsen, A. , Nybom, O. , Obr, S. , Réal, P. , Sýkora, J. ,
        Tsuda, M. , Ujhelyi, S. , Ulmer, G.
    Ethiopian: Jacquemart, S. , Kimmins, D. E. , Scott, K. M. F. , Ulmer, G.
    Oriental: Kobayashi, M. , Ulmer, G.
    Australian: Kimmins, D. E. , McFarlane, A. G. , Neboiss, A. , Ulmer, G. , Wise, K. A. J.
    Oceania: Neboiss, A. , Ulmer, G.
Larvae: Botosăneanu, L. (P), Dolan, T. (N), Flint, O. S. , Jr. (W), Henson, E. B. (N), Hickin,
    N. E. (W), Lepneva, I. (P), Mackenthun, K. M. (N), Marlier, G. (P, E), Moretti,
    G. P. (P), Sýkora, J. (P).
Fossils: Ross, H. H. (W).
* * * * *
Helicopsychidae: Machado, A. B. M. (Nt).
Hydropsychidae, larvae: Badcock, R. M. (P).
Phryganeidae: Wiggins, G. B. (W).

Lepidoptera

No other data: Adamczewski, S. , Adkin, G. T. , Alexinschi, A. , Allander, H. , Allcard, H. G. ,
Andersen, S. L. , Anderson, W. A. , Autard, L. F. , Bayard, A. , Bellinger, P. F. , Bengry,
R. , Blackman, T. M. , Bollmann, H. G. , Bruckova, B. , Buholzer, R. , Burt, J. W. ,
Caldwell, E. , Cargnelutti, J. , Carlsson, M. , Charbonnier, J. R. , Clarke, R. D. ,
Courtenay, J. , Crow, P. N. , Danilevsky, A. S. , van Deurs, W. , Dickson, C. G. C. ,
Dufrane, A. D. A. , Dumigan, E. J. , Ekengren, B. R. , van Eldik, H. C. L. , Ellison,
R. E. , Evers, H. , de Folliart, G. , de Gahan, A. C. , Gaillard, F. J. , Gardiner, F. P. ,
Gerris, V. J. , Gonzalo, P. H. , Harman, I. , Harris, L. E. , Jr. , Hasbrouck, F. ,
Hashimoto, I. , Heslop-Harrison, G. , Holik, O. , Hunt, C. J. , Jarvis, F. V. L. ,
Jorgensen, L. , Kaye, W. J. , Klinzig, E. , Knaben, N. , Kostrowicki, S. , Kovács, L. ,
Krogerus, H. , Kruger, E. , Legras, L. , Lempke, B. J. , Lepigre, A. L. , Lewis, C. B. ,
Lindenthal, J. G. , Loibl, H. , Matsumura, S. , McCubbin, C. , Meise, A. , Noak, H. ,
Nordman, A. , Opheim, M. , Paul, F. , Pease, R. W. , Jr. , Pescott, R. T. M. , Pohl, B. ,
Prüffer, J. , Raebel, H. , Recchia, C. , do Rego-Barros, A. R. , Ricci, M. , Schaaf, E. ,
von Schantz, M. , Schmidlin, A. , Shajovskoy, S. S. , Smith, V. T. H. , Sołtys, E. ,
Storace, L. , Suire, J. , Sundby, R. , Suzuki, -, Swatschek, B. , Szmyt, A. M. , Thomann,
H. , Travassos, L. P. , Filho, Trebilcoch, R. E. , Turner, J. R. , Ureta Rojas, E. ,
Vanek, J. , Weber, P. , Wehrli, E. , Widen, C. J. , Wilcox, J. , Zielaskowski, H.
World: Alspaugh, R. D. , Atkins, E. L. , Bucciarelli, I. , Durand, G. , Remington, C. L. ,
Smith, A. , Smith, E. A.
Nearctic: Brower, A. E. , Eff, J. D. , Forbes, W. T. M. , Gray, P. H. H. , Kimball, C. P. ,
Krivda, A. W. , de Lattin, G. , Réal, P. , Sheppard, A. C. , Syme, P. D. , Voss, E. G. ,
Williams, J. L.
Neotropical: Benson, W. P. , de Biezanko, C. M. , Forbes, W. T. M. , Heimlich, W. ,
Heineman, B. , Réal, P.
Palearctic: Agenjo, R. , Alfieri, A. , Azuma, M. , Bentinck, G. A. , de Biezanko, C. M. ,
Birkett, N. L. , Błeszyński, S. , Brinkmann, R. , Bureš, I. , Camping, M. W. , Cleu, H. ,
Fiori, A. , Florin, J. , Gremminger, A. , Hackman, W. L. V. , Hartig, F. , Höne, H. ,
Huggins, H. C. , Issekutz, L. , Johansson, S. , Kuchlein, J. H. , Lacreuze, C. , de Lattin,
G. , Mell, R. , Menhofer, H. , Mere, R. M. , Mihara, M. , Miwa, Y. , Moucha, J. ,
Palm, N-B. , Pelham-Clinton, E. C. , Popescu-Gorj, A. , Prola, G. , Razowski, J. ,
Réal, P. , Sauter, W. , Suomalainen, E. , Svensson, I. , Tuleskof, K. , Valletta, A. ,
Williams, J. L. , Wolff, N. L. , de Worms, C. , Zangheri, S.
Ethiopian: Barnes, B. D. , Janse, A. J. T. , Pinhey, E. C. G. , Réal, P. , Sevastopulo, D. G. ,
Vari, L. , Viette, P. , de Worms, C.
Oriental: Miwa, Y. , Sevastopulo, D. G.
Australian: Allaway, A. , Angel, F. M. , Haines, L. C. , Hateley, K. , Salmon, J. T.
Oceania: Bradley, J. D. , Viette, P.
Leaf-miners: Gregor, F. (P), Hartig, F. (P).
Of economic importance: Collins, R. J. (W).
Larvae: Anderson, L. D. (N), Atkins, E. L. (N), Capps, H. W. (W), Comstock, J. A. (N),
Hattori, I. , MacKay, M. R. (N), Mathur, R. N. (O), Patocka, J. (P), Réal, P. (P, E),
Timlin, J. S. (A).
Fossils: Fairey, K. D.

* * * * *

MACROLEPIDOPTERA, no locality: Bank, G.
World: Jacobs, S. N. A.
Nearctic: Buchholz, O. , Ferguson, D. C. , Lewis, R. E. , Miller, A. , Newman, J. H. ,
Mueller, J. , Rawson, G. W.
Neotropical: Alayo Dalmau, P. , Breyer, A.
Palearctic: Baynes, E. S. A. , Beirne, B. P. , Betz, J. T. , Brander, T. , de Bros, E. ,
Bruun, H. , Burmann, K. , Bytinski-Salz, H. , Dabrowski, J. , Goncalves, T. , Goodson,
A. L. , Heydemann, F. , Issiki, S. , Jackh, E. , Janmoulle, E. W. A. , Kaisila, J. ,
Mariani, M. , Michieli, Š. , Monteiro, R. P. T. , Nicolesco, E. V. , Nordström, F. ,
Petersen, B. , Sheljuzhko, L. , Torstenius, S. , Urbahn, E. , Wolfsberger, J. ,
Zukowski, R.
Paleotropical: Brandt, W. (Oc), Cunningham, J. R. (A), LeSouef, J. C. (A).
Larvae: Jancik, O. (W), Sarlet, L. (P).
MICROLEPIDOPTERA, World: Clarke, J. F. G.
Nearctic: Braun, A. F. , Freeman, T. N. , Powell, J. A. , Tilden, J. W.
Neotropical: Amsel, H. G. , Pastrana, J. A.
Palearctic: Amsel, H. G. , Beirne, B. P. , Benander, P. , Bradley, J. D. , Bruun, H. ,
Burmann, K. , De Lucca, C. , Ford, L. T. , Fust, B. , Hartig, F. , Kasy, F. , Klimesch,
J. , Parenti, U. , Schultz, V. G. M. , Sternlicht, M. , Wakely, S.
Paleotropical: Bradley, J. D. (E), Common, I. F. B. (A), Crook, F. P. (O, Oc),
Diakonoff, A. (O, Oc), Wilson, J. O. (A).

* * * * *

BARONIAE: Epstein, H. (N, P).
GEOMETROIDEA: Frazier, C. W. (A).
HESPERIOIDEA: Ehrlich, P. R. (W), Fleming, H. (Nt), Freeman, H. A. (N, Nt), Gillham,
    N. W. (N), Lindsey, A. W.
HETEROCERA, World: Tams, W. H. T.
    Nearctic: Baker, N. W., Griewisch, L., Martin, L. M.
    Neotropical: de la Torre y Callejas, S. L.
    Palearctic: Blom, W. L., De Lucca, C., Inoue, H., Kennard, A., Pinker, R.,
        da Silva Cruz, D. M. A.
    Paleotropical: Angel, F. M. (A), Brown, A. L. (A), Harslett, J. (A), Nieuwenhuis,
        E. J. (O, Oc), Roepke, W. (O, Oc), Stoneham, H. F. (E).
NOCTUOIDEA: Fleming, H. (Nt), Franclemont, J. G. (N, Nt, P, O, Oc), Orfila, R. M. (Nt).
NYMPHALOIDEA: Fox, R. M. (W).
PAPILIONOIDEA: Adelphe-David, -. (N), Ehrlich, P. R. (W), Fleming, H. (Nt), MacLeod,
    E. G. (N), Marks, L. S. (W).
PYRALOIDEA: Ford, R. J., Marion, H. (P, E, O, A, Oc).
RHOPALOCERA: Mizoguchi, O.
    World: Blom, W. L., Forster, E. W., Hovanitz, W., Macy, R. W., McAlpine, W. S.,
        Price, H. F., Riley, N. D.
    Holarctic: Epstein, H., Hemming, F., Warren, B. C. S.
    Nearctic: Arnhold, F. R., Brown, F. M., Burdick, W. N. Chermock, R. L., De Foliart,
        G. R., Freeman, T. N., Garth, J. S., Griewisch, L., Hessel, S. A., Macy, R. W.,
        Meiners, E. P., Mattoni, R. H. T., dos Passos, C. F., Preston, F. W., Reinthal, W. J.,
        Sala, F. P., Slater, C. P., Syme, P. D., Thorne, F. T.
    Neotropical: Bates, M., Field, W. D., Gabriel, A. G., Garth, J. S., Hayward, K. J.,
        Herrera, J., Llano, R. J., McAlpine, W. S., Shoumatoff, N., de la Torre y Callejas, S. L.
    Palearctic: Blom, W. L., Bousseau, J., Bradley, J. D., Clench, H. K., Dujardin, F.,
        Forcher-Mayr, H., Friese, G., Hayashi, K., Hellman, E. A., Iwase, T., Kennard, A.,
        Krzywicki, M., Kurentzov, A. J., Lempke, B. J., Lordovic, Z., Michieli, Š., Murayama,
        S., Nikitin, M. I., Okagaki, H., Okano, M., Parvis, A., Reinthal, W. J., Shirôzu, T.,
        Shoumatoff, N., Sibatani, A., da Silva Cruz, D. M. A., Verity, R., Wiltshire, E. P.,
        Yamamoto, H., Yoshida, M.
    Ethiopian: Carcarson, R. H., Gabriel, A. G., Jackson, T. H. E, Paulian, R. M. A.,
        van Son, G., Stoneham, H. F., Swanepoel, D. A., Van Someren, V. G. L.
    Oriental: Gabriel, A. G., Hayashi, K., Nieuwenhuis, E. J., Okano, M., Ong, S. K.,
        Shirôzu, T., Sibatani, A., Tongyai, M. R. C., Wegner, A. M. R., Yoshida, M.
    Australian: Angel, F. M., Angel, S., Brown, A. L., Burns, A. N., Couchman, L. E.,
        Crosby, D., Edwards, E. O., Fisher, R. H., Frazier, C. W., Gabriel, A. G., Harris,
        E. J. W., Kerr, J. R., Landy, J., Macqueen, J., Nikitin, M. I., Ong, S. K., Skreen, E.,
        Tindale, N. B., Wright, W. E.
    Oceania: Couchman, L. E., Nieuwenhuis, E. J., Ong, S. K., Tindale, N. B.
    Larvae: Iwase, T. (P).
SATURNIOIDEA: Bauer, D. L. (N, Nt), Fleming, H. (Nt), Oiticica-Filho, J., (N, Nt),
    Orfila, R. N. (Nt).
TINEINA: Vari, L. (E).
ZYGAENOIDEA: Ford, R. J.

* * * * *

Adelidae: Lewandowski, M. R. (W), Okano, M. (P, O), Zagulajev, A. K. (P).
Aegeriidae: Brower, A. E. (N), Henne, C. (N), Issekutz, L. (P), Lewandowski, M. R. (W),
    Nicolesco, E. V. (P), Parvis, A. (P), Schnaider, Z. (P).
Agaristidae: Ogata, M. (P).
Agromyžidae: Hering, E. M. (P).
Agrotidae: Schultz, V. G. M. (P).
Arctiidae: Birket-Smith, J. (E), Daniel, F. (P), Dufay, C. (P), Ford, R. J., Franclemont,
    J. G. (N, Nt, P, O, Oc), Gardiner, B. O. C. (P), Knowlton, C. B. (N), Okagaki, H. (P),
    Okano, M. (P, O), Ryszka, H. (P), Smith, M. E. (N), de Toulgoet, H. (P, E), Wiltshire,
    E. P. (P).
Argynnidae: Heydemann, F. (P), Schulte, A. (P).
Blastobasidae: Selander, R. B. (N, Nt).
Bombycidae: Daniel, F. (P).
Caradrinidae: Gardiner, B. O. C. (P), Warnecke, G. H. G. (P).
Ceratiidae: Maruyama, K. (P).
Ceratocampidae: Jancik, O. (W).
Coleophoridae: Glaser, W. (P), Lewandowski, M. R. (W), McDunnough, J. R. H. (N), Toll, S. (P).
Cosmopterygidae: Hodges, R. W. (N), Kuroko, H. (P, O).
Cossidae: Clench, H. K. (W), Daniel, F. (P), Lewandowski, M. R. (W), Schnaider, Z. (P),
    Tindale, N. B. (A, Oc).

Fossils: Kozhanchikov, I. V. (F:P).
Crambidae: Khan, M. R. (O), de Lattin, G. (P), Okano, M. (P, O).
Ctenuchidae: Obraztsov, N. S. (P, O, A).
Cymatophoridae: Daniel, F. (P).
Danaidae: d'Almeida, R. F. (N, Nt), Slater, C. P. (N),
Drepanidae: Watson, A. (W).
Elachistidae: Kumata, T. (P), Lewandowski, M. R. (W).
Eriocraniidae: Lewandowski, M. R. (W).
Eucosmidae: McDunnough, J. R. H. (N).
Gelechiidae: Common, I. F. B. (A), Gozmany, L. (W), Povolný, D. (P), Sattler, K. (P),
   Zukowski, R. (P).
Geometridae, World: Fletcher, D. S. , de Laever, E.
   Nearctic: Bauer, W. R. , Kirkwood, C. W. , Okagaki, H. , Rindge, F. H. , Sala, F. P.
   Palearctic: Albers, T. , Aubert, J. F. , Grosz, F. J. , Heydemann, F. , Herbulot, C. ,
      Homberg, R. , Juul, K. , Kuznetzov, V. I. , Okagaki, H. , Povolný, D. , Reisser, H. , Sarlet,
      L. , Schultz, V. G. M. , Schütze, E. , Urbahn, E. , Vardikian, S. A. , Wiltshire, E. P. ,
      Zangheri, S.
   Ethiopian: Herbulot, C.
   Larvae: Haggett, G. (P), McGuffin, W. C. (N), Pinker, R. (P).
Gracilariidae: Common, I. F. B. (A), Gregor, F. (W), Kumata, T. (P), Kuznetzov, V. I. (P),
   Povolný, D. (P), Wise, K. A. J. (A).
Hepialidae: Daniel, F. (P), Harris, E. J. W. (A), Holmes, D. R. (A), King, C. , Lewandowski,
   M. R. (W), Mules, M. W. (A), Paclt, J, (W), Quick, W. N. B. (A), Tindale, N. B. (W).
Hesperiidae, World: Alberti, B.
   New World: Bell, E. L. , MacNeill, C. D. , Nicolay, S. S.
   Nearctic: Burns, J. M. , Hulbrit, E. R. , Miller, L. D. , Tilden, J. W. , Warren, B. C. S.
   Neotropical: Etcheverry, M. , Hayward, K. J.
   Palearctic: Dujardin, F. , Gallivanone, M. , Kauffman, G. , Mac Neill, C. D. , Prose, H. ,
      Ogata, M. , Tilden, J. W. , Verity, R. , Warren, B. C. S. , Wiltshire, E. P.
   Paleotropical: Berger, L. A. (E), Couchman, L. E. (A, Oc), Harslett, J. (A), Mac Neill,
      C. D. (A).
Hyponomeutidae: Friese, G. (P).
Incurvariidae: Lewandowski, M. R. (A), Zagulajev, A. K. (P).
Ithomiidae: d'Almeida, R. F. (N, Nt), Fox, R. M. (Nt).
Lasiocampidae: Tams, W. H. T. (W), Wiltshire, E. P. (P).
Lemoniidae: Wiltshire, E. P. (P).
Limacodidae: Clench, H. K. (N, E), Fairey, K. D. (A).
Lycaenidae, no locality: Ford, R. J.
   World: Clench, H. K. , Downey, J. C. , Mattoni, R. H. T.
   Nearctic: Epstein, H. , Freeman, H. A. , Hower, T. W. , Hulbirt, E. R. , Huntington, E. I. ,
      Miller, L. D. , Nabokov, V. , Nicolay, S. S. , Philip, K. W. , Thorne, F. T. , Tilden, J. W. ,
      Ziegler, J. B.
   Neotropical: Huntington, E. I. , Nicolay, S. S.
   Palearctic: Bernardi, G. , Beuret, H. , Epstein, H. , Gallivanone, M. , Hayashi, K. ,
      Heydemann, F. , Howarth, T. G. , Nabokov, V. , Schulte, A. , Tilden, J. W.
   Paleotropical: Bennett, N. H. (E), Brandt, W. (Oc), Harslett, J. (A), Murray, D. P. (E),
      Stempffer, H. (E).
Lymantriidae: Collenette, C. L. (W), Gardiner, B. O. C. (P), Wiltshire, E. P. (P).
   Larvae: Kumata, T. (P).
Lyonetiidae: Klimesch, J. (P).
Megalopygidae: Clench, H. K. (Nt).
Megathymidae: Freeman, H. A. (N, Nt), Miller, L. D. (N), Stallings, D. B. (N, Nt).
   Larvae: Stallings, D. B. (N, Nt).
Melitaeidae: Higgins, L. G. (W).
Micropterygidae: Lewandowski, M. R. (W).
Mimallonidae: Pearson, H. R. (N, Nt).
Morphidae: Seiler, D. (N, Nt, P, E).
Nepticulidae: Carolsfeld-Krausé, A. G. (P), Klimesch, J. (P).
Noctuidae, no locality: Kashiwagi, M. , Vasič, K.
   World: Arnhold, F. R. , Boursin, C. , Brower, A. E. , Dufay, C. , Tams, W. H. T.
   Nearctic: Adelphe-David, -, Bauer, W. R. , Berio, E. , Ferguson, D. C. , Franclemont, J. G. ,
      Hardwick, D. F. , Hessel, S. A. , McElvare, R. R. , Newman, J. H. , Rees, W. A. , Reid,
      R. H. , Sala, F. P. , Wyatt, A. K.
   Neotropical: Franclemont, J. G. , Köhler, P. E. , McElvare, R. R. , Petrowsky, B.
   Palearctic: Berio, E. , Classey, E. W. , Dufay, C. , Franclemont, J. G. , Fust, B. , Hanson,
      R. B. , Heydemann, F. , Kuznetzov, V. I. , de Lajonquiere, Y. , de Lattin, G. , Michieli, Š. ,
      Ogata, M. , Rjabov, M. A. , Rungs, C. , Sugi, S. , Urbahn, E. , Warnecke, G. H. G. ,
      Wiltshire, E. P.

57

Paleotropical: Berio, E. (E, O), Bowden, J. (E), Common, I. F. B. (A), Franclemont, J. G. (O, Oc).
Larvae: Classey, E. W. (P), Haggett, G. (P), Pinker, R. (P).
Fossils: Kozhanchikov, I. V. (F:P).
Nolidae: Warnecke, G. H. G. (P).
Notodontidae: Daniel, F. (P), Franclemont, J. G. (N, Nt, P, O, Oc), Kiriakoff, S. G. (E), Okano, M. (P, O), Okagaki, H. (P), Nakamura, M. (P, O), Wiltshire, E. P. (P).
Nymphalidae, Nearctic: Bauer, D. L., Dusek, R. V., Epstein, H., Gillham, N. W., Grey, L. P., Hovanitz, W., Hower, T. W., Klots, A. B., Krivda, A. W., Réal, P., Reinthal, W. J., Seiler, D., Slater, C. P.
Neotropical: Bauer, D. L., Grey, L. P., Potts, R. W. L., Réal, P., Seiler, D.
Palearctic: Bauer, D. L., Epstein, H., Gallivanone, M., Gillham, N. W., Grey, L. P., Issekutz, L., Seiler, D.
Ethiopian: Grey, L. P., Seiler, D.
Oecophoridae: Common, I. F. B. (A), Gozmany, L. (P), Hannemann, H-J. (P).
Orgyidae - fossils: Kozhanchikov, I. V. (F:P).
Orneodidae:˙ Schwarz, R. (P).
Papilionidae, no locality: Johnson, F. L.
World: Fox, R. M., Wilson, K. H.
Nearctic: Brower, L. P., Dusek, R. V., Seiler, D., Wyatt, C. W.
Neotropical: Seiler, D., Vazquez Garcia, L.
Palearctic: Gallivanone, M., Ryszka, H., Seiler, D., Wyatt, C. W.
Ethiopian: Berger, L. A., Seiler, D.
Parnassiidae: Bousseau, J. (W), Eisner, C. (N, Nt, P), Ryszka, H. (N, P), Zelný, J. (P).
Phalaenidae: Cook, W. C. (N), Heinicke, W. (P), Henne, C. (N), Kostrowicki, A. (P), Povolný, D. (P), Reid, R. H. (N), Todd, E. L. (N, Nt).
Phycitidae: Tiedemann, O. (W).
Pieridae, World: Bari, B., Berger, L. A., Hovanitz, W.
Nearctic: d'Almeida, R. F., Krivda, A. W., Petersen, B., Wyatt, C. W.
Neotropical: d'Almeida, R. F., Brown, F. M., Vazquez Garcia, L.
Palearctic: Benz, F., Bernardi, G., Froitzheim, J., Gallivanone, M., Moucha, J., Petersen, B., Schulte, A., Zelný, J.
Ethiopian: Berger, L. A., Bernardi, G.
Plusiidae: Gardiner, B. O. C. (P).
Psychidae: Betrem, J. G. (O, A, Oc), Bourgogne, J. (W), Das, G. M. (O), Davis, D. (N, Nt), Lewandowski, M. R. (W), Meier, H. (P), Monteiro, R. P. T. (P), Pinker, R. (P), Sauter, W. (W), Schwarz, R. (P), Sieder, L. (P), Torstenius, S. (P), Vazquez Garcia, L. (Nt).
Fossils: Kozhanchikov, I. V. (F:P).
Pterophoridae: Baynes, E. S. A. (P), Bigot, L. (N, Nt, P, E), Gaj, A. J. (P), Huggins, H. C. (P).
Pyralidae, no locality: Le Charles, L.
World: Błeszyński, S., Janse, A. J. T., Kuchlein, J. H., Lange, W. H., Jr., Martin, E. L., Munroe, E. G.
New World: Box, H. E., Klots, A. B.
Palearctic: Baynes, E. S. A., Gardiner, B. O. C., Helmers, G., Huggins, H. C., Inoue, H., Kuznetzov, V. I., Matuura, A., Schwarz, R., Soffner, J., Wojtusiak, R.
Paleotropical: Helmers, G. (E, O, Oc), Kapur, A. P. (O), Martin, E. L. (E).
Pterophoridae: Lange, W. H., Jr. (N), Schwarz, R. (P).
Pyraustidae: Capps, H. W. (N, Nt), Munroe, E. G. (W).
Riodinidae: Ford, R. J., McAlpine, W. S. (N, Nt).
Saturnidae: Escalante, T. (Nt), Gallivanone, M. (P), Hoock, J. M. L., Jancik, O. (W), Wandschneider, W. (W).
Satyridae, New World: Brown, F. M. (Nt), Christensen, G. (N), Ehrlich, P. R. (N), de Lesse, H. J. L. (N), Miller, L. D. (N), Wyatt, C. W. (N).
Palearctic: Christensen, G., Grosz, F. J., de Lattin, G., de Lesse, H. J. L., Varin, G., Wagener, S., Wyatt, C. W.
Paleotropical: Condamin, M. (E), Couchman, L. E. (A, Oc), Quick, W. N. B. (A).
Scythridae: Hannemann, H-J. (P).
Sesiidae: Schwarz, R. (P).
Sphingidae: Benz, F. (P), Cary, C. R. (N, Nt), Escalante, T. (Nt), Gallivanone, M. (P), Lichy, R., Mooser-Barendun, O. (Nt), Oiticica-Filho, J. (N, Nt), Sieker, W. (W), Wiltshire, E. P. (P), Zopp, J. (W).
Stenomidae: Duckworth, W. D. (N).
Stigmelidae: Lewandowski, M. R. (W).
Syntomidae: Daniel, F. (P).
Talaeporiidae: Torstenius, S. (P).
Thyatiridae: Okano, M. (P, O).

Thyretidae: Kiriakoff, S. G. (E).
Tineidae: Petersen, G. (P), Zagulajev, A. K. (P).
Tortricidae, no locality: Hoshino, M.
    Nearctic: Obraztsov, N. S. , Powell, J. A.
    Palearctic: Huggins, H. C. (P), Kuznetzov, V. I. , Obraztsov, N. S. , Oku, T. , Prose, H. ,
        Razowski, J. , Sauter, W. , Yasuda, T.
    Paleotropical: Common, I. F. B. (A), Diakonoff, A. (E, O, Oc).
Trypetidae: Hering, E. M. (W).
Uraniidae: Altena, C. O. R.
Zygaenidae, no locality: Droit, P. A. , Le Charles, L.
    World: Alberti, B. , Tremewan, W. G.
    Palearctic: Dabrowski, J. , Daniel, F. , Dujardin, F. , Gallivanone, M. , Meier, H. , Reichl,
        E. , Reiss, H. , Verity, R. , Wiltshire, E. P.
    Paleotropical: Reiss, H. (E, O).

Diptera

No other data: Abe, Y. , Adler, S. , Afshar, J. , d'Andretta Jor. , C. , Beck, E. C. , Beyer, E. ,
    Blanchard, E. E. , Breuer, M. , Capoor, V. N. , Carney, M. P. , Chagnon, G. , Cordero,
    I. O. , Damasceno, R. M. G. , Davis, G. J. , Deane, M. P. , De Leon, J. R. , Diaz-Najara, A. ,
    Dineley, D. A. , Dinulescu, G. , Dreyfus, A. , Drummond, F. H. , Edashige, T. , Eshghy, N. ,
    Fellton, H. L. , Field, G. , Finelle, P. , Fira, V. , Friend, R. B. , Frota-Pessoa, O. ,
    Gabaldon, A. , Gandara, A. F. , Garcia, M. , Goetghebuer, M. , Grjebine, M. A. , Heinz,
    H. J. , Hodgkin, E. P. , Hoyt, C. P. , Jones, C. G. , Keilin, D. , Kishida, K. , Lariviere, M. ,
    Lenko, K. , Lima, M. M. , Linsdale, D. D. , Lips, M. A. H. , Logan, L. , Lupascu, G. ,
    Mackod, J. , Makino, S. , Mangabeiro, O. , Filho, Mani, M.S. , Marshall, J.F. , Masters, C. O. ,
    Montshadskij, A. S. , Mouchet, J. , Nash, T. A. , Neghme-Rodriguez, A. , Niblett, M. ,
    Nozawa, K. , Paramonov, S. J. , Peller, W. , Perry, W. J. , Peterffi, F. , Pinto, C. ,
    Pugh, C. H. W. , Quisenberry, B. F. , Rachou, R. , Rahman-Ansari, M. A. , Redlinger,
    L. M. , Ringdahl, O. , Schmid, F. , Roubaud, E. , Ryberg, O. , Scossiroli, R. E. , Shute,
    P. G. , da Silva Ramos, A. , Spassky, B. , Spence, T. , Spiller, D. , Thienemann, A. ,
    Thuneberg, E. , Travassos, L. P. , Filho, Vanderplank, F. L. , Vincke, I. , Wahlgren, E. ,
    Watt, M. N. , White, O. M. , Yoshimoto, C. M. Zangheri, P. , Zeledon, R. , Zilahi-Sebess, G.
    World: Melander, A. L.
    New World: Allen, D. G. (N), Brooks, A. R. (N), Cole, F. R. (N), de Medina, F. (Nt).
    Palearctic: Brauns, A. , van Bruggen, A. C. , Collin, J. E. , Doorman, G. , Edwards, J. ,
        Fonseca, E. C. M. A. , Grensted, L. W. , Hammond, C. O. , Kim, K. C. , Ouchi, Y. , Smith,
        K. G. V. , Bonne-Wepster, J.
    Paleotropical: van Bruggen, A. C. (E), Bryan, E. H. (Oc), Lever, R. J. A. W. (Oc),
        Miller, D. (A).
Coprophilous: Laurence, B. R. (P).
Medically important: Bacon, M. (N), Blanton, F. S. (W), Britz, L. (P), Ryckman, R. E. (N).
Shore-inhabiting: Ardö, P. (W).
Social: Kabos, W. J. (P).
Larvae: Brauns, A. (P), Tate, P. (P).
Fossils: Rohdendorf, B. B. (M:?).
* * * * *
ACALYPTRATAE: da Costa Lima, A. M. (Nt), Doskočil, J. (P), Harrison, R. A. (A, Oc),
    McAlpine, D. K. (A), Sturtevant, A. H. (N), Wheeler, M. R. (N).
BRACHYCERA: Curran, C. H. (W), Lyneborg, L. (P), Oldroyd, H. (W), Teschner, D. (P),
    Venturi, F. (P).
CYCLORRHAPHA, larvae: Townsend, L. H.
MUSCOIDEA: da Costa Lima, A. M. (Nt), Jones, D. T. (N), Reinhard, H. J. (N, Nt), Sleeper,
    D. A. (N).
NEMATOCERA: da Costa Lima, A. M. (Nt), Downes, J. A. , Frizzi, -. (P), Obrecht, C. B. (N),
    Teschner, D. (P).
PUPIPARA: Del Ponte, E. (Nt), Gumiarães, L. R. , Prouty, J. M.
THECOSTOMATA: Čepelák, J. (P).
* * * * *
Acroceridae: Cole, F. R. (N). FOSSILS: Schlinger, E. I. (F:W).
Agromyzidae, Nearctic: Frick, K. E. , Frost, S. W. , Ryden, N. S.
    Neotropical: de Oliveira, S. J. , Spencer, K. A.
    Palearctic: Griffiths, G. G. D. , Kangas, E. , Kato, S. , Kuroda, M. , Lundqvist, A. ,
        Nowakowski, J. T. , Rohdendorf, E. , Ryden, N. S. , Sasakawa, M. , Spencer, K. A.
    Paleotropical: Frick, K. E. (Oc), Griffiths, G. G. D. (E, O, A, Oc), Kleinschmidt, R. P. (A),
        Sasakawa, M. (O, A, Oc), Spencer, K. A. (E, O, A, Oc).
Anisopodidae: Lane, J. (Nt).

Anthomyidae: Johnson, P. (E), Kabos, W. J. (P), Kato, S. (P), Lambrecht, F. L. (E), Machada, A. B. (E), Maillot, L. (E), Potts, W. H. (E), Rageau, J. G. F. (E), Rickenbach, A. (E), Snyder, F. M. (W).
Anthomyzidae: Sabrosky, C. W. (W).
Apioceridae: Cazier, M. A. (N), Hull, F. M. (W), Painter, R. H. (N, Nt).
Asilidae, no locality: Dyte, C. E., Stahl, E. V.
    World: Hull, F. M., Pritchard, A. E.
    Nearctic: Burdick, W. N., Cloyd, W. J., Cole, F. R., Hays, K., Johnson,. D. E., Martin, C. H., Wilcox, J.
    Neotropical: Carrera, M., Farr, T. H.
    Palearctic: Castellani, O., Hradský, M., Ionescu, M. A., Janssens, E., Kimura, T., Parmenter, L., Timon-David, J., Weinberg, M.
    Ethiopian: Hobby, B. M.
    Larvae: Dyte, C. E. (W).
Asteiidae: Sabrosky, C. W. (W).
Bibionidae: Hardy, D. E. (Nt, E, O, A, Oc), Lane, J. (Nt), Okada, I. (P).
Blepharoceridae: Lane, J. (Nt), Mannheims, B. (W), Stuckenberg, B. R. (W).
Bombyliidae, no locality: Dyte, C. E.
    World: Hull, F. M., Paramonov, S. J.
    Nearctic: Cole, F. R., Hall, J. C., Johnson, D. E., Johnson, L. M., Kellen, W. R., Marston, N., Painter, R. H., Priddy, R. B., Schlinger, E. I.
    Neotropical: Hall, J. C., Marston, N., Painter, R. H.
    Palearctic: Ionescu, M. A., Takahasi, H., Weinberg, M.
    Paleotropical: Bowden, J. (E), Dyte, C. E. (E), Hesse, A. J. (E), Takahasi, H. (O).
Borboridae: See Sphaeroceridae.
Calliphoridae, Nearctic: Bargren, W. C., Cross, W. H., Eastwood, J. P., James, M. T., Peris, S. V., Siverly, R. E., Trivette, E. C.
    Neotropical: Del Ponte, E., James, M. T., Peris, S. V.
    Palearctic: Day, C. D., Gregor, F. Hori, K., Kano, R., Kirchberg, E., Lehrer, A., Nuorteva, P., Peris, S. V., Povolný, D., Rohdendorf, E.
    Paleotropical: Hardy, G. H. (A), James, M. T. (Oc), Joyce, C. R. (Oc), Murray, M. D. (A), Peris, S. V. (E, O, A, Oc), Rickenbach, A. (E), Theowald, -. (O, A, Oc), Zumpt, F. (E).
    Larvae: Bennett, G. F. (N).
Calobatidae: Aczel, M. (Nt, O, A).
Cecidomyiidae: Möhn, E. (W), Moser, J. C. (W), Nyveldt, W. C. (W), Pritchard, A. E. (W), Rao, S. N. (O), Stelter, H. (P), Weinberg, M. (P).
    Larvae: Möhn, E. (W).
    Galls: Möhn, E. (W).
Celiphidae: Vanschuytbroeck, P. (E).
Ceratopogonidae (Heleidae), no locality: Mirsa, A.
    World: Saunders, L. G., Wirth, W. W.
    Nearctic: Boesel, M. W., Coher, E. I., Curtis, L. C., Downes, J. A., Hubert, A. A., Jones, R. H., Khalaf, K., Lewis, F. B., Pelham-Clinton, E. C., Williams, R. W.
    Neotropical: Barbosa, F. A. S., Coher, E. I., Floch, H., Forattini, O. P., Fox, I., Lane, J., Ortiz Cordero, I.
    Palearctic: Amosova, I. S., Clastrier, J., Downes, J. A., Gutsevich, A. V., Harant, H., Hubert, A. A., Khalaf, K., Mayer, K., Pehlam-Clinton, E. C., Remm, H., Rivosecchi, L., Takahasi, H., Tokunaga, M., Vaillant, F.
    Ethiopian: Clastrier, J., Das Gupta, S. K., de Meillon, B.
    Oriental: Coher, E. I., Delfinado, M. D., Lee, D. J., Reye, E. J., Sen, P., Takahasi, H., Tokunaga, M.
    Australia: Dyce, A. L., Lee, D. J., Reye, E. J., Waterhouse, E. J.
    Oceania: Lee, D. J., Reye, E. J., Tokunaga, M.
    Larvae: Mayer, K. (P, E), Saunders, L. G. (W), Vaillant, F. (P).
Chaoboridae: Cook, E. F. (N), Verbeke, J. (E).
Chironomidae (Tendipedidae): Gouin, F. (P), Guyer, G., Lenz, F., Storå, R.
    World: Brundin, L., Caspers, H., Codreanu, R., Strenzke, K.
    Nearctic: Beck, W. M., Jr., Boesel, M. W., Dendy, J. S., Grodhaus, G., Neff, S. E., Rempel, J. G., Roback, S. S., Strenzke, K., Sublette, J. E., Townes, H. K.
    Neotropical: Freeman, P., de Oliveira, S. J., Roback, S. S.
    Palearctic: Albu, P., Birkett, N. L., Botnariuc, N., Dahl, J., Fittkau, E. I., Freeman, P., Kalugina, N. S., Kettle, D. S., Palmen, E., Romaniszyn, W., Strenzke, K., Tokunaga, M., Wülker, W.
    Paleotropical: Fittkau, E. I. (E), Freeman, P. (E, O, A, Oc), Marks, E. N., Tokunaga, M. (O, Oc).
    Larvae: Botnariuc, N. (P), Cindea-Cure, V. (P), Curry, L. L. (N), Kalugina, N. S. (P),

Neff, S. E. (N), Roback, S. S. (N, Nt), Wülker, W. (P).
Fossils: Paine, G. H. , Jr. (N).
Chloropidae: Andersson, H. (P), Antunes, P. C. S. (Nt), Brauns, A. (P), Nartshuk, E. P. (P),
  Nishijima, Y. (P), Sabrosky, C. W. (N, Nt, E, O, A, Oc), Southwood, T. R. E. (N, P).
Clusiidae: Sasakawa, M. (P).
Coenomyiidae: Pechuman, L. L. (N).
Conopidae: Camras, S. (W), Chvala, M. (P), Cole, F. R. (N), Nakao, S. (P), Smith, K. G. V. (W),
  Takahasi, H. (P, O), Tanaka, A. , Trojanowa-Bańkowska, R. (P), Zimina, L. W. (P).
Culicidae, no locality: Acosta, M. J. , Asanuma, K. , Barreto-Reyes, P. , Bejarano, J. C. R. ,
  Boese, J. L. , Castro, M. P. , Cerqueira, N. L. , Galliard, H. L. , Iyenger, M. O. T. ,
  Klein, J. M. , Lassmann, G. , Lyman, F. E. , Natvig, L. R. , Peeters, E. M. E. , Philipps,
  D. J. , Rees, D. M. , Roberts, T. S. , Woke, P. A. , Woodfield, B. R. G.
  World: Barr, A. R. , Belkin, J. N. , Knight, K. L. , Martinez, A. , Mattingly, P. F. , Micks,
    D. W. , Senevet, G. , Stone, A.
  Nearctic: Aitken, T. H. G. , Bacon, M. , Bargren, W. C. , Barnes, R. G. , Barr, A. R. ,
    Barrera, A. , Belkin, J. N. Bellamy, R. E. , Bickley, W. E. , Bradley, G. H. , Branch, N. ,
    Breland, O. P. , Brennan, J. M. , Brookman, B. , Burbutis, P. , Carpenter, S. J. , Coher,
    E. I. , Curtis, L. C. , Darsie, R. F. , Dickinson, W. E. , Edmunds, L. R. , Evans, B. R. ,
    Freeborn, S. B. , Garth, J. S. , Gjullin, C. M. , Grant, C. D. , Graves, R. C. , Griffith,
    M. E. , Grodhaus, G. , Harmston, F. C. , Hartley, C. F. , Hathaway, E. S. , Hecht, O. ,
    Hedeen, R. A. , Hopla, C. E. , Joyce, C. R. , King, W. V. , Knutson, H. , LaCasse, W. J. ,
    Laffoon, J. L. , Long, J. D. , Martinez-Palacios, A. , Mead, F. W. , Miller, A. , Murray,
    W. S. , Nielson, L. T. , Owen, W. B. , Pratt, H. D. , Rempel, J. G. , Roberts, R. H. ,
    Rozeboom, L. E. , Ryckman, R. E. , Smith, M. E. , Thurman, E. B. , Tilden, J. W. ,
    Vockeroth, J. R. , Williams, R. W.
  Neotropical: Aitken, T. H. G. , Anduze, F. J. , Antunes, P. C. S. , Barrera, A. , Bates, M. ,
    Bonne-Wepster, J. , Bruijning, C. F. A. , Coher, E. I. , Correa, R. R. , De Biagi, A. M. B. ,
    Duret, J. P. , Forattini, O. P. , Galindo, P. , Hecht, O. , Lane, J. , Levi-Castillo, R. ,
    Martinez-Palacios, A. , de Oliveira, S. J. , Rozeboom, L. E. , Vargas, L.
  Palearctic: Aitken, T. H. G. , Bohart, R. M. , Britz, L. , Callot, J. , Canamares, F. T. ,
    Classey, E. W. , Coher, E. I. , Feng, L. C. , Ghaffary, E. N. , Gutsevich, A. V. , Hedeen,
    R. A. , Kano, R. , Kettle, D. S. , Kirchberg, E. , Kramář, J. , LaCasse, W. J. , Mariani, M. ,
    Mihályi, F. , Miyazaki, I. , Murdoch, W. P. , Nakagawa, H. , Omori, N. , Peus, F. ,
    de Prada, J. , Salem, H. H. , Sasa, M. , Shahgudian, E. R. , Takahasi, H. , Trivette, E. C. ,
    Ungureanu, E. M. , Yamaguti, S.
  Ethiopian: Adam, M. J-P. , Briscoe, M. S. , Burgess, R. W. , Doucet, J. , Gillett, J. D. ,
    Haddow, A. J. , Hamon, M. J. , Lane, J. E. , Lumsden, W. H. R. , McDonald, W. A. ,
    Muspratt, J. , Peters, W. , Rageau, J. G. F. , Senevet, G. , Wolfs, J.
  Oriental: Baisas, F. E. , Bonne-Wepster, J. , Chow, C. Y. , Colless, D. , Feng, L. C. ,
    Griffith, M. E. , MacDonald, W. W. , Menon, M. A. U. , Rao, T. R. , Sen, P. , Shahgudian,
    E. R. , Takahasi, H. , Thurman, E. B. , Wharton, R. H.
  Australian: Bonne-Wepster, J. , Colless, D. , Dobrotworsky, N. V. , Douglas, G. W. , Laird,
    M. , Lee, D. J. , Marks, E. N. O'Gower, A. K. , Waterhouse, E. J. , Wharton, R. H. ,
    Woodhill, A. R.
  Oceania: Belkin, J. N. , Bohart, R. M. , Bonne-Wepster, J. , Christian, S. H. , Coher, E. I. ,
    Colless, D. , Joyce, C. R. , King, W. V. , Laird, M. , Lee, D. J. , Menon, M. A. U. ,
    O'Gower, A. K. , Peters, W. , Rageau, J. G. F. , Wharton, R. H. , Woodhill, A. R.
  Larvae: Bellamy, R. E. , Cross, C. G. , Horsfall, W. R. , Hull, W. B. , Penn, G. H.
                              * * * * *
Anophelinae, no locality: Corradetti, A.
  World: Rozeboom, L. E. , Senevet, G.
  New World: Abonnenc, E. (Nt), Cova-Garcia, P. (Nt), Deane, L. (Nt), Del Ponte, E. (Nt),
    Frizzi, -. (N), Hack, W. H. (Nt), de Lucena, D. T. (Nt), Ricciardi, I. (Nt).
  Palearctic: Duport, M. , Kuhlhorn, F. , Łukasiak, J. , Otsuru, M. , Toumanoff, C.
  Ethiopian: Abonnenc, E. , Adam, M. J-P. , Bailly-Choumara, H. , Holstein, M. , Lambrecht,
    F. L. , Senevet, G. , van Someren, E. C. C.
  Oriental: Büttiker, W. , Christophers, R. , King, W. V. , Otsuru, M. , Qutubuddin, M. , Reid,
    J. A. , Sandosham, A. A.
Culicinae, World: Laven, H.
  Neotropical: Abonnenc, E. , Del Ponte, E.
  Palearctic: Hara, J. , Lukasiak, J. , Rioux, J. , Sztankay-Gulyás, M.
  Ethiopian: Abonnenc, E. , Machado, A. B. , van Someren, E. C. C.
  Oriental: Hara, J. , Laffoon, J. L. , Qutubuddin, M. , Trapido, H.
  Arctic: Jenkins, D. W.
Dixinae: Rioux, J. (P).
Megarhininae: Qutubuddin, M. (O), van Someren, E. C. C. (E).
                              * * * * *
Cuterebridae: Dalmat, H. T. (N), Penner, L. R. (W).

61

Cyrtidae: Hull, F. M. (W), Plomley, N. J. B. (A).
Diopsidae: Ardö, P. (W), Collart, A., (E), Shillito, J. F. (W).
Dixidae: Garrett, C. B. D. (N), Peus, F. (P).
Dolichopodidae, no locality: Fukuhara, N.
    World: Cowley, J., Harmston, F. C., Stackelberg, A. A.
    Palearctic: Dyte, C. E., Giordani-Soika, A., Parmenter, L., Vaillant, F.
    Paleotropical: Adachi, M. (Oc), Giordani-Soika, A. (E), Nardy, G. H. (A),
      Vanschuytbroeck, P. (E).
  Larvae: Dyte, C. E. (W), Vaillant, F. (P).
Drosophilidae, no locality: Spencer, W. P.
    World: Burla, H., Miller, D. D., Wheeler, M. R.
    Nearctic: de Barros, R., Carson, H. L., Dobzhansky, T., Hackman, W. L. V., Heed,
      W. B., Levitan, M., Stalker, H., Wasserman, M.
    Neotropical: de Barros, R., Brncic, D., Burla, H., Carson, H. L., Cordeiro, A. R.,
      da Cunha, A. B., Dobzhansky, T., Freire-Maia, N., Frydenburg, O., Heed, W. B.,
      Koref, S., de Magalhaes, L. E., Pavan, C., Petersen, J. A., Salzano, F. M., Townsend,
      J. I., Wasserman, M.
    Palearctic: Basden, E. B., Burla, H., Frydenburg, O., Hackman, W. L. V., Kanellis, A.,
      Okada, T., Pipkin, S. B., Sobels, F. H.
    Paleotropical: Burla, H. (E), Dharmarajan, M. (O), Hollingsworth, M. (E), Mather,
      W. D. (A, Oc), Nolte, D. S. (E), Pipkin, S. B. (Oc).
Dryomyzidae: Parmenter, L. (P).
Empididae: Baretto, M. P. (Nt), Chillcott, J. G. (N), Collin, J. E. (W), Dyte, C. E., Farr,
    T. H. (Nt), Ito, S. (P), Maddock, D. R., Smith, K. G. V. (Nt, P, A), Vaillant, F. (N, P, E).
  Larvae: Dyte, C. E. (W), Vaillant, F. (N, P, E).
Ephydridae: Dahl, L. R. (P), Giordani-Soika, A. (P, E), Jorgenson, E. C. (N), Koizumi, K. (P),
    Maddock, D. R., de Oliveira, S. J. (Nt), Wirth, W. W. (W).
Errinidae: Stuckenberg, B. R. (E).
Eumyidae: Åbro, A. (P).
Fungivoridae: See Mycetophilidae.
Gastrophilidae: Capelle, K. J. (N).
Heleidae: See Ceratopogonidae.
Helomyzidae: Garrett, C. B. D. (N), Gill, G. D. (N).
Hippoboscidae: Ash, J. S. (P), Bequaert, J. C. (W), Chapulsky, J. (P), Herman, C. M. (N),
    Leclercq, M. (P, E), MacArthur, K. W. (N), Peus, F. (P), Povolný, D. (P), Takahasi,
    H. (P, O), Tarshis, I. B. (W).
Hylophilidae: Bucciarelli, I. (W).
Itonididae: Foote, R. H. (N), Harde, K. W., Inouye, M. (P), Johnson, N. E. (N), Nayar,
    K. K. (O), Skuhrava, M. (P).
Larvaevoridae: Čepelák, J. (P), Day, C. D. (P), Monko, A. (P), Sellers, W. F. (N, P),
    Takano, S. (P).
Lauxaniidae (Sapromyzidae): Kato, S. (P, Oc), Shewell, G. E. (W), Stuckenberg, B. R. (E).
Leptidae: Hardy, G. H. (A), Takahasi, H. (P, O).
Limoniidae: Nielsen, P. (P).
Liriopeidae: Peus, F. (P).
Lonchaeidae: Hackman, W. L. V. (P), McAlpine, J. F. (N, Nt, E, A, Oc), Morge, G. (P, E, O),
    Sasakawa, M. (P).
  Larvae: Morge, G. (P, E, O).
Lonchopteridae: Coe, R. L. (W).
Micropezidae (Tylidae): Aczel, M. (Nt, O, A), Verbeke, J. (E).
Milichiidae: Sabrosky, C. W. (W).
Muscidae, World: Albuquerque, D. O., Chillcott, J. G., Saccà, G., Snyder, F. M.,
    Vockeroth, J. R.
    Nearctic: Chillcott, J. G., Eldridge, B. J., Huckett, H. C., Siverly, R. E., West, L. S.
    Palearctic: Dobreanu, E., Fonseca, E. C. M. A., Gregor, F., Hafez, M., Hennig, W.,
      Hori, K., Huckett, H. C., Kano, R., Kirchberg, E., Peris, S. V., Peus, F., Povolný,
      D., Salem, H. H., Sztankay-Gulyás, M., Tiensuu, L.
    Paleotropical: Hiregaudar, L. S. (O), Paterson, H. E. (E), Peris, S. V. (E, O, A, Oc).
Mycetophilidae: Barendrecht, G. (P), Fisher, E. (N), Garrett, C. B. D. (N), Hardy, G. H. (A),
    Kjellander, E. (P), Laffoon, J. L. (N, P), Lane, J. (Nt), Mikołajczyk, W. (P), Okada,
    I. (P), Shaw, F. R. (N, Nt), Tollet, R. (W).
  Fossils: Coher, E. I. (W).
Mydaidae: Hull, F. M. (W).
Nemestrinidae: Bequaert, J. C. (W), Hull, F. M. (W), Stuardo-Ortiz, C. (Nt).
Neriidae: Aczel, M. (W).
Nothybidae: Aczel, M. (O).

Nycteribiidae: Aellen, V. (P), Chapulsky, J. (P), Hoffmann-Sandoval, A. (Nt), Hŭrka, K. (P), Karaman, Z. (P), Povolný, D. (P), Theodor, O, (P, E, O, A, Oc), Wenzel, R. L. (W).
Oestridae: Capelle, K. J. (N), Grunin, K. J. (P, E), Hiregaudar, L. S. (O), Laurence, B. R. (E), Leclercq, M. (P, E), Takahasi, H. (P, O).
    Larvae: Bennett, G. F. (N).
Otitidae: Foote, R. H. (N), Namba, R. (N), Parmenter, L. (P), Steyskal, G. C. (W).
Pallopteridae: Morge, G. (P). LARVAE: Morge, G. (P).
Pantophthalmidae: Carrera, M. (Nt).
Pelecorhynchidae: Pechuman, L. L. (N, Nt).
Phasiidae: Dupuis, C. (P).
Phlebotomidae: See Psychodidae.
Phoridae: Borgmeier, T. (Nt), Colyer, C. N. (W), Schmitz, H. (W).
Pipunculidae: Coe, R. L. (P), Hardy, D. E. (Nt, E, O, A, Oc), Koizumi, K. (P).
Platypezidae: Aczel, M. (Nt), Collart, A. (W), Kessel, E. L. (W).
Psilidae: Capelle, K. J. (N), Verbeke, J. (E).
Psychodidae: Messer, C. C. V., Messghali, A.
    World: Fairchild, G. B., Jung, H. F., Quate, L. W.
    Nearctic: Haseman, L., Hertig, M.
    Neotropical: Abonnenc, E., Barretto, M. P., Biagi, F., Deane, L., Del Ponte, E., Duret, J. P., Floch, H., Forattini, O. P., Hanson, W. J., Hertig, M., Ortiz Cordero, I., Vargas, L.
    Palearctic: Duport, M., Lewis, D. J., Mariani, M., Parrot, L., Saccà, G., Sara, M., Shinoda, O., Theodor, O., Tokunaga, M., Vaillant, F., Zivkovic, V.
    Paleotropical: Abonnenc, E. (E), Guggisberg, C. A. W. (E), Kirk, R. (E), Lewis, D. J. (E, O, A, Oc), Parrot, L. (E, O, A, Oc), Qutubuddin, M. (E), Rageau, J. G. F. (E), Theodor, O. (E, O, A, Oc), Tokunaga, M. (O, Oc).
    Larvae: Vaillant, F. (P).
Ptychopteridae: Bellamy, R. E. (N).
    Larvae: Bellamy, R. E. (N).
Pyrgotidae: Aczel, M. (Nt, E), Keiser, F. (W).
Rhagionidae: El-Moursy, A. A. (P), Hull, F. M. (W), Nagatomi, A. (P), Parmenter, L. (P), Stuckenberg, B. R. (E).
Rhinophoridae: Herting, B. (W).
Rhyphidae: Hardy, G. H. (A).
Sapromyzidae: See Lauxaniidae.
Sarcophagidae (Cordyluridae), World: Dodge, H. R., Downes, W. L., Jr., Hall, D. G., Lopes, H. S., Roback, S. S., Snyder, F. M.
    Nearctic: Newhouse, V. F.
    Palearctic: Collart, A., Hori, K., Kano, R., Kirchberg, E., Lehrer, A., Rohdendorf, B. B., Saccà, G., Salem, H. H.
    Paleotropical: Collart, A. (E), Hardy, G. H. (A), Joyce, C. R. (Oc), Rohdendorf, B. B. (E), Thomas, H. T. (O).
    Larvae: Sanjean, J. (N).
Scatophagidae: Hackman, W. L. V. (P).
Scatopsidae: Cook, E. F. (W), Tollet, R. (P, E).
Scenopinidae: Dyte, C. E.
Sciaridae: Bentinck, W. C. (N), Lane, J. (Nt), Lengersdorf, F. (P), Shaw, F. R. (N, Nt, Oc), Tuomikoski, R. K. (W).
Sciomyzidae: Berg, C. O. (N), Foote, B. A. (N), Hamrum, C. (N), Neff, S. E. (N), Steyskal, G. C. (W), Verbeke, J. (E).
    Larvae: Berg, C. C. (N), Foote, B. A. (N), Neff, S. E. (N).
Sepsidae: Smith, H. W. (W).
Simuliidae, World: Martinez, A., Smart, J., Stone, A.
    Nearctic: Coher, E. I., Davies, D. M., Davies, L., De Foliart, G. R., Hartley, C. F., Jamnback, H., Jr., McComb, C. W., Peterson, B., Roberts, R. H., Shewell, G. E., Sleeper, D. A., Sommerman, K. M., Wood, D. M.
    Neotropical: Anduze, P. J., Coher, E. I., Dalmat, H. T., D'Andretta, M. A. V., Elishewitz, H., Floch, H., Iriarte, D. R., Ortiz Cordero, I., Vargas, L.
    Palearctic: Davies, L., Dorier, A. H., Grenier, P., Novak, V., Ogata, K., Ossiannilsson, F., Rivosecchi, L., Rubtzov, I. A., Sasa, M., Shewell, G. E., Takahasi, H., Zivkovic, V.
    Paleotropical: Coher, E. I. (O), Crosskey, R. W. (E), Grenier, P. (E), Mackerras, I. M. (A, Oc), Mackerras, M. J. (A), de Meillon, B. (E), Ovazza, M. (E), Rageau, J. G. F. (E, Oc), Takahasi, H. (O), Waterhouse, E. J. (A).
    Larvae: De Foliart, G. R. (N).
Sphaeroceridae: Richards, O. W. (W), Vanschuytbroeck, P. (E).
Stratiomyiidae: Dahl, L. R. (P), Hanson, W. J. (N), Hull, F. M. (W), James, M. T. (W), Kraft, K. J. (N), Lindner, E. (Nt, P, E, O, A, Oc), McFadden, M. W. (N), Parmenter, L. (P), Quist, J. A. (N).

Streblidae: Aellen, V. (P), Dybas, H. S. (N, Nt), Hoffmann-Sandoval, A. (Nt), Thurman,
  E. B. (N, Nt), Wenzel, R. L. (W).
Syrphidae, no locality: Ashby, C. F., Meeuse, A. D. J.
  World: Coe, R. L., Hull, F. M., Stackelberg, A. A.
  Nearctic: Bean, J. L., Cole, F. R., van Doesburg, P. H., Hamrum, C., Sedman, Y.,
    Telford, H. S., Vockeroth, J. R., Weems, H. V., Jr.
  Neotropical: van Doesburg, P. H., Sedman, Y., Weems, H. V., Jr.
  Palearctic: Bańkowska, R., Brauns, A., Čepelák, J., van Doesburg, P. H., Glumac, S.,
    Hammond, C. O., Hodson, W. E. H., Keiser, F., Kempŕy, L., Malski, K., Mihályi, F.,
    Ninomija, E., Parmenter, L., Rogerson, J. P., Schneider, F., Shiraki, T., Spuris, Z.,
    Stys, P., Trojanska-Bankowska, R., Van der Goot, V. S., Zimina, L. W.
  Paleotropical: van Doesburg, P. H. (E, A), Hardy, G. H. (A), Keiser, F. (E, O, A, Oc),
    Shiraki, T. (O, Oc), Stuckenberg, B. R. (E).
  Larvae: Ninomija, E. (P).
Tabanidae, no locality: Bouvier, G., Kobayashi, H., Philip, C. B.
  World: Bequaert, J. C., Fairchild, G. B., Pechuman, L. L., Stone, A.
  Nearctic: Bailey, N. S., Bargren, W. C., Belkin, J. N., Blickle, R. L., Coher, E. I.,
    Davies, D. M., Hays, K., Heid, G., Hull, F. M., McAlpine, J. F., Middlekauff, W. W.,
    Roberts, R. H.
  Neotropical: Barretto, M. P., Coher, E. I., Hays, K., Heid, G., Roberts, R. H.
  Palearctic: Åbro, A., Chvala, M., Glumac, S., Kauri, H., Leclercq, M., Lyneborg, L.,
    Moucha, J., Murdoch, W. P., Nikitin, M. I., Oldroyd, H., Otsuru, M., Parmenter, L.,
    Peus, F., Takahasi, H., Trojan, P., Yajima, A.
  Ethiopian: Crosskey, R. W., Dias, J. A. T. S., Doucet, J., Leclercq, M., Oldroyd, H.,
    Ovazza, M., Potts, W. H., Rageau, J. G. F.
  Oriental: Coher, E. I., Hiregaudar, L. S., Mackerras, I. M., Takahasi, H.
  Australian: English, K. M. I., Mackerras, I. M., Nikitin, M. I.
  Oceania: Mackerras, I. M., Rageau, J. G. F.
Tachinidae, World: Rohdendorf, B. B.
  Nearctic: Arnaud, P. H., Jr., Beneway, D. F., Cole, F. R., Downes, W. L., Jr.,
    McAlpine, J. F.
  Neotropical: Arnaud, P. H., Jr., Cortes, P. R., Rettenmeyer, C. W., Thompson, W. R.
  Palearctic: d'Aguilar, J., Fonseca, E. C. M. A., Herting, B., Kennaugh, J. H., Mesnil,
    L. P., Mihályi, F., Sisojevič, P., Spooner, G. M., Tiensuu, L.
  Paleotropical: Hardy, G. H. (A), Mesnil, L. P. (E, O, A, Oc), Verbeke, J. (E).
Tanyderidae: Bellamy, R. E. (N).   LARVAE: Bellamy, R. E. (N).
Tendipedidae: See Chironomidae.
Tephritidae: Blanc, F. L. (N), Foote, R. H. (N, Nt), Hardy, D. E. (O, Oc).
  Larvae: Blanc, F. L. (N).
Thaumaleidae: Vaillant, F. (N, P, E).
Therevidae: Barnes, A. M. (W), Cole, F. R. (N), Dyte, C. E., Hildebrand, C. W. (N),
    Hull, F. M. (W), Schlinger, E. I. (N, Nt).
Tipulidae, no locality: Wood, H. G.
  World: Alexander, C. P. (W).
  Nearctic: Bellamy, R. E., Byers, G. W., Dickinson, W. E., Foote, B. A.
  Palearctic: Erhan, E., Ishida, H., Mannheims, B., Slipka, J., Theowald, -, Tjeder,
    B. C. H., Tokunaga, M.
  Paleotropical: Mannheims, B. (E), Tokunaga, M. (O, Oc).
  Larvae: Bellamy, R. E. (N), Chiswell, J. R. (P), Theowald, -. (P).
Trypetidae, no locality: Keifer, H. H., Munro, H. K.
  Nearctic: Britten, H., Jones, S. C.
  Neotropical: Aczel, M., Bates, M., Britten, H., Bush, G., Wille, J. E.
  Palearctic: Britten, H., Ito, S., Mihályi, F., Shiraki, T.
  Paleotropical: Britten, H. (E, O, A, Oc), May, A. W. S. (A, Oc), Perkins, F. A. (O, A, Oc),
    Shiraki, T. (O, Oc).
  Larvae: Bush, G. (Nt).
Tylidae: See Micropezidae.

Hymenoptera

No other data: Arle, R., Athur, A. P., Bakke, A., Barbotim, F., Bare, O. S., Belizin, V. I.,
  Benoit, P. L. G., Berland, L., Bischoff, H., Blanchard, E. E., Blüthgen, P.,
  Bruniquel, S., Casal, O. H., Cavro, E., Ceresa, L., Chen, C-W., Cherian, M. C.,
  Crévecoeur, A., Del Junco, J. J., Downes, D. J., Dutu-Lăcătusu, M., Fischer, C. R.,
  Forsius, R., Fullaway, D. T., Fulnek, L., de Germond, J. D., Granger, C., Gupta,
  V. K., Hacker, H., Hammer, K., Huba, A., Koscielska, M., Lal, K. B., Mao, Y-T.,
  Masi, L., Matsumura, S., Merisuo, A. K., Nagase, H., Panfilov, D. V.,

Pearson, J. F. W. , Perkins, J. F. , Ramakrishna-Ayayr, T. V. , Rao, V. P. , Schmitz, G. ,
Seabra, C. A. C. , Stancati, M. F. , Sustera, O. , Tomsik, B. , Trebilcoch, R. E. ,
Tsinowskii, Y. P. , Viktorov, G. A. , Wagenknecht, R. , Yarrow, I. H. H.
New World: Barnes, J. W. (N), Daly, H. V. (N, Nt), Krombein, K. V. (N), Mayer, F. (N, Nt).
Palearctic: Alfieri, A. , Bytinski-Salz, H. , Daly, H. V. , Diniz, M. A. , Gyorfi, J. , Hedwig,
K. , Lehmann, W. , Šedivý, J. , Wiebes, J.
Paleotropical: Alam, S. M. (O), Cheesman, L. E. (Oc), Daly, H. V. (E, O, A, Oc),
Krombein, K. V. (Oc), Menon, M. G. R. (O), Merino, G. (O), Plant, J. (A), Rayment,
T. (A, Oc), Taylor, R. (A).
Arctic: Petersen, B.
Parasitic: Beardsley, J. W. (Oc), Claridge, M. F. (P), Fernando, W. (O), Glowacki, J. (P),
Graham, M. W. R. V. (N, P), Hellén, W. (P), Ishii, T. , Moser, J. C. (W), Schmidt,
E. (P, E, O, A, Oc).
Social: Araujo, R. L. (N, Nt).
Gall wasps: Mehes, G. (P), Monzen, K. (O), Sternlicht, M. (P).
Fossils: Daly, H. V. (F:W).

* * * * *

ACULEATA: Balthasar, V. (P), Erlandsson, S. (P), Kjellander, E. (P), Richards, O. W. (P),
Sato, O. (P), Spooner, G. M. (P), Yasumatsu, K. (P, Oc).
APOIDEA, no locality: Benoist, R.
Nearctic: Bohart, G. E. , Cross, E. A. , Daly, H. V. , Fischer, R. L. , Gittins, A. R. ,
Hurd, P. D. , Jr. , Lanham, U. N. , Lindsley, E. G. , Michener, C. D. , Pengelly, D. H. ,
Shinners, L. H. , Timberlake, P. H.
Neotropical: Alayo Dalmau, P. , Cross, E. A. , Fischer, R. L. , Lanham, U. N. ,
Michener, C. D. , Moure, P. J. S.
Palearctic: Baker, D. B. , Clarke, K. U. , Elfving, R. , Hirashima, Y. , Lanham, U. N. ,
Mavromoustakis, G. A. , Ponomareva, A. A. , Popov, V. B.
Paleotropical: Baker, D. B. (O), Hirashima, Y. (O, Oc), Lanham, U. N. (E, O, A, Oc),
Lieftinck, M. A. (O, A, Oc).
BETHYLOIDEA: Ghesquière, J. (W), Kurian, C. (O).
CEPHOIDEA: Benson, R. B. (W), Maa, T-C. (W).
CHALCIDOIDEA: Burks, B. D. , (W), Grandi, G. (W), Hoffer, A. (W), Kerrich, G. J. (W),
Yasumatsu, K. (W).
Nearctic: Peck, O. , Szabó, J. B.
Neotropical: De Santis, L. , Gomes, J. G. , Szabó, J. B.
Palearctic: Andriescu, I. , Constanţa, C. , Domenichini, G. , Erdös, J. , Ferriere, C. ,
Graham, M. W. R. V. , Jansson, A. , Novicky, S. , Sachtleben, H. , Schmutterer, H. ,
Suciu, I. , Szabó, J. B. , Szelényi, G.
Paleotropical: Kurian, C. (O), Mathur, R. N. (O), Nikolskaya, M. N. (E, O), Riek, E. F. (A).
CHRYSIDOIDEA: Nikolskaya, M. N. (E, O).
CYNIPOIDEA: Ionescu, M. A. (P), Kerrich, G. J. (W), Peck, O. (N), Riek, E. F. (A), Weld,
L. H. (N).
ICHNEUMONOIDEA: Kurian, C. (O), Mason, W. R. M. (W), Rao, S. N. (O), Sachtleben, H. (P).
ORUSSOIDEA: Benson, R. B. (W).
PROCTOTRUPOIDEA (Serphoidea): Ghesquière, J. (W), Jansson, A. (P), Masner, L. (W),
Peck, O. (N), Soyka, W. (W), Szabó, J. B. (N, Nt, P, E, Oc), Szelényi, G. (P).
SCOLIOIDEA: Benno, P. (P), Jacot-Guillarmod, C. F. (E).
SERPHOIDEA: See Proctotrupoidea.
SIRICOIDEA: Benson, R. B. (W), Maa, T-C. (W).
SPHECOIDEA: Alayo Dalmau, P. (Nt), de Andrade, N. F. (P, E), Callan, E. M. (E), Ferguson,
G. R. (W), Miller, C. D. F. (N), Riek, E. F. (A), Tsuneki, K. (P), van der Vecht,
J. (O, Oc).
SYMPHYTA (Chalastogastra): Barendrecht, G. (P), Beer, R. E. (W), Benson,
R. B. (P, A, Oc, Arc), Burks, B. D. (W), Hellén, W. (P), Kontuniemi, T. (P),
Middlekauff, W. W. (N), Okutani, T. (P), Takeuchi, K. (P), Wong, H. R. (N, P),
Woollatt, L. H. (P), Zhelochovtsev, A. N. (P).
Larvae: Hotchkiss, D. E. (N, P, A), Okutani, T. (P).
TENTHREDINOIDEA: Pádr, Z. (P), Pasteels, J. J. (E), Precupetu, A. (P), Ross, H. H. (N),
Stritt, W. (P), Weiffenbach, H. (P), Will, H. C. (N), Zirngiebl, L. (P).
VESPOIDEA: Alayo Dalmau, P. (Nt), Ferguson, G. R. (W), Miller, C. D. F. (N), Ribaut, H. (P).
XYELOIDEA: Benson, R. B. (W).

* * * * *

Agaontidae: Grandi, G. (W), Joseph, K. J. (P, E), Kuttamathiathu, J. (P, E, A), Wiebes, J. T. (O).
Andrenidae: Rozen, J. G. (W), Shinn, A. F. (N, Nt).
Anthophoridae: Baker, D. B. (E), Iuga-Raica, V. G. (P), Sivik, F. P. (P, E, O), Snelling,
R. R. (N, Nt).
Aphelinidae: Alam, S. M. (O), Bachmaier, F. (P), Compere, H. (W), Ghesquière, J. (W),
Jasnosh, V. A. , Mahan, M. (O), Soyka, W. (W).

Apidae, no locality: Marzoratti, O.
    World: Kocourek, M., Maa, T-C., Mavromoustakis, G. A.
    New World: LaBerge, W. E. (N, Nt).
    Palearctic: Bandeira, L., Diniz, M. A., Enslin, E., Erlandsson, S., Faester, K., Knechtel,
        W., Kocourek, M., van Lith, J. P., Löken, A., Móczár, M., Noskiewicz, J., Sakagami,
        S. F., Sivik, F. P., Stoeckhert, F. K., Teunissen, H. G. M., Valkeila, E., Wiering, H.,
        Wolf, H.
    Paleotropical: Lieftinck, M. A. (O, A, Oc), Pagden, H. T. (O), Sivik, F. P. (E, O).
Apterogynidae: Invrea, F. (W), Suárez, F. J. (W).
Bembicidae: Duncan, C. D. (N), Ferguson, G. R. (N, Nt), Gillaspy, J. E. (N, Nt).
Bethylidae: Evans, H. E. (N, Nt), Ogloblin, A. A. (Nt).
Bombidae, no locality: Babiy, P.
    World: Clarke, K. U., Kruseman, G., Maina, B. A., Stephen, W. P.
    New World: Chandler, L. (N), Hobbs, G. A. (N), Neave, F. (N), Milliron, H. E. (N, Nt).
    Palearctic: Brian, A. D., Dylewska, M., Ishikawa, R., Sakagami, S. F.
Braconidae, World: Mackauer, M., Muesebeck, C. F. W., Shenefelt, R. D.
    Nearctic: Fischer, M., Mason, W. R. M., McComb, C. W., Riegel, G. T., Schlinger, E. I.
    Neotropical: Heqvist, K-J., Nixon, G. E. J.
    Palearctic: Beyr, J., Čapek, M., Eady, R. D., Fischer, M., Gyorfi, J., Hedwig, K.,
        Johansson, S., Königsmann, E., Lăcătusu, M., Nixon, G. E. J., Papp, E., Starý, P.,
        Telenga, N. A., Tobias, V. I., Watanabe, C., Wiackowski, S.
    Paleotropical: Bhatnagar, S. P. (O), De Saeger, H. (E), Heqvist, K-J. (O), Mathur, R. N. (O),
        Nixon, G. E. J. (E, O, A, Oc), Parrott, A. W. (A, Oc).
    Larvae: Short, J. R. T. (P).
Cephidae: Anca, P. (P), Ries, D. T.
Chalcididae: Bachmaier, F. (P), Bouček, Z. (P), Habu, A. (P), Jasnosh, V. A., Menon,
    M. G. R. (O), Steffan, J. R. (W).
Chrysididae, World: Cooper, K. W., Linsenmaier, W., Zimmermann, S.
    Nearctic: Cooper, K. W.
    Palearctic: Balthasar, V., Benno, P., Erlandsson, S., Harant, H., Invrea, F., Negru, S.,
        Noskiewicz, J., Nouvel, H., Preuss, G., Teunissen, H. G. M., Tsuneki, K., Valkeila, E.,
        Zirngiebl, L.
    Ethiopian: Edney, E. B.
Cimbicidae: Kapuścinśki, S. (P).
Cleonymidae: Heqvist, K-J. (W), Wallace, G. E. (W).
Cleptidae: Riek, E. F. (A), Zimmermann, S. (W).
Colletidae: Noskiewicz, J. (P), Stephen, W. P. (N, Nt).
Crabronidae: Tanaka, E. (P).
Cynipidae: Eady, R. D. (P), Lyon, R. (N), Masuda, H. (P), Yasumatsu, K. (P).
Diapriidae: Priesner, H. (P), Sundholm, A. (P).
Dryinidae: Brown, H. E. (W), Richards, O. W. (W).
Elasmidae: Bachmaier, F. (P).
Encyrtidae, World: Compere, H., Ghesquière, J., Hoffer, A., Skinner, F. E.
    Nearctic: Hagen, K. S., Miller, C. D. F., Timberlake, P. H.
    Palearctic: Bachmaier, F., Tachikawa, T., Trjapitzin, V. A., Zinna, G.
    Oriental: Alam, S. M., Mahan, M.
Eucharitidae: Bachmaier, F. (P), Bouček, Z. (P).
Eulophidae: Bachmaier, F. (P), Bouček, Z. (P), Delucchi, V. (P).
Eumenidae: Willink, A. (Nt), van der Vecht, J. (O, Oc).
Eupelmidae: Bachmaier, F. (P), Eady, R. D. (W).
Eurytomidae: Bouček, Z. (P), Bugbee, R. E. (N, Nt), Claridge, M. F. (W).
Evaniidae: Edmunds, L. R. (N), Townes, H. K. (W).
Formicidae, no locality: Bibikoff, M., Brangham, A. N., Enzmann, E. V., Furukawa, H.,
    Jones, E. L., Okano, K., Patrizi, S., Stumper, R.
    World: Baba, Y., Brown, W. L., Jr., Creighton, W. S., Gregg, R. E., O'Rourke, F. J.,
        Weber, N. A., Wing, M. W.
    New World: LaBerge, W. E., Potts, R. W. L., Smith, M. R.
    Nearctic: Cloyd, W. J., Cole, A. C., Creighton, W. S., Grundmann, A. W., Gunn, W. B.,
        Ingham, C., Kannowski, P. B., King, R. L., Mallis, A., Miller, C. D. F., Rettenmeyer,
        C. W., Van Pelt, A. F., Jr., Wheeler, G. C.
    Neotropical: Borgmeier, T., Creighton, W. S., Gonçalves, C. R., Kannowski, P. B., Kempf,
        W. W., Kusnezov, N., Rettenmeyer, C. W., Van Pelt, A. F., Jr.
    Palearctic: Azuma, M., Begdon, J., Bernard, F., Betrem, J. G., van Boven, J. K. A.,
        Brian, M. V., Bytinski-Salz, H., Collingwood, C. A., Forsslund, K. H., Gösswalk, K.,
        Hayashida, K., Holgersen, H., Holzel, E., Kholova, H., Kloft, W., Knechtel, W.,
        Koehler, W., Kutter, H., Le Masne, G., Lemke, U., Markl, W., Morisita, M.,

Novak, V. , Pisarski, B. , Preuss, G. , Raignier, R. P. A. , Samšiňák, K. , Šilhavý, V. ,
Soyer, B. , Sweeney, R. C. H. , Tsuneki, K. , Wolf, H.
Ethiopian: Bernard, F. , van Boven, J. K. A. , Raignier, R. P. A. , Sweeney, R. C. H.
Oriental: Mukerji, D.
Australian: Douglas, A. M. , Freeland, J. , Greaves, T. , Kingma, J. T. , Lowery, B. B. ,
McAreavey, J. J. , Mercovich, T. C. , Ray, J. R. , Taylor, R.
Oceania: Potts, R. W. L. , Wilson, E. O.
Larvae: Wheeler, G. C.
Gasteruptionidae: Pasteels, J. J. (W), Šedivý, J. (P).
Gasteruptiidae: Crosskey, R. W. (W), Townes, H. K. (W).
Halictidae: Ordway, E. (N).
Heloridae: Pschorn-Walcher, H. (W), Riek, E. F. (A).
Ichneumonidae, no locality: Ozols, E. , Pisică, G. C. , Vasič, K.
World: Czartoryski, S. A. , Kerrich, G. J. , Macek, J. , Townes, H. K.
Nearctic: Heinrich, G. , Mason, W. R. M. , Mitchell, R. T. , Smith, L. K. , Walkley, L. M. ,
Walley, G. S. , Zwölfer, H.
Neotropical: Walkley, L. M.
Palearctic: Aerts, W. , Aubert, J. F. , Bachmaier, F. , Bajári, E. , Ceballos, G. , Chiu, S. ,
Constantineanu, M. I. , Glowacki, J. , Gyorfi, J. , Hedwig, K. , Heinreich, G. , Hinz, R. ,
Iwata, K. , Johansson, S. , Kim, C-W. , Leclercq, J. , Lehmann, W. , Obrtel, R. ,
Teunissen, H. G. M. , Uchida, T. , Zwölfer, H.
Paleotropical: Baltazar, C. R. (O), Betrem, J. G. (O, A, Oc), Chiu, S. (O), Heinreich,
G. (E, O), Leclercq, J. (E, O, A, Oc), Parrott, A. W. (A, Oc).
Larvae: Short, J. R. T. (N, P).
Leucospididae: Bachmaier, F. (P).
Masaridae: Willink, A. (Nt).
Megachilidae: Hill, R. E. (N), Hobbs, G. A. (N), Mitchell, T. B. (W), Móczár, M. (P), Sinha,
R. N. (W).
Meliponidae: Moure, P. J. S. (W), Schwarz, H. F. (N, Nt, O).
Melittidae: Móczár, M. (P), Stage, G. I. (N).
Methocidae: Pagden, H. T. (O).
Mutillidae, World: Ferguson, W. E. , Kocourek, M. , Suárez, F. J.
New World: Ferguson, W. E. (N), Hurd, P. D. , Jr. (N), Mickel, C. E. (N, Nt).
Palearctic: Invrea, F. , Nonveiller, G. , Nouvel, H. , Valkeila, E.
Paleotropical: Invrea, F. (E), Mickel, C. E. (Oc), Pagden, H. T. (O).
Mymaridae: Bakkendorf, O. (P), Debauche, H. R. (W), Doutt, R. L. (N, Oc), Hincks, W. D. (P),
Ogloblin, A. A. (Nt), Soyka, W. (N, Nt, P, O).
Myrmosidae: Suárez, F. J. (W).
Nomadidae: Rodeck, H. G. (W).
Ormyridae: Bachmaier, F. (P).
Oryssidae: Guiglia, D. (P, E).
Pamphiliidae: Anca, P. (P).
Perilampidae: Bachmaier, F. (P), Bouček, Z. (P), Steffan, J. R. (W).
Platygastridae: Sundholm, A. (P).
Pompilidae: See Psammocharidae.
Proctotrupidae: Debauche, H. R. (W), Ogloblin, A. A. (Nt), Pschorn-Walcher, H. (W),
Rief, E. F. (A).
Psammocharidae (Pompilidae): Babiy, P.
World: Dreisbach, R. R. , Townes, H. K. , Wahis, R.
Nearctic: Dreisbach, R. R. , Evans, H. E. , Hurd, P. D. , Jr.
Neotropical: Argañaras, J. , Dreisbach, R. R. , Evans, H. E.
Palearctic: Grozdanovič-Simič, J. , Ishikawa, R. , Móczár, L. , Nouvel, H. , Preuss, G. ,
Scobiola-Palade, X. , Soyer, B. , Valkeila, E. , Wolf, H.
Paleotropical: van der Vecht, J. (O, Oc).
Pteromalidae: Bouček, Z. (P), Delucchi, V. (N, P), Mahan, M. (O), von Rosen, H. (W),
Wallace, G. E. (W).
Roproniidae: Townes, H. K. (W).
Sapygidae: Bechtel, R. C. (W), Valkeila, E. (P).
Scelionidae: Hagen, K. S. (N), Yasumatsu, K. (P, Oc).
Sclerogibbidae: Schlinger, E. I. (W).
Scoliidae: Betrem, J. G. (P, O, A, Oc), Bradley, J. C. (N, Nt, E), Guiglia, D. (P, E), Hurd,
P. D. , Jr. (N), Nouvel, H. (P), Steinberg, D. D. M. (P).
Serphidae: See Proctotrupidae.
Siricidae: Anca, P. (P), Ries, D. T.
Sphecidae, no locality: Nielsen, E. T.
World: Leclercq, J.
Nearctic: Bohart, R. M. , Ferguson, G. R. , Fritz, M. A. , Murray, W. D. , Schlinger, E. I. ,
Scullen, H. A. , Strandtmann, R. , Williams, F. X.

   Neotropical: Ferguson, G. R. , Fritz, M. A. , Schlinger, E. I. , Scullen, H. A. , Williams,
      F. X. , Willink, A.
   Palearctic: Balthasar, V. , de Beaumont, J. , Faester, K. , Fahlander, K. , Iwata, K. ,
      van Lith, J. P. , Móczár, L. , Preuss, G. , Pulawski, W. J. , Scobiola-Palade, X. ,
      Valkeila, E. , Verhoeff, P. M. F. , Wolf, H.
   Paleotropical: Arnold, G. (E), van Lith, J. P. (O, A, Oc).
Sphegidae: Åbro, A. (P), Grozdanovič-Simič, J. (P), Nouvel, H. (P), Roth, P. (P),
      Teunissen, H. G. M. (P).
Stephanidae: Townes, H. K. (W).
Tenthredinidae: Benson, R. B. (W), Čingovski, J, (P), Enslin, E. (P), Iuga-Raica, V. G. (P),
      Lindqvist, M. E. (P), Malaise, R. E. (Nt, P), Papp, E. (P), Scobiola-Palade, X. (P).
Tetrastichidae: Gradwell, G. R. (W), Mahan, M. (O).
Thysanidae: Bachmaier, F. (P).
Thynnidae: Salter, K. E. W. (Nt, O, A, Oc).
Tiphiidae: Allen, H. W. , Ishikawa, R. (P), Jacot-Guillarmod, C. F. (E), Valkeila, E. (P).
Torymidae: Eady, R. D. (P), Hobbs, K. R. (N), Hussey, N. W. (W), Joseph, K. J. (P, E),
      Kuttamathiathu, J. (P, E, A), Lienk, S. E. (N), Milliron, H. E. (N), Steffan, J. R. (W).
Trichogrammatidae: Bakkendorf, O. (P), Doutt, R. L. (N, Oc), Guesquière, J. (W), Quednau,
      W. (W), Soyka, W. (W).
Trigonalidae: Riek, E. F. (A), Townes, H. K. (W).
Vespidae, World: Bequaert, J. C. , Giordani-Soika, A. , Miller, C. D. F.
   Nearctic: Bechtel, R. C. , Bohart, R. M. , Cooper, K. W. , Duncan, C. D. , Neave, F. ,
      Snelling, R. R.
   Neotropical: Benno, P. , Snelling, R. R. , Willink, A.
   Palearctic: Åbro, A. , Bandeiro, L. , Benno, P. , Faester, K. , Ishikawa, R. , Kim, C-W. ,
      Löken, A. , Teunissen, H. G. M. , Valkeila, E. , Weyrauch, W. , Wolf, H.
   Paleotropical: Pagden, H. T. (O), Riek, E. F. (A), van der Vecht, J. , (O, Oc).
Vipionidae: Bhatnagar, S. P. (O).
Xiphydriidae: Ries, D. T.
Xyelidae: Burdick, D. (N).
Xylocopidae: Maa, T-C. (O, A).

                              Coleoptera

No other data: Anfossi, R. , Antoine, M. , Arambourg, Y. , Audibert, M. , Baker, A. W. ,
      Balderson, J. , Balty, J. A. , Barajon, M. , Barro, M. , Boitel, A. G. , Bollow, H. ,
      Borodin, D. , Bosq, J. M. , Bossong, H. , Boudan, R. , Breurken, W. F. , Brimley, J. F. ,
      Bruniquel, S. , Bureau, P. L. , Busulini, E. , Butovitsch, V. , Cachan, P. , Clarke, R. D. ,
      Clarke-MacIntyre, W. , Clement, P. , Coulter, W. K. , Courtenay, J. , Crandall, R. H. ,
      David, R. , Deane, C. , Deleve, J. , Descarpentries, A. , Diringshofen, R. V. , Dozier,
      B. K. , Eastin, J. , Ekbom, P. J. , Ekengren, B. R. , van Eldik, H. C. , Eliescu, G. , Erb,
      J. , Farcu, E. , Fragoso, S. S. , Gaillard, F. J. , Grundmann, E. , Guerin, J. , Hashimoto,
      I. , Hepper, H. C. , Holdhaus, K. , Hoshino, M. , Jakob, H. , Kajiharo, E. S. , Kangas, Y. ,
      Kato, Y. , Korbel, L. , Krauss, N. L. H. , Kult, K. , Leach, E. R. , Legros, C. , Levasseur,
      L. , Lopez, P. R. , Manfrini, M. , Mateu, J. , Mathieu, J. M. , Matsumura, S. , Mendes,
      D. , Mequignon, A. , Metsävainio, K. , Mouchet, J. , de Muizon, J. , Nyholm, T. , Oke,
      C. G. , van Ootstroom, S. J. , Owen-Campbell, J. , Padron, A. G. , Pavan, M. ,
      Pérez Alcalá, R. , Pickard-Cambridge, D. , Podtiaguin, B. , Porta, A. , Purtoy, M. ,
      Rebmann, O. , Reitter, E. , Saenz Sanguinetti, A. , de Saint-Albin, E. , Sanchez Ruiz, C. ,
      Schjøtz-Christensen, K. B. , Seabra, C. A. C. , Servaas, M. , Smedley, D. N. , Sokolowski,
      K. , Straneo, S. L. , Sutton, E. , Tanner, V. M. , Tempere, G. , Terán, A. , Thuneberg, E. ,
      Ting, P. C. , Tordo, G. , Verhalha, M. M. , Veyret, P. , Wichmann, H. E., Wilcke, H. ,
      Woodcock, A. T. A. , Yamasaki, K.
   World: Bowman, J. R. , Crowson, R. A. , Salkilld, B. W.
   Nearctic: Alspaugh, R. D. , Barnes, J. W. , Brown, W. J. , Dietrich, H. , Dimmitt, W. A. ,
      Downie, N. M. , Dury, R. , Fender, K. M. , Frost, C. A. , Karren, J. B. , Malkin, B. ,
      McReynolds, J. W. , Meiners, E. P. , Nelson, G. H. , Papp, C. S. , Parker, F. H. , Robert, A.
   Neotropical: Kay, R. G. W. , Sawaya, M. P.
   Palearctic: Alfieri, A. , Allen, A. A. , Baguena Corella, L. , Balazuc, J. , Blomqvist, G. ,
      Brakman, P. J. , Bytinski-Salz, H. , Cleu, H. , Dahl, J. , Derenne, E. , Franco, B. ,
      Gspan, A. , Hansen, V. , van Heerdt, P. F. , Hervé, P. , Holzel, E. , Horion, A. , de Jong,
      C. , Kangas, E. , Kocher, L. F. J. , Kono, H. , Kryzhanovsky, O. L. , Lazorko, W. ,
      Lohse, G. A. , Marcu, O. , Massee, A. M. , Miwa, Y. , Moscardini, C. , Muller, G. ,
      Nakane, T. , Novak, P. , von Peez, A. , Pretner, E. , Sage, B. L. , Stančič, J. , Stockmann,
      S. , Strand, A. , Weise, E. , Zecchini, R.
   Ethiopian: Andreae, H. , Botto, G. , Bruneau de Mire, P. , Gedye, A. F. J. , Vinson, J. L. J.·

                                 68

Oriental: Miwa, Y.
Australian: Brooks, J. G. , Cunningham, J. R. Fricke, F. , Gourlay, E. S. , Hallgarten, F. ,
    Hornabrook, R. , McMillan, R. P. , Plant, J. , Smith, A.
Oceania: Crook, F. P. , Ford, E. J. , Jr.
Aquatic: Anderson, J. B. (N), Balfour-Browne, F. (P), Bertrand, H. (W), Naumann, H. (P),
    Young, F. N. , Jr. (N).
Cavernicolous: Agazzi, G. (P), Balazuc, J. (P), Demaux, J. (P), Forti, M. A. L. (P), Jeannel,
    R. , Meggiolaro, G. (P), Muller, G. (P), Ochs, J. (W), Pretner, E. (P), Uéno, S-I. (P).
Inquiline: McMillan, R. P. (A).
Of stored products: Howe, R. W. (W).
Wood borers: Twinn, D. C. (P).
Larvae: d'Aguilar, J. (P), Burakowski, B. (P), Daggy, T. (N), Garner, W. V. (N), Hayashi,
    N. (P), Kurosa, K. (P), Larsson, S. G. (W), Mathur, R. N. (O), Rees, B. E. (N), Rozen,
    J. G. , Jr. (W), Ting, P. C. , Viado, G. B.
Fossils: Crowson, R. A. (F:W), Schweiger, H. (C:P).
* * * * *

ADEPHAGA: Brelih, S. (P).
CLAVICORNIA: Hisamatsu, S. (P), Lechanteur, F.
COLYDIOIDEA: Armstrong, J. W. T. (A).
HETEROMERA: Buck, F. D. (W), Smith, E. T. (A).
HYDRADEPHAGA: Popham, E. J. (P).
LAMELLICORNIA: Endrodi, S. (W), Goljan, A. , Kuyten, P. (W), Martinez, A. (W), Nomura,
    S. (P), Von Bloeker, J. C. , Jr. (W).
MALACODERMATA: Ieniştea, M. A. (P).
RHYNCHOPHORA: Cockerham, K. L. , Hayes, W. P. (N), Sleeper, E. L. (N, Nt).
TENEBRIONOIDEA: Armstrong, J. W. T. (A).
* * * * *

Aderidae: Werner, F. G. (N).
Alleculidae (Cistelidae); Maŕan, J. (P), Papp, C. S. (N, Nt).
Amphizoidae: Edwards, J. G. (W), Leech, H. B. (N).
Anistomidae: See Leiodidae.
Anobiidae: Dominik, J. (P), Ford, E. J. , Jr. (Oc), Palm, T. (P), Ruckes, H. , Jr. (N),
    Saraiva, -. (P).
Anthicidae: Bonadona, P. (W), Bucciarelli, I. (W), Craig, W. S. (N), Hagen, K. S. (W), Smith,
    E. T. (A), Van Hille, J. C. (E), Werner, F. G. (N, Oc).
Anthribidae: Frieser, R. (W), Jôraku, T. (P), Uno, M. (P), Valentine, B. D. (W).
Attelabidae: Ter-Minasian, M. E. (P), Voss, E. (W).
Biphyllidae: Parsons, C. T. (N).
Bostrichidae: Belkin, J. N. (W), Chujo, M. (P, Oc), Dominik, J. (P), Gerberg, E. J. (W),
    Saraiva, -. (P), Vrydagh, J. M. (W), Wood, S. L. (W).
Brenthidae: Haedo, J. A. (W), Schedl, K. (W), Soares, B. (Nt).
Bruchidae (Mylabridae, Lariidae): Beal, R. S. , Jr. (N), Bottimer, L. J. (W), Chujo, M. (P, Oc),
    Decelle, J. (E), Southgate, B. J. (W), Zacher, F. (P).
Buprestidae, no locality: Paul, F. , Richter, A. A.
    World: Cobos Sanchez, A. , Gemmell, A. , Gerini, F. , Helfer, J. R. , Nelson, G. H. ,
        Obenberger, J. , Tongyai, M. R. C.
    Nearctic: Barr, W. F. , Beer, F. M. , Benoit, P. , Capelouto, R. , Cazier, M. A. , Chamberlin,
        W. J. , Figg-Hoblyn, J. P. , Good, H. G. , Knull, J. N. , Nelson, G. H. , Parker, F. H. ,
        Tilden, J. W. , Vogt, G. B.
    Neotropical: Cazier, M. A. , Figg-Hoblyn, J. P. , Vogt, G. B. , de Zayas Muños, F.
    Palearctic: Alexeev, A. V. , Baudon, A. , Kurosawa, Y. , Robin, M. , Saraiva, -, Schaefer, L.
    Ethiopian: Ferreira, M-C.
    Oriental: Kurosawa, Y. , Tongyai, M. R. C. , Vogt, G. B.
    Australian: Deuquet, C. F. , Gemmell, A. , Hateley, K. , LeSouef, J. C. , Macqueen, J. ,
        McMillan, R. P. , Mules, M. W.
    Oceania: Kurosawa, Y.
  Larvae: Alexeev, A. V. (P).
Byrrhidae: El-Moursy, A. A. (N), Fiori, G.
Byturidae: Parsons, C. T. (N).
Cantharidae (Telephoridae): Fender, K. M. (N), Green, J. W. (N), Hicker, R. (P, E), Magis,
    N. (P, E), McKey-Fender, D. (N), Miskimen, G. W. (N, Nt), Moscardini, C. (P),
    Wittmer, W. (W).
Carabidae, no locality: Blazejewski, F. , Cauchois, P. , Colas, G. , Jeannel, R. , Robinson, J. H. ,
    Tanaka, K. , Winston, P. W. , Yoshida, A.
    World: Bänninger, M. , Blumenthal, C. L. , Bomans, H. E. , Breuning, S. , Brivio, P. C. ,
        Darlington, P. J. , Jr. , Endy, E. T. , Fassati, M. , Heinz, W. , Korell, A. , Laneyrie, R. ,
        Mandl, K. , McReynolds, J. W. , Puisségur, C. , Schönmann, R. , Schweiger, H. ,
        Van Dorsselaer, R. , Van Hoegarden, A.

69

Holarctic: Negre, J. , Lindroth, C. H. , Van Hoegarden, A.
Nearctic: Ball, G. E. , Bell, R. T. , Benschoter, C. A. , Dozier, H. L. , Everly, R. T. , Hacker,
  H. , Hatch, M. H. , Lindroth, C. H. , Madge, R. , Stehr, W. C.
Neotropical: Bell, R. T. , Bolívar y Pieltain, C. , Negre, J. , Schweiger, H.
Palearctic: Antoine, M. , Bari, B. , Blumenthal, C. L. , Bourgin, P. , Bucciarelli, I. ,
  Burmeister, F. , Cabidoche, M. , De Monte, T. , Durand, G. , Fassati, M. , Gallivanone,
  M. , Habu, A. , Hürka, K. , Ieniştea, M. A. , Ishida, H. , Jedlička, A. , Kryzhanovsky, O. L. ,
  Kurosa, K. , Lagar, A. , Lazorko, W. , Magistretti, M. , Maŕan, J. , Meggiolaro, G. ,
  de Monte, T. , Moore, B. P. , Morgante, G. C. , Ohkura, M. , Panin, S. , Pŕívora, M. ,
  Puisségur, C. , Sǎvulescu, N. , Schuler, L. , Schultz, V. G. M. , Seiler, D. , Uéno, S-I.
Ethiopian: Basilewsky, P. , Bruneau de Mire, P. , de Monte, T. , Schuler, L.
Oriental: Landin, B. O. , Louwerens, C. J.
Australian: Britton, E. B. , Darlington, P. J. , Jr. , Moore, B. P. , Salkilld, B. W.
Oceania: Darlington, P. J. , Jr. , Salkilld, B. W. , Schweiger, H.
Antarctic: Schweiger, H.
Cavernicolous: Karaman, Z. (P), Krekeler, C. H. (N), Valentine, J. M. (W).
Larvae: Boldori, L. , Cerruti, M. (P), Garner, W. V. (N), Hürka, K. (P), Kurosa, K. (P).
Fossils: Fassati, M. (W).
Catopidae: Cabidoche, M. (P), Henrot, H. (W), Jeannel, R. , Schweiger, H. (W), Szymczakowski,
  W. (W), Uéno, S-I. (P).
Cerambycidae: Arnau, J. M. , Harde, K. W. , Matsuda, K. , da Veiga Ferreira, G.
World: Bomans, H. E. , Breuning, S. , Chemsak, J. A. , Dillon, L. S. , Franz, E. , Gilmour,
  E. F. , Quentin, R. M. , Tippmann, F. F.
Nearctic: Bouseman, J. , Chemsak, J. A. , Firmin, F. , Fuchs, E. , Genung, W. , Good, H. G. ,
  Hicks, S. D. , Hopping, G. R. , Knull, J. N. , Linsley, E. G. , McNeel, W. , Nishio, Y. ,
  Olson, R. E. , Seiler, D. , Simon, A. , Tilden, J. W. , Vogt, G. B.
Neotropical: Čekalović Kuschević, T. , Chemsak, J. A. , Fuchs, E. , Lane, F. , Prosen, A. F. ,
  Rosales, C. J. , Seiler, D. , de Zayas Muños, F.
Palearctic: Boos, H. , Chang, S. , Chemsak, J. A. , Durand, G. , Ehara, S. , Fuchs, E. ,
  Fujimura, T. , Gallivanone, M. , Hayashi, M. , Heyrovsky, L. , Ieniştea, M. A. ,
  Kapušciński, S. , Karpiński, J. J. , Lagar, A. , Markl, W. , Mitono, T. , Nishio, Y. ,
  Ohbayashi, K. , Panin, S. , Plavitstshikov, N. N. , Robin, M. , Saraiva, -, Sǎvulescu, N. ,
  Schaefer, L. , Seiler, D. , Seki, K. , Simon, A. , Villiers, A. M.
Ethiopian: Ferreira, M-C. , Fuchs, E. , Gilmour, E. F. , Hunt, J. W. , Quentin, R. M. , Seiler,
  D. , Villiers, A. M.
Oriental: Chang, S. , Fuchs, E. , Fujimura, T. , Gilmour, E. F. , Gressitt, J. L. , Mitono, T. ,
  Salkilld, B. W. , Seki, K.
Australian: Fuchs, E. , Harslett, J. , Salkilld, B. W.
Oceania: Chemsak, J. A. , Gressitt, J. L. , Mitono, T. , Salkilld, B. W.
Larvae: Duffy, E. A. J. (W).
Chelonariidae: Nelson, H. G. (W).
Chrysomelidae, no locality: Cantonnet, P. , Heinz, E. , Medvedev, L. N. , Shapiro, D. S. ,
  Springer, H. , Stirrett, G. M. , White, B. E. , Wood, G. C.
World: Bechynê, J. , Bryant, G. E. , Demaux, J. , Edwards, J. G. , Goecke, H. , Gressitt,
  J. L. , Hincks, W. D. , Jolivet, P. , Kocher, L. F. J. , Král, J. , Madar, J. , Shaw, S. ,
  Uhmann, E.
New World: Marx, E. J. F. , Pallister, J. C. , Wilcox, J. A.
Nearctic: Blake, D. H. , Brown, W. J. , Gentner, L. G. , Hill, R. E. , Lawson, F. A. , McClay,
  A. T. , Nishio, Y. , Papp, C. S. , Sanderson, M. W. , Scherer, G. , Smith, R. F. , Thomas,
  G. W. , Vogt, G. B. , Ward, J. L. , Weidhaas, J. A. , Jr. , Weisman, D. M. , Wilcox, J. N.
Neotropical: Bechynê, J. , Blake, D. H. , Navajas, E. , Papp, C. S. , Rosales, C. J. , Scherer,
  G. , Smith, R. F.
Palearctic: Bari, B. , Brivio, P. C. , Burlini, M. , Chujo, M. , Demaux, J. , Fongond, R. ,
  Franz, H. , Goto, M. , Kimoto, S. , Kontkanen, P. , Machatschke, J. W. , Nishio, Y. ,
  Nonveiller, G. , Ruffo, S. , Volgin, V. I. , Yasutomi, K.
Ethiopian: Bechynê, J. , Dahl, J. , Scherer, G.
Oriental: Chujo, M. , Gressitt, J. L. , Kimoto, S. , Shukla, S. P.
Oceania: Chujo, M. , Gressitt, J. L.
Larvae: Volgin, V. I. (P).
Cicindelidae, no locality: Brouerius van Nidek, C. M. C. , Robinson, J. H.
World: Korell, A. , Mandl, K. , Rivalier, E. , Van Dorsselaer, R.
Nearctic: Beer, F. M. , Cazier, M. A. , Duncan, D. K. , Graves, R. C. , Spiegler, P. E. ,
  Wallis, J. B.
Neotropical: Cazier, M. A. , Hummelinck, P. W.
Palearctic: Ieniştea, M. A. , Ohkura, M. , Panin, S.
Oriental: Tongyai, M. R. C.

Ciidae (Cisidae, Cioidae): Chujo, M. , (P, O, Oc), Miyatake, M. (P), Nobuchi, A. (P).
Cleridae: Barr, W. F. (N), Iga, M. , Sedlacek, J. (A), Soares, B. (Nt), Winkler, J. R. (W).
Coccinellidae, World: Chapin, E. A. , Dieke, G. H. , Fürsch, H. , Pope, R. D.
    Nearctic: Dozier, H. L. , Malkin, B. , Stehr, W. C. , Timberlake, P. H. , Watson, W. Y. ,
       Weidhaas, J. A. , Jr. , Wingo, C.
    Neotropical: Malkin, B.
    Palearctic: Bielawski, R. , Capra, F. , Ehara, S. , de Gunst, J. H. , Kamiya, H. , Kapur,
       A. P. , Miyatake, M.
    Paleotropical: Bielawski, R. (O, A, Oc), de Gunst, J. H. (O), Kamiya, H. (O), Kapur,
       A. P. (E, O, A, Oc).
Colydiidae: King, E. W. (N), Parsons, C. T. (N), Pope, R. D. (E, A, Oc).
Corylophidae (Orthoperidae): Paulian, R. M. A. (E).
Cossyphodidae: Andreae, H. (E).
Cryptophagidae: Bruce, N. (W), Coombs, C. W. (N, P), Parsons, C. T. (N), Woodroffe,
    G. E. (P, N).
Cucujidae: King, E. W. (N), Lefkovitch, L. P. (W), Parsons, C. T. (N).
Cupedidae: Neboiss, A. (A).
Curculionidae, no locality: Arnoldi, L. V. , Darge, R. , Gomez, M. , Konishi, M. ,
    Rohmer Lintzmann, C. G. , Viana, M. J.
    World: Balfour-Browne, J. , Cawthra, E. , Gilbert, E. E. , Gonzales Gutierrez, M. ,
       Janczyk, F. , Kingsolver, J. M. , Roudier, A. J. , Sleeper, E. L.
    Nearctic: Anderson, D. M. , Brezner, J. , Burke, H. R. , Gilbert, E. E. , Howden, A. T. ,
       Kissinger, D. G. , Marsh, G. A. , McCowan, V. F. , O'Brien, C. W. , Pierce, W. D. ,
       Schoof, H. F. , Stockton, W. D. , Tuttle, D. M. , Valentine, B. D. , Vaurie, P. , Vazquez, A. ,
       Warner, R. E.
    Neotropical: Burke, H. R. , Gilbert, E. E. , Günther, K. , Hornabrook, R. , Kissinger, D. G. ,
       Kuschel, G. , Papp, C. S. , Schoof, H. F. , Vazquez, A. , Warner, R. E.
    Palearctic: Bari, B. , Dieckmann, L. , Ferragu, M. , Franz, H. , Frieser, R. , Gilbert,
       E. E. , Hirano, C. , Hoffmann, A. , Lona, C. , Magnano, L. , Morimoto, K. , Palau Camps,
       J. M. , Roudier, A. J. , Saraiva, -, Sleeper, E. L. , Smreczynski, S. , Stančič, J. ,
       Ter-Minasian, M. E. , Voss, E.
    Ethiopian: Ferragu, M. , Günther, K. , Haaf, E. , Hornabrook, R. , Roudier, A. J. ,
       van Schalkwyk, H. A. D. , Voss, E.
    Oriental: Günther, K. , Hertel, R. , Hornabrook, R. , Sleeper, E. L. , Voss, E.
    Australian: Baker, F. H. U. , Chadwick, C. E. , Gowing-Scopes, E. , Günther, K. , Hertel,
       R. , Hornabrook, R.
    Oceania: Ferragu, M. , Günther, K. , Hertel, R. , Hornabrook, R. , Zimmerman, E. C.
    Larvae: Anderson, W. H. (N), Brezner, J. (N).
    Fossils: Smreczynski, S. (F:P), Voss, E.
Cyphonidae: See Helodidae.
Dascillidae: Armstrong, J. W. T. (W).
Denticollidae: Kishii, T. (P).
Dermestidae: Armstrong, J. W. T. (A), Beal, R. S. , Jr. (W), Kalik, V. (N, Nt, P, E, O, A),
    Mroczkowski, M. (W), Papp, C. S. , Strong, R. G.
Discolomidae: John, H. (W).
Drilidae: Magis, N. (P), Wittmer, W. (W).
Dryopidae: Guéorguiev, V. B. (P), Hinton, H. E. (W), Ieniştea, M. A. (P), Nelson, H. G. (W),
    Steffan, W. , Zeck, E. H.
Dytiscidae, no locality: Kamiya, K.
    World: Balfour-Browne, J. , Guignot, F. , Mouchamps, R. , Sanfilippo, N.
    Nearctic: Firmin, F. , Leech, H. B. , Spangler, P. J. , Wallis, J. B. , Zimmerman, J. R.
    Neotropical: Young, F. N. , Jr.
    Palearctic: Franciscolo, M. E. , Galewski, K. , Guéorguiev, V. B. , Hoch, K. , Hrbáček, J. ,
       Ieniştea, M. A. , Lagar, A. , Ohkura, M. , Riha, P. , Schaefer, L. , Uéno, S-I.
    Ethiopian: Omer-Cooper, J.
    Larvae: Boese, J. L. , Galewski, K. (P).
Elateridae, no locality: Begg, J. A. , Olexa, A. , Quelle, F.
    World: Becker, E. C. , Glen, R. , von Hayek, C. M. F. , Kulash, W. M. , Lanchester, H. P. ,
       Quirsfeld, E. D.
    Nearctic: Adelson, B. J. , Brooks, A. R. , Good, H. G. , Knull, J. N. , Kring, J. B. , Lane,
       M. C. , Quate, L. W. , Quist, J. A. , Tsherepanov, A. I.
    Neotropical: Adelson, B. J. , Arnett, R. H. , Jr. , Jeuniaux, C. , Navajas, E. , Pallister, J. C.
    Palearctic: Binaghi, G. , Boguleanu, G. , Burakowski, B. , Ghilarov, M. S. , von Hayek,
       C. M. F. , Jagemann, E. , Jeuniaux, C. , Kishii, T. , Leseigneur, -, Markl, W. , Ohira, H. ,
       Stepanov, E. M. , Tsherepanov, A. I.
    Paleotropical: Kishii, T. (O), Leseigneur, -. (E), Neboiss, A. (A), Ohira, H. (O),
       Van Zwaluwenburg, R. H. (Oc).
    Larvae: Glen, R. (N), Kurosa, K. (P), Ohira, H. (P, O).

Elmidae: Guéorguiev, V. B. (P), Hinton, H. E. (W), Janssens, E. (P), Nelson, H. G. (W).
    Larvae: Nelson, H. G. (N, Nt).
Endomychidae: Chujo, M. (P, O, Oc), Strohecker, H. F. (W).
Erotylidae: Alvarenga, M. (W), Boyle, W. W. (W), Chujo, M. (P, O, Oc), Delkeskamp, K. (W),
    Nobuchi, A. (P), Pallister, J. C. (Nt), Parsons, C. T. (N), Yoro, T. (P).
Eucnemidae: Hisamatsu, S. (P), Knull, J. N. (N).
Euglenidae: Craig, W. S. (N).
Georyssidae: Guéorguiev, V. B. (P).
Gyrinidae, no locality: Kamiya, K., Ochs, G.
    World: Brinck, P., Mouchamps, R., Sanfilippo, N.
    Nearctic: Spangler, P. J., Wallis, J. B.
    Palearctic: Franciscolo, M. E., Guignot, F., Guéorguiev, V. B., Hoch, K., Hrbáček, J.
      Ieniştea, M. A., Lagur, A., Ohkura, M., Schaefer, L.
    Ethiopian: Guignot, F., Omer-Cooper, J.
Haliplidae, World: Guignot, F., Mouchamps, R.
    Nearctic: Leech, H. B., Spangler, P. J., Wallis, J. B., Zimmerman, J. R.
    Palearctic: Franciscolo, M. E., Guéorguiev, V. B., Hoch, K., Hrbáček, J., Ohkura, M.,
      Pearce, E. J., Sanfilippo, N.
Helodidae (Cyphonidae): Armstrong, J. W. T. (W), Parsons, C. T. (N).
Hemipeplidae: Lefkovitch, L. P. (W).
Heteroceridae: Miller, W. V. (N, Nt), Nelson, H. G. (W), Pacheco, F. (W), Papp, C. S. (N, Nt).
Histeridae, World: Herzer, A., Wenzel, R. L.
    New World: Reichensperger, A. (Nt), Ross, E. S. (N), Therond, J. (N, Nt).
    Palearctic: Kryzhanovsky, O. L., Moro, G. B., Muller, G., Panin, S., Rotter, J.,
      Stockmann, S., Therond, J.
    Paleotropical: Andreae, H. (E), Therond, J. (E, Oc).
Hydraenidae: See Limnebiidae.
Hydrophilidae, World: Balfour-Browne, J., Mouchamps, R.
    New World: Leech, H. B. (N), Richmond, E. A. (N), Spangler, P. F. (N, Nt),
      Zimmerman, J. R. (N).
    Palearctic: Chiesa, A., Guéorguiev, V. B., Hoch, K., Hrbáček, J., Ienistea, M. A.,
      Pretner, E., Zecchini, R.
    Larvae: Richmond, E. A. (N).
Ipidae: See Scolytidae.
Languriidae: Boyle, W. W. (W), Chujo, M. (P, O, Oc), Villiers, A. M. (P, E, O, A, Oc).
Lagriidae: Borchmann, F. (W), Gressitt, J. L. (O, Oc), Pardo Alcaide, A. (P), Parsons,
    C. T. (N).
Lampyridae: Fender, K. M. (N), Green, J. W. (N), Magis, N. (P), McDermott, F. A. (N, Nt),
    Okada, Y. K. (P).
Lathridiidae: Walkley, L. M. (N).
Leiodidae (Anisotomidae, Liodidae): Hisamatsu, S. (P), Uéno, S-I. (P), Yoro, T. (P).
Leptinidae: Wood, D. M. (W).
Limnebiidae (Hydraenidae): Binaghi, G. (P), Janssens, E. (P).
Limnichidae: Nelson, H. G. (W).
Limulodidae: Dybas, H. S. (W).
Lucanidae, no locality: Didier, R., Haberaecker, L.
    World: Benesh, B., Bomans, H. E., de Lisle, M. O., Pereira, F. S., Weinreich, E.
    New World: Seiler, D. (N, Nt).
    Palearctic: Gallivanone, M., Seiler, D.
    Paleotropical: Carne, P. B. (A), Holloway, B. A. (A), Salkilld, B. W. (A, Oc), Seiler, D. (E).
Lycidae: Green, J. W. (N), Magis, N. (P), Ohbayashi, K. (P), Winkler, J. R. (P).
Lyctidae: Chujo, M. (P, O, Oc), Dominik, J. (P), Gerberg, E. J. (W), Santoro, F. H. (W),
    Saraiva, -. (P), Vrydagh, J. M. (W).
Lymexylonidae: Dominik, J. (P), Lane, F. (Nt), Palm, T. (P).
Malachiidae: Evers, A. M. J. (W), Pardo Alcaide, A. (P), Wittmer, W. (N).
Melasidae: Adelson, B. J. (N, Nt), Cobos Sanchez, A. (W), Olexa, A.
Meloidae, World: Battoni, S., Freude, H., Kaszab, Z., Pardo Alcaide, A., Selander, R. B.,
    Werner, F. G.
    New World: Carruth, L. A. (N), Dillon, L. S. (N), Enns, W. R. (N, Nt), Martinez, A. (Nt),
      Parker, F. H. (N), Tilden, J. W. (N), Werner, F. G. (N).
    Old World: Enns, W. R. (P, E, O, A, Oc), Gallivanone, M. (P), Magistretti, M. (P),
      Pardo Alcaide, A. (P).
    Larvae: MacSwain, J. W. (N).
Monommidae: Freude, H. (W).
Mordellidae: Chujo, M. (P, O, Oc), Ermisch, K., Franciscolo, M. E. (W), Kato, A. (P), Nomura,
    S. (P), Ray, E., Thomas, G. W. (N), Tokeji, M. (P, O, Oc).

Mycetophagidae: King, E. W. (N), Miyatake, M. (P), Parsons, C. T. (N).
Mylabridae: See Bruchidae.
Nitidulidae: Connell, W. A. (N, Nt), Dobson, R. M. (W), Easton, A. M. (W), Gillogly, L. R. (W),
    Hisamatsu, S. (P), Howden, H. F. (N), Parsons, C. T. (N), Walkley, L. M. (N).
  Larvae: Dorsey, C. K. (N).
Oedemeridae: Arnett, R. H., Jr. (W), Hicker, R. (P), Magistretti, M. (P), Pardo Alcaide,
    A. (P).
Passalidae: van Doesburg, P. H. (W), Endrodi, S. (W), Hincks, W. D. (W), Pereira, F. S. (W),
    Roze, J. A. (Nt).
Paussidae: Luna de Carvalho, E. A. (W), Reichensperger, A. (Nt, E, O).
Pedilidae: Craig, W. S. (N).
Phalacridae: Lewis, E. (W).
Phengodidae: Miskimen, G. W. (N, Nt), Wittmer, W. (W).
Plastoceridae: Bechtel, R. C. (N).
Platypodidae: Johnson, N. E. (N), Murayama, J. J. (P), Nunberg, M. (W), Schedl, K. (W),
    Wood, S. L. (W).
  Fossils: Schedl, K. (F:W).
Pselaphidae, no locality: Cauchois, P., Jeannel, R., Schubert, F.
    World: Coiffait, H.
    New World: Marsh, G. A. (N), Park, O. (N, Nt), Quirsfeld, E. D. (N, Nt), Schuster,
      R. O. (N).
    Palearctic: Besuchet, C., Karaman, Z., Kubota, M., Meggiolaro, G., Ochs, J., Pearce,
      E. J., Sawada, K., Uéno, S-I.
    Ethiopian: Andreae, H., Cerruti, M., Jeannel, R., Meggiolaro, G.
Psephenidae: Armstrong, J. W. T. (W), Nelson, H. G. (W).
  Larvae: Nelson, H. G. (N, Nt).
Ptiliidae (Trichopterygidae): Dybas, H. S. (W), Franz, H. (P, E), Kubota, M. (P), Paulian,
    R. M. A. (E), Sawada, K. (P), Sundt, E. (W).
Ptilodactylidae: Armstrong, J. W. T. (W), Nelson, H. G. (W).
Ptinidae: Andreae, H. (E), Palm, T. (P).
Rhinomaceridae: Kuschel, G. (W).
Rhipiceridae: Dahl, J. (E).
Rhipiphoridae: Besuchet, C. (W), Selander, R. B. (W).
Rhizophagidae: Parsons, C. T. (N).
Salpingidae: Spilman, T. J. (N).
Scaphidiidae: Bouseman, J. (W).
Scarabaeidae, no locality: Janssens, A. M. J. J., Ortoya Arboleda, F. J., Tsukamoto, K.
    World: Auber, L., Balthasar, V., Bari, B., von Bloeker, J. C., Jr., Bourgin, P.,
      Cartwright, O. L., Endrodi, S., Frey, G., Gemmell, A., Gibson, W. W., Howden,
      H. F., Landin, B. O., de Lisle, M. O., Machatschke, J. W., Pereira, F. S., Petrovitz,
      R., Ruter, G., Schein, H., Whicher, L. S., Woodruff, R.
    New World: Gibson, W. W., Matthews, E. G., Robinson, M., Sanderson, M. W.,
      Saylor, L. W.
    Nearctic: Bottimer, L. J., Carrilo, J. L., Cazier, M. A., Davis, J. J., Dawson, R. W.,
      Dewailly, P., Halffter, G., Hayes, W. P., Hoffmann, C. H., Howden, H. F., Langston,
      J. M., Mikšič, R., Owens, V. H., Papp, C. S., Parsons, C. T., Potts, R. W. L., Vaurie,
      P., Wade, J. S., Wallis, J. B.
    Neotropical: Carrillo, J. L., Halffter, G., Islas S., F., Navajas, E., Papp, C. S.,
      Wade, J. S.
    Palearctic: Agazzi, G., Bourgin, P., Dewailly, P., Gallivanone, M., Ghilarov, M. S.,
      Goto, M., Ienistea, M. A., Mackauer, M., Mikšič, R., Millo, B., Murayama, J. J.,
      Nonveiller, G., Panin, S., Petrovitz, R., Pilleri, G., Robin, M., Sawada, H.,
      Szijj, L., Tesař, Z.
    Ethiopian: Dewailly, P., Ferreira, M-C., Gedye, A. F. J., Haaf, E., Paulian, R. M. A.,
      Schein, H.
    Oriental: Sawada, H. (O).
    Australian: Bourke, T. V., Britton, E. B., Carne, P. B., Haaf, E., Hoy, J. M., Mulder,
      R. H., Richards, A.
  Larvae: Ritcher, P. O. (N).
Scolytidae, no locality: Curti, M., Stark, V. N., Zinowiew, G. A.
    World: Nunberg, M., Schedl, K., Thatcher, T. O., Wood, S. L.
    Nearctic: Allen, D. G., Anderson, W. H., De Leon, D., Hopping, G. R., Johnson, N. E.,
      Kingborn, J. M., McCowan, V. F., Thatcher, T. O., Washburn, R. I., Wright, K. H.
    Neotropical: Thatcher, T. O.
    Palearctic: Karpiński, J. J., Kurentzov, A. J., Murayama, J. J., Negru, S., Nobuchi, A.,
      Nosek, J., Palm, T., Pfeffer, A., Sokanovsky, B. V., Thatcher, T. O., Živojinović, S.,
      Zocchi, R., Zwolfer, -.
    Oriental: Kalshoven, L. G. E.
  Larvae: Thatcher, T. O. (W).
  Fossils: Schedl, H. (F:W).

Scydmaenidae: Besuchet, C. (W), Franz, H. (P, E), Pearce, E. J. (P), Quirsfeld, E. D. (N, Nt), Sawada, K. (P).
Serropalpidae (Melandryidae, Hallomenidae): Hayashi, M. (P), Kato, A. (P), Nomura, S. (P), Tokeji, M. (P).
Silphidae: Bliss, R. Q. (W), Dorsey, C. K. (N), Ieniştea, M. A. (P), Karaman, Z. (P), Madge, R. (W), van der Wiel, P. (P).
Silvanidae: Parsons, C. T. (N).
Smicripidae: Parsons, C. T. (N).
Sphaeriidae: Paulian, R. M. A. (E).
Staphylinidae, no locality: Renkonen, O. , Székessy, V.
    World: Blackwelder, R. E. , Coiffait, H. , Dvořák, R. , Moore, I. , Scheerpeltz, O. , Seevers, C. H. , Steel, W. O. , Tottenham, C. E. , Wendeler, H.
    Nearctic: Hacker, H. , Kistner, D. H. , Lohse, G. A. , Miller, W. V. , Sanderson, M. W.
    Neotropical: Martinez, A. , Miller, W. V.
    Palearctic: Adachi, T. , Benick, G. , Boelens, W. C. , Cerruti, M. , Coiffait, H. , Fagel, G. , Jarrige, J. , Kistner, D. H. , Lohse, G. A. , Ochs, J. , Sawada, K. , Schultz, V. G. M. , Smetana, A. , Szujecki, A. , Watanabe, Y.
    Paleotropical: Adachi, T. (O), Fagel, G. (E), Jarrige, J. (E), Kistner, D. H. (E), Last, H. R. (E), Tottenham, C. E. (E, Oc).
  Myrmecophilous: Borgmeier, T. (Nt), Seever, C. H. (W).
  Termitophilous: Borgmeier, T. (Nt), Seevers, C. H. (W).
  Larvae: Cerruti, M. (P).
Stylopidae (Xenidae, Strepsiptera): Bohart, R. M. (W), Luna de Carvalho, E. A. (E), Pasteels, J. J. (E, P), Riek, E. F. (A), Ulrich, W. (W).
Tenebrionidae, World: Ardoin, P. , Kulzer, H. , Molinari, H.
    New World: Kaszab, Z. , Koch, C. , Triplehorn, C. A.
    Nearctic: Boddy, D. W. , LaRivers, I. , McCowan, V. F. , Parsons, C. T. , Spilman, T. J. , Wade, J. S.
    Neotropical: Freude, H. , Marcuzzi, G. , Molinari, H. , Peña, L. E. , Wade, J. S.
    Palearctic: Antoine, M. , Devidts, J. , Español C. , F. , Ghilarov, M. S. , Kaszab, Z. , Kelejnikova, S. I. , Koch, C. , Kühnelt, W. , Pierre, F. , Skopin, N. G.
    Paleotropical: Fricke, F. (A), Kaszab, Z. (E, O, Oc), Koch, C. (E, A), Pierre, F. (O), Salkilld, B. W. (A, Oc).
  Larvae: Skopin, N. G. (W).
Thorictidae: Andreae, H. (E).
Trixagidae (Throscidae): Adelson, B. J. (N, Nt), Cobos Sanchez, A. (W).
Trogositidae (Temnochilidae, Ostomidae): Parsons, C. T. (N).

Siphonaptera

No other data: Good, N. E. , Guimarães, L. R. , Rosický, B. , Shaftesbury, A. D. , Sharif, M. , Złotorzycki, J.
    World: George, R. S. , Holland, G. P. , Hopkins, G. H. E. , Johnson, P. T. , Rapp, W. F. , Jr. , Sakaguti, K. , Smit, F. G. A. M. , Traub, R.
    New World: Barrera, A. , Hecht, O. , Hopla, C. E. , Mendez, E. , Stewart, M. A. , Tipton, V. J.
    Nearctic: Augustson, G. F. , Bacon, M. , Barnes, A. M. , Beck, D. E. , Benton, A. H. , Branch, N. , Brinck, P. , Brown, N. R. , Burbutis, P. , Davies, D. M. , Eads, R. B. , Edwards, R. L. , Ellis, L. L. , Jr. , Fox, I. , Geary, J. M. , Hefley, H. M. , Holland, G. P. , Hubbard, C. A. , Jameson, E. W. , Jr. , Jellison, W. L. , Joyce, C. R. , Lane, J. E. , Layne, J. N. , Lewis, R. E. , Morlan, H. B. , Pratt, H. D. , Prince, F. M. , Ryckman, R. E. , Russell, H. G. , Jr. , Senger, C. M. , Stark, H. E. , Wilson, N.
    Neotropical: Anduze, P. J. , Diaz-Ungria, C. , Eads, R. B. , Fox, I. , Ryckman, R. E.
    Palearctic: Brinck, P. , Burtt, E. T. , Conci, C. , Darskaya, N. F. , Dunnet, G. M. , Freeman, R. B. , Jameson, E. W. , Jr. , Kumada, N. , Mikulin, M. A. , Nagahana, M. , Nakagawa, H. , Peus, F. , Rostigayev, B. A. , Rothschild, M. , Skalon, O. I. , Skuratowicz, W. , Tiflov, V. E. , Yasumatsu, K.
    Ethiopian: Davis, D. H. S. , Freeman, R. B. , de Meillon, B.
    Oriental: Beck, D. E. , Freeman, R. B. , Hiregaudar, L. S.
    Australian: Dunnet, G. M. , Freeman, R. B. , Holland, G. P. , Mules, M. W.
    Oceania: Freeman, R. B.
  Larvae: Elbel, R. E. (W).

* * * * *

Ceratophillidae: Darskaya, N. F. (P).
Hystricopsyllidae: Rostigayev, B. A. (N, P, E).
Ischnopsyllidae: Hůrka, K. (P).

CHAETOGNATHA

No other data: Baldasseroni, D. V. (W), Bieri, R. (W), Colman, H. (AO, P), David,
P. M. (AO, PO, IO), Fraser, J. H. (AO), Furnestin, M-L. (AO, P), Gamulin, T. (P),
Ghirardelli, E. (P), Hamon, M. (AO, P, PO), Hure, J. (P), de Leira, A. (AO, P),
Massuti, M. (P), Owre, H. B. (AO), van Oye, P., Pierce, E. L. (AO), Rao, T. S. S. (IO),
Suárez-Caabro, J. A. (Nt), Tchindonova, J. G. (PO, IO), Thomson, J. M. (W),
Tokioka, T. (W), Vannucci, M. (AO).

POGONOPHORA

No other data: Burdon-Jones, C. (W), Ivanov, A. V. (W), Jägersten, G., Kirkegard, J. B. (W),
Southward, E. C. (W).

ECHINODERMATA

No other data: Baranova, Z. I. (PO, Arc, Ant), Belihov, D.V., Brattström, H. O. (AO),
Burdon-Jones, C. (AO), Chang, F-Y., Cherbonnier, G., Cotton, B. C. (A), Cumano,
H. B., Dollfus, R. P. (P), Grainger, E. H. (N, Arc), Hamond, R. (P), Llabador, F. (P),
Millott, N. (Nt, P), Morishita, A., Mu, A. T., Parker, R. H. (Nt), Pearson, J. F. W.,
Rivera Gallo, A., Skalkin, V. A., Tortonese, E. (W), Vevers, H. G. (AO), Zavodnik,
D. (P).
Fossils: Bairstow, L., Deflandre-Rigaud, M. (M-T:?), Kopf, M. J. (P:N), Pope, J. K. (P:N),
Sinclair, G. W., Strimple, H. L. (P:N).
* * * * *
CYCLOCYSTOIDEA - fossils: Pope, J. K.
PELMATOZOA - fossils: Ubaghs, G. (F:P).

ASTEROIDEA

No other data: Aldrich, F. A. (N), Bernasconi, I. (Nt, Ant), Casa-Muñoz, M. E. (Nt), Clark,
A. (W), Delavault, R. (P), Domantay, J. S. (O), Endean, R. (A), Engel, H. (P),
Fell, H. B. (A, Oc, Ant), Hayashi, R. (P), Madsen, F. J. (W), Swan, E. F. (N), Tortonese,
E. (W), Uchida, T. (PO), Ziesenhenne, F. C. (PO).
Abyssal: Beliaev, G. M. (PO, IO), Madsen, F. J. (W).
Fossils: Fell, H. B. (M-T:A, Oc, Ant), Hess, H. (M:P), Müller, A. H. (M:P), Rasmussen,
H. W. (M:P), Wright, C. W. (M:?).
* * * * *
Porcellanasteridae: Beliaev, G. M. (W).

AULUROIDEA

(None)

BLASTOIDEA

Fossils: Armstrong, A. K. (P:?), Beaver, H. H. (P:?), Bowsher, A. L. (P:W), Cline, L. M.,
Conkin, J. E. (P:N), Fay, R. O. (P-R:W), Galloway, J. J. (P:N, Nt), Horowitz, A. C. (P:N).
Joysey, K. A. (P:P), Kopf, R. W. (P:N), Reimann, I. G. (P:?).

CARPOIDEA

Fossils: Caster, K. E. (F:W), Gill, E. D. (P:A, Oc), Melendez, B. (P:P), Regnell, G. (P:?).

CRINOIDEA

No other data: Clark, A. (W).
Fossils, no age: Doreck, H.
    Paleozoic: Bowsher, A. L. (W), Graffham, A. A. (N), Gutschick, R. C. (N), Kier, P. M.,
    Laudon, L. R., McBee, W., Jr., Moore, R. C. (W), Parks, J. M., Jr., Strimple,
    H. L. (N), Ubaghs, G. (P), Yakovlev, N. N. (P).
    Mesozoic: Bowsher, A. L. (N), Hess, H. (P), Moore, R. C. (W), Rasmussen, H. W. (W).
* * * * *

ECHINODERMATA, CRINOIDEA (continued)

ARTICULATA - fossils: Sieverts-Doreck, H. (M-T:W).
CAMERATA (Adunata): Lane, N. G.
COMATULIDA - fossils: Perkins, B. F. (M:N, Nt).
* * * * *
Allagecrinidae - fossils: Koenig, J. W. (P:N).
Calceocrinidae - fossils: Kopf, R. W. (P:N).
Codiacrinidae - fossils: Koenig, J. W. (P:N).
Dolatocrinidae - fossils: Kopf, R. W. (P:N).
Melocrinitidae - fossils: Kopf, R. W. (P:N).
Poteriocrinitidae - fossils: Kopf, R. W. (P:N).
Rhodocrinitidae - fossils: Kopf, R. W. (P:N).
Roveacrinidae - fossils: Peck, R. E. (M:W).
Thallocrinidae - fossils: Kopf, R. W. (P:N).

CYSTOIDEA

Fossils: Bowsher, A. L. (P:W), Melendez, B (P:P), Regnell, G. (P:?).

ECHINOIDEA

No other data: Cherbonnier, G. , Krau, L.
  Nearctic: Crane, F. , Glen, W. , Swan, E. F.
  Neotropical: Bernasconi, I. , Caso-Muñoz, M. E. , Millott, N.
  Palearctic: Engel, H. (P), Millott, N. , Nisiyama, S.
  Paleotropical: Bernasconi, I. (Ant), Domantay, J. S. (O), Endean, R. (A), Fell,
    H. B. (A, Oc, Ant), Knox, G. A. (A, Oc, Ant), Nisiyama, S. (Oc), Utinomi, H. (PO),
    Ziesenhenne, F. C. (PO).
Spines: Cutress, Mrs. C. E. (N, Nt).   FOSSILS: Cutress, Mrs. C. E. (M-C:N, Nt).
Fossils, no age: Desio, A. (P), Moskvin, M. M. , Santos, M. E.
  Paleozoic: Kier, P. M. , Nisiyama, S. (P).
  Mesozoic: Collignon, G. (P, E), Cooke, C. W. (N), Fell, H. B. (A, Oc, Ant), Kier, P. M. ,
    Kongiel, R. (P), Maccagno, A. M. (P, E), Melville, R. V. , Nisiyama, S. (M:P).
  Cretaceous: Brunnschweiler, R. O. (A, Oc), Kermack, K. A. (P), Marchesini-Santos,
    M. E. C. (Nt), Richards, E. F. (N), Smith, D. J. (N), Wright, C. W. (P).
  Cenozoic: Cooke, C. W. (N), Glen, W. (N), Grant, U. S. , 4th. (N), Nisiyama, S. (P).
  Tertiary: Brunnschweiler, R. O. (A, Oc), Fell, H. B. (A, Oc, Ant), Hoppinger, J. J. , Kier,
    P. M. , Maccagno, A.   (P, E), Marchesini-Santos, M. E. C. (Nt), Nisiyama, S. (Oc),
    Raup, D. M. (N), Smith, D. J. (N).
  Quaternary: Nisiyama, S. (Oc).
                              * * * * *
CLYPEASTROIDEA: Limbaugh, C. (N).
IRREGULARIA (Exocyclica): Durham, J. W. (W).
  Fossils: Connell, J. F. L. (T:N), Durham, J. W. (F:W), Joysey, K. A. (M-T:P), O'Gara,
    W. T. (M:N, Nt).
SPATANGOIDA: Nichols, D. (P).
                              * * * * *
Clypeastridae - fossils: Kalabis, V. (T:?).
Micrasteridae - fossils: Nichols, D. (M:?).

EDRIOASTEROIDEA

Fossils: Kesling, R. V. (P:?), Pogue, J. (F:W), Regnell, G. (P:?).
                              * * * * *
Agelacrinitidae - fossils: Emielity, J. G. (P:N).

EOCRINOIDEA

(None)

HAPLOZOA

(None)

HOLOTHURIOIDEA

No other data: Arnold, D. C. (P), Caso-Muñoz, M. E. (Nt), Cherbonnier, G. , Cutress,
  Mrs. C. E. , Deichmann, E. (W), Domantay, J. S. (Trop), Ekman, S. P. , Endean, R. (A),
  Engel, H. (P), Filice, F. P. (PO), Wootton, D. (N).
Abyssal: Beliaev, G. M. (PO, IO), Hansen, B.
Fossils: Sambe Gowda, S. (M-C:O, A, Oc).
Sclerites - fossils: Frizzell, D. L. (W), Frizzell, H. E. , Gutschick, R. C. (P:N), Hampton,
  J. S. (F:W).

* * * * *

ASPIDOCHIROTA: Panning, A. (W).
DENDROCHIROTA: Panning, A. (W).

* * * * *

Cucumariidae: Hampton, J. S. (W).
Holothuriidae: Hampton, J. S. (W).

MACHAERIDIA

Fossils: Kopf, M. J. (P:N).

OPHIOCYSTOIDEA

Fossils: Pope, J. K.

OPHIUROIDEA

No other data: Berry, C. T. (N, P), Casa-Muñoz, M. E. (Nt), Clark, A. (W), Domantay, J. S. (O),
  Endean, R. (A), Fell, H. B. (A, Oc, Ant), Fontaine, A. R. (N, AO, P), Kjennerud, H. (AO),
  Matsumoto, H. (PO), Murakami, S. (PO), Swan, E. F. (N), Ziesenhenne, F.C. (PO, AO, IC).
Abyssal: Beliaev, G. M. (PO, IO).
Fossils: Berry, C. T. (T:N, P), Fell, H. B. (M-T:A, Oc, Ant), Hess, H. (M:P), Johnson,
  R. B. (P:N), Kopf, R. W. (P:N), Müller, A. H. (M:P), Rasmussen, H. W. (M:P).

* * * * *

Amphiuridae: Thomas, L. P. (N).

PARACRINOIDEA

(None)

SOMASTEROIDEA

(None)

GRAPTOZOA

Fossils, Paleozoic: Ball, H. W. , Bouček, B. (P), Bulman, O. M. B. , Burnaby, T. P. (P),
  Cumming, L. M. (N), Decker, C. E. (W), Desio, A. (P), Dodge, H. W. , Jr. (N), Gortani,
  M. (P), Jaanusson, V. , Jaeger, H. , Kozlowski, R. , Kühne, W. G. , Přibyl, A. (P),
  Rigby, J. K. (N), Strachan, I. (W), Thomas, D. E. (A), Thorsteinsson, R. , Waite,
  R. H. (N), Whittington, H. B.

* * * * *

DENDROIDEA: Berry, W. B. N.
GRAPTOLOIDEA: Berry, W. B. N. , Holland, C. H. (P:P).

PTEROBRANCHIA

No other data: Burdon-Jones, C. (W)

HEMICHORDATA

No other data: Burdon-Jones, C. (W), Ray, D. L.

ENTEROPNEUSTA

No other data: Brambell, F. W. R. , Bullock, T. H. (W), Gustafson, G. (P), Rao, K. P. (W), Sawaya, P. (Nt), Silén, L. (P), Woodwick, K. H. (N).
Larvae: Björnberg, T. K. S. (W).

* * * * *

Ptychoderidae: Björnberg, T. K. S. (W).

TUNICATA

No other data: Carlisle, D. B. (W), Das, S. M. (O), Hamond, R. (P).
Pelagic: Berner, L. , Jr. (W), Tokioka, T. (W).
Fossils: Deflandre-Rigaud, M. (M-T:?).

Copelata
(Larvacea)

No other data: Bjornberg, T. K. S. (N, Nt), Plough, H. H. (W).

* * * * *

Appendiculariidae: Udvardy, M. D. F. (AO, PO).

Ascidiacea

No other data: Abbott, D. P. (PO, Oc), Bjornberg, T. K. S. (N, Nt), Brewin, B. I. (A), Kott, P. (P, IO, A, Ant), Millar, R. H. (W), Mulicki, Z. (P), Peres, J. M. (AO, P), Plough, H. H. (W), Salfi, M. (W), Tokioka, T. (PO), Trason, W. J. B. (N), Zinn, D. J. (N, Nt).

* * * * *

Didemnidae: Carlisle, D. B. (W).

Thaliacea

No other data: Fraser, J. H. (W), Plough, H. H. (W).

* * * * *

Salpidae: Yount, J. L. (W).

CEPHALOCHORDATA

No other data: Fort, G. , Webb, J. E. (W).

VERTEBRATA

No other data: Chai, J-C. , Flerow, C. (P), Mack, G. (A).
Cavernicolous: Mohr, C. E. (N).
Sub-fossil: Guilday, J. E. (N), Möhl, U. (P, Arc), Parmalee, P. W. (N).
Fossils, no age, no locality: Aichinger, J. , de Alvarez, E. F. , d'Assignies, S. , Bakr, A. , Barry, T. , Bondesio, P. , Boni, A. , Bordas, A. , Cambridge, P. , Cardini, L. , Chang, H-C. , Chiu, C-T. , Collins, R. L. , Del Campana, D. , DeLise, K. C. , Dubrovo, I. A. , Eaton, T. H. , Jr. , van Frank, R. , Greenwood, M. , Gureev, A. A. , Hu, C-K. , Huang, W-L. , Hughes, J. T. , Kitts, D. B. , Kozlowski, R. , Lane, H. H. , Mook, C. C. , Nagao, T. , Pasa, A. , Pei, W-C. , Piveteau, J. , de Ringuelet, A. B. , Robinson, J. T. , Sawin, H. J. , Saint-Seine, P. , Schröder, J. , Sun, A-L. , Truyols-Santonja, J. , Turnbull, W. D. , Weiler, W.
No age: Cattoi, N. V. (Nt), Degerbol, M. (Arc, P), Deraniyagala, P. E. P. (O), Edinger, T. (W), Flerow, C. (P), Lewis, E. (W), MacAlpin, A. J. (N), Malez, M. (P), Nath, B. (O).
Paleozoic: Obruchev, D. V. , Ørvig, T. , Sieber, R. (W).
Permo-Triassic (Karroo): Boonstra, L. D. (E), Haughton, S. H. (E).
Mesozoic: Russell, L. S. (N), Sieber, R. (W), Young, C-C. (P).
Cenozoic: Dehm, R. (P, E, O, A, Oc), Rusconi, C. (Nt), Russell, L. S. (N), Sieber, R. (W), Strain, W. S. (N), Young, C-C. (P).

No other data: Ahmad, N. , Aleev, I. G. , Alm, G. , Angel, F. , Aurich, H. J. , Bagge, O. ,
Bălărescu, P. , Barros Valenzuela, R. , Belloc, G. J. J. , Bhargava, H. N. , Blache, J. ,
Blanc, M. A. , von Bonde, C. , Boscá Berga, F. , Brown, W. C. , Caldwell, D. K. ,
Carneiro, E. J. , Cassie, R. M. , Catala, R. L. A. , Cavinato, E. , Chi, P. , Chu, K. Y. ,
Chu, Y. T. , Colton, J. , Crawford, S. C. , Curtis, L. , Dardignac, J. , Deckert, K. ,
Desbrosses, P. , Devasundaram, M. P. , Devincenzi, G. J. , Diem, K. L. , Durand, J. M. ,
Ebina, K. , Eggert, B. , El-Zarka, S. , Fabricius, E. , Fourmanoir, P. , Fraser-Brunner,
A. , Fridriksson, A. , Frost, G. A. , Geisler, R. , Ginsburg, I. , Gneri, F. S. ,
Gonçalves Sanches, J. , Groenewald, A. A. J. , Gundersen, K. , Hardenberg, J. D. F. ,
Harrison, A. C. , Hassler, W. W. , Jr. , Heldt, J. H. , Hellier, T. E. , Herman, S. ,
Hiyama, Y. , Hulot, A. , Ikeda, H. , Inaba, D. , Johnson, W. E. , Kadam, K. M. ,
Kaganovsky, A. G. , Kapoor, B. G. , Karandikar, K. R. , Kewalramani, H. G. , Kimura, S. ,
Klak, G. E. , Kulikova, E. B. , Kulkarni, C. V. , Lagueux, R. , Lebedev, V. D. , Le Danois,
E. , Le Danois, Y. , Lehman, B. A. , Luethy, D. R. , Maar, A. , Mallory, J. , Marshall,
N. B. , Marshall, T. C. , Mayer, R. , Miles, C. B. , Misra, K. S. , Mitani, F. , Moitra,
S. K. , Monod, T. , Mori, T. , Morice, J. , Mukerji, D. D. , Nalbant, T. , Navano, L. ,
Nybelin, O. , Oliver, M. , Oshima, M. , Oureishi, M. R. , Pappenheim, P. , Petit, G. ,
de Plaza, M. L. F. , Rollefsen, G. , Rullan, J. B. , Sandon, M. , Shlubsky, -, Sinclair, H. ,
Slack, H. D. , Soeser, F. , Soetersdal, G. , Soljan, T. , Spanowskaja, V. D. , Sparta, A. ,
Steinbach, G. , Storey, M. H. , Sunde, L. A. , Suvatti, C. , Takai, T. , Tanner, V. M. ,
Taylor, A. G. , Tenison, W. P. C. , Thines, G. , Tsukahara, H. , Tubb, R. A. , Vaz-Ferreira,
R. , Vincent, A. , Wade, C. B. , Wakiya, Y. , Wales, J. H. , Walker, E. T. , Watanabe, M. ,
Waterman, T. H. , Wolski, T. , Yabe, H. , Yamoto, T. , Yanez Andrade, P. A. , Young, M. W.
World: Fowler, H. W. , Hubbs, C. L. , Kanazawa, R. H. , Kühlmann, D. , Myers, G. S. ,
Schultz, L. P. , Taylor, W. R.
Nearctic: Bailey, J. R. , Berdegué, J. , Bond, C. E. , Dempster, L. J. , Eaton, S. W. , Flury,
A. G. , Follett, W. I. , Freeman, H. W. , Gerking, S. D. , Harville, J. P. , Hildebrand, H. H. ,
Jean, Y. , Legendre, V. , McFarland, W. N. , McMillin, H. C. , Mengel, R. M. , Miller,
R. G. , Myers, E. C. , New, J. G. , Pfaff, J. R. , Ross, R. D. , Squires, H. J. , Walters, V. ,
Wilimovsky, N. J.
Neotropical: Alonso de Aramburu, A. S. , Berdegué, J. , Berst, A. , Boeseman, M. ,
Carvalho, J. P. , Fernandez-Yepez, A. , Gordon, M. , Koepcke, H-W. , Leitão de Carvalho,
A. , Lin, S. Y. , McMillin, H. C. , de Menezes, R. S. , de Miranda-Ribeiro, P. ,
Soriano-Senorans, J. , Travassos, H. P.
Palearctic: Berziņś, B. V. A. , Curry-Lindahl, K. , Dollfus, R. P. , Drenski, P. S. ,
Kähsbauer, P. , Klausewitz, W. , Lin, S. Y. , Matheson, C. , Misik, V. , Nikolskij, G. V. ,
Orkin, P. A. , Pravdin, I. F. , Shindo, S. , de Silva, P. H. D. , Slastenenko, E. P. , Staff, F. ,
Tambs-Lyche, H. , Wilimovsky, N. J.
Ethiopian: Crass, R. S. , Curry-Lindahl, K. , Hey, D. , Klausewitz, W. , Marlier, G. , Maul,
G. E. , Travassos, H. P. , Whitehead, J. P. ,
Oriental: Chacko, P. I. , Chen, J. T. F. , Chopra, B. N. , Delsman, H. C. , Klausewitz, W. ,
Kurian, C. V. , Mahendra, B. C. , Picciolo, A. , Raj, B. S. , Whitley, G. P.
Australian: Graham, D. , Klausewitz, W. , Kurian, C. V. , Parrott, A. W. , Phillipps, W. J. ,
Whitley, G. P.
Oceania: Boeseman, M. , Brock, V. E. , Gosline, W. A. , Klausewitz, W. , Kurian, C. V. ,
Legand, M. , Rapson, A. M. , Strasburg, D. W. , Whitley, G. P.
Antarctic: Whitley, G. P.
Marine, no locality: Walford, L. A.
World: Gordon, B. L. , Holly, M. , Tucker, D. W.
Nearctic: Alverson, D. L. , Clemens, W. A. , Fitzgerald, J. W. , Gordon, B. L. , Gordon,
M. S. , Gray, I. E. , Houck, W. J. , Krefft, G. , Leim, A. H. , Mansueti, R. , Miller, R. J. ,
Newman, M. , Pinto, S. Y. , de Sylva, D. P. , Templeman, W. , Williams, G. C. ,
Woolcott, W. S.
Neotropical: Amato, F. L. , Carranza, J. , Erdman, D. S. , Gunter, G. , Hildebrand, H. H. ,
Hoese, H. D. , Howell-Rivero, L. , Leitão de Carvalho, A. , Martin S. , F. , Meinken, H. ,
Newman, M. , Pinto, S. Y. , Rivas, L. R. , Roberts, C. R. , Shoemaker, H. H. , Suttkus,
R. D. , Tee-Van, J.
Atlantic Ocean: Cadenat, J. , Day, L. R. , Fahy, W. E. , Letaconnoux, R. , McKenzie, R. A. ,
Perlmutter, A. , Postel, E. , Roux-Esteve, R. , Scattergood, L. W. , Schnakenbeck, -,
Smith, J. L. B. , Springer, V. G. , Tåning, Å. V. , Tortonese, E. , Wheatland, S. B. ,
Wise, J. P.
Palearctic: Aksiray, F. , Al-Hussaini, A. H. , Gohar, H. A. F. , Hikita, T. , Karlovac, O. ,
Lindberg, G. U. , Müller, G. I. , Okada, Y. , Poll, M. , Steinitz, H. , Svetovidov, A. N. ,
Zei, M.
Ethiopian: Correia da Costa, F. , Davies, D. H. , Meinken, H. , Poll, M. , Roux, C. , Talbot, F.
Tropical oceans: Randall, J. E. , Jr. , Woods, L. P.

PISCES (continued)

Indian Ocean: Abe, T. , Aoyagi, H. , Bapat, S. V. , Mees, G. F. , Munro, I. S. R. , Nayak,
P. D. , Palmer, G. , Rofen, R. R. , Silas, E. G. , Smith, J. L. B. , Tinker, S. W.
Oriental: de Beaufort, L. F. , Chandy, M. , Meinken, H. , Nair, R. V. , Vijayaraghavna, P.
Australian: de Beaufort, L. F. , McKenzie, M. K. , Munro, I. S. R.
Pacific Ocean: Abe, T. , Aoyagi, H. , de Beaufort, L. F. , Brock, V. E. , Munro, I. S. R. ,
Palmer, G. , Rofen, R. R. , Rutenberg, E. P. , Silas, E. G. , Smith, J. L. B. , Stephens,
J. S. , Jr. , Tee-Van, J. , Tinker, S. W.
Arctic & Antarctic: Abe, T. (Ant), Andriashev, A. P. (Arc, Ant), Miller, R. G. (Ant),
Munro, I. S. R. (Ant).
Littoral: Böhlke, J. (Nt), Briggs, J. C. (N, Nt), Clark, E. (N), Dawson, C. E. (N, IO), Gordon,
M. S. (N), Herre, A. W. (IO, PO), Joseph, E. B. (N), Limbaugh, C. (N), Rechnitzer,
A. B. (N), Reid, G. K. (N), Smith, C. L. (Nt), Walker, B. W. (PO), Winn, H. E. (N),
Yerger, R. W. (N, Nt).
Pelagic: Herre, A. W. (IO, PO), Mead, G. W. (Nt).
Abyssal: Backus, R. H. (AO), Ebeling, A. W. (PO), Grey, M. (W), Koefoed, E. (AO), Mead,
G. W. (Nt), Rass, T. S. (PO), Rechnitzer, A. B. (W).
Estuarine: Fahy, W. E. (N), Fehlmann, H. A. (Oc), Harrington, R. W. , Jr. (N), Hoedeman,
J. J. (Trop), Kilby, J. D. (N), Mansueti, R. (N), Massmann, W. H. (N), McLane,
W. M. (N).
Fresh-water, no locality: Jonasson, P. M.
World: Holly, M. , Stoye, F. H. , Trewavas, E.
Nearctic: Bailey, R. M. , Banta, B. H. , Beckman, W. C. , Boschung, H. T. , Jr. , Brown,
C. J. D. , Burton, E. M. , Cleary, R. E. , Clemens, W. A. , Cook, F. A. , Cooper, G. P. ,
Creaser, C. W. , Cross, F. , Cuerrier, J. P. , Dalquest, W. W. , Dence, W. A. , Dendy,
J. S. , DeWitt, J. W. , Dickinson, W. E. , Dolan, T. , Eddy, S. , Fitzgerald, J. W. , Gibbs,
R. H. , Jr. , Gilbert, C. R. , Greenbank, J. , Hall, G. E. , Hass, R. L. , Hemphill, A. ,
Hubbs, C. , Johnson, R. E. , Keleher, J. J. , Kilby, J. D. , Kooyman, B. H. , Koster, W. J. ,
Lachner, E. A. , Lagler, K. F. , Mansueti, R. , McLane, W. M. , Miller, R. B. , Miller,
R. R. , Moore, G. A. , Obrecht, C. B. , Raney, E. C. , Reid, G. K. , Riel, A. D. , Riggs,
C. D. , Rivas, L. R. , Robinson, D. , Scott, D. C. , Scott, W. B. , Shapavalov, L. ,
Shoemaker, H. H. , Simon, J. R. , Simpson, J. C. , Suttkus, R. D. , Trautman, M. B. ,
Tryon, C. A. , Jr. , Warner, E. N. , Williams, G. C. , Winn, H. E. , Witt, A. , Jr. , Woolcott,
W. S. , Yerger, R. W.
Neotropical: Alvarez, J. , Boschi, E. E. , Hoedeman, J. J. , Martin S. , F. , Meinken, H. ,
Miller, R. R. , de Mirando-Ribeiro, P. , Rivas, L. R. , Schindler, O.
Palearctic: Aoyagi, H. , Balon, E. K. , Beckman, W. C. , Berinkey, L. , Florin, J. , Frank,
S. , Gasowska, M. , Hikita, T. , Karaman, S. K. , Kosswig, C. , Libosvárský, J. , Miyadi,
D. , Müller, G. I. , Okada, Y. , Oliva, O. , Poll, M. , Popescu-Gorj, A. , Schindler, O. ,
Schnakenbeck, -, Shiraishi, Y. , Sivertsen, E. , Sømme, S. , Stoica, N. , Svetovidov, A. N. ,
Thumann, M. E. , Worthingon, E. B. , Wu, H-W.
Oriental: de Beaufort, L. F. , Chandy, M. , Das, S. M. , Deraniyagala, P. E. P. , Herre,
A. W. , Hoedeman, J. J. , Inger, R. F. , Jayaram, K. C. , Meinken, H. , Munro, I. S. R. ,
Rendahl, H. , Silas, E. G. , Villadolid, D.
Ethiopian: d'Aubenton, F. , Daget, J. , De Bont, A. F. , FitzSimons, V. , Gosse, J. P. ,
Greenwood, P. H. , Hoedeman, J. J. , Holly, M. , Johnels, A. G. , Jubb, R. , Meinken, H. ,
Poll, M. , Roux, C. , Worthington, E. B.
Australian: Hoedeman, J. J. , Munro, I. S. R. , Shipway, B.
Oceania: de Beaufort, L. F. , Fehlmann, H. A. , Hoedeman, J. J. , Munro, I. S. R.
Otoliths: Fitch, J. E. (N), Frizzell, D. L. (N), Rullan, J. B.
Fossil otoliths: Dante, J. H. (T:N), Frizzell, D. L. (F:N, Nt), Simmons, E. G. , Stinton, F. C. (C:W).
Skeletons: Follett, W. I. (N).
Scales: Fujita, S. (P). FOSSILS: David, L. D. (M-T:N, Nt), Rothwell, W. T. , Jr. (M-C:?).
Blood sera: Gemeroy, D. G. (N, Nt, P, E).
Luminescence: Iwai, T. (PO).
Larvae: Ahlstrom, E. H. (AO, PO), Ball, O. P. , Jr. (N, P, PO), Balon, E. K. (P), Bruun, A. F. (W),
Kuthalingam, M. D. K. (O), de Leira, A. (AO, P), Mańkowski, W. , Mito, S. (P), Munro,
I. S. R. (O, A, Oc, Ant), Vijayaraghavna, P. (O), Voss, N. A. (Nt), Wheatland, S. B. (AO),
Williams, G. C.
Fossils: Fowler, H. W. (F:W), Gilbert, C. R. (F:N), MacAlpin, A. J. (F:N), Oberhelová, N. ,
White, E. I. (F:W).
Paleozoic: Arambourg, C. (E), Bystrow, A. (P), Dunkle, D. H. , Gross, W. , Lehman, J. P. ,
McAlester, A. L. , Nielsen, E. (Arc), Schaeffer, B. , Stensiö, E. A. , Teixeira, C. (E),
Thomas, G. (P), Watson, D. M. S. (W), Westoll, T. S.
Mesozoic: Accordi, B. (P), Applegate, S. P. , Arambourg, C. (E), Brough, J. , Dunkle,
D. H. , d'Erasmo, G. , Gardiner, B. G. (P), Kuhn-Schnyder, E. , Lehman, J. P. , Nielsen,
E. (Arc), Nybelin, O. , Schaeffer, B. , Stensiö, E. A. , Teixeira, C. (E), Watson,
D. M. S. (W). , Westoll, T. S.

Cenozoic: Applegate, S. P. , Berinkey, L. (P), Daniltchenko, P. G. , David, L. D. (N), d'Erasmo, G. , Hayasaka, S. (P), Jerzmańska, A. (P), Kalabis, V. (P), Nikolskij, G: V. (P), Schaeffer, B. , Wilimovsky, N. J. (N).

* * * * *

ACTINOPTERYGII: Saxena, D. B. (O).
    Fossils: Casier, E. M. (M-T:?), Griffith, J. (P-M:W), Lindsey, C. C. L. (F:N).
AGNATHA - fossils: Bystrow, A. (P:P), Fahlbusch, K. (F:P), Gross, W. (P:?), White, E. I. (F:W).
AMPHIOXI: Legeza, M. J. (PO).
ANGUILLIFORMES (Apodes): Clark, E. (P), Rosenblatt, R. H. (PO).
APODOIDEA: Böhlke, J. (W).
ARTHRODIRA - fossils: Heintz, A. (P:?), Mark, E. (P:P), Ørvig, T. (P:?).
BATOIDEI: Daiber, F. C. (N).
BLENNIOIDEI: Milward, N. (A), Olsen, Y. H. (N, Nt).
BRACHYTHORACI - fossils: Kulczycki, J. (P:?).
CERATIOIDEA: Bertelsen, E. (W).
CHONDRICHTHYES: Bigelow, H. B. (W), Hargis, W. J. , Jr. (AO).
CLUPEIFORMES: Ben-Tuvia, A. (P), Cohen, D. M. (W), Svetovidov, A. N. (P).
CLUPEOIDEA: Dannevig, G. , Hourston, A. S. (N).
COTTOIDEA: Wilimovsky, N. J. (W).
    Fossils: Wilimovsky, N. J. (F:W).
CROSSOPTERYGII - fossils: Jarvik, E. (P:?).
CYATHASPIDA - fossils: Flower, R. H. (P:?).
CYCLOSTOMATA: Holly, M. (W).
CYPRINIFORMES: Menon, A. G. K. (O, A, Oc).
CYPRINODONTIFORMES: Barlow, G. W. (N, Nt), Hoedeman, J. J.
DIPNOI - fossils: Kulczycki, J. (P:?),
ELASMOBRANCHII: Backus, R. H. (AO), Budker, P. , Flechsig, A. (PO), Garrick, J. A. F. (A, PO), Krefft, G. (AO, PO), Siccardi, E. (Nt), Welander, A. D. (N, Oc), White, E. G. (AO, O), Ximenez-Trianon, I.
    Fossils: Casier, E. M. , Hotton, N. , III. (P:N).
EXOCOETINA: Imai, S. (PO).
GADIFORMES: Svetovidov, A. N. (P).
GOBIOIDEA: Barlow, G. W. (PO), Dôtu, Y. (P), Takagi, K. (P, O, Oc), Tomiyama, I. (P, O, Oc).
GYMNOTOIDEA: Dahl, G. (Nt).
HETEROMI: McDowell, S. (W).
HETEROSOMATA: See Pleuronectiformes.
HOLOCEPHALI: Legeza, M. J. (PO), Schroeder, W. C. (AO).
HOLOSTEI - fossils: da Silva Santos, R. (M-C:Nt).
HYBODONTIDA - fossils: Seilacher, A. (M:P).
INIOMI: Krefft, G. (AO), Rofen, R. R.
    Fossils: Rofen, R. R. (M-C:?).
ISOSPONDYLI: Krefft, G. (AO), Scott, T. D. (O, A, Oc).
    Fossils: da Silva Santos, R. (M-C:Nt).
LEPTOCEPHALI: Nair, R. V. (O).
LYOPOMI: McDowell, S. (W).
MACROPETALICHTHYIDA - fossils: Reinhard, R. H. (P:W).
MUGILIFORMES: Ben-Tuvia, A. (P).
NEMATOGNATHOIDEA: Nikolskij, G. V. (P), van der Stigchel, J. W. (Nt).
    Fossils: Nikolskij, G. V. (C:P).
OSTEICHTHYES: Boschung, H. T. , Jr. (N, Nt), Branson, B. A. (N), Countryman, W. D. (N), Hargis, W. J. , Jr. (AO, Outten, L. M. (N), Schroeder, W. C. (AO), Welander, A. D. (N).
    Fossils: Liu, H-T. (P-T:?).
OSTRACODERMI- fossils: Denison, R. H. (P:?), Dineley, D. L. (F:P), Heintz, A. (P:?), Ørvig, T. (P:?), Robertson, G. M. (P:?).
PERCIFORMES (Percomorphi): Garnaud, J. (P, O, A, Oc), Maurin, C. M. J. E. (AO), Scott, T. D. (O, A, Oc).
PHARYNGOGNATHI: Garnaud, J. (P, O, A, Oc).
PLACODERMI - fossils: Denison, R. H. (P:?), Karatajute-Talimaa, V. (F:P), Liu, H-T. (P-T:?).
PLEURONECTIFORMES (Heterosomata): Chabanaud, P. (W), Deubler, E. E. (N, Nt), Ketchen, K. S. (PO), Kotthaus, A. (AO), Kuronuma, K. (P), Rathjen, W. F. (AO).
    Fossils: Chabanaud, P. (F:W).
RHIPIDISTIA - fossils: Kulczycki, J. (P:?).
SCLEROPAREI: Ketchen, K. S. (PO).
SCOMBRIFORMES: Aasen, O. (P), Correia da Costa, F. (E), Vilela, H. (P, E).
SELACHII: Cadenat, J. (AO), D'Ancona, U. (P), Ketchen, K. S. (PO), Springer, S. (W), Thompson, J. R. (AO), Tortonese, E. (AO, P).
    Fossil teeth: Avnimelech, M. (M-C:?).
SILUROIDEA: Hoedeman, J. J. , Jayaram, K. C. (P, E, O), Menon, A. G. K. (O, A, Oc), Srinivasachar, H. R. (O), Weitzman, S. H. (Nt).

SOLENICHTHYES: Wheeler, A. C. (W).
SQUALOIDEA: Aasen, O. (P).
SYNENTOGNATHI: Berry, F. H. (AO), Breder, C. M., Jr. (W), Jones, S. (IO).
    Larvae: Jones, S. (IO).
SYNGNATHIFORMES: Clark, E. (P).
TELEOSTEI: D'Ancona, U. (P), Garrick, J. A. F. (A, Oc), MacDonagh, E. J. (Nt), Merriman,
    D. (AO), Moreland, J. (A), Srivastava, P. N. (O), Wigley, R. L. (N).
    Blood sera: Suyehiro, Y.
    Larvae: Masuda, T. (P), Rass, T. S. (AO, PO, Arc).
TELEOSTOMI: Breder, C. M., Jr. (N, Nt), Nani, A. (Nt).
TETRODONTIFORMES: Clark, E. (P, Oc).
ZEOIDEI: Kamohara, T. (P, IO, PO).

* * * * *

Acanthuridae: Randall, J. E., Jr. (Trop).
Acipenseridae: Murgoci, A. (P), Roussow, G. (N, P), Vladykov, V. D. (N, P).
Ageniosidae: Dahl, G. (Nt).
Agonidae: Barraclough, W. E. (PO), Legeza, M. J. (W).
Albulidae: Gehringer, J. W. (AO),   LARVAE: Gehringer, J. W. (AO).
Amblyopsidae: Clay, W. M. (N).
Anabantidae: Myint, T. (O), Picciolo, A. (O).
Anarrhichadidae: Barsukov, V. V. (AO, PO).
Anguillidae: Ege, V. (W), Matsui, I. (IO, PO).
Apogonidae: Lachner, E. A. (W).
Astronesthidae: Gibbs, R. H., Jr. (W).
Bagridae: Jayaram, K. C. (P, E, O), Qasim, S. Z. (O).
Berycidae: Kotthaus, A. (AO).
Birgeriidae - fossils: Griffith, J. (P-M:W).
Blenniidae: Chapman, W. M. (IO, PO), Cohen, D. M. (Nt), Honma, Y. (PO), Qasim, S. Z. (P),
    Steinitz, H. (P), Strasburg, D. W. (IO, PO), Tomiyama, I. (PO).
Brotulidae: Walker, B. W. (W).
Bunocephalidae: Dahl, G. (Nt), Orces V., G. (Nt).
Callionymidae: Murgoci, A. (P).
Caproidae: Berry, F. H. (W).
Carcharhinidae: Baldwin, W. J. (PO).
Carangidae: Berry, F. H. (AO), Gibbs, R. H., Jr. (AO), Mather, F. J. (AO), Suzuki, K. (P),
    de Sylva, D. P. (W).
Carapidae: Arnold, D. C. (AO, IO, PO).
Catostomidae: Lindsey, C. C. L. (N), Robins, C. R. (W).
Centrarchidae: Crawford, R. W. (N), Daiber, F. C. (N), Dineen, C. F. (N).
Centriscidae - fossils: Rozhdestvensky, A. K. (T:P).
Centropomidae: Pai, M. V. (O).
Characidae: Böhlke, J. (Nt), Dahl, G. (Nt), Ladiges, W. (Nt, E), Myers, G. S. (W),
    Weitzman, S. H. (Nt).
Chauliodontidae: Ege, V. (W), Haffner, R. E. (W).
Chirocentridae: Prabhu, M. S. (O).
Cichlidae: Greenwood, P. H. (E), Kähsbauer, P. (Nt), McConnell, R. H. (Nt, E), Peters, H. M.,
    Pinto, S. Y. (W), Steinitz, H. (P), Trewavas, E. (E), Weibezahn, F. H. (Nt).
    Fossils: Greenwood, P. H. (C:?).
Clariidae: Myint, T. (O).
Clinidae: Springer, V. G. (W).
Clupeidae, no locality: Devold, F., Furnestin, J.
    Nearctic: Cating, J. P., Peterson, C., Sykes, J. E.
    Neotropical: Peterson, C., Pozzi, A. J. S.
    Palearctic: Aasen, O., Andreu, B., Dragersund, O., Hoestlandt, H., Molander, A.,
    Navarro-Martin, F., Østvedt, O. J., Otterlind, G.
    Paleotropical: Rossignol, M. (E), Sekharan, K. V. (O).
Cobitidae: Bănărescu, P. (P), Minamori, S. (P), Niwa, H. (P), Rendahl, H. (O).
Coccosteidae - fossils: Obrucheva, O. P. (P:?).
Congridae: Castle, P. H. J. (A), Kanazawa, R. H. (W).
Coregonidae: Dottrens, E. (P), Dymond, J. R. (N), Gaswoska, M. (P), Lawler, G. H. (N),
    Lindsey, C. C. L. (N).
Corvaspidae - fossils: Tarlo, L. B. (P:?).
Coryphaenidae: Gibbs, R. H., Jr. (W), Mather, F. J. (AO).
Cottidae: Bond, C. E. (N), Čihař, J. (P), Honma, Y. (PO), Kobayashi, K. (P), Lindsey,
    C. C. L. (N), Robins, C. R. (W).
    Larvae: Kobayashi, K. (PO).

Cyclopteridae: Legeza, M. J. (W), Ueno, T. (PO).
Cynoglossidae: Cadenat, J. (AO), Mahadeva, N. , Ochiai, A. (P).
Cyprinidae, no locality: Kerswill, C. J.
    Nearctic: Breed, H. I. , Brittan, M. R. , Collette, B. B. , Gibbs, R. H. , Jr. , Johnson, R. E. ,
       Lachner, E. A. , Lindsey, C. C. L. , Outten, L. M. , Schwartz, F. J. , Suttkus, R. D. ,
       Underhill, J. C. , Uyeno, T.
    Palearctic: Bănărescu, P. , Čihař, J. , Gyurkó, S. , Gasowska, M. , Holčík, J. , Kafuku, T. ,
       Kulawczyková-Obrhelová, N. , Kuronuma, K. , Müller, G. I. , Nakamura, M. , Steinitz,
       H. , Uyeno, T. , Vasiliu, G. D.
    Paleotropical: Brittan, M. R. (E, O, Oc), Kafuku, T. (O), Sachlan, M. (O, A, Oc),
       Whitehead, J. P. (E).
Cyprinodontidae: Aksiray, F. (P), Brown, J. L. (N, Nt), Chipman, R. K. , Egami, N. (P),
    Kosswig, C. (P), Myers, G. S. (W), Steinitz, H. (P), Weibezahn, F. H. (Nt).
Doradidae: Dahl, G. (Nt), Orces V. , G. (Nt).
Echeneidae: Lachner, E. A. (W).
Edestidae - fossils: Obruchev, D. V. (P-M:?).
Eleotridae: Lachner, E. A. (PO).
Elopidae: Gehringer, J. W. (AO).   LARVAE: Gehringer, J. W. (AO).
Emblemariidae: Stephens, J. S. , Jr. (W).
Engraulidae: Peterson, C. (N, Nt), de Plaza, M. L. F. (Nt), Pozzi, A. J. S. (Nt).
Erythrinidae: Hoedeman, J. J.
Esocidae: Čihař, J. (P), Hourston, A. S. (N), Kulawczyková-Obrhelová, N. (P), Lawler,
    G. H. (N).
Exocoetidae: Abe, T. (IO, PO, Ant), Bruun, A. F. (W), Parin, N. V. (AO, IO, PO).
Gadidae: Bratberg, E. , Maurin, C. M. J. E. (AO, P).
Galaxiidae: Scott, E. O. G. (A), Stokell, G. (Nt, E, A).
Galeidae: Olsen, A. M. (A).
Gempylidae: Iwai, T. (IO, PO), Tucker, D. W. (W).
Girellidae: Norris, K. S. (AO, PO).
Gobiesocidae: Briggs, J. C. (W), Murgoci, A. (P).
Gobiidae: Bănărescu, P. (P), de Buen, F. (W), Herre, A. W. (O, Oc), Kulawczyková-Obrhelová,
    N. (P), Lachner, E. A. (PO), Scott, E. O. G. (A).
Goodeidae: Turner, C. L. (Nt).
Haemulidae: Courtenay, W. R. , Jr. (AO), Robins, C. R. (AO), Rosenblatt, R. H. (N, Nt).
Helicoprinidae - fossils: Obruchev, D. V. (P-M:?).
Heterenchelidae: Ben-Tuvia, A. (P).
Heteropneustidae: Myint, T. (O).
Hexagrammidae: Quast, J. C. (PO), Sato, S. (PO).
Hippocampidae: Kähsbauer, P. (Nt).
Istiophoridae: Howard, J. K. (W), LaMonte, F. (Nt), Morrow, J. E. , Jr. (W), Nakamura,
    H. (IO, PO), de Sylva, D. P. (W).
    Larvae: Gehringer, J. W. (AO).
Labridae: Bauchot-Boutin, M. L. (P), Bruns, P. M. (P, IO, PO), Randall, J. E. , Jr. (Trop).
Leptolepidae - fossils: Nybelin, O. (M:?).
Leptoscopidae: Moreland, J. (A).
Lethrinidae: Akazaki, M. (O, Oc), Prabhu, M. S. (O).
Loricariidae: Dahl, G. (Nt), Orces V. , G. (Nt).
Lutianidae: Akazaki, M. (O, Oc), Juhl, R. (Nt), Talbot, F. (E).
Macrorhamphosidae: Pozzi, A. J. S. (AO).
Macruridae: Makushok, V. M. (AO, IO, PO).
Makairidae: LaMonte, F. (Nt).
Mastacembelidae: Sufi, S. M. K. (O).
Megalopidae: Gehringer, J. W. (AO).   LARVAE: Gehringer, J. W. (AO).
Melamphaidae: Ebeling, A. W. (W).
Mugilidae: Delais, M. (P, E), Murgoci, A. (P), Thomson, J. M. (W).
Mullidae: Lachner, E. A. (W).
Myctophidae: Bolin, R. L. (W), Gibbs, R. H. , Jr. (AO), Tåning, Å. V. (AO, IO, PO), Wisner,
    R. L. (W).
Nemichthyidae: Castle, P. H. J. (A).
Nemipteridae: Akazaki, M. (O, Oc).
Neoscopelidae: Bolin, R. L. (W).
Ogcocephalidae: Bradbury, M. (W).
Ophidiidae: Robins, C. R. (AO).
Ophiocephalidae: Myint, T. (O), Qasim, S. Z. (O).
Opisthognathidae: Thomas, L. P. (N).
Osmeridae: Hamada, K. (N, Nt, P).
Palaeoniscidae - fossils: Heyler, D. (P: P).
Paneidae: Martin S. , F. (Nt).

Paralepididae: Ege, V. (W).
Parapercidae: Kamohara, T. (P, O, Oc).
Pentapodidae: Akazaki, M. (O, Oc).
Percidae: Bănărescu, P. (P), Cole, C. F. (N), Collette, B. B. (N), Crawford, R. W. (N), Daiber,
       F. C. (N), Kulawczyková-Obrhelová, N. (P), Lachner, E. A. (N), Strawn, K. (N).
Peristediidae: Kamohara, T. (P, IO, PO).
Petromyzontidae: Clay, W. M. (N), Creaser, C. W. (N), Lindsey, C. C. L. (N), Sato, S. (P),
       Vladykov, V. D. (N, P), Zanandrea, G. (P).
Phallostethidae: Herre, A. W. (O, Oc).
Pholididae: Wilimovsky, N. J. (W).   FOSSILS: Wilimovsky, N. J. (F:W).
Pimelodidae: Dahl, G. (Nt).
Platycephalidae: Lynch, D. D. (A).
Pleuronectidae: Hourston, A. S. (N), Molander, A. (P).
   Larvae: Ostroumova, T. A. (PO).
Poeciliidae: Rosen, D. E. (N, Nt), Weibezahn, F. H. (Nt).
Psammosteidae - fossils: Mark, E. (P:P), Tarlo, L. B. (P:?).
Pteropsaridae: Tomiyama, I. (P, O, Oc).
Ptychodontidae - fossils: Reinhard, R. H. (M:W).
Pygidiidae: Dahl, G. (Nt).
Rajidae: Ishiyama, R. (PO), Steven, G. A. (P).
Retropinnidae: Stokell, G. (A).
Salmonidae, no locality: Kerswill, C. J.
      Nearctic: Ball, O. P., Jr., Dymond, J. R., Everhart, W. H., Fitzgerald, J. W., Lindsey,
         C. C. L., Morton, W. M., Needham, P. R., Slastenenko, E. P., Vladykov, V. D.,
         Welander, A. D., Withler, F. C.
      Neotropical: Gonzalez Regalado, T.
      Palearctic: Berry, J., Friend, G. F., Hikita, T., Kaj, J., Kulawczyková-Obrhelová, N.,
         Kuronuma, K., Morton, W. M., Nakamura, N., Nomura, M., Svärdson, G., Ueno, T.,
         Vasiliu, G. D., Vladykov, V. D.
      Atlantic & Pacific Oceans: Berry, J. (AO), Neave, F. (PO), Nomura, M. (PO).
Saurichthyidae - fossils: Griffith, J. (P-M:W).
Sciaenidae: Collignon, J. (E), Daiber, F. C. (N), Fitch, J. E. (PO), Walker, B. W. (W).
Scombridae: Angot, M. (PO), Duarte-Bello, P. P. (Nt), Gibbs, R. H., Jr. (AO), Jones, S. (IO),
       Koh, T. P. (W), Mather, F. J. (AO), Radhakrishnan, N. (O), Serventy, D. L. (A, Oc),
       Steven, G. A. (P), de Sylva, D. P. (W).
   Larvae: Jones, S. (IO), Klawe, W. L. (W).
Scorpaenidae: Barraclough, W. E. (PO), Kotthaus, A. (AO), Matsubara, K., Phillips, J. B. (N),
       Rasmussen, B. (AO), Welander, A. D. (N), Westrheim, S. J. (N, PO).
Serranidae: Katayama, M. (P, IO, PO), Miller, R. J. (N, Nt), Smith, C. L. (Nt), Sykes, J. E. (N),
       de Sylva, D. P. (W).
Serrivomeridae: Bauchot-Boutin, M. L. (W), Castle, P. H. J. (A).
   Larvae: Bauchot-Boutin, M. L. (W).
Sillaginidae: Lynch, D. D. (A), Radhakrishnan, N. (O).
Siluridae: Haig, J. (P, O), Ladiges, W. (Nt, P, E), Qasim, S. Z. (O).
Sisoridae: Sufi, S. M. K. (O).
Soleidae: Cadenat, J. (AO).
Sparidae: Akazaki, M. (IO, PO), Coupé, R. J. F.
Sphyraenidae: de Sylva, D. P. (W).
Sternoptychidae: Haig, J. (N), Maruyama, K. (P).
Stichaeidae: Makushok, V. M. (AO, PO), Wilimovsky, N. J. (W).
   Fossils: Wilimovsky, N. J. (F:W).
Stomiatidae: Ege, V. (W), Haffner, R. E. (W), Imai, S. (P), Morrow, J. E., Jr. (AO).
Stromateidae: Prabhu, M. S. (O).
Synaphobranchidae: Castle, P. H. J. (A).
Syngnathidae: Herald, E. S. (W), Joseph, E. B. (N), Kähsbauer, P. (Nt), Pozzi, A. J. S. (AO),
       Scott, E. O. G. (A), Strawn, K. (AO).
Synodontidae: Gehringer, J. W. (AO).   LARVAE: Gehringer, J. W. (AO).
Tetraodontidae: Abe, T. (IO, PO, Ant), Baldwin, W. J. (PO), Fujita, S. (P).
   Larvae: Fujita, S. (P).
Thonidae: Rossignol, M. (AO).
Thymallidae: Lindsey, C. C. L. (N).
Thunnidae: Clemens, H. B. (PO), Juhl, R. (Nt), Nakamura, H. (IO, PO).
Trachypteridae: Fitch, J. E. (PO), Palmer, G. (P).
Trichiuridae: Prabhu, M. S. (O), Tucker, D. W. (W).
Tripterygiidae: Moreland, J. (A), Rosenblatt, R. H. (W).
Uranoscopidae: Moreland, J. (A).

Xiphiidae: LaMonte, F. (Nt).   LARVAE: Gehringer, J. W. (AO).
Zeidae: Myers, G. S. (W).
Zoarcidae: Andriashev, A. P. (W), Bayliff, W. (PO), Ege, V. (P), Honma, Y. (PO), Ueno,
    T. (PO).

TETRAPODA

No other data: Bernis, F. (P), Bowman, R. I. (Nt), Dehner, E. W. (N).
Fossils: Jarvik, E. (P: ?).
Fossil tracks: Baird, D. (P-M: ?), Faul, H. (P-M: ?), Leonardi, P. (P: P), Stokes, W. L. (F:N).

AMPHIBIA

No other data: Abe, Y. , Avel, -, Bailey, J. W. , Bang, A. P. B. , Baumann, F. , Baxter, M. A. ,
    Birkenmeier, E. , Breukelman, J. W. , Brooks, M. , Brown, E. E. , Brown, W. C. ,
    Cognetti, G. , Cook, F. R. , Curtis, L. , Downes, M. C. , Gans, C. , Herre, W. , Inukai, T. ,
    Isemonger, R. M. , Juszczyk, W. , Kassing, E. , Kattouw, S. H. , Klemmer, K. ,
    Langelbartel, D. A. , Littlewood, W. H. , Liu, C. C. , Main, A. R. , McConkey, E. H. ,
    Mittleman, M. B. , Müller, K. , Neill, W. T. , Newth, D. R. , Palmer, E. L. , Pascenko,
    U. I. , Raitt, R. J. , Ramsey, L. W. , Raney, E. C. , Sinclair, H. , Storey, M. H. , Storm,
    R. M. , Tanner, V. M. , Tarastshuk, W. T. , Wager, V. , Werler, J. E. , Whitsell, J. S. ,
    Wilmoth, G.
World: Lanza, B. , Mertens, R. , Myers, G. S. , Orton, G. L. , Sokol, O. M. , Svilha, A.
Nearctic: Anderson, G. P. , Anderson, P. K. , Babbitt, L. H. , Bailey, J. R. , Banta, B. H. ,
    Barbour, R. M. , Barton, A. J. , Bleakney, J. S. , Bragg, A. N. , Brandt, B. B. ,
    Brattstrom, B. H. , Breckinridge, W. J. , Britt, N. W. , Brown, C. , Bumzahem, C. B. ,
    Burger, W. L. , Burns, D. M. , Burt, C. E. , Camp, C. L. , Chaney, A. H. , Chermock,
    R. L. , Clarke, R. , Cliff, F. S. , Conant, R. , Cook, S. F. , Jr. , Countryman, W. D. ,
    Crenshaw, J. W. , Jr. , Dalquest, W. W. , Dammann, A. E. , Davis, W. B. , Degenhardt,
    W. G. , Denman, N. S. , Dowling, H. G. , Driver, E. C. , Duellman, W. E. , Dury, R. ,
    Edgren, R. A. , Etheridge, R. , Ferguson, D. E. , Flury, A. G. , Forsyth, J. W. , Fox,
    W. , Jr. , Freeman, H. W. , Gehlbach, F. R. , Gentry, G. , Giltz, M. L. , Goin, C. J. ,
    Hagmeier, E. , Hecht, B. M. , Hensley, M. M. , Howard, W. E. , Howell, T. , Humphrey,
    F. L. , Hutchison, V. H. , Isenberg, C. , Jameson, D. L. , Kauffeld, C. F. , Kennedy, J. P. ,
    Klimstra, W. D. , Liner, E. A. , List, J. C. , Livezey, R. L. , Logier, E. B. S. , Loomis,
    R. B. , Lowe, C. H. , MacMahon, J. A. , Mansueti, R. , Maslin, T. P. , McCarley, W. H. ,
    McCauley, R. H. , Jr. , Mecham, J. S. , Milstead, W. W. , Minton, S. A. , Moore, J. A. ,
    Moore, J. E. , Murray, K. , New, J. G. , Obrecht, C. B. , Pahl, G. , Parker, M. V. , Payne,
    K. E. , Perkins, R. M. , Pettus, D. , Potter, F. E. , Jr. , Pyburn, W. F. , Richmond, N. D. ,
    Riemer, W. J. , Russell, R. W. , Schwartz, A. , Shank, M. C. , Shannon, F. A. , Slater,
    J. R. , Smith, P. W. , Sochurek, E. , Stebbins, R. C. , Stille, W. T. , Swanson, P. L. ,
    Tanner, W. W. , Tihen, J. A. , Tinkle, D. W. , Triplehorn, C. A. , Walker, W. F. , Webb,
    R. G. , Wright, A. A. , Zweifel, R. G.
Neotropical: Alvarez del Toro, M. , Anderson, J. D. , Bailey, J. R. , Banta, B. H. , Berst,
    A. , Bokerman, W. C. A. , Brattstrom, B. H. , Brongersma, L. D. , Bumzahem, C. B. ,
    Burger, W. L. , Cliff, F. S. , Cochran, D. M. , Conant, R. , Dalquest, W. W. , Davis, W. B. ,
    Duellman, W. E. , Etheridge, R. , Figg-Hoblyn, J. P. , Firschein, I. L. , Gehlbach, F. R. ,
    Grant, C. , Greenhall, A. M. , Hardy, J. D. , Jr. , Hecht, B. M. , Humphrey, F. L. ,
    Klappenbach, M. A. , Leitão de Carvalho, A. , Lowery, G. H. , Jr. , Lynn, W. G. ,
    Martin del Campo, R. S. , Milstead, W. W. , Myers, G. S. , Parker, M. V. , Peters, J. A. ,
    Roze, J. A. , Ruibal, R. , Sawaya, M. P. , Sawaya, P. , Schwartz, A. , Shannon, F. A. ,
    Shreve, B. , Smith, H. M. , Stuart, L. C. , Taylor, E. H. , Thompson, F. G. , Webb, R. G. ,
    Zweifel, R. G.
Palearctic: Aellen, V. , Alekperov, A. M. , Balcells R. , E. , Basoglu, M. , Buchholz, K. F. ,
    Bureš, I. , Capocaccia, L. , Cei, J. M. , Cherchi, M. A. , Curry-Lindahl, K. , Darewski,
    I. S. , Dely, O. G. , Eiselt, J. , Fuhn, I. E. , Ghaffary, E. N. , Hellmich, W. , Herter, K. ,
    Hillenius, D. , Jenni, W. , Kaisila, J. , Karaman, S. K. , Kauri, H. , Kawamura, T. ,
    Knoepffler, P. L. , Koba, K. , Llabador, F. , Malnate, E. V. , Marcus, A. , Munsterman,
    H. E. , Myers, G. S. , Okada, Y. , Panchen, A. L. , Papanjan, S. , Pope, C. H. ,
    Radovanović, M. , Rotter, J. , Schiøtz, A. , Scortecci, G. , Shannon, F. A. , de Silva,
    P. H. D. , Sochurek, E. , Steinitz, H. , Štěpánek, O. , Støp-Bowitz, C. , Stugren, B. ,
    Szarski, H. , Terentjev, P. V. , Vancea, S.
Ethiopian: Braestrup, F. W. , Capocaccia, L. , Cherchi, M. A. , Curry-Lindahl, K. ,
    FitzSimons, V. F. M. , Grandison, A. G. C, , Guibé, J. , Hewitt, J. , Hoffman, A. C. ,
    Kauffeld, C. F. , Laurent, R. F. , Perret, J. L. , Pitman, C. R. S. , Power, J. H. , Rose,
    S. , Rose, W. , Schiøtz, A. , Scortecci, G. , de Witte, G. F.

Oriental: Abdulali, H. , Brongersma, L. D. , Cochran, D. M. , Hendrickson, J. R. ,
Kawamura, T. , Kripalani, M. B. , Mitchell, F. J. , Okada, Y. , Rabor, D. S. , Romer,
J. D. , Silas, E. G. , Taylor, E. H.
Australian: Cogger, H. G. , Condon, H. T. , Mackay, R. D. , Mitchell, F. J. , Moore, J. A. ,
Parker, M. V. , Stephenson, N. G.
Oceania: Brongersma, L. D. , Hecht, B. M. , Mackay, R. D. , Mitchell, F. J. , Zweifel, R. G.
Tadpoles: Orton, G. L. (W).
Fossils, no age: Dalquest, W. W. (N, Nt), Dely, O. G. (P).
Paleozoic: Brough, M. C. , Bystrow, A. (P), Colbert, E. H. , Efremov, I. A. , Gregory,
J. T. , Hotten, N., III. (N), Konzhukova, E. D. , Langston, W. , Jr. (N),
Maldonado-Koerdell, M. (Nt), Olson, E. C. , Romer, A. S. , Seltin, R. J. (W), Vaughn,
P. P. (N), Watson, D. M. S. (W), Wilson, J. A.
Mesozoic: Camp, C. L. (N, P, E), Colbert, E. H. , Efremov, I. A. , Gregory, J. T. ,
Konzhukova, E. D. , Langston, W. , Jr. (N), Maldonado-Koerdell, M. (Nt), Romer, A. S. ,
Watson, D. M. S. (W), Wilson, J. A.
Cenozoic: Brattstrom, B. H. , Carreck, J. N. (P), Tatarinov, L. P. (P), Tihen, J. A. (N),
Uzzell, T. M. (N, Nt).

* * * * *

ANURA: See Salientia.
APODA: Ramaswami, L. S. (O).
CAUDATA, no locality: Stull, W. D.
World: Brame, A. H. , Jr.
Nearctic: Allyn, W. P. , Bragg, A. N. , Ferguson, D. E. , Fowler, J. A. , Gosner, K. L. ,
Grobman, A. B. , Highton, R. , Hilton, W. A. , Hutchison, V. H. , Jopson, H. G. M. , Lantz,
J. P. , Moore, E. F. , Netting, M. G. , Sinclair, R. M. , Snyder, R. C. , Stewart, M. M. ,
Von Bloeker, J. C. , Jr. , Zenisek, C. J.
Neotropical: Hilton, W. A. , Lantz, J. P. , Maldonado-Koerdell, M. , Von Bloeker, J. C. , Jr.
Palearctic: Lantz, J. P.
Fossils: Brame, A. H. , Jr. (F:W).
CRYPTOBRANCHOIDEA: Obst, J. (P).
GYMNOPHIONA: Blanc, M. G. , Freytag, G. E. (W).
Fossils: Hecht, M. K. (M-T:?).
LABYRINTHODONTIA - fossils: Baird, D. (P:?), von Huene, F. (P-M:?), Panchen, A. L. (P:P),
Shishkin, M. A. (P-M:?), Welles, S. P. (M:?).
LEPOSPONDYLI - fossils: Baird, D. (P:?).
SALAMANDROIDEA: Obst, J. (P).
SALIENTIA (Anura), no locality: Reig, O. A.
World: Freytag, G. E. , Savage, J. M.
Nearctic: Axtell, R. W. , Blair, W. F. , Bragg, A. N. , Fouquette, M. J. , Jr. , Fowler, J. A. ,
Gosner, K. L. , Jacobs, G. J. , Johnson, F. C. , Lindsay, H. L. , McAlister, W. H. , Reedy,
J. J. , Walker, C. F. , Wright, A. H. , Zenisek, C. J.
Neotropical: Axtell, R. W. , Capurro, L. F. , Cei, J. M. , Cochran, D. M. , Codoceo, M. R. ,
Fouquette, M. J. , Jr. , Leviton, A. E. , Lutz, B. , Rivero, J. A. , Vellard, J. , Walker, C. F.
Palearctic: Bannikov, A. G. , Frommhold, E. , Inger, R. F. , Jacobs, G. J. , Leviton, A. E. ,
Obst, J.
Ethiopian: Bush, S. F. , Inger, R. F. , Poynton, J. , Visser, J. D.
Oriental: Alcala, A. C. , Bhaduri, J. L. , Inger, R. F. , Ramaswami, L. S.
Australian: Leviton, A. E.
Tadpoles: Starrett, P. (N, Nt).
Fossils: Hecht, M. K. (M-T:?), Reig, O. A. , Savage, J. M. (F:W), Zweifel, R. G. (F:W).
SEYMOURIAMORPHA - fossils: Špinar, Z. V. (F:P).
STEGOCEPHALIA - fossils: Heyler, D. (P:P), Lehman, J. P. (P-M:?), Pfannenstiel, M. (M:P).
URODELA: Bannikov, A. G. (P), Cei, J. M. (P), Estes, R. (N), Freytag, G. E. (N, Nt, P), Jacobs,
G. J. (N, O), Obst, J. (P), Tsutsui, Y. (P), von Wahlert, G. (W), Walker, C. F. (N, Nt).
Fossils: Auffenberg, W. (C:N, Nt), Estes, R. (M-C:N), Hecht, M. K. (M-C:?), Herre, W.

* * * * *

Ambystomidae: Anderson, J. D. (N, Nt), Holle, P. A. (N).
Brachycephalidae: Griffiths, I. (Nt, Oc).
Brachyopidae - fossils: Panchen, A. L. (P-M:?).
Bufonidae: Avelino, B. , Baldauf, R. J. (W), Blair, A. P. (N), Dent, J. N. (N, Nt), Karlstrom,
E. L. (N, Nt), Sanders, O. (N), Schuierer, F. , Thornton, W. A. (N), Turner, F. B. (N),
Volpe, E. P. (N).
Centrolepidae: Starrett, P. (Nt).
Discoglossidae: Knoepffler, P. L. (P).
Hylidae: Dent, J. N. (N, Nt), Fouquette, M. J. , Jr. (N, Nt), Funkhouser, A. (Nt), Goin, C. J. (Nt),
Gorman, J. (N), Harper, F. (N), Lantz, J. P. (N, Nt, P), Littlejohn, M. J. (A),
Martof, B. S. (N).

Hynobiidae: Shibata, Y. (P).
Hyperoliidae: Laurent, R. F. (E).
Leptodactylidae: Dent, J. N. (N, Nt), Dixon, J. R. (N, Nt), Littlejohn, M. J. (A).
Microhylidae - larvae: Griffiths, I. (P, E).
Palaeobatrachidae - fossils: Špinar, Z. V. (F:P).
Pelobatidae: Chrapliwy, P. S. (N), Savage, J. M. (W).
 Fossils: Špinar, Z. V. (F:P).
Plethodontidae: Dent, J. N. (N, Nt), Gordon, R. E. (N), Gorman, J. (N), Grenn, N. B. (N),
 Hairston, N. G. (N), Highton, R. (N), Knepton, J. C., Jr. (N), Martof, B. S. (N),
 Muchmore, W. B. (N), Pope, C. H. (N), Potter, F. E., Jr. (N), Rabb, G. B. (Nt),
 Tanner, W. W. (N, Nt), Thurow, G. R. (N), Valentine, B. D. (N), Wood, J. T. (N).
Ranidae: Berger, L. (P), Dunlap, D. G. (N), Martof, B. S. (N), Ruibal, R. (N, Nt), Turner,
 F. B. (N), Volpe, E. P. (N).
Salamandridae: Jopson, H. G. M. (N), Twitty, V. C. (N).
Scaphiopodidae: Wasserman, A. (N).
Sirenidae: Goin, C. J.   FOSSIL: Goin, C. J. (P-R:?).

REPTILIA

No other data: Abalos, J. W., Abel, E., Adams, W. E., Aleman, C., Anthony, J., Arnoult, J.,
 Bailey, J. W., Barwick, R., Bell, L. N., Bogdanov, O. P., Breukelman, J. W., Brown,
 W. C., Clausen, R. T., Cook, F. R., Cooper, J. E., Copland, S. J., Curtis, L., Dundee,
 H., Edelstam, C., Freiberg, M. A., Gans, C., George, J. C., Hadsall, S., Harrison,
 J. S., Hoge, A. R., Isemonger, R. M., Jones-Burdick, W. H., Juszczyk, W., Kassing,
 E., Kattouw, S. H., Klemmer, K., Knoepffler, P. L., Lác, J., Langelbartel, D. A.,
 Littlewood, W. H., Main, A. R., Manacas, S., Mathur, P. N., McConkey, E. H., Mead,
 A. P., Mittleman, M. B., Müller, K., Neill, W. T., Palmer, E. L., Parker, H. W.,
 Pfeiffer, R., Prakash, R., Raitt, R. J., Ramsey, L. W., Robinson, P., Rodgers, T. L.,
 Shaw, C. E., Sinclair, H., Smith, A. G., Storey, M. H., Tanner, V. M., Tarastshuk,
 W. T., Themido, A. A., Tien, D. V., Werler, J. E., Whitsell, J. S., Wilmoth, G.
 World: Battersby, J. C., Bogert, C. M., Lanza, B., Mertens, R., Myers, G. S., Old,
 W. E., Jr., Svilha, A., Wermuth, H.
 Nearctic: Abbott, W. G., Anderson, G. P., Anderson, P. K., Babbitt, L. H., Bailey, J. R.,
 Banta, B. H., Barbour, R. M., Barton, A. J., Bleakney, J. S., Brandt, B. B.,
 Breckenridge, W. J., Brattstrom, B. H., Britt, N. W., Brown, B. C., Bumzahem, C. B.,
 Burger, W. L., Burns, D. M., Burt, C. E., Camp, C. L., Carpenter, C. C., Chaney,
 A. H., Clarke, R., Cliff, F. S., Conant, R., Cook, F. A., Cook, S. F., Jr., Countryman,
 W. D., Crenshaw, J. W., Jr., Dalquest, W. W., Dammann, A. E., Davis, W. B., Davis,
 W. K., Degenhardt, W. G., Dickinson, W. E., Dixon, J. R., Dowling, H. G., Driver,
 E. C., Duellman, W. E., Dury, R. M., Edgren, R. A., Etheridge, R., Ferguson, D. E.,
 Flury, A. G., Forsyth, J. W., Fox, W., Jr., Freeman, H. W., Gehlbach, F. R., Gentry,
 G., Gorman, J., Hagmeier, E., Hecht, B. M., Hensley, M. M., Howard, W. E.,
 Humphrey, F. L., Isenberg, C., Jameson, D. L., Johnson, M. L., Johnson, R. M.,
 Kauffeld, C. F., Kennedy, J. P., Klimstra, W. D., Legler, J. M., Liner, E. A., List,
 J. C., Livezey, R. L., Logier, E. B. S., Loomis, R. B., Lowe, C. H., MacMahon, J. A.,
 Mansueti, R., Maslin, T. P., Mattlin, R. H., McCauley, R. H., Jr., Mecham, J. S.,
 Milstead, W. W., Minton, S. A., Moore, J. E., Murray, K., New, J. G., Obrecht, C. B.,
 Parker, M. V., Perkins, R. M., Potter, F. E., Jr., Pyburn, W. F., Richmond, N. D.,
 Riemer, W. J., Russell, R. W., Schwartz, A., Shannon, F. A., Slater, J. R., Smith,
 P. W., Snyder, R. C., Sochurek, E., Stebbins, R. C., Stille, W. T., Storm, R. M.,
 Swanson, P. L., Tanner, W. W., Tinkle, D. W., Triplehorn, C. A., Walker, W. F., Webb,
 R. G., Woodin, W. H., Wright, A. A., Zweifel, R. G.
 Neotropical: Alayo Dalmau, P., Alvarez del Toro, M., Anderson, J. D., Berst, A., Bailey,
 J. R., Banta, B. H., Brattstrom, B. H., Brongersma, L. D., Bumzahem, C. B., Burger,
 W. L., Cliff, F. S., Cochran, D. M., Collette, B. B., Conant, R., Dalquest, W. W., Davis,
 W. B., Davis, W. K., Dixon, J. R., Duellman, W. E., Etheridge, R., Figg-Hoblyn, J. P.,
 Gehlbach, F. R., Grant, C., Greenhall, A. M., Hardy, J. D., Jr., Hecht, B. M.,
 Humphrey, F. L., Legler, J. M., Leitão de Carvalho, A., Martin, P. S.,
 Martin del Campo, R. S., Milstead, W. W., Myers, G. S., Niceforo Maria, -, Norris,
 K. S., Parker, M. V., Peters, J. A., Richmond, N. D., Ruibal, R., Roze, J. A., Saporiti,
 E., Schwartz, A., Shannon, F. A., Shreve, B., Smith, H. M., Stuart, L. C., Taylor, E. H.,
 Thompson, F. G., Underwood, G., Vanzolini, P. E., Webb, R. G., Williams, E. E.,
 Zweifel, R. G.
 Palearctic: Aellen, V., Alekperov, A. M., Andrushko, A. M., Balcells R., E., Basoglu, M.,
 Brelih, S., Buchholz, K. F., Bureš, I., Capocaccia, L., Cherchi, M. A., Curry-Lindahl,
 K., Darewski, I. S., Dely, O. G., Dixon, J. R., Eiselt, J., Fuhn, I. E., Ghaffary, E. N.,
 Hellmich, W., Heptner, W. G., Herter, K., Hillenius, D., Hoofien, J. H., Inger, R. F.,

REPTILIA (continued)

Jenni, W. , Kaisila, J. , Karaman, S. K. , Koba, K. , Llabador, F. , Malnate, E. V. , Marx,
H. , Moore, N. W. , Munsterman, H. E. , Myers, G. S. , Okada, Y. , Panchen, A. L. , Pope,
C. H. , Radovanović, M. , Rotter, J. , Schiøtz, A. , Scortecci, G. , Shannon, F. A. , de Silva,
P. H. D. , Sochurek, E. , Štěpánek, O. , Støp-Bowitz, C. , Stugren, B. , Szarski, H. ,
Terentjev, P. V. , Vancea, S. , Verner, P. H.

Ethiopian: Braestrup, F. W. , Broadley, D. G. , Capocaccia, L. , Cherchi, M. A. ,
Curry-Lindahl, K. , FitzSimons, V. F. M. , Guibé, J. , Hellmich, W. , Hewitt, J. ,
Hoffman, A. C. , Inger, R. F. , Kauffeld, C. F. , Laurent, R. F. , Lesage, M. C. , Perret,
J. L. , Pitman, C. R. S. , Power, J. H. , Rose, W. , Scortecci, G. , de Witte, G. F.

Oriental: Alcala, A. C. , Brongersma, L. D. , Cochran, D. M. , Deraniyagala, P. E. P. , Haas,
G. , Hendrickson, J. R. , Inger, R. F. , Okada, Y. , Rabor, D. S. , Romer, J. D. , Saxena,
D. B.

Australian: Cogger, H. G. , Condon, H. T. , Glauert, L. , LeSouef, J. C. , Mack, G. , Mackay,
R. D. , Mitchell, F. J. , Parker, M. V.

Oceania: Brongersma, L. D. , Hecht, B. M. , Mackay, R. D. , Mitchell, F. J.

Of deserts: Dammann, A. E. (W), Mayhew, W. (N), Norris, K. S. (N).

Fossils; no age: Bock, W. , Dalquest, W. W. (N, Nt), Dely, O. G. (P), Kermack, K. A. ,
Royo y Gomez, J. (Nt, P), Wang, T-Y. (P).

Paleozoic: Baird, D. , Brough, M. C. , Bystrow, A. (P), Colbert, E. H. , Efremov, I. A. ,
Gregory, J. T. , Hotten, N. , III (N), von Huene, F. , Langston, W. , Jr. (N), Olson, E. C. ,
Romer, A. S. , Seltin, R. J. , Sukhanov, V. B. (P), Vaughn, P. P. (N), Watson,
D. M. S. (W), Whittard, W. F. (E), Wilson, J. A.

Mesozoic: Camp, C. L. (N, P, E), Colbert, E. H. , Efremov, I. A, Gregory, J. T. , Haas,
G. (P), von Huene, F. , Kuhn-Schnyder, E. , Langston, W. , Jr. (N), Peyer, B. , Price,
L. I. (Nt), Romer, A. S. , Sukhanov, V. B. (P), Swinton, W. E. , Watson, D. M. S. (W),
Whittard, W. F. (E), Wilson, J. A.

Cenozoic: Auffenberg, W. (N, Nt), Brattstrom, B. H. , Deraniyagala, P. E. P. (E),
Młynarski, M. (P), Tihen, J. A. (N), Uzzell, T. M. (N, Nt).

* * * * *

ANOMODONTIA - fossils: Barry, T. (P-M:E), Tatarinov, L. P. (P-M:P)

ARCHOSAURIA - fossils: Charig, A. J. (M:?), Khozatsky, L. T. (M-C:?).

CHELONIA, World: Carr, A. F. , Hartweg, N. , Młynarski, M. , Poglayen, I. , Savage, J. M. ,
Wermuth, H. , Williams, E. E.

New World: Cagle, F. R. , Crenshaw, J. W. , Jr. , Legler, J. M. , Smith, R. A.

Nearctic: Fowler, J. A. , MacMahon, J. A. , Mosimann, J. E. , Tinkle, D. W.

Neotropical: Freiberg, M. A. , Medem, F. , Mosimann, J. E.

Palearctic: Hunt, T. J.

Paleotropical: Acharji, M. N. (O), Bhaduri, J. L. (O), Brain, C. K. (E), Hunt, J. T. (E, O).

Fossils: Bergounioux, F. M. (F:P), Bräm, H. (F:P), Khozatsky, L. T. (M-C:?), Koerner,
H. E. (T:?), Milstead, W. W. , Oelrich, T. (F:N), Roberts, D. (T:N), Staesche,
K. (M-C:W), Tatarinov, L. P. , Zangerl, R. (F:W), Zhou, M-Z. (M-C:P).

COTYLOSAURIA - fossils: Tschudinov, P. K. (P-M:P).

CROCODILIA: Bhaduri, J. L. (O), Brain, C. K. (E), Freiberg, M. A. (Nt), Lavocat, R. J. M. (P, E),
McDowell, S. (W), Medem, F. (Nt, P, E, A), Smith, R. A. (N, Nt), Wermuth, H. (W).

Fossils: Hecht, M. K. (M-T:?), Langston, W. , Jr. (C:W), Price, L. I. (M-C:Nt).

CRYPTODIRA: McDowell, S. (W).

DEINOCEPHALIA - fossils: Orlov, J. A. (P:?).

DICYNODONTIA - fossils: Cox, C. B. (F:W), Cruickshank, R. I. (M:E), Walker, A. D. (P:P).

DINOSAURIA - fossils: Brown, B. (M:?), Edmund, A. G. (M:N), Kay, J. L. (M:N), Langston,
W. , Jr. (M:W), Lavocat, R. J. M. (F:P, E), Maleev, E. A. (M:P), Rozhdestvensky,
A. K. (F:P), Sternberg, C. M. (M:N), Stokes, W. L. (M:N), Zhou, M-Z. (M-C:P).

LACERTILIA: See Sauria.

NOTHOSAURIA - fossils: Zangerl, R. (F:W).

OPHIDIA: See Serpentes.

PLESIOSAURIA - fossils: Welles, S. P. (M:?).

PSEUDOSUCHIA - fossils: Walker, A. D. (M:P).

PTERODACTYLOIDEA - fossils: Brown, B. (F:W).

SAURIA, World: Burt, C. E. , Underwood, G.

Nearctic: Axtell, R. W. , Bell, E. L. , Blair, W. F. , Camp, C. L. , Dixon, J. R. , Fowler,
J. A. , Gloyd, H. K. Hotton, N. , III, Lantz, J. P. , Tihen, J. A. , Von Bloeker, J. C. , Jr.

Neotropical: do Amaral, A. , Axtell, R. W. , Cunha, O. R. , Dixon, J. R. , Donoso, R. ,
Hellmich, W. , Hummelinck, P. W. , Lantz, J. P. , Mahendra, B. C. , Rand, A. S. ,
Von Bloeker, J. C. , Jr.

Palearctic: Chernov, S. A. , Dixon, J. R. , Lantz, J. P. , von Wettstein, O.

Paleotropical: Abdulali, H. (O), Bhaduri, J. L. (O), Biswas, B. (O), Brain, C. K. (E),
Mitchell, F. J. (O, A, Oc), Schiøtz, A. (E), Stephenson, N. G. (A), Visser, J. D. (E).

Fossils: Etheridge, R. (Q:N, Nt), Hecht, M. K. (M-T:?), Hoffstetter, R. (F:W), Tihen,
   J. A. (C:N).
SERPENTES (Ophidia), World: Hoffstetter, R., Minton, S. A.
   New World: Axtell, R. W., Burger, W. L., McDowell, S., Oliver, J. A.
   Nearctic: Allyn, W. P., Dixon, J. R., Fouquette, M. J., Jr., Fowler, J. A., Gloyd, H. K.,
      Grobman, A. B., Klauber, L. M., Ortenburger, A. I., Reilly, E. M., Jr., Von Bloeker,
      J. C., Jr.
   Neotropical: do Amaral, A., Dixon, J. R., Emsley, M. G., Fouquette, M. J., Jr.,
      Leviton, A. E., Młynarski, M., Netting, M. G., Olrog, C. C., Von Bloeker, J. C., Jr.,
      Walker, W. F.
   Palearctic: Chernov, S. A., Dixon, J. R., Kramer, E., Leviton, A. E., Malnate, E. V.
   Ethiopian: Brain, C. K., Colley, W. E., Condamin, M., Doucet, J., Lesage, M. C.,
      McDowell, S., Pringle, J. A., Stegmann, D. O., Sweeney, R. C. H., Vesey-Fitzgerald,
      L. D. E. F., Visser, J. D.
   Oriental: Abdulali, H., Acharji, M. N., Behura, B. K., Bergman, R. A. M., Bhaduri, J. L.,
      Mahendra, B. C., Młynarski, M., Wegner, A. M. R.
   Australia: Leviton, A. E., Stephenson, N. G.
   Oceania & Antarctica: McDowell, S. (Oc), Olrog, C. G. (Ant).
   Fossils: Hecht, M. K. (M-T:?).
SQUAMATA: Estes, R. (N), Frommhold, E. (P), Grandison, A. C. C. (E), McAlister, W. H. (N),
   Savage, J. M. (W).
   Fossils: Estes, R. (M-C:N), Savage, J. M. (F:W).
STEGOSAURIA - fossils: Hoffstetter, R. (F:W).
TESTUDINATA: See Chelonia.
THERAPSIDA - fossils: Crompton, A. W. (P-M:E), Kühne, W. G. (M:?).
THERIODONTIA - fossils: Brink, A. S. (P-M:E), Estes, R. (P-M:?), Orlov, J. A. (P:?),
   Parrington, F. R. (P-M:E).
                          * * * * *
Agamidae: Braestrup, F. W. (P, E), Harris, V. (E).
Amphisbaenidae: Gans, C.. FOSSIL: Walker, M. V. (T:?).
Anguidae: Fitch, H. S. (N).
Boidae: Collette, B. B. (Nt), Davis, O. S. (W).
Chamaeleonidae: Hillenius, D. (W), Rand, A. S. (E).
Colubridae: Bailey, J. R., Clay, W. M. (N), Dowling, H. G. (W), Fitch, H. S. (N), Fox, W., Jr. (N),
      Fuller, T. C., Gehlbach, F. R. (N, Nt), Stickel, W. H.
   Fossils: Dowling, H. G. (F:W).
Crocodilidae: Kalin, J.
Crotalidae: Brattstrom, B. H., Gloyd, H. K. (N, Nt, P), Klauber, L. M. (N), Vellard, J. (Nt).
   Fossils: Brattstrom, B. H.
Dasypeltidae: Gans, C.
Elapidae: Dickinson, W. H. (P, E), Mackay, R. D. (A), Misra, D. S. (O), Orces V., G. (Nt).
Gekkonidae: Kluge, A. G., Štěpánek, O. (Nt).
   Fossils: Kluge, A. G.
Hydrophiidae: Griffiths, I. (O, A, Oc).
Iguanidae: Codoceo, M. R. (Nt), Gordon, R. E. (N), Hardy, J. D., Jr. (Nt), Rabb, G. B. (Nt),
      Savage, J. M. (W), Wilhoft, D. C. (N, Nt).
   Fossils: Savage, J. M. (F:W).
Lacertidae: van Bree, P. J. H. (P), Klemmer, K., Peters, G. (P).
Leptodactylidae: Savage, J. M. (W). FOSSILS: Savage, J. M. (F:W).
Mosasauridae - fossils: Dowling, H. G. (M:?).
Pelobatidae: Savage, J. M. (W). FOSSILS: Savage, J. M. (F:W).
Plasmodiidae: Peláez Fernández, D. (W).
Pliosauridae - fossils: Tarlo, L. B. (M:?).
Polycotylidae - fossils: Walker, M. V. (M:N).
Pteranodontidae - fossils: Walker, M. V. (M:N).
Rhizodontidae - fossils: Cruickshank, A. R. I. (P:?).
Rhynchosauridae - fossils: Walker, A. D. (M:P).
Scincidae: Tanner, W. W. (N, Nt).
Teiidae: Orces V., G. (Nt), Ruibal, R. (Nt).
Testudinidae: Hunt, T. J. (W), Knepton, J. C., Jr. (N).
Trionychidae - fossils: Winters, H. H. (F:W).
Uropeltidae: Gans, C.
Viperidae: Bernström, J., Dickinson, W. H. (P, E), Misra, D. S. (O), Saint Girons, H. (P),
      Schwarz, E. (P, E).
Xantusiidae: Savage, J. M. (W). FOSSILS: Savage, J. M. (F:W).

No other data: Alabaster, J. S. , Aldrich, E. C. , Alexander, A. G. , Alexander, H. G. , Amadon,
D. , Andrew, D. G. , Arne, P. , Axtell, H. , Barros Valenzuela, R. , Beecher, W. J. ,
Bellrose, F. C. , Berlioz, J. , Bomp, G. , van der Borg, H. H. , Brouwer, G. A. ,
Carricker, D. O. , Colls, D. G. , de Costa, M. J. P. , Croockewit, H. W. E,
De Schauensee, R. M. , Earnshaw, E. M. , Edelstam, C. , Engel, H. , Engelbach, P. ,
Falla, R. A. , Ferens, B. , Ficken, R. , da Fonseca, S. , Frade, F. , Frith, H. J. , Gavio,
H. S. , Gebhardt, E. , Goodwin, D. , Greenway, J. C. , Jr. , Griscom, L. , Grönvall, J. S. ,
Gyldenstolpe, N. , Hartshorne, J. M. , Haverschmidt, F. , Heim de Balsac, H. , Igalffy,
K. , Iredale, T. , Issel, W. P. , Jouanin, C. , Judin, K. A. , Junge, G. C. A. , Kenyon,
K. W. , Kleinschmidt, A. , MacDonagh, E. J. , Marien, D. , McLacklan, G. F. ,
Metsävainio, K. , Moynihan, M. H. , Mumford, R. E. , Munro, G. C. , Novatti, R. , Okada,
Y. , Opsahl, J. F. , Papadepol, A. , Paulian, P. , Raitt, R. J. , Richdale, L. E. ,
Robertson, W. B. , Jr. , Slud, P. , Smith, H. D. , Tinbergen, N. , Tomkins, I. R. , Vertse,
A. , West, D. A. , Williams, G. R. , Wolk, R. G. , Zusi, R.
World: Bock, W. , Brown, J. L. , Crandall, L. S. , Dilger, W. C. , Friedmann, H. ,
Gilliard, E. T. , Glenny, F. H. , Handley, C. O. , Jr. , Macdonald, J. D. , Meise, W. ,
Rogers, C. H. , Short, L. A. , Jr. , Sibley, C. G. , Stresemann, E. , Timmerman, G. ,
Wetmore, A.
New World: Lanyon, W. E. , Miller, A. H. , Oberholser, H. C. , Parkes, K. C. , Paynter,
R. A. , Twomey, A. C.
Nearctic: Abbott, W. G. , Alcorn, G. D. , Aldrich, J. W. , Austin, O. L. , Jr. , Baker, R. H. ,
Banks, R. C. , Behle, W. H. , Bole, B. P. , Bond, G. M. , Booth, E. S. , Breckenridge,
W. J. , Brodkorb, P. , Burton, E. M. , Cook, F. A. , Dalquest, W. W. , Davis, W. B. ,
Dickerman, R. W. , Dickinson, J. C. , Jr. , Drury, W. H. , Dusi, J. , Eisenmann, E. , Fox,
W. , Jr. , Gabrielson, I. N. , Godfrey, W. E. , Good, H. G. , Gross, A. O. , Guiguet, C. J. ,
Harper, F. , Harrell, B. E. , Hemphill, D. V. , Howard, W. E. , Howell, T. R. , Hudson,
G. E. , Huey, L. M. , Imhof, T. A. , Jaeger, E. C. , Johnson, J. C. , Jr. , Johnston, R. F. ,
Kemsies, E. , Lidicker, W. Z. , Jr. , Lincoln, F. C. , Lowery, G. H. , Jr. , Martin, P. ,
Mayhew, W. , McCarley, W. H. , McNeel, W. , Mead, F. W. , Mengel, R. M. , Miller,
L. H. , Miller, R. J. , Myers, E. C. , Nero, R. W. , New, J. G. , Niedrach, R. J. , Norris,
R. A. , Orr, R. T. , Palmer, R. S. , Parmelee, D. , Patten, J. A. , Pettingill, O. S. , Jr. ,
Phillips, A. R. , Pitelka, F. A. , Rapp, W. F. , Jr. , Reilly, E. M. , Jr. , Rett, E. Z. ,
Ross, J. B. , Salt, N. R. , Snyder, L. L. , Squires, W. A. , Sutton, G. M. , Todd, W. E. C. ,
Tordoff, H. B. , Trautman, M. B. , Wallace, G. J. , Warner, D. W. , Webster, J. D.
Neotropical: Alvarez del Toro, M. , Austin, O. L. , Jr. , Berst, A. , Biaggi, V. , Blake,
E. R. , Bond, J. , Brodkorb, P. , Brown, J. L. , Carriker, M. A. , Jr. , Dalquest, W. W. ,
Davis, W. B. , Dickerman, R. W. , Diesselhorst, G. , Dorst, J. , Edwards, E. P. ,
Eisenmann, E. , Gilliard, E. T. , Harrell, B. E. , Howell, T. R. , Huey, L. M. , Johnston,
R. F. , Koepcke, H-W. , Koepcke, M. , Martin del Campo, R. S. , Medina, D. R. ,
Medina P. , G. , Mees, G. F. , Moreno, A. , Nicéforo Maria, -, Novaes, F. C. , Olrog,
C. C. , Orr, R. T. , Partridge, W. H. , Phelps, W. H. , Jr. , Philippi, R. , Phillips, A. R. ,
Pinto, O. M. O. , Pitelka, F. A. , Sick, H. , Stager, K. E. , Steinbacher, F. , Sutton, G. M. ,
Tashian, R. E. , Todd, W. E. C. , Trautman, M. B. , Voous, K. H. , Warner, D. W. ,
Watson, G. E. , 3rd, Webster, J. D.
Old World: Deignan, H. G. , Oberholser, H. C. , Traylor, M. A.
Palearctic: Al-Hussaini, A. H. , Allouse, B. E. , Austin, O. L. , Jr. , Barth, E. K. , Bauer,
K. , Bērziņs, B. V. A. , von Boetticher, H. , Braaksma, S. , Brinkman, H. , Černý, W. ,
Clancey, P. A. , Curry-Lindahl, K. , Czarnecki, Z. , De Bont, A. F. , Delacour, J. ,
De Lucca, C. , Dementiev, G. P. , Drury, W. H. , Durand, G. , Fontaine, V. , Hagen, Y. ,
Hall, B. P. , Hamelink, K. C. , Hzrrison, J. G. , Harrison, J. M. , Heptner, W. G. ,
Holgersen, H. , Johansen, H. , Johnston, R. F. , von Jordans, A. , Kozlova, E. V. ,
Kroneisl-Rucner, R. , Lepiksaar, J. , Løppenthin, B. , Loukashkin, A. S. , Marle, J. G. ,
Majvejev, S. D. , Mayaud, N. , Mees, G. F. , Meinertzhagen, R. , Moltoni, E. , Moore,
N. W. , Mörzer Bruijns, M. F. , Nagy, E. , Niethammer, G. , Palmgren, P. , Paludan, K. ,
Portenko, L. A. , Rokitansky, G. , Rudebeck, G. E. , Sacarrão, G. F. , Sage, B. L. ,
Salomonsen, F. , Shaw, T. H. , Smith, H. M. , Sokołowski, J. B. , Steinbacher, F. , Sutter,
E. , Sutton, G. M. , Tutman, I. , Vaurie, C. , Voipio, P. T. , Voous, K. H. , Watson,
G. E. , 3rd, Willgohs, J. F. , Wynne, O. E. , Yamashina, Y.
Atlantic Islands: Hagen, Y. , Volsøe, H.
Ethiopian: Anciaux de Faveaux, F. , Benson, C. W. , von Boetticher, H. , Boulton, R. ,
Bowen, W. W. , Broekhuysen, G. J. , Chapin, J. P. , Clancey, P. A. , Courtenay-Latimer,
M. , Curry-Lindahl, K. , Davies, D. H. , De Bont, A. F. , Dekeyser, P. L. , Diesselhorst,
G. , Granvik, H. , Hall, B. P. , Hey, D. , Irwin, M. P. S. , Liversidge, R. ,
Mackworth-Praed, C. W. , Malbrant, R. , Moltoni, E. , Moreau, R. E. , Niethammer, G. ,
Paterson, M. , Petter, J. J. , Petter-Rousseaux, A. , Pitman, C. R. S. , Prigogine, A. ,
Rand, A. L. , da Rosa Pinto, A. A, , Rudebeck, G. E. , Salomonsen, F. , Schouteden, H. ,

Skead, C. J. , Smithers, R. H. N. , Steinbacher, F. , Stoneham, H. F. , Verheyen, R. K. ,
Vincent, J. , White, C. M. N. , Winterbottom, J. M.
Oriental: Abdulali, H. , Biswas, B. , Coomans de Ruiter, L. , Deraniyagala, P. E. P. , Dorst,
J. , Harrison, J. G. , Harrison, J. M. , van Heurn, W. C. , Husson, V. M. , Manuel, C. G. ,
van Marle, J. G. , Mayr, E. , Mees, G. F. , Parkes, K. C. , Rabor, D. S. , Rand, A. L. ,
Ripley, S. D. , Sálim, A. , Salomonsen, F. , Sims, R. W. , Smith, H. M. , Smythies, B. E. ,
Stager, K. E. , Sutter, E. , Vaurie, C. , Voous, K. H. , Wynne, O. E. , Yamashina, Y.
Australian: Fleming, C. A. , Keast, J. A. , Lindsay, C. J. , Mack, G. , Mayr, E. , McEvey,
A. R. , Mees, G. F. , Serventy, D. L. , Sibson, R. B. , Sims, R. W. , Turbott, E. G.
Oceania: Baker, R. H. , Bryan, E. H. , Dorst, J. , Galbraith, I. C. J. , Gilliard, E. T. , Mees,
G. F. , Rand, A. L. , Sims, R. W. , van Deusen, H. M. , Warner, D. W. , Yamashina, Y.
Arctic: Gudmundsson, F. , Holgersen, H. , Parmelee, D. , Salomonsen, F.
Antarctic: Holgersen, H. , Olrog, C. C.
Sub-fossils: Dawson, E. W. (A), Lepiksaar, J. (P), Scarlett, R. J. (A), Schwabe, A. (P).
Fossils: Brodkorb, P. (M-C:W), Burtschak-Abramovitsch, N. I. (F:P), Carreck, J. N. (Q:P),
Compton, L. V. (C:?), Dalquest, W. W. (F:N, Nt), Harrell, B. E. (Q:N), Howard, H. (C:N),
Jánossy, D. (Q:P), Lunk, W. A. (F:W), Mengel, R. M. (Q:N), Miller, A. H. (C:N),
Miller, L. H. (C:N), Swinton, W. E. (M:?), Tordoff, H. B. (F:N), Verheyen,
R. K. (F:P, E, O, A, Oc), Wang, T-Y. (F:P), Wetmore, A. (F:W).
Marine: Alverson, D. L. (N), Gordon, M. S. (N), Gordon, M. S. (Nt), Hubbs, C. L. (PO), Murphy,
R. C. (W), Pfaff, J. R. (E), Rand, R. W. (E).
Fossils: Murphy, R. C. (F:W).
Water-fowl: Benzon, B. (P), Delacour, J. , Gollop, J. B. (N), Harris, R. D. (N).
Game birds: Delacour, J. , Lehmann V. , F. C. (Nt).
Wild-fowl: Harrison, J. G. (W), Harrison, J. M. (W).
Birds of prey: Lehman V. , F. C. (Nt).
Eggs: Makatsch, W. (W), Pitman, C. R. S. (E), Price, H. F. (N).
Bones: Lüttschwager, J. (P), Storer, R. W. (N, Nt).
Hybrids: Sibley, C. G. (W).
* * * * *
ACCIPITRES: Condon, H. T. (A), Starck, D. (P, E).
ANSERIFORMES: Cooch, G. (Arc), Griswold, J. A. (W), Szczepski, J. B. (P).
CHARADRIIFORMES: Sibson, R. B. (Oc), Stettenheim, P. (N), Szczepski, J. B. (P).
DINORNITHIFORMES: Scarlett, R. J. (A).
FALCONIFORMES: Cade, T. J. (Arc), Marčetić, M. (P), Rudebeck, G. E. (W).
GRUIFORMES: Condon, H. T. (A).
LARIFORMES: Szczepski, J. B. (P).
LARO-LIMICOLAE: Condon, H. T. (A), Hitchcock, W. B. (W).
PASSERIFORMES: Baird, J. (N), Condon, H. T. (A), Davis, J. (Nt), Graber, R. R. (N, Nt),
Norris, R. A. (N), Simmons, K. E. L. (W), Szijj, L. (P), Wolters, H. E. (P, E).
PODICIPITIFORMES: Simmons, K. E. L. (W).
PROCELLARIIFORMES: Bourne, W. R. P. (W), Mayaud, N. (W), Sibson, R. B. (Oc).
PSITTACIFORMES: Condon, H. T. (A), Orfila, R. N. (Nt), Turbott, E. G. (A).
STRIGIFORMES: Cade, T. J. (Arc), Starck, D. (P, E).
TUBINARES: Condon, H. T. (A), Serventy, D. L. (W).
* * * * *

Alaudidae: Tutman, I. (P).
Alcidae: Stettenheim, P. (N), Storer, R. W. (W).
Anatidae: Berry, J. (W), Coombes, R. A. H.(P), Cotter, W. B. (W), Dusek, R. V. (N), Dzubin,
A. (N), Dusek, R. V. (N), Humphrey, P. S. (W), Jackson, M. (N), Johnsgard, P. A. (W),
Kuroda, N. (W), Lumsden, H. G. (W), MacKay, R. H. (N), Matthews, G. V. T. , McKinney,
F. (N, P), Munro, J. A. (N), Scott, P. (W).
Apodidae: Rogers, C. H. (W).
Ardeidae: Bo, N. A. (Nt), Meyerreicks, A. J. (N).
Fossils: Adams, C. (F:W).
Caprimulgidae: Selander, R. K. (N, Nt).
Carduelidae: Hinde, R. A. (P), Nicolai, J. (P, E), Wolters, H. E. (W).
Charadriidae: McGill, A. R. (A).
Corvidae: Johnston, D. W. (N), Keve, A. (P).
Cuculidae: Berger, A. J. (W).
Drepaniidae: Baldwin, P. H. (Oc).
Estrildidae: Wolters, H. E. (W).
Falconidae: Bond, R. M. (N).
Fringillidae: Baldwin, P. H. (N), Bonne, W. D. , Bowman, R. I. (Nt), Davis, J. (N, Nt), Hinde,
R. A. (P), Marler, P. (N, P, E), Marshall, J. T. (N, Nt), Nelson, G. E. , Jr. (N),
Oakeson, B. B. (N), Tutman, I. (P).
Gruidae: Walkinshaw, L. (W).
Hirundinidae: Lunk, W. A. (N, Nt).

Icteridae: Collier, G. (N, Nt), Huntington, C. E. (N), Selander, R. K. (N, Nt).
Jacanidae: Collier, G. (Nt, O).
Laniidae: Hamilton, T. H. (W), Olivier, G. (N, P, E).
Laridae: Johnston, D. W. (N), Macpherson, A. (Arc), Olivier, G. (W).
Meliphagidae: Salomonsen, F. (W).
Motacillidae: Tutman, I. (P).
Muscicapidae: Löhrl, H. (P).
Nectariniidae: Williams, J. G. (E).
Odobenidae: Loughrey, A. J. (Arc).
Paridae: Åbro, A. (P), Dixon, K. L. (N), Hinde, R. A. (P), Lunk, W. A. (N), Snow,
   D. W. (N, P, E), Tutman, I. (P).
Parulidae: Eaton, S. W. (N), Vincent, J. (E).
Phalacrocoracidae: Bo, N. A. (Nt), van Tets, G. F. (W).
Picidae: Alexander, G., Baldwin, P. H. (N), Bodenstein, G. (P, E, O, A, Oc), Dusek, R. V. (N),
   Von Bloeker, J. C., Jr. (N, E, O).
Pipridae: Snow, D. W. (Nt).
Podicipitidae: Storer, R. W. (W).
Procellariidae: McGill, A. R. (A).
Sittidae: Löhrl, H. (N, P).
Spheniscidae, Fossils: Marples, B. J. (T:?).
Strigidae: Marshall, J. T. (N, Nt).   FOSSILS: Marshall, J. T. (N, Nt).
Sturnidae: von Jordans, A. (P).
Sylvidae: Åbro, A. (P), Tutman, I. (P).
Tetraonidae: Law, C. E. (N).
Thraupidae: Storer, R. W. (W).
Trochilidae: Lehman V., F. C. (Nt), Ruschi, A. (Nt).
Troglodytidae: Selander, R. K. (N, Nt).
Turdidae: Tutman, I. (P), Wallace, G. J. (Nt).
Tryannidae: Johnson, N. K. (N), Phillips, A. R. (N), Stein, R. C. (N).
Vireonidae: Hamilton, T. H. (N, Nt).

MAMMALIA

No other data: Andersen, S., Anderson, R. M., Aramburu, R., Artimo, A., Bang, A. P. B.,
   Beck, H., Beidleman, R. G., Blancou, L., Bohlke, H., Bomp, G., Bradt, G. W.,
   van Bree, J. H., Broadbooks, H. E., Brown, R. Z., Brust, J., Bunichro, A., Cabrera,
   A., Cameron, A. W., Carpenter, R., Caubere, B., Colls, D. G., Constant, P., Corbet,
   G. B., Cringan, A. J., Dawbin, W. H., Dehnel, A., Della Serra, O., DeVos, A., Edge,
   E. R., Ehik, G. Y., Erickson, E., Falla, R. A., Fautin, R. E., van der Feen, P. J.,
   Finlayson, H. H., Fleetwood, D., Frade, F., Frich, H., Frick, C., Fugler, C. M.,
   Gibson-Hill, C. A., Gordon, K. L., Hatter, J., Hooper, J., Hrubesch, K., Kean, M. A.,
   Kenyon, K. W., Kleinschmidt, A., Kretzoi, M., Kuyt, E., Llanos, A. C., Lundholm,
   B. G., Marelli, C. A., McLaren, I. A., Mead, A. P., Metsävainio, K., Mislin, H.,
   Mondolfi, E., Müller-Using, D., Opsahl, J. F., Pohle, H. E., Rainey, D. G., Raitt, R. J.,
   Rojas, P., Ryberg, O., Schnapp, B., Schroeder, N., Sugden, L., Tomkins, I. R.,
   Troughton, E. L., Ursin, T., Vachold, J., Van Rooyen, R. J., Vornatscher, J., Webb,
   R., Weigel, I., Winogradow, B., Yedid, H., Zalkin, V. I.
World: Chapskiy, K. K., Crandall, L. S., Handley, C. O., Jr., Hayman, R. W., Hershkovitz,
   P., Johnson, D. H., Lawrence, B., Old, W. E., Jr., Schwarz, E., Simpson, G. G.,
   Svihla, A., Van Gelder, R. G.
Nearctic: Anderson, P. K., Anthony, H. E., Baker, R. H., Barbour, R. M., Barkalow, F. S.,
   Benson, S. B., Blair, W. F., Bloedel, P., Bole, B. P., Booth, E. S., Breckenridge, W. J.,
   Bryant, J., Burt, W. H., Clothier, R. R., Cockrum, E. L., Coleman, R. H.,
   Commissaris, L., Cowan, I. M., Dalquest, W. W., Davis, J. A., Jr., Davis, W. B.,
   Doutt, J. K., Downing, S. C., Driver, E. C., Durrant, S. D., Dusi, J., Fay, F. H.,
   Finley, R. B., Jr., Flook, D. R., Fox, W., Jr., Frum, W. G., Fuller, W. A., Glass,
   B. P., Guiguet, C. J., Gunderson, H. L., Gut, H. J., Hagmeier, E., Hall, E. R.,
   Hamilton, W. J., Jr., Harper, F., Hemphill, D. V., Heppenstall, C. A., Hoffmeister,
   D. F., Hooper, E. T., Howard, W. E., Hudson, G. E., Ingles, L. G., Jackson, C. F.,
   Jackson, H. H. T., Jaeger, E. C., Johnson, M. L., Jones, J. K., Jr., Klimstra, W. D.,
   Layne, J. N., Lee, M. R., Lidicker, W. Z., Jr., Martin, P., McLaughlin, C. A.,
   McNeel, W., Moore, J. E., Naora, N., Nero, R. W., New, J. G., Orr, R. T., Palmer,
   R. S., Pearson, P. G., Peterson, R. L., Quay, W. B., Rasmussen, D. I., Reilly,
   E. M., Jr., Ross, J. B., Schantz, V. S., Schwartz, A., Sealander, J. A., Stevens, W. E.,
   Wetzel, R. M., Yerger, R. W., Youngman, P. M.

Neotropical: Anthony, H. E. , Baker, R. H. , Berst, A. , Booth, E. S. , Burt, W. H. ,
Castellanos, A. , Dalquest, W. W. , Davis, W. B. , Enders, R. K. , Goodwin, G. G. ,
Greenhall, A. M. , Hooper, E. T. , Husson, A. M. , Kelson, K. R. , Koopman, K. F. ,
Mann, G. , Pearson, O. P. , Pirlot, P. L. , Reig, O. A. , Russell, R. J. , Jr. , Schwartz,
A. , Sogandares B. , F. , Vieira, C. O. C. , Villa Ramirez, B.
Palearctic: Ausländer, D. , Balcells R. , E. , Barth, E. K. , Bauer, K. , van Bemmel,
A. C. V. , von Boetticher, H. , Bird, P. F. , van den Brink, F. H. , Calinescu, R. ,
Carter, T. D. , Curry-Lindahl, K. , Czarnecki, Z. , Dementiev, G. , Frechkop, S. ,
da Gama, M. M. , Grodziñski, W. , Hagen, Y. , Hellwing, S. A. , Heptner, W. G. ,
Hooijer, D. A. , Husson, A. M. , Jensen, P. V. , Jones, J. K. , Jr. , Lepiksaar, J. , Ling,
H. , Matheson, C. , Mirić, D. , Morrison-Scott, T. C. S. , Nagy, E. , Naora, N. , Ondrias,
J. C. , Osborn, D. J. , Paaver, K. L. , Pelikan, J. , Reinwaldt, E. , Schaefer, H. ,
Scheygrond, A. , Setzer, H. W. , Siivonen, L. , Skuratowicz, W. , Stroganov, S. U. ,
Todorovic, M. , Toschi, A. , Tsutsui, Y. , Verschuren, J. , de Villalta Comella, J. F. ,
Voipio, P. T. , von Wettstein, O.
Ethiopian: Ansell, W. F. H. , Bateman, J. A. , von Boetticher, H. , Braestrup, F. W. ,
Carter, T. D. , Clancey, P. A. , Curry-Lindahl, K. , Dekeyser, P. L. , Frechkop, S. ,
Hayman, R. W. , Hey, D. , Kuhn, H-J. , Malbrant, R. , Meester, J. , Morrison-Scott,
T. C. S. , Pirlot, P. L. , Pitman, C. R. S. , Rosevear, D. R. , Smithers, R. H. N. ,
Stegmann, D. O. , Swynnerton, G. H. , Verheyen, W. , Verschuren, J. ,
Vesey-Fitzgerald, L. D. E. F.
Oriental: Anthony. H. E. , Biswas, B. , Davis, D. D. , Deraniyagala, P. E. P. , van Heurn,
W. C. , Hill, J. E. , Khajuria, H. , Nath, B. , Pirlot, P. L. , Rabor, D. S. , Ripley, S. D. ,
Romer, J. D.
Australian: Mack, G. , Pirlot, P. L. , Scott, E. O. G.
Oceania: Hill, J. E. , Husson, A. M. , Pirlot, P. L.
Arctic: Jensen, P. V. , Kelsall, J. P. , McEwen, E. H. , Osborn, D. J. , Rausch, R. , Vibe, C.
Bones: Enlow, D. H. , Lüttschwager, J. (P).
Teeth: Ijiri, S.   FOSSILS: Ijiri, S.
Hair: Mayer, W. V. (W).
From bird pellets: Bauer, K. (P), Becker, K. (P).
Marine: Hubbs, C. L. (PO), Pfaff, J. R. (E), Silas, E. G. (IO).
Cavernicolous - fossils: Dumitrescu, M. (Q:P).
Blood sera: Gemeroy, D. G. (N, Nt, P, E).
Subfossil/domestic: Ambros, C. (P), Boessneck, J. (P), Bökönyi, S. (P), Gandert, O. F. ,
Kuhn-Schnyder, E. (P), Lepiksaar, J. (P), Muller, H. H. (P), Paaver, K. L. (P),
Riedel, D. A. (P), Spahni, J-C. (P).
Fossils, no age, no locality: Apostol, L. , Aramburu, R. , Aubert, S. F. , Augusta, J. , Bajanov,
V. S. , Bauzs, D. J. , Blanc, A. C. , Cabrera, A. , Caria, I. C. , Dal Piaz, G. B. ,
Dechaseaux, C. , Evans, G. L. , Gabunia, I. K. , Gadjiew, D. V. , Garevski, R. , Geist,
O. W. , de Graaff, G. , Hills, E. S. , Hürzeler, J. , Jatzko, I. J. , Marcus, L. F. , Marelli,
C. A. , Meade, G. , Meiring, A. J. D. , Pidoplichko, I. G. , Reynolds, T. E. , Serre, B. ,
Seton, H. , Sternberg, G. F. , Studer, F. V. , Tanaka, R. , Taylor, B. E. , Tokuda, M. ,
Topachevsky, V. M. , Trevisan, L. , Van Houten, F. B. , Wernert, P. , Westphal, F. ,
Yanovskoya, N. M.
World: Chapskiy, K. K. , Simpson, G. G.
Nearctic: Dalquest, W. W. , Morris, W. J. , Patterson, B. , Stirton, R. A.
Neotropical: Arellano, A. R. V. , Castellanos, A. , Cattoi, N. V. , Chaffee, R. G. , Dalquest,
W. W. , Pascual, R. , Patterson, B. , Reig, O. A. , Royo y Gomez, J. , Spillman, F. ,
Stirton, R. A.
Palearctic: Burtschak-Abramovitsch, N. I. , Crusafont Pairo, M. , Koby, F. E. , Lavocat,
R. J. M. , Risto, G. , Royo y Gomez, J. , Takai, F. , Viret, J. F. E, Want, T-Y.
Paleotropical: Lavocat, R. J. M.(E), Stirton, R. A. (A).
All ages: Cook, H. J. (N), Enlow, D. H. , Naora, N. (N, P).
Mesozoic: Arambourg, C. (E), Clemeñs, W. A. , Hormann, K. , Kermack, K. A. , McKenna,
M. C. , Parrington, F. R. (E), Russell, L. S. (N).
Cenozoic: Downs, T. (N, Nt), Gazin, C. L. , Hopwood, A. T. (E), Lance, J. F. (N), Lehmann,
U. (P), Matsumoto, H. (P), Maxson, J. H. , Mottl, M. (P), de Paula Couto, C. (Nt),
Ray, C. E. (N, Nt), Savage, D. E. , Schwarz, E. (P, E), Winters, H. H. (N, Nt), Zapfe,
H. (P, E, O, A, Oc).
Tertiary: Alf, R. (N), Arambourg, C. (E), Bump, J. D. (N), Chaffee, R. G. (N), Donohoe,
J. C. (N), Dorr, J. A. , Jr. (N), Fields, R. W. (Nt), Green, M. , Gregory, J. T. ,
Hormann, K. , Jepsen, G. L. , Kay, J. L. (N), Konizeski, R. (N), MacInnes, D. J. (E),
McGrew, P. O. (N), McKenna, M. C. , McWhirter, N. (N), Russell, D. E. (W), Schaefer,
H. (P), Schaub, S. , Tobien, H. (P), Untermann, B. R. (N), Untermann, G. E. (N),
Wilson, J. A. , Wilson, R. W. (N), Zhou, M-Z. (P).
Quaternary: Anelli, F. (P), Anthony, H. E. (Nt), Bird, P. F. (P), Cannonge, B. (P),
Deraniyagala, P. E. P. (E), Gromova, V. (P), Gut, H. J. (N), Hooijer, D. A. (P),

Hopkins, M. L. (N), von Königswald, G. H. R. (O), Koopman, K. F. (Nt), Kortenbout van der Sluijs, G. (P), Leonardi, P. (P), Lewis, E. (N), Lundelius, E. (N, A), Maccagno, A. M. (P), Maldonado-Koerdell, M. (Nt), Musil, R. (P), Nelson, E. R. (N), Olsen, S. (N), Schaub, S., Schultz, C. B. (N), Spencer, H. E. P. (P), Starrett, A. (N), Sutcliffe, A. J. (P), Vialli, V. (P), de Villalta Comella, J. F. (P), Zeuner, F. E., Zhou, M-Z. (P).

Small mammals: Anciaux de Faveaux, F. (E), Becker, K. (P), Davis, D. H. S. (E), Davis, W. H. (N), Delany, M. J. (P), Djulić, B. (P), Felten, H. (W), Frank, F. (P), van Heurn, W. C. (P), Kratochvíl, J. (P), Serafinski, W. (P), von Wettstein, O. (P).

Fossils: Heller, F. (C:P), von Wettstein, O. (Q:P).

* * * * *

ANTHROPOIDEA: Lewis, E. (P, E, O, A, Oc).

ARTIODACTYLA: Edwards, R. Y. (N), Vereschagin, H. K. (P), Wodzicki, K. (A).
   Fossils: Adam, K. D. (Q:P), Cook, H. F. (F:N), Cooke, H. B. S. (Q:E), Macdonald, J. R. (T:?), Rakovec, I. (Q:P), Trofimov, B. A. (F:P), Vereschagin, H. K. (C:P), Whitmore, F. C., Jr. (C:?).

CARNIVORA: Fiedler, W., Ginsburg, L. (W), Harrison, D. L. (P), Loukashkin, A. S. (P), McCarley, W. H. (N), Reig, O. A. (Nt), Vereschagin, H. K. (P), Von Bloeker, J. C., Jr. (N, E, O).
   Sub-fossils: Boessneck, J. (P), Erdbrink, D. P. (P, E, O, A, Oc).
   Fossils: Adam, K. D. (Q:P), Clark, J. (T:?), Cook, H. J. (M-C:N), Dietrich, W. O. (Q:P), Erdbrink, D. P. (C:P, E, O, A, Oc), Ewer, R. F. (F:E), Fejfar, O. (C:P), Hough, M. J. (T:?), Macdonald, J. R. (T:?), Olsen, S. (T:N), Orlov, J. A. (T:?), Rakovec, I. (Q:P), Reig, O. A. (F:Nt), Savage, R. J. G. (T:P, E, O, A, Oc), Shikama, T. (Q:P), Singer, R. (Q:E), Vereschagin, H. K. (C:P).

CAVICORNIA: Bannikov, A. G. (P).   FOSSILS: Bohlin, B. (T:P).

CERCOPITHECOIDEA - fossils: Freedman, L. (F:E).

CETACEA: Brown, S. G. (W), Budker, P., Clarke, R. (W), Deinse, A. B. (P), Fraser, F. C. (W), Gilmore, R. M., Hale, H. M. (A), Harrison-Matthews, L. (W), Junge, G. C. A., Ichihara, T. (PO, Ant), Jonsgård, Å., Kellogg, R. (W), Moore, J. C. (AO), Nemoto, T. (PO, Ant), Ohsumi, S. (PO, Ant), Omura, H. (P, PO, Ant), Pike, G. C. (PO), Schevill, W. E. (W), Slijper, E. J. (W), Starrett, A. (N, Nt), Ulmer, F. A., Jr. (N).
   Fossils: Barwick, A. R. (F:N), Deinse, A. B. (F:P), Kellogg, R. (F:W).

CHIROPTERA, no locality: Goodwin, C. G., Issel, W. P., Jennings, W. L., Sanborn, C. C.
   World: Felten, H., Lawrence, B., Stager, K. E.
   Nearctic: Bee, J. W., Benson, S. B., Bradshaw, G. V., Cockrum, E. L., Davis, W. H., Gentile, J., Glass, B. P., Hall, J. S., Heppenstall, C. A., Krutzsch, P. H., Murray, K., Negus, N. C., Orr, R. T., Rudd, R. L., Wilson, N., Winkelmann, J. R.
   Neotropical: Bee, J. W., Ceballos-Bendesú, I., Greenhall, A. M., Koopman, K. F., Negus, N. C., Niceforo Maria, -, Ruschi, A., Russell, R. J., Jr., Schaldach, W. J., Jr., de la Torre, L., Villa Ramirez, B., Winkelmann, J. R.
   Palearctic: Aellen, V., Bels, L., Bird, P. F., Blackmore, M., Cannonge, B., Casteret, N., Djulić, B., Dumitrescu, M., Eisentraut, M., Gaisler, J., Gallocher, R. P., Hanák, V., Harrison, D. L., van Heerdt, P. F., Imaizumi, Y., Kahmann, H., Kaisila, J., Kowalski, K., Krzanowski, A., Lanza, B., Okada, H., Sluiter, J. W., Strinati, P., Topál, G., Wassif, K.
   Paleotropical: Aellen, V. (E), Anciaux de Faveaux, F. (E), Douglas, A. M. (A), Eisentraut, M. (E), Harrison, D. L. (E), Van Deusen, H. M. (O, A, Oc).
   Fossils: Dietrich, W. O. (Q:P), Koopman, K. F. (Q:Nt), Kowalski, K. (C:P), Topál, G. (C:P).

CREODONTA - fossils: Gromova, V. (F:P), Matthes, H. W.

DEINOTHERIOIDEA - fossils: Crouzel, F. (F:P).

DESMOSTYLIA - fossils: Reinhard, R. H. (M-C:W), Shikama, T. (F:P).

DINOCERATA - fossils: Wheeler, W. H. (T:?).

EDENTATA - fossils: von der Osten, E. (F:Nt).

ELEPHANTOIDEA - sub-fossils: Erdbrink, D. P. (P, E, O, A, Oc).
   Fossils: Crouzel, F. (F:P), Erdbrink, D. P. (C:P, E, O, A, Oc).

FERAE - fossils: Kretzoi, M. (M-T:?).

FISSIPEDIA - fossils: Tedford, R. H. (T:N).

GLIRES: Moojen, J. (Nt).

GRAVIGRADA - fossils: Orr, P. C. (Q:N, Nt).

HOMINOIDEA: Singer, R. (E).

HYRACOIDEA: Hatt, R. T. (N, E).   FOSSILS: Churcher, C. S. (F:E).

INSECTIVORA, Nearctic: Bee, J., Gentile, J., Hoffmeister, D. F., Murray, K., Rudd, R. L., Ulmer, F. A., Jr., Von Bloeker, J. C., Jr.
   Neotropical: Bee, J.

94

Palearctic: Crowcroft, W. P., Hanák, V., Hanzák, J., Harrison, D. L., Imaizumi, Y., Kahmann, H., Kowalski, K., Markov, G., Wassif, K., Wolf, H.
Paleotropical: Harrison, J. L. (O, A, Oc), Von Bloeker, J. C., Jr. (E, O).
Fossils: Butler, P. M. (F:E), Clark, J. (T:?), Fejfar, O. (C:P), Hibbard, C. W. (C:N), Jánossy, D. (Q:P), Kowalski, K. (C:P), Reed, C. A. (C:N), Robinson, P. (T:N), Trofimov, B. A. (F:P).
LAGOMORPHA: Murray, K. (N), Severaid, J. H. (N).
Fossils: Bohlin, B. (T:P), Dawson, M. R. (F:N, P, E), Wood, A. E. (T:?).
MARSUPIALIA: Glauert, L. (A), Guiler, E. (A), Marcus, L. F. (Nt, A, Oc), Marlow, B. J. (A), Plomley, N. J. B. (A), Reig, O. A. (Nt), Ride, W. L. D. (A), Scott, E. O. G. (A), Van Deusen, H. M. (O, A, Oc).
Fossils: Reig, O. A. (F:Nt), Ride, W. L. D. (F:A), Scott, E. O. G. (F:A), Tedford, R. H. (C:O, A, Oc).
MONOTREMATA: Van Deusen, H. M. (O, A, Oc).
MYOMORPHA: Kennerly, T. E. (N).
MYSTACOCETI: Jablokov, A. V. (PO, Arc), Tomilin, A. G. (AO, PO, Arc).
NOTOUNGULATA - fossils: Pascual, R. (T:Nt).
ODONTOCETI: Jablokov, A. V. (PO, Arc), Ogawa, T. (PO), Sergeant, D. E. (W), Tomilin, A. G. (AO, PO, Arc), Yamada, M. (P).
OREODONTOIDEA - fossils: Schultz, C. B. (T:N).
PANTODONTA - fossils: Simons, E. L. (C:N, P).
PERISSODACTYLA: Vereschagin, H. K. (P).
Fossils: Adam, K. D. (Q:P), Cook, H. J. (M-C:N), Cooke, H. B. S. (Q:E), Rakovec, I. (Q:P), Singer, R. (Q:E), Vereschagin, H. K. (C:P).
PINNIPEDIA: van Bemmel, A. C. V. (AO), Fay, F. H. (PO, Arc), Fisher, H. D. (N, Arc), Fujino, K. (AO, PO, Ant), Harrison-Matthews, L. (W), King, J. E. (W), Mohr, E. (W), Rand, R. W. (E), Scheffer, V. B. (W), Sivertsen, E. (Arc, Ant), Vaz-Ferreira, R.
PRIMATES: Dandelot, P. (P, E), Dart, R. A. (E), Fiedler, W., Gilmore, R. M., Haddow, A. J. (E), Hill, W. C. O. (W), Kalin, J., Khajuria, H. (O), Kuhn, H-J., Leakey, L. S. B. (P, E, O, A, Oc), Lumsden, W. H. R. (E), Starck, D. (E), Wells, L. H. (E).
Sub-fossils: Bay, R. (P, Oc).
Fossils: Fejfar, O. (C:P), von Königswald, G. H. R. (F:P, E, O, A, Oc), Leakey, L. S. B. (C:P, E, O, A, Oc), Robinson, P. (T:N), Simons, E. L. (C:W), Zapfe, H. (C:P, E, O, A, Oc).
PROBOSCIDEA: Adam, K. D. (P, E), Beliajeva, E. I. (P), Vereschagin, H. K. (P).
Fossils: Arellano, A. R. V. (F:N, Nt), Cooke, H. B. S. (Q:E), Coppens, Y. (F:P, E), Dietrich, W. O. (F:P), d'Erasmo, G. (M-C:?), Garutt, W. E. (M-C:?), Makiyama, J. (C:P), Rakovec, I. (Q:P), Shikama, T. (F:P), Vereschagin, H. K. (C:P).
RHINOCEROTOIDEA: Wood, H. E. (W).   FOSSILS: Wood, H. E. (F:W).
RODENTIA, no locality: Gilmore, R. M., Hrubesch, K.
Nearctic: Bee, J. W., Bradshaw, W. N., Brooks, A. C., Degenhardt, W. G., Donohoe, J. C., Durham, F. E., Edwards, R. Y., Gentile, J., Hatt, R. T., Manville, R. H., McCarley, W. H., Murray, K., Reedy, J. J., Sheppe, W., Jr., Tryon, C. A., Jr., Von Bloeker, J. C., Jr.
Neotropical: Bee, J. W., Crespo, J. A., Landry, S. O., Jr., Reig, O. A.
Palearctic: Andrushko, A. M., Crowcroft, W. P., Hanák, V., Hansen-Melander, E., Hanzák, J., Harrison, D. L., Kahmann, H., Kowalski, K., von Lehmann, E., Loukashkin, A. S., Marcheş, G., Markov, G., Osborn, D. J., Paspaleff, G. W., Petter, F., Shaw, T. H., Vereschagin, H. K., Wassif, K., Wolf, H.
Ethiopian: Brooks, A. C., Davis, D. H. S., Guggisberg, C. A. W., Hatt, R. T., Landry, S. O., Jr., von Lehmann, E., Petter, F., Pirlot, P. L., Von Bloeker, J. C., Jr.
Oriental: Harrison, J. L., Landry, S. O., Jr., Van Deusen, H. M., Von Bloeker, J. S., Jr.
Australian: Harrison, J. L., Landry, S. O., Jr., Mahoney, J. A., Van Deusen, H. M., Wodzicki, K.
Oceania: Harrison, J. L., Landry, S. O., Jr., Van Deusen, H. M.
Arctic: Bee, J. W., Osborn, D. J.
Bones: Lavocat, R. J. M. (W).
Fossils: Black, C. C. (T:N), Burke, J. J. (T:N, P), Carreck, J. N. (Q:P), Dietrich, W. O. (Q:P), Donohoe, J. C. (C:N), Fejfar, O. (C:P), Galbreath, E. C. (T:?), Hibbard, C. W. (C:N), Hough, M. J. (T:?), Jánossy, D. (Q:P), Kowalski, K. (C:P), Misonne, X. (T:?), Reig, O. A. (F:Nt), Schaldach, W. J., Jr. (Q:N), Schaub, S. (C:?), Shotwell, J. A. (T:N), Stout, T. M., Vereschagin, H. K. (C:P), White, J. A. (C:?), Wilson, R. W. (T:N), Wood, A. E. (T:?).
SCIUROMORPHA: Gromov, Y. M. (P).   FOSSILS: Gromov, Y. M. (C:P).
SIRENIA: Hatt, R. T. (N, E), Moore, J. C. (W).
Fossils: Reinhart, R. H. (M-C:W), VanderHoof, V. L. (T:?).
TAPIROIDEA - fossils: Bader, R. (Q:?).

MAMMALIA (continued)

THERIA - fossils: Thenius, E. (C:P).
TYLOPODA: Herre, W.
UNGULATA: Bourliere, F. (E), Brooks, A. C. (N, E), Dandelot, P. (P, E), Flook, D. R. (N),
      Markov, G. (P), Olivier, G. (N, P, E, O, A, Oc).
  Sub-fossils: Boessneck, J. (P).
  Fossils: Shikama, T. (Q:P).
XENARTHRA: Hoffstetter, R. (F:W).

* * * * *

Amynodontidae - fossils: Gromova, V. (F:P).
Arvicolidae - fossils: Kretzoi, M.
Balaenopteridae: Nishiwaki, M. (W).
Balaenidae: Nishiwaki, M. (W).
Bovidae: Benzon, B. (E), Bubeník, A. B. (P), Coolidge, H. J. (P, O), Tener, J. S. (N).
  Fossils: Frankforter, W. D. (F:N), Leakey, L. S. B. (Q:E), Mottl, M. (C:P), Singer, R. (Q:E),
      Skinner, M. F. (Q:W), Sokolov, I. I. (F:P), Wells, L. H. (Q:?).
Camelidae - fossils: Bader, R. (Q:?), Havesson, J. I. (C:P), Macdonald, J. R. (T:?).
Canidae: Churcher, C. S. (W), Jackson, H. H. T (N), Joliecoeur, P. (N), Lawrence, B. (W),
      Loughrey, A. J. (N), Rohrs, M., Szunyoghy, J. (P).
  Fossils: Cadeo, G. C. (F:P), VanderHoof, V. L. (T:?).
Cercopithecidae: Dandelot, P. (P, E), Vlcek, E. (P).
Cervidae: Banfield, A. W. F. (N), van Bemmel, A. C. V. (P), Bubeník, A. B. (W), Coombes,
      R. A. H. (P), Cowan, I. M. (N), Hummelinck, P. W. (Nt), Kelsall, J. P. (N),
      von Lehmann, E. (P), Szunyoghy, J. (P).
  Sub-fossils: Erdbrink, D. P. (P, E, O, A, Oc).
  Fossils: Azzaroli, A. (T:?), Erdbrink, D. P. (C:P, E, O, A, Oc), Kahlke, H. D. (Q:P), Sokolov,
      I. I. (F:P).
Chalicotheriidae: Beliajeva, E. I. (P).   FOSSILS: Butler, P. M. (F:P, E, O, A, Oc).
Cricetidae, no locality: Magalhaes, H., Wetzel, R. M.
  World: Quay, W. B., Vorontsov, N. N.
    Nearctic: Anderson, S., Clark, W. K., Davis, J. A., Jr., Dice, L. R., Edwards, R. L.,
      Finley, R. B., Jr., Hardy, R., Hoffmeister, D. F., Hooper, E. T., Justice, K. E.,
      Larrison, E. J., Lyman, C. P., Negus, N. C., Packard, R. L., Schaldach, W. J., Jr.,
      Stombaugh, T. A., Zimmermann, K.
    Neotropical: Hooper, E. T., Olrog, C. C., Pearson, O. P.
    Palearctic: Prychodko, W., Wahrman, J., Zimmermann, K.
    Arctic & Antarctic: Manning, T. H. (Arc), Olrog, C. C. (Ant).
  Fossils: Bader, R. (Q:?), Davis, J. A., Jr. (F:N), Heller, F. (C:P), Wetzel, R. M. (Q:?).
Dasypodidae: Russell, R. J., Jr. (N, Nt).
Dasyuridae: Mahoney, J. A. (A).   FOSSILS: Mahoney, J. A. (Q:A).
Daubentoniidae: Petter, J. J. (E), Petter-Rousseaux, A. (E).
Deinotheriidae - fossils: Bergounioux, F. M. (F:P).
Delphinidae: Cadenat, J. (E), Nishiwaki, M. (W).
Desmostylidae - fossils: Ijiri, S. (T:PO).
Dipodidae: Vorontsov, N. N. (W).
Elephantidae - fossils: de Aguirre, E. (Q:P), Musil, R., Orr, P. C. (Q:N), Singer, R. (Q:E).
Equidae: Bannikov, A. G. (P), Quinn, J. H. (N, P).
  Fossils: Bader, R. (C:?), Clark, J. (T:?), Gromova, V. (Q:P), Howe, J. A. (Q:?), Morris,
      W. J. (T:N), Mooser-Barendun, O. (C:Nt), Mottl, M. (C:P), Quinn, J. H. (F:N, P),
      Skinner, M. F. (T:W), Sokolov, I. I. (F:P), Tedford, R. H. (T:N), Wehrli, H. (F:P).
Erinaceidae: Szunyoghy, J. (P).   FOSSILS: Butler, P. M. (T:P).
Felidae: Haltenorth, T. (W), Hibben, F. C. (N), Rohrs, M.
  Sub-fossils: Schwabe, A. (P).
Geomyidae: Kennerly, T. E. (N), McLaughlin, C. A. (N), Russell, R. J., Jr. (Nt).
  Fossils: Russell, R. J., Jr. (C:Nt).
Giraffidae - fossils: Boné, E. (C:E), Bohlin, B. (T:P), Singer, R. (Q:E).
Gliridae: Prychodko, W. (P).
Helaletidae - fossils: Wood, H. E. (N).
Heteromyidae: Benson, S. B. (N), Butterworth, B. B., Hardy, R. (N), Huey, L. M. (N, Nt),
      Justice, K. E. (N).
Hippopotamidae - fossils: Accordi, B. (Q:P).
Hominidae: Boné, E., Clemente, L. S. (O), Woo, J-K. (P, O).
  Fossils: Dart, R. A. (Q:?), Oakley, K. P.
Hyaenidae: Kurtén, B. (P, E, O, A, Oc).   FOSSILS: Kurtén, B. (C:P, E, O, A, Oc).
Hyracodontidae: Beliajeva, E. I. (P).
Indricotheriidae - fossils: Gromova, V. (F:P).
Indridae: Petter, J. J. (E), Petter-Rousseaux, A. (E).

Ischyromyidae - fossils: Howe, J. A. (T:?).
Lemuridae: Petter, J. J. (E), Petter-Rousseaux, A. (E).
Leporidae: Hummelinck, P. W. (Nt), Manning, T. H. (Arc), Szunyoghy, J. (P).
Mastodontidae - fossils: Bergounioux, F. M. (F:P), Mottl, M. (C:P).
Merycoidodontidae - fossils: Falkenbach, C. H. (T:N), Koerner, H. E. (T:?).
Muridae: Harrison, J. L. (W), Hill, J. E. (P), Imaizumi, Y. (P), Kuroda, N. (P, O), Poots,
    L. (P), Ride, W. L. D. (A), Zimmermann, K. (P).
    Fossils: Mahoney, J. A. (Q:A), Ride, W. L. D. (F:A).
Mustelidae: Van Gelder, R. G. (N, Nt), Wright, P. L. (N).
    Fossils: Mottl, M. (C:P).
Ochotonidae: Gromov, Y. M. (P).   FOSSILS: Gromov, Y. M. (Q:P).
Odobenidae: Mansfield, A. W. (Arc).
Ovidae: Cowan, I. M. (N).
Phocidae: Doutt, J. K. (AO, PO), Laws, R. M. (W), Mansfield, A. W. (Arc, Ant), Rasmussen,
    B. (AO).
Physeteridae: Nishiwaki, M. (W).
Pongidae: Coolidge, H. J. (P, E), Woo, J-K. (P, O).
    Fossils: Mottl, M. (C:P).
Rhinocerotidae: Beliajeva, E. I. (P).
Rhinolophidae: Djulić, B. (P).
Sciuridae: Barkalow, F. S. , Jr. (N), Dobroruka, L. J. (P, E), Hansen, R. M. (N), Hardy, R. (N),
    Harris, W. P. (W), Larrison, E. J. (N), Moore, J. C. (O), Schaldach, W. J. , Jr. (N),
    Smith, R. E. (N), Snyder, D. P. (N), Wade, O. (N), White, J. A. (N).
    Fossils: Barkalow, F. S. , Jr. (F:N), Wehrli, H. (Q:P, N).
Soricidae: Clothier, R. R. (N), Findley, J. S. (N, P), Jackson, H. H. T. (N, Nt), von Lehmann,
    E. (P, E), Meester, J. (E), Pruitt, W. O. , Jr. (Arc), Schaldach, W. J. , Jr. (Nt),
    Szunyoghy, J. (P).
    Fossils: Meester, J. (Q:E).
Spalacidae: Szunyoghy, J. (P).
Suidae - fossils: Ewer, R. F. (F:E), Leakey, L. S. B. (Q:?).
Talpidae: Jackson, H. H. T. (N), Szunyoghy, J. (P).
    Fossils: Reed, C. A. (C:W).
Tayassuidae - fossils: Bader, R. (Q:?).
Ursidae: Kurtén, B. (W).
    Sub-fossils: Schwabe, A. (P).
    Fossils: Cadeo, G. C. (F:P), Ehrenberg, K. (Q:P), Kurtén, B. (C:W), Mottl, M. (C:P),
    Musil, R.
Vespertilionidae: Bauer, K. (P), Djulić, B. (P), Frum, W. G. (N), Nicholas, G. (N),
    Poots, L. (P).
Viverridae: Wenzel, E. (W).
Zapodidae: Krutzsch, P. H. (N).
Ziphiidae: Nishiwaki, M. (W).

ALPHABETICAL LIST

AASEN, O. Institute of Marine Research, Bergen, Norway. [Pisces: Squaloidea & Clupeoidea of Europe (Yes); Scombriformes of Europe (No)]
*ABALOS, Dr. Jorge W. Address unknown. (Hemiptera, Reptilia)
ABBASSIAN-LINTZEN, Mrs. Rosemarie. Faculty of Veterinary Sciences, Avenue Kakh, Teheran, Iran. [Acarina: Ixodoidea of Iran (Yes)] [Institute of Parasitology & Malariology]
* ABBOTT, Miss Betty. Department of Biology, Virginia Polytechnic Institute, Blacksburg, Va., U.S.A. [Annelida: Polychaeta]
ABBOTT, Dr. Donald P. Hopkins Marine Station, Pacific Grove, Calif., U.S.A. [Tunicata: Ascidiacea of Pacific N. America, Polynesia, Micronesia (Yes)] [Stanford University]
ABBOTT, R. Tucker. Academy of Natural Sciences, Philadelphia 3, Penna., U.S.A. [Marine Mollusca of Indo-Pacific (Yes); f-w. Gastropoda of medical inportance of World (Yes)]
ABBOTT, Waldo G. Santa Barbara Museum of Natural History, Santa Barbara, Calif., U.S.A. [Aves of w. U.S. (Yes); Reptilia of California (Yes)]
ABDEL-MALEK, E. See MALEK, E. T. Abdel.
ABDULALI, Humayun. c/o Messrs. Faiz & Co., 75 Abdul Reham Street, Bombay 3, India. [Birds, snakes, lizards, amphibians, of Peninsular India & Pakistan s. of Himalayas (Yes)] [Bombay Natural History Society]
ABDUSSALAM, M. 8-A Tapp Road, Lahore, Pakistan. [Acarina: Mesostigmata, Ixodoidea, of Indo-Pakistan (Yes)] [College of Animal Husbandry]
ABE, Dr. Tokihoru. Tokaiku Suisan Kenkyujo, Tsukishima, Kyobashi, Tokyo, Japan. [Pisces, espec. Exocoetidae & Tetraodontidae, of Indopacific & Antarctic Oceans (Yes)]
* ABE, Yoshio. Zoological Laboratory, Hiroshima University, Hiroshima, Japan. [Diptera; Amphibia]
* ABEL, Dr. Erich. Zoologisches Institut der Universität, Wien I, Austria. [Reptiles]
ABONNENC, Emile. École Nacionale de Médecine, Dakar, Senegal. [Diptera: Phlebotomidae, Culicinae, Anophelinae, of Neotropical & Ethiopian (Yes)]
ABOUL-ELA, Dr. I. Department of Zoology, Faculty of Science, University of Cairo, Giza, Egypt. [Gastropoda: Nudibranchiata of Red Sea (Yes)]
ABRICOSSOV, G. G. Biological Faculty, University of Moscow, Leninskiy Gory, Moscow B234, U.S.S.R. [F-w. Bryozoa of Europe, Asia, Africa; g. Victorella of World (Yes)]
ÅBRO, Arnold, cand. real. Gard, Haugesund, Norway. [Odonata; Orthoptera: Saltatoria; Diptera: Tabanidae & Eumyidae; Hymenoptera: Sphegidae & Vespidae; Hemiptera: Hydrometridae (Yes); Acarina: Hydrachnidae; Chilopoda (No); Aves: Sylvidae & Paridae (Yes); all of Scandinavia & n.w. Europe]
ABSELL, Alfred. Died January 1957.
* ABSOLON, Prof. S.K. Vsetickova 31, Brno, Czechoslovakia. [Insecta: Apterygota]
*ABULADZE, Cand. Vet. Sci. K.I. Moscow Veterinary Academy, Kuzjminki Moscow reg., Moscow, U.S.S.R. [Cestodea of birds of U.S.S.R.]
ACCORDI, Prof. Bruno, Direttore dell' Instituto di Geologia dell' Universitá, Corso Italia 21, Catania, Italy. [L. Triassic fishes of Europe (No); Pleistocene Mammalia: Hippopotamidae of Europe (Yes)]
ACHARJI, Mr. M.N. Zoological Survey of India, 34 Chittaranjan Avenue, Calcutta 12, India. [Snakes & chelonians of India (Yes)]
*ACHMEROV, Cand.Biol.Sci. A.H. Pond Institute of Fish Economy, Podsosensky 26, Moscow, U.S.S.R. [Helminths of fishes of U.S.S.R.]
ACKERT, J.E. (Manhattan, Kans.; Nematoda) Not now active in taxonomy.
ACOSTA, Dr. José T. Calle Goss 317, Vibora, Habana, Cuba. [Foraminifera of Cuba] [Universidad de Habana]
* ACOSTA, M.J. Address unknown. [Diptera: Culicidae]
ACZEL, Dr. Martin. Instituto Miguel Lillo, Calle Miguel Lillo 205, Tucumán, Argentina. [Diptera: Trypetidae & Clythiidae of S. & C. America; Neriidae of World; Tylidae of S. & C. America, Oriental, Australian; Pyrgotidae of S. & C. America & Ethiopian; Nothybidae of Orient (Yes)]
ADACHI, Miss Marian. Department of Entomology, University of Arizona, Tucson, Ariz., U.S.A. [Diptera: Dolichopodidae of Hawaii (Yes)]
ADACHI, Prof. Tsunamitsu. Biological Laboratory, Tôyô University, 17 Haramachi, Bunkyoku, Tokyo, Japan. [Terr. Oligochaeta of Japan (Yes); Coleoptera: Staphylinidae of Japan, Formosa, Korea (No)]
ADAM, M. J-P. Laboratoire d'Entomologie, O.R.S.T.O.M., 47 Blvd. des Invalides, Paris (VII), France. [Diptera: Culicidae of Ethiopian (No); g. Anopheles of Ethiopian (Yes)] [Office de la Recherche Scientifique et Technique Outre-Mer]
ADAM, Dr. Karl Dietrich. Museum für Naturkunde, Archivstrasse 3, Stuttgart, Germany. [Mammalia: Proboscidea of Europe, Asia, Africa (Yes); Quaternary Carnivora, Perissodactyla, Artiodactyla, of Europe (Yes)]

101

ADAM, Dr. W. Directeur de Laboratoire, Department de Malacologie, Institut Royal des Sciences Naturelles, 31 rue Vautier, Bruxelles, Belgium. [Recent & Quaternary Mollusca of Belgium (Yes); Recent & Quaternary terr. & f-w. Mollusca of C. Africa (Yes); Cephalopoda (Yes)]

ADAMCZAK, F. Zakład Paleontologii, Uniwersytetu Warszawskeigo, Nowy-Swiat 67, Warszawa, Poland. [Paleozoic Ostracoda: Beyrichiacea of Europe (No), of Poland (Yes)]

* ADAMCZEWSKI, S. Instytut Zoologiczny, Polska Akademia Nauk, Słowkowska 17, Krakow, Poland. [Lepidoptera]

ADAMOVIĆ, Dr. Z. R. Prirodnjački Musej Srpske Zemlje, Njegoševa 51, Beograd, Yugoslavia. [Odonata of Yugoslavia; Orthoptera: Acrididae of Yugoslavia (Yes)]

ADAMS, C. F. Died January 21, 1950. (Jefferson City, Mo., Diptera)

ADAMS, Dr. C. G. Department of Zoology, British Museum (Natural History), Cromwell Road, London, S. W. 7, England. [Jurassic Foraminifera: Lagenidae of Europe (Yes)]

ADAMS, Dr. Claude T., Sr. Wright-Patterson Air Force Base, 5240 Access Road, Dayton 31, Ohio, U. S. A. [Fossil birds: Ardeidae of World (Yes)]

ADAMS, Dr. James R. Department of Zoology, University of British Columbia, Vancouver, B. C., Canada. [Parasites of f-w. fish & game of n. w. N. America (Yes)]

ADAMS, L. E. (University Park, Pa.; Homoptera) Not now active in taxonomy.

ADAMS, P. A. Biological Laboratories, Harvard University, Cambridge 38, Mass., U. S. A. [Neuroptera: Chrysopidae & Myrmeleonidae of N. America & Micronesia (Yes)]

* ADAMS, Mr. W. E. Department of Anatomy, University of Otago, Dunedin, New Zealand. [Reptiles]

ADDICOTT, Mr. W. O. 1742 Oxley Street, South Pasadena, Calif., U. S. A. [Recent & Tertiary Mollusca (No)] [General Petroleum Corp.]

ADELPHE-DAVID, Frére, s. c. 135 King Ouest, Sherbrooke, P. Q., Canada. [Lepidoptera: Papilionoidea of n. e. U. S. & e. Canada (Yes); Noctuidae of Quebec (No)] [École de Génie, Université de Sherbrooke]

ADELSON, Mr. Bernard J. 112 Agriculture Hall, University of California, Berkeley 4, Calif., U. S. A. [Coleoptera: Elateridae, Throscidae, Melasidae; of N. America (Yes); of C. & S. America (No)]

* ADHAMI, Mr. A. R. Iraq Ministry of Agriculture, Abu Graib Farm, Abu Graib, Iraq. [Nematoda]

* ADKIN, G. T. Address unknown. (Lepidoptera)

* ADLER, Prof. S. Hebrew University, Jerusalem, Israel. [Diptera]

AECHTER, Dr. Dr. Rupert. Theodor Körnerstrasse 79, Graz, Austria. [Araneae of Austria (No)]

AELLEN, Dr. V. Muséum d'Histoire Naturelle, Genève, Switzerland. [Mammalia: Chiroptera of Europe & Africa (Yes); Reptilia & Amphibia of Europe (No); Diptera: Nycteribiidae & Streblidae of Europe (No)]

AERTS, W. In der Gracht 3, Köln-Poll, Germany. [Hymenoptera: Ichneumonidae of Palearctic (Yes)] [Museum Alexander Koenig, Bonn]

► * AFSHAR, Prof. Jalal. Ministry of Agriculture, Kerej School of Agriculture, Teheran, Iran. [Diptera]

* AGARWAL, J. P. School of Entomology, St. John's College, Agra, India. [Odonata]

AGAZZI, Giorgio. Cannaregio 4889 B, Venezia, Italy. [Coleoptera: Scarabaeidae of Europe (No), of Italy (Yes); cave beetles of Eur. Alps (Yes)]

AGENJO, Ramon. Marques de Urquijo 17, Madrid, Spain. [Lepidoptera of Spain (Yes)] Instituto Español de Entomologia]

AGER, Dr. D. V. Department of Geology, Imperial College of Science and Technology, London, S. W. 7, England. [Jurassic Brachiopoda of Europe & env. (Yes), Triassic & Cretaceous of same (No)]

AGERSBORG, Dr. H. P. K. 1212 North Maple Street, Centralia, Ill., U. S. A. [Mollusca: Nudibranchiata of World (Yes)] [Agersborg Biological Laboratory]

► * AGRELL, Dr. Ivar. Zoologiska Institution, Lund, Sweden. [Collembola]

AGUAYO, Carlos Guillermo, Director, Museo Poey, 4 No. 554, Vedada, Habana, Cuba. [Mollusca of West Indies (No); of Cuba (Yes)] [Universidad de Habana]

AGUESSE, Pierre. Station Biologique de la Tour du Valet, Le Sambuc, Camargue (B. du R.), France. [Odonata of Europe & N. Africa (Yes)]

d'AGUILAR, Jacques. Station Centrale de Zoologie Agricole, Route de St. Cyr, Versailles (S. et. O.), France. [Diptera: Tachinidae of Europe (Yes); Coleoptera (Larvae) of Europe]

de AGUIRRE, Emiliano. Instituto "Lucas Mallada", Castellana 84, Madrid, Spain. [Quaternary Mammals: g. Elephas of Europe (Yes)]

AHLBERG, Dr. Olof. Statens Vaxtskyddsanstalt, Stockholm 19, Sweden. [Thysanoptera of Scandinavia (Yes)]

AHLSTROM, Dr. Elbert H. Box 271, La Jolla, Calif., U. S. A. [Larval marine Pisces of Atlantic & Pacific Ocean (Yes); planktonic Rotifera of World (Yes)] [U. S. Fish & Wildlife Service]

AHMAD, Dr. M. Department of Zoology, University of the Punjab, Lahore, Pakistan. [Isoptera of Indomalaya (Yes)]

* AHMAD, Dr. Nazir. East Pakistan Fisheries Department, Eden Building, Dacce, East Pakistan. [Pisces)]

* AHMAD, Dr. T. , Director of Plant Protection, 20 Pakistan Secretariat, Karachi, Pakistan. [Insecta: Exopterygota]

AHRENS, Carsten. 3461 Harrisburg Street, Pittsburgh 4, Penna. , U.S.A. [Odonata of N. America (Yes)] [South Hills High School]

* AICHINGER, J. Zoologisches Museum der Universität, Künstlergasse 16, Zürich, Switzerland. [Fossil vertebrates]

AITKEN, Mr. T.H.G. Trinidad Regional Virus Laboratory, P. O. Box 164, Port of Spain, Trinidad. [Diptera: Culicidae of N. America (Yes); of n. S. America & Trinidad (Yes); of Mediterranean (Yes)] [The Rockefeller Foundation]

AIZENBERG, Dr. E.E. Biological Laboratory, Biological-Pedological Faculty, Moscow State University, Moscow B-234, U.S.S.R. [Homoptera: Aphidoidea of U.S.S.R. (Yes), of World (No)]

AKATOVA, N.A. Zoological Institute, Academy of Sciences, Leningrad B-164, U.S.S.R. [Ostracoda & Phyllopoda of Palearctic (Yes)]

AKAZAKI, M. Department of Fisheries, Kyoto University, Kyoto, Japan. [Pisces: Sparidae, Nemipteridae, Lethrinidae, Pentapodidae, Lutjanidae; of Indo-Pacific (Yes)]

AKERS, Mr. W.H. The California Co. , The California Co. Bldg. , New Orleans, La. , U.S.A. [Cenozoic Foraminifera of World (Yes)]

AKIMUSCHKIN, J.J. Institute of Oceanology, Academy of Science USSR, Lujnikovskaja 8, Moscow Y-127, U.S.S.R. [Cephalopoda, excl. Sepiidae, of nw. Pacific Ocean (Yes); their beaks from predator stomachs (Yes)]

AKIYAMA, Masahiko. Geological & Mineralogical Institute, Tokyo Kyôiku Daigaku, Otsuka-Machi, Bunkyô-ku, Tokyo, Japan. [Cenozoic Pelecypoda: Pectinidae of Japan (Yes)]

➤ * AKRAMOWSKI, Nikolai N. Zoological Institute, Akademia Nauk of the Armenian SSR, Erevan, Armenian S.S.R. [Odonata]

AKSIRAY, Dr. Fethi, Hidrobiologi Enstitüsü, Emirgân, Istanbul, Turkey. [Cyprinodontid Pisces of Turkey & Near East (Yes); marine Pisces of Turkey (Yes)]

* ALABASTER, J.S. 46 Fitzgeorge Avenue, London, W.14, England. [Aves]

ALAM, Dr. S.M. Department of Zoology, Muslim University, Aligarh, U. P. , India. [Hymenoptera of India & Pakistan (Yes): Encyrtidae of Ceylon & Burma (Yes); Aphelinidae of Malaya (Yes)]

ALAYO DALMAU, Dr. Pastor. Museo de Historia Natural, Universidad de Oriente, Santiago, Cuba. [Hymenoptera: Vespoidea, Sphecoidea, Apoidea of Cuba (Yes); Lepidoptera, excl. microlepidoptera, from Cuba (Yes); Reptilia of Cuba (Yes); terr. & f-w. Mollusca of Cuba (No)]

ALBERS, C.C. Pan-American Petroleum Corp. , P. O. Box 14085, Houston 21, Texas, U.S.A. [Tertiary Foraminifera of Louisiana Gulf Coast (No)]

ALBERS, Dr. Jürgen. Mobil Oil A. G. , Celle, Germany. [L. Cretaceous Foraminifera: g. Vaginulina of Germany (No)]

* ALBERS, Th. Finksweg 54, Hamburg-Finkenwerder, Germany. [Lepidoptera: Geometridae of Europe (Yes)]

ALBERTI, Dr. Burchard. Zoologisches Museum, Invalidenstrasse 43, Berlin N.4, German Dem. Republic. [Lepidoptera: Zygaenidae & Hesperiidae (Hesperiidi) of World (Yes)]

* ALBRECHT, F.O. Laboratoire d'Evolution des Etres Organises, 105 Boulevard Raspail, Paris (VI), France. [Orthoptera]

ALBRIGHT, Mr. Philip N. 943 E. Mistletoe Avenue, San Antonio 12, Texas, U.S.A. [Odonata: Anisoptera of Texas (Yes); Zygoptera of Texas (No)]

ALBRITTON, Claude C. , Jr. 3436 University Blvd. , Dallas 5, Texas, U.S.A. [Cretaceous smaller Foraminifera (No)] [Southern Methodist University]

ALBU, Paula, asistent univ. , Facultatea de Ştiinţe Naturale, Splaiul Independentei Nr. 91-93, Bucureşti, Rumania. [Diptera: Chironomidae (imago) of Rumania (Yes)]

* ALBUQUERQUE, Dalcy de O. Departmento de Entomologia, Museu Nacional, Quinta da Boa Vista, Rio de Janeiro, Brazil. [Diptera: Muscidae of World]

ALCALA, Prof. Angel C. Department of Biology, Silliman University, Dumaguete City, Negros Oriental, Philippines. [Amphibia: Anura of P.I. (Yes); Reptilia, excl. snakes, of Negros (Yes)]

ALCORN, Prof. Gordon D. Department of Biology, College of Puget Sound, Tacoma 6, Wash. , U.S.A. [Aves of n. w. U.S. (Yes)]

ALDRICH, Dr. Frederick A. Department of Limnology, Academy of Natural Sciences, Philadelphia 3, Penna. , U.S.A. [Pelecypoda: Unionidae of U.S. (Yes); Asteroidea of e. U.S. (Yes)]

* ALDRICH, E.C. 5631 Camellia Avenue, Sacramento, Calif. , U.S.A. [Aves]

ALDRICH, Dr. John W. Fish & Wildlife Service, U.S. Department of Interior, Washington 25, D.C. , U.S.A. [Aves of N. America (Yes)]

* ALEV. Iuri Glebovitch. Biological Station of Sevastopol, Primorskii Bulvard, Sevastopol, Krymskaja Oblast, U. S. S. R. [Pisces]
* ALEINIKOVA, M. M. Address unknown, except U. S. S. R. [Myriapoda]
* ALEKPEROV, A. M. Department of Zoology, State University, Baku, Caucasus, U. S. S. R. [Amphibia, Reptilia]
* ALEMAN, C. Museo de Historia Natural La Salle, Caracas, Venezuela. [Reptilia]
* ALEMANY PROENZA, Dra. M. Instituto de la Vibora, 14 No. 709 Repto. Almondares, Marianao, Habana, Cuba. [Fossil Foraminifera]
ALENCÁSTER de CSERNA, Sra. Gloria. Instituto Geológico, Ciudad Universitaria, Mexico 20, D. F., Mexico. [Mesozoic Pelecypoda & Gastropoda of Mexico (No)]
* ALEXANDER, A. G. Edward Grey Institute, Botanic Garden, Oxford, England. [Aves]
ALEXANDER, Anne J. Rhodes University, Grahamstown, Union of South Africa. [Scorpionida: g. Opisthophthalmus of S. Africa (Yes); Onychophora: Peripatopsidae of S. Africa (No)] [Zoological Laboratories, Downing Street, Cambridge, England]
ALEXANDER, Dr. Claude G. Department of Biology, San Francisco State College, 1600 Holloway, San Francisco 27, Calif., U. S. A. [Tetraphyllidean Cestoda of w. N. America (Yes)]
ALEXANDER, Charles I. (Dallas, Tex.; fossils) Not now active in taxonomy.
ALEXANDER, Dr. Charles P. Department of Entomology, University of Massachusetts, Amherst, Mass., U. S. A. [Diptera: Tipulidae of World (Yes)]
ALEXANDER, Gordon. University of Colorado, Boulder, Colo., U. S. A. [Orthoptera, espec. Acrididae, of Colorado (Yes); Aves: g. Colaptes]
* ALEXANDER, H. G. Address unknown. [Aves]
ALEXANDER, Robert C. 423 Warwick Road, Wynnewood, Penna., U. S. A. [Marine Gastropoda & Pelecypoda of New Jersey (No)]
ALEXANDER, Dr. Richard D. Museum of Zoology, University of Michigan, Ann Arbor, Michigan. [Homoptera: Cicadidae of e. U. S. (Yes): Orthoptera: Tettigoniidae & Gryllidae of e. U. S. (No)]
ALEXEEV, Anatolii V. Zoological Museum, University of Moscow, Hertzen Str. 6, Moscow K-9, U. S. S. R. [Coleoptera: Buprestidae of Europe & U. S. S. R. (No); g. Agrilus, Imago & larva, of Europe (Yes)]
* ALEXINSCHI, Alexandru. Str. Uzinei nr. 20, Iasi, Rumania. [Lepidoptera]
ALF, Ray. Webb School, Claremont, Calif., U. S. A. [Mammals of White River Oligocene, U. S. (Yes)]
ALFIERI, Dr. A. P. O. Box 430, Cairo, Egypt. [Coleoptera, Lepidoptera, Hemiptera-Heteroptera, Hymenoptera excl. of Chalcidoidea & Braconidae; of Egypt (Yes)]
ALFIREVIC, Prof. Slobodan. Institut za Oceanografiju i Ribarstvo, Split, Yugoslavia. [Recent Foraminifera of Adriatic Sea & Yugoslavia (Yes)]
* ALFONSO RIBERA, Dr. Hector. Calle Fernando de Castro 33, Leon, Spain. [Hemiptera of Spain (Yes)]
AL-HUSSAINI, Prof. A. H. Department of Zoology, Faculty of Science, Ain Shams University, Abbassiah, Cairo, Egypt. [Aves of Egypt (No); Pisces of Red Sea (Yes)]
ALICATA, Dr. Joseph E. Agricultural Experiment Station, University of Hawaii, Honolulu 14, Hawaii. [Helminths of man & domest. animals of N. America & Hawaiian Is. (Yes)]
* ALIKUNHI, Dr. K. H. Central Inland Fisheries Research Sub-Station, 28 Cantonment Road, Cuttack, India. [Crustacea]
* ALKINS, W. E. Address unknown. (Terr. & f-w. mollusks; fossils of carboniferous limestone)
ALLABOUGH, Edwin A., Jr. 2686 Anza Trail, Palm Springs, Calif., U. S. A. [Fossil & Recent Mollusca (No)]
* ALLAN, Miss Joyce. 72 Cremorne Road, Cremorne, N. S. W., Australia. [Mollusca]
ALLAN, Prof. R. S. University of Canterbury, Christchurch, New Zealand. [Recent Brachiopoda of s. Hemisphere (Yes); Tertiary Brachiopoda of New Zealand & Australia (Yes); Devonian Brachiopoda of New Zealand (Yes)]
* ALLANDER, H. Landsvagen 49, Sundbyberg, Stockholm, Sweden. [Lepidoptera]
ALLAWAY, Alan L. Telford Street, Yarrawonga, Vict., Australia. [Lepidoptera of e. Australia (Yes)]
* ALLCARD, H. G. Ravenswood Wythenshawe Road. Northenden, Manchester, England. [Lepidoptera]
ALLEGRE, Prof. Charles. Department of Science, Iowa State Teachers College, Cedar Falls, Iowa, U. S. A. [Protozoa: g. Phacus of U. S. (Yes)]
ALLEN, A. A. The Tiled House, 63 Blackheath Park, London, S. E. 3, England. [Coleoptera of Brit. Isles (Yes)]
* ALLEN, Mr. Charles A. 1125 10th Avenue, Honolulu 16, Hawaii. [Mollusca]
ALLEN, Donald G., Research Entomologist, Oregon Forest Lands Research Institute, Corvallis, Ore., U. S. A. [Coleoptera: Scolytidae of Oregon (Yes); Diptera of w. Oregon forests (Yes)]

* ALLEN, Dr. H. W.   Research Laboratories, U. S. Department of Agriculture, Box 150, Moorestown, N. J. , U. S. A.   [Hymenoptera: Tiphiidae]
ALLEN, Dr. J. A.   Dove Marine Laboratory, King's College, Newcastle-upon-Tyne, Cullercoats, Northumberland, England. [Gastropoda & Lamellibranchia of Europe (Yes); Crustacea: Decapoda of Europe (Yes)]
ALLEN, Dr. J. Frances. Systematic Biology Program, National Science Foundation, Washington 25, D. C. , U. S. A. [Estuar. Gastropoda & Pelecypoda of Atlantic Cst. & Chesapeake Bay (Yes)]
ALLEN, Prof. Dr. M. W.   112 Agriculture Hall, University of Calif. , Berkeley 4, Calif. , U. S. A. [F-w. & plant parasitic Nematoda of World (Yes); insect parasitic Nematoda of N. America (Yes)]
ALLEN, Rex W.   P. O. Box 518, University Park, N. Mex. , U. S. A. [Nematoda, Cestoda, helminth parasites of ruminants, of N. & S. America (Yes)] [U. S. Department of Agriculture; Animal Disease & Parasite Research Division]
ALLEN, William R.   (Lexington, Ky. , U. S. A.) Deceased.
ALLEN, William T.   (Dallas, Texas; Paleozoic Cephalopoda) Not now active in taxonomy.
ALLGÉN, Lektor Dr. Carl. Stallmästaregatan 21 CII, Malmö V, Sweden. [Free-living Nematoda, espec. Marine, of World (Yes)]
ALLISON, E. C.   Museum of Paleontology, University of California, Berkeley 4, Calif. , U. S. A. [Cretaceous-Recent Mollusca & Foraminifera of w. N. America (Yes)]
ALLISON, Mrs. Frances   (Miss F. R. Nurse), Lecturer in Zoology, Canterbury University College, Christchurch, New Zealand. [Turbellaria: Tricladida, paludicolous, navicolous, of New Zealand outlying is. (Yes)]
ALLISON, Ray. Department of Zoology, Entomology, & Physiology, Louisiana State University, Baton Rouge, La. , U. S. A. [Monogenetic Trematoda of f-w. fish of s. e. U. S. (Yes)]
ALLOITEAU, James, Directeur de Recherches, Laboratoire de Géologie, Sorbonne, 1 rue Victor-Cousin, Paris (V), France. [Jurassic & Cretaceous Madreporaria of World (Yes)]
ALLOUSE, Bashir E.   Iraq Natural History Museum, Baghdad, Iraq. [Aves of Iraq & Middle East (Yes)]
ALLRED, Dorald M. Department of Zoology & Entomology, Brigham Young University, Provo, Utah. [Acarina: Dermanyssidae of w. U. S. (Yes)]
ALLYN, William P.   2223 College Avenue, Terre Haute, Indiana. [Snakes & salamanders of Indiana (Yes)] [Indiana State Teachers College]
* ALM, Dr. Gunnar. Sotvattenslaboratories, Drottningholm, Sweden. [Pisces]
de ALMEIDA, W. Ferreira. See FERREIRA de ALMEIDA, Waldemar.
d' ALMEIDA, Romualdo Ferreira. Rua Viana Junior 25, Encantado, Rio de Janeiro, Brazil. [Lepidoptera: Danaidae, Ithomiidae, Pieridae, of America (Yes)] [Museu Nacional do Rio de Janeiro]
ALONSO de ARAMBURU, Dra. Armonía S. Encargada de la Sección Ictiologia, Museo de Ciencias Naturales, Paseo del Bosque, La Plata, Argentina. [Fishes of Argentina (Yes)]
* ALSPAUGH, Ronald D.   521 17th Street, n. w. , Canton, Ohio. [Lepidoptera of World (Yes); Coleoptera of m. w. U. S. (Yes)]
ALTENA, Dr. C. O. van Regteren. Rijksmuseum van Natuurlijke Historie, Leiden, Netherlands. [Gastropoda, Bivalvia (Yes); Gastropoda: Limacidae, Arionidae (Yes); Lepidoptera: Uraniidae: g. Nyctalemon˙ (Yes)]
ALTHAUS, Dr. B.   Om Pfaffenstieg 7, Jena, Thuringia, German Democratic Republic. [Rotatoria & Nemathelminthes of Europe (Yes)]
ALTHERR, Dr. Edm. , Directeur des Écoles, Aigle, Switzerland. [F-l. Nematoda of Europe & Africa (Yes)]
ALTIMIRA ALÉU, Carlos. Av. Rep. Argentina 54, Prol. 2a, Barcelona, Spain. [Terr. & f-w. mollusks of Spain, N. Africa, France, Canaries (Yes); Pupillidae & Hebiellidae of Spain (Yes)]
ALTNER, Helmut. Zoologisches Institut Luisenstrasse 14, München 2, Germany. [Collembola of c. Europe & Mediterranean (Yes)]
ALVARENGA, M. Rua Eduardo Guinle 41, Ap. 101, Botafogo, Rio de Janeiro, Brazil. [Coleoptera: Erotylidae of World (Yes)] [Fundação Campos Seabra]
* ALVAREZ, Mrs. Clemencia. Instituto Nacional de Biologia, Apartado Postal 19186, Mexico, D. F. , Mexico. [Collembola of World]
* de ALVAREZ, Dra. Elsa Fernandez. Facultad de Ciencias, Universidad de Buenos Aires, Cabrera 5455, Buenos Aires, Argentina. [Fossil vertebrates]
ALVAREZ, Dr. José. Calle 27, Num. 71, S. Pedro de los Pinos, D. F. , Mexico. [F-w. fishes of Mexico (Yes)] [Escuela Nacional de Ciencias Biológicas]
* ALVAREZ A. , Javier. Laboratorio de Paleontologia, Gerencia de Exploracion, Petroleos Mexicanos, Cipres Nr. 176, Mexico 4, D. F. , Mexico. [Fossil Foraminifera]

ALVAREZ del TORO, Prof. M. Director del Museo Zoologico de Chiapas, Apartado Postal 6, Tuxtla Gutierrez, Chiapas, Mexico. [Aves, Reptilia, Amphibia, of Chiapas (Yes)]

ALVAREZ SANCHEZ, Dr. Julio. Instituto de Edafologia, Calle Serrano 113, Madrid, Spain. [Gastropoda: Pulmonata of w. Europe (Yes); f-w. Gastropoda of Mediterranean (No)]

* ALVERSON, Dayton Lee. 17916 Brittany Drive, Seattle 66, Wash., U.S.A. [Marine birds of w.U.S., marine fishes of w.U.S.]

* ALVES, Dr. William, Director, Malaria & Bilharzia Research Laboratory, P.O.Box 8105, Causeway, Salisbury, Southern Rhodesia. [Mollusca]

ALZONA, Dr. C. Via dei Colombo N. 1, Quinto, Genova, Italy. [Terr. Mollusca of Holarctic]

AMADON, DEAN. Department of Birds, American Museum of Natural History, New York 24, N.Y., U.S.A. [Aves (Yes)]

AMANO, Assist. Prof. M. Geological Institute, Kumamoto University, Kumamoto, Japan. [Cretaceous Pelecypoda of Japan (No)]

* AMAR, Dr. Raymond. Departement de Zoologie, Université de Damas, Damascus, Syria. [Crustacea]

do AMARAL, Dr. Afranio. Rua Bela Sintra 755, São Paulo, Brazil. [Serpentes of Neotropics (Yes); Lacertilia of Brazil (Yes)] [Instituto Butantan]

AMATO, F.L. Apartado del Este 4991, Caracas, Venezuela. [Cretaceous-Tertiary Foraminifera of Peru, Ecuador, Colombia, Venezuela (Yes); marine fishes of Venezuela (Yes)]

AMBROS, C. Archeologicky ústav, Nitra-Hrad, Czechoslovakia. [Post-glacial mammalian bones of c. Europe (Yes)]

AMEEL, Dr. Donald J. Department of Zoology, Kansas State College, Manhattan, Kansas. [Trematoda of U.S. (Yes)]

AMIO, Mr. Masaru. Shimonoseki College of Fisheries, Yoshimi, Shimonoseki City, Japan. [Marine Gastropoda of Japan (Yes)]

AMOS, William H. St. Andrews School, Middletown, Del., U.S.A. [Sessile & Benthic Hydrozoa, Anthozoa, Bryozoa, Annelida, Pelecypoda, Gastropoda, Amphipoda of Atlantic U.S. estuaries (Yes)]

AMOSOVA, Dr. I.S. Institute of Cytology, Academy of Sciences, Macklin 32, Leningrad F-121, U.S.S.R. [Diptera: Heleidae; g. Culicoides of U.S.S.R. (Yes)]

* AMREIN, Yost U.L. Address unknown. (Nematoda)

AMSDEN, Mr. T.W. Oklahoma Geological Survey, Norman, Okla., U.S.A. [Silurian & L. Devonian Brachiopoda (No)]

AMSEL, Dr. H.G. Landessammlungen für Naturkunde, Erbprinzenstrasse 13, Karlsruhe, Baden, Germany. [Microlepidoptera of palearctic & neotropics (Yes)]

ANANTARAMAN, Prof. M., Professor of Parasitology, Veterinary College, Madras 7, India. [Parasitic helminths & Acarina of India (Yes)]

ANANTHAKRISHNAN, T.N., Professor of Zoology, Loyola College, Madras 31, India. [Thysanoptera of India (Yes)]

ANASTOS, Dr. George. Department of Zoology, University of Maryland, College Park, Md., U.S.A. [Acarina: Ixodoidea of World (Yes)]

ANCA, Precupeţu. Str. Splaiul Independentei 91-95, Bucureşti, Rumania. [Hymenoptera: Cephidae, Pamphilidae, Siricidae of Rumania (Yes)]

ANCIAUX de FAVEAUX, R.P. Dom. Félix, o.s.b. Mission Ste.-Thérese, B.P. 96, Jadotville, Belgian Congo. [Bats of Katanga (Yes); cave animals of Katanga (No); birds & small mammals of Katanga (No)]

d'ANCONA, Umberto. See D'ANCONA, Umberto.

ANDER, Fil. Dr. Kjell. Biologiska Institutionen, Folkskoleseminarium, Danmarksgatan 4 E, Linköping, Sweden. [Orthoptera: Tettigoniidae of Old World (Yes); Gryllacrididae of World (Yes); Odonata of Palearctic (No)]

AN DER LAN, Dr. Hannes. Zoologisches Institut der Universität, Innsbruck, Austria. [Turbellaria of World (Yes)]

ANDERSEN, Harold V. School of Geology, Louisiana State University, Baton Rouge, La., U.S.A. [Tertiary Foraminifera of Gulf Coast of Ala., Miss., La. (Yes)]

* ANDERSEN, Mag. Jhs. Kalö pr. Rönde, Denmark. [Mammals]

ANDERSEN, Cand. Mag. Svend, Director, Zoological Gardens, Roskildevej 32, København F, Denmark. [Mammals]

* ANDERSEN, S.L. Hoendiepstraat 56, Amsterdam, Netherlands. [Lepidoptera]

ANDERSON, Donald M. Department of Science, New York State University Teachers College, Buffalo 22, N.Y., U.S.A. [Coleoptera: Curculionidae of N.America (No); g. Smicronyx of N.America (Yes)]

ANDERSON, F.S. [Springforbi, Denmark; Diptera) Not now active in taxonomy.

ANDERSON, Dr. F.W. Geological Survey & Museum, Exhibition Road, London, S.W.7, England. [Carboniferous & Jurassic-Cretaceous Ostracoda (Yes); post-Tertiary Ostracoda (No)]

ANDERSON, G. Paul. 604 West College, Independence, Mo., U.S.A. [Amphibia & Reptilia of U.S., espec. Mo. (Yes)]

ANDERSON, J.B. Department of Health, Education and Welfare, 9th Floor, Santa Fe Bldg., Dallas, Texas, U.S.A. [Aquatic Coleoptera & Hemiptera (No)]

ANDERSON, Mr. James D. Museum of Vertebrate Zoology, University of California, Berkeley 4, Calif., U.S.A. [Amphibia: Ambystomidae of N.America & Mexico (Yes); Amphibia & Reptilia of n.w.Mexico (Yes)]

ANDERSON, L.D. Department of Entomology, University of California, Riverside, Calif., U.S.A. [Hemiptera: Gerridae of N.America (Yes); Lepidopterous larvae of N.America (No)]

ANDERSON, Prof. Marlowe G. P.O.Box 97, State College, N.Mex., U.S.A. [Trematoda: Azygiidae of N.America (Yes): Cestoda of N.America (No)] [New Mexico College of Agriculture & Mechanical Arts]

ANDERSON, N.H. Entomology Laboratory, Belleville, Ont., Canada. [Heteroptera: Anthocoridae of n.w.U.S. (Yes); of Canada & U.S. (No)] [Canada Department of Agriculture]

ANDERSON, Dr. Paul K. Nevis Biological Station, Irvington-on-Hudson, N.Y., U.S.A. [Mammalia, Reptilia, Amphibia of N.America (Yes)] [Columbia University]

ANDERSON, Dr. Roy C. Department of Parasitology, Ontario Research Foundation, 43 Queen's Park, Toronto 5, Ont., Canada. [Nematoda: Filarioidea of World (Yes)]

* ANDERSON, Dr. Rudolph M. National Museum of Canada, Ottawa, Ont., Canada. [Mammalia]

ANDERSON, Mr. Sydney. Museum of Natural History, University of Kansas, Lawrence, Kansas, U.S.A. [Mammalia: Rodentia: Microtinae of N.America (Yes)]

* ANDERSON, Dr. William A. 509 Spring Avenue, Lutherville, Md., U.S.A. [Lepidoptera]

ANDERSON, Dr. William H. Division of Insects, U.S. National Museum, Washington 25, D.C., U.S.A. [Coleoptera: Scolytidae of N.America (Yes); larvae of Curculionoidea of N.America (Yes)] [U.S. Department of Agriculture]

ANDERSSON, Mr. Hugo. Universitetets Zoologiska Institution, Lund, Sweden. [Diptera: Chloropidae of Scandinavia (Yes)]

ANDOH, Takashi. Teppo-cho 4-23, Gifu, Gifu-ken, Japan. [Odonata of Japan (Yes)]

de ANDRADE, N.F. R. Marques de Subserra, 15-5o. Dto., Lisboa, Portugal. [Hymenoptera: Sphecoidea of w.Palearctic & s. Ethiopian (Yes)]

ANDRÁSSY, Dr. I. Egyetemi Állatrendszertani, Intézet, Puskin u. 3, Budapest VIII, Hungary. [Free-living Nematoda of World (Yes); plant parasitic Nematoda of Europe & N.America (Yes)]

ANDRE, Floyd. Iowa State College, Ames, Iowa, U.S.A. [Thysanoptera of N.America (Yes)]

ANDRÉ, Prof. Dr. Marc. 8bis Avenue Thiers, La Varenne, (Seine) France. [Acarina: Thrombidions of Europe & Africa (Yes)]

ANDREAE, Dr. H. South African Museum, P.O.Box 61, Cape Town, Union of South Africa. [Coleoptera: Pselaphidae, Histeridae, Thorictidae, Cossyphodidae, Ptinidae, g.Ageniosa, of S.Africa (No)]

* d'ANDRETTA JOR., Dr. Carlos. Escola Paulista de Medicina, Caixa Postal 7144, São Paulo, Brazil. [Diptera]

ANDREU, Dr. B. Institución de Investigaciones Pesqueras, Vigo, Spain. [Mollusca: Lamellibranchiata of n.w.Spain (No); Pisces: Clupeidae of Europe (Yes)]

* ANDREW, Dr. D.G. Department of Zoology, Downing Street, Cambridge, England. [Aves]

ANDREWS, Glenn Collins (Mrs. L.E.Andrews). 20 Neptune Place, Nassau Shores, Massapequa, N.Y., U.S.A. [Cretaceous & Tertiary Foraminifera of N.America (Yes)]

ANDREWS, H.W. (Christchurch, England; Diptera) Died April 9, 1955.

ANDREWS, Dr. Jay D. Virginia Fisheries Laboratory, Gloucester Point, Va., U.S.A. [Mollusca of Chesapeake Bay (Yes)]

ANDREWS, Dr. John S. Animal Parasite Laboratory, Animal Disease & Parasite Research Division, Agricultural Research Service, Beltsville, Md., U.S.A. [Parasitic Nematoda of sheep, cattle, swine of U.S. (Yes); Nematoda of horses & cattle in Puerto Rico (No)]

ANDREWS, Dr. Ted F. Professor of Biology, Kansas State Teachers College, Emporia, Kans., U.S.A. [F-w. Copepoda & Cladocera of Kansas (Yes)]

ANDRIASHEV, Dr. A.P. Zoological Institute, Academy of Sciences, Leningrad 164, U.S.S.R. [Marine fishes of Arctic & Antarctic (Yes): Zoarcidae of all seas (Yes)]

ANDRIESCU, Ionel. Str. Taetoarei Nr. 31, Iasi, Rumania. [Hymenoptera: Chalcidoidea of Rumania & Europe (Yes)] [Universitatea "Al.I. Cuza"]

ANDROSSOVA, Mme. H. Zoologischeski Institut, Akademii Nauk, Leningrad 164, U.S.S.R. [Bryozoa of w.Pacific (Yes)]

ANDRUSHKO, A. M. Department of Zoology, Leningrad State University, Leningrad 164, U.S.S.R. [Reptilia & Mammalia: Rodentia of c.Asia (No)]

* ANDUZE, Pablo J. Creole Petroleum Corporation, Apartado 889, Caracas, Venezuela.
  [Diptera: Culicidae, Simuliidae; Hemiptera: Reduviidae; Siphonaptera; of Neotropics]
ANELLI, Prof. Dr. Franco. Istituto Italiano di Speleologia, Castellana-Grotte, Bari, Italy.
  [Quaternary Mammalia of Italy (No)]
* ANFOSSI, Romano. Via Chenna 6, Alessandria, Italy. [Coleoptera]
* ANGEL, Fernand. Musée Océanographique, Monaco. [Pisces]
ANGEL, F. (Paris, France; Reptilia) Died 1950.
ANGEL, Frank M. 34 Fullerton Road, Parkside, S. Austr., Australia. [Lepidoptera of Aus-
  tralia (No); Rhopalocera of South Australia (Yes)]
ANGEL, Miss L. M. Zoology Department, University of Adelaide, Adelaide, S. Austr., Aus-
  tralia. [Trematoda: Digenea of South Australia (No); Endoprocta of World (No)]
ANGEL, Mr. S. 24 Burgess Avenue, Moonah, Tasmania, Australia. [Lepidoptera: Rhopa-
  locera of Australia (No); of Tasmania (Yes)]
ANGELIER, Eugène.   Laboratoire de Zoologie Général, Faculté des Sciences, Alées Jules-
  Guesde, Toulouse, France. [Hydracarina of Europe & Africa (Yes)]
ANGERMANN, H. Hoberge 41a, ü. Bielefeld 2, Germany. [Scorpionida: Chactidae of Medi-
  terranean (Yes)] [Zoologisches Institut der Universität Mainz]
ANGOT, M. Institut Français d'Océanie, B. P. 4, Nouméa, New Caledonia. [Pisces: Scom-
  bridae of trop. Pacific (Yes)]
ANISGARD, Harry W. C/o Carter Oil Co., Box 318, Billings, Mont., U.S.A. [Cretaceous
  & Tertiary Foraminifera of W. Hemisphere (Yes)]
* ANKEL, Dr. W. E., Dirktor des Zoologischen Institute der Technischen Hochschule,
  Darmstadt, Germany. [Porifera: Spongillidae; Mollusca]
* ANNEREAUX, Ralph F. Animal Pathology Laboratory, Division of Animal Industry, Sacra-
  mento 14, Calif., U.S.A. [Trematoda of World; Nematoda of World]
ANRAKU, Mr. Masateru. Faculty of Fisheries, Hokkaido University, Hakodate, Japan.
  [Crustacea: pelagic Copepoda of Japan & N. Pacific (Yes)]
* ANSARI, Dr. M. A. R. Institute of Hygiene & Preventive Medicine, 6 Birchwood Avenue,
  Lahore, Pakistan. [Diptera, Mallophaga]
ANSELL, Mr. W. F. H. Department of Game & Tsetse Control, c/o P. O. Box 1, Chilanga,
  Northern Rhodesia. [Mammals of C. Africa (Yes)]
ANTHONY, Dr. Harold E. Department of Mammals, American Museum of Natural History,
  New York 24, N. Y., U.S.A. [Recent Mammals of N. & S. America & Burma; Pleis-
  tocene Mammals of West Indies. Retired]
* ANTHONY, Mr. J. Laboratoire d'Anatomie Comparée, Muséum National d'Histoire Natur-
  elle, rue Cuvier 57, Paris (V), France. [Reptilia]
ANTHONY, Prof. James D. Department of Zoology, University of Wisconsin, Milwaukee 11,
  Wis., U.S.A. [Cestoda: Lytocestidae of World (Yes)]
* ANTIPIN, Dr. Vet. Sc., Prof. D. N. All-Union Skrjabin Institute of Helminthology, Staro-
  pansky 3, Moscow K-12, U.S.S.R. [Helminths of animals]
ANTOINE, Maurice. See Addenda.
ANTUNES, Prof. P. C. A. Faculdade de Higiene e Saúde Pública, Caixa Postal 8099, São
  Paulo, Brazil. [Diptera: Culicidae of Neotropics (Yes); Chloropidae of Neotropics
  (No)]
AOKI, Shigeru. Institute of Geology and Mineralogy, Tokyo University of Education, Bunkyo-
  ku, Otsukakubo-machi, Tokyo, Japan. [Miocene & Pliocene Pelecypoda, Gastropoda,
  Scaphopoda, of Japan (Yes)]
AOYAGI, Hyoji. Kyokasho-ka, Monbu-sho, Chiyodo-ku, Tokyo, Japan. [Pisces of Indo-Pa-
  cific coral reefs (Yes); of inland waters of Asia (Yes)]
APOSTOLESCU, V. Institut Francais du Petrole, 4 Place Bir-Hacheim, Rueil-Malmaison
  (S. & O.), France. [Crustacea: Mesozoic-Recent Ostracoda of France (Yes)]
APPELGATE, Shelton Pleasants. 5427 University Avenue, Chicago, Ill., U.S.A. [Mesozoic
  & Tertiary Pisces (Yes)] [Walker Museum, University of Chicago]
APPLIN, Mrs. Esther R. U.S. Geological Survey, 1202 1/2 N. State Street, Jackson 2,
  Miss., U.S.A. [Cretaceous & Eocene smaller Foraminifera of s.e. U.S. (No)]
APT, Dr. Walter. Nematology Section, Western Washington Experiment Station, Puyallup,
  Wash., U.S.A. [Plant parasitic & saprophytic Nematoda of N. America (Yes)] [U.S.
  Department of Agriculture]
* ARAGÃO, H. B. Departmento de Entomologia, Instituto Oswaldo Cruz, Caixa Postal 926,
  Rio de Janeiro, Brazil. [Acarina]
ARAI, Mr. Hisao P. Department of Zoology, University of California, Los Angeles 24, Calif.,
  U.S.A. [Trematoda: marine Digenea of n. e. Pacific (Yes)]
ARAMBOURG, Prof. C., Directeur Honoraire, Laboratoire de Paléontologie, 13 Place Val-
  hubert, Paris (V), France. [Paleozoic & Mesozoic Pisces & Mammalia of Africa
  (Yes)]
* ARAMBOURG, Y. 37 Boulevard de Grenelle, Paris (XV), France. [Coleoptera]
de ARAMBURU, A. Alonso. See ALONSO DE ARAMBURU, A. S.

* ARAMBURU, Raúl H. Museo de Ciencias Naturales, Paseo del Bosque, La Plata, Argentina. [Recent & Fossil Mammalia]

ARAUJO, R. L. Instituto Biologico, Caixa Postal 7.119, São Paulo, Brazil. [Hymenoptera: social wasps; Isoptera; of W. Hemisphere (Yes)]

* ARCANGELI, Dr. Alceste. Istituto di Zoologia della Universitá, Via Academia Albertina 17, Torino, Italy. [Crustacea: Isopoda]

ARCHER, Allan F. Biology Department, Box 160, Union University, Jackson, Tenn., U.S.A. [Araneae: Argiopidae, Mimetidae, of Neotropics, Ethiopian, Indopacific, Nearctic (Yes); Crustacea: Decapoda: Grapsidae, Gecarcinidae, Ocypodidae of Neotropics (No); Gastropoda: Camaenidae, Cepoliidae, Polygyridae of Nearctic & Neotropics (No)]

ARDÖ, Dr. Paul. Entomologiska Avdelningen, Universitetets Zoologiska Institution, Lund, Sweden. [Diptera: Diopsidae of World (No); shore flies of World (No)]

ARDOIN, P. 20, rue du Casino, Arcachon, Gironde, France. [Coleoptera: Tenebrionidae of N.& S. America (No); of Africa, Europe, Madagascar, India, Malaisie (Yes)]

ARELLANO, A.R.V. Instituto Geologico de Mexico, Oficina de Estratigrafia, Apartado 19066, Mexico 4, D. F., Mexico. [Mammalia: fossil Proboscidea Cenozoic mammals of N. America, espec. Mexico]

de la ARENA y FERNANDEZ, Julio. Department of Morphology & Genetics, School of Sciences, University of Habana, Habana, Cuba. [Protozoa: f-w. amoebae of Cuba (No)]

AREVAD, Kr. Statens Skadedyrlaboratorium, Springforbi, Denmark. [Entotrophi of n.Europe (No)]

ARGAÑARÁS, Dr. Jorge. Libertad 912, Santiago del Estero, Argentina. [Hymenoptera: Psammocharidae of S. America (No)]

ARIAS, C., Dr. Sergio. Museo Historia Natural La Salle, Apartado 681, Caracas, Venezuela. [Terr. & f-w. Mollusca: Helicinidae of Venezuela; Pomatiasidae of V.; Cyclophoridae of V. & Trinidad; Ampullariidae of V. & T.; Pleuroceridae of V.; Thiaridae of V.; Lymnaeidae of V., Physidae of V.; Planorbidae, Succinidae of V.; Pupillidae of V., T., Colombia; Vitrinidae of V.; Camaenidae of V., Strophocheilidae of V., T.; Orthalicidae of V.; Clausiliidae of V.; Urocoptidae of V.; Streptaxidae of V., T.; Veronicellidae of V. (Yes)] [Fundación La Salle de Ciencias Naturales]

ARKELL, W. J. (Cambridge, England; Ammonites) Deceased.

* ARLÉ, Dr. R. Museo Nacional, Quinta da Boa Vista, Rio de Janeiro, Brazil. [Hymenoptera]

ARMSTRONG, Augustus K. Department of Geology, University of Cincinnati, Cincinnati 21, Ohio, U.S.A. [Mississippian Foraminifera: endothyroids (Yes); Mississippian Brachiopoda (Yes); Mississippian Blastoidea (No)]

* ARMSTRONG, John C. 1165 Fifth Avenue, New York 29, N.Y., U.S.A. [Crustacea: Decapoda of World]

ARMSTRONG, J. W. T. "Cullingera", Nyngan, N.S.W., Australia. [Coleoptera: Helodidae, Dascillidae, Psephenidae, Ptilodactylidae, of World (Yes); Dermestidae, Tenebrionoidea, Colydioidea, of Australia (Yes)]

ARNAL, Dr. Robert E. Department of Physical Science, San Jose State College, San Jose 14, Calif., U.S.A. [Cretaceous to Recent Foraminifera of California (Yes)]

* ARNAU, Prof. J.M. Almirante Brown 568, Buenos Aires, Argentina. [Coleoptera: Cerambycidae]

ARNAUD, Mr. Paul H., Jr. Bureau of Entomology, 1220 "N" Street, Sacramento 14, Calif., U.S.A. [Diptera: Tachinidae of N. & S. America (Yes)]

* ARNE, P., Directeur, Musée de la Mer à Biarritz, Villa Haliotis, Guethary (B.-P.), France. [Aves]

ARNETT, Dr. Ross H., Jr. Department of Biology, Catholic University of America, Washington 17, D.C., U.S.A. [Onychophora of World (Yes); Coleoptera: Oedemeridae of World (Yes); Elateridae of Neotropics (No)]

ARNHOLD, F.R. Route 3, Chippewa Falls, Wis., U.S.A. [Lepidoptera: Rhopalocera of N. America (No); Heterocera: g. Catocala of World (Yes)]

ARNOLD, Mr. D.C. Department of Zoology, University College, Singleton Park, Swansea, Wales. [Pisces: Carapidae of Atlantic & Indo-Pacific (Yes); Holothurioidea of n.e. Atlantic & Mediterranean (No)]

ARNOLD, Dr. George. National Museum of Southern Rhodesia, P. O. Box 240, Bulawayo, Southern Rhodesia. [Hymenoptera: Sphecidae of Ethiopian (No)]

ARNOLD, Prof. John G., Jr. Department of Medical Technology, Loyola University, New Orleans 18, La., U.S.A. [Trematoda & Cestoda of fishes & rabbits of U.S. (No)]

ARNOLD, John R. (Stockton, Calif.) Not now active in taxonomy.

ARNOLD, Dr. Zach M. Museum of Paleontology, University of California, Berkeley 4, Calif., U.S.A. [Recent Foraminifera: Allogromiidae (Yes); fossil (Possibly)]

* ARNOLDI, Dr. L.V. Zoological Institute, Academy of Science, Leningrad 164, U.S.S.R. [Coleoptera: Curculionidae]

* ARNOULD, Dr. Michel. Société Geologique de France, 28 rue Serpente, Paris (VI), France. [Fossil invertebrates]

ARNOULD-SAGET, Mme. 80 Allée K Jules Verne, La Celle Saint Cloud, (S. & O.), France. [Jurassic Ammonitoidea (No)]

* ARNOULT, J. Muséum National d'Histoire Natural, 57 rue Cuvier, Paris (V), France. [Reptilia]

ARTHUR, Dr. Don R. Department of Zoology, King's College, Strand, London, W. C. 2, England. [Acarina: Ixodoidea: g. Ixodes of World (Yes); g. Dermacentor of Europe & Asia (Yes)]

ARTUSY, Prof. Raymond L. Department of Geology, New York University, Washington Square College, New York, N. Y., U. S. A. [Crustacea: Tertiary Ostracoda (No); Eocene Ostracoda (Yes); Cretaceous to Recent small Foraminifera (No)]

* ARVY, Dr. Lucie. Laboratoire d'Anatomie et d'Histologie Comparées, Sorbonne, 1 rue Victor Cousin, Paris (V), France. [Bryozoa]

* ASADOV, Cand. Biol. Sc. S. L. Zoological Institute of the Academy of Sciences of Azerbaijan S. S. R., Lokbatanskoe Highway, I, Baku, Azerbaijan, U. S. S. R. [Nematoda of animals of U. S. S. R.]

ASAHINA, Dr. Syoziro. Totsuka-3 chome, 123, Shinjuku-ku, Tokyo, Japan. [Recent & fossil Odonata of Asia (Yes); Neuroptera, excl. Chrysopidae & Hemerobiidae, of n. e. Asia (Yes); Orthoptera: Grylloblattoidea & Blattaria of Japan (Yes)] [Department of Medical Entomology, National Institute of Health]

ASANO, Dr. Kiyoshi. Institute of Geology & Paleontology, Tôhoku Daigaku, Katahira-chô, Sendai City, Japan. [Cretaceous-Recent Foraminifera of Japan (Yes); Tertiary-Recent of Pacific (Yes)]

* ASANUMA, Kiyoshi, Chief of Entomology Section, Research Institute for Natural Resources, Hyakunin-chô, Shinjuku-ku, Tokyo, Japan. [Diptera: Culicidae]

ASH, Mr. Charles. Arizona Fertilizer Inc., P. O. Box 2191, Phoenix, Ariz., U. S. A. [Hemiptera: Tingidae & Piesmidae of s. w. U. S. (Yes)]

ASH, Dr. J. S. Game Research Station, Burgate Manor, Fordingbridge, Hants, England. [Diptera: Hippoboscidae: g. Ornithomyia of Europe (Yes)]

* ASHBY, C. F. 33 Dan Street, Graceville, Queensl., Australia. [Diptera: Syrphidae]

ASHE, G. H. (Colyton, England; Coleoptera) Not now active in taxonomy.

ASHE, William A. (Harbel, Liberia; Acarina) Not now active in taxonomy.

ASHWORTH, Edwin T. International Petroleum Co., Talara, Peru. [Paleocene & Eocene Foraminifera of Peru (Yes); Pennsylvanian Fusulinidae of Texas (No)]

* d'ASSIGNIES, S. Muséum National d'Histoire Naturelle, 3 Place Valhubert, Paris (V), France. [Fossil Vertebrates]

d'ASSIS-FONSECA, E. See FONSECA, E. A.

ASTROVA, G. G. Paleontological Inst., Academy of Sciences, Leninsky Prospect 33, Moscow W-71, U. S. S. R. [Ordovician-Silurian Bryozoa of U. S. S. R. (Yes)]

* ATHEARN, Herbert D. Address unknown. (Pelecypoda: Unionidae)

ATKINS, Dr. Daphne. The Marine Laboratory, Citadel Hill, Plymouth, Devon, England. [Crustacea: Brachyura: g. Pinnotheres of Britain (No); Entoprocta: Loxosomatidae of Britain (No); Brachiopoda of n. e. Atlantic (Yes)]

ATKINS, Dr. E. L. Department of Entomology, University of California, Riverside, Calif., U. S. A. [Lepidoptera of World (No); larval stages from N. America (Yes)]

* ATKINSON, Kathleen Muriel. Entomology Department, National Agricultural Advisory Service, Government Buildings, Lawnswood, Leeds, 16, England. [Nematoda]

ATODA, Prof. Kenji. Department of Biology, Tôhoku University, Kawauchi Branch, Kawauchi, Sendai City, Miyagi Pref., Japan. [Actiniaria of n. Japan (No)]

ATTIAH, Hassan H. Entomological Section, Ministry of Agriculture, Dokky, Egypt. [Acarina: Tetranychidae, Tenuipalpidae, Eriophyidae, Tyroglyphidae, of Egypt (Yes)]

* ATTLEE, H. G. 4, Combermere Road, St. Leonards-on-Sea, Sussex, England. [Odonata]

ATTRIDGE, Mrs. Mildred. 270 Third Street, Midland, Ont., Canada. [Crustacea: Marine Copepoda of N. America (Yes)]

ATYEO, Warren T. Department of Entomology, University of Kansas, Lawrence, Kans., U. S. A. [Acarina: Bdellidae & Calyptostomidae, of World (Yes)]

ATZ, James W. (New York, N. Y.; Pisces) Not now active in taxonomy.

d'AUBENTON, F. Laboratoire des Pêches d'Autre Mer, 57 Rue Cuvier, Paris (V), France. [F-w. Pisces of E. Africa (Yes) [Muséum National d'Histoire Naturelle]

AUBER, Jacques, Assistant au P. C. B., Laboratoire de Biologie Animale, 12 rue Cuvier, Paris (V), France. [Neuroptera: of France (Yes); of Madagascar (No)]

AUBER, Mr. L. 7 bis Avenue des Ailantes, Saint-Maur (Seine), France. [Coleoptera: Scarabaeidae: Coprinae of World (Yes)]

* AUBER, Mme. M. Laboratoire d'Anatomie Comparée, Sorbonne, 1 rue Victor Cousin, Paris (V), France. [Arachnida]

AUBERT, Dr. J. Musée Zoologique, Lausanne, Switzerland. [Plecoptera of Europe, Asia, S. America (Yes); Ephemeroptera of Europe (No)]

AUBERT, Jacques-F. Laboratoire d'Evolution des Etres Organises, Faculté des Sciencés, 105 Blvd. Raspail, Paris (VI), France. [Hymenoptera: Ichneumonidae of Europe (Yes)]; Lepidoptera: Geometridae: Larentiinae of Europe & c. Asia (Yes)]
* AUBERT, Prof. S. F. Licencié des Sciences, Yverdon, Switzerland. [Fossil Mammalia]
AUDCENT, H. (Diptera) Died 1948.
* AUDIBERT, M. 6 Avenue Antoinette, La Garenne-Colombes (Seine), France. [Coleoptera]
AUDY, Dr. J.R. Institute for Medical Research, Kuala Lumpur, Malaya. [Acarina: Trombiculidae of Old World excl. U. S. S. R. (Yes)]
AUERBACH, Dr. Stanley I. 125 W. Vanderbilt Drive, Oak Ridge, Tenn., U. S. A. [Chilopoda: Geophilidae, Lithobiidae, Scolopendridae, of N. America, Africa, Europe (Yes)] [Oak Ridge National Laboratory]
AUFFENBERG, Mr. Walter. Biological Sciences Curriculum Studies, Hale Science Bldg., University of Colorado, Boulder, Colo., U. S. A. [Cenozoic Reptilia, espec. snakes, & Amphibia, espec. urodeles, of N. America & West Indies (Yes)]
* AUGUSTA, J. Geological Faculty, Universita Karlova, Albertov 6, Praha II, Czechoslovakia. [Fossil Mammalia]
AUGUSTON, Mr. G. F. 820 South Street, Madera, Calif., U. S. A. [Siphonaptera of N. America (Yes); Acarina: Ixodidae & Argasidae of N. America (No)]
AURICH, Dr. Horst Joachim. Biologische Anstalt Helgoland, (24 b) List, Sylt, Germany. [Coelenterata: Medusae & Crustacea: Copepoda of N. Atlantic (Yes); Zooplankton (No)]
AUSLÄNDER, D. Muzeul National de Istorie Naturala "Grigore Antipa", Kisselef No. 1, Bucureşti III, Rumania. [Mammalia of Rumania & Europe (Yes)]
* AUSTIN, M. D. Address unknown. (Acarina)
AUSTIN, Dr. Oliver L., Jr. Florida State Museum, Gainesville, Fla., U. S. A. [Aves of N. & C. America & e. Asia (Yes)]
* AUTARD, Luis F. Sarmiento 805, Santa Lucia, San Juan, Argentina, [Lepidoptera]
AUTRUM, Prof. H. Zoologisches Institut der Universität, Luisenstrasse 14, München 2, Germany. [Hirudinea (Yes)]
* AVELINO, Dr. Barrio. Inst. Bact. Malbran, Minist. Salud Publica, Buenos Aires, Argentina. [Amphibia: Physalaemus]
AVES, Mr. C. A. Gulf Oil Corp., 5311 Kirby Drive, Houston 5, Texas, U. S. A. [Recent Foraminifera of Gulf Cst. (Yes); Pleistocene, Pliocene, Miocene Foraminifera of Gulf Cst. (Yes); Oligocene (No)]
AVNIMELECH, Dr. M., Professor of Paleontology and Historical Geology, Hebrew University, Jerusalem, Israel. [Recent & Quaternary Gastropoda of Middle East (Yes); Tertiary Pteropoda of Mediterranean (Yes); Cretaceous & Tertiary Serpulida (Yes); Cretaceous & Tertiary Nautiloidea (No); Cretaceous & Tertiary teeth of Selachia (Yes)]
AX, Dr. Peter. Zoologisches Institut. der Universität, Hegewischstrasse 3, Kiel, Germany. [Marine Turbellaria of Europe (No); Archiannelida: Nerillidae of World (Yes)]
* AXTELL, Harold. Department of Ornithology, Buffalo Museum of Science, Buffalo, N. Y., U. S. A. [Aves]
AXTELL, Mr. Ralph W. Department of Biology, East Texas State College, Commerce, Tex., U. S. A. [Reptilia: Lacertilia of N. & C. America (Yes); Serpentes of N. & C. America (Yes); Amphibia: Anura of s. U. S. & Mexico (Yes)]
AYALA C., Biol. Agustin. Apartado Postal 24706, Mexico 11, D. F., Mexico. [Fossil Foraminifera of Mexico (Yes); microfossils of Mexico (Yes)]
AYRES, W. S. Lakes Entrance, Victoria, Australia. [Marine shells of Australia (Yes)]
* AZEVEDO MARTINS, Dr. Emmanoel. Departmento de Moluscos, Museu Nacional, Quinta da Boa Vista, Rio de Janeiro, Brazil. [Mollusca; fossil invertebrates]
AZUMA, Prof. Masao. 80 Araebisu-chô, Nishinomiya, Hyogo Pref., Japan. [Hymenoptera: Formicidae of Japan & Palearctic (Yes); Mollusca, shells of Japan (Yes); Lepidoptera of Japan (Yes)]
AZZAROLI, Prof. Augusto. See Addenda.

* BABA, Dr. Kikutaró. Biological Institute, Osaka Gakugei Daigaku, Tennoji-ku, Osaka, Japan. [Opisthobranchiate Mollusca]
BABA, Mr. Yoshiyuki. 3569, 6 chôme, Itabashi-ku, Tokyo, Japan. [Hymenoptera: Formicidae of World]
BABBITT, Lewis H. Petersham, Mass., U. S. A. [Reptilia & Amphibia of N. America (Yes)] [Herpetology Department, Worcester Natural History Society]
BABERO, Dr. Bert B. Department of Zoology, Fort Valley State College, Fort Valley, Ga., U. S. A. [Trematodes of Canidae & Mustelidae of Georgia & Alaska (Yes)]
BABIY, Dr. Peter. Salzburg-Parsch, Rettenpacherstrasse 17, Salzburg, Austria. [Hymenoptera: g. Bombus, g. Psithyrus, Pompilidae (Yes)]
*BABNIK, P. Physiological Institute, Zaloska c. 4, Ljubljana 5, Yugoslavia [Coelenterata]
BACCETTI, Dott. B. Stazione di Entomologia Agraria, Via Romana 15, Firenze, Italy. [Orthoptera of Palearctic (Yes)]

* BACELAR, Dr. Amelia. Museu Nacional de Historia Natural, Museu Bocage, Lisboa, Portugal [Arachnida]

BĂCESCU, Dr. Mihai, Directeur de la Section Carcinologique et Ichthyologique du Musée, Muzeul National de Istorie Naturala "Grigori Antipa", Sos. Kisselef 1, Bucuresti III, Rumania. [Crustacea: Mysidacea, Apseudidae, Cumacea, of Mediterranean (Yes); Decapoda, Cirolanidae, g. Cobitis, of Mediterranean (Yes)]

BACHMAIER, Franz. Entomologische Abteilung, Sammlung des Bayerischen Staates, Menzingerstrasse 67, München 19, Germany. [Hymenoptera: Chalcidoidea: Leucospidae, Chalcididae, Ormyridae, Perilampidae, Eucharitidae, Encyrtidae, Elyrelmidae, Thysanidae, Aphelinidae, Elasmidae of Palearctic (Yes); Eulophidae: g. Tetrastichus of Palearctic (No); Ichneumonoidea: Ichneumonidae: g. Gelis of Palearctic (No)]

BACHMANN, Dr. F. CIBA Aktiengesellschaft, Basel, Switzerland. [Homoptera: Diaspidinae of Europe (Yes)]

BACHMAYER, Dr. Friedrich. Naturhistorisches Museum, Burgring 7, Wien I, Austria. [Triassic to Pleistocene Crustacea: Decapoda of Europe (Yes); Isopoda of same (No)]

* BACIGALUPO, Dr. Juan. Jefe del Instituto de Parasitologia, Facultad de Ciencias Medicas, Paraguay 2155, Buenos Aires, Argentina. [Parasites]

BACKLUND, Dr. H. O. Villa Rukwa, Alster, Sweden. [Oligochaeta: Lumbricidae of Scandinavia (Yes); Enchytraeidae of Scandinavia (No)]

BACKUS, Dr. Richard H. Woods Hole Oceanographic Institution, Woods Hole, Mass., U. S. A. [Sharks of Atlantic Ocean (Yes); bathypelagic fishes of Atlantic (No)]

BACON, Dr. John. 1136 Mulberry, Ottawa, Kans., U. S. A. [Hemiptera: Veliidae: g. Rhagovelia of W. Hemisphere (Yes)] [Ottawa University]

BACON, Mr. Marion. 411 S. 41st Street, Apartment 3, Omaha 31, Nebr., U. S. A. [Diptera: Culicidae; other biting Diptera; Siphonaptera; all of w. U. S. (No)] [University of Nebraska, College of Medicine]

* BADANIN, Dr. Vet. Sci. Prof. N. V. Uzbek Institute of Agriculture, K. Marx Street 83, Samarkand, U. S. S. R. [Helminths of camels of U. S. S. R.]

BADCOCK, Miss Ruth M. University College of North Staffordshire, Keele, Staffs, England. [Trichoptera: Hydropsychidae, espec. larvae, of Europe (Yes)]

BADEN POWELL, Dr. A. W. P. O. Box 9027, Newmarket, Auckland, New Zealand. [Mollusca of Antarctic & Subantarctic (Yes); terr. & marine Mollusca of N. Z. (Yes); Tertiary Mollusca of N. Z. (Yes)] [Auckland Institute & Museum]

* BADEN-POWELL, D. F. W. University Museum, Oxford, England. [Fossil & Recent Mollusca]

BADER, Dr. Carl. Naturhistorisches Museum, Augustinergasse 2, Basel, Switzerland. [Acarina: Hydrachnellae of Switzerland, Alps, Africa (Yes)]

BADER, Dr. Robert. Department of Zoology, University of Illinois, Urbana, Ill., U. S. A. [Miocene Mammalia: Equidae: g. Parahippus & g. Merychippus (Yes); Pleistocene peccary, tapir, llama, g. Peromyscus (all Yes)]

BADONNEL, Prof. André. 4 rue Ernest Lavisse, Paris (XII), France. [Psocoptera of World (No)]

BAER, Dr. Jean G. Institute de Zoologie, Université de Neuchâtel, Neuchâtel, Switzerland. [Cestoda, Trematoda, other parasites of World (Yes)]

BAETA NEVES, Prof. C. M. L. Instituto Superior de Agronomia, Entomologia Agricola e Forestal, Tapada da Ajuda, Lisboa, Portugal. [Insects & mites of stored products of Portugal & Portuguese Africa (Yes)]

BAGDASARIAN, A. T. Zoological Institute, Academy of Sciences of Armenian S. S. R., Avanskoje shosse 18, Erevan, U. S. S. R. [Acarina: Tetranychidae & Bryobiidae of Armenia (Yes)]

* BAGGE, Mr. O. Danmarks Fiskeri og Havundersøgelser, Charlottenlund Slot, Charlottenlund, Denmark. [Fishes]

* BAGNALL, Sir Richard S. 2 W. Cromwell Road, London, S. W. 7, England. [Collembola]

BĂGUENA CORELLA, Dr. L. Instituto Español de Entomologia, Hipodromo, Madrid, Spain. [Coleoptera of Iberian Pen. (Yes)]

BAHAMONDE NAVARRO, Prof. J. N., Jefe de Laboratorio de Hidrobiologia, Museo Nacional de Historia Natural, Casilla 787, Santiago, Chile. [Crustacea: Decapoda of w. cst. S. America (Yes)]

BAHAMONDES, Dr. Luis. Juan B. Justo 162 Dto. 4º IO P., Godoy Cruz, Mendoza, Argentina. [Homoptera: Aphidoidea; Thysanoptera; both of Argentina (Yes)] [Dirección General de Sanidad Vegetal, Ministerio de Agricultura de la Nación, Facultad Ciencias Agrarias, Cátedra Entomologia Agricola Investigador]

* BAI, Sye-o. Fisheries Research Institute, Ministry of Fisheries, Peking, Peoples Republic of China. [Crustacea: Copepoda]

BAIJAL, H. N. Zoology Department, Agra College, Agra, India. [Collembola, espec. Onychiurinae, Hypogastrurinae, Neanurinae, Entomobryidae, Isotomidae, of India (Yes); Odonata: Anisoptera of India (Yes); Dermaptera of India (No)]

112

BAILEY, Joseph R. Department of Zoology, Duke University, Durham, N. C., U. S. A.
[Reptilia & Amphibia of N. C., s. e. U. S., trop, America (Yes); Colubrid snakes (Yes);
Pisces of N. C. (Yes)]
*BAILEY, Col. John Wendell. 27 Willway Road, Richmond 26, Va., U. S. A. [Reptilia & Am-
phibia of Virginia]
BAILEY, Dr. Norman S., Chairman, Department of Natural Science, Bradford Junior Col-
lege, Bradford, Mass., U. S. A. [Heteroptera: Tingidae of New England (Yes); Dip-
tera: Tabanidae of New England (No)]
BAILEY, Reeve M. Museum of Zoology, University of Michigan, Ann Arbor, Mich., U. S. A.
[F-w. Pisces of N. America (Yes)]
BAILEY, Prof. Stanley F. Department of Entomology, University of California, Davis,
Calif., U. S. A. [Thysanoptera of N. America (Yes)]
BAILLY-CHOUMARA, Dr. H. S. G. H. M. P., Bobo Dioulasso, Upper Volta (French West Af-
rica). [Diptera: Anophelinae of Ethiopian (Yes)] [Office de Recherche Scientifique
et Technique Outre-Mer]
BAILY, Dr. Joshua L., Jr. 4435 Ampudia Street, San Diego 3, Calif., U. S. A. [F-w. Mol-
lusca of w. U. S. (Yes)]
* BAINTON, Jack D. 1744 Camino Sierra, Bakersfield, Calif., U. S. A. [Fossil inverte-
brates]
BAIRD, Dr. Donald. Department of Geology, Princeton University, Princeton, N. J., U. S. A.
[Carbonif. to Triassic reptile & amphibian footprints (Yes); Carbonif. Amphibia: Le-
pospondyli (Yes); Carbonif. Amphibia: Labyrinthodontia & Reptilia (No)]
BAIRD, Mr. James. Norman Bird Sanctuary, Third Beach Road, Middletown, R. I., U. S. A.
[Aves: Passerines of N. America (Yes)]
BAIRSTOW, L. Department of Palaeontology, British Museum (Natural History), Cromwell
Road, London, S. W. 7, England. [Fossil Dibranchiata; Fossil Echinoderma, espec.
of England]
BAISAS, Francisco E. 828 Dos Costillas, Sampaloc, Manila, Philippines. [Diptera: Culici-
dae of Oriental (Yes)] [Division of Malaria Control, Department of Health]
BAITSELL, Dr. G. A. (New Haven, Conn.; Protozoa) Not now active in taxonomy.
* BAJANOV, V. S. Zoological Institute, Academy of Sciences of the Kazakh S. S. R., Schev-
chenko str., Alma-Ata, U. S. S. R. [Fossil Mammalia]
BAJÁRI, Mrs. Elizabeth, Curator of Hymenoptera, Hungarian National Museum, Baross u.
13, Budapest VIII, Hungary. [Hymenoptera: Ichneumonidae of Hungary & c. Europe
(Yes)]
BAKER, Dr. A. D. In charge, Nematode Investigations, Science Service Bldg., Carling Ave-
nue, Ottawa, Ont., Canada. [Plant-parasitic & soil Nematoda: Tylenchoidea, Aphe-
lenchoidea, Rhabditoidea, Dorylaimoidea; of N. America (Yes)]
* BAKER, A. W. Address unknown. (Coleoptera)
BAKER, D. B. 67 Cheam Road, Ewell, Surrey, England. [Hymenoptera: Apoidea excl. Ha-
lictidae of Palearctic & India (Yes); Anthophoridae of Africa (Yes)]
BAKER, Dr. Edward W. Division of Insects, U. S. National Museum, Washington 25, D. C.,
U. S. A. [Acarina: Agricultural mites of World (No)] [U. S. Department of Agriculture]
BAKER, Dr. Horace B., Acting Chairman, Zoological Laboratory, University of Pennsyl-
vania, Philadelphia 4, Penna., U. S. A. [Mollusca, espec. terr. Pulmonata, of World
(No)]
BAKER, Mr. Nelson W. 279 Sherwood Drive, Santa Barbara, Calif., U. S. A. [Lepidoptera:
Heterocera of Calif. (Yes); molluscan shells of Calif. cst. (Yes); marine inverte-
brates of c. Calif. cst. (Yes)] [Santa Barbara Museum of Natural History]
BAKER, Mr. R. (London, England; fossil Arthropoda) Not now active in taxonomy.
BAKER, Rollin H. The Museum, Michigan State University, East Lansing, Mich., U. S. A.
[Mammalia of N. & C. America (Yes); Aves of Micronesia & U. S. (Yes)]
* BAKKE, Alf. Zoologisk Museum, Sarsgatan 1, Oslo, Norway. [Hymenoptera]
BAKKENDORF, O. Bogtrykkerrej 26, København, NV, Denmark. [Hymenoptera: Mymari-
dae & Trichogrammatidae of n. Palearctic (Yes)]
* BAKR, Mr. Abu. Museum of Comparative Zoology, Cambridge 38, Mass., U. S. A. [Fossil
vertebrates; Rotifera]
* BAL, D. V. Department of Zoology, Institute of Science, Mayo Road, Fort, Bombay 1,
India. [Acarina]
BALACHOWSKY, A. Institut Pasteur, 25 rue Dr. Roux, Paris (XV), France. [Homoptera:
Coccoidea of Palearctic, Ethiopian, Neotropical (No); Diaspididae of same regions
(Yes)]
BALAMUTH, Dr. William. Department of Zoology, University of California, Berkeley 4,
Calif., U. S. A. [Protozoa: f-l. & parasitic Amoebae & Ciliata of World (Yes)]
*BĂLĂRESCU, Petru. Institutul de Cercetări Piscicole, Bul. A. Ipătescu, Bucuresti, Ru-
mania. [Pisces]
BALASHOV, J. S. Zoological Institute, Academy of Sciences, Leningrad Centre, U. S. S. R.
[Acarina: Ixodoidea of U. S. S. R. (Yes)]

BALÁT, Dr. František. Minská 14, Brno 16, Czechoslovakia. [Mallophaga of Europe (Yes)] [Czechoslovak Academy of Sciences]
BALAZUC, Dr. J. 16, Avenue de Lowendal, Paris (XV), France. [Coleoptera, esp. cavernicole, of Cévennes Mts., France (No); Crustacea: Amphipoda of caves of w. Europe (No)]
* BALAVOINE, P. Department de Geologie, Museum National d'Histoire Naturelle, 61 rue de Buffon, Paris (V), France. [Bryozoa]
BALCELLS R., Dr. E. Laboratorio de Fisiología, Facultad de Ciencias, Universidad de Barcelona, Barcelona, Spain. [Reptilia, Amphibia, Mammalia, of Iberian Pen. (Yes)] [Consejo Superior de Investigaciones Cientificas]
BALCH, Robert F. 1107 E. Glendale Avenue, Appleton, Wis., U.S.A. [Plecoptera, Trichoptera, Ephemeroptera (No)] [The Institute of Paper Chemistry]
BALDASSERONI, Prof. Dott. V. Museo Zoologico de "La Specola", Via Romana 17, Firenze, Italy. [Chaetognatha of World; Oligochaeta: Lumbricidae of Europe]
BALDAUF, Dr. Richard J. Department of Wildlife Management, Agricultural & Mechanical College of Texas, College Station, Tex., U.S.A. [Amphibia: Bufonidae of World (No)]
* BALDERSTON, Mr. Buele C. Address unknown. (Arachnida)
BALDWIN, Prof. Ewart M. Department of Geology, University of Oregon, Eugene, Ore., U.S.A. [Eocene & Oligocene Mollusca of Oregon Coast Range (No)]
BALDWIN, P.H. Department of Zoology, Colorado State University, Fort Collins, Colo., U.S.A. [Aves: Picinae of Rocky Mts. (Yes); g.Acanthis of Alaska (Yes); Drepaniidae of Hawaii (Yes)]
BALDWIN, Mr. Wayne J. Department of Zoology, University of California, Los Angeles 24, Calif., U.S.A. [Pisces: Tetraodontidae & Carcharhinidae of e. Pacific (Yes)]
* BALECH, Prof. Enrique. Casilla 64, Necochea, Argentina. [Planktonic Protozoa] [Colegio Nacional de Necochea]
BALFOUR-BROWNE, Prof. F. Brocklehirst, Collin, Dumfries, Scotland. [Aquatic Coleoptera of Britain (No)]
BALFOUR-BROWNE, Mr. J. Department of Entomology, British Museum (Natural History), Cromwell Road, London, SW.7, England. [Coleoptera: Hydrophilidae, Dytiscidae, Curculionidae: Apioninae of World (Yes)]
BALINSKY, Prof. Dr. B.I. Department of Zoology, University of the Witwatersrand, Johannesburg, Union of South Africa. [Odonata & Plecoptera of s.Africa (Yes)]
BALK, C. Lochman. See LOCHMAN BALK, C.
* BALKE, N.P.W. Jericholaan 64a, Rotterdam, Netherlands. [Crustacea: Malacostraca]
BALL, George E. Department of Entomology, University of Alberta, Edmonton, Alta., Canada. [Coleoptera: Carabidae of N. America (Yes)]
BALL, Gordon H. Department of Zoology, University of California, Los Angeles 24, Calif., U.S.A. [Protozoa: Gregarines of marine Crustacea of World (No)]
BALL, Dr. H.W. Department of Palaeontology, British Museum (Natural History), Cromwell Road, London, S.W.7, England. [Mesozoic-Tertiary Decapod Crustacea of World (Yes); Paleozoic-Tertiary Annelida of World (Yes); Silurian Graptolithida (Yes)]
BALL, Mr. Orville P., Jr. Supervisor of Recreation (Fish & Game), Water Department, City of San Diego, San Diego, Calif., U.S.A. [Pisces: Salmonidae of N. America (Yes); marine fish larvae of e. Pacific Ocean & N. Hemisphere (No)]
BALL, S.C. (New Haven, Conn.; Birds) Died August 16, 1956.
BALOGH, János I. Institutum Zoosystematicum Universitatis, Puskin-u, 3, Budapest VIII, Hungary. [Terr. Acarina of Europe (No); of Africa & S. America (Yes)]
BALON, Dr. Eugeniusz K. Ichtyologické Laboratorium SAV, Železná Studienka, Bratislava IX, Czechoslovakia. [F-w. fishes & larvae of Danube, Vistula, Oder (Yes)]
BALSEIRO, Lina Mercedes. c/o Texas Petroleum Co., Apartado 267, Caracas, Venezuela. [Miocene, Oligocene, Cretaceous smaller Foraminifera of n.S. America (No)]
BALSS, H. (München, Germany; Crustacea) Died September, 1957.
BALTAZAR, Dr. Clare R. Bureau of Plant Industry, Manila, Philippines. [Hymenoptera: Ichneumonidae of Philippines (Yes)]
BALTHASAR, Dr. Vladimir. Lublańská17, Praha II, Czechoslovakia. [Coleoptera: Scarabaeidae: Laparosticti, Coprophagi, Cetoniinae;of World (Yes); Hymenoptera: Aculeata, excl. Formicidae, espec. Sphecidae & Chrysididae of Palearctic (Yes)]
* BALTY, Prof. J.A. 123 Avenue Albert, Bruxelles, Belgium. [Coleoptera]
BAMFORTH, Stuart S. Zoology Department, Newcomb College of Tulane University, New Orleans 18, La., U.S.A. [Protozoa: f-l. Phytomastigina, excl. Chlamydomonas & Euglena, of U.S. Gulf Cst. (Yes)]
BĂNĂRESCU, Dr. Petru. Institutul de Cercetări Piscicole al României, Boulv. Ana Ipătescu 46, Bucureşti IV, Rumania. [Pisces: Cyprinidae: Gobioninae & g.Cobitis of Europe, Siberia, e.Asia (Yes); Cyprinidae & Cobitidae of Europe & Anatolia (Yes); Percidae of Europe & Siberia (Yes); Gobiidae of Black Sea (Yes); Crustacea: Copepoda: Diaptomidae of s.e. Europe (Yes)]

BANDEIRA, Luiz. (Veterinary) Av. Defensores de Chaves, No. 27-2 D, Lisboa, Portugal. [Hymenoptera: Vespinae of Portugal (Yes); Apinae of Portugal (No)]
* BANDY, Prof. Orville L. Department of Geology, University of Southern California, Los Angeles 7, Calif., U.S.A. [Protozoa: Recent & fossil Foraminifera]
BANE, Ray. Placid Oil Co., 1401 Carondelet Bldg., New Orleans, La., U.S.A. [Miocene & Oligocene Foraminifera of La. & Texas Gulf Coast (Yes)]
BANFIELD, A.W.F., Chief Mammalogist, Canadian Wildlife Service, Ottawa, Ont., Canada. [Mammalia: Artiodactyla: Cervidae: g. Rangifer of N. America (Yes)]
* BANG, A.P.B., Cand.Mag. Statens Skadedyrlaboratorium, Springforbi, Denmark. [Mammalia, Amphibia]
BANGHAM, Ralph V. Department of Biology, College of Wooster, Wooster, Ohio, U.S.A. [Parasites of f-w. Pisces of N. America (Yes); Acanthocephala of same (Yes)]
* BANK, G., Jr. Konig Williamstraat 36, Zaandam, Netherlands. [Lepidoptera: Macrolepidoptera]
BAŃKOWSKA, Mrs. Regina. Institute of Zoology, Polish Academy of Sciences, ul. Wilcza 64, Warszawa, Poland. [Diptera: Syrphidae & Conopidae of Europe (Yes)]
BANKS, Maxwell Robert. Department of Geology, University of Tasmania, Hobart, Tasmania. [Ordovician Coelenterata of Australia (Yes); Permian invertebrates of e. Australia (Yes); Fossil invertebrates of Tasmania (Yes)]　　　　　　　　・
BANKS, Richard C. Museum of Vertebrate Zoology, University of California, Berkeley 4, Calif., U.S.A. [Aves of N. America (No)]
BANNER, Dr. A.H. Department of Zoology, University of Hawaii, Honolulu 14, Hawaii. [Crustacea: Decapoda: Alpheidae of Indo-Pacific (Yes); Mysidacea of N. Pacific (Yes); Euphausiacea of n. Pacific (Yes)]
* BANNERMAN, David A. Address unknown. (Birds)
BANNER, Dr. F.T. The British Petroleum Co., Research Station, Cordbury Road, Sunbury on Thames, Middlesex, England. [Mesozoic - Cenozoic Foraminifera (Yes)]
BANNIKOV, Prof. Dr. A.G. Zoological Museum, Herzenstr. 6, Moscow, K-9, U.S.S.R. [Amphibia: Urodela & Anura of c. Asia (Yes); Mammalia: Artiodactyla: Cavicornia & Perissodactyla: Equidae; of c. Asia (Yes)]
BÄNNINGER, Max. Susenbergerstrasse 206, Zürich 6, Switzerland. [Coleoptera: Carabidae: Pamborini, Omophronini, Elaphrini, Siagonini, Scaritina, Pasimachina, of World (Yes)]
* BANNINK, Dr. D.D. c/o Weestra, Tiel (Guelder), Netherlands. [Fossil Foraminifera]
BANSE, Dr. K. Institut für Meereskunde der Universität Kiel, Hohenbergstrasse 2, Kiel, Germany. [Polychaeta of Europe & India (Yes); Polychaeta: Thoracogoneate Fabriciinae of World (Yes)]
BANTA, Mr. Benjamin H. Natural History Museum, Stanford University, Stanford, Calif., U.S.A. [Amphibia & Reptilia of w. U.S. & n. Mexico (Yes); f-w. Pisces of w. U.S. Great Basin (Yes)]
BAO-LING WU. See WU, Bao-ling.
BAPAT, Mr. S.V. Central Marine Fisheries, Research Sub-Station, 3rd Floor, Botawalla Chambers, Sir P.M. Road, Bombay 1, India. [Marine Pisces of Bay of Bengal, Arabian Sea, Indian Ocean (Yes)]
* BARAJON, Mario. Viale Brianza 26, Milano, Italy. [Coleoptera]
BARANOV, M. Not now active in taxonomy.
BARANOVA, Mrs. Zoja I. (Also as S.J. Baranova) Zoological Institute, Academy of Sciences, Leningrad 164, U.S.S.R. [Echinodermata of Polar Basin, n.w. Pacific, trop. Pacific, Antarctic Ocean (Yes)]
BARAT, Carol A. Muzeul de Istorie Naturală "Grigore Antipa", Secţia Paleontologie, Şos. Kisselef Nr. 1, Bucureşti 1, Rumania. [Fossils of Rumania (Yes)]
BARATTINI, Prof. Luis P. R. Masini 2932, Montevideo, Uruguay. [Homoptera: Auchenorhyncha of S. America (No)] [Museo Dámaso A. Larrañaga]
BARBAT, William Franklin. (San Francisco, Calif.; fossil Foraminifera) Not now active in taxonomy.
BARBER, Mr. H.G. Division of Insects, U.S. National Museum, Washington 25, D.C., U.S.A. [Hemiptera: Lygaeidae of New World] Died January 27, 1960.
BARBOSA, Dr. F.A.S. Instituto Aggeu Magalhaes, Caixa Postal 459, Recife, Pernambuco, Brazil. [Diptera: Heleidae: g. Culicoides of Neotropics (No); Mollusca: f-w. Planorbidae of Neotropics & Africa (Yes)]
BARBOSA, Prof. Maria Martha. Divisão de Geologia, Museu Nacional, Quinta da Boa Vista, Rio de Janeiro, Brazil. [Carboniferous Bryozoa (Yes); L. Miocene (Yes)]
* BARBOTIM, F. Licencié ès Sc. Nat. Contrôleur Service, 12 rue E. Renan, Rennes, France.[Hymenoptera]
BARBOUR, Dr. Roger M. 433 Clifton Avenue, Lexington, Ky., U.S.A. [Mammalia, Reptilia, Amphibia, of Kentucky (Yes)] [University of Kentucky]
BARCELO, J. Cuerda. See CUERDA BARCELO, J.

* BARE, Prof. Orlando Smith. College of Agriculture, University of Nebraska, Lincoln 3, Neb., U.S.A. [Hymenoptera]
BARENDRECHT, Dr. G. Zoological Laboratory, University of Amsterdam, Pl. Doklaan 44, Amsterdam C, Netherlands. [Hymenoptera: Symphyta of Palearctic (Yes); Diptera: Fungivoridae of Palearctic (Yes)]
BARGREN, Mr. William C. Department of Zoology, Comer Hall, Alabama Polytechnic Institute, Auburn, Ala., U.S.A. [Diptera: Culicidae of N.America (Yes); Calliphorinae & Pangoniinae of s.e.U.S. (Yes); Acarina: Ixodidae of s.e.U.S. (Yes)]
BARI, Bruno. Via Zezio 35, Como, Italy. [Coleoptera: Carabidae, Chrysomelidae, Curculionidae, of Italy (Yes); Scarabaeidae: Cetoniinae of World (Yes); Lepidoptera: g. Colias of World (Yes)]
BARKALOW, F.S., Jr. Department of Zoology, North Carolina State College, Raleigh, N.C., U.S.A. [Recent Mammalia of s.e.U.S. (Yes); Recent & fossil Sciurus niger of U.S. (Yes)]
BARKER, Mr. C.E. 27 Willcott Street, Mount Albert, Auckland, New Zealand. [Marine shells of Australia (No); terr. & marine shells of N.Z. (Yes)]
BARKER, Prof. D. Department of Zoology, University of Hong Kong, Hong Kong. [Crustacea: Thermosbaenacea of Mediterranean (Yes)]
BARKER, Mr. R.W. Shell Development Co., 3737 Bellaire Blvd., Houston, Tex., U.S.A. [Recent Foraminifera (Yes); Tertiary Foraminifera of Caribbean & Gulf Cst. (Yes); marine Gastropoda, excl. micro-forms (Yes); Mollusca of Caribbean & Gulf of Mexico]
BARLOW, Mr. George W. Department of Zoology, University of Illinois, Urbana, Ill., U.S.A. [Pisces: Gobioidea of e.Pacific (Yes); of World (No); Cyprinodontes of N. & S.America (No)]
BARNARD, J. Laurens. Beaudette Foundation for Biological Research, R. F.D. 1, Box 482, Solvang, Calif., U.S.A. [Crustacea: Recent Amphipoda: Gammaridae of e.Pacific ($3.50/hour); Tertiary - Recent Scleractinia of e.Pacific ($3.50/hour)]
BARNARD, Dr. K.H. South African Museum, Cape Town, Union of South Africa. [Marine & f-w. Crustacea: Phyllopoda, Cirripedia, Isopoda, Amphipoda, Decapoda, Stomatopoda, of S.Africa (Yes)]
BARNARD, Mr. Robert A.S. Department of Zoology, Sydney University, Sydney, N.S.W., Australia. [Araneae: Mygalomorphae, espec. Dipluridae of Australia (Yes)]
* BARNARD, T. 7 Telegraph Lane, Claygate, Surrey, England. [Fossil invertebrates]
BARNES, Allan M. Bureau of Vector Control, California Department of Public Health, 2151 Berkeley Way, Berkeley 4, Calif., U.S.A. [Diptera: Therevidae of World (Yes); Siphonaptera of N.America (No); of California (Yes)]
BARNES, B.D. P.O.Box 54, Umtali, Southern Rhodesia. [Lepidoptera of Southern Rhodesia (Yes)]
BARNES, Dr. H. Marine Station, Keppel Pier, Millport, Isle of Cumbrae, Scotland. [Crustacea: Cirripedia of World (Yes)] [Scottish Marine Biological Association]
BARNES, Dr. H.F. Rothamsted Experimental Station, Harpenden, Herts, England. [Diptera: Cecidomyidae of World] Died February 5, 1960.
BARNES, John W. Department of Biology, Wisconsin State College, Stevens Point, Wis., U.S.A. [Coleoptera & Hymenoptera of Wisconsin & Minnesota (No)]
BARNES, Ralph C. Communicable Disease Center Services, U.S. Public Health Service, Region VIII, 551 First National Bank Bldg., Denver 2, Colo., U.S.A. [Diptera: Culicidae of U.S. (Yes)]
BARNES, Robert D. Biology Department, Gettysburg College, Gettysburg, Penna., U.S.A. [Arachnida: Araneida of N.America (Yes)]
* BARNETT, Mr. Peter. Department of Zoology, University of Southampton, Southampton, England. [Crustacea: Copepoda]
BARNETT, Dr. S.F. East African Veterinary Research Organization, P.O.Box 32, Kikuyu, Kenya. [Protozoa: Sporozoa of vertebrates of E.Africa (Yes)]
BARNUM, Andrew H. Department of Entomology, Iowa State College, Ames, Iowa. [Orthoptera: Acrididae & Oedipodae of N.America (Yes); Acrididae of S.America (No)]
BARR, Dr. A. Ralph. California State Department of Public Health, 5545 E. Shields Avenue, Fresno 27, Calif., U.S.A. [Diptera: Culicidae of World (No); of N.America (Yes)]
BARR, William F. Department of Entomology, University of Idaho, Moscow, Idaho, U.S.A. [Coleoptera: Cleridae of N.America (Yes); Buprestidae of N.America (Yes)]
BARRACLOUGH FELL, H. See FELL, H. Barraclough.
BARRACLOUGH, William E. Fisheries Research Board of Canada, Pacific Biological Station, Nanaimo, B.C., Canada [Pisces: Scorpaenidae, g. Sebastodes of n.e.Pacific (Yes); Agonidae of n.e.Pacific (Yes)]
BARRATT, Peter R. 2 Blackwell Mill Cottages, Miller's Dale, Buxton, Derbyshire, England. [Collembola of Britain (Yes); Insecta of stored products of Britain (No)] [British Transport Commission]

116

BARRERA, Alfredo. Retorno 201-7B, Unidad Modelo, Mexico 13, D. F., Mexico. [Siphonaptera of N. & C. America (Yes); of S. America (No); Diptera: Culicidae of N. & C. America (No)] [Laboratorio de Parasitologia, Escuela Nacional de Ciencias Biológicas (I. P. N.)]

* BARRETO-REYES, Dr. Pablo. Instituto Carlos Finlay, Apartado Aereo 3950, Bogotá, Colombia. [Diptera: Culicidae]

BARRETT, James M. Biology Department, Marquette University, Milwaukee 3, Wis., U. S. A. [Protozoa: Heliozoa: Actinophryidae of World (No)]

BARRETTO, Prof. Mauro Pereira. Departmento de Parasitologia, Faculdade de Medicina, Ribeirao Preto, S. P., Brazil. [Diptera: Psychodidae & Tabanidae of Neotropics (Yes); Empididae of Neotropics (No)]

* BARRIOS, Miss Margot, Museo Geológico Nacional, Carrera, 15, No. 9-63, Bogotá, Colombia. [Fossil invertebrates]

* BARRO, Manuel. Address unknown. (Coleoptera)

* BARROETA, Luis Flores. Laboratorio de Helmintologia, Escuela Nacional de Ciencias Biológicas I. P. N., Prolongacion de Carpio, Mexico 4, D. F., Mexico. [Trematoda]

* BARROSO, Manuel Jeronimo. Universidad de Salamanca, Salamanca, Spain. [Rotifera]

* BARROS VALENZUELA, Raphael. Casilla 174, Linares, Chile. [Aves; f-w. Pisces]

BARRY, Dr. T. Albany Museum, Grahamstown, Union of South Africa. [Permian-Triassic (Karroo) Anomodontia of S. Africa (No)]

BARSUKOV, V. V. Zoological Institute, Academy of Sciences, Leningrad Centre, U. S. S. R. [Pisces: Anarhichadidae of N. Atlantic & N. Pacific (Yes)]

BARTENSTEIN, Dr. Helmut. c/o Mobil Oil A. G. in Deutschland, P. O. Box 110, (20a) Celle, Germany. [Jurassic & L. Cretaceous Foraminifera of World (Yes); fossil Foraminifera in general (No); marine & br-w. Holocene Foraminifera of Europe (Yes); Paleozoic marine & br-w. Foraminifera of Germany (Yes)]

BARTH, Dr. E. K. Zoological Museum, Sarsgatan 1, Oslo NO, Norway. [Aves of Norway (Yes); of Sweden & Denmark (No); land Mammalia of Norway (Yes)] [University of Oslo]

* BARTHA, Dr. Ferenc. Magyar Állami Földtani Intézet, Vorosilov-ut 14, Budapest XIV, Hungary. [Gastropoda]

BARTHEL, Dr. K. W. Bayerische Staatssammlung für Paläontologie und Historische Geologie, Richard Wagnerstrasse 10/11, München 2, Germany. [Mesozoic Cephalopoda: Ammonoidea of Bavaria (Yes)]

BARTLETT, H. A. Geology Department, University of Tasmania, P. O. Box 647 C, G. P. O., Hobart, Tasmania. [Permian Bryozoa: Fenestellidae of Tasmania (No)]

* de BARTOLOMÉ, J. F. M. Ranmoor Residential Chambers, 405 Fulwood Road, Sheffield 10, England. [Mollusca]

BARTON, Mr. A. James. Shadyside, Stony Brook, L. I., N. Y., U. S. A. [Amphibia & Reptilia of N. America (Yes)] [The Stony Brook School]

BARTOŠ, Prof. Dr. Emanuel. Zoological Institution, Viničná 7, Praha II, Czechoslovakia. [Rhizopoda: Thecata; Rotatoria; Tardigrada; Megaloptera; Mecoptera; Raphidioptera; Neuroptera; all of Czechoslovakia (No)]

BARTSCH, Dr. Paul. Lebanon, Lorton, Va., U. S. A. [Recent & Tertiary Mollusca of World] Died April 24, 1960.

BARWICK, Arthur R. 10 Wessex Road, Sligo Park Hills, Silver Spring, Md., U. S. A. [Tertiary Mollusca of Atlantic Cst. U. S. (Yes); Tertiary Cetacea of mid. Atlantic U. S. (Yes)] [Department of Geology & Geography, Howard University]

* BARWICK, Mr. R. Victoria University College, Box 196, Wellington, New Zealand. [Reptilia]

BARY, Dr. B. McK. Oceanographic Laboratory, 78 Craighall Road, Edinburgh 6, Scotland. [Copepoda: Calanoida; Euphausiacea; Mysidacea; all of s. w. Pacific (Yes)]

BASCH, Mr. Paul F. Department of Zoology, University of Michigan, Ann Arbor, Mich., U. S. A. [Gastropoda: Ancylidae of N. America (No)]

BASDEN, Mr. E. B. Institute of Animal Genetics, West Mains Road, Edinburgh 9, Scotland. [Diptera: Drosophilidae of Palearctic (Yes)]

* BASHKIROVA, Cand. Vet. Sci. E. Ja. Moscow State University, Moscow B-234, U. S. S. R [Trematoda & Cestoda of animals]

BASILEWSKY, P., Chef de la Section d'Entomologie, Musée Royal du Congo Belge, Tervuren, Belgium. [Coleoptera: Carabidae of Africa s. of Sahara & Madagascar (Yes)]

* BASIR, Dr. M. A. Department of Zoology, Muslim University, Aligarh, U. P., India. [Nematoda]

BASOGLU, Prof. Dr. Muthar. Zoologi Enstitüsü, Ege Üniversitesi, Bornova, Izmir, Turkey. [Reptilia & Amphibia of Turkey (Yes)]

BASSE de MÉNORVAL, Dr. E. 10 Avenue Paul Appell, Paris (XIV), France. [Jurassic - Cretaceous Ammonoidea (No); Nautiloidea (No)] [Centre National de la Recherche Scientifique]

117

BASSINDALE, R. Department of Zoology, University of Bristol, Bristol, England. [Crustacea: Cirripedia of Britain (No); marine invertebrates of Britain (No)]
BASSLER, Mr. R. S., Associate in Paleontology, U. S. National Museum, Washington 25, D. C., U. S. A. [Paleozoic Bryozoa & Ostracoda of America (No)]
BASSUS, Diplom-Biologe W. Forstzoologisches Institut, Schicklerstrasse 5, Eberswalde, Germany. [Soil Nematoda of c. Europe (Yes)]
* BATALLER, Prof. J. -R. University of Barcelona, Barcelona, Spain. [Fossil invertebrates]
BATCHELOR, Gordon Stanley. R. D. 4, Box 4409-A, Wenatchee, Wash., U. S. A. [Acarina: Eriophyidae of World (Yes)]
BATEMAN, J. A. Kaffrarian Museum, 3 Lower Albert Road, King Williams Town, Union of South Africa. [Mammalia of e. Cape Prov. (Yes)]
BATES, Mr. Marston. Department of Zoology, University of Michigan, Ann Arbor, Mich., U. S. A. [Lepidoptera: Rhopalocera of West Indies (Yes), Diptera: Culicidae & Trype-- tidae of Neotropics (No)]
BATHAM, Dr. Elizabeth J. (Portobello, New Zealand; Cirripedia, Mollusca, Actiniaria) Not now active in taxonomy.
BATIE, William A. (Centralia, Wash.; Invertebrates) Not now active in taxonomy.
BATJES, Dr. D. A. J. c/o Shell Trinidad Ltd., Point Fortin, Trinidad. [Tertiary Foraminifera of Europe (No)]
* BATOR, Dr. A. Zoologisches Institut der Universität, Innsbruck, Austria. [Hemiptera: Heteroptera]
BATTAGLIA, Dr. Bruno. Istituto di Zoologia e Anatomia Comparata, della Università di Padova, Padova, Italy. [Genetics & Ecology]
BATTAGLIA, Raffaello. (Padova, Italy; fossils) Died March 18, 1958.
BATTEN, Dr. Roger L. Geology Department, University of Wisconsin, Madison, Wis., U. S. A. [Paleozoic - Mesozoic Gastropoda: Pleurotomaria (Yes)]
BATTERSBY, Mr. J. C. British Museum (Natural History), Cromwell Road, London, S. W. 7, England. [Reptilia of World (Yes)]
BATTONI, Dr. Silvano. Via Ugo Foscolo 26, Macerata, Italy. [Coleoptera: Meloidae of World (No); g. Mylabris of Mediterranean (Yes)]
BAUCHOT-BOUTIN, Mme. M. L. Laboratoire de Zoologie (Ichthyologie), Museum National d'Histoire Naturelle, 57 Rue Cuvier, Paris (V), France. [Pisces: Nemichthyoidei: Serrivomeridae of World, adults & Larvae (Yes); Perciforma: Labroidei: Labridae of cst. France (No)]
BAUDON, Andre. 265 Blvd. Wattin, Ain-es-Sebaa, Morocco. [Coleoptera: Buprestidae of N. Africa (Yes)]
BAUER, David L. 1103 Ballew Avenue, Everett, Wash., U. S. A. [Lepidoptera: Nymphalidae: Melitaeini, espec. g. Chlosyne & Microtia, of Palearctic (No); of New World (Yes); Saturnioidea: g. Coloradia, Hemileuca, Pseudohazis, of America (Yes)]
BAUER, Dr. Dipl. Ing. K. Zoologisches Forschungsinstitut und Museum Alexander Koenig, Koblenzer Strasse 162, Bonn, Germany. [Aves of Europe (Yes); Mammalia of c. & s. e. Europe (Yes); mammal remains from bird pellets of Europe (Yes); Chiroptera: Vespertilionidae of Palearctic (No)]
BAUER, Mr. O. N. All-Union Research Institute of Lake & River Fishery, Leningrad W-164, U. S. S. R. [Parasites of f-w. fishes of Holarctic (Yes)]
BAUER, William R. 235 Liberty Street, Petaluma, Calif., U. S. A. [Lepidoptera: Noctuidae & Geometridae of N. America (Yes)] [California State Department of Agriculture]
* BAUGHMAN, J. L. Rockport, Texas, U. S. A. [Mollusca]
* BAUMANN, Dr. F. Naturhistorisches Museum, Bern, Switzerland. [Amphibia]
BAUMANN, Dr. H. Übersee Museum, Bahnhofsplatz, Bremen, Germany. [Tardigrada (Yes); Crustacea (No)]
BAUZA, Juan. See RULLAN, Juan Bauza.
* BAXTER, M. A. Croydon Polytechnic, Scarbrook Road, Croydon, England. [Amphibia]
BAY, Prof. Dr. Roland. Socinstrasse 38, Basel, Switzerland. [Jaws & teeth of Primates of Europe & Melanesia (Yes)]
* BAYARD, Andre. 34 Blvd. Arago, Paris (XVII), France. [Lepidoptera]
BAYER, Frederick M. Division of Marine Invertebrates, U. S. National Museum, Washington 25, D. C., U. S. A. [Octocorallia of World (No); Gorgonacea of W. Indies & Oceania (Yes)]
BAYLIFF, William H. Washington Department of Fisheries, 4015 20th Avenue W., Seattle 99, Wash., U. S. A. [Pisces: Zoarcidae of n. e. Pacific (Yes)]
BAYNES, E. S. A. 2 Arkendale Road, Glenageary, Co. Dublin, Eire. [Lepidoptera: Pyralidae & Pterophoridae of Ireland (No); Macrolepidoptera of Ireland (Yes)]
* BAZICALOVA, A. N. Station Limnologique du lac Baikal, Listventchnoe, Irkoutsk, U. S. S. R. [Crustacea]
BAZYLUK, Dr. Wɫadysɫaw. Zoological Institute, Polish Academy of Science, ul. Wilcza 64, Warszawa, Poland. [Orthoptera of Palearctic (Yes); Blattoidea & Mantoidea of Europe (Yes); Dermaptera of Europe (Yes)]

BÉ, Dr. Allan W. H. Lamont Geological Observatory, Palisades, N. Y. , U. S. A. [Recent & Pleistocene planktonic Foraminifera of World (Yes)]
BEACH, Neil W. Department of Biology, Gettysburg College, Gettysburg, Penna. , U. S. A. [Planktonic Rotifera of N. America (Yes)]
BEACH, Paul R. P. O. Box 1249, Houston 1, Texas, U. S. A. [Oligocene & Miocene Foraminifera of Texas Cst. (No)]
BEAL, Dr. R. S. , Jr. Division of Insects, U. S. National Museum, Washington 25, D. C. , U. S. A. [Coleoptera: Dermestidae of World (Yes); Bruchidae of U. S. (Yes)] [Section of Insect Identification and Parasite Introduction, Entomological Research Division, Agricultural Research Service, U. S. Department of Agriculture]
BEAMER, R. H. (Lawrence, Kans. , U. S. A. ; Homoptera) Died November 21, 1957.
BEAN, J. L. 1811 Simpson Street, St. Paul 13, Minn. , U. S. A. [Diptera: Syrphidae of N. America (Yes)] [University of Minnesota]
BEARDSLEY, Mr. J. W. Hawaiian Sugar Planters Association Experiment Station, 1527 Keeaumoku Street, Honolulu 14, Hawaii. [Parasitic Hymenoptera of Hawaii (Yes); Homoptera: Coccoidea of Hawaii & Micronesia (Yes)]
BEATTY, Alice F. (Mrs. George H. Beatty). P. O. Box 281, State College, Penna. , U. S. A. [Odonata, larvae & imagines, of World (Yes)]
BEATTY, George H. III. P. O. Box 281, State College, Penna. , U. S. A. [Odonata, larvae & imagines, of World (Yes)] [Pennsylvania State University]
de BEAUCHAMP, Prof. P. Laboratoire d'Evolution des Etres Organisés, 105 Blvd. Raspail, Paris (VI), France. [Turbellaria: Tricladida: Paludicola, Terricola, Maricola; of America (No); of Europe, Africa, Oceania (Yes); Rhabdocoela: Polycladida (No); Rotifera: Ploima, Rhizota (Yes); Bdelloida (No)]
BEAUDRY, J. R. (Montreal, Canada; Orthoptera) Not now active in taxonomy.
de BEAUFORT, Dr. L. F. De Hooge Kley, Amersfoort, Netherlands, [Marine & f-w. Pisces of Indo-Australia Arch. (Yes)] [Zoological Museum, Amsterdam]
de BEAUMONT, Prof. J. Musée Zoologique, Lausanne, Switzerland. [Hymenoptera: Sphecidae of Palearctic (Yes)]
de BEAUX, O. (Genova, Italy; Aves, Mammalia) Died in 1955.
BEAVER, Prof. Harold Hartman. Department of Geology, Baylor University, Waco, Texas, U. S. A. [Mississippian & Pennsylvanian Blastoidea (Yes)]
BEAVER, Dr. Paul C. Department of Tropical Medicine and Public Health, Tulane University School of Medicine, 1430 Tulane Avenue, New Orleans 12, La. , U. S. A. [Trematoda: Echinostomatidae of N. & S. America (Yes); Nematode tissue stages in man (Yes)]
* BEAVER, Prof. William C. Department of Biology, Wittenberg College, Springfield, Ohio, U. S. A. [Pisces]
BECHET, Ion. Catedra de Zoologie, Universitatea Cluj, Str. Miko 5-7, Cluj, Rumania. [Mallophaga of Europe (Yes)]
BECHTEL, Robert C. 2230 Ward Place, Reno, Nev. , U. S. A. [Hymenoptera: Sapygidae of World (Yes); Vespidae: Vespinae, Polistinae, Polybiinae of California (Yes); Coleoptera: Plastoceridae of Nearctic (Yes)]
BECHYNÉ, Dr. Jan. Museum G. Frey, Tutzing, bei München, Germany. [Coleoptera: Chrysomelidae: Alticinae of World excl. c. Europe (Yes); Chrysomelinae of World excl. Australia (Yes); Eumolpinae & Galerucinae of C. & S. America, Madagascar (Yes)]
BECK, Dr. D. Elden. Department of Zoology & Entomology, Brigham Young University, Provo, Utah, U. S. A. [Siphonaptera of w. U. S. & Formosa (Yes)]
* BECK, Elizabeth C. Bureau of Entomology, Florida State Board of Health, Jacksonville, Fla. , U. S. A. [Diptera]
* BECK, H. Museum of Natural History, Regina, Sask. , Canada. [Mammalia]
BECK, R. Stanley. 621 Truxtun, Bakersfield, Calif. , U. S. A. [Fossil Foraminifera of w. cst. N. America (No)]
BECK, William M. , Jr. P. O. Box 210, Jacksonville 11, Fla. , U. S. A. [Diptera: Tendipedidae of Florida (Yes)] [Florida State Board of Health]
BECKER, Dr. Edward C. Systematic Entomology, Science Service Bldg. , Ottawa, Ont. , Canada. [Coleoptera: Elateridae of World (No); of N. America (Yes)]
BECKER, Prof. Elery R. Division of Life Sciences, Arizona State College, Tempe, Ariz. , U. S. A. [Protozoa: Coccidia]
BECKER, Dr. K. Bundesgesundheitsamt, Correnplatz 1, Berlin-Dahlem, Germany. [Small mammals of Europe (Yes); from owl pellets of Europe (Yes)]
BECKER, J. Departmento de Entomologia, Museu Nacional, Quinta da Boa Vista, Rio de Janeiro, Brazil. [Heteroptera: Miridae of Neotropics (Yes)]
* BECKER, Leroy E. Creole Petroleum Corp. , Maracaibo, Venezuela. [Fossil invertebrates]
BECKLUND, W. W. Georgia Coastal Plain Experiment Station, Tifton, Ga. , U. S. A. [Nematoda of livestock in N. America (Yes)] [U. S. Department of Agriculture]

119

BECKMAN, Dr. Heinz. Firma Preüssag Erdöl, Ludwig Brückstrasse 53, München 61, Germany. [Paleozoic-Triassic conodonts of Europe (Yes)]

BECKMAN, Dr. W. C. Food & Agriculture Organization, United Nations, Box 256, Damascus, Syria. [F-w. Pisces of Colorado & Syria (no)]

BECKMANN, Mr. Jean Pierre. c/o Cuban Stanolind Oil Co., Apartado 2651, Habana, Cuba. [Cretaceous-Tertiary Foraminifera of N. & S. America (Yes); of Europe (No)]

BEE, James William. Museum of Natural History, University of Kansas, Lawrence, Kans., U. S. A. [Mammalia: Insectivora, Chiroptera, Rodentia, of Arctic Alaska, U. S., Guatemala, West Indies (No)]

BEECHER, Dr. William J. 3048 N. Troy Street, Chicago 18, Ill., U. S. A. [Aves] [Chicago Natural History Museum]

BEER, Prof. Frank M. 510 N. 13th Street, Corvallis, Ore., U. S. A. [Coleoptera: Buprestidae & Cicindelidae of N. America (Yes)] [Oregon State College]

BEER, Robert E. Department of Entomology, University of Kansas, Lawrence, Kans., U. S. A. [Acarina: Trombidiformes of World (No); Tarsonemidae & Tetranychidae of World (Yes); Hymenoptera: Symphta of N. America (No)]

BEERS, Prof. C. Dale. Department of Zoology, University of North Carolina, Chapel Hill, N. C., U. S. A. [Protozoa: Ciliata (No)]

BEETLE, Dorothy E. 609 Russell Street, Laramie, Wyo., U. S. A. [Terr. Mollusca of N. America (No)]

* BEETS, Dr. C. c/o Shell Venezuelan Oil Co., Geology Department, Apartado 809, Caracas, Venezuela. [Mollusca]

BEGDON, Jerzy. Instytut Zoologiczny, ul. Głowackiego 2, Lublin, Poland. [Hymenoptera: Formicoidea of Poland (No)] [Uniwersytet Marie Curie Skłodowskiej]

* BEGG, J. A. Entomology Laboratory, 10 Park Avenue East, Chatham, Ont., Canada. [Coleoptera: Elateridae (Wireworms)]

BEGG, J. L. 3 Mansionhouse Road, Mount Vernon, Glasgow, E. 2, Scotland. [Ordovician & Silurian Trilobita (No)]

BEHLE, Prof. William H. Division of Biological Sciences, University of Utah, Salt Lake City 12, Utah. [Aves of Utah & Great Basin (Yes)]

* BEHM, Mr. Hans. Department of Micropaleontology, American Museum of Natural History, New York 24, N. Y., U. S. A. [Fossil invertebrates]

BEHURA, Dr. Basanta Kumar. Department of Zoology, Ravenshaw College, Cuttack, Orissa, India. [Homoptera: Aphididae & Membracidae of Orissa (Yes); Acari: Tyroglyphoidea of Orissa (Yes); Reptilia: Serpentes of Orissa (Yes)]

* BEIDLEMAN, Richard G. Department of Zoology, Colorado Agricultural & Mechanical College, Fort Collins, Colo., U. S. A. [Mammalia]

BEIER, Dr. Max. Naturhistorisches Museum, Burgring 7, Wien 1, Austria. [Pseudoscorpionidea of World (Yes); Orthoptera: Mantidae: Pseudophyllinae]

* BEINGOLEA, Ing. Oscar. Estación Experimental de Agricultura de la Molina, Casilla 2791, Lima, Peru. [Nematoda]

BEIRNE, Dr. Bryan P. Box 179, Belleville, Ont., Canada. [Homoptera: Cicadellidae of Canada & Alaska (No); Microlepidoptera of Ireland (No); Macrolepidoptera of British Isles (No)] [Entomology Laboratory, Canada Department of Agriculture]

* BEJARANO, Maj. Dr. Juan C. R. Instituto de Entomologia Sanitaria, Av. Parral 652, Buenos Aires, Argentina. [Diptera: Culicidae]

BEKLEMISCHEV, Prof. W. N. Novo Peschanaya 3, kv. 100, Moscow D. 57, U. S. S. R. [Turbellaria of Palearctic seas (No)]

BELFIELD, Dr. W. 153 Windsor Rd., Oldham, Lancs., England. [Scorpionida of West Africa (Yes)]

BELFORD, D. J. Bureau of Mineral Resources, Canberra, A. C. T., Australia. [Up. Cretaceous Foraminifera of W. Australia (Yes); Tertiary of New Guinea (Yes)]

BELIAEV, G. M. Institute of Oceanology, Academy of Sciences, Lujnicovskaja 8, Moscow 127, U. S. S. R. [Asteroidea, Ophiuroidea, Holothurioidea; of abyssal Pacific & Indian Oceans (No); Asteroidea: Porcellanasteridae of World (Yes)]

BELIAJEVA, E. I. Palaeontological Museum of the Academy of Sciences of U. S. S. R., Lenin Prospectus 16, Moscow, U. S. S. R. [Mammalia: Rhinocerotidae: Alloceropinae & Dicerorhininae of U. S. S. R.: Coenopinae, Aceratheriinae, Teleoceratinae, Elasmotheriinae, of U. S. S. R. & Mongolia; Hyracodontidae, Chalicotheriidae, of U. S. S. R. & Mongolia; Proboscidea: Gomphotheriinae, of U. S. S. R. & Mongolia; Platybelodontinae, Elephantinae, of U. S. S. R. (all Yes)]

* BELIHOV, D. V. Department of Zoology, Kasan University, Kasan, U. S. S. R. [Echinodermata]

* BELIZIN, V. I. Liebnich Strasse 16, Kursk, U. S. S R [Hymenoptera]

BELKIN, Dr. John N. Department of Entomology, University of California, Los Angeles 24, Calif., U. S. A. [Diptera: Culicidae of N. America, S. Pacific (Yes); Tabanidae of N. America (Yes); Coleoptera: Bostrichidae of World (Yes)]

BELL, Dr. A. Weir. Life Sciences Department, Los Angeles City College, 855 N. Vermont, Avenue, Los Angeles 29, Calif., U.S.A. [Oligochaeta: Enchytraeidae of World (Yes)]

BELL, Mr. Ernest L. 150-17 Roosevelt Avenue, Flushing 54, N.Y., U.S.A. [Lepidoptera: Hesperiidae of New World (Yes)] [American Museum of Natural History]

BELL, Dr. Edwin L. Department of Biology, Albright College, Reading, Penna., U.S.A. [Reptilia: Sauria: g. Sceloperus of U.S. (Yes)]

* BELL, Mr. F. Heward. Fisheries Hall No. 2, University of Washington, Seattle 5, Wash., U.S.A. [Hydrozoa]

* BELL, Ian L. Address unknown. (Anoplura)

* BELL, Mr. L. Neil. P.O.Box 306, Tamiami Station, Miami, Fla., U.S.A. [Reptilia]

BELL, Ross T. Department of Zoology, University of Vermont, Burlington, Vt., U.S.A. [Coleoptera: Carabidae of U.S. & Canada (Yes); of Mexico (No)]

BELL, Prof. W.C. Department of Geology, University of Texas, Austin 12, Texas, U.S.A. [Cambrian Brachiopoda (Yes)]

BELLAMY, Dr. R.E. Encephalitis Laboratory, P.O.Box 1564, Bakersfield, Calif., U.S.A. [Diptera: adult & larval Tipulidae, Ptychopteridae, Tanyderidae, Culicidae of N. America (Yes)]

* BELLIDO, Antonio Garcia. Museo de Sciencias Naturales, Madrid 6, Spain. [Rotifera]

BELLINGER, Dr. Peter F. Department of Natural Sciences, San Fernando Valley State College, Northridge, Calif., U.S.A. [Collembola, espec. Isotomidae, of World (Yes); Lepidoptera (No)]

* BELLOC, G.J.J., Sous-Directeur, Musée Océanographique de Monaco, Monaco. [Pisces]

BELLON, Dr. L. [Malaga, Spain; Pisces) Died 1954.

* BELLROSE, F.C. Illinois Natural History Survey, Urbana, Ill., U.S.A. [Aves]

BELOPOLSKAIA, M.M. Leningrad State University, Leningrad W-164, U.S.S.R. [Trematoda: Microphallidae of birds of sea-coasts of Eurasia (Yes)]

BELS, Dr. L. Velserstraat 101, Haarlem, Netherlands. [Mammalia: Chiroptera: Microchiroptera of w. Europe (No)]

BELTRAN, Prof. Enrique. Apartado Postal 1079, Mexico 1, D.F., Mexico. [Protozoa parasitic in man (Yes)] [Universidad de Mexico]

BELYSHEV, Dr. B.F., C.B.S. Necrasovsky by-street 50, Bijsk, Altai, U.S.S.R. [Odonata of U.S.S.R. & N. Asia (Yes)]

van BEMMEL, Dr. A.C.V. Koninklijke Rotterdamse Diergaarde · (Blijdorp Zoo), Rotterdam, Netherlands. [Mammalia of e.Asia (No); Asiatic deer, g.Rusa, Hyelaphus, Muntiacus, of e.Asia (Yes); seals of Atlantic (No)]

BENANDER, Dr. Per. Höör, Malmöhus, Sweden. [Microlepidoptera of Scandinavia (Yes)]

BENAVIDES-CACERES, Victor E. Apartado 1081, Lima, Peru. [Cretaceous Cephalopoda: Ammonoidea (No)]

BENAZZI, Prof. Mario. Istituto di Zoologia, Universitá di Pisa, Via A, Volta 4, Pisa, Italy. [Turbellaria: Tricladida Paludicola of Europe (Yes)]

BENEDICT, Dr. Frances A. (Fresno, Calif.; Chiroptera, Marsupialia) Not now Active in taxonomy.

BENESH, Mr. Bernard. Burrville, Tenn., U.S.A. [Coleoptera: Lucanidae of World (Yes)]

* BENGRY, Mr. Ronald. Institute of Jamaica, Kingston, Jamaica. [Lepidoptera]

BENICK, Dr. G. Wakenitzstrasse 69, Lübeck, Germany. [Coleoptera: Staphylinidae: g. Atheta, Amischa, Meotica, of Palearctic (Yes)]

BENING, A.L. (Leningrad, U.S.S.R.: Crustacea) Deceased.

BENNETCH, Leonard M. 827 W. Market Street, Bethlehem, Penna., U.S.A. [Rotifera of World (Yes)]

* BENNETT, Mr. A.A. Foreign Department, Phillips Petroleum Co., Room 730, Adams Bldg., Bartlesville, Okla., U.S.A. [Fossil invertebrates]

BENNETT, Gordon F. Department of Parasitology, Ontario Research Foundation, 43 Queens Park, Toronto 5, Ont., Canada. [Immature Diptera: Calliphoridae: g. Protocalliphora; Oestridae: g. Cuterebra & g. Cephenemyia; of N. America (Yes)]

BENNETT, Dr. H.J. Department of Zoology, Louisiana State University, Baton Rouge, La., U.S.A. [Digenetic Trematoda of cold-blooded hosts of s.e. U.S. (No)]

BENNETT, Miss Isobel. Department of Zoology, University of Sydney, Sydney, N.S.W., Australia. [Intertidal invertebrates of New South Wales (Yes)]

BENNETT, Mr. N.H. Department of Entomology, The Zoological Museum, Tring, Hert , England. [Lepidoptera: Lycaenidae of Africa (Yes)] [British Museum (Natural History)]

BENNISON, Mr. G.M. Department of Geology & Mineralogy, Marischal College, Aberdeen, Scotland. [Fossil (Dinantian, Namurian, L.Westphalian) non-marine Pelecypoda, g. Carbonicola & Naiadites, of Scotland & n. England (Yes)]

BENNO, P. Beekseweg 3, Babberich (G.), Netherlands. [Hymenoptera: Vespidae of Surinam & Dutch Antilles (No); Vespidae, Chrysididae, Scolioidea, of Netherlands (Yes); solitary Vespidae of S. America & "tropics" (No)]

* BENOIST, Raymond. Address unknown. (Hymenoptera: Apoidea)

* BENOIT, Ing. P. L. G. Musée du Congo Belge, Tervuren, Belgium. [Hymenoptera].
BENSCHOTER, C. A. Laboratorio Entomologico, U. S. Department of Agriculture, Apartado
    Postal 28970, Mexico 17, D. F., Mexico. [Coleoptera: Carabidae: g. Omophron of N.
    America (Yes)]
BENSON, C. W. Department of Game & Tsetse Control, P. O. Box 1, Chilanga, near Lusaka,
    Northern Rhodesia. [Aves of N. Rhodesia & Nyasaland (Yes)]
BENSON, D. A. (Ottawa, Canada; Mammalia) Not now active in taxonomy.
BENSON, Mr. R. B. Department of Entomology, British Museum (Natural History), Crom-
    well Road, London, S. W. 7, England. [Hymenoptera: Symphyta of Europe, Mediter-
    ranean, Arctic & montane, Australia, New Guinea (Yes); Siricoidea, Cephoidea, Xye-
    loidea, Orussoidea, Tenthredinoidea: Nematinae: g. Athalia, Tenthredopsis, Rhogo-
    gaster; of World (Yes)]
BENSON, Prof. Richard H. Department of Geology, University of Kansas, Lawrence, Kans.,
    U. S. A. [Mississippian & post-Paleozoic Ostracoda (Yes)]
BENSON, Dr. Seth B. Museum of Vertebrate Zoology, University of California, Berkeley 4,
    Calif., U. S. A. [Mammalia: Chiroptera, Rodentia: Heteromyidae, of w. N. America]
BENSON, W. Pedro. See Addenda.
BENTINCK, G. A. Kasteel Amerongen, Amerongen, Netherlands. [Lepidoptera of Nether-
    lands (Yes)]
* BENTINCK, Mr. William C. Department of Entomology, University of California, Berke-
    ley 4, Calif., U. S. A. [Diptera: Sciaridae of N. America (Yes)]
BENTON, Dr. Allen H. Department of Biology, New York State College for Teachers, Al-
    bany, N. Y., U. S. A. [Siphonaptera of e. N. America (Yes)]
BEN-TUVIA, A., Biologist, Sea Fisheries Research Station, P. O. Box 699, Haifa, Israel.
    [Pisces: Clupeiformes, Mugiliformes, Heterenchelidae, of e. Mediterranean & n. Red
    Sea (Yes)]
BENZ, Dr. F. 17 Bollwerkstrasse, Binningen, Switzerland. [Lepidoptera: Sphingidae of
    Europe (Yes); g. Colias of Europe (No)]
BENZON, Dr. Bøje, President du Zoo, Springforbi, København, Denmark. [Water fowl of
    Europe; Antelopes & buffalo of Africa]
BEQUAERT, Joseph C. Museum of Comparative Zoology, Cambridge 38, Mass., U. S. A.
    [Diptera, Hymenoptera, Acarina, Mollusca (No)]
* BERDAN, Dr. Jean M. U. S. Geological Survey, Washington 25, D. C., U. S. A. [L. Pale-
    ozoic Ostracoda]
BERDEGUÉ, Mr. Julio, Director, Departamento de Investigaciones Cientificas, Apartado
    Postal 32, Los Mochis, Sinaloa, Mexico. [Fishes of Pacific Cst. of N. & S. America
    (Yes)]
BERE, Miss Ruby. (Madison, Wis.; Copepoda) Not now active in taxonomy.
BERENGUER, C. G. See GALLEGO BERENGUER, C.
BERG, Dr. Clifford O. Department of Entomology, Cornell University, Ithaca, N. Y., U. S. A.
    [Diptera: Sciomyzidae, espec. immature, of N. America (Yes)]
BERG, L. S. (Leningrad, U. S. S. R; Pisces) Deceased.
BERG, Robert Raymond. (Denver, Colo.; fossils) Not now active in taxonomy.
BERGER, Dr. Andrew J. Department of Anatomy, East Medical Bldg., Ann Arbor, Mich.,
    U. S. A. [Aves: Cuculidae of World (No)] [University of Michigan Medical School]
BERGER, Leszek. Instytut Zoologiczny, Polska Akademia Nauk, ul. Swierczewskiego 19,
    Posnán, Poland. [Amphibia: Ranidae of c. Europe (Yes); Mollusca: Bivalvia: Sphaeri-
    idae: g. Pisidium of Europe (Yes); Gastropoda: Ellobiidae & Cochlicopidae of c. Europe
    (Yes)]
BERGER, L. A. Department d'Entomologie, Musée Royal du Congo Belge, Tervuren, Bel-
    gium. [Lepidoptera: Hesperiidae of Africa (Yes); Papilionidae & Pieridae of Africa
    (No); Pieridae: g. Colias of World (Yes)]
BERGESON, G. Botany & Plant Pathology Department, Purdue University, Lafayette, Ind.,
    U. S. A. [Soil & plant parasitic Nematoda of U. S. (Yes)]
van den BERGHE, L. See Appendix.
BERGMAN, Prof. Dr. R. A. M. Afdeling Cult. Phys. Anthropologie, Linnaeusstraat 2a, Am-
    sterdam, Netherlands. [Reptilia: snakes of Java (No)] [Royal Tropical Institute]
BERGOUNIOUX, Pere F. M., Professeur, Institut Catholique, 31 rue de la Fonderie, Tou-
    louse, France. [Mastodontidae & Deinotheridae of c. & w. Europe (Yes); fossil (?)
    Chelonia of N. Africa (Yes)]
BERGQUIST, Harlan Richard. Room 2644, Interior Bldg., Washington 25, D. C., U. S. A.
    [Cretaceous Foraminifera of N. America (Yes)] [U. S. Geological Survey]
BERGSTROM, David W. Zoology Department, Miami University, Oxford, Ohio, U. S. A.
    [Acarina: Hydracarina of c. U. S. (No)]
BERINKEY, Laszló. Section Zoologique, Magyar Nemzeti Múzeum, Baross-utca 13, Buda-
    pest VIII, Hungary. [F-w. Pisces of Europe & U. S. S. R (Yes); Pleistocene f-w. Pis-
    ces of c. Europe (Yes)]

122

BERIO, E. Museo de Storia Naturale, Via Grigata Liguria 9, Genova, Italy. [Lepidoptera: Noctuidae of Europe, Asia, Africa, Indomalaya, N. America (Yes)]

BERKELEY, Alfreda. (Toronto, Canada; Crustacea) Deceased.

BERKELEY, Cyril J. Marine Biological Station, Nanaimo, B. C., Canada. [Polychaeta of w. cst. N. America (Yes)]

* BERLAND, L. Laboratoire d'Entomologie, Muséum National d'Histoire Naturelle, 45bis rue de Buffon, Paris (V), France. [Araneida: Hymenoptera]

BERLIOZ, Prof. J. Muséum National d'Histoire Naturelle, 55 rue de Buffon, Paris (V), France. [Aves (Yes)]

* BERLY, J. A. Division of Entomology, Clemson College, Clemson, S. C., U. S. A. [Odonata]

BERMUDEZ, Dr. P. J. Geological Laboratory, Creole Petroleum Corporation, Jusepin, Venezuela. [Foraminifera of Antilles-Caribbean (Yes)]

BERNARD, Prof. F. Faculté des Sciences, Université d'Algiers, Alger, Algeria. [Hymenoptera: ants of Europe & Africa (Yes); Protozoa: coccolithophorids of Mediterranean & warm seas (Yes)]

BERNARDI, Dr. Georges, Attaché au Laboratoire d'Entomologie du Muséum National d'Histoire Naturelle, 45 bis rue de Buffon, Paris (V), France. [Lepidoptera: Pieridae of Palearctic & Africa (Yes); Lycaenidae of Palearctic (Yes)]

BERNASCONI, Profesora Irene. Rosario 127, Buenos Aires, Argentina. [Echinoidea & Asteroidea of S. America & Antarctica (Yes)] [Museo Argentino de Ciencias Naturales]

* BERNATH, Robert J. The Clapp Laboratories, Inc., Washington Street, Duxbury, Mass., U. S. A. [Invertebrate marine borers]

BERNER, Mr. Leo, Jr. Scripps Institution of Oceanography, La Jolla, Calif., U. S. A. [Pelagic Tunicata excl. Larvacea, of World (Yes)]

BERNER, Prof. Lewis. Department of Biology, University of Florida, Gainesville, Fla., U. S. A. [Ephemeroptera of N. A. espec. s. e. U. S. (Yes)]

BERNHARD, Dr. Friedrich. Obertor 5, Meisenheim-Glan, Germany. [Acarina: Mesostigmata: Typhlodromidae & Ascaidae of Europe (Yes)]

BERNIS, F. Museo Nacional de Ciencias Naturales, Madrid, Spain. [Vertebrates, excl. marine, of Iberian Peninsula (No)]

* BERNSTRÖM, J. Tidö Castle, Westeras, Sweden. [Reptilia: Viperidae]

* ĐEROUŠEK, J. Address unknown. [Fossil Copepoda]

* BERRILL, N. J. Department of Zoology, McGill University, Montreal, Que., Canada. [Coelenterata]

BERRY, Dr. Charles T. A 1 Harvey Road, Stonington, Conn., U. S. A. [Tertiary & Recent Ophiuroidea of N. America & Europe (Yes)]

BERRY, Dr. Elmer G. Laboratory of Tropical Diseases, National Institutes of Health, Bethesda 14, Md., U. S. A. [Mollusca: Planorbidae & Hydrobiidae of medical importance of Africa & W. Hemisphere (Yes)]

BERRY, Prof. E. W. Department of Geology, Duke University, Box 6665, College Station, Durham, N. C., U. S. A. [Mesozoic & Tertiary Foraminifera (Yes)]

BERRY, Mr. Frederick H. Bureau of Commercial Fisheries, U. S. Fish & Wildlife Service, P. O. Box 283, Brunswick, Ga., U. S. A. [Pisces: Carangidae & Hemiramphidae of w. N. Atlantic (Yes); Caproidae of World (Yes)]

BERRY, Dr. J., Director, The Nature Conservancy, 12 Hope Terrace, Edinburgh 9, Scotland. [Pisces: Salmonidae of Atlantic & Europe (No); Aves: Anatidae: g. Anser of World (No); of N. Hemisphere (Yes)]

BERRY, Dr. J. E. Prairie View Agricultural & Mechanical College of Texas, Prairie View, Texas, U. S. A. [Trematoda: Monogenea: Gyrodactyloidea of N. America (No); f-w. Dactylogyridae of N. America (Yes)]

BERRY, Dr. S. Stillman. 1145 W. Highland Avenue, Redlands, Calif., U. S. A. [Cephalopoda of World (Yes); chitons of World (Yes), fossil chitons of w. N. America (Yes); Pliocene - Recent marine Mollusca excl. Nudibranchiata; Pliocene to Recent Brachiopoda of w. N. America (Yes)]

BERRY, W. B. N. Geology Department, University of Houston, Houston 4, Texas, U. S. A. [Fossil Graptolithina: Graptoloidea (Yes); Dendroidea (No)]

BERSIER, Dr. Arnold. (Lausanne, Switzerland; microfossils) Not now active in taxonomy.

BERST, Prof. Antonio. Calle San Lorenzo 2087, Santa Fe, Argentina. [Mammalia, Aves, Reptilia, of S. America (Yes); Amphibia & Fishes of Argentina (Yes)] [Collegio Immaculada de Santa Fe]

BERTELSEN, Dr. E. Marinbiologisk Laboratorium, Charlottenlund Slot, Denmark. [Pisces: Ceratioidea of World (Yes)]

BERTHELSEN, Mr. Ole. Danmarks Geologiske Undersøgelse, Tranegårdsvej 20, Hellerup, Denmark. [Cheilostomatous Bryozoa of Danian-Paleocene of n. Europe (Yes)]

BERTIN, L. (Paris, France; Pisces) Died 1956.

BERTOLANI, M. Address unknown. (Tardigrada)

BERTRAM, C. K. Ricardo. (Cambridge, England; Acarina) Not now active in taxonomy.

BERTRAM, D. S. (London, England; Acarina) Not now active in taxonomy.
BERTRAND, Dr. Henri. 6 rue du Guignier, Paris (XX), France. [Developm. stages of aquatic Coleoptera of World, excl. Hydraenidae, Chrysomelidae, Curculionidae (Yes)] [Laboratoire d'Entomologie du Muséum National d'Histoire Naturelle]
BERZINŠ, Bruno V. A. Ugglehult, Sweden. [Rotatoria of World (Yes); Aves, Pisces, Odonata, of Europe (No)] [South Swedish Fishery Association, Institute of Research, Aneboda]
BESAIRIE, H., Chef du Service Géologique du Madagascar, B. P. 322, Tananarive, Madagascar. [Ammonites & Belemnites of Madagascar (No)]
BESSELING, A. J. President Rooseveltweg 102 B, Utrecht, Netherlands. [Acarina: Hydrachnellae of Netherlands (Yes)]
* BESSIÈRE, Dr. C., Professeur de Zoologie-Parasitologie, Faculté de Pharmacie, Montpellier, France. [Parasitology]
BEST, Mr. R. V. McMaster University, Hamilton, Ont., Canada. [Trilobita: Olenellidae of N. America & Greenland (Yes)]
BESUCHET, Dr. Claude. Muséum d'Histoire Naturelle, Les Bastions, Genève, Switzerland. [Coleoptera: Pselaphidae of w. Palearctic (Yes); Scydmaenidae: Cephenniini of World (Yes); Rhipiphoridae: Rhipidiinae of World (Yes)]
BETHUNE, Winona J. See TRASON, W. J. B.
BETREM, Dr. J. G. Duymaer van Twiststraat 2, Deventer, Netherlands. [Hymenoptera: Scoliidae of Palearctic & Indo-Australia (Yes); Formicidae: g. Formica of Palearctic (Yes); Ichneumonidae of Indo-Australia (No); Lepidoptera: Psychidae of Indo-Australia (No)] [Government College for Tropical Agriculture]
BETTEN, Dr. Cornelius. 405 Central Ave., Highland Park, Ill., U. S. A. [Trichoptera of N. America (Yes)]
* BETTENSTAEDT, Dr. Franz. Preussiche Bergwerks- und Hütten-A. G., Postfach 1103, Hannover, Germany. [Fossil Foraminifera]
BETZ, J. T. 35 Avenue de Gaulle, Croix (Nord), France. [Macrolepidoptera of w. Europe & Mediterranean (No)]
BEURET, Dr. H. 3 Birkenstrasse, Münchenstein I, Switzerland. [Lepidoptera: Lycaenidae of Palearctic (Yes)]
* BEVAN, W. J. Government Buildings, Ministry of Agriculture, Fisheries & Food, Lawnswood, Leeds 16, England. [Nematoda]
BEY-BIENKO, Prof. Dr. G. Ya. Zoological Institute, Academy of Sciences of U. S. S. R., Leningrad B-164, U. S. S. R. [Dermaptera of Europe & Asia (Yes); Orthoptera: Blattoidea of Europe & Asia (Yes); Acridoidea of Palearctic (Yes); Tettigonioidea of Europe & Asia (Yes)]
* BEYER, Erwin. Department of Zoology, University of Bonn, Bonn, Germany. [Diptera]
BEYR, Ing. Jaroslav. Polska 36, Král. Vinohrady, Praha XII, Czechoslovakia. [Hymenoptera: Braconidae of Palearctic (No)]
BEZUBIK, Dr. Bernard. Katedra Parazytologii, Ul. Akademicka 11, Lublin, Poland. [Helminths of birds of Poland (Yes); setariosis of horses of Poland (Yes)]
BHADURI, Prof. J. L. Department of Zoology, University of Calcutta, 35 Ballygunge Circular Road, Calcutta 19, India. [Amphibia: Salientia of India (Yes); Reptilia: Sauria, Serpentes, Chelonia, Crocodilia of India (No)] [Zoological Survey of India]
BHARGAVA, H. N. Address unknown. (Pisces)
* BHATIA, Dr. M. L., Head, Zoology Department, Delhi University, Delhi 8, India. [Hirudinea of India (Yes)]
BHATIA, Dr. S. B. Department of Geology, University of Lucknow, Lucknow, India. [Foraminifera, fossil & Recent, of Indo-Pacific Ocean (Yes); Tertiary of India & I. of Wight (Yes); Paleozoic of India (Yes)]
BHATNAGAR, Dr. S. P. Department of Zoology, Government College, Naini Tal, U. P., India. [Hymenoptera: Vipionidae & Braconidae of Oriental (Yes)]
BIAGGI, Virgil. Biology Department, College of Agriculture & Mechanical Arts, Mayaguez, Puerto Rico. [Aves of West Indies (No)]
BIAGI, Dr. Francisco. Apartado 25788, Mexico 12, D. F., Mexico. [Hemiptera: Reduviidae: Triatominae of Mexico (Yes); Diptera: Psychodidae: g. Phlebotomus of Mexico] [Jefe de la Seccion de Parasitologia, Escuela de Medicina, Universidad de Mexico]
BIANCHERI, Dr. E. Salita San Gerolamo 8/9, Genova, Italy. [Ephemeroptera, Eur.(Yes)]
BIANCHI, Dr. C. Instituto di Zoologia dell'Universitá, Parma, Italy. [Arthropoda]
BIANCHI, Mr. F. A. Hawaiian Sugar Planters Association Experiment Station, 1527 Keeaumoku Street, Honolulu, Hawaii. [Thysanoptera of America, Pacific, India (Yes)]
* BIBIKOFF, M. Edmoncote Manor, Warwick Road, Leamington Spa, England. [Hymenoptera: Formicidae]
BICK, Dr. George H. Biology Department, Southwestern Louisiana Institute, Box 139, S. L. I. Station, Lafayette, La., U. S. A. [Odonata of U. S., espec. s.e. U. S. (Yes)]
*BICK, Dr. H. Zoologisches Institut der Universität, Bonn, Germany. [Protozoa: Ciliata]

BICKLEY, Dr. Wm. E. Department of Entomology, University of Maryland, College Park, Md., U.S.A. [Neuroptera: Chrysopidae of N. America (Yes); Diptera: Culicidae of N. America (No)]

BICZOK, Dr. Francis. Zoological and Biological Institute of the University, Tancsics Mihaly ut. 2, Szeged, Hungary. [Protozoa: soil Flagellata, Rhyzopoda, Ciliata, of Hungary]

BIDDER, Miss Anna. The Zoological Laboratory, Downing Street, Cambridge, England. [Large squids from stomack of spermwhales of Antarctic (Yes)]

BIEDA, Prof. Dr. Franciszek. Katedra Paleontologii, Akademia Gorniczo-Hutnicza, al. Mickiewicza 30, Kraków, Poland. [Paleogene Foraminifera: Nummulitidae of Europe (Yes); of America, Asia, Africa (No)]

BIEGEL, Dr. Maria. Mainzerstrasse 113, Ingelheim (Rhein), Germany. [Protozoa: Peritricha: f-w. Sessilia of Europe (No)]

BIELAWSKI, Dr. Ryszard. Instytut Zoologiczny, Polska Akademia Nauk, ul. Wilcza 64, Warszawa, Poland. [Coleoptera: Coccinellidae, espec. Epilachninae, of Palearctic, Indo-Malayia, Australia, Pacific Is. (Yes)]

* BIELECKA, W. Instytut Geologiczny, Rakowiecka 4, Warszawa, Poland. [Protozoa: Flagellata]

BIELENIN, Irena. Maly Rynek 4/6, Krakow, Poland. [Homoptera: Coccidae of Poland (Yes)] [Katedra Zoologii Wyzszej Szkoły Rolniczej]

BIERI, Mr. Robert. Personnel Department, Antioch College, Yellow Springs, Ohio, U.S.A. [Chaetognatha of World (Yes)]

BIERNAT, Dr. G. Zakład Paleozoologii, Polskiej Akademii Nauk, ul. Nowy-Swiat 67, Warszawa, Poland. See Addenda.

de BIEZANKO, Prof. C.D., Eng. Agr., Palacio de Comercio, Apt. 501 Caixa Postal 15, Pelotas, Rio Grande do Sul, Brazil. [Lepidoptera of Brazil, Uruguay, Argentina, (Yes); Lepidoptera, excl. Micropterygoidea, Incurvarioidea, Nepticuloidea, Tineoidea, Tortricoidea, Pterophoroidea, of C. Europe (Yes)]

BIGELOW, Prof. Henry B. Museum of Comparative Zoology, Cambridge 38, Mass., U.S.A. [Pisces: Chondrichthyes of all oceans (Yes)]

BIGELOW, Dr. R.S. Macdonald College, McGill University, Montreal, Que., Canada. [Orthoptera of Canada (Yes); Thysanoptera of Canada (No)]

BIGGS, Rev. H.E.J. 19 Siward Road, Bromley, Kent, England. [Terr. & f-w. Mollusca of Near East & Middle East (Yes)]

BIGOT, L. Station Biologique de la Tour de Valat, Le Sambuc, I. Camargue, Bouches du Rhône, France. [Lepidoptera: Pterophoridae of Palearctic (Yes); of America & Africa (No)] [Centre National de la Recherche Scientifique]

BIGUET, Prof. Jean. Institut de Parasitologie, Faculté de Medecine et Pharmacie, Lille (Nord), France. [Trematoda: Microphallidae of World (Yes); Cestoda: Anoplocephalidae of Europe & Madagascar (No)]

* BIJVANK, Dr. Gerhard. c/o Deilmann-Bergbau Guibtt, Bentheim, Germany. [Protozoa: Flagellata]

BILEK, Alois. Zoologische Staatssammlung, Menzingerstrasse 67, München 19, Germany. [Odonata of Europe (Yes)]

BINAGHI, Mr. G. Via Peshiera 30A, Genova, Italy. [Coleoptera: Elateridae & Hydraenidae of Palearctic (Yes)] [Osservatorio Malattie delle Piante]

BINGEFORS, Dr. Sven. Swedish Seed Association, Uppsala 1, Sweden. [Nematoda: g. Dityleuchus (No)]

BIOCCA, Prof. Ettore. Istituto di Parassitologia, Città Universitaria, Roma, Italy. [Nematoda, espec. Strongylata, from mammals of Europe, Africa, Asia (Yes)]

BIRABEN, Prof. Dr. Max. Calle 47, No. 215, La Plata, Argentina. [Araneae of Neotropics (Yes); Crustacea: Branchiopoda of Neotropics (Yes) [Museo de la Plata]

BIRCH, R.L. Department of Biology, West Virginia University, Morgantown, W. Va., U.S.A. [Acarina: Oribatidae (No)]

BIRCHFIELD, Dr. Wray. P.O. Box 3777, University Station, Gainesville, Fla., U.S.A. [Nematoda: Tylenchida of s.U.S. (Yes)] [State Plant Board of Florida]

BIRD, P.F., Curator of Zoology & Botany, The City Museum, Bristol, England. [Pleistocene & Recent Mammalia, excl. Rodentia, of Britain (No); of Somerset, Glouchestershire, Bristol (Yes); Recent Chiroptera of Britain (Yes)]

* BIRD, Ralph D. P.O. Box 250, Brandon, Man., Canada. [Odonata]

BIRKENMEIER, Dr. Elmar. Zoologisches Institut der Universität, Wien I, Austria. [Amphibia]

BIRKET-SMITH, Dr. J. Nigerian College A.S.T., Ibadan, Nigeria. [Lepidoptera: Arctiidae: Lithosiinae of w. & c. Africa (Yes)]

BIRKETT, Dr. Neville L. 3 Thorny Hills, Kendal, Westmoreland, England. [Diptera: Chironomidae of Gr. Brit. (Yes); Lepidoptera of Gr. Brit. (No)]

BIRSTEIN, Prof. Dr. J.A. Faculty of Biology, Moscow State University, Leninskiye Gory, Moscow W-234, U.S.S.R. [Crustacea: Malacostraca, espec. Amphipoda, Isopoda, Decapoda, Mysidacea, of Pacific deeps & f-w. of U.S.S.R. (No)]

125

BISAT, W.S. "Leighton", Crabtree Hill, Collingham, Wetherby, Yorks, England. [Carboniferous Goniatites of England (Yes)]

BISCHOFF, Dr. Günther. Gewerkschaft Elwerath, Betrieb Osterwald, Osterwald über Neuenhaus (Grafschaft Bentheim), Germany. [Devonian-Triassic Conodonts of w. Europe & N. Africa (Yes)]

BISCHOFF, Prof. Dr. Hans. Address Unknown. [(Hymenoptera)

BISHAL, Y. Geological Department, Shell House, P.O. Box 228, Cairo, Egypt. [Fossil larger Foraminifera of Middle East & Europe (Yes)]

* BISHOPP, Dr. Fred C. Box 1033, Brownsville, Texas, U.S.A. [Acarina: Ixodoidea]

BISWAS, B. Zoological Survey of India, Indian Museum, 27 Chowringhee, Calcutta 13, India. [Aves & Mammalia of Orient (Yes); Reptilia: Sauria of Orient (No)]

BISWAS, Mr. S. Crustacea Section, Zoological Survey of India, 34 Chittaranjan Avenue, Calcutta 12, India. [Crustacea of India (Yes)]

BITSCH, Dr. J. Laboratoire de Zoologie, Dijon (Cote d'Or), France. [Thysanura: Machilidae of World (Yes)]

BJÖRNBERG, Tagea K.S. Instituto Oceanografico, Caixa Postal 9075, São Paulo, Brazil. [Enteropneusta: Ptychoderidae of World (Yes); tornaria larvae (Yes); Tunicata: Asciacea & Copelata of N. & S. America (Yes)]

* BLACHE, J. Centre d'Études des Pêches, B.P. 447, Fort Lamy, Tchad (French Equatorial Africa). [Pisces]

BLACK, Mr. C.C. Museum of Comparative Zoology, Cambridge 38, Mass., U.S.A. [Mid-Tertiary Rodentia of N. America (Yes)]

BLACK, Donald Milton. (Tupelo, Miss.; fossils) Not now active in taxonomy.

BLACK, Dr. John D. (Kirksville, Mo.; Pisces) Not now active in taxonomy.

BLACK, Dr. W.F. Department of Biology, Sir George Williams College, Drummond Street, Montreal, Que., Canada. [Crustacea: Mysidacea, Isopoda, Decapoda, of N. Atlantic (Yes)]

BLACKBURN, Dr. Maurice. Scripps Institution of Oceanography, La Jolla, Calif., U.S.A. [Hydrozoa: Calyptoblastea & Gymnoblastea of Australia (No); Trachymedusae & Narcomedusae of Australia (Yes)]

* BLACKMAN, Thomas M. 2450 Vista Drive, Upland, Calif., U.S.A. [Macrolepidoptera]

BLACKMORE, M. 72 Woodfield Road, Ealing W-5, England. [Mammalia: Microchiroptera of Europe (Yes)]

BLACKWELDER, Dr. R.E. Department of Zoology, Southern Illinois University, Carbondale, Ill., U.S.A. [Coleoptera: Staphylinidae of World (No)]

BLAGOVESHTCHENSKY, Dr. D.I. Zoological Institute, Academy of Sciences of U.S.S.R., Leningrad 164, U.S.S.R. [Mallophaga & Anoplura of U.S.S.R. (Yes)]

BLAIR, Dr. Albert P. Department of Zoology, University of Tulsa, Tulsa 4, Okla., U.S.A. [Amphibia: g. Bufo of U.S. (Yes)]

BLAIR, W. Frank. Department of Zoology, University of Texas, Austin 12, Texas, U.S.A. [Amphibia: Anura of N. America (Yes); Reptilia: Lacertilia of s.w. U.S. (Yes); Mammalia of U.S. (Yes)]

BLAKE, Charles H. (Hillsboro, N.C.; Aves) Not now active in taxonomy.

BLAKE, Mrs. Doris H. 3416 N. Glebe Road, Arlington 7, Va., U.S.A. [Coleoptera: Chrysomelidae of N.& S. America (No)]

BLAKE, Mr. Emmet R. Chicago Natural History Museum, Chicago 5, Ill., U.S.A. [Aves of Neotropics (Yes)]

BLAKE, Oliver Duncan. Oil & Gas Conservation Commission, 15 Poly Drive, Billings, Mont., U.S.A. [Upper Paleozoic Bryozoa: Trepostomata (Yes); Cryptostomata (No)]

*BLANC, Dr. Albert Carlo. Via F. Caccioni 1, Città Universitaria, Roma, Italy. [Fossil Mammalia]

BLANC, Mr. F.L. Bureau of Entomology, California Department of Agriculture, 1220 "N" Street, Sacramento 14, Calif., U.S.A. [Diptera: Tephritidae of Calif. (Yes); g. Rhagoletis, adults & larvae, of N. America (Yes)]

BLANC, Dr. M.A., Sous-Directeur au Muséum, Laboratoire de Zoologie (Poissons), Muséum National d'Histoire Naturelle, 57 rue Cuvier, Paris (V), France. [Pisces]

* BLANC, M.G. Address unknown. (Amphibia: Gymnophiones)

* BLANCAS, Dr. Fortunato. Museo de Historia Natural "Javier Prado", Casilla Correo 1109, Lima, Peru. [Nematoda]

* BLANCHARD, Dr. Everard E. Instituto de Sanidad Vegetal, Paseo Colon 922, Piso 4, Buenos Aires, Argentina. [Diptera, Hymenoptera, Thysanoptera]

* BLANCOU, L. Correspondant du Muséum National d'Histoire Naturelle (Mammifères), 55 rue de Buffon, Paris (V), France. [Mammalia]

BLANTON, Dr. F.S. Department of Entomology, University of Florida, Gainesville, Fla., U.S.A. [Diptera of medical importance of World (No)]

BŁAŻEJEWSKI, Mr. Franciszek. Zakład Zoologii, Uniwersytet Mikołaja Kopernika, ul. Danielewskiego 6, Torun, Poland. [Coleoptera: Carabidae of c. Europe (No); Nitulidae g. Meligethes of c. Europe (Yes)]

BLEAKNEY, John Sherman. Department of Biology, Acadia University, Wolfville, N. S., Canada. [Amphibia & Reptilia of Canada (Yes)]

BLESIO, Franco. See FRANCO, Blesio.

BLEST, Dr. A. D. University College, Gower Street, London, W. C. 2, England. [Araneae: Linyphiidae of Europe (No)]

BŁESZYŃSKI, Dr. Stanislaw. Instytut Zoologiczny, Polska Akademia Nauk, Sławkowska 17, Kraków, Poland. [Lepidoptera of Poland (Yes); g. Crambus of Palearctic (Yes); of Nearctic, etc. (No)]

BLICKLE, Prof. Robert Louis. Department of Entomology, University of New Hampshire, Durham, N. H., U. S. A. [Diptera: Tabanidae of N. America (Yes); Trichoptera of N. America (Yes); Acarina; Ixodidae of n. e. U. S. (Yes)]

BLISS, Mr. Raymond Q. 417 W. Rittenhouse Street, Philadelphia 44, Penna., U. S. A. [Coleoptera: Silphidae of U. S. (Yes); g. Necrophorus of World (Yes)]

BLIVEN, B. P. P. O. Box 98, Eureka, Calif., U. S. A. [Heteroptera: Gymnocerata of w. U. S. (Yes); Pentatomidae of India (No); Homoptera: Cicadellidae & Psyllidae of w. N. America (No)]

BLOEDEL, P. P. O. Box 274, Williams, Ariz., U. S. A. [Mammalia of s. w. U. S. (Yes)]

BLOK, Mr. A. "Downs Cot", Falmer Road, Rottingdean, Sussex, England. See Addenda.

BLOKLANDER, A. Terweeweg 73, Oegstgeest, Netherlands. [Recent Mollusca & Bryozoa of w. Europe (Yes); Pliocene-Pleistocene of England, Belgium, Holland (Yes); Miocene of Germany, Belgium, Netherlands (Yes); Miocene of Loire-Bassin, France (Yes)]

BLOM, W. L. Westerbinnensingel 3ᵃ, Groningen, Netherlands. [Macrolepidoptera Rhopalocera of w. Europe (Yes); Heterocera of Netherlands (Yes); Rhopalocera of World (No)]

BLOMQVIST, G. Joutseno, Finland. [Coleoptera of Finland (No)]

* BLOOMER, H. Howard. Longdown, Sunnydale Road, Swanage, Dorset, England. [Mollusca]

BLOSSOM, Philip M. (Orlando, Fla.; Mammalia) Died February 21, 1960.

BLÖTE, Dr. H. C. Entomology Department, Museum van Natuurlijke Historie, Leiden, Netherlands. [Hemiptera]

BLOW, Dr. W. H. c/o D'Arcy Exploration Co. (Africa) Ltd., P. O. Box 325, Tripoli, Libya. [Cretaceous-Recent planktonic Foraminifera: Orbulinidae, Heterohelicidae, Globorotalidae, Globotruncanidae (Yes)]

BLOWER, Mr. J. G. Department of Zoology, The University, Manchester 13, England. [Diplopoda & Chilopoda of Europe (Yes)]

BLUME, Prof. Dr. Werner. Wilhelm Weberstrasse 6, Göttingen, Germany. [Terr. & f-w. shells (No)]

BLUMENTHAL, Major Carl L. Gudestrasse 3, (20a) Uelzen/Hannover, Germany. [Coleoptera: Carabidae, g. Carabus of World (Yes); g. Pterostichus of Europe (No)]

* BLÜTHGEN, Dr. Paul. Hallische Strasse 58, Naumberg (Saale), Deutsche Demokratische Republik. [Hymenoptera]

BO, Dra. Nelly A. Departmento de Zoologia, Museo de Ciencias Naturales de La Plata, Paseo del Bosque, La Plata, Argentina. [Aves: Pelecaniformes: Phalacrocoracidae of Argentina (Yes); Ciconiiformes: Ardeidae of Argentina (Yes)]

* BOADA, Luis Via. Faculdad de Ciencias, La Universidad, Barcelona, Spain. [Fossil invertebrates]

BOARDMAN, Richard S. Division of Invertebrate Paleontology, U. S. National Museum, Washington 25, D. C., U. S. A. [Paleozoic Bryozoa (Yes)]

BOBIES, Carl A. (Wien, Austria: invertebrates) Deceased.

* BOBIN, Dr. Geneviève, Laboratoire d'Anatomie et Histologie Comparées, Sorbonne, 1 rue Victor Cousin, Paris (V), France. [Bryozoa]

BOCK, Dr. K. J. Griesheimerstrasse 16, Marl (Kr. Recklinghausen), Germany. [Protozoa: Ciliata, marine & f-w., excl. Tintinnida & Parasitica (Yes)]

BOCK, Walter. Biological Laboratories, Harvard University, Cambridge 38, Mass., U. S. A. [Aves of World (No)]

* BOCK, Mr. Wilhelm. Box 161, North Wales, Penna., U. S. A. [Fossil Reptilia & Amphibia]

BOCQUET, Prof. Charles. Laboratoire de Zoologie, Nouvelle Université, Rue de Gaillon, Caen (Calvados), France. [Crustacea: Isopoda of Europe (No); Copepoda parasitic on invertebrates of Europe (No)]

BOCQUET-VEDRINE, Jacqueline. Service de Zoologie, Faculté de Sciences, Caen (Calvados) France. [Crustacea: Cirripedia: Rhizocephala of France (No)] [Centre National de la Recherche Scientifique]

BODDY, Dr. Dennis W. Columbia Basin College, Pasco, Wash., U. S. A. [Coleoptera: Tenebrionidae of w. N. America (Yes)]

BODEN, Dr. Brian P. Scripps Institution of Oceanography, La Jolla, Calif., U. S. A. [Crustacea: Euphausiacea of World (Yes)]

BODENHEIMER, Prof. Dr. F. S. (Jerusalem, Israel; Homoptera; Orthoptera; Mammalia of Middle East) Died in 1959.
BODENSTEIN, Dr. G. Binger Strasse 65/p, Ingelheim am Rhein, 1, Germany. [Aves: Picidae, g. Dendroscopus of Old World (Yes)]
* BODMER, Walter. Kunstmaler, Missionsstrasse 41, Basel, Switzerland. [Fossil invertebrates]
BÖDVARSSON, Dr. Högni. Zoologiska Institutionen, Lund, Sweden. [Collembola of Scandinavia (No)]
BOELENS, W. C. Paul Krugerstraat 48, Hengelo (O), Netherlands. [Coleoptera: Staphylinidae of Mid-Europe (Yes)]
BOERMAN, D. J. Sonoystraat 51, DenHaag, Netherlands. [Mollusca, espec. Recent marine (No)]
BOERNER, Charles H. 2940 Oahu Avenue, Honoluly 14, Hawaii. [Mollusca of Hawaii (No); g. Cypraea of Hawaii (Yes)]
* BOERO, Juan J. Division de Profilaxis, Direction de Sanidad Animal, Ministerio de Agricultura, Buenos Aires, Argentina. [Acarina: Ixodidae]
BOESE, J. L. R. R. 1, Alpine, Ind., U. S. A. [Coleoptera: larvae of Dytiscidae (No); Diptera: Culicidae (No)] [Indiana University]
BOESEL, Prof. M. W. 5141 Oxford-Milford Road, R. R. 2, Oxford, Ohio, U. S. A. [Diptera: Tendipedidae & Heleidae of Nearctic (Yes)] [Miami University]
BOESEMAN, Dr. M., Curator of Fishes, Rijksmuseum van Natuurlijke Historie, Leiden, Netherlands. [Pisces of n. S. America & New Guinea (Yes); Orthoptera, no longer active]
BOESSNECK, Priv. Dozent Dr. Joachim. Tieranatomisches Institut der Universität, Schwere Reiterstrasse 9, München, Germany. [Sub-fossil Mammalia: Ungulata of Europe & Carnivora of c. Europe (Yes); domestic animals of ancient world (Yes)]
BOETTGER, Prof. Dr. Caesar R. Zoologisches Institut, Pockels Strasse 10a, Braunschweig (Niedersachsen),Germany. [Tertiary-Recent Mollusca (Yes); Trematoda, g. Schistosoma & Fasciola, espec. of Africa (No)] [Technical University]
von BOETTICHER, Dr. H., Directeur emeritus du Naturwissenschaftliches Museum, Hinterm Glockenberg 1b, Coburg, Germany. [Aves of Palearctic & Africa (Yes); Mammalia of same (No)]
* BOEV, Dr. S. N. Zoological Institute, Academy of Sciences of the Kazakh S. S. R., Ujgurskaja Street 85, Alma-Ata, 12, U. S. S. R. [Nematoda of sheep of U. S. S. R.]
* BOGDANOV, O. P. Zoological Institute, Academy of Sciences, Taschkent, Uzbek, U. S. S. R. [Reptilia]
BOGERT, Charles M. Department of Amphibians & Reptiles, American Museum of Natural History, New York 24, N. Y., U. S. A. [Reptilia of World (Yes)]
BÖGGILD, Ole. Poppelhegnet 5, Lyngby, Denmark. [Araneida of Denmark (Yes)] [Zoophysiological Laboratory, København University]
BOGHOSSIAN, Miss H. E. Zoological Institute, Academy of Science of Armenian SSR, Avanckoe Shosse, No. 20, Erivan, U. S. S. R. [Nematoda: Tylenchidae, Neotylenchidae, Heteroderidae, Aphelenchidae, of Armenia (Yes)]
BOGITSH, Dr. B. J. Department of Biology, Georgia Teachers College, Collegeboro, Ga., U. S. A. [Trematoda & Cestoda of N. America (Yes); espec. Strigeidae & parasites of f-w. fish & amphibians]
BOGOESCU, Constantin. Facultatea de Biologie, Splaiul Independentei, Nr. 93-95, Bucureşti, Rumania. [Ephemeroptera & Plecoptera of c. & s. e. Europe (Yes)]
BOGOSLOVSKY, Dr. A. S. Biological Laboratory, Moscow State University, Moscow B-234, Lengora, U. S. S. R. [Rotatoria of U. S. S. R. (Yes)]
BOGULEANU, Ing. Gheorghe. Institutul Agronomic "Nicolaie Bălcescu", B-dul Mărăşti 59, Bucureşti, Rumania. [Coleoptera: Elateridae of Rumania (Yes)]
BOHART, Dr. George Edward. Campus Box 80, Utah State University, Logan, Utah, U. S. A. [Hymenoptera: Apoidea of N. America (Yes)] [U. S. Department of Agriculture]
BOHART, Richard M. Department of Entomology, University of California, Davis, Calif., U. S. A. [Hymenoptera: Vespidae; Sphecidae of N. America (Yes); Diptera: Culicidae of Pacific & Ryukyu Is. (Yes); Strepsiptera of World (Yes)]
BOHLIN, Dr. Birger. Luthagsesplanaden 24E, Uppsala, Sweden. [Mammalia: Pontian Cavicornia & Giraffidae of c. Asia; Up. Oligocene Lagomorpha of c. Asia]
* BOHLKE, Dr. H. Institut für Haustierkunde, Hegeurschstrasse 1, Kiel, Germany. [Mammals]
BÖHLKE, J., Asst. Curator of Fishes, Academy of Natural Sciences, Philadelphia 3, Penna., U. S. A. [Pisces: Characidae of S. America (No); marine eels, excl. Congridae, of World (Yes); shore fishes of West Indies (Yes)]
BÖHM, Prof. Dr. L. K., Lehrkanzel für Allgemeine Zoologie und Parasitologie, Tierärztlichen Institut der Hochschule, Linke Bahngasse 11, Wien III, Austria. [Parasitic Nematoda of birds & mammals of c. Europe (Yes)]

128

BOHMANN, Dr. rer. nat. habil. Ludwig. (Heidenheim, Germany; Rodentia) Not now active in taxonomy.

BOHNSACK, Dr. Kurt K. Department of Zoology, San Diego State College, San Diego 15, Calif., U.S.A. [Acarina: Oribatei of Nearctic (No)]

BOITEL, A.G.P.M. 2 rue A. de Musset, Sidi-bel-Abbès, Algeria. [Coleoptera]

BOKERMAN, Mr. Werner C.A. Rua Anita Garibaldi N. 45, 5º, 501, São Paulo, Brazil. [Amphibia of Neotropics (Yes)]

BÖKÖNYI, S. Magyar Nemzeti Muzeum, Muzeum Krt. 14-16, Budapest VIII, Hungary. [Subfossil domestic animals of Europe & w. Asia; Mammalia of same]

van den BOLD, Dr. W. Louisiana State University, Baton Rouge, La., U.S.A. [Post-Paleozoic Crustacea: Ostracoda; smaller Foraminifera (Yes)]

BOLDORI, Leonida. Via Procaccini, 73, Milano, Italy. [Coleoptera: larvae of Carabidae; cave faunas]

BOLE, Mr. B.P., Jr. Biology Laboratory, 2080 Adelbert Road, Western Reserve University, Cleveland 6, Ohio. [Birds & Mammals of N. America (Yes)]

BOLÉ, Dr. Jōze. Biološki Inštitut Medicinske Fakultete, Lipičeva 2, Ljubljana, Yugoslavia. [Gastropoda of Yugoslavia(Yes)]

BOLIEK, Dr. M.Irene. Department of Biological Sciences, Florida State University, Tallahassee, Fla., U.S.A. [Crustacea: Copepoda & Cladocera of n.w. Florida (No); Acarina: Hydracarina of n.w. Florida (No)]

BOLIN, Dr. Rolf L. Hopkins Marine Station, Pacific Grove, Calif., U.S.A. [Pisces: Osteichthyes: Myctophidae & Neoscopelidae of World (Yes)]

BOLÍVAR y PIELTAIN, Prof. Cándido. Apartado Postal 19186, Escuela Nacional de Ciencias Biológicas, Instituto Politécnico Nacional, Mexico 17, D.F., Mexico. [Orthoptera, espec. Eumastacidae, of World (Yes) ; Zoraptera of America (Yes); Arachnida: Ricinulidea of America (Yes); Coleoptera: Carabidae of Mexico (Yes)]

BOLLI, Dr. Hans M. Venezuelan Atlantic Refining Co., Apartado Postal 893, Caracas, Venezuela. [Planktonic Foraminifera of New World, Europe, N. Africa (Yes)]

BOLLING, Werner. Luitpoldstrasse 33, Bamberg, Bavaria, Germany. [Gastropoda: Bythinellidae of c. Europe (Yes)]

* BOLLMAN, Hans Gunther. Deutsches Entomologisches Institut, Waldowstrasse 1, Berlin-Friedrichshagen, Germany. [Lepidoptera]

* BOLLOW, Dr. H. Engelschalkingerstrasse 67, München 27, Germany. [Coleoptera]

BOLSTER, Mr. George C. Fisheries Laboratory, Ministry of Agriculture, Fisheries & Food, Lowestoft, Suffolk, England. [Crustacea: Copepoda: Clausiidae: g. Mytilicola of Europe (Yes)]

* BOLTON, Dr. T.E. Geological Survey of Canada, Department of mines and Technical Surveys, Ottawa, Ont., Canada. [Fossil invertebrates]

BOLTOVSKOY, Dr. E. Lucio Vicente Lopez 712, Temperley, Argentina. [Foraminifera of Argentine seas (Yes)] [Museo Argentino de Ciencias Naturales "Bernardina Rivadavia"]

BOMANS, Hughes E. P.O.Box 59, Albertville, Katanga, Belgian Congo. [Coleoptera: Lucanidae of Africa (Yes), Lucanidae, Cerambycidae, Carabidae, of World (No)]

BOMFORD, Brig. G. Hainton Lodge, Sutton Courtenay, Berks, England. [Ammonoidea of "Inferior Oolite" of England (Yes)]

* BOMP, Dr. G. U.S. Fish & Wildlife Service, Washington 25, D.C., U.S.A. [Aves, Mammalia]

BONA, Dr. Franco. Istituto di Zoologia, 17 Via Accademia Albertina, Torino, Italy. [Cestoda: Cyclophillidea of birds of World (Yes); Cestoda & Trematoda of World (No)]

BONADONA, Paul. Villa Stella Maria, Chemin de la Baronne, Le Cannet, France. [Coleoptera: Anthicidae of World (No); of Palearctic, Africa, Madagascar (Yes)]

BOND, Prof. Carl E. Department of Fish & Game, Oregon State College, Corvallis, Ore., U.S.A. [Pisces of Pacific N.W. of U.S. (No); g. Cottus (Yes)]

BOND, Dr. G. National Museums of Southern Rhodesia, P.O.Box 240, Bulawayo, Southern Rhodesia. [Permian-Triassic (Karroo) non-marine Lamellibranchia, Gastropoda, Phyllopoda, Ostracoda of c. Africa (Yes)]

BOND, Gorman M. U.S. National Museum, Washington 25, D.C., U.S.A. [Aves of U.S. & Canada (Yes)]

BOND, James. Department of Birds, Academy of Natural Sciences, Philadephia 3, Penna., U.S.A. [Aves of West Indies, C.& S. America (Yes)]

BOND, Prof. Ralph H. Department of Geology, Capital University, Columbus 9, Ohio. [Devonian-Mississippian Conodonts of e. U.S. (Yes)]

BOND, Dr. Richard M. Virgin Islands Agricultural Program, Kingshill, St. Croix, Virgin Islands. [Aves: Falconidae, espec. g. Falco of N. America (No)]

BONDAR, Gregorio. (Bahia, Brazil; Coleoptera, Pseudoscorpionida) Died February 1959.

* BONDAREVA, V.I. Institute of the Kazakh Branch of the All-Union Lenin Academy of Agricultural Sciences, Taschkentskaya Street 207, Alma-Ata, U.S.S.R. [Helminths of animals of U.S.S.R.]

von BONDE, Cecil. Beach Road, Seapoint, Capetown, Union of South Africa [Pisces]

129

BONDESEN, P. (Aarhus, Denmark; Gastropoda) Not now active in taxonomy.
* BONDESIO, Pedro. Departmento de Paleontologia, Museo de La Plata, Paseo del Bosque,
    La Plata, Argentina. [Fossil vertebrates]
BONÉ, Rev. Dr. E. Département des Sciences, Collège Philosophique, 95, Route de Mont-
    St. Jean, Louvain, Belgium. [Mammalia: Hominidae (Yes); Oligocene-Pleistocene
    Giraffidae of Africa (Yes)]
* BONÉ, Dr. G. V. I. R. S. A. C., B. P. 217, Costermansville, Belgian Congo. [Parasites]
BONET, Dr. F. Guty Cárdenas 69, Mexico 20, D. F., Mexico. [Protura, Pauropoda, Col-
    lembola, of World (Yes); fossil Ciliata: Tintinnidae of World (Yes); fossil calcisphae-
    rids of World (Yes)]
BONHAM, Kelshaw. (Seattle, Wash.; Trematoda & Pisces) Not now active in taxonomy.
* BONI, Dr. A. Istituto di Geologia, Universitá di Pavia, Pavia, Italy. [Fossil vertebrates]
* BONNE, W. D., Jr. Bilderdijkstraat 9I, Amsterdam W, Netherlands. [Aves: Fringillidae]
BONNET, L., Professeur agrégé au Lycée Bellevue, Toulouse, France. [Protozoa: soil
    Thecamoebae of Europe (Yes)]
BONNET, Dr. P., professeur, Laboratoire de Zoologie, Faculté des Sciences, Toulouse,
    France. [Araneida of World (No)] [Université de Toulouse]
BONNE-WEPSTER, Mrs. J. Mauritskade 57, Amsterdam O, Netherlands. [Diptera: Culi-
    cidae of Surinam & Indo-Australia (Yes); of Netherlands (No)] [Instituut voor Trop-
    ische Hygiene en Geographische Pathologie]
BONNOT, P. (Stanford, Calif.; marine mammals, Gastropoda) Deceased.
BOOLOOTIAN, Mr. R. A. Department of Zoology, University of California, Los Angeles 24,
    Calif., U. S. A. [Cephalopoda of all oceans (Yes)]
BOONSTRA, Dr. L. D. South African Museum, Cape Town, Union of South Africa. [Permian
    - Triassic (Karroo) Vertebrates of Africa (Yes)]
* van den BOORN, Dr. M. C. J. Dr. Schaepmanlaan 4, Eindhoven, Netherlands. [Hemiptera:
    Heteroptera]
BOOS, Father Heinrich, M. S. C. Ostenallee 88, Hamm, Westfalen, Germany. [Coleoptera:
    Cerambycidae of C. Europe (Yes)]
BOOTH, A. H. (Accra, Ghana; Mammalia) Died 1958.
BOOTH, Dr. Ernest S. Department of Biological Science, Walla Walla College, College
    Place, Wash., U. S. A. [Aves & Mammalia of Pacific n. w. U. S. (Yes); Mammalia of
    Mexico (No)]
BORATYNSKI, Dr. K. L. Department of Zoology & Applied Entomology, Imperial College of
    Science & Technology, Prince Consort Road, London, S. W. 7, England. [Homoptera:
    Coccoidea of Europe (Yes)]
BORCEA, Paul. Facultatea Stiinte Naturale, Universitatea "Al. I. Cuza", Iasi, Rumania.
    [Heteroptera of Europe (Yes); Homoptera: Auchenorhyncha of Europe (No)]
* BORCHMANN, F. Zoologische Forschungsinstitut und Museum A. Koenig, 150 Koblenzer-
    strasse, Bonn, Germany. [Coleoptera: Lagriidae of World (Yes)]
BORCHSENIUS, Prof. Dr. N. S. Zoological Institute, Academy of Sciences, Leningrad B-164,
    U. S. S. R. [Homoptera: Coccoidea of e. Palearctic & Indo-China (Yes)]
* BORDAS, Dr. Alejandro. Figueroa 575, Buenos Aires, Argentina. [Fossil vertebrates]
van der BORG, H. H. Deventerstraat 3, Apeldoorn, Netherlands. [Aves]
BORGMEIER, Dr. T., O. F. M. Estrada Rio Grande 2116, Jacarepaguá, D. F., Brazil.
    [Hymenoptera: Formicidae of Neotropics (Yes); Diptera: Phoridae of Neotropics (Yes);
    Coleoptera: Staphylinidae, myrmecoph. & termitoph., of Neotropics (Yes)]
* BORGHORST, G. Address unknown. (Crustacea: Malacostraca)
BÖRJE, Dr. Carlin. Baldersvägen 14, Sundsvall, Sweden. [Rotifera (Yes)]
* BORODIN, D. Address unknown. (Coleoptera)
BORRO, Sr. Primitivo. Coloma 4, Casa Blanca, Habana, Cuba. [Foraminifera "in general"
    (Yes)]
BORROR, Dr. Donald J. Department of Zoology and Entomology, Ohio State University,
    Columbus 10, Ohio. [Odonata of n. e. U. S. (Yes); Libellulidae of N. & S. America
    (No); g. Oligoclada & Erythrodiplax of N. & S. America (Yes)]
* BORUTSKY, Prof. E. B. Zoological Museum, Moscow State University, Hertzena 6, Mos-
    cow K-9, U. S. S. R. [Crustacea: Copepoda]
* BORZA, Dr. Al. Str. Grădinilor 39, Cluj, Rumania. [Crustacea]
* BOSCÁ BERGA, F. Facultad de Ciencias, Valencia, Spain. [Pisces]
BOSCHI, Dr. Enrique Eduardo. Calle Nahuel Huapi 2251, Capital, Buenos Aires, Argentina.
    [Crustacea: Palaemonidae & Penaeidae of Neotropics (Yes); f-w. Pisces of Neo-
    tropics (No)] [Departamento de Investigaciones Pesqueras]
BOSCHMA, Dr. H. Rijksmuseum van Natuurlijke Historie, Leiden, Netherlands. [Rhizo-
    cephala of World (Yes); Coelenterata: Stylasterina of World (Yes)]
BOSCHUNG, Dr. H. T., Jr. Department of Biology, University of Alabama, University,
    Ala., U. S. A. [Pisces: bony fishes of shore of Gulf of Mexico (Yes); of f-w. of s. e.
    U. S. (No)]
* BOSQ, Juan M. Almirante Brown 161, Ramos Mejia, B. A., Argentina. [Coleoptera]

* BOSSONG, H. 7 Avenue des Templiers, Epinal (Vosges), France. [Coleoptera]
BOSWELL, Mrs. H. P. O. Box 8081, Johannesburg, Union of South Africa. [Gastropoda:
    Volutidae, Conidae, Muricidae, of World (No)]
BOTERO-ARANGO, Gerardo. Carrera Balboa 63-13, Medellin, Colombia. [Cretaceous
    Mollusca of n. w. S. America (No)] [Facultad Nacional de Minas]
BOTNARIUC, Dr. Nicolae. Facultatea de Stiinte Naturale, Splaiul Independentei Nr. 91-93,
    Bucureşti, Rumania. [Diptera: Chironomidae, larvae & imagines, of Rumania (Yes);
    Crustacea: Phyllopoda of Rumania (Yes)]
BOTOSĂNEANU, Lazar. Institut de Spéologie de Bucarest, Str. Dr. Capsa 8, Bucureşti 15,
    Rumania. [Trichoptera, larvae, pupae, imagines, of Europe (Yes); Crustacea:
    Bathynellacea of Rumania (No)]
BOTT, Dr. Richard. Senckenbergische Naturforschende Gesellschaft, Natur-Museum und
    Forschungsinstitut, Senckenberg-Anlage 25, Frankfurt am Main, Germany. [Crusta-
    cea: Decapoda: Astacidae & Potamonidae, of World (Yes), Stomatopoda of World (Yes)]
* BOTTAZZI, Dr. Elsa, Assistant, Istituto di Zoologia, Università di Parma, Parma, Italy.
    [Acarina]
BOTTIMER, L. J. 310 Hummingbird Lane, Kerrville, Texas, U. S. A. [Coleoptera: Bruchi-
    dae of World (No), Scarabaeidae of U. S. (No)]
BOTTO, Dr. G. Via Rosine 8, Torino, Italy. [Coleoptera of South Africa]
BOUČEK, Prof. Bedřich. Geologické Fakulty, Karlova Universita, Albertov 6, Praha II,
    Czechoslovakia. [Silurian & Ordovician Graptolithina of c. Europe (Yes); Sil. & Dev.
    Ostracoda of Bohemia (Yes); Paleozoic Pteropoda: Hyolithida & Tentaculitida of
    Europe (Yes); Ord. & Sil. Conularida of c. Europe (Yes)]
BOUČEK, Dr. Zdeněk. Národni Museum, Václavské Náměsti 1700, Praha II, Czechoslovakia.
    [Hymenoptera: Chalcidoidea of w. Palearctic (No), Perilampidae, Eucharitidae, Chal-
    cididae, Eurytomidae, Eulophidae, Pteromalidae, of w. Palearctic (Yes)] [Entomolo-
    gy Department, National Museum]
* BOUCHARD, Prof. J. Louis. Department of Biology, Northwestern State College, Alva,
    Okla., U. S. A. [Helminths of Amphibia of n. e. U. S.]
BOUCOT, A. J. Department of Geology, Massachusetts Institute of Technology, Cambridge
    39, Mass., U. S. A. [Silurian & Devonian Brachiopoda & Gastropoda of World (Yes)]
* BOUDAN, R. 85 rue de Nouzonville, Charleville, Ardennes, France. [Coleoptera]
BOUDREAUX, Dr. Henry Bruce. Deparment of Zoology, Louisiana State University, Baton
    Route 3, La., U. S. A. [Homoptera: Aphidae of N. America (Yes); Acarina: Tetrany-
    chidae of World (Yes)]
BOUET, Georges. (Paris, France; Aves) Died 1957.
BOUILLON, Dr. J. Laboratoire de Zoologie et de Biologie Animale, Université Libra de
    Bruxelles, 50 Avenue Franklin Roosevelt, Bruxelles, Belgium. [Gastropoda: Melani-
    idae of Africa (Yes); Coelenterata: Limnomedusa (Yes)]
BOULTON, Mr. Rudyerd. 3234 Reservoir Road n. w., Washington 7, D. C., U. S. A. [Aves
    of Africa (Yes)]
BOURDEAU, Dr. Flora G. (also as Flora B. Gorirossi). 360 Prospect Street, New Haven
    11, Conn., U. S. A. [Acarina: Mesostigmata of World (Yes)] [Hartford Yale Founda-
    tion]
BOURDILLON, Dr. A. Station Marine d'Endoume, Rue de La Batterie des Lions, Marseil-
    les 7, France. [Pycnogonida of Atlantic & Mediterranean (Yes)]
BOURDON, Marc. c/o C. P. T. L., 230 g. Istiklal, Tripoli, Liyba. (also 101 Boulevard
    Péreire, Paris (XVII), France) [Post-Paleozoic Foraminifera (No)]
BOURGIN, P., , Assistant au Muséum National d'Histoire Naturelle, 55 rue de Buffon,
    Paris (V), France. See Addenda.
BOURGOGNE, Jean, Sous-Directeur au Museum, Laboratoire d'Entomologie, 45bis rue de
    Buffon, Paris (V), France. [Lepidoptera: Psychidae, excl. Micropsychidae, of
    World (No), of Palearctic & Ethiopian (Yes)] [Muséum National d Histoire Naturelle]
BOURKE, Mr. T. V. Entomological Branch, Department of Agriculture, Box 36, G. P. O.,
    Sydney, N. S. W., Australia. [Coleoptera: Scarabaeidae of e. Australia (Yes)]
BOURLIERE, Prof. F. Laboratoire de Biologie, Faculté de Médicine, 45 rue des Saints
    Pères, Paris (VI), France. [Mammalia: Ungulata of Africa (Yes)] [Université de
    Paris]
BOURNE, Dr. W. R. P. 46 Wilbury Road, Hove 3, Sussex, England. [Aves: Procellarii-
    formes of World (Yes)] [Edward Grey Institute of Field Ornithology]
BOURNIER, Dr. A. 10 rue Abert, Montpellier, France. [Thysanoptera of Europe & Medi-
    terranean (Yes)] [Ecole Nationale d Agriculture de Montpellier]
BOURRELLY, Dr. P., Sous Directeur, Laboratoire de Cryptogamie, Muséum National
    d'Histoire Naturelle, 12 rue de Buffon, Paris (V), France. [Euglenophyceae/Phyto-
    flagellata (Yes)]
BOURSIN, Charles. 11 rue des Écoles, Paris (V), France. [Lepidoptera: Noctuidae: Trifi-
    nae of World espec. Palearctic (Yes)]

131

BOUSEMAN, J. Department of Entomology, University of Illinois, Urbana, Ill., U.S.A. [Coleoptera: Cerambycidae of N. America (Yes); Scaphidiidae of World (No); Mecoptera: Panorpidae of World (No)]

BOUSFIELD, Dr. E.L. National Museum of Canada, Ottawa, Ont., Canada. [Crustacea: f-w. Amphipoda of N. America (Yes); marine intertidal Amphipoda of Canada (Yes); terr. Talitridae of World (Yes); Cirripedia of N. America (No)]

BOUSKA, Josef. (Praha, Czechoslovakia; fossils) Died 1957.

BOUSSEAU, Colonel Jacques. 20 Boulevard Joseph Vallier, Grenoble, France. [Lepidoptera: Rhopalocera of France & N. Africa (No), g. Parnassius of World (No)]

* BOUVIER, Dr. G. Institut Veterinaire, rue Dr. Cesar Roux 37, Lausanne, Switzerland. [Diptera: Tabanidae]

* BOUXIN, Dr. H.L. Laboratoire Maritime du Collège de France, Concarneau (Finistère), France. [Fossil invertebrates]

BOVEE, Dr. Eugene C. Department of Biology, University of Florida, Gainesville, Fla., U.S.A. [Sarcodina: Amoebida of N. America (Yes), Ciliata: g. Euplotes of N. & S. America (No), Sporozoa: Coccidia: g. Eimeria of N. America (No)]

van BOVEN, Prof. Dr. J.K.A. Institut de Zoologie, Rue de Namur 71, Louvain, Belgium. [Hymenoptera: Formicidae of w. Europe (Yes), g. Dorylus of Africa (Yes)]

BØVING, Adam G. (Washington, D.C.; larvae of Coleoptera) Died March 16, 1957.

BOWDEN, J. Kawanda Research Station, P.O. Box 265, Kampala, Uganda. [Diptera: Bombylidae & Lepidoptera: Noctuidae of Ethiopian (Yes)]

BOWEN, Dr. R.N.C. University of California, Institute of Technology & Engineering, La Jolla, Calif., U.S.A. See Addenda.

BOWEN, Mr. W. Wedgewood. Dartmouth College Museum, Hanover, N.H., U S.A. [Aves of Africa (No)]

BOWER, Harold M. (Wausau, Wis.; Lepidoptera) Not now active in taxonomy.

BOWMAN, Dr. John R. Technological Institute, Northwestern University, Evanston, Ill., U.S.A. [Coleoptera of World (No)]

BOWMAN, Mrs. Mollie. (Queensland, Australia; Mollusca) Not now active in taxonomy.

BOWMAN, Dr. Robert I. Department of Biological Science, San Francisco State College, San Francisco, Calif., U.S.A. [Aves: Geospizinae of Galapagos Is. (Yes); Vertebrates of Galapagos excl. fishes (Yes)]

BOWMAN, Dr. Thomas E. Division of Marine Invertebrates, U.S. National Museum, Washington 25, D.C., U.S.A. [Crustacea: Copepoda: marine Calanoida; Amphipoda: Hyperiidea: Cyamidae; Isopoda: Cymothoidae; all of World (Yes)]

BOWSHER, Mr. Arthur L. Box 521, Tulsa, Okla., U.S.A. [Paleozoic Crinoidea, Blastoidea of World (Yes), Upper Paleozoic Gastropoda of U.S. & Alaska (Yes); Mesozoic Crinoidea of U.S. & Alaska (Yes)]

BOX, Dr. Harold E. 2 First Avenue, Cascade, Port of Spain, Trinidad. [Lepidoptera: Pyralidae: Crambinae: g. Diatraea of W. Hemisphere (Yes)]

BOYD, Elizabeth M. Department of Zoology, Mount Holyoke College, South Hadley, Mass., U.S.A. [Parasites of N. American birds, espec. Passeriformes (No)]

BOYER, Dr. Cecilia Dagert. Escuela de Biologia, Universidad Central de Venezuela, Caracas, Venezuela. [Parasites of man & mammals]

* BOYER, Miss Frenseuie Dagert. Escuela de Biologia, Universidad Central de Venezuela, Caracas, Venezuela. [Scorpiones]

BOYLE, Dr. W. Wayne. Department of Zoology & Entomology, Frear Laboratory, Pennsylvania State University, University Park, Penna., U.S.A. [Coleoptera: Erotylidae of World (No), of N. America (Yes), Languriidae of World (No), of w. Hemisphere (Yes)]

* BOZIE, B. Station Biologique, Roscoff (Finistère), France. [Crustacea: Copepoda]

* BOZZINI, Mlle. M. Laboratoire de Anatomie Comparée, 1 rue Victor Cousin, Paris (V), France. [Arachnida] [Sorbonne]

* BOZZO, Dr. Bianco. Museo Civico di Storia Naturale, 9 Via Brigata Liguria, Genova, Italy. [Orthoptera]

BRAAKSMA, S. Administration Forestière, J.M. Kemperstraat 3, Utrecht, Netherlands. [Aves of n.w. Europe (Yes)]

BRAARUD, T. Institute for Marine Biology, Blindern-Oslo, Norway. [Dinoflagellates of northern waters; Coccolithophorids] [University of Oslo]

BRADBURY, Margaret. Hopkins Marine Station, Pacific Grove, Calif., U.S.A. [Pisces: Ogcocephalidae of World (No); of Gulf of Mexico (Yes)]

BRADE-BIRKS, The Reverend Dr. S.G. The Vicarage, Godmersham, by Canterbury, Kent, England. [Chilopoda of Brit. Is. (Yes); Recent & fossil Diplopoda of Britain (Yes)]

BRADLEY, G.A. Forest Biology Laboratory, Box 156, University of Manitoba, Winnipeg 9, Man., Canada. [Homoptera: Aphididae: g. Cinara of Canada (Yes)]

BRADLEY, Dr. George H. U.S. Public Health Service, Department of Health, Education & Welfare, Washington 25, D.C., U.S.A. [Diptera: Culicidae of s.e. U.S. (No)]

BRADLEY, Prof. J. Chester. Comstock Hall, Cornell University, Ithaca, N.Y., U.S.A. [Hymenoptera: Scoliidae of W. Hemisphere & Ethiopian (Yes)]

BRADLEY, Mr. J. D. Department of Entomology, British Museum (Natural History), Crom-
well Road, London, S. W. 7, England. [Microlepidoptera, excl. Pyraloidea, of Brit.
Is., African Commonw. Terr., Atlantic Is., Melanesia (Yes)]
BRADLEY, John S. (Dallas, Texas; fossils]) Not now active in taxonomy.
BRADSHAW, Prof. A. S. Department of Zoology, Ohio Wesleyan University, Delaware,
Ohio, U. S. A. [Crustacea: Cladocera of e. U. S. (Yes), Copepoda of e. U. S. (No)]
BRADWHAW, Mr. Gordon V. Department of Zoology, University of Arizona, Tucson, Ariz.,
U. S. A. [Mammalia: Chiroptera of N. America (No)]
BRADSHAW, John S. Marine Foraminifera Laboratory, Scripps Institution of Oceanography,
La Jolla, Calif., U. S. A. [Recent planktonic Foraminifera: Globigerinidae, Globoro-
talidae of World (Yes)]
BRADSHAW, W. N. Department of Biology, McMurry College, Abilene, Texas, U. S. A.
[Mammalia: Rodentia of Texas (No)]
* BRADT, Dr. G. W. Address unknown. (Mammals)
BRADY, Lionel Francis. Museum of Northern Arizona, Flagstaff, Ariz., U. S. A. [Fossils
of Kaibab Form. of w. U. S. (No)]
BRAENDEGAARD, Dr. Jens. Egernvej 73, København, Denmark. [Araneida of Greenland,
Iceland, Faroe Is., n. w. Europe espec. Denmark (Yes)]
BRAESTRUP, Dr. F. W. Universitets Zoologiske Museum, Krystalgade, København K, Den-
mark. [Reptilia: g. Agama of Africa, w. Asia (Yes); Mammalia, Reptilia, Amphibia
excl. Hyperoliidae, of Africa (No)]
BRAGA, Dr. José M. Musée Zoologique Augusto Nobre, Faculdade de Ciencias de Porto,
Porto, Portugal. [Crustacea: Asellidae of Europe, Asia, Africa (Yes), Syncarida:
Bathynellidae of same (Yes)]
BRAGG, Dr. Arthur N. Department of Zoology, University of Oklahoma, Norman, Okla,
U. S. A. [Amphibia of N. America (Yes), espec. Salientia of U. S. & Caudata of Okla-
homa, Kansas, Arkansas, Texas]
BRAIN, Dr. C. K. Transvaal Museum, P. O. Box 413, Pretoria, Union of South Africa.
[Reptilia of s. Africa (Yes)] [Transvaal Museum]
BRAKMAN, P. J. Wilhelminastraat 21, Nieuw- en St. Joosland, Netherlands. [Hemiptera-
Heteroptera of w. Europe (No); Coleoptera of w. Europe (Yes)] [Zoölogisch Museum,
Amsterdam]
BRÄM, Dr. Heinrich. Langackerstrasse, Embrach, Zürich, Switzerland. [Fossil Chelonia
of Europe (Yes)]
BRAMBELL, Prof. F. W. R. University College of North Wales, Bangor, Caernarvonshire,
Wales. [Enteropneusta]
BRAME, Mr. Arden H., Jr. 340 South Clark Drive, Beverly Hills, Calif., U. S. A. [Am-
phibia: Recent & fossil Caudata of World (Yes)]
BRAMKAMP, Richard Allan. (New York, N. Y., fossils) Died September 1, 1958.
BRANCH, Mrs. Nina. Entomological Research Center, Florida State Board of Health, Box
308, Vero Beach, Fla., U. S. A. [Diptera: Culicidae of s. e. U. S. (Yes); Siphonaptera,
Acarina, Anoplura, of Florida (No)]
BRAND, Dr. E. c. c. Wintershall A. G., August-Rosterg-Haus, Kassel, Germany. [Juras-
sic-L. Cretaceous Foraminifera & Crustacea: Ostracoda (Yes)]
* BRAND, Dr. John P. Geology Department, Texas Technological College, Lubbock, Texas,
U. S. A. [Fossil invertebrates]
van den BRANDE, Prof. J. Rijkslandbouwhogeschool, Coupure Links 233, Gent, Belgium.
[Plant parasitic Nematoda of Belgium & Belg. Congo (Yes)]
BRANDER, T. Raikko, Matku, Finland. [Macrolepidoptera, excl. g. Eupithecia, of Fennos-
candia (Yes); Mollusca: Unionacea of Fennoscandia (Yes)]
BRANDES, Dr. Carl-Heinz. Institut für Meeresforschung, Am Handelshafen 12, Bremer-
haven-G, Germany. [Crustacea: Copepoda of Atlantic & Baltic (Yes)]
BRANDT, Prof. B. B. Department of Zoology, North Carolina State College, Raleigh, N. C.,
U. S. A. [Reptilia & Amphibia of s. e. U. S. (Yes)]
BRANDT, Mr. Rolf, Medico. Poste Restante, Benghazi, Libya. [Terr. & f-w. Mollusca,
espec. Claurilidiidae, of Palearctic, espec. c. Europe & n. e. Africa (Yes)]
BRANDT, Mr. W. Division of Entomology, Commonwealth Scientific and Industrial Research
Organization, P. O. Box 109, Canberra, A. C. T., Australia. [Macrolepidoptera,
espec. Lycaenidae of Papuan]
* BRANGHAM, Lt. Col. A. Norman. Address unknown. (Hymenoptera: Formicidae)
BRANSON, Branley A. Department of Biology, Kansas State College, Pittsburg, Kansas,
U. S. A. [Terr. & f-w. Gastropoda of N. America (Yes); Pisces: f-w. Osteichthyes of
N. America (Yes); Araneida of Oklahoma & Texas (No)]
BRANSON, Dr. Carl C. Department of Geology, University of Oklahoma, Norman, Okla.,
U. S. A. [Mollusca: Pelecypoda: Paleozoic g. Conocardium (Yes); Pennsylvanian &
Permian Invertebrates of N. America (No)]
BRANSON, Mrs. Herberta V. P. (Tulsa, Okla.; fossils) Not now active in taxonomy.

133

BRATTSTROM, Bayard H. Department of Biology, Orange County State College, Fullerton, Calif., U.S.A. [Cenozoic & Recent Amphibia & Reptilia of New York, California, Nicaragua, Revillagigedo Is. (Yes); Reptilia: Recent & fossil Crotalidae (Yes)]

BRATTSTRÖM, Prof. Dr. H.O., Director, Zoologisk Museum, Bergen, Norway. [Crustacea: Ascothoracida of all seas (Yes); Echinodermata of n. Atlantic (No); Crustacea: Cirripedia of Scandinavia (No)] [Also Director, Biological Station, Espegrend]

BRAUN, Dr. Annette F. 5956 Salem Road, Cincinnati 30, Ohio, U.S.A. [Microlepidoptera, espec. g. Bucculatrix, of N. America (Yes)]

BRAUN, Dr. R. Zoologisches Institut der Johannes Gutenberg Universität, Mainz, Germany. [Araneida of c. Europe (Yes)]

BRAUNS, Privatdozent Dr. rer. nat. Adolf. Staatliches Naturhistorisches Museum, Pockelsstrasse 10a, (20b) Braunschweig, Germany. [Diptera: terricole larvae & pupae of Palearctic (Yes); imagines of Palearctic, espec. Syrphidae & Chloropidae (Yes)]

BRAUNSTEIN, Jules. Shell Oil Corp., P.O. Box 193, New Orleans 3, La., U.S.A. [Cretaceous Foraminifera of Gulf Cst. of U.S. (Yes)]

BRAVO-HOLLIS, Margarita. Laboratorio de Helmintologia, Instituto de Biologia, Ciudad Universitaria, Mexico 30, D.F., Mexico. [Marine Trematoda (Yes); marine helminths in general (No)]

BRAZENOR, C.W. (Melbourne, Australia; Vertebrates) Not now active in taxonomy.

BRECKENRIDGE, Dr. W.J. Minnesota Museum of Natural History, University of Minnesota, Minneapolis 14, Minn., U.S.A. [Aves of U.S. (Yes); Mammalia, Reptilia, Amphibia, of e.U.S. (Yes)]

BREDER, Dr. Charles M., Jr. Department of Fishes & Aquatic Biology, American Museum of Natural History, New York 24, N.Y., U.S.A. [Pisces: Synentognathi of World (Yes); Teleostomi of e. N. America & West Indies (No)]

van BREE, P.J.H. Zoologisch Museum, Plantage Middenlaan 53, Amsterdam, Netherlands. [Reptilia: Lacertidae of Europe (Yes); Mammalia in general (No)]

BREED, Dr. Helen Illick. Department of Conservation, Fernow Hall, Cornell University, Ithaca, N.Y., U.S.A. [Pisces: Cyprinidae of N. America (No)]

BREGANTE, Hugo. Camarones 2631, Buenos Aires, Argentina. [Mantodea of Neotropics (Yes)]

BREGETOVA, Mrs. Nina G. Zoological Institute, Academy of Sciences, Leningrad B-164, U.S.S.R. [Acarina: Gamasoidea of U.S.S.R. (Yes)]

BREHM, Dr. Vincenz. Biologische Station, Lunz am See, N.Ö., Austria. [Crustacea: f-w. Copepoda: Calanidae of S. Hemisphere (Yes); Cladocera of S. Hemisphere (Yes)]

BREISTROFFER, Maurice, Conservateur, Muséum d'Histoire Naturelle, Rue Dolomieu, Grenoble, Isère, France. [Cephalopoda: Cretaceous Ammonoidea of "Albien=Gault mondial" (Yes); of France & Mediterranean (No)]

BREKKE, Director Reidar. Søndre Gate 14, Trondheim, Norway. [Ephemeroptera, Plecoptera, Trichoptera, of Scandinavia (Yes)] [Det Kongelige Norske Videnskabers Selskab]

BRELAND, Dr. Osmond P. Department of Zoology, University of Texas, Austin 12, Texas, U.S.A. [Diptera: Culicidae of N. America (Yes); Orthoptera: Mantidae, egg cases of U.S. (Yes)]

BRELIH, Savo. Prirodoslovni Muzej v Ljubljani, Prešernova 20, Ljubljana, Yugoslavia. [Coleoptera: Adephaga of Slovenia (Yes); Reptilia of Yugoslavia (Yes); Mallophaga of Yugoslavia (No)]

BRENNAN, James M. Rocky Mountain Laboratory, U.S. Public Health Service, Hamilton, Mont., U.S.A. [Acarina: Trombiculidae of W. Hemisphere (Yes); Ixodides of N. America (No); Diptera: Culicidae of N. America (No)]

BRETET, Roger. Villa "La Falaise", Blvd. General de Gaulle, Saint-Jean-Cap-Ferrat, France. [Mollusca] Not now active in taxonomy.

* BREUER, Mrs. Marta Erps. Departmento de Biologia Geral, Universidad de São Paulo, Caixa Postal 8105, São Paulo, Brazil. [Diptera]

* BREUKELMAN, J.W. Department of Biology, Kansas State Teachers College, Emporia, Kans., U.S.A. [Reptilia, Amphibia]

BREUNING, Mr. S. 7 rue Durantin, Paris (XVIII/67), France. [Coleoptera: Carabini of World (Yes); Cerambycidae: Lamiinae of World (Yes)] [Muséum National d'Histoire Naturelle]

* BREURKEN, W.F. Zoologisch Museum, Afd. Entomologische, Zeeburgerdijk 21, Amsterdam, Netherlands. [Coleoptera]

BREWIN, Dr. Beryl I. University of Otago, c/o Museum, King Street, Dunedin, New Zealand. [Ascidiacea of New Zealand (Yes)]

BREYER, Alberto. Maipu 267, Buenos Aires, Argentina. [Lepidoptera, excl. microlepidoptera, of Argentina (Yes)] [Museo Argentino de Ciencias Naturales]

BREZNER, Mr. Jerry. Entomology Department, University of Missouri, Columbia, Mo., U.S.A. [Coleoptera: larval & adult g. Curculio of c. U.S. (Yes)]

BRIAN, Prof. Alessandro. Istituto de Zoologia, dell'Universitá Genova, Via Balbi 5,

Genova, Italy. [Crustacea: Copepoda of Mediterranean & Italy (Yes); terr. Isopoda, espec. cavernicole, of "Apenin et Alpes italiennes" (Yes)]
BRIAN, A. D. Woolgarston, Corfe Castle, Dorset, England. [Hymenoptera: g. Bombus of Gr. Britain (Yes)]
BRIAN, M. V. Nature Conservancy, Furzebrook Research Station, Wareham, Dorset, England. [Hymenoptera: Formicidae of Brit. Is. (Yes); Collembola of Brit. Is. (Yes)]
BRIDGE, Josiah. (Washington, D. C.; fossils) Died 1953.
BRIGGS, John C. Department of Anatomy, University of British Columbia, Vancouver 8, B. C., Canada. [Pisces of shore of w. Atlantic (Yes); Gobiesocidae of World (Yes)]
BRIGHT, Mr. Robert C. Department of Geology, University of Minnesota, Minneapolis 14, Minn., U. S. A. [Cambrian Trilobita of N. America (Yes); Ordovician Trilobita & Conodonts of Great Basin of U. S. (No); Cambrian & Ordovician Conodonts of N. America (No)]
BRILL, Dr. Kenneth G., Jr. Department of Geology, St. Louis University, St. Louis 3, Mo., U. S. A. [Permo-Carboniferous Brachiopoda (No)]
BRIMBLECOMBE, Mr. A. R., Senior Entomologist, Department of Agriculture & Stock, Brisbane B 7, Australia. [Homoptera: Coccoidea of Australia (Yes)]
BRIMLEY, J. F. Wellington, Ont., Canada. [Hemiptera & Coleoptera (No)]
BRINCK, Dr. Per. Zoologiska Institution, Lunds Universitets, Lund, Sweden. [Coleoptera: Gyrinidae of World (Yes); Plecoptera of World (Yes); Anoplura of World (No); Siphonaptera of Holarctic (No)]
BRINCKMANN, Dr. Anita. See Addenda.
BRINK, Dr. A. S. Bernard Price Institute (Palaeontology), University of the Witwatersrand, Johannesburg, Union of South Africa. [Permian-Triassic (Karroo) Reptilia: Theriodontia of S. Africa (Yes)]
van den BRINK, F. H. 6 Bieruma Oostingweg, Oranjewoud, Netherlands. [Mammalia of Europe (Yes)]
BRINKHURST, Dr. R. O. Department of Zoology, University of Liverpool, Liverpool 3, England. [Oligochaeta: Naididae, Tubificidae, espec. f-w., of w. Europe (Yes)]
BRINKMAN, Mej. Dra. H., conservator, Gemeentelijk Museum voor het Onderwijs, Den Haag, Netherlands. [Aves of Netherlands (No)]
BRINKMANN, Dr. A., Jr. Zoological Laboratory, University of Bergen, Bergen, Norway. [Trematoda of World (No); Monogenea of N. Atlantic & Arctic (Yes)]
BRINKMANN, Rudolf. Albauweg 31, Essen, Germany. [Lepidoptera, macro & micro, of Europe (No)]
BRINTON, Edward. Scripps Institution of Oceanography, La Jolla, Calif., U. S. A. [Crustacea: Euphausiacea of World (Yes)]
BRISCOE, Dr. M. S. School of Medicine, Howard University, Washington 1, D. C., U. S. A. [Diptera: Culicidae of Liberia, W. Africa (Yes)]
BRISTOWE, Dr. W. S. Beech Hanger, Ashurst, Near Tunbridge Wells, Kent, England. [Araneida of Gr. Britain (No)]
BRITT, N. W. Department of Zoology, Ohio State University, Columbus 10, Ohio. [Ephemeroptera of Ohio (Yes); Reptilia & Amphibia of Ohio (No)]
BRITTAN, Dr. Martin R. Department of Biology, Sacramento State College, Sacramento 19, Calif., U. S. A. [Pisces: f-w. Cyprinidae of w. N. America, Oriental, Ethiopian (Yes); marine of Indo-Pacific (Yes)]
BRITTEN, Harry. 21 Tollers Lane, Old Coulsdon, Surrey, England. [Diptera: Trypetidae of Africa, Australia, N. & S. America, Asia, Micronesia (No); of Europe (Yes)]; g. Anastrepha of W. Hemisphere (Yes)]
BRITTON, Mr. E. B. Department of Entomology, British Museum (Natural History), Cromwell Road, London, S. W. 7, England. [Coleoptera: Carabidae of New Zealand (Yes); Scarabaeidae: Melolonthinae of Australia (Yes)]
BRITZ, Dr. Lothar. Funkenburgstrasse 7/II, Leipzig C 1, German Democratic Republic. [Diptera: Culicidae of c. Europe (Yes); medical spp. of Diptera, Anoplura, Acarina: Ixodides, of c. Europe (No)]
BRIVIO, Dr. P. Carlo, Director, Museo Entomologico del Pontificio Istituto Missioni Estere, Via Lecco 45, Monza (Milano), Italy. [Coleoptera: Carabidae of World (No); of Italy (Yes); Chrysomelidae of Italy (Yes)]
BRNCIC, Dr. Danko. Catedra de Biologia, Instituto de Biologia "Juan Noe", Escuela de Medicina, Universidad de Chile, Santiago, Chile. [Diptera: Drosophilidae of Neotropics (No); of Chile, Argentina, Peru, Bolivia (Yes)]
BROAD, Dr. A. Carter. Department of Zoology & Entomology, Ohio State University, Columbus 10, Ohio. [Crustacea: Decapoda: Penaeidae of s. e. U. S. (Yes); Palaemonidae: marine & estuarine larvae of g. Palaemonetes of U. S. (No)]
* BROADBOOKS, Dr. Harold E. Address unknown. (Mammals)
BROADHEAD, Dr. E. Zoology Department, The University, Leeds 2, England. [Corrodentia of Europe (Yes)]

* BROADHURST, F. M. Department of Geology, The University, Manchester 13, England. [Fossil invertebrates]
BROADLEY, D. G. , Honorary Keeper of Herpetology, National Museum of Southern Rhodesia, P. O. Box 240, Bulawayo, Southern Rhodesia. [Reptilia of Rhodesia & Nyasaland (Yes)]
BROCH, Prof. Hjalmar, Gustav Vigelands vei 9, Oslo, Norway. [Hydrozoa: polyps & hydrocorals of Arctic & Subantarctic-Antarctic (No); Octocoralla: Pennatularia of all oceans (No); Alcyonaria & Gorgonaria of Arctic & Antarctic (No); Crustacea: Cirripedia of World (No)]
* BROCK, J. A. P. O. Box 693, Tripoli, Libya, [Fossil invertebrates]
BROCK, Mr. Vernon E. P. O. Box 5425, Pawaa Substation, Honolulu, Hawaii. [Pisces of Hawaii (Yes); marine fishes of trop. Pacific (No)]
BRODKORB, Dr. Pierce. Department of Biology, University of Florida, Gainesville, Fla. , U. S. A. [Fossil birds of World (Yes); Recent birds of N. & S. America (Yes)]
* BRODSKY, Dr. K. A. Academy of Sciences of the U. S. S. R. , Pushkinsky Proyezd, Leningrad V-164, U. S. S. R. [Crustacea]
BROEKHUYSEN, Dr. G. J. Department of Zoology, University of Cape Town, Cape Town, Union of South Africa. [Aves of Cape Prov. (Yes)]
BRO LARSEN, Dr. Ellinor. Zoologisk Laboratorium og Studiesamling, Nørregade 10, København, Denmark. [Arthropoda]
BRONGERSMA, Dr. L. D. Rijksmuseum van Natuurlijke Historie, Raamsteeg 2, Leiden, Netherlands. [Reptilia & Amphibia of s. e. Asia, New Guinea, Surinam (Yes)]
* BRÖNNIMANN, Dr. Paul. Esso Standard, S. A. , Apartado 4087, Habana, Cuba. [Protozoa]
* BRONSON, Albert B. Address unknown. (Mollusca)
* BRØNSTED, H. V. University of København, Krystalgade, København, Denmark. [Coelenterata]
* BROOKES, Albert E. 178 Balmoral Road, Mt. Eden, S. 2, Auckland, New Zealand. [Mollusca]
BROOKES, Miss H. M. Waite Agricultural Research Institute, Private Mail Bag, G. P. O. , Adelaide, S. A. , Australia. [Homoptera: Coccoidea, espec. Pseudococcidae, of Australia (Yes)]
* BROOKLEY, Arthur. International Petroleum Ltd. , Exploration Department, Bogotá, Colombia. [Fossil invertebrates]
BROOKMAN, Dr. Bernard. Division of Research Grants, National Institute of Health, U. S. Public Health Service, Bethesda, Md. , U. S. A. [Diptera: Culicidae of N. America (No)]
BROOKS, A. C. P. O. Box 12, Masindi, Uganda. [Mammalia: Ungulata & Rodentia of Brit. Columbia & East Africa (Yes)] [Game & Fisheries Department]
BROOKS, Mr. A. R. Canada Agriculture Research Laboratory, University Sub Post Office, Saskatoon, Sask. , Canada. [Prairie insects of Alberta, Saskatchewan, Manitoba (No)]
BROOKS, F. G. (Mt. Vernon, Iowa; parasites) Died March 4, 1955.
BROOKS, G. S. Deceased.
* BROOKS, Dr. George T. Texas Southern University, Houston, Texas , U. S. A. [Heteroptera]
BROOKS, Prof. H. K. Department of Geology, University of Florida, Gainesville, Fla. , U. S. A. [Paleozoic Crustacea: Malacostraca (Yes); Paleozoic Crustacea in general]
BROOKS, James Elwood. (Dallas, Texas; fossils) Not now active in taxonomy.
BROOKS, Mr. J. G. P. O. Box 354, Cairns, Queensland, Australia. [Coleoptera of Australia (Yes)]
BROOKS, Dr. John L. J. W. Gibbs Laboratory, Yale University, New Haven, Conn. , U. S. A. [Crustacea: Cladocera, espec. g. Daphnia of N. & S. America (Yes)]
* BROOKS, Maurice. Department of Forestry, West Virginia University, Morgantown, W. Virginia, U. S. A. [Amphibia]
de BROS, E. "La Fleurie", 28 Rebgasse, Binningen (Baselland), Switzerland. [Macrolepidoptera, excl. Lycaenidae, Hesperiidae, Psychidae, of Switzerland (Yes)]
BROTZEN, Dr. Fritz. Sveriges Geologiska Undersökning, Stockholm 50, Sweden. [Mesozoic Foraminifera of World (Yes)]
* BROUERIUS van NIDEK, C. M. C. Vogelkersstraat 28, Bussum, Netherlands. [Coleoptera: Cicindelidae]
* BROUGH, Prof. James. Department of Zoology, University College, Cardiff, Wales. [Mesozoic Pisces]
* BROUGH, Mrs. Margaret C. Department of Zoology, University College, Cardiff, Wales. [Carboniferous Reptilia & Amphibia]
* BROUWER, Dr. G. A. Department of Ornithologie, Rijksmuseum van Natuurlijke Historie, Leiden, Netherlands. [Birds]
* BROUWER, J. Apartado Aereo 3439, Bogota, Colombia. [Mollusca]
BROWER, Dr. Auburn E. 8 Hospital Street, Augusta, Maine, U. S. A. [Macrolepidoptera of e. N. America (Yes); Microlepidoptera of e. N. America (Yes in part); Aegeriidae of Nearctic (Yes); g. Catocala of New World (Yes)]

BROWER, Dr. Lincoln P. Department of Zoology, Yale University, New Haven 11, Conn.,
U. S. A. [Lepidoptera: Papilio glaucus group of N. America (Yes)]
BROWN, Dr. A. C. Department of Zoology, Capetown University, Capetown, Union of South
Africa. [Crustacea: Isopoda: Tanaidacea of Ethiopean (No); of s. Africa (Yes)]
BROWN, Mr. A. L. "Delias", 5 Creek, Road, Mitcham, Vict., Australia. [Lepidoptera:
Rhopalocera & Heterocera, excl. of Microlepidoptera, of Australia, espec. Victoria
(Yes)]
BROWN, Dr. Barnum. American Museum of Natural History, New York 24, N. Y., U. S. A.
[Mesozoic Dinosauria (Yes), Pterodactyls (Yes)]
BROWN, Prof. Bryce C. Strecker Museum, Baylor University, Waco, Texas, U. S. A. [Rep-
tilia & Amphibia of Texas (Yes)]
BROWN, DR. C. J. D. Department of Zoology & Entomology, Montana State College, Boze-
man, Mont., U. S. A. [Fishes of Montana (No)]
BROWN, D. A. Geology Department, Canberra University College, P. O. Box 197, Canberra,
Australia. [Tertiary & Recent Bryozoa, Cyclostomata, Cheilostomata, of New Zealand,
Australia, Antarctica (Yes)]
* BROWN, David E. "The Craft", Caunton, Newark, Notts, England. [Mollusca]
* BROWN, E. E. Department of Zoology, Davidson College, Davidson, N. C., U. S. A. [Am-
phibia]
BROWN, Mr. E. S. Commonwealth Institute of Entomology, British Museum (Natural History)
Cromwell Road, London, S. W. 7, England. [Aquatic & semi-aquatic Heteroptera of Old
World (No); Coreidae of World (Yes)]
BROWN, Mr. F. Martin. Fountain Valley School, Colorado Springs, Colo., U. S. A. [Lepi-
doptera: Rhopalocera of Rocky Mts. (Yes); Satyridae & Pieridae of Neotropics (Yes)]
BROWN, Miss G. L. Nematode Investigations, Science Service Laboratory, Carling Avenue,
Ottawa, Ont., Canada. [Nematoda: Tylenchida of Canada (Yes)]
BROWN, Harry E. Department of Entomology, University of Missouri, Columbia, Mo.,
U. S. A. [Hymenoptera: Dryinidae of World (No); of N. America (Yes); Homoptera: Ci-
cadellidae of N. America (No)]
BROWN, Prof. Harley P. Department of Zoology, University of Oklahoma, Norman, Okla.,
U. S. A. [Neuroptera: Sisyridae of U. S. e. of Rocky Mts. (No)]
BROWN, H. W. (Sydney, Australia; Coleoptera) Deceased.
BROWN, Mr. Jerram L. Museum of Vertebrate Zoology, University of California, Berkeley
4, Calif., U. S. A. [Pisces: Cyprinodontidae: g. Fundulus of New World (Yes); Aves of
World, espec. Mexico (No)]
BROWN, Mr. Noel K., Jr. Gulf Oil Corp., New York Exploration Division, P. O. Box 35,
Bowling Green Station, New York 4, N. Y., U. S. A. [Cretaceous-Tertiary Foramini-
fera (Yes)]
BROWN, Prof. N. R. University of New Brunswick, Fredericton, N. B., Canada. [Siphonap-
tera of e. N. America (Yes); Anoplura of e. Canada (No); Acarina: Ixodoidea of e.
Canada (Yes)]
BROWN, Prof. Paul L. Department of Zoology, Southern University, Baton Rouge, La.,
U. S. A. [Crustacea: Decapoda: crayfish of Illinois (Yes); of Louisiana (No)]
* BROWN, Philip M. U. S. Geological Survey, Box 2857, Raleigh, N. C., U. S. A. [Fossil
invertebrates]

BROWN, Dr. R. L. 3956 Oakwood Place, Riverside, Calif., U.S.A. [Protozoa, Platyhelminthes, Nemathelminthes, of man (Yes)]
* BROWN, Robert Z. Colorado College, Colorado Springs, Colo., U.S.A. [Mammals]
BROWN, Mr. S.G. National Institute of Oceanography, Wormley, Godalming, Surrey, England. [Mammalia: Cetacea of all oceans (Yes)]
* BROWN, Dr. Walter C. Address unknown.(Vertebrates)
BROWN, W.J. Division of Entomology, Canadian Department of Agriculture, Ottawa, Ont., Canada. [Coleoptera of N. America (Yes); Chrysomelidae (Yes)]
BROWN, William L., Jr. Dept. of Entomology, Cornell University, Ithaca, N.Y., U.S.A. [Hymenoptera: Formicidae of World (No); Dacetini of World (Yes)]
BROWNING, E. (London, England; Arachnida) Not now active in taxonomy.
* BROWNING, John L. 2851 Vuelta Grande, Long Beach 15, Calif., U.S.A. [Fossil invertebrates]
BRTEK, Dr. Jan. Reg. Museum Bojnice, Distr. Prievidza, Czechoslovakia. [Crustacea: Copepoda: f-w. Calanoida of c. Europe (Yes); Anostraca of Europe (Yes); f-w. Isopoda of c. Europe (Yes)]
BRUCE, Dr. Nils. Gardby, Oland, Sweden (May - Sept.), Odalvägen 22-26, Hässelby Villastad, Sweden (Oct. - April). [Coleoptera: Cryptophagidae: g. Cryptophagus, Micrambe, Mnionomus, of World, excl. N. America (Yes)]
* BRUCKOVA, B. Entomologicky ústav, Národni Museum Praze, Václavské Náměsti 1700, Praha II, Czechoslovakia. [Lepidoptera]
van BRUGGEN, Mr. A.C. (biol.drs.). Division of Entomology, P.O. Box 513, Pretoria, Union of South Africa. [Mollusca of World (No); Diptera of Europe, S. Africa (No)]; Ephemeroptera of World (No)]
BRUIJNING, Dr. C.F.A. Rijksmuseum van Natuurlijke Historie, Leiden, Netherlands. [Orthoptera: Blattidae (Yes); Diptera: Culicidae of Neotropics (Yes)]
BRUNDIN, Prof. Lars. Entomology Department, Swedish Museum of Natural History, Stockholm 50, Sweden. [Diptera: Chironomidae of World (Yes)]
BRUNEAU de MIRÉ, P. Muséum National d'Histoire Naturelle, 57 rue Cuvier, Paris (V), France. [Coleoptera of Sahara & trop. arid Africa (No); Carabidae of same (Yes)]
BRUNEL, Pierre. Station de Biologie Marine, Grande-Riviére, Gaspé-sud, Que., Canada. [Crustacea: Amphipoda of Arctic & N. Atlantic Oceans (Yes)]
* BRUNETTI, Prof. Dr. B. Istituto di Zoologia, Via Romano 17, Firenze, Italy. [Nematoda]
* BRUNIQUEL, S. Station Centrale de Boukoko, M'Baiki, par Bangui, Oubangui-Chari, French Equatorial Africa. [Coleoptera, Hymenoptera]
BRUNNSCHWEILER, Dr. R.O. c/o Timor Oil Limited, 67 York Street, Sydney, N.S.W., Australia. [Mesozoic Ammonoidea: Neocretaceous & Tertiary Echinoidea; Aucelliidae; all of Australasia (No)]
BRUNOLD, Dr. E. Zoologisches Institut der Eidg. Technischen Hochschule, Universitätsstrasse 2, Zürich, Switzerland. [F-l. soil Nematoda of Switzerland (No)]
BRUNS, Mr. Paul M. Reedley College, Reedley, Calif., U.S.A. [Pisces: Labridae of Red Sea, Pacific, Indian, Mediterranean Oceans (Yes)]
BRUNSON, Prof. Royal B. Department of Zoology, Montana State University, Missoula, Mont., U.S.A. [Gastrotricha of World (Yes)]
* BRUST, Miss J. Department of Zoology, The University, Leeds 2, England. [Mammalia]
BRUUN, Dr. Anton F. Universitetets Zoologiske Museum, København K, Denmark. [Pisces: Exocoetidae of World (Yes); leptocephalus stages of apodal fishes of World (Yes)]
BRUUN, Dr. Henrik H. Abo Akademi, Abo, Finland. [Microlepidoptera & Macrolepidoptera of n. Europe (Yes)]
BRUŸNS, Dr. M.F. Mörzer. State Institute for Nature Conservation Research (R.I.V.O.N.) Staatsbosbeheer, Soestdijkseweg 33 N, Bilthoven, Netherlands. [Aves of n.w. Europe (Yes)]
BRYAN, Dr. D.E. Department of Entomology, Oklahoma Agricultural & Mechanical College, Stillwater, Okla., U.S.A. [Thysanoptera: Thripidae of N. America (No)]
BRYAN, Edwin H., Jr. Bernice P. Bishop Museum, Honolulu 17, Hawaii. [Aves of Hawaii & Guam (Yes); Diptera of Hawaii (Yes); marine Mollusca of Hawaii (No)]
BRYANT, Miss E.B. (Cambridge, Mass.; Arachnida) Deceased.
BRYANT, Mr. G.E. Commonwealth Institute of Entomology, British Museum (Natural History), Cromwell Road, London, S.W.7, England. [Coleoptera: Chrysomelidae of World (Yes)]
BRYANT, J. P.O. Box 176, Fort Smith, N.W.T., Canada. [Mammalia of n. Canada (No)]
BRYDEN, Dr. Robert R. Biology Department, High Point College, High Point, N.C., U.S.A. [Hydrozoa: Hydridae of N. America (Yes)]
BRYK, Felix. (Stockholm, Sweden; Lepidoptera) Deceased.
BRZĘK, Prof. Dr. Gabriel. Al. Racławickie 20, Lublin, Poland. [Crustacea: Cladocera of Poland (Yes)] [Wyzszej Szkoły Rolniczej]
BUBENÍK, Dr. A.B. Radlická 22, Praha 16, Smichov, Czechoslovakia. [Mammalia: Cervidae of World (Yes); Bovidae of Palearctic (No)] [National Museum]

BUCCIARELLI, Italo. Museo Civico de Storia Naturale, Corso Venezia 55, Milano, Italy. [Coleoptera: Anthicidae & Hylophilidae of World (No), of Europe & N. Africa (Yes); Carabidae: Pterostichinae & Scaritinae of Palearctic (No), of Europe (Yes); Lepidoptera of World (No)]

BUCHANAN, L. L. (Washington, D. C.; Coleoptera) Died February, 1958.

BUCHER, Walter H. (New York, N. Y.; fossils) Not now active in taxonomy.

BÜCHERL, Prof. Dr. Wolfgang. Instituto Butantan, São Paulo, Brazil. [Chilopoda: Scolopendromorpha of S. America (Yes); Geophilomorpha of S. America (No); Scutigeromorpha of S. America (Yes); Orthognatha of S. America (Yes); Araneida: Ctenidae & Lycosidae of S. America (Yes); Scorpionida of S. America (Yes)]

BUCHHOLTZ, Frau Dr. Christiane. Zoologisches Institüt, der Universität, Ketzerbach 63, Marbürg/Lahn, Germany. [Odonata, espec. Calopterygidae, of Germany, Lebanon, Syria, Turkey (Yes)]

BUCHHOLZ, Dr. Horst A. Wanderndes Museum, Geologisches Institut der Universität, Olshausenstrasse 40-60, Kiel, Schleswig-Holstein, Germany. [Crustacea: Copepoda: marine Calanoidea of North Sea & Baltic (Yes); f-w. of C. Europe (Yes); Cirripedia: Thoracica, incl. larvae, of North Sea & Baltic (No); Rotatoria: marine Monogononta of North Sea & Baltic (Yes); f-w. of c. Europe (Yes)]

BUCHHOLZ, Dr. K. F. Zoologisches Forschungsinstitut und Museum Alexander Koenig, Herpetologische Abteilung, Koblenzer Strasse 154-162, Bonn, Germany. [Odonata of World (No); of Palearctic (Yes); Amphibia & Reptilia of Palearctic (Yes)]

BUCHHOLZ, Otto. 493 Markthaler Place, Roselle Park, N. J., U. S. A. [Macrolepidoptera of N. America (No)]

BUCHNER, Prof. Dr. H. Zoologisches Institut der Universität, Luisenstrasse 14, München 2, Germany. [Rotatoria, g. Brachionus of c. Europe (No)]

* BUCK, Dr. E. Geological Lamtesamt, Schutzenstrasse 4, Stuttgart, Germany. [Fossil invertebrates]

BUCK, Mr. F. D. 36 Besant Court, Newington Green Road, London, N. 1, England. [Coleoptera: Heteromera of World (No); of Australia (Yes)]

BUCKLEY, Prof. J. J. C. Department of Parasitology, London School of Hygiene & Tropical Medicine, London, W. C. 1, England. [Nematoda: Filarioidea of man & animals of Tropics (Yes)]

BUCKUP, Erica Helena. Museo Riograndense de Ciencias Naturais, Rua Coronel Vicente 430, Pôrto Alegre, R. G. do S., Brazil. [Chilopoda & Scorpionida of Neotropics (Yes); Araneida of Neotropics (No)]

BUCKUP, Prof. Ludwig. Museu Riograndense de Ciencias Naturais, Rua Coronel Vicente 430, Pôrto Alegre, R. G. do S., Brazil. [Heteroptera: Pentatomidae of Neotropics (Yes)]

BUDKER, P., Sous-Directeur du Laboratoire des Pêches Coloniales, Muséum National d'Histoire Naturelle, 57 rue Cuvier, Paris (V), France. [Pisces: sharks (Yes); Mammalia: whales (No)]

BUDZIER, Dr. H. H. An der Hasenbäk 11, Rostock, Germany. [Nematoda: g. Heterodera of Germany (No); Protozoa of ruminants (No)]

BUEHLER, Mr. Edward John. Department of Geology, University of Buffalo, Buffalo 14, N. Y., U. S. A. [Anthozoa: paleozoic tabulate & rugose corals (Yes)]

* de BUEN, Fernando. Servicio Oceanografia y Pesca, 18 de Julio 953, Montevideo, Uruguay. [Pisces: Gobiidae of World (Yes)]

BUETTNER, Dr. K. Reichenbacherstrasse 33, Zwickau i Sa, Germany. [Heteroptera of Germany]

BUGBEE, Robert E. Department of Biology, Allegheny College, Meadville, Penna., U. S. A. [Hymenoptera: Eurytomidae of New World (Yes)]

BUGE, Dr. E. Service d'Information Géologique, Bureau de Recherches Géologiques, Géophysiques et Minières, 74 rue de la Fédération, Paris (XV), France. [Post-Paleozoic Bryozoa]

* BUHOLZER, R. Bleicherstrasse 1, Lucerne, Switzerland. [Lepidoptera]

BUHRER, Miss Edna M. Nematology Section, Plant Industry Station, U. S. Department of Agriculture, Beltsville, Md., U. S. A. [Plant Nematoda (Yes)]

BUICK, W. G. See Addenda.

BULL, P. C. Animal Ecology Section, Department of Scientific & Industrial Research, Wellington, New Zealand. [Coccidia & Nematoda of rabbits of New Zealand (No)]

BULLIS, Harvey. U. S. Fish & Wildlife Service, P. O. Box 630, Pascagoula, Miss., U. S. A. [Abyssal Gastropoda of Atlantic (Yes); marine Gastropoda of Tropics & Subtropics (Yes)]

BULLOCK, Dr. Theodore H. Department of Zoology, University of California, Los Angeles 24, Calif., U. S. A. [Enteropneusta of World (No)]

BULLOCK, Prof. Wilbur L. Department of Zoology, University of New Hampshire, Durham, N. H., U. S. A. [Acanthocephala of fishes of World (Yes); blood Protozoa of marine fishes of N. America (No); Trematoda of marine fishes of N. America (No)]

BULMAN, O. M. B. Sedgwick Museum, Cambridge University, Cambridge, England. [Grap-
tolithina (Yes)]
* von BÜLOW, Dr. Thekla. Ginsterweg 17, Lüneburg, Germany. [Oligochaeta]
* BULYCHEVA, Mme. A. Zoological Institute, Academy of Sciences, Leningrad-centre,
U. S. S. R. [Crustacea: Amphipoda]
BUMP, Prof. James D. Museum of Geology, South Dakota School of Mines & Technology,
Rapid City, S. D., U. S. A. [Oligocene Mammalia of U. S. (Yes)]
BUMZAHEM, Mr. C. B. 1929 N. Bissell Street, Chicago 14, Ill., U. S. A. [Amphibia &
Reptilia of N. & C. America (No)] [University of Illinois College of Medicine]
* BUNICHRO, A. Gifu University, Nakamachi, near Gifu-shi, Japan. [Mammalia]
BUNING, Dr. W. L. Paleontological Laboratory, N. V. de Bataafsche Petroleum Maat schap-
pij, Den Haag, Netherlands. [Smaller Foraminifera (No)]
BURAKOWSKI, Mr. Bolesław. Instytut Zoologiczny, Polska Akademia Nauk, ul. Wilcza 64,
Warszawa, Poland. [Coleoptera: Elateridae of Europe (Yes); larvae of Coleoptera of
c. Europe (No)]
BURBUTIS, Paul. Department of Entomology, University of Delaware, Newark, Del., U. S. A.
[Siphonaptera of e. U. S. (Yes); Diptera: Culicidae of c. Atlantic U. S. (No)]
BURCH, John Bayard. Museum of Zoology, University of Michigan, Ann Arbor, Mich.,
U. S. A. [Mollusca: Pulmonata of N. America (Yes); Protozoa: Ciliophora: Colpodidae
of World (Yes); Ciliophora parasites & commensals of pulmonate Mollusca of World
(Yes)]
BURCH, John Q. 4206 Halldale Avenue, Los Angeles 62, Calif., U. S. A. [Marine Mollusca
of e. Pacific (Yes)]
BURCH, Paul R. (Rockville, Va.; Mollusca) Died 1958.
* BURD, Mr. Anthony C. Fisheries Laboratory, Lowestoft, Suffolk, England. [Crustacea:
Copepoda]
* BURDELEV, Dr. T. E. Timirjasev Academy of Agriculture, Moscow, U. S. S. R. [Parasitic
Nematoda of U. S. S. R.]
* BURDEN, Mr. J. H. 1 Havilah Street, Chatswood, Sydney, N. S. W., Australia. [Neurop-
tera]
BURDICK, Mr. Don. Department of Entomology, University of California, Berkeley 4,
Calif., U. S. A. [Hymenoptera: Xyelidae & Argidae of N. America (Yes)]
BURDICK, William N. 1108 S. Harvard Blvd., Los Angeles 6, Calif., U. S. A. [Lepidoptera:
Rhopalocera of w. U. S. (Yes); Diptera: Asilidae of w. U. S. (No)]
BURDON-JONES, Dr. C., Deputy Director, Marine Biology Station, Menai Bridge, Anglesey,
Wales. [Hemichordata incl. Pterobranchia of World (Yes); Mollusca & Echinoder-
mata of N. Atlantic (Yes); Pogonophora of World (Yes)] [University of Wales]
* BUREAU, P. L. 7 rue Legoff, Paris (V), France. [Coleoptera]
BUREŠ, Dr. Ivan. Institut Zoologique et Musée d'Histoire Naturelle, Académie des Sciences
de Bulgarie, Boulevard Rouski 1, Sofia I, Bulgaria. [Reptilia & Amphibia of Balkan
Pen. (Yes); fauna cavernicola, "Canica"; Lepidoptera of Bulgaria (Yes)]
van der BURG, W. J. van Galenstraat 28, Oss, Netherlands. [Pliocene Gastropoda & Pele-
cypoda of w. Europe (Yes); Tertiary Mollusca of w. Europe (No); Recent Mollusca of
Netherlands (Yes)]
* BURGER, Dr. André. Rue de Corcelles 46, Peseux, Switzerland. [Rotatoria]
BURGER, W. Leslie. Department of Biology, College of William and Mary, Williamsburg,
Va., U. S. A. [Amphibia & Reptilia of Virginia & Venezuela (Yes); rattleless pit
vipers of w. Hemisphere (Yes)]
BURGESS, Dr. C. M. 2502 Manoa Road, Honolulu 14, Hawaii, U. S. A. [Gastropoda: Cyprae-
idae of World (No); of Hawaii (Yes)]
BURGESS, Dr. R. W. Liberian Institute of the American Foundation for Tropical Medicine,
Harbel, Liberia. [Diptera: Culicidae: Anopheles gambiae-A. melas of W. Africa (No);
mosquitoes in latex cups of Liberia (No)]
BÜRGL, Dr. Hans. Apartado Nac. 2599, Bogotá, Colombia. [Cretaceous Ammonites of
Colombia (Yes); Miocene, Pliocene, Quaternary Pelecypoda & Gastropoda of Colom-
bia (Yes); U. Cretaceous & Tertiary Foraminifera of Caribbean (No)] [Instituto Geoló-
gico Nacional]
BURK, Creighton Alvin. Box 696, Casper, Wyo., U. S. A. [Paleozoic & Mesozoic fossils of
n. Rocky Mts. (No)]
BURKE, Horace R. Department of Entomology, Agricultural & Mechanical College of Texas,
College Station, Texas, U. S. A. [Coleoptera: Curculionidae of s. w. U. S. (Yes); of
Mexico (No); g. Anthonomus of N. America (No)]
BURKE, Mr. J. J. 176 Grant Avenue, Vandergrift, Penna., U. S. A. [Eocene & Oligocene
Mammalia: Rodentia of N. America & Asia (Yes)]
BURKENROAD, Martin D. Apartado 3318, Panama, Rep. de Panama. [Crustacea: Deca-
poda: Penaeidea of World (Yes)]
BURKS, B. D. Division of Insects, U. S. National Museum, Washington 25, D. C., U. S. A.
[Hymenoptera: Chalcidoidea & Symphyta of World (Yes)]

BURLA, Dr. Hans. Zoologisches Institut der Universität, Künstlergasse 16, Zürich, Switzerland. [Diptera: Drosophilidae of World (No); of Europe & Africa (Yes); g. Zygothrica of S. America (Yes)]

BURLINI, Milo. Ponzano Veneto, (Treviso), Italy. [Coleoptera: Chrysomelidae: g. Cryptocephalus of Palearctic (Yes)]

BURMA, Benjamin H. California Exploration Co., Room 615, 320 Market Street, San Francisco, Calif., U. S. A. [Fossil Foraminifera of World (Yes); fossil Radiolaria of World (No)]

* BURMANN, Karl. Anichstrasse 34, Innsbruck, Austria. [Macrolepidoptera of Austria; Microlepidoptera of Palearctic]

BURMEISTER, Dr. Fritz. Föhrenwald 25, Kleinmachnow-Berlin, German Democratic Republic. [Coleoptera] See Addenda.

BURN, Mr. Robert F. 34 Autumn Street, Geelong, West Victoria, Australia. [Mollusca: Opisthobranchia, excl. Pteropoda, of Australia (Yes), of S. Pacific (No)]

BURNABY, T. P. Department of Geology, University College, Keele, N. Staffs, England. [Cenomanian benthonic Foraminifera of E. Anglia (Yes); Graptolithina of Welsh Borderland (Yes)]

BURNS, Mr. A. N. National Museum of Victoria, Russell Street, Melbourne C. 1, Vict., Australia. [Lepidoptera: Rhopalocera of Australia (Yes); Homoptera: Cicadidae of Australia (No)]

BURNS, Mr. Douglas M. 2235 N. E. 28th Avenue, Portland 12, Ore., U. S. A. [Reptilia & Amphibia of w. N. America (Yes)] [University of Oregon Medical School]

BURNS, John M. Department of Zoology, University of California, Berkeley 4, Calif., U. S. A. [Lepidoptera: Hesperiidae, espec. g. Erynnis, of Nearctic (Yes)]

BURRI, Dr. Fritz, Gymnasiallehrer, Peter Rot-Strasse 106, Basel, Switzerland. [Brachiopoda: L. Cretaceous & Jurassic Rhynchonellidae of Jura Mts. & Normandie (Yes)]

BURSA, Adam S. 505 Pine Avenue West, Montreal, Que., Canada. [Dinoflagellates of Polar Ice Cap (Yes)]

BURSCH, Dr. J. George. c/o Phillips Petroleum Co., Apartado de Correos 1031, Caracas, Venezuela. [Cretaceous-Recent non-planktonic smaller Foraminifera of Venezuela (Yes); larger Foraminifera of e. Moluccas (No)]

BURT, Dr. Charles E. Quivira Specialties Co., 4204 W. 21st Street, Topeka, Kans., U. S. A. [Amphibia & Reptilia of U. S. (Yes); lizards of World (Yes)]

* BURT, David R. R. Department of Zoology, The University, St. Andrews, Fife, Scotland. [Cestoidea of birds of Ceylon (Yes); of wading birds of N. America (Yes)]

* BURT, Mr. J. W. 19 James Street, Danenong, Vict., Australia. [Lepidoptera]

BURT, William H. Museum of Zoology, University of Michigan, Ann Arbor, Mich., U. S. A. [Mammalia of N. & C. America (Yes)]

BURTON, A. J. Department of Zoology, University of Natal, Pietermaritzburg, Union of South Africa. [Not a taxonomist.

BURTON, Mr. E. Milby, Director, The Charleston Museum, Charleston, S. C., U. S. A. [Pisces & Aves of S. C. (Yes)]

BURTON, Dr. Maurice. (London, England; Coelenterata, Porifera) Not now active in taxonomy.

BURTSCHAK-ABRAMOVITSCH, Dr. N. I. Museum of Natural History, 9 Shaumyan Street, Baku, U. S. S. R. [Fossil birds & mammals of Palearctic (Yes)]

BURTT, Dr. E. T. Zoology Department, Kings College, Newcastle-upon-Tyne 1, England. [Siphonaptera; Siphunculata; Acarina: Ixodoidea of Great Britain (Yes)]

BUSH, E. A. R. (London, England; Echinodermata) Deceased.

BUSH, Mr. Guy. Box 2804, Virginia Polytechnic Institute, Blacksburg, Va., U. S. A. [Diptera: Trypetidae, espec. larvae, of Mexico (No)]

BUSH, Prof. S. F. Department of Zoology, University of Natal, Pietermaritzburg, Union of South Africa. [Amphibia: Anura of s. Africa (Yes); Protozoa: Gregarinoidea of s. Africa (No)]

BUSH, Dr. James. 2243 Stanmore Drive, Houston 19, Texas, U. S. A. [Later Cenozoic Foraminifera of W. Hemisphere (Yes); Cenozoic Bryozoa of W. Hemisphere (Yes)]

BUSHEY, Dr. Clinton J. Department of Zoology, Olivet Nazarene College, Kankakee, Ill., U. S. A. [Terr. Gastropoda of Illinois (Yes)]

* BUSULINI, Dr. Enzo. S. Marco 4518 A, Venezia, Italy. [Coleoptera]

BUTLER, Mrs. Elizabeth Ann. Louisiana Geological Survey, Baton Rouge 3, La., U. S. A. [Oligocene-Miocene Foraminifera of e. U. S. & Gulf Cst. (Yes); Oligocene & Miocene Ostracoda of Gulf Coast (Yes); Up. Cretaceous cheilostome Bryozoa of same (No)]

BUTLER, Mr. L. S. G. 3 Los Angeles Court, St. Kilda, Melbourne S. 2, Australia. [Araneida of Australia (No)]

BUTLER, P. M. Royal Holloway College, Englefield Green, Surrey, England. [Fossil Insectivora of Africa (Yes); Tertiary Erinaceidae of Europe (Yes); Perissodactyla: fossil Chalicotheriidae of Old World (Yes)]

BUTLER, T. H. Pacific Biological Station, Nanaimo, B. C., Canada. [Crustacea: Decapoda: Macrura of Pacific Cst. of Canada]

BUTOT, L. J. M. Nassaustraat 10, Vleuten (Utrecht), Netherlands. [Gastropoda: Prosobranchia: Pulmonata of Indonesia (Yes); Pelecypoda of Netherlands (Yes)] [Rijksinstituut voor Veldbiologisch Onderzoek ten Behoeve van het Natuurbehoud (RIVON)]

* BUTOVITSCH, Prof. Dr. V. Entomology Department, State Institute of Forest Research, Experimentalfältet, Sweden. [Coleoptera]

BUTTERLIN, Jacques. Institut Française d'Amerique Latine, Calle del Nazas 43, Mexico 5, D. F., Mexico. [Cretaceous-Miocene larger 'Foraminifera of Caribbean (Yes)] [Instituto de Geologia, Universidad Nacional Autonoma de Mexico]

BUTTERWORTH, Dr. Bernard B. Department of Biology, University of Wichita, Wichita 14, Kansas, U. S. A. [Mammalia: Heteromyidae (Yes)]

BUTTIKER, Dr. W. C/o J. R. Geigy S. A., Basle, Switzerland. [Diptera: Culicidae: Anophelini of s. e. Asia (Yes)]

BUTTNER, Dr. Alice. Institut de Parasitologie, Rue de l'Ecole-de-Medecin 15, Paris (VI), France. [Trematoda: Schistosomatidae of Africa & S. America (Yes); of Orient (No)]

BUTTREY, Prof. Benton W. Department of Zoology, State University of South Dakota, Vermillion S. D., U. S. A. [Protozoa: Mastigophora: g. Trichomonas of Amphibia (Yes)]

* BUTUROVIĆ, Adem. Biološki Institut, Sarajevo Museum, Sarajevo, Yugoslavia. [Crustacea: Isopoda]

BUYS, John L. (Canton, N. Y.; Homoptera) Died May 24, 1955.

BYCHOVSKAJA-PAVLOVSKAJA, Mrs. I. E. Zoological Institute, Academy of Sciences, Leningrad W-164, U. S. S. R., [Trematoda of birds, fishes, mammals, of Europe, Asia (Yes); of N. Africa (No)]

BYERS, Dr. C. Francis. Department of Biology, University of Florida, Gainesville, Fla., U. S. A. [Odonata of N. America (Yes)]

BYERS, George W. Department of Entomology, University of Kansas, Lawrence, Kans., U. S. A. [Mecoptera of N. America (Yes); Diptera: Tipulidae of e. N. America (Yes)]

BYRD, Elon E. Department of Zoology, University of Georgia, Athens, Ga., U. S. A. [Trematoda & Cestoda of W. Hemisphere (Yes)]

* BYRD, Mr. Rodgers. Department of Zoology, University of Michigan, Ann Arbor, Mich., U. S. A. [Protozoa]

BYSTROW, Prof. Alexius. Astrachanskaja 6/8, lodg. 13, Leningrad K-175, U. S. S. R. [Paleozoic Agnatha, Pisces, Amphibia, Reptilia of U. S. S. R. (Yes)] [Leningrad State University]

BYTINSKI-SALZ, Dr. H., Head, Plant Quarantine Service, Ministry of Agriculture, P. O. Box 8393, Tel Aviv, Israel. [Coleoptera & Hymenoptera of Near East (Yes); Macrolepidoptera & Hymenoptera: Formicidae of Europe & Near East (Yes)]

CABALLERO y CABALLERO, Prof. Dr. Eduardo. Apartado Postal 692, Mexico 1, D. F., Mexico. [Trematoda of N. America; Nematoda of C. America; Hirudinea of S. America & West Indies (all Yes)]

CABIDOCHE, Michel. 20 rue Cézanne, Tarbes (Htes-Pyr.), France. [Coleoptera: Carabidae: Trechitae & Pterostichinae: g. Haptoderus, of Pyrenees (Yes); Catopidae: Bathyscinae of Pyrenees (No)]

CABLE, Dr. R. M. Department of Zoology, Purdue University, Lafayette, Ind., U. S. A. [Digenetic Trematoda (No); Acanthocephala of turtles (Yes)]

* CABRERA, Dr. Angel. Museo de La Plata, Paseo del Bosque, La Plata, Argentina. [Fossil & Recent Mammalia] Died July 7, 1960.

CADE, Tom J. Department of Zoology, University of California, Los Angeles 24, Calif,, U. S. A. [Aves: Falconiformes & Strigiformes of Arctic & Subarctic]

CADENAT, Mr. J., Chef, Section Biologie Marine, Institut Française Afrique Noire, Goree, Sénegal. [Pisces of trop. Atlantic (Yes); Selachii: Requins & Raies of trop. Atlantic (Yes); Heterosomata: Soleidae & Cynoglossidae of trop. Atlantic (Yes); Mammalia: Cetacea: Delphinidae of w. cst. Africa (No)]

CADEO, Dr. Gian Carlo. Via Ceradini 14, Milano, Italy. [Fossil Carnivora: Ursidae & Canidae of Europe (Yes)]

CAGLE, Fred R. Department of Zoology, Tulane University, New Orleans 15, La., U. S. A. [Reptilia: turtles of N. & S. America (No)]

CAIRNS, Dr. Eldon J. Department of Botany & Plant Pathology, Alabama Polytechnic Institute, Auburn, Ala., U. S. A. [Nematoda: Tylenchida: Dorylaimidae of N. America (Yes)]

CAIRNS, John, Jr., Associate Curator of Limnology, Academy of Natural Sciences, Philadelphia 3, Penna., U. S. A. [Protozoa of coastal f-w. streams of Temperate Zone (Yes)]

* CALABRO, F. J. Seven Seas Mercantile Co., 15 Moore Street, New York 4, N. Y. [Fossil invertebrates]

142

CALABY, Mr. J.H. Wildlife Survey Section, Commonwealth Scientific & Industrial Research Organization, P.O. Box 109, Canberra, A.C.T., Australia. [Isoptera of Australia & Tasmania (Yes)]

* CALDWELL, David K. Address unknown. (Pisces)

* CALDWELL, Mrs. E. 628 So. Yewdell Street, Philadelphia 43, Penna., U.S.A. [Lepidoptera]

CALDWELL, Dr. John S. R.D. 3, Circleville, Ohio. [Homoptera: Fulgoroidea of Mexico & West Indies (Yes); Psyllidae of W.I. (Yes); of Mexico (No); Membracidae: Ceresini of N. America & Mexico (No)]

CALINESCU, Prof. Dr. Raul. Laboratorul de Biogeografie, Universitatea "C.I. Parhon", Bulevard N. Balcescu 1, Bucureşti, Rumania. [Mammalia of Rumania (Yes)]

CALLAN, Dr. Edward McC. Department of Zoology & Entomology, Rhodes University, Grahamstown, Union of South Africa. [Hymenoptera: Sphecoidea of S. Africa (Yes)]

CALLOMAN, J.H. Department of Chemistry, University College, Gower Street, London, W.C.1, England. [Cephalopoda: M. & Up. Jurassic Ammonites (Yes)]

CALLOT, Prof. Jacques. Institut de Parasitologie, Faculté de Medecine, 3 rue Koeberle, Strasbourg (Bas Rhin), France. [Diptera: Culicidae of Europe & N. Africa (Yes)]

* CALVER, M.A. Geological Survey, Exhibition Road, London, S.W. 7, England. [Fossil invertebrates]

CALVERT, Prof. Philip P. P.O. Box 14, Cheyney, Penna., U.S.A. [Odonata (No)]

* CALVINO, Eva Mameli. Stazione Sperimentale de Floricoltura, Cas. Post. 214, Sanremo, Italy. [Nematoda]

CAMACHO, E. c/o Shell Oil Co., P.O. Box 1748, Baton Rouge, La., U.S.A. [Fossil Foraminifera of Cuba, Haiti, Dominican Rep., Louisiana Gulf Cst. (No)]

* CAMACHO, Horacio. Direccion Nacional de Mineria, Paseo Colon 751, Buenos Aires, Argentina. [Fossil Foraminifera]

* CAMARGO, Dr. Helio F. de Almeido. Departmento de Zoologia, Caixa Postal 7172, São Paulo, Brazil. [Arachnida]

CAMARGOS LOUREIRO, Prof. Milgar. Escola Superior de Agricultura, Vicosa (Minas), Brazil. [Scorpionidea: Buthidae of New World (Yes)]

CAMBRIDGE, Philip. 21 Wilson Road, Ely, Cardiff, Wales. [Pliocene-Recent marine Mollusca excl. Pteropoda & Nudibranchia of n.w. Europe (Yes); Pliocene-Pleistocene marine fossils excl. Mollusca, Foraminifera, Polyzoa, Mammalia, of n.w. Europe (No)]

* CAMERON, Austin W. Zoological Section, National Museum of Canada, Ottawa, Ont., Canada. [Mammals]

CAMERON, Mrs. H. 19 Clarke Street, Yarralumla, Canberra, A.C.T., Australia. [Orthoptera: Blattariae of Australia (No)]

CAMERON, Dr. Malcolm. (London, England; Coleoptera) Deceased.

* CAMERON, Prof. Thomas W.M. P.O. Box 231, Macdonald College, Que., Canada. [Parasites]

CAMIN, Dr. Joseph H. Department of Entomology, University of Kansas, Lawrence, Kansas. [Acarina: Mesostigmata of World (No); Trigynaspida of World (Yes)]

CAMP, Dr. Charles L. Museum of Paleontology, University of California, Berkeley 4, Calif., U.S.A. [Mesozoic Reptilia & Amphibia of N. America, e. Asia, S. Africa (Yes); Reptiles, espec. lizards of w. N. America (No)]

CAMPANA-ROUGET, Dr. Yvonne. Institut de Parasitologie, Faculté de Médecine de Paris, 15 rue de l'École de Médecine, Paris (VI), France. [Nematoda of marine & f-w. fishes, espec. Spirurida of World, espec. Africa (Yes)]

CAMPAU, Donald E. 440 Yellowstone, Billings, Mont., U.S.A. [Ordovician-Mississippian Chitinozoa of N. America (Yes); Devonian Ostracoda of Michigan Basin (No); Mississippian Foraminifera: g. Millerella of Michigan Basin (Yes)]

CAMPBELL, A. Richard. Shell Development Co., 3737 Bellaire Blvd., Houston, Texas, U.S.A. [Devonian Ostracoda (Yes); Tertiary Foraminifera of Gulf Cst. U.S. (Yes)]

CAMPBELL, Prof. A.S. 3011 Regent Street, Berkeley 5, Calif., U.S.A. [Fossil & Recent Radiolaria of World (Yes); Fossil & Recent Tintinnida of World (Yes)]

CAMPBELL, Miss J. Zoology Department, University, Glasgow, Scotland. [Heteroptera of Britain (No)]

CAMPBELL, Mr. J.D. University of Canterbury, Christchurch, New Zealand. [Triassic & Liassic Brachiopoda of New Zealand & New Caledonia (Yes)]

CAMPBELL, K.S.W. Department of Geology, University of New England, Armidale, N.S.W., Australia. [Up. Paleozoic Brachiopoda (Yes)]

CAMPING, M.W. Robert Kochstraat 25, Leeuwarden, Netherlands. [Lepidoptera of Netherlands (Yes)]

del CAMPO, Rafael S. Martin. See MARTIN del CAMPO, R.S.

CAMRAS, Dr. Sidney. 4407 N. Milwaukee Avenue, Chicago 30, Ill., U.S.A. [Diptera: Conopidae of World (Yes)]

ČANADJIJA, Dr. Stjepan, Direktor Muzeja Zagreb, Hrvatski Narodni, Zoološki Muzej, Demetrova ul. 1/II, Zagreb, Yugoslavia. [Tardigrada & Gordioidea of Yugoslavia & Balkan Pen. (Yes)]

CANAMARES, Dr. F. Torres. Jefe Provincial de Sanidad, Cuenca, Spain. [Diptera: Culicinae of med. import. of Iberian Pen., Balearic Is., Canaries, Marruecos (Yes)]

CANDEIAS, A. R. das Enfermeiras da Grande Guerra, No. 6-3ºE, Lisboa, Portugal. [Marine Copepoda, excl. Cyclopoida, of N. & S. Atlantic (Yes); Copepoda parasitic on sardine of Mediterranean (Yes)]

* CANELLA, Mario F. Department of Zoology, Ferrara University, 14 Via Boldini, Ferrara, Italy. [Protozoa: Ciliata]

* CANER, Alan. Geological Survey of Victoria, Mines Department, Melbourne, Vict., Australia. [Fossil invertebrates]

CANNICCI, Prof. Dr. Gabriella. Laboratoria Centrale di Idrobiologia de Roma, Piazza Borghese 91, Roma, Italy. [Marine & f-w. Crustacea: Malacostraca of Italy (No); planktonic Cladocera, marine & f-w., of Italy (Yes)]

CANNONGE, Bernard. 33 rue Georges Bizet, Dijon (Cote d'Or), France. [Mammalia: Chiroptera of Europe (Yes); Quaternary Mammalia of Europe (Yes)]

CANSDALE, G. S. (London, England ;mammals, reptiles) Not now active in taxonomy.

CANTELL, Dr. C. Aug. Nilsson. Skepparegatan 16, Visby, Sweden. [Crustacea: Cirripedia thoracica of World (Yes)]

* CANTONNET, Dr. P. 232 Blvd. St. Germain, Paris (VII), France. [Coleoptera: Chrysomelidae]

CANTOREANU, Margareta. Statiunea Zoologică, Sinaia, Ploesti, Rumania. [Homoptera: Cicadoidea of c. & e. Europe (No)]

CANTRALL, Dr. Irving J. Museum of Zoology, University of Michigan, Ann Arbor, Mich., U.S.A. [Orthoptera & Dermaptera of New World (Yes)]

CAPART, Dr. André. Institut Royal des Sciences Naturelle de Belgique, Rue Vautier 31, Bruxelles 4, Belgium. [Crustacea: Decapoda: Brachyura of e. N. Atlantic (No); of e. S. Atlantic (Yes); of c. Africa (No); marine Copepoda Parasitica (No); f-w. (Yes)]

ČAPEK, Mir. State Forest Research Institute, Banska Stiavnica, Czechoslovakia. [Hymenoptera: reared Braconidae of c. Europe excl. Aphidiinae, Cheloninae, Opiinae, g. Bracon (Yes)]

CAPELLE, Kenneth J. 2107 Park Street, Missoula, Mont., U.S.A. [Diptera: Oestridae; Gasterophilidae; Psilidae: g. Loxocera; all of N. America (Yes)] [U.S. Fish & Wildlife Service]

CAPELOUTO, Reuben. Orkin Exterminating Co., Inc., 936 West Brevard Street, Tallahassee, Fla., U.S.A. [Coleoptera: Buprestidae of s. U.S., espec. Florida (No)]

CAPENER, Mr. A. L. St. George's Home for Boys, P. O. Box 4, Cleveland, Johannesburg, Union of South Africa. [Homoptera: Membracidae of Africa (Yes)]

CAPOCACCIA, Lilia. Museo Civico di Storia Naturale Giacomo Doria, Via Brigata Liguria 9, Genova, Italy. [Reptilia & Amphibia of Liguria & E. Africa]

* CAPOOR, V. N. University, Allahabad, India. [Diptera]

CAPORIACCO, L. (Florence Italy; Acarina) Deceased.

CAPPS, Mr. Hahn W. Division of Insects, U.S. National Museum, Washington 25, D.C., U.S.A. [Lepidoptera, larvae of all families of World (No); Pyraustidae, adults of New World (No)] [U.S. Department of Agriculture]

CAPRA, Dr. F., Conservatore anoz., Museo Civico di Storia Naturale, Via Brigata Liguria 9, Genova (116), Italy. [Orthopteroidea & Coleoptera: Coccinellidae, of Europe & Mediterranean (No)]

CAPURRO, Prof. Luis F. Casilla 10135, Santiago, Chile. [Amphibia: Anura of Chile (Yes)] [Centro de Investigaciones Zoologicas, Universidad de Chile]

CARALP, Michelle-Hélène, Assistante de Géologie, Centre de 3ºCycle de Géologie Approfondie, 351 cours de la Libération, Talence (Gironde), France. [Miocene Foraminifera of Bassin d'Aquitaine (Yes)]

CĂRĂUŞU, Prof. Dr. Sergiu. Statiunea Zoologică Marină "Prof. Ioan Borcea", Agigea, Constanța, Rumania. [Crustacea: Amphipoda: Gammaridea of Black Sea & Mediterranean (Yes)]

CARAYON, Mr. Jaques. Museum National d'Histoire Naturelle, 57 rue Cuvier, Paris (V), France. [Hemiptera: Anthocoridae of World (Yes); Nabidae, espec. Prostemminae of World (Yes)]

CARBONELL, Carlos S. See Addenda.

CARCASSON, R. H. The Coryndon Museum P. O. Box 658, Nairobi, Kenya. [Lepidoptera: Rhopalocera of Ethiopian, excl. Madagascar (Yes)]

* CARCELLES, Alberto R. Prim 366, Alta Gracia, Cordoba, Argentina. [Up. Tertiary & Quaternary marine & fluvial Mollusca of Argentina, Uruguay, Paraguay, Brazil]

* CARDINI, Prof. Luigi. Via del Proconsolo 12, Firenze, Italy. [Fossil vertebrates]

CAREY, Mr. L. E. Department of Entomology, British Museum (Natural History), Cromwell Road, London, S. W. 7, England. [Homoptera]

* CARGNELUTTI, Jan. Biološki Institut Slovenske Akademije Znanosti i Umetnosti, Ljubljana, Yugoslavia. [Lepidoptera]
* CARIA, Dr. Ida Comaschi. Istituto di Geologia, Universitá, Cagliari, Italy. [Fossil mammalia]
CARL, G. Clifford. (Victoria, B. C.; lower vertebrates) Not now active in taxonomy.
CARL, Mrs. G. C. See HART, J. F. L.
CARLISLE, Dr. D. B. Marine Biological Laboratory, Citadel Hill, Plymouth, England. [Tunicata, excl. Larvacea of World (No); of Europe & Mediterranean (Yes); Didemnidae of World (Yes)]
de CARLO, J. See DeCARLO, J.
CARLSON, Stanley A. Richfield Oil Corp., Paleontology Laboratory, P. O. Box 147, Bakersfield, Calif., U. S. A. [Tertiary & Cretaceous Foraminifera of California (Yes)]
* CARLSSON, Matte. Bergsunds Strand 9, Stockholm, Sweden. [Lepidoptera]
CARNE, Dr. P. B. Division of Entomology, Commonwealth Scientific & Industrial Research Organization, P. O. Box 109, Canberra, A. C. T., Australia. [Coleoptera; Scarabaeidae: Dynastinae & Rutelinae of Australia (Yes); Coprinae & Geotrupinae of Australia (No); Lucanidae of Australia (No)]
* CARNEIRO, Ephigenio Jose. Instituto de Biologia e Pesquisas, Caixa Postal 357, Curitiba, Parana, Brazil. [Pisces]
* CARNEY, M. P. Viale Tunisia 43, Milano, Italy. [Diptera]
* CAROLI, Dr. E. Stazione Zoologica, Villa Comunale, Naples, Italy. [Crustacea]
CAROLSFELD-KRAUSÉ, A. G. Slotsherrens Have 97, København Van, Denmark. [Lepidoptera: Nepticulidae of Europe (Yes)]
CARON, J. R. Hindelaan 27, Hilversum, Netherlands. [Crustacea]
CARPENTER, Mr. Charles C. Department of Zoology, University of Oklahoma, Norman, Okla., U. S. A. [Reptilia of Oklahoma (Yes)]
CARPENTER, Prof. F. M. Biological Laboratories, Harvard University, Cambridge 38, Mass., U. S. A. [Neuroptera: Hemerobiidae & Mecoptera, of N. America (Yes); Neuroptera: Coniopterygidae of New World (Yes); fossil Insecta of World (Yes)]
* CARPENTER, Mr. Robert. Address unknown. (Mammalia)
CARPENTER, Col. Stanley J. 6th Army Medical Laboratory, Fort Baker, Calif., U. S. A. [Diptera: Culicidae of N. America (Yes)]
CARR, Mr. A. F. Department of Biology, University of Florida, Gainesville, Fla., U. S. A. [Marine turtles of World (Yes)]
CARRANZA, Jorge. Estacion de Biologia Marina, Instituto Tecnologico de Vera Cruz, Apartado 539, Veracruz, Ver., Mexico. [Marine Pisces of Gulf of Mexico (No)]
CARRECK, Mr. J. N. "Old Stones", Elmstead Glade, Chislehurst, Kent, England. [Quaternary Mammalia, espec. Rodentia; Aves; Reptilia; of n. w. Europe (Yes)] [Queen Mary College, University of London]
CARRERA, Messias. Departmento de Zoologia, Caixa Postal 7172, São Paulo, Brazil. [Diptera: Asilidae & Pantophtalmidae of C. & S. America (Yes)]
* CARRICK, Louis. Franz Theodore Stone Institute, Ohio State University, Put-in-Bay, Ohio, U. S. A. [Aquatic invertebrates]
* CARRICKER, David O. Everglades National Park, Homestead, Fla., U. S. A. [Aves]
CARRIKER, M. A., Jr. Apartado No. 82, Popayan, Colombia. [Aves of C. & S. America, espec. Costa Rica, Colombia, Venezuela, Peru, Bolivia (Yes); Mallophaga of World (No); of Neotropics (Yes)]
CARRIKER, Dr. Melbourne R. Department of Zoology, University of North Carolina, Chapel Hill, N. C., U. S. A. [Life history stages of Mollusca of economic importance of e. cst. of U. S. (Yes)]
CARRILLO, Jose L., Oficina de Estudios Especiales, S. A. G., Londres 40, Mexico 6, D. F., Mexico. [Coleoptera: Scarabaeidae: g. Macrodactylus of N. & C. America (Yes); of S. America (No)]
CARROLL, Prof. J. University College Dublin, Faculty of Agriculture, Glasnevin, Dublin, Eire. [Plant parasitic Nematoda of Ireland (No)]
* CARRUTH, Dr. L. A. Department of Entomology, University of Arizona, Tucson, Ariz., U. S. A. [Coleoptera: Meloidae of Arizona (No)]
CARSON, Carlton M. 455 E. Main Street, Ventura, Calif., U. S. A. [Miocene & Pliocene Foraminifera of Ventura & Sta. Maria basins, Calif. (Yes)]
CARSON, Prof. Hampton L. Department of Zoology, Washington University, St. Louis 5, Mo., U. S. A. [Diptera: Drosophilidae of New World (Yes)]
CARTER, Dr. Alan N. 70 Madeline Street, Burwood E. 13, Vict., Australia. [Tertiary Foraminifera of s. e. Australia (Yes); Recent Cephalopoda: Sepiidae of s. e. Australia (Yes)] [Geological Survey of Victoria, Mines Department]
CARTER, Mr. D. J. Imperial College, London, S. W. 7, England. [Pliocene-Recent smaller Foraminifera of n. w. Europe (Yes); Cretaceous & Tertiary larger & smaller Foraminifera of Europe & Middle East (Fee)]

CARTER, Dr. G. F. E. c/o Pan Venezuelan Oil Co., Apartado 5498, Correos del Este, Caracas, Venezuela. [Ordovician Ostracoda of s. Quebec (Yes)]
CARTER, Miss Marjorie Estelle. Valdosta State College, Valdosta, Ga., U. S. A. [Crustacea: Copepoda: f-w. harpacticoids (Yes)]
CARTER, Mr. T. Donald. American Museum of Natural History, New York 24, N. Y., U. S. A. [Mammalia of Africa & Asia (Yes)]
CARTWRIGHT, Mr. O. L. Division of Insects, U. S. National Museum, Washington 25, D. C., U. S. A. [Coleoptera: Scarabaeidae of World (No); of W. Hemisphere (Yes)]
de CARVALHO, Antenor Leitao. See LEITAO de CARVALHO, A.
CARVALHO, J. C. M., Director, Museu Nacional, Quinta da Boa Vista, Rio de Janeiro, Brazil. [Hemiptera: Miridae & Isometopidae of World (Yes)]
CARVALHO, Mr. J. de Paiva. Caixa Postal 9075, São Paulo, Brazil. [Parasitic Copepoda of fishes of Brazil (Yes); Pisces of Brazil (No)] [Oceanographic Institute, University of São Paulo]
CARVER, Dr. Mary. 28 Coranderrk Street, Reid, Canberra, A. C. T., Australia. [Homoptera: Aphidoidea, excl. Adelgidae & Chermidae, of Australia (Yes)] [Division of Entomology, Commonwealth Scientific & Industrial Research Organization]
CARY, Mrs. C. Reed. Ellet Lane & Wissahickon, Mt. Airy, Philadelphia 19, Penna., U. S. A. [Lepidoptera: Sphingidae of W. Hemisphere; of Galapagos Is. (Yes)]
CARY, Charles W. Union Oil Co. of California, Box 613, Bakersfield, Calif., U. S. A. [Fossil Foraminifera of Pacific Cst. of U. S. (Yes)]
* CASAL, Osvaldo H. Barros Pazos 6347, Buenos Aires, Argentina. [Hymenoptera]
CASEMIR, H. Lerchenstrasse 3, Hüls/Krefeld, Germany. [Araneida: Araneidae: Erigoninae & Linyphiinae of Europe (Yes); of N. America (No)]
* CASEY, R. Geological Survey, Exhibition Road, London, S. W. 7, England. [Fossil invertebrates]
CASIER, Dr. Edgard M. Department of Vertebrate Palaeontology, Institut Royal des Sciences Naturelles, 31 rue Vautier, Bruxelles 4, Belgium. [Pisces: Fossil Elasmobranchii (Yes); Jurassic-Pliocene Actinopterygii (No)]
CASO MUÑOZ, Srita. Maria Elena. Instituto de Biologia, Apartado Postal 29817, Mexico 18, D. F., Mexico. [Asteroidea, Ophiuroidea, Echinoidea, Holothuroidea, of Atlantic & Pacific Cst. of Mexico (Yes)]
CASPERS, Prof. Dr. H. Zoologisches Staatsinstitut, Bornplatz 5, Hamburg 13, Germany. [Diptera: marine Chironomidae of World (Yes)] [University of Hamburg]
CASSAGNAU, P. Laboratoire de Zoologie, Faculté des Sciences, Allees St. Michel, Toulouse, France. [Collembola of s. Europe (No)]
* CASSIE, Mr. R. Morrison. New Zealand Oceanographic Institute, Department of Scientific & Industrial Research, Box 8009, Wellington, New Zealand [Pisces]
CASTELL, Mr. C. P. Department of Palaeontology, British Museum (Natural History), Cromwell Road, London, S. W. 7, England. [Cenozoic Mollusca of Britain (Yes)]
CASTELLANI, Ins. Omero. Piazza dei Sicani 4, Borgata Acilia (Roma), Italy. [Orthoptera: Blattoidea, Mantoidea, Phasmoidea; Dermaptera & Diptera: Asilidae; of Italy (Yes)]
CASTELLANOS, Alfredo. Instituto de Fisiografia y Geologia de Rosario, Leandro Alem 1626, Rosario de Santa Fe, Argentina. [Recent & fossil Mammalia of S. America (Yes)]
CASTER, Dr. Kenneth E. Old Tech. Bldg., University of Cincinnati, Cincinnati 20, Ohio, U. S. A. [Devonian invertebrate faunas of World, espec. S. America & S. Africa (Yes); Echinodermata: Carpoidea of World (Yes)] [Department of Geology]
CASTERET, Norbert. Le Mourlon, St. Gaudens (Hte-Garonne), France. [Mammalia: Chiroptera of Fr. Pyrenees]
CASTLE, Dean Gordon B. Montana State University, Missoula, Mont., U. S. A. [Plecoptera & Isoptera of w. U. S.]
CASTLE, Mr. P. H. J. Zoology Department, Victoria University of Wellington, P. O. Box 196, Wellington, New Zealand. [Deep-sea Pisces: Apodes: Synaphobranchidae, Nemichthyidae, Congridae, Serrivomeridae, of New Zealand (Yes)]
* CASTLE, Prof. William A. Department of Biology, Mary Washington College, Fredericksburg, Va., U. S. A. [Turbellaria]
de CASTRO, A. Lemos. See LEMOS de CASTRO, A.
* CASTRO, Dr. Manuel P. Instituto de Entomologia Sanitaria, Av. Parral 652, Buenos Aires, Argentina. [Diptera: Culicidae] Mail returned from above address...."Unknown".
* CATALA, Dr. Rene L. A. Boite Postale 15, Noumea, New Caledonia. [Pisces]
CATE, Mr. Crawford N. 12719 San Vicente Blvd., Los Angeles 49, Calif., U. S. A. [Gastropoda: g. Cypraea of World (Yes); Mollusca of Hawaii (Yes)]
CATING, James P. U. S. Fish & Wildlife Service, 1530 S. W. 4th Street, Beaufort, N. C., U. S. A. [Pisces: Clupeidae of e. U. S. (No)]
CATTLEY, Mr. J. G. The Fisheries Laboratory, Lowestoft, Suffolk, England. [Crustacea: planktonic Copepoda of s. North Sea (Yes); marine Tanaidacea & Isopoda of Indian Oc. (Yes); pelagic Isopoda of Dana Exp. area (Yes)]

CATTOI, Dra. Noemi V. Nazca 2330, Buenos Aires, Argentina. [Fossil vertebrates of S. America (No); fossil Mammalia of S. America (Yes)] [Museo Argentino de Ciencias Naturales]

* CAUBERE, Bertrand. 1 Avenue Moderne, Paris (XIX), France. [Mammalia]

* CAUCHOIS, Dr. P. Font Romeu (Pyr. Or.), France. [Coleoptera: Carabidae & Pselaphidae]

CAUDRI, Dr. C. M. Bramine. c/o Texas Petroleum Co., Apartado 267, Caracas, Venezuela. [Tertiary Foraminifera of Caribbean & Indo-Pacific (Yes); Tertiary Mollusca of Caribbean & Indo-Pacific (Yes); Devonian (Eiffel) Mollusca (Yes)]

CAUSEY, Prof. David. Box 42, University Station, Fayetteville, Ark., U.S.A. [Oligochaeta, espec. Microdrili, of Mississippi Valley (Yes); parasitic Crustacea, espec. marine Copepoda of Gulf of Mexico & C. America (Yes); from f-w. hosts of s.U.S. (Yes)] [University of Arkansas]

CAUSEY, Nelle B. Box 42, University Station, Fayetteville, Ark., U.S.A. [Diplopoda & Chilopoda of N. America (Yes)] [University of Arkansas]

CAVAZZA, C. F. (Bologna, Italy; Mammalia) Deceased.

CAVE, Mrs. R. Department of Geology, Bedford College, London, N.W.1, England. [Fossil Brachiopoda: g. Lingula of Silurian & Downtonian (Yes)]

CAVENESS, Dr. Fields E. Plant Pathology Department, South Dakota State College, Brookings, S.D., U.S.A. [Soil & plant parasitic Nematoda of U.S. (Yes)]

* CAVINATO, Dr. E. Istituto di Zoologia, Universitá di Padova, Padova, Italy. [Pisces]

* CAVRO, Prof. E. 106 rue J-B. Hosselet, Féchain (Nord), France. [Hymenoptera]

CAWTHRA, E. (Mrs. P. Belton) Department of Zoology, University of Glasgow, Glasgow W.2, Scotland. [Coleoptera: Curculionidae: Erirrhininae of World (Yes); Eugnominae of World (Yes)]

CAZIER, Dr. Mont A. Department of Insects & Spiders, American Museum of Natural History, New York 24, N.Y., U.S.A. [Coleoptera: Cicindelidae of New World (Yes); Buprestidae of N. America & Mexico (Yes); Scarabaeidae of N. America (Yes); Diptera: Apioceratidae of N. America (Yes)]

CEBALLOS, Dr. Gonzalo. Instituto Español de Entomologia, Palacio del Hipodromo, Madrid 6, Spain. [Hymenoptera: Ichneumonidae, espec. Ichneumoninae & Cryptinae, of Palearctic]

CEBALLOS-BENDEZÚ, Prof. Dr. Ismael. Apartado Postal 423, Cuzco, Peru. [Mammalia: Chiroptera of S. America (Yes)] [Museo de Historia Natural de la Universidad Nacional del Cuzco]

CECIONI, Dr. Giovanni. Empresa Nacional del Petroleo, Casilla 507, Iquique, Chile. [Ordovician orthoconic or cyrtoconic Nautiloidea of S. America (Yes); all L. Paleozoic of America (No)]

CEI, Dr. J.M. Instituto de Biologia, Facultad Ciencias Medicas, Universidad Nacional de Cuyo, Mendoza, Argentina. [Amphibia: Salientia of Argentina, Chile, Chaco, Andes, Europe (Yes); Urodela of Europe (Yes)]

ČEJCHAN, Dr. A. Zoological Department, Hradec Králové Region Museum, Malé Náměsti 125, Hradec Králové, Czechoslovakia. [Orthoptera of Europe (Yes); Acrididae: Catantopinae of Palearctic (Yes); Blattoidea of c. Europe (No); Dermaptera of C. Europe (No)]

ČEKALOVIČ KUSCHEVIČ, Rte. Tomás. Casilla 214, Punta Arenas, Magallanes, Chile. [Insecta of Magallanes Prov. (No); Coleoptera: Cerambycidae of same (Yes)]

ČEKANOVSKAJA, O. Zoological Institute, Academy of Sciences, University Quay 2, Leningrad-Centre, U.S.S.R. [Aquatic Oligochaeta of U.S.S.R. (Yes); terr. Oligochaeta of U.S.S.R. (No)]

ČEPEK, P. Spálená 49, Praha 2, Czechoslovakia. [Cretaceous Foraminifera of Czechoslovakia (Yes)] [Paleontologicka Laboratoř, Československa Akademie Věd]

ČEPELÁK, Doc. RNDr. Jiři. Vysoká Škola Pol'nohospodárska, Dobšinského 6, Nitra, Czechoslovakia. [Diptera: Larvaevoridae & Syrphidae excl. Chilosia of c. Europe (Yes); Thecostomata of c. Europe (No)]

* CERCERO, Dra. Maria Cristina. Instituto de Biologia, Ciudad Universitaria, Villa Obregon 20, D.F., Mexico. [Trematoda; Nematoda]

* CERDA GONZÁLEZ, Dr. M., Entomologo, Museo Nacional de Historia Natural, Casilla 787, Santiago, Chile. [Insects]

* CERESA, L. Address unknown. [Hymenoptera]

ČERNÝ, Vladimir. Department of Parasitology, Biological Institute, Czechoslovakian Academy of Sciences, Na cvičišti 2, Praha XIX, Czechoslovakia. [Acarina: Ixodoidea of c. Europe (Yes)]

ČERNÝ, Docent Dr. Walter. Institute of Systematic Zoology, Biological Faculty, Charles University, Viničná 7, Praha II, Czechoslovakia. [Aves of c. Europe (Yes); Crustacea: Isopoda: Oniscoidea of c. Europe (Yes)]

* CERQUEIRA, N. L., Chefe de Laboratorio, Servicio Nacional Febre Amarela, Caixa Postal 830, Rio de Janeiro, Brazil. [Diptera: Culicidae]

CERRUTI, Marcello. 116 Via della Stazione Tuscolana, Roma, Italy. [Coleoptera: Staphy-
linidae: Staphylininae of Europe (Yes); Pselaphidae of e. Africa (Yes), larve of Cara-
bidae & Staphylinidae of Europe (Yes); cave faunas]
CERVENKOVA, E. H. See HEJSKOVA-CERVENKOVA, E.
CEUCA, Mr. T. Catedra de Zoologia, Universitatea "Victor Babeş", Str. Mikó 5-7, Cluj,
Rumania. [Diplopoda of Rumania & s. e. Europe (Yes); Polydesmidae & Blaniulidae of
Europe (Yes)]
CHABANAUD, Dr. Paul. Muséum National d'Histoire Naturelle, 57, rue Cuvier, Paris (V),
France. [Pisces: Recent & fossil Pleuronectiformes of World (No)]
CHABAUD, Dr. Alain. 15 rue de l'Ecole-de Medecine, Paris (VI), France. [Nematoda of
vertebrates of World (Yes)]
CHACE, Mr. E. P., Curator of Conchology, Natural History Museum, Balboa Park, San
Diego 1, Calif., U. S. A. [Terr. & Marine Mollusca, Pleistocene & Recent, of w. cst.
N. America (Yes)]
CHACE, Dr. Fenner A., Jr. Division of Marine Invertebrates, U. S. National Museum,
Washington 25, D. C., U. S. A. [Crustacea: Decapoda & Stomatopoda of World (Yes)]
CHACKO, P. I. Fisheries Biological Station, 6 Menads Street, Puraswalham, Vepery, Mad-
ras 7, India. [Pisces of s. India (No)] [Department of Fisheries of Madras State]
CHADWICK, C. E. Entomological Branch, Department of Agriculture, Box 36, G. P. O.,
Sydney, N. S. W., Australia. [Coleoptera: Curculionidae of econ. import., espec.
g. Perperus, of N. S. W. (No)]
CHADZIBEJLI, Mme. Z. Institut pour la Protection des Plantes, Tshavtschavadze Avenue
No. 17, Tbilisi, U. S. S. R. [Homoptera: Coccoidea of e. Mediterranean (Yes)]
CHAFFEE, Dr. Robert G. Dartmouth College Museum, Hanover, N. H., U. S. A. [Oligocene
Mammalia of U. S. (Yes); fossil Mammalia of Argentina (Yes)]
* CHAGNON, Gustav. 1124 Demontigny Street, Montreal, Que., Canada. [Diptera]
CHAKRAVARTY, M. Zoology Department, Calcutta University, 35 Ballygunge Circular
Road, Calcutta 19, India. [Coccidia, Myxosporidia, Haemosporidia, Gregarinida,
Heterotrichida, Oligotrichida, Polymastigida, Hypermastigida, of Bengal, India (Yes)]
* CHAMBERLAIN, R. Agricultural Entomology Division, Ministry of Agriculture, Elmwood
Avenue, Belfast, N. Ireland. [Plant parasitic Nematoda]
CHAMBERLIN, Dr. Joseph C. Box 278, Forest Grove, Ore., U. S. A. [Chelonethida of
World (No)] [Entomology Research Branch, U. S. Department of Agriculture]
CHAMBERLIN, J. Lockwood. 509 Franklin Street, Alexandria, Va., U. S. A. [Pelecypoda:
Mactridae of World (No); marine Mollusca of Arctic (Yes)]
CHAMBERLIN, Dr. R. V. Department of Biology, University of Utah, Salt Lake City 1, Utah.
[Chilopoda & Diplopoda of World (Yes); Arachnida of New World (No); Annelida of
World (No)]
CHAMBERLIN, Dr. W. J. Department of Entomology, Oregon State College, Corvallis,
Ore., U. S. A. [Coleoptera: Buprestidae of U. S. (No)]
CHAMNEY, T. Potter. Shell Oil Co., Calgary, Alta., Canada. [Cretaceous & Jurassic
Foraminifera of w. Canada (Yes); Jurassic Ostracoda & other microfossils of w.
Canada]
CHANDLER, Asa C. (Houston, Texas; helminths) Died Summer 1958.
CHANDLER, Harry P. (Red Bluff, Calif.; Coleoptera) Deceased.
CHANDLER, Dr. Leland. Entomology Department, Purdue University, Lafayette, Ind.,
U. S. A. [Hymenoptera: Bombini of Nearctic (Yes)]
CHANDY, Dr. Miss M. Department of Zoology, University of Delhi, Delhi, India. [F-w.
& marine Pisces of India (Yes)]
* CHANEY, Mr. Allan H. 1708 S. Boston Place, Russellville, Ark., U. S. A. [Reptilia &
Amphibia of s. & s. w. U. S.]
* CHANG, Feng-Ying. Institute of Marine Biology, Academia Sinica, Tsingtao, People's
Republic of China. [Echinodermata]
* CHANG, Hsi-Chih. Institute of Vertebrate Paleontology, Academia Sinica, P. O. Box 643,
Peking, People's Republic of China. [Fossil vertebrates]
CHANG, Li-Sho. Geological Survey of Taiwan, P. O. Box 31, Taipei, Taiwan, Formosa.
[Tertiary-Recent smaller Foraminifera of Taiwan (Yes)]
CHANG, Shu-chen. Department of Entomology, Taiwan Provincial College of Agriculture,
Taichung, Taiwan, Formosa. [Coleoptera: Cerambycidae of Taiwan (Yes); of China
mainland (No)]
* CHANNON, P. J. Bureau of Mineral Resources, Canberra, A. C. T., Australia. [Fossil
invertebrates]
CHANT, Dr. D. A. Entomology Laboratory, Box 179, Belleville, Ont., Canada. [Acarina:
Phytoseiidae of World (Yes)]
* CHAO, Dr. Hsiu-fu. Fukien Agricultural College, Foochow, Fukien, People's Republic of
China. [Odonata]
CHAPIN, Dr. Edward A. P. O. Box 17, West Medway, Mass., U. S. A. [Coleoptera: Cocci-

nellidae excl. Epilachninae & Scymninae, of New World (Yes); Chilocorinae & Psylloborinae of World (Yes)]
* CHAPIN, Dr. James P. c/o Institut pour la Recherche Scientifique en Afrique Centrale, B. P. 217, Bukavu, Belgian Congo. [Aves of Belgian Congo]
* CHAPMAN, Harold. Address unknown. (Heteroptera)
* CHAPMAN, K. H. Department of Zoology, University of Manchester, Manchester 13, England. [Orthoptera]
CHAPMAN, Dr. P. J. New York State Agricultural Experiment Station, Cornell University, Box 462, Geneva, N. Y., U. S. A. [Corrodentia of N. America (No)]
* CHAPMAN, Mrs. R. F. Merryways, Chalk Lane, Ashtead, Surrey, England. [Crustacea]
* CHAPMAN, Stella M. Entomology Department, National Agricultural Advisory Service, Block II, Government Bldgs., Lawnswood, Leeds 16, England. [Nematoda]
CHAPMAN, Dr. Wilbert M. American Tunaboat Association, 1 Tuna Lane, San Diego, Calif., U. S. A. [Pisces: Blenniidae of Indo-Pacific (No)]
CHAPPARS, Michael S. (Washington, D. C.; fossils) Not now active in taxonomy.
CHAPPUIS, Dr. P. A. Laboratoire de Zoologie, Faculté des Sciences, Allies Saint-Michel, Toulouse, France. [Subterr. f-w. harpacticoid Crustacea: Copepoda & Isopoda of World (Yes)]
CHAPSKIY, Dr. K. K. Zoological Institute, Academy of Sciences, Leningrad B-164, U. S. S. R. [Fossil & Recent Mammalia: Pinnipedia, espec. Phocidae & Odobenidae of World (Yes)]
CHAPULSKY, Josef. Department of Parasitology, Charles University, Viničná ul. 7, Praha II, Czechoslovakia. [Diptera: Hippoboscidae of c. Europe (No); Nycteribiidae of Europe (Yes)]
* CHARBONNIER, J. R. 5 Montée du Change, Lyon, France. [Lepidoptera]
CHARDEZ, D. 21 Av. Florent Becker, Heusy-Verviers, Belgium. [Rhizopoda: Thecamoeba of Europe (Yes)]
* CHARDOME, M. Institut pour la Recherche Scientifique en Afrique Centrale, B. P. 217, Bukavu, Belgian Congo. [Platyhelminthes]
CHARIG, Dr. A. J. Department of Palaeontology, British Museum (Natural History), Cromwell Road, London, S. W. 7, England. [Triassic Reptilia: Archosauria (Yes); Tertiary & Quaternary Mollusca, excl. Cephalopoda (Yes)]
CHARLES, Bro. L., F. S. C. (St. Louis, Mo.; Coleoptera, Myriapoda) Not now active in taxonomy.
* CHATTERJI, Dr. A. K. Geological Survey of India, 27 Chowringhee, Calcutta 13, India. [Fossil Foraminifera]
* CHATWIN, C. P. (St. Austell, England, ; Fossils) Not now active in taxonomy.
CHAUDHURI, Dr. D. N. Ray. St. Xavier's College, Park Street, Calcutta 16, India. [Homoptera: Aphididae of s. e. Asia (Yes); Greenideinae of Melanesia (Yes)]
CHAUHAN, Dr. B. S. Zoological Survey of India, 34 Chittaranjan Avenue, Calcutta 12, India. [Trematoda: Monogenea: Gasterostomata: Hemiuridae (fish parasites) of World (Yes)]
CHAVAN, Prof. André. Chantermerle à Seyssel (Ain), France. [Fossil & Recent marine Mollusca, espec. Pelecypoda: Heterodonta (Yes)]
* CHAVARRIA y CHAVARRIA, Dr. Manuel. Escuela Nacional de Veterinaria, Calzada Tacuba No. 213, Tacuba 17, D. F., Mexico. [Nematoda, Trematoda]
CHEATUM, E. P. Southern Methodist University, Dallas 5, Texas, U. S. A. [Terr. & f-w. Gastropoda of Texas (Yes)]
CHEESMAN, Miss L. Evelyn. Department of Entomology, British Museum (Natural History), Cromwell Road, London, S. W. 7, England. [Hymenoptera of New Caledonia, New Hebrides, Loyalty Is. (Yes)]
CHEETHAM, Alan H. Department of Geology, Louisiana State University, Baton Rouge, La., U. S. A. [Cretaceous-Recent cheilostome Bryozoa (Yes)]
CHEISSIN, Eugen M. Petropavlovskaja 8, kv. 13, Leningrad P-22, U. S. S. R. [Infusoria: Astomata & Hysterocinetidae, of L. Baical (Yes); Thygmotricha (No); Sporozoa: Coccidia, espec. g. Eumeria of Leningrad (Yes)] [Zoological Laboratory, University of Leningrad]
▸ CHEMSAK, Mr. John A. 112 Agriculture Hall, University of California, Berkeley 4, Calif., U. S. A. [Coleoptera: Cerambycidae of World (No); of N. & S. America, s. Pacific, China (Yes)]
* CHEN, Chin-Wen. Taiwan Farmers' Association, Taipei, Taiwan, Formosa. [Hymenoptera]
CHEN, Miss Ling-chu. Department of Entomology, University of Kansas, Lawrence, Kans., U. S. A. [Hemiptera: Corixidae: g. Micronecta of Asia (Yes)]
CHEN, Prof. Johnson T. F., Head, Department of Biology, Tunghai University, Taichung, Taiwan, Formosa. [Pisces of Formosa & s. China (Yes)]
* CHEN, Dr. T. T. Department of Zoology, University of Southern California, Los Angeles 7, Calif., U. S. A. [Protozoa: Opalinidae]
CHENG, Fung-Ying. Department of Entomology, National Taiwan University, Taipeh, Taiwan, Formosa. [Mecoptera: Panorpidae & Bittacidae of Asia (Yes)]

149

CHENG, Mr. Thomas. Department of Histology & Embryology, School of Dentistry, University of Maryland, Baltimore 1, Md., U.S.A. [Trematoda: Digenea: Lecithodendriidae, Brachycoeliidae, Dicrocoeliidae, Allocreadiidae, Plagiorchiidae, of N. & S. America (Yes); Cestoidea: Hymenolepidae of New World]

CHERBONNIER, G., Assistant au Laboratoire de Malacologie, Muséum National d'Histoire, Naturelle, 55 rue de Buffon, Paris (V), France. [Echinoderms, espec. Holothurioidea & Echinoidea (Yes)]

CHERCHI, Prof. Maria Adelaide. Istituto di Zoologia, Universitá di Genova, Via Balbi 5, Genova, Italy. [Reptilia & Amphibia of Italy & Somaliland (Yes)]

* CHERIAN, Sri. M. C., Government Entomologist, Research Institute, Lawley, Road, Coimbatore, India. [Hymenoptera]

CHERMOCK, R. L. Box 1927, University, Ala., U.S.A. [Lepidoptera: Rhopalocera of N. America (Yes); Amphibia of s. e. U. S. (Yes)] [University of Alabama]

CHERNOV, Prof. Dr. S. A. Zoological Institute, Academy of Sciences, Leningrad-Centre, U.S.S.R. [Reptilia: Sauria & Serpentes of Palearctic (Yes)]

* CHERTKOVA, A. N. All-Union Skrjabin Institute of Helminthology, Staropansky 3, Moscow K-12, U.S.S.R. [Animal helminths]

* CHESTNUT, Dr. A. F. Institute of Fisheries Research, Morehead City, N. C., U.S.A. [Mollusca] [University of North Carolina]

CHEVALIER, J. P. Recherches Laboratoire de Géologie, Sorbonne, 1 rue Victor Cousin, Paris (V), France. [Neogene corals (Yes); Recent corals (Yes)]

* CHEW, Robert M. (Los Angeles, Calif., Arachnida) Not now active in taxonomy.

CHHAPGAR, Mr. B. F. Taraporevala Marine Biological Station, Netaji-Subhash Road, Bombay 2, India. [Crustacea: marine Brachyura of India (Yes)]

* CHI, Dr. Ping, Director, Fan Memorial Institute of Biology, Peking, People's Republic of China. [Pisces]

CHIBA, Dr. Takuo. Shimonoseki College of Fisheries, Yoshimi, Shimonoseki, Japan. [Crustacea: Copepoda: Gymnoplea & Podoplea of c. Pacific & Indian Oceans (No)]

CHICKERING, A. M. Albion College, Albion, Mich., U.S.A. [Araneida of C. America & West Indies (Yes)]

CHIESA, Dr. Aldo. Via S. Stefano 1, Bologna, Italy. [Coleoptera: Hydrophilidae of Palearctic]

* CHIHARA, Ayako. Address unknown. [Thysanoptera]

CHIJI, Manzo. Osaka Museum of Natural History, Utsubo, Park, Nishiku, Osaka, Japan. [Tertiary-Recent smaller Foraminifera (Yes)]

CHILLCOTT, J. G. Systematic Entomology, Science Service Bldg., Carling Avenue, Ottawa, Ont., Canada. [Diptera: Muscidae of N. America (No); Empididae of N. America (Yes); Muscidae: Fanniinae of World (Yes)]

CHIN, Ju-Huang. See SHAW, Tsen Hwang.

CHINA, Dr. W. E. Keeper of Entomology, British Museum (Natural History), Cromwell, Road, London, S. W. 7, England. [Heteroptera & Homoptera of World (No)]

CHIPMAN, Robert K. Department of Zoology, Tulane University, New Orleans 18, La., U.S.A. [Pisces: Cyprinodontidae (No)]

CHISWELL, Dr. J. R. East Malling Research Station, Maidstone, Kent, England. [Homoptera: Cicadellidae of Gr. Britain (Yes); Diptera: Tipulidae: larvae of Tipulinae of Gr. Brit. (Yes)]

CHITWOOD, Dr. B. G. Kaiser Foundation Research Institute, S. 14th & Cutting Blvd., Richmond, Calif., U.S.A. [Plant parasitic Nematoda (Fee); arthropod & saprozoic aquatic Nematoda (Fee); Gordiacea, Kinorhyncha, Tardigrada (Yes)]

CHITWOOD, Mrs. May Belle. Helminth Parasite Section, Animal Disease & Parasite Research Division, U. S. Department of Agriculture, Agricultural Research Center, Beltsville, Md., U.S.A. [Parasitic Nematoda of animals of World (Yes); Linguatulida of World (Yes)]

* CHIU, Chung-tang. Institute of Vertebrate Paleontology, Academic Sinica, P. O. Box 643, Peking, People's Republic of China. [Fossil Vertebrates]

CHIU, Miss Shui-chen. Division of Applied Zoology, Taiwan Agricultural Research Institute, Taipeh, Taiwan, Formosa. [Hymenoptera: Ichneumonidae of Taiwan, China mainland, Japan, Korea (Yes)]

CHLEBOWITCH, V. Zoological Institute, Academy of Sciences, Leningrad-Centre, U.S.S.R. [Polychaeta of Arctic & Pacific seas of U.S.S.R. (No); Nereidae (Yes)]

CHOPARD, Prof. L. Department d'Entomologie, Muséum National d'Histoire Naturelle, 45bis, rue de Buffon, Paris (V), France. [Orthoptera: Gryllodea of World (Yes); cavernicolous Orthoptera]

CHOPRA, Dr. B. N. See Addenda.

CHOUMARA, H. See BAILLY-CHOUMARA, H.

* CHOURDHURI, D. K. Entomology Department, Imperial College of Sciences, London, S. W. 7, England. [Apterygota]

CHOW, Dr. C. Y. c/o World Health Organization, 3 Teuku Umar, Djakarta, Indonesia. [Diptera: Culicidae of Orient (No)]
CHOW, Minchen. See ZHOU, Ming-zhen.
CHRAPLIWY, Mr. Peter S. Department of Zoology, University of Illinois, Urbana, Ill., U. S. A. [Amphibia: Pelobatidae of N. America (Yes)]
CHRISTENSEN, Bent. Zoologisk Laboratorium, Nørregade 10, København K, Denmark. [Microdrili: Encytraeidae of Europe (cytotaxonomy of live material only)]
CHRISTENSEN, George. Staenget 2, Gentofte, Denmark. [Lepidoptera: Satyridae of Holarctic (No)]
CHRISTIAN, Dr. Paul J. Department of Biology, University of Louisville, Louisville 8, Ky., U. S. A. [Homoptera: Cicadellidae: g. Typhlocyba, Edwardsiana, Empoa, Ossiannilssonola, Ribautiana, Henribautia, Eupteryx, Hymetta, of N. America (Yes)]
CHRISTIAN, Mr. S. H. Malaria Control Section, Department of Public Health, Minj, Western Highlands, New Guinea. [Culicidae: Culicinae of New Guinea (Yes)]
CHRISTIANSEN, Mr. Bengt. Zoologisk Avdeling, Tromsö Museum, Tromsö, Norway. [Recent Foraminifera & Hydroida of n. e. Atlantic & e. Arctic (Yes)]
CHRISTIANSEN, Kenneth A. Department of Biology, Grinnell College, Grinnell, Iowa. [Collembola of Lebanon-Syria reg. (Yes), Entomobryinae of World (Yes)]
* CHRISTIE, Dr. J. R. Agricultural Experiment Station, University of Florida, Gainesville, Fla., U. S. A. [Nematoda]
CHRISTL, Hans, Jun., Praktische Tierarzt, Griesbach i. Rottal, Germany. [Infusoria: Ophryoscolecidae of rumens (Yes)]
CHRISTOPHERS, Bt. -Col. Sir. R. Zoological Laboratory, The Museums, Cambridge, England. [Diptera: Culicidae: Anophelini of India (No)]
CHRONIC, Dr. John. Department of Geology, University of Colorado, Boulder, Colo., U. S. A. [Pennsylvanian & Permian Foraminifera: Fusulinidae; Bryozoa; Brachiopoda; Mollusca; (Yes)]
CHRYSANTHUS, FR., O. F. M. Cap. Warandelaan 5, Oosterhout (N. Br.), Netherlands. [Araneida of n. w. Europe (Yes); of New Guinea (No)]
* CHU, K. Y. Department of Zoology, National Taiwan University, Taipei, Taiwan, Formosa. [Pisces]
* CHU, Prof. Yuanting T. Address unknown. (Pisces)
CHUANG, S. H. Zoology Department, University of Malaya in Singapore, Singapore 10, Malaya. [Brachiopoda: Inarticulata of World (No); Recent Lingulidae, larvae & adults, of World (Yes); fossil g. Lingula of Britain & N. America (No)]
CHUJO, Prof. Dr. Michio. Laboratory of Entomology, Faculty of Liberal Arts, Kagawa University, Kagawa-ken, Shikoku, Japan. [Coleoptera: Chrysomelidae, Mordellidae, Ciidae, Erotylidae, Languriidae, Endomychidae, Bruchidae, Bostrychidae, Lyctidae, of Japan, Korea, Saghalien I., China, Formosa, Micronesia (Yes); Odonata of Formosa & Hainan (No)]
CHURCH, Clifford C. 15 Montrose Street, Bakersfield, Calif., U. S. A. [Cretaceous-Recent Foraminifera of Pacific Cst. (Yes)] [Tidewater Oil Co.]
CHURCHER, Dr. C. S. Department of Zoology, University of Toronto, Toronto 5, Ont., Canada. [Mammalia: g. Vulpes of World (Yes); Pleicene & Pleistocene Hyracoidea of Africa (No)]
* CHURCHILL, E. P. 415 S. University Street, Vermillion, S. D., U. S. A. [Crustacea of Chesapeake Bay (Yes); f-w. Pelecypoda: mussels (Yes)]
CHUTE, R. M. (Middlebury, Vt.; parasites) Not now active in taxonomy.
CHVALA, M. Department of Systematic Zoology, Charles University, Vinična 7, Praha II, Czechoslovakia. [Diptera: Tabanidae of Palearctic (Yes); Conopidae of Europe (Yes)]
CIFELLI, R. Department of Geology, Brown University, Providence, R. I., U. S. A. [Jurassic smaller Foraminifera, espec. Lagenidae, of Britain (Yes); of w. cst. N. America Tertiary-Pliocene (Yes)]
ČIHAŘ, Jiři. Department of Systematic Zoology, Charles University, Viničná 7, Praha, Czechoslovakia. [Pisces: Cyprinidae: g. Carassius; Esocidae; Cottidae; of Palearctic (Yes)]
CINDEA-CURE, Victoria. Institutul de Piscicultura, B-dul Ana Ipatescu Nr. 46, Bucureşti, Rumania. [Diptera: larvae of Tendipedidae of Rumania (Yes)]
ČINGOVSKI, Jonče. Prirodonaučen Muzej, Orce Nikolov 11, Skopje, Yugoslavia. [Hymenoptera: Tenthredinidae of Yugoslavia, Macedonia, Balkan Pen. (Yes)]
CIORDIA, Honorico. Regional Animal Disease Research Laboratory, c/o Georgia Experiment Station, Experiment, Ga., U. S. A. [Trematoda (Yes)] [U. S. Department of Agriculture]
* ĈIRDEI, Prof. Facultatea de Stiinte Naturale, Str. Vovidenie Nr. 4, Iaşi, Rumania. [Odonata]
CIRY, Prof. R. Faculté des Sciences, Boulevard Gabriel, Dijon, France. [Cretaceous Foraminifera, espec. Fusulinidae, of w. Europe, n. Africa, Turkey (Yes)]

151

* CITA, Prof. Maria Bianca. Istituto di Geologia dell'Università, Piazzale Gorini 15, Milano, Italy. [Mesozoic-Tertiary smaller Foraminifera, espec. planktonic, of Italy (Yes)]

de CIVRIEUX, J. M. S. See SELLIER de CIVRIEUX, J. M.

CLANCEY, Mr. P. A. The Durban Museum, Durban, Natal, Union of South Africa. [Aves of s. & e. Africa, Europe, n. Africa (Yes); Mammalia of s. Africa (Yes)]

* CLAPHAM, Dr. P. A. Game Research Station, Burgate Manor, Fordingbridge, Hants, England. [Nematoda]

CLARIDGE, Mr. M. F. Hope Department of Entomology, University Museum, Oxford, England. [Hymenoptera: Eurytomidae of World (No); of Palearctic (Yes); Parasitica of Palearctic (No)]

CLARK, Miss Ailsa. British Museum (Natural History), Cromwell Road, London, S. W. 7, England. [Asteroidea, Ophiuroidea, Crinoidea, of World (Yes)]

CLARK, Austin H. (Washington, D. C.; Echinodermata, Onychophora, Rhopalocera) Died 1954.

* CLARK, Charles A. Address unknown. (Odonata)

CLARK, Mr. D. J. Department of Zoology, British Museum (Natural History), Cromwell Road, London, S. W. 7, England. [Araneae: of Africa (Yes); Salticidae of Africa & Europe (Yes)]

CLARK, Prof. David L. Department of Geology, Southern Methodist University, Dallas 5, Texas. [Mesozoic Cephalopoda: Lytoceratidae (Yes); Upp. Paleozoic Goniatitina (Yes); Up. Paleozoic-Triassic conodonts (Yes)]

CLARK, David T. Department of Microbiology, College of Veterinary Medicine, Michigan State University, East Lansing, Mich., U. S. A. [Nematoda of domestic animals (Yes); Cestoda of birds (Yes)]

CLARK, Dr. Eugenie. Cape Haze Marine Laboratory, Placida, Fla., U. S. A. [Pisces: Plectognaths, Apodes, Syngnathids, of Red Sea (Yes); Plectognaths of Micronesia (No); shallow-w. marine fishes of w. cst of Florida (Yes)]

CLARK, Dr. Gordon Marston. Patuxent Research Refuge, Laurel, Md., U. S. A. [Parasitic Acarina of N. America (Yes)]

CLARK, J. (Mooroolbark, Australia; Ants) Died June 1, 1956.

CLARK, Dr. J. Department of Geology, South Dakota School of Mines, Rapid City, S. D., U. S. A. [U. Eocene-Oligocene Carnivores & Insectivores (Yes); Oligocene Equidae (Yes)]

CLARK, Robert B. Department of Zoology, University of Bristol, Bristol 8, England. [Polychaeta (No); Nephtyidae (Yes)]

CLARK, Mr. T. H. Department of Geological Sciences, McGill University, Montreal, Que., Canada. [Ordovician invertebrates, excl. Bryozoa, of e. Canada (No)]

CLARK, Dr. W. C. Entomology Division, Department of Scientific & Industrial Research, P. O. Box 223, Nelson, New Zealand. [Soil Nematoda of N. Z. (Yes); Mollusca: Trochidae of N. Z. & Australia (No); Pycnogonida of S. Pacific (Yes)]

CLARK, Dr. William K. Department of Biology, Sam Houston State Teachers College, Huntsville, Texas, U. S. A. [Mammalia: g. Peromyscus of s. e. U. S. (Yes)]

CLARKE, Arthur H., Jr. Museum of Comparative Zoology, Cambridge 38, Mass., U. S. A. [Marine Mollusca of n. e. N. America (Yes); abyssal marine Mollusca of World (Yes); f-w. Mollusca, excl. Sphaeriidae & Pleuroceridae, of N. America (Yes)]

CLARKE, C. H. D. (Toronto, Canada; Mammalia) Not now active in taxonomy.

CLARKE, Dr. J. F. Gates. Division of Insects, U. S. National Museum, Washington 25, D. C,, U. S. A. [Microlepidoptera of World (Yes)]

CLARKE, Dr. K. U. Department of Zoology, University of Nottingham, Nottingham, England. [Hymenoptera: Apoidea of Europe (No); g. Bombus & Psithyrus of World (No)]

* CLARKE, M. Hughes. Central Micropaleontological Laboratory, Bataafsche Petroleum, Carel v. Bylandlaan 30, Den Haag, Netherlands. [Fossil invertebrates]

CLARKE, Dr. R. National Institute of Oceanography, Wormley, Godalming, Surrey, England. [Mammalia: Cetacea, excl. Delphinidae of World (Yes)]

CLARKE, Robert. Biology Department, Kansas State Teachers College, Emporia, Kans., U. S. A. [Reptilia & Amphibia of Kansas (Yes)]

* CLARKE, Mr. R. D. 36 Acacia Street, Box Hill, Vict., Australia. [Lepidoptera; Coleoptera]

CLARKE, V. Department of Health, Research Laboratory, P. O. Box 8105, Causeway, Southern Rhodesia. [Mollusca: Planorbidae of Ethiopian (Yes)]

CLARKE, Mr. William D. Department of Marine Biology, Scripps Institution of Oceanography, La Jolla, Calif., U. S. A. [Crustacea: Mysidacea of World (Yes)]

* CLARKE-MacINTYRE, William. Cojimies, Manabi, Ecuador. [Coleoptera]

CLASSEN, Willard J., Jr. P. O. Box 278, Oildale, Calif., U. S. A. [Tertiary Foraminifera of w. cst. U. S. (Yes)]

CLASSEY, E. W. 22 Harlington Road East, Feltham, Middlesex, England. [Lepidoptera: Noctuidae, incl. larvae, of Britain (Yes); Diptera: Culicidae of Britain (Yes)]

CLASTRIER, Dr. J. Institut Pasteur, Alger, Algeria. [Diptera: Ceratopogonidae of Europe & Africa (Yes)]

CLAY, Dr. Theresa. Department of Entomology, British Museum (Natural History), Cromwell Road, London, S. W. 7, England. [Mallophaga of birds & mammals (Yes); Anoplura of mammals (No)]

CLAY, Prof. William M. Department of Biology, University of Louisville, Louisville 8, Ky., U. S. A. [Pisces: Petromyzontidae & Amblyopsidae of N. America (Yes); Reptilia: Colubridae: g. Natrix of N. America (Yes)]

CLEARY, Robert E. 514 4th Street S. E., Independence, Iowa, U. S. A. [F-w. Pisces of Great Lakes reg. (No)]

CLEAVES, Arthur Bailey. [(St. Louis, Mo.; fossils) Not now active in taxonomy.

CLEGG, John. Haslemere Educational Museum, Haslemere, Surrey, England. [F-w. invertebrates, excl. Protozoa & Rotifera, of Britain (Yes)]

CLEMENS, Mr. H. B. 7237 E. Lanai Street, Long Beach, Calif., U. S. A. [Pisces: Thunnidae of e. Pacific (Yes)] [California Department of Fish & Game]

* CLEMENS, Howard P. Department of Zoology, University of Oklahoma, Norman, Okla., U. S. A. [Crustacea: Amphipoda]

CLEMENS, W. A. Department of Paleontology, University of California, Berkeley 4, Calif., U. S. A. [Mesozoic Mammalia (Yes)]

CLEMENS, W. A. Department of Zoology, University of British Columbia, Vancouver 8, B. C., Canada. [F-w. & marine Pisces of Br. Columbia (Yes)]

* CLEMENT, Pierre. Address unknown. [Coleoptera]

* CLEMENTE, Prof. Leopoldo S. Department of Zoology, University of the Philippines, Quezon City, Philippines. [Insects; races of Homo; P. I. & Indomalaya]

CLENCH, Harry K. Carnegie Museum, Pittsburgh 13, Penna., U. S. A. [Lepidoptera: Cossidae of World (Yes); Limacodidae of N. America & Africa (Yes); Lycaenidae of World (Yes); Megalopygidae of S. & C. America (No); Rhopalocera of Afghanistan (Yes)]

CLENCH, William J. Museum of Comparative Zoology, Cambridge 38, Mass., U. S. A. [Marine Mollusca of w. Atlantic (Yes); f-w. Mollusca of N. America (Yes); terr. Mollusca of Melanesia & West Indies (Yes)]

CLEU, Dr. H. 18 Fbg. Gambetta, Aubenas (Ardèche), France. [Lepidoptera & Coleoptera of France (No)]

CLEVELAND, Merrill. U. S. Department of Agriculture, Agricultural Research Service, Entomology Research Branch, Fruit Insects, 1237 Washington Avenue, Vincennes, Ind., U. S. A. [Acarina: phytoph. mites of deciduous fruit trees of N. America (Yes)]

CLIFF, Mr. Frank Samuel. Department of Zoology, Chico State College, Chico, Calif., U. S. A. [Reptilia of w. U. S., Mexico, Baja. Calif. (Yes); Amphibia of w. U. S. & Mexico (No)]

CLIFFORD, Carleton M. Department of Zoology, University of Maryland, College Park, Md., U. S. A. [Acarina: Ixodidae, incl. nymphs & larvae, of s. e. U. S. (Yes)]

CLIFFORD-JONES, Dr. W. Department of Zoology, University College of North Wales, Bangor, Wales. See JONES, W. Clifford.

CLINE, Mr. L. M. Department of Geology, University of Wisconsin, Madison, Wis., U. S. A. [Fossil Blastoidea (Yes)]

* CLINTON, H. F. Address unknown. (Mallophaga)

CLOGSTON, Mr. Fred L. Department of Biological Science, University of California at Santa Barbara, Goleta, Calif., U. S. A. [Crustacea: marine harpacticoid Copepoda of e. N. Pacific (Yes)]

CLOTHIER, Prof. Ronald R. Department of Biological Science, Arizona State College, Tempe, Ariz., U. S. A. [Mammalia of Arizona (Yes); Soricidae of Rocky Mt. states (Yes)]

CLOUD, Dr. Preston E., Jr. U. S. Geological Survey, Washington 25, D. C., U. S. A. [Fossil & recent Brachiopoda of World (Yes)]

CLOUDSLEY-THOMPSON, Dr. J. L. Glendoone, 10 Lower Green Road, Esher, Surrey, England. [Chilopoda of Britain (No); Arachnida, excl. Acari & Linyphiidae, of Britain (No)] [King's College, University of London]

CLOYD, Mr. Will John. Carson-Newman College, Jefferson City, Tenn., U. S. A. [Hymenoptera: Formicidae of N. America (Yes); Diptera: Asilidae of s. e. U. S. (Yes)]

COATNEY, Dr. G. Robert, Chief, Laboratory of Parasite Chemotherapy, National Institute of Allergy & Infectious Diseases, National Institutes of Health, Bethesda 14, Md., U. S. A. [Blood Protozoa of World (No)]

COATON, Dr. W. G. H. Division of Entomology, P. B. 134, P. O. Vallis, Pretoria, Union of South Africa. [Isoptera of Ethiopian (No)] [Department of Agriculture]

COATS, Ruth E. 3846 Skyline Blvd., Carlsbad, Calif., U. S. A. [Gastropoda: Trochidae of World (Yes)]

COBB, Mrs. Grace S. Nematology Section, Plant Industry Station, Beltsville, Md., U. S. A. [Plant parasitic Nematoda: g. Heterodera of World (Yes)] [Agricultural Research Service, U. S. Department of Agriculture]

COBBAN, Mr. W. A. U. S. Geological Survey, Federal Center, Denver 14, Colo., U. S. A. [Up. Cretaceous Cephalopoda of w. U. S. (Yes)]

COBBEN, René H. Entomological Laboratory, Gen. Foulkesweg 37, Wageningen, Netherlands. [Heteroptera of w. Europe & Dutch Antilles (Yes); Saldidae of World (Yes); Homoptera: Auchenorhyncha of w. Europe & Dutch Antilles (Yes)]

COBOS SANCHEZ, Mr. Antonio. Instituto de Aclimatacion, Almeria, Spain. [Coleoptera: Buprestidae, Eucnemidae, Trixagidae, of World (Yes)]

COCHRAN, Dr. Doris M. Division of Reptiles & Amphibians, U. S. National Museum, Washington 25, D. C., U. S. A. [Reptilia & Amphibia of West Indies (Yes); of Thailand (Yes); frogs of Brazil (Yes)]

COCHRAN, Wendell A. Route 2, Carthage, Mo., U. S. A. [Devonian Brachiopoda, espec. g. Atrypa, of c. U. S. (Yes)]

COCKAYNE, E. A. (London, England; Lepidoptera) Died November 1956.

COCKERHAM, Mr. K. L. Agricultural Extension Service, Louisiana State University, Baton Rouge, La., U. S. A. [Coleoptera: Rhynchophora]

* COCKINGS, K. L. East African Medical Survey & Research Institute, P. O. Box 162, Mwanza, Tanganyika. [Acarina]

COCKRUM, Dr. E. Lendell. Department of Zoology, University of Arizona, Tucson, Ariz., U. S. A. [Mammals of U. S. (Yes); Chiroptera of N. America (Yes)]

CODOCEO, Miss Maria R. Museo Nacional de Historia Natural, Casilla 787, Santiago, Chile. [Reptilia: Iguanidae; Batrachia: Salientia; both of S. America (Yes)]

CODREANU, Prof. Radu. Laboratoire de Zoologie (Invertébrés), Faculté des Sciences Naturelles, Splaiul Independentei 93, Bucuresţi 35, Rumania. [Turbellaria: f-w. Tricladida of World (Yes); Crustacea: Isopoda: Epicaridea & Asellidae of World (Yes); Diptera: parasitic & epizoic Chironomidae of World (Yes)]

COE, Mr. R. L. Department of Entomology, British Museum (Natural History), Cromwell Road, London, S. W. 7, England. [Diptera: Syrphidae of World (No), of Palearctic (Yes); Pipunculidae of Palearctic (No); Lonchopteridae of World (No)]

COE, Dr. Wesley R. (La Jolla, Calif.; Mollusca) Not now active in taxonomy.

COFFIN, Harold G. 22 E. Whitman Drive, College Place, Wash., U. S. A. [Crustacea: Decapoda: Paguridae of w. cst. of N. & C. America (Yes)]

COGGER, Harold G. Department of Herpetology, Australian Museum, College Street, Sydney, N. S. W., Australia. [Reptilia & Amphibia of Australia (Yes)]

COGGESHALL, Arthur S. (Santa Barbara, Calif.; dinosaurs) Deceased.

* COGNETTI, G. Departmento di Zoologia, dell'Universitá, Bologna, Italy. [Amphibia]

COGSWELL, Mr. Howard L. (Oakland, Calif.; Aves) Not now active in taxonomy.

* COHEN, A. Muzeul National de Istorie, "Grigore Antipa", Kisselef No. 1, Bucureşti III, Rumania. [Araneida]

COHEN, Daniel M. U. S. National Museum, Washington 25, D. C., U. S. A. [Opisthoproctoid & Stomiatoid fishes of World (Yes); Blenniidae of w. S. America (Yes)] [U. S. Fish & Wildlife Service]

COHER, Dr. Edward I. 557 California Street, Newtonville, Mass., U. S. A. [Diptera: fossil Mycetophilidae of World (Yes); Recent Culicidae of New World, Asia, Pacific, (Yes); Tabanidae, Simuliidae, Ceratopogonidae, of New World & s. e. Asia (No)] [World Health Organization, Nepal]

COHIC, F., Maitre de Recherches, Laboratoire d'Entomologie Agricole, Institut Français d'Oceanie, B. P. 4, Noumea, New Caledonia. [Homoptera: Coccoidea of S. Pacific (Yes)]

COHN, Theodore J. Insect Division, Museum of Zoology, University of Michigan, Ann Arbor, Mich., U. S. A. [Orthoptera: Tettigoniidae, espec. Decticinae, of New World (Yes)]

COIFFAIT, Dr. H. Laboratoire Souterrain de Moulis, Faculté des Sciences, Toulouse, France. [Coleoptera: Staphylinidae: Leptotyphlinae of World (Yes); Xantholinae of Palearctic (Yes); Pselaphidae, g. Mayetia of World (Yes)]

COIL, William H. Department of Zoology, University of Nebraska, Lincoln 8, Neb., U. S. A. [Cestoda of birds & mammals (Yes); Trematoda of World (Yes)]

COKER, Prof. R. E. Department of Zoology, University of North Carolina, Chapel Hill, N. C., U. S. A. [Crustacea: cyclopoid & harpacticoid Copepoda of New World (Yes)]

* COLAS, G. Museum National d'Histoire Naturelle, 45bis rue de Buffon, Paris (V), France. [Coleoptera: Carabidae]

* COLAS-BELCOUR, Jaques. Service de Parasitologie, Institut Pasteur, 96 rue Falquiere, Paris (XV), France. [Acarina: Argasidae]

COLBERT, Dr. Edwin H. American Museum of Natural History, New York 24, N. Y. [Late Paleozoic & Mesozoic Amphibia & Reptilia (Yes)]

COLBRAN, Mr. R. C. Science Branch, Head Office, William Street, Brisbane B. 7, Queensland, Australia. [Nematoda]

COLE, Dr. A. C., Jr. Department of Zoology & Entomology, University of Tennessee, Knoxville, Tenn., U. S. A. [Hymenoptera: Formicidae of U. S. (Yes)]

COLE, Dr. Charles F. Zoology Department, University of Arkansas, Fayetteville, Ark., U. S, A. [Pisces: Percidae: g. Etheostoma: sg. Boleosoma of N. America (Yes)]

COLE, Dr. Frank R. 454 Gill Avenue, Port Hueneme, Calif., U. S. A. [Diptera of N. America,

154

espec. w. N. A.: Acroceridae, Therevidae, Bombyliidae, Conopidae, Syrphidae, Tachinidae, Asilidae (No)]

* COLE, Dr. Gerald A. Department of Zoology, Arizona State University, Tempe, Ariz.,
U. S. A. [Crustacea: microcrustacea]

COLE, Prof. W. Storrs. Department of Geology, McGraw Hall, Cornell University, Ithaca,
N. Y., U. S. A. [Cretaceous-Recent larger Foraminifera of New World & Indo-Pacific
(Yes)]

COLEMAN, Mr. Robert Hemphill. Route 8, Box 615, Charleston, S. C., U. S. A. [Mammalia
of S. C. (Yes)]

COLES, John W. British Museum (Natural History), Cromwell Road, London, S. W. 7, England. [Free-living Nematoda of Europe (No); of Britain (Yes)]

COLL, Francisco E. See ESPANOL C., F.

COLLADO, Juan Gil. Avenida General Mola 95, Madrid, Spain. [Acarina & Insecta of med.
interest of Spain (Yes)]

COLLART, A., Directeur de Laboratoire, Institut Royal des Sciences Naturelles, 31 rue
Vautier, Bruxelles, Belgium. [Diptera: Diopsidae of Africa (Yes); g. Microsania of
World (Yes); Sarcophagidae of Europe & Africa (No)]

COLLENETTE, Mr. C. L. Department of Entomology, British Museum (Natural History),
Cromwell Road, London, S. W. 7, England. [Lepidoptera: Lymantriidae of World (Yes)]

COLLESS, Dr. D. Department of Parasitology, University of Malaya, Sepoy Lines, Singapore
3, Malaya. [Diptera: Culicidae of Orient (Yes); of Australasia (No)]

COLLETTE, Bruce B. 235 Lang Road, Sam Houston Village No. 2, San Antonio 9,
Texas, U. S. A. [Pisces: Percidae: sg. Hololepis of e. U. S. (Yes); Etheostomatinae of
U. S. (No); Reptilia: Serpentes, g. Tropidophis of West Indies (Yes); Reptilia of West
Indies (No)]

COLLEY, Wm. 6 Plainfield Terrace, Newtown St. Boswells, Roxburghshire, Scotland. [Reptilia: snakes of Brit. E. Africa & Sudan (No)]

COLLIER, Mr. Gerald. Department of Zoology, University of California, Los Angeles 24,
Calif., U. S. A. [Aves: Icteridae of New World (No); Jacanidae of s. e. Asia, C. America (No)]

COLLIGNON, G. 7 rue de l'Isère, Gières (Isère), France. [Jurassic-Cretaceous Ammonitoidea, Echinoidea, Gastropoda, Lamellibranchia, of France & Madagascar (Yes)]

COLLIGNON, J. Laboratoire d'Oceanographie de l'Institut d'Etudes Centrafricaines, B. P.
322, Pointe-Noire, Moyen Congo, French Equatorial Africa. [Marine Mollusca, excl.
Cephalopoda, of w. Africa (Yes); Pisces: Sciaenidae of w. Africa (Yes)]

* COLLIN, Mr. Jas. E. Raylands, Newmarket, Suffolk, England. [Diptera of Britain; Diptera excl. Nematocera, of Palearctic; Empididae of World (all Yes)]

COLLINGWOOD, C. A. Shardlow Hall, Shardlow, Derby, England. [Hymenoptera: Formicidae
of Europe & c. Asia (Yes)] [Ministry of Agriculture]

COLLINS, Mr. A. C. 9 Olympic Avenue, Newtown, Geelong, Vict., Australia. [Tertiary
Foraminifera of Australia (No); Quaternary & Recent (Yes)]

COLLINS, Mr. R. J. Department of Entomology, British Museum (Natural History), Cromwell
Road, London, S. W. 7, England. [Economic Lepidoptera of World (No)] [Commonwealth
Institute of Entomology.]

* COLLINS, Prof. R. Lee. Geology Department, Louisiana State University, Baton Rouge 3,
La., U. S. A. [Tertiary invertebrates & vertebrates]

COLLINSON, Dr. Charles W. Illinois State Geological Survey, Urbana, Ill., U. S. A. [Ordovician & Mississippian Cephalopoda of New World & Europe (Yes); Paleozoic Chitinozoa
of World (Yes); Pennsylvanian invertebrates of Illinois (Yes)]

* COLLS, D. G. Canadian Wildlife Service, 900 Dominion Public Bldg., Winnipeg, Man.,
Canada. [Aves & Mammalia]

COLMAN, Mr. J. Marine Biological Station, Port Erin, Isle of Man, Great Britain. [Chaetognatha of N. Atlantic (Yes); of Middle East (No)]

COLOM, Mr. Guillermo. Isabel II, No. 19, Soller (Mallorca), Spain. [Tertiary Microforaminifera of Spain (Yes); fossil Tintinnidae (Yes)]

COLOMBO, G. Istituto di Zoologia, Universitá de Padova, 10 Via Loredan, Padova, Italy.
[Orthoptera: Acridoidea of Europe (No)]

COLOSI, Prof. G. Istituto de Zoologia, Via Romana 17, Firenze, Italy. [Crustacea: Potamonidae of World (No); Mollusca: Veronicellidae of World (No)]

COLTER, Dr. V. S. (Guatemala City; fossils) Not now active in taxonomy.

* COLTON, Mr. John. U. S. Fish & Wildlife Service, Woods Hole, Mass., U. S. A. [Pisces]

COLYER, Mr. C. N. Upton Don, Long Lane, Upton-by-Chester, Cheshire, England. [Diptera:
Phoridae of World (No); of British Isles (Yes)]

COMAN, Dr. Daniel. Institutul de Speleologie, Str. Miko 5, Cluj, Rumania. [Free-living
Nematoda of Rumania (Yes); Mermithidae of World (Yes)]

COMELLINI, Andre. Musée d'Histoire Naturelle, Genève, Switzerland. [Araneida: Thomisidae of Europe & Africa (Yes)]

COMFORT, Dr. Alex. 44 The Avenue, Loughton, Essex, England. [Gastropoda: Helicidae: Cepaea nemoralis of World (Yes)]

COMITA, Prof. G. W. Department of Zoology, North Dakota Agricultural College, Fargo, N. D., U. S. A. [Crustacea: f-w. Copepoda of N. America (Yes)]

COMMISSARIS, Mr. Larry. Department of Zoology, University of Arizona, Tucson, Ariz., U. S. A. [Mammalia of s. w. U. S. (Yes)]

COMMON, Mr. I. F. B. Division of Entomology, Commonwealth Scientific & Industrial Research Organization, P. O. Box 109, Canberra, A. C. T., Australia. [Lepidoptera: Tortricidae; Noctuidae: g. Heliothis, g. Agrotis, Hadeninae; Gelechiidae: g. Pectinophora; Gracilariidae; Oecophoridae; & other microlepidoptera; all of Australia (Yes)]

COMPERE, Harold. Citrus Experiment Station, University of California, Riverside, Calif., U. S. A. [Hymenoptera: Encyrtidae & Aphelinidae, parasitic in coccids & mealy bugs, of World (Yes)]

* COMPTON, Mr. Lawrence V., Head Biologist, Soil Conservation Service, Washington 25, D. C., U. S. A. [Miocene to Pleistocene birds (No)]

COMSTOCK, Dr. John A. P. O. Box 158, Del Mar, Calif., U. S. A. [Lepidoptera, life histories, of N. America (No)]

COMSTOCK, William P. (Newark, N. J., Lepidoptera) Deceased.

CONANT, Mr. Roger. Taunton Lakes, Marlton, N. J., U. S. A. [Reptilia & Amphibia of e. N. America (Yes); of Mexico (No)]

CONCI, Dr. Cesare. Museo Civico di Storia Naturale, Corso Venezia 55, Milano, Italy. [Odonata of Europe (Yes); Mallophaga of Europe (No); Anoplura & Siphonaptera of Italy (Yes)]

CONDAMIN, Mr. Michel. Institut Français d'Afrique Noire, Université de Dakar, Dakar, Senegal. [Lepidoptera: Satyridae: g. Mycalesis of Africa (Yes); Reptilia: Ophidia of E. Africa (Yes)]

CONDÉ, Dr. Bruno. 30 rue Sainte-Catherine, Nancy (M-M.), France. [Protura; Entotrophi: Campodeidae & Procampodeidae; Diplopoda: Pselaphognatha; Palpigradi; all of World (Yes)] [Université de Nancy]

CONDON, H. T., Curator of Birds, South Australian Museum, North Terrace, Adelaide, Australia. [Aves: Tubinares, Laro-limicolae, Grues, Psittaci, Accipitres, Passeres, of Australian (Yes); Reptilia & Amphibia of Australian (No)]

de CONINCK, L. A. P. See DE CONINCK, L. A. P.

CONKIN, James E. Department of Geology, University of Louisville, Louisville 8, Ky., U. S. A. [Mississippian Foraminifera of N. America (Yes); Cretaceous-Tertiary Foraminifera of Gulf Cst. of U. S. (Yes); L. Mississippian Blastoidea of N. America (Yes); Mississippian invertebrates, Paleozoic Foraminifera, Pleistocene land snails (No)]

CONLIN, James P. 3617 Baldwin Street, Fort Worth 10, Texas, U. S. A. [Pennsylvanian-Cretaceous Cephalopoda, espec. Comanchean & Gulf Ammonitoidea, of World (Yes)]

CONNELL, Prof. James F. L. Department of Geology, Southwestern Louisiana Institute, Lafayette, La., U. S. A. [Eocene Echinoidea: Irregularia of e. & s. U. S. (Yes); Eocene Pelecypoda of e. & s. U. S. (Yes)]

CONNELL, Dr. Joseph H. Department of Biological Sciences, University of California, Santa Barbara College, Goleta, Calif., U. S. A. [Cirripedia of w. Europe & w. N. America (Yes); epizoic Cirripedia of e. Pacific (Yes)]

CONNELL, Dr. Walter A. Department of Entomology, University of Delaware, Newark, Del., U. S. A. [Coleoptera: Nitidulidae of New World (Yes)]

CONSANI, Mario. (Firenze, Italy; Hymenoptera) Deceased.

CONSIGLIO, Dott. Carlo. Istituto di Zoologia, Viale Regina Elena 326 (Policlinico), Roma, Italy. [Plecoptera of Europe & N. Africa (Yes); Odonata of Italy (No)]

* CONSTANT, Pierre. 16 Blvd. de la Fontaine-des-Suisses, Dijon, France, [Mammalia]

CONSTANTA, Constandache. Str. Splaiul Independenţei 91-95, Bucureşti, Rumania. [Hymenoptera: Chalcidoidea of Rumania (Yes)]

CONSTANTINEANU, Prof. Mihai I. Str. Vovidenie Nr. 4, Iasi, Rumania. [Hymenoptera: Ichneumonidae of Romania (Yes)] [Universitatea "Al. J. Cuza"]

CONTRERAS, Dr. Prof. F. Zaragoza No. 141, Mexico 3, D. F., Mexico. [Crustacea: Brachyura of Mexico; Fossil & Recent marine & f-w. Mollusca of Gulf of Calif. & Pacific]

COOCH, G. Canadian Wildlife Service, Ottawa, Ont., Canada. [Aves: Anseriformes of Arctic N. America (Yes)]

COOGAN, Alan Hall. Department of Geology, Cornell College, Mount Vernon, Iowa, U. S. A. [Up. Carboniferous-Permian fusulinid Foraminifera of w. U. S. & Carnic Alps, Austria (Yes); Permian productid & spiriferid Brachiopoda of California & Oregon (Yes)]

COOK, Mr. Carl. Crailhope, Ky., U. S. A. [Odonata of World (Yes)]

COOK, Dr. David R. Department of Biology, Wayne State University, Detroit 1, Mich., U. S. A. [Acarina: Hydracarina of North America & Africa (Yes)]

COOK, Dr. Edwin F. Department of Entomology & Economic Zoology, University of Minnesota, St. Paul 1, Minn., U. S. A. [Diptera: Scatopsidae of World (Yes); Chaoborinae of N. America (Yes); Anoplura & Mallophaga: Trichodectidae of N. America (Yes)]

COOK, Fannye A., Director, Mississippi Game & Fish Commission Museum, 111 N. Jefferson Street, Jackson, Miss., U.S.A. [Birds, f-w. fishes, reptiles, of Mississippi (Yes)]

COOK, Dr. Harold J. Agate, Neb., U.S.A. [Fossil Mammalia of w. N. America, espec. Oligocene & later Carnivora, Perissodactyla, Artiodactyla, (Yes)] [Cook Museum of Natural History]

COOK, Paul P., Jr. 152 Lincoln Street, Reedley, Calif., U.S.A. [Homoptera: Membracidae of World (Yes)]

COOK, Mr. S. F., Jr. 715 Bear Creek Road, Orinda, Calif., U.S.A. [Reptilia & Amphibia of California (Yes)]

* COOK, Theodore D. Shell Oil Co., P.O. Box 1861, Corpus Christi, Texas, U.S.A. [Fossil invertebrates]

COOK, Dr. William C. P.O. Box 616, Walla Walla, Wash., U.S.A. [Lepidoptera: Phalaenidae of N. America (Yes)] [U.S. Department of Agriculture]

COOKE, C. Montague. (Honolulu, Hawaii; Mollusca) Died October 29, 1948.

COOKE, C. Wythe. U.S. National Museum, Washington 25, D.C., U.S.A. [Mesozoic & Cenozoic Echinoidea of e. U.S. (Yes); Cenozoic Mollusca of e. U.S. (No)]

COOKE, Dr. H.B.S. Department of Geology, University of Witwatersrand, Johannesburg, Union of South Africa. [Quaternary Mammalia: Proboscidea, Perissodactyla, Artiodactyla, of c. & s. Africa (Yes)]

COOKE, Mr. J.A. 123 Woodstock Road, Oxford, England. [Arachnida, excl. Acarina, of Europe & Turkey (Yes); of Tanganyika (No)] [University Museum]

COOLIDGE, Mr. Harold J. 2101 Constitution Avenue N.W., Washington 25, D.C., U.S.A. [Mammalia: Pongidae of Africa & Asia (No); Bovidae: g. Novibos, Bibos, Bos, of s. & s. e. Asia (No)] [National Research Council]

COOMANS, Drs. H.E. Marine Biological Institute, Piscadero Bay, Curaçao, Netherlands West Indies. [Marine Gastropoda of West Indies (Yes); marine Lamellibranchia of W.I. (Yes)]

COOMANS de Ruiter, Drs. L. Graaf Florislaan 24, Hilversum, Netherlands. [Aves of Malaysia & W. Borneo, espec. Celebes (Yes)]

COOMBES, Mr. R.A.H. Zoological Museum, Tring, England. [Aves: Anserinae of Palearctic (Yes); Mammalia: deer of Palearctic (Yes)]

* COOMBS, Burton. Department of Paleontology, University of California, Berkeley 4, Calif., U.S.A. [Fossil invertebrates]

COOMBS, C.W. Pest Infestation Laboratory, London Road, Slough, Bucks, England. [Coleoptera: Cryptophagidae: g. Cryptophagus of Europe & N. America (Yes)]

* COOPER, Dr. B.A. Regional Advisory Entomologist, Shardlow Hall, Shardlow, Derby, England. [Nematoda]

COOPER, Mr. C.L. U.S. Geological Survey, Washington 25, D.C., U.S.A. [Up. Paleozoic Ostracoda, Foraminifera, Conodonts (all No)]

COOPER, Dr. G. Arthur. Division of Invertebrate Paleontology, U.S. National Museum, Washington 25, D.C., U.S.A. [Fossil & Recent Brachiopoda of World (Yes)]

COOPER, Dr. Gerald P. University Museums Annex, University of Michigan, Ann Arbor, Mich., U.S.A. [Pisces of Michigan (No)]

* COOPER, John E. Address unknown. (Reptilia)

COOPER, Janet L. (Mrs. W. F. Rapp, Jr.) Not now active in taxonomy.

COOPER, Prof. Kenneth W. Department of Biology, University of Florida, Gainesville, Fla., U.S.A. [Hymenoptera: Vespidae of N. America (Yes); Chrysididae of N. America (Yes to genus); g. Ceratochrysis of World (Yes)]

COOPER, Wm. C. Standard Oil Co. of California, Exploration Department, P.O. Box 606, La Habra, Calif., U.S.A. [Mesozoic & Cenozoic Foraminifera of N. America (Yes)]

COOPEY, R.W. 2034 N.E. Multnomah Street, Portland 12, Ore., U.S.A. [Crustacea: Anostraca of Oregon (Yes)]

COOREMAN, Jean. Section d'Entomologie, Institut Royal des Sciences Naturelles de Belgique, 31 rue Vautier, Brussels 4, Belgium. [Acarina, excl. Ixodidae & Tetrapodili, of World (Yes); Hydrachnellae of Belgium]

COPELAND, Dr. M.J. Geological Survey of Canada, Department of Mines & Technical Surveys, Ottawa, Ont., Canada. [Carboniferous non-marine Arthropoda, excl. Insecta, of Canada (Yes); Jurassic & Paleozoic Ostracoda of Canada (No)]

COPELAND, T.P. Department of Biology, East Tennessee State College, Johnson City, Tenn., U.S.A. [Protura & Collembola of s. e. U.S. (No)]

* COPLAND, Stephen J. Address unknown. (Reptilia)

COPPENS, Yves. Museum National d'Histoire Naturelle, 13 place Valhubert, Paris (V), France. [Fossil Proboscidia of Africa & Eurasia (Yes)]

COPSEY, Jack E. 1666 Chester Avenue, Arcata, Calif., U.S.A. [Trematoda: Capsalidae of Pacific Cst. U.S. (Yes); Trematoda of marine fishes of Calif. cst. (No)]

* CORBET, G. B.   Queen's College, University of St. Andrews, Dundee, Scotland.   [Mammalia]
* CORBET, Dr. Philip S.   Virus Research Institute, Box 49, Entebbe, Uganda.   [Odonata; Trichoptera]
CORDEIRO, Dr. A. R.   Instituto de Ciencias Naturais, Av. Paulo Gama, Porto Alegre, R. S.,
    Brazil.   [Diptera: Drosophila of S. America (Yes)]
CORDELL, Robert James.   503 N. Central Expressway, Richardson, Texas, U. S. A.   [Mississippian-Permian Crustacea: Ostracoda (No)]   [Sun Oil Co., Production Research
    Laboratory]
CORDERO, Ergasto H.   (Montevideo, Uruguay; Annelida) Died 1951.
* CORDERO, Dr. Ignacio Ortiz.   Ministerio de Sanidad y Asistencia Social, Instituto Nacional
    de Higiene, Caracas, Venezuela.   [Diptera]
CORELLA, Luis Baguena.   See BAGUENA CORELLA, Luis.
CORLISS, Dr. John O.   Department of Zoology, Natural History Bldg., University of Illinois
    Urbana, Ill., U. S. A.   [Holotrichous ciliated Protozoa, espec. Hymenostomatida, of
    World (Yes)]
CORNWALL, Mr. Ira E.   1951 Argyle Avenue, Victoria, B. C., Canada.   [Crustacea: Cirripedia of World (Yes)]
CORONADO, Srita. Biol. Luz.   Apartado Postal 19186, Mexico 17, D. F., Mexico.   [Ricinulidea of W. Hemisphere (Yes); Orthoptera, espec. Eumastacidae, of World (No)]   [Instituto Politecnico Nacional, Escuela Nacional de Ciencias Biologicas]
* CORRADETTI, Dr. Augusto.   Istituto Superiore di Sanità, Viale Regina Margherita 299,
    Roma, Italy.   [Diptera: Culicidae: Anophelini]
CORRÊA, Dra. Diva Diniz.   C/o Prof. Marcus, Caixa Postal 6994, São Paulo, Brazil.
    [Nemertinea of Brazil, w. & e. csts. of U. S. A. (Yes)]   [University of São Paulo]
CORREA, Dr. Renato R.   P. O. Box 2543, São Paulo, Brazil.   [Diptera: Culicidae of S.
    America (Yes); Hemiptera: Triatomidae of C. & S. America (Yes); Gastropoda:
    Planorbidae of S. America (No)]
CORREIA da COSTA, Dr. F.   See Addenda.
CORRINGTON, J. D.   (Miami, Fla.; herpetology) Not now active in taxonomy.
* CORT, Prof. W. W.   School of Public Health, University of North Carolina, Chapel Hill,
    N. C., U. S. A.   ([Parasites])
CORTES, Mr. P. Raúl.   Casilla 5577, Santiago, Chile.   [Diptera: Tachinidae of Chile (Yes)]
    [Universidad Católica de Chile]
CORTI, Prof. Dott. Alfredo.   (Torino, Italy; Hymenoptera) Not now active in taxonomy.
CORYELL, Mr. H. N.   3477 Far Hills Avenue, Dayton 29, Ohio, U. S. A.   [Paleozoic-Recent
    Foraminifera, Ostracoda, Bryozoa (Yes)]   [University of Dayton]
COSCARÓN, Dr. S.   1185 Calle 46, La Plata, Argentina.   [Chilopoda: Escolopendromorpha of
    Argentina (Yes)]   [Museo de la Plata]
* de COSTA, Dra. Maria Juana P.   División de Zoología Agrícola, Paseo Colón 922, Buenos
    Aires, Argentina.   [Aves]
da COSTA LIMA, Prof. A. M.   Instituto Oswaldo Cruz, Rio de Janeiro, Brazil.   [Diptera:
    Acalyptratae; Muscoidea; Nematocera of economic importance; of Neotropics (No)]
da COSTA NOVAES, F.   See NOVAES, F. da Costa.
* COSTELLO, Mr. Leslie C.   Department of Zoology, University of Maryland, College Park,
    Md., U. S. A.   [Endoparasitic Protozoa of tropical regions]
* COSTLOW, J. D., Jr.   Marine Laboratory, Duke University, Beaufort, N. C., U. S. A.
    [Crustacea: Cirripedia]
COTT, Dr. H. Edwin.   Biological Sciences Department, California State Polytechnic College,
    San Luis Obispo, Calif., U. S. A.   [Thysanoptera: Tubulifera of World (No); of N. America (Yes)]
COTTER, Dr. William B., Jr.   College of Charleston, Charleston, S. C., U. S. A.   [Aves:
    Anatidae of World (No)]
COTTIER, Dr. W.   Entomology Division, P. O. Box 223, Nelson, New Zealand.   [Homoptera:
    Aphididae & Coccidae of New Zealand (Yes)]   [Department of Scientific & Industrial Research]
COTTON, Bernard C.   166 Wellington Road, Payneham, Adelaide, Australia.   [Mollusca of
    s. Australia (Yes); Echinodermata & Bryozoa of Tasmania (Yes); Brachiopoda of w.
    Australia (Yes); Tertiary Mollusca of S. Australia]   [South Australian Museum]
COUCHMAN, Mr. L. E. . 35 Browne Street, West Hobart, Tasmania.   [Lepidoptera: Rhopalocera, espec. Satyridae & Hesperiidae, of Australia, New Guinea, & adjacent islands
    (Yes)]
* COULTER, William K.   Pacific Northwest Forest & Range Experiment Station,   P. O. Box
    4059, Portland 8, Oregon, U. S. A.   [Coleoptera]
COUNTRYMAN, Prof. William D.   Department of Biology, Norwich University, Northfield,
    Vt., U. S. A.   [Pisces: Osteichthyes; Reptilia; Amphibia; all of Vermont (Yes)]
* COUPÉ, R. J. F.   Institut Scientifique des Pêches, Casablanca, Morocco.   [Pisces: Sparidae]
* COURTENAY, Mr. J.   P. O. Box 95, Morwell, Vict., Australia.   [Lepidoptera; Coleoptera]

COURTENAY, Mr. Walter Rowe, Jr. Marine Laboratory, 1 Rickenbacker Causeway, Miami 49, Fla., U.S.A. [Pisces: Haemulidae of w. N. Atlantic (Yes)]
COURTENAY-LATIMER, Miss M., Director, East London Museum, East London, Union of South Africa. [Birds of s. Africa (Yes)]
COURTNEY, Mr. Wilbur D. Western Washington Experiment Station, Puyallup, Wash., U.S.A. [Nematoda: g. Ditylenchus of w. U.S. (No)]
COUVREUR, J. B.P. 224, Elizabethville, Belgian Congo. [Hydrobiology]
COVA-GARCIA, Dr. Pablo. Division de Malariologia, Maracay, Aragua, Venezuela. [Diptera: Anophelinae of S. America, espec. Venezuela (Yes)]
COWAN, Dr. Ian McT. Department of Zoology, University of British Columbia, Vancouver 8, B.C., Canada. [Mammals of w. & n. Canada (Yes); Cervidae & Ovidae of N. America (Yes)]
COWIE, Dr. J.W. Geology Department, The University, Bristol 8, England. [L. Cambrian Trilobita & Brachiopoda (Yes); L. Paleozoic Trilobita (Yes)]
COWLEY, Mr. J. Holywell House, Edington, Bridgewater, Somerset, England. [Odonata of World (Yes); Diptera: Dolichopodidae, g. Dolichopus of World (Yes); Neuroptera: Nemopteridae of World (Yes)]
COWPER, Mr. T.R. (Cronulla, Australia; Pisces) Not now active in taxonomy.
* COX, Ben B. P.O. Box 219B, R.D. 1, Cheswick, Penna., U.S.A. [Fossil invertebrates]
COX, Dr. C.B. Department of Zoology, King's College, Strand, London, W.C. 2, England. [Permo-Triassic Reptilia: Synapsida: Dicynodontia of World (Yes)]
COX, Mr. Keith W. California Department of Fish & Game, North Rotunda, Museum Building, Stanford University, Stanford, Calif., U.S.A. [Gastropoda: g. Haliotis of w. cst. U.S. (Yes)]
COX, Dr. Leslie Reginald. Senior Principal Scientific Officer, British Museum (Natural History), London, S.W. 7, England. [Cambrian-Pliocene, espec. Mesozoic, Lamellibranchia & Gastropoda of World (Yes)]
COXHEAD, Peter. 12 Cambridge Square, London, W. 2, England. [Marine littoral Mollusca of Britain (Yes)]
* COZART, Duane E. Minneapolis Department of Health, University Campus, Minneapolis 14, Minn., U.S.A. [Aquatic Invertebrates]
CRABILL, Dr. Ralph E., Jr. Division of Insects, U.S. National Museum, Washington 25, D.C., U.S.A. [Chilopoda of World, espec. U.S. (Yes)]
CRAIG, Mr. G.Y. Grant Institute of Geology, West Mains Road, Edinburg 9, Scotland. [Carboniferous invertebrates (No)] [Edinburgh University]
CRAIG, Lawrence Carey. (Denver, Colo.; fossils) Not now active in taxonomy.
CRAIG, Dr. W.S. Department of Zoology & Entomology, Iowa State College, Ames, Iowa, U.S.A. [Coleoptera: Anthicidae, Euglenidae, Pedilidae of n. c. U.S. (Yes)]
CRAIK, Dr. David Warren. (Abilene, Texas; Belostomatidae) Not now active in taxonomy.
CRAM, Eloise. (Bethesda, Md.; Helminths) Deceased.
CRANDALL, Lee S., General Curator Emeritus, New York Zoological Park, New York 60, N.Y., U.S.A. [Mammals & birds of world (No)]
* CRANDALL, R.H. 1992 Mar Vista Avenue, Altadena, Calif., U.S.A. [Coleoptera]
CRANE, Frank. 6507 Sondra Drive, Dallas 14, Texas, U.S.A. [Echinoidea of N. America (Yes)]
CRANE, Jocelyn. New York Zoological Park, New York 60, N.Y., U.S.A. [Crustacea: Brachyura: Ocypodidae of marine littoral of World, excl. Europe & Orient (No); g. Uca (Yes)]
CRASS, R.S. P.O. Box 662, Pietermaritzburg, Union of South Africa. [Ephemeroptera of s. Africa (Yes); f-w. Pisces of Natal (Yes)]
* CRASTIN, N.I. Far-Eastern Scientific Research Veterinary Institute, Severnaja Street 112, Blagoveschensk, U.S.S.R. [Animal helminths of U.S.S.R.]
* CRAWFORD, F.D. Union Oil Co. of California, P.O. Box 1365, Orcutt, Calif., U.S.A. [Fossil invertebrates]
CRAWFORD, George Ivor. (Carshalton, England; Amphipoda) Not now active in taxonomy.
CRAWFORD, Ronald W. Department of Zoology, San Diego State College, San Diego 15, Calif., U.S.A. [Pisces: Percidae & Centrarchidae of U.S. (Yes)]
* CRAWFORD, Dr. Stanton Chapman. Department of Zoology, University of Pittsburg, Pittsburg 13, Penna., U.S.A. [Pisces]
CREASER, Dr. Charles W. Department of Biology, Wayne State University, Detroit 2, Mich., U.S.A. [F-w. Pisces of N. America (No), espec. lampreys (Yes)]
* CREASER, Dr. Edwin P. Hofstra College, Hempstead, N.Y., U.S.A. [Crustacea]
CREIGHTON, Prof. W.S. Department of Biology, College of the City of New York, 139th Street & Convent Avenue, New York, N.Y., U.S.A. [Hymenoptera: Formicidae of s. w. U.S. & n. Mexico (Yes); g. Polyrhachis of World (Yes)]
CRENSHAW, Dr. John W., Jr. Dept. of Biology, Southern Illinois University, Carbondale, Ill., U.S.A. [Reptilia: Testudinata: Emydidae: g. Pseudemys of New World (Yes); Reptilia & Amphibia of s. e. U.S. (No)]

159

* CRESPIN, Irene. Bureau of Mineral Resources, Canberra, Australia. [Fossil inverte-
brates]
CRESPI SALOM, A. (Mallorca, Spain; Protozoa) Not now active in taxonomy.
CRESPO, Dr. Jorge A. Departamento de Mamiferos, Museo Argentino de Ciencias Naturales,
Avda.Angel Gallardo 470, Buenos Aires, Argentina. [Mammals: Rodentia of Argentina
(No)]
* CRÉVECOEUR, A. 9 rue de la Reforme, Bruxelles, Belgium. [Hymenoptera]
CRICHTON, Dr. M. I. Zoology Department, The University, Reading, England. [Trichoptera
of Gr. Britain (Yes)]
CRICKMAY, Dr. C. H. 525 Salem Avenue, Calgary, Alta., Canada. [Devonian-Jurassic An-
thozoa; Ordovician-Cretaceous Brachiopoda; Devonian-Cretaceous Ammonoidea; all of
w. N. America (No)] [Imperial Oil Limited]
* CRINGAN, A. J. Department of Zoology, Ontario Agricultural College, Guelph, Ont., Can-
ada. [Mammalia]
CRISP, Dr. D. J., Director, Marine Biology Station, Menai Bridge, Anglesey, Wales. [Crus-
tacea: Cirripedia of Europe (Yes)] [University College of North Wales]
CROCKER, Dr. Denton W. Dept. of Biology, Skidmore College, Saratoga Springs, N. Y., U. S. A.
[Crustacea: Decapoda: Astacidae of n. e. U. S. & e. Canada (Yes)]
* CROFTS, Miss Doris R. Queen Elizabeth College, London, W. 8, England. [Mollusca]
CROFTS, John. 2 Rose Street, Sandringham, Vict., Australia. [Mollusca of Australia & N. Z.
[Yes)]
CROME, Dr. Wolfgang. Zoologisches Museum, Invalidenstrasse 43, Berlin N. 4, German
Democratic Republic. [Araneae of World (No)]
CROMPTON, Dr. A. W., Director, The South African Museum, Cape Town, Union of South
Africa. [Permo-triassic Reptilia: Therapsida: Cynodontia of s. Africa (Yes)]
CROMROY, Dr. Harvey L. Assoc. Prof. of Biology, College Station, Mayaguez, Puerto Rico.
[Acarina: Eriophyidae & Tarsonemidae of Caribbean (Yes)]
CROOCKEWIT, H. W. E. J. J. Viottastraat 27, Amsterdam Z, Netherlands. [Birds] [Amster-
dam Zoological Museum]
CROOK, Frederick P., Hon. Secretary, Society of Entomologists, P. O. Box 6, Epping,
N. S. W., Australia. [Isoptera of Oceania (Yes); Lepidoptera of Oceania & E. Indies
(Yes); Coleoptera of Oceania (Yes)]
* CROSBIE, J. M. 110 Athania Place, Metairie, La., U. S. A. [Fossil invertebrates]
CROSBY, Mr. D. 52 Longview Road, North Balwyn E. 9, Vict., Australia. [Lepidoptera:
Rhopalocera of Australia (Yes)]
* CROSS, Clarence G. Address unknown. (Mosquito larvae)
CROSS, Earle A. Department of Entomology, Purdue University, West Lafayette, Ind., U. S. A.
[Hymenoptera: Apoidea: g. Nomia of New World (Yes); Acarina: Trombidiformes: Scut-
acaridae of World (Yes)]
CROSS, Dr. Frank. Museum of Natural History, University of Kansas, Lawrence, Kans.,
U. S. A. [F-w. Pisces of Great Plains of N. America (Yes)]
* CROSS, Mr. Hansell F. Northeast Louisiana State College, Monroe, La., U. S. A. [Acarina]
CROSS, Dr. William H. P. O. Box 821, Sebring, Fla., U. S. A. [Odonata: Anisoptera of s. e.
U. S. (Yes); Orthoptera & Diptera: Calliphoridae of s. e. U. S. (No)]
CROSSKEY, Mr. R. W. Commonwealth Institute of Entomology, c/o British Museum (Natural
History), Cromwell Road, London, S. W. 7, England. [Diptera: Simuliidae & Tabanidae
of Ethiopian (Yes); Hymenoptera: Gasteruptiidae of World (Yes)]
CROSSLEY, Dr. D. A., Jr. Oak Ridge National Laboratory, Building 9711-1, Y-12, P. O. Box
Y, Oak Ridge, Tenn., U. S. A. [Acarina: Trombiculidae of U. S. (Yes); Trombidiidae of
U. S. (No); Speleognathidae of U. S. (No); Rhinonyssidae of U. S. (No)]
* CROUCH, Robert W. 3427 Broadmead, Houston 25, Texas, U. S. A. [Fossil invertebrates]
CROUZEL, Abbe F., Professeur, Institut Catholique, 31 rue de la Fonderie, Toulouse, France.
[Fossil Mastodontes & Deinotherides of c. & w. Europe & n. Africa (Yes)]
* CROW, Peter N. 11 Roundwood Park, Harpenden, Herts, England. [Lepidoptera]
CROWCROFT, Dr. W. P. Dept. of Zoology, British Museum (Natural History), Cromwell Road,
London, S. W. 7, England. [Mammalia: Insectivora & Rodentia of Palearctic (Yes)]
* CROWDER, Prof. H. W. 447 W. Lennox Street, Fort Wayne, Ind., U. S. A. [Homoptera:
Cicadellidae]
CROWELL, Robert M. Department of Biology, St. Lawrence University, Canton, N. Y.,
U. S. A. [Hydracarina of e. U. S. (Yes)]
CROWELL, Dr. Sears. Department of Zoology, Indiana University, Bloomington, Ind., U. S. A.
[Hydrozoa: hydroids of e. cst. N. America (Yes)]
CROWSON, R. A. Department of Zoology, The University, Glasgow, Scotland. [Fossil or
Recent Coleoptera of doubtful assignment of World (Yes)]
CRUICKSHANK, A. R. I. University Museum of Zoology, Cambridge, England. [Carboniferous
Reptilia: Rhizodontidae (No); Triassic Dicynodonts of Africa (Yes)]
CRUSAFONT-PAIRÓ, Dr. M. Colon 13, Sabadell, Spain. [Fossil Mammalia of Spain (Yes)]

CRUSZ, Dr. Hilary. **Department of Zoology, University** of Ceylon, Colombo 3, Ceylon. [Terr. & Marine Trematoda of mammals of India, Ceylon, Burma (Yes); Cestoda: Taeniidae of World (No); Nematoda of vertebrates of India, Ceylon, Burma (Yes); Protozoa: cephaline Gregarinida of Apterygota of World (Yes)]

CRUZ, M. A. da SILVA. See da SILVA CRUZ, M. A.

CUCKLER, Dr. Ashton C. 31 Hawthorne Drive, Westfield, N. J., U. S. A. [Nematoda: Oxyuridae (No)] [Merck Institute for Therapeutic Research]

CUERDA BARCELÓ, J. Calle Antonio Planas 11, Palma de Mallorca, Spain. [Quarternary & Recent marine Mollusca of Meditterranean (Yes)]

CUERRIER, Mr. J. P. Limnologiste en chef, Service Canadien de la Faune Sauvage, Edifice Norlite, Ottawa, Ont., Canada. [F-w. Pisces of N. America (Yes)]

* CUMANO, H. B., Naturaliste, Faculté des Sciences, Rua da Escola Politecnica, Lisboa, Portugal. [Echinodermata]

CUMBER, Dr. Ronald Alan. Entomology Division, Department of Scientific & Industrial Research, Palmerston North, New Zealand. [Psocoptera of N. Z. (Yes); Gastropoda: Pulmonata of N. Z. (Yes)]

CUMMING, Leslie M. Victoria Memorial Museum, Ottawa, Ont., Canada. [Paleozoic Graptolithida of Canadian Appalachian Mts. (Yes)] [Geological Survey of Canada]

* CUMMING, Robert B. Biology Department, University of Florida, Gainesville, Fla., U. S. A. [Odonata of New World (Yes), nymphs (No)]

CUMMINGS, Dr. Robert H. Department of Geology, The University, Glasgow W 2, Scotland. [Foraminifera (Yes); Up. Paleozoic Protozoa (Yes); other Protozoa (No)]

da CUNHA, Prof. A. B. Departamento de Biologia Geral, Faculdade de Filosofia, Caixa Postal 8105, São Paulo, Brasil. [Diptera: Drosophilidae of S. America (Yes)]

da CUNHA, Prof. A. X. Museu e Laboratório Zoológico, Universidade de Coimbra, Coimbra, Portugal. [Protura of Europe & Africa (Yes)]

CUNHA, O. R. Museu Paraense Emilio Goeldi, Belém, Pará, Brazil. [L. Miocene marine Mollusca of Pará (Yes); Reptilia: Lacertilia of Amazonia (Yes)]

CUNLIFFE, Frederick. R. F. D. 2, Buzzards Bay, Mass., U. S. A. [Acarina: Trombidiformes of New World (Yes)]

* CUNNINGHAM, Hugh B. Section of Economic Entomology, Illinois Natural History Survey, Natural Resources Bldg., Urbana, Ill., U. S. A. [Homoptera: Cicadellidae]

CUNNINGHAM, Mr. J. R. Tasmanian Museum & Art Gallery, Hobart, Tasmania, Australia. [Insecta of Tasmania (No); Coleoptera & Lepidoptera (Yes)]

CURRAN, Dr. C. H. American Museum of Natural History, New York 24, N. Y., U. S. A. [Diptera: Brachycera of World (Yes)]

CURRIE, Dr. E. Department of Geology, The University, Glasgow W 2, Scotland. [Carboniferous Goniatites of Scotland (Yes)]

CURRY, Mr. D. 50 Cuckoo Hill Road, Pinner, Middlesex, England. [L. Tertiary Mollusca of n. w. Europe (Yes)]

CURRY, Dr. LaVerne L. Department of Biology, Central Michigan College, Mt. Pleasant, Mich., U. S. A. [Diptera: Tendipedidae, larvae & pupae, of N. America (Yes)]

CURRY-LINDAHL, Dr. Kai. Nordiska Museet & Skansen, Stockholm, Sweden. [Mammals, birds, reptiles, amphibians, fishes, of Europe & Belgian Congo (No)]

* CURTI, M. Promenade gasse 29, Kaltenleutgeben, Wien, Austria. [Coleoptera: Scolytidae]

CURTIN, Dr. Charles B. 1628 Rose Hill Drive, Charlottesville, Va., U. S. A. [Tardigrada of World (Yes); Trematoda & Cestoda of f-w. fish of U. S. (No); f-w. invertebrates of U. S. (No)]

CURTIS, Lawrence. Forest Park Zoo, Fort Worth, Texas, U. S. A. [Reptilia, Amphibia, Pisces (Yes)]

CURTIS, L. C. Livestock Insect Laboratory, Box 210, Kamloops, B. C., Canada. [Diptera: Ceratopogonidae: g. Culicoides of n. w. America (Yes); Culicidae of n. w. America (No)]

CURTIS, Dr. M. L. K. City Museum, Bristol 8, England. [Trilobites]

CURTIS, Dr. W. C. (Columbia, Mo.; Turbellaria) Not now active in taxonomy.

CUTRESS, Charles E. Division of Marine Invertebrates, U. S. National Museum, Washington 25, D. C., U. S. A. [Actiniaria, Corallimorpharia, Ceriantharia, Zoantharia, of World (Yes)]

CUTRESS, Mrs. Charles E. Division of Marine Invertebrates, U. S. National Museum, Washington 25, D. C., U. S. A. [Holothurians of Pacific (Yes); Cretaceous-Recent spines of Echinoidea of W. Hemisphere (No)]

CUVILLIER, Prof. J. Laboratoire de Micropaléontologie de l'Université, 191 rue St. Jacques, Paris (V), France. [Foraminifera & microfossils of Mediterranean basin (No)]

CUYLER, Mr. R. Duncan. North Carolina Orthopedic Hospital, Gastonia, N. C., U. S. A. [Megaloptera: Corydalidae of World (No); of U. S. (Yes); Odonata of N. America (Yes)]

* CZAPIK, Dr. Anna. Zakład Zoologii, Uniwersytet Jagielloński, SW. Anny 6, Kraków, Poland. [Protozoa: f-l. Ciliata; Rotifera]

CZAPLINSKI, Dr. Bogdan. Zakład Parazytologii, Polskiej Akademii Nauk, ul. Pasteura 3, Warszawa 22, Poland. [Cestoda: Hymenolepididae of Anseriformes of Poland (Yes)]

CZARNECKI, Mr. Zygmunt. Uniwersytet im. Adama Mickiewicza, ul. Fredry 10, Poznań, Poland. [Aves & Mammalia of Poland (Yes)]

CZARTORYSKI, Stephan A. (Prince of Pogoń). Ul. Ratajczaka 28/55, Poznań I, Poland. [Hymenoptera: Ichneumonidae of World (No)]

DABROWSKI, Mgr. J. Grabówskiego 8/4, Kraków, Poland. [Lepidoptera: Zygaenidae, espec. g. Zygaena of C. Europe (Yes); Zygaenidae of Palearctic (No); Macrolepidoptera of Poland (Yes)] [Polska Akademia Nauk, Oddziat Instytutu Zoologicznego w Krakowie]

DAGET, J. Laboratoire d'Hydrobiologie, Diafarabe, French Sudan. [F-w. fishes of w. Africa (Yes)] [Institut Français d'Afrique Noire]

* DAGGY, Dr. Richard H. Arabian American Oil Co., Dhahran, Saudi Arabia. [Ephemerida]

DAGGY, Dr. Tom. Box 626, Davidson, N. C., U.S.A. [Immature stages of Coleoptera of e. U.S. (Yes)]

D' AGUILAR, J. See d'AGUILAR, J.

DAHL, Dr. Erik. Universitets Zoologiska Institution, Lund, Sweden. [Crustacea, espec. Amphipoda (No)]

DAHL, George. Instituto de Ciencias Naturales, Apartado Postal 2535, Bogotá, Colombia. [Pisces: Ostariophysoidea: Characidae, Gymnotoidea, Pimelodidae, Doradidae, Ageniosidae, Pygididae, Loricariidae, Bunocephalidae; all of Panama, Colombia, Venezuela, excl. Amazonas (Yes)] [Liceo Bolivar]

* DAHL, Mrs. Ingerlise. Carlshøjvej 40, Lyngby, Denmark. [Oligochaeta]

DAHL, Jørgen. Department of Freshwater Fisheries, Danmarks Fiskeri- og Havundersøgelser, Charlottenlund Slot, Charlottenlund, Denmark. [Coleoptera: Rhipiceridae & Galerucidae of Africa (No); Coleoptera of Denmark (No); Diptera: Chironomidae of Denmark (No)]

DAHL, Lektor Richard. Zoologiska Institut, Lunds Universitets, Lund, Sweden. [Diptera: Ephydridae of Palearctic (Yes); Stratiomyiidae of Palearctic (No)]

* DAHL, S. O. Address unknown. (Oligochaeta)

DAHM, Anders, Amanuensis, Zoologiska Institution, Lunds Universitets, Lund, Sweden, [Turbellaria: Tricladida: Paludicola of Europe (Yes)]

DAIBER, Dr. Franklin C. Department of Biological Sciences, University of Delaware, Newark, Del., U.S.A. [F-w. Pisces: Centrarchidae & Percidae of n.e. U.S. (Yes); marine Sciasnidae of N.Y.-Va.cst. (Yes); Elasmobranchia: Batoidei of N.Y.-Va.cst. (Yes)]

* DAIN, L. G. W. O. Sjesdorskaja 27, Wsesoyuzny Neftyanoy Nachnoissledovatelsky Geologo-Rasvedochny Institut (W. N. I. G. R. I.), Leningrad, U. S. S. R. [Protozoa]

DALBIEZ, F. Esso Rep., 210 Cours Victor Hugo, Bègles (Gironde), France. [Cretaceous Foraminifera: Globotruncanidae of Europe & Africa (Yes); Paleocene & Eocene Globorotaliidae (Yes)]

* DALE, P. S. Entomology Division, Department of Scientific & Industrial Research, Nelson, New Zealand. [Insects]

DALENIUS, Fil. Lic. Per. Hallbygatan 38b, Uppsala, Sweden. [Acarina: Oribatidae of Sweden, Pyrenees, Antarctic, Subantarctic Is. (Yes)]

DALES, Dr. R. Phillips. Department of Zoology, Bedford College, Regent's Park, London, N.W.1, England. [Pelagic Polychaeta of World (Yes)] [University of London]

DALL, Mr. W. Zoology Department, University of Queensland, Brisbane, Australia. [Crustacea: Penaeidae of Indo-Pacific (Yes); Euphausiacea of s.w. Pacific (Yes); Copepoda: Calanoida of s.w. Pacific (Yes)]

DALMAT, Dr. Herbert T. Laboratory of Tropical Diseases, National Institutes of Health, Bethesda 14, Md., U.S.A. [Diptera: Simuliidae of C. America (Yes); Cuterebridae of N. America (Yes)]

DALQUEST, W. W. Midwestern University, Wichita Falls, Texas, U.S.A. [Mammalia & Reptilia of N. America & Mexico (Yes); Aves & Amphibia of N. America & Mexico (No); f-w. Pisces of N. America (No); of Texas (Yes); all, Pleistocene & Recent]

DALY, Howell V. Department of Zoology, Louisiana State University, Baton Rouge, La., U.S.A. [Hymenoptera: Apoidea of N. America (Yes); Fossil & Recent Hymenoptera of World (No)]

van DAM, Dr. A. J. (Amsterdam, Netherlands; Crustacea) Not now active in taxonomy.

* DAMAS, Prof. Dr. H. F. C. Department of Zoology, University of Liège, Liège, Belgium. [Rotifera]

* DAMASCENO, Dr. R. M. G. Departmento Nacional de Endemia Rurais, Praça Batista Campos 145, Belém, Pará, Brazil. [Diptera]

DAMIAN, Miss Andriana. Centrul de Cercetári Biologice al Academiei R. P. R., Spl. Independentei 93, Raion Lenin, Bucureşti, Rumania. [Crustacea: f-w. Copepoda of Rumania (Yes)]

DAMMANN, Arthur E. Poisonous Animals Research Laboratory, Arizona State University, Tempe, Ariz., U.S.A. [Reptilia & Amphibia of N. America & Deserts of World (Yes); other poisonous terr. animals of World (Yes)]

van DAMME, E. N. G. Ericaweg 7, Huizen, N. H., Netherlands. [Collembola of Europe (Yes)]

DANCE, S. P. Zoology Department, British Museum (Natural History), Cromwell Road, London, S. W. 7, England. [Non-marine Gastropoda & Pelecypoda of India, Ceylon, Burma, Cyprus (Yes); marine Gastropoda & Pelecypoda of Indian Ocean (Yes); Sphaeriidae & Xenophoridae of World (Yes)]

D'ANCONA, Prof. Umberto. Istituto di Zoologia e Anatomia Comparata, Via Loredan 10, Padova, Italy. [Pisces: Teleosteans & Selachians of Mediterranean (Yes)] [Università Padova]

DANDELOT, Mr. P. Laboratoire des Mammifères, Muséum National d'Histoire Naturelle, 55 rue de Buffon, Paris (V), France. [Mammalia: Primates, espec. g. Cercopithecus & Semnopithecus, of Africa & Asia (Yes); Ungulata of Africa & Asia (Yes)]

D'ANDRETTA, Mrs. M. A. Vulcano. Departamento de Zoologia, Secretaria da Agricultura, Caixa Postal 7172, São Paulo, Brazil. [Diptera: Simuliidae of Neotropics (Yes)]

DANIEL, F. Entomologische Abteilung, Zoologisches Sammlung des Bayerischen Staates, Menzingerstrasse 67, München 38, Germany. [Lepidoptera: Zygaenidae, Syntomidae, Arctiidae, Bombyces, Notodontidae, Cymatophoridae, Cossidae, Hepialidae, of Palearctic (Yes)]

DANIEL, Milan. Biological Institute, Czechoslovakian Academy of Sciences, Na cvičišti 2, Praha XIX, Czechoslovakia. [Acarina: Trombiculidae, Trombidiidae, Parasitiformes, of Europe (Yes)]

* DANILEVSKY, A. S. Kathedra Entomologii, Leningrad State University, Leningrad-Centre 164, U. S. S. R. [Lepidoptera]

* DANILTCHENKO, Paul G. Paleontological Institute, Academy of Sciences, B. Kaluzhskaja, Moscow B-71, U. S. S. R. [Tertiary marine fishes]

DANKS, Miss Lydia. Dabas Muzeja, Kr. Barona iela 4, Riga, Latvia. [Corrodentia of U. S. S. R. (Yes)]

DANNER, Wilbert R. Department of Geology, University of British Columbia, Vancouver, B. C., Canada. [Permian Foraminifera: Fusulinidae of Asia; fossils of Br. Columbia & Washington]

DANTE, John H. 4501 Woodfield Road, Kensington, Md., U. S. A. [Tertiary otoliths of fishes of N. America (Yes)]

* DARDIGNAC, Jean, Institut des Pêches, Casablanca, Morocco. [Pisces]

DAREWSKI, Dr. I. S. Zoological Institute, Academy of Sciences, Leningrad-Centre, U. S. S. R. [Reptilia of Palearctic (Yes); Amphibia of U. S. S. R. (Yes)]

* DARGE, R. Address unknown. [Coleoptera: Curculionidae]

DARLINGTON, Dr. Julian T. Department of Biology, Shorter College, Rome, Ga., U. S. A. [Turbellaria: f-w. Tricladida of U. S. (Yes); mesostomine Rhabdocoela & prorhynchid Alloeocoela of N. America (Yes)]

DARLINGTON, Dr. P. J., Jr. Museum of Comparative Zoology, Cambridge 38, Mass., U. S. A. [Coleoptera: Carabidae of World (No), of New Guinea (Yes), of Australia (No)]

DARSIE, Prof. Richard F., Jr. Department of Entomology, University of Delaware, Newark, Del., U. S. A. [Diptera: Culicidae of Nearctic (Yes)]

DARSKAYA, N. F. Parasitological Laboratory, Sovietskaya 13-15, Stavropol, Caucasas, U. S. S. R. [Siphonaptera of U. S. S. R. (Yes); g. Ceratophyllus of Palearctic (Yes)]

DART, Dr. R. A. Medical School, University of the Witwatersrand, Hospital Street, Johannesburg, Union of South Africa. [Pleistocene Homo (Yes); higher Primates of Africa (Yes)]

DARTEVELLE, E. (Leopoldville, Belgian Congo) Died October 1956.

DAS, Dr. G. M. Tocklai Experiment Station, Cinnamara P. O., Assam, India. [Lepidoptera: Psychidae of India (Yes)]

DAS, Dr. S. M. Department of Zoology, Lucknow University, Lucknow, India. [F-w. fishes of India (Yes); Tunicata of India, Burma, Pakistan, Ceylon (Yes)]

DASGUPTA, Dr. J. Reader in Biology, Medical College, Pondicherry, India. [Odonata & Hemiptera of India (Yes)]

DATTA, Mr. A. K. Fish Section, Zoological Survey of India, 34 Chittaranjan Avenue, Calcutta 12, India. [Helminths of India]

D'ATTILIO, Anthony. 44 Lynwood Drive, Valley Stream, N. Y., U. S. A. [Marine Gastropoda: g. Conus & Muricidae of Indo-Pacific (Yes)]

* DAUGHERTY, Jack. Department of Zoology, Rice Institute, Houston, Texas, U. S. A. [Trematoda]

* DAUGUET, P. 43 rue Claude-Bernard, Paris (V), France. [Hemiptera]

* DAULTON, Dr. K. A. C. Tobacco Research Board, P. O. Box 1909, Salisbury, Southern Rhodesia. [Nematoda]

DAVE, Miss M. J. Indian Cancer Research Centre, Hospital Avenue, Parel, Bombay 12, India. [Anthozoa: Actiniaria: Athenaria, Thenaria, Acontiaria, of India (Yes)]

DAVID, Dr. Lore R. 5427 Dorchester, Chicago 15, Ill., U. S. A. [Tertiary fishes of California (Yes); Cretaceous-Tertiary fish scales of America (Yes)] [Crerar Library]

DAVID, P. M. National Institute of Oceanography, Wormley, Godalming, Surrey, England. [Planktonic Chaetognatha of Southern Ocean & subtropics of S. Hemisphere (Yes)]

* DAVID, R. Department d'Entomologie, Muséum National d'Histoire Naturelle, 45bis rue de Buffon, Paris (V), France. [Coleoptera]

DAVID, S. Kanakaraj. Agricultural College and Research Institute, Coimbatore, India. [Homoptera: Aphididae of India (Yes)]

DAVIDSON, John A. Department of Entomology, University of Maryland, College Park, Md., U.S.A. [Homoptera: Coccoidea: Diaspididae & Pseudococcidae of N. America (Yes)]

DAVIDSON, Dr. Ralph H. Department of Entomology, Ohio State University, Columbus 10, Ohio, U.S.A. [Homoptera: Cicadellidae of N. America (Yes)]

* DAVIES, A.M. Arngrove, Station Road, Amersham, Bucks, England. [Fossil invertebrates]

DAVIES, Dr. D.H. Scripps Institution of Oceanography, La Jolla, Calif., U.S.A. [Aves of S. Africa (Yes); marine Pisces of S. Africa (Yes)] [Institute of Marine Resources, University of California]

DAVIES, Dr. Douglas M. Department of Biology, McMaster University, Hamilton, Ont., Canada. [Diptera: Simuliidae & Tabanidae of n. c. & e. U.S. & Canada (Yes); Siphonaptera of Ontario (No)]

DAVIES, Dr. Lewis. Research Branch, Department of Agriculture, K.W. Neatby Bldg., Ottawa, Ont., Canada. [Diptera: Simuliidae: g. Prosimulium of Holarctic (Yes)]

DAVIS, Dr. Charles C. Department of Biology, Western Reserve University, Cleveland 6, Ohio, U.S.A. [Pelagic f-w. marine Crustacea: Copepoda (No)]

DAVIS, Don. Department of Entomology, Cornell University, Ithaca, N.Y., U.S.A. [Lepidoptera: Psychidae of W. Hemisphere (Yes)]

DAVIS, Mr. D. Dwight. Chicago Natural History Museum, Chicago 5, Ill., U.S.A. [Mammalia of Indo-Malaya (Yes)]

DAVIS, Mr. D.H.S. Medical Ecology Centre, P.O. Box 1038, Johannesburg, Union of South Africa. [Small Mammalia, espec. Rodentia, of s. Africa (Yes); Siphonaptera, Anoplura, Acarina (ectoparasitic), of s. Africa (No)]

DAVIS, G.J. 417 George Washington Way, Richland, Wash., U.S.A. [Diptera]

DAVIS, Dr. John. Hastings Reservation, Jamesburg Route, Carmel Valley, Calif., U.S.A. [Aves: Passeriformes of Mexico (No); Emberizinae: g. Pipilo of U.S. & Mexico (Yes)]

DAVIS, Joseph A., Jr. New York Zoological Park, New York 60, N.Y., U.S.A. [Non-marine Mammalia of N. America (Yes); recent & fossil Neotominae of N. America (Yes)]

DAVIS, J.J., Professor Emeritus, Department of Entomology, Purdue University, Lafayette, Ind., U.S.A. [Coleoptera: Scarabaeidae: g. Phyllophaga of N. America (Yes); Homoptera: Aphididae of N. America (Yes)]

DAVIS, Dr. Norman W. R.D.2, Dansville, N.Y., U.S.A. [Arachnida: Opiliones of U.S. (No)]

DAVIS, Dr. Olive Stull. Department of Veterinary Science, Purdue University, Lafayette, Ind., U.S.A. [Reptilia: Boidae of World (No)]

DAVIS, Dr. William B. Box 254, F.E., College Station, Texas, U.S.A. [Mammalia, Aves, Reptilia, Amphibia of w. U.S. & Mexico (Yes)] [Department of Wildlife Management, Texas Agricultural & Mechanical College]

DAVIS, Wayne H. Department of Entomology & Economic Zoology, University of Minnesota, St. Paul, Minn., U.S.A. [Small land Mammalia of N. America; Chiroptera, espec. g. Myotis, of N. America (Yes)]

* DAVIS, Wm. K. Biology Department, Southwest Texas Teachers College, San Marcus, Texas, U.S.A. [Reptilia of s.w. U.S. & n. Mexico]

* DAVISON, D.B. Address unknown. (Gastrotricha)

* DAVISON, Martin L. Address unknown. (Parasitology)

* DAVTJAN, Dr. E.A. Zoological & Veterinary Institute, Nalbandjan Street 128, Erevan, U.S.S.R. [Helminths of animals of U.S.S.R.]

* DAWBIN, W.H. Zoology Department, Victoria College, Wellington, New Zealand. [Mammalia]

DAWES, Dr. Ben. King's College, University of London, London, W.C. 2, England. [Trematoda of Europe (Yes)]

DAWLEY, Dr. Charlotte. Woman's College, University of North Carolina, Greensboro, N.C., U.S.A. [F-w. Mollusca of Mississippi Valley (Yes); terr. Mollusca of e. U.S. (Yes)]

DAWSON, C.E. Bears Bluff Laboratories, Wadmalaw Island, S.C., U.S.A. [Marine littoral fishes of s.e. & s. U.S. (Yes); of Persian Gulf (No)]

DAWSON, Dr. Elliot W. New Zealand Oceanographic Institute, Department of Scientific & Industrial Research, P.O. Box 8009, Wellington, New Zealand. [Diplopoda of N.Z. & s.w. Pacific (No); marine Nemertinea of N.Z. & s. oceans (Yes); subfossil birds of Australia & N.Z. (Yes)]

* DAWSON, Prof. James A. City College of New York, New York 31, N.Y., U.S.A. [Protozoa]

DAWSON, Mrs. J.W. See MACKEN, Miss Judith.

DAWSON, Dr. Mary R. 543 West Woodland, Ferndale 20, Mich., U.S.A. [Fossil Mammalia: Lagomorpha of N. America, Europe, Africa (Yes)]

DAWSON, Dr. R.W. 14 Desert Lane, Rt. 2, Mesa, Ariz., U.S.A. [Coleoptera: Scarabaeidae: g.Serica of N. America (Yes)]

DAY, Dr. C.D. 7 Weymouth Avenue, Dorchester, Dorset, England. [Diptera: Larvaevoridae & Calliphoridae of Britain (Yes)]

DAY, John H. Department of Zoology, University of Cape Town, Rondebosch, Union of South Africa. [Polychaeta of S. Africa (Yes)]

DAY, L.R. Fisheries Research Board of Canada, Biological Station, St. Andrews, N.B., Canada. [Marine fishes of n. Atlantic (Yes)]

DAY, W.C. 1021 Hubert Road, Oakland 10, Calif., U.S.A. [Ephemeroptera of w. N. America (Yes)]

DEAN, Dr. W.T. Department of Paleontology, British Museum (Natural History), Cromwell Road, London, S.W.7, England. [M. & Up. Ordovician Trilobita & Brachiopoda of Britain (Yes)]

* DEANE, C. Rothley Entomological Museum, Montville, Queensland, Australia. [Coleoptera]

DEANE, Dr. Leonidas. Faculdade de Medicina de São Paulo, Caixa Postal 8100, São Paulo, Brazil. [Diptera: Culicidae: Anophelini; Psychodidae: g. Phlebotomus; Hemiptera: Reduviidae: Triatominae; all of S. America (Yes)]

* DEANE, Maria Baumgartten. Faculdade de Medicina, Caixa Postal 8100, São Paulo, Brazil. [Diptera]

DEASON, Hilary J. (Washington, D.C.; Pisces) Not now active in taxonomy.

DEAY, Prof. Howard O. Department of Entomology, Purdue University, Lafayette, Ind., U.S.A. [Heteroptera: Coreidae of U.S. (Yes); Corixidae: g. Tenagobia of New World (Yes)]

DEBAUCHE, Prof. H.R. Laboratoire de Zoologie Systématique, Université de Louvain, 71 rue de Namur, Louvain, Belgium. [Diptera: Mymaridae & Proctotrupidae of World (Yes)]

De BIAGI, Sra. Ana Maria de Buen. Apartado 25788, Mexico 12, D.F., Mexico. [Diptera: Culicidae of Mexico (No)]

* De BONA, Arlete. Instituto Oswaldo Cruz, Caixa Postal 926, Rio de Janeiro, Brasil. [Nematoda]

De BONT, Dr. A.F. Université de Leopoldville, P.O.Box 118, Leopoldville XI, Belgian Congo. [Aves of Europe & Africa (Yes); f-w. fishes of Africa (Yes)] [Directeur de la Station de Recherches Piscicoles]

* DEBOURLE, Mr. A. Société Nacionale des Pétroles d'Aquitaine, Pau (B-Pyr), France. [Fossil invertebrates]

De CARLO, Prof. José. Pedro Lozano 3591, Buenos Aires, Argentina. [Aquatic Hemiptera]

DECELLE, J., Entomologiste a l'Institut National pour l'Étude Agronomique du Congo Belge, B.P. 18, Yangambi 1, par Stanleyville, Belgian Congo. [Coleoptera: Bruchidae of Africa s. of Sahara (Yes)]

DECHASEAUX, Mlle. Colette. Laboratoire de Paléontologie, Sorbonne, 1 rue Victor Cousin, Paris (V), France. [Fossil Mammalia,"paléoneurologie" (Yes)]

DECKER, Charles E. Faculty Exchange, University of Oklahoma, Norman, Okla., U.S.A. [Paleozoic Graptolithida of World (Yes)]

DECKER, Heinz. Institut Phytopathologie der Universität Rostock, Rostock, German Democratic Republic. [Soil Nematoda: Tylenchidae of Europe (Yes)]

* DECKERT, Dr. Kurt. Department of Ichthyology, Zoologisches Museum, Invalidenstrasse 43, Berlin N 4, German Democratic Republic. [Pisces]

DECLOITRE, L. 55 Avenue du Maine, Paris (XIV), France. [Protozoa: Thecamoebae of World (Yes)]

De CONINCK, Prof. L.A.P. "De Peppels", Verschansingstraat, Mariakerke bij Gent, Belgium. [F-l. Nematoda of World (Yes)] [Laboratory of Zoology, State University]

De COSTA, John. Zoology Department, Indiana University, Bloomington, Ind., U.S.A. [Crustacea: f-w. Decapoda (Yes); f-w. Amphipoda & Isopoda (No)]

DeCOURSEY, R.M. Department of Zoology, University of Connecticut, Storrs, Conn., U.S.A. [Nymphs of Hemiptera of N. America (No)]

DEDE, E. Ludwig Brückstrasse 53, München 61, Germany. [Triassic Conodonts of Europe (Yes); M. Triassic Foraminifera of Europe (Yes)]

* DEDMAN, Miss M. 15 Camira Street, Oakleigh, Vict., Australia. [Mollusca]

DEELMAN, Mr. John Jaxon. Department of Zoology, University of California, Los Angeles 24, Calif., U.S.A. [Trematoda: Opecoelidae & Allocreadiidae of marine fishes of w. N. America (No)]

DEEVEY, Edward S., Jr. Osborn Zoological Laboratory, Yale University, New Haven, Conn., U.S.A. [Hydroidea of World, espec. N. America (Yes)]

DEEVEY, Dr. Georgiana Baxter. Bingham Oceanographic Laboratory, 55 Hillhouse Avenue, New Haven, Conn., U.S.A. [Marine Zooplankton of N. Atlantic, Gulf of Mexico, Peru Current (No); marine Copepoda & Cladocera of N. Atlantic, Gulf of Mexico (Yes); of Pacific (No)] [Yale University]

DEFLANDRE, Pr. Georges. Laboratoire de Micropaléontologie de l'École Pratique des Hautes Études, 105 Boulevard Raspail, Paris (VI), France. [F-l. Jurassic-Recent Flagellata (No); Fossil & Recent Rhizopoda (No); Cambrian - Quaternary Radiolaria (No); Chitinozoa & Hystrichosphaerida] [Centre National de la Recherche Scientifique]

DEFLANDRE-RIGAUD, Marthe. Laboratoire de Micropaléontologie de l'École Pratique des Études, 105 Boulevard Raspail, Paris (VI), France. [Jurassic-Tertiary Spongia, Tunicata, Echinodermata (No)] [Centre National de la Recherche Scientifique]

De FOLIART, Dr. Gene R. Department of Entomology & Parasitology, University of Wyoming, Laramie, Wyo., U.S.A. [Lepidoptera: Rhopalocera of Wyoming (Yes); Diptera: Simuliidae, adults & larvae & pupae, of w.U.S. (Yes)]

DEGENHARDT, Mr. William G. Department of Biology, Agricultural & Mechanical College of Texas, College Station, Texas, U.S.A. [Amphibia & Reptilia of N.America (No), of Texas (Yes); Mammalia: Rodentia of New England states (Yes)]

DEGERBØL, Prof. Dr. M., Director of Laboratory of Quaternary Zoology, Universitets Zoologiske Museum, København, Denmark. [Quarternary Vertebrata of n. Europe & Greenland (Yes)]

De GIUSTI, Prof. Dominic. Department of Biology, Wayne State University, Detroit 1, Mich., U.S.A. [Acanthocephala of World (Yes); Nematoda of fishes of World (Yes)]

DEGNER, Prof. Dr. Ehrard. (Hamburg, Germany; Mollusca) Not now active in taxonomy.

DEGRANGE, Mr. Charles. Institut d'Hydrobiologie, rue des Dauphins 1, Grenoble, France. [Ephemeroptera, Plecoptera, Odonata, of France (Yes)]

DEHM, Dr. Richard. Institut für Paläontologie und Historische Geologie, Richard Wagnerstrasse 10, München 2, Germany. [Tertiary-Pleistocene Mammalia; Pleistocene terr. & f-w. Mollusca; both of Old World (Yes)]

* DEHNEL, Dr. August. Zakład Badania Ssaków,Polska Akademia Nauk, Białowieza, Poland. [Mammalia]

* DEHNEL, P.D. Department of Zoology, University of British Columbia, Vancouver 8, B.C., Canada. [Parasites]

DEHNER, Prof. Eugene W., O.S.B. Department of Zoology & Entomology, St. Benedict's College, Atchison, Kans., U.S.A. [Vertebrates, excl. fishes, of Kansas (Yes); Orthoptera of Kansas (No)]

DEICHMANN, Elizabeth. Curator of Marine Invertebrates, Museum of Comparative Zoology, Cambridge, 38, Mass., U.S.A. [Holothurians of World (Yes); Alcyonaria of West Indies (Yes)]

DEIGNAN, H.G. Division of Birds, U.S. National Museum, Washington 25, D.C., U.S.A. [Aves of Old World (Yes)]

van DEINSE, Dr. A.B. West Sidelinge 68, Rotterdam, Netherlands. [Mammalia: Fossil & Recent Cetacea of Europe, espec. Netherlands (No)]

DEISS, Charles F. Department of Geology, Owen Hall, University of Indiana, Bloomington, Ind., U.S.A. [L. & M. Cambrian Trilobita of N.American cordillera (No)]

DEKEYSER, Dr. P.L. Institut Français d'Afrique Noire, Dakar, Sénégal. [Mammalia of Fr.W.Africa (No); Aves of same (Yes)]

DELACOUR, Jean. Los Angeles County Museum, Los Angeles 7, Calif., U.S.A. [Birds of Asia, game birds, waterfowl (Yes)]

DELAIS, M. Institut Scientifique et Technique des Pêches Maritimes, 59 av. Raymond Poincaré, Paris (XIV), France. [Pisces: Mugilidae of Mediterranean & Africa]

DELAMARE DEBOUTTEVILLE, Dr. C. Laboratoire Arago, Banyuls-sur-Mer (Pyr.-Or.), France. [Crustacea: Mystacocarida, Copepoda, Syncarida, Thermosbaenacea, of World (Yes); Collembola of World (Yes); & Zoraptera of World (No)]

* DELAMURE, Dr. S.L. Crimean Medical Institute, Lenin Street 5/7, Simferopol, U.S.S.R. [Helminths of sea mammals]

DELANY, Mr. M.J. Department of Zoology, The University, Southampton, England. [Thysanura of Brit.Isles (Yes); small mammals of Brit.Isles (Yes)]

* De La PAZ, Justo. College of Liberal Arts, University of the Philippines, Quezon City, Philippines. [Hemiptera: Pentatomidae]

DELAVAULT, Dr. Robert. Laboratoire de Biologie Animale, Faculté des Sciences, 12 rue Cuvier, Paris (V), France. [Asteroidea of cst. of France & Italy]

* Del CAMPANA, Prof. Domenico. San Godenze, Firenze, Italy. [Fossil vertebrates]

De LEON, Dr. Donald. c/o Harry Wallace, Pensacola, N.C., U.S.A. [Coleoptera: Scolytidae of U.S. (Yes); Acarina: Phytoseiidae, Tenuipalpidae, Tarsonemidae, of N.America (Yes)]

* De LEON, Dr. J.Romeo. Director General of Health, Guatemala City, Guatemala. [Diptera]

DÉLÉPINE, Prof. G. Laboratoire de Géologie, Université Libre de Lille, 13 rue de Toul, Lille, France. [Paleozoic Fossils of Europe & N.Africa (No)]

* DELÈVE, J. 29 rue Robert Goldschmidt, Bruxelles, Belgium. [Coleoptera]

DELFINADO, Miss Mercedes D. Division of Malaria, Department of Health, Manila, Philippines. [Diptera: Ceratopogonidae of Philippines (Yes)]

* DeLISE, Knixie C. Address unknown. (Fossil vertebrates)
* Del JUNCO y REYES, J. J. Piamonte 14, Madrid, Spain. [Hymenoptera]
DELKESKAMP, K. , Kustos, Zoologisches Museum, Invalidenstrasse 43, Berlin N. 4, German
      Democratic Republic. [Coleoptera: Erotylidae of World (Yes)]
DELL, Dr. R. K. Dominion Museum, Wellington, New Zealand. [Mollusca of New Zealand
      (Yes); of Pacific & Antarctic (No)]
DELLA SANTA, Prof. Dr. E. Versoix, Genève, Switzerland, [Cestoda of Europe (Yes)]
* DELLA SERRA, Octavio. Address unknown. (Mammalia)
DeLONG, Prof. Dwight M. 203 Botany & Zoology Bldg. , Ohio State University, Columbus 10,
      Ohio. [Homoptera: Cicadellidae of N. America & Mexico (Yes)]
De LOTTO, Mr. G. Scott Agricultural Laboratories, Department of Agriculture, P. O. Box
      30028, Nairobi, Kenya. [Homoptera: Coccoidea of Africa s. of Sahara (Yes)]
Del PONTE, Prof. Dr. E. Florenzia Balcarce 81, Buenos Aires, Argentina. [Diptera: Culi-
      cidae, espec. g. Anopheles, Psorophora, Aëdes, Haemagogus; Psychodidae: Fleboto-
      mus; Pupipara; Calliphoridae; of S. America (Yes); Hemiptera: Triatominae of S.
      America (Yes); Anoplura] [Instituto de Entomologia Sanitaria, Facultad Agronomia y
      Veterinaria]
DELPHY, L. Villa Miro Castro, Blvd. des Pins, Cannes (A. M.), France. [Acarina; Ixodidae:
      g. Hyalomma of Mid. East (Yes)]
DELSMAN, Prof. Dr. H. C. Laan van Vogelenzang 12, Hilversum, Netherlands. [Pisces of
      Indonesia (Yes)]
De LUCCA, Dr. C. 10 Church Square, Gharghur, Malta. [Aves of Europe & Mediterranean
      (Yes); Lepidoptera: Heterocera & Microlepidoptera of Mediterranean, espec. Malta
      (Yes)]
DELUCCHI, Dr. Vittorio. European Laboratory, Commonwealth Institute of Biological Con-
      trol, 36 rue de Chêtre, Delémont (Bern), Switzerland. [Hymenoptera: Chalcidoidea:
      Pteromalidae & Eulophidae of Palearctic (Yes); Pteromalidae of Nearctic (No)]
DELY, O. Gy. Department of Amphibia & Reptiles, Magyar Nemzeti Muzeum, Baross-utca.
      13, Budapest VIII, Hungary. [Fossil & Recent Amphiba & Reptilia of c. Europe (Yes)]
* DELYE, Mr. Gerard. Zoologie Generale, Faculté des Sciences, Université, Alger, Algeria.
      [Crustacea]
DEMANGE, J. M. Laboratoire de Zoologie, Muséum National d'Histoire Naturelle, 61 rue de
      Buffon, Paris (V), France. [Diplopoda & Chilopoda of World (No); of France (Yes)]
* DEMAUX, J. 59 Avenue Franklin Roosevelt, Paris (VIII), France. [Coleoptera: Chrysome-
      lidae of France (Yes); Hispinae of World (No); cave beetles of Europe (Yes)]
DEMEL, Prof. Dr. Kazimierz. Morski Instytut Rybacki, Al. Zjednoczenia 1, Gdynia, Poland.
      [Benthic invertebrates of Baltic Sea]
DEMENTIEV, Prof. Dr. Georges. Zoologicheski Muzei, University of Moscow, W. Gercena
      6, Moscow K 9, U. S. S. R. [Aves of Palearctic (Yes); Mammalia of Palearctic (No)]
* De MESA, Pedro. 44 B Camerino Street, Quezon City, Philippines. [Mollusca]
De MONTE, Dr. Med. Tiziano. 16 Via S. Lazzaro, Trieste, Italy. [Coleoptera: Carabidae:
      Bembidiini of Palearctic (Yes)]
DeMOTT, Lawrence L. Geology Department, Oberlin College, Oberlin, Ohio, U. S. A. [M. Or-
      dovician Trilobita of N. America (Yes)]
DEMOULIN, Dr. Georges. Rue des Fusillés 22, Ottignies, Belgium. [Recent & fossil Ephem-
      eroptera of World (Yes); fossil Archodonata of World (Yes)] [Institut Royal des
      Sciences Naturelles de Belgique]
DEMPSEY, Mr. James E. Department of Paleontology, Sohio Petroleum Co. , P. O. Box 624,
      Houston 1, Texas, U. S. A. [Paleocene Foraminifera of U. S. Gulf Cst. (No)]
DEMPSTER, Lillian J. Department of Fishes, California Academy of Sciences, San Francisco
      18, Calif. , U. S. A. [Pisces of California (Yes)]
DENCE, Mr. W. A. R. D. 4, Syracuse 7, N. Y. , U. S. A. [F-w. Pisces of e. U. S. (Yes)]
DENDY, Dr. Jack S. Fisheries Building, Alabama Polytechnic Institute, Auburn, Ala. ,
      U. S. A. [F-w. fishes of s. e. U. S. (Yes); Diptera: Tendipedidae of Alabama (Yes)]
DENIS, J. 103 rue Jean-Jaures, Denain (Nord), France. [Araneida, espec. Zodariidae,
      Erigonidae, Linyphiidae, of Palearctic, espec. w. (Yes)]
DENISON, Dr. Robert H. Chicago Natural History Museum, Chicago 5, Ill. , U. S. A. [Paleo-
      zoic Ostracodermi & Placodermi (Yes)]
DENMAN, Mr. N. S. 291 Riverside Drive, St. Lambert, Apt. 3, Montreal 23, Que. , Canada.
      [Amphibia of Quebec (No)]
DENMARK, H. A. Florida State Plant Board, Seagle Building, Gainesville, Fla. , U. S. A.
      [Homoptera: Aphidae of Florida (Yes); Acarina: Tetranychidae of Florida (Yes)]
DENNING, Dr. D. G. 2016 Donald Drive, Moraga, Calif. , U. S. A. [Trichoptera of N. America
      (Yes)]
DENNIS, Dr. Clifford J. (Ada, Okla. ; Membracidae) Not now active in taxonomy.
DENT, Dr. J. N. Department of Biology, University of Virginia, Charlottesville, Va. , U. S. A.
      [Amphibia: g. Leptodactylus, Hyla, Eleutherodactylus, Plethodon, Gyrinophilus, of
      U. S. & West Indies (Yes)]

167

DENTON, J. Fred. Department of Microbiology, Medical College of Georgia, Augusta, Ga.,
U.S.A. [Dicrocoeliid Trematoda of N. America (Yes)]
DERANIYAGALA, Mr. P.E.P. 59 Castle Street, Colombo 8, Ceylon. [Fishes, reptiles,
birds, mammals, of Ceylon (Yes); Pleistocene mammals & reptiles of Africa (No)]
* DERBENEVA, N.N. Zoological Institute, Academy of Sciences, Leningrad 164, U.S.S.R.
[Embioptera]
* DERBYSHIRE, Dr. Russel Clay. Department of Zoology, University of Omaha, Omaha,
Neb., U.S.A. [Protozoa, Trematoda, Cestoda, Nematoda, of U.S. (Yes)]
DERENNE, Monsieur E. 3 avenue du Kouter. Auderghem, B.16, Belgium. [Coleoptera of
Belgium (Yes)]
De RIDDER, Miss Margaretha. Laboratorium voor Systematische Dierkunde, Rijsuniversiteit
te Gent, 14 Universiteit Straat, Gent, Belgium. [Marine & br-w. Rotifera of World
(Yes)]
* DERJAVIN, A.N. Zoological Institute, Academy of Sciences of the Azerbaijan SSR, Kar-
ganova 15, Baku, U.S.S.R. [Crustacea]
DEROO, G., Paleontologist. 5 rue Pasteur, Viroflay (S. & O.), France. [Cretaceous Ostra-
coda of Europe (Yes)]
De SAEDELEER, H. E. 31 Van Beversquare, Bruxelles 18, Belgium. [Protozoa: Flagellata &
Rhizopoda (No)]
De SAEGER H. 184 Avenue de Messidor, Bruxelles 18, Belgium. [Hymenoptera: Braconidae of
Ethiopian (No)] [Institut des Parcs Nationaux du Congo Belge]
De SANTIS, Prof. Luis. Facultad de Ciencias Naturales y Museo, La Plata, Argentina. [Hy-
menoptera: Chalcidoidea of S. America (Yes); Thysanoptera of S. America (Yes)]
* DESBROSSES, P. Office des Pêches Maritimes, 59 Avenue R. Poincaré, Paris (XVI),
France. [Pisces]
* DESCARPENTRIES, A. Muséum National d'Histoire Naturelle, 45bis rue de Buffon, Paris
(V), France. [Coleoptera]
* De SCHAUENSEE, R.M. Academy of Natural Sciences, Philadelphia 3, Penn., U.S.A.
[Birds]
De SEABRA, A.F. (Lisboa, Portugal; Heteroptera) Deceased.
DESIO, Prof. Ardito. Istituto di Geologia, Piazzale Gorini 15, Milano, Italy. [Tertiary Mol-
lusca & Echinoidea of Libya (Yes); Silurian (Fezzan) Graptolitida of Libya (Yes)] [Uni-
versity of Milan]
DESJARDINS, Max. Laboratoire de Malacologie, Muséum National d'Histoire Naturelle, 55
rue de Buffon, Paris (V), France. [Fossil & Recent Gastropoda: Prosobranchia: Risso-
inae (Yes)]
* DESLANDES, Dr. N. Instituto Oswaldo Cruz, Rio de Janeiro, Brazil. [Mollusca]
De SYLVA, Donald P. Bayside Laboratory, P.O.Box 514, Lewes, Del., U.S.A. [Pisces:
Scombridae, Sphyraenidae, Istiophoridae, of w. Atlantic, Gulf, Caribbean (Yes);
marine fishes of s.e.U.S. (Yes); marine Sphyraenidae, Istiophoridae, Serranidae,
Scombridae, Carangidae of World (No)]
DEUBLER, Dr. Earl E., Jr. Institute of Fisheries Research, University of North Carolina,
Morehead City, N.C., U.S.A. [Pisces: Pleuronectiformes of New World (Yes)]
DEUNFF, J., Attaché de Recherches au Centre National de la Recherche Scientifique, Institut
de Géologie, Rue du Thabor, Rennes (I. et V.), France. [Fossil Ciliata of Africa (No);
Paleozoic Hystrichosphaeridea of N.America & Europe (Yes)]
DEUQUET, Mr. C.F. 123 Hurstville Street, Oatley, N.S.W., Australia. [Coleoptera: Bupre-
stidae of Australia, espec. g. Stigmodera (Yes)]
* van DEURS, Mr. Wilhelm. Frugtparken 7, Gentofte, Denmark. [Lepidoptera]
* DEVASUNDARAM, M.P., Officer in Charge, Chilka Biological Station, Balugaon (Puri Dis-
trict), Orissa, India. [Pisces]
DEVIDTS, J. Croix du Sud, Hameau de la Garde, La Ciotat, (B. de Rhône), France. [Coleop-
tera: Tenebrionidae of France (Yes); terr. & f-w. Mollusca of France (Yes); of Palearc-
tic (No)]
* DEVINCENZI, Dr. G.J. (Montevideo, Uruguay; Pisces) Died 1942.
DEVINEY, Miss Ezda M. Coker College, Hartsville, S.C., U.S.A. [Invertebrates of s.e.
U.S. (No)]
* DEVOLD, F. Institute of Marine Research, Bergen, Norway. [Pisces: Herring]
DeVOS, A. Department of Entomology & Zoology, Ontario Agricultural College, Guelph, Ont.,
Canada. [Mammalia of Canada (No)]
DEW, Miss Barbara. 80 Carrington Avenue, Hurstville, N.S.W., Australia. [Polychaeta:
Serpulidae of Australia & Indo-Pacific (Yes)]
* DEWAILLY, Dr. Vet. P., Attaché au Muséum National d'Histoire Naturelle, 94 Avenue de
Suffren, Paris (XV), France. [Coleoptera: Scarabaeidae: Melolonthinae of Holarctic &
Madagascar]
DeWITT, Prof. J.W., Jr. Fisheries Department, Humboldt State College, Arcata, Calif.,
U.S.A. [F-w. Pisces of n.w.U.S. (No)]

* DeWITT, Dr. Robert M. Department of Biology, University of Florida, Gainesville, Fla.,
U.S.A. [Terr. & f-w. Gastropoda]
DEXTER, Dr. Ralph W. Department of Biology, Kent State University, Kent, Ohio, U.S.A.
[Crustacea: Anostraca of N. America (Yes)]
DHARMARAJAN, Dr. M. Department of Animal Genetics, Madras Veterinary College, Madras
7, India. [Diptera: g. Drosophila of s. India (Yes)]
D'HERDE, J. Rijkslandbouwhogeschool, Coupure Links 233, Gent, Belgium. [Plant-parasitic
Nematoda of Belgium (No)] [Rijksstation voor Insektenkunde]
DIAKONOFF, Dr. A. Rijksmuseum van Natuurlijke Historie, Leiden, Netherlands. [Micro-
lepidoptera, espec. Tortricidae, of tropical s. Asia & New Guinea (Yes); Tortricidae of
Madagascar (No)]
DIAS, J. A. Travassos Santos. Missão de Combate às Tripanosomiases, 2a Subsecção de Ento-
mologia, Maputo, Mozambique. [Acarina: Ixodoidea of World (Yes); Diptera: Tabanidae
of Ethiopian (Yes)]
* DIAZ-NÁJARA, A. Entomologo del Instituto de Salubridad, Av. Instituto Técnico 266, Mexi-
co 17, D. F., Mexico. [Diptera]
DIAZ-UNGRIA, Dr. Carlos. Sociedad de Ciencias Naturales La Salle, Apartado 681, Caracas,
Venezuela. [Parasitic helminths of Venezuela (Yes); Siphonaptera of Venezuela (No);
Acarina: Ixodidae of Venezuela (Yes); Acanthocephala of Venezuela (Yes)]
DICE, Dr. Lee R. Laboratory of Vertebrate Zoology, University of Michigan, Ann Arbor,
Mich., U.S.A. [Mammalia: Rodentia; g. Peromyscus of N. America (No)]
DICKERMAN, E. Eugene. Department of Biology, Bowling Green State University, Bowling
Green, Ohio, U.S.A. [Trematoda of L. Erie & tributaries (No)]
DICKERMAN, Robert W. Minnesota Museum of Natural History, University of Minnesota,
Minneapolis 14, Minn., U.S.A. [Birds of s. w. U.S. & Mexico (No)]
DICKINS, Mr. J. M. Bureau of Mineral Resources, Geology & Geophysics, Childers Street,
Turner, Canberra, Australia. [Permian Pelecypoda of S. Hemisphere (Yes); Owenian,
Carboniferous, Mesozoic Pelecypoda of Australia (Yes); Up. Paleozoic Gastropoda of
Australia (Yes); Permian fossils of Australia; Permian Pelecypoda & Gastropoda of
World]
DICKINSON, Dr. J. C., Jr. Department of Biology, University of Florida, Gainesville, Fla.,
U.S.A. [Aves of N. America (Yes)]
DICKINSON, Mr. W. E. 730 E. Euclid Avenue, Milwaukee 11, Wis., U.S.A. [Diptera: Culici-
dae & Tipulidae of Wisconsin (Yes); Reptilia & Pisces of Wisconsin (Yes)]
DICKINSON, W. H. 2510 Olive Avenue, Long Beach, Calif., U.S.A. [Reptilia: Elapidae &
Viperidae of Asia & Africa (Yes)]
DICKSON, C. G. C. "Blencathra" Cambridge Ave., St. Michael's Estate, Cape Town, Union of
South Africa. [Lepidoptera (No)]
DICKSON, R. C. Citrus Experiment Station, Riverside, Calif., U.S.A. [Homoptera: Aphididae
& Diaspididae of World, espec. America (Yes)]
* DIDIER, Dr. Robert. Laboratoire d'Entomologie, Muséum National d'Histoire Naturelle,
45bis rue de Buffon, Paris (V), France. [Coleoptera: Lucanidae]
DIEBEL, Dr. Kurt. Paläontologisches Museum der Humboldt Universität, Invalidenstrasse 43,
Berlin, N 4, German Democratic Republic. [Triassic Conodonts of c. Europe (No); Up.
Cretaceous Conodonts of Africa (Yes)]
DIECKMANN, Lothar. Crednerstrasse 9, Leipzig 039, German Democratic Republic. [Coleop-
tera: Curculionidae of c. Europe (No); sg. Pseudorchestes of Palearctic (Yes)]
DIEKE, Dr. G. H. Johns Hopkins University, Baltimore 18, Md., U.S.A. [Coleoptera: Cocci-
nellidae of World, espec. Latin Amer., (Yes)]
* DIEM, Kenneth L. Department of Wildlife Research, Utah State University, Logan, Utah,
U.S.A. [Pisces]
DIESSELHORST, Dr. G. Zoologische Sammlung der Bayerischen Staates, Menzingerstrasse
67, München 19, Germany. [Aves of Tanganyika & Paraguay (Yes)]
* DIETRICH, Mrs. Alice S. Entomology Department, Comstock Hall, Cornell University,
Ithaca, N.Y., U.S.A. [Odonata]
DIETRICH, Dr. Henry. Department of Entomology, Cornell University, Ithaca, N.Y., U.S.A.
[Coleoptera of n. e. U.S. (Yes)]
DIETRICH, Prof. Dr. W. O. Geologisch-Paläontologishes Institut der Universität, Invaliden-
strasse 43, Berlin N 4, German Democratic Republic. [Fossil Proboscidea of Europe
(Yes); Pleistocene Mammalia: Carnivora, Chiroptera, Rodentia, of Germany (Yes)]
DIETZ, Curt. (Stanford, Calif.; Echinoidea) Not now active in taxonomy.
DIEUZEIDE, Dr. R., Directeur de la Station d'Aquiculture et de Pêche, Castiglione (Alger),
Algeria. [Marine biology of Algeria (Yes)]
* DIGBY, Dr. P. S. B. Department of Biology, St. Thomas' Hospital Medical School, London,
S. W. 1, England. [Crustacea: Copepoda]
DIKMANS, Dr. Gerard. (Ionia, Mich.; Nematoda) Not now active in taxonomy.
DILGER, Prof. William C. Laboratory of Ornithology, Cornell University, Ithaca, N.Y.,
U.S.A. [Aves of World (Yes), to species)]

* DILLER, Dr. William F., Jr. Department of Zoology, University of Pennsylvania, Philadelphia, Penna., U.S.A. [Protozoa]
* DILLINGHAM, Hervie. Department of Paleontology, Atlantic Refining Co., Oil Center Station, Lafayette, La., U.S.A. [Fossil invertebrates]
* DILLON, Mrs. Elizabeth. 1008 Harrington Street E., College Station, Texas, U.S.A. [Coleoptera: Cerambycidae: Lamiinae of World (Yes)]
DILLON, Lawrence S. Agricultural & Mechanical College of Texas, College Station, Texas, U.S.A. [Coleoptera: Cerambycidae of World (Yes); Meloidae of Texas (Yes)]
DIMMITT, W.A. Department of Entomology, Iowa State College, Ames, Iowa, U.S.A. [Coleoptera of N. America (No)]
DINEEN, Dr. Clarence F. Chairman, Biology Department, Saint Mary's College, Notre Dame, Ind., U.S.A. [Pisces: Centrarchidae of N. America (Yes)]
* DINELEY, Mrs. Daphne Aubertin. The Priory, Berwick St. John, Shaftesbury, Dorset, England. [Diptera]
DINELEY, Dr. D.L. Department of Geology, University of Exeter, Exeter, England. [Ostracoderms of n.w. Europe & Svalbard (Spitzbergen) (Yes); Devonian Conodonts of s.w. England (Yes)]
DINIZ, Dr. M.A. Museu e Laboratório Zoológico, Universidade de Coimbra, Coimbra, Portugal. [Hymenoptera of Pen. Iberica (No); Apidae of Palearctic (Yes)]
DINNIK, DR. J.A. East African Veterinary Research Organization, P.O. Box 32, Kikuyu, Kenya. See Addenda.
* DINULESCU, Mr. Gheorghe. Facultatea de Medicina Veterinara, Arad, Rumania. [Diptera]
* DION, Y. Laboratoire de Biologie Générale, Faculté des Sciences, Toulouse, France. [Crustacea]
* DIRINGSHOFEN, Richardo V. Caixa Postal 2131, São Paulo, Brasil. [Coleoptera]
* DIRKSE van SCHALKWYK, Hester A. See van SCHALKWYK, H.A.D.
DIRSH, Dr. V.M. Department of Entomology, British Museum (Natural History), Cromwell Road, London, S.W.7, England. [Orthoptera - Acridoidea of World (Yes)] [Anti-Locust Research Centre]
DISPONS, Paul. Int. Général, 10 Rue Saint-Dominique, Paris (VII), France. [Heteroptera: Reduviidae of Palearctic and Ethiopian (Yes)]
DISSANAIKE, A.S. Department of Parasitology, Faculty of Medicine, University of Ceylon, Kynsey Road, Colombo 8, Ceylon. [Parasitic Protozoa: Microsporidia, Gregarinida: Acephalina, Schizogregarinina, of Ceylon (Yes); parasitic helminths of Ceylon (No)]
DIXON, James R. Box 254 FE, College Station, Texas, U.S.A. [Amphibia: Leptodactylidae, espec. g. Tomodactylus, Syrrhophus, Eleutherodactylus, Microbatrachylus, Pternohyla, Hyla, of s.w. U.S. & Mexico (Yes); Reptilia, espec. lizards & snakes of s.w. U.S., Mexico, Japan, Korea (Yes)]
DIXON, Dr. Keith L. Department of Wildlife Management, Agricultural & Mechanical College of Texas, College Station, Texas, U.S.A. [Aves: Paridae of N. America (Yes)]
DJULIĆ, Prof. Beatrica. Voje Kovačevića 5, Zagreb, Yugoslavia. [Mammalia: Microchiroptera: Vespertilionidae & Rhinolophidae of Europe (Yes); Micromammalia of Balkan Pen. (No)] [Yugoslavian Academy of Sciences & Arts]
DLABOLA, Dr. Jiri. Nitranska 26/III p, Praha XII, Czechoslovakia. [Homoptera: Auchenorhyncha of World (No); of Palearctic (Yes)]
* DOANE, George H. 2080 Obispo St., Long Beach, Calif., U.S.A. [Fossil invertebrates]
DOBREANU, Ecaterina. Centrul de Cercetári Biologice, Splaiul Independentei 93, Raionul Lenin, Bucureşti, Rumania. [Crustacea: f-w. Amphipoda; Homoptera: Aleyrodinea & Psylloidea; Diptera: Muscidae; all of Rumania (Yes)]
* DOBROLUBOA, T.A. Paleontological Institute, Academy of Sciences, Leninskii Prospekt 33, Moscow B-71, U.S.S.R. [Carboniferous tetracorals]
DOBRORUKA, RNDr. L.J. Zoologická Zahrada, Praha Troja, Czechoslovakia. [Chilopoda of World (Yes); Symphyla of Europe, Asia, Africa (Yes); Mammalia: Sciuridae, Cervidae, Felidae, of Palearctic & Africa (Yes)]
DOBROTWORSKY, Mr. N.V. Department of Zoology, University of Melbourne, Carlton N.3, Vict., Australia. [Diptera: Culicidae of Australia (Yes)]
* DOBROVOLNY, Dr. Charles G. Laboratory of Tropical Diseases, National Institutes of Health, Bethesda 14, Md., U.S.A. [Parasites]
DOBŠÍK, Dr. Bohuslav. Zoologický Ústav V.Š.Z., Zemědělská 1, Brno, Černá Pole, Czechoslovakia. [Heteroptera of Palearctic (No); Lygaeidae (Yes)] [Universitas Agriculturae et Sylviculturae]
DOBSON, Mr. R. c/o National Provincial Bank, Jersey, Channel Islands, Great Britain. [Odonata of Australia (Yes)]
DOBSON, Dr. R.M. Department of Entomology, Rothamsted Experiment Station, Harpenden, Herts, England. [Coleoptera: Nitidulidae, g. Carpophilus of the World (Yes)]
DOBZHANSKY, Prof. Th. Department of Zoology, Columbia University, New York 27, N.Y., U.S.A. [Diptera: g. Drosophila of New World (Yes)]

170

* DODGE, Henry. 6 Rochambeau Road, Scarsdale, N.Y., U.S.A. [Marine Mollusca of World (No)]
DODGE, Dr. Harold R. Intermountain Forest Experiment Station, Federal Building, Missoula, Mont., U.S.A. [Diptera: Sarcophagidae of the World (Yes)]
DODGE, Harry W., Jr. Department of Geology, University of Massachusetts, Amherst, Mass., U.S.A. [Up. Pennsylvanian - L. Permian Foraminifera: Fusulinidae of c.N. America (No); L. Ordovician Graptolithina (Deepkill & Normanskil) of New Jersey (No)]
DODSON, Edward O. (Ottawa, Canada; birds, mammals) Not now active in taxonomy.
DOEKSEN, Dr. Ir. J. Bornesteeg 67, Wageningen, Netherlands. [Thysanoptera of Netherlands (Yes); Oligochaeta: Lumbricidae of w. Europe (Yes)]
* DOELLO-JURADO, Prof. M. Museo de Historia Natural, Peru 208, Buenos Aires, Argentina. [Mollusca]
DOERING, Dr. Kathleen. Department of Entomology, University of Kansas, Lawrence, Kans., U.S.A. [Homoptera: Cercopidae of N. America (Yes); Fulgoridae: Acanaloniinae, Issinae, Dictyopharinae, Flatinae: g. Mistharnophantia; all of N. America (Yes)]
van DOESBURG, P.H. Cantonlaan 1, Baarn, Netherlands. [Coleoptera: Passalidae of World (Yes); Diptera: Syrphidae of Europe, Asia, Africa, Australia (Yes), of New World (No)] [Zoologisch Museum]
DOETSCHMAN, Willis H. 1320 Woodrow Street, Oildale, Calif., U.S.A. [Parasitic Acarina of World (No)]
* DÖHLER, Dr. Walter. Wilhemstrasse 133, Klingenberg am Main, Germany. [Trichoptera]
* DOHRN, Dr. P.F.R. Stazione Zoologica di Napoli, Villa Comunale, Napoli 101, Italy. [Coelenterata of Mediterranean]
DOLAN, Thomas. Consulting Biologist, 610 Commercial Trust Building, Philadelphia 2, Pa., U.S.A. [Larvae of Ephemerida, Plecoptera, Trichoptera, Odonata, of e.N. America (No); f-w. Pisces of e.N. America (No)]
DOLLFUS, Dr. Robert Ph. Muséum National d'Histoire Naturelle, 57 Rue Cuvier, Paris (V), France. [Helminths (No), Distomata & Tetrarhyncha (Yes); Crustacea: parasitic Copepoda & Isopoda (No); Pisces of Morocco, Red Sea (No); Echinodermata & Anthozoa: Hexacoralla of Red Sea (No)]
DOMANTAY, Prof. Jose S. 31 Bernardo Avenue, S. Francisco del Monte, Quezon City, Philippines. [Holothurioidea of P.I. & tropics (Yes); Asteroidea, Echinoidea, Ophiuroidea, of P.I. (Yes)] [University of Santo Tomas]
DOMENICHINI, Prof. Dr. G. Istituto di Entomologia Agraria, Universitá di Milano, Via Celoria 2, Milano, Italy. [Hymenoptera: Chalcidoidea of Europe & Mediterranean (Yes)]
DOMINIK, Jan. Zarzad Lasów Doświadczalnych Szkoły Głównej Gospodarstwa Wiejskiego, Rogów koło Koluszek, Poland. [Coleoptera: Anobiidae, Lyctidae, Bostrychidae, Lymexylonidae, of C. Europe (Yes)]
DOMROW, Mr. Robert. Queensland Institute for Medical Research, Herston Road, Herston N 9, Brisbane, Queensland, Australia. [Parasitic Acarina of Mammals of Australia (Yes)]
DONCASTER, Mr. J.P. Department of Entomology, British Museum (Natural History), Cromwell Road, London, S.W.7, England. [Homoptera: Aphididae of World (Yes); Aleyrodidae & Psyllidae of World (No)]
DONDALE, Mr. C.D. Science Service Laboratory, Box 400, Kentville, N.S., Canada. [Araneida: Erigonidae: g. Grammonota of Nearctic (Yes); Thomisidae: g. Philodromus of N. America (Yes)]
DONEY, Hugh Holt. Department of Geology, Del Mar College, Corpus Christi, Texas, U.S.A. [Tertiary marine Mollusca of N. America (No); Pennsylvanian Pelecypoda of N. America (No)]
DONNELLY, Thomas W. Department of Geology, The Rice Institute, Houston, Texas, U.S.A. [Odonata of World (Yes)]
DONNER, Josef. Wichtelgasse 74, Wien 17, Austria. [Rotatoria, espec. of soil (Yes)]
DONOHOE, Mr. John C. Walker Museum, University of Chicago, Chicago 37, Ill., U.S.A. [Tertiary-Recent Mammalia: Rodentia of N. America (Yes); Tertiary Mammalia of N. America (Yes)]
DONOSO, Prof. Roberto. Escuela de Medicina Veterinaria, Catedra de Biologia General, Universidad de Chile, Santiago, Chile. [Amphibia: lizards of S. America (Yes); Acarina: Ixodoidea of New World (Yes)]
DONOVAN, D.T. Brewery House, South Stoke, Bath, England. [Jurassic Ammonoidea (Yes)]
DOORMAN, G., Entomologist, Flat "De Akker" B20, De Bilt, Netherlands. [Diptera of Netherlands (No)]
* DORAN, Dr. David J. Zoological Division, Bureau Animal Industry, Beltsville, Md., U.S.A. [Trematoda: Aposcoelidae of United States (Yes)]
* DORECK, Dr. Hertha. Reichenberger Strasse 12, Stuttgart-Möhringen, Germany. [Fossil Crinoidea]
DORIER, Prof. Dr. A.H. Laboratoire de Zoologie, 14 rue Hébert, Grenoble, France. [Diptera: Simuliidae of France (No); Gordiacea of World (Yes)]

171

DORMAN, James Hubert. The California Company, 800 The California Bldg., New Orleans
  12, La., U.S.A. [Tertiary Foraminifera of Gulf Coast (Yes)]
DORR, Prof. John A., Jr. Department of Geology, University of Michigan, Ann Arbor, Mich.,
  U.S.A. [L. & M. Cenozoic Mammalia of Rocky Mts. (Yes)]
DORSEY, Dr. C.K. College of Agriculture, West Virginia University, Morgantown, W.Va.,
  U.S.A. [Coleoptera: immature Nitidulidae & Silphidae of N. America (No)]
DORST, Dr. J. Sous-directeur de Laboratoire, Muséum National d'Histoire Naturelle, 55 rue
  de Buffon, Paris (V), France. [Aves of S. America & Indo-Pacific (Yes)]
DOSKOČIL, Dr. J. Zoologie ústav Biologické, Karlovy University Fakulty, Viničná 7, Praha
  II, Czechoslovakia. [Diptera: Acalyptrata of c. Europe (No)]
DOSSE, Prof. Dr. Gudo. Institut für Pflanzenschutz der Landwirtschaftlichen Hochschule
  Hohenheim, Stuttgart-Hohenheim, Germany. [Acarina: Tetranychidae, Phytoseiidae,
  Phytoptipalpidae, of Europe (Yes)]
DOTTRENS, Dr. Emile, Directeur, Muséum d'Histoire Naturelle, Genève, Switzerland.
  [Pisces: Coregonidae of w. Europe (Yes)]
DÔTU, Mr. Yosie. Fisheries Laboratory, Faculty of Agriculture, Kyushu University, Fukuoka,
  Japan. [Pisces: Gobioidea of Japan (Yes)]
DOUCET, Dr. J. Idert-Adiopodoume, B.P. 20, Abidjan, Ivory Coast. [Diptera: Tabanidae &
  Culicidae: Culicinae, of Ivory Coast (Yes), Anophelinae (No); Reptilia: Ophidia of Ivory
  Coast (Yes); Pentastomida of World (Yes)]
DOUGHERTY, Dr. Ellsworth C. Lab. for Gnotobiotic Studies, 2428 Bancroft Way, Berke-
  ley, 4, Calif., U.S.A. [Crustacea: Amphipoda: Caprellidea of World (Yes); Nematoda:
  Metastrongylidae of World (Yes), Rhabditidae of World (No)]
DOUGLAS, Mr. A.M. Western Australian Museum, Perth, Australia. [Hymenoptera: Formi-
  cidae: Ponerinae, espec. g. Myrmecia, of W. Australia (Yes); Mammalia: Chiroptera
  of Australia (Yes)]
DOUGLAS, Mr. G.W. Walter & Eliza Hall Institute, Royal Melbourne Hospital, Parkville,
  N.2., Vict., Australia. [Diptera: Culicidae of Australia (Yes)]
DOUGLAS, Prof. Lee T. Box 112, Emory, Virginia, U.S.A. [Cestoda: Nematotaeniidae of
  World (Yes)] [Emory and Henry College]
DOUGLASS, Raymond C. U.S. Geological Survey, U.S. National Museum, Washington 25,
  D.C., U.S.A. [Jurassic to Recent larger Foraminifera (No); Cretaceous to Tertiary
  Orbitolinidae (Yes); Pennsylvanian to Permian Fusulinidae of N. America (Yes)]
DOULL, Mr. K.M. Department of Entomology, University of Adelaide, Waite Agricultural Re-
  search Institute, P.B. Adelaide, S. Australia. [Thysanoptera of Australasian (No)]
DOUTT, Dr. J. Kenneth. Carnegie Museum, Pittsburgh 13, Pa., U.S.A. [Mammalia of Penn-
  sylvania (Yes); Phocidae of n. Atlantic & n. Pacific (Yes)]
DOUTT, Dr. Richard L. 1050 San Pablo Avenue, Albany 6, Calif., U.S.A. [Hymenoptera:
  Mymaridae & Trichogrammatidae of California & Micronesia (Yes)]
* DOUVRES, Frank William. Address unknown. (Parasitic Nematoda: g. Rictularia of World)
DOW, Dr. Richard P. (Logan, Utah, U.S.A.; Hymenoptera) Not now active in taxonomy.
DOWLING, Dr. Herndon G. Department of Zoology, University of Arkansas, Fayetteville,
  Ark., U.S.A. [Recent & Fossil Reptilia: Colubridae of World (Yes); Recent Amphibia
  & Reptilia of s.e. United States (Yes); Up. Cretaceous Reptilia: Mosasauridae (No)]
* DOWNES, D.J. Address unknown. (Hymenoptera)
DOWNES, Mr. J.A. Science Service Building, Carling Avenue, Ottawa, Ont., Canada. [Dip-
  tera: Heleidae of N. America & Britain (Yes); Nematocera: biting forms (No)]
* DOWNES, Mr. M.C. Fisheries & Game Department, Flinders Street Extension, Melbourne,
  Vict., Australia. [Aves]
DOWNES, W. 2056 Granite Street, Victoria, B.C., Canada. [Heteroptera of British Columbia
  (Yes)]
DOWNES, William L. Department of Entomology, University of Illinois, Urbana, Ill., U.S.A.
  [Diptera: Sarcophagidae of World (Yes), Tachinidae of N. America (No)]
DOWNEY, Dr. John C. Department of Zoology, Southern Illinois University, Carbondale, Ill.,
  U.S.A. [Lepidoptera: Lycaenidae of World (No), of N. America (Yes)]
DOWNIE, Dr. N.M. 1621 Purdue Street, Lafayette, Ind., U.S.A. [Coleoptera of c. & n.e.
  U.S. (Yes)] [Purdue University]
DOWNING, Stuart C. Division of Mammalogy, Department of Zoology & Palaeontology, Royal
  Ontario Museum, 100 Queen's Park, Toronto 5, Canada. [Mammalia of e. Canada (Yes)]
DOWNS, Dr. H.R. Shell Oil Company, Box 1191, Tulsa, Okla., U.S.A. [Fossil Foraminifera:
  Fusulinidae; Conodonts of N. America (No)]
DOWNS, Dr. Theodore. Los Angeles County Museum, Exposition Park, Los Angeles 7, Calif.,
  U.S.A. [M. & Up. Cenozoic Mammalia of N. America & Mexico (Yes)]
DOWNS, Dr. Wilbur G. (Port of Spain, Trinidad; Diptera) Not now active in taxonomy.
* DOZIER, Mr. Byrd K. Box 5215, State College Station, Raleigh, N.C., U.S.A. [Coleoptera]
DOZIER, Herbert L. 36 Henry Street, Hampton, Va., U.S.A. [Coleoptera: Carabidae & Coc-
  cinellidae of e. U.S. (Yes)]

172

DRAESEKE, J. (Dresden, German Democratic Republic; Lepidoptera: Lycaenidae) Not now active in taxonomy.
* DRAGE, Kevin L. 87 Port Road, Southwark, S. Australia. [Mollusca]
DRAGERSUND, O. Institute of Marine Research, Bergen, Norway. [Pisces: Clupeidae of n. e. Atlantic (Yes)]
DRAGESCO, Dr. Jean. Laboratoire d'Evolution, 105 Blvd. Raspail, Paris (VI), France. [Ciliata of World (Yes)]
DRAKE, Dr. Carl John. Division of Insects, U. S. National Museum, Washington 25, D. C., U. S. A. [Hemiptera: Tingidae, Piesmidae, Saldidae, Leptopodidae, Ochteridae, Thaumastocoridae of World (Yes); Gerridae, Veliidae, Mesoveliidae, Hebridae, Hydrometridae, Pleidae, Nepidae of New World (Yes)]
DRAKE, Robert J. Dept. of Zoology, Univ. of British Columbia, Vancouver 8, B. C., Canada. [Recent & Pleistocene nonmarine Mollusca & nonmarine Mollusca from human prehistory of w. N. America (Yes)]
DREISBACH, Mr. R. R. 301 Helen Street, Midland, Mich., U. S. A. [Hymenoptera: Psammocharidae of World (No); New World (Yes); Insecta of Michigan]
DRENSKI, Dr. P. St. Institut Zoologique, Académie des Sciences, 1 Boul. Rouski, Sofia, Bulgaria. [Araneida; Acarina: Ixodoidea; Pisces; all of the Balkan Pen. (Yes)]
DRESCO, Ed. 30 rue Boyer, Paris (XX), France. [Cavernicolous Araneae & Opiliones of France, Spain, Portugal, Italy, Switzerland (Yes)] [Museum National d'Histoire Naturelle]
DRESSCHER, Th. G. N. Geneeskundige Dienst, Nieuwe Achtergracht 100, Amsterdam, Netherlands. [Hirudinea of Europe (Yes)]
DREW, Leslie Clinton. The Museum, Michigan State University, East Lansing, Mich., U. S. A. [Arachnida: Araneae of c. U. S. & Durango, Mexico (Yes)]
* DREYFUS, Andre. Facultad de Filosofia, Universidad de São Paulo, São Paulo, Brazil. [Diptera]
DRIVER, Dr. Ernest C. 119 Prospect Street, Northampton, Mass., U. S. A. [Mollusca, Amphibia, Reptilia, Mammalia, of New England (Yes)] [Smith College]
* DROIT, Dr. P. A. 5bis avenue de Maréchal Foch, Gap (Hautes-Alpes) France. [Lepidoptera: Zygaenidae of Palearctic]
DROOGER, Prof. Dr. C. W. Wentlaan 11, Utrecht, Netherlands. [Tertiary Foramininfera (No), Oligocene-Miocene Miogypsinidae & Lepidocydinidae of World (Yes)] [Geological Institute]
DROOP, Dr. M. R. Marine Station, Millport, Scotland. [F-l. marine & f-w. Flagellata (Yes)]
DROPKIN, Dr. Victor H. U. S. Nematode Research Laboratory, 3985 Union Ave., Seaford, N. Y., U. S. A. [Root Knot Nematoda of World (Yes)] [U. S. Department of Agriculture]
DROUANT, Ronald. Geology Department, Louisiana State University, Baton Rouge 3, La., U. S. A. [Cretaceous Ostracoda (Yes)]
DROZDOWSKI, Mgr. Arnold. Zakład Zoologii Systematycznej, Uniwersytet Mikołaja Kopernika, ul. Danielewskiego 6, Torún, Poland. [Gastropoda of Poland (Yes)]
* DRUMMOND, F. H. Zoology Department, University of Melbourne, Melbourne, Australia. [Diptera]
DRUMMOND, Dr. R. O. Entomology Research Laboratory, Box 232, Kerrville, Texas, U. S. A. [Acarina of N. America (No)]
DRURY, Dr. W. H. Louise Ayer Hatheway School, Drumlin Farm, So. Lincoln, Mass., U. S. A. [Aves of Holarctic (Yes)] [Harvard University]
DRUSHITS, V. V. Department of Geology, Moscow State University, Moscow B-234, U. S. S. R. [L. Cretaceous Ammonoidea of Caucasus, Crimea, S. Europe (Yes)]
DUARTE, Mr. Eliseo. Casilla de Correo 1401 Central, Montevideo, Uruguay. [Mollusca of World (No), of Uruguay (Yes)]
DUARTE-BELLO, Dr. Pedro P. Research Associate Professor, Laboratorio de Biologia Marina, Universidad de Villanueva, Apartado 6, Marianao, Habana, Cuba. [Pisces: Scombridae of West Indies (Yes)]
DU BAR, Jules R. Geology Department, University of Houston, Houston 4, Texas, U. S. A. [Late Cenozoic Pelecypoda & Gastropoda of e. U. S. (Yes)]
DUBININ, V. B. (Leningrad, U. S. S. R.; Acarina) Died May 8, 1958.
DUBININA, Mrs. M. N. Zoological Institute, Academy of Sciences, Leningrad W-164, U. S. S. R. [Cestoda of vertebrates of Europe & Asia (Yes), of n. Africa (No)]
DUBOIS, Dr. Georges. Grand-Rue 12, Corcelles (Neuchâtel), Switzerland. [Trematoda: Strigeida of World (Yes)]
* DuBOIS, John J. (Turlock, Calif.; Coleoptera) Not now active in taxonomy.
DuBOSE, William Perry, Jr. Pee Dee Experiment Station, Florence, S. C., U. S. A. [Homoptera: Delphacidae, espec. Delphacodes of Nearctic (Yes)]
DUBOURDIEU, G. Laboratoire de Géologie, Collège de France, Place Marcellin-Berthelot, Paris (V), France. [M. Cretaceous Ammonites, espec. Turrilites, of N. Africa]
* DUBROVO, I. A. Paleontological Institute, Academy of Sciences, 33 Lenin Prospectus, Moscow B-71, U. S. S. R. [Fossil vertebrates]

DUCASSE, Dr. Janine. Centre de 3º Cycle de Géologie Approfondie, 351 Cours de la Libera-
tion, Talence (Gironde), France. [Cretaceous Bryozoa of the Basin d'Aquitaine (Yes)]
DUCKWORTH, Walter Donald. North Carolina State College, Box 5215, Raleigh, N. C.,
U. S. A. [Microlepidoptera: Stenomidae of N. America (Yes)]
DUDICH, Prof. Dr. Andrew. Allatrendszertani Intezet, Institute of Zoological Systematics,
Pushkin u. 3, Budapest VIII, Hungary. [F-w. Crustacea: Amphipoda of Europe (No)]
DUDLEY, Dr. Patricia L. Zoology Department, University of Washington, Seattle 5, Wash.,
U. S. A. [Crustacea: Copepoda: Notodelphyidae, Enterocolidae, Botryllophilidae, of all
oceans (Yes)]
DUELLMAN, Mr. William E. Museum of Zoology, University of Michigan, Ann Arbor, Mich.,
U. S. A. [Reptilia & Amphibia of N. & C. America (Yes)]
DUFAY, C. Observatoire de Lyon, Saint-Genis-Laval (Rhône), France. [Lepidoptera: Noctui-
dae: Quadrifinae of Europe (Yes), espec. g. Abrostola of World (Yes) & g. Nycteola of
Palearctic (Yes); Arctiidae: Nolinae of Palearctic, espec. China (No)]
DUFFY, Mr. E. A. J. Commonwealth Institute of Entomology, British Museum (Natural His-
tory), Cromwell Road, London, S. W. 7., England. [Coleoptera: larvae of Cerambyci-
dae of World (Yes)]
* DUFRANE, Abel D. A. Department d'Entomologie, Musée d'Histoire Naturelle, Avenue du
Tir 69, Mons, Belgium. [Lepidoptera]
DUGGAN, J. J. Experimental Farm, Glasnevin, Dublin, Ireland. [Plant Parasitic Nematoda
espec. g. Heterodera, of Republic of Ireland (No)] [University College]
* DUGGAN, Prof. T. L. Biology Department, Loyola University, New Orleans 18, La., U. S. A.
[Parasites]
DUJARDIN, F. 25 Rue Guiglia, Nice (A. M.) France. [Lepidoptera: Zygaenidae, incl. g. Pro-
cris, of Palearctic (Yes), Rhopalocera of France (No), Hesperiidae of Europe (Yes)]
[Zoo of Cap Ferrat]
DULIC, B. Zavod za biologiju, Medicinskog Fakulteta u Zagrebu, Zagreb, Yugoslavia. [Chi-
roptera of Europe (Yes); Micromammalia of Balkan Pen. (Yes)] See DJULIĆ, B.
DUMBLETON, Mr. L. J. Lincoln Agricultural College, Christchurch, New Zealand. [Homop-
tera: Aleyrodidae of Australia, New Zealand, S. Pacific (Yes); Acarina: Trombiculidae
& Ixodidae of New Zealand (Yes)]
* DUMIGAN, Mr. E. J. 10 High Street, Toowoomba, Queensland, Australia. [Lepidoptera]
* DUMITRESCU, D. Muzeul National de Istorie Naturala, "Grigore Antipa", Kisselef No. 1,
Bucureşti III, Rumania. [Nematoda]
DUMITRESCU, Margareta. Institutul de Speologie al RPR, Str. Dr. Marinescu 7, Bucureşti,
Rumania. [Recent Mammalia: Chiroptera of caves of Rumania (Yes); Quaternary Mam-
malia of caves of Rumania (Yes)]
DUNBAR, Dr. Carl O. Peabody Museum of Natural History, Yale University, New Haven,
Conn., U. S. A. [Pennsylvanian & Permian Foraminifera: Fusulinidae & Brachiopoda
(No)]
DUNBAR, Dr. M. J. Department of Zoology, McGill University, Montreal 2, Que., Canada.
[Amphipoda of Arctic & Subarctic (Yes)]
DUNCAN, Dr. Carl D., Chairman, Division of Natural Sciences, San Jose State College, San
Jose 14, Calif., U. S. A. [Hymenoptera: Vespidae & Bembicidae of N. America (No)]
DUNCAN, Donald Cave. U. S. Geological Survey, Washington 25, D. C., U. S. A. [Upper Cam-
brian Trilobita of N. America (No)]
DUNCAN, D. K. P. O. Box 412, Globe, Ariz., U. S. A. [Coleoptera: Cicindelidae of N. America
(Yes)]
DUNCAN, Helen M. U. S. Geological Survey, Room 326, U. S. National Museum, Washington
25, D. C., U. S. A. [Paleozoic, espec. Ordovician, Carboniferous, Permian, Corals:
Rugosa & Tabulata (No); Paleozoic, espec. Carboniferous & Permian, Bryozoa: Cyclo-
stomata, Trepostomata & Cryptostomata (No)]
* DUNDEE, Mr. H. 101 Hiawatha Blvd., Lake Hiawatha, N. J., U. S. A. [Reptilia]
DUNHAM, Dr. D. W. Department of Biology, Evansville College, Evansville, Ind., U. S. A.
[Acarina: Ixodidae (Yes)]
DUNKLE, Dr. David H. U. S. National Museum, Washington 25, D. C., U. S. A. [Late Paleo-
zoic & Mesozoic Pisces (Yes)]
DUNLAP, Dr. Donald G. Department of Biology, Ripon College, Ripon, Wis., U. S. A. [An-
ura: Ranidae of N. America, espec. w. & c. (Yes)]
DUNLOP, Grace. Department of Geology, Bedford College, Regent's Park, London, N. W. 1,
England. [Carboniferous Brachiopoda: Spiriferidae of Britain (No)]
DUNN, Mr. A. P. Lewers Street, Creswick, Vict., Australia. [Arachnida (Yes)]
* DUNN, E. College of Agriculture, 13 George Square, Edinburgh 8, Scotland. [Nematoda]
* DUNN, Dr. E. R. (Haverford, Pa.; Herpetology) Died 1956.
DUNN, Margaret E. See WATSON, Mrs. Margaret E.
DUNN, Mr. R. A. 60 Mimosa Road, Carnegie S. E. 9, Vict., Australia. [Araneae & Pedipalpi
of Australia (Yes); Scorpiones of Australia (No); Arachnida, excl. Acarina, of Aus-
tralia]

174

DUNNET, Dr. G. M. Culterty Field Station, University of Aberdeen, Natural History Department, Newburgh, Aberdeenshire, Scotland. [Siphonaptera of Australia (Yes), of Britain & n. Europe (No)]

* DUNNINGTON, H. V., Paleontologist, 38 College Road, Maidenhead, Berks, England. [Mesozoic-Tertiary Foraminifera of s. w. Asia & Mid-East (No)] [Iraq Petroleum Co.]

DUPORT, Maria. Institutul Dr. I. Cantacuzino, Splaiul Independentei 108, Bucureşti, Rumania. [Diptera: Culicidae: Anophelini; Psychodidae: Phlebotominae; both of Rumania (Yes)]

* DUPRÉ, Helen Mugard. Laboratoire de Biologie Animale, Université de Paris, 12 rue Cuvier, Paris (V), France. [Protozoa: Ciliata]

DUPUIS, Dr. C. École des Hautes Études, 57 rue Cuvier, Paris (V), France. [Diptera: Phasiinae of Palearctic (Yes); Heteroptera of Palearctic (No)]

DUGUET, C. F. See DEUQUET, C. F.

DURAN, M. Laboratorio Oceanográfico de Baleares, Paseo Maritimo (S' Aigo Dolça), Palma de Mallorca, Spain. [Ciliata: Tintinnoinea of w. Mediterranean & temp. & trop. Atlantic (Yes); Crustacea: Copepoda: Calanoida & marine planktonic Cyclopoida, of same (No)] [Instituto Espanol de Oceanografia]

DURAND, G. Beautour, Le Bourg, La Roche-sur-Yon, (Vendée), France. [Aves of Europe (Yes); Lepidoptera of World (No); Coleoptera: Carabidae & Cerambycidae of France (Yes)]

* DURAND, Dr. J. M. Chef du Laboratoire d'Ichthyologie, Institut Océanographique de l'Indochine, Nhatrang, Viet-Nam. [Pisces]

DURBIN, Dr. Charles G. Food & Drug Administration, Department of Health, Education & Welfare, Washington 25, D. C., U. S. A. [Lungworms & Capillarids (No)]

DURCHON, Prof. M. Université d'Alger, Faculte des Sciences, Laboratoire de Zoologie P. C. B., Alger, Algeria. [Polychaeta: Nereidae & Syllidae of W. Mediterranean (Yes)]

DURET, Dr. José Pedro. Oficina Sanitaria Panamericana, Apartado 3469, Panama, D. F., Panamá. [Diptera: Culicidae & Flebotominae of Neotropics (Yes)]

DURHAM, Dr. Floyd E. 1822 N. Potrero Grande Drive, South San Gabriel, Calif., U. S. A. [Mammalia: Rodentia of s. California deserts (No)] [Hancock Foundation, University of Southern California]

DURHAM, Prof. J. Wyatt. Department of Paleontology, University of California, Berkeley 4, Calif., U. S. A. [Fossil & Recent irregular Echinoidea of World (Yes); Cretaceous - Recent Hexacorala of N. America (Yes); Tertiary Gastropoda & Pelecypoda of New World (Yes)]

* DURKOP, A. H. Tönning Eider 24b, Germany. [Collembola]

DURRANT, Prof. Stephen D. Department of Zoology, University of Utah, Salt Lake City 12, Utah, U. S. A. [Mammalia of Utah (Yes)]

DURY, RALPH. Cincinnati Museum of Natural History, Central Parkway at Walnut, Cincinnati 10, Ohio, U. S. A. [Coleoptera of s. w. Ohio (Yes); Reptilia & Amphibia of e. N. America (Yes)]

DUSEK, R. Val. 16 Lenox Avenue, Lynbrook, N. Y., U. S. A. [Lepidoptera: Papilionidae & Nymphalidae; Aves: Picidae, Anatinae, Fuligulinae; all of e. N. America (No)]

DUSENBURY, Arthur N., Jr. Creole Petroleum Corporation, Maracaibo, Venezuela. [Cretaceous - Recent Foraminifera & Ostracoda (No); Fossil Mollusca of Venezuela (No)]

DUSI, Julian. Zoology Department, Alabama Polytechnic Institute, Auburn, Ala., U. S. A. [Mammalia & Aves of Alabama (Yes)]

DUŠKOVÁ, Dr. Františka. Zoologicky ústav, Karlova University, Viničná 7, Praha II, Czechoslovakia. [Coccoidea: Diaspididae of c. Europe (Yes)]

* DUSSART, B. H. Station de Recherches Lacustres, Thonon-les-Bains (Haute Savoie),. France. [Copepoda]

DUSZYNSKA, S. Zakład Paleontologii, Uniwersytet Warszawski, Nowy-Swiat 67, Warszawa, Poland. [Devonian Foraminifera of Holy Cross Mountains (No)]

* DUTHOIT, Cecily M. C. Ministry of Agriculture, Fisheries & Food, "Woodthorne", Wolverhampton, Staffs., England. [Nematoda]

* DUTHY, Barbara L. Address unknown. [Nematoda]

DUTRO, Mr. J. T., Jr. Room 332, U. S. National Museum, Washington 25, D. C., U. S. A. [Up. Devonian-Permian Brachiopoda of Pacific U. S. & Alaska (Yes); Up. Devonian & Mississippian Brachiopoda of Rocky Mts. (Yes); Fossil and Recent Brachiopoda (No)]

* DUTU-LĂCĂTUSU, Dr. M. Facultatea de Stiinte Naturale, Bucureşti, Rumania. [Hymenoptera]

* DUVALL, Allen J. (Laurel, Md.; Aves) Not now active in taxonomy.

DÜZGÜNES, Dr. Zeliha. Ankara Universitesi Ziraat Fakültesi, Ankara, Turkey. [Acarina: Tetranychidae & Phytoptipalpidae; Homoptera: Aphididae, Eriosomatidae, Coccoidea: Coccidae & Pseudococcidae; all of Turkey (Yes)]

DVOŘÁK, Mr. Rudolf. Jerevanská 16, Praha 13, Czechoslovakia. [Coleoptera: Staphylinidae of World (Yes)]

* DYAL, S. Department of Entomology, Punjab University, Lahore, Pakistan. [Araneida]

175

DYBAS, Henry S. Division of Insects, Chicago Natural History Museum, Chicago 5, Ill.,
U. S. A. [Coleoptera: Ptiliidae of World (No), Limulodidae of World (Yes); Diptera:
Streblidae of New World (Yes)]

DYCE, Mr. A. L. Wildlife Survey Section, Commonwealth Scientific & Industrial Research
Organization, P. O. Box 109, Canberra, A. C. T., Australia. [Diptera: Ceratopogonidae:
g. Alluaudomyia & g. Macropeza of Australia (Yes)]

DYLEWSKA, Mirosɫawa. Instytut Zoologiczny, Polska Akademia Nauk, ul. Sɫawkowska 17,
Kraków, Poland. [Hymenoptera: g. Bombus & Psithrus of Europe (Yes)]

DYMOND, Dr. J. R. University of Toronto, Department of Zoology, Toronto 5, Canada. [Pis-
ces: Salmonidae of Canada (Yes); Coregonidae of Canada (No)]

DYTE, Mr. C. E. Orlando, 14 Linchfield Road, Datchet, Bucks, England. [Diptera: Bombyliidae: g. Thyridanthrax, espec. Tsetse parasites, of Africa (Yes); Dolichopodidae,
pupae of World (Yes); adults of Europe & Africa (No); Asiloidea & Empidoidea, pupae
of World (No), Asilidae, Therevidae, Scenopinidae, Empididae] [A. R. C. Pest Infestation Laboratory]

DZUBIN, A. c/o Canadian Wildlife Service, University of Saskatchewan, Saskatoon, Sask.,
Canada. [Aves: Anatidae, espec. g. Anas, of Canada (Yes)]

EADES, David. Museum of Zoology, University of Michigan, Ann Arbor, Mich., U. S. A.
[Orthoptera: Saltatoria of U. S. & Canada (No), Gryllacrididae, incl. Rhaphidophoridae,
of World (Yes)]

EADIE, Dr. J. M. Rowett Research Institute, Bucksburn, Aberdeenshire, Scotland. [Ciliata:
Ophryoscolecidae of rumens (Yes)]

EADS, Richard B. Division of Entomology, Texas State Department of Health, Austin 2, Texas,
U. S. A. [Siphonaptera of U. S. & Mexico (Yes); Acarina: mammal parasites of U. S. &
Mexico (No)]

EADY, Mr. R. D. Commonwealth Institute of Entomology, British Museum (Natural History),
Cromwell Road, London, S. W. 7, England. [Hymenoptera: Braconidae: Aphidiinae;
Chalcidoidea: Torymidae; Cynipidae: Cynipinae; all of Europe (Yes); Eupelmidae of
World (No)]

EAGER, Dr. R. M. C. The Manchester Museum, University, Manchester 13, England. [Up.
Carboniferous non-marine Pelecypoda: Anthracosiidae & Myalinidae (Yes)]

EALES, Dr. N. B. Littledown, Kingwood, Henley-on-Thames, England. [Gastropoda: Opisthobranchiata of World (No), Aplysiidae (Yes)] [University of Reading]

EAMES, Dr. F. E. Research Station, British Petroleum Co. Ltd., Cadbury Road, Sunbury-on-
Thames, Middlesex, England. [Larger Foraminifera & Mollusca of Europe, Middle
East, Far East, Caribbean (Yes)]

EARL, Mr. Paul. Wistar Institute, 36th & Spruce Street, Philadelphia 4, Pa., U. S. A. [Pro-
tozoa: Phytomastigina: g. Euglena of World (Yes); Ciliata of World (Yes)]

* EARNSHAW, E. M. Estancia San Isidro, Magdalena, Argentina. [Aves]

EASON, Dr. E. H. Bourton Far Hill Farm, Moreton-in-Marsh, Gloucestershire, England.
[Chilopoda of British Isles (Yes); Diplopoda of British Isles (No)]

* EASTIN, Mr. James. 168 West 3rd North, Logan, Utah, U. S. A. [Coleoptera]

EASTON, Dr. Alan M. Roadside Cottage, 173 Lower Road, Great Bookham, Surrey, England.
[Coleoptera: Nitidulidae: g. Meligethes of World (Yes)]

EASTON, Mr. W. H. University of Southern California, Los Angeles 7, Calif., U. S. A. [Car-
boniferous corals of N. America (Yes)]

EASTOP, Dr. V. F. Department of Entomology, British Museum (Natural History), Cromwell
Road, London, S. W. 7, England. [Homoptera: Aphididae, Aleyrodidae, Psyllidae of
World (Yes)]

* EASTWOOD, John P. Address unknown. (Diptera)

EATON, Dr. Stephen W. Biology Department, St. Bonaventure University, St. Bonaventure,
N. Y., U. S. A. [Aves: Parulidae of n. U. S. and Canada (Yes); f-w. Pisces of upper Allegheny River system (Yes)]

EATON, Dr. Theodore H., Jr. Zoology Department, University of Kansas, Lawrence, Kans.,
U. S. A. [Fossil vertebrates]

EBELING, Alfred W. Scripps Hall, Scripps Institution of Oceanography, La Jolla, Calif.,
U. S. A. [Bathypelagic Pisces of e. Pacific (Yes); Berycomorphi: Melamphaidae of World
(Yes)]

EBERLY, William R. Manchester College, North Manchester, Ind., U. S. A. [Crustacea: Entomostraca of Indiana (No); Isopoda of N. America (Yes); Amphipoda & Decapoda: crayfish, of Indiana & e. c. U. S. (Yes)]

EBERZIN, Prof. Dr. A. G. Paleontologcal Institute Academy of Sciences, Lenin Str. 33, Moscow B-71, U. S. S. R. [Fossil & Recent Pelecypoda: Cardiidae, espec. Limnocardiinae
& Dreissenidae of Eurasia (Yes); Miocene-Pliocene Pelecypoda of World (No)]

EBINA, Ken-ichi. Zoological Laboratory, Tokyo University of Fisheries, Shiba-Kaigandori 6,
Minato-ku, Tokyo, Japan. [Pisces]

EBNER, Dr. Richard. Beethovengasse 3, Wien IX, Austria. [Orthoptera of the Palearctic (Yes)]

ECHOLS, Mrs. D. J. Department of Geology, Washington University, St. Louis 5, Mo.,
  U. S. A. [Fossil marine Ostracoda; fossil & Recent Foraminifera, excl. Fusulinidae
  (Yes)]
ECKERLEIN, Dr. Hans. Elsasser-Strasse 5, Coburg, Germany. [Heteroptera of Europe,
  N. Africa, Asia minor (Yes)]
* EDASHIGE, Tadao. Entomology Laboratory, Matsuyama Agricultural College, Matsuyama
  City, Ehime Pref., Japan. [Diptera]
EDDY, Prof. Samuel. Department of Zoology, University of Minnesota, Minneapolis 14,
  Minn., U. S. A. [F-w. Pisces of U. S. (Yes)]
* EDELSTAM, C. Östermalmsgatan 61, Stockholm 5, Sweden. [Aves & Reptilia]
EDELSTEN, Mr. H. M. (London, England; Lepidoptera) Died May 2, 1959.
* EDGE, Elton R. Address unknown. (Pelecypoda & Mammalia)
EDGELL, Dr. Henry S. c/o Iranian Oil Exploration Company, Masjid-I-Sulaiman, via Abadan,
  Iran. [Jurassic to Recent Foraminifera of Middle East (Yes); Cretaceous to Oligocene
  Foraminifera of Australia & N. America (Yes); Devonian Trilobita: Lichacea of World
  (No)]
EDGREN, Dr. Richard A. Division of Biological Research, G. D. Searle & Company, P. O.
  Box 5110, Chicago 80, Ill., U. S. A. [Reptilia & Amphibia of c. U. S. (Yes)]
EDINGER, Dr. Tilly. Museum of Comparative Zoology, Cambridge 38, Mass., U. S. A.
  [Brains of fossil vertebrates of World (Yes)] [Harvard University]
* EDMONDS, J. M. Department of Geology, University Museum, Oxford, England. [Fossil
  invertebrates]
EDMONDS, Dr. S. J. Department of Zoology, University of Adelaide, Adelaide, Australia.
  [Acanthocephala, Sipunculoidea, Echiuroidea; all of Indo-Pacific (Yes)]
EDMONDSON, Prof. C. H. Bernice P. Bishop Museum, Honululu 17, Hawaii, U. S. A. [Crus-
  tacea: Brachyura & marine wood-boring Mollusca of c. Pacific]
EDMONDSON, W. T. Department of Zoology, University of Washington, Seattle 5, Wash.,
  U. S. A. [Rotifera of World (Yes)]
EDMUND, Dr. A. Gordon. Altona Road, R. R. 2, Pickering, Ont., Canada. [Cretaceous
  Dinosauria of N. America (Yes)] [Royal Ontario Museum]
EDMUNDS, George F., Jr. Division of Biological Sciences, University of Utah, Salt Lake
  City 12, Utah, U. S. A. [Ephemeroptera of World, espec. N. America (Yes)]
EDMUNDS, Dr. Lafe R., Principal Entomologist, Engineer Research & Development Labora-
  tory, Fort Belvoir, Va., U. S. A. [Diptera: Culicidae; Orthoptera: Blattidae; Hymen-
  optera: Evaniidae; all of U. S. (No)]
EDNEY, Prof. E. B. Zoology Department, University College, Salisbury, Southern Rhodesia.
  [Isopoda: Oniscoidea of Britain (Yes); Hymenoptera: Chrysididae of s. Africa (Yes)]
* EDWARDS, Mr. A. B. c/o Royal Society of Tasmania, Tasmanian Museum, Hobart, Tas-
  mania, Australia. [Corrodentia]
EDWARDS, Mr. C. Marine Station, Millport, Isle of Cumbrae, Scotland. [Marine and br-w.
  Crustacea: Amphipoda: g. Gammarus of w. Europe & N. Atlantic (Yes); Hydrozoa: An-
  thomedusae & Leptomedusae of w. European cst. & e. N. Atlantic (Yes)]
EDWARDS, Dr. C. A. T. National Agricultural Advisory Service, Government Buildings,
  Westbury-on-Trym, Bristol, England. [Symphyla of World (Yes)]
EDWARDS, Prof. E. E. University College of Ghana, Achimota, Ghana. [Plant Parasitic
  Nematoda; Trematoda & Cestoda; Nematoda of vertebrates; all of Africa (Yes)]
EDWARDS, Mr. E. O. "Myimbarr", Cummins Rd., Menangle Park, N. S. W., Australia.
  [Lepidoptera: Rhopalocera of New South Wales (Yes)]
EDWARDS, Dr. Ernest P. Museum of Natural History of Houston, Box 8175, Houston 4,
  Texas, U. S. A. [Aves of Mexico (Yes)]
EDWARDS, Mr. James. 81 Hassam Parade, Newcastle, Staffs., England. [Diptera, excl.
  Cecidomysidae, of Britain (Yes)]
EDWARDS, Dr. J. Gordon. Department of Biology, San Jose State College, San Jose, Calif.,
  U. S. A. [Coleoptera: Chrysomelidae: g. Syneta, of World (Yes); Amphizoidae of
  World (Yes)]
* EDWARDS, Mr. J. S. Department of Zoology, Auckland University, Auckland, New Zealand.
  [Homoptera: Cicadellidae]
EDWARDS, Dr. Richard A. Department of Geology, University of Florida, Gainesville, Fla.,
  U. S. A. [Cenozoic Ostracoda]
* EDWARDS, Dr. Robert J. Address unknown. (Arachnida)
EDWARDS, Dr. Robert L. Box 505, Woods Hole, Mass., U. S. A. [Mallophaga of World
  (No); Mammalia: Cricetidae of e. Canadian Arctic & e. U. S. (No); Siphonaptera of e. N.
  America (Yes)]
EDWARDS, R. Y. Parks Branch, Department of Recreation & Conservation, Victoria, B. C.,
  Canada. [Mammalia: Rodentia of British Columbia (Yes), Artiodactyla (No)]
EFF, J. Donald. 820 Grant Place, Boulder, Colo., U. S. A. [Lepidoptera of N. America (Yes)]
EFFLATOUN, H. C. (Cairo, Egypt; Diptera) Died March 1957.

EFREMOV, Prof. I. A. Paleontological Institute, Academy of Science, Lenin Prospekt 33, Moscow B-71, U.S.S.R. [Permian to Cretaceous Amphibia & Reptilia (Yes)]

EGAMI, Dr. N. Zoological Institute, Science Faculty, Tokyo University, Motofuju-cho, Bunkyo-Ku, Tokyo, Japan. [Pisces: Cyprinodontoidae of Asia (No); Crustacea: Copepoda of Japan (No)]

EGE, Dr. Volh. Marine Biological Laboratory, Charlottenlund Slot, Charlottenlund, Denmark. [Pisces: g. Anguilla, Paralepididae, g. Stomias, g. Chauliodus, of all Oceans (No); g. Zoarces of n. Europe (No)]

* EGGERT, Bruno. Address unknown. (Pisces)

EGGLESTON, Dr. Harla Ray. Biology Department, Marietta College, Marietta, Ohio, U.S.A. [F-w. Pelecypoda of Ohio R. drainage (Yes)]

* EGGLETON, Prof. Frank E. Department of Zoology, University of Michigan, Ann Arbor, Mich., U.S.A. [Gastropoda of Michigan; Pelecypoda: Sphaeriidae of N. America]

* EGLITIS, V. K. Department of Entomology & Microbiology, Latvian Research Institute of Agriculture, Riga, Latvia, [Arachnida]

* EGUCHI, Dr. Motoki. Department of Mining, Faculty of Technology, Tohoku University, Sendai, Japan. [Mesozoic-Recent Hydrozoa & Anthozoa]

EHARA, Shôzô. Zoological Institute, Faculty of Science, Hokkaido University, Sapporo, Japan. [Acarina: Tetranychoidea, Raphignathoidea, Tydeoidea, Cunaxoidea, Phytoseiidae, all of Japan (Yes); Coleoptera: Cerambycidae of Japan (No), Coccinellidae: Epilachninae of Japan (Yes)]

* EHIK, Dr. G. Y. Zoological Department, Hungarian National Museum, Baross-u. 13, Budapest VII, Hungary. [Mammalia]

* EHLERS, Mr. G. M. Museum of Paleontology, University of Michigan, Ann Arbor, Mich., U.S.A. [Fossil invertebrates]

EHRENBERG, Prof. Dr. K. Döblinger Hauptstrasse 66/1o, Wien XIX/117, Austria. [Pleistocene Mammalia: Carnivora: Ursidae: g. Ursus of Europe (Yes)]

EHRLICH, Dr. Paul R. Department of Biological Sciences, Stanford University, Stanford, Calif., U.S.A. [Lepidoptera: Papilionoidea & Hesperioidea of World (No); Satyrinae: g. Erebia of Nearctic (Yes)]

EICHER, D. L. Geology Department, University of Colorado, Boulder, Colo., U.S.A. [L. Cretaceous Foraminiferá of w. U.S. (Yes)]

EICHLER, Prof. Dr. Wolfdietrich. Clara-Zetkin-Strasse 23, Kleinmachnow, German Democratic Republic. [Mallophaga & Anoplura of World (Yes)] [Parasitologische Abteilung des Bezirks-Hygiene-Instituts Potsdam]

* EIGENBRODT, Dr. H. Address unknown. (Porifera)

EISELT, Dr. J. Kustos, Zoologische Abteilung, Naturhistorisches Museum, Burgring 7, Wien I, Austria. [Amphibia & Reptilia of Europe, w. Asia & N. Africa (Yes); Crustacea: Copepoda: Cyclopoida: Siphonostoma (Yes)]

EISENACK, Prof. Dr. A. Urbanstrasse 24, Reutlingen, Germany. [Ordovician & Silurian Hystrichosphaeridea of Europe (No); Ordovician & Silurian Chitinozoa of Europe (Yes)]

EISENMANN, Eugene. American Museum of Natural History, New York 24, N.Y., U.S.A. [Aves of n.S. America, C. America & New York (Yes)]

EISENTRAUT, Prof. Dr. M. Hauptkonservator am Staatliches Museum für Naturkunde, Archivstrasse 3, Stuttgart, Germany. [Mammalia: Chiroptera of Europe & w. Africa (Yes)]

EISNER, Curt. Kwekerijweg 5, Den Haag, Netherlands. [Lepidoptera: Parnassiidae of Europe, Asia, & America (Yes)]

EKBLOM, Tore. (Stockholm, Sweden; Hemiptera) Deceased.

* EKBOM, P. J. A. Auroragatan 15 B, Helsingfors, Finland. [Coleoptera]

* EKENGREN, B. R. Marie Dalsvägen, 60, B, Malmö, Sweden. [Lepidoptera, Coleoptera]

EKMAN, Prof. Dr. S. P. Zoologiska Institutionen, Uppsala, Sweden. [Terr. Entomostraca (No); Holothurioidea (No)]

ELBEL, Robert E. Department of Zoology, University of Oklahoma, Norman, Okla., U.S.A. [Siphonaptera: reared larvae of World; Mallophaga of Old World Tropics (Yes)]

* van ELDIK, H.C.L. Van der Woertstraat 20, Den Haag, Netherlands. [Lepidoptera, Coleoptera, Odonata]

ELDRIDGE, Lt. B. F. Department of Preventive Medicine, A. M. S. S., Fort Sam Houston, Texas, U.S.A. [Diptera: Muscinae of N. America (Yes)]

ELFVING, R. Ylä-Aatala, Kuopio, Finland. [Hymenoptera: Apoidea of Europe (No), of Finland (Yes)]

* ELGEE, Mr. Donald E. Forest Biology Laboratory, College Hill, Fredericton, N. B., Canada. [Insecta of maritime Canada]

* EL-GINDY, Dr. M.S. Address unknown. (Parasites)

ELIAS, Dr. Maxim K. 103 Nebraska Hall, University of Nebraska, Lincoln 8, Neb., U.S.A. [Carboniferous-Permian Bryozoa, Goniatites, Brachiopoda, Conodonts, of N. Hemisphere (Yes)]

ELIASON, A. Naturhistoriska Museet, Göteborg C, Sweden. [Polychaeta (No)]

* ELIESCU, Grigore. Institutul Forestier, Bucureşti, Rumania. [Coleoptera]

178

* ELISHEWITZ, Dr. Harold. Address unknown. [Diptera: Simuliidae of Neotropical; Acarina: Ixodoidea of World]
ELKADY, Mr. E. A. Faculty of Agriculture, Ein Shams University, Saray El-Koubbeh, Egypt. [Homoptera: Aphididae of Egypt (Yes)]
ELKINS, Joe C. 7010 Alderney Drive, Houston 24, Texas, U. S. A. [Heteroptera: Reduviidae of N. America (Yes); Harpactorinae of N. America (No), of C. & S. America (Yes); Saicinae of World (Yes)]
ELLER, Dr. E. R. Carnegie Museum, Pittsburgh 13, Penna., U. S. A. [Polychaeta: Scolecodonts of all periods (Yes)]
* ELLERMAN, Sir John R., Bart. (London, England; Mammalia) Not now active in taxonomy.
ELLIOTT, Prof. Alfred M. Zoology Department, University of Michigan, Ann Arbor, Mich., U. S. A. [F-l. Protozoa: Ciliata (Yes)]
ELLIOTT, Mr. G. F. Iraq Petroleum Company Ltd., 214 Oxford Street, London, W. 1, England. [Fossil & Recent Brachiopoda: Terebratellacea (Yes); Tertiary Brachiopoda of Europe (Yes)]
ELLIS, A. D., Jr. Pan-American Petroleum Corporation, P. O. Box 14085, Houston 21, Texas, U. S. A. [Tertiary Foraminifera of Gulf Coast U. S.]
* ELLIS, A. E. Epsom College, Epsom, Surrey, England. [Mollusca]
ELLIS, Prof. B. F. Geology Department, 920 Main, 100 Washington Square East, New York 3, N. Y., U. S. A. [Mesozoic & Cenozoic Foraminifera (Yes)] [New York University]
ELLIS, Leslie L., Jr. Box 983, Mississippi State College, State College, Miss., U. S. A. [Aquatic Hemiptera of s. e. U. S. (Yes); Siphonaptera of s. e. & s. w. U. S. (No)]
* ELLISON, Mr. R. E. Youll Grange, Links, Road, Eastbourne, Sussex, England. [Lepidoptera]
ELLISON, Robert Lee. 226 S. Allen Street, State College, Penna., U. S. A. [Devonian Brachiopoda, Mollusca, Bryozoa, Trilobitomorpha, of Hamilton group of Pennsylvania (Yes)]
ELLISON, Mr. S. P., Jr. Department of Geology, University of Texas, Austin 12, Texas, U. S. A. [Paleozoic & Mesozoic Conodonts & Foraminifera (Yes)]
EL-MOURSY, A. A. Department of Entomology, Faculty of Science, University of Cairo, Giza, Egypt. [Coleoptera: Byrrhidae of N. America (Yes); Neuroptera: Nemopteridae & Myrmeleonidae of Egypt (Yes); Diptera: Rhagionidae of Mediterranean (Yes)]
ELOFSON, O. Ludvigsvägen 3, Sundsvall, Sweden. [Crustacea: marine Ostracoda of n. w. Europe (No)] [Institute of Zoology, Uppsala]
* ELSTER, Prof. Dr. H. J. Hydrobiologische Station, Falkau Schwarzwald (17b), Germany. [Copepoda of Europe (No)]
* ELTYSHEVA, Mrs. R. S. Paleontological Laboratory, Leningrad State University, 16th Line 29, Leningrad B-178, U. S. S. R. [Fossil invertebrates]
* EL-ZARKA, Dr. Salah. Department of Ichthyology, Alexandria Institute of Hydrobiology, Kayet Bay, Alexandria, Egypt. [Pisces]
van EMDEN, F. (London, England; Insecta) Deceased.
* EMEIS, J. D. 37 van Wijngaerdenstraat, Den Haag, Netherlands. [Fossil invertebrates]
EMERSON, Prof. A. E. Department of Zoology, University of Chicago, Chicago 37, Ill., U. S. A. [Isoptera of World (Yes)]
EMERSON, Dr. K. C. Department of Entomology, Oklahoma Agricultural & Mechanical College, Stillwater, Okla., U. S. A. [Mallophaga & Anoplura of World (Yes)]
EMERSON, Dr. William K. Department of Fishes & Aquatic Biology, American Museum of Natural History, New York 24, N. Y., U. S. A. [Scaphopoda of e. Pacific (Yes); fossil Scaphopoda of N. America (No)]
EMIELITY, Joseph George. Milwaukee Public Museum, Milwaukee 3, Wis., U. S. A. [Devonian Edrioasteroidea: Agelacrinitidae of N. America (Yes)]
EMSLEY, M. G. Imperial College of Tropical Agriculture, St. Augustine, Trinidad. [Reptilia: Serpentes of Trinidad & Tobago (Yes); Heteroptera of British Isles (No)]
* EMURA, Shigeo. Faculty of Science, Niigata University, Ohatamachi, Niigata, Japan. [Mollusca]
ENBYSK, Betty Joyce. 2027 E. 135th Place, Seattle 55, Wash., U. S. A. [Pleistocene & Recent benthonic Foraminifera of n. e. Pacific (Yes)] [University of Washington]
ENDEAN, Dr. R. Department of Zoology, University of Queensland, George Street, Brisbane, Australia. [Asteroidea, Ophiuroidea, Echinoidea, Holothurioidea, of Queensland (Yes)]
* ENDERLEIN, Gunther. (Hamburg, Germany; Sarcophagidae) Not now active in taxonomy.
ENDERS, Mr. Robert K. Swarthmore College, Swarthmore, Penna., U. S. A. [Mammalia of Panama (Yes)]
ENDO, Riuji. Laboratory of Earth Sciences, Saitama University, Urawa City, Saitama Pref., Japan. [Cambrian Trilobites (No)]
ENDRODI, Dr. S. Orlay u. 9, Budapest XI, Hungary. [Coleoptera: Lamellicornia of World (No); Scarabaeidae: Dynastinae & Aphodiinae; Passalidae; of World (Yes)] [University of Agricultural Sciences, Gödällö]
ENDY, Mr. Edward T. 24 W. Gravers Lane, Philadelphia 18, Penna., U. S. A. [Coleoptera: Carabidae of World (Yes)]

ENGEL, Prof. Dr. H. Zoologisch Museum, Plantage Middenlaan 53, Amsterdam C, Netherlands. [Echinoidea, Asteroidea, Holothurioidea, Gastropoda: Nudibranchia; Hirudinea of Netherlands (No)]

* ENGEL, Dr. H. Zoologisches Staatssammlung, Menzingerstrasse 67, München 38, Germany. [Aves]

* ENGELBACH, P. , Ornithologist, 10 rue Copernic, Paris (XVI), France. [Aves]

ENGELHARDT, Dr. Wolfgang, Konservator an der Zoologischen Staatssammlung, Menzingerstrasse 67, München 19, Germany. [Araneida of Europe (Yes)]

ENGLISH, Miss K. M. I. Department of Zoology, University of Sydney, Sydney, N. S. W. , Australia. [Diptera: Tabanidae, immature stages, of Australia (Yes)]

* ENIGK, Karl. (Hanover, Germany; Acarina, Trematoda, Nematoda) Not now active in taxonomy.

ENLOW, Dr. D. H. Department of Anatomy, University of Michigan, Ann Arbor, Mich., U. S. A. [Fossil & Recent vertebrate bones (Yes)]

ENNS, Dr. W. R. Department of Entomology, University of Missouri, Columbia, Mo. , U. S. A. [Coleoptera: Meloidae: Nemognathinae of W. Hemisphere (Yes); of E. Hemisphere (No); Acarina: Caeculidae of U. S. (Yes)]

ENSLIN, Dr. E. 27 Schliessfach, Furth i. B. , Germany. [Hymenoptera: Tenthredinidae & Apidae of Europe (Yes)]

* ENZMANN, Dr. Ernest V. 4000 Lincoln Place Drive, Des Moines, Iowa, U. S. A. [Hymenoptera: Formicidae]

EPSTEIN, Dr. Hans. 7997 Composite Group, APO 757, c/o P. M. , New York, N. Y. , U. S. A. [Lepidoptera: Rhopalocera, espec. Lycaeninae, Charaxidi, Apaturidi, Baroniae, of the Holarctic (Yes)]

EPSTEIN, W. M. Kharkov Zootechnical Institute, Prospect Pravdy 5, kv. 282, Kharkov 22, U. S. S. R. [Hirudinea: f-w. & marine Ichthyobdellidae of Europe & n. Asia (Yes)]

d'ERASMO, Prof. Geremia. Istituto di Geologia, Universita di Napoli, Largo S. Marcellino 10, Napoli (405), Italy. [Mesozoic & Cenozoic Pisces (Yes); Neozoic Proboscidea (No)]

* ERB, J. 3 Place Esquirol, Toulouse, France. [Coleoptera]

ERBEN, Prof. Dr. Heinrich Karl. Geologisch-Palaeontologisches Institute der Universität, Nussallee 2, Bonn, Germany. [Cephalopoda: L. Devonian Goniatitacea & Devonian Bactritacea; Silurian & Devonian Trilobita (Yes)]

ERCOLINI, Dr. Antonio. Istituto di Museo della Universitá di Torino, Via Academia Albertina 17, Torino, Italy. [Oligochaeta: Aeolosomatidae & Naididae of New World (Yes)]

ERDBRINK, D. P. Geological Institute, University of Utrecht, Oude Gracht 320, Utrecht, Netherlands. [Tertiary & Quaternary Carnivora, excl. Pinnipedia; Elephantoidea; Cervidae; all of Old World (Yes)]

ERDMAN, D. S. Box 412, Lajas, Puerto Rico. [Marine Pisces of West Indies (Yes)]

ERDÖS, Dr. J. Szentháromság-tér 3, Tompa, Hungary. [Hymenoptera: Chalcidoidea of Europe (Yes)]

ERHAN, Eleonora. Centrul de Cercetari Biologice, Splaiul Independentei Nr. 93-95, Bucureşti, Rumania. [Diptera: Tipulidae of Rumania (Yes); of c. Europe & Balkans (No)]

* ERICKSON, C. W. Curator of Conchology, Worcester Museum of Natural History, 12 State Street, Worcester, Mass. , U. S. A. [Mollusca]

* ERICKSON, E. Harvard Medical School, Department of Anatomy, Cambridge, Mass., U. S. A. [Mammalia]

ERICSON, Mr. D. B. Lamont Geological Observatory, Palisades, N. Y. , U. S. A. [Pleistocene & Recent plankton Foraminifera of Atlantic Ocean (Yes)]

* ERK, Dr. A. Suat. Department of Geology, University of Ankara, Ankara, Turkey. [Fossil Foraminifera]

ERLANDSSON, Fil. Dr. S. Sibyllegatan 7, Stockholm, Sweden. [Hymenoptera: Apidae of Scandinavia (Yes); Chrysididae of Scandinavia (No); Aculeata of s. Europe (No)]

* ERMISCH, K. An den Märchenweise 47, Leipzig S 3, German Democratic Republic. [Coleoptera: Mordellidae]

ERNST, Dr. E. Schweiz. Tropeninstitut, Socinstrasse 57, Basel, Switzerland. [Isoptera of Africa (Yes)]

* ERSHOV, DR. V. S. All-Union Skrjabin Institute of Helminthology, Staropansky 3, Moscow K-12, U. S. S. R. [Helminths of animals]

ERTL, Dr. Milan. Oddelenie zoológie S. A. V. , Sienkiewiczova 1, Bratislava, Czechoslovakia. [F-w. Rhizopoda of Europe (Yes)]

ESAKI, Teiso. (Fukuoka City, Japan; Insecta) Died December 14, 1957.

ESCALANTE, Dr. Tarsicio. Mariano Escobedo No. 63, Tacuba 17, D. F. , Mexico. [Lepidoptera: Sphingidae & Saturnidae of Mexico (Yes)]

* ESHGHY, Nosratollah. Institute of Parasitology, University of Téhéran, Téhéran, Iran. [Diptera]

ESHLEMAN, Dr. S. K. , III. Norristown State Hospital, Norristown, Pa. , U. S. A. [F-w. Porifera of Atlantic Cst. U. S. (Yes)]

ESPAÑOL C., Francisco. Museo de Zoologia, Apartado Correos 593, Barcelona, Spain. [Coleoptera: Tenebrionidae of Mediterranean (Yes)]

ESSER, Mr. R. P. Plant Pathology Laboratory, P. O. Box 3777, University Station, Gainesville, Fla., U. S. A. [Nematoda: Tylenchida of s. U. S. (Yes)] [State Plant Board of Florida]

ESSIG, E. O. Department of Entomology & Parasitology, University of California, Berkeley 4, Calif., U. S. A. [Homoptera: Aphididae (Yes)]

ESSLINGER, Dr. Jack Houston. Department of Tropical Medicine & Public Health, Tulane University School of Medicine, New Orleans 12, La., U. S. A. [Parisites of animals]

ESTES, Richard. Museum of Paleontology, University of California, Berkeley 4, Calif., U. S. A. [Triassic to Recent Urodela & Squamata of N. America (Yes); Permian to Triassic Theriodontia (Yes)]

ESTEVE, Mlle. Rolande. See ROUX-ESTEVE, R.

ETCHEVERRY, Prof. Maria. Instituto Pedagógico, Universidad de Chile, Casilla 147, Santiago, Chile. [Lepidoptera: Hesperidae of Chile (Yes)]

ETGES, Prof. Frank J. Department of Zoology, University of Cincinnati, Cincinnati 21, Ohio, U. S. A. [Digenetic Trematoda of N. America (Yes)]

ETHERIDGE, Mr. R. Museum of Zoology, University of Michigan, Ann Arbor, Mich., U. S. A. [Recent Reptilia of U. S., Mexico, W. Indies (Yes); Recent Amphibia of U. S. & Mexico (No); Pleistocene Lizards of &. S. & Mexico (Yes)]

ETHINGTON, Dr. Raymond L. Department of Geology, Arizona State University, Tempe, Ariz., U. S. A. [Cambrian-Triassic Conodonts, espec. Ordovician (Yes)]

ETTER, John. Sinclair Oil & Gas Company, P. O. Box 1167, Oil Center Station, Lafayette, La., U. S. A. [Plio-miocene Foraminifera of the Louisiana Gulf Coast (Yes); Up. Cretaceous to Oligocene Foraminifera of Mississippi (Yes)]

EUZET, Dr. Louis. Station Biologique, Sete (Herault), France. [Cestoda: Tetraphyllidea of World (Yes); Trematoda: Monogenoidea of Europe (No)]

* EVANS, A. G. T. Kingsley Hall, Central Wall Road, Canvey Island, Essex, England. [Mollusca]

EVANS, Burton Robert. U. S. Quarantine Station, New Orleans (Algiers), La., U. S. A. [Diptera: Culicidae of N. America (No)]

* EVANS, F. Dove Marine Laboratory, Cullercoats, Northumberland, England. [Crustacea]

EVANS, Prof. Frederick R. Department of Zoology, University of Utah, Salt Lake City 12, Utah, U. S. A. [F-l. Ciliata of lakes & streams of Utah; Intestinal Flagellata of Rodents of Utah (Yes)]

* EVANS, Mr. Glen L. 2204 Sinclair Street, Midland, Texas, U. S. A. [Fossil Mammalia]

EVANS, Dr. G. Owen. British Museum (Natural History), Cromwell Road, London S. W. 7, England. [Acarina: Mesostigmata: Parasitoidea & Uropodoidea of Europe, Africa, s. e. Asia (Yes); New World (No)]

EVANS, Howard E. Department of Entomology, Cornell University, Ithaca, N. Y., U. S. A. [Hymenoptera: Pompilidae & Bethylidae of N. & C. America (Yes)]

EVANS, Mr. J. 33 Queensville Street, West Footscray W 12, Victoria, Australia. [Rotifera of Victoria & s. New South Wales (Yes)]

EVANS, Dr. J. W., Director, Australian Museum, Hyde Park, Sydney, N. S. W., Australia. [Homoptera: Jassoidea of World (No), of Australia & New Zealand (Yes); Paleozoic & Mesozoic Homoptera of World (Yes)]

► EVERETT, Robert W., Jr. 6511 General Diaz, New Orleans, La., U. S. A. [Cenozoic Foraminifera (Yes)] [Texaco Paleontological Laboratory]

EVERHART, W. Harry. Department of Zoology, 7 Coburn Hall, University of Maine, Orono, Maine, U. S. A. [Inland Pisces: Salmonidae of n. e. U. S. (Yes)]

EVERLY, Prof. Ray T. Experiment Station, Purdue University, West Lafayette, Ind., U. S. A. [Coleoptera: Carabidae of U. S. (Yes)]

EVERS, Mr. A. M. J. Durerstrasse 13, Krefeld, Germany. [Coleoptera: Malachiidae of World (Yes)]

* EVERS, Hans. Bahrenfeld, Pfitznerstrasse 74, Hamburg, Germany. [Lepidoptera]

EVITT, Dr. W. R. The Carter Oil Company, P. O. Box 801, Tulsa, Okla., U. S. A. [Ordovician Trilobita (Yes)]

EWART, Dr. William. University of California, Riverside, Calif., U. S. A. [Thysanoptera of s. w. U. S. (Yes)]

EWER, Dr. R. F. Department of Zoology & Entomology, Rhodes University, Grahamstown, Union of South Africa. [Pleistocene Carnivora & Suidae of Africa (Yes)]

EWING, H. E. (Washington, D. C.; Arachnida) Deceased.

EXLINE, Dr. Harriet (Mrs. D. L. Frizzell). 6 Rolla Gardens, Rolla, Mo., U. S. A. [Araneida of n. w. U. S. & w. cst. of S. America (Yes)]

EYERDAM, Walter J. 7531 19th St. n. e., Seattle 15, Wash., U. S. A. [Scaphopoda: Dentaliidae & Gastropoda: g. Placostylus of New Zealand & Melanesia (Yes); land shells of S. America (No); Alaska marine shells (Yes)]

van EYNDHOVEN, G. L. Zoologische Museum, Zeeburgerdijk 21, Amsterdam, Netherlands. [Acarina, espec. Bryobia, of World (Yes); Rhinonyssidae & fur mites of mammals of World (Yes)]

EZZAT, Dr. Y. M. 7 Ali Gallad Street, Midan Soliman Goher, Dokki-Cairo, Egypt. [Homoptera: Diaspididae & Pseudococcidae of Egypt (Yes); Planococcini of World (Yes)] [University of Assyout]

* FABRICIUS, Eric. Kungl. Fiskeristyrelsen, Sötvattenslaboratoriet, Drottningholm, Sweden. [Pisces]

FAESTER, Dr. K. Universitetets Zoologiske Museum, Krystalgade, København K, Denmark. [Hymenoptera: Aculeata: Apidae, Vespidae, Sphecidae; all of n. & c. Europe (Yes)]

FAGE, Prof. L. Muséum d'Histoire Naturelle, Laboratoire de Zoologie, 61 Rue de Buffon, Gobelins 28-64, Paris, France. [Pycnogonidea; Crustacea: Cumacea, Pelagic Amphipoda]

FAGEL, G. Institut des Parcs Nationaux du Congo Belge, 31 rue Vautier, Bruxelles 4, Belgium. [Staphylinidae of Palearctic (No); Staphylinidae: Paederinae, Oxytelinae, Omaliinae, Piestinae, Proteininae, of Ethiopian (Yes)]

FAGERSTROM, J. A. Department of Geology, Morrill Hall, University of Nebraska, Lincoln, Nebr., U. S. A. [Mid. Devonian Tetracoralla & Brachiopoda (Yes)]

FAHLANDER, Dr. Kjell. Danmarksgatan 4, B, Linkoping, Sweden. [Hymenoptera: Sphecidae of Fennoskandia (Yes)]

FAHLBUSCH, Dr. K. Geologische Institut, Technische Hochschule, Alexanderstrasse 35, Darmstadt, Germany. [Fossil Agnatha of c. Europe (Yes)]

FAHRENBACH, Mr. Wolf H. Zoology Department, University of Washington, Seattle 5, Wash., U. S. A. [Crustacea: harpacticoid Copepoda parasitic in red marine algae of Europe & N. America (Yes)]

FAHY, Dr. William E. Institute of Fisheries Research, University of North Carolina, Morehead City, N. C., U. S. A. [Marine & br-w. Pisces of w. N. Atlantic (Yes)]

FAIN, Dr. A, Professor of Medical Zoology, Institute de Medecine Tropicale, 155 Rue Nationale, Anvers, Belgium. [Endoparasitic mites of vertebrates, excl. chiggers, of World (Yes); other parasitic mites from vertebrates of Ethiopian (No)]

FAIRCHILD, Dr. G. B. Box 42, Balboa Heights, Canal Zone. [Diptera: Tabanidae of World (No), of Neotropics (Yes), Psychodidae: g. Phlebotomus of World (Yes)] [Gorgas Memorial Laboratory]

FAIRCHILD, William Wert. Standard Oil Company of Texas, P. O. Box 1249, Houston, Texas, U. S. A. [Tertiary Foraminifera (No)]

FAIREY, Mr. K. D. Box 1176, G. P. O., Sydney, N. S. W., Australia. [Lepidoptera: Limacodidae of Australia (Yes); fossil Lepidoptera (No)]

FALKENBACH, Mr. Charles H. American Museum of Natural History, New York 24, N. Y., U. S. A. [L. Oligocene to Up. Pliocene Mammalia: Merycoidodontidae of N. America (Yes)]

* FALLA, Dr. Robert A., Director, Dominion Museum, Buckle Street, Wellington, New Zealand. [Mammalia, Aves]

FALLIS, Prof. A. Murray. Ontario Research Foundation, 43 Queens Park, Toronto 5, Ont., Canada. [Blood Protozoa & Trematoda (No)]

* FARCU, Dr. Eduardo. Instituto de Entomologia, Hippodromo, Madrid, Spain. [Coleoptera]
* FARIS, R. C. Farrinseer, Cornafean, Cavan Co., Ireland. [Odonata]

FARNER, Donald S. Laboratory of Zoophysiology, State College of Washington, Pullman, Wash., U. S. A. [Acarina: Analgesidae (No)]

FARR, Miss Marion M. Animal Disease & Parasite Research Division, Agricultural Research Center, Beltsville, Md., U. S. A. [Protozoa: Coccidia of birds of N. America (Yes)] [U. S. Department of Agriculture]

FARR, Dr. T. H. c/o Institute of Jamaica, Kingston, Jamaica. [Diptera: Empididae & Asilidae of West Indies (No)]

FARRAN, G. P. (Dublin, Ireland; Copepoda) Died 1949.

FARRELL, Charles E. Box 1511, Vanderbilt University, Nashville 5, Tenn., U. S. A. [Acarina: g. Euschöngastia of U. S. (No)]

FARRIER, Dr. Maurice H. Box 5215, State College Station, Raleigh, N. C., U. S. A. [Acarina: Veigaiidae of World (Yes), Tetranychidae of U. S. (No)] [North Carolina State College]

FASSATI, Dr. Milos. Societas Entomologica Čechosloveniae, Viničná 7, Praha II, Czechoslovakia. [Coleoptera: Carabidae of Europe (Yes); g. Amara of Palearctic (Yes); Fossil & Recent g. Bembidion of World (Yes)]

FASSULIOTIS, Mr. G. Nematode Research Laboratory, 3985 Union Avenue, Seaford, N. Y., U. S. A. [Nematoda: Tylenchida of n. e. U. S. (Yes)]

FAUL, Henry. U. S. Geological Survey, Washington 25, D. C., U. S. A. [Paleozoic & Mesozoic fossil footprints (Yes)]

FAURE, Dr. J.C. Private Bag 134, Vallis, Pretoria, Union of South Africa. [Thysanoptera of Africa (Yes)] [Department of Agriculture]

FAUST, Prof. Ernest C. School of Medicine, Tulane University, New Orleans 12, La., U.S.A. [Protozoa & helminths of man (Yes)]

FAUTIN, Dr. Reed W. Department of Zoology & Fhysiology, University of Wyoming, Laramie, Wyo., U.S.A. [Mammalia of Wyoming]

FAUVEL, P. (Angers, France; Polychaeta) Deceased.

FAVRE, Dr. Jules. (Museum d'Histoire Naturelle, Geneva, Switzerland; Fossil & Recent Mollusca) Deceased 1959 (?).

FAY, Dr. F.H. Arctic Health Research Center, P.O. Box 960, Anchorage, Alaska, U.S.A. [Mammalia of Alaska (Yes), Pinnipeds of N. Pacific Ocean, Bering & Chukchi Seas (Yes)]

FAY, Robert. O. Geology Department, University of Oklahoma, Norman, Okla., U.S.A. [Blastoidea & Conodonts of World (Yes)]

FEDDERSEN, T.G. (Hellerup, Denmark; Lepidoptera) Died February 1959.

* FEDOTOV, D.M. Goskova 22A kv. 7, Moscow, U.S.S.R. [Myzostomida]

* van der FEEN, P.J. Zoologisch Museum, Plantage Middenlaan 53, Amsterdam, Netherlands. [Mammalia]

van der FEEN, Mrs. W.S.S. (née van Benthem Jutting), Conservatrice, Zoologisch Museum, Plantage Middenlaan 53, Amsterdam, Netherlands. [Mollusca of Netherlands & North Sea; terr. f-w. & marine Mollusca of Indonesia & New Guinea (Yes)]

FEHLMANN, Mr. Herman Adair. Natural History Museum, Stanford University, Stanford, Calif., U.S.A. [Br-w. & f-w. Pisces of Oceania (No)]

FEIDER, Prof. Dr. Z. Laboratorul de Zoologie, Universitatea "Al. I. Cuza", Iaşi, Rumania. [Acarina: Trombidoidea of Eurasia, Africa, America (Yes); Trombiculidae & Ixodoidea of Eurasia (Yes)]

* FEIO, Jose Lacerda de Araujo. Museu Nacional, Quinta da Boa Vista, Rio de Janeiro, Brazil. [Araneida & Pseudoscorpionida of Neotropics (Yes); Gordiacea]

FEJFAR, Dr. Oldřich. Ústředni Ústav Geologický, Hrabedni 9, Praha I, Czechoslovakia. [Miocene - Pleistocene (espec. Villafranchien) Mammalia: Rodentia, Carnivora, Insectivora, Primates; all of c. Europe (Yes)]

FELDMAN-MUHSAM, B. The Hebrew University, Hadassah Medical School, Box 1255, Jerusalem, Israel. [Acarina: Ixodidae, excl. g. Ixodes, of World (Yes); g. Ixodes of Middle East (Yes)]

FELDMESSER, Dr. Julius. U.S. Department of Agriculture, 2120 Camden Road, Orlando, Fla., U.S.A. [Nematoda: Tylenchidae & Oxyuridae of U.S. (No)]

* FELIKSIAK, Prof. Dr. Stanisław. Instytut Zoologiczny, Polska Akademia Nauk, ul. Wilcza 64, Warszawa, Poland. [Mollusca]

FELL, Prof. H. Barraclough. Department of Zoology, Victoria University of Wellington, P.O. Box 196, Wellington, New Zealand. [Triassic-Recent Echinoidea, Asteroidea, Ophiuroidea, of deep & shallow water of New Zealand, Australia, S. Pacific, Antarctic (Recent Yes, fossil only of New Zealand)]

* FELLTON, H.L. R.F.D., Marietta, Ga., U.S.A. [Diptera]

FELTEN, Dr. Heinz. Natur-Museum Senckenberg, Senckenberg-Anlage 25, Frankfurt am Main, Germany. [Small Mammalia, espec. Chiroptera, of the World (Yes)]

FENDER, Kenneth M. Route 3, McMinnville, Ore., U.S.A. [Coleoptera of Pac. n.w.U.S.; Cantharidae of N. America; Lampyridae: g. Ellychnia of N. America (No)]

FENG, Prof. L.C. Institute of Parasitic Diseases, Chinese Academy of Medical Sciences, Shanghai, People's Republic of China. [Diptera: Culicidae of Palearctic & Orient (No)]

FENNAH, Mr. R.G. Commonwealth Institute of Entomology, c/o British Museum (Natural History), London, S.W.7, England. [Fossil & Recent Homoptera: Fulgoroidea of World (Yes); Recent Cercopoidea: g. Aeneolamia, Prosapia, Delassor, Zulia, Panabrus, of trop. America & U.S. (Yes)]

FENNEL, W.E. Department of Biology, Brooklyn College, Brooklyn, N.Y., U.S.A. [Nematoda: Dorylaimidae of Great Lakes (No)]

* FEOFANOVA, Yu. M. Neftjanoj Institut imeni Gubkina, Leninsky Prospect 33, Moscow V-71, U.S.S.R. [Fossil Bryozoa]

FERENS, Dr. Bronisław. Institute of Zoology, Polska Akademia Nauk, ul. Slawkowska 1, Kraków, Poland. [Aves]

FERGUSON, Mr. D.C. Nova Scotia Museum of Science, Halifax, Nova Scotia, Canada. [Macrolepidoptera of N. America (No); of n.e.U.S. & e. Canada (Yes); Macrolepidoptera: Plusiinae of N. America (Yes)]

FERGUSON, Dr. Denzel E. Department of Zoology, Mississippi State University, State College, Miss., U.S.A. [Salamanders of Oregon (Yes); Amphibia & Reptilia of Mississippi (Yes)]

FERGUSON, Dr. Edward, Jr. 747 Locust Street, Jefferson City, Mo., U.S.A. [F-w. & f-l. Ostracoda of N. America (Yes)]

FERGUSON, Dr. F. F. Communicable Disease Center, U.S. Public Health Service, 50 Seventh Street, Atlanta, Ga., U.S.A. [Turbellaria of World (Yes)]

FERGUSON, George R. 21 Hadden Road, Scarsdale, N.Y., U.S.A. [Hymenoptera: Schecoidea & Vespoidea of World (No); Bembicinae & Sphecinae of New World (Yes)]

FERGUSON, William E. 112 Agriculture Hall, University of California, Berkeley 4, Calif., U.S.A. [Hymenoptera: Mutillidae of World (No), nocturnal Mutillidae of N. America (Yes)]

FERNÁNDEZ, Dr. R. Museo Poey, Cátedra "U", University of Habana, Habana, Cuba. [Foraminifera]

FERNANDEZ-GALIANO, Prof. Dimas. Centro de Investigaciones Zoológicas, Instituto José de Acosta, Teruel, Spain. [Ciliata: Ophryoscolecidae, Cycloposthiidae, Balantiidae; Flagellata: Opalinidae (all Yes)]

* FERNANDEZ MARTINEZ, Prof. José. Basualdo 191, Buenos Aires, Argentina. [Protozoa]

FERNANDEZ YEPEZ, Prof. Agustin. Apartado 4232 del Este, Caracas, Venezuela. [Pisces of Neotropics & Caribbean Sea (Yes)] [Museo de Ciencias Naturales]

FERNANDO, Prof. Wilfred. Department of Zoology, University of Ceylon, Colombo 3, Ceylon. [Turbellaria: Temnocephalida; Trematoda; parasitic Hymenoptera of Ceylon (Yes)]

FERRAGU, M. 58 rue Dulong, Paris (XVII), France. [Coleoptera: Curculionidae: Apioninae of Palearctic, Madagascar, Oceania (Yes); Baridini of Palearctic (Yes)]

FERREIRA, C.S. Museu Nacional, Quinta da Boa Vista, Rio de Janeiro, Brazil. [Oligocene to Pleistocene Mollusca of Caribbean (Yes)]

FERREIRA, Dra. Maria-Corinta. Museu Dr. Alvaro de Castro, Lourenço Marques, Mozambique, Portuguese East Africa. [Coleoptera: Scarabaeidae: Scarabaeini, Onitini, Coprini, Oniticellini, Gymnopleurini, Canthonini, Onthophagini, Sisyphini; Cerambycidae: Prioninae; Buprestidae: Julodini; all of Africa s. of Sahara (Yes)]

* FERREIRA de ALMEIDA, Dr. Waldemar. Museu Nacional, Quinta da Boa Vista, Rio de Janeiro, Brazil. [Protozoa]

* FERRER y GALDIANO, M. Departmento de Acarinos, Museo National de Madrid, Madrid, Spain. [Acarina]

* FERRERO, Dr. L. Laboratorio Centrale de Idrobiologia, Piazza Borghese 91, Roma, Italy. [Rotifera]

FERRIERE, Dr. C. 57 route de Florissant, Genève, Switzerland. [Hymenoptera: Chalcidoidea of Palearctic (Yes)] [Muséum d'Histoire Naturelle]

FERRIS, Prof. G. F. (Stanford, Calif.; Anoplura, Coccoidea) Died May 21, 1958.

FERRIS, John. Department of Entomology, Purdue University, Lafayette, Ind., U.S.A. [Plant parasitic Nematoda of N. America (No)]

FEYLING-HANSSEN, Rolf W. Norges Geologiske Undersökelse, Josefines gate 34, Oslo, N.V., Norway. [Up. Pleistocene Pelecypoda & Foraminifera of Arctic & Subarctic (Yes)]

de FEZ SANCHEZ, Siro. See SANCHEZ, Siro de Fez.

* FICKEN, Robert. Address unknown. (Aves)

FIEDLER, Carl. Suhl, Germany; Coleoptera] Deceased.

FIEDLER, Dr. O. G. H. Agricultura Laboratoria Ltd., Silverton, Transvaal, Union of South Africa. [Anoplura of game mammals of Africa (Yes)]

FIEDLER, Dr. Walter. Anatomisches Institude, L. Rehn-strasse 14, Frankfurt am Main, Germany. [Mammalia: Primates & Carnivora (No)]

* FIELD, Dr. Gordon. Address unknown. (Diptera)

FIELD, Mrs. Louise Randall. 914 E. 40th St., Austin, Texas, U.S.A. [Coelenterata: Anthozoa of c. Atlantic Coast (Yes)]

FIELD, Dr. William D. Division of Insects, U.S. National Museum, Washington 25, D.C., U.S.A. [Lepidoptera: Rhopalocera of Neotropics (No)]

FIELDING, M.J. E.I. du Pont Chemical Company, Experimental Station, Building 268, Wilmington, Del., U.S.A. [Parasitic & f-l. soil Nematoda]

FIELDS, Prof. Gordon. Department of Biology, Victoria College, Victoria, B.C., Canada. [Cephalopoda: Decapoda of n.e. Pacific Ocean (Yes)]

FIELDS, Dr. R.W. Department of Geology, Montana State University, Missoula, Mont., U.S.A. [Tertiary Hystricomorpha of S. America (Yes)]

FIGG-HOBLYN, Dr. John P. Natural History Museum, Stanford University, Stanford, Calif., U.S.A. See Addenda.

FIGUEIRA, Mr. Armando J.G. Museu Municipal do Funchal, Madeira Islands. [Crustacea: Decapoda of Atlantic & Mediterranean (Yes); Natantia of World (Yes)]

FIGUEIRAS, Mr. Alfredo. Agustin Abreu No. 2385, Montevideo, Uruguay. [Mollusca, excl. Pteropoda & Nudibranchiata, of Uruguay & Patagonia (Yes)]

FIGUERAS, Antonio. Instituto de Investigaciones Pesqueras, General Aranda 66, Vigo, Spain. [Mollusca: Lamellibranchiata of Spanish Atlantic (Yes)]

* FIGUEROA, Mauro C. Address unknown. (Aquatic invertebrates)

184

FILATOVA, Dr. Z. A. Institute of Oceanology, Academy of Sciences, Lujnikovskaja 8, Moscow 127, U.S.S.R. [Marine bivalve Mollusca of deep-sea Pacific & Northern Seas (Yes)]

FILICE, Francis P. 976 Southgate Avenue, Daly City, Calif., U.S.A. [Flagellata: Zoomastigophora & Holothuroidea of e. Pacific (Yes)]

FILIPPI, Prof. Natale. S. Polo 2878, Venice, Italy. [Heteroptera of Europe, espec. Mediterranean (Yes)]

FILIPPONI, Prof. Ales. Laboratorio de Parassitologia, Istituto Superiore di Sanità, Viale Regina Elena 299, Roma, Italy. [Sporozoa: Gregarinida of Europe (No); Turbellaria: Polycystidea of Europe (No); "Gamalina, Macrochelidae" of Italy (Yes)]

FILIPPOVA, Miss N. A. Zoological Institute, Academy of Sciences, Leningrad 164, U.S.S.R. [Acarina: Ixodoidea of U.S.S.R. (Yes)]

FINDENEGG, Prof. Dr. Ingo. Biologische Station, Lunz, Austria. [Crustacea: planktonic Cladocera of Europe (Yes)]

FINDLEY, Dr. James S. Department of Biology, University of New Mexico, Albuquerque, N. Mex., U.S.A. [Mammalia: Soricidae: g. Sorex of N. America & Eurasia (Yes)]

* FINELLE, P. Service de l'Elevage, Bouar, Oubangui, French Equatorial Africa. [Diptera]

FINELY, Harold E. Department of Zoology, Howard University, Washington 1, D.C., U.S.A. [Peritrichida of World (Yes); f-w. Ciliata of N. America (Yes)]

FINKS, Robert M. Department of Geology, Brooklyn College, Brooklyn 10, N.Y., U.S.A. [Paleozoic Porifera of World (Yes), Mesozoic (No)]

* FINLAYSON, Dr. H. H. c/o South Australian Museum, North Terrace, Adelaide, Australia. [Mammalia]

FINLEY, Dr. Robert B., Jr. 7 Blackhawk Drive, Forest Heights, Washington 21, D.C., U.S.A. [Mammalia of N. America (No), Cricetidae of N. America (Yes)]

FIORI, Dott. Attilio. Via Gualandi 5, Bologna, Italy. [Lepidoptera of Europe (No)] [Università di Bologna]

* FIORI, G. Istituto di Entomologia, Via Filippo Re 6, Università di Bologna, Bologna, Italy. [Coleoptera: Byrrhidae]

* FIRA, Valeria. Facultatea de Biologie, Splaiul Independentei Nr. 93-95, Bucureşti, Rumania. [Diptera]

FIRMIN, Rev. F. 807 Avenue Royale, St. Jean, Ile d'Orléans, Que., Canada. [Coleoptera: Cerambycidae & Dytiscidae of Quebec (Yes)]

* FIRSCHEIN, Mr. I. Lester. Address unknown. [Amphibia of Mexico]

FISCHER, F.C.J. Lumeystraat 7c, Rotterdam, Netherlands. [Trichoptera of World (Yes)]

* FISCHER, Dr. Carlos R. Instituto Biologico, Caixa Postal 75, Campinas, São Paulo, Brazil. [Hymenoptera]

FISCHER, Guillermo Mann. See MANN, Guillermo.

FISCHER, Heinz. Vogelmauer 33, Augsburg, Germany. [Orthoptera of Germany (Yes)]

FISCHER, Dr. Max. Naturhistorisches Museum, Zoologische Abteilung, Burgring 7, Wien I, Austria. [Hymenoptera: Braconidae: Opiinae of Europe & Nearctic (Yes); g. Meteorus of Europe (No)]

FISCHER, Dr. P. H. Ecolé des Mines de Paris, 38 Boulevard St. Michel, Paris (VI), France. [Marine Mollusca of Europe & Indo-Pacific (No); Eocene, Miocene, Pleistocene marine Mollusca of France (Yes); Intertidal Gastropoda of World (Yes)]

FISCHER, Dr. Roland L. Department of Entomology, Michigan State University, East Lansing, Mich., U.S.A. [Hymenoptera: Apoidea of N. America (Yes), of Neotropics (No)]

FISCHER-PIETTE, Prof. E. Muséum National d'Histoire Naturelle, 55 rue de Buffon, Paris (V), France. [Mollusca: Veneridae, espec. g. Tivela, Sunetta, Meretrix, Donax, Heterodonax (Yes); terr. & f-w. of Madagascar (Yes)]

FISCHTHAL, Prof. Jacob H. Harpur College, Endicott, N.Y., U.S.A. [Trematoda of U.S., Canada, N. Africa (No)]

FISH, Dr. Charles J. 1291 Kingstown Road, Kingston, R.I., U.S.A. [Pelagic marine Crustacea: devel. stages of Entomostraca of c. & w. N. Atlantic (No)]

FISHELSON, L. University of Tel-Aviv, Herzel Street, Abu-Kabir, Tel-Aviv, Israel. [Orthoptera: Acridoidea of Israel (Yes)]

FISHER, Dr. Donald W. State Paleontologist, New York State Museum & Science Service, Albany 1, N.Y., U.S.A. [Cambrian-Devonian Trilobites & Gastropods of New York (Yes); Mollusca: Cambrian-Silurian Hyolithidae of New York (Yes), Ordovician-Devonian Tentaculitidae of New York (Yes)]

FISHER, Miss Edna M. (San Francisco, Calif.; Mammalia) Died July 1954.

FISHER, Dr. Elizabeth. 4204 Somerset Place, Baltimore 10, Md., U.S.A. [Diptera: Mycetophilidae of N. America (Yes); Odonata of Maryland (Yes)]

FISHER, Dr. H. D. Arctic Unit, Fisheries Research Board of Canada, 505 Pine Avenue, West, Montreal, Que., Canada. [Mammalia: Pinnipedia of Arctic & e. Canada (Yes)]

FISHER, Mr. J. M. Waite Research Institute, Private Mail Bag, Adelaide, S. Australia. [Nematoda: Tylenchida of s. Australia (Yes)]

FISHER, Mr. R. H. 21 Seaview Road, Lynton, S. Australia. [Lepidoptera: Rhopalocera of s. Australia (Yes)]

FISHER, Waltèr Ҟ. (Pacific Grove, Calif.; Echinodermata, etc.) Died November 2, 1953.

FITCH, Prof. Henry S. Department of Zoology, University of Kansas, Lawrence, Kans., U. S. A. [Reptilia: garter snakes & alligator lizards of g. Gerrhonotus, of w. U. S. (Yes)]

FITCH, John E. State Fisheries Laboratory, Terminal Island, San Pedro, Calif., U. S. A. [Otoliths of marine Pisces of Pacific Cst. of N. America (Yes); Trachipteridae of Pacific Ocean (Yes); Sciaenidae of e. Pacific (No), g. Cynoscion (Yes)]

FITTKAU, E. J. Hydrobiologische Anstalt, Plön (Schleswig-Holstein), Germany. [Diptera: Chironomidae of Palearctic & Africa (Yes)]

FITZGERALD, James W. Washington Department of Fisheries, Olympia, Wash., U. S. A. [F-w. & marine Pisces of Puget Sound (Yes); Salmonidae of w. cst. of N. America (Yes)]

FitzSIMONS, Dr. V., Director, Transvaal Museum, Box 413, Pretoria, Union of South Africa. [Reptilia, Amphibia, f-w. Pisces of s. Africa (Yes)]

* FIZE, A. Institut Oceanographique de Nhatrang, Cauda, Nhatrang, Viet-Nam. [Decapoda]

* FJELD, Per. Department of Zoology, University of California, Berkeley 4, Calif., U. S. A. [Protozoa]

FLAHAUT, Martha R. (Seattle, Wash.; Aves, Mammalia) Died January 1, 1956.

FLECHSIG, Arthur. Scripps Institution of Oceanography, La Jolla, Calif., U. S. A. [Pisces: Elasmobranchs of n. e. Pacific (Yes)]

FLEETWOOD, Mr. L. D. L. Department of Mammals, The Coryndon Museum, P. O. Box 658, Nairobi, Kenya. [Mammalia: Rodentia & Chiroptera of e. Africa (Yes)]

FLEMING, Dr. C. A. New Zealand Geological Survey, Wellington, New Zealand. [Fossil & Recent Mollusca: Pelecypoda & Gastropoda of New Zealand (Yes); Aves of New Zealand (Yes)]

FLEMING, Henry. New York Zoological Society, 185th Street & Southern Boulevard, New York 60, N. Y., U. S. A. [Lepidoptera: Papilionoidea, Hesperoidea, Saturnioidea, Noctuoidea, of n. S. America (Yes)]

FLEMINGER, Dr. Abraham. 3785 Mt. Everest Blvd., San Diego, Calif., U. S. A. [Crustacea: Copepoda: Calanoida of Gulf of Mexico, equatorial & w. N. Atlantic (Yes)]

FLEROW, Prof. Dr. Constantin C., Head, Paleontological Museum, Academy of Sciences of U. S. S. R., 16 Lenin Prospectus, Moscow W-71, U. S. S. R. [Fossil & Recent Vertebrates of U. S. S. R., Europe & Asia (Yes)]

FLETCHER, Mr. D. S. c/o Department of Entomology, British Museum (Natural History), Cromwell Road, London, S. W. 7, England. [Lepidoptera: Geometridae of World (Yes)]

FLINT, O. S., Jr. Department of Entomology, Cornell University, Ithaca, N. Y., U. S. A. [Immature & adult Trichoptera of N. America (Yes); immature of World (No)]

FLOCH, Hervè, Directeur, Institut Pasteur de la Guyane Française, Cayenne, French Guiana. [Diptera: Psychodidae: g. Phlebotomus; Ceratopogonidae; Simuliidae; all of Neotropics (Yes); Acarina: Trombiculidae of Neotropics (Yes), Ixodoidea of Neotropics (Yes)]

FLOCK, Dr. Robert A. Department of Entomology, University of California, Riverside, Calif., U. S. A. [Homoptera: Cicadellidae, Membracidae, Fulgoridae of s. w. U. S. (Yes)]

FLOOK, Donald R. Canadian Wildlife Service, Federal Building, Edmonton, Alta., Canada. [Mammalia, espec. Ungulata, of w. Canada (No)]

FLORIN, Dr. J. Direction de la pêche du Canton de S. Galle, Laboratoire Cantonal, Saint Galle, Switzerland. [Pisces of Switzerland (Yes); Lepidoptera & Trichoptera of Switzerland (No)]

FLOWER, Mr. Rousseau H. New Mexico Bureau of Mines, Socorro, N. Mex., U. S. A. [Paleozoic Cephalopoda: Nautiloidea & Coleoidea (Yes); Silurian Cyathaspida (Yes)]

FLÜGEL, Dr. E. Naturhistorisches Museum, Burgring 7, Wien I, Austria. [Paleozoic Stromatoporoidea (Yes); Mesozoic & Cenozoic polypoid Hydrozoa (Yes); Triassic Scleractinia (Yes)]

FLUKE, Dr. C. L. College of Agriculture, University of Wisconsin, Madison 6, Wis., U. S. A. [Diptera: Syrphidae of New World] Died in 1959.

* FLUNO, John A. 1550 Grove Terrace, Winter Park, Fla., U. S. A. [Odonata]

FLURY, Mr. Alvin G. Box 552, Mathis, Texas, U. S. A. [Reptilia & Amphibia of N. America (Yes); f-w. Pisces of Texas (Yes)]

FOERSTER, R. E., Principal Scientist, Pacific Biological Station, Nanaimo, B. C., Canada. [Hydromedusae, Scyphomedusae, Ctenophora, of Pacific Cst. of N. America (No)] [Fisheries Research Board of Canada]

de FOLIART, G. R. See De FOLIART, Gene R.

FOLKMANOVA, Doc. Dr. B. Zoologisches Institut, Masaryk Universität, Brno, Czechoslovakia. [Chilopoda of Czechoslovakia & U. S. S. R. (Yes); of Europe (No)]

FOLLETT, W. I. Department of Ichthyology, California Academy of Sciences, San Francisco 18, Calif., U. S. A. [Recent Pisces of California, incl. skeletons (Yes)]

FONGOND, R. 16 rue Larrey, Paris (V), France. [Coleoptera: Chrysomelidae of France (No)]

FONSECA, Mr. E. C. M. d'Assis. 58 Woodstock Road, Redland, Bristol 6, England. [Diptera, excl. Nematocera, of Britain (Yes); Tachinidae & Muscidae of Palearctic (Yes)]

da FONSECA, Prof. Flavio. Caixa Postal 7144, São Paulo, Brazil. [Acarina parasitic on vertebrates of World (Yes); Protozoa parasitic on vertebrates of Neotropics (No); "Porocephalida" of Neotropics & Nearctic (Yes)] [Escola Paulista de Medicina]

* FONSECA, Dr. Olympio, Filho. Marques de Olinda No. 18, Rio de Janeiro, Brazil. [Parasites]

da FONSECA, Jose Pinto. See PINTO da FONSECA, J.

* da FONSECA, Prof. Secundino. Museo Argentino de Ciencias Naturales, Av. Angel Gallardo 921, Buenos Aires, Argentina. [Aves]

FONTAINE, A. R. Victoria College, 3155 Richmond Road, Victoria, B. C. , Canada. [Echinodermata: Ophiuroidea of Pacific n. w. U. S. , N. Atlantic, Mediterranean (Yes)]

FONTAINE, Mme. J. 16 Quai Claude-Bernard, Lyon, France. [Ephemeroptera of France (Yes); of Madagascar (No)]

FONTAINE, Mrs. Marion. Department of Biology, Victoria College, 3155 Richmond Rd. , Victoria, B. C. , Canada. [Crustacea: Copepoda: Calanoida of n. & s. Atlantic & n. e. Pacific (Yes)]

FONTAINE, Dr. Viking. Naturhistoriska Museet, Slottsskogen, Göteborg 11, Sweden. [Aves of Scandinavia]

FOOTE, Mr. Benjamin A. Department of Entomology, Cornell University, Ithaca, N. Y. , U. S. A. [Diptera: adult & immature Sciomyzidae of N. America (Yes); Tipulidae of N. America (No)]

FOOTE, Dr. Richard H. Division of Insects, U. S. National Museum, Washington 25, D. C. , U. S. A. [Diptera: Itonididae & Otitidae of N. America (Yes), Tephritidae of New World (Yes)]

FORATTINI, Dr. O. P. Departamento de Entomologia, Universidade de São Paulo, São Paulo, Brazil. [Diptera] See Addenda.

FORBES, Dr. C. L. Sedgwick Museum, Downing Street, Cambridge, England. [Carboniferous & Permian Coelenterata & Foraminifera: Fusulinidae of World (Yes)]

FORBES, Prof. William T. M. 16 Garden Street, Cambridge 38, Mass. , U. S. A. [Lepidoptera of n. e. U. S. (Yes); of Neotropics (No)]

FORCART, Dr. Lothar. Naturhistorisches Museum, 2 Augustinergasse, Basel, Switzerland. [Gastropoda: Systellomatophora, Veronicellidae of World (No); of Africa (Yes); Styllomatophora: Vitrinidae & Zonitidae of Palearctic (Yes)]

FORCHER-MAYR, Hanns, Conservator, Natural History Museum, Via Osvaldo 77, Bolzano-Bozen, Italy. [Lepidoptera: Rhopalocera of Italy (Yes)]

FORD, Mr. E. J. , Jr. 1173 A Neal Avenue, Wahiawa, Oahu, Hawaii, U. S. A. [Coleoptera of Hawaiian Is. (Yes); Anobiidae of Pacific Is. (Yes)] [Bernice P. Bishop Museum]

FORD, Mr. L. T. 28 Park Hill Road, Bexley, Kent, England. [Microlepidoptera of England (Yes)]

FORD, Richard F. (Stanford, Calif. , Pisces). Not now active in taxonomy.

* FORD, Mr. Robert J. 3266 Ardmore Ave. , South Gate, Calif. , U. S. A. [Lepidoptera: Riodinidae, Lycaenidae, Arctiidae, Zygaenoidea, Pyraloidea]

* FORD, W. K. City of Liverpool Public Museums, Carnatic Hall, Elmswood Road, Liverpool 18, England. [Odonata of Britain (Yes)]

FOREMAN, Mrs. Helen. 131 South Professor Street, Oberlin, Ohio, U. S. A. [Devonian Radiolaria: g. Spumellina of Ohio (No)]

FOREST, Mr. Jacques. Laboratoire de Zoologie, Muséum National d'Histoire Naturelle, 61 Rue de Buffon, Paris (V), France. [Marine Decapoda: Macrura of e. Atlantic (No), Anomura (Yes); Brachyura of Indo-Pacific (No), Paguridae (Yes)]

FORMAN, McLain J. 424 Whitney Bank Bldg. , New Orleans, La. , U. S. A. [Fossil invertebrates (No)]

FORREST, J. E. Department of Zoology, Queen Mary College, Mile End Road, London, E. 1, England. [Mollusca] See Addenda.

* FORSIUS, Dr. Runar. Sampsav 22, Helsingfors-Kottby, Finland. [Hymenoptera]

FORSMAN, Mr. Bror. Styrmansgatan Y, Kalmar, Sweden. [Crustacea: Isopoda & Cumacea of Swedish Coasts (No); Amphipoda: g. Gammarus of Swedish Coasts (No); marine invertebrates of Baltic (No)] [Zoologiska Institutionen, Uppsala]

FORSSLUND, Assist. Prof. Dr. Karl H. St. Skogsforskningsinstitut, Stockholm 51, Sweden. [Acarina: Oribatei; Trichoptera; Hymenoptera: Formicidae; all of n. Europe (Yes)]

FORSTER, Miss A. Rae. (Harpenden, England; Nematoda) Not now active in taxonomy.

FORSTER, Dr. E. W. Zoologische Sammlung des Bayerischen Staates, Menzingerstrasse 67, München 38, Germany. See FORSTER, Dr. Walter.

FORSTER, G. R. Marine Biological Association Laboratory, Citadel Hill, Plymouth, England. [Porifera of British coasts (Yes)]

FÖRSTER, Dr. Horst. Andruperstrasse 122, Haselünne Kr. Meppen, Germany. [Heteroptera of Germany (No); Corixidae of Germany (Yes)]

FORSTER, Dr. R.R. Otago Museum, Dunedin, New Zealand. [Phalangida of New Zealand & Australia (Yes); Araneida of New Zealand (Yes)]

FORSTER, Dr. Walter, Direktor, Zoologische Sammlung des Bayerischen Staates, Menzinger-strasse 67, München 19, Germany. [Lepidoptera: Rhopalocera of World (Yes)]

FORSYTH, Dr. John W. Department of Biology, Texas Christian University, Fort Worth 9, Texas, U.S.A. [Amphibia & Reptilia, excl. turtles, of Texas (Yes)]

* FORT, G. Licencié ès Sciences, Laboratoire de Zoologie, Toulouse, France. [Cephalochor-
* data]

* FORTI, M.A. Livio, Entomologist, Club Alpino Italiano, Commissione Grotte, via Milano 2, Trieste, Italy. [Coleoptera & Crustacea of caves of n.e. Italy (Yes)]

FOSTER, A.O. (Beltsville, Md.; parasites) Not now active in taxonomy.

FOSTER, Glen Lloyd. Humble Oil & Refining Company, Exploration Department, 612 Barfield Building, Amarillo, Texas, U.S.A. [Near-Recent & Fossil Ostracoda (Yes)]

FOSTER, Mr. Richard W. 50 Glezen Lane, Wayland, Mass., U.S.A. [Marine Mollusca of Bermuda (Yes); Pelecypoda of W.Indies (Yes); Cephalopoda of w.N. Atlantic (No)]

FOTT, Jan. Biological Faculty, Universita Karlova, Viničná ul. 7, Praha II, Czechoslovakia. [Rotatoria: Monogononta of World (No)]

* FOUNTAIN, H.C. (Torpoint, England; Acarina) Died March 19, 1958.

FOUQUETTE, M.J., Jr. Department of Zoology, University of Texas, Austin, Texas, U.S.A. [Amphibia: Anura, espec. Hylidae, & Reptilia: Serpentes, all of Panama & s.w.U.S. (Yes)]

* FOURMANOIR, P. Institut de Recherche Scientifique, B.P. 434, Tananarive, Madagascar. [Pisces]

* FOURNIER, G. Department of Paleontology, c/o Mene Grande Oil Company, Apartado Postal 709, Caracas, Venezuela. [Tertiary Foraminifera of S. America (Yes)]

* FOURNIER, Prof. Ovila. 11385 Dorchester East., Montreal, Que., Canada. [Aquatic Insecta]

FOWLER, Mr. Henry W. Department of Fishes, Academy of Natural Sciences, Philadelphia 3, Penna., U.S.A. [Fossil & Recent Pisces of World (No)]

FOWLER, Mr. J.A. Cranbrook Institute of Science, Bloomfield Hills, Mich., U.S.A. [Amphibia: salamanders, frogs, toads, of N. America (Yes); Reptilia: snakes, lizards, turtles, of e.N.America (Yes)]

* FOWLER, T.G. Carn Eve, Sennen, near Penzance, Cornwall, England. [Mollusca]

FOX, Dr. Irving. Department of Microbiology, School of Tropical Medicine, San Juan, Puerto Rico. [Ectoparasites in general (Yes); Acarina of Neotropics (Yes); Diptera: Ceratopogonidae of Neotropics (Yes); Siphonaptera of Neotropics & Nearctic (Yes)]

* FOX, J.P. Department of Paleontology, California Ecuador Petroleum Company, Casilla 1256, Quito, Ecuador. [Fossil invertebrates]

FOX, Dr. Richard M. Department of Insects, Carnegie Museum, Pittsburg 13, Penna., U.S.A. [Lepidoptera: Ithomiidae of trop. America (Yes); Nymphaloidea & Papilionidae of World (Yes); parasitic Insecta & Vector Insecta of World (No)]

* FOX, Mr. Stephen K., Jr. Box 136, Princeton, N.J., U.S.A. [Fossil invertebrates]

FOX, Dr. Wade, Jr. Louisiana State University School of Medicine, New Orleans 12, La., U.S.A. [Reptilia & Amphibia, espec. g.Thamnophis, of N.America (Yes); Aves & Mammalia of N.America]

FRACKER, S.B. (Washington D.C.; Lepidoptera & Heteroptera) Not now active in taxonomy.

* FRADE, Prof. Dr. F. Missão Zoológica de Moçambique, c/o Almoxarifado da Fazenda, Lourenço Marques, Mozambique, Portuguese East Africa. [Arachnida, Aves, Mammalia]

FRAGA de AZEVEDO, Dr. J. Instituto de Medicina Tropical, Lisboa, Portugal. [Mollusca: f-w. snails of Portugal & trop. Africa]

FRANC, André, Sous-directeur du Laboratoire de Malacologie, Muséum National d'Histoire Naturelle, 55 rue de Buffon, Paris (V), France. [Pelagic Mollusca (Yes); Terr. & f-w. Mollusca of New Caledonia (Yes)]

FRANCESCHI, Dr. T. Istituto di Zoologia, Università di Genova, Via Balbi 5, Genova, Italy. [Tardigrada & Ciliata: g. Colpoda (Yes)]

FRANCISCOLO, Dr. M.E. c/o Museo di Storia Naturale, Via Brigata Liguria No. 9, Genova, Italy. [Coleoptera: Mordellidae of World (Yes); Haliplidae, Gyrinidae, Dytiscidae, of Palearctic (No); cave animals of Italy, France, Jugoslavia (No)]

FRANCLEMONT, John G. Department of Entomology, Cornell University, Ithaca, N.Y., U.S.A. [Lepidoptera: Noctuoidea, espec. Noctuidae, Notodontidae, Arctiidae, of New World (Yes); of Orient, Japan, Philippines, Solomon Is., New Guinea (No)]

* FRANCO, Dra. Asela B. Cebu City, Cebu, Philippines. [Mollusca]

FRANCO, Blesio. Via Musei 44, Brescia, Italy. [Coleoptera of Brescia Prov., Italy (Yes)] [Museo di Storia Naturale "G.Ragazzoni"]

FRANCOIS, Donald Davis. Department of Conservation, Cornell University, Ithaca, N.Y., U.S.A. [Crustacea: Astacidae of N. Hemisphere (Yes); Parastacidae of S. Hemisphere (Yes)]

* FRANCOISE, Dr. Yves. Laboratoire de Zoologie, Muséum National d'Histoire Naturelle, 57 rue Cuvier, Paris (V), France. [Crustacea: Copepoda]

FRANK, Dr. Fritz. Philosophenweg 16, Oldenburg i. O., Germany. [Small Mammalia of c. Europe]

* van FRANK, Mr. Richard. Department of Vertebrates, Museum of Comparative Zoology, Cambridge 38, Mass., U.S.A. [Fossil vertebrates]

FRANK, Stanislav. Department of Systematic Zoology, Charles University, Viničná 7, Praha II, Czechoslovakia. [Pisces of c. Europe (Yes)]

FRANKE, Alfred. Kolner Strasse 39, 22 (a) Remscheid-Lennep, Germany. [Acarina: Oribatidae & Trombidiidae of Germany (No)]

FRANKEL, Larry. Department of Geology, University of Connecticut, Storrs, Conn., U.S.A. [Pleistocene Gastropoda: Pulmonata of c.N. America (Yes)]

FRANKENBERGER, Prof. Dr. Zdenko. Embryologicky ustav Universitá Karlova, Albertov 4, Praha II, Czechoslovakia. [Crustacea: Isopoda: Oniscoidea of Palearctic (No)]

FRANKFORTER, Mr. Weldon D., Director, Sanford Museum, Cherokee, Iowa, U.S.A. [Pleistocene Mammalia: g. Bison of N. America (Yes)]

FRANKLIN, Mary T. Rothamsted Experimental Station, Harpenden, Herts, England. [Soil & plant-parasitic Nematoda: Tylenchida of World (Yes)]

FRANSSEN, Dr. C.J.H. Entomologisch Laboratoriu, Instituut voor Plantenziektenkunding Onderzoek, Binnenhaven No. 4a at Wageningen, Netherlands. [Thysanoptera of Netherlands (No)]

FRANTIŠEK, Prof. Krkavec. Slezský ústav ČSAV, 31 Nádražni okruh, Opava, Czechoslovakia. [Trichoptera of Czechoslovakia (Yes)]

FRANZ, Dr. Elli. Senckenbergische Naturforschende Gesellschaft, Senckenberg Anlage 25, Frankfurt am Main, Germany. [Coleoptera: Cerambycidae of World (Yes)]

FRANZ, Prof. Dr. Ing. Herbert. Institut für Geologie und Bodenkunde, Gregor Mendelstrasse 33, Vienna XVIII/110, Austria. [Acarina: Caeculidae (No); Coleoptera: Scydmaenidae & Ptiliidae of Europe & Africa (No); Curculionidae & Chrysomelidae: Cryptocephalinae & Chrysomelinae of Europe (No)]

FRANZEN, Dorothea. Illinois Wesleyan University, Bloomington, Ill., U.S.A. [Cenozoic f-w. Mollusca (No); terrestrial (Yes)]

FRASER, Dr. F.C. Department of Zoology, British Museum (Natural History), Cromwell Road, London, S.W.7, England. [Mammalia: oceanic & coastal Cetacea (Yes)]

FRASER, Lt. Col. F.C. 55 Glenferness Avenue, Bournemouth, Hants, England. [L. Permian to Recent Odonata of Old World & S. America (Yes); Recent Neuroptera of Old World (No)]

FRASER, Dr. J.H. Scottish Home Department Marine Laboratory, P.O. Box 101, Victoria Road, Torry, Aberdeen, Scotland. [Tunicata: Thaliacea of World (Yes); Chaetognatha & Siphonophora of n.e. Atlantic (Yes); marine pelagic Copepoda & marine zooplankton of n.e. Atlantic (No)]

* FRASER-BRUNNER, A. 11 Bushwood Road, Kew, Surrey, England. [Pisces of Indo-Pacific (Yes); Plectognathi of trop. & temp. seas (Yes); g. Barbus of Asia & Africa (Yes)]

* FRAUNFELTER, George. Department of Paleontology, Creole Petroleum Corporation, Apartado 172, Maracaibo, Venezuela. [Fossil invertebrates]

FRAYNE, Dr. Nathaniel Z. 2768 Hudson Blvd., Jersey City 6, N.J., U.S.A. [Trematoda, "Choricotyle", of e. cst.U.S. (Yes)]

FRAZIER, C.W. 178 Marsh Street, Armidale, N.S.W., Australia. [Rhopalocera of Australia (Yes); Heterocera: g. Geometroidea of Australia (Yes)]

FREBOLD, Dr. Hans. Geological Survey of Canada, Department of Mines & Technical Surveys, Ottawa, Ont., Canada. [Jurassic to L. Cretaceous Ammonites of N. America, n. Europe, Arctic Regions (Yes); L. Jurassic of World (Yes)]

FRECHKOP, Serge, Directeur de Laboratoire, Institut Royal des Sciences Naturelle de Belgique, 31 Rue Vautier, Bruxelles, Belgium. [Mammalia of Europe & Africa (No)]

FREDERICKSON, Prof. E.A. School of Geology, University of Oklahoma, Norman, Okla., U.S.A. [Cambrian Trilobita of New World (Yes)]

FREEBORN, Dr. S.B. Department of Entomology, University of California, Davis, Calif., U.S.A. [Diptera: Culicidae of Nearctic] Died July 17, 1960.

FREEDMAN, L. Department of Anatomy, Medical School, University of the Witwatersrand, Hospital Street, Johannesburg, Union of South Africa. [Plio-pleistocene Cercopithecoidea, espec. Cercopithecinae, of Africa (Yes)]

FREELAND, Mr. J. 19 Central Avenue, Como, N.S.W., Australia. [Hymenoptera: Formicidae: g. Myrmecia of New South Wales (Yes)]

FREEMAN, Hugh Avery. 1605 Lewis Drive, Garland, Texas, U.S.A. [Lepidoptera: Hesperioidea, espec. Megathymidae, of N. America & Mexico (Yes); Theclinae of U.S. & Canada (Yes)]

FREEMAN, Harley L. 353 South Atlantic Avenue, Ormond Beach, Fla., U.S.A. [Mollusca of w. Atlantic & Gulf of Mexico]

FREEMAN, Prof. Harry W. 3006 Dennis Drive, Columbia, S.C., U.S.A. [Pisces, Amphibia, Reptilia, of s.e.U.S. (Yes)]

FREEMAN, Mr. Paul. Department of Entomology, British Museum (Natural History), Cromwell Road, London, S.W.7, England. [Diptera: Chironomidae of World, excl. N. America (Yes)]

FREEMAN, Mr. R.B. Department of Zoology, University College, Gower Street, London, W.C.1, England. [Siphonaptera of Old World (Yes)]

FREEMAN, Dr. Reino S. Ontario Research Foundation, 43 Queens Park, Toronto 5, Ont., Canada. [Cestoda: Cyclophyllidea: Taeniidae & Anoplocephalidae of N. America (Yes)]

FREEMAN, Dr. T.N. Insect Systematics & Biological Control Unit, Division of Entomology, Science Service Building, Ottawa, Ont., Canada. [Lepidoptera: Arctic butterflies of Canada (Yes); Microlepidoptera of Canada (Yes)]

FREIBERG, Prof. Marcos A. Calle Ghigliazza 166, José C. Paz, (B.A.), Argentina. [Reptilia: turtles & caymans of Argentina] [Ministerio de Agricultura y Ganaderia]

FREIRE-MAIA, Prof. N. Universidade de Paraná, Faculdade de Filosofia, Laboratorio de Genetica, Curitiba, Paraná, Brazil. [Diptera: Drosophila, "domestic species" of Brazil (Yes)]

de FREITAS, Dr. J.F. Teixeira. Instituto Oswaldo Cruz, Laboratorio de Helmintologia, Caixa Postal 926, Rio de Janeiro, Brazil. [Nematoda of Vertebrates of S. America (Yes); parasitic Trematoda of S. America (Yes)]

* FRENCH, R.A. Rothamsted Experimental Station, Harpenden, Herts, England. [Odonata]

* FRETTER, Dr. V. Department of Malacology, The University, Reading, England. [Mollusca]

FREUDE, Heinz. Konservator, Zoologische Sammlung des Bayerischen Staates, Entomologische Abteilung, Menzingerstrasse 67, München 38, Germany. [Coleoptera: Monommidae of World (Yes); Tenebrionidae of S. America (Yes); Meloidae of World (No)]

FREY, Dr. David G. Jordan Hall, Indiana University, Bloomington, Ind., U.S.A. [Pleistocene to Recent Cladocera in lake & bog sediments of Europe & N. America (Yes); Chydoridae of Europe & N. America (Yes); Decapoda: Atyidae & Palaemonidae of Indo-Pacific (No)]

FREY, Mr. Georg. Osterwaldstrasse 60a, München 23, Germany. [Coleoptera; Scarabaeidae: Onthophagini & Onitini of World, excl. Australia & Oceania (Yes)] [Museum G. Frey]

FREYTAG, Günther E. Chausseestrasse 116, Berlin N.4, German Democratic Republic. [Amphibia: Urodela of America, Europe, Asia (Yes); Anura of World (No), of Europe & Asia (Yes); Gymnophiona of World (No)]

FRIAUF, Dr. James J. Department of Zoology, Vanderbilt University, Nashville 4, Tenn., U.S.A. [Orthoptera of s.e.U.S. (Yes); Polyphagine roaches of s.w.U.S. & Mexico (Yes); Gastrotricha of coastal U.S. (No)]

* FRICH, Dr. H. Ludwig Rehnstrasse 16, Frankfurt am Main, Germany. [Mammalia]

* FRICK, Dr. Childs. Roslyn, N.Y., U.S.A. [Mammalia]

FRICK, Dr. Kenneth E. Irrigation Experiment Station, Prosser, Wash., U.S.A. [Diptera: Agromyzidae of N. America, Micronesia, Hawaii (Yes)]

FRICKE, Mr. F.T. 36 Ruthven Street, Bondi Junction, Sydney, Australia. [Coleoptera of Australia (No); Tenebrionidae: g. Cardiothorax of e. Australia (Yes)]

* FRIDRIKSSON, Arni. The University Research Institute, Fishery Department, Reykjavik, Iceland. [Pisces]

FRIEDMANN, Dr. Herbert. Division of Birds, U.S. National Museum, Washington 25, D.C., U.S.A. [Aves of World (Yes)]

FRIEDRICH, Prof. Dr. H. Institut für Meeresforschung, Am Handelshafen 12, Bremerhaven, Germany. [Nemertinea of World, espec. Northern Seas (Yes)]

FRIEDRICH, Dr. Hans. Schneckenburgerstrasse 15/I, München 8, Germany. [Terr., f-w., marine Mollusca of World (Yes)]

FRIEND, Mr. G.F. Department of Zoology, University of Edinburgh, Edinburgh 9, Scotland. [Pisces: Salmonidae, espec. Charr, of Europe (Yes); Crustacea: parasitic Copepoda: Lernaeopodidae of Salmonidae of World (Yes)]

* FRIEND, Dr. R.B. Connecticut Agricultural Experiment Station, 123 Huntington Street, New Haven, Conn., U.S.A. [Diptera]

FRIESE, Dipl.-Biol. Gerrit. Deutches Entomologisches Institut, Waldowstrasse 1, Berlin-Friedrichshagen, German Democratic Republic. [Lepidoptera: Hyponomeutidae of Palearctic (Yes); Rhopalocera of Europe (Yes)]

FRIESER, Robert. Maximilianstrasse 7, Starnberg, Germany. [Coleoptera: Anthribidae of World (Yes), Curculionidae of Europe (Yes)]

FRITCHMAN, Dr. Harry. Boise Junior College, Boise, Idaho, U.S.A. [Gastropoda: Acmaeidae of Pacific Cst. of Alaska & U.S. (Yes)]

* FRITH, H.J. Wildlife Survey Section, Commonwealth Scientific & Industrial Research Organization, P.O. Box 109, Canberra, Australia. [Aves]

FRITZ, Prof. Madeleine A. Department of Geological Sciences, University of Toronto, 388 Brunswick Avenue, Toronto, Ont., Canada. [Paleozoic Bryozoa & Anthozoa of N. America (Yes); Paleozoic Stromatoporoidea of N. America (No)]

FRITZ, Manfredo A. Casilla de Correo 2607, Buenos Aires, Argentina. [Hymenoptera: Sphe-
cidae: Bembicini, Nyssonini & Heliocausini of Neotropics (Yes); Bembicini of Nearctic
(Yes)]
FRIZZELL, Dr. Don L. 6 Rolla Gardens, Rolla, Mo., U.S.A. [Fossil & Recent Foramini-
fera, excl. Fusulinidae, of World (No); Fossil Holothurian sclerites of World (Yes);
Fossil Fish otoliths of New World (No)]
FRIZZELL, Dr. Harriet E. (Mrs. D. L.; also as EXLINE, H.). 6 Rolla Gardens, Rolla, Mo.,
U.S.A. [Araneida of New World (No); Fossil Holothurian sclerites (No); Micro-
fossils (No)]
FRIZZI, Prof. Istituto Spallanzani, Palazzo Botta, Pavia, Italy. [Diptera: Nematocera of
Europe (Yes); Culicidae: g. Anopheles of N. America (Yes)]
FROEHLICH, Dr. Claudio G. Caixa Postal 6994, São Paulo, Brazil. [Turbellaria: Tricladida
terricola of World (Yes)]
FROEHLICH, Dra. Eudoxia Maria. Departmento de Zoologia, Caixa Postal 6994, São Paulo,
Brazil. [Turbellaria: Tricladida terricola of World (Yes)]
FROESCHNER, Dr. Richard C. Department of Zoology, Montana State College, Bozeman,
Mont., U.S.A. [Hemiptera of N. America (Yes): Cydnidae of World (Yes); Neuroptera
of N. America (No); Homoptera: Auchenorhyncha of N. America (No)]
FROITZHEIM, Rev. J. Sonderfeld 85, Essen-Überruhr, Germany. [Lepidoptera: Pieridae of
Palearctic (No)]
FROMMHOLD, Zoodirektor E. Tierpark Cottbus, Wichernstrasse 7, Radebeul 1, Dresden,
German Democratic Republic. [Amphibia: Salientia; Reptilia: Squamata; both of
Europe (Yes)]
FROST, C. A. 67 Henry Street, Framingham, Mass., U.S.A. [Coleoptera of N. America (Yes)]
* FROST, G. Allen. Address unknown. (Pisces)
FROST, Dr. S.W. 465 E. Foster Avenue, State College, Penna., U.S.A. [Diptera: Agro-
myzidae of N. America (Yes)] [Pennsylvania State University]
* FROTA-PESSOA, Dr. O. Address unknown. [Diptera]
FRUM, W. Gene. 311 Holswade Drive, Huntington, W. Va., U.S.A. [Mammalia of West
Virginia (Yes); g. Myotis of N. America (Yes)]
FRYDENBERG, Dr. Ove. Institute of Genetics, Institute of Biology, Farimagsgade, Køben-
havn, Denmark. [Diptera: Drosophila of Europe (Yes), of S. America (No)]
FRYER, Dr. G. East African Fisheries Research Organization, P. O. Box 343, Jinja, Uganda.
[Crustacea: f-l., f-w. Cyclopoida & Harpacticoida of Britain & Africa (Yes); f-w. para-
sitic Copepoda of World, espec. Africa (Yes); f-w. Branchiura of World, espec. Africa
(Yes)]
FUCHS, Dipl. Ernest. Weimarerstrasse 4, Vienna 18, Austria. [Coleoptera: Cerambycidae
of Palearctic, Neotropics, Oriental, Ethiopian (Yes), of Nearctic & Australian (No)]
FUDAKOWSKI, Dr. Józef. Instytut Zoologiczny, Polska Akademia Nauk, ul. Sławkowska 17,
Krakow, Poland. [Larvae of Odonata, espec. Agrionica & Calopterygidae of Palearctic
(Yes)] [Jagiellonian University]
* FUGLER, Charles M. Department of Biology, Agricultural & Mechanical College of Texas,
College Station, Texas, U.S.A. [Mammalia of Neotropics]
FUHN, I. E. Academia R. P. R., Centrul de Cercetari Biologice, Laboratorul de Sistematică,
Splaiul Independentei 93, Bucureşti, Rumania. [Amphibia & Reptilia of Europe, N.
Africa, Near East (Yes)]
FUJIE, Tsutomu. Department of Geology & Mineralogy, Hokkaido University, Sapporo, Japan.
[Tertiary-Recent marine Gastropoda & Pelecypoda of n. Japan (Yes)]
FUJIMOTO, Prof. Haruyoshi. Department of Geology, Faculty of Education, University of
Yamagata, Yamagata Pref., Japan. [Paleozoic Foraminifera: Fusulinidae of Japan
& e. Asia (Yes); Paleozoic Anthozoa: Rugosa & Tabulata of Japan & e. Asia (Yes)]
FUJIMURA, T. Shimane Agricultural Experiment Station, Izumo City, Shimane Prefecture,
Japan. [Coleoptera: Cerambycidae of Japan (Yes), of s. e. Asia (No)]
FUJINO, Mr. Kazuo. Whales Research Institute, 4, 12 Chome, Nishigashi-Dori, Tsukishima,
Chuo-ku, Tokyo, Japan. [Mammalia: Cetacea: Pinnipedia of n. Pacific, Atlantic &
Antarctic (Yes)]
FUJITA, Mr. Shiro. Moji Municipal Aquarium, Kyu-Moji 5, Moji City, Fukuoka Pref., Japan.
[Pisces: Tetraodontidae of Japan, incl. immature stages (Yes); Scales of Teleostomi of
Japan (No)] [Kyushu University]
* FUKUHARA, Mr. N. Laboratory of Insect Identification, National Institute of Agricultural
Sciences, Nishigahara, Tokyo, Japan. [Diptera: Dolichopodidae]
FUKUI, Mr. T. Biological Institute, Yokohama Municipal University, Mutsuara, Kanazawa-Ku,
Yokohama, Japan. [Acanthocephala & Trematoda: Digenea: Paramphistomatidae; of
Japan (Yes)]
* FUKUZUMI, Dr. Sadakichi. Kitasato Institute for Infectious Diseases, 138 Shiba-Shirokane-
Sanko-chô, Minato-ku, Tokyo, Japan. [Acarina: Trombiculidae]
* FULLAWAY, Mr. D. T. Territorial Board of Agriculture, P. O. Box 5425, Pawaa Substation,
Honolulu, Hawaii, U.S.A. [Hymenoptera]

FULLER, Mr. Tom C. 1247 S. Floyd Street, Louisville 3, Ky., U.S.A. [Reptilia: Serpentes: g. Pituophis of Kentucky (Yes)]
FULLER, Henry S. Department of Rickettsial Diseases, Walter Reed Army Institute of Research, Washington 12, D.C., U.S.A. [Acarina: Parasitic mites of Vertebrates of World (No)]
FULLER, Dr. W.A. Canadian Wildlife Service, P.O. Box 2357, Whitehorse, Yukon Territory, Canada. [Mammalia of Yukon & N.W. Terr., Canada (No)]
FULMER, Charles V. c/o Standard Oil Company, Room 250, 557 Roy Street, Seattle 9, Wash., U.S.A. [Tertiary calcareous Foraminifera of California, Oregon, Washington (Yes)]
* FULNEK, Dr. Leopold. Mariengasse 48, Wien-Mauer, Austria. [Hymenoptera]
* FULTON, Dr. Bentley Ball. Department of Entomology, North Carolina State College, Raleigh, N.C., U.S.A. [Orthoptera: Gryllidae of U.S.]
FUNKHOUSER, Anne. Life Sciences Department, University of Tulsa, Tulsa, Okla., U.S.A. [Amphibia: Hylidae: g. Phyllomedusa (Agalychnis) of trop. America (Yes)]
FUNNELL, Mr. B.M. Sedgwick Museum, Cambridge, England. [Pleistocene Foraminifera of North Sea Basin (Yes)]
FURGASON, Dr. Waldo H. Department of Zoology, University of California, Los Angeles 24, Calif., U.S.A. [Holotrichous f-w. Ciliata, espec. Tetrahymenidae (Yes)]
FURMAGA, Dr. Stefan. Zakład Parazytologii, Wyzsza Szkoła Rolnicza, ul. Akademicka 11, Lublin, Poland. [Helminths of rodents, helminths of birds of prey, Nematoda: g. Setaria of horses; all of Poland (Yes)]
FURMAN, Dr. Deane P. Department of Entomology & Parasitology, University of California, Berkeley 4, Calif., U.S.A. [Acarina: parasitic Mesostigmata of Nearctic & Neotropics (Yes)]
FURNESTIN, Mme. M-L. Institut Scientifique et Technique des Pêches Maritimes, 59 av. Raymond Poincaré, Paris (XVI), France. [Chaetognatha of e. Atlantic (N. & S.) & Mediterranean (Yes)]
* FURNESTIN, Dr. J., Directeur, Institut des Pêches Maritimes du Maroc, Casablanca, Morocco. [Pisces: Clupeidae]
FURNISH, Prof. W.M. Department of Geology, State University of Iowa, Iowa City, Iowa, U.S.A. [Up. Paleozoic to Cretaceous Ammonoidea & L. Paleozoic Conodonts (Yes)]
FÜRSCH, H. Dachauerstrasse 425, München 54, Germany. [Coleoptera: Coccinellidae of World (No), of Palearctic & Africa (Yes)]
* FURUKAWA, Haruo. Biological Laboratory, Tokyo Gakugei University, Setagaya College, Tokyo, Japan. [Orthoptera: Hymenoptera: Formicidae]
FUST, Bernh. Rellinghauserstrasse 246, Essen, Germany. [Lepidoptera: Noctuidae of Europe (Yes); Microlepidoptera (No)]
FYFE, Marian. Department of Zoology, University of Otago, The Museum, King Street, Dunedin, New Zealand. [Turbellaria: terr. Planaria of New Zealand & Australia (Yes)]

* GABALDON, Dr. Arnoldo. Division de Malariologia, Ministeria de Sanidad y Asistencia Social, Maracay, Aragua, Venezuela. [Diptera]
* GABÉ, Dr. M. Laboratoire d'Anatomie Comparée, Sorbonne, 1 rue Victor Cousin, Paris (V), France. [Arachnida]
GÁBOR, Jenser. Tudományos Munkatárs, Természettudományi Muzeum Allattár, Baross u. 13, Budapest VIII, Hungary. [Thysanoptera of Hungary (Yes)]
GABRIEL, Mr. A.G. Department of Entomology, British Museum (Natural History), Cromwell Road, London, S.W.7, England. [Lepidoptera: Rhopalocera of Africa, Indo-Australia, S. America (No)]
* GABRIEL, Mr. C.J. 9 Glen Road, Toorak, Vict., Australia. [Mollusca]
GABRIELSON, Dr. Ira N. 709 Wire Building, Washington 5, D.C., U.S.A. [Aves of N. America, espec. Alaska (Yes)] [Wildlife Management Institute]
* GABUNIA, I.K. Paleontological Laboratory, Academy of Science, Tbilisi, U.S.S.R. [Fossil Mammalia]
* GADEA, Dr. E. Consejo Superior de Investigaciones Cientificas, Instituto de Biologia Aplicada, Universidad de Barcelona, Barcelona, Spain. [Nematoda]
* GADJIEV, D.V. Museum of Natural History, Academy of Science of the Azerbaijan SSR, Schaumjan Str. 9, Baku, U.S.S.R. [Fossil Mammalia]
* GAGARIN, V.G. Zoological Institute, Academy of Sciences of the Kirghiz SSR, Dzerjinskaja Street 38, Frunze, U.S.S.R. [Helminths of animals of U.S.S.R.]
* de GAHAN, Prof. Angelina Chiarelli. Facultad de Ciencias, Universidad de Buenos Aires, Calle Viamonte 444, Buenos Aires, Argentina. [Lepidoptera]
* GAILLARD, F.J. 5 cité du Midi, Paris (XVIII), France. [Coleoptera & Lepidoptera]
GAILLARD, Mr. Jean M., Assistant, Laboratoire de Malacologie, Museum National d'Histoire Naturelle, 55 rue de Buffon, Paris (V), France. [Mollusca: Cerithiidae (Yes)]
GAISLER, Jiři, Prom. biolog., Vertebratological Laboratories, Czechoslovak Academy of Sciences, Plotni 25a, Brno, Czechoslovakia. [Mammalia: Chiroptera: Microchiroptera of Europe (Yes)]

GAJ, A. J. Warszawska 14/5, Krakow 2, Poland. [Lepidoptera: Pterophoridae of Palearctic (No), of Europe (Yes)]

GAJEVSKAJA, Prof. Dr. N. S. Katedra Hydrobiologii, Institute Rybnoj Promislennosti i Hozjajstva, Moscow A-8, U. S. S. R. [F-w. Ciliata & Suctoria (Yes), Marine (No)]

GALBRAITH, Mr. I. C. J. British Museum (Natural History) Cromwell Road, London, S. W. 7, England. [[Resident non-marine Aves of n. Melanesia (Yes); Cephalopoda (No)]

GALBREATH, Dr. Edwin C. Department of Zoology, Southern Illinois University, Carbondale, Ill., U. S. A. [Oligocene & Miocene Rodents (Yes)]

GALE, Hoyt Rodney. 1775 Hill Drive, Eagle Rock, Los Angeles 41, Calif., U. S. A. [Pliocene & Pleistocene Mollusca of California (Yes)]

GALEWSKI, Mgr. Kazimiers. Institut Zoologiczny, ul. Wilcza 64, Warszawa, Poland. [Coleoptera: immature & adult Dytiscidae of Europe (Yes)]

GALINDO, Pedro. Gorgas Memorial Laboratory, Apartado 1252, Panama, Rep. Panama. [Diptera: Culicidae of Neotropics (Yes)]

* GALKIN, U. I. Murman Marine Biological Institute, Academy of Sciences of the U. S. S. R., Dalnie Zelentsy, Murman Region, U. S. S. R. [Gastropoda]

GALLAGHER, Dr. John J. 1716 E. Terry St., Pocatello, Idaho, U. S. A. [Rotifera of World (Yes)]

* GALLEGO BERENGUER, Dr. G. Laboratoria de Parasitologia Animal, Faculdad de Farmacia, Ciudad Universitaria, Madrid, Spain. [Nematoda]

* GALLIARD, Prof. Dr. H. L. Faculté de Médicine, 15 rue de l'Ecole de Medicine, Paris, France. [Diptera: Culicidae]

GALLIFORD, Mr. A. L. Portinscale, 46 Trevor Drive, Crosby, Liverpool 23, England. [Rotifera of World (Yes); Crustacea: Cladocera of British Isles (Yes)]

GALLINGANI, Dr. Maria Grasia. (Genova, Italy; Copepoda) Not now active in taxonomy.

GALLITELLI, Dr. E. Montanaro. Istituto de Paleontologia, Università di Modena, Modena, Italy. [Paleozoic-Tertiary Coelenterata of Mediterranean & Red Sea; Miocene-Pliocene Gastropoda of Mediterranean; Secondary-Quaternary micro-Foraminifera of Mediterranean]

GALLIVANONE, Rag. Franco M. Piazza S. S. Pietro e Lino 4, Milano 119, Italy. [Lepidoptera: Rhopalocera: Papilionidae, Pieridae, Nymphalidae, Lycaenidae of Italy (Yes), Sphingidae & Saturnidae of Italy (Yes), Hesperidae & Zygaenidae of Italy (No), Saturnidae of Europe & Asia (No); Coleoptera: Lucanidae & Cerambycidae of Italy (Yes), Scarabaeidae, Carabidae, Meloidea, of Italy (No)]

GALLOCHER, R. P. 1 Place de l'Archange, Marseille (V), France. [Mammalia: Chiroptera of s. e. France (Yes)]

GALLOWAY, Dr. J. J. Department of Geology, Indiana University, Bloomington, Ind., U. S. A. [Ordovician-Devonian Stromatoporoidea of World (Yes); Mississippian Blastoidea: g. Pentremites of America (Yes); Ordovician Bryozoa of World (Yes); Ordovician-Recent Foraminifera of World (Yes)]

GALVAGNI, Dr. Antonio. Corso Rosmini 54, Rovereto, Trento, Italy. [Orthoptera & Dermaptera of Europe (Yes)]

da GAMA, Dr. Maria Manuela. Museu e Laboratorio Zoologico, Universidad de Coimbra, Coimbra, Portugal. [Mammalia of Iberian Pen. (Yes)]

GAMULIN, Dr. Tomo, Director, Institut Biologique, P. p. 17, Dubrovnik, Yugoslavia. [Hydrozoa: Siphonophora; Chaetognatha; Crustacea: Copepoda; all of Adriatic Sea (Yes)]

* GANDARA, A. F. Address unknown. (Diptera)

* GANDERT, Dr. O. F. Museum für Vor- & Fruhgeschichte, Stresemannstrasse 110, Berlin SW, Germany. [Domestic Mammalia]

* GANGER, David. Sohio Petroleum Company, Adams Petroleum Company Building, Houston, Texas, U. S. A. [Fossil invertebrates]

GANGWERE, Dr. S. K. Biology Department, Wayne State University, Detroit 2, Mich., U. S. A. [Orthoptera & Dermaptera of c. U. S. (No)]

GANS, Carl. Department of Biology, University of Buffalo, Buffalo 14, N. Y., U. S. A. [Amphibia & Reptilia (No); Uropeltidae, Amphisbaenidae, Dasypeltidae (Yes)]

GANTES, Mlle. Hélène. Institut Scientifique Cherifien, Avenue Biarney, Rabat, Morocco. [Gastropoda: Opisthobranchiata of Atlantic cst. of Morocco (No)]

* GARAPATI, Mr. 95 Poonamak High Road, Kilpank, Madras 10, India. [Protozoa]

* GARCIA, Dr. Miguel. Instituto de Entomologia Sanitaria, Av. Parral 652, Buenos Aires, Argentina. [Diptera] Mail returned unclaimed from above address.

* GARCIA-DIAZ, Dr. Julio. Department of Entomology, University of Puerto Rico, Rio Piedras, Puerto Rico. [Odonata]

GARDINER, B. G. Queen Elizabeth College, London W. 8, England. [Up. Triassic-M. Jurassic Pisces of Europe (Yes)]

GARDINER, Brian O. C. Entomology Field Station, 34A Storeys Way, Cambridge, England. [Lepidoptera: Arctiidae, Plusiidae, Lymantridae, Pyralidae, of British Isles (Yes), Caradrinidae (No)]

* GARDINER, Mrs. Frances P. Address unknown. [Lepidoptera]

GARDNER, Mr. A. E. 29 Glenfield Road, Banstead, Surrey, England. [Odonata of World (Yes), immature stages, of Europe (Yes)]
* GARDNER, Julia. U. S. Geological Survey, U. S. National Museum, Washington 25, D. C. [Tertiary Mollusca of s. Atlantic & Gulf Cst. (Yes)]
GARDNER, Norman W. 4 Kauri Glen Road, Birkenhead, Auckland, New Zealand. [Terrestrial Mollusca of New Zealand (Yes); Gastropoda: Volutidae of World (No), of New Zealand (Yes); g. Placostylus of s. w. Pacific (Yes)]
* GAREVSKI, R., Kustos, Prirodonaučen Musej, Orce Nikolov 11, Skopje, Yugoslavia. [Fossil Mammalia]
GARMAN, Philip. The Connecticut Agriculture Experiment Station, New Haven, Conn., U. S. A. [Acarina: Tetranychidae & Phytoseiinae of n. e. U. S. (No); Odonata of n. e. U. S. (No)]
GARMON, Mr. George. Sun Oil Company, Box 1270, McAllen, Texas, U. S. A. [Tertiary Foraminifera of Texas Gulf Coast (No)]
GARNAUD, Dr. J. Institut Océanographique, Musée de Monaco, Monaco. [Pisces: Percomorphi & Pharyngognathi of Mediterranean & Indo-Australian Arch. (No)]
GARNER, W. E. 20 Vincent Road, Highams Park, London, E. 4, England. [Rotatoria of British Isles (Yes)]
GARNER, Dr. William V. Department of Biology, Monmouth College, West Long Branch, N. J., U. S. A. [Larval Coleoptera, espec. Carabidae, of N. America (Yes); Plecoptera naiads of N. America (Yes)]
GARNHAM, P. C. C. London School of Hygiene & Tropical Medicine, University of London, Gower Street, London, W. C. 1, England. [Sporozoa: Haemosporidia of World (Yes)]
GAROIAN, Dr. George. Department of Zoology, Southern Illinois University, Carbondale, Ill., U. S. A. [Cestoda: Dibothriocephalidae: g. Schistocephalus of N. America (Yes)]
GARRETT, Mr. C. B. D. P. O. Box 8, Horseshoe Bay, Canada. [Diptera: Fungivoridae, Helomyzidae & Dixidae of N. America (Yes)]
GARRETT, J. B., Jr. Pan American Petroleum Corporation, P. O. Box 3092, Houston 1, Texas, U. S. A. [Cenozoic smaller Foraminifera of Gulf Coast U. S. (No)]
GARRICK, Mr. J. A. F. Department of Zoology, Victoria University College, P. O. Box 196, Wellington, New Zealand. [Pisces: Elasmobranchii & Teleostei of S. Pacific, espec. New Zealand (Yes)]
GARRISS, Mr. Howard R. North Carolina State College, P. O. Box 5397, State College Station, Raleigh, N. C., U. S. A. [Nematoda: Tylenchoidea of New World (Yes)]
GARTH, John S. Allan Hancock Foundation, University of Southern California, Los Angeles 7, Calif., U. S. A. [Decapoda: Brachyura of e. Pacific (Yes), of w. Pacific (No); Lepidoptera: Rhopalocera of s. w. U. S. (Yes), Tropical America (No); Diptera: Culicidae of N. America (No)]
GARUTT, W. E. Zoological Institut, Academy of Sciences, Leningrad 164, U. S. S. R. [Fossil Proboscidea (Yes)]
GASOWSKA, Dr. Matylda. Instytut Zoologiczny, Polska Akademia Nauk, ul. Wilcza 64, Warszawa, Poland. [F-w. Pisces of Europe; Coregoninae & Cyprinidae of Europe (Yes)]
* GASULL, L. Via Augusta 65-5, Barcelona, Spain. [Crustacea]
GATES, Dr. G. E. 251 Silver Road, Bangor, Maine, U. S. A. [Oligochaeta of World, excl. Africa & S. America (Yes)]
GAUD, Dr. Jean. Institut d'Hygiene du Maroc, B. P. 769R, Rabat, Morocco. [Acarina: Sarcoptiformes: Analgesoidea of World (No), of Europe & Africa (Yes)]
GAUFIN, A. R. Department of Zoology, University of Utah, Salt Lake City, Utah, U. S. A. [Plecoptera of N. America (Yes)]
GAULD, Dr. D. T. Department of Zoology, University College of Ghana, Achimota, Ghana. [Crustacea: marine planktonic Calanoida of Gulf of Guinea & British Waters (No)]
* GAUMONT, R. L. Institut National Agronomique, 16 rue Claude-Bernard, Paris (V), France. [Insecta: Endopterygota]
GAUN, Sven E., Veterinary, Stoholm (Jylland), Denmark. [Hemiptera of Denmark]
* GAUNITZ, Sven. Vadsbrogatan 14, Töreboda, Sweden. [Odonata]
GAUTHIER, Henri. Villa Les Strelitzias, 16 avenue Lyautey, Ancien Golf La Redoute, Alger, Algeria. [Crustacea: Branchiopoda, Ostracoda, Copepoda, of Continental Waters (No)]
* GAUTHIER-LIEVRE, Mme. L. Laboratoire de Botanique, Faculté des Sciences, Alger, Algeria. [Sarcodina: Thecamoeba]
GAUTIER, Dr. Yves. Laboratoire de Biologie Animale, Faculté des Sciences, Marseille, France. [Tertiary & Quaternary Bryozoa: Gymnolaemata of s. Europe & n. Africa ("Tethys") (Yes); Recent Gymnolaemata of Mediterranean (Yes)]
GAVALA, Juan. Goya 6, Madrid, Spain. [Marine Lamellibranchiata & Gastropoda of World (Yes); g. Cypraea of World (Yes)]
* GAVIO, Prof. Hector S. Medrano 1922, Buenos Aires, Argentina. [Aves]
GAVRILOV, Dr. Konstantin. Instituto Miguel Lillo, Calle Miguel Lillo 205, Tucumán, Argentina. [Oligochaeta] [Universidad Nacional de Tucumán]
GAY, Mr. F. J. Division of Entomology, Commonwealth Scientific & Industrial Research Or-

ganization, P. O. Box 109, Canberra, A. C. T., Australia. [Isoptera of Australia (Yes), of New Guinea & Pacific Is. (No)]

GAZIN, Dr. C. L. Division of Vertebrate Paleontology, U. S. National Museum, Washington 25, D. C., U. S. A. [Cenozoic Mammalia, espec. Eocene & Paleocene (Yes)]

GEARY, Major John M., U. S. A. F., Office of the Surgeon, Hq. U. S. Air Forces, Europe, APO 633, New York, N. Y., U. S. A. [Siphonaptera of New York State (Yes)]

* GEBHARDT, Dr. Erwin. Meisterleinplatz 5, Nurnberg, Germany. [Aves]

GEDYE, A. F. J. Coryndon Museum, P. O. Box 7342, Nairobi, Kenya. [Coleoptera, espec. Cetoniinae, of Africa (Yes)]

GEHLBACH, Frederick R. 2706 Tremont Road, Columbus 21, Ohio. [Amphibia & Reptilia of s. w. U. S. & Mexican plateau (Yes); opisthoglyph snakes, espec. g. Trimorphodon & g. Oxybelis of New World (Yes)]

GEHRINGER, Mr. Jack W. U. S. Fish & Wildlife Service, Bureau of Commercial Fisheries, Biological Laboratory, P. O. Box 283, Brunswick, Ga., U. S. A. [Larval & adult marine Pisces: Elopidae, Megalopidae, Albulidae, Synodontidae; larval & immature Istiophoridae & Xiphiidae; all of w. N. Atlantic Ocean (Yes)]

* GEHWEILER, Mr. William J. Zoology Department, North Carolina State College, Raleigh, N. C., U. S. A. [Odonata; f-w. Oligochaeta]

* GEIER, Dr. P. Muséum d'Histoire Naturelle, Ville de Genève, Switzerland. [Hemiptera]

GEIJSKES, Dr. D. C. P. O. Box 306, Paramaribo, Surinam. [Odonata & Plecoptera of Guyanas (Yes); Acarina: Tetranychidae, of Guyanas (No)] [Surinaams Museum]

* GEISLER, Dr. Rolf. Lerchenstrasse 40, Freiburg, Germany. [Pisces]

* GIEST, Otto William. Department of Paleontology, University of Alaska, College, Alaska, U. S. A. [Fossil Mammalia]

* von GELEI, Prof. G. Zoologisches Institut, Luisenstrasse 14, München 2, Germany. [Protozoa]

GELLÉRT, Dr. József. Magyar Tudományos Akadémia, Biológiai Kutatóintézete, Tihany, Hungary. [Protozoa: Ciliata of Hungary (Balaton Sea) (Yes)]

GEMEROY, Dr. D. G. Department of Zoology, Rutgers University, New Brunswick, N. J., U. S. A. [Blood sera of Pisces & Mammalia (Yes)]

GEMIGNANI, E. V. Deceased.

GEMMELL, Alexander. "Braemar", P. O. Box 53, Glen Alpin, Queensland, Australia. [Coleoptera: Buprestidae: g. Stigmodera of Australia (Yes); Buprestidae, Cetonidae, Rutelidae of World (No)]

GENTILE, Mr. Joseph. Address unknown. (Insectivora, Chiroptera, Rodentia of Maryland)

GENTNER, Dr. Louis G. Southern Oregon Branch Experiment Station, 5595 Pacific Highway S., Medford, Ore., U. S. A. [Coleoptera: Chrysomelidae: Alticinae of N. America (Yes)]

GENTRY, Dr. Glenn. Tennessee Game & Fish Commission, 212 Cordell Hull Building, Nashville, Tenn., U. S. A. [Amphibia & Reptilia of Tennessee (Yes)]

GENUNG, Mr. William. P. O. Box 37, Belle Glade, Fla., U. S. A. [Coleoptera: Cerambycidae of Florida (Yes); Locustidae, excl. Melanopli of Florida (No), Oedipodinae & Tryxalinae of Florida (Yes)] [Everglades Experiment Station, University of Florida]

* GEORGE, Dr. J. C. Department of Zoology, University of Baroda, Baroda (Bombay), India. [Reptilia]

GEORGE, Mr. R. S. 1 Podsmead Place, Gloucester, England. [Siphonaptera of World (No), of Europe (Yes)]

GEORGE, Dr. R. W. Western Australian Museum, Perth, W. Australia. [Marine Crustacea of n., w., s. coasts of Australia & Indian Ocean (Yes); Crustacea: adult & larval Palinuridae of World (Yes)]

GEORGE, Prof. T. Neville. Department of Geology, The University, Glasgow W 2, Scotland. [Up. Paleozoic Brachiopoda: g. Spirifer (Yes)]

GEORGEVICH, Prof. Jivoin. (Beograd, Yugoslavia, Protozoa) Deceased.

* GEORGIEVSKI, Dr. Mitko. Cretan Dimov 5, Skopje, Yugoslavia. [Acarina: Hydrachnellae]

* GEPTNER, W. G. See HEPTNER, W. G.

* GERBER, Eduard. (Bern, Switzerland; fossils) Deceased.

GERBERG, Dr. Eugene J. Insect Control & Research Inc., 6601 Johnnycake Road, Baltimore 7, Md., U. S. A. [Coleoptera: Lyctidae & Bostrychidae of World (Yes)]

* GERHARD, William J. (Chicago, Ill.; Insecta) Died December 15, 1958.

* GERICHTER, Dr. C. B. Department of Parasitology, Hebrew University, Jerusalem, Israel. [Nematoda]

GERING, Dr. Robert L. Wells College, Aurora, N. Y., U. S. A. [Chelonethida & Araneida: Agelenidae of N. America (No)]

GERINI, Dr. Francesco. Via S. Carlo 94, Livorno, Italy. [Coleoptera: Buprestidae of World (No), of Italy (Yes), terr. Mollusca, espec. Clausiliidae, of World (No)]

GERKING, Dr. Shelby D. Department of Zoology, University of Indiana, Bloomington, Ind., U. S. A. [Pisces of c. U. S. (Yes)]

GERLACH, Dr. S. Zoologisches Institut der Universität, Hegewischstrasse 3, Kiel, Germany.

[Marine f-l. Nematoda of World (Yes); marine Gastrotricha of World (No); Archiannelida of World (No)]

* de GERMOND, J. D.   7 Boulevard Beau-Site, Sainte-Maxime-sur-Mer (Var), France. [Hy-
menoptera]

GEROULD, John H. (Hanover, N. H.: Sipunculoidea) Not now active in taxonomy.

* GERRIS, V. J. A. M. Jansveld 30bis, Utrecht, Netherlands. [Lepidoptera]

GERSCHMAN, B. J. See de PIKELIN, B. G.

GERTSCH, Dr. W. J. American Museum of Natural History, New York 24, N. Y., U. S. A.
[Araneida of N. America (Yes)]

* GERWEL, Dr. Czesław. Zakład Biologii ogolnej, Akademia Medyczna, ul. Fredry 10, Poznań, Poland. [Anoplura]

* GEYER, J. W. C. Department of Entomology, University of Pretoria, Pretoria, Union of
South Africa. [Insecta: Endopterygota]

GHAFFARY, E. Nezam. Assistant Professor, Department of Biology, Teheran University
School of Medicine, Teheran, Iran. [Reptilia; Amphibia; Diptera: Culicidae; Acarina:
Ixodidae: all of Iran (Yes)]

GHESQUIÈRE, Ing. J. Stella Mare, Menton, France. [Hymenoptera: Chalcidoidea: Encyrtidae, Aphelinidae, Trichogrammatidae; Proctotrupoidea; Bethyloidea; all of World (Yes);
Homoptera: Aleurodoidea of World (Yes)]

GHIDINI, Prof. Gian Maria. Via Montevideo 1/9, Genova, Italy. [Isoptera of Africa (Yes)]

GHIGI, Prof. Alessandro. (Bologna, Italy; Mammalia) Not now active in taxonomy.

GHILAROV, Prof. Dr. M. S. Laboratory of Soil Zoology, Institute of Animal Morphology,
Academy of Sciences, Lenin Ave. 33, Mowcow W-71, U. S. S. R. [Coleoptera: Elateridae
& Scarabaeidae of W. Europe (No), Tenebrionidae of w. Europe & c. Asia (Yes)]

GHIRARDELLI, Prof. Elvezio. Istituto di Zoologia, Università, San Giacomo 9, Bologna,
Italy. [Chaetognatha of Mediterranean (Yes)]

GHORAB, M. A.   Geological Department, Shell House, P. O. Box 228, Cairo, Egypt. [Fossil
invertebrates] See Addenda.

GIANOTTI, Dr. Agostino. c/o Ausonia Mineraria S. P. A., Via P. S. Mancini 27, Roma, Italy.
[Miocene (Tortonian) Foraminifera of Italy (Yes); Mesozoic microfacies of Italy (Yes)]

GIBBS, Dr. Robert H., Jr. Department of Biology, Boston University, Boston 15, Mass.,
U. S. A. [Recent f-w. Pisces, espec. Cyprinidae, of Atlantic Cst. of U. S. (Yes); Astronesthidae of World (Yes); Myctophidae & Scombridae of Atlantic (Yes); Carangidae
of w. N. Atlantic (Yes); Coryphaenidae of World (Yes); Odonata of N. America (Yes)]

GIBSON, Lee. Creole Petroleum Corporation, Maracaibo, Venezuela. [Ostracoda of New
World & Europe (Yes); Tertiary & Mesozoic Foraminifera of New World (Yes)]

GIBSON, Mr. Thomas G. Department of Geology, Guyot Hall, Princeton University, Princeton, N. J., U. S. A. [Tertiary & Recent Gastropoda: Turridae of w. Atlantic & Carribean
(Yes)]

GIBSON, Dr. W. W. Rockefeller Foundation, Calle Londres 40, Mexico 6, D. F., Mexico.
[Coleoptera: Scarabaeidae: Coprinae of World (No); g. Phanaeus of W. Hemisphere (Yes)]

* GIBSON-HILL, C. A. Raffles Museum, Singapore, Malaya. [Mammalia]

GIEYSZTOR, Prof. Dr. M. Katedra Hydrobiologii, Uniwersytetu Warszawskiego, Krak Przedmiescie 26/28, Warszawa 64, Poland. [F-w. Turbellaria of World (Yes)]

* GIGLIOLI, Marco E. C. Address unknown. (Mollusca, Insecta)

GIGON, Dr. Walter O. c/o Bielstrasse 14, Oberwil (Bld.), Switzerland. [Up. Cretaceous-
Eocene Foraminifera (Yes)]

GILBERT, Mr. Carter R. Museum of Zoology, University of Michigan, Ann Arbor, Mich.,
U. S. A. [Upland F-w. Pisces of e. U. S. (Yes); fossil f-w. Pisces of N. America (Yes)]

GILBERT, Edward E. 425 Pennsylvania Avenue, Freeport, N. Y., U. S. A. [Coleoptera: Curculionidae: Baridinae of New World & Eurasia (Yes), Raymondionyminae of World (Yes)]

GILBERT, M. See GILBERT, M.

* GILES, D. E. Oregon State College, Corvallis, Oregon. [Coelenterata]

GILES, Dr. E. T. Department of Zoology, University of New England, Armidale, N. S. W.,
Australia. [Dermaptera of Australia & New Zealand (Yes); Orthoptera of Australia
(Yes)]

GILL, Edmund Dwen. National Museum of Victoria, Russell Street, Melbourne C. 1, Australia. [Up. Silurian & L. Devonian Brachiopoda, Trilobita, Carpoidea, of Australia
(Yes)]

GILL, Mr. Gordon D. Department of Biology, Northern Michigan College, Marquette, Mich.,
U. S. A. [Diptera: Heleomyzidae of N. America (Yes)]

GILLARD, A. Rijkslandbouwhogenschool, Coupure Links 233, Ghent, Belgium. [Plant parasitic Nematoda of Belgium (No); Nematoda: Heteroderinae of Belgium & Belg. Congo
(Yes); Rotatoria: Brachionidae of World (Yes)]

GILLASPY, James E. Division of Science, San Bernardino Valley College, San Bernardino,
Calif., U. S. A. [Hymenoptera: Bembicidae: Bembicini of New World (Yes)]

* GILLETT, Dr. J. D. East African Virus Research Institute, P. O. Box 49, Entebbe, Uganda.
[Diptera: Culicidae of Ethiopian (No)]

GILLHAM, Nicholas W. Biological Laboratories, Harvard University, Cambridge 38, Mass.,
U. S. A. [Lepidoptera: Nymphalidae of Palearctic (No), of Nearctic (Yes); Hesperiidae
of N. America (Yes)]
GILLIARD, Dr. E. Thomas. American Museum of Natural History, New York 24, N. Y.,
U. S. A. [Aves of World, espec. New Guinea & Amazonia (Yes)]
GILLOGLY, Lorin R. 202 Amesti Road, Watsonville, Calif., U. S. A. [Coleoptera: Nitidulidae
of World (Yes)]
* GILMORE, Dr. Raymond M. Fish & Wildlife Service, Scripps Institution of Oceanography,
La Jolla, Calif., U. S. A. [Mammalia: Rodentia, Cetacea, Primates]
GILMOUR, Mr. E. F. Museum & Art Gallery, Waterdale, Doncaster, England. [Coleoptera:
Cerambycidae: Prioninae, Lamiinae, Cerambycinae, of World, espec. Borneo (Yes);
espec. Prioninae of Africa]
GILTZ, Dr. M. L. Department of Zoology & Entomology, Ohio State University, Columbus 10,
Ohio, U. S. A. [Amphibia of Ohio (Yes)]
* GINES, Rvdo. Hno. H. C. Apartado de Correos 681, Caracas, Venzuela. [Mollusca]
GINET, R. Laboratoire de Zoologie Générale, 16 Quai Claude Bernard, Lyon 1, France.
[Crustacea: Amphipoda: g. Niphargus of caves of France (Yes)]
GINETZINSKAJA, Miss T. A. Department of Invertebrate Zoology, Leningrad State University,
Leningrad W-164, U. S. S. R. [Trematoda of birds of Palearctic (Yes); cercariae of
Trematoda, espec, Strigeidae, of Palearctic (No)]
* GINSBURG, Mr. Isaac. Division of Fishes, U. S. National Museum, Washington 25, D. C.,
U. S. A. [Pisces] [U. S. Fish & Wildlife Service]
GINSBURG, L. Muséum National d'Histoire Naturelle, 3 place Valhubert, Paris (V), France.
[Mammalia: Carnivora of Old World (Yes); of New World (No)]
GIORDANI-SOIKA, Prof. Dr. A. Museo Civico Storia Naturale, Fontego dei Turchi, Venezia,
Italy. [Hymenoptera: solitary Vespidae, espec. Eumenidae of World (Yes); Diptera:
Ephydridae & Dolichopodidae of Palearctic & Ethiopian (Yes)]
GISIN, Dr. Hermann. Musée d'Histoire Naturelle Ville de Genève, Genève, Switzerland.
[Collembola of Europe (Yes)]
GISLEN, R. E. (Lund, Sweden; Crinoidea) Died 1954.
GITTINS, Arthur Richard. Department of Entomology, University of Idaho, Moscow, Idaho,
U. S. A. [Hymenoptera: Apoidea of N. America (No)]
GIVEN, Mr. B. B. (Nelson, New Zealand; Hymenoptera & Coleoptera) Not now active in tax-
onomy.
GIVEN, Robert Reed. 710 W. 27th Street, Los Angeles 7, Calif., U. S. A. [Marine Porifera
of s. Calif. (Yes)] [University of Southern California]
GJESSING, Helen W. Box 112, San Juan, Puerto Rico. [Trematoda of bats of N. America (No);
ectoparasites of bats, espec, Acarina: Spinturnicidae & Myobiidae, of N. America (No)]
GJULIC, B. See DJULIĆ, B.
GJULLIN, Mr. C. M. Box 332, Corvallis, Ore., U. S. A. [Diptera: Culicidae of N. America
(No)] [Entomology Research Branch, U. S. Department of Agriculture]
GLAESSNER, Dr. M. F. Department of Geology, University of Adelaide, Adelaide, S. Aus-
tralia. [Fossil Crustacea: Malacostraca, espec. Decapoda (Yes); Mesozoic-Tertiary
Foraminifera (No)]
GLANCE, Grace. (Washington, D. C.; Apterygota) Not now active in taxonomy.
GLASER, Ing. Wolfgang. Walfischgasse 4/4/18, Wien I, Austria. [Lepidoptera: Coleophori-
dae of Europe (No)]
GLASS, Prof. Bryan P. Department of Zoology, Oklahoma Agricultural & Mechanical College,
Stillwater, Okla., U. S. A. [Mammalia of Oklahoma (Yes), Chiroptera of N. America
(Yes)]
* GLASSELL, Steve A. Address unknown. (Crustacea)
GLAUERT, Mr. L. Western Australian Museum, Perth, W. A., Australia. [Reptilia & Mam-
malia: Marsupialia of W. Australia (Yes); Scorpionida of Australia]
GLEN, Dr. Robert, Director-General, Research Branch, Department of Agriculture, Carling
Avenue, Ottawa, Ont., Canada. [Coleoptera: Elateridae: g. Corymbites of World (No);
larvae of Elateridae of Canada (No)]
GLEN, Mr. William. Department of Geology, College of San Mateo, San Mateo, Calif., U. S. A.
[Miocene to Recent Pelecypoda, Gastropoda, Echinoidea, of Calif., Ore., Wash. (Yes)]
GLENNY, Dr. Fred H. Youngstown University, Youngstown 2, Ohio, U. S. A. [Aves of World,
espec. Psittaciformes (No)] [Blue Sea Lake Biological Laboratory, Messines, Que.]
GLIBERT, Dr. Maxime. Institut Royal des Sciences Naturelles, 31 rue Vautier, Bruxelles,
Belgium. [Cenozoic marine Gastropoda of Belgium & France (Yes); Cenozoic marine
Pelecypoda & Gastropoda of Europe (No)]
GLOWACKI, Dr, J. Kepinska 32, Brwinow k. Warszawa, Poland. [Hymenoptera: Ichneumoni-
dae & egg parasites of Europe (Yes)]
GLOYD, Dr. Howard K. Department of Zoology, University of Arizona, Tucson, Ariz.,
U. S. A. [Reptilia: Crotalidae of N. America (Yes), of S. America & Asia (No); Sauria
& Serpentes of s. w. N. America (No)]

GLOYD, Leonora K. Natural Resources Building, Illinois State Natural History Survey, Urbana, Ill., U.S.A. [Odonata, espec. g. Argia & Gomphoides, of New World (Yes)]
GLUDE, John B. U.S. Fish & Wildlife Service, 800 Dreams Landing, Annapolis, Md., U.S.A. [Pelecypoda: Myidae, Veneridae, Ostreidae, of e. U.S. (Yes)]
GLUMAC, Dr. Slobodan. Poljoprivredni Fakultet, Novi Sad, Yugoslavia. [Diptera: Syrphidae of Balkans & s. Europe (Yes), Tabanidae of Balkans (No)]
GNANAMUTHU, Prof. C.P. University Zoological Research Laboratory, University of Madras, Madras 5, India. [Crustacea: parasitic Copepoda of marine fishes: Caligoida: Caligidae, Lernaeopodidae, Lernaeidae, Dichelesthiidae & Ergasilidae; of India (Yes)]
* GNEDINA, M.P. All-Union Skrjabin Institute of Helminthology, Staropansky 3, Moscow K-12, U.S.S.R. [Animal Helminths of U.S.S.R.]
* GNERI, Prof. Francisco S. Departamento de Ictiologia, Museo de Ciencias Naturales, Avda. Angel Gallardo 470, Buenos Aires, Argentina. [Pisces]
GOCHT, H. c/o Wintershall Aktiengesellschaft Erdölwerke Niedersachsen, (23) Barnstorf Bez. Bremen, Germany. [Fossil Hystricosphaeridea, Dinoflagellata, Peridineae, chiefly Cretaceous & Tertiary, of Europe]
GODFREY, Mr. W. Earl. National Museum of Canada, Ottawa, Ont., Canada. [Aves of Canada & Alaska (Yes)]
GODSIL, Mr. H.C. (San Pedro, Calif,; Pisces) Not now active in taxonomy.
GOECKE, H. v. Beckerathplatz 9, Krefeld, Germany. [Coleoptera: Chrysomelidae: Donaciinae of World (Yes)]
* GOERGES, Julius. (Kassel, Germany; fossils) Deceased.
GOERLICH, Dr. Franz. Postfach 20, (23) Bentheim, Germany. [Mesozoic to Tertiary Ostracoda: Cytherideinae (Yes)]
* GOETGHEBUER, M. Rue Nouve-St. Jacques 39, Gand, Belgium. [Diptera]
GOFFART, Prof. Dr. H. Biologische Bundesanstalt, Institut für Hackfruchtkrankheiten und Nematodenforschung, Toppheideweg 88, Münster (Westfalen), Germany. [Plant parasitic Nematoda of Europe (Yes)]
GOGOLCZYK, Mgr. W. Paleozoological Institute, Swierczewskiego 19, Poznań, Poland. [Devonian Stromatoporoidea of Poland (Yes)]
GOHAR, Prof. Hamed A.F. Director, Oceanographical Institute, Al-Ghardaqa, Red Sea, Egypt. [Coelenterata: Alcyonaria: Xeniidae & Stolonifera of Red Sea (Yes); Pisces of Red Sea (Yes); Gastropoda: Nudibranchiata of Red Sea (No)]
GOHEEN, Dr. A.C. Department of Plant Pathology, University of California, Davis, Calif., U.S.A. [Plant parasitic Nematoda: g. Pratylenchus] [U.S. Department of Agriculture]
GOHRBANDT, Klaus A.H. Rohöl-Gewinnungs AG., Schwarzenbergplatz 16, Wien I, Austria. [Eocene & Paleocene Foraminifera (Yes); Oligocene & Miocene (No)]
GOIN, Coleman J. Department of Biology, University of Florida, Gainesville, Fla., U.S.A. [Amphibia of N. America (Yes); Hylidae of S. America (Yes); Carboniferous to Recent Sirenidae (Yes)]
GOJDICS, Dr. Mary. Barat College, Lake Forest, Ill., U.S.A. [Flagellata: Euglenoidena (Yes)]
GOLDBERG, Mr. Aaron. Animal Parasite Laboratory, Agricultural Research Center, Beltsville, Md., U.S.A. [Parasitic Nematoda of livestock, espec. Ruminants, of U.S. (No)]
GOLDBERG, Robert Jack. Department of Biological Sciences, Chicago Teachers College, North Side Branch, 2216 W. Hirsch Street, Chicago 22, Ill., U.S.A. [F-w. Gastrotricha (Yes)]
GOLDEN, Dr. A. Morgan. U.S. Agricultural Research Station, P.O. Box 98, Alisal Branch, Salinas, Calif., U.S.A. [Plant parasitic Nematoda: Tylenchida, excl. Neotylenchidae, g. Ditylenchus, g. Aphelenchoides, of World (Yes); Longidorinae of World (Yes)] [U.S. Department of Agriculture]
GOLDEN, Thelma S. U.S. Agricultural Research Station, P.O. Box 98, Alisal Branch, Salinas, Calif., U.S.A. [Nematoda: Tylenchoidea, excl. Ditylenchus, g. Aphelenchoides & Neotylenchidae, of World (Yes)]
GOLDRING, Dr. Roland. Department of Geology, The University, Reading, Berks, England. [Up. Devonian-Permian Trilobita (Yes); Up. Devonian-L. Carboniferous productid Brachiopoda of Europe (Yes)]
* GOLDRING, Winifred. (Slingerland, N.Y.; fossils) Not now active in taxonomy.
* GOLIGHTLY, W.H. National Agricultural Advisory Service, Elswick Hall, Elswick Park, Newcastle-on-Tyne 4, England. [Nematoda]
GOLIKOV, Mr. A.N. Zoological Institute, Academy of Sciences, Leningrad 164, U.S.S.R. [Gastropoda: Prosobranchia of seas of U.S.S.R. & adjacent waters (Yes), espec. Buccinidae, Muricidae, Littorinidae, Nassidae, of Boreal & Arctic regions of Atlantic, Pacific, Arctic]
* GOLJAN, Mgr. Antoni. Instytut Zoologiczny, Polska Akademia Nauk, ul. Wilcza 64, Warszawa, Poland. [Coleoptera: Lamellicornia]
GOLLOP, J.B. C/o Canadian Wildlife Service, 313 Field Husbandry Building, University of Saskatchewan, Saskatoon, Sask., Canada. [Aves: waterfowl of Alberta, Manitoba, Saskatchewan (No)]

GOLVAN, Dr. Yves. Institut de Parasitologie, 15 rue Ecole-de-Medecine, Paris (VI), France. [Acanthocephala of World (Yes)]

GOMES, Jalmirez Guimarães. Ministerio de Agricultura, Divisão de Defesa Sanitaria Vegetal, Rio de Janeiro, Brazil. [Hymenoptera: Chalcidoidea of S. America (Yes)]

* GOMEZ, Prof. Mateo. Olta, La Rioja, Argentina. [Coleoptera: Curculionidae]

GOMEZ-MENOR, Dr. J. Residencia de Profesores, Calle del Ministro Ibañez Martin 2.6ºA, Ciudad Universitaria, Madrid, Spain. [Hemiptera: Coccoidea, Aleurodidae, Cicadidae, of Europe & n. Africa (Yes)]

GONÇALVES, Prof. Cincinnato Rory. Universidade Rural, Escola Nacional de Agronomia, Caixa Postal 25, Rio de Janeiro, Brazil. [Hymenoptera: Formicidae of Neotropics (No), g. Atta & Acromyrmex (Yes)]

GONCALVES, Timoteo. Trav. Dionisio dos Santos, Silva-Porto, Portugal. [Macrolepidoptera of n. Portugal]

* GONÇALVES SANCHES, Dr. J. Missão Zoologica de Moçambique, c/o Almoxarifado da Fazenda, Lourenço Marques, Moçambique, Portuguese East Africa [Pisces]

GONOR, Jefferson J. (Seattle, Wash.; Polychaeta & Crustacea) Not now active in taxonomy.

* GONZALEZ, Mr. Juan G. Box 6805, College Station, Texas, U.S.A. [Crustacea]

GONZALEZ GUTIERREZ, Manuel. Viladomat, 234, 6º, 4ª, Barcelona, Spain. [Coleoptera: Curculionidae of World (No), of Iberian Pen. (Yes)]

GONZALEZ REGALADO, Dr. Thomas. Director de Piscicultura, Ministerio de Agricultura, Canning 2362, Buenos Aires, Argentina. [Pisces: Salmonidae of S. America] [Ministerio de Agricultura y Ganaderia]

GOOD, Prof. Henry G. Dept. of Zoology, Alabama Polytechnic Institute, Auburn, Ala., U.S.A. [Coleoptera: Cerambycidae, Buprestidae, Elateridae; Aves; all of s.U.S. (Yes)]

GOOD, Dr. J.M. Nematology Field Laboratory, U.S. Deparment of Agriculture, Tifton, Ga., U.S.A. [Nematoda of soil of s.e.U.S. (No); parasitic Tylenchidae, Criconematidae, Aphelenchidae, of s.e.U.S. (Yes)]

* GOOD, Dr. Newell E. Philadelphia Department of Public Health, Philadelphia 7, Penn., U.S.A. [Siphonaptera]

GOODCHILD, Dr. Chauncey G. Department of Biology, Emory University, Atlanta 22, Ga., U.S.A. [Digenetic Trematoda of e.U.S. (Yes)]

GOODEY, Dr. J.Basil. Rothamsted Experimental Station, Harpenden, Herts, England. [Nematoda: Rhabditida & Tylenchida of World (Yes)]

GOODING, Mr. R.U. Department of Zoology, Johnson Hall, University of Washington, Seattle 5, Wash., U.S.A. [Copepoda: Clausidiidae of World (Yes)]

GOODMAN, Dr. John D. Department of Biology, University of Redlands, Redlands, Calif., U.S.A. [Trematoda: Digenea of reptiles of World, espec. U.S. (Yes); f-w. cercariae of World, espec. U.S. (Yes); Cestoda & Nematoda of World (No)]

GOODNIGHT, Clarence J. Department of Biological Sciences, Purdue University, W. Lafayette, Ind., U.S.A. [Opiliones of U.S. & C. America (Yes); f-w. Oligochaeta of U.S. (No)]

GOODNIGHT, Marie L. Biology Annex, Purdue University, W. Lafayette, Ind., U.S.A. [Opiliones of N. & C. America (Yes)]

GOODSON, A.L. 26 Park Road, Tring, England. [Macrolepidoptera of Great Britain (Yes)] [The Zoological Museum]

* GOODWIN, D. Toft, Monks Road, Virgina Water, Surrey, England. [Aves]

GOODWIN, G.G. American Museum of Natural History, New York 24, N.Y., U.S.A. [Mammalia of C. America (Yes); Chiroptera (Yes)]

GORDON, Mr. Bernard L. 9 Washington Street, Westerly, R.I., U.S.A. [Marine Pisces of World (No), of Rhode Island (Yes)] [Rhode Island College of Education]

GORDON, Dr. Isabella. British Museum (Natural History), Cromwell Road, London, S.W.7, England. [Crustacea: Malacostraca, espec. Decapoda of World (No); Pycnogonida of Britain & Antarctic (No); Isopoda & Amphipoda of Britain (No)]

* GORDON, Dr. K.L. Department of Zoology, Oregon State College, Corvallis, Ore., U.S.A. [Mammalia]

GORDON, Myron. Genetics Laboratory, American Museum of Natural History, New York 24, N.Y., U.S.A. ["Xiphophorin" Pisces of C. America (Yes)]

GORDON, Malcolm S. Department of Zoology, University of California, Los Angeles 24, Calif., U.S.A. [Marine Pisces of e. Canadian Arctic (Yes); costal marine Pisces of e.N. America (No); Aves, espec. shore & pelagic, of N. America & Mexico (No)]

GORDON, Dr. Robert E. Department of Pure & Applied Science, Northeast Louisiana State College, Monroe, La., U.S.A. [Amphibia: Plethodontidae of N. America (Yes); Reptilia: Iguanidae of N. America (Yes)]

GORIROSSI, Dr. Flora Bourdeau. See BOURDEAU, Flora G.

GORMAN, Dr. Joe. Department of Biology, St. Louis University, 1400 S. Grand Boulevard, St. Louis 4, Mo., U.S.A. [Reptilia; Amphibia: Hylidae & Plethodontidae; all of Nearctic (No)]

* GORSAC, S.A. Place de la Gare 61, St. Trond (V.S. Truiden), Belgium. [Nematoda]

*GORSHKOV, Dr. I. P. Veterinary Academy, Kuzjminki, Moscow reg. , U.S.S.R. [Helminths of pigs & horses of U.S.S.R.]

GORTANI, Prof. De.Michele, Istituto di Geologia e Paleontologia dell'Università, Via Zamboni 63, Bologna, Italy. [Paleozoic fossils, espec. Graptolithida of Sardinien & Carnic Alps (No)]

* GORTLER, A. Department of Entomology, Zoological Institute, Vinicna 7, Praha II, Czechoslovakia. [Odonata]

GOSLINE, Dr. William A. Department of Zoology, University of Hawaii, Honolulu 14, Hawaii, U.S.A. [Pisces of Hawaii (Yes)]

GOSNER, K. L. Newark Museum, 43-49 Washington Street, Newark, N.J., U.S.A. [Amphibia: Salientia of N.America (Yes), Caudata of N.America (No)]

GOSSE, Mr. J.P. Institut National pour l'Étude Agronomique du Congo Belge, Station de Yangambi, Belgian Congo. [F-w. Pisces of Belgian Congo (Yes)]

GOSSLER, Dr. O. Haydnstrasse 4, St. Pölten, Austria. [Rotatoria of plankton of c. Europe (Yes)]

GÖSSWALD, Professor Dr. Karl, Direktor des Instituts für Angewandte Zoologie der Universität Würzburg, Röntgenring 10, Würzburg (Bavaria), Germany. [Hymenoptera: Formicidae of c. Europe (Yes)]

GOSTILOVSKAIA, M. Zoological Institute, Academy of Sciences, Leningrad 164, U.S.S.R. [Bryozoa: Cheilostomata of Arctic Seas of U.S.S.R. (Yes)]

GOTO, H. E. Department of Zoology, Imperial College, London, S.W.7, England. [Collembola of World (Yes)]

GOTO, Mitsuo. Kita 609, Takaishi-cho, Senhoku-gun, Osaka, Japan. [Coleoptera: Scarabaeidae: Coprophagides of Japan (Yes); Chrysomelidae of Japan (No)]

GOTOH, Akira. Aino Potato Pest Laboratory, Nagasaki Prefectural Agricultural Experiment Station, Aino, Nagasaki Pref., Japan. [Nematoda: g. Pratylenchus of Japan (No)]

GOTTLIEB, Dr. E. Sea Fisheries Research Station, P.O.Box 699, Haifa, Israel. [Crustacea: Amphipoda & Decapoda of the e. Mediterranean (No)]

GOTTO, Dr. R.V. Department of Zoology, Queens University, Belfast, N. Ireland. [Crustacea: Ascidicolous Copepoda: Cyclopoida & Notodelphyoida of World (Yes)]

GOUIN, Fr. Musée Zoologique de l'Université et de la Ville de Strasbourg, Strasbourg (Bas Rhin), France. [Diptera: Chironomidae of Europe (No)]

* GOULD, Dr. Douglas J. Army Medical Service Graduate School, Army Medical Center, Washington 12, D.C., U.S.A. [Acarina: Trombiculidae & Ixodoidea of w.N.America]

GOULD, Prof. George E. Department of Entomology, Purdue University, Lafayette, Ind., U.S.A. [Heteroptera: Veliidae & Gerridae of N.America (No)]

GOURLAY, E.S. Entomology Division, Department of Scientific & Industrial Research, Box 223, Nelson, New Zealand. [Coleoptera of New Zealand (Yes)]

* GOUX, Prof. Dr. L. Sciences Naturelles, Lysée Périer, Marseille, France. [Hemiptera: Coccoidea]

GOWING-SCOPES, Mr. Eric. Oakhurst, Oakwood Road, Crofton, Orpington, Kent, England. [Coleoptera: Curculionidae of Australia (Yes)]

GOZMANY, Dr. Lancelot. Magyar Nemzeti Museum, Baross-u. 13, Budapest (VIII), Hungary. [Lepidoptera: Gelechiidae: g.Symmoca of World (Yes); Gelechiidae & Oecophoridae of Palearctic (No)]

de GRAAF, De Heer Fr. Willemsparkweg 147, Amsterdam, Netherlands. [Rotatoria & Rhizopoda of Europe (Yes)]

* de GRAAFF, G. Department of Anatomy, University of the Witwatersrand, Johannesburg, Union of South Africa. [Fossil Mammalia]

GRABAU, Myles C. Department of Biology, Northwest Missouri State College, Maryville, Mo., U.S.A. [Odonata: Anisoptera, incl. nymphs, of N.America (Yes)]

*GRABDA, Prof. Dr. Eugeniusz. Zakład Zoologii, Wyzsza Szkoła Rolnicza, Olsztyn-Kortowo, Poland. [Parasites of fish]

GRABDA, Jadwiga. Instytut Weterynarii, Olsztyn-Kortowo, Poland. [F-w. Copepoda: Lernaeidae & Lernaeopodidae of Europe (Yes)]

GRABER, Richard R. Illinois Natural History Survey, Division of Wildlife Research, Urbana, Ill., U.S.A. [Aves: Passeriformes, espec. juvenile plumages, of N.America (Yes); of Mexico (No)]

GRADWELL, Mr. G.R. Hope Department of Entomology, University Museum, Oxford, England. [Hymenoptera: Tetrastichinae of World (No), of Europe (Yes)]

GRAF, A. Eidg. Landw. Versuchsanstalt, Birchstrasse 95, Zürich 50, Switzerland. [Nematoda: g. Ditylenchus, Pratylenchus, Hoplolaimus, Heterodera, of c. Europe (Yes)]

GRAFF, Dr. Otto. Institut für Humuswirtschaft der Forschung für Landwirtschaft, Braunschweig-Völkenrode, Germany. [Oligochaeta: Lumbricidae of Palearctic (Yes); Megascolecidae, excl. g.Pheretima, of New World & Australia (Yes)]

GRAFFAM, Albert Allen. Box 1188, Ardmore, Okla., U.S.A. [Paleozoic Crinoidea of N.America (Yes); Tertiary pelagic Foraminifera of New World (No)]

* GRAHAM, Prof. A. Department of Zoology, University of Reading, Reading, England.
[Mollusca]

GRAHAM, David H. 28 Whites Line East, Lower Hutt, New Zealand. [Pisces of New Zealand
(No)]

GRAHAM, Dr. G. L. Department of Parasitology, University of Pennsylvania, School of
Veterinary Medicine, Philadelphia 4, Penn., U. S. A. [Parasitic Nematoda: g. Strongy-
loides (Yes)]

* GRAHAM, Dr. Herbert W. U. S. Fish & Wildlife Service, Woods Hole, Mass., U. S. A.
[Protozoa: Dinoflagellata]

GRAHAM, Dr. Joseph J. School of Mineral Sciences, Stanford University, Stanford, Calif.,
U. S. A. [Fossil Foraminifera of California & Philippine Is. (Yes)]

GRAHAM, Dr. M. W. R. de V. Hope Department of Entomology, University Museum, Oxford,
England. [Hymenoptera: Chalcidoidea of Europe (Yes); Hymenoptera: Parasitica of
Holarctic (No)]

GRAHAM, Dr. T. W. U. S. Department of Agriculture, Tobacco, Medicinal & Special Crops,
Bureau of Plant Industry, Florence, S. C., U. S. A. [Nematoda of s. e. U. S. (Yes)]

GRAINGER, Dr. E. H. Arctic Unit, 505 Pine Avenue West, Montreal, Que., Canada. [Echi-
nodermata & Polychaeta of Arctic N. America (No)]

GRAINGER, Dr. J. West of Scotland Agricultural College, Auchincruive by Ayr, Scotland.
[Plant parasitic Nematoda of crops of Scotland (No)]

GRAINGER, Dr. J. N. R. Department of Zoology, The University, Hull, England. [Crustacea:
parasitic Copepoda of w. Europe (Yes); F-w. Calanoid Copepoda of Britain (No)]

GRANDI, Prof. Dott, Guido, Direttore, Istituto di Entomologia della Universitá, Via Filippo
Re 6, Bologna 117, Italy. [Hymenoptera: Chalcidoidea: Agonidae & g. Philotrypesis of
World (Yes)]

GRANDI, Prof. Marta. Istituto di Entomologia della Universitá, Via Filippo Re 6, Bologna
117, Italy. [Ephemerida of Europe (No), of Italy (Yes)]

GRANDISON, Miss A. G. C. British Museum (Natural History), Cromwell Road, London, S. W.
7, England. [Amphibia of Africa (Yes); Reptilia: Squamata of Africa, espec. n. Africa
(Yes)]

GRANDJEAN, Francois. Muséum National d'Histoire Naturelle, 61 rue de Buffon, Paris (V),
France. [Acarina: Oribatidae of World (No)]

GRANDORI, Remo. (Milano, Italy; Aphidoidea) Died August 6, 1955.

* GRANGER, Charles. 26 rue Vineuse, Paris (XVI), France. [Hymenoptera]

GRANOVSKY, Dr. A. A. Division of Entomology, University of Minnesota, St. Paul 1, Minn.,
U. S. A. [Homoptera: Aphidae of World (Yes)]

GRANT, Chapman. Rt. 1, Box 80, Escondido, Calif., U. S. A. [Reptilia & Amphibia of West
Indies (Yes)]

GRANT, Charles Donald. 865 Sherman Ave., Menlo Park, Calif., U. S. A. [Acarina: Laelaptidae of N. America (Yes); Diptera: Culicidae of w. U. S. (No)]

GRANT, Capt. C. H. B. (London, England; Aves) Died January 9, 1958.

GRANT, Mr. Harold J., Jr. Academy of Natural Sciences, Philadelphia 3, Penna., U. S. A.
[Orthoptera of New World (Yes); Tetrigidae of World (Yes)]

GRANT, Richard E. U. S. National Museum, Washington 25, D. C., U. S. A. [Up. Cambrian
Trilobita of Minnesota, Montana, Wyoming (Yes); Permian Brachiopoda of w. Texas
(No)]

GRANT, Dr. U. S., 4th. Department of Geology, University of California, Los Angeles 24,
Calif., U. S. A. [Cenozoic Mollusca & Echinoidea of w. N. America (No)]

GRANVIK, Dr. Hugo. Vejbystrand, Sweden. [Aves of c. Africa (No)]

GRASSÉ, Pierre Paul. Laboratoire d'Evolution, 105 Blvd. Raspail, Paris (VI), France.
[Protozoa: Zooflagellata (No); Isoptera of Europe & Africa (No)] [Université de Paris]

GRAU, Gilbert. 2457 Claremont Avenue, Hollywood 27, Calif., U. S. A. [Pelecypoda: Pectinidae of World (Yes)]

GRAVES, Dr. Robert C. Flint Community College, Flint 3, Mich., U. S. A. [Coleoptera: Cicindelidae of N. America (Yes); Diptera: Culicidae of N. America (No)]

GRAVESTEIN, W. H. Rubensstraat 87, Amsterdam Z, Netherlands. [Heteroptera & Homoptera
of Netherlands]

GRAY, I. E. Department of Zoology, Duke University, Durham, N. C., U. S. A. [Marine Pisces of N. Carolina (Yes)]

GRAY, Dr. P. H. H. R. R. 2, Digby, Nova Scotia, Canada. [Lepidoptera of Nova Scotia (No)]

GRAY, Dr. Peter. Department of Biological Science, University of Pittsburgh, Pittsburgh 13,
Penna., U. S. A. [Crustacea: parasitic Copepoda of invertebrates & protochordates
(Yes)]

GREAVES, T. Division of Entomology, Commonwealth Scientific & Industrial Research Organization, P. O. Box 109, Canberra, A. C. T., Australia. [Isoptera & Hymenoptera: For-
midae of Australia (No)]

GREEN, Carleton. See GREENE, Karl W.

201

GREEN, C. D. Zoology Department, Royal Holloway College, Englefield Green, Surrey, England. · [Collembola of w. Africa (No)]
GREEN, Dr. J. Zoology Department, Bedford College, Regent's Park, London, N. W. 1, England. [Acarina: Halacaridae of Palearctic (Yes); Crustacea: Cladocera of Europe & Africa (Yes); Protozoa: Peritricha of Europe (No)]
GREEN, J. W. California Academy of Sciences, San Francisco 18, Calif., U. S. A. [Coleoptera: Lycidae, Lampyridae, Cantharidae, of Nearctic (Yes)]
GREEN, Dr. Morton. South Dakota School of Mines & Technology, Rapid City, S. D., U. S. A. [Oligocene-Pliocene Mammalia (Yes)]
GREEN, Prof. N. Bayard. Marshall College, Huntington, W. Va., U. S. A. [Amphibia: Plethodontidae of e. U. S. (Yes)]
GREENBANK, Dr. John. Olathe, Colorado, U. S. A. [F-w. Pisces of N. America (No)]
GREENBERG, Dr. Bernard. College of Pharmacy, University of Illinois, Chicago 12, Ill., U. S. A. [Acarina: Labidostommatidae of World (Yes); Trombiculidae: g. Acomatacarus of Nearctic & Neotropics (Yes)]
* GREENE, Charles T. (College Park, Md., Diptera) Deceased.
GREENE, Karl W. P. O. Box 3751, Honolulu 11, Hawaii, U. S. A. [Gastropoda: g. Conus of Hawaiian Is. & Micronesia (Yes)]
GREENHALL, Dr. Arthur M. Royal Victoria Institute Museum, Port of Spain, Trinidad. [Mammalia of West Indies & Trinidad (Yes); Chiroptera of West Indies, C. & S. America (Yes); Reptilia & Amphibia of West Indies, C. & S. America (No)]
GREENWAY, James C., Jr. Museum of Comparative Zoology, Harvard University, Cambridge 38, Mass., U. S. A. [Aves (Yes)]
GREENWOOD, P. H. Department of Zoology (Fish Section), British Museum (Natural History), Cromwell Road, London, S. W. 7, England. [F-w. Pisces, espec. Cichlidae, of Africa (Yes); Miocene-Holocene Cichlidae (Yes)]
GREGG, Dr. Robert E. Department of Biology, University of Colorado, Boulder, Colo., U. S. A. [Hymenoptera: Formicidae of World (No); of N. America (Yes)]
GREGG, Dr. Wendell O. 2200 S. Harvard Blvd., Los Angeles 18, Calif., U. S. A. [Marine Mollusca of w. N. America (No); nonmarine (Yes)]
GREGOR, Ing. Dr. František. Biological Institute, Parasitology, Czechoslovak Academy of Sciences, 1 Zemědělská, Brno, Czechoslovakia. [Leaf-mining Lepidoptera of Europe (Yes), g. Lithocolletis of World (Yes); Diptera: Muscidae & Calliphoridae of Europe (Yes)]
GREGORY, Dr. Joseph T. Peabody Museum, Yale University, New Haven, Conn., U. S. A. [Permian-Triassic Reptilia & Amphibia (Yes): Miocene-Pliocene Mammalia (No)]
GREGORY, William K. (Woodstock, N. Y.; Vertebrate fossils) Not now active in taxonomy.
GREGSON, Mr. J. D. Veterinary & Medical Entomology Laboratory, P. O. Box 210, Kamloops, B. C., Canada. [Acarina: Ixodoidea of Canada (Yes)]
GREKOFF, Dr. N. 60 Av. d'Iena, Paris (XVI), France. [Paleozoic-Recent Crustacea: Ostracoda of Europe & Africa (Yes)] [Institut Français du Pètrole]
GREKULINSKI, Mr. Edmund. 165 Avenue B. New York 9, New York, U. S. A. [Paleozoic-Recent Foraminifera & Ostracoda (No)]
GRELL, Prof. Dr. Karl G. Zoologisches Institut, Hölderlinstrasse 12, Tübingen, Germany. [Recent Foraminifera (No)]
GREMMINGER, A. Gottesauer Platz 1, Karlsruhe (Baden), Germany. [Lepidoptera of Palearctic (No)]
GRENIER, P. Service d'Entomologie Medicale, Institute Pasteur, 25 rue du Docteur Roux, Paris (XV), France. [Diptera: Simuliidae of Europe, N. Africa, Ethiopian (Yes)]
GRENSTED, Prof. L. W. Oriel College, Oxford University, Oxford, England. [Mollusca of Britain (No); Diptera of Britain (No)]
GRESSITT, Dr. J. Linsley. Bernice P. Bishop Museum, Honolulu 17, Hawaii, U. S. A. [Coleoptera: Chrysomelidae of Pacific & s. e. Asia (Yes); Cryptocephalinae of World (Yes); Cerambycidae & Lagriidae of Pacific & s. e. Asia (Yes)]
GRETILLAT, Etienne H. S. Laboratoire Central Elevage, Boite Postal 4, Tananarive RP, Madagascar. [Acarina: Gamasidae & Tyroglyphidae of Madagascar]
GREY, Mrs. Marion. Division of Fishes, Chicago Natural History Museum, Chicago 5, Ill., U. S. A. [Abyssal Pisces of World (Yes)]
GREY, L. Paul. R. F. D. 1, Box 216, Lincoln, Maine, U. S. A. [Lepidoptera: Nymphalidae of S. America, Africa, Europe, Asia (No); Argynninae of N. America (Yes)]
GRICE, Dr. George D., Jr. U. S. Fish & Wildlife Service, Box 2021, Juneau, Alaska, U. S. A. [Crustacea: neritic Copepoda: Calanoida & Cyclopoida of Florida (Yes)]
GRIDELLI, Dr. E. (Trieste, Italy; Coleoptera) Deceased.
GRIESBACH, Frederick. Shell Oil Company, Grand Junction, Colo., U. S. A. [Up. Cretaceous Foraminifera of Rocky Mts., U. S. (No)]
* GRIEVE, Mrs. Evelyn G. 4035 Harvard Avenue, Montreal 28, Que., Canada. [Odonata]
GRIEWISCH, Louis. 1181 Reed Street, Green Bay, Wis., U. S. A. [Lepidoptera of N. America (No), of Wisconsin (Yes)]

GRIFFIN, F. J. 29 Bushey Park Gardens, Teddington, Middlesex, England. [Isoptera of World (No)]

GRIFFITH, Dr. J. Biology Department, Medical School, Guy's Hospital, London, S. E. 1, England. [Permian-L. Jurassic Pisces: Actinopterygia, espec. Saurichthyidae & Birgeriidae, of World (Yes)]

GRIFFITH, Dr. Melvin E. United States Oriental Mission, American Embassy, Bangkok, Thailand. [Diptera: Culicidae of Thailand & Oklahoma (No)]

GRIFFITHS, G. G. D. 13 Woodlands Avenue, Finchley, London, N. 3, England. [Diptera: Agromyzidae of Europe, espec. Britain, (Yes); of rest of Old World (No)]

GRIFFITHS, Dr. I. Department of Zoology, Birkbeck College, University of London, Malet Street, London, W. C. 1, England. [Amphibia: Salientia: Brachycephalidae of S. America & E. Indies (No); Microhylidae, larval stages, of Africa & Asia (Yes); Reptilia: Hydrophidae of India & Australasia (Yes)]

GRIFFITHS, Lt. Col. R. J. 287 Whitehorse Road, Ringwood, Vict., Australia. [Mollusca: Cypraeidae of World (Yes)]

GRIGG, Mrs. James A. Wiston, 21 Dalrymple Street, Edgehill, Cairns, Queensland, Australia. [Marine Gastropoda of Australia Cst. (Yes)]

GRILL, Dr. Rudolf. Geologische Bundesanstalt, Rasumofskygasse 23, Wien (III), Austria. [Tertiary Foraminifera of Austria (No)]

GRIMSDALE, T. F. 61 Harestone Hill, Caterham, Surrey, England. [Cambrian-Recent Foraminifera, espec. Orbitoididae & planktonic groups, espec. Tertiary (Yes)]

* GRISCOM, Mr. Ludlow. Museum of Comparative Zoology, Harvard University, Cambridge 38, Mass., U. S. A. [Aves]

GRISWOLD, Mr. John A. Philadelphia Zoological Garden, 34th Street & Girard Avenue, Philadelphia 4, Penna., U. S. A. [Aves: Anseriformes of World (Yes)]

* GRJEBINE, M. A. Institut de Recherche Scientifique, Boite Postale 434, Tsimbazaza-Tananarive, Madagascar. [Diptera]

GROBMAN, Dr. Arnold. Biological Sciences Curriculum Study, University of Colorado, Boulder, Colo., U. S. A. [Amphibia: salamanders & Reptilia: snakes, of e. N. America (Yes)]

GROCOTT, Robert G. Board of Health Laboratory, Box 503, Balboa Heights, Canal Zone. [Trematoda & Nematoda, excl. plant parasitic, of Panama (Yes)]

GRODHAUS, Gail. California Department of Public Health, Bureau of Vector Control, 2151 Berkeley Way, Berkeley 4, Calif., U. S. A. [Diptera: Culicidae of w. N. America (Yes); g. Tendipes of California (Yes); Trematoda: Schistosomatidae of N. America (No)]

GRODZIŃSKI, Dr. Władysław. Department of Evolution, The Jagiellonian University, ul. św. Anny 6, Kraków 4, Poland. [Mammalia of Poland, Czechoslovakia, D. D. R. (No)]

* GROENEWALD, A. A. J. Provincial Fisheries Institute, Lydenburg (Transvaal), Union of South Africa. [Pisces]

GROMADSKA, M. Universytet Mikołaja Kopernika, ul. Sienkiewicza 30/32, Torun, Poland. [Thysanoptera of Europe (Yes); of Holarctic (No)]

GROMOV, Y. M. Zoological Institute, Academy of Sciences, Leningrad B-164, U. S. S. R. [Tertiary-Recent Mammalia: Rodentia: Sciuromorpha; Quaternary-Recent Lagomorpha: Ochotonidae; all of Eurasia (Yes)]

GROMOVA, Dr. Vera. Paleontological Institute, Academy of Sciences, Moscow W-71, U. S. S. R. [Pleistocene Mammalia, espec. Equidae, Indricotheriidae, Amynodontidae, of e. Europe & n. Asia (Yes); Creodonta of c. Asia (No)]

* GRÖNVALL, J. S., Preparator Konstnär, Museum Zoologicum Universitatis, Helsinki, Finland. [Aves]

de GROOT, A. A. Onderlangs 13, Arnhem, Netherlands. [Rhizopoda of fresh water & mosses of World (Yes)]

GROSS, Dr. A. O. Laboratory of Ornithology, Bowdoin College, Brunswick, Maine, U. S. A. [Aves of N. America (Yes)]

GROSS, Mr. G. F. South Australian Museum, Adelaide, Australia. [Heteroptera of Australia, New Guinea, New Zealand, all S. Pacific islands (Yes)]

GROSS, Prof. Dr. Walter. Geological-Paleontological Institute, Humboldt University, Invalidenstrasse 43, Berlin N. 4, German Democratic Republic. [Paleozoic Pisces & Agnatha (No); Paleozoic Conodonts (No)]

* GROSSMAN, Stewart. Department of Geology, University of Kansas, Lawrence, Kans., U. S. A. [Fossil Ostracoda]

GROSPIETSCH, Dr. Th. Hydrobiologische Anstalt der Max-Planck-Gesellschaft, Plön (Holstein), Germany. [Rhizppoda: Testacea of World (Yes); subfossil forms from peat (Yes)]

GROSSU, Prof. Dr. Alexandru. Facultatea de Biologie, Splaiul Independentei 93, Bucureşti, Rumania. [Gastropoda of Rumania (Yes); g. Alopia of Rumania & Balkan Pen. (Yes)]

GROSZ, Franz Josef. Zoologisches Forschunginstitut und Museum A. Koenig, Bonn, Germany. [Lepidoptera: Satyridae & Geometridae of Palearctic (Yes)]

203

GROZDANOVIČ-SIMIČ, Jelena. Zoološki zavog Prirodno-matematičnog Faculteta, Studen-
skitrg, Beograd, Yugoslavia. [Hymenoptera: Sphegidae & Pompilidae of Yugoslavia
(Yes)]
GRUNDMANN, Dr. Albert W. Department of Zoology, University of Utah, Salt Lake City 12,
Utah, U. S. A. [Hymenoptera: Formicidae of w. U. S. (Yes); Nematoda & Platyhel-
minthes of animals of w. U. S. (No)]
* GRUNDMANN, E. Address unknown. (Coleoptera]
GRUNER, Dr. Hans-Eckhard. Zoologisches Museum, Invalidenstrasse 43, Berlin N. 4, Ger-
man Democratic Republic. [Crustacea of c. Europe, Baltic & North Seas, n. Atlantic
Ocean (Yes); marine Isopoda of World (Yes)]
GRUNIN, K. J. Zoological Institute, Academy of Sciences, Leningrad-164, U. S. S. R. [Dip-
tera: Oestridae of Europe, Asia, Africa (Yes)]
GSPAN, Alfonz. Prirodoslovni Muzej, Prešernova 20, Ljubljana, Yugoslavia. [Coleoptera
of Slovenia (No)]
* GUBANOV, N. M. Jakut Branch of the Academy of Sciences of USSR, Jakutsk, U. S. S. R.
[Helminths of animals of U. S. S. R.]
* GUBERLET, John E. Department of Zoology, University of Washington, Seattle, Wash.,
U. S. A. [Trematoda of fishes of Pacific]
GUDMUNDSSON, Dr. Finnur. Natural History Museum, P. O. Box 532, Reykjavik, Iceland.
[Aves of Arctic & Subarctic (Yes)]
GUÉORGUIEV, Vassil B. Institut Zoologique et Musée d'Histoire Naturelle, 1 Boulevard
Rouski, Sofia, Bulgaria. [Coleoptera: Haliplidae, Dytiscidae, Gyrinidae, Hydro-
philidae, Dryopidae, Helmidae, Georyssidae; of Europe (Yes); Dytiscidae of Asia
(No)]
* GUERIN, Jacintho. Rua Braz de Cubas 116, São Paulo, Brazil. [Coleoptera]
GUEVARA POZO, D. Instituto "López-Neyra" de Parasitologia, San Jerónimo 64, Granada,
Spain. [Cestoda & Nematoda of Spain (Yes)]
GUGGISBERG, C. A. W. Medical Research Laboratory, P. O. Box 30141, Nairobi, Kenya. [Dip-
tera: Phlebotominae of Ethiopian (Yes); Acarina: Ixodidae, excl. g. Ixodes, of e. Africa
(Yes); Mammalia: Rodentia of Kenya (Yes)]
GUIBÉ, Dr. J., Professeur, Laboratoire de Zoologie (Reptiles & Poissons), Muséum National
d'Histoire Naturelle, 57 Rue Cuvier, Paris (V), France. [Reptilia & Amphibia of w.
Africa & Madagascar (Yes)]
GUIGLIA, Dr. D. Museo Civico di Storia Naturale, via Brigata Liguria 9, Genova, Italy. [Hy-
menoptera: Scoliidae of Palearctic & Ethiopian (No); Oryssidae of Palearctic & Ethiop-
ian (Yes)]
GUIGNOT, Dr. F. 23 rue des Trois-Faucons, Avignon, France. [Coleoptera: Haliplidae &
Dytiscidae of World (Yes); Gyrinidae of Europe & Africa (Yes)]
GUIGUET, Charles J. Provincial Museum, Victoria, B. C., Canada. [Aves & Mammalia of
British Columbia (Yes)]
* GUILCHER-SKREB, Yvette. Address unknown. (Suctoria)
GUILDAY, Mr. John E. Department of Mammalogy, Carnegie Museum, Pittsburgh 13, Penna.,
U. S. A. [Up. Pleistocene archeological faunas of e. U. S. (Yes)]
GUILER, Dr. Eric. Department of Zoology, University of Tasmania, P. O. Box 647c, Hobart,
Tasmania. [Mammalia: Marsupiala of Tasmania (Yes)]
* GUIMARÃES, Lindolpho R. Departmento de Zoologia, Caixa Postal 7172, São Paulo, Brazil.
[Mallophaga; Siphonaptera; Diptera: Pupipara]
GUIMARAES GOMES, Jalmirez. See GOMES, J. G.
GULIČKA, Dr. Ján. Katedra Zoologie, Comenius University, Moskovaská 2, Bratislava,
Czechoslovakia. [Diplopoda of Palearctic (Yes); Chilopoda of Europe (Yes)]
GULLENTOPS, Prof. Frans. Institut Geologique de l'Université de Louvain, 10 rue Saint-
Michel, Louvain, Belgium. [Tertiary-Recent Foraminifera: Lagenidae (Yes)]
* GUNDERSON, K. Institute of Marine Research, Bergen, Norway. [Pisces]
GUNDERSON, Harvey L. Museum of Natural History, University of Minnesota, Minneapolis 14,
Minn., U. S. A. [Mammalia of n. c. U. S. (Yes)]
GUNHOLD, Dr. P. Landwirtschaftlich-chemische Bundes-Versuchsanstalt, Trunnerstrasse 1,
Wien, Austria. [Nematoda (Yes); Acarina: Oribatei of Europe (No)]
* GUNN, Willis B. Address unknown. (Hymenoptera: Formicidae)
de GUNST, J. H. 35 Meyenhage, De Bilt, Netherlands. [Coleoptera: Coccìnellidae of Indo-
nesia & Netherlands (Yes)]
GUNTER, Dr. Gordon, Director, Gulf Coast Research Laboratory, Ocean Springs, Miss.,
U. S. A. [Pisces & Pelecypoda: Ostreidae, of n. Gulf of Mexico (Yes)]
GUNTHER, Dr. C. E. M. 29 Flaumont Avenue, Lane Cove, N. S. W., Australia. [Acarina:
Trombiculidae: Trombiculinae of Asia & Australia (No); of New Guinea (Yes); Listro-
phoridae of New Guinea (Yes)]
GÜNTHER, Prof. Dr. Klaus. Zoologisches Institut, Freie Universitat, Königin Luise-Strasse
13, Berlin-Dahlem, Germany. [Orthoptera: Phasmatodea of World (Yes); Tetrigidae

of World, excl. Holarctic (Yes); Coleoptera: Curculionidae: Otiorrhynchinae & Rhynchophorinae of World, excl. Holarctic (No)]

* GUPTA, V. K. Insect Section, Zoological Survey of India, 34 Chittaranjan Avenue, Calcutta 12, India. [Hymenoptera]

* GUREEV, A. A. Zoological Institut, Academy of Sciences, Leningrad B-164, U. S. S. R. [Fossil vertebrates]

GURJANOVA, Prof. Dr. E. F. Zoological Institute, Academy of Sciences, Universitetskaya Nabereznaya 1, Leningrad B-164, U. S. S. R. [Crustacea: marine Amphipoda: Gammatoidea & Isopoda of N. Atlantic, Arctic, N. Pacific Oceans (Yes)]

GURNEY, Dr. Ashley B. Division of Insects, U. S. National Museum, Washington 25, D. C., U. S. A. [Orthoptera, Dermaptera, Zoraptera, Psocoptera, of World (Yes)]

GUSHANSKAJA, L. H. Laboratory of Helminthology, Academy of Sciences, Lenin Highway 33, Moscow, B-71, U. S. S. R. [Trematoda of animals]

GUSSEV, Dr. A. V. Zoological Institute, Academy of Sciences, Leningrad B-164, U. S. S. R. [F-w. Trematoda: Monogenea of World (No); f-w. Dactylogyridae of Europe & Asia (Yes); Parasitic Copepoda from fishes (No)]

GUSTAFSON, Dr. Gunner. Rosvik, Lysekil, Sweden. [Amphineura: Solenogastres; Enteropneusta; Annelida: Polychaeta; all of Sweden (No)] [Kristineberg Zoological Station]

GUSTAFSON, Paul V. (Seattle, Wash.; Nematoda) Not now active in taxonomy.

* GUT, Mr. H. James. P. O. Box 700, Sanford, Fla., U. S. A. [Pleistocene & Recent Mammalia of Florida]

GUTENTAG, Edwin D. Box 8516, University Station, Baton Rouge 3, La., U. S. A. [Pliocene-Recent f-w. Ostracoda (Yes)]

GUTIERREZ, M. Gonzalez. See Gonzalez-Gutierrez, M.

GUTIERREZ, Dr. Ricardo O. Instituto Nacional de Tecnologia Agropecuaria, Dirección de Ganaderia, Rivadavia N. 1439 - Piso 2, Buenos Aires, Argentina. [Helminths of Argentina(No); Acarina: Ixodoidea of S. America, espec. Argentina (Yes)]

GUTIERREZ-ALONZO, R. (Santiago, Chile; Coleoptera) Died 1953.

GUTSCHICK, Prof. R. C., Head, Department of Geology, University of Notre Dame, Notre Dame (South Bend), Ind., U. S. A. [Arenaceous Foraminifera, Ostracoda, sclerites of Holothurioidea, spicules of Porifera; all of Paleozoic of c. & w. U. S. (Yes); Mississippian Cephalopoda, Crinoidea (micro), Brachiopoda (Yes)]

GUTSEVICH, Dr. A. V. Entomological Society, Universitetskaja nab. 1, Leningrad B-164, U. S. S. R. [Diptera: Culicidae & bloodsucking Heleidae of Palearctic (Yes)]

GUYER, Gordon. Department of Entomology, Michigan State University, East Lansing, Mich., U. S. A. [Diptera: Tendipedidae (Yes)]

*GVOZDEV, E. V. Zoological Institute, Academy of Sciences of the Kazakh SSR, Ujgurskaja street 85, Alma-Ata 12, U. S. S. R. [Helminths of birds & rodents of U. S. S. R.]

GWILLIAM, Dr. G. F. Department of Biology, Reed College, Portland 2, Oregon, U. S. A. [Scyphozoa of e. Pacific (No); Stauromedusae (Yes)]

GYGER, Dr. H. P. Leonhardstrasse 55, Basel, Switzerland. [Diplura: Japygidae of Europe (Yes); Myriapoda of World (No)]

* GYLDENSTOLPE, Dr. Nils. Naturhistoriska Riksmuseet, Stockholm 50, Sweden. [Aves]

GYORFI, Prof. Janos. Zrinyi utca 44, Sopron, Hungary. [Hymenoptera, espec. Ichneumonidae & Braconidae, of Palearctic (Yes)]

GYURKÓ, Stefan. Catedra de Zoologie, Universitatea "Babes-Bolyai," Cluj, Rumania. [Pisces: Cyprinidae: g. Chondrostoma of Europe (Yes)]

HAAF, Dr. E. Museum G. Frey, Tutzing, bei München, Germany. [Coleoptera: Curculionidae: Brachycerinae of Africa (Yes); Scarabaeidae: Troginae of Africa & Australia (Yes)]

HAAN, Mr. C. 23 Coolullah Avenue, South Yarra, Vict., Australia. [Amphineura: Polyplacophora of Australia & New Zealand (Yes); Patelliformia: Fissurellidae, Patellidae, Lottiidae, Hipponidae, Capulidae, Galeridae, of Australia (Yes)]

HAARLØV, Dr. Niels. Zoologisk Laboratorium, Den kgl. Vetr.-og Landbohajskole, Bülosvej 13, København V, Denmark. [Acarina: Oribatei, Mesostigmata, Prostigmata, of Arctic & n. Europe (Yes); Collembola of Greenland & Scandinavia (No)]

HAAS, Dr. Fritz. Chicago Natural History Museum, Chicago 5, Ill., U. S. A. [F-w. & terr. Mollusca of World (Yes)]

HAAS, Georg. Zoological Institute, Hebrew University, Jerusalem, Israel. [Recent Reptilia of s. w. Asia (Yes); M. Triassic Reptilia of Israel (No)]

HAAS, Merrill W. c/o Carter Oil Co., P. O. Box 801, Tulsa 2, Okla., U. S. A. [Tertiary Foraminifera of the New World (No)]

HAAS, Dr. Otto H. American Museum of Natural History, New York 24, N. Y., U. S. A. [Fossil Invertebrates, espec. Mesozoic (Yes)]

* HAAS, Wilbert H. See HASS, Wilbert H.

HABE, Dr. Tadashige. Amakusa Marine Biological Laboratory, Tomioka, Reihoku-cho, Amakusa, Kyushu, Japan. [Shell-bearing Opisthobranchia, Lamellibranchia, Scaphopoda, Prosobranchia (excl. Mitridae & Turridae), all of Japan (Yes)] [Kyushu University]
HABEEB, Dr. Herbert. Grand Falls, N. B., Canada. [Acarina: Hydrachnellae, espec. Thyasidae, Oxidae, Torrenticolidae, Teutoniidae, Sperchonidae, Hygrobatinae, Feltriidae, Tiphysinae, Foreliinae, Axonopsidae, Aturidae, g. Xystonotus, Acalyptonotidae, g. Truncaturus, of N. America (Yes)]
* HABERAECKER, Leonhard. Ottostrasse 3, München 2, Germany. [Coleoptera: Lucanidae]
HABIB, Dr. A. Faculty of Agriculture, Ein Shams University, Saray El-Koubbeh, Egypt. [Homoptera: Coccoidea: Lecaniinae & Asterolecaniinae of Egypt (Yes)]
HABU, Akinobu. Division of Entomology, National Institute of Agricultural Science, Nishigahara, Kita-Ku, Tokyo, Japan. [Coleoptera: Carabidae of Japan (Yes); Hymenoptera: Chalcididae of Japan (Yes)]
HACK, Dr. Walter H. Ayacucho 230, Resistencia, Argentina. [Diptera: Culicidae: Anophelini of Argentina (Yes); Heteroptera: Triatominae of Argentina (Yes)]
* HACKER, H. Butterfield Street, Herston, Queensland, Australia. [Hemiptera, Hymenoptera]
HACKER, Miss Hilary. 1922 N. E. Weidler, Portland 12, Ore., U. S. A. [Coleoptera: Carabidae & Staphylinidae of Oregon (No)]
HACKMAN, Dr. Phil. Walter L. V. Chief, Entomology Department, Zoological Museum, Helsinki, Finland. [Diptera: Drosophilidae, Lonchaeidae, Scatophagidae of n. Europe (Yes); Drosophilidae: g. Scaptomyza of Holarctic Region (Yes); Araneae & Lepidoptera of n. Europe (No)]
HADA, Prof. Dr. Hoshine. Suzugamine College, Hiroshima, Japan. [Rotatoria of Far East (Yes); f-l. Protozoa of Far East & Pacific (Yes)]
HADDOW, Dr. A. J. East African Virus Research Institute, P. O. Box 49, Entebbe, Uganda. [Mammalia: Primates of trop. Africa (Yes); Diptera: Culicidae of trop. Africa (Yes)]
HADERLIE, Dr. E. C. Department of Zoology, Monterey Peninsula College, Monterey, Calif., U. S. A. [Trematoda, Cestoda, Acanthocephala, all parasitic in f-w. fishes of Pacific Cst. U. S. (Yes)]
HADLEY, Prof. Charles E. 52 Warfield Street, Upper Montclair, N. J., U. S. A. [Hydrozoa: g. Hydra (Yes)] [Upsala College, East Orange]
* HADLEY, Wade H., Jr. Mene Grande Oil Co., Apartado 709, Caracas, Venezuela. [Fossil invertebrates]
* HADSALL, Prof. S. Department of Zoology, Fresno State College, Fresno, Calif., U. S. A. [Reptilia]
* HADŽI, Prof. Dr. Jovan. Ljubljana Zoological Laboratory, University, Ljubljana, Yugoslavia. [Hydrozoa; Crustacea; Ostracoda; Pseudoscorpiones; Scorpiones; Ciliata: Folliculinidae; all of s. Europe]
HADZISSARANTOS, Prof. H., Directeur, Laboratoire de Zoologie Agricole de l'Ecole d'hautes études Agronomique. Kapsalie 11, Kolonaki, Athens, Greece. [Araneida of Balkans (Yes)]
HAEDO, Dr. Jose Antonio. Jardin Zoologico Municipal, Acevedo y Cabello, Buenos Aires, Argentina. [Coleoptera: Brenthidae of World, espec. Neotropics (Yes)]
HAFEZ, Prof. Dr. Mahmoud. Department of Entomology, Faculty of Science, University of Cairo, Giza, Cairo, Egypt. [Diptera: Muscidae of Egypt (No)]
HAFFNER, Dr. Rudolph E. Bucknell University, Lewisburg, Pa., U. S. A. [Pisces: Stomiatidae & Chauliodontidae of World (No)]
HAGEN, Kenneth S. Department of Biological Control, 1050 San Pablo Avenue, Albany 6, Calif., U. S. A. [Coleoptera: Anthicidae: g. Notoxus of New World (Yes); g. Mecynotarsus of Old World (Yes); Hymenoptera: Scelionidae & Encyrtidae of Nearctic (Yes)] [University of California]
HAGEN, Dr. Yngvar. Statens Viltundersokelser, Zoologisk Museum, Sarsgatan 1, Oslo, Norway. [Aves of n. Europe (Yes); terrestrial Mammalia of n. Europe (No); Aves of Tristan da Cunha (No)]
HAGGETT, Mr. G. 1 Torton Hill, Arundel, Sussex, England. [Lepidoptera: Larvae of Noctuidae & Geometridae of Great Britain (Yes)]
HAGMEIER, Mr. Edwin. Department of Biology, University of New Brunswick, Fredericton, N. B., Canada. [Mammalia of Brit. Columbia & E. Canada (No); Amphibia & Reptilia of E. Canada (No)]
HAGN, Dr. Herbert, Dipl. Geol., Priv. Doz. Mettingstrasse 4 - 1 M, München 19, Germany. [Up. Cretaceous-Tertiary benthonic or pelagic smaller Foraminifera of Alps & Mediterranean (Yes)] [Institut für Palaontologie und historische Geologie]
HAGUE, Florence S. (Sweet Briar, Va.; Oligochaeta) Not now active in taxonomy.
HAHNERT, Prof. W. F. Department of Zoology, Ohio Wesleyan University, Delaware, Ohio, U. S. A. [F-l. Protozoa; Oligochaeta; f-w. Crustacea; terr. & f-w. Gastropoda & Pelecypoda; Hirudinea; all of c. U. S. (Yes)]

HAIG, Janet. Hancock Foundation, University of Southern California, Los Angeles 7, Calif., U. S. A. [Crustacea: Porcellanidae of w. N. America (Yes); Pisces: Siluridae of Palearctic & Oriental (Yes); Sternoptychidae of w. N. America (Yes)]

HAIRSTON, N. G. Department of Zoology, University of Michigan, Ann Arbor, Mich., U. S. A. [Amphibia: Plethodontidae of s. Appalachian Mts. (Yes); Protozoa: Paramecium aurelia var. of Michigan (Yes)]

HALÁSZFY, Dr. Eva. Magyar Nemzeti Muzeum, Természettudományi Muzeum, Baross u. 13, Budapest VIII, Hungary. [Heteroptera: Pentatomidae of c. Europe (Yes); Coreidae of Europe (Yes)]

HALE, Mr. Herbert M., Director, The South Australian Museum, North Terrace, Adelaide, S. Australia. [Crustacea: Decapoda, Isopoda, Cumacea, of Australia & Antarctic (No); Mammalia: Cetacea: whales of S. Australian cst. (No)]

HALFFTER, Gonzalo. Medellin 344-14, Colonia Roma-Sur, Mexico 7, D. F., Mexico. [Scarabaeidae: Coprinae, espec. g. Canthon, of N. America & Mexico (Yes)] [Escuela Nacional de Ciencias Biologicas]

* HALIBURTON, William. (Ottawa, Canada; Coleoptera) Not now active in taxonomy.

* HALIK, Dr. L. Zitua 36, Praha II, Czechoslovakia. [Acarina: Hydrachnellae]

HALL, Mrs. Beryl Patricia. Bird Room, British Museum (Natural History), Cromwell Road, London, S. W. 7, England. [Aves of Africa & Asia (Yes)]

* HALL, Clarence. Department of Geology, University of California, Los Angeles 24, Calif., U. S. A. [Fossil invertebrates]

HALL, C. C., Jr. Department of Entomology, University of Kansas, Lawrence, Kans., U. S. A. [Acarina: Eriophyidae of N. America, espec. Kansas, (Yes); Trichoptera of N. America, espec. Texas (No)]

HALL, David G. U. S. Department of Agriculture, Room 5145 South Bldg., Washington 25, D. C., U. S. A. [Diptera: Sarcophagidae of World (No)]

HALL, Dr. E. Raymond. Department of Zoology, University of Kansas, Lawrence, Kans., U. S. A. [Mammalia of N. America (Yes)]

HALL, Mr. Gordon E. 6245 Round Oak Lane, Jacksonville 11, Fla., U. S. A. [F-w. Pisces of Oklahoma (Yes)]

HALL, Jack C. Department of Biological Control, University of California, Riverside, Calif., U. S. A. [Diptera: Bombyliidae of New World (Yes); Acarina: Phytoseiidae of N. America (No)]

HALL, John S. Museum of Natural History, University of Illinois, Urbana, Ill., U. S. A. [Mammalia: Chiroptera of N. America (Yes)]

* HALL, Prof. Richard P. Department of Biology, New York University, New York 53, N. Y., U. S. A. [Protozoa]

HALL, Dr. W. J. Commonwealth Institute of Entomology, 56 Queen's Gate, London, S. W. 7, England. [Homoptera: Coccoidea of World (Yes)]

* HALLAM, A. 29 Guthlaxton Street, Leicester, England. [Fossil invertebrates]

HALLGARTEN, F. 6 Park Street, Pascoe Vale, W. 8, Vict., Australia. [Coleoptera of Australia (Yes)]

HALSTEAD, Dr. Bruce W. World Life Research Institute, 22022 Center Street, Reche Canyon, Colton, Calif., U. S. A. [Venomous & poisonous marine animals of World (Yes)]

HALSTEAD, Morris E. Amerada Petroleum Corp., 1811 Niels Esperson Bldg., Houston 2, Texas, U. S. A. [Microfossils]

HALTENORTH, Dr. Th. Zoologische Staatssammlung, Menzingerstrasse 67, München 38, Germany. [Mammalia: Felidae of World (Yes)]

HAMADA, Keikichi. Faculty of Fisheries, Hokkaido University, Minato-Machi 253, Hakodate City, Japan. [Pisces: Teleostei: Osmeridae of Japan, The Amur, Bering Sea, N. & C. America (Yes)]

HAMELINK, K. C. Bastionstraat 16, Delfzijl, Netherlands. [Aves of Europe (Yes)]

* HAMILL, James M. 753 So. Ogden Drive, Los Angeles, Calif., U. S. A. [Fossil invertebrates]

HAMILTON, Mr. Edwin L. Navy Electronics Laboratory, San Diego 52, Calif., U. S. A. [Planktonic Foraminifera of World (No)]

* HAMILTON, I. B. Sun Oil Co., Box 2880, Dallas, Texas, U. S. A. [Fossil invertebrates]

HAMILTON, Prof. John Meacham. Department of Biology, Park College, Parkville, Mo., U. S. A. [Protozoa: Ciliophora: Peritrichida: f-w. Loricata (Yes)]

HAMILTON, Mr. Terrell H. Biological Laboratories, Harvard University, Cambridge 38, Mass., U. S. A. [Aves: Vireonidae of New World (Yes); Aves: Laniinae of World (No)]

HAMILTON, Dr. W. J., Jr. Department of Conservation, Cornell University, Ithaca, N. Y., U. S. A. [Mammalia of e. U. S. (Yes)]

van der HAMMEN, Dr. L. Rijksmuseum van Natuurlijke Historie, Leiden, Netherlands. [Acarina: Oribatidae of Europe (Yes); of New Guinea (No)]

* HAMMER, Karl. Zimmermanngasse 22, Wien IX, Austria. [Hymenoptera]

HAMMER, Dr. Marie. Strødam, Hillerød, Denmark. [Acarina: Oribatidae of Greenland, n. Europe, Andes Mts. (No)] [Zoological Museum, København]

HAMMOND, C. O. 34 Passmore Gardens, New Southgate, London, N. 11, England. [Diptera, espec. Syrphidae, of Brit. Isles (No); Odonata of Brit. Isles (No)]

HAMON, J. 82 rue A. Briand, Orsay (S. et O.), France. [Diptera: Culicidae of trop. Africa (Yes)] [Office de la Recherche Scientifique et Technique Outre Mer]

HAMON, Mlle. Maryvonne. Laboratoire de Biologie Générale, Faculté des Sciences, Université, d'Alger, Alger, Algeria. [Copepoda: Chaetognatha of e. Atlantic, Mediterranean, w. Pacific (Yes)]

HAMOND, Mr. R. "Scaldbeck," Morston, Holt, Norfolk, England. [Hydrozoa: Calyptoblastea & Gymnoblastea of World (Yes); Coelenterata, Crustacea, Polychaeta, Bryozoa, Suctoria, Tunicata, Echinodermata; all of s. North Sea (Yes)]

HAMPTON, Mr. John S. 13 Holland Way, Hayes, Bromley, Kent, England. [Paleozoic-Mesozoic Holothurian sclerites, espec. Achistridae & Stichopitidae, of World; Jurassic-Cretaceous Stichopitidae, Cal "Calclamnidae", Achistridae, Etheridgellidae, Theeliidae, of n. Europe; Recent Aspidochirotida, Dendrochirotida, g. Holothuria, g. Cucumaria, of World; Up. Cretaceous Porifera: Calcispongea: Solenida: Porosphaeridae of n. Europe; (all Yes)]

HAMRUM, Prof. Charles. Department of Biology, Gustavus Adolphus College, St. Peter, Minn., U.S.A. [Diptera: Sciomyzidae & Syrphidae of N. America (Yes)]

HANÁK, Dr. V. Zoological Institute, Charles University, Viničná 7, Praha II, Czechoslovakia. [Mammalia: Insectivora, Rodentia, Chiroptera, of c. & s. Europe (Yes)]

HANAOKA, Dr. T. Nakai Regional Fisheries Research Laboratory, Ujina, Hiroshima, Japan. [Copepoda, nauplius larvae, of Japan (No)]

HANCOCK, Dr. J. M. Department of Geology, King's College, London, W.C. 2, England. [Up. Cretaceous Ammonites of Europe (Yes); Cretaceous Belemnites of Europe (Yes); Up. Cretaceous Brachiopoda of n. w. Europe (Yes)] [University of London]

HAND, Dr. Cadet. Department of Zoology, University of California, Berkeley 4, Calif., U.S.A. [Anthozoa: Actiniaria of World (Yes); Hydrozoa: Hydroida of N. America (Yes)]

HANDFORD, Dr. R. H., Officer in Charge, Entomology Laboratory, P. O. Box 210, Kamloops, D. C., Canada. [Orthoptera: nymphs of Acrididae of w. Canada (No)]

HANDLEY, Dr. Charles O., Jr. Division of Mammals, U.S. National Museum, Washington 25, D. C., U.S.A. [Mammalia of World (Yes); Aves of World (No)]

HANDSCHIN, Prof. Dr. E., Directeur, Naturhistorisches Museum, Augustinergasse 2, Basel, Switzerland. [Neuroptera; Megaloptera; Mecoptera, excl. g. Chrysopa; all of World (Yes)]

HANKS, Robert W. U.S. Fish & Wildlife Service, Boothbay Harbor, Maine, U.S.A. [Marine Mollusca & Polychaeta of n. New England Cst. (Yes)]

HANNA, Dr. G. Dallas. Department of Mollusks, California Academy of Sciences, San Francisco 18, Calif., U.S.A. [Fossil terr. & f-w. Mollusca of World (Yes)]

HANNA, Dr. Marcus A. Gulf Oil Co., 5311 Kirby Drive, Houston 5, Texas, U.S.A. [Lower Cretaceous smaller Foraminifera of U.S. Gulf Coast (Yes); Tertiary larger Foraminifera of U.S. Gulf Coast (Yes)]

HANNEMANN, Dr. Hans-Joachim. Zoologisches Museum, Invalidenstrasse 43, Berlin N. 4, German Democratic Republic. [Lepidoptera: Depressariini of Palearctic (No); g. Scythris of Europe (No)]

HANNERZ, Dr. Lennart. Sötvattens Laboratoriet, Drottningholm, Sweden. [Polychaeta: Spionidae, Disomidae, Poecilochaetidae, of North Sea (No)]

HANNON, Chancellor I. Citrus Experiment Station, Lake Alfred, Fla., U.S.A. [Plant parasitic Nematoda of World, esp. Tropics (Yes)]

HANNUM, Dr. C. A. Department of Zoology, University of Wichita, Wichita 14, Kans., U.S.A. [Trematoda, Cestoda, parasitic Nematoda, of N. America & Pacific (Yes)]

HANSEN, Bent. Zoological Museum, Krystalgade, København, Denmark. [Holothurioidea of deep-sea (Yes)]

HANSEN, Dr. M. F. Department of Zoology, Kansas State College, Manhatten, Kans., U.S.A. [Helminths of domestic animals of N. America (Yes)]

HANSEN, Richard M. Experiment Station, Colorado State University, Fort Collins, Colo., U.S.A. [Mammalia: Sciuridae, espec. g. Citellus, of Rocky Mts. U.S. (Yes)]

HANSEN, Vagn. Danmarks Fiskeri og Havundersøgelser, Planktonlaboratoriet, Charlottenlund Slot, Denmark. [Crustacea: marine Copepoda: Gymnoplea of N. Atlantic & adjacent seas (Yes)]

HANSEN, Dr. Phil. Victor. J. E. Ohlsensgade 4, København, Denmark. [Coleoptera of Denmark (Yes)] [Zoologisk Museum]

HANSEN-MELANDER, Fil. lic. Eva. Institute of Genetics, Lund, Sweden. [Mammalia: Rodentia of Scandinavia (No)]

HANSENS, Elton J. Department of Entomology, Rutgers University, New Brunswick, N. J., U.S.A. [Ectoparasites of mammals of New Jersey]

HANSMAN, Robert H. 1215 Avenue F, For Madison, Iowa, U.S.A. [Pennsylvanian Nautiloidea of N. America (No)]

HANSON, B. H.   Naturhistoriska Riksmuseum, Stockholm 50, Sweden.   [Lepidoptera: Noctuidae of Europe (Yes)]

HANSON, Dr. John F.   Department of Entomology, University of Massachusetts, Amherst, Mass., U. S. A.   [Plecoptera of World (Yes)]

HANSON, Mary Louise.   See PRITCHARD, Mrs. Claremont G.

HANSON, Wilford J.   Department of Entomology, University of Kansas, Lawrence, Kans., U. S. A.   [Diptera: Stratiomyiidae: g. Nemotelus, of N. America (Yes); Psychodidae: g. Phlebotomus of Panama (No)]

* HANTKE, Dr. René.   Geologisches Institute, Sonneggstrasse 5, Zurich 6, Switzerland.   [Cretaceous Mollusca]

HANZÁK, Jan.   National Museum, Department of Zoology, Václavské náměsti, Praha 2, Czechoslovakia.   [Mammalia: Insectivora & Rodentia of c. Europe (Yes)]

HANZAWA, Prof. Shoshiro.   Institute of Geology & Paleontology, Tohoku University, Sendai, Japan.   [Fossil larger Foraminifera: Carboniferous-Permian Fusulinidae of Japan; Cretaceous-Tertiary Orbitoididae of Indo-Pacific; Tertiary Discocyclinidae & Miogypsinidae of Indo-Pacific; Tertiary-Recent Nummulitidae of Indo-Pacific (all Yes)]

HAQUE, A. F. M. Mohsenul.   Geological Survey of Pakistan, Quetta, West Pakistan.   [Up. Cretaceous & Up. Tertiary smaller Foraminifera of Pakistan & U. S. A. (Yes)]

HARA, Dr. Jun, Chief, Department of Biology, School of Physical Education, Juntendo University, Narashino-Shi, Chiba Pref., Japan.   [Diptera: Culicinae of Japan, Korea, Formosa, Far East (Yes)]

HARADA, Dr. Isokiti.   Shimoda Marine Biological Station, Shimoda, Shizuoka Pref., Japan.   [Crustacea: Cumacea of N. Pacific (Yes); f-w. Copepoda of Formosa (No); Acanthocephala of Japan & Formosa (No)]

* HARAMOTO, Frank H.   Department of Entomology, University of Hawaii, Honolulu 14, Hawaii, U. S. A.   [Acarina]

HARANT, Prof. H.   Faculté de Medecine, Institut de Parasitologie, Rue Auguste Broussonet, Montpellier, France.   [Diptera: Heleidae of Palearctic (No); Hymenoptera: Chrysididae & Mallophaga of Palearctic (Yes)]

* HARBISON, Miss Anne.   Academy of Natural Sciences, Philadelphia 3, Penna., U. S. A.   [Mollusca]

* HARBISON, Charles F.   Museum of Natural History (Entomology), Balboa Park, San Diego 1, Calif., U. S. A.   [Odonata]

* HARDE, Dr. Karl Wilhelm.   Staatliches Museum für Naturkunde, Schloss Rosenstein, Stuttgart O, Germany.   [Coleoptera: Cerambycidae; Diptera: Itonididae]

* HARDEN, P. C.   Department of Entomology & Zoology, Pasadena College, Pasadena 7, Calif., U. S. A.   [Odonata]

* HARDENBERG, Dr. J. D. F.   [Pisces]

HARDING, Dr. J. P.   British Museum (Natural History), Cromwell Road, London, S. W. 7, England.   [Crustacea: Entomostraca of World (Yes)]

HARDWICK, Dr. D. F.   Insect Systematics & Biological Control Unit, Entomology Division, Science Service Bldg., Ottawa, Ont., Canada.   [Lepidoptera: Noctuidae of N. America (Yes)]

HARDY, D. Elmo.   Agricultural Experiment Station, University of Hawaii, Honolulu 14, Hawaii, U. S. A.   [Diptera: Pipunculidae & Bibionidae of Tropics & Orient (Yes); Tephritidae of Pacific & Orient (Yes)]

HARDY, G. A.   (Victoria, Canada; Coleoptera & Lepidoptera) Not now active in taxonomy.

HARDY, G. H.   "Karambi" Letitia St., Katoomba, N. S. W., Australia.   [Diptera: Mycetophilidae & Tachinidae of Australia (No); Rhyphidae, Leptidae, Dolichopodidae, Syrphidae, g. Calliphora, g. Sarcophaga, of Australia (Yes)]

HARDY, Jerry D., Jr.   22 Wade Ave., Baltimore 28, Md., U. S. A.   [Reptilia, espec. g. Leiocephalus & Alsophis of W. Indies (Yes); Reptilia & Amphibia of C. America (No)]

HARDY, Dr. Ross, Professor of Zoology, Long Beach State College, Long Beach 15, Calif., U. S. A.   [Mammalia: Rodentia: Sciuridae, Heteromyidae, Cricetidae, of w. U. S. A. (Yes)]

HARGIS, Dr. William J., Jr.   Virginia Fisheries Laboratory, Gloucester Point, Va., U. S. A.   [Trematoda: Monogenea of World (Yes); Pisces: Osteichthyes & Chondrichthyes of Gulf of Mexico & w. N. Atlantic (No)]

* HARKEMA, Dr. Reinard.   North Carolina State College, Raleigh, N. C., U. S. A.   [Trematoda & Cestoda of U. S.]

* HARKER, J.   Department of Zoology, The University, Manchester 13, England.   [Odonata]

HARKER, Dr. Peter.   Geological Survey of Canada, Ottawa, Ont., Canada.   [Carboniferous-Permian Brachiopoda, Anthozoa, Cephalopoda: Ammonoidea, Foraminifera: Fusulinidae; all of w. Canada & Arctic (Yes)]

HARLOW, Francis H., Jr.   1071 Piñon Loop, Los Alamos, N. Mex., U. S. A.   [Pennsylvanian Brachiopoda of N. America (Yes)]

HARMAN, I.   Address unknown.   (Lepidoptera)

HARMANN, Dr. Gerd. See HARTMAN, G.
HARMSTON, Fred C. P. O. Box 334, Logan, Utah, U. S. A. [Diptera: Dolichopodidae of World (Yes); Culicidae of N. America (Yes)]
* HAROLD, A. Gulf Oil Corp., 17 Battery Place, New York, N. Y., U. S. A. [Fossil invertebrates]
HARPER, Dr. A. M. Canada Agricultural Research Station, Lethbridge, Alta., Canada. [Homoptera: Aphididae: Eriosomatinae of Canadian prairies (No)]
HARPER, Dr. Francis. 115 Ridgway Street, Mount Holly, N. J., U. S. A. [Aves & terr. Mammalia of n. Canada (Yes); Amphibia: Hylidae of e. N. America (Yes)]
HARPER, J. C. Department of Geology, The University, Liverpool 3, England. [Ordovician Faunas of Britain (No)]
* HARRASSOWITZ, Otto. Friedrichstrasse 14, Wiesbaden, Germany. [Fossil invertebrates]
HARRELL, Byron E. Department of Zoology, State University of South Dakota, Vermillion, S. D., U. S. A. [Aves of S. Dakota (Yes); cloud forest Aves of Mexico & n. C. America (No); Pleistocene Aves of N. America (No)]
* HARRELL, Mrs. D. C. 1003 Pecan Blvd., Jackson, Miss., U. S. A. [Mesozoic & Tertiary Foraminifera]
* HARRELL, Glen C. Humble Oil & Refining Co., P. O. Box 1271, Corpus Christi, Texas, U. S. A. [Fossil invertebrates]
HARRINGTON, George L. 566 Washington Ave., Palo Alto, Calif., U. S. A. [Foraminifera of Pacific (Yes)] [Stanford University]
* HARRINGTON, Dr. Horacio J. Facultad de Ciencias Naturales de Buenos Aires, Ayacucho 1364, Buenos Aires, Argentina. [Trilobita]
HARRINGTON, Dr. Robert W., Jr. Entomological Research Center, Florida State Board of Health Laboratory, P. O. Box 308, Vero Beach, Fla., U. S. A. [Estuarine Invertebrates & Pisces of Atlantic Cst. of Florida (Yes)]
HARRIS, E. J. W. Range Road, Kuranda, N. Qld., Australia. [Lepidoptera: Rhopalocera of Australia (Yes); Hepialidae of s. e. Australia (Yes)]
HARRIS, Dr. Halbert M., Head, Department of Zoology & Entomology, Iowa State College, Ames, Iowa, U. S. A. [Heteroptera: Nabidae & Rhopalidae of World (Yes); Anthocoridae of N. America (Yes); Gerridae of New World (Yes)]
* HARRIS, James Z. Gulf Oil, 5311 Kirby Drive, Houston, Texas, U. S. A. [Fossil invertebrates]
* HARRIS, Lester E., Jr. Washington Missionary College, Takoma Park 12, Md., U. S. A. [Lepidoptera]
HARRIS, R. D., Ornithologist, Canadian Wildlife Service, Federal Bldg., Edmonton, Alta., Canada. [Waterfowl of N. America (Yes)]
HARRIS, R. W. Faculty Exchange, Box 177, University of Oklahoma, Norman, Okla., U. S. A. [Microfossils of New World & Europe (Yes)]
HARRIS, Dr. V. "South Lodge," Buchan Hill, nr. Crawley, Sussex, England. [Reptilia: Agamidae of W. Africa (Yes)]
HARRIS, Wray. (Honolulu, Hawaii; Mollusca) Died December 17, 1953.
HARRIS, William P., Jr. 309 Rivard Blvd., Grosse Pointe, Mich., U. S. A. [Mammalia: Sciuridae of World (Yes)]
HARRIS, Mr. W. V. c/o Department of Entomology, British Museum (Natural History), London, S. W. 7, England. [Isoptera of Palearctic & Paleotropical (Yes)]
* HARRISON, A. C. 73 St. Georges Street, Cape Town, Union of South Africa. [Pisces]
HARRISON, Abner C. U. S. Navy Hydrographic Office, Washington 25, D. C., U. S. A. [Marine & f-w. Crustacea: Cladocera of World (No), of New World (Yes)]
HARRISON, Dr. David L. Bowerwood House, St. Botolph's Road, Sevenoaks, Kent, England. [Mammalia: Rodentia, Insectivora, Carnivora, of s. w. Asia (Yes); Chiroptera of Europe, s. w. Asia, Africa (Yes)]
HARRISON, Dr. Jeffery G. Merriewood, St. Botolph's Road, Sevenoaks, Kent, England. [Aves of Palearctic & Oriental (Yes); wildfowl of World (Yes)]
HARRISON, Dr. J. L. Queensland Institute of Medical Research Field Station, District Hospital, Innisfail, Queensland, Australia. [Mammalia: Rodentia & Insectivora of s. e. Asia & Australasia (Yes); g. Rattus associated with man of World (Yes)]
HARRISON, Dr. James M. Bowerwood House, St. Botolph's Road, Sevenoaks, Kent, England. [Aves of Palearctic & Oriental (Yes); wildfowl of World (Yes)]
* HARRISON, Julian S. Department of Zoology, Duke University, Durham, N. C., U. S. A. [Reptilia]
HARRISON, Dr, M. B. Cornell University Nematode Research Laboratory, 3985 Union Avenue, Seaford, N. Y., U. S. A. [Plant parasitic Nematoda of n. e. U. S. (No)]
HARRISON, Roy A. Plant Diseases Division, Department of Scientific Industrial Research, Private Bag, Auckland C 1, New Zealand. [Diptera: Acalyptrata of New Zealand & Pacific (Yes)]

HARRISON-MATTHEWS, Dr. L. Zoological Society of London, Regent's Park, London, N.W. 1, England. [Mammalia: Cetacea & Pinnipedia of World (No)]

* HARRY, Dr. Harold W. Department of Medical Zoology, Walter Reed Army Institute of Research, Washington 12, D.C., U.S.A. [Mollusca of e. & s.U.S.]

HARSLETT, Mrs. J. P.O. Box 15, Amiens, Queensland, Australia. [Lepidoptera: Lycaenidae, Hesperiidae, moths; Coleoptera: Cerambycidae; all of Australia (Yes)]

HART, Josephine F.L. (Mrs. G.C. Carl). 410 Queen Anne Hts., Victoria, B.C., Canada. [Crustacea: Marine Decapoda Reptantia of B.C. (Yes); Cumacea of B.C. (Yes)] [Provincial Museum]

HART, Dr. J.F. 2406 Gorman Rd., Longview, Wash., U.S.A. [Cestoda of elasmobranch fishes (No)] [Longview Fibre Co.]

HARTIG, Prof. Count Fred. Partschins (Bolzano), Italy. [Microlepidoptera of Paleactic (Yes); Lepidoptera of Mediterranean (Yes); leaf miners of Europe & Mediterranean (No)]

HARTLAND-ROWE, R. Calgary, Alta., Canada; Symphyla) Not now active in taxonomy.

HARTLEY, C.F. U.S. Public Health Service, Communicable Disease Center, Tropical Diseases Laboratory, Box 769, Savannah, Ga., U.S.A. [Diptera: Culicidae & Simuliidae of e.N. America (No)]

HARTLEY, Mrs. T. 351 Glenferrie Road, Malvern, Vict., Australia. [Mollusca (No)]

HARTMAN, Dr. Olga. Allan Hancock Foundation, University of Southern California, Los Angeles 7, Calif., U.S.A. [Annelida: Polychaeta of World (Fee)]

HARTMAN, Willard D. Peabody Museum of Natural History, Yale University, New Haven, Conn., U.S.A. [Porifera of Indo-Pacific & America (Yes)]

HARTMAN, G.· Museum der Stadt, Hegertorwall 28, Osnabrück, Germany. [Cenozoic & Recent Ostracoda of World (Yes)]

HARTMAN-SCHRÖDER, G. Städtisches Museum, Hegertorwall 28, Osnabrück, Germany. [Polychaeta of World, excl. planktonic (Yes)]

* HARTSHORNE, James M. 108 Kay Street, Ithaca, N.Y., U.S.A. [Aves]

HARTWEG, Dr. Norman. Museum of Zoology, University of Michigan, Ann Arbor, Mich., U.S.A. [Reptilia: Testudinea of New World (Yes), of Old World (No)]

HARTWICH, Dr. G. Zoologisches Museum, Invalidenstrasse 43, Berlin N.4, German Democratic Republic. [Parasitic Nematoda of vertebrates of Europe (Yes); Nematoda: Ascaroidea of World (Yes)]

HARTWIG, Dr. E.K. College of Agriculture, Glen, Orange Free State, Union of South Africa. [Thysanoptera of Africa, espec. Orange Free State & n. Cape (Yes)]

* HARUHIKO, Trie. Faculty of Fisheries, University of Nagasaki, Sakibe-machi, Saseho, Nagasaki-ken, Japan. [Crustacea]

HARVILLE, Dr. John P. San Jose State College, San Jose, Calif., U.S.A. [Pisces of California (Yes)]

HARWOOD, Philip H. (Wimborne, England; Heteroptera & Coleoptera) Died August 17, 1957.

HARWOOD, Dr. Paul D. R.D. 1, Ashland, Ohio, U.S.A. [Odonata of Ohio (Yes); Trematoda: Telorchiidae of World (Yes)] [Hess & Clark, Inc.]

* HARWOOD, Dr. Robert D. Department of Zoology, San Diego State College, San Diego, Calif., U.S.A. [Neuroptera]

HARZ, Kurt. Nüdlingweg 4, Kreis Bad Kissingen, (13A) Münnerstadt (Bavaria), Germany. [Dermaptera, Orthoptera, Blattoidea, of c. Europe (Yes)]

* HASBROUCK, F. Department of Entomology, Oregon State College, Corvallis, Ore., U.S.A. [Lepidoptera]

* HASE, Albrecht. (Berlin, Germany; Acarina) Not now active in taxonomy.

HASEGAWA, Megumi. Hokkaido Institute of Public Health, Sapporo, Hokkaido, Japan. [Cercaria larvae of Trematoda of e. Asia (Yes); medical entomology (Yes)]

* HASEGAWA, Hiroshi. Division of Entomology, National Institute of Agricultural Sciences, Nishigahara, Kiti-Ku, Tokyo, Japan. [Heteroptera]

HASEMAN, Leonard. Professor Emeritus of Entomology, Whitten Hall, University of Missouri, Columbia, Mo., U.S.A. [Diptera: Psychodidae of N. America (Yes)]

* HASHIMOTO, Isao. 1-22 Haracachi, Shinjukuku, Tokyo, Japan. [Coleoptera & Lepidoptera]

HASS, Robert L. 2215 S. California Avenue, Chicago 8, Ill., U.S.A. [F-w. Pisces of N. America (Yes)] [Chicago Natural History Museum]

HASS, Wilbert H. (Washington 25, D.C., U.S.A., L. Ordovician-Triassic Conodonts of 'N. America) Died November 30, 1959.

* HASSAN, Dr. A.I. Zoology Department, Cairo University, Giza, Egypt. [Araneida]

HÄSSLEIN, Ludwig. Bertleinstrasse 3, Lauf am Pegnitz, Bei Nürnberg (Bayern), Germany. [Pleistocene & Recent terr. & f-w. Gastropoda & Pelecypoda of c. Europe (Yes)]

* HASSLER, Dr. William W., Jr. Box 5215, State College Station, Raleigh, N.C., U.S.A. [Pisces]

HASTINGS, Dr. Anna B. British Museum (Natural History), Cromwell Road, London, S.W.7, England. [Marine & f-w. Bryozoa (No)]

HATAI, Prof. Dr. Kotora. Department of Geology, College of Education, Tohoku University, Kita 7-Bancho, Sendai, Japan. [Cenozoic Brachiopoda of Pacific (Yes); Cenozoic Pelecypoda, Gastropoda, Scaphopoda, of Pacific (Yes)]
HATCH, Dr. Melville H. Department of Zoology, University of Washington, Seattle 5, Wash., U.S.A. [Coleoptera & Isopoda of British Columbia, Washington, Idaho, Oregon (Yes)]
HATCHETT, Stephen P. (Washington, D.C.; Isopoda) Not now active in taxonomy.
HATELEY, K. Main Western Highway, Kiata, Vict., Australia. [Lepidoptera & Coleoptera: Buprestidae of S. Australia & Victoria (Yes)]
HATHAWAY, Prof. Edward S. Department of Zoology, Tulane University, New Orleans 18, La., U.S.A. [Diptera: Culicidae of U.S. Gulf Cst. (No)]
HATT, Dr. Robert T. Cranbrook Institute of Science, Bloomfield Hills, Mich., U.S.A. [Mammalia: Rodentia, Hyracoidea, Sirenia, of N. America & Africa (No)]
* HATTER, J. Department of Parks, Game Branch, 567 Burrard St., Vancouver, B.C., Canada. [Mammalia]
* HATTORI, Miss Isoko. Division of Entomology, National Institute of Agricultural Science, Nishigahara, Kita-Ku, Tokyo, Japan. [Larvae of Lepidoptera]
HAUER, Dr. J. Karlstrasse 88, Karlsruhe 17a, Germany. [Rotatoria: Monogononta of World, espec. Eurasia, S. America, S. Africa, Sunda Arch.(Yes)]
HAUGHTON, Dr. S.H. P.O. Box 401, Pretoria, Union of South Africa. [Permian-Triassic (Karroo) vertebrates of trop. Africa]
HAUPT, Dr. H.C.H. (Halle, Germany; Hymenoptera) Not now active in taxonomy.
* HAVERSCHMIDT, F. Paramaribo, Surinam. [Aves]
HAVESSON, J.I. Dairy Institute of Vologda, Cabinet of Zoology, Vologda, Molochnoje, U.S.S.R. [Pliocene & Pleistocene Mammalia: Tylopoda: Camelidae of Eurasia & N. Africa (Yes)]
HAVLIČEK, Dr. V. Ustředni ústav geologický, Hradebni 9, Praha I, Czechoslovakia. [Paleozoic Brachiopoda of Europe (Yes)]
* HAVLIK, Dr. O. Ustav Microbiologie, Srobarova 48, Praha XII, Czechoslovakia. [Gordiacea]
* HAWKINS, Prof. H.L. 63 Tilehurst Road, Reading, England. [Fossil invertebrates]
HAY, William W. School of Mineral Sciences, Stanford University, Stanford, Calif., U.S.A. [Tertiary marine Ostracoda of Europe (Yes); Cretaceous-Tertiary Foraminifera (Yes)]
HAYAMI, Itaru. Geological Institute, Faculty of Science, Tokyo University, Tokyo, Japan. [Jurassic Lamellibranchia of Japan (Yes), Cretaceous (No)]
HAYASAKA, Dr. Ichiro, President, Shimane University, Matsue City, Shimane Pref., Japan. [Carboniferous-Permian Mollusca, Brachiopoda, Corals (Yes)]
HAYASAKA, Shozo. Institute of Geology & Paleontology, Faculty of Science, Tohoku University, Sendai, Japan. [Tertiary-Pleistocene marine Pelecypoda, Gastropoda, Scaphopoda, of Japan (Yes)]
HAYASHI, Kei. 23 Minami-cho, Itabashi-ku, Tokyo, Japan. [Lepidoptera: Rhopalocera of Saghalien I., Japan, Korea, Ryukyu Is., Formosa, Manchuria (Yes); Lycaenidae of Palaearctic (No)]
HAYASHI, Masao. 71 3-chôme, Sumie-Nishi, Sumiyoshi, Osaka, Japan. [Coleoptera: Cerambycidae & Melandryidae of Japan (Yes)] [Osaka Municipal Museum of Natural History]
HAYASHI, Nodoka. 530-9 Kikunamachi, Kohoku-Ku, Yokohama, Japan. [Coleoptera, larvae, of Japan (Yes)]
HAYASHI, Dr. Ryoji. Biological Institute, Toyama University, Toyama, Japan. [Asteroidea of Japan (Yes)]
HAYASHIDA, Kazuo. Zoological Institute, Faculty of Science, Hokkaido University, Sapporo, Japan. [Hymenoptera: Formicidae of Japan (No)]
von HAYEK, Miss C.M.F. Department of Entomology, British Museum,(Natural History), Cromwell Road, London, S.W.7, England. [Coleoptera: Elateridae of World, espec. Europe (Yes)]
HAYES, Prof. William P. 301 W. Delaware, Urbana, Ill., U.S.A. [Coleoptera: Scarabaeidae & Rhynchophora of c. U.S. (No)] [University of Illinois]
HAYMAN, Mr. R.W. Department of Zoology (Mammals), British Museum (Natural History), Cromwell Road, London, S.W.7, England. [Terrestrial Mammalia of World, espec. Africa (Yes)]
HAYNES, Dr. John. 4 Oxford Avenue, Llandrindod Wells, Radnorshire, Wales. [Tertiary Foraminifera of Europe & Middle East (Yes); Mesozoic of Canada (Yes)]
HAYNES, Winthrop P. (Boxford, Mass.; Devonian fossils) Not now active in taxonomy.
HAYS, Kirby. Department of Zoology & Entomology, Alabama Polytechnic Institute, Auburn, Ala., U.S.A. [Diptera: Tabanidae of New World (Yes); Asilidae of U.S. (Yes); Acarina: Ixodidae & Laelaptidae of N. America (Yes)]
HAYWARD, Dr. K.J. Instituto Miguel Lillo, Miguel Lillo 205, Tucumán, Argentina. [Lepidoptera: Rhopalocera of Argentina (Yes); Hesperiidae of Neotropics (Yes)] [National University of Tucumán]

HAZELTINE, Wm. (Dallas, Texas; Coleoptera: Scarabaeidae) Not now active in taxonomy.
HAZEN, William E. Address unknown. (Tubellaria: Rhabdocoelida)
HEACOCK, Robert L. Box 720, Casper, Wyo., U.S.A. [Mesozoic Foraminifera of U.S.
   Rocky Mts. & Gr. Plains (No)]
HEALY, Dr. George R. Communicable Disease Center, Parasitology Training Laboratory,
   P.O. Box 185, Chamblee, Ga., U.S.A. [Trematoda of New World (Yes)]
HEASLIP, Prof. William G. Department of Geology, Syracuse University, Syracuse 10, N.Y.,
   U.S.A. [Cenozoic Pelecypoda: g. Venericardia of N. America (Yes)]
HEBARD, Dr. William B. (New York, N.Y., gartersnakes) Not now active in taxonomy.
* HEBERER, G. Zoologisches Institut, Bahnhofstrasse 28, Göttingen, Germany. [Copepoda]
* HECHT, Bessie M. American Museum of Natural History, New York 24, N.Y., U.S.A.
   [Amphibia & Reptilia of New Guinea, N. America, W. Indies]
HECHT, Max K. Department of Biology, Queens College, Flushing, N.Y., U.S.A. [Triassic-
   Oligocene Amphibia & Reptilia (frogs, salamanders, caecilians, lizards, snakes, cro-
   codilians (Yes)]
HECHT, Dr. Otto. Rio Pánuco Núm. 83, México 5, D.F., Mexico. [Siphonaptera & Diptera:
   Culicidae of New World (No)]
HECK, O.B. Department of Biology, Coe College, Cedar Rapids, Iowa, U.S.A. [Cestoda:
   Cyclophyllidea of N. America (No)]
HEDBERG, Dr. H.D. 1037 Hulton Road, Oakmont, Penna., U.S.A. [Cretaceous-Tertiary
   Foraminifera of Caribbean (No)]
HEDEEN, Capt. R.A. Entomology Branch, Department of Preventive Medicine, Army Medi-
   cal Service School, Fort Sam Houston, Texas, U.S.A. [Diptera: Culicidae of N. Ameri-
   ca & Palearctic, espec. Europe & Middle East (Yes)]
HEDGPETH, Joel W. Pacific Marine Station, Dillon Beach, Calif., U.S.A. [Devonian-
   Recent Pycnogonida of World (Yes)] [College of the Pacific]
HEDIGER, Dr. Heini. (Zürich, Switzerland; Reptilia) Not now active in taxonomy.
HEDLEY, Dr. R.H. British Museum (Natural History), Cromwell Road, London, S.W.7,
   England. [Protozoa: Foraminifera (Yes)]
HEDWIG, Karl., Rektor i.R. Königsberger Strasse 2, (21a) Minden i. W., Germany. [Hy-
   menoptera of Palearctic (Yes); Ichneumonidae of Palearctic (Yes); Braconidae of
   Palearctic (No)]
HEED, William B. Department of Zoology, University of Arizona, Tucson, Ariz.,
   U.S.A. [Diptera: Drosophilidae of New World (Yes)]
HEEGAARD, Prof. Dr. Poul. Department of Zoology, University of Indonesia, P.O. Box 25,
   Bandung, Java. [Crustacea: parasitic Copepoda of World (Yes)]
van HEERDT, Dr. P.F. Zoologisch Laboratorium, Janskerkhof 3, Utrecht, Netherlands.
   [Chiroptera of w. Europe (Yes); Coleoptera & Homoptera of n.w. Europe (No)]
HEFLEY, Dr. Harold M. P.O. Box 147, Goodwell, Okla., U.S.A. [Siphonaptera of N. Ameri-
   ca (Yes)]
HEFNER, Dr. R.A. Department of Zoology, Miami University, Oxford, Ohio, U.S.A. [Diplo-
   poda & Chilopoda of n.c. U.S. (Yes)]
HEID, Graham. Communicable Disease Center, U.S. Public Health Service, Audio-Visual
   Section, Box 185, Chamblee, Ga., U.S.A. [Diptera: Tabanidae of N. & C. America
   (No); g. Chrysops of s.e. U.S. (Yes)]
HEILMAN, Mr. R.A. 533 Spruce Street, Lebanon, Pa., U.S.A. [Mollusca: Sphaeriidae,
   excl. g. Pisidium, of N. America (Yes)]
* HEIM de BALSAC, Prof. H. 34 rue Hamelin, Paris (XVI), France. [Aves]
HEIMLICH, Wilhelm. Casilla 10123, Santiago, Chile. [Lepidoptera of Chile (No)]
* HEINAJOKI, Martha. Zoologischen Museum der Universität, Helsinki, Finland. [Opiliones]
* HEINDL-MENGERT, Dr. Herta. Bogenstrasse 32, Nürnberg, Germany. [Nematoda]
HEINEMAN, Bernard. 175 West 72nd Street, New York 23, N.Y., U.S.A. [Lepidoptera of
   Jamaica (Yes)]
HEINICKE, Wolfgang. Louis-Schlutter-Strasse 16a, Gera, German Democratic Republic.
   [Lepidoptera: Noctuidae: g. Apamea of Europe & Asia (Yes)]
HEINREICH, Gerd. Dryden, Maine, U.S.A. [Hymenoptera: Ichneumonidae: Ichneumoninae
   of Canada, Palearctic, Oriental, Ethiopian (Yes)]
HEINTZ, Prof. Dr. Anatol. Paleontologisk Museum, Sarsgatan 1, Oslo 45, Norway. [Siluri-
   an-Devonian Ostracodermi (Yes); Devonian Arthrodira (No)] [University of Oslo]
* HEINZ, E. Bank für Handel und Industrie A-G., Uhlandstrasse 9/11, Berlin-Charlottenburg,
   Germany. [Coleoptera: Chrysomelidae]
* HEINZ, Mr. H.J. South African Institute for Medical Research, Johannesburg, Transvaal,
   Union of South Africa. [Diptera]
HEINZ, Walter, Diplom-ingenieur, Amoberen langen Rain, Wilhelmsfeld b. Heidelberg,
   Germany. [Coleoptera: Carabidae of World (No); of Palearctic (Yes)]
HEINZE, Dr. K. Biologische Bundesanstalt, Königin-Luise-Strasse 19, Berlin-Dahlem,
   Germany. [Homoptera: Aphidoidea of Europe (Yes)]

* HEISCH, R. B.   Division of Insect-Borne Diseases, Medical Research Laboratory, P. O. Box
    141, Nairobi, Kenya.   [Acarina]
HEJSKOVA-ČERVENKOVÁ, Eva.   Ustav Hygieny, Hydrobiologie, Scobarova 48, Praha XII,
    Czechoslovakia.   [Porifera & Bryozoa of Czechoslovakia (Yes)]
* HELDT, J. H.   Station Oceanographique, Salammbô, Tunisia.   [Pisces]
* HELDT, Mme. J. H.   Institut des Hautes Etudes, Rue Rome, Tunis, Tunisia.   [Copepoda]
HELFER, Jacques R.   Mendocino, Calif., U. S. A.   [Coleoptera: Buprestidae of World (No);
    of California (Yes)]
HELLÉN, Phil. Dr. Wolter, Curator, Museum of Zoology, University of Helsingfors, Hel-
    sinki, Finland.   [Hymenoptera: Symphata & Parasitica of c. & n. Europe (Yes)]
* HELLER, Miss Anita F.   Institute of Parasitology, MacDonald College, McGill University,
    Montreal 2, Que., Canada.   [Copepoda]
HELLER, Prof. Dr. Florian.   Geologisches Institut, Schlossgarten 5, Erlangen, Germany.
    [Pliocene-Pleistocene Mammalia: Micromammals, espec. Microtinae, of c. Europe
    (Yes)]
HELLER, Robert Leo.   Department of Geology, University of Minnesota at Duluth, Duluth,
    Minn., U. S. A.   [L. Paleozoic Fossils of U. S. (Yes)]
* HELLIER, T. E.   Institute of Marine Science, University of Texas, Port Aransas, Texas,
    U. S. A.   [Pisces]
HELLMAN, E. A.   Iittala, Finland.   [Macrolepidoptera, espec. Rholalocera, g. Pieris, g.
    Brenthis, of Fennoscandia (Yes)]
HELLMICH, Dr. W.   Zoologische Staatssammlung, Menzingerstrasse 67, München 19, Ger-
    many.   [Amphibia & Reptilia of Europe (Yes); Sauria, espec. g. Liolaemus, of S.
    America (Yes); Reptilia of Angola (Yes)]
HELLWING, Salo A.   Muzeul de Istorie Naturală "Grigore Antipa", Soš. Kisselef Nr. 1,
    Bucureşti I, Rumania.   [Mammalia of Europe, espec. Rumania (Yes)]
HELMCKE, .Prof. Dr. Johann-Gerhard.   Max Planck Gesellschaft, Faradayweg 16, Berlin-
    Dahlem, Germany.   [Brachiopoda of World (Yes)]
HELMERS, G.   van Koetsvelstraat 8bis, Amsterdam, Netherlands.   [Lepidoptera: Pyralidae of
    Europe (Yes), of S. Africa, Indonesia, N. Guinea (No)]
HELMS, Herr J.   Geologisch-Paläontologisches Institut und Museum der Humboldt Universität,
    Invalidenstrasse 43, Berlin N. 4, German Democratic Republic.   [Devonian Conodonts of
    Thuringia & Harz Mts., Germany (Yes)]
HELSON, Gordon A. H.   Superintendent, Plant Quarantine Service, Department of Agriculture,
    Wellington, New Zealand.   [Homoptera: Jassidae of N. Zealand (No)]
HELWIG, Dr. Edwin R.   Department of Biology, University of Colorado, Boulder, Colo.,
    U. S. A.   [Orthoptera: Acridioidea of N. America (No)]
HEMMING, C. F.   The Desert Locust Survey, P. O. Box 30023, Nairobi, Kenya.   [Mollusca of
    arid e. Africa (No)]
* HEMMING, Francis.   28 Park Village East, Regent's Park, London, N. W. 1, England.
    [Lepidoptera: Rhopalocera of Holarctic]
HEMPHILL, Mr. Andrew.   Department of Biology, Spring Hill College, Mobile, Ala., U. S. A.
    [F-w. Pisces of Alabama coastal plain (No)]
* HEMPHILL, Prof. Donald V.   Biology Department, Pacific Union College, Angwin, Calif.,
    U. S. A.   [Aves & Mammalia of w. N. America]
HENBEST, Lloyd G.   U. S. National Museum, Washington 25, D. C., U. S. A.   [Fossil & Recent
    Foraminifera of World (No)]   [U. S. Geological Survey]
* HENDERSON, V. E.   Nematode Investigations, Science Service Laboratory, Carling Avenue,
    Ottawa, Ont., Canada.   [Nematoda]
HENDRICKSON, John R.   Department of Zoology, University of Malaya, Singapore, Malaya.
    [Amphibia & Reptilia of s. e. Asia & Malay Arch. (Yes)]
HENDRIX, W. E.   6261 N. Sultana, Temple City, Calif., U. S. A.   [Tertiary benthonic Fora-
    minifera of s. California (Yes)]
HENNE, Christopher.   231 24th Place, Manhattan Beach, Calif., U. S. A.   [Lepidoptera: Aegeri-
    idae & Phalaenidae: g. Copicucullia, Annaphila, Heliothiinae; all of s. w. U. S. (Yes)]
HENNIG, Prof. Dr. W.   Deutsches Entomologisches Institut, Josef-Nawrocki Str. 10, Berlin-
    Friedrichshagen, German Democratic Republic.   [Diptera: Muscidae of Palearctic (Yes)]
HENNINGSMOEN, Dr. Gunnar.   Universitetets Paleontologiske Museum, Sarsgate 1, Oslo
    N. O., Norway.   [Ordovician-Silurian Ostracoda: Paleocopa of Norway (Yes); Cambrian-
    Ordovician Trilobita of Norway (Yes)]
HENROT, Dr. Henri.   5 rue Ancelle, Neuilly-sur-Seine, France.   [Coleoptera: Catopidae of
    World (Yes)]
HENRY, Dora.   Oceanographic Laboratories, University of Washington, Seattle 5, Wash.,
    U. S. A.   [Cirripedia: Lepadomorpha, Verrucomorpha, Balanomorpha (Yes)]
HENSLEY, Jack R.   Department of Zoology, University of Arizona, Tucson, Ariz., U. S. A.
    [Acanthocephala]
HENSLEY, Dr. M. M.   Department of Zoology, Michigan State University, East Lansing, Mich.,
    U. S. A.   [Reptilia & Amphibia of N. America, espec. s. w. U. S. (Yes)]

214

HENSON, Dr. E. B. Department of Zoology, University of Maryland, College Park, Md.,
U.S.A. [Aquatic stages of Plecoptera, Ephemeroptera, Trichoptera, of c.e.U.S.
(Yes); Crustacea: Amphipoda & Isopoda of c.e.U.S. (Yes)]
HENSON, Dr. F. R. S. (London, England; fossil Foraminifera) Not now active in taxonomy.
HEPNER, Leon W. Ft. Hays Kansas State College, Hays, Kans., U.S.A. [Homoptera: Cica-
dellidae of N. America (No)]
HEPPENSTALL, Miss C.A., Assistant Curator of Mammals, Carnegie Museum, Pittsburgh
13, Penna., U.S.A. [Mammalia of Pennsylvania (Yes); Chiroptera of e.N. America
(Yes)]
HEPPER, Hector C. Nueva York 4480, Buenos Aires, Argentina. [Coleoptera: Chrysomelidae
& Coccinellidae of Argentina]
HEPTNER, Prof. Dr. W.G. Zoological Museum of the University, ul. Gerzena 6, Moscow
K-9, U.S.S.R. [Mammalia of U.S.S.R. & c. & s.w. Asia (Yes); Aves & Reptilia of
U.S.S.R. (No)]
HEQVIST, Karl-Johan. Amanuens Statens Skogsforskningsinstitut, Stockholm 51, Sweden.
[Hymenoptera: Braconidae of Oriental & Neotropical (Yes); Chalcidoidea: Cleonymidae
of World (Yes)]
HERALD, Dr. Earl S. California Academy of Sciences, San Francisco 18, Calif., U.S.A.
[Pisces: Syngnathidae of World (Yes)]
HERBER, Dr. E.C. 416 W. South Street, Carlisle, Pa., U.S.A. [Trematoda: Monostomes of
World (Yes)] [Dickinson College]
HERBST, Dr. Hans Volkmar, Limnologische Station, Niederrhein, Krefeld, Germany. [Crus-
tacea: f-l. Cyclopoida (Yes)]
HERBULOT, Claude. 31 Avenue d'Eylau, Paris (XVI), France. [Lepidoptera: Geometridae of
w. Europe & Africa (No), of Madagascar & E. African islands (Yes), Larentiinae & En-
nominae of Africa (Yes)]
HERING, Prof. Dr. E.M. Reichensteiner Weg. 21, Berlin-Dahlem, Germany. [Leaf-mining
Insecta of Palearctic (Yes); Diptera: Trypetidae of World (Yes); Agromyzidae of
Palearctic (No)]. [Zoological Museum, Humboldt University]
HERLICH, H. Regional Animal Disease Research Laboratory, P. O. Drawer 952, Auburn, Ala.,
U.S.A. [Nematoda: Trichostrongylidae of ruminants of U.S. (Yes)]
HERMAN, Dr. Carlton M. Patuxent Research Refuge, Laurel, Md., U.S.A. [Blood Protozoa
of birds of World (Yes); Diptera: Hippoboscidae of N. America (No)] [U.S. Fish & Wild-
life Service]
* HERMAN, Mr. Sydney. Narragansett Marine Laboratory, University of Rhode Island, Kings-
ton, R.I., U.S.A. [Pisces]
* HEROLD, W. Zoologische Institut der Universität, Holderlinstrasse 12, Tübingen, Germany.
[Isopoda]
HERPIN, Dr. R., Conservateur du Musée d'Histoire Naturelle, 39 rue Amiral d'Aboville,
Cherbourg (Manche), France. [Annelida: Polychaeta]
HERRE, Dr. Albert W. School of Fisheries, University of Washington, Seattle, Wash., U.S.A.
[Littoral & pelagic Pisces of trop. Indo-Pacific; F-w. Pisces of trop. Orient; Gobiidae
& Phallostethidae of Indo-Pacific; (all Yes)]
HERRE, Prof. Dr. W., Direktor, Instituts für Haustierkunde, Hegewischstrasse 1, Kiel,
Germany. [Fossil & Recent Amphibia: Urodela (Yes); Mammalia: domesticated Tylo-
poda (Yes)]
HERRERA, Prof. José. Casilla Correo 147, Santiago, Chile. [Lepidoptera: Rhopalocera of
Andes Mts. (Yes)]
HERRICK, Prof. C.A. (Madison, Wis.; parasitology) Died October, 1955.
HERRICK, Glenn W. (Ithaca, N.Y., Thysanoptera) Not now active in taxonomy.
HERRICK, Stephen M. 306 Mimosa Drive, Decatur, Ga., U.S.A. [Smaller Foraminifera of
Claiborne formation of Georgia (Yes)]
HERRING, Jon L. Division of Entomology, University of California, Berkeley 4, Calif.,
U.S.A. [Aquatic Heteroptera of Tropics (Yes); marine Heteroptera of World (Yes)]
HERRINGTON, Rev. H.B. Westbrook Heights, Westbrook, Ont., Canada. [Fossil & Recent
Pelecypoda: Sphaeriidae of N. America (Yes)]
HERSHKOVITZ, Philip. Chicago Natural History Museum, Chicago 5, Ill., U.S.A. [Mam-
malia of World (No)]
HERTEL, Dr. Rolf. Staatliches, Museum für Tierkunde, Zwinger, Dresden A 1, German
Democratic Republic. [Coleoptera: Pachyrrhynchini of Indo-Pacific (Yes); Odonata of
c. Europe (Yes); Pelecypoda: Unionidae of Germany (No)]
HERTER, Prof. Dr. K., Direktor am Zoologischen Institut der Freien Universität Berlin,
Königin Lüisestrasse 13, Berlin-Dahlem, Germany. [Amphibia & Reptilia of Germany
(Yes); Hirudinea of Germany (Yes)]
HERTIG, Dr. Marshall. Gorgas Memorial Laboratory, Apartado 1252, Panama, Rep. Panama.
[Diptera: Phlebotomus of New World (Yes)]
HERTING, Dr. B. Landesmuseum für Naturkunde, Himmelreichallee, Münster i.w., Germany.
[Diptera: Tachinidae of Europe (Yes); Rhinophorinae of World (Yes)]

215

HERTLEIN, Leo G. Department of Geology, California Academy of Sciences, San Francisco 18, Calif., U.S.A. [Cenozoic marine Mollusca of w. N. America (No)]

* HERTZOG, Dr. L. A. 12 rue Ch. Grad, Strasbourg (B.-Rh.), France. [Copepoda]

HERVÉ, Mr. Pierre, Eaux et Forêts, 2 rue Valperga, Nice, France. [Coleoptera of Gallo-Rhénane & Provence (France) (No)]

HERZER, Dr. Albert. Offentlich chemisches Handels-Laboratorium, Nadorster Strasse 124, Oldenburg, Germany. [Coleoptera: Histeridae of World (Yes)]

* HESLOP-HARRISON, Dr. G. Department of Agricultural Zoology, King's College, New-castle-on-Tyne, England. [Homoptera: Psyllidae; Lepidoptera]

HESS, Dr. Hans. Hauptstrasse 121, Binningen, near Basel, Switzerland. [Jurassic Asteroidea, Ophiuroidea, Crinoidea, of c. Europe (Yes)]

HESSE, Dr. A. J. South African Museum, Cape Town, Union of South Africa. [Diptera: Bombyliidae of s. Africa (Yes)]

HESSEL, Sidney A. Nettleton Hollow Road, Washington, Conn., U.S.A. [Lepidoptera: Noctuidae & Rhopalocera of Mid-Atlantic U.S. (Yes)]

HESSLAND, Dr. Ivar. Kungstensgatan 45, Stockholm, Sweden. [Paleozoic Ostracoda (No)] [Geologiska Institutet, University of Stockholm]

* HESTER, Mr. S.W. H. M. Geological Survey, Exhibition Road, London, S.W.7, England. [Fossil invertebrates]

HEUER, Prof. Edward. Departments of Geology & Biology, Texas Christian University, Fort Worth 9, Texas, U.S.A. [Pennsylvanian marine invertebrates of c. N. America (No)]

van HEURN, Drs. W.C. "Kleine Noordijk", Wilp, bij Deventer (Guelders), Netherlands. [Small Mammalia of Netherlands (Yes); Aves & Mammalia of Java & surrounding islands (No)]

HEWATT, Willis G. Department of Biology, Texas Christian University, Fort Worth 9, Texas, U.S.A. [Marine invertebrates of Texas & Gulf of Mexico (Yes)]

HEWITT, Dr. John. Albany Museum, Grahamstown, Union of South Africa. [Reptilia; Amphibia; Araneida, espec. Aviculariidae; Scorpiones; all of S. Africa (Yes)]

HEWITT, Prof. Philip Cooper. Geology Department, Union College, Schenectady 8, N.Y., U.S.A. [Larger Foraminifera, espec. Orbitoididae, of Gulf of Mex. & Caribbean (Yes); Up. Paleozoic Endothyridae & Fusulinidae of Appalachian Mts. (Yes)]

HEY, Dr. D. Department of Nature Conservation, Provincial Administration of Cape of Good Hope, Private Bag, Stellenbosch, Union of South Africa. [Pisces of s. Africa; Aves & Mammalia of Cape Prov. of Africa]

HEYDEMANN, Prof. Dr. F. Lütjenburger Strasse 25, 24b Plön (Holstein), Germany. [Lepidoptera of Palearctic (Yes); Rhopalocera: Argynnidae, Lycaenidae of Europe (Yes); Heterocera: Noctuidae: g. Apamea, Procus, Miana, Crino, of Palearctic (Yes); Geometridae: g. Dysstroma, Larentia, Ortholitha, Boarmia, Ematurga of Palearctic (Yes)]

HEYLER, D. Laboratoire de Paleontologie, 13 Place Valhubert, Paris (V), France. [Permian Pisces: Paleoniscidae & Permian Amphibia: Stegocephalia, both of France (Yes)]

HEYNEMAN, Donald. Department of Zoology, University of California, Los Angeles 24, Calif., U.S.A. [Trematoda & Cestoda (Yes)]

HEYROVSKY, Dr. L. Platnerska 7, Praha I, Czechoslovakia. [Coleoptera: Cerambycidae of Palearctic (Yes)]

HEYSIN, E.M. See CHEISSIN, E.M.

HIATT, Dr. R.W. Department of Zoology & Entomology, University of Hawaii, Honolulu 14, Hawaii, U.S.A. [Crustacea: Brachyura of c. Pacific]

HIBBARD, Dr. Claude W. Museum of Paleontology, University of Michigan, Ann Arbor, Mich., U.S.A. [Pliocene-Pleistocene Rodentia & Insectivora of N. America (Yes)]

HIBBARD, Raymond R. (Buffalo, N.Y., Fossil invertebrates) Deceased.

HIBBEN, Dr. F.C. Department of Anthropology, University of New Mexico, Albuquerque, New Mexico, U.S.A. [Mammalia: "mountain lion" of N. America (Yes)]

HICKER, Regierungsrat Richard. Mauerbacherstrasse 123, Wien-Hadersdorf, Austria. [Coleoptera: Cantharidae of Europe, Asia, Africa (Yes); Oedemeridae of Palearctic (Yes)]

HICKIN, Dr. Norman E. Home Farm, Fetcham, Leatherhead, Surrey, England. [Trichoptera larvae of World (Yes); woodboring Insecta of World (No)]

HICKMAN, Prof. V.V. University of Tasmania, Box 647 C, G.P.O., Hobart, Tasmania, Australia. [Araneida: Apneumonomorphae of Tasmania (Yes)]

HICKS, Dr. Ellis A. Department of Zoology & Entomology, Iowa State College, Ames, Iowa, U.S.A. [Acarina: Diplogyniidae of N. America (Yes)]

HICKS, S.D. Room 336, Science Service Building, Ottawa, Ont., Canada. [Coleoptera: Cerambycidae, g. Oberea of e. N. America (Yes)]

HIDAKA, Mr. T. Entomological Laboratory, Faculty of Agriculture, Kyushu University, Fukuoka, Japan. [Terr. Heteroptera of Japan & Ryukyu Is. (Yes); Lygaeidae of Japan, Formosa, Ryukyu Is. (Yes)]

HIGGINS, Harold. 2965 South 14th East, Salt Lake City 6, Utah, U.S.A. [Acarina: Oribatei of N. America (Yes); Caeculidae of N. America & Korea (Yes)]

HIGGINS, Dr. L. G. Gracious Pond Farm, Chobham, Surrey, England. [Lepidoptera: Melitaei-
dae of World (Yes)]
HIGGS, Prof. William R. P. O. Box 338, Louisiana Polytechnic Institute, Ruston, La., U.S.A.
[Mesozoic-Cenozoic Foraminifera, excl. Fusulinidae, of N. America (Yes); Paleozoic-
Cenozoic marine invertebrates, excl. graptolites, of N. America (Yes)]
HIGHBY, Dr. P.R. 1056 West 79th Street, Los Angeles 44, Calif., U.S.A. [Nematoda: Fila-
rioideae of N. America (No)] [George Pepperdine College]
HIGHTON, Dr. Richard. Department of Zoology, University of Maryland, College Park, Md.,
U.S.A. [Amphibia: salamanders of N. America (No); g. Plethodon of N. America (Yes)]
HIKITA, Mr. Toyohiko. Hokkaido Salmon Hatchery, Nakanoshima, Sapporo City, Hokkaido,
Japan. [Pisces: Salmonidae of n. Japan & Hokkaido (Yes); other marine & f-w. Pisces
of n. Japan & Hokkaido (No)]
* HILDEBRAND, Mr. Charles W. 1738 39th Avenue, San Francisco 22, Calif., U.S.A. [Dip-
tera: Therevidae of N. America]
HILDEBRAND, Dr. Henry H. University of Corpus Christi, Corpus Christi, Texas, U.S.A.
[Pisces of Gulf of Mexico & arctic cst. of Canada (No)]
HILL, Dr. A.R. Department of Zoology, University of Glasgow, Glasgow, Scotland. [Heter-
optera: Anthocoridae of World (Yes); Homoptera: Aphidoidea of Europe (No)]
HILL, Bernard Louis, Jr. The California Company, 800 The California Co. Bldg., New
Orleans 12, La., U.S.A. [Cretaceous-Recent Foraminifera & Ostracoda (No)]
HILL, Dorothy. Department of Geology, University of Queensland, Brisbane, Australia.
[Ordovician-Permian Anthozoa: Rugosa & Tabulata of World (Yes)]
HILL, Dr. Howard R. Los Angeles Museum, Los Angeles 7, Calif., U.S.A. [Mollusca &
Linguatulida of World (Yes)]
HILL, Mr. J.E. Mammal Section, British Museum (Natural History), Cromwell Road,
London, S.W.7, England. [Mammalia of s.e. Asia, Malaysia, Celebes, New Guinea,
Pacific (Yes); g. Rattus of Asia (Yes)]
HILL, Dr. R.E. Department of Entomology, University of Nebraska, Lincoln 1, Nebr.,
U.S.A. [Hymenoptera: Megachilidae: g. Coelioxys of N. America (Yes); Coleoptera:
Halticinae of N. America (No)]
HILL, Dr. W.C. Osman. Zoological Society of London, London, N.W.1, England. [Mam-
malia: Primates of World (Yes)]
HILLE RIS LAMBERS, Mr. D. Edescheweg 139, Bennekom, Netherlands. [Homoptera:
Aphididae of World (Yes)]
HILLENIUS, Mr. D. Department of Herpetology, Zoologisch Museum, Plantage Middenlaan
53, Amsterdam, Netherlands. [Amphibia & Reptilia of Europe (Yes); chameleons of
World (Yes)]
HILLIARD, Prof. John R., Jr. Department of Biology, McMurry College, Abilene, Texas,
U.S.A. [Orthoptera: Acrididae of Texas (Yes)]
* HILLS, Prof. E.S. Department of Geology, University of Melbourne, Carlton, N. 3, Vict.,
Australia. [Fossil Mammalia]
HILTERMANN, Dr. Heinrich. Amt für Bodenforschung, Wiesenstrasse 1, Hannover, Germany.
[Fossill small Foraminifera, espec. g. Neoflabellina & Bolivinaides of World (Yes)]
HILTON, Dr. William A. 1263 Dartmouth Avenue, Clarement, Calif., U.S.A. [Amphibia:
salamanders of Western Hemisphere (No); of N. America (Yes)] [Pomona College]
HINCHEY, Prof. M. Catherine. Biology Department, Temple University, Philadelphia 22,
Penna., U.S.A. [Mastigophora: Hexamitidae of amphibians & reptiles (Yes)]
HINCKS, Dr. W.D. Manchester Museum, The University, Manchester 13, England. [Der-
maptera; Coleoptera: Passalidae & Chrysomelidae: Cassidinae; all of World (Yes);
Hymenoptera: Mymaridae of Europe (Yes)]
HINDE, Dr. R.A. Department of Zoology, Downing Street, Cambridge, England. [Aves:
Fringillidae, Carduelinae, Paridae of Britain (No)]
HINSCH, Dr. W. Salingtwick 3 B, Hamburg 26, Germany. [Oligocene-Miocene Gastropoda &
Pelecypoda of n. Europe, es pec. Astartidae (Yes)]
HINSCHERBERGER, Prof. P. Department de Zoologie, Université de Nancy, 30 rue Sainte-
Catherine, Nancy, France. [Symphyla] Not now active in taxonomy.
HINSHAW, Merton E., Curator, Pathology Museum, University of California Medical Center,
San Francisco 22, Calif., U.S.A. [Terr. Mollusca of N. America (Yes)]
HINTON, Dr. H.E. Department of Zoology, University of Bristol, Bristol, England. [Coleop-
tera: Elmidae of World (No), of S. America (Yes); Dryopidae of World (No)]
HINTZE, Prof. Lehi F. Department of Geology, Brigham Young University, Provo, Utah,
U.S.A. [L. Ordovician Trilobita of N. America (Yes)]
HINZ, Rolf. Munsterkamp 11, Einbeck, Germany. [Hymenoptera: Ichneumonidae, espec.
g. Dusona, of Germany (Yes)]
* HIRAIWA, Dr. Yoshi Kuni. Faculty of Agriculture, Kyushu University, Fukuoka, Japan.
[Crustacea]
HIRAMATSU, Mr. Tatsuo. Fukuoka Fisheries Experimental Station, Suzakiur.. machi, Fukuo-
ka, Fukuoka Pref., Japan. [Pelecypoda: Taxodonta: Anadara of E. Jushima Channel
(Yes); Dysodonta: g. Pecten & Heterodonta: g. Meretrix of E. Jushima Channel (No)]

217

HIRANO, Chisato. Division of Entomology, National Institute of Agricultural Sciences, Nishi-gahara, Kita-ku, Tokyo, Japan. [Coleoptera: Curculionidae, espec. Attelabinae, of Japan (Yes)]

HIRASHIMA, Yoshihiro. Entomological Laboratory, Faculty of Agriculture, Kyushu University, Fukuoka City, Kyushu, Japan. [Hymenoptera: Apoidea of Japan, Korea, China, Ryukyus, Formosa (Yes); of Micronesia (No)]

* HIRAYAMA, Katsumi. Institute of Geology & Mineralogy, University of Tokyo, Bunkyo-ku, Tokyo, Japan. [Fossil invertebrates]

HIREGAUDAR, L. S. Bombay Veterinary College, Parel, Bombay 12, India. [Protozoa: Amoebida, Rhizomastigina, Protomonadina, Coccidia, Haemosporidia of India (Yes); Platyhelminthes: Digenea & Cyclophyllidea, of India (Yes); Nemathelminthes: Strongy-loidea, Ascaroidea, Trichenelloidea, Spiruroidea of India (Yes); Acarina: Ixodidae, Argasidae, Mesostigmata, Trombidiformes, of India (Yes); Hemiptera; Siphonaptera, Diptera: Muscidae, Oestridae, Tabanidae, of India (No)]

HIROMATSU, Seichiro. Laboratory for Bacteriology, Aki Health Center, Aki-Machi, Kochi-Ken, Shikoku, Japan. [Acarina; Trombiculidae of Asia & Japan (Yes)]

HIRSHFIELD, Prof. H. I. Department of Biology, New York University, New York 3, N. Y., U. S. A. [Marine Protozoa: Peritricha: Urceolariidae & Scyphiidae of s. California (Yes); Foraminifera, Radiolaria, Tintinnidae, Dinoflagellata of trop. Pacific (Yes)]

HIRSCHMANN, Dr. Hedwig. Department of Plant Pathology, North Carolina State College, Raleigh, N. C., U. S. A. [F-l. & plant parasitic Nematoda of N. America & Europe (Yes)]

HIRSCHMANN, Werner. Am Kavierlein 26/I, Fürth/Bayern, Germany. [Acarina: Mesostig-mata: g. Uropodina, Gamasides, Digamasellus, Dendrolälaps (Yes)]

HISAMATSU, Sadanari. Entomology Laboratory, College of Agriculture, Ehime University, Matsuyama City, Ehime Pref., Japan. [Coleoptera: Eucnemidae & Nitidulidae of Japan (Yes); Clavicornia & Leiodidae of Japan (No)]

HITCHCOCK, Mr. W. B. P. O. Box 315, City, Canberra, A. C. T., Australia. [Aves: Laro-limicolae, espec. Sterninae, of World (Yes)]

HIURA, Mr. Isamu. Osaka Municipal Museum of Natural History, Utsubo-Park, Nishi-ku, Osaka, Japan. [Heteroptera: Anthocoridae of Japan & s. e. Asia (Yes)]

* HIYAMA, Dr. Yoshio. Fisheries Institute, Tokyo University, Bunkyo-ku, Tokyo, Japan. [Pisces]

HOARE, Dr. Cecil A. Wellcome Laboratories of Tropical Medicine, 183 Euston Road, London, N. W. 1, England. [Protozoa: g. Trypanosoma of mammals of World (Yes)]

HOARE, Dr. Richard D. Department of Geology, Bowling Green State University, Bowling Green, Ohio, U. S. A. [Crustacea: Ostracoda: g. Metacypris of N. America (Yes); Pennsylvanian Brachiopoda of N. America (Yes)]

HOBART, J. Department of Agricultural & Forest Zoology, University College of North Wales, Bangor, Caerns, Wales. [Acarina: soil mites & marine mites of Britain (No)]

HOBBS, Prof. Horton H., Jr. Dept. of Biology, Univ. of Virginia, Charlottesville, Va., U. S. A. [Crustacea: Decapoda: Astacidae; Ostracoda: g. Entocythere; both of N. America (Yes)]

HOBBS, Dr. G. A. Canada Agriculture Research Station, Lethbridge, Alta., Canada. [Hy-menoptera: g. Megachile & Bombus of w. N. America (Yes)]

HOBBS, Dr. Kenneth R. Department of Horticulture Services & Inspection, California State Polytechnic College, Pomona, Calif., U. S. A. [Hymenoptera: Torymidae: g. Torymus of w. cst. U. S. (No)]

HOBBY, Dr. B. M. University Museum, Oxford, England. [Diptera: Asilidae of Ethiopian (Yes)]

HOBERLANDT, Dr. L. Department of Entomology, Narodni Museum, Vaclavsté Námĕsti 1700, Prague II, Czechoslovakia. [Heteroptera of Palearctic, espec. c. & s. w. Asia (Yes); Aradoidea, aquatics, semiaquatics, of Old World (Yes)]

HOCH, Rektor i. R. Karl. Römerstrasse 148, Bonn, Germany. [Coleoptera: Haliplidae, Dy-tiscidae, Gyrinidae, Hydrophilidae (excl. Sphaeridiinae); all of Europe (excl. Russia) & North Africa (Yes)]

HOCH, Dr. Ursula (nee Ursula Tatge). Bödekerstrasse 12, Hannover, Germany. [M. Triassic (Muschelkalk) Conodonts of Germany (No)]

HOCKLEY, Mr. A. R. Department of Zoology, The University, Southampton, England. [Crus-tacea: Isopoda: g. Limnoria & commensal & parasitic Copepoda, of European shores (Yes)]

HODGES, Ronald W. Department of Entomology, Cornell University, Ithaca, N. Y., U. S. A. [Lepidoptera: Cosmopterygidae of N. America (No)]

* HODGKIN, E. P. 6 Princes Street, Mosman Park, W. Austr., Australia. [Diptera]

HODSON, Mrs. Floyd (Helen K. Hodson). Box 368, Hallandale, Fla., U. S. A. [Tertiary Mol-lusca & Foraminifera of Venezuela & Caribbean]

HODSON, Prof. F. Department of Geology, The University, Southampton, England. [Carboni-ferous Cephalopoda: g. Goniatites (Yes)]

HODSON, W. E. H. Government Buildings, Coley Park, Reading, Berks, England. [Diptera: Syrphidae of Europe (Yes)]

HOEDEMAN, Mr. J. J. Curator of Fishes, Ichthyology Department, Zoological Museum, Plantage Middenlaan 53, Amsterdam (C), Netherlands. [F-w. & estuarine Pisces of Tropics (No); of Surinam & Caribbean (Yes); Siluriformes, Cyprinodontiformes, Erythrinidae (Yes)]

HOENIGMAN, Prof. Janez. P. P. 281, Sarajevo, Yugoslavia. [Mastigophora: Ellobiopsidae, g. Ellobiopsis & Amallocystis, of World (Yes); Crustacea: Cladocera of Adriatic (Yes); plantonic Copepoda of Adriatic (Yes); Mysidacea & Amphipoda: Oxycephalidae of Mediterranean (Yes) [Biološki Institut Univerziteta]

van HOEPEN, Dr. E. C. N. P. O. Box 6, Hluhluwe, Natal, Union of South Africa. [Cretaceous Ammonitoidea of S. Africa (Yes); Cretaceous Mollusca & invertebrates (No); Recent marine Mollusca of S. Africa (Yes)]

* HOEPPLI, Prof. R. Department of Parasitology, University of Malaya, Singapore, Malaya. [Nematoda]

HOESE, Mr. H. D. Marine Laboratory, Rockport, Texas, U. S. A. [Marine Pisces of Gulf of Mexico, espec. Texas (Yes)]

HOESTLANDT, Prof. Dr. H. Faculté Libre des Sciences, Laboratoire de Zoologie, 13 rue de Toul, Lille (Nord), France. [Pisces: Clupeidae; Crustacea: Isopoda: "Sphéronnéres"; Brachyura: "Brachrhynques"; all of Atlantic cst. of Europe (Yes)]

HOFF, Prof. C. Clayton. Department of Biology, University of New Mexico, Albuquerque, N. Mex., U. S. A. [Pseudoscorpiones of W. Hemisphere (Yes); f-w. Ostracoda of c. U. S. (Yes)]

HOFFER, Dr. Augustin. Jičinská 4, Praha XII, Czechoslovakia. [Hymenoptera: Chalcidoidea, espec. Encyrtidae, of World (No); of Palearctic (Yes)] [Entomologické odděleni, Národni Museum v Praze]

HOFFMAN, Dr. A. C. National Museum, Bloemfontein, Union of South Africa. [Amphibia of s. Africa (Yes); Reptilia of s. Africa (No)]

HOFFMAN, Prof. Glen L. 1802 Fourth Avenue North, Grand Forks, N. D., U. S. A. [Trematoda: Strigeida of N. America (Yes)]

HOFFMAN, Richard L. Box 749, Blacksburg, Virginia. [Diplopoda, espec. Polydesmida, Spirobolida, Spirostreptida, of Nearctic, Neotropical, Ethiopian, Pacific (Yes)]

HOFFMAN, A. 15 Avenue Marshal de Lattre de Tassigny, Boulogne-Billancourt (Seine), France. [Coleoptera: Curculionidae of Palearctic, excl. Japan & e. Russia (Yes)]

HOFFMANN, Anita. See HOFFMANN-SANDOVAL, Anita.

HOFFMANN, Dr. Clarence H. Entomology Research Division, Beltsville, Md., U. S. A. [Coleoptera: Scarabaeidae: g. Trichiotinus & Osmoderma of N. America (No)]

HOFFMANN-SANDOVAL, Biol. Anita. Apartado Postal 8026, Mexico, D. F., Mexico. [Acarina: Trombiculidae & Ixodoidea of Mexico (Yes); Diptera: Streblidae & Nycteribiidae of Mexico (Yes)] [Escuela Nacional de Ciencias Biológicas, I. P. N.]

* HOFFMANN, William E. 805 Rhode Island Avenue, Lawrence, Kans., U. S. A. [Aquatic Hemiptera]

HOFFMEISTER, Dr. Donald F. Museum of Natural History, University of Illinois, Urbana, Ill., U. S. A. [Mammalia of Arizona & Illinois; Rodentia: g. Peromyscus of N. America; Insectivora: g. Blarina of N. America; (all Yes)]

* HOFFMEISTER, Prof. J. Edward. Department of Geology, University of Rochester, Rochester 3, N. Y., U. S. A. [Fossil Corals]

HOFFSTETTER, Dr. R. Maitre de Recherches au Centre National de la Recherche Scientifique, Laboratoire de Paleontologie du Museum, 13 Place Valhubert, Paris (VI), France. [Fossil lizards & snakes; Stegosauria; Mammalia: fossil Edentata: Xenarthra; all of World (Yes)]

* HOFKER, Dr. J. Scheveningse Laan 157, 's Gravenhage, Netherlands. [Fossil Foraminifera]

* HOFMÄNNER, B. (La Chaux de Fonds, Switzerland; Orthoptera) Died June 1957.

* HOGE, A. R. Address unknown. (Reptilia)

HÖGLUND, Dr. Hans. Kungliga Fiskeristyrelsen, Havsfiskelaboratoriet, Lysekil, Sweden. [Foraminifera of the "Skagerak (North Sea)" (No)]

HOLČÍK, Juraj. Department of Systematic Zoology, Charles University, Viničná 7, Praha II, Czechoslovakia. [Pisces: Cyprinidae: g. Rhodeus of Palearctic (Yes)]

HOLCOMB, L. D. Shell Oil Co., 314 North Auburn, Farmington, N. Mex., U. S. A. [Cretaceous-Recent Foraminifera of Washington, Oregon, California, New Mexico, Arizona, Colorado, Utah (Yes)]

HÖLDER, H. Geologische Institut der Universität, Sigwartstrasse 10, Tübingen, Germany. [Jurassic Ammonites of Europe]

* HOLDHAUS, Dr. Karl. Naturhistorisches Museum, Burgring 7, Wien 1, Austria. [Coleoptera]

HOLGERSEN, H., Chief, Department of Zoology, Stavanger Museum, Stavanger, Norway. [Hymenoptera: Formicidae of Europe (No); Homoptera: Auchenorrhyncha of Scandinavia (No); Aves of Antarctic, Europe, Arctic of Old World (Yes)]

* HOLIK, Otto. Loschiwitzer Strasse 23, Dresden A53, German Democratic Republic. [Lepidoptera]

HOLLAND, C. H. Department of Geology, Bedford College, Regent's Park, London, N. W. 1, England. [Silurian Nautiloidea of Britain (Yes); Upper Silurian (Ludlovian) of Britain (No)]

HOLLAND, F. D., Jr. Geology Department, University of North Dakota, Grand Forks, N. D., U. S. A. [Paleozoic Brachiopoda, espec. Devonian & Mississippian, of N. America (Yes); fossil Crustacea: Decapoda of n. c. U. S. (Yes)]

HOLLAND, George P. Entomology Division, Science Service, Department of Agriculture, Ottawa, Ont., Canada. [Siphonaptera of World, espec. N. America & Australasia (Yes)]

HOLLANDE, Prof. André. Laboratoire de Biologie Générale, Faculté des Sciences, Alger, Algeria. [Protista (No); Radiolaria & Flagellata (Yes)]

HOLLE, Dr. Paul A. 7 Mars Drive, Shrewsbury, Mass., U. S. A. [Amphibia: Ambystomidae of N. America (No); Mollusca: g. Melampus of w. Atlantic (Yes)]

HOLLINGSWORTH, Dr. M. Zoology Department, University College of Ghana, Achimota, Accra, Ghana. [Diptera: Drosophilidae of Ethiopian (No)]

HOLLINGSWORTH, R. V. Paleontological Laboratory, Incorporated, P. O. Box 51, Midland, Texas, U. S. A. [Mississippian-Permian Foraminifera: Fusulinidae (Yes)]

HOLLINSWORTH, Miss H. R. Systematic Entomology, Science Service Building, Carling Avenue, Ottawa, Ont., Canada. [Homoptera: Cicadellidae of Canada (Yes)]

HOLLIS, Prof. J. P. Department of Plant Pathology, Louisiana State University, Baton Rouge, La., U. S. A. [Plant parasitic Nematoda of Louisiana (No); g. Tylenchorhynchus of Louisiana (Yes)]

HOLLOWAY, Dr. Beverley A. Dominion Museum, Wellington C. 3, New Zealand. [Coleoptera: Lucanidae of New Zealand (Yes); Diplopoda: Sphaerotheridae of New Zealand (Yes); Mallophaga: g. Rallicola of World (No)]

HOLLOWAY, Prof. Harry L. Department of Biology, Roanoke College, Salem, Va., U. S. A. [Acanthocephala of New World (Yes)]

HOLLOWDAY, Mr. Eric. 45 Manor Road, Aylsbury, Bucks, England. [Rotifera of World (No); of Europe (Yes)]

HOLLY, Dr. Maximilian, Kustos, Museum of Natural History of Vienna i. P., Hetsgasse 23/19, Wien III, Austria. [Marine & f-w. Cyclostomata & Pisces of World (Yes); f-w. Pisces of Africa (Yes)]

HOLM, Dr. Åke. Zoologiska Institutionen, Uppsala, Sweden. [Araneae of Arctic, Europe, Africa (Yes)]

HOLMES, Mr. D. R. Red Hill, Vict., Australia. [Lepidoptera: Hepialidae of Victoria (No)]

HOLMQUIST, Dr. Charlotte. Zoologiska Institutionen, Lund, Sweden. [Crustacea: Mysidacea (Yes); "Marine-glacial relicts," g. Mysis (Yes)]

HOLSTEIN, Dr. M. Malaria Eradication Division, World Health Organization, Palais des Nations, Génève, Switzerland. [Diptera: Culicidae: Anophelinae of Africa (Yes)]

HOLT, Dr. Perry C. Department of Biology, Virginia Polytechnic Institute, Blacksburg, Va., U. S. A. [Oligochaeta: Branchiobdellidae of N. America (Yes)]

HOLTHUIS, Dr. L. B. Rijksmuseum van Natuurlijke Historie, Leiden, Netherlands. [Crustacea: Stomatopoda & Decapoda: Macrura of World (Yes); Isopoda of Netherlands (Yes)]

HOLTZMANN, Dr. Oliver. Plant Pathology Department, University of Hawaii, Honolulu 14, Hawaii, U. S. A. [Plant parasitic Nematoda of Hawaii (No); g. Rotylenchulus of Hawaii (Yes)]

HOLWILL, F. J. W. Department of Geology, Imperial College, London, S. W. 7, England. [Devonian corals]

HOLZEL, Major E. Museumgasse 2, Klagenfurt, Austria. [Hymenoptera: Formicidae of c. Europe (No); Coleoptera of c. Europe (Yes); Orthoptera of c. Europe (No)]

HOLZMANN, Dr. Christiane. Breidenbornerstrasse 8, Kaiserslautern, Germany. [Acarina: Parasitiformes of Germany (Yes); g. Veigaia of Bavaria (No)]

HOMBERG, Rodolphe. 13 Avenue d'Eylan, Paris (XVI), France. [Lepidoptera: Geometridae of France (Yes); Sterrhinae (Acidaliinae) of Palearctic (Yes)]

HOMOLÁČ, Ing. M. E. Pod Hájem 67, Kyje u Praha, Czechoslovakia. [Dipolopda of Palearctic (No); of Europe (Yes)]

HÖNE, Dr. Hermann. Zoologisches Forschungsinstitut & Museum Alexander Koenig, Koblenzerstrasse 160, Bonn am Rhein, Germany. [Lepidoptera of Far East (No)]

* HONEGGER, Carol. Biology Department, Temple University, Philadelphia 22, Pa., U. S. A. [Protozoa: g. Pelomyxa]

HONESS, Mr. Ralph F. Agriculture Hall, University of Wyoming, Laramie, Wyoming, U. S. A. [Helminths of domestic & game animals of w. U. S.]

* HONEYMAN, A. M. Department of Geology, The University, Nottingham, England. [Fossil invertebrates]
HONIGBERG, Prof. Bronislaw M. Department of Zoology, University of Massachusetts, Amherst, Mass., U.S.A. [Protozoa: parasitic Zoomastigophora, espec. Polymastigida: Trichomonadidae, Oxymonadidae, Hexamitidae, g. Retortamonas; all of World (Yes)]
* HONJO, K. Tôkai Regional Fisheries Research Laboratory, Tsukishima, Chuoku, Tokyo, Japan. [Copepoda]
HONMA, Mr. Yoshiharu, Department of Biology, Faculty of Science, Niigata University, Niigata City, Japan. [Pisces: Zoarcidae & Blennidae of Sea of Japan & N. Pacific (Yes); Cottidae of Sea of Japan & N. Pacific (No)]
* HOOCK, Jean M. L. Department de Zoologie, Université de Paris a la Sorbonne, 12 rue Cuvier, Paris (V), France. [Lepidoptera: Saturnidae]
* HOOD, Prof. J. Douglas. Roberts Hall, Cornell University, Ithaca, N.Y., U.S.A. [Thysanoptera of New World]
HOOFIEN, J. H. Bank Leumi Le-Israel B.M., P.O. Box 2, Tel-Aviv, Israel. [Reptilia of Israel & Near East (Yes)]
HOOGENRAAD, H.R. (Deventer, Netherlands: Protozoa) Deceased.
HOOGSTRAAL, Mr. Harry. U.S. Naval Medical Research Unit Number 3, American Embassy, Cairo, Egypt. [Acarina: Ixodidae & Argasidae of World (Yes)]
HOOIJER, Dr. D.A. Rijksmuseum van Natuurlijke Historie, Leiden, Netherlands. [Quaternary Mammalia of Asia & Europe (Yes)]
HOOPTER, Mr. D.J. Nematology Department, Rothamsted Experiment Station, Harpenden, Herts, England. [F-l. soil & f-w. Nematoda of World (Yes); plant parasitic Nematoda of World (Yes)]
* HOOPER, J. 92 Station Crescent, Ashford, Middlesex, England. [Mammalia]
HOOPER, Prof. Emmet T. Museum of Zoology, University of Michigan, Ann Arbor, Mich., U.S.A. [Mammalia, espec. Rodentia: Cricetidae, of N. America, espec. Mexico & U.S. (Yes)]
HOPE, Mr. D. Department of Zoology, Colorado State University, Fort Collins, Colo., U.S.A. [F-l. soil & plant parasitic Nematoda of Colorado (Yes)]
HOPKINS, Mr. G.H.E. Zoological Museum, Tring, Herts, England. [Siphonaptera of World (Yes)]
HOPKINS, Miss Marie L. Department of Zoology, Idaho State College, Pocatello, Idaho, U.S.A. [Up. Pleistocene larger Mammalia of s.e. Idaho (No)]
HOPKINS, Dr. Sewell H. Biology Department, Agricultural & Mechanical College of Texas, College Station, Texas, U.S.A. [Digenetic Trematoda, espec. parasites of fishes & molluscs, of World (Yes)]
HOPLA, Prof. Cluff E. Department of Zoology, University of Oklahoma, Norman, Okla., U.S.A. [Diptera: Culicidae of N. America (No); Siphonaptera of New World (No); Acarina: Argasidae & Ixodidae of New World (Yes)]
HOPPER, Mr. Bruce E. Department of Botany & Plant Pathology, Alabama Polytechinic Institute, Auburn, Ala., U.S.A. [F-l. marine Nematoda of Atlantic & Gulf of Mexico (Yes); f-l. soil & f-w. Nematoda of U.S. & Canada (Yes); plant parasitic Nematoda of U.S. & Canada (Yes)]
HOPPING, George R. Dominion Forest Biology Laboratory, Customs Building, Calgary, Alta., Canada. [Coleoptera: Cerambycidae & Scolytidae of w. Canada (No)]
HOPPINGER, John J. Apartment 505, 11720 Edgewater Drive, Lakewood 7, Ohio, U.S.A. [Tertiary Echinoidea (Yes); Ordovician-Pennsylvanian Trilobita (Yes)]
HOPWOOD, Dr. A.T. 99 Clifton Hill, St. John's Wood, London, N.W. 8, England. [Tertiary-Pleistocene Mammalia of Africa (No)]
* HORA, Sundar L. (Calcutta, India; Pisces) Deceased.
HÖREGOTT, Dr. Heinz. Technische Hochschule, Zoologisches Institut, Zellescher Weg 40, Dresen, German Democratic Republic. [Araneae, excl. Micryphantidae, of c. Europe (Yes)]
HORI, Katsushige. Institute of Biology, Faculty of Science, Kanazawa University, Kanazawa City, Ishikawa Pref., Japan. [Diptera: Muscidae & Calliphoridae of Japan & Korea (No); Sarcophagidae: g. Sarcophaga of Japan & Korea (Yes)]
* HORI, Masaru. Osaka Municipal Museum of Natural History, Utsubo-Park, Nishi, Osaka, Japan. [Pelecypoda]
HORIKOSHI, Masuoki. c/o Misaki Marine Biological Station, Koajiro, Misaki-machi, Miura City, Kanagawa Pref., Japan. [Marine Mollusca of Indo-Pacific (Yes)] [Ochanomizu University]
HORION, Msgr. Dr. Adolf. Stein 36, Überlingen/Bodensee, Germany. [Coleoptera of c. Europe (Yes)]
HORMANN, K. Esso Standard (Libya) Inc., Sciara Mohammed Ben Ali Senussi, P.O. Box 385, Tripoli, Libya. [Cretaceous-Tertiary Mammalia (Yes)]
HORNABROOK, Dr. R. C/o National Hospital, Queen's Square, London, W.C. 2, England. [Coleoptera of New Zealand (Yes); Curculionidae of S. Hemisphere (No); of N.Z. (Yes)]

HORNADAY, Gordon Raymer. Department of Paleontology, University of California, Berkeley 4, Calif., U.S.A. [Tertiary Foraminifera of Pacific Cst. U.S. (Yes)]

* HORNELL, J. (Madras, India; Pisces) Deceased.

HORNIBROOK, Mr. N. de B. P.O.Box 268, Lower Hutt City, New Zealand. [Cretaceous-Recent Foraminifera & Ostracoda of New Zealand (Yes)]

HORNÝ, Dr. R. Ústřední ústav geologický, Hradebni 9, Praha I, Czechoslovakia. [Paleozoic Gastropoda: Loxonematacea & Bellerophontacea; Paleozoic Polyplacophora; Paleozoic Cephalopoda: Nautiloidea: Dawsonoceratidae & Bactritidae; all of Europe (Yes)]

HOROWITZ, Alan S. Box 269, Littleton, Colo., U.S.A. [Mississippian Blastoidea: g. Pentremites of N. America (Yes)]

HORSFALL, Dr. William R. Department of Entomology, University of Illinois, Urbana, Ill., U.S.A. [Diptera: eggs of Culicidae of U.S. (No)]

HORVATH, Dr. A. Institut für Systematische Zoologie, Adytér 2, Szeged, Hungary. [Quaternary & Recent Mollusca of World (No), of c. Europe (Yes)]

* HORVATH, Charles. 8649 Clifton Way, Beverly Hills, Calif., U.S.A. [Boring Mollusca]

HORVATH, Prof. Dr. F. Institut für Mikrobiologie, Universität für Landwirtschaft, Gödöllö, Hungary. [Protozoa: Hypotricha of Hungary (No)]

* HOSHINO, Masaya. 14, 2-chôme, Higashi-Rokugo, Otaku, Tokyo, Japan. [Lepidoptera: Tortricidae; Coleoptera]

HOSKINS, Donald M. Department of Internal Affairs, Bureau of Topographical & Geological Survey, Harrisburg, Penna., U.S.A. [M.Silurian Ostracoda of Pennsylvania]

HOSMER, Mrs. Fell, Jr. Scripps Institution of Oceanography, La Jolla, Calif., U.S.A. [Recent smaller Foraminifera of Gulf of Mexico (Yes); of Gulf of California (No)]

HOTCHKISS, Doreen E. 2440 Longest Avenue, Louisville, Ky., U.S.A. [Hymenoptera: Symphyta: larval sawflies of N.America, Australia, Europe (Yes)]

HOTTES, F.C. 357 Orchard Avenue, Grand Junction, Colo., U.S.A. [Homoptera: Aphidae of U.S. (Yes)]

HOTTINGER, Lukas. C/o Geologisch-Palaeontologisches Institut Bernoullianum, Basel, Switzerland. [Eocene Foraminifera: g. Alveolina of India, Indonesia, Japan (No); of Mediterranian, Turkey, Persia (Yes)]

HOTTON, Dr. Nicholas, III. Department of Anatomy, University of Kansas, Lawrence, Kans., U.S.A [Permian Tetrapoda & sharks of N.America (Yes); Recent lizards of N.America (No)]

HOUCK, Warren J. Box 3499, Route 3, Arcata, Calif., U.S.A. [Marine Pisces of n.California (Yes)] [Humboldt State College]

* HOUGH, Dr. Margaret Jean. See Addenda.

HOURSTON, Dr. Alan S. Fisheries Research Board of Canada, Biological Station, Nanaimo, B.C., Canada. [Pisces: Pleuronectidae & Clupeidae: g. Clupea of Pacific cst. of N. America (No); Esocidae of Canada (No)]

HOUŠA, Dr. Václav. Paleontological Laboratory, Czechoslovakian Academy of Science, National Museum, Vaclavské námesti 1700, Praha II, Czechoslovakia. [Secondary-Tertiary Decapoda of Europe (Yes)]

HOUSE, M.R. Department of Geology, Science Laboratories, South Road, Durham, England. [Devonian Ammonoidea of Europe (Yes)]

HOVANITZ, Dr. William. Division of Biology, California Institute of Technology, Pasadena, Calif., U.S.A. [Lepidoptera: Rhopalocera of World (No); g. Colias of World (Yes); g. Argynnis of N.America (Yes)]

HOVASSE, Prof. R. Faculte des Sciences, 1 Avenue Vercingetorix, Clermont-Ferrand, France. [Protozoa: Phytoflagellata of Europe (Yes)]

HOWARD, Dr. Arthur D. 6427 Eglise Avenue, Rivera, Calif., U.S.A. [Minute Pelecypoda of Pacific cst. U.S.; Unionidae of Mississippi R. & Iowa; Pteropoda of Pacific cst. U.S. [University of Southern California]

HOWARD, Dr. Hildegarde. Los Angeles County Museum, Exposition Park, Los Angeles 7, Calif., U.S.A. [Pleistocene Aves, excl. Passeriformes & Anseriformes, of w.N. America (Yes); Miocene-Pliocene Aves, excl. Anseriformes, of California (Yes)]

HOWARD, Mr. John K. Marine Laboratory, University of Miami, 1 Rickenbacker Causeway, Miami 49, Fla., U.S.A. [Pisces: Istiophoridae of World (Yes)]

HOWARD, Dr. Robert Stearns. Department of Biological Sciences, University of Delaware, Newark, Del., U.S.A. [Intertidal Dermaptera of e. & s.coasts of N.America (Yes); Bryozoa of Cape Cod (Yes)]

HOWARD, Dr. Walter E. Field Station Administration, University of California, Davis, Calif., U.S.A. [Mammalia, Aves, Amphibia, Reptilia, of e.side of San Joaquin Valley, California (Yes)]

HOWARTH, Dr. M.K. Department of Palaeontology, British Museum (Natural History), Cromwell Road, London, S.W.7, England. [Jurassic-Cretaceous (espec. Liassic) Ammonoidea of Europe (Yes)]

HOWARTH, Mr. T.G. Department of Entomology, British Museum (Natural History), Cromwell Road, London, S.W.7, England. [Lepidoptera: Lycaenidae: Theclini of Asia (Yes)]

HOWDEN, Mrs. Anne T. C/o Insect Systematics, Science Service, Department of Agriculture, Ottawa, Ont., Canada. [Coleoptera: Curculionidae: Pandeleteini of N. America (Yes)]

HOWDEN, Henry F. Insect Systematics, Science Service, Department of Agriculture, Ottawa, Ont., Canada. [Coleoptera: Scarabaeidae of N. America (Yes); Geotrupinae of World (Yes); Nitidulidae of N. America (Yes)]

HOWE, Mr. H. V. Department of Geology, Louisiana State University, Baton Rouge, La., U. S. A. [Mesozoic-Cenozoic Ostracoda & Foraminifera (No)]

HOWE, John Alfred. University of Nebraska State Museum, University of Nebraska, Lincoln, Neb., U. S. A. [Oligocene Mammalia: Rodentia: g. Ischyromys (Yes); Pleistocene Equidae: g. Equus (No)]

HOWE, R. W. Department of Scientific & Industrial Research, Pest Infestation Laboratory, London Road, Slough, Bucks, England. [Coleoptera of stored products of World (Yes)]

HOWELL, Prof. B. F. Department of Geology, Princeton University, Princeton, N. J., U. S. A. [Cambrian Trilobites of World (Yes); fossil worms & sponges of World (Yes)]

HOWELL, Prof. Thelma. Department of Biology, Wesleyan College, Macon, Ga., U. S. A. [Amphibia: salamanders of s. Appalachian Mts., U. S. (No)]

HOWELL, Dr. Thomas R. Department of Zoology, University of California, Los Angeles 24, Calif., U. S. A. [Aves of N. & C. America (Yes)]

HOWELL-RIVERO, Dr. Luis, Curator, Department of Fishes, Museo Poey, University of Habana, Habana, Cuba. [Pisces of Caribbean (Yes)]

HOWER, Theo. W. R. 1, 11921 Santigo Avenue, Orange, Calif., U. S. A. [Lepidoptera: Nymphalidae: g. Euphydryas & g. Melitaea; Lycaenidae: Theclinae & Plebeinae; all of s. California, w. Arizona, w. Nevada (Yes)]

HOY, Mr. J. M. Entomology Division, Department of Scientific & Industrial Research, P. O. Box 623, Palmerston North, New Zealand. [Coleoptera: larvae of Scarabaeidae; insect parasitic Nematoda: Dactylopiidae; all of New Zealand (Yes)]

* HOYT, Mr. Charles P. 1970 Ualakaa Street, Honolulu 14, Hawaii, U. S. A. [Diptera]

HOYT, Dr. J. S. Y. (Etna, N. Y.: Aves) Died 1951.

HOZATSKIJ, L. T. See KHOZATSKY, L. T.

HRABĚ, Prof. Dr. Sergěj. Kotlářská 2, Brno, Czechoslovakia. [Oligochaeta: Tubificidae & Lumbriculidae of World (Yes)]

HRADSKÝ, Dr. Milan. Korunni 46, Praha XII, Czechoslovakia. [Diptera: Asilidae of Palearctic (Yes)]

HRBÁČEK, Dr. Jaroslav. Department of Hydrobiology, Biological Institute, Czechoslovakian Academy of Sciences, Viničná 7, Praha II, Czechoslovakia. [Crustacea: Cladocera: g. Daphnia of World (Yes); Coleoptera: Hydrophilidae of Palearctic (No); g. Hydraena (Yes); Dytiscidae, Haliplidae, Gyrinidae, of Europe (No)]

* HRISAFI, Cornelia. Institutul de Cercetari Agronomice, B-dul, Miciurin, Bucureşti, Rumania. [Insecta]

HRUBESCH, DR. K. Nagelschmiedg. 5, Mühldorf / Inn, Germany. [Mammalia, espec. Rodentia (Yes)]

* HSIAO, Dr. Sidney C. Address unknown. [Crustacea: Copepoda]

HSIAO, Tsai-Yu. Department of Biology, Nankai University, Tientsin, People's Republic of China. [Hemiptera: Miridae & Coreidae of China (Yes)]

HSÜ, Dr. S. Y. Li (also as H. F.) Department of Hygiene & Preventive Medicine, College of Medicine, State University of Iowa, Iowa City, Iowa, U. S. A. [Trematoda: Schistosomatidae & Opisthorchiidae of World (Yes); Nematoda of vertebrates of World (No)]

* HU, Chang-kang. Institute of Vertebrate Paleontology, Academia Sinica, P. O. Box 643, Peking, People's Republic of China. [Fossil vertebrates]

* HU, Dr. Yung-Tsu. Address unknown. [Crustacea: Copepoda]

HUANG, T. Y. Taiwan Petroleum Exploration Office, Chinese Petroleum Corporation, Miaoli, Taiwan, Formosa. [Tertiary smaller Foraminifera of Taiwan (Yes)]

* HUANG, Wei-Lung. Institute of Vertebrate Paleontology, Academia Sinica, P. O. Box 643, Peking, People's Republic of China. [Fossil vertebrates]

* HUBA, A. Staroturskich Hodnik 45, Bratislava, Czechoslovakia. [Hymenoptera]

HUBBARD, Dr. C. A. 15115 S. W. 74th Avenue, Tigard 23, Ore., U. S. A. [Siphonaptera of Pacific Northwest U. S. (Yes)] [Pacific College]

HUBBELL, Prof. Theodore H. Museum of Zoology, University of Michigan, Ann Arbor, Mich., U. S. A. [Orthoptera & Dermaptera of New World (Yes); Orthoptera: Rhaphidophorinae of World (Yes)]

HUBBS, Dr. Clark. Department of Zoology, University of Texas, Austin, Texas, U. S. A. [F-w. Pisces of Texas (Yes)]

HUBBS, Dr. Carl L. Scripps Institution of Oceanography, La Jolla, Calif., U. S. A. [Pisces of World; marine Mammalia & Aves of Pacific]

HUBENDICK, Dr. Sc. Bengt. Naturhistoriska Museet, Göteburg 11, Sweden. [Gastropoda: Lymnaeidae of World (Yes); Planorbidae "of certain areas" (Yes)]

HUBER, Dr. F. Zoophysiologisches Institut der Universität, 12 Hölderlinstrasse, Tübingen, Germany. [Orthoptera: Gryllidae of Germany (Yes); of s. Europe (No)]

HUBER, Ivan. Department of Zoology, University of Maryland, College Park, Md., U.S.A. [Acarina: Trombiculidae: Leeuwenhoekiinae of World; Neuroptera of Nearctic (Yes)]

HUBERT, Capt. A.A. Department of Entomology, Walter Reed Army Institute of Research, Walter Reed Army Medical Center, Washington D.C., U.S.A. [Diptera: Ceratopogonidae of N. America & e. Asia (No)]

HUBRICHT, Leslie. 2111 Kenilworth Avenue. Louisville 5, Ky., U.S.A. [Gastropoda: land snails of-e. U.S. (Yes); Crustacea: f-w. Amphipoda of N. America (Yes); f-w. Isopoda of N. America (No)]

HUCKETT, Dr. H.C. Box 38, R.F.D., Riverhead, N.Y., U.S.A. [Diptera: Muscidae of Holarctic (No); of N. America (Yes)]

HUCKRIEDE, Dr. Reinhold. Geologische-Palaontologische Institut, Deutschhausstrasse 10, (16) Marburg, Germany. [Triassic Conodonts (Yes)]

HUDDLE, J.W. (Washington, D.C.; fossils) Not now active in taxonomy.

HUDSON, Dr. Gerda B. (Johannesburg, Union of South Africa; Odonata) Not now active in taxonomy.

HUDSON, Dr. George E. Department of Zoology, State College of Washington, Pullman, Wash., U.S.A. [Aves & Mammalia of Nearctic (No)]

HUDSON, Joy J. (Brisbane, Australia; Decapoda) Not now active in taxonomy.

HUDSON, Dr. R.G.S. Department of Geology, University College, Gower Street, London, W.C.1, England. [Carboniferous-Mesozoic Stromatoporoidea (Yes); Carboniferous-Permian Hydroidea & Tetracoralla (Yes)]

von HUENE, Prof. F. Geologische-Palaontologische Institut, Universität Tübingen, Sigwartstrasse 10, Tübingen, Germany. [Paleozoic-Mesozoic Labyrinthodontia & Reptilia, excl. turtles (Yes)]

HUEY, Laurence M. Natural History Museum, Balboa Park, San Diego 1, Calif., U.S.A. [Aves & Mammalia: kangaroo rats & pocket mice of s. California & Baja California (Mexico) (Yes)]

HUFF, Dr. Clay G. Naval Medical Research Institute, Bethesda 14, Md., U.S.A. [Protozoa: g. Plasmodium of animals of World (Yes)]

HUGGHINS, Dr. E.J. Department of Entomology-Zoology, South Dakota State College, Brookings, S.D., U.S.A. [Trematoda, Cestoda, Nematoda, of cattle, sheep, f-w. fishes, fish-eating birds; all of N. America (Yes)]

HUGGINS, Mr. H.C. 65 Eastwood Boulevard, Westcliffe-on-Sea, Essex, England. [Lepidoptera, espec. Pyralidae, Pterophoridae, Tortricidae, of Britain (No)]

HUGHES, Dr. A.Margaret. Royal Free Hospital School of Medicine, 8 Hunter Street, London, W.C. 1, England. [Acarina: Tyroglyphidae of World (Yes)]

HUGHES, David D. P.O.Box 385, Tripoli, Libya. [Mesozoic-Recent smaller Foraminifera (Yes); Paleozoic Animals incertae sedis (Yes)] [Ess o Standard (Libya), Inc.]

HUGHES, Jack T. Panhandle-Plains Historical Museum, Canyon, Texas, U.S.A. [Fossil vertebrates] [West Texas State College]

HUGHES, Dr. Roscoe D. Department of Biology & Genetics, Medical College of Virginia, Richmond 19, Va., U.S.A. [Acarina: Anoetidae of World (Yes)]

HULBIRT, Dr. E.R. 622 North Bright Avenue, Whittier, Calif., U.S.A. [Lepidoptera: Lycaenidae & Hesperiidae of w. U.S. (Yes)]

HULINGS, Dr. N. Departments of Biology & Geology, Texas Christian University, Ft. Worth, Texas, U.S.A. [Miocene-Pliocene & Recent marine Ostracoda, Miocene-Recent marine Mollusca of e. & s. csts. U.S. (Yes)]

HULL, Prof. Frank M. P.O.Box 413, University, Miss., U.S.A. [Diptera: Syrphidae, Asilidae, Bombyliidae, Nemestrinidae, Mydaidae, Therevidae, Rhagionidae, Stratiomyidae, Apioceridae, Cyrtidae; all of World (Yes); Tabanidae of N. America (Yes)] [University of Mississippi]

* HULL, Rev. J.E. Normandale House, High Spen, Rowlands Gill, Durham, England. [Araneida]

HULL, Dr. R.W. Department of Biological Sciences, Northwestern University, Evanston, Ill., U.S.A. [Protozoa: Suctoria of N. America (Yes)]

HULL, Lt. Cdr. W.B., MSC, USN. Disease Vector Control Center, Naval Air Station, Jacksonville, Fla., U.S.A. [Acarina: parasitic Mesostigmata of Mediterranean (Yes), Halarachnidae of World (Yes), g. Pneumonyssus of primates (Yes); Diptera: Culicidae: larvae of g. Aedes of Philippines (Yes)] [U.S. Navy Department]

* HULOT, A. Address unknown. [Pisces]

HULT, J., Director-in-chief, Board of Fisheries, P.O. Box 2126, Göteborg 2, Sweden. [Crustacea: marine Isopoda & Decapoda of n.w. Europe (No)]

HUMES, Prof. Arthur G. Department of Biology, Boston University, 675 Commonwealth Avenue, Boston 15, Mass., U.S.A. [Crustacea: parasitic Copepoda: Harpacticoida, Cyclopoida, Caligoida, Lernaeopodoida, of World (Yes); espec. Tisbidae, Diosaccidae, Ameiridae, Clausidiidae, Lichomolgidae, Myicolidae, Ergasilidae, Lamippidae, Caligidae]

HUMMELINCK, Dr. P. Wagenaar. Zoological Laboratory, Janskerkhof 3, Utrecht, Netherlands. [Coelenterata: Hydroidea of Caribbean (No); Rhizostomeae: g. Cassiopea of Caribbean (Yes); Scorpiones of Caribbean (Yes); Pseudoscorpiones of Caribbean (No); Pedipalpi & Tarantulinae of Neotropics (Yes); Gastropoda: Mesogastropoda: Pomatiasidae; Stylommatophora: Cerionidae & Urocoptidae; all of Caribbean (No); Coleoptera: Cicindelinae of Caribbean (Yes); Reptilia: Lacertilia of Antillean (No); Mammalia: Cervidae & Leporidae of Neotropics (No)]
HUMPHREY, Miss Frances L. Box 276, Wickenburg, Ariz., U.S.A. [Reptilia & Amphibia of s.w. U.S. & Mexico (Yes); Scorpiones of Arizona (Yes)]
HUMPHREY, Dr. Philip S. Peabody Museum of Natural History, Yale University, New Haven, Conn., U.S.A. [Aves: Anatidae of World (Yes)]
HUMPHREY, William E. Pan American International Oil Co., 630 Fifth Avenue, Suite 450, New York 20, N.Y., U.S.A. [Neocomian-L. Albian Ammonites]
HUNGERFORD, Prof. H.B. 323 Snow Hall, University of Kansas, Lawrence, Kansas, U.S.A. [Aquatic & semiaquatic Hemiptera of World (Yes)]
* HUNT, Charles J. 7 Avenue de la Victoire, Nice, France. [Lepidoptera]
HUNT, Rev. J.W., Principal, the Missionary Institution, P.O. Indaleni, Natal, Union of South Africa. [Coleoptera: Cerambycidae: Lamiinae of s. Africa (Yes)]
HUNT, O.E. 7300 Wingate Street, Houston 11, Texas, U.S.A. [Acarina: Gamasides: Entonyssidae, Rhinonyssidae, Dermanyssidae, all of New World (Yes); parasitic Laelaptidae of World (Yes)] [U.S. Department of Agriculture]
HUNT, Timothy J. C/o Zoological Society of London, Regent's Park, London, N.W.1, England. [Reptilia: Testudines of Palearctic, Ethiopian, Oriental (Yes); Testudinidae of World (Yes)]
HUNTER, Rev. Elwood B. 1965 S.E. 21st Avenue, Portland 14, Ore., U.S.A. [Amphineura of Mexico & N. America, espec. Alaska (Yes)]
HUNTER, George W., III. (Gainesville, Fla.; parasites) Not now active in taxonomy.
HUNTER, Dr. W.D. Russell. Department of Zoology, University of Glasgow, Glasgow W.2, Scotland. [F-w. Mollusca of British Is. (Yes); marine Pelecypoda: g. Hiatella of Europe & N. Atlantic (Yes); Gastropoda: Neritacea of Greater Antilles (No)]
HUNTER, Wanda S. Box 6007, College Station, Durham, N.C., U.S.A. [Trematoda of U.S. (Yes)] [Duke University]
HUNTINGTON, Dr. Charles E. Department of Biology, Bowdoin College, Brunswick, Maine, U.S.A. [Aves: Icteridae: Quiscalus quiscula of N. America (Yes)]
HUNTINGTON, Mr. E. Irving, Research Associate, American Museum of Natural History, New York 24, N.Y., U.S.A. [Lepidoptera: Lycaenidae of W. Hemisphere (No)]
HUPÉ, Pierre Renè. Laboratoire de Geologie de la Sorbonne, 1 rue Victor Cousin, Paris (V), France. [Cambrian Trilobita of Africa & s. Europe (Yes)]
HURD, Dr. Paul D., Jr. 112 Agriculture Hall, University of California, Berkeley 4, Calif., U.S.A. [Aculeate Hymenoptera: g. Pepsis, Scoliidae, diurnal Mutillidae, Apoidea of N. America (Yes)]
HURE, Dr. Jure, kustos, Institut Biologique, Put Ispod Petke 4, Dubrovnik, Yugoslavia. [Chaetognatha & Crustacea: Copepoda of Adriatic Sea (Yes)]
HŮRKA, K. Department of Entomology, Universita Karlova, Viničná ul. 7, Praha II, Czechoslovakia. [Coleoptera: Carabidae, larvae & adults, of c. Europe (Yes); Diptera: Nycteribiidae & Aphaniptera: Ischnopsyllidae, of Palearctic (Yes)]
HURLEY, Dr. D.E. New Zealand Oceanographic Institute, Department of Scientific & Industrial Research, P.O. Box 8009, Wellington, New Zealand. [Crustacea: Amphipoda & Isopoda of s. Pacific (Yes)]
HÜRZELER, Dr. Johannes. Section Osteologique, Museum d'Histoire Naturelle, Augustinergasse 2, Basel, Switzerland. [Fossil Mammalia of Europe]
HUSSAKOF, Dr. Louis. (Brooklyn, N.Y.; fossil Pisces) Not now active in taxonomy.
HUSSEY, Dr. Keith M. Geology Department, Iowa State College, Ames, Iowa, U.S.A. [Tertiary Foraminifera of U.S. Gulf Cst. (Yes); Pleistocene Foraminifera of Arctic Alaska (Yes)]
HUSSEY, Dr. N.W. Glasshouse Crops Research Institute, Worthing Road, Rustington, Littlehampton, Sussex, England. [Hymenoptera: Chalcidoidea: Torymidae: g. Megastigmus of World (Yes)]
HUSSEY, Prof. Roland F. Department of Biology, University of Florida, Gainesville, Fla., U.S.A. [Hemiptera: Heteroptera of W. Hemisphere (Yes)]
HUSSON, Dr. A.M., Curator of Mammals, Rijksmuseum van Natuurlijke Histoirie, Leiden, Netherlands. [Mammalia of Europe, espec. the Netherlands; Surinam; West Indies; Dutch New Guinea; Indonesia (all Yes)]
HUTCHESON, R.B. Superior Oil Co., P.O. Box 1031, Bakersfield, Calif., U.S.A. [Fossil Foraminifera (Yes)]
HUTCHINS, Louis W. (Woods Hole, Mass.; Bryozoa & Cirripedia) Deceased.
HUTCHINSON, Prof. G. Evelyn. Osborn Zoological Laboratory, Yale University, New Haven 11, Conn., U.S.A. [Heteroptera: Corixidae & Notonectidae of Old World (No)]

HUTCHINSON, Dr. M. T. Department of Entomology, Agricultural Experiment Station, New
Brunswick, N. J., U. S. A. [Nematoda: Tylenchida of n. e. U. S. (No)]
HUTCHISON, Dr. Victor H. Department of Zoology, Duke University, Durham, N. C., U. S. A.
[Amphibia of e. N. America (No); Caudata of N. America (Yes)]
HUTTEL, Wladimir. (Montpellier, France; Diptera) Deceased.
HYATT, K. H. British Museum (Natural History), Cromwell Road, London, S. W. 7, England.
[Araneae & Acarina: Mesostigmata of Britain & Himalaya, espec. Nepal (Yes)]
HYLAND, Mr. K. E., Jr. Department of Zoology, University of Rhode Island, Kingston, R. I.,
U. S. A. [Acarina: Trombiculidae: g. Hannemania of World (Yes); Trichoptera of
Nearctic (No)]
HYMAN, Dr. Libbie H. American Museum of Natural History, New York 24, N. Y., U. S. A.
[Turbellaria of World (Yes)]
HYNES, Dr. H. B. N. Zoology Department, University of Liverpool, Liverpool, England.
[Plecoptera of Europe & Africa (Yes); Crustacea: f-w. Amphipoda of Europe (Yes)]

IACOB, Ing. N. Institutul de Cercetări Horti-Viticole, Bd. N. Bălcescu Nr. 4-6, Bucureşti-
Băneasa, Rumania. [Acarina: Tetranychidae of Rumania]
* IBARRA-GRASSO, Addalberto. División Zoologia Agricola, Paseo Colón 922-4º piso, Buenos
Aires, Argentina. [Acarina: Phytophagous Acari, Phytoseiidae, Oribatei]
ICHIHARA, Mr. Tadayoshi. The Whales Research Institute, 4, 12-Chome, Nishigashi-Dori,
Tsukishima, Chuo-Ku, Tokyo, Japan. [Mammalia: Cetacea: whales of n. Pacific &
Antarctic (Yes)]
ICHIKAWA, Dr. K. Department of Geosciences, Faculty of Science, Osaka City University,
Osaka, Kita-ku, Japan. [Mesozoic Pelecypoda, espec. Triassic (Yes); Permian-
Triassic Radiolaria (No)]
ICHINOHE, Mr. M. Hokkaido National Agricultural Experiment Station, Kotoni, Sapporo,
Japan. [Nematoda: g. Heterodera, Meloidogyne, Aphelenchoides, of Japan (Yes)]
* IDA, Mr. Kazuyoshi. Petroleum Section, Geological Survey of Japan, 8 Kawada-cho, Shin-
juku, Tokyo, Japan. [Fossil invertebrates]
IDE, Prof. F. P. Department of Zoology, University of Toronto, Toronto 5, Ont., Canada.
[Ephemeroptera of n. e. N. America (Yes); Diplopoda, Chilopoda, Crustacea: Isopoda &
Amphipoda, of Ontario (No)]
IENIŞTEA, Dr. Mircea Al.. Staţiunea Zoologică, Sinaia (reg. Ploeşti), Rumania. [Coleop-
tera: Cicindelidae, Carabidae, Dytiscidae, Gyrinidae, Hydrophilidae, Silphidae,
Malacodermata, Dryopidae, Scarabaeidae, Cerambycidae; all of c. & e. Europe (Yes)]
* IGA, Masahiro. 10, 5-chome, Abenosuji, Abeno, Os aka, Japan. [Coleoptera: Cleridae]
* IGALFFY, Prof. K., Custos-Directeur, Ornitholoski Institut, Ilirskitrg 9, Zagreb, Yugo-
slavia. [Aves]
IGNOFFO, Dr. Carlo Michael. Department of Biology, Iowa Wesleyan College, Mt. Pleasant,
Iowa, U. S. A. [Anoplura of World (Yes); Homoptera: Aphididae: Eriosomatinae of N.
America (Yes)]
IGO, Mr. Hisayoshi. Geological & Mineralogical Institute, Faculty of Science, Tokyo Kyoiku
Daigaku, Otokakubo-machi, Bunkyo-ku, Tokyo, Japan. [Carboniferous Fusulinidae of
Japan; Silurian-Permian Rugosa & Tabulata of Japan]
IHAROS, G. Balatonfenyves V, Hungary. [Tardigrada of e. Europe (Yes)]
IHLE, J. E. W. (Rotterdam, Netherlands; Tunicata) Deceased.
II, Dr. Naoyoshi. 515 Matsubara-cho, Hikone City, Shiga-ken, Japan. [Crustacea: Mysidacea
of n. w. Pacific (Yes)]
IJIRI, Shôji. C/o Paleontological Society of Japan, Geological Institute, Faculty of Science,
University of Tôkyô, Tôkyô, Japan. [Tertiary Mammalia: Desmostylidae of Pacific
rim (Yes); Fossil & Recent mammal teeth (No)]
* IKEBE, Nubuo. Geological Institute, Kyoto University, Kyoto, Japan. [Mollusca]
* IKEDA, Hyôzi. Zoological Institute, Tokyo University, Tokyo, Japan. [Pisces]
IKEZAKI, Dr. Francis M. 2447 Oahu Avenue, Honolulu 14, Hawaii, U. S. A. [Trematoda:
Gyrodactylus eucaliae of North Dakota (Yes)]
IKONOMOV, Dr. Peter. Prirodo-matematički fakultet, Skopje, Yugoslavia. [Ephemeroptera of
Yugoslavia & Balkans (Yes)]
* ILIFFE, Lady Charlotte. Yattenden Court, near Newbury, Berks, England. [Mollusca]
ILLG, Dr. Paul L. Department of Zoology, University of Washington, Seattle 5, Wash.,
U. S. A. [Parasitic & commensal Copepoda]
* ILLICK, Helen J. See BREED, H. J. I.
* ILLICK, J. Theron. Address unknown. [Coelenterata]
ILLIES, Gisela. Technische Hochschule Karlsruhe, Institut für Geologie, Kaiserstrasse 12,
Karlsruhe, Germany. [Jurassic Bryozoa, espec. Cyclostomata, of s. Germany (Yes)]
ILLIES, Dr. Joachim. Fuldastation, Schlitz (Oberhessen), Germany. [Plecoptera of Europe
& S. America (Yes); Ephemeroptera of Germany (Yes)]
* ILYIN, Prof. B. S. (Moscow, U. S. S. R.; Pisces) Deceased.

IMADATÉ, Gentaro. Gozaemon-Zaka, Koryiyama, Nara, Japan. [Protura of Asia & Mela-
nesia (Yes); Collembola: Onychiuridae of Japan (No)] [Kyoto University]
IMAI, Dr. Sadahiko. Zoological Laboratory, Kagoshima University, Shimoarata-Machi 470,
Kagoshima City, Japan. [Pisces: Exocoetina of n. w. Pacific (Yes); Stomiatina of
Japan (Yes)]
IMAIZUMI, Rikizo. Institute of Geology & Paleontology, Faculty of Science, Tohoku Univer-
sity, Kawauchi, Sendai, Japan. [Crustacea: Decapoda: Reptantia & Brachyura of Japan,
Europe, New World (all Yes)]
IMAIZUMI, Y., Scientific Officer, Department of Zoology, National Science Museum, Ueno
Park, Tokyo, Japan. [Mammalia: Insectivora, Microchiroptera, Rodentia: Muridae;
all of Japan (Yes)]
IMAMURA, Prof. Taiji. Biological Institute, Ibaraki University, Mito, Ibaraki pref., Japan.
[Symphyla of Japan (Yes); Acarina: Hydrachnellae of Japan & China (Yes); Halacaridae
& Spinturnidae of Japan (Yes)]
* IMANISHI, Shigeru. Institute of Geology & Paleontology, Tôhoku University, Katahire-chô,
Sendai City, Japan. [Ostracoda]
IMBRIE, Prof. John. Department of Geology, Columbia University, New York, N. Y., U. S. A.
[Devonian Brachiopoda (Yes)]
IMHOF, Thomas A. 307 38th Street, Fairfield, Ala., U. S. A. [Aves of Alabama (Yes)]
IMLAY, Mr. R. W. Room 331, U. S. National Museum, Washington 25, D. C., U. S. A. [Jura-
ssic-Cretaceous Ammonites of N. America (Yes)] [U. S. Geological Survey]
INABA, Akihiko. Mukaishima Marine Biological Station, Mukaishima, Onomichi, Hiroshima
Pref., Japan. [Mollusca of Inland Sea of Seto (No); Opisthobranchia of Japan (Yes)]
[Hiroshima University]
* INABA, Densaburo. Tokyo University of Fisheries, Shiba Kaigandori 6, Minato-ku,
Tokyo, Japan. [Pisces]
INGER, Robert F. Chicago Natural History Museum, Chicago 5, Ill., U. S. A. [Reptilia &
Amphibia: Salientia of Africa, Asia, Malaysia (Yes); f-w. Pisces of Malaysia (Yes)]
INGHAM, Charles. Department of Zoology, University of Utah, Salt Lake City, Utah, U. S. A.
[Hymenoptera: Formicidae of N. America (Yes)]
INGLE, Robert M. (Tallahassee, Fla.; Mollusca) Not now active in taxonomy.
INGLES, Prof. L. G. Department of Biology, Fresno State College, Fresno, Calif., U. S. A.
[Mammalia of N. America (Yes)]
INGLIS, Dr. W. G. Department of Zoology, British Museum (Natural History), Cromwell
Road, London, S. W. 7, England. [Nematoda of vertebrates of World (Yes); Nemato-
morpha of Europe (No); Acanthocephala of World (No)]
INGRAM, H. A. P. Emmanuel College, Cambridge, England. [Terr. & f-w. Mollusca of
Britain (Yes); of Europe, excl. Russia (No)]
INGRAM, Dr. William M. Public Health Service, 4675 Columbia Parkway, Cincinnati 26,
Ohio, U. S. A. [Mesozoic-Recent Gastropoda: Cypraeidae (Yes); Recent terr. Gastro-
poda of California (No)]
INO, Dr. Takashi. Tokai Regional Fish Research Laboratory, Tsukishima, Tokyo, Japan.
[Gastropoda: Haliotidae of n. Pacific (Yes)]
INOUE, Hiroshi. Eiko High School, Funakoshi, Yokosuka, Kanagawa Pref., Japan. [Lepidop-
tera: Macroheterocera of Japan, Korea, Manchuria (Yes); Pyralididae of Japan (No)]
INOUE, Mr. I. Biological Institute, Tokyo Gakugei University, Koganei City, Tokyo, Japan.
[Gordiacea of Japan & Asia (Yes)]
INOUYE, Dr. Motonori, Chief Forest Entomologist, Government Forest Experiment Station,
Hokkaido Branch, No. 13 Avenue, 5 Street, Toyohira, Sapporo, Hokkaido, Japan.
[Homoptera: Aphididae & Eriosomatidae of Hokkaido & n. Japan (No); Adelgidae of
Japan (Yes); Diptera: Itonididae of Japan (No)]
* INUKAI, Prof. Tetsuo. Zoological Institute, Hokkaido University, Sapporo, Japan. [Am-
phibia]
INVREA, Dr. Fabio. Museo Civico di Storia Naturale, via Brigata Liguria 9, Genova, Italy.
[Hymenoptera: Mutillidae of Palearctic & e. Africa (No); Apterogynidae of World (Yes);
Chrysididae of Palearctic (No)]
IONEL, A. See ANDRIESCU, I.
IONESCU, C. N. (Bucureşti, Rumania; Collembola) Deceased.
IONESCU, Prof. Dr. M. A. Facultatea de Stiinte Naturale, Splaiul Independentei 95, Bucureş-
ti, Rumania. [Diptera: Asilidae & Bombiliidae of Europe (Yes); Hymenoptera: Cynipoi-
dea of Europe (Yes); Apterygota, espec. Protura, of Europe (No)]
* IREDALE, T. Department of Ornithology, Australian Museum, Hyde Park, Sydney, N. S. W.,
Australia. [Aves & Mollusca]
IRELAND, Prof. H. A. Department of Geology, University of Kansas, Lawrence, Kans.,
U. S. A [Paleozoic arenaceous Foraminifera of World (Yes)]
IRIARTE, Dr. D. R. Laboratorio de la Clinica Luis Razetti, Box 1744, Caracas, Venezuela.
[Diptera: Simuliidae of Venezuela (Yes)]

IRIE, Prof. H. Faculty of Fisheries, Nagasaki University, Sasebo, Nagasaki Pref., Japan. [Crustacea; marine pelagic Amphipoda: Hyperiidea of Japanese seas (Yes)]
IRWIN, M. P. S. C/o National Museum, P. O. Box 240, Bulawayo, Southern Rhodesia. [Aves of Ethiopian (Yes)]
* ISEMONGER, R. M. 5 Charles Bullock Avenue, Belvedere, Salisbury, Southern Rhodesia. [Amphibia & Reptilia]
ISENBERG, Carl. 19500 Skyline Boulevard, Redwood City, Calif., U. S. A. [Reptilia & Amphibia of Santa Cruz Mts. of California (Yes)]
ISHIDA, Hiroshi. No. 1929, Goshikiyama, Nishi-Tarumi-chô, Tarumi-ku, Kobe, Japan. [Coleoptera: Caraboidea of Japan (Yes); Diptera: Tipulidae of Japan (No)] [Hyogo Agricultural College]
ISHIHARA, Prof. Tamotsu. Entomological Laboratory, College of Agriculture, Ehime University, Matsuyama, Japan. [Homoptera: Auchenorrhyncha of e. Asia (Yes)]
* ISHII, Tei, Dean, Faculty of Agriculture, Tokyo University of Agriculture & Technology, Fuchu-Machi, Tokyo, Japan. [Parasitic Hymenoptera]
ISHII, Dr. Y. Department of Parasitology, Faculty of Medicine, Kyushu University, Fukuoka, Japan. [Acarina: Erythraeidae of c. & w. Japan (Yes)]
ISHIKAWA, Ryôsuke. 756 Yoyogi-Hommachi, Shibuya-Ku, Tokyo, Japan. [Hymenoptera: Pompilidae of Japan (Yes); Apidae: Bombini; Tiphiidae; Vespidae; Vespinae; all of Japan (No)]
ISHIYAMA, Prof. Reizo. Shimonoseki College of Fisheries, Yoshimi, Shimonoseki City, Yamaguchi Pref., Japan. [Pisces: Rajidae of w. N. Pacific (Yes); of e. N. & S. Pacific (No)]
ISLAS, S., Federico. Oficina de Entomologia, Dirección General de Defensa Agricola, Balderas No. 94 - 2nd Piso, Mexico 1, D. F., Mexico. [Coleoptera: Scarabaeidae: Aphodiinae of Mexico (Yes); Coprinae & Melolonthinae of Mexico (No)]
* ISOSSIMOW, W. See IZOSIMOV, W.
ISRAELSKY, Mr. Merle C. U. S. Geological Survey, 4 Homewood Place, Menlo Park, Calif., U. S. A. [Eocene Foraminifera of California (No)]
ISSEKUTZ, Dr. László. Kohfidisch, Burgenland, Austria. [Lepidoptera of c. Europe (No); Nymphalidae: g. Melitaea of Palearctic (Yes); Aegeriidae of Europe & n. Africa (Yes)]
* ISSEL, Dr. W. P. Address unknown. [Mammalia: Chiroptera; Aves]
ISSIKI, Syuiti. Entomology Laboratory, University of Osaka Prefecture, Sakai City, Osaka, Japan. [Microlepidoptera & Mecoptera of Japan (Yes)]
ITAGAKI, Hiroshi. 342 Taishido-machi, Setagaya-ku, Tokyo, Japan. [Gastropoda: Lymnaeidae of Japan (Yes); Thiaridae of Japan (No)]
ITO, J. Hygiene Laboratory, Faculty of Education, Shizuoka University, Shizuoka, Japan. [Trematoda: Digenea, larvae, of Japan (Yes)]
ITO, Dr. Syusiro. Entomology Laboratory, College of Agriculture, University of Osaka Prefecture, Sakai City, Osaka, Japan. [Diptera: Trypetidae & Empididae of Japan (Yes)]
ITO, Dr. Takashi. The Faculty of Fisheries, Prefectural University of Mie, 11 Otanimachi, Tsu, Mie Pref., Japan. [Crustacea: f-w. & br-w. Copepoda of Japan (Yes), of E. Asia (No)]
ITÔ, Dr. Takeo. Department of Biology, Ehime University, Matsuyama City, Ehime Pref., Japan. [Hydrozoa: f-w. & br-w. Hydroida of Japan (Yes); Sipunculoidea, Echiuroidea, Priapuloidea, of Japan (Yes)]
ITOIGAWA, Junji. Department of Earth Sciences, Nagoya University, Chikusa-ku, Nagoya, Japan. [Cenozoic Mollusca of Japan (Yes)]
IUGA-RAICA, Dr. Victoria G. Muzeul de Istorie Naturală "Grigore Antipa Şoseana," Kisselef No. 1, Bucureşti III, Rumania. [Hymenoptera: Apidae: Anthophorinae of c. Europe (Yes); Tenthredinidae: Tenthredininae of c. Europe (Yes)]
▸ IVANOV, Prof. A. V. Zoological Institute, Academy of Sciences, Leningrad 164, U. S. S. R. [Pogonophora of World (Yes); Turbellaria: Acoela (No); parasitic Gastropoda of World (Yes)]
▸ * IVASHKIN, V. M. Laboratory of Helminthology, Academy of Sciences of U. S. S. R., Lenin Highway, 33, Moscow B-71, U. S. S. R. [Helminths of animals of U. S. S. R.]
IVIE, Mr. Wilton. P. O. Box 56, Furlong, Penna., U. S. A. [Araneida of N. America (Yes)]
IWAI, T. Department of Fisheries, Kyoto University, Maizuru, Japan. [Pisces: Gempylidae: g. Scombrina of Indo-Pacific (Yes); luminous fishes of Pacific (Yes)]
IWASI, Prof. Masao. Biological Institute, Seikei University, Tokyo, Japan. [Crustacea: Amphipoda & Isopoda, marine, f-w., terr., of Japan (Yes)]
IWASE, Mr. Taro. 4 Shinhana-cho, Hongo, Tokyo, Japan. [Lepidoptera: Rhopalocera, espec. larvae, of Japan (No)]
IWATA, Prof. Kunio. Hyogo University of Agriculture, Sasayama, Hyogo Pref., Japan. [Hymenoptera: Sphecidae & Ichneumonidae of Honshu, Japan (No)]
IWATA, Prof. S. Department of Biology, Nara Gakugei University, Nara, Japan. [Cestoda of Japan (Yes)]

228

IYATOMI, Prof. K. Faculty of Agriculture, Nagoya University, Anjyo, Aichi-Ken, Japan. [Nematoda: Tylenchida: Tylenchidae & Neotylenchidae of Japan (Yes)]
* IYENGAR, Dr. M. O. T. South Pacific Commission, Post Box No. 9, Noumea, New Caledonia. [Diptera: Culicidae]
IZOSIMOV, Prof. W. Laboratory of Biology, Medical Institute, Kasanj, U. S. S. R. [Oligochaeta of U. S. S. R. (No)]
* IZZARD, Mr. R. J. Department of Entomology, British Museum (Natural History), Cromwell Road, London, S. W. 7, England. [Heteroptera]

JAANUSSON, Dr. Valdar. Paleontological Institute, Uppsala University, Uppsala, Sweden. [Ordovician Trilobita (Yes); Ordovician-Silurian Graptoloidea & Brachiopoda: Articulata (No); Ordovician Crustacea: Ostracoda: Palaeocopa (Yes)]
JABLOKOV, A. V. Institute of Animal Morphology, Academy of Science, Leninsky prospect 33, Moscow V-71, U. S. S. R. [Mammalia: Odontoceti & Mysticeti of Arctic (Yes); of N. Pacific (No)]
JACHONTOV, V. V. See YAKHONTOV, V. V.
JACK, Kenneth M. Warwick Lodge, 643 London Road, Thornton Heath, Surrey, England. [Acarina: Pterygosomidae of World (Yes)]
JACKH, Mr. Eberhard. Joseph-Haydn-Platz 11, Bremen, Germany. [Microlepidoptera of Europe (Yes); Neuroptera: Planipennia of Europe (No)] [Übersee Museum]
JACKIEWICZ, Maria. Zakład Zoologii Ogólnej, Uniwersytet im Adam Mickiewicza, ul. Fredry 10, Poznań, Poland. [Gastropoda: Lymnaeidae of Europe (Yes)]
JACKSON, Prof. C. F. Department of Zoology, University of New Hampshire, Durham, N. H., U. S. A. [Mammalia of n. e. U. S. & Quebec (Yes)]
JACKSON, Dr. Daniel F. Department of Biology, Western Michigan University, Kalamazoo, Mich., U. S. A. [Crustacea: Cladocera of N. America (Yes); Hydrozoa: Hydroida & Trachylina of N. America (Yes)]
JACKSON, Dr. Hartley H. T. Room 61, U. S. National Museum, Washington 25, D. C., U. S. A. [Mammalia of Wisconsin (Yes); Insectivora: Soricidae of New World (No); g. Sorex (Yes); Talpidae of N. America (No); Carnivora: Canidae: g. Canis of N. America (Yes)]
JACKSON, Dr. J. S. National Museum of Ireland, Kildare Street, Dublin, Eire. [Mississippian (Dinantian) Anthozoa: Rugosa of Ireland (Yes)]
JACKSON, Mary. Department of Zoology, University of British Columbia, Vancouver, B. C., Canada. [Aves: Anatidae of N. America (No)]
JACKSON, Mr. T. H. E. Kapretwa Estate, Box 129, Kitale, Kenya. [Lepidoptera: Rhopalocera of trop. Africa (Yes)]
JACOB, F. H. Ministry of Agriculture, Fisheries and Food, Plant Pathology Laboratory, Harpenden, England. [Homoptera: Aphididae of Britain (Yes)]
JACOBS, Frank E. 274 Stantonville Drive, Oakland 19, Calif., U. S. A. [Intertidal Mollusca of n. California (Yes)]
JACOBS, Dr. George J. 800 Rural Avenue, Williamsport 4, Penna., U. S. A. [Amphibia: Urodela of N. America & Oriental (Yes); Anura of N. America & Japan (Yes)]
JACOBS, Dr. Leon. Laboratory of Tropical Diseases, National Institute of Health, Bethesda 14, Md., U. S. A. [Protozoa: parasitic Amoebae of World (No); Protozoa of uncertain position of World (Yes)]
JACOBS, S. N. A. 54 Hayes Lane, Bromley, Kent, England. [Microlepidoptera of World (Yes)]
* JACOBS, W. Zoologisches Institut der Universität, 14 Luisenstrasse, München 2, Germany. [Orthoptera]
JACOBSON, Mr. Morris K. 455 139th Street, Rockaway Beach 94, N. Y., U. S. A. [Marine Mollusca of e. cst. N. America (Yes); terr. Mollusca of World (No)]
JACOT-GUILLARMOD, Charles Frédéric. Albany Museum, Grahamstown, Union of South Africa. [Thysanoptera of World (No); Hymenoptera: Scolioidea of Africa & Madagascar (No); Tiphiidae of Africa & Madagascar (Yes)]
JACQUEMART, Serge. C/o Institut Royal des Sciences Naturelles de Belgique, Rue Vautier 31, Bruxelles 4, Belgium. [Trichoptera of Europe, Africa, New World, (Yes); Collembola of Europe (No)]
JACZEWSKI, Prof. Dr. Tadeusz. Instytut Zoologiczny, Polskiej Akademii Nauk, ul. Wilcza Nr. 64, Warszawa, Poland. [Aquatic & semi-aquatic Heteroptera of World (No); Corixidae, Notonectidae, Mesoveliidae, Hydrometridae, Ochteridae of World (Yes)]
* JACZO, Dr. Imre. Biológiai Kutatóintézete, Magyar Tudományos Akadémia, Tihany, Hungary. [Copepoda]
JAECKEL, Dr. Siegfried G. A., Jr. Dorfstrasse 16, Kiel-Heikendorf, Germany. [Pleistocene -Recent Mollusca of World (No), of Palearctic (Yes)]
JAECKEL, Prof. Dr. Siegfried H. Zoologisches Museum, Invalidenstrasse 43, Berlin N. 4, German Democratic Republic. [Terr. & f-w. Mollusca of Palearctic (Yes)]
JAEGER, Edmund C. 4465 6th Street, Riverside, Calif., U. S. A. [Aves & Mammalia of deserts of N. America (No)]

JAEGER, Dr. H. Geologisch-Paläontologisches Institut & Museum, Invalidenstrasse 43, Berlin N 4, German Democratic Republic. [Graptoloidea of "Upper to Lower Ludlow; Wenlock & Valent partim" (g. Monograptus, Retiolites, Abiesgraptus, Linograptus, Cyrtograptus) (Yes)]

JAGEMANN, Dr. Emil. Horákova 4, Brno-Žabovřesky, Czechoslovakia. [Coleoptera: Elateridae of Palearctic (Yes)] [Institute of Plant Pathology]

JÄGERSTEN, Prof. G. Zoological Institute, University of Uppsala, Uppsala, Sweden. [Annelida: Myzostomida (Yes); Pogonophora (Yes)]

JAGO, N. D.; Lecturer in Entomology, Zoology Department, University College of Ghana, Achimota, Accra, Ghana. [Dermaptera, Orthoptera, Dictyoptera of Ethiopian (No); Orthoptera: Acrididae: g. Calliptamus of Palearctic & Ethiopian (Yes)]

JAHN, Prof. Theodore L. Department of Zoology, University of California, Los Angeles 24, Calif., U.S.A. [Protozoa: Flagellata & Suctoria (No)]

JAHODA, William J. (Hartford, Conn.; Copepoda) Not now active in taxonomy.

* JAKOB, Dr. H. Mollardg. 13, Wien VI, Austria. [Coleoptera]

JAKOBI, Prof. Dr. Hans. Instituto de Pesquisas, Faculdade de Filosofia da Universidade do Paraná, Curitiba, Brazil. [Crustacea: Copepoda: Harpacticoida; Syncarida: Bathynellacea; both of World (Yes)]

JAKOVLEVA, A. M. Medical Institute, Chernovitsi, Ukraine, U.S.S.R. [Mollusca: "Loricata of seas of U.S.S.R." (Yes)]

JAKOWSKA, Dr. Sophia, Associate Professor of Biology, College of Mount St. Vincent, Mount St. Vincent-on-the-Hudson, New York 71, N.Y., U.S.A. [Sporozoa: non-pigmented Haemosporidia in cold-blooded vertebrates (Yes); Myxosporidia in fishes (Yes)]

JAKUBSKI, Dr. A.W. Penrhos Polish Home, Pwllheli, Wales. [Rotatoria; Gastrotricha; Homoptera: Underground Margarodidae]

JAMES, Dr. Maurice T. Department of Zoology, State College of Washington, Pullman, Wash., U.S.A. [Diptera: Stratiomyidae of World (Yes); Calliphoridae of New World & Micronesia (Yes)]

JAMESON, David L. Department of Zoology, San Diego State College, San Diego, Calif., U.S.A. [Amphibia & Reptilia of w.U.S. (Yes)]

JAMESON, Dr. E.W., Jr. Department of Zoology, University of California, Davis, Calif., U.S.A. [Siphonaptera of N. America, Japan, Korea (Yes); Acarina: Laeleptidae, Trombiculidae, Myobiidae, of N. America, Japan, Korea (Yes)]

JAMIESON, Dr. B. C/o Annelida Section, British Museum (Natural History), Cromwell Road, London, S.W.7, England. [Oligochaeta of Neotropics & Paleotropics (Yes, after 1961)]

JAMNBACK, Dr. Hugo, Jr. State Education Building, Albany 1, N.Y., U.S.A. [Diptera: Simuliidae of n.e.U.S. (Yes)] [New York State Museum]

JANCIK, Otto. Furth-Göttweig Nr. 78, N-Ö., Austria. [Lepidoptera: Saturniidae & Ceratocampidae of World (No); devel. stages of Marcolepidoptera of World (Yes)]

JANCZYK, Dr. F. Zoologische Sammlung, Naturhistorisches Museum, Burgring 7, Vienna 1, Austria. [Coleoptera: Curculionidae of World (Yes); Arachnida: Opiliones: Sironidae of s. Europe (No)]

JANETSCHEK, Prof. Dr. H. Zoologisches Institut der Universität Innsbruck, Universitätstrasse 4, Innsbruck, Austria. [Thysanura: Machilidae of Europe (Yes)]

JANGI, Dr. B.S., Lecturer in Zoology, College of Science, Nagpur, India. [Chilopoda: Scolopendromorpha of World (Yes)]

* JANISCH, Miklós. Institutum Zoologiae Generalis et Parasitologiae Veterinarium, Landler Jenö u 2, Budapest VII, Hungary. [Acarina]

JANISZEWSKA, Dr. Janina. Instytut Zoologiczny, Uniwersytet im. Bolesława Bieruta, ul. Sienkiewicza 21, Wrocław, Poland. [Sporozoa: Cnidosporidia: Actinomyxidia of World (Yes); Rhizopoda: Testacea of World (Yes)]

JANMOULLE, Mr. E.W.A. 2 rue Ernotte, Watermael, Belgium. [Microlepidoptera of w. Europe (Yes)]

JANNONE, Prof. G., Direttore, Osservatorio Fitopatologico, Via Pescheira 30 A, Genova, Italy. [Orthoptera: Acridioidea of Europe & e. Africa (Yes)]

JÁNOSSY, Dr. D. Paleontology Department, Hungarian Natural History Museum, Museum krt. 14-16, Budapest VIII, Hungary. [Pleistocene Mammalia: Insectivora & Rodentia of c. Europe (No); Pleistocene Aves of c. Europe (Yes)]

JANSE, Prof. A.J.T. 541 Adcock Street, Gezina, Pretoria, Transvaal, Union of South Africa. [Lepidoptera of S. Africa (No); Pyralidae of World (No)]

* JANSSENS, Dr. A. M. J. J. (Bruxelles 4, Belgium. Coleoptera). Deceased.

JANSSENS, Prof. Dr. Em. 31 Avenue des Coccinelles, Bruxelles-Boitsfort, Belgium. [Coleoptera: Helmidae & Hydraenidae of Palearctic (No), of Greece (Yes); Diptera: Asilidae of Palearctic (No), of Greece (Yes)] [Universite Libre de Bruxelles]

JANSSON, A. Sturegatan 52, Örebro, Sweden. [Hymenoptera: Chalcidoidea & Proctotrupoidea of n. Europe (No)]

JARRIGE, J. 1 Place de l'Eglise, Vintry-sur-Seine (Seine), France. [Coleoptera: Staphylinidae of Palearctic & Malgache (Yes)]
JARVI, Prof. T. H. Calonius Str. 9 C, Helsinki, Finland. [Araneida of n. Europe]
JARVIK, Dr. Erik. Paleozoologiska Avdeling, Naturhistoriska Riksmuseum, Stockholm 50, Sweden. [Devonian Crossopterygii (Yes); Devonian Tetrapoda (Yes)]
JARVIS, Daniel. Box 55, Azle, Texas, U. S. A. [L. Permian Fusulinidae (No)] [Texas Christian University]
* JARVIS, F. V. L. 33 Greencourt Drive, Bognor Regis, Surrey, England. [Lepidoptera]
JARVIS, Hubert, (Toowang, Australia; Aphididae) Not now active in taxonomy.
JASCHNOV, Prof. W. A. Kiprenskogo 10, Moscow D-80, U. S. S. R. [Hydromedusae of n. seas & Black Sea (Yes); Crustacea: Copepoda: Calanoida of n. seas, Black Sea, Atlantic Ocean (Yes)]
JASKOSKI, Dr. Benedict J. Biology Department. Loyola University, 6525 Sheridan Road, Chicago 26, Ill., U. S. A. [Nematoda: Ascaridae of N. America (No)]
JASNOSH, V. A. Address unknown. [Hymenoptera: Chalcididae & Aphelinidae]
* JATZKO, I. J. Laboratory of Paleontology, University of Odessa, Peter the Great Street 1, Odessa, U. S. S. R. [Fossil Mammalia]
JAUME, Mr. Miguel. Calle 13 entre H y G, No. 351, Vedado, Habana, Cuba. [Terr., f-w., marine Mollusca of West Indies (Yes)] [Museo y Biblioteca de Zoologia de la Habana]
JAWLOWSKI, Prof. Dr. H. Zakład Biologii Akademii, Medycznij Polska, ul. Krolewska 15, Lublin, Poland. [Diplopoda of Poland, Rumania, Bulgaria, Latvia, Lithuania, Estonia (Yes)]
JAXON-DEELMAN, J. See DEELMAN, John Jaxon.
JAYARAM, Mr. K. C., Zoological Assistant, Zoological Survey of India, Indian Museum, Calcutta 13, India. [F-w. Pisces of India (Yes); f-w. Siluroidea, espec. Bagridae, of Oriental, Ethiopian, Palearctic (Yes)]
* JEAN, Yves. Biological Station, St. Andrews, N. B., Canada. [Pisces & Crustacea of e. N. America]
JEANNEL, Prof. Rene. Muséum National d'Histoire Naturelle, 45bis rue de Buffon, Paris (V), France. [Coleoptera: Carabidae, Pselaphidae, Catopidae; cave faunas (Yes); Pselaphidae of Africa (Yes)]
JEANNENOT, Mme. F. Laboratoire de Zoologie, Faculté des Sciences de Dijon, Dijon (Côte d'Or), France. [Collembola of France (Yes)]
JEDLIČKA, Ing. Arnošt. Ul. Národni Obrany č. 31, Praha-Bubeneč, Czechoslovakia. [Coleoptera: Carabidae, excl. g. Carabus, of Europe, Asia, N. Africa (Yes)]
JEEKEL, C. A. W. Zoologisch Museum, Zeeburgerdijk 21, Amsterdam-O, Netherlands. [Diploda of World (Yes); Arachnida, excl. Acarina, of w. Europe (No); Chilopoda of Europe (No)]
JEFFORDS, Mr. R. M. Humble Oil & Refining Co., P. O. Box 2180, Houston 1, Texas, U. S. A. [Paleozoic corals (Yes), Paleozoic-Mesozoic marine invertebrates, hystrichosperids, dinoflagellates, silicoflagellates (No)]
JELETZKY, Mr. J. A. Geological Survey of Canada, Ottawa, Ontario, Canada. [Carboniferous-Pleistocene Cephalopoda: Dibranchiata (Yes); Up. Jurassic-Cretaceous Ammonoidea of N. America (No); Up. Jurassic-Cretaceous Pelecypoda: g. Aucella & Inoceramus of N. Hemisphere (No)]
JELLISON, Dr. William L. Rocky Mountain Laboratory, Hamilton, Montana, U. S. A. [Siphonaptera & Anoplura of N. America (Yes)] [U. S. Public Health Service]
JENKINS, Dale W., Chief, Entomology Branch, Fort Detrick, Frederick, Md., U. S. A. [Acarina: g. Eutrombicula of New World (Yes); Diptera: Culicidae: g. Aedes of Arctic (No)]
JENKINS, Dr. W. R. Department of Botany, University of Maryland, College Park, Md., U. S. A. [Soil Nematoda of N. America (No)]
JENNI, Dr. Werner. Ottenbergstrasse 36, Zürich 49, Switzerland. [Amphibia & Reptilia of Europe (Yes)]
* JENNINGS, W. L. Florida State Board of Health, Jacksonville, Fla., U. S. A. [Mammalia: Chiroptera]
JENSEN, Dr. D. D. Department of Entomology, University of California, Berkeley 4, Calif., U. S. A. [Homoptera: Psyllidae of Old World (No), of New World (Yes)]
JENSEN, Harold J. Department of Botany & Plant Pathology, Oregon Agricultural Experiment Station, Corvallis, Ore., U. S. A. [Nematoda: plant parasitic, soil, f-w., all of World (Yes); marine of w. cst. U. S. (Yes)]
JENSEN, Cand. Mag. Poul Valentin. Universitets Zoologiske Museum, Krystalgade 27, København, Denmark. [Terr. Mammalia of Denmark, Sweden, Norway, Finland, Iceland, Faröe Is., Greenland (Yes)]
JEPPS, Dr. Margaret W. Department of Zoology, The University, Glasgow, Scotland. [Protozoa, espec. Foraminifera & those of medical importance]
JEPPSON, Lee R. University of California, Citrus Experiment Station, Riverside, Calif., U. S. A. [Acarina: citrus mites, Tetranychidae, g. Brevipalpus, Phytosciidae, of s. California (No)]

231

JEPSON, Prof. Glenn L. Department of Geology, Princeton University, Princeton, N. J.,
 U. S. A. [L. Tertiary Mammalia (Yes)]
JERZMAŃSKA, Mgsr. Anna. Zakład Paleozoologii, Universytetu Wrocłskiego, Ul. Sienkie-
 wicza 21, Wrocław, Poland. [Tertiary Fishes of Carpathian Flysch]
JEUNIAUX, Charles. Institut L. Fredericq, 17 place Delcour, Liège, Belgium. [Coleoptera:
 Elateridae of Palearctic (Yes); Chalcolepidiinae of S. America (Yes)]
JEWELL, Dr. Minna E. Department of Biology, Thornton Junior College, Harvey, Ill., U. S. A.
 [F-w. Porifera: Spongillidae of U. S. & Canada (Yes)]
JEWETT, Dr. John Mark. State Geological Survey, University of Kansas, Lawrence, Kans.,
 U. S. A. [Up. Paleozoic marine invertebrates of c. U. S.]
JEWETT, Mr. Stanley G., Jr. 7742 S. E. 27th Avenue, Portland 2, Ore., U. S. A. [Plecop-
 tera of World, excl. Europe ; espec. New World, India, Philippines; all (Yes)]
JIROVEC, Prof. Dr. Otto. Department of Parasitology, Charles University, Vinična 7,
 Praha (II), Czechoslovakia. [Sporozoa: Cnidosporidia, Haplosporidia, g. Taxolpasma,
 g. Penumocystis; all of World (Yes)]
* JOAN, Dra. Teresa. Canning 2471, Buenos Aires, Argentina. [Platyhelminthes]
* JOBE, Mrs. Thomas C. C/o Samedan Oil Corp., Oil Center Station, Lafayette, La., U. S. A.
 [Fossil Foraminifera]
* JOBLING, Mr. B. Welcome Laboratory of Tropical Medicine, 183-193 Euston Road, London,
 W. C. 1, England. [Anoplura]
JOBSON, Mrs. A. E. 3 Wellington Street, East Lindfield, N. S. W., Australia. [Araneida of
 New South Wales (Yes)]
▸* JODOT, Paul. 12 Rue du Regard, Paris (VI), France. [Mollusca]
JOHANSEN, Dr. Carl. Entomology Department, State College of Washington, Pullman, Wash.,
 U. S. A. [Homoptera: Aphididae of w. U. S. (No)]
JOHANSEN, Prof. Dr. H. Department of Ornithology, Zoological Museum of the University of
 Copenhagen, København, Denmark. [Aves of n. Eurasia (Yes)]
* JOHANSON, E. Statens Växtskyddsanstalt, Stockholm 19, Sweden. [Nematoda]
JOHANSSON, Sven. Zoologiska Institution, Lunds Universitets, Lund, Sweden. [Hymenoptera:
 Ichneumonidae & Braconidae of n. & c. Europe (Yes); Lepidoptera of Sweden (No)]
JOHN, Dr. D. D. (Cardiff, Wales; Echinodermata) Not now active in taxonomy.
JOHN, Hans. Karlstrasse 58, Bad Nauheim (16), Germany. [Coleoptera: Discolomidae of
 World (Yes)]
JOHN, Margaret E. Ministry of Agriculture, Fisheries & Food, Wye, Ashford, Kent, England.
 [Nematoda of economic importance]
JOHNELS, Dr. A. G. Zoologiska Institutet, Rådmansgatan 70 A, Stockholm V, Sweden. [F-w.
 Pisces of w. Africa (Yes)]
JOHNS, Mr. P. M. Department of Zoology, University of Canterbury, Christchurch, New
 Zealand. [Amphineura: Chitonidae of New Zealand (Yes); Diplopoda: Sphaerotrichopo-
 dae of New Zealand (Yes)]
JOHNSEN, Palle. Box 394 Ndola, Northern Rhodesia. [Diptera: Glossinidae: g. Glossina of
 Africa (No)] [Game & Tsetse Control Department]
JOHNSGARD, P. A. Department of Conservation, Cornell University, Ithaca, N. Y., U. S. A.
 [Aves: Anatidae of World (Yes)]
* JOHNSON, Bert M. Address unknown. [Diploda & Chilopoda of N. America]
JOHNSON, Mr. D. Elmer. P. O. Box 334, Dugway, Utah, U. S. A. [Diptera: Bombyliidae of N.
 America (Yes); Asilidae of N. America (No)]
JOHNSON, Dr. David H. Division of Mammals, U. S. National Museum, Washingon 25, D. C.,
 U. S. A. [Mammalia of World (Yes)]
JOHNSON, D. S. Department of Zoology, University of Malaya in Singapore, Bukit Timah
 Road, Singapore 10. [Crustacea] See Addenda.
JOHNSON, Fred C. Department of Zoology, University of Texas, Austin, Texas, U. S. A.
 [Amphibia: Anura of N. America (Yes)]
* JOHNSON, F. L. 25 Fermoy Road, Thorpe Bay, Essex, England. [Lepidoptera: Papilionidae]
JOHNSON, Dr. G. A. L. Department of Geology, Science Laboratories, South Road, Durham,
 England. [Carboniferous (Up. Viséan) Brachiopoda & rugose corals of n. England (Yes)]
 [University of Durham]
* JOHNSON, Grace Phillips. Address unknown. [Fossil invertebrates]
JOHNSON, Dr. J. C., Jr. Department of Biological Science, Kansas State Teachers College,
 Pittsburg, Kans., U. S. A. [Aves, excl. oceanic, of N. America (Yes); Mallophaga
 from Piciformes of N. America (Yes)]
JOHNSON, Lucile Maughan. Box 334, Dugway, Utah, U. S. A. [Diptera: Bombyliidae of U. S.
 (Yes)]
JOHNSON, Dr. Leland P. College of Liberal Arts, Drake University, Des Moines 11, Iowa,
 U. S. A. [Protozoa: Phytomastigina: g. Euglena of World (Yes)]
JOHNSON, Mr. Melvin A., Jr. (Grambling, La.; Mammalia) Not now active in taxonomy.
JOHNSON, Dr. Murray L. 501 North Tacoma Avenue, Tacoma 3, Wash., U. S. A. [Mammalia
 & Reptilia of Pacific n. w. U. S. (Yes)]

JOHNSON, Martin W. Scripps Institution of Oceanography, La Jolla, Calif., U.S.A. [Crustacea: Copepoda & Euphausiacea of Pacific & Arctic Oceans (Yes); larvae of Decapoda of e. Pacific (No)]

JOHNSON, N. E., Entomologist, Weyerhaeuser Timber Co., P. O. Box 420, Centralia, Wash., U.S.A. [Coleoptera: Scolytidae & Platypodidae of Pacific n.w. U.S. & Canada (Yes); Diptera: Itonididae of Douglas fir cones of Pacific n.w. (Yes)]

JOHNSON, Ned K. Museum of Vertebrate Zoology, University of California, Berkeley 4, Calif., U.S.A. [Aves: Tyrannidae: g. Empidonax of w. N. America (Yes)]

JOHNSON, Dr. Phyllis T. Box 2033, Balboa Heights, Canal Zone. [Siphonaptera & Anoplura of World (Yes)]

JOHNSON, Prof. Robert Britten. Division of Geology, Purdue University, Lafayette, Indiana. [Devonian Brachiopoda, Ophiuroidea, corals of e. & c. U.S. (Yes)]

JOHNSON, Dr. R. E. U.S. Fish & Wildlife Service, 1006 W. Lake Street, Minneapolis 8, Minn., U.S.A. [F-w. Pisces of N. America (No); Cyprinidae of Great Plains of N. America (Yes)]

JOHNSON, Mr. Richard I. Museum of Comparative Zoology, Cambridge 38, Mass., U.S.A. [Mollusca: Unionidae of World (No); of N. America (Yes)]

JOHNSON, Mr. Richard M. Biology Department, Tennessee Wesleyan College, Athens, Tenn., U.S.A. [Reptilia of e. N. America (Yes)]

* JOHNSON, W. E. Biological Station, Fisheries Research Board, Nanaimo, B. C., Canada. [Pisces]

JOHNSTON, Donald E. Department of Zoology, University of Maryland, College Park, Md., U.S.A. [Acarina: Trachytoidea of Holarctic (Yes)]

JOHNSTON, Dr. David W. Department of Biology, Mercer University, Macon, Ga., U.S.A. [Aves: Laridae & Corvidae of N. America (Yes)]

JOHNSTON, E. B. W. 130 Bispham Road, Blackpool, Lancs., England. [Rotatoria of Britain (Yes)]

JOHNSTON, Francis Newlands. Comus, Montgomery County, Md., U.S.A. [Triassic marine Cephalopoda of World]

JOHNSTON, H. B. (Frome, England; Orthoptera) Not now active in taxonomy.

JOHNSTON, Ian McKay. 1129A 10th Street, Albany 6, Calif., U.S.A. [Protozoa: Foraminifera: Pelecypoda: g. Pecten; Gastropoda: g. Turritella; all of west cst. U.S. (No)] [University of California]

JOHNSTON, Dr. Richard F. Museum of Natural History, University of Kansas, Lawrence, Kans., U.S.A. [Aves of N. America, Japan, Korea, Peru, Chile (Yes)]

* JOHNSTON, Titus. Department of Plant Pathology, Louisiana State University, Baton Rouge, La., U.S.A. [Nematoda]

JOHRI, Prof. L. N. Department of Zoology, University of Delhi, Delhi 8, India. [Cestoda of India, Burma, Thailand (Yes)]

JOLICOEUR, Pierre. C/o Department of Geology, University of Chicago, Chicago 37, Ill., U.S.A. [Wolves of n.w. Canada (No)]

JOLIVET, Dr. P. Institut Royal des Sciences Naturelles de Belgique, 31 Rue Vautier, Bruxelles 4, Belgium. [Coleoptera: Chrysomeloidea of World (No); parasites of insects (Gregarinidae, Trichomycetes, Gordiacea) of Africa (No); wings of insects of World]

* JONASSON, P. M. Freshwater Biological Laboratory, University of Copenhagen, Hillerod, Denmark. [Invertebrates; Pisces]

JONES, Dr. Arthur W. Department of Zoology & Entomology, University of Tennessee, Knoxville, Tenn., U.S.A. [Cestoda (No)]

JONES, Bradford C. Paleontology Laboratory, Union Oil Co., 17905 S. Central Avenue, Compton, Calif., U.S.A. [Fossil smaller Foraminifera (No)]

JONES, Mr. Bernard R. Minnesota Department of Conservation, 400 Shubert Building, St. Paul, Minn., U.S.A. [F-w. bottom Fauna]

* JONES, C. Garrett. Division of Malaria Eradication, World Health Organization, Palais des Nations, Genève, Switzerland. [Diptera]

JONES, D. G. Department of Geology, King's College, Strand, London, W. C. 2, England. [Namurian & Westphalian Cephalopoda, Pelecypoda, Gastropoda, Brachiopoda of S. Wales (No)]

* JONES, Prof. Daniel J. Department of Geology, University of Utah, Salt Lake City, Utah, U.S.A. [Fossil invertebrates]

JONES, David L. Paleontology & Stratigraphy Branch, U.S. Geological Survey, Menlo Park, Calif., U.S.A. [Cretaceous Mollusca, espec. Inoceraminae, of w. N. America (Yes)]

JONES, Dr. David T. P.O. Box 264, Bourbonnais, Ill., U.S.A. [Pleistocene-Recent terr. & f-w. Gastropoda of n.c. U.S. (No); f-l. f-w. Amoebae of n.c. U.S. (No); Diptera: Muscoidea of n.c. U.S. (No)] [Olivet Nazarene College, Kankakee]

JONES, Everet C. Pacific Oceanic Fishery Investigations, U.S. Fish & Wildlife Service, Post Office Box 3830, Honolulu, Hawaii, U.S.A. [Crustacea: marine Copepoda: Calanoida of tropical & temperate waters (Yes)]

233

* JONES, Mr. Ed L. 491 Alfred Street, North Sydney, N.S.W., Australia. [Hymenoptera: Argentine ants].

JONES, Prof. E. Ruffin, Jr. Department of Biology, University of Florida, Gainesville, Fla., U.S.A. [Turbellaria: Rhabdocoela & Alloeocoela; Archiannelida: g. Dinophilus; all of N. America (Yes)]

JONES, Frank Norton. (Wilmington, Del.; Lepidoptera) Not now active in taxonomy.

JONES, J. Knox, Jr. Museum of Natural History, University of Kansas, Lawrence, Kans., U.S.A. [Mammalia of N. America & n.e. Asia (Yes)]

* JONES, Dr. Myrna Frances. Laboratory of Tropical Diseases, National Institutes of Health, Bethesda 14, Md., U.S.A. [Parasites]

JONES, Dr. N.S. Marine Biological Station, Port Erin, Isle of Man, Great Britain. [Crustacea: Cumacea of World (Yes); Tanaidacea & Amphipoda of Britain (No)] [University of Liverpool]

JONES, P.J. Bureau of Mineral Resources, Childers Street, Turner, Canberra, Australia. [Up. Paleozoic Ostracoda of w. Australia (Yes)]

JONES, Dr. Robert Henry. Insects Affecting Man & Animals, P.O. Box 232, Kerrville, Texas, U.S.A. [Diptera: Heleidae of N. America (No); g. Culicoides of N. America (Yes)]

JONES, Dr. S., Chief Research Officer, Central Marine Fisheries Research Station, Mandapam Camp, S. India. [Pisces: Scrombridae & Synentognathi, larvae & adults, of Indian Ocean (Yes)]

JONES, Prof. S.C. Department of Entomology, Oregon State College, Corvallis, Ore., U.S.A. [Diptera: Trypetidae of U.S. (No)]

* JONES, Miss S.E. Address unknown. [Araneida]

* JONES, Victor E. Address unknown. [Odonata]

JONES, Dr. W. Clifford. Department of Zoology, University College of North Wales, Bangor, Wales. [Porifera: Calcarea: Homocoela: g. Leucosolenia of Britain (Yes)]

JONES, Prof. Woodrow H. Department of Biology, Fisk University, Nashville, Tenn., U.S.A. [Crustacea: Branchiopoda: Cladocera of s.U.S. (Yes)]

* JONES-BURDICK, William H. Address unknown. [Reptilia]

JONESCU, Mihail A. See IONESCU, M.A.

de JONG, Drs. B. C/o Peter Stuyvesant College, Willemstad, Curaçao. [Araneae of Netherlands & Curaçao (Yes)]

de JONG, Dr. C. Bilderdjklaan 69, Bilthoven, Netherlands. [Coleoptera of Europe, espec. Netherlands; Orthoptera: Tettigoniidae of Asia; insects from stored products of World; (all No)]

JONSGÅRD, Mr. Å. Universitets Biologiske Laboratorium og Statens Institut Hvalforskning, Frederiksgate 3, Oslo, Norway. [Mammalia: Cetacea: whales (Yes)]

JOPSON, Dr. Henry G.M. Department of Biology, Bridgewater College, Bridgewater, Va., U.S.A. [Amphibia: salamanders of s.w.U.S. (No); g. Diemyctylus of e.U.S. (Yes)]

JÔRAKU, Takeo. Toyama Agricultural Experiment Station, Tarômaru, Toyama, Japan. [Coleoptera: Anthribidae of Japan (Yes)]

JORDAN, H.E. Karl. (Tring, England; Coleoptera, Lepidoptera) Died 1958.

JORDAN, Prof. Dr. K.H.C. Zoologisches Institut der Technisches Hochschule, Zellescher Weg 40, Dresden A 20, German Democratic Republic. [Fossil & Recent Heteroptera of c. Europe (Yes)]

JORDAN, Louise. (Norman, Okla.; Fossil Foraminifera) Not now active in taxonomy.

JORDANO, Prof. Dr. Diego. Laboratorio de Biologia, Facultad de Veterinaria, Cordoba, Spain. [Cestoda of birds & domestic mammals of Spain & S. America (Yes)]

von JORDANS, Prof. Dr. A., Museums-Director, Zoologisches Forschungsinstitut & Museum Alexander Koenig, Bonn, Germany. [Aves of Palearctic (No), of Balearic Is. & Spain (Yes); g. Sturnus (Yes)]

JORGE, Prof. Dr. A. Ricardo. Museu de Zoologia, Faculdade de Ciencias, Universidade de Lisboa, Portugal. [Polychaeta of Lusitania (Yes); Chrysopetalidae of World (Yes); Sipunculoidea & Echiuroidea of Portugal, Spain, France, w. Mediterranean (No)]

JORGENSEN, Clive D. Department of Entomology, Oregon State College, Corvallis, Ore., U.S.A. [Acarina: Ixodoidea of N. America (No)]

* JORGENSEN, Lester. Address unknown. [Lepidoptera]

JORGENSON, Mr. Edsel C. U.S.D.A. Nematology Section, 477 Federal Building, Salt Lake City, Utah, U.S.A. [Nematoda: Tylenchida & Dorylaimoidea of New World & Europe (No); Diptera: Ephydridae of Utah (No)] [U.S. Department of Agriculture]

JOSEPH, Dr. Edwin B. Department of Biology, Birmingham-Southern College, Birmingham 4, Ala., U.S.A. [Shallow water marine Pisces of Gulf of Mexico & s. Atlantic (Yes); Syngnathidae of N. American csts. [Yes)]

JOSEPH, Dr. K.J. (See also KUTTAMATHIATHU, J.) Laboratoire de l'Evolution, 105 Boulevard Raspail, Paris, France. [Hymenoptera: Agaontidae & Torymidae: Idarninae of Asia & Africa (Yes)]

JOSIFOV, Dr. Michail. Institute & Museum of Zoology, Academy of Sciences, Ruski 1, Sofia, Bulgaria. [Terr. Heteroptera of Balkan Pen. (Yes); aquatic & semiaquatic Heteroptera of Balkan Pen. (No)]
* JOTWANI, M. G. Division of Entomology, Indian Agricultural Research Institute, New Delhi 12, India. [Insecta: Exopterygota]
* JOUANIN, Mr. C. Department d'Ornithologie, Museum National d'Histoire Naturelle, 55 rue de Buffon, Paris (V), France. [Aves]
JOYCE, Dr. C. R., Scientist (R), U. S. Public Health Service, P. O. Box 1410, Honolulu, Hawaii, U. S. A. [Acarina: Ixodoidea of N. America & Pacific Is. (Yes); Mallophaga, of mammals, & Anoplura of N. America & Pacific Is. (Yes); Siphonaptera of m. w. & e. U. S. (Yes); Diptera: Calliphoridae & Sarcophagidae of Pacific Is. (Yes); Culicidae of U. S. & Pacific Is. (Yes)]
JOYON, J. 1 Avenue Vercingétorix, Clermont-Ferrand, France. [Flagellata of France (No); Chrysomonadina of France (Yes)]
JOYSEY, Dr. K. A. University Museum of Zoology, Downing Street, Cambridge, England. [Paleozoic Blastoidea of Europe (Yes); Mesozoic-Tertiary Echinoidea: Irregularia of Middle East (No)]
JUBB, R. A. Department of Ichthyology, Rhodes University, Grahamstown, Union of South Africa. [F-w. Pisces of s. Africa (Yes)]
JUBERTHIE-JUPEAU, Mme. L. Laboratoire souterrain, Moulis (Ariège), France. [Symphyla of trop. America & Oceania (Yes); of Asia, Europe, Africa (No)]
JUDD, Prof. W. W. Department of Zoology, University of Western Ontario, London, Ont., Canada. [Aquatic insects]
* JUDIN, K. A. Zoological Institute, Academy of Sciences, Leningrad B-164, U. S. S. R. [Aves]
JUHL, Rolf. Box 186, Playa Ponce, Puerto Rico. [Marine Pisces: Thunnidae & Lutianidae of West Indies (Yes)]
JUNG, Dr. Herbert F. Burscheid-Maxhahn, Bezirk Düsseldorf, Germany. [Diptera: Psychodidae of World (No); of Palearctic (Yes)] [Biologisches Institut, Farbenfabriken Bayer]
JUNGE, Dr. G. C. A. Rijksmuseum van Natuurlijke Historie, Leiden, Netherlands. [Aves & Mammalia: Cetacea (Yes)]
JUSTICE, Mr. Keith E. Department of Zoology, University of Arizona, Tucson, Ariz., U. S. A. [Mammalia: Rodentia: Cricetidae & Heteromyidae of Arizona (Yes)]
* JUSZCZYK, Dr. Włodzimierz. Uniwersyte tu Marii Curie-Skłodowskiej, ul. Bart. Głowackiego 2, Lublin, Poland. [Amphibia & Reptilia]
JUUL, Overlaerer Knud. Provstebakken 24, Aarhus, Denmark. [Lepidoptera: Geometridae: g. Eupithecia of Denmark & Scandinavia (Yes)]

* KAAS, P. Mient 2, Den Haag, Netherlands. [Mollusca]
KAASSCHIETER, J. P. H. Grote Haarsekade 21, Gorinchem, Netherlands. [Cenozoic smaller Foraminifera of Europe (Yes)]
KABATA, Z. Scottish Home Department, Marine Laboratory, P. O. Box 101, Victoria Road, Torry, Aberdeen, Scotland. [Crustacea: Copepoda: Lernaeopodidae & Lernaeidae of e. N. Atlantic (Yes)]
KABOS, W. J. Van Baerlestraat (26), Amsterdam Z-1, Netherlands. [Diptera: Acalyptratae: Anthomyidae of Netherlands & Belgium; social Diptera of Netherlands & Belgium]
* KABURAKI, Prof. Tokio. Zoological Institute, College of Agriculture, University of Tokyo, Tokyo, Japan. [Turbellaria]
* KACZMAREK, Jadwiga. Zaklad Zoologii Ogólnej, Uniwersytet im. Adama Mickiewicza, ul. Fredry 10, Poznań, Poland. [Chilopoda]
* KADAM, K. M. Department of Zoology, Central College, Bangalore, Madras, India. [Pisces]
* KADENATSII, A. N. Omsk Veterinary Institute, Rabinovitcha Street 55, Omsk, U. S. S. R. [Helminths of animals]
KAESTNER, Prof. Dr. A., Direktor der Wissenschaftlichen Sammlungen des Bayerischen Staates, Menzinger Strasse 67, München 19, Germany. [Araneae & Pseudoscorpiones of c. Europe (No)]
KAEVER, Dr. Mathias. C/o Germany Embassy, Kabul, Afghanistan. [Cretaceous Foraminifera of n. w. Europe, n. N. America, Afghanistan (Yes)] [Deutsche geologische Mission Afghanistan]
KAFUKU, Dr. Takeichiro. Freshwater Fisheries Research Laboratory, Hino-Machi, 399 Minamitama-Gun, Tokyo, Japan. [Pisces: Cyprinidae of s. Asia (No); of Japan (Yes)]
KAGAN, Dr. Irving G. Communicable Disease Center, P. O. Box 185, Chamblee, Ga., U. S. A. [Trematoda: Schistosomatidae & Leuchochloridiinae of World (No)]
* KAGANOVSKY, A. G. Pacific Institute of Fisheries and Oceanography, Vladivostok, U. S. S. R. [Pisces]
KAHLER, Prof. Dr. Franz. Tarviserstrasse 28, Klagenfurt, Austria. [Carboniferous-Permian Fusulinidae of Eurasia (Yes)] [Landesmuseum für Kärnten]
KAHLER, Dr. Gustava. Tarviserstrasse 28, Klagenfurt, Austria. [Carboniferous-Permian Fusulinidae of Eurasia (Yes)] [Landesmuseum für Kärnten]

KAHLKE, Dr. H. D. Museum für Ur- und Frühgeschichte Thüringens, Humboldstrasse 11, Weimar, German Democratic Republic. [Pleistocene Cervidae of Europe & China (Yes)]

KAHMANN, Prof. Dr. Herman. Zoologisches Institut der Univers ität, Luisenstrass e 14, München 2, Germany. [Mammalia: Chiroptera, Insectivora, Rodentia of Europe & Mediterranean Is. (Yes); of N. Africa (No)]

KÄHSBAUER, Dr. Paul, Curator of Fishes, Naturhistorisches Museum, Burgring 7, Wien 1, Austria. [Pisces of Europe (Yes); Hippocampidae, Cichlidae, Syngnathidae of S. & C. America (Yes)]

KAISER, Makram N. Department of Medical Zoology, U. S. Naval Medical Research Unit No. 3, c/o American Embassy, Cairo, Egypt. [Acarina: Ixodoidea of N. Africa & Near East (Yes)]

KAISER, Dr. Peter. Zoologische Museum, Bornplatz 5, Hamburg 13, Germany. [Gastropoda: Pulmonata of Europe (Yes)]

KAISILA, Jouko. Zoological Institute of the University, Rautatiek 13, Helsinki, Finland. [Pseudoscorpiones; Macrolepidoptera; Reptilia; Amphibia; Mammalia, espec. Chiroptera; all of n. Europe (No)]

KAJ, Dr. Józef. ul. Wojska Polskiego 71c, Poznań, Poland. [Pisces: Salmonidae of c. & n. Europe (Yes)] [Wyzsza Szkoła Rolnicza]

* KAJIHARO, E. S. Address unknown. [Coleoptera]

* KAKTINA, Mr. Dz. K. Institute of Soil & Agricultural Sciences, Riga, Latvia, U. S. S. R. [Nematoda]

KALABIS, Doc. RNDr. Vladimir. Husitská 14, Brno 12, Czechoslovakia. [Miocene Echinoidea: g. Clypeaster & Tertiary Pisces of Carpathian Flysch (Yes)]

KALELA, Dr. Olavi. (Helsinki, Finland; Aves & Mammalia) Not now active in taxonomy.

KALÍK, Vladimir. Na Okrouhliku 837, Pardubice, Czechoslovakia. [Coleoptera: Dermestidae of Palearctic, Ethiopian, Oriental, Australian (Yes); of New World (No)]

KALIN, Prof. Dr. Joseph. Zoologisches Institut der Universität, Fribourg, Switzerland. [Mammalia: Primates (No); Reptilia: Crocodilidae (Yes)]

KALSHOVEN, Dr. L. G. E. Rotondeweg 2, Blaricum, Netherlands. [Coleoptera: Scolytoidea of Java (No); Isoptera: Termitidae of Java (No)]

KALTENBACH, Dr. H. Falkensteinerstrasse 8, Königstein (Taunus), Germany. [Mollusca of n. Africa (Yes)]

KALUGINA, Miss N. S. Zoological Museum, Moscow State University, Hertzen Street 6, Moscow K-9, U. S. S. R. [Diptera: Chironomidae of Palearctic (No); g. Glyptotendipes & Endochironomus of Palearctic (Yes); immature forms of these genera of European part of U. S. S. R. (Yes)]

KAMADA, Yasuhiko. Department of Geology, Nagasaki University, Nagasaki, Japan. [Up. Cretaceous-Cenozoic marine Pelecypoda & Gastropoda of Japan (Yes)]

KAMBE, Dr. Nobukazu. Geological Survey of Japan, No. 135 Hisamoto-cho, Kawasaki City, Kanagawa Pref. , Japan. [Triassic Pelecypoda: g. Myophoria of Japan (Yes)]

KAMIYA, Hiroyuki. Entomological Laboratory, Faculty of Agriculture, Kyushu University, Fukuoka, Japan. [Coleoptera: Coccinellidae of Japan, Loochoo Is. , Formosa (Yes); of E. Asia (No)]

* KAMIYA, Kazuo. Laboratory of Entomology, Aichi University of Liberal Arts, Okazaki, Aichi Pref. , Japan. [Coleoptera: Dytiscidae, Gyrinidae]

KAMO, Dr. Hajime. Department of Parasitology, Kyushu University, Fukuoka, Japan. [Acarina: Trombiculidae of Japan (Yes)]

KAMOHARA, Dr. Prof. T. Biological Laboratory, Liberal Arts Faculty, Kochi University, Kochi, Japan. [Pisces: Cataphracti: Peristediidae; Jugulares: Parapercidae; Zeoidei; all of Japan & Indo-Pacific Oceans (Yes)]

KÄMPFE, Dr. Lothar. Zoologisches Institut, Domplatz 4, Halle/S. C. 1., German Democratic Republic. [Nematoda:Heteroderidae: g. Heterodera of Europe (Yes)]

* KAMPTNER, Prof. Dr. Erwin. Geologisch-Paleontologische Abteilung, Naturhistorisches Museum, Burgring 7, Wien 1, Austria. [Protozoa: Coccolithophorides]

KANAKOFF, George P. Los Angeles County Museum, Los Angeles 7, Calif. , U. S. A. [Cenozoic invertebrates of California (Yes); Recent Gastropoda of w. cst. of N. America (Yes)]

KANAMARU, Mr. Tajima. Miyake, Suzuka City, Mie-Ken, Japan. [Sea shells of Japan (Yes)]

KANAZAWA, Robert H. Division of Fishes, U. S. National Museum, Washington 25, D. C. , U. S. A. [Pisces of World, espec. Congridae (Yes)]

KANEHARA, Kinji. Geological Survey of Japan, Kawadacho-8, Shinjuku-ku, Tokyo, Japan. [Neogene marine Mollusca of Japan (Yes)]

KANEKO, Dr. Kiyotoshi. Department of Medical Zoology, Tokyo Medical & Dental University, Yushima, Bunkyo-ku, Tokyo, Japan. [Acarina: Trombiculidae; Anoplura: Haematopinidae & Hoplopleuridae; Mallophaga: Menoponidae: g. Myrsidea; all of Japan (Yes)]

KANELLIS, A. Universitat, Thessaloniki, Greece. [Chilopoda of Palearctic (No); Diptera: Drosophilidae of Palearctic (No)]

KANGAS, Prof. Esko. Institute of Agriculture & Forest Zoology, Snellmanink 5III, Helsinki, Finland. [Coleoptera of Fennascandia (No); Diptera: Agromyzidae: g. Phytobia of Palearctic] [University of Helsinki]
* KANGAS, Yrjö. Patola 15, Oulunkyla, Helsinki, Finland. [Coleoptera]
KANNO, Dr. Saburo. Institute of Geology & Mineralogy, Tokyo University of Education, Otsukakubo-machi, Bunkyo-ku, Tokyo, Japan. [Cenozoic Mollusca of Japan (Yes)]
KANNOWSKI, Dr. Paul B. Department of Biology, University of North Dakota, Grand Forks, N. D., U.S.A. [Hymenoptera: Formicidae of N. & C. America (Yes)]
KANO, Prof. Rokuro. Department of Medical Zoology, Tokyo Medical & Dental University, Yushima, Bunkyo-ku, Tokyo, Japan. [Diptera: Muscidae, Calliphoridae, Sarcophagidae, Culicidae; Acarina: Trombiculidae; all of Japan (Yes)]
* KAPOOR, B. G. Zoology Department, Delhi University, Delhi, India. [Pisces]
KAPUR, Dr. A. P. Zoological Survey of India, 34 Chittaranjan Avenue, Calcutta 12, India. [Coleoptera: Coccinellidae of Old World (Yes); Lepidoptera: Pyralidae: Crambinae of Oriental (Yes); Embioptera of Indo-Malayan (No)]
KAPUŚCIŃSKI, Prof. Dr. Stanisław. ul. Zduńska 12, Kraków 11, Poland. [Hymenoptera: Cimbicidae of Palearctic (Yes); Coleoptera: Cerambycidae of c. Europe (Yes)] [Instytut Badawczy Leśnictwa, Zakład Ochrony Lasów Górskich]
KARABAG, Prof. Dr. Tevfik. Zoologi Enstitüsü, Fen Fakültesi, Ankara, Turkey. [Orthoptera: Tettigonidae of Anatolia & Near East (Yes)]
* KARAFIAT, Prof. Address unknown. [Acarina: Scutacaridae]
KARAMAN, Dr. Stanko L. Cas. Post. 138, Skopje, Yugoslavia. [Crustacea: Amphipoda & Isopoda, espec. subterranean, Thermosbaenacea, Ingolfielida, Anaspidacea; f-w. Pisces; Amphibia; Reptilia; all of Palearctic (Yes)]
KARAMAN, Dr. Zora. Cas. Post. 138, Skopje, Yugoslavia. [Diptera: Nycteribiidae of Palearctic (Yes); Coleoptera: Pselaphidae of Palearctic (Yes); subterranean Coleoptera (Silphidae & Trechinae)·of Europe & Asia Minor (Yes)]
* KARANDIKAR, Dr. K. R. Department of Zoology, Karmatak College, Dharwar (Bombay), India. [Pisces]
* KARATAJUTE-TALIMAA, V. Lietuvos T. S. R. Mokslu Akademija, Geologijos ir Geografijos, Kosciuškos g-vè 14a, Vilnius, Lietuvos T. S. R., U. S. S. R. See Addenda.
KARCZEWSKI, L. Instytut Geologiczny, Rakowiecka 4, Warszawa, Poland. [Fossil Gastropoda: Nerineidae of Poland (Yes)]
KÁRDOS, Mr. Ervin H. 2041 North Pepper Street, Burbank, Calif., U. S. A. [Acarina: Trombiculidae of N. America & e. Asia (No); larval stages of N. America (Yes)]
* KÅRE, Dr. Elgmerk. Limnologisk Institut, University of Oslo, Blindern, Oslo, Norway. [Crustacea: Copepoda]
KARLIN, Dr. Edward J. Biology Department, Bowling Green State University, Bowling Green, Ohio, U. S. A. [Gastropoda: land slugs of N. America & Europe (Yes)]
KARLING, Dr. Phil. Tor Gustav. Naturhistoriska Riksmuseet, Stockholm 50, Sweden. [Turbellaria (No)]
KARLOVAC, Dr. Otmar. Institut za Oceanografiju, 1 Ribarstvo, Split, Yugoslavia. [Crustacea: Decapoda of Adriatic Sea (Yes); Pisces of Adriatic Sea (No)]
KARLSTROM, Prof. E. L. Department of Biology, Augustana College, Rock Island, Ill., U. S. A. [Amphibia: Bufonidae of w. N. America & Mexico (Yes)]
* KARNY, Dr. H. H. Zoological Museum, Buitenzorg, Java, Indonesia. [Orthoptera]
KARPIŃSKI, Prof. Dr. Jan Jerzy. Instytut Badawczy Leśnictwa, ul. Nowoopaczewska 3, Warszawa 22, Poland. [Coleoptera: Scolytidae & Cerambycidae of Europe (Yes)]
KARPPINEN, Dr. E. O. Zoological Institute, P. -Rautatiekatu 13, Helsinki, Finland. [Acarina: Oribatei; Oligochaeta: Lumbricidae; both of Fennoscandia (No)]
KARREN, Mr. J. B. Zoology Department, Brigham Young University, Provo, Utah, U. S. A. [Coleoptera of N. America (No)]
* KASAKOVA, V. P. Department of Geology, Moscow State University, Moscow B-234, Lengory, U. S. S. R. [Cephalopoda: Ammonoidea]
* KASHIWAGI, Masana. Zoology Institute, Faculty of Science, Hokkaido University, Sapporo, Hokkaido, Japan. [Lepidoptera: Noctuidae]
KASIM, S. Z. See QASIM, S. Z.
* KASIMOV, Dr. G. B. S. Zoological Institute, Academy of Sciences of Azerbaijan S. S. R., Karganova Street 15, Baku, U. S. S. R. [Helminths of animals]
KASKA, Harold V. Cia Guatemala-California de Petroleos, Apartado 1307, Guatemala City, Guatemala. [Mesozoic-Tertiary Foraminifera of Caribbean & n. S. America (Yes)]
KASSAI, T. Állatorvostudományi Föiskola, Landler Jenő u. 2, Budapest VII, Hungary. [Nematoda: Strongylata of Europe (No); Protostrongylidae (Yes)]
* KASSING, Mrs. Edith. Address unknown. [Amphibia & Reptilia]
KÄSTNER, Alfred. See KAESTNER, A.
KASTON, B. J. Department of Biology, Teacher's College of Connecticut, New Britain, Conn., U. S. A. [Araneae of New England (Yes)]

KASY, Dr. F. Theresiengasse 40/10, Wien XVIII, Austria. [Microlepidoptera of c. & s.e. Europe (No)]

KASZAB, Dr. Zoltan. Zoological Department of the Hungarian National Museum, Baross-u 13, Budapest VIII, Hungary. [Coleoptera: Meloidae of World (Yes); Tenebrionidae of Palearctic, Oriental, Papuan, Oceania (Yes); of New World & Africa (No)]

KATASHIMA, R. Zoological Laboratory, Faculty of Science, University of Hiroshima, Hiroshima, Japan. [F-w. Ciliata of Japan (No); Astomata of Oligochaeta of Japan (Yes); marine & f-w. Spirotricha: g. Euplotes of Japan (Yes)]

KATAYAMA, Dr. Masao. Hofu Educational College of Yamaguchi University, Hofu City, Yamaguchi Pref., Japan. [Pisces: Serranidae of Japan (Yes); of trop. Indian & Pacific Oceans (No)]

KATES, Kenneth C. Animal Disease & Parasite Research Division, Agricultural Research Center, Beltsville, Md., U.S.A. [Nematoda of ruminants of U.S. (Yes)]

KATO, Akiro. Yoyogi-Hatsudai 523, Shibuya-ku, Tokyo, Japan. [Coleoptera: Mordellidae of Japan (Yes); Melandryidae of Japan (No)]

KATO, Prof. Dr. Kojiro. Department of Biology, Saitama University, Saitama Prefecture, Urawa, Japan. [Turbellaria: Polycladida of Indo-Pacific (Yes); Acoela of Indo-Pacific (No)]

KATO, Masayo. Kato's Cicadidae Museum, 1800 2-chome, Kamishakujii, Nerima-ku, Tokyo, Japan. [Homoptera: Cicadoidea of World (No); of Indo-China & Manchuria (Yes)]

KATO, Shizuo. National Institute of Agricultural Science, Nishigahara, Kita-Ku, Tokyo, Japan. [Diptera: Muscidae (Anthomyiidae) of Japan (Yes); Agromyzidae of Japan (No); Lauxaniidae of Japan & Micronesia (No)]

* KATO, Yukio. Entomological Institute, Government Experiment Station of Forestry, Shimomeguro, Meguro-ku, Tokyo, Japan. [Coleoptera]

* KATTOUW, S.H. Landstraat 46, Delfzijl, Netherlands. [Amphibia & Reptilia]

KAUFFELD, Mr. C.F. Staten Island Zoological Society, Staten Island 10, N.Y., U.S.A. [Reptilia & Amphibia of N. America & Africa (Yes)]

KAUFFMAN, E.G. Museum of Paleontology, Museums Building, University of Michigan, Ann Arbor, Mich., U.S.A. [Cretaceous invertebrates of w. U.S. (Yes); Ordovician Trilobita, espec. Calymenidae, of e. U.S. (Yes)]

KAUFFMAN, Guido. Via Nassa 21, Lugano, Switzerland. [Lepidoptera: Hesperiidae of Palearctic (No); of Europe (Yes)]

KAURI, Dr. Hans. Zoologiska Institutionen, Lund, Sweden. [Opiliones of Europe, S. Africa, Australia (No); Amphibia of Palearctic (No); Diptera: Tabanidae of Scandinavia (Yes)]

* KAVEDA, M. Zoological Laboratory, University of Hiroshima, Hiroshima, Japan. [Protozoa]

KAWAI, Mr. Teizi. Zoological Laboratory, Nara Women's University, Nara, Japan. [Plecoptera of Japan & c. Asia (Yes); of Far East (No)]

KAWAMURA, Prof. Toshijiro. Zoological Laboratory, Hiroshima University, Hiroshima, Japan. [Amphibia of Japan, Formosa, Korea (Yes)]

KAWASHIMA, Kenjirô. Department of Parasitology, Faculty of Medicine, Kyushu University, Fukuoka, Japan. [Acarina: Trombidiformes, Mesostigmata, Sarcoptiformes; Neuroptera; all of Japan (Yes)]

KAWECKI, Prof. Dr. Zbigniew. Zakład Zoologii, Szkoła Głowna Gospodarstwa Wiejskiego, Rakowiecka 8, Warszawa, Poland. [Homoptera: Coccidae of Palearctic (Yes)]

KAY, Miss E.A. Zoology Department, University of Hawaii, Honolulu 14, Hawaii, U.S.A. [Gastropoda: Cypraeidae of Pacific (Yes)]

KAY, Dr. J. LeRoy. Carnegie Museum, Pittsburgh 13, Penna., U.S.A. [Up. Eocene Mammalia & Jurassic Dinosauria of w. N. America (Yes)]

KAY, Marshall. Department of Geology, Columbia University, New York 27, N.Y., U.S.A. [Ordovician Ostracoda (No)]

KAY, R.G. Webster. Casilla de Correo No. 1539. Montevideo, Uruguay. [Coleoptera of Uruguay (No)]

KAYASHIMA I. Takanabe Nôgyo, Kôtô-Gakko, Takanabe-machi, Miyazaki, Japan. [Araneida of Far East (Yes); of Micronesia (No)]

* KAYE, Mr. W.J. Chantry Lodge, Guildford, Surrey, England. [Lepidoptera]

KAZUBSKI, Mr. Stanisław Leszek. Akademia Nauk, ul. Pasteura 3, Warszawa, Poland. [Protozoa: parasitic Ciliata of land snails of Europe (Yes)]

* KEAN, Mary Alice. Address unknown. [Mammalia]

KEAST, Dr. J. Allen. Australian Museum, Hyde Park, Sydney, Australia. [Aves of Australia (Yes)]

KEATHLEY, Mrs. Kathleen Stephens. 1706 North Weatherford, Midland, Texas, U.S.A. [Permo-Pennsylvania & Tertiary Foraminifera (Yes)]

* KEEGAN, H.L. Address unknown. [Linguatulida: Acarina: Laelapidae & Dermanyssidae]

KEEN, Prof. Myra. Department of Geology, Stanford University, Stanford, Calif., U.S.A. [Tertiary invertebrates (megascopic) of California (Yes); Cretaceous-Recent Pelecypoda: Cardiidae (Yes); Recent Pelecypoda & Gastropoda of e. Pacific (Yes)]

238

KEETON, William T. Department of Entomology, Cornell University, Ithaca, N.Y., U.S.A.
[Diplopoda of World (No); of N. America (Yes)]
KEFERMÜLLER, Maria. Zakład Zoologii Systematycznej, Uniwersytet im. Adama Mickiewicza,
ul. Fredry 10, Poznań, Poland. [Ephemeroptera of Poland (Yes)]
KEH, Benjamin. California State Department of Public Health, Bureau of Vector Control, 2151
Berkeley Way, Berkeley 4, Calif., U.S.A. [Acarina: Ixodidae & Argasidae of Califor-
nia (Yes)]
KEIDING, Mr. Johs. (Springforbi, Denmark; Hydrachnellae) Not now active in taxonomy.
* KEIFER, H. H. State Department of Agriculture, 1220 North Street, Sacramento, Calif.,
U.S.A. [Acarina: Eriophyidae; Diptera: Trypetidae]
KEIJ, Dr. A.J. C/o Brunei Shell Petroleum Co. Ltd., Seria, Brunei. [Eocene-Oligocene
marine Ostracoda of France & Belgium (Yes); Neogene of Indonesia (No)]
KEIJZER, Dr. C.J. Rijksmuseum van Natuurlijke Historie, Leiden, Netherlands. [Recent
Foraminifera of World (Yes)]
KEILIN, Mr. David. Cambridge University, Cambridge, England. [Diptera (No)] [Molteno
Institute]
KEISER, Dr. Fred. Naturhistorisches Museum, Augustinergasse 2, Basel, Switzerland.
[Diptera: Pyrgotidae of World (Yes); Syrphidae of Old World (Yes)]
KEKENBOSCH, Jean. Institut Royal des Sciences Naturelles de Belgique, 31 rue Vautier,
Bruxelles, Belgium. [Araneae of Belgium (Yes)]
KELEHER, Mr. J.J. Fisheries Research Board of Canada, Biological Station, 539 Richmond
Street, London, Ont., Canada. [F-w. Pisces of Canada (No)]
KELEJNIKOVA, Mme. S.I. Zoological Museum, University of Moscow, Herzen street 6,
Moscow K-9, U.S.S.R. [Coleoptera: Tenebrionidae of U.S.S.R. (No)]
von KELER, Dr. Stefan, Kustos. Zoologisches Museum, Invalidenstrasse 43, Berlin N.4,
German Democratic Republic. [Mallophaga & Anoplura of World (Yes); Corrodentia of
Europe (Yes)]
KELLEN, William R. 5138 North Mason Avenue, Chicago 30, Ill., U.S.A. [Aquatic Hemip-
tera of Oceania (No); Diptera: Bombyliidae of Nearctic (No)]
KELLER, O.P. Estrada de Itu 10297, Caixa Postal 46, Osasco, São Paulo, Brazil. [Homop-
tera: Cicadidae of World (Yes)]
* KELLNER, Stephen. 174 Phillip Street, Sydney, N.S.W., Australia. [Mollusca]
KELLOGG, Dr. Remington. U.S. National Museum, Washington 25, D.C., U.S.A. [Fossil &
Recent Cetacea of World]
KELLUM, Lewis B. Museum of Paleontology, University of Michigan, Ann Arbor, Mich.,
U.S.A. [Mesozoic-Cenozoic Mollusca of N. America (Yes)]
KELSALL, Mr. J.P., Supervising Wildlife Biologist, Mackenzie District, Canadian Wildlife
Service, Box 117, Yellowknife, Northwest Territories, Canada. [Arctic Mammalia of
Canada (No); Caribou (Yes)]
KELSON, Dr. Keith R. National Science Foundation, Washington 25, D.C., U.S.A. [Mam-
malia of N. & C. America (No)]
KELTON, Dr. L.A. Insect Systematics & Biology, Science Service Building, Ottawa, Ont.,
Canada. [Heteroptera, espec. Miridae, of World (Yes)]
* KEMPEL, J.G. Department of Zoology, University of Saskatchewan, Saskatoon, Sask.,
Canada. [Araneida]
KEMPF, Dr. Walter W., Ofm. Provincialado dos Franciscanos, Caixa Postal 5650, São
Paulo, Brazil. [Hymenoptera: Formicidae of Neotropics (Yes)]
KEMPNÝ, Dr. Ladislav. Československá Akademie Věd-Slezský ústav, Nádražni Okruh 31,
Opava, Czechoslovakia. [Diptera: Syrphidae of Palearctic (Yes)]
KEMSIES, Emerson. Department of Zoology, University of Cincinnati, Cincinnati 21, Ohio,
U.S.A. [Aves of Ohio (Yes); of Yellowstone Park (No)]
KENK, Dr. Roman. 810 Ramsey Street, Alexandria, Va., U.S.A. [Turbellaria: Tricladida
paludicola of World (Yes)]
KENNARD, Alan. St. Peter's Hall, Oxford, England. [Lepidoptera: Rhopalocera of Britain
& France (Yes); Heterocera, excl. Tortricidae & Tineanidae, of Britain (Yes)]
KENNAUGH, J.H. Zoological Department, The University, Manchester 13, England. [Dip-
tera: Tachinidae of Britain (Yes)]
KENNEDY, Dr. J.P. Department of Biology, University of St. Thomas, Houston 6, Texas,
U.S.A. [Amphibia & Reptilia of Texas (Yes)]
* KENNELLY, D.H. 33 Catton Street, Uittenhage, Union of South Africa. [Mollusca]
KENNERLY, Prof. T.E. Department of Biology, Baylor University, Waco, Texas, U.S.A.
[Mammalia: Rodentia: Geomyidae & Myomorphi of U.S. (Yes)]
KENT, Dr. Lois Schoonover. 1003 Lincolnshire Drive, Champaign, Ill., U.S.A. [Miocene
Mollusca of Maryland (No); Pennsylvanian fossils of Illinois, espec. Brachiopoda &
Gastropoda (No)]
* KENYON, Mr. K.W. U.S. Fish & Wildlife Service, 2725 Montlake Boulevard, Seattle 2,
Wash., U.S.A. [Aves & Mammalia]
KEPKA, Dr. Phil. Otto. Zoologisches Institut der Universität, Graz, Austria. [Acarina:
Trombiculidae of World (No), of Europe (Yes)]

KERMACK, Dr. K.A. Department of Zoology, University College, Gower Street, London, W.C.1, England. [Cretaceous Echinoidea of w. Europe (No); Mesozoic Mammalia (Yes); fossil Reptilia (Yes)]

KERNEY, Mr. M.P. Department of Geology, Imperial College, London, S.W.7, England. [Quaternary-Recent non-marine Gastropoda & Pelecypoda of Europe (Yes)]

KERR, Dr. J.R. 29 Hipwood Street, Hamilton, Brisbane, Australia. [Lepidoptera: Rhopalocera of Australia (Yes)]

KERR, Dr. K.B. 910 Hildreth Street, Charles City, Iowa, U.S.A. [Cestoda & Nematoda of poultry of U.S. (No)]

KERRICH, Mr. G.J. C/o Department of Entomology, British Museum (Natural History), Cromwell Road, London, S.W.7, England. [Hymenoptera: Ichneumonidae, parasitic Cynipoidea, Chalcidoidea; of British Commonwealth (Yes)]

KERSLAKE, Mrs. J. 29 Nundah Street, Lane Cove, N.S.W., Australia. [Gastropoda: Epitoniidae of New South Wales (Yes), of Queensland (No)]

* KERSWILL, Dr. C.James. Atlantic Biological Station, St. Andrews, N.B., Canada. [Pisces: Cyprinidae & Salmonidae]

KERTÉSZ, G. Institut Zoosystematicum Universitatis, Puskin-u 3, Budapest VIII, Hungary. [Rotifera of Europe & Africa (Yes); Crustacea: Anostraca, Notostraca, Conchostraca, of Europe & Asia (Yes)]

KESLING, Mr. R.V. Museum of Paleontology, University of Michigan, Ann Arbor, Mich., U.S.A. [Paleozoic Crustacea: Ostracoda (No); Paleozoic Edrioasteroidea (No)]

KESSEL, Prof. Edward L. Department of Biology, University of San Francisco, San Francisco 17, Calif., U.S.A. [Diptera: Platypezidae of World (Yes)]

KESSINGER, Walter Paul, Jr. Box 109, Southwestern Louisiana Institute, Lafayette, La., U.S.A. [Fossil Foraminifera of w. Texas (Kiamichi & Duck Creek) (Yes)]

KETCHEN, Dr. K.S. Biological Station, Fisheries Research Board, Nanaimo, B.C., Canada. [Pisces: Selachii of n.e. Pacific Ocean (Yes); Heterosomata of n.e. Pacific & Bering Sea (Yes); Scleroparei of n.e. Pacific & Bering Sea (No)]

* KETTERER, Charles. 6 rue du Seex, Sion (Valais), Switzerland. [Araneida]

KETTERER, Prof. John J. Monmouth College, Monmouth, Ill., U.S.A. [Protozoa: Trypanosomatidae (Yes)]

KETTLE, Dr. D.S. Department of Zoology, West Mains Road, Edinburgh 9, Scotland. [Diptera: Chironomidae; g. Culicoides of Britain (Yes); Culicidae of Europe & Middle East (Yes)]

KEVAN, Dr. D.Keith McE. P.O. Box 268, Macdonald College, Que., Canada. [Orthoptera, espec. Acrididae of World, espec. n.w. Europe & tropical Africa (Yes); Pyrogomorphidae of World (Yes); Trigonopterygidae of s.e. Asia (Yes); Lathiceridae & Xyronotidae of Africa & America (Yes)]

KEVE, Assist. Prof. Dr. Andrew. Hungarian Institute of Ornithology, Garas u. 14, Budapest II, Hungary. [Aves: Corvidae of Europe (Yes); of Tjan-Shan & Asia (No)]

KEVEKLEINER, A. See KEVE, Andrew.

KEW, W.S.W. 1100 Union Street, San Francisco 9, Calif., U.S.A. [Fossil invertebrates]

* KEWALRAMANI, H.G. Taraporevala Aquarium, Marine Drive, Bombay 2, India. [Pisces]

KEY, Dr. A.J. Brunei Shell Petroleum Co., Seria, Brunei. [Tertiary marine Ostracoda of n.w. Europe (Yes)] (See KEIJ, A.J.)

KEY, Dr. K.H.L. Division of Entomology, Commonwealth Scientific & Industrial Research Organization, P.O.Box 109, Canberra City, A.C.T., Australia. [Orthoptera: Acridoidea of Australia (Yes), of S. Africa (No); Phasmatodea: Podacanthinae & Phasmatinae of Australia (Yes)]

KHAJURIA, Mr. H., Assistant Zoologist, Zoological Survey of India, 34 Chittaranjan Avenue, Calcutta 12, India. [Mammalia, espec. Primates, of India, Pakistan, Burma, Ceylon (Yes)]

KHALAF, Kamel. Higher Teachers College, Baghdad, Iraq. [Diptera: Heleidae: g. Culicoides of N. America (No), of Iraq (Yes)]

* KHALAF el-DUWEINI, Dr. A., Lecturer in Zoology, Faculty of Science, University of Cairo, Cairo, Egypt. [Okigochaeta]

KHAMBATA, Dr. F.S. C/o Mrs. Gazdar, Family House, 794 Parsi Colony, Dadar, Bombay-14, India. [Tetraphyllidean Cestoda of marine fishes of Bombay, India (Yes)] [Bombay Veterinary College]

KHAN, M.A. Livestock Insect Section, Science Service Laboratory, Canada Department of Agriculture, Lethbridge, Alta., Canada. [Nematoda associated with insects of World (Yes); Ecto-parasites of domestic animals of World (Yes)]

KHAN, Dr. M.H. C/o Pakistan Petroleum Ltd., P.I.D.C. House, Kutchery Road, Karachi, Pakistan. [Cretaceous-Tertiary larger Foraminifera of Pakistan & India (Yes); Cretaceous smaller Foraminifera of Pakistan & India (Yes)]

KHAN, Mr. Mohammad Rashid. Department of Plant Protection, Malir Halt, Jinnah Avenue, Karachi 27, W. Pakistan. [Lepidoptera: Crambidae of Indo-Pakistan (Yes)]

KHAN, S.A. Department of Plant Pathology, Louisiana State University, Baton Rouge, La.,
U.S.A. [Nematoda: g. Pratylenchus of Louisiana & E. Pakistan (Yes)]
* KHATIB, Dr.S.M. Husain, Head of the Department of Zoology, College of Science, Raipur,
India. [Insecta]
* KHEISSIN, E.M. See CHEISSIN, E.M.
KHOLOVÁ, Helene. Institute of Economic Entomology, Strnady 167, Zbraslav II, Czechoslo-
vakia. [Hymenoptera: Formicidae of c. & n. Europe (Yes); Collembola of Europe (Yes)]
* KHOZATSKY, Dr. L.T. Department of Vertebrate Zoology, Leningrad University, Univer-
sity Embankment I, Leningrad 164, U.S.S.R. [Mesozoic-Cenozoic Chelonia & Archo-
sauria]
KIEFER, Prof. Dr. Friedrich. Anstalt für Bodenseeforschung, Schiffstrasse 56, Konstanz-
Staad, Germany. [Crustacea: f-w. Copepoda of World]
KIELAN, Dr. Z. Paleontological Institute, Polish Academy of Sciences, 67 Nowy Swiat, War-
saw, Poland. [Up. Ordovician (Ashgillian) Trilobites of Bohemia, Poland, Scandinavia
(Yes); Ordovician Scolecodonts of same (Yes)]
KIELHORN, Mr. William V. U.S. Navy Laboratory of Oceanography, c/o Woods Hole Oceano-
graphic Institution, Woods Hole, Mass., U.S.A. [Zooplankton of Labrador Sea (Yes)]
KIER, Mr. P.M. U.S. National Museum, Washington 25, D.C., U.S.A. [Paleozoic-Tertiary
Echinoidea (Yes); Devonian Crinoidea (Yes)]
KIERSTEAD, Prof. Caroline Heminway (Mrs. Friend H. Kierstead). 41 Harrison Avenue,
Northampton, Mass., U.S.A. [Tertiary Foraminifera of West Indies (Yes); Recent
Foraminifera of antarctic & S. Pacific (Yes)] [Smith College]
KILBY, Dr. John D. Biology Department, University of Florida, Gainesville, Fla., U.S.A.
[Br-w. & f-w. Pisces of s.e.U.S. (Yes)]
KILGORE, J.E. Standard Oil Co. of Texas, P.O. Box 1249, Houston, Texas, U.S.A. [Ter-
tiary Foraminifera of Gulf cst. U.S. (No)]
KILIAN, Dr. E.F. Instituto de Zoologia, Universidad Austral, Valdivia, Chile. [Porifera of
S. America (Yes)]
KIM, Chang-Whan. Department of Biology, Korea University, Anam-Dong, Seoul, Korea.
[Hymenoptera: Ichneumonidae & Vespidae of S. Korea (Yes)]
KIM, Ke Chung. Room 303, Department of Entomology & Economic Zoology, University of
Minnesota, St. Paul 1, Minn., U.S.A. [Araneida of Korea (Yes); Diptera of Palearctic
(No)]
KIMBALL, Charles P. 7340 Point of Rocks Road, Sarasota, Fla., U.S.A. [Lepidoptera of
Florida (Yes)]
KIMMINS, Mr. D.E. C/o Department of Entomology, British Museum (Natural History),
Cromwell Road, London, S.W.7, England. [Trichoptera of Europe, Africa, Australia
(Yes); Neuroptera, excl. Mantispidae; Ephemeroptera; Plecoptera; Odonata]
KIMOTO, Mr. Shinsaku. Entomological Laboratory, Faculty of Agriculture, Kyushu Univer-
sity, Fukuoka, Kyushu, Japan. [Coleoptera: Chrysomelidae of e. & s.e. Asia (Yes)]
* KIMURA, Dr. Shigeru. Address unknown. [Pisces]
KIMURA, Mr. T. 41 Nishikujô-Okunicho, Minami-ku, Kyoto, Japan. [Diptera: Asilidae of
Japan (Yes)]
KINCAID, Prof. Trevor. 1904 East 52nd, Seattle 5, Wash., U.S.A. [Crustacea: Copepoda:
f-w. Calanidae of N. America (Yes); marine Gastropoda: g. Thais (sg. Nucella) of Paci-
fic cst. of N. America] [University of Washington]
KINDLE, C.H. Geology Department, The City College, Convent Avenue & 139th Street, New
York 31, N.Y., U.S.A. [Cambrian Trilobita (Yes)]
* KING, C. 23 Bush Street, Windsor, Brisbane, Australia. [Lepidoptera: Hepialidae]
KING, Dr. Edwin W. Department of Entomology & Zoology, Clemson College, Clemson, S.C.,
U.S.A. [Coleoptera: Mycetophagidae, Colydiidae, Cucujidae, of N. America (Yes)]
* KING, Mr. Joseph E. P.O. Box 3830, Honolulu, Hawaii, U.S.A. [Crustacea: Copepoda]
KING, Miss Judith E. Department of Zoology, British Museum (Natural History), Cromwell
Road, London, S.W.7, England. [Mammalia: Pinnipedia of World (Yes)]
KING, Dr. L.C. Geology Department, University of Natal, Durban, Union of South Africa.
[Cretaceous-Cenozoic Pelecypoda & Gastropoda of S. Africa (Yes)]
KING, Robert E. (New York, N.Y., Fossils) Not now active in taxonomy.
KING, Dr. Robert L. Department of Zoology, State University of Iowa, Iowa City, Iowa, U.S.A.
[Hymenoptera: Formicidae of Iowa (Yes); Orthoptera: Acrididae of Iowa (Yes)]
KING, Dr. W.V. 1336 Seabreeze Avenue, Fort Lauderdale, Fla., U.S.A. [Diptera: Culicidae
of U.S.A. & New Guinea (No), g. Anopheles of Philippines (No)]
KINGHORN, Mr. J.M. Forest Biology Laboratory, 409 Federal Building, Victoria, B.C.,
Canada. [Coleoptera: Scolytidae of N. America (Yes)]
KINGHORN, J.R. (Sydney, Australia: Reptilia) Not now active in taxonomy.
KINGMA, Dr. J. Th. New Zealand Geological Survey, P.O. Box 368, Lower Hutt, New Zealand.
[Hymenoptera: Ants of New Zealand (Yes); Up. Cretaceous-Tertiary Ostracoda & Fora-
minifera of New Zealand (No)] Not now active in taxonomy.

KINGSOLVER, J. M. Illinois Natural History Survey, Urbana, Ill., U. S. A. [Coleoptera: Curculionidae of World (No); Cleoninae: g. Lixus, fossil & Recent (No); Recent of N. America (Yes)]

KINGSTON, Mr. Newton. Ontario Research Foundation, 43 Queens Park, Toronto 5, Ont., Canada. [Trematoda: Eucotylidae & Dicrocoeliidae (of birds) of N. America (Yes)]

KINNE, Dr. O. Department of Zoology, University of California, Los Angeles 24, Calif., U. S. A. [Br-w. Coelenterata (Yes); Crustacea: br-w. Amphipoda of Baltic Sea (Yes)]

* KINOSHITA, Toraichiro. Hokkaido Fisheries Research Laboratory, Yoichiekimae, Hokkaido, Japan. [Mollusca]

KINSEY, Alfred C. (Bloomington, Ind.; Cynipidae) Died August 25, 1956.

* KIPS, R. H. Rijkslandbouwhogeschool, Coupure Links 233, Ghent, Belgium. [Nematoda]

KIRBY, Harold. (Berkeley, Calif.; Protozoa) Died February 21, 1952.

KIRBY, Louie C. Box 281, Tyler, Texas, U. S. A. [Cretaceous-Tertiary Foraminifera of New World (Yes)]

KIRCHBERG, Dr. Erich. Max von Pettenkofer Institut, Corrensplatz 1, Berlin-Dahlem, Germany. [Diptera: Culicidae of Europe (No); Muscidae, Tachinidae, Calliphoridae, Sarcophagidae, of Europe (Yes)]

KIRIAKOFF, Dr. S. G., Curator, Zoological Museum, University of Ghent, 14 Universiteitsstraat, Ghent, Belgium. [Lepidoptera: Thyretidae & Notodontidae of Ethiopian (Yes)]

KIRITSHENKO, Prof. Dr. A. N. Zoological Institute, Academy of Sciences, Leningrad B-164, U. S. S. R. [Heteroptera of World (Yes)]

KIRJANOVA, Dr. E. S. Zoological Institute, Academy of Sciences, Leningrad 164, U. S. S. R. [Nematomorpha: Chordodida & Paragordiida of World (Yes); plant-parasitic & soil Nematoda of U. S. S. R. (No)]

KIRK, Dr. R. Faculty of Medicine, University of Malaya, Singapore. [Diptera: Psychodidae: Phlebotominae of Ethiopian (Yes)]

* KIRKALDY, Dr. J. F. Department of Geology, Queen Mary College, Mile End Road, London E. 1, England. [Fossil invertebrates]

KIRKEGÅRD, J. B. Zoological Museum, København, Denmark. [Pogonophora & Polychaeta of all oceans (Yes)]

KIRKPATRICK, T. W. (St. Augustine, Trinidad; Diptera) Not now active in taxonomy.

KIRKWOOD, Mr. Carl W. P. O. Box 47, Summerland, Calif., U. S. A. [Lepidoptera: Geometridae of N. America (No); of s. w. U. S. (Yes)]

* KIRTISINGHE, Dr. P., Lecturer in Zoology, University of Ceylon, Colombo, Ceylon. [Copepoda]

KIS, B. Universitatea Bolyai, str. Arany J. 11, Cluj, Rumania. [Orthoptera & Dermaptera of c. & s. e. Europe (Yes); Neuroptera of Rumania (Yes)]

KISCH, Mr. B. S. Villa Alba, 38 Boulevard Thiers, Saint-Jean-de-Luz (B. -P), France. [Marine Mollusca of Bay of Biscay (No)]

KISER, R. W. Centralia Junior College, Centralia, Wash., U. S. A. [Crustacea: Cladocera of World (Yes)]

* KISHIDA, Kyukichi. 2352 Kotake-cho, Nerima-Ku, Tokyo, Japan. [Acarina; Diptera]

KISHII, Takashi. 21-2 Miyashita-cho, Daigakuji-Monzen, Saga, Ukyo-ku, Kyoto, Japan. [Coleoptera: Elateridae of Japan, Loo-Choo Is., Saghalien, Korea, Formosa; Denticollidae of Japan & Saghalien (all Yes)]

* KISSELOVA, M. Marine Biological Institute, Academy of Science, Sevastopol, U. S. S. R. [Annelida]

KISSINGER, Dr. D. G. Box 832, South Lancaster, Mass., U. S. A. [Coleoptera: Curculionidae: g. Apion of New World (Yes); Baridinae & Cryptorhynchinae of Mexico (Yes)]

KISTNER, Dr. David H. Department of Biology, Chico State College, Chico, Calif., U. S. A. [Coleoptera: Staphylinidae: Pygostenini of Africa & Far East (Yes); Omalinae of U. S. & Europe (Yes)]

KITAHARA, Prof. K. 117 Yamashitacho, Kagoshima-shi, Kyushu, Japan. [Acarina: Trombiculidae of Japan (Yes)] [Kagoshima University]

KITAKAMI, Shiro. (Kumamoto City, Japan; Diptera) Deceased.

* KITTS, Dr. David B. School of Geology, University of Oklahoma, Norman, Okla., U. S. A. [Fossil vertebrates]

KJELLANDER, Eric, Assistant, Naturhistoriska Riksmuseet, Stockholm 50, Sweden. [Hymenoptera: Aculeata of n. & c. Europe (No); Diptera: Mycetophilidae of Europe (Yes)]

KJELLESVIG-WAERING, Erik N. Pan Venezuelan Oil Co., Apartado 5498 este, Caracas, Venezuela. [Paleozoic Eurypterida of World (Yes)]

KJENNERUD, Johanne, Curator, Zoological Museum, Bergen, Norway. [Crustacea: Isopoda of n. Atlantic (No); Ophiuroidea of n. Atlantic (Yes)]

* KLAK, Prof. George E. 185 Clinton Avenue, Apt. 10-G, Brooklyn 5, N. Y., U. S. A. [Pisces]

KLAPPENBACH, Miguel A. Museo Nacional de Historia Natural, Casilla de Correo 399, Montevideo, Uruguay. [Terr. & f-w. Mollusca of S. America (No); Mollusca of Uruguay (Yes); Amphibia of Uruguay (Yes)]

* de KLASZ, Dr. Jan. Address unknown. (Microfossils)
KLAUBER, L. W. 233 West Juniper Street, San Diego 1, Calif., U.S.A. [Reptilia: snakes,
    espec. rattlesnakes, of s. w. U.S. (Yes)]
KLAUS, Dr. J. C/o Institut de Géologie, Université de Fribourg, Fribourg, Switzerland.
    [Cretaceous Foraminifera: Globotruncanidae (Albian-Maestrichtian) of Alpino-Medi-
    terranean) (Yes)]
KLAUSEWITZ, Dr. W. Senckenbergische Naturforschende Gesellschaft, Senckenberg-Anlage
    25, Frankfurt am Main, Germany. [Pisces: of Europe, s. Asia, Africa, Indo-Austra-
    lian Arch. (Yes)]
KLAWE, Witold L. Inter-American Tropical Tuna Commission, Scripps Institution of Oceano-
    graphy, La Jolla, Calif., U.S.A. [Pisces: larval & juvenile Scombroidae of all oceans
    (Yes)]
KLEIN, Dr. Bruno M. Schlossgasse 55, St. Andrä-Wördern b. Wien, Austria. [Ciliata (No)]
* KLEIN, Dr. J. M. Institut d'Enseignement et de Recherches Tropicales, 80 Route d'Aulnay,
    à Bondy (Seine), France. [Diptera: Culicidae]
KLEINPELL, Prof. R. M. Department of Paleontology, University of California, Berkeley 4,
    Calif., U.S.A. [Oligocene-Pliocene smaller Foraminifera of Washington, Oregon,
    California (Yes); Neogene smaller Foraminifera of Fiji Is. & Philippines (Yes)]
KLEINSCHMIDT, Dr. A., Hauptkonservator, Museum für Naturkunde Stuttgart, Zoologische
    Abteilung, Schloss Rosenstein, Stuttgart, Germany. [Aves & Mammalia]
KLEINSCHMIDT, Mrs. R. P. Kersley Road, Kenmore, S. W. 11, Brisbane, Australia. [Dip-
    tera: leaf-mining Agromyzidae of Australia (Yes)]
KLEMENT, Volker. Bahnhofstrasse 2, Asperg (Wttbg.), Germany. [Rotifera: Monogononta,
    excl. Bdelloidea, of Germany (No)]
KLEMM, Walter. Mollardgasse 12 B, Wien VI, Austria. [Terr. & f-w. Mollusca of World
    (No); of Europe (Yes)]
KLEMMER, Dr. K. Natur-Museum und Forschungs-Institut Senckenberg, Senckenberg An-
    lage 25, Frankfurt am Main, Germany. [Amphibia & Reptilia (No); Reptilia: Lacertidae
    (Yes)]
*KLESOV, M. D. Ukrainian Institute of Experimental Veterinary Science, Kharkov, U.S.S.R.
    [Helminths of animals of U.S.S.R.]
KLIE, W. (Pyrmont, Germany: Copepoda) Died April, 1951.
KLIMASZEWSKA, Mgr. Helena. Zakład Ekologii, Polskiej Akademii Nauk, ul. Nowy Swiat 72,
    Warszawa, Poland. [Odonata of Poland (Yes); Acarina: Tyroglyphoidea of Poland (No)]
KLIMESCH, Dr. Joseph. Donatusgasse 4, Linz a. d. Donau, Austria. [Microlepidoptera,
    espec. g. Nepticula & Bucculatrix, of Palearctic (No), of Europe (Yes)]
KLIMOWICZ, Mgr. Henryk. Katedra Hydrobiologii, Uniwersytetu, Warszawa, Krak. Przed-
    mieście 26/28, Warszawa, Poland. [F-w. Rotatoria of World (Yes); f-w. Mollusca of
    Poland (Yes)]
KLIMSTRA, Prof. W. D. Department of Zoology, Southern Illinois University, Carbondale,
    Ill., U.S.A. [Amphibia & Reptilia of c. U.S. (Yes); Mammalia of c. U.S. (No)]
* KLINZIG, E. 35 place de la Réunion, Mulhouse (Haut-Rhin), France. [Lepidoptera]
KLOFT, Dr. W., Privatdozent, Institut für Angewandte Zoologie, Universität Würzburg,
    Röntgenweg 10, Würzburg, Germany. [Hymenoptera: Formicidae of c. Europe (Yes);
    Homoptera: Aphididae of c. Europe (No)]
KLOTS, Dr. Alexander B. Department of Insects & Spiders, American Museum of Natural
    History, New York 24, N.Y., U.S.A. [Lepidoptera: Pyralididae: Crambinae of New
    World (Yes); Nymphalidae: g. Boloria of N. America (Yes)]
KLOTS, Dr. Elsie. 215 Young Avenue, Pelham, N.Y., U.S.A. [Odonata of N. America &
    West Indies (Yes); of China & Africa (No)]
KLUGE, Arnold G. Department of Biology, University of Southern California, Los Angeles
    7, Calif., U.S.A. [Fossil & Recent Reptilia: Gekkonidae (Yes)]
KLUGE, H. (Leningrad, U.S.S.R.; Bryozoa) Died in 1957.
* KNABEN, Dr. Nils. Universitetets Zoologiske Museum, Sarsgatan 1, Oslo 45, Norway.
    [Lepidoptera, Mollusca]
KNAPP, Frank T. (Brunswick, Ga.; Pisces) Not now active in taxonomy.
* KNAPP, Mr. S. E. Address unknown. [Crustacea: Copepoda & Turbellaria: Rhabdocoelida,
    of Pacific n. w. U.S.]
KNECHTEL, Prof. Dr. Wilhelm. Vila Sylvana, Calea Codrului 34, Sinaia, Rumania. [Hy-
    menoptera: Formicidae & Apinae of Rumania (No); Thysanoptera of Rumania (No)]
* KNEPTON, James C., Jr. Address unknown. [Reptilia: Testudinidae & Amphibia: Pletho-
    dontidae, of s. e. U.S.]
KNIGHT, Dr. Harry H. Department of Zoology, Iowa State College, Ames, Iowa, U.S.A.
    [Heteroptera: Miridae of N. America (Yes)]
KNIGHT, Dr. J. Brookes. 5965 Gulf of Mexico Drive, Longboat Key, Fla., U.S.A. [Paleozoic
    Gastropoda & Monoplacophora] Died March 21, 1960.
KNIGHT, Dr. Kenneth L. Division of Preventive Medicine, Bureau of Medicine & Surgery,
    Dept. of the Navy, Washington 25, D. C., U.S.A. [Diptera: Culicidae of World (Yes)]

KNIGHT, R. A. Mississippi State College, Box 186, State College, Miss., U.S.A. [Nematoda of ruminants of U.S. (Yes)]
KNIGHT-JONES, Prof. E.W. Department of Zoology, University College of Swansea, Singleton Park, Swansea, Wales. [Hirudinea: marine Piscicolidae (Yes)]
* KNIKER, Hedwig T. 761 Baker Avenue, Seguin, Texas, U.S.A. [Fossil invertebrates]
KNIPPER, Dr. H. Übersee-Museum, Bahnhofsplatz, Bremen, Germany. [Orthoptera of c. & s. Europe & Africa (Yes); terr. & f-w. Mollusca of c., s., s.e. Europe & Africa (Yes)]
KNOEPFFLER, Ludovic Philippe. Palais Ophelia 501, 13 Avenue Shakespeare, Nice, France. [Reptilia & Amphibia, espec. Discoglossidae, of Mediterranean (Yes)]
KNOWLTON, Mr. Carroll B. Department of Entomology, Cornell University, Ithaca, N.Y., U.S.A. [Lepidoptera: Arctiidae of N.America (Yes)]
KNOWLTON, George F. Utah State University, Logan, Utah, U.S.A. [Homoptera: Aphidae of w.U.S. (Yes)]
KNOX, Mr. G.A. Department of Zoology, University of Canterbury, Christchurch, New Zealand. [Polychaeta & Echinoidea of New Zealand, S.Pacific, Antartica (Yes)]
KNUDSEN, Cand. Mag. J. Zoological Museum, Krystalgade 27, København, Denmark. [Marine Mollusca of w.Africa (Yes)]
KNULL, Dorothy J. (Mrs. Joseph N. Knull). 330 E. Dunedin Road, Columbus 14, Ohio, U.S.A. [Homoptera: Cicadellidae of U.S. (Yes)] [Ohio State University]
KNULL, Prof. Josef N. Department of Zoology & Entomology, Ohio State University, Columbus 10, Ohio, U.S.A. [Coleoptera: Elateridae, Eucnemidae, Buprestidae, Cerambycidae, of N.America (Yes)]
KNÜLLE, Willi. Biologische Bundesanstalt, Königin-Luise- Strasse 19, Berlin-Dahlem, Germany. [Acariformes]
KNUTSON, Dr. Herbert. Department of Entomology, Kansas State College, Manhattan, Kans., U.S.A. [Orthoptera: Acrididae, & Diptera: Culicidae, both of c.U.S. (Yes)]
KOBA, Prof. Kazuo. Biological Laboratory, Faculty of Education, Kumamoto University, Kumamoto, Japan. [Reptilia & Amphibia of Loo Choo Is. (Yes), of Japan (No)]
* KOBAYASHI, Prof. H. Institute of Medical Zoology, Kyoto Medical University, Kyoto, Japan. [Diptera: Tabanidae]
KOBAYASHI, Mr. Kiyu. Faculty of Fisheries, Hokkaido University, Minato-Machi 253, Hakodate, Japan. [Pisces: larvae of Cottidae of n.Pacific (Yes); f-w. Cottus of Japan (Yes)]
KOBAYASHI, Mr. Mineo. Department of Zoology, National Science Museum, Ueno Park, Tokyo, Japan. [Trichoptera of Japan, Formosa, Korea, China (Yes)]
KOBAYASHI, Prof. Teichi. Geological Institute, University of Tokyo, Tokyo, Japan. [Cambrian Trilobita & Ordovocian Nautiloidea of e.Asia (Yes)]
KOBJAKOVA, Z.I. Department of Hydrobiology & Ichthyology, Leningrad State University, Leningrad-Centre 164, U.S.S.R. [Marine Decapoda, espec. Macrura, of Arctic & Pacific, espec. "East Sea" (Yes)]
KOBULEJ, Tibor. Állatorvostudományi Föiskola, Általános állattani és parasitologiai intézete, Landler Jeno-u 2, Budapest VII, Hungary. [Acarina: Trombidiidae & Trombiculidae of c.Europe (Yes)]
KOBY, Fred. Edouard. Feierabenstrasse 6, Basel, Switzerland. [Up. Pleistocene Mammalia of c.Europe & France (Yes)]
KOCH, C. Professional Officer, Entomological Department, Transvaal Museum, P.O. Box 413, Pretoria, South Africa. [Coleoptera: Tenebrionidae of Ethiopian, & Madagascar (Yes); general only of New World, Australia, Asia (Yes)]
* KOCH, H,J. P.O. Box 1122, Johannesburg, Union of South Africa. [Marine Mollusca]
KOCH, Wilhelm. C/o Landesamt für Bodenforschung, Wiesenstrasse 1, Hannover, Germany. [Cretaceous Foraminifera; espec. Up. Cretaceous g.Neoflabellina, Bolivinoides, Globotruncana, of c.Europe (all Yes)]
KOCHER, L.F.J. Institut Scientifique Chérifien, Rabat, Morocco. [Coleoptera of Morocco (Yes); Chrysomelidae, excl. Halticinae, of World (No); Eumolpinae, Galerucinae, Cassidinae, of Europe & N.Africa (Yes)]
KOCOUREK, Miroslav. Stalingradská 96, Hodonin, Czechoslovakia. [Hymenoptera: Apidae of Palearctic (Yes); g.Nomada of World (Yes); Mutillidae of World (Yes)]
KOEFOED, Dr. Einar. Fjøsanger, Norway. [Deep-sea Pisces of Atlantic Ocean (No)]
KOEHLER, Prof. Dr. Witold Koehler, Instytut Badawczy Leśnictwa, ul. Nowoopaczewska 3, Warszawa 22, Poland. [Hymenoptera: Formicidae of Palearctic (No); of c. & n. Europe (Yes)]
KOENIG, Mr. John Waldo. Missouri Geological Survey, Box 250, Rolla, Mo., U.S.A. [Mississippian Bryozoa: Cryptostomata of c.N.America (Yes); Crinoidea: Inadunata: Allagecrinidae & Codiacrinidae of c.N.America (Yes)]
von KOENIGSWALD, G.H.R. See von KÖNIGSWALD, Prof. Dr. G.H.R.
KOEPCKE, Dozent Dr. Hans-Wilhelm. Museo de Historia Nacional "Javier Prado", Universidad Nacional Mayor de San Marcos, Casilla 1109, Lima, Peru. [Pisces of S. America, espec. Peru (Yes); Aves of Peru (No)]

KOEPCKE, Dr. Maria. Casa Humboldt, Casilla 1932, Lima-Miraflores, Peru. [Aves of Peru (Yes)] [Museo de Historia Nacional "Javier Prado"]

KOERNER, Dr. Harold E. Department of Geology, University of Colorado, Boulder, Colo., U.S.A. [Oligocene-Miocene Merycoidodontidae & Chelonia (No)]

KOH, Prof. T.P. Taiwan Normal University, Taipei, Taiwan, Formosa. [Pisces: tunas of World (Yes)]

KÖHLER, Pablo E. Gral. Urguiza 1546, Florida, B.A., Argentina. [Lepidoptera: Noctuidae of trop. S. America (Yes)] [Ministerio de Agricultura]

KOHLS, Glen M. Rocky Mountain Laboratory, Hamilton, Mont., U.S.A. [Acarina: Ixodoidea of World (Yes)]

KOHN, Dr. Alan J. Department of Biological Sciences, Florida State University, Tallahassee, Fla., U.S.A. [Gastropoda: g. Conus of trop. Pacific & Indian Oceans (Yes)]

KOHNO, Mrs. Mitsuko. Zaimoku-cho, Aizu-Wakamatsu City, Fukushima Pref., Japan. [Plecoptera of Japan (Yes)]

KOIZUMI, Dr. K. Department of Entomology, Faculty of Agriculture, Okayama University, Okayama, Japan. [Diptera: Ephydridae & Dorilaidae of Japan (Yes)]

* KOJIMA, Toshibumi. Address unknown. [Coleoptera: Cerambycidae]

KOLLMANN, Dr. Kurt. C/o Rohoel-Gewinnungs A.G., Schwarzenbergplatz 16, Vienna I, Austria. [Tertiary Ostracoda: Cytherideinae of Europe (Yes)]

KOLOSVÁRY, Prof. Dr. Gabriel. Systematic Zoology Institute, University at Szeged, Táncsics Mihály utca 2, Szeged, Hungary. [Fossil & Recent Madreporaria & Balanidae (Yes)]

KOMAI, T. (Kyoto, Japan: Coelenterata) Not now active in taxonomy.

KOMAKI, Yuzo. Fisheries Department, Faculty of Agriculture, Tokyo University, Hongo, Tokyo, Japan. [Crustacea: Euphausiacea of w. Pacific & Sea of Japan (Yes); Copepoda of same (No)]

KOMAREK, J. (Praha, Czechoslovakia; Turbellaria) Died in 1955.

KOMAROVSKY, Dr. B. Sea Fisheries Research Station, P.O. Box 699, Haifa Israel. [Protozoa: Marine microplankton: Tintinnina & Dinoflagellata; Crustacea: marine Cladocera; all of Mediterranean & Red-Seas (No)]

KOMATSU, T. 3170 2-chome, Suehiro-machi, Kamisuwa, Suwa-shi, Nagano, Japan. [Araneida of Japan (No); of caves in Japan (Yes)]

KOMIYA, Dr. Y. Department of Parasitology, National Institute of Health, Kamiosaki, Chojamaru, Shinagawaku, Tokyo, Japan. [Trematoda of man & domestic animals: Heterophydae, Fasciolydae, Schistosomatidae, Cyathocotylidae, of Japan (Yes); other Trematoda of Japan (No)]

KOMP, W.H.W. (Bethesda, Md.; Culicidae) Died December 7, 1955.

KONDO, Yoshio. Bernice P. Bishop Museum, Honolulu 17, Hawaii, U.S.A. [Gastropoda: Pulmonata of Inner Pacific (Yes)]

KONGIEL, Prof. Dr. R. Ogrodowa 4-10, Warszawa, Poland. [Jurassic-Cretaceous Echinoidea & Up. Cretaceous Belemnoidea of Poland (No)] [Muzeum Liemi]

KÖNIGSMANN, Dr. E. Deutsches Entomologisches Institut, Josef-Nawrockistrasse 10, Berlin-Friedrichshagen, German Democratic Republic. [Hymenoptera: Braconidae, espec. Alysiinae, of Palearctic (Yes)]

von KÖNIGSWALD, Prof. Dr. Gustav H.R. Department of Paleontology, Mineralogisch-Geologisch Instituut, Rijks-Universiteit, Oude Gracht 320, Utrecht, Netherlands. [Fossil higher Primates of Old World (Yes); Pleistocene Mammalia of s.e. Asia (No)]

* KONISHI, Masayasu. Entomological Institute, Hokkaido University, Sapporo, Hokkaido, Japan. [Coleoptera: Curculionidae]

KONIZESKI, Dr. Richard. U.S. Geological Survey, c/o Montana State University, Missoula, Mont., U.S.A. [Tertiary Mammalia of N. America (No)]

KONJUKOVA, E.D. See KONZHUKOVA, E.D.

KONO, Hiromichi. (Sapporo City, Japan; Coleoptera) Deceased.

KONO, Hiroshi. 34 Nagaike, Moriguchi, Osaka Pref., Japan. [Crabs, land shells, sea shells, Coleoptera, all of Japan (No)] [Osaka Municipal Museum of Natural History]

KONTKANEN, Dr. P. Zoological Museum, P.-Rautatiekatu 13, Helsinki, Finland. [Homoptera: Cicadelloidea of Palearctic (Yes); Coleoptera: Chrysomelidae of Palearctic (No)]

KONTUNIEMI, Dr. Tahvo. Koskelantie 42 F 46, Helsinki, Finland. [Hymenoptera: Symphyta of Fennoskandia (Yes); g.Pamphilius (No)]

KONZHUKOVA, E.D. Paleontological Museum, Leninsky Prospect 16, Moscow, B-71, U.S.S.R. [Permian-Triassic Amphibia (Yes); Recent Brachiopoda of Pacific (No)]

KOOPMAN, Dr. Karl F. 511 West 113th Street, New York 25, N.Y., U.S.A. [Pleistocene-Recent Mammalia of West Indies (Yes); Pleistocene-Recent Chiroptera of Neotropics (Yes)] [Queens College]

KOOYMAN, Mr. Burt H. Fisheries Branch, 200 Memorial Boulevard, Winnipeg 1, Man., Canada. [F-w. Pisces of Manitoba (Yes)]

KOPF, Max J. 750 Elmwood Avenue, Buffalo 22, N.Y., U.S.A. [Paleozoic Echinodermata of N. America (No), Machaeridia (Yes)] [Buffalo Museum of Science]

KOPF, Rudolph William. P.O. Box 3, Monticello, Utah, U.S.A. [Devonian Echinodermata: Blastoidea of e. U.S. (Yes); Devonian Crinoidea: Calceocrinidae, Poteriocrinitidae, Rhodocrinitidae, Melocrinitidae, Dolatocrinidae, Thallocrinidae, of e. U.S. (Yes); Paleozoic Ophiuroidea of e. U.S. (Yes); Devonian Gastropoda: g. Platyceras of U.S. & Canada (No); Paleozoic Crustacea: Cirripedia of N. America (Yes)]

* KOPYRIN, A.V. Siberian Scientific-Research Veterinary Institute, Lermontova Street 93, Omsk, U.S.S.R. [Helminths of animals of U.S.S.R.]

KORATHA, K.J. Kuzhivelipuram, Tiruvalla, Kerala State, India. [Monogenetic Trematoda of World (Yes); parasitic Trematoda, Cestoda, Acanthocephala, Nematoda, of India, Pakistan, Malaya, Burma, Ceylon (Yes); Crustacea: Penaeidae of World (No)]

* KORBEL, Dr. Ladislav. Katedra Zoológie, Moskovska 1, Bratislava, Czechoslovakia. [Coleoptera]

KOREF, Dr. Susi. Catedra de Biologia, Instituto de Biologia "Juan Noe", Escuela de Medicina, Universidad de Chile, Santiago, Chile. [Diptera: Drosophilidae of S. America (No), of Chile (Yes)]

* KOREJWO, K. Zakład Geologii Historycznej, Obzna 3, Warszawa, Poland. [Pelecypoda]

KORELL, Armin. Bühlchenweg 3, Kassel-Nordshausen 16, Hessen, Germany. [Coleoptera: Carabidae: g. Carabus & Calosoma; Cicindelidae: g. Cicindela of World (Yes)]

KORMILEV, Dr. Nicholas A. 67-43 Central Avenue, Glendale 27, N.Y., U.S.A. [Heteroptera: Phymatidae & Aradidae of World (Yes); Colobathristidae of World (No)]

KORMONDY, Dr. Edward J. Department of Zoology, Oberlin College, Oberlin, Ohio, U.S.A. [Immature & adult Odonata of N. America (Yes); adults of C. America (Yes)]

KORMOS, Dr. J. Sejtgenetikai Laboratórium, Aradi Vértanúk tere 1 sz, Szeged, Hungary. [Suctoria of Hungary (Yes)]

KORNICKER, Dr. Louis S. Institute of Marine Science, University of Texas, Port Aransas, Texas, U.S.A. [Fossil & Recent Ostracoda: Myodocopa & Cladocopa (Yes), Recent Podocopa (Yes), fossil (No)]

KOROBKOV, Prof. Dr. I.A. Moskovskij Prospect 206, Apt. 58, Leningrad M-70, U.S.S.R. [Cenozoic Pelecypoda & Gastropoda of Europe (Yes)]

* KORONEOS, Mr. Jean. Rue Kaftadjoglou 15, Athens 8, Greece. [Homoptera: Coccoidea]

KOROTKEVITSCH, Miss V.S. Zoological Institute, Academy of Sciences, Leningrad W-164, U.S.S.R. [Pelagic Nemertinea of World (Yes); bottom Nemertinea of Far East Seas of U.S.S.R. (No)]

KORT, J. Plantenziektenkundige Dienst, Wageningen, Netherlands. [Nematoda: g. Heterodera of Netherlands (No); f-l. Nematoda in meadows of Netherlands (No)]

KORTENBOUT VAN DER SLUIJS, G. Rijksmuseum van Mineralogisch en Geologisch, 1 van der Werffpark, Leiden, Netherlands. [Pleistocene Mammalia of w. Europe (Yes)]

KOS, Fran. (Ljubljana, Yugoslavia; Apterygota) Died in 1958.

* KOSAROFF, Prof. Dr. G. Institut Zoologique, Academie des Sciences, 1 Boulevard Rouski, Sofia, Bulgaria. [Insecta: Diplura]

* KOSCIELSKA, M. Instytut Zoologiczny, ul. Sienkiewicza 21, Wrocław, Poland. [Hymenoptera]

KOSSWIG, Prof. Dr. Curt. Zoologische Staatsinstitut & Museum, Bornplatz 5, Hamburg 13, Germany. [Pisces of Asia Minor, espec. Cyprinodontidae (Yes)]

KOSTER, Prof. William J. Biology Department, University of New Mexico, Albuquerque, N. Mex., U.S.A. [Pisces of New Mexico (Yes)]

KOSTROWICKI, Andrzej. Boremlowska 19 m 9, Warszawa 26, Poland. [Lepidoptera: Phalaenidae of Palearctic (Yes)]

* KOSTROWICKI, Samuel. Instytut Zoologiczny Polska Akademia Nauk, ul. Wilcza 64, Warszawa, Poland. [Lepidoptera]

KOSZTARAB, M. 12 Merrill Road, Apt. A, Baltimore 28, Md., U.S.A. [Homoptera: Coccoidea of c. Europe & N. America (Yes)]

KOTAKA, Tamio. Institute of Geology & Paleontology, Tohoku University, Sendai. Japan. [Cenozoic shell-bearing Mollusca of Japan; Cenozoic Gastropoda: Turritellidae of Pacific (Yes)]

* KOTLÁN, Prof. A. Állatorvostudományi Fōiskola, Landler Jenō u.2, Budapest VII, Hungary. [Trematoda, Acarina]

KOTT, Miss P. Department of Zoology, University of Queensland, Brisbane, Australia. [Tunicata: Ascidiacea of Antarctic, Sub-Antarctic, Australian, Indian Ocean, English Channel (Yes); Polychaeta: Eunicidae & Nereidae of w. Australia (No)]

KOTTHAUS, Regierungsrat Dr. Adolf. Biologische Anstalt Helgoland, Abteilung Fischereibiologie, Friedrich-Albert-Pust-Platz 23, Bremerhaven 4, Germany. [Pisces: Berycidae & Scorpaenidae of N. Atlantic (Yes), Heterosomata of N. Atlantic (No)]

KOTTHOFF, Dr. P. Pflanzenschutzamt, Studstrasse 16, Munster i.W, Germany. [Helminths of Westphalia]

KOUMANS, F.P. (Den Haag, Netherlands; Pisces) Not now active in taxonomy.

* KOVÁCS, Dr. L. Kléh István u 3/a. III. 1, Budapest XII, Hungary. [Lepidoptera]

246

* KOVAL, V. P. Kiev State University, Vladimirskaja Street 58, Kiev, U. S. S. R. [Trematoda of animals of U. S. S. R.]

KOWALSKI, Dr. Kazimierz. Zoological Institute, Polish Academy of Science, Sławkowska 17, Krakow, Poland. [Pliocene-Recent Mammalia: Rodentia, Insectivora, Chiroptera, of Europe (Yes)]

KOYAMA, Dr. T. Anatomical Laboratory, Tokyo Medical & Dental University, Yushima, Bunkyo-ku, Tokyo, Japan. [Gastropoda of Antarctic, Subantarctic, e. Asia, Oceania (Yes)]

KOZHANCHIKOV, I. V. Zoological Institute, Academy of Sciences, Leningrad 164, U. S. S. R. [Fossil Lepidoptera: Noctuidae, Psychidae, Orgyidae, Cossidae, of U. S. S. R.]

KOZICKA, Dr. Jadwiga. Polska Akademia Nauk, ul. Pasteura 3, Warszawa, Poland. [Helminths of fish]

KOZLOFF, Prof. Eugene N. Department of Biology, Lewis & Clark College, Portland 1, Ore., U. S. A. [Protozoa: Ciliata: commensal & parasitic Holotricha in mollusks & oligochaetes, of World, espec. N. America (Yes); Sporozoa: Gregarines of N. America (No); Flagellata: Cryptobiidae of N. America & Europe (Yes)]

KOZLOVA, Mrs. E. V. Zoological Institute, Academy of Sciences, Leningrad 164, U. S. S. R [Aves of U. S. S. R. (No)]

* KOZLOWSKI, Roman. Zakład Paleontologii, Universytet Warszawski, Wawelska 17, Warszawa, Poland. [Graptolites; fossil vertebrates]

KRACH, W. Zakład Paleontologii, Akademia Gorniczo-Hutnicza, Al. Mickiewicza 30, Krakow, Poland. [Eocene-Miocene Gastropoda & Lamellibranchiata of Poland (Yes)]

KRADEL, K. (Berlin-Kleinmachnow, German Democratic Republic; Nematoda) Not now active in taxonomy.

KRAFT, Dr. John C. Geological Department, Shell Oil Co., Calgary, Alta., Canada. [Ordovician Ostracoda of N. America (No)]

KRAFT, Mr. Kenneth J. Department of Biology, University of Minnesota, Duluth 11, Minn., U. S. A. [Diptera: Stratiomyidae: Pachygasterinae of N. America (Yes)]

KRÁL, J. Italská 2, Praha 12, Czechoslovakia. [Coleoptera: Chrysomelidae: Halticinae of World (No); of Palearctic (Yes)] [Zoological Gardens of Prague]

KRALL, Mr. E. Eesti NSV Teaduste Akadeemia, Zoologia Instituut, Vanemuise 21, Tartu, Estonia, U. S. S. R. [Soil & f-w. Nematoda of Estonia (Yes)]

KRAMANY, Dr. H. (St. Pölten, Austria; Trichoptera) Died in 1955.

KRAMÁŘ, Doz, Dr. J. Universita Karlova, Parasitologie, Viničná ul. 7, Praha 2, Czechoslovakia. [Diptera: Culicidae of c. Europe (Yes)]

KRAMER, Dr. Eugen. Lindenbuck, Kollbrunn, Switzerland. [Reptilia: Serpentes of Europe & n. Africa (Yes)] [Naturhistorisches Museum, Basel]

KRAMER, James P. Division of Insects, U. S. National Museum, Washington 25, D. C., U. S. A. [Homoptera: Cicadellidae & Fulgoroidea of N. America & West Indies (Yes)] [U. S. Department of Agriculture]

KRAMP, Dr. P. L. Zoologiske Museum, Krystalgade 27, København, Denmark. [Coelenterata: of the World (No); Medusae of World (Yes); marine borers (No)]

KRANTZ, Dr. G. W. Department of Entomology, Oregon State College, Corvallis, Ore., U. S. A. [Acarina of N. America (Yes); of stored products of World (Yes)]

KRASCHENINNIKOW, Dr. Serhij. Zoological Laboratory, University of Pennsylvania, Philadelphia 4, Penna., U. S. A. [Ciliata: g. Balantidium (Yes); Ophryoscolecidae (Yes)]

KRATOCHVÍL, Prof. Dr. Josef. Jiráskova 47, Brno, Czechoslovakia. [Micromammalia of Europe (Yes); cavernicolous Arachnida: Araneida of World (Yes); Arachnida: Opilionidea of Europe (Yes)] Czechoslovakian Akademy of Science] [Not V. Kratochvil; not Hymenoptera]

* KRAU, Luiza. Instituto Oswaldo Cruz, Caixa Postal 926, Rio de Janeiro, Brasil. [Echinoidea]

KRAUS, Dr. O. Senckenbergische Naturforschende Gesellschaft, Senckenberg Anlage 25, Frankfurt am Main, Germany. [Chilopoda & Diplopoda of World (Yes); Arachnida: Araneae, Scorpiones, Pedipalpi, Solifugae, of World (Yes)]

KRÄUSEL, Dr. Wolfgang. Geologisch-Paläontologisches Institut der Goethe-Universität, Senckenberg-Anlage 32, Frankfurt am Main, Germany. [Bryozoa, espec. Cryptostomata, of Germany, espec. Devon (Yes)]

* KRAUSS, Mr. N. L. H. 2437 Parker Place, Honolulu 14, Hawaii, U. S. A. [Coleoptera]

KRCZAL, Dr. Herbert. Wielandstrasse 3, Heidelberg, Germany. [Acarina: Pyemotidae of c. Europe (Yes)] [Biologische Bundensanstalt Institut für Obstbau]

KREFFT, Dr. Gerhard. Bundesforschungsanstalt für Fischerei, Institut für Seefischerie, Neuer Wall 72, Hamburg 36, Germany. [Marine Pisces of Greenland (Yes); Elasmobranchii of Atlantic & trop. e. Pacific (Yes); Isospondylida & Iniomida of N. Atlantic (Yes)]

KREIS, Dr. Hans A. Eidgenossisches Gesundheitsamt, Bollwerk 27, Bern, Switzerland. [F-l. & parasitic Nematoda (Yes)]

KREKELER, Prof. Carl H. Department of Biology, Valparaiso University, Valparaiso, Ind.,
U.S.A. [Coleoptera: cave Carabidae of N. America (Yes)]
KRETZOI, Dr. Miklós. Magyar Állami Földtani Intézet, Vorosilov ut.14, Budapest XIV,
Hungary. [Neozoic Mammalia, espec. Ferae; fossil Arvicolidae (Yes)]
KRICHELDORFF, Adolf. (Berlin, Germany; Coleoptera) Not now active in taxonomy.
* KRIEGER, Dr. Felix. Schellingstrasse 110/4, München, Germany. [Odonata]
KRIMHOLZ, Docent G. Ja. Department of Geology, Leningrad State University, Leningrad
B-164, U.S.S.R. [Jurassic-L. Cretaceous Cephalopoda: Belemnoidea of w. Europe &
U.S.S.R. (Yes); L.-M. Jurassic Ammonitoidea of U.S.S.R. (Yes)]
KRING, James B. Connecticut Agricultural Experiment Station, P.O. Box 1106, New Haven
14, Conn., U.S.A. [Homoptera: Aphidae of N. America (Yes); Coleoptera: Elateridae
of New England (No)]
KRIPALANI, Miss M.B. Herpetological Section, Zoological Survey of India, 34 Chittaranjan
Avenue, Calcutta 12, India. [Amphibia of India, Ceylon, Burma (Yes)]
KRISHNA, K. Department of Zoology, University of Chicago, Chicago, Ill., U.S.A. [Isoptera
of World (Yes)]
KRISHNASWAMY, Dr. S. Department of Zoology, University of Madras, Madras 5, India.
[Marine Crustacea: Copepoda: Calanoida, Cyclopoida, Harpacticoida (f-l., commensal,
parasitic) of Madras, India & British Is. (Yes)]
KRITSCHER, Dr. E. Naturhistorisches Museum, Burgring 7, Wien 1, Austria. [Araneae of
Europe (Yes)]
KRIVDA, V.W. P.O. Box 864, The Pas, Man., Canada. [Lepidoptera: g. Colias, Boloria,
Erebia, of N. America (Yes)]
KRÖBER, O. (Hamburg, Germany; Diptera) Not now active in taxonomy.
* KROGERUS, Dr. Harry. Mannerheimvägen 25A, Helsinki, Finland. [Lepidoptera]
KROLOPP, Dr. Endre. Magyar Állami Földtani Intézet, Vorosilov-ut 14, Budapest XIV,
Hungary. [Pleistocene & Recent non-marine Gastropoda of c. Europe (Yes); Recent
non-marine Pelecypoda of c. Europe (No)]
KROMBEIN, Karl V. Division of Insects, U.S. National Museum, Washington 25, D.C., U.S.A.
[Hymenoptera: wasps of U.S., Micronesia, s.w. Pacific, Bahamas (Yes); bees of
Micronesia, Bahamas, Solomon Is. (Yes)] [U.S. Department of Agriculture]
KRÖMMELBEIN, Karl. Geologisch-Paläontologisches Institut der Universität, Senckenberg-
Anlage 32, Frankfurt am Main, Germany. [M. Devonian Ostracoda of Germany (Yes);
Wealden Ostracoda of Brasil (Yes); Devonian macrofossils of Rhenish Schiefergebirge,
Germany (Yes); Devonian & Carboniferous macrofossils of S. America, espec. Amazon
Basin (No)]
KRONEISL-RUCNER, Prof. Renata. Ornitholoski Institut, Ilirski Trg. 9, Zagreb, Yugoslavia,
[Aves of Yugoslavia (Yes)]
* KRONMARK, H. Address unknown. [Orthoptera]
*KROTOV, A.I. Institute of Malaria, Medical Parasitology & Helminthology, M. Pirogovskaja
Street 20, Moscow, U.S.S.R. [Helminths of animals]
KROTT, Dr. G. Steinbrückstrasse 6, Säckingen/Rh., Baden, Germany. [Acarina: Eriophyi-
* KROZAL, Herbert. See KRCZAL, H.   dae of c. Europe]
* KRUGER, Erich. Renteilichung 71, Essen, Germany. [Lepidoptera]
KRUIDENIER, Prof. Francis J. Department of Zoology, University of Illinois, Urbana, Ill.,
U.S.A. [Digenetic Trematoda of World (No); Nematoda of rodents of N. America (No);
Sporozoa: g. Eimeria of rodents of N. America (No)]
* KRUSBERG, Mr. Lorin. Box 5397, North Carolina State College, Raleigh, N.C., U.S.A.
[Nematoda]
KRUSEMAN, Dr. G. Zoölogisch Museum, Zeeburgerdijk 21, Amsterdam (Oost), Netherlands.
[Hymenoptera: Bombidae: g. Bombus & Psithyrus of World (Yes)]
KRUTZSCH, P.H. Department of Anatomy, University of Pittsburgh School of Medicine,
Pittsburgh 3, Penn., U.S.A. [Mammalia: Chiroptera & Rodentia: Zapodidae of N.
America (Yes)]
KRYZHANOVSKY, Oleg L. Zoological Institute, Academy of Sciences, Leningrad 164,
U.S.S.R. [Coleoptera of c. Asia (Yes); Carabidae & Histeridae of Palearctic (No),
of U.S.S.R. (Yes)]
KRZANOWSKI, Dr. Adam. Instytut Biologii Doświadczalnej, Michałowka 1, Puławy, Poland.
[Mammalia: Chiroptera of Europe (Yes)]
KRZYWICKI, Mgr. Mieczysław, Ośrodek Metod. Plac, Litewski 1, Lublin, Poland. [Lepidop-
tera: Rhopalocera of Europe (Yes)]
KRZYWIEC-RAJSKA, Mgr. Danuta. Polska Akademia Nauk, Instytut Zoologiczny, Oddział w
Poznaniu, ul. Swierczewskiego 19, Poznań, Poland. [Homoptera: "Aphidina" of c.
Europe (Yes)]
KUBICEK, Dr. F. Institut de Zoologie de l'Université Masaryk, Kotlárská z, Brno, Czecho-
slovakia. [Crustacea]
KUBO, Prof. Dr. Itsuo. Tokyo University of Fisheries, Shiba Kaigandori 6, Minato-Ku,
Tokyo, Japan. [Crustacea: Macrura of Japan (Yes)]

KUBOTA, Masao. Sôyô High School, Komine, Odawara-shi, Kanagawa-ken, Japan. [Coleoptera: Pselaphidae of Japan (Yes); Ptiliidae of Japan (No)]
KUCHLEIN, J. H. Zoölogisch Museum, Zeeburgerdÿk 21, Amsterdam (O), Netherlands. [Lepidoptera: Pyralidae of World (No); Microlepidoptera & Macrolepidoptera of Europe & N. Africa (No)]
KUDO, Prof. R. R. Department of Zoology, Southern Illinois University, Carbondale, Ill., U. S. A. [Sarcodina: Amoebidae & Endamoebidae of World (No); Sporozoa: Myxosporidia & Microsporidia of World (No)]
KUFFERATH, Hubert. (Bruxelles, Belgium; Protozoa) Died in 1958.
KÜHLHORN, Dr. Friedrich, Konservator, Zoologisches Sammlung, des Bayerischen Staates, Menzingerstrasse 67, München 38, Germany. [Diptera: Culicidae: g. Anopheles of Germany (Yes)]
KÜHLMANN, Dietrich. Fritsche Strasse 8, Leipzig N. 22, German Democratic Republic. [Pisces of World (No), of Europe (Yes); Odonata of c. Europe (Yes)]
KUHN, Cand. med. Hans- Jürg. Wilckensstrasse 41, Heidelberg, Germany. [Mammalia of Liberia (Yes); Primates (No)]
KÜHN, H. Biologische Zentralanstalt, Weissenfelser Strasse 57a, Naumburg/Saale, German Democratic Republic. [Plant-parasitic & soil Nematoda, excl. Dorylaimoidea, of Germany (Yes)]
KÜHN, Prof. Dr. Oth. Paläontologisches Institut der Universität, Wien 1, Austria. [Fossil Pelecypoda: Rudistacea of World (Yes); Triassic-Up. Cretaceous Ammonitoidea (Yes); Cretaceous-Tertiary Hexacoralla & Bryozoa (No)]
KÜHNE, Dr. Walter G. Geologisch-Paläontologisches Institut, Freie Universität Berlin, Altensteinstrasse 33, Berlin-Dahlem, Germany. [Mesozoic Mammalia: Therapsida (Yes); Silurian Graptolitoidea (Yes)]
KÜHNELT, Prof. Dr. Wilhelm. Zoologisches Institut der Universität, Wien 1, Austria. [Terr. Mollusca of Europe (No); Coleoptera: Tenebrionidae of Palearctic (Yes)]
KUHN-SCHNYDER, Prof. Dr. Emil, Direktor des Paläontologischen Institutes und Museums der Universität, Künstlergasse 16, Zürich 6, Switzerland. [Fossil Mammalia of Europe (No); Triassic marine Pisces & Reptilia (Yes)]
KUIPER, Mr. J. G. J. 121 rue de Lille, Paris (VII), France. [Pelecypoda: Sphaeriidae: g. Pisidium of World (Yes)]
KUIPER, Ir. K. Plantenziektenkundige Dienst, Geertjesweg 15, Wageningen, Netherlands. [Plant-parasitic Nematoda: Tylenchida of w. Europe (Yes)]
KUITERT, Dr. Louis C. Agricultural Experiment Station, University of Florida, Gainesville, Fla., U. S. A. [Hemiptera: Nepidae & Gerridae of W. Hemisphere (Yes)]
KUKALOVÁ, Dr. Jarmila. Department of Paleontology, Geological-Geographical Faculty of the Charles University, Albertov 6, Praha II, Czechoslovakia. [Paleozoic & Secondary Insecta of World (Yes); Paleozoic Diplopoda of World (Yes)]
KULASH, Walter M. P. O. Box 5215, State College Station, Raleigh, N. C., U. S. A. [Coleoptera: Elateridae of World (No); of s. e. U. S. (Yes)]
KULAWCZYKOVÁ-OBRHELOVÁ, Mrs. Naděžda, Assistent of Paleontological Laboratory, Academy of Sciences, National Museum, Václavské náměsti 68, Praha 2, Czechoslovakia. [F-w. Pisces: Cyprinidae, Salmonidae, Gobiidae, Percidae, Esocidae of c. Europe]
KULCZÝCKI, Dr. Julian. Polska Akademia Nauk, Zakład Paleozoologii, ul. Nowy-Świat 67, Warszawa, Poland. [Paleozoic Pisces: Brachythoraci, Rhipidistia, Dipnoi (Yes)]
KULHAVÝ, V. Křižova 273, Praha XVI, Czechoslovakia. [Crustacea: Harpacticoida from subterr. waters of World (Yes); Bathynellacea of World (Yes) [Charles University]
* KULIKOVA, E. B. Institute of Oceanology, Academy of Sciences, Lujnicovskaja 8, Moscow, U. S. S. R. [Pisces]
* KULKARNI, C. V., Director of Fisheries, Tareporevala Aquarium, Bombay 2, India. [Pisces]
KULLMANN, Dr. E. Parasitologisches Institut, Endenicher Allee 19, Bonn, Germany. [Araneida: "Netzbauende Spinnen" of Germany & s. Europe (No)]
* KULT, Dr. Karel. Department of Entomology, Universitá Karlova, Viničná ul. 7, Praha II, Czechoslovakia. [Coleoptera]
KULZER, Herr Hans. Museum G. Frey, Hofrat Beisele Strasse 8, Tutzing, bei München, Germany. [Coleoptera: Tenebrionidae of World (Yes)]
KUMADA, Dr. Nubuo. Department of Medical Zoology, Tokyo Medical & Dental University, Yushima, Bunkyo-Ku, Tokyo, Japan. [Siphonaptera of Japan & e. Asia (Yes); Acarina: Trombiculidae of Japan (Yes)]
KUMADA, Toshio. (Odawara, Japan; Pisces) Deceased.
KUMATA, Mr. T. Entomological Institute, Faculty of Agriculture, Hokkaido University, Sapporo, Japan. [Lepidoptera: Gracilariidae & Elachistidae of Japan (Yes); larvae of Lymantriidae of Japan (No)]
KUMMEL, Dr. Bernhard. Museum of Comparative Zoology, Cambridge 38, Mass., U. S. A. [Triassic Ammonitoidea (Yes); Mesozoic-Recent Nautiloidea (Yes)] [Harvard University]
KUMPF, Herman E. Marine Laboratory, 1 Rickenbacher Causeway, Miami 49, Fla., U. S. A. [Cephalopoda: Octopoda of N. Atlantic (Yes); Cephalopoda of Carribbean (Yes)]

* KUNDU, Dr. Hirendra L. Department of Zoology, Birla College of Science, Pilani (Rajasthan), India. [Coleoptera: larvae of Elateridae]
* KUNG, Dr. C. C. Address unknown. (Nematoda).
KUNST, Dr. Miroslav. Katedra Systematické Zoologie, Karlovy University Fakulty, Viničná 7, Praha II, Czechoslovakia. [Acarina: Oribatei of Palearctic (Yes); Oligochaeta of Europe (Yes)]
KUNTZ, Dr. R. E. Department of Parasitology, U. S. Naval Medical Research Unit 2, APO 63, San Francisco, Calif., U. S. A. [Trematoda & other helminths (No)]
KUNZ, Dr. Helmut. Im Allmet 8, Bischmisheim/Saar, Germany. [Marine & br-w. Copepoda: Harpacticoida of World (Yes); of f-w. of Germany (No)]
KUPPER, Dr. Inge. C/o Rohoel-Gewinnungs A. G., Schwarzenbergplatz 16, Wien I, Austria. [Tertiary Foraminifera of Europe (Yes); Miogypsinidae of Nigeria & Br. W. Africa (Yes)]
*KURASHVILI, Dr. B. E. Zoological Institute, Academy of Sciences of the Georgian SSR, Dzerginskaja Street 8, Tbilisi, U. S. S. R. [Helminths of animals of World]
KURENTZOV, Prof. A. J. Lenin Street 50, Vladivostok, U. S. S. R. [Coleoptera: Ipidae & Lepidoptera: Rhopalocera of Ussuri, Amur, e. Siberia (Yes)] [Far Eastern Branch of the Academy of Sciences of U. S. S. R.]
KURIAN, Dr. Chandy. Entomologist. Central Coconut Research Station, Oachiri P. O., Kerala State, India. [Hymenoptera: Bethyloidea of Oriental (Yes); Chalcidoidea & Ichneumonoidea of Oriental (No)]
KURIAN, Dr. C. V., Research Officer (Biology), Oceanographic Laboratory, Cochin -4, Kerala, India. [Crustacea: larvae of Decapoda of Atlantic & Mediterranean (Yes); Cumacea & parasitic Copepoda of Indian Ocean (Yes); Pisces of Indo-Australian (No)]
KURODA, Prof. Matsuo. Yazu High School, Yazu-gun, Koge-town, Tottori Pref., Honshu, Japan. [Diptera: Agromyzidae of Japan (Yes)]
KURODA, Dr. Nagamichi. 1 Fukuyoshi-cho, Akasaka, Minato-ku, Tokyo, Japan. [Aves: Anatidae of World (Yes); Mammalia: Muridae of Japan, Ryukyu Is., Formosa, Korea, n. China (Yes)]
KURODA, Dr. T. Zoological Institute, Kyoto University, Kyoto, Japan. [Shelled Mollusca of Japan, Formosa, Ryukyu Is., Korea, Saghalien I. (Yes)]
KUROKO, Hiroshi. Hikosan Biological Laboratory, Kyushu University, Hikosan, Soeda Machi, Tagawa-gun, Fukuoka Pref., Japan. [Lepidoptera: Cosmopterygidae: g. Cosmopteryx of Japan & Formosa (Yes)]
KURONUMA, Dr. Katsuzo. Freshwater Fisheries Research Laboratory, Hino-machi, Minamitama-gun, Tokyo, Japan. [Pisces: Salmonoidea, Cyprinidae, flatfish, of Japan (No)]
KUROSA, Kazuyoshi. Kanamecho 1-15, Toshima-ku, Tokyo, Japan. [Coleoptera: Carabidae of Japan (Yes); beetle larvae, espec. of Carabidae & Elateridae, of Japan (Yes)]
* KUROSAWA, Mikio. Nihon Tokushu Noyaku Production Co., Agricultural Experiment Station, Toyoda, Hino-Machi, Tokyo, Japan. [Thysanoptera]
KUROSAWA, Mr. Yoshihiko. Division of Zoology, National Science Museum, Ueno Park, Tokyo, Japan. [Coleoptera: Buprestidae of Far East & Micronesia (Yes); of tropical Asia (No)]
KURTÉN, Dr. Björn. Institute of Geology & Paleontology, Snellmansgatan 5, Helsinki, Finland. [Miocene-Recent Mammalia: Hyaenidae & Ursidae of Old World (Yes); Miocene-Recent Ursidae of New World (No)]
KURTPINAR, Hasib. Laboratory of Parasitology, Bacteriological & Serological Institute, Etlik, Ankara, Turkey. [Acarina: Ixodidae of Mediterranean (Yes)]
KURTZ, Vincent Ellsworth. 1107 Union National Bldg., Wichita, Kans., U. S. A. [Up. Cambrian (Franconian) Trilobita of Missouri (Yes)]
KUSCHEL, Dr. Guillermo. Casilla 4150, Santiago, Chile. [Coleoptera: Curculionidae of Neotropics (Yes); Rhinomaceridae (Nemonychidae) of World (Yes)]
KUSNEZOV, Prof. N. Instituto Miguel Lillo, Calle Miguel Lillo 205, Tucumán, Argentina. [Hymenoptera: Formicidae of S. America (No), of Argentina (Yes)]
KUSSAKIN, O. G. Zoological Institute, Academy of Sciences, Leningrad - Centre, U. S. S. R. [Crustacea: Isopoda of n. w. Pacific & Arctic oceans (Yes)]
KUTHALINGAM, Dr. M. D. K. Central Marine Fisheries Research Unit, 50 A. Theatre Road, Calcutta 16, India. [Pisces: eggs & larvae of fishes of Bay of Bengal (Yes)]
KUTTAMATHIATHU, Dr. Joseph. (See also Joseph, K. J.) Laboratoire d'Evolution, 105 Boulevard Raspail, Paris (VI), France. [Hymenoptera: Agaontidae & Callimomidae: Idarninae, of Asia, Australia, Africa (Yes)]
KUTTER, Dr. H. Apotheke Flawil, Kanton St. Gallen, Switzerland. [Hymenoptera: Formicidae of Europe (Yes)]
KUWAYAMA, Dr. Satoru, Director, Hokkaido National Agricultural Experiment Station, Kotoni, Sapporo, Hokkaido, Japan. [Neuroptera, Trichoptera, Homoptera: Psyllidae; all of Japan (Yes)]
KUYT, E. Game Branch. Department of Natural Resources, Regina, Sask., Canada. [Mammalia]
* KUZIN, B. S. Address unknown. [Coleoptera]

KUZNETZOV, V. I. Zoological Institut, Academy of Sciences, Universitetsskaja Naberezhnaja 1, Leningrad 164, U. S. S. R. [Lepidoptera: Tortricidae & Gracilariidae of Palearctic (Yes); Pyralidae, Noctuidae, Geometridae, of c. Asia (Yes)]

LaBERGE, Dr. W. E. Department of Zoology & Entomology, Iowa State College, Ames, Iowa, U. S. A. [Hymenoptera: Apidae of New World (Yes); Formicidae of New World (No)]

* LAC, Jan. Faunistické Laboratórium, Slovenska Akademia Vied, Sienkiewiczova 1, Bratislava, Czechoslovakia. [Reptilia]

LaCASSE, W. J. 388 2nd School Group, Gunter Air Force Base, Ala., U. S. A. [Diptera: Culicidae of N. America, Japan, Korea, Okinawa, Morocco (Yes)]

LĂCĂTUSU, Mathilda. Str. Splaiul Independentei No. 91-95, Bucureşti, Rumania. [Hymenoptera: Braconidae of Europe (Yes)]

* LACEY, R. J. Department of Parasitology, State Teachers College, Cedar Falls, Iowa, U. S. A. [Cestoda]

LACHNER, Dr. Ernest A. Division of Fishes, U. S. National Museum, Washington 25, D. C., U. S. A. [F-w. Pisces of e. U. S. (No); Apogonidae, Mullidae, Echeneidae of World (Yes); Cyprinidae & Percidae of e. N. America (No); Eleotridae & Gobiidae of c. Pacific (No)]

LACK, David. (Oxford, England; Aves) Not now active in taxonomy.

LACKEY, James B. Department of Civil Engineering, University of Florida, Gainesville, Fla., U. S. A. [Marine & f-w. Ciliata & Flagellata of World (Yes)]

LACKMAN, Fredda Jean Bullard. Geology Department, Lone Star Producing Co., Dallas 1, Texas, U. S. A. [Cretaceous-Tertiary Foraminifera of Texas Gulf Cst. (No)]

LACOURT, A. W. Merelstraat 33, Leiden, Netherlands. [Marine Bryozoa of w. Europe (No); Bryozoa: Phylactolaemata of World (Yes)]

LACREUZE, Charles. Avenue des Arpillières 19, Chêne-Bougeries, Genève, Switzerland. [Lepidoptera of Palearctic]

LADD, Dr. Harry S. Room 405, U. S. National Museum, Washington 25, D. C., U. S. A. [Tertiary Mollusca of Pacific Is. (Yes)]

LADIGES, Dr. W., Kustos. fur niedere Wirbeltiere, Zoologisches Staatsinstitut u. Zoologisches Museum, Bornplatz 5, Hamburg 13, Germany. [Pisces: Characidae of S. America & Africa (Yes); Siluridae of S. America, Africa, Asia (Yes)]

de LAEVER, E. 171 Rue de Fragnee, Liège, Belgium. [Lepidoptera: Geometridae: g. Eupithecia of World (No), of Europe, China, Japan (Yes)]

LAFOON, Dr. Jean L. Department of Zoology & Entomology, Iowa State College, Ames, Iowa, U. S. A. [Diptera: Mycetophilidae & Culicidae of Nearctic (No); g. Fungivora of Holarctic (Yes); g. Aëdes of Philippines (Yes)]

LAGAAIJ, Dr. Robert. Doormanlaan 46, Wassenaar, Netherlands. [Bryozoa of Gulf of Mexico & Caribbean (Yes); Cenozoic Bryozoa of w. Europe, Gulf of Mexico, Caribbean (No)]

LAGAR, A. Sanjuanistas 20, Barcelona, Spain. [Coleoptera: Carabidae: g. Carabus & Cychrus of Europe & N. Africa (Yes); Dytiscidae & Gyrinidae of Europe & N. Africa (Yes); Cerambycidae: g. Dorcadion of Spain (Yes)]

LAGLER, Dr. Karl F. 2122 Natural Science Bldg., University of Michigan, Ann Arbor, Mich., U. S. A. [F-w. Pisces of c. N. A. (Yes)]

La GRECA, Dr. M. Istituto di Zoologia, Università di Napoli, 8 Via Mezzacannone, Napoli, Italy. [Orthoptera of Palearctic (Yes); Mantodea of World (Yes)]

* LAGUEUX, Dr. Robert. Quebec Department of Fish & Game, Tadoussac Salmon Hatchery, Tadoussac, Saguenay Co., Que., Canada. [Pisces]

LAIDLOW, Dr. F. F. The Rectory, Foxearth, Sudbury, Suffolk, England. [Land shells of s. e. Asia]

LAIMING, Boris. C/o The Texas Company, 3350 Wilshire Boulevard, Los Angeles 5, Calif., U. S. A. [Up. Cretaceous-Tertiary smaller Foraminifera of U. S. Pacific Cst. (No)]

LAING, F. 17 Luttrell Avenue, Putney, London, S. W. 15, England. [Homoptera: Aphididae, Coccidae, Psyllidae, of World]

LAIRD, Dr. Marshall. Institute of Parasitology, Macdonald College, P. O. Box 102, Macdonald College P. O., Que., Canada. [Diptera: Culicidae of Australia & Oceania (No); blood Protozoa of s. e. Asia & Oceania (Yes); parasites of mosquitoes of World (Yes)]

LAIRD, Wilson M. (Grand Forks, N. D., U. S. A.; Fossils) Not now active in taxonomy.

de LAJONQUIERRE, Y. 24 Avenue de Mirmont, Cauderan (Gironde), France. [Lepidoptera: Noctuidae of France (No)]

* LAL, Dr. K. B. Department of Entomology, Agricultural Research Institute, New Delhi, India. [Hymenoptera]

* LAL, Dr. M. B. Department of Zoology, University of Lucknow, Lucknow, India. [Parasites]

LALICKER, Cecil Gordon. P. O. Box 991, McAllen, Texas, U. S. A. [Jurassic-Cretaceous Foraminifera (No)]

LALLEMAND, Mr. V. 4 Avenue Winston Churchill, Uccle, Belgium. [Homoptera: Laternari-
idae of World, espec. Africa (Yes)]
LAMB, Dr. K. P. Department of Scientific & Industrial Research, Plant Diseases Division,
Private Bag, Auckland, New Zealand. [Acarina: Eriophyidae, espec. gall formers, of
New Zealand (Yes); Phytoseiinae of New Zealand (No); Tetranychidae of Australasia
(No), of New Zealand (Yes)]
LAMBERT, Dr. Robert. (Ottawa, Canada; Hymenoptera & Lepidoptera) Died October 21, 1957.
LAMBRECHT, F. L. Institu pour la Recherche Scientifigue en Afrique Centrale, Bukavu,
Belgian Congo. [Diptera: g. Glossina & Anopheles of Africa (Yes)]
LAMONT, Dr. Archie. Jess Cottage, Carlops, Penicuik, Midlothian, Scotland. [Ordovician-
Silurian Brachiopoda, Mollusca, Trilobita, Chelicerata, of Scotland & Ireland, espec.
Llandeilian, Caradocian, Ashgillian, Llandoverian, Gala-Tarannon, & Wenlockian;
Arenigian & Llandeilian Conodonts of Scotland; Gala-Tarannon fossils of Scotland (all
Yes)]
LaMONTE, Miss Francesca. American Museum of Natural History, New York 24, N. Y.,
U. S. A. [Pisces: Istiophoridae, Makairidae, Xiphiidae, of Caribbean & w. S. America
(No)]
LANCE, Dr. John F. Department of Geology, University of Arizona, Tucson, Ariz., U. S. A.
[Pliocene-Pleistocene Mammalia, excl. Rodentia of N. America (Yes)]
LANCE, Mr. James R. Scripps Institution of Oceanography, La Jolla, Calif., U. S. A. [Gas-
tropoda: Nudibranchiata of Pacific Cst. N. America (Yes); Crustacea: Copepoda: g. Tigri-
opus of World (Yes)]
LANCHESTER, Horace P. Entomology, Agricultural Research Center, Beltsville, Md., U. S. A.
[Coleoptera: Elateridae: Cardiophorinae of World (No); of N. America (Yes)]
LANDA, Dr. V. Czechoslovak Academy of Science, Institute of Entomology, 7 Viničná, Praha
2, Czechoslovakia. [Ephemeroptera of Palearctic (Yes)]
LANDIN, Dr. B. O. Entomologiska Avdelningen, Universitetets Zoologiska Institution, Lund,
Sweden. [Coleoptera: Scarabaeidae: Aphodiini of World (No); of Ethiopian & n. w. Europe
(Yes); Carabidae of Burma & British India (No), g. Colpodes (Yes)]
LANDON, Mr. L. R. University of Wisconsin, Madison, Wis., U. S. A. [Paleozoic Crinoidea
(Yes)] See LAUDON, L. R.
LANDRY, Stuart O., Jr. Department of Biology, Louisiana State University in New Orleans,
New Orleans 22, La., U. S. A. [Mammalia: Rodentia of S. America & trop. Old World
(No)]
LANDY, Mr. J. 60 Central Park Road, East Malvern, Vict., Australia. [Lepidoptera: Rhopa-
locera of Australia (Yes)]
LANE, Frederico. Departmento de Zoologia, Secretaria da Agricultura, Caixa Postal 7172,
São Paulo, Brasil. [Coleoptera] See Addenda.
* LANE, Dr. H. H. 1241 West Empire Street, Freeport, Ill., U. S. A. [Fossil vertebrates]
LANE, Prof. John. Faculdade de Higiene, Caixa Postal 8099, São Paulo, Brasil. [Diptera:
Sciaridae, Mycetophilidae, Anisopodidae, Bibionidae, Ceratopogonidae, Blepharoceridae,
all of Neotropical (Yes); Culicidae (No)]
LANE, John E. USOM/E, c/o American Embassy, Addis Ababa, Ethiopia. [Fleas, lice, ticks,
mites of mammals & man of U. S. (Yes); Diptera: Culicidae of E. Africa]
LANE, Merton C. P. O. Box 616, Walla Walla, Wash., U. S. A. [Coleoptera: Elateridae of N.
America (Yes)]
LANE, Norman Gary. Department of Geology, University of California, Los Angeles 24, Calif.,
U. S. A. [Paleozoic Crinoidea: Camerata (Yes)]
LANEYRIE, R. 5 Boulevard Bineau, Levallois (Seine), France. [Coleoptera: Carabidae: Tre-
chinae & Bathysciinae of caves & subterranean of World (Yes)]
LANG, Doc. Dr. Jaroslaw. Zoologisches Institut der Universität, Viničná 7, Praha II, Czecho-
slovakia. [Diplopoda of Czechoslovakia & Bulgaria (Yes)]
LANG, Prof. Dr. Karl G. H. Naturhistoriska Riksmuseum, Stockholm 50, Sweden. [Crustacea:
Harpacticoida & Tanaidacea of World (Yes)]
LANG, Veleslav. Puškinova 7, Vyškov, Czechoslovakia. [Homoptera: Cicadina & Aleurodina
of c. Europe (Yes)]
* LANGE, Mr. A. B. Section of Entomology, Moscow State University, Leninskije Gory,
Moscow V-234, U. S. S. R. [Acarina]
LANGE, Prof. Frederico Waldemar. Caixa Postal 16, Ponta Grossa, Paraná, Brazil. [Paleo
zoic microfossils: Chitinozoa, Scoledoconts, Hystrichosphaeridae, of S. America (Yes)]
[Petróleo Brasileiro S. A.]
LANGE, Dr. W. Harry, Jr. Division of Entomology & Parasitology, University of California,
Davis, Calif., U. S. A. [Lepidoptera: Pterophoridae of Nearctic (Yes); Pyralididae of
World (Yes)]
* LANGELBARTEL, David A. Natural History Museum, University of Illinois, Urbana, Ill.,
U. S. A. [Amphibia & Reptilia]
LANGENHEIM, Mr. R. L. Jr. Museum of Paleontology, University of California, Berkeley,
Calif., U. S. A. [Devonian-Permian marine invertebrates of Utah, Nevada, California,
Arizona (Yes)]

252

LANGSTON, J. M. 310 Green Street, Starkville, Miss., U.S.A. [Coleoptera: Scarabaeidae: g. Phyllophaga of Mississippi (No)]

LANGSTON, Dr. Wann, Jr. National Museum of Canada, Ottawa, Ont., Canada. [Permian-Mesozoic Reptilia & Amphibia of N. America (Yes); Dinosaurs of World (Yes); Cenozoic Crocodilia of World (Yes)]

LANTHAM, Prof. U. N. Saline Valley Farms, Saline, Mich., U.S.A. [Hymenoptera: Apoidea: g. Andrena of World (No)]

LANSBURY, Ivor. 11-A Battlefield Road, St. Albans, Herts, England. [Hemiptera: Heteroptera: Corixidae of Palearctic, Ethiopian, Oriental (Yes); Gerridae of Palearctic & Ethiopian (Yes); Notonectidae of Palearctic & Ethiopian (Yes); of New World (No)]

* LANSING, Dr. A. I. Department of Anatomy, Medical School, University of Pittsburg, Pittsburgh, Penna., U.S.A. [Rotifera]

LANTZ, Mr. John Perry. Box 8793, University of Miami, Miami 46, Fla., U.S.A. [Amphibia, espec. tree-frogs & salamanders, of Europe & New World (Yes); Reptilia: lizards of Europe & New World (No)]

LANYON, Dr. Wesley E. Department of Birds, American Museum of Natural History, New York 24, N. Y., U.S.A. [Aves of New World (Yes)]

LANZA, Prof. Dr. Benedetto. Istituto di Zoologia, Via Romana 17, Firenze, Italy. [Reptilia & Amphibia of World (No); of Mediterranean (Yes); cave faunas of Italy; Mammalia: Chiroptera of Mediterranean (Yes)]

* LARIOS, Prof. Ignacio. Instituto de Biologia, Ciudad Universitaria, Villa Obregón 20, D. F., Mexico. [Trematoda]

La RIVERS, Ira. Department of Biology, University of Nevada, Reno, Nev., U.S.A. [Coleoptera: Tenebrionidae of w. U.S. (Yes); Hemiptera: Naucoridae of World (No), of New World (Yes)]

* LARIVIÈRE, Dr. M. Faculté de Medicine (Parasitologie), Dakar, Senegal (Afrique Orient. Française). [Diptera]

* LARKIN, Dr. P. A. Department of Zoology, University of British Columbia, Vancouver, B. C., Canada. [Crustacea: Amphipoda & Mysidacea]

* LARNOWSKI, Eugeniusz. See ZARNOWSKI.

La ROCQUE, Prof. A. Department of Geology, Ohio State University, Columbus 10, Ohio, U.S.A. [Paleozoic Pelecypoda of N. America (Yes); Mesozoic-Cenozoic non-marine Mollusca of N. America (Yes)]

LARRISON, Prof. Earl J. Department of Biological Science, University of Idaho, Moscow, Idaho, U.S.A. [Mammalia: Sciuridae: g. Eutamias of Pacific n. w. U.S. (Yes); Cricetidae: Microtinae of Pacific n. w. U.S. (Yes)]

LARSEN, Wesley P. Biology Department, Carbon College, Price, Utah, U.S.A. [Odonata: Anisoptera of Utah (Yes)]

LARSON, Prof. E. R. Department of Geology, University of Nevada, Reno, Nev., U.S.A. [Paleozoic Brachiopoda of Great Basin of U.S. (No)]

LARSSON, Dr. Sv. G. Department of Entomology, Københavns Universitets Zoologiske Museum, Krystalgade 27, København, Denmark. [Larvae of Coleoptera of World (Yes)]

La RUÉ, Prof. George R. 7203 Wells Parkway, Hyattsville, Md., U.S.A. [Cestoda: Proteocephalidae & digenetic Trematoda of N. America (Yes)]

LARWOOD, Gilbert P. Department of Geology, Kings College, Newcastle-upon-Tyne, England. [Cretaceous Bryozoa: Cheilostomata: Cribrimorpha (Yes); Tertiary-Quaternary Bryozoa (No)]

LASERON, Mr. C. F. 15 Hill Street, Fairlight, N. S. W., Australia. [Mollusca, espec. minute Gastropoda, of Australia (Yes)]

LÁSKA, Dr. František. Zoology Department, Masaryk University, Kotlářska 2, Brno, Czechoslovakia. [Acarina: Hydrachnellae of Europe (Yes)]

* LASSMANN, Dr. Gunther. Independencia 3, Jalapa Enriquez, V. C., Mexico. [Diptera: Culicidae]

LAST, H. R. 12 Winkworth Road, Banstead, Surrey, England. [Coleoptera: Staphylinidae: g. Zyras, espec. of Africa, (Yes)]

* LATIMER, M. Courtenay. See COURTENAY-LATIMER, M.

de LATTIN, Prof. Dr. Gustaf. Zoologisches Staatsinstitut und Zoologisches Museum, Bornplatz 5, Hamburg 13, Germany. [Lepidoptera of Holarctic (No); Satyridae, Acronictinae, Crambidae, of Palearctic (Yes)]

LATTIN, John D. Department of Entomology, Oregon State College, Corvallis, Ore., U.S.A. [Heteroptera: Pentatomidae: Scutellerinae of World (Yes); Pentatomoidea of N. America (Yes); Heteroptera, excl. Miridae, of Pacific n. w. U.S. (Yes)]

de LAUBENFELS, M. W. (Corvallis, Ore., U.S.A.; Porifera) Died February 4, 1958.

LAUBMANN, A. (München, Germany; Aves) Not now active in taxonomy.

LAUDON, Mr. L. R. Department of Geology, University of Wisconsin, Madison, Wis., U.S.A. [Paleozoic Crinoidea (Yes)]

LAURENCE, B. R. London School of Hygiene & Tropical Medicine, Keppel Street - Gower Street, London, W. C. 1, England. [Coprophilous Diptera of Europe (Yes); Diptera: Oestridae of Africa (No)]

LAURENT, Mr. R. F.   B. P. 2908, Elisabethville, Belgian Congo.   [Amphibia & Reptilia of c.
    Africa (Yes); Reptilia & Amphibia of e. s. & w. Africa (No), Amphibia: Hyperoliidae
    (Yes)] [Universite Officialle du Congo Belge et du Ruanda Urundi]
LAURIE, E. M. O.   (London, England; Mammalia) Not now active in taxonomy.
LAURSEN, Dr. Dan. Juliusvej 6, Gentofte, Denmark. [Pleistocene Mollusca of Arctic (Yes);
    Recent Mollusca: larvae of Prosobranchia of Florida & n. w. Atlantic currents (No); g.
    Ianthina of World (Yes)]
LAUTERER, P. Náměsti Rudé armády 12, Brno, Czechoslovakia. [Homoptera: Auchenorrhyn-
    cha of c. Europe (Yes); Tettigellidae: Tettigellinae & Proconiinae of World (No)]
LAVEN, Mr. H. Max-Planck-Institut für Biologie, Spemannstrasse 34, Tübingen, Germany.
    [Diptera: Culicidae: g. Culex of World (No)]
LAVOCAT, Dr. Réné J. M., Directeur de Laboratoire a l'Ecole des Hautes Etudes, Galerie de
    Paleontologie du Museum, Place Valhubert 13, Paris (V), France. [Mammalia: rodent
    bones of World (No), of Europe & Africa (Yes); fossil Mammalia & Dinosauria of Europe
    & Africa (Yes); Reptilia: Crocodilia of Europe & Africa (No)]
LAW, C. E. Defense Research Board, Ottawa, Ont., Canada. [Aves: Tetraonidae: g. Lagopus of
    N. America (Yes)]
LAWLER, Mr. G. H. Biological Station, 539 Richmond Street, London, Ont., Canada. [Pisces:
    Coregonidae: g. Coregonus of N. America (No); Esocidae of w. Canada (Yes)]
LAWRENCE, Barbara. Museum of Comparative Zoology, Cambridge 38, Mass., U. S. A.
    [Mammalia of World (No); of Africa, Near East, East Indies, Philippines, S. America
    (Yes); Canidae & Chiroptera of World (Yes)]
LAWRENCE, Dr. R. F. Natal Museum, Pietermaritzburg, Natal, Union of South Africa. [Ara-
    chnida, excl. Acarina: Mesostigmata, Hydrachnellae, Ixodides, Oribatei, of Africa (No);
    Onychophora of Africa (No); Myriopoda, excl. Symphyla, Pauropoda, Diplopoda: Psela-
    phognatha, of Africa (No)]
* LAWS, Dr. C. R. Department of Zoology, Auckland University College, Box 2553, Auckland,
    New Zealand. [Fossil invertebrates]
LAWS, Dr. Richard M. National Institute of Oceanography, Wormley, Godalming, Surrey,
    England. [Mammalia: Pinnipedia: Phocidae of S. Hemisphere (Yes); of N. Hemisphere
    (No)]
LAWSON, Dr. Fred A. Department of Entomology, Kansas State College, Manhattan, Kansas,
    U. S. A. [Coleoptera: Chrysomelidae of N. America (Yes)]
LAWSON, Dr. J. D. Department of Geology, The University, Birmingham 15, England. [Up.
    Silurian Brachiopoda of Britain (Yes)]
LAYNE, Dr. James N. Department of Biology, University of Florida, Gainesville, Fla., U. S. A.
    [Mammalia of N. America (Yes); Siphonaptera of e. U. S. (Yes)]
LAZORKO, Dr. W. 2596 East 18th Avenue, Vancouver, B. C., Canada. [Coleoptera of Ukraine
    (Yes); Carbaidae of Europe (No)]
* LEACH, Mr. E. R. 415 Hillside Avenue, Piedmont, Calif., U. S. A. [Coleoptera]
LEAKEY, Dr. L. S. B. P. O. Box 658, Nairobi, Kenya. [Pleistocene Mammalia: Suidae (Yes);
    Miocene-Recent Primates of Old World (Yes); Pleistocene Bovidae (Yes)] [The Coryndon
    Museum]
LEANZA, Dr. Armando F. Peru 684, Buenos Aires, Argentina. [Ordovician Trilobita of World
    (Yes); Up. Jurassic-L. Cretaceous Ammonitoidea of World (Yes)] [Dirección Nacional
    de Mineria]
* LEBEDEV, V. D. Ichthyological Laboratory, Biological Faculty, University of Moscow,
    Moscow, U. S. S. R. [Pisces]
* LEBIS, M. E. (Domfront, France; Scarabaeidae) Not now active in taxonomy.
* Le BLANC, Rufus J. 3737 Bellaire Boulevard, Houston, Texas, U. S. A. [Fossil invertebrates]
LEBOUR, Marie V. (Plymouth, England; Decapoda) Not now active in taxonomy.
Le CALVEZ, Madame Y. 75 Boulevard Soult, Paris (XII), France. [Tertiary Foraminifera of
    Europe (Yes); Recent Foraminifera of Mediterranean & Atlantic (Yes); espec. Miliolidae]
    [Bureau Recherches Géologiques-Géophysiques et Minières]
* LECHANTEUR, Dr. F. F. Address unknown. [Coleoptera: Clavicornia]
Le CHARLES, Louis. 22 Avenue des Gobelins, Paris (V), France. [Lepidoptera: Zygaenidae &
    Pyralidae]
LECLERCQ, Dr. Jean. 17 Place Delcour, Liège, Belgium. [Hymenoptera: Sphecidae: of World
    (No), Crabroninae of World (Yes); Ichneumonidae of Old World (No)] [Université de
    Liège]
LECLERCQ, Dr. Marcel. Rue du Prof. E. Malvoz 41, Beyne Heusay, Liège, Belgium. [Dip-
    tera: Tabanidae, Oestridae, Hippoboscidae, of Palearctic & Ethiopian (Yes)] [Institut
    Royal des Sciences Naturelles de Belgique]
* Le DANOIS, E. LeValmore 3, Rue Quinault, St. Germain-en-Laye, (S. et O.), France. [Pis-
    ces]
* Le DANOIS, Yseult. LeValmore 3, Rue Quinault, St. Germain-en-Laye, (S. et O.), France.
    [Pisces]
* LEDERER, Dr. Gustav. Zoologische Garten, Schellingstrasse 6, (16) Frankfurt am Main,
    Germany. [Odonata]

* LEE, Dr. C. Bruce. Museum of Zoology, University of Michigan, Ann Arbor, Mich., U.S.A. [Mollusca]
LEE, Mr. D.J. School of Public Health & Tropical Medicine, University of Sydney, Sydney, N.S.W., Australia. [Diptera: Culicidae & Ceratopogonidae of Australasia (Yes)]
* LEE, Mr. J. Warren. Southern University, Southern Branch P.O., Baton Rouge, La., U.S.A. [Protozoa] Died April 1, 1960.
LEE, Kenneth E. Department of Scientific & Industrial Research, Soil Bureau Experiment Station, Eastern Hutt Road, Lower Hutt, New Zealand. [Oligochaeta: Megascolecidae & Lumbricidae of New Zealand (Yes)]
LEE, M. Raymond. Department of Zoology, University of Utah, Salt Lake City, Utah, U.S.A. [Mammalia of N. America (Yes)]
LEE, Mr. Robert D. School of Tropical & Preventive Medicine, Loma Linda, Calif., U.S.A. [Hemiptera: Cimicidae of New World (Yes)]
LEECH, Hugh B. California Academy of Sciences, San Francisco 18, Calif., U.S.A. [Coleoptera: Amphizoidae, Haliplidae, Dytiscidae, Hydrophilidae, of N. America (Yes)]
LEENE, Dr. Jentina E. Laboratory of Fibre Technology (Textile Department), Technical University, Delft, Holland. [Crustacea: Decapoda: Portunidae: g. Charybdis of Indo-Pacific (No)]
LEESON, H.S. (London, England; Diptera) Not now active in taxonomy.
van LEEUWEN, T. See THEOWALD, Dr. Br.
van LEEUWEN, Prof. Dr. W.M. Docters. Burgemeester van den Boschlaan 52, Leersum, Netherlands. [Galls of the Netherlands & Indonesia (Yes)]
LEFKOVITCH, L.P. Department of Scientific & Industrial Research, Pest Infestation Laboratory, London Road, Slough, Bucks, England. [Coleoptera: Hemipeplidae & Cucujidae, espec. Laemophloeinae, of World (Yes)]
* Le GAC, P. Laboratoire de Zoologie du Muséum, 61 rue de Buffon, Paris (V), France. [Acarina: Trombiculidae]
LEGAND, M. Institut Français d'Oceanie, B.P. 4, Noumea, New Caledonia. [Pisces of New Caledonia & New Hebrides (No)]
LEGENDRE, Prof. Dr. R. Laboratoire de Zoologie, Faculté des Sciences, Institut des Hautes Etudes de Madagascar, Tananarive, Madagascar. [Arachnida: Araneida of Madagascar (No)]
LEGENDRE, Vianney. G3 Université de Montreal, 2900 Mt. Royal Boulevard, C.P. 6128 Montreal, Que., Canada. [Pisces of N. America (Yes)]
LEGEZA, M.J. Zoological Institute, Academy of Sciences, Leningrad-Centre, U.S.S.R. [Pisces: Agonidae & Cyclopteridae of World (Yes); Amphioxi & Holocephali of the Japan Sea (Yes)]
LEGLER, Mr. John M. Museum of Natural History, University of Kansas, Lawrence, Kans., U.S.A. [Reptilia of U.S. & C. America (Yes); Chelonia of New World (Yes)]
LEGRAND, Prof. J.J. Faculté des Sciences, Poiters, France. [Crustacea: Isopoda: Oniscoidea of World (No); of France & n. Europe (Yes)]
* LEGRAS, Leon. 5 rue August Bailly, Courbevoie (Seine), France. [Lepidoptera]
* LEGROS, C. Museum National d'Histoire Naturelle, 45 bis Rue de Buffon, Paris V, France. [Coleoptera]
* LEHMAN, Burton A. U.S. Fish & Wildlife Service, Beaufort, N.C., U.S.A. [Pisces]
LEHMAN, J.P., Directeur, Laboratoire de Paleontologie, Museum National d'Histoire Naturelle, 13 Place Valhubert, Paris (VI), France. [Paleozoic & Mesozoic Pisces & Stegocephalia (No)]
von LEHMANN, Dr. Ernst. Nettekoven, bei Bonn, Germany. [Mammalia: Rodentia & Soricidae of Europe, China, s.w. Africa (Yes); Cervidae: g. Capreolus of Palearctic (Yes)] [Zoologisches Forschungsinstitut und Museum Alexander Koenig]
LEHMANN V., Prof. F. Carlos, Jefe, Departamento de Zoologia, Universidad del Valle, Apartado 680, Cali, Colombia. [Aves: Trochilidae, birds of prey, game birds, of Neotropical (Yes)]
LEHMANN, Dr. Ulrich. Geologisches Staatsinstitut, Esplanade lb, Hamburg (36), Germany. [Pliocene & Pleistocene Mammalia, excl. Rodentia, of Europe (Yes); Up. Paleozoic Ammonitoidea (Yes); Up. Paleozoic corals (No)]
LEHMANN, Dr. Wolfram. Technische Hochschule, Zoologisches Institut, Zellescher Weg 40, Dresden, German Democratic Republic. [Hymenoptera of Germany (No); Ichneumonidae of Germany (No)]
LEHRER, Andy. Str. Platon Nr. 1, Iasi, Rumania. [Diptera: Sarcophagidae: g. Miltogramma (No); Sarcophagidae & Calliphoridae of Palearctic (Yes)]
LEIGH, Dr. W. Henry. Zoology Department, University of Miami, Coral Gables 46, Fla., U.S.A. [Trematoda of N. America (No)]
LEIM, A.H. Biological Station, Fisheries Research Board, St. Andrews, N.B., Canada. [Marine Pisces & Crustacea: Decapoda: g. Spirontocaris of e. Canadian cst. (Yes)]
LEIPER, Prof. R.T. 18 Palfrey Close, St. Albans, Herts, England. [Helminths (Yes)] [Commonwealth Bureau of Helminthology]

de LEIRA, Dr. Alvarino. Doce de Octubre 11, Madrid, Spain. [Chaetognatha & Hydrozoa: Siphonophora of Atlantic & Mediterranean (Yes); Coelenterata: Medusae & Pisces: larvae of same (No)] [Instituto Español de Oceanografia]

LEIST, Claude. (Pittsburg, Kansas, U.S.A.) Not now active in taxonomy.

LEITÃO de CARVALHO, Antenor. Departmento de Herpetologia, Museu Nacional, Quinta da Boa Vista, Rio de Janeiro, Brazil. [Amphibia & Reptilia of Brazil (Yes); f-w. Pisces of Brazil (Yes); marine Pisces of s. Atlantic cst. (Yes)]

▸ LELOUP, Dr. Eugene. Institut Royal des Sciences Naturelles de Belgique, Rue Vautier 31, Bruxelles 4, Belgium. [Amphineura; Hydrozoa: Hydroidea & Siphonaphora: Anthozoa: Ceriantharia]

Le MAITRE, Prof. Dr. Dorothée. Faculté Libre des Sciences, 13 rue de Toul, Lille (Nord), France. [Devonian Brachiopoda, corals, Stromatoporoidea, of Europe & N. Africa]

Le MASNE, Georges. Faculté des Sciences, Place Victor Hugo, Marseille (3º), France. [Hymenoptera: Formicidae of s. France (No)]

LEMCHE, Dr. Henning. Zoologisk Museum, Krystalgade 27, København K, Denmark. [Gastropoda:\Opisthobranchiata, excl. Pteropoda & Pyramidellidae, of World (Yes); Monoplacophora of World (Yes)]

LEMKE, Dr. Ursula. Geltorf über Schleswig, Germany. [Hymenoptera: Formicidae of c. & n. Europe (No)]

* LEMON, R. 1 Bromwall Road, Billesley, Birmingham, England. [Fossil invertebrates]

LEMOS de CASTRO, A. Museu Nacional, Quinta da Boa Vista, Rio de Janeiro, Brazil. [Terr. Crustacea: Isopoda: Oniscoidea of Neotropical (Yes); Isopoda: Cymothoidea & Argulidae of Neotropical (Yes); Decapoda of Brazil (Yes)]

* LEMPKE, B.J. Oude Yselstraat 12 (II), Amsterdam Z-2, Netherlands. [Lepidoptera: Rhopalocera & Macrolepidoptera of Netherlands] [Zoologische Museum]

LENGERSDORF, Mr. F. 26 Combahnstrasse, Beuel-Bonn am Rhein, Germany. [Diptera: Sciaridae of Palearctic (No)]

* LENKO, Karol. C/o Faculdade de Higiene, Caixa Postal 8099, São Paulo, Brazil. [Diptera]

LENT, Dr. Herman. Instituto Oswaldo Cruz, Caixa Postal 926, Rio de Janeiro, Brazil. [Hemiptera: Reduviidae: Triatominae of World (Yes); Piratinae of New World (Yes); Reduviinae of S. America (Yes); g. Zelurus of World (Yes)]

LENZ, Prof. Dr. Frederick. Hydrobiologische Anstalt, Ploen, Schleswig-Holstein, Germany. [Diptera: Tendipedidae (Yes)]

LEON, Luis A. Laboratorio de Parasitologia y Medicina Tropical, Apartado de Correos 457, Quito, Ecuador. [Protozoa & helminths of man of New World (Yes)]

LEONARD. Dr. Justin W. Michigan Department of Conservation, Lansing 26, Mich., U.S.A. [Odonata of New World & Melanesia (No); Trichoptera of N. America (No); Ephemeroptera of Great Lakes region of U.S. (No)]

LEONARD, Dr. Mortimer D. 2480 16th Street, N.W., Washington 9, D.C., U.S.A. [Homoptera: Aphidae of U.S. (Yes)]

LEONARDI, Prof. Dr. Piero. Istituto di Geologia dell'Università, Via Boldini 14, Ferrara, Italy. [Triassic Mollusca of Alps (Yes); Permian Tetrapoda (tracks) of Alps (Yes); Pleistocene Macromammalia of Europe (No)]

LEONE, Dr. Charles A. Department of Zoology, University of Kansas, Lawrence, Kans., U.S.A. [Sera of Decapoda of World (No)]

* Le PELLEY, Dr. R. Entomological Laboratory, Department of Agriculture, P.O. Box 338, Nairobi, Kenya. [Homoptera: Coccidae]

* Le PAGE, Helio Sermeha. Instituto Biologico, Rua Aguiar de Andrade 117, Santos, Brazil. [Homoptera: Coccidae]

* LEPESME, P.C. (Paris, France: Coleoptera; Cerambycidae) Deceased.

* LEPIGRE, A.L. Directeur de Jardin d'Essais, Alger, Algeria. [Lepidoptera]

LEPIKSAAR, Johannes. Naturhistoriska Museet, Göteborg, Sweden. [Subfossil & Recent Aves & Mammalia of Europe (Yes)]

LEPNEVA, Prof. I. Zoological Institute, Academy of Sciences, Leningrad 164, U.S.S.R. [Trichoptera larvae of U.S.S.R. (No)]

LEPSI, Prof. Dr. I. Muzeul National de Istorie "Grigore Antipa", Sos. Kisselef No. 1, Bucuresti 3, Rumania. [F-w. Protozoa: Amoebina, Testacea, non-parasitic Euciliata (Yes)]

Le QUESNE, Dr. W.J. Millbury, Millshot Drive, Chequers Hill, Amersham, Bucks, England. [Hemiptera: Heteroptera of Britain (No); Homoptera: Auchenorhyncha of Britain (Yes)]

* de LERMA, Dr. B. Istituto di Zoologia, Università di Napoli, Via Mezzocannone 8, Napoli, Italy. [Opiliones]

Le ROUX, Mr. P.J. Box 2, Kleinmondstrand, Union of South Africa. [Marine Mollusca of S. Africa cst. (No)]

* LeROUX, Mr. P.L. Department of Parasitology, London School of Tropical Medicine, Gower Street - Keppel Street, London, W.C.1, England. [Nematoda]

LESAGE, (Rev.) Fr. M.C., S.V.D. Aquinas College, Osu - Accra, Ghana. [Reptilia of Ghana (No); Ophidia of W. Africa, espec. Ghana (Yes)]

LESEIGNEUR, M., Professeur. 1 rue Président Carnot, Grenoble, France. [Coleoptera: Elateridae of Europe & Africa (Yes)]

LeSOUEF, J. C. P. O. Blairgowrie, Vict., Australia. [Coleoptera: Buprestidae & Lepidoptera of Australia & Tasmania (Yes); Reptilia & Mollusca of Australia & Tasmania (No)]

de LESSE, H. J. L. Laboratoire d'Entomologie, Muséum d'Histoire Naturelle, 45 bis rue de Buffon, Paris (V), France. [Lepidoptera: Satyridae of Palearctic & Nearctic (Yes)]

LESTON, Mr. D. 44 Abbey Road, London, N. W. 8, England. [Mesozoic-Recent Heteroptera of Britain (Yes); Recent Pentatomoidea of World (Yes)]

LETACONNOUX, R. Institut des Pêches Maritimes, 74 Allées du Mail, La Rochelle, Charente-Maritime, France. [Pisces of N. Atlantic (No)]

LETH, K. O., Viceskoleinspector, Solvaenget 34, Herning, Denmark. [Odonata & Hemiptera: aquatic Heteroptera of Denmark (Yes)]

LEUTZE, Willard P. Department of Geology, Earlham College, Richmond, Ind., U. S. A. [Paleozoic Eurypterida of N. America (Yes); Up. Silurian fossils of Salina Basin, n. e. U. S. (Yes)]

* LEVASSEUR, Mr. L. 3 rue Victor Considérent, Paris (XIV), France. [Coleoptera]

LEVENSTEIN, R. J. Institute of Oceanology, Academy of Science of U. S. S. R., Prospect Lomo-nossova 18 kv. 94, Moscow B-296, U. S. S. R. [Non-pelagic Polychaeta of Bering Sea & N. Pacific (Yes)]

LEVER, Prof. J. Vrije Universiteit, Zoologisch Laboratorium, Rapenburgerstraat 128, Am-sterdam, Netherlands. [Gastropoda of Netherlands (No)]

LEVER, Mr. R. J. A. W. C/o Lloyds Bank, 164 Finchley Road, London, N. W. 3, England. [Diptera of Melanesia, espec. Solomon Is. (No)]

LEVI, Prof. Dr. Claude. Laboratoire de Biologie générale, Faculté des Sciences, 12 Rue de l'Université, Strasbourg, France. [Marine Porifera: Acalcarea (Yes); Gastrotricha: Macrodasyoidea]

LEVI, Dr. Herbert W. Museum of Comparative Zoology, Cambridge 38, Mass., U. S. A. [Araneida: Theridiidae of N. & C. America & West Indies (Yes); spiders of Rocky Mts., n. U. S., Canada, Alaska (Yes)]

* LEVI, Mrs. Lorna R. Museum of Comparative Zoology, Cambridge 38, Mass., U. S. A. [Araneida: spiders of N. America (Yes)]

* LEVI-CASTILLO, Prof. Dr. Roberto. P. O. Box 3606, Guayaquil, Ecuador. [Diptera: Culici-dae of Neotropics] [Centro Ecuatoriano de Investigaciones Entomológicas]

LEVINE, Dr. Norman D. College of Veterinary Medicine, University of Illinois, Urbana, Ill., U. S. A. [Protozoa: Coccidiomorpha of World (Yes); Protozoa, Nematoda, Platyhel-minthes; all of domestic animals of World (No)]

LEVINSON, Dr. Stuart A. Humble Oil & Refining Co., P. O. Box 2180, Houston 1, Texas, U. S. A. [Fossil & Recent Crustacea: Ostracoda of World (Yes); Tertiary Foraminifera of Gulf cst. U. S. (Yes)]

LEVITAN, Dr. M. Anatomy Department, Women's Medical College of Pennsylvania, Phila-delphia 29, Penna., U. S. A. [Diptera: Drosophilidae of e. U. S. (Yes)]

LEVITON, Mr. Alan Edward. Department of Herpetology, California Academy of Sciences, San Francisco 18, Calif., U. S. A. [Reptilia: snakes & Amphibia: frogs & toads, of Australia, Asia, S. America (Yes)]

LEVITT, Miss V. C. 94 Rossmore Avenue, Punchbowl, N. S. W., Australia. [Araneida: g. Atrax, Pseudatrax, of N. S. W., g. Missulena of Australia (all No)]

LEWANDOWSKI, Mr. M. R. Ul. Grodziska 21 m. 3, Poznań, Poland. [Lepidoptera: Hepiali-dae, Eriocranidae, Micropterygidae, Adelidae, Incurvariidae, Stigmelidae, Psychidae, Coleophoridae, Elachistidae, Cossidae, Aegeriidae, of World (Yes)]

LEWIS, Alan. Department of Zoology, University of Hawaii, Honolulu 14, Hawaii, U. S. A. [Crustacea: f-w. & marine Copepoda of fish of Hawaii, Florida, Gulf of Mexico, Carib-bean (Yes)]

* LEWIS, Mr. C. B., Director, Institute of Jamaica, Kingston, Jamaica, B. W. I. [Lepidoptera]

LEWIS, Dr. D. J. C/o British Museum (Natural History), Cromwell Road, London, S. W. 1, England. [Diptera: g. Phlebotomus of Old World (Yes)] [Medical Research Council]

LEWIS, Mr. E. 8 Parry Road, South Norwood, London, S. E. 25, England. [Coleoptera: Phala-cridae of World (No); of Palearctic (Yes)]

LEWIS, Edward. U. S. Geological Survey, Paleontology & Stratigraphy Branch, Federal Center, Denver, Colo., U. S. A. [Vertebrate fossils of World (No); Cenozoic faunas of N. Ameri-ca (No); Pleistocene Mammalia of N. America (Yes); anthropoid apes of Old World (Yes)]

LEWIS, Dr. Franklin B. 335 Prospect Street, New Haven, Conn., U. S. A. [Diptera: Ceratopo-gonidae of e. U. S. (Yes)] [Northeastern Forest Experiment Station]

LEWIS, Mr. Robert E. Department of Entomology, 303 Harker Hall, University of Illinois, Urbana, Ill., U. S. A. [Siphonaptera & Macrolepidoptera of U. S. (Yes)]

* LeZOTTE, Lloyd A., Jr. Department of Biological Sciences, Purdue University, W. Lafay-ette, Ind., U. S. A. [Trematoda]

LIBERTY, Bruce A. (Ottawa, Canada; Fossils) Not now active in taxonomy.

LIBOSVÁRSKÝ, J. Czechoslovak Academy of Science, Plotni 25a, Brno, Czechoslovakia.
[F-w. Pisces of Czechoslovakia (Yes)]
LICHAREV, Dr. I. M. Zoological Institute, Academy of Sciences, Leningrad-Centre, U. S. S. R.
[Mollusca: terr. Pulmonata & Prosobranchia of U. S. S. R. (Yes)]
* LICHY, Rene. Address unknown. [Lepidoptera: Sphingidae]
LIDICKER, William Z., Jr. Museum of Vertebrate Zoology, University of California, Berkeley
4, Calif., U. S. A. [Mammalia of N. America (Yes); Aves of N. America (No)]
LIEB, Prof. Dr. Fritz. Aescherstrasse 25, Basel, Switzerland. [Jurassic Ammonitoidea of
Inferior Dogger (Yes); Jurassic Brachiopoda of Inferior Oolite]
LIEBERMANN, Dr. José. Manuela Pedraza 2618, Buenos Aires, Argentina. [Orthoptera:
Acrididae of Neotropical (Yes)]
* LIEDER, Dr. U. Waldostrasse 22, Berlin-Friedrichshagen, German Democratic Republic.
[Crustacea: Copepoda: Cladocera]
LIEFTINCK, Dr. M. A. Rijksmuseum van Natuurlijke Historie, Leiden, Netherlands. [Odonata
of Asia, Australia, Pacific (Yes); Hymenoptera: Apoidea, espec. Apidae, of Indo-Aus-
tralian (Yes)]
LIENK, Dr. S. E. New York State Agricultural Experiment Station, Geneva, N. Y., U. S. A.
[Hymenoptera: g. Torymus of N. America (Yes)]
LIEU, K. O. Victoria. (Columbus, Ohio; Coleoptera) Deceased.
LIGHT, W. I. S. Ministry of Agriculture, Fisheries & Food, Wye, Ashford, Kent, England.
[Nematoda of economic importance (No)]
LIKHAREV, Dr. I. M. Zoological Institute, Academy of Sciences, Universitetskaja nab. 1,
Leningrad B-164, U. S. S. R. [Terr. Mollusca of U. S. S. R. (Yes)]
LILIEFELT, K. G. Gustaf Nydbergsgatan 2, Malmö, Sweden. [Mollusca of N. Atlantic & Br.
Isles; Gastropoda: Prosobranchia of North Sea; Pelecypoda of e. cst. Africa-India, w.
cst. America (all Yes)]
* LIMA, Milton Moura. Departamento Nacional de Endemias Rurais, Avenida Rio Branco 80
(18), Rio de Janeiro, Brazil. [Diptera]
LIMBAUGH, Conrad. Scripps Institution of Oceanography, La Jolla, Calif., U. S. A. [Marine
Pisces of California cst. (Yes); Echinoidea: Clypeastroidea of California cst. (Yes)]
* LIMON-GUTTIERREZ, L. Laboratorio de Paleontologia, Gerencia de Exploración, Petroleos
Mexicanos, Cipres 176, Mexico 4, D. F., Mexico. [Fossil Foraminifera]
* LIN, C. C. Department of Geology, National Taiwan University, Taipei, Taiwan, Formosa.
[Fossils]
LIN, S. Y. Food and Agriculture Organization Mission, Apartado Postal 289, Tegucigalpa,
D. C., Honduras. [Pisces of Asia & C. America]
LINARES, Dra. A. Laboratorio de Geologia, Facultad de Ciencias, Universidad de Granada,
Granada, Spain. [Jurassic-Tertiary smaller Foraminifera of w. Mediterranean & Alps
(No); Eocene (Yes)]
LINCICOME, Dr. D. R. 7118 Cedar Avenue, Takoma Park, Washington 12, D. C., U. S. A.
[Acanthocephala of World (Yes)]
LINCOLN, Dr. Frederick C. U. S. Fish & Wildlife Service, Washington 25, D. C., U. S. A.
[Aves of N. America (No)]
LINDBERG, Prof. Dr. G. U. Zoological Institute, Academy of Sciences, Leningrad 164,
U. S. S. R. [Marine Pisces of Okhotsk, Japan, Yellow & East China Seas (Yes)]
LINDBERG, Prof. Dr. Hakan. Zoological Institute, Helsinki, University, Helsinki, Finland.
[Heteroptera & Homoptera of Palearctic & Micronesia (Yes)]
LINDBERG, Dr. Knut. 5 Gladstonvägen, Lund, Sweden. [F-w. & marine Crustacea: Cyclopoi-
da: Gnathostoma (Yes)]
LINDBERG, Dr. Robert G. Atomic Energy Project, University of California, Los Angeles 24,
Calif., U. S. A. [Crustacea: Palinuridae of w. cst. N. America (Yes), of Hawaii (No)]
van der LINDE, Dr. W. J. Department of Agriculture, Box 513, Pretoria, Union of South
Africa. [F-l. soil plant parasitic Nematoda of World (Yes)]
* LINDENMANN-NEBIKER, Dr. W. Münchenstein bei Basel, Switzerland. [Collembola]
* LINDENTHAL, Dr. Jos. Grob. Zoologisches Institut der Universität, Kemperstrasse 13,
Köln, Germany. [Lepidoptera]
LINDER, Dr. Folke. Hälsinborg, Sweden. [Crustacea: Anostraca (No); Notostraca (Yes)]
[Zoological Institution, Uppsala]
LINDINGER, Dr. Philos. Leonhard, Alsterdorfer Strasse 191, Hamburg 39, Germany.
[Homoptera: Coccidae of World (No)]
LINDNER, Prof. Dr. Erwin. Staatliches Museum für Naturkunde, Archivstrasse 4, Stuttgart,
Germany. [Diptera: Stratiomyiidae of World, excl. N. America (Yes)]
* LINDQUIST, Dr. A. Box 2126, Göteborg, Sweden. [Br-w. Copepoda of Baltic plankton]
[Kungliga Fiskeristyrelsen]
LINDQUIST, Dr. W. D. Department of Bacteriology & Public Health, Michigan State University,
East Lansing, Mich., U. S. A. [Nematoda of domestic animals of N. America & W.
Africa (Yes)]

LINDQVIST, Magister E. Bredviksvägen 10, Helsinki-Munksnäs, Finland. [Hymenoptera: Phytophaga: Nematinae of n. Eurasia (Yes)]

LINDROTH, Prof. Dr. Carl H. Lund University, Zoologiska Institutionen, Lund, Sweden. [Coleoptera: Carabidae of Canada & Alaska (Yes); circumpolar area (No)]

LINDSAY, Charles John. Dominion Museum, Wellington, New Zealand. [Aves of New Zealand (Yes)]

LINDSAY, Hague L. Department of Zoology, University of Tulsa, Tulsa, Okla., U.S.A. [Amphibia: Anura of U.S. (Yes)]

* LINDSEY, Dr. A.W. Department of Biological Sciences, Denison University, Granville, Ohio, U.S.A. [Lepidoptera: Hesperioidea]

LINDSEY, Dr. Casimir C. Lindsey. Institute of Fisheries, University of British Columbia, Vancouver 8, B.C., Canada. [Pisces: Fossil Actinopterygii of Br. Columbia (No); Recent Petromyzonidae, Coregonidae, Salmonidae, Catostomidae, Cyprinidae, Cottidae, all of w. Canada & Alaska (Yes); Thymallidae of N. America (Yes)]

LINDSTRÖM, Dr. Maurits. Geological-Paleontological Institute, Lund, Sweden. [Ordovician Conodonts of Scandinavia & Britain (Yes)]

LINER, Ernest A.   P.O. Box 468, Hammond, La., U.S.A. [Amphibia & Reptilia of Louisiana (Yes)]

LING, Dr. Harry. Zoological Museum, Academy of Sciences, Vanemuise 21, Tartu, Estonian S.S.R., U.S.S.R. [Mammalia of Baltic (Yes)]

LINNAVUORI, Mr. R.   Turun linna, Åbo (Turku), Finland. [Homoptera: Auchenorrhyncha of Palearctic (Yes); Cicadellidae of Africa, Oceania, S. America (Yes)]

* LINSDALE, Donald D. 112 Agriculture Hall, University of California, Berkeley 4, Calif., U.S.A. [Diptera]

LINSDALE, Dr. Jean M. (Carmel Valley, Calif.; Mammalia) Not now active in taxonomy.

LINSENMAIER, W. Ebikon, Luzern, Switzerland. [Hymenoptera: Chrysididae of World (Yes)]

LINSLEY, Prof. E. Gorton. Department of Entomology & Parasitology, University of California, Berkeley 4, Calif., U.S.A. [Coleoptera: Cerambycidae of N. America (Yes); Hymenoptera: Apoidea of N. America (No)]

LINSLEY, Robert M. Department of Geology, Colgate University, Hamilton, N.Y., U.S.A. [Paleozoic (espec. Devonian) Gastropoda of N. America (Yes)]

LINTZ, Dr. Joseph, Jr. Mackay School of Mines, Reno, Nev., U.S.A. [Pennsylvanian marine invertebrates of Appalachian & Cordilleran Prov. (Yes)]

LIPOVSKY, Louis J. Department of Entomology, Walter Reed Army Institute of Research, Walter Reed Army Medical Center, Washington 12, D.C., U.S.A. [Acarina: Trombiculidae of World, larvae (No), nymphs & adults (Yes)]

* LIPS, M.A.H. B.P. 1190, Elisabethville, Belgian Congo. [Diptera]

* LISENKO, I.M. Laboratory of Invertebrate Zoology, University of Tartu, Tartu, Estonian S.S.R., U.S.S.R. [Invertebrates]

de LISLE, Mr. M.O. 29 Boulevard Raspail, Paris 7, France. [Coleoptera: Lucanidae & Cetoninae of World (Yes)]

LIST, Dr. James C. Department of Science, Ball State Teachers College, Muncie, Ind., U.S.A. [Amphibia & Reptilia of Kentucky, Illinois, Indiana (U.S.A.) (Yes)]

van LITH, J.P. Allard Piersonstraat 28 c, Rotterdam W, Netherlands. [Hymenoptera: Sphecidae: Pseninae of Palearctic & Indo-Australia (Yes); Apidae: g. Epeolus of Palearctic (No)]

* LITTLEFORD, Robert A. (College Park, Md., U.S.A.; Pisces, Amphibia, Reptilia) Not now active in taxonomy.

LITTLEJOHN, Murry J. Zoology Department, University of Melbourne, Carlton N 3, Vict., Australia. [Amphibia: Leptodactylidae of s.w. & s.e. Australia (Yes); Hylidae of s.w. & s.e. Australia (No)]

* LITTLEWOOD, Wm. H. Address unknown. [Amphibia & Reptilia]

* LIU, Ch'eng Chao. Yenching University, Peiping, People's Republic of China. [Amphibia]

LIU, H.T. Institute of Vertebrate Paleontology, Academia Sinica, P.O. Box 643, Peking, People's Republic of China. [Devonian-Tertiary Placodermi & Osteichthyes (Yes)]

* LIU, Dr. J.Y. Tsingtao Marine Biological Laboratory, Academia Sinica, 28 Laiyang Road, Tsingtao, People's Republic of China. [Crustacea: Decapoda]

LIVANOW, Prof. N. Department of Zoology, Kasan State University, Komleva 20, Kasan, U.S.S.R. [Turbellaria: Tricladida of U.S.S.R. (Yes); Polychaeta: Terebelloidea of Europe (No); Hirudinea of U.S.S.R. (No)]

LIVERSIDGE, R. Museum & Snake Park, Port Elizabeth, Union of South Africa. [Aves of s. Africa (Yes)]

LIVEZEY, Dr. Robert L. Division of Life Sciences, Sacramento State College, Sacramento 19, Calif., U.S.A. [Amphibia & Reptilia of N. America (Yes)]

* LIZER y TRELLES, Dr. Carlos. Gasper Campos 1683, Vicente López, Argentina. [Homoptera: Coccidae]

* LJUBIMOV, M.P. Gertsena Street 44-b, Moscow, U.S.S.R. [Helminths of animals of World]

LLABADOR, Dr. Francis. 1 Rue Gambetta, Nemours, Algeria. [Terr. & f-w. shelled Mollusca of n. w. Africa (Yes); Echinodermata of Oran cst. (No); Reptilia & Batrachia of Nemours (w. Algeria) (No)]

LLANO, Raúl Jorge. Casilla de Correos 198, Tandil FCNGR, Argentina. [Lepidoptera of Argentina (Yes)]

* LLANOS, Dr. Augusto C. Cordoba 2761, Olivos, Buenos Aires, Argentina. [Mammalia]

LLEWELLYN, Dr. J. Department of Zoology, The University, Edgbaston, Birmingham 15, England. [Trematoda: Monogenea of marine fishes (Yes)]

LLOYD, Dr. A. J. Department of Geology, University College, Gower Street, London, W. C. 1, England. [Up. Jurassic Foraminifera: rotaliform & arenaceous Lagenidae & Polymorphinidae of n. w. Europe (Yes); Permian Schwagerininae of n. Iraq (Yes)]

LOCHMAN-BALK, Christina. Box 1421, Socorro, N. M., U. S. A. [Cambrian Trilobita and other fossils of New World (Yes)] [New Mexico Institute of Mining & Technology]

LOCKET, Mr. G. H. Atner's Tower, Stockbridge, Hampshire, England. [Araneida of Britain (Yes)]

* LOEBLICH, Dr. Alfred R., Jr. California Research Corp., P. O. Box 446, LaHabra, Calif., U. S. A. [Fossil Foraminifera of World]

* LOEBLICH, Helen T. California Research Corp., P. O. Box 446, La Habra, Calif., U. S. A. [Fossil Foraminifera]

LOESCH, Harold C. Alabama Marine Laboratory, Bayou LaBatre, Ala., U. S. A. [Mollusca: oysters: g. Donax of Gulf of Mexico (Yes)]

LOEWEN, Prof. S. L. 517 South Lincoln Street, Hillsboro, Kans., U. S. A. [Cestoda: Cyclophyllidea: g. Oochoristica & Taenia (Yes); Trematoda: g. Phyllodistomum & Catoptroides (Yes)] [Tabor College]

LOFFLER, Dr. Heinz. Zoologisches Institut der Universität, 1 Dr. Karl Lueger-Ring 1, Wien I, Austria. [Crustacea: f-w. Ostracoda of World (No), of Eurasia (Yes); Entomostraca: Boeckellidae (Calanidae) of World (Yes); f-w. Harpacticoidea of World (Yes)]

* LOGAN, Lucile. Florida State Board of Health. Bureau of Entomology, P. O. Box 210, Jacksonville, Fla., U. S. A. [Diptera]

LOGIER, E. B. S., Associate Curator, Department of Ichthyology & Herpetology, Royal Ontario Museum of Zoology, 100 Queen's Park, Toronto 5, Canada. [Amphibia & Reptilia of Canada & Alaska (Yes)]

LOGINOVA-DUDYKINA, M. M. Zoological Institute, Academy of Sciences, Leningrad 164, U. S. S. R. [Homoptera: Psylloidea of U. S. S. R. & Europe (Yes)]

LOGVINENKO, V. N. Zoological Institute, Academy of Science of Ukrainian S. S. R., ul. Wladimirskaja 55, Kiev, U. S. S. R. [Homoptera: Cicadina of Palearctic (No); of European U. S. S. R. (Yes)]

LOHMANDER, Hans. Naturhistoriska Museet, Göteborg, Sweden. [Diplopoda of s. e. Europe, U. S. S. R., Scandinavia, Canaries, Madeira, Azores, Cape Verdes; Chilopoda, Pseudoscorpionida, Opiliones, terr. Mollusca, terr. Crustacea: Isopoda, of Scandinavia; Araneida: Gnaphosidae, Clubionidae, Thomisidae, Salticidae, Lycosidae, Hahniidae, of Scandinavia]

LÖHRL, Dr. Hans. Favoritepark 1, Ludwigsburg, Germany. [Aves: Sittidae of Europe, N. America, Asia (Yes); Muscicapini of Europe & Asia (No)] [Staatliche Vogelschutzwarte für Baden-Württemburg]

LOHSE, Dr. Gustav Adolf. Lehmweg 56, Hamburg 20, Germany. [Coleoptera of c. Europe (Yes); Staphylinidae: g. Lesteva, Tevales, Paralesteva, of Palearctic & Nearctic (Yes)] [Verein für Naturwissenschaftliche Heimatforschung zu Hamburg]

* LOIBL, H. Steinstrasse 15, Hamburg, Germany. [Lepidoptera]

LÖKEN, Astrid, Curator of Entomology, Zoological Museum, University of Bergen, Bergen, Norway. [Hymenoptera: Apidae & Vespidae of Palearctic (No); g. Bombus & Vespa of Scandinavia (Yes)]

LOKKE, Donald H. Pan American Petroleum Corporation, P. O. Box 591, Tulsa 2, Okla., U. S. A. [Fossil Foraminifera: Fusulinidae of N. America (Yes)]

LOKSA, Dr. Imre. Institutum Zoosystematicum Universitatis, Puskin-utca 3, Budapest VIII, Hungary. [Myriapoda of Palearctic & s. Asia (Yes); Araneida of Palearctic (No), of Africa & S. America (Yes)]

LOM, Dr. Jiri. Protozoologická laborator, Československá Akademie Ved, Vinična 7, Praha II, Czechoslovakia. [Parasitic Ciliata of c. Europe (Yes)]

LOMAKINA, N. B. Zoological Institute, Academy of Sciences, Leningrad-Centre, U. S. S. R. [Crustacea: Malacostraca: Mysidacea & Cumacea of Arctic, Antarctic, Pacific (Yes); Euphausiacea of World (Yes)]

LOMBARDINI, Giocondo. Via G. M. Cecchi 25, Florence, Italy. [Acarina: Parasitidae of Italy (Yes)]

LONA, Prof. Carlo. Museo Civico di Storia Naturale, 4 Piazza A. Hortis, Trieste, Italy. [Coleoptera: Curculionidae: g. Otiorrhynchus of Palearctic (Yes)]

LONG, Prof. James D. Department of Biology, Illinois College, Jacksonville, Ill., U. S. A. [Diptera: Culicidae of s. w. U. S. (Yes)]

LONGFIELD, Miss C. E. The Park House, Cloyne, County Cork, Ireland. [Odonata: Libelluli-
dae: g. Orthetrum of Africa (Yes)]
LONGHURST, Mr. Alan R. Fisheries Development & Research Unit, Freetown, Sierra Leone.
[Crustacea: Notostraca of World (Yes)]
LOOF, Mr. P. A. A. Plantenziektenkundige Dienst, Wageningen, Netherlands. [Free-living &
plant-parasitic Nematoda, excl. marine, of Europe (Yes)]
LOOKIN, E. See LUKIN, E. J.
LOOMIS, H. F. 5355 S. W. 92nd Street, Miami 56, Fla., U. S. A. [Diplopoda of N. America,
C. America, Colombia (Yes)]
LOOMIS, Dr. Richard B. Department of Biology, Long Beach State College, Long Beach 15,
Calif., U. S. A. [Acarina: Trombiculidae of N. America (Yes); Amphibia & Reptilia of
U. S. (Yes)]
LOOS, Clive. Chiriquie Land Corp., Almirante, Panama. [Free-living & plant-parasitic
Nematoda of tropics & sub-tropics (Yes)]
LOOSJES, Dr. F. E. Vossenlaan 4, Wageningen-Hoog, post Bennekom, Netherlands. [Gastro-
poda: Clausiliidae of World (Yes)]
LOPES, H. de Souza. Instituto Oswaldo Cruz, Caixa Postal 926, Rio de Janeiro, Brazil.
[Diptera: Sarcophagidae of World (Yes)]
LOPEZ, Miss M. T. Centro de Investigaciones Zoologicas, Universidad de Chile, Casilla
10135, Santiago, Chile. [F-w. Crustacea: Decapoda of Chile (Yes)]
* LÓPEZ, Rev. P. R. Escolasticado Teatinos, So'n Espanyolet, Palma, Majorca, Spain.
[Coleoptera]
LÓPEZ-NEYRA, Prof. Dr. C. R. Instituto Nacional de Parasitologia, Universidad de Granada,
Granada, Spain. [Helminths of World (Yes)]
LØPPENTHIN, Bernt. Universitetsbiblioteket, Nørre alle 49, København N., Denmark. [Aves
of Scandinavia (Yes), of Persia (No)]
LORANGER, Miss Diane M. 300 9th Avenue West, Calgary, Alta., Canada. [Ordovician-Cre-
taceous Ostracoda of w. Canada & n. w. Terr. (Yes); Paleozoic Foraminifera: Charophy-
ta of w. Canada] [Imperial Oil Ltd.]
LORDELLO, Dr. Luiz Gonzaga E. Escuela Superior de Agricultura Louis de Queiros, Univer-
sidade de São Paulo, Piracicaba, S. P., Brazil. [Plant parasitic & s oil Nematoda: Ty-
lenchoidea, Aphelenchoidea, Dorylaimoidea of São Paulo (Yes)]
LORKOVIĆ, Prof. Dr. Zdravka. Bioloski Institut, Zagreb, Salata, Yugoslavia. [Lepidoptera:
Rhopalocera of s. e. Europe (Yes); g. Leptidea, Everes, Erebia of tyndarus group, of
Palearctic (Yes)]
LOUGHREY, Alan G. Canadian Wildlife Service, Norlite Building, Ottawa, Ont., Canada.
[Mammalia: Canidae of Arctic & Subarctic N. America (No); Odobenidae of Arctic (Yes)]
LOUKASHKIN, Mr. Anatole S. 1210 23rd Avenue, San Francisco 22, Calif., U. S. A. [Aves of
n. e. Asia (Yes); Rodentia & Carnivora of Manchuria, Ussuriland, E. Mongolia, Trans-
baikalia (Yes)]
LOUWERENS, C. J. Neuweg 399, Hilversum, Netherlands. [Coleoptera: Carabidae of Oriental
(Yes)]
LOVEGROVE, Mr. T. Scottish Home Department, Marine Laboratory, Victoria Road, Torry,
Aberdeen, Scotland. [Crustacea: Cirripedia larvae & marine zooplankton of North Sea
(Yes)]
LOVERIDGE, Mr. A. (St. Helena Island, South Atlantic; Reptilia & Amphibia of E. Africa) Not
now active in taxonomy.
* LOWE, Charles H., Jr. Department of Zoology, University of Arizona, Tucson, Ariz.,
U. S. A. [Amphibia & Reptilia of N. America]
* LOWENSTAM, Mr. Heinz A. Division of Geological Sciences, California Institute of Tech-
nology, Pasadena, Calif., U. S. A. [Fossil invertebrates]
LOWERY, Rev. B. B. St. Ignatius College, Riverview, Sydney, N. S. W., Australia. [Hymen-
optera: Formicidae of Australia (Yes)]
LOWERY, Dr. George H., Jr. Museum of Zoology, Louisiana State University, Baton Rouge,
La., U. S. A. [Aves of N. & C. America (Yes)]
LOWNSBERY, Mr. B. F. Department of Plant Nematology, University of California, Davis,
Calif., U. S. A. [Nematoda: Tylenchida & plant parasitic Dorylaimoidea of World (No)]
LOWRIE, Dr. Donald C. Los Angeles State College, 855 North Vermont, Los Angeles 29,
Calif., U. S. A. [Araneida of w. N. America, Chicago, (Ill.), Pensacola (Fla.) (Yes)]
LOŽEK, Dr. Vojen. Central Institute of Geology, Hradebni 9, Praha I, Czechoslovakia.
[Quaternary-Recent nonmarine Gastropoda & Pelecypoda of c. Europe (Yes), of Neogene
(No)]
LUBINSKY, George. P. O. Box 90, Macdonald College, Que., Canada. [Ciliata: Ophryoscole-
cidae of World (Yes)]
LUC, Mr. M. Office de la Recherche Scientifique Outre-Mer, Boite postale 20, Abidjan, Cote
d'Ivoire, French West Africa. [Plant-parasitic Nematoda of tropics (Yes); free-living
marine Nematoda of Europe (No)]

LUCAS, J. A. W. Rijksmuseum van Natuurlijke Historie, Leiden, Netherlands. [Polychaeta of cst. of w. Europe (Yes); of w. Mediterranean (No)]
de LUCENA, Dr. Durval T. Rua Jader de Andrede 57, Poco, Recife, Pernambuco, Brazil. [Gastropoda: Planorbidae of Brazil (Yes); Diptera: Anophelini of Brazil (Yes); Hemiptera: Triatominae of Brazil (No)]
LUCKER, John T. Parasite Laboratory, Animal Disease & Parasite Research Division, Agricultural Research Center, Beltsville, Md., U. S. A. [Nematoda parasitic in vertebrates, espec. in ruminants, of N. America (Yes)]
LUCZAK, Jadwiga. Polska Akademia Nauk, ul. Nowy Świat 72, Warszawa, Poland. [Araneida, excl. Micryphantidae, of Poland (Yes)]
LUCZKOWSKA, E. Zakład Paleontologii, Akademia Gorniczo-Hutnicza, Al Mickiewicza 30, Krakow, Poland. [Miocene Foraminifera of Poland (Yes)]
LUDBROOK Dr. N. H. Department of Mines, Box 38, Rundle Street P. O., Adelaide, Australia. [Tertiary Mollusca of S. Australia (Yes); Mesozoic-Tertiary Foraminifera of S. Australia (No)]
* LUDFORD, A. 269 Luton Road, Harpenden, Herts, England. [Fossil invertebrates]
LUDVÍK, Dr. J. Laboratory for Electron Microscopy in Biology, Czechoslovak Academy of Sciences, Albertov 4, Praha 2, Czechoslovakia. [Parasitic Mastigophora & Sporozoa (Yes)]
* LUETHY, Don R. Florida Game & Fish Commission, Tallahassee, Fla., U. S. A. [Pisces]
LUGINBILL, Philip. (West Lafayette, Ind., U. S. A.; Insects) Deceased.
LUKASIAK, Dr. J. 10 Marszatkowska 34/50-1, Warszawa 10, Poland. [Diptera: Culicidae: Anophelini & Culicini of Poland (Yes); Nematoda of mammals of Poland (No)] [Parasitologia PZH]
LUKIN, Prof. Dr. E. I. Dom Specialists 65, Kharkov 22, U. S. S. R. [F-w. Hirudinea of Europe & n. Asia (Yes)]
* LÜLING, Dr. H. Institut für Küsten und Binnenfischerei, Neuer Wall 70/74, Hamburg 36, Germany. [Nematoda & Crustacea: Copepoda]
* LÜLING, Dr. K. H. Ichthyology Department, Zoologisches Forschungsinstitut und Museum Alexander Koenig, Koblenzerstrasse 150-164, Bonn, Germany. See Addenda.
LULL, Richard S. (New Haven, Conn., U. S. A.; fossils) Died April 22, 1957.
LUMSDEN, Mr. H. G. Ontario Department of Lands & Forests, Maple, Ont., Canada. [Aves: Anatidae of World (Yes)]
LUMSDEN, Prof. William. Physical Science Department, Long Beach State College, Long Beach 11, Calif., U. S. A. [Up. Tertiary Ostracoda of S. Calif. (No); Up. Tertiary Pelecypoda & Gastropoda of S. Calif. (No)]
LUMSDEN, Dr. W. H. R. East African Trypanosomiasis Research Organization, Box 96, Tororo, Uganda. [Diptera: Culicidae of e. Africa (No); Mammalia: Primates of e. Africa (No)]
LUNA de CARVALHO, Eduardo A. Museo do Dundo, Dundo, Lunda, Angola. [Coleoptera: Paussidae of World (Yes); Strepsiptera of World (Yes)]
LUNDBLAD, Prof. Dr. C. O. Naturhistoriska Riksmuseum, Entomologiska Avdelningen, Stockholm 50, Sweden. [Acarina: Hydrachnellae of World (Yes)]
LUNDELIUS, Dr. Ernest. Department of Geology, University of Texas, Austin, Texas, U. S. A. [Pleistocene Mammalia of w. Australia & Texas (Yes)]
* LUNDHOLM, Dr. B. G. Mammalogist, Transvaal Museum, P. O. Box 413, Pretoria, Union of South Africa. [Mammalia]
LUNDQVIST, Dr. Arne. Genetiska Institutionen, Lunds Universitet, Lund, Sweden. [Diptera: Agromyzidae of Scandinavia (No)]
LUNK, Dr. William A. Museum of Zoology, University of Michigan, Ann Arbor, Mich., U. S. A. [Aves: Paridae: g. Parus of N. America (Yes); Hirundinidae of New World (No); fossil birds of World (No)]
* LUNZ, G. Robert. Bears Bluff Laboratories, Wadmalaw Island, S. C., U. S. A. [Crustacea: Decapoda & Stomatopoda of s. e. U. S.; Pelecypoda: oysters of s. e. U. S.]
* LUPASCU, Gheorghe. Department d'Entomologie, Institutul Dr. I. Cantacuzino, Splaiul Independentei Nr. 108, Bucureşti 35, Rumania. [Diptera]
LUPO, Prof. Dr. V. Istituto d'Entomologia Agraria, Università di Catania, via Valdisavoia 5, Catania, Italy. [Homoptera: Coccidae: Diaspinae of Mediterranean (Yes)]
LUPU, D. Muzeul National de Istorie Naturala "Grigore Antipa", Kiselev No. 1, Bucuresti III, Rumania. [Mollusca: Limacidae of Rumania (Yes)]
LUTHER, Prof. Alexander. Djurgårdsvillan 8, Helsinki, Finland. [Turbellaria: Rhabdocoelida of World & Tricladida paludicolá of n. Europe (No)] [Zoological Institute]
* LUTTERMOSER, Dr. George W. Laboratory of Tropical Disease, National Institutes of Health, Bethesda 14, Md., U. S. A. [Trematoda, Cestoda]
LÜTTIG, Dr. Gerd. Amt für Bodenforschung, Wiesenstrasse 1, Hannover, Germany. [Quaternary-Recent non-marine Ostracoda of c. Europe (Yes); Gastropoda: Valvatinae of c. Europe (No)]
LÜTTSCHWAGER, Dr. J. Zoologisches Institut der Universität Heidelberg, Sophienstrasse 6, Heidelberg, Germany. [Bones of birds & mammals of Europe (Yes)]

LUTZ, Dr. Bertha. Museu Nacional, Quinta da Boa Vista, Rio de Janeiro, Brazil. [Amphibia: Salientia of S. America (Yes)]
LUTZ, John C. 6623 Landsdowne Avenue, Philadelphia 31, Penna., U.S.A. [Heteroptera, excl. Miridae & Anthocoridae, of New World, Asia, Africa, Australia (Yes)]
* LUX, Miss E. Address unknown. [Orthoptera]
* LYAIMAN, Dr. E.M. Moscow Fish Institute, Pryanishnikova Street 2-a, Moscow, U.S.S.R. [Helminths of fishes of World]
LYMAN, Dr. Charles P. Museum of Comparative Zoology, Cambridge 38, Mass., U.S.A. [Mammalia: Rodentia: g.Synaptomys of N. America (Yes)]
* LYMAN, F. Earle. Address unknown. [Ephemerida & Diptera]
* LYNCH, Ing. Alberto. Escuela Experimental Agricola Molina, Casilla 2791, Lima, Peru. [Nematoda]
LYNCH, D.D. Fisheries Game Department, 605 Flinders Street, Melbourne, Vict., Australia. [Pisces: Platycephalidae & Sillaginidae of Australia (Yes)]
LYNCH, Prof. James E. College of Fisheries, University of Washington, Seattle 5, Wash., U.S.A. [Crustacea: Anostraca & Notostraca of N. America (Yes)]
LYNEBORG, Leif. Statens Skadedyrlaboratorium, Strandvejen 740, Springforbi, Denmark. [Diptera: Brachycera of n. & w.Europe (Yes); Tabanidae of Palearctic (Yes)]
LYNN, Prof. W.Gardner. Department of Biology, The Catholic University of America, Washington 17, D.C., U.S.A. [Amphibia of West Indies (Yes)]
LYNSDALE, Prof. Jean. Department of Zoology, University of Rangoon, Rangoon, Burma. [Cestoda of Burma (Yes)]
LYON, Robert. Department of Biology, Los Angeles City College, 855 North Vermont Avenue, Los Angeles, Calif., U.S.A. [Hymenoptera: Cynipidae of Pacific U.S. (Yes)]
LYONS, Richard B. 5850 S.W. Terwilliger Boulevard, Portland 1, Ore., U.S.A. [Mollusca: Polyplacophora of Oregon (Yes); Mopaliidae of w.cst. of N. America (Yes)]
LYS, Mr. M. 4 Place Bir Hakeim Rucil. Malmaison, Seine et Oise, France. [Paleozoic & Cretaceous-Paleocene Foraminifera (No); Paleozoic Conodonts (No)] [Institut Français du Petrole]
LYTLE, Mr. Charles F. Dept. of Zoology, Tulane University, New Orleans 18, La., U.S.A. [Hydrozoa: Olindiidae of World (Yes)]

* MA, Prof. Ting Ying H. Department of Geology, College of Science, National Taiwan University, Taipei, Taiwan, Formosa. [Fossil invertebrates]
MAA, Prof. Tsing-chao. 32 Nanking Road East, Taipeh, Taiwan, Formosa. [Hymenoptera: Siricoidea, Cephoidea, g.Apis, of World (Yes); g.Xylocopa of Oriental & Australian (Yes); Hemiptera: Phymatidae, Machaerotinae, Urostylidae, of Old World (Yes)]
* MAAR, Dr. A. Henderson Research Station, P.O.Box 4, Mazoë, Southern Rhodesia. [Pisces]
MABBOTT, T.W. Department of Agriculture for Scotland, Scientific Services, East Craigs, Corstorphine, Edinburgh 12, Scotland. [Plant-parasitic Nematoda of Britain (Yes)]
MACALESTER, A.L. See McALESTER, A.L.
MacALPIN, Archie J. Department of Geology, University of Notre Dame, Notre Dame, Ind., U.S.A. [Fossil vertebrates, espec. fishes, of U.S. (Yes)]
MACAN, Dr. T.T. Freshwater Biological Association, Ferry House, Ambleside, Westmoreland, England. [Ephemeroptera nymphs of w.Europe (Yes)]
MacARTHUR, K.W. Department of Invertebrate Zoology, Milwaukee Public Museum, Milwaukee 3, Wis., U.S.A. [Diptera: Hippoboscidae of N. America (Yes)]
MACCAGNO, Dr. A.M. Istituto di Geologia, Universitá di Roma, Roma, Italy. [Quaternary vertebrates of c. Italy & Mediterranean (No); Mesozoic-Tertiary Echinoidea of Italy & E. Africa (No); Mesozoic-Tertiary microfossils of c. Italy (No)]
* MACCAGNO, Dr. T. Paulucci. Istituto di Zoologia della Universitá, Torino, Italy. [Crustacea: Decapoda]
* MacCORMICK, James R. 57 Aylesbury Road, Walworth, London, S.E. 17, England. [Mollusca]
MacDONAGH, Dr. E.J. Calle 15, No. 1163, La Plata, Argentina. [Pisces: Teleostei of Argentina (Yes); Aves, excl. Passeres (Yes)] [Universidad Católica Argentina]
MACDONALD, Dr. J.R. Box 52, Buhl, Idaho, U.S.A. [Mammalia: Miocene & Pliocene Camelidae (Yes); Pliocene Carnivora (Yes); Oligocene & Miocene Bunodont Artiodactyla (Yes)]
MACDONALD, Mr. J.D. In charge of Bird Section, British Museum (Natural History), Cromwell Road, London, S.W.7, England. [Aves of World (Yes)]
MacDONALD, W.W. Institute for Medical Research, Kuala Lumpur, Malaya. [Diptera: Culicidae of s.e.Asia (Yes)]
MACEK, J. Na Moráni 6, Praha II, Czechoslovakia. [Hymenoptera: Ichneumonidae of World (No); Heteroptera: Cydnidae of World (No)]
MACFADYEN, Mr. A. Department of Zoology, University College of Swansea, Singleton Park, Swansea, Glamorganshire, Great Britain. [F-l. Acarina, espec. soil, of n.Europe & Arctic (Yes)]

MACFADYEN, Mrs. L. M. I. (London, England; Coelenterata) Not now active in taxonomy.
MACFADYEN, Dr. W. A. Hope's Grove, Tenterden, Kent, England. [Jurassic & Pleistocene-Holocene Foraminifera of Britain]
* MacFARLAND, Mrs. Olive H. 775 Santa Ynez Street, Stanford, Calif., U. S. A. [Mollusca]
MACFARLANE, D. Commonwealth Institute of Entomology, British Museum (Natural History), Cromwell Road, London, S. W. 7, England. [Acarina, excl. Ixodidae, of Old World]
*MacFARQUHAR, Wm. K. Sinclair Oil & Refining Co., Apartado 1706, Santa Barbara Camp, Caracas, D. F., Venezuela. [Fossil invertebrates]
Mac GILLAVRY, Prof. Dr. H. J. Geologisch Instituut, Nieuwe Prinsengracht 130, Amsterdam, Netherlands. [Cretaceous Pelecypoda: Rudistae (Yes); Cretaceous-Tertiary larger Foraminifera (Yes)]
MacGILLIVRAY, Mrs. M. E. Field Crop Insect Laboratory, P. O. Box 248, Fredericton, N. B. Canada. [Aphidae of Canada (Yes)]
MacGINITIE, Mrs. Nettie. Kerkhoff Marine Laboratory, 101 Dahlia Street, Corona Del Mar, Calif., U. S. A. [Marine Mollusca of Arctic Alaska (Yes)]
MACHADO, Mr. A. de Barros. Laboratório de Biologia, Museu do Dundo, Lunda, Angola. [Diptera: g. Glossina of Africa (Yes); Culicinae of Ethiopian (No); Isoptera: g. Apicoter-mes of Africa (Yes); Araneae apneumonae (No)]
MACHADO, Dr. Angelo Barbosa M. Avenida Olegario Maciel 2323, Apartamento 202, Belo Horizonte, Minas Gerais, Brazil. [Odonata & Trichoptera: Helicopsychidae of Neo-tropics (Yes)]
* MACHADO, Joaquim Pinheiro, Filho. Departmento de Entomologia, Museo Nacional, Quinta da Boa Vista, Rio de Janeiro, Brazil. [Orthoptera]
MACHATSCHKE, Prof. Dr. Johann W. Deutsches Entomologisches Institut, Waldowstrasse 1, Berlin-Friedrichshagen, German Democratic Republic. [Coleoptera: Clytrinae & Cryp-tocephalinae of Palearctic (Yes); Rutelinae of World (Yes)]
* MACHIN, J. Queen Mary College, Mile End Road, London, E. 1, England. [Mollusca]
* MACHON, Rogelio P. Address unknown. [Mollusca]
MacINNES, Dr. D. G. Triangle Cottage, Old Boars Hill, Oxford, England. [Miocene Mammalia of Africa (Yes)]
MacINTOSH, G. Department of Agricultural Zoology, North of Scotland College of Agriculture, Marischal College, Aberdeen, Scotland. [Nematoda: g. Heterodera (No)]
MacINTYRE, Mr. J. Division of Fisheries & Oceanography, Commonwealth Scientific & In-dustrial Research Organization, Box 21, Cronulla, N. S. W., Australia. [Crustacea: Amphipoda: littoral Talitridae of New Zealand; g. Gammarus of Arctic & Subarctic; marine bottom invertebrates of New South Wales (all No)]
MACK, G. Queensland Museum, Brisbane, Australia. [Vertebrates of Australia, espec. Aves, Mammalia, Reptilia (Yes)]
MACKAUER, Dr. Manfred. Zoologisches Institut der Universität, Siesmayerstrasse 70, Frank-furt am Main, Germany. [Hymenoptera: Braconidae: Aphidiinae of World (Yes); Cole-optera: S carabaeidae: Laparostictae of Europe (Yes); Melolonthinae of Europe (No)]
MacKAY, Miss M. R. Systematic Entomology, Science Service Building, Ottawa, Ont., Canada. [Lepidoptera larvae of N. America (Yes)] [Canadian Department of Agriculture]
MACKAY, Mr. Roy D. Australian Museum, College Street, Sydney, Australia. [Amphibia & Reptilia, espec. Elapidae, of New Guinea & Australia, espec. New South Wales & Queensland (Yes)]
MacKAY, Mr. R. H. Canadian Wildlife Service, Department of Zoology, University of British Columbia, Vancouver, B. C., Canada. [Aves: Anatidae of N. America (Yes)]
MACKE, William Bernard. 1325 Avenue F, Billings, Mont., U. S. A. [Mississippian micro-fossils of Williston Basin, U. S. (Yes)]
MACKEN, Judith. (Mrs. J. W. Dawson) Dominion Museum, Wellington, New Zealand. [Bryo-zoa of Australia, New Zealand, Pacific (Yes)]
MacKENSIE, G. P. (San Marino, Calif.; Coleoptera) Died November 3, 1958.
MACKENTHUN, Kenneth M., Public Health Biologist, Wisconsin State Board of Health, 453 State Office Building, Madison 2, Wis., U. S. A. [Aquatic invertebrates, espec. Trichop-tera, of Wisconsin (Yes)]
MACKERETH, Mrs. Jean C. (Westmoreland, England, Trichoptera) Not now active in taxo-nomy.
MACKERRAS, Dr. I. M., Director, Queensland Institute of Medical Research, Herston Road, Herston N. 9, Queensland, Australia. [Diptera: Simuliidae & Tabanidae of Australasian & Pacific (Yes)]
MACKERRAS, Dr. M. Josephine. Queensland Institute of Medical Research, Herston Road, Herston N. 9, Queensland, Australia. [Diptera: Simuliidae of e. Australia (Yes)]
MACKIN, Dr. J. G. Department of Biology, Agricultural & Mechanical College of Texas, College Station, Texas, U. S. A. [Crustacea: Isopoda: Asellidae & Anostraca of U. S. & Canada (Yes); Protozoa parasitic on oysters of World (Yes)]
* MACKOD, Dr. J. Field Research Laboratory, Blackford, Carlisle, Cumberland, England. [Diptera]

MACKWORTH-PRAED, C. W. Castletop, Burley, Ringord, Hants, England. [Aves of Africa (Yes)] [British Museum (Natural History)]

MacLEOD, Ellis G. 209 Howe Drive, Olney, 'Md., U.S.A. [Mecoptera, Rhaphidioidea, Lepidoptera: Papilionoidea, of Nearctic (Yes); Neuroptera: larvae & adults of Nearctic (Yes); Megaloptera of World (Yes)] [University of Maryland]

MacMAHON, Mr. James A. Dayton Museum of Natural History, Dayton 2, Ohio, U.S.A. [Amphibia & Reptilia of N. America (Yes); Chelonia: g. Clemmys of N. America (Yes)]

MacMICHAEL, Don. See McMICHAEL, D. F.

MacMILLAN, Gordon K. 169 Glenfield Drive, Pittsburgh 35, Penna., U.S.A. [Mollusca: terr. Pulmonata, espec. g. Anguispira & Discus, of e. N. America (No)]

MACMILLIAN, R. P. See McMillan, R. P.

MACNAB, Dr. James A. Biology Department, Portland State College, 1620 S.W. Park Ave., Portland, Ore., U.S.A. [Oligochaeta: Megascolescidae of Pacific cst. U.S. (Yes)]

MACNAE, W. Department of Zoology, University of the Witwatersrand, Wilner Park, Johannesburg, Union of South Africa. [Crustacea: Amphipoda & Decapoda of Indo-West Pacific (Yes); Gastropoda: Nudibranchiata, Saccoglossa, Aplysiacea of Indo-West Pacific (Yes)]

MacNEIL, Mr. F. Stearns. U.S. Geological Survey, Menlo Park, Calif., U.S.A. [Tertiary Gastropoda & Pelecypoda of U.S. Atlantic & Gulf Coastal Plains, Pacific Ocean (No) Alaska (Yes)]

Mac NEILL, C. Don, Assistant Curator, Department of Entomology, California Academy of Sciences, San Francisco 18, Calif., U.S.A. [Lepidoptera: Hesperiidae of Europe, Asia, Australia (No); of New World (Yes)]

MacNEILL, Col. Niall. Ordnance Survey, Phoenix Park, Dublin, Ireland. [Odonata of Ireland (Yes)]

* MACOMBER, Donald. 110 Athania Place, Metairie, La., U.S.A. [Fossil invertebrates]

MACPHERSON, Mr. Andrew. 535 Percy Street, Ottawa, Ont., Canada. [Aves: g. Larus of Arctic N. America (Yes)]

MACPHERSON, Miss J. Hompe, Curator of Molluscs, National Museum of Victoria, Melbourne, Australia. [Marine Mollusca of Australia (Yes); Patellidae & Acmaeidae of Indo-Pacific (Yes)]

* MACQUART, M. Address unknown. [Crustacea]

MACQUEEN, Mr. J. "Amaroo", Via Milmerran, Queensland, Australia. [Lepidoptera: Rhopalocera of Australia (Yes); Coleoptera: Buprestidae of Australia (No)]

MacSWAIN, Dr. J. W. Department of Entomology, University of California, Berkeley 4, Calif., U.S.A. [Coleoptera: larvae of Meloidae of N. America (Yes)]

MACY, Prof. Ralph W. Department of Biology, Portland State College, 1620 S.W. Park Ave., Portland 1, Ore., U.S.A. [Lepidoptera: Rhopalocera of World, espec. U.S.A.; helminths, espec. Trematoda, of World, espec. U.S.A.]

MADAR, Doc. Dr. Jindřich. Žateckých 14, Praha XIV, Czechoslovakia. [Coleoptera: Chrysomelidae: Halticinae of World (No), of Palearctic (Yes)]

* MADDOCK, D. R. 450 Cross Street, Ogden, Utah, U.S.A. [Diptera: Empididae & Ephydridae]

MADER, Leopold. (Wien, Austria; Coleoptera) Not now active in taxonomy.

* MADGE, Dr. E. H. 43 Hornsey Lane Gardens, London, N.6, England. [Terr. Mollusca of Mauritius, Reunion, Rodriguez, Chagos Arch. (Yes)]

MADGE, R. Department of Entomology, University of Alberta, Edmonton, Alberta, Canada. [Coleoptera: Silphidae: g. Necrophorus of World (Yes); Carabidae; g. Lebia of N. America (Yes)]

MADRIGAL, Rodrigo Brenes. Laboratorio de Parasitologia, Escuela de Microbiologia, Universidad de Costa Rica, San José, Costa Rica. [Trematoda, Cestoda, Nematoda of C. America (Yes)]

MADSEN, Dr. F. Jensenius. Universitetets Zoologiske Museum, København, Denmark. [Anthozoa: Octocorallia of N. Atlantic (No); Echinodermata of deep sea (Yes); Asteroidea of all oceans (Yes)]

MADSEN, Dr. Holger. Jagtfondens Vildtbiologiske Undersøgelser, Nörregade 10, København, Denmark. [Parasitic Nematoda of birds (Yes)]

MAGALHAES, Dr. Hulda. Box 496, Bucknell University, Lewisburg, Pa., U.S.A. [Mammalia: Rodentia: g. Mesocricetus of laboratories (Yes); Gastropoda: g. Busycon of Atlantic Cst. of U.S. (Yes)]

de MAGALHAES, Mr. Luiz Edmundo. Departamento de Biologia Geral, Universidade de São Paulo, Caixa Postal 8105, São Paulo, Brazil. [Diptera: g. Drosophila of S. America (Yes)]

MAGGENTI, Armand R. 231 Soils & Plant Nutrition, University of California, Davis, Calif., U.S.A. [Nematoda: Plectidae: g. Plectus of N. America & Europe (Yes)]

MAGIS, Dr. Noel. 13 Blvd. Saucy, Liège, Belgium. [Coleoptera: Drilidae, Lycidae, Lampyridae, Cantharidae, of Palearctic (Yes); Cantharidae of Ethiopian & Madagascar (Yes)]

MAGISTRETTI, Dr. Mario. Via Tonale 9, Milano, Italy. [Coleoptera: Carabidae, Oedermeridae, Meloidae, of Europe & Mediterranean basin (Yes)]

MAGNANO, Luigi. Piazzetta Scala 4, Verona, Italy. [Coleoptera: Curculionidae of Palearctic (No); of Mediterranean (Yes)]

MAGNÉ, M. Jean. C/o S.N. Repal, Boite Postale 105, Alger, Algeria. [Fossil & Recent smaller Foraminifera, planctonic forms, of w. Mediterranean (Yes); Tertiary smaller Foraminifera of n. Africa (Yes)]

* MAHADEVA, N. Address unknown. [Pisces: Cynoglossidae]

MAHAN, Man. Section of Entomology, Department of Zoology, Aligarh University, Aligarh, India. [Hymenoptera: Chalcidoidea: Encyrtidae, Aphelinidae, Pteromalidae, Tetrastichidae, all of India, Pakistan, Burma, Ceylon (Yes)]

* MAHDIHASSAN, Dr. S. Department of Biochemistry, Cipla Laboratories, 289 Bellasis Road, Bombay 8, India. [Homoptera: Coccidae]

MAHENDRA, Prof. B.C. Department of Zoology, Agra College, Agra, India. [Fishes, lizards, snakes, of India, Ceylon, Burma, Pakistan (Yes)]

MAHLER, Friedrich. (Salzburg, Austria; Gastropoda) Deceased.

MAHON, Dr. June. Department of Zoology, Bedford College, Regent's Park, London, N.W.1, England. [Cestoda: Cyclophyllidea of World (Yes)] [University of London]

MAHON, Mr. J.A. Western Australian Regional Laboratory, Commonwealth Scientific & Industrial Research Organization, University Grounds, Nedlands, W. Australia. [Acarina: Bdellidae & Penthaleidae of s.w. Australia (Yes); Collembola of s.w. Australia (No)]

MAHONY, Mr. J.A. Department of Geology & Geophysics, University of Sydney, Sydney, N.S.W., Australia. [Quaternary-Recent Rodentia: Murinae of Australia (Yes); Quaternary-Recent Marsupialia: Dasyuridae of Australia (Yes)]

MAI, Prof. W.F. Department of Plant Pathology, Cornell University, Ithaca, N.Y., U.S.A. [Plant pathogenic & soil Nematoda: Tylenchida, Dorylaimina, Rhabditina, Enoplina, of New World (Yes)]

* MAIELLO, Daniel G. Department of Zoology, University of Rhode Island, Kingston, R.I., U.S.A. [Acarina]

MAILLET, P., Maitre de Conferences, Laboratoire de Biologie Animale, P.C.B., Faculté des Sciences, Rennes (IV), France. [Homoptera: Jassidae of France (Yes)]

MAILLOT, L. Institut d'Etudes Centrafricaines, B.P. 181, Brazzaville, French Equatorial Africa. [Diptera: g. Glossina of Africa (Yes)].

* MAIN, Mr. A.R. Zoology Department, University of Western Australia, Nedlands, Australia. [Amphibia & Reptilia]

MAIN, Dr. Barbara York. Department of Zoology, University of Western Australia, Nedlands, W. Australia. [Arachnida: Mygalomorphae & Scorpionida: Buthidae of Australia (Yes)]

MAINA, Mr. Barth A. 2245 West Jackson Boulevard, Chicago 12, Ill., U.S.A. [Hymenoptera: Apidae: Bombini of World (Yes)] [Chicago City Junior College]

MAKATSCH, Dr. Wolfgang. Martin Hoop Strasse 31, Bautzen (Oberlausitz), Germany. [Bird eggs of World (Yes)]

* MAKINO, Prof. Sajiro. Institute of Zoology, Hokkaido University, Sapporo, Japan. [Diptera]

MAKIYAMA, Dr. J. Geological Institute, Kyoto University, Kyoto, Japan. [Tertiary Mollusca of Japan (Yes); Tertiary & Pleistocene Mammalia: Proboscidea of Asia (Yes)]

* MAKOWSKI, H. Zakład Geologii Historycznej, Obozna 8, Warszawa, Poland. [Fossil Bryozoa]

* MAKRIDIN, V.P. Department of Geology, Kharkov State University, Kharkov, U.S.S.R. [Fossil Brachiopoda]

MAKUSHOK, V.M. Institute of Oceanology, Academy of Sciences, Moscow 127, U.S.S.R. [Pisces: Stichaeoidae of N. Pacific & N. Atlantic (Yes); Macruridae of "All three oceans" (Yes)]

MALAISE, Dr. René E. Naturhistoriska Riksmuseet, Stockholm 50, Sweden. [Hymenoptera: Tenthredinidae of Asia & Neotropics (Yes)] [Swedish Museum of Natural History]

MALATESTA, Dr. A. Servizio Geologico d'Italia, Largo Santa Susanna 13, Roma, Italy. [Miocene-Recent marine Mollusca: Conchifera of Mediterranean (Yes)]

MALBRANT, Dr. René. 31 Rue Vineuse, Paris (XVI), France. [Aves & Mammalia of French Equatorial Africa (Yes)] [Museum National d'Histoire Naturelle]

MALCOLM, Dr. David R. Biology Department, Portland State College, 1620 S.W. Park Avenue, Portland 1, Ore., U.S.A. [Acarina: Tetranychidae of w. U.S. (No); Chelonethida of N. America (Yes)]

MALDONADO-CAPRILES, Dr. J. College of Agriculture, Mayaguez, Puerto Rico. [Homoptera: Cicadellidae: Idiocerinae of World (Yes); Heteroptera: Reduviidae of Neotropics (Yes)]

* MALDONADO-KOERDELL, Dr. Manuel. Culiacán 74, Mexico 11, D.F., Mexico. [Amphibia: Caudata of Mexico; Quaternary Mammalia of Mexico; Permo-Triassic Amphibia of Mexico]

MALECKI, J. Zaklad Paleontologii, Akademia Gorniczo-Hutnicza, Al. Mickiewicza 30, Krakow, Poland. [Tertiary Bryozoa of Poland (Yes)]

MALEEV, Dr. E.A. Paleontological Museum, Academy of Sciences of U.S.S.R., Leninsky Prospect 16, Moscow B-71, U.S.S.R. [Mesozoic Dinosauria of Asia (Yes)]

MALEK, E. T. Abdel. University of Khartoum, P. O. Box 32, Khartoum North, Sudan. [Gastropoda: Planorbidae of Africa (Yes)]
* MALEVICH, Y. J. Gr. Bzonnaja 7, fl. 3, Moscow K-104, U. S. S. R. [Annelida]
MALEZ, Dr. Mirko. Geološko-paleontološka zbirka, Jugoslavenška Akademija, Demetrova 18/II. kat., Zagreb, Yugoslavia. [Fossil Vertebrates of Balkan Pen. (Yes)]
MALICOAT, Arthur F. 3921 Cut-Off Road, New Orleans 14, La., U. S. A. [Fossil Invertebrates, Oligocene-Recent (No)]
* MALJKOVSKIJ, M. P. Ul. 8 Marta 65, Alma-Ata 2, Kazakh S. S. R. [Orthoptera]
MALKIN, Borys. Department of Anthropology, University of Minnesota, Minneapolis 14, Minn., U. S. A. [Coleoptera of n. w. U. S. & w. Canada; Coccinellidae of N. & C. America (Yes)]
MALLIS, Mr. Arnold. P. O. Drawer 2038, Pittsburgh 30, Penna., U. S. A. [Hymenoptera: Formicidae of California (No); household insects of U. S. (Yes)] [Gulf Research & Development Company]
MALLOCH, J. R. (Tampa, Fla.; Diptera) Not now active in taxonomy.
* MALLORY, Mr. Jack. Department of Biology, University of Alabama, University, Ala., U. S. A. [Pisces]
MALLORY, Prof. V. S. Department of Geology, University of Washington, Seattle 5, Wash., U. S. A. [L. Tertiary smaller Foraminifera of w. cst. N. America (Yes); L. Tertiary Orbitoidea of w. cst. N. America (No)]
MALMBERG, G. Zootomiska Institutet, Radmansgatan 70A, Stockholm Va, Sweden. [Trematoda: Gyrodactylidae of World (No); of Holarctic, espec. Scandinavia (Yes)]
MALNATE, Mr. Edmond V. West Lake Road, Lake Pine, Marlton, N. J., U. S. A. [Amphibia & Reptilia, espec. g. Natrix, of e. Asia (Yes)] [Academy of Natural Sciences of Philadelphia]
MALSKI, Krzysztof. Instytut Zoologiczny, Polska Akademia Nauk, ul. Sławkowska 17, Krakow, Poland. [Diptera: Syrphidae of Palearctic (No); g. Chilosia (Yes)]
MALZ, Dr. H. Forschungs-Institut & Natur Museum Senckenberg, Senckenberg Anlage 25, Frankfurt am Main, Germany. [Jurassic Crustacea: Ostracoda of Europe (Yes); of N. America (No)]
MAMET, Mr. J. R. Dr. Roux Street, Rose Hill, Mauritius. [Homoptera: Coccoidea of Madagascar, Mascarenes, w. Indian Oc. islands (Yes); Conchaspididae of World (Yes)]
MAMONTOVA-SOLUCHA, Mrs. V. A. Institute of Zoology, Academy of Science of Ukrainian SSR, Kiev, U. S. S. R. [Homoptera: Aphidoidea of Palearctic (No); European U. S. S. R. (Yes)]
* MAMMEN, Dr. T. A. Department of Zoology, University of Travancore, Trivandrum, Madras, India. [Coelenterata]
* MANACAS, Sara. Centro Zoologia, Rua da Junqueira 14, Lisboa, Portugal. [Reptilia]
* MANCINI, Dr. Cesare. Museo Civico di Storia Naturale, Via Brigata Liguria 9, Genova, Italy. [Hemiptera: Auchenorrhyncha]
MANDAHL-BARTH, Dr. Georg. Danmarks Akvarium, Charlottenlund, Denmark. [Terr. & f-w. Mollusca of n. Europe (Yes); f-w. Mollusca of Africa, espec. E. Africa (Yes)]
MANDL, Prof. Dipl. Ing. Dr. Karl. Weissgerberlande 26/13, Wien III, Austria. [Coleoptera: Cicindelidae of World (Yes); Carabidae: g. Carabus, Calosoma, Cychrus of World (Yes)]
MĂNDRU, Dr. Constantin. Muzeul de Istorie Naturală, Strada Gh. Dimitrov Nr. 72, Iaşi (Jassy), Rumania. [Orthoptera of Rumania (Yes)]
MAÑÉ-GARZÓN, Fernando. Museo de Historia Natural, Casilla de Correo 399, Montevideo, Uruguay. [Crustacea: Tanaidacea & Isopoda; Arachnida: Pycnogonida]
MANFREDI, Dr. P., Vice Direttore, Museo Civico di Storia Naturale, Corso Venezia 55, Milano, Italy. [Diplopoda & Chilopoda of Palearctic (No)]
* MANFRINI, Miss M. Department of Zoology, Instituto Miguel Lillo, Calle Miguel Lillo 205, Tucumán, Argentina. [Coleoptera]
*. MANGABEIRA, Dr. Octavio, Filho. Instituto Oswaldo Cruz, Caixa Postal 926, Rio de Janeiro, Brazil. [Diptera]
MANGIN, Dr. Jean Philippe. Laboratoire de Geologie, Boulevard Gabriel, Dijon (Côte d'Or), France. [Paleogene & Neogene Foraminifera (Yes)]
* MANI, Mr. M. S. Zoological Survey of India, 34 Chittaranjan Avenue, Calcutta 12, India. [Diptera]
MANKAU, Dr. Reinhold. Department of Plant Nematology, University of California, Riverside, Calif., U. S. A. [Nematoda: Tylenchoidea of s. w. U. S. & India (Yes); Dorylaimoidea of s. California (Yes)]
* MANKAU, Mrs. Sarojam K. Department of Nematology, Riverside Experiment Station, Riverside, Calif., U. S. A. [Cestoda]
* MAŃKOWSKI, Dr. Władyslaw. Morski Instytut Rybacki, Al. Zjednoczenia 1, Gdynia, Poland. [Larvae of fishes]
MANN, Guillermo. Ladislao Errázuriz 2157, Santiago, Chile. [Mammals of Chile (Yes)] [Centro de Investigaciones Zoológicas]

MANN, Dr. K.H. Department of Zoology, The University, Reading, England. [Hirudinea of Europe (Yes); of N. America (Yes)]
MANNHEIMS, Dr. B. Zoologisches Forschungsinstitut und Museum A. Koenig, Koblenzer-strasse 150, Bonn, Germany. [Diptera: Tipulidae of Palearctic & African (Yes); Blepharoceridae of World (Yes)]
MANNING, Raymond B. The Marine Laboratory, University of Miami, Virginia Key, Miami 49, Fla., U.S.A. [Crustacea: Stomatopoda of w. Atlantic (Yes)]
MANNING, Mr. T.H. 37 Linden Terrace, Ottawa 1, Ont., Canada. [Mammalia: g. Dicrostonyx, Clethrionomys, Lepus, of Arctic Canada (Yes)]
MANOLACHE, Prof. Dr. Constantin. Institutul de Cercetări Agronomice, Bul. Mărăşti 61, Bucureşti, Rumania. [Homoptera: Aphididae, Psyllidae, Aleurodidae, of Europe (Yes)]
* MANOLACHE, Florica. Institutul de Cercetări Biologice, Boulevard Miciurin, Bucureşti, Rumania. [Hemiptera]
MANSFIELD, Dr. A.W. Arctic Unit, Fisheries Research Board of Canada, 505 Pine Avenue West, Montreal 18, Que., Canada. [Mammalia: Pinnepedia: Odobenidae of e. Canadian Arctic (Yes); Phocidae of Arctic & Antarctic (Yes)]
MANSUETI, Dr. Romeo. Chespeake Biological Laboratory, Department of Research & Education, Solomons, Md., U.S.A. [Pisces, marine, f-w., estuarine, of Mid. Atlantic U.S. (Yes); Amphibia & Reptilia of Mid. Atlantic U.S. (Yes)]
MANTER, Prof. H.W. Department of Zoology, University of Nebraska, Lincoln 8, Neb., U.S.A. [Trematoda: Monogenea & Digenea of marine & f-w. fishes (Yes)]
* MANTOVANI, M.P. Istituto di Geologia, Universitá di Modena, Modena, Italy. [Fossil Foraminifera]
MANUEL, Dr. C.G. Institute of Science & Technology, Herran Street, Manila, Philippines. [Aves of Philippines (Yes)]
MANVILLE, Dr. Richard H. U.S. Fish & Wildlife Service, U.S. National Museum, Washington 25, D.C., U.S.A. [Mammalia: Rodentia of N. America (No)]
MANWELL, Reginold D. Department of Zoology, Syracuse University, Syracuse, N.Y., U.S.A. [Protozoa: esp. parasitic & blood (Yes)]
* MAO, Ying-tou. Food & Agriculture Administration, United Nations, Via della Terma di Caracalla, Roma, Italy. [Hymenoptera]
MAŘAN, Dr. J. Department of Entomology, National Museum, Praha II-1700, Czechoslovakia. [Orthoptera of Palearctic (Yes); Coleoptera: Carabidae & Alleculidae of Palearctic (Yes)]
MARČETIĆ, Prof. Milorad. Sv. Markovića 1, Sremski Karlovci, Yugoslavia. [Aves: Falconi-formes of Vojvodina (Yes)] [Prirodnjačke Odeljenje, Vojvodanski Muzeja Novi Sad]
MARCHE-MARCHAD, I. Goree, Senegal. [Marine Pelecypoda & Gastropoda of w. Africa (Yes)] [Institut Français d'Afrique Noire]
MARCHEŞ, Gervin. Str. Gr. Alexandrescu 11/A, Bucureşti III, Rumania. [Mammalia: Rodentia of Rumania & Balkans (Yes); of Near & Middle East (No)] [Institutul de Igienă si Sănătate Publică]
MARCHESINI-SANTOS, Mrs. Maria E.C. Div. Geologia e Mineralogia, Av. Pasteur 404, Praia Vermelha, Rio de Janeiro, Brazil. [Cretaceous & Tertiary Echinoidea of Brazil (Yes)] [Conselho Nacional de Pesquisas]
* MARCHETTE, Nyven J. Address unknown. [Crustacea: Cirripedia & Amphipoda of Pacific Cst. U.S.]
* MARCOCI, Simona. Facultatea de Biologie, Splaiul Independentei Nr. 93-95, Bucureşti, Rumania. [Hemiptera]
MARCU, Prof. Orest. Catedra de Geografie, Universitatea Cluj, Str. Kogilniceau 1, Cluj, Rumania. [Coleoptera of Rumania (Yes)]
MARCUS, Mrs. Amelia. Muzuel de Istorie Naturala "Gr. Antipa", Sos Kisselef 1, Bucureşti III, Rumania. [Crustacea: Planktonic Copepoda of Black Sea (Yes); Amphibia of Rumania]
MARCUS, Dr. Ernesto. Caixa Postal 6994, São Paulo, Brazil. [Gastropoda: Opisthobranchiata of World (Yes); Bryozoa, Tardigrada, Oligochaeta, Onychophora, Pycnogonida, Turbellaria, Phoronidea (No)] [University of São Paulo]
MARCUS, Eveline du Bois-Reymond. Caixa Postal 6994, São Paulo, Brazil. [Gastropoda: Opisthobranchiata, Tardigrada, Turbellaria, Bryozoa, f-w. Oligochaeta (No)]
* MARCUS, Leslie F. Department of Paleontology, University of California, Berkeley 4, Calif., U.S.A. [Mammalia: Marsupialia of Australia, New Guinea, C. America; fossil Mammalia]
MARCUZZI, Prof. Giorgio. Department of Zoology, Universitá, via Loredan 10, Padova, Italy. [Coleoptera: Tenebrionidae, excl. "Melasomes", of Venezuela, Colombia, West Indies (Yes)]
* MARELLI, Dr. Carlos A., Director del Instituto Conservacionista "Gama", Calle 35, esquina 58, La Plata, Argentina. [Mammalia, Recent & Fossil]
MARGALEF, Dr. Ramon. Instituto de Investigaciones Pesqueras, Universidad de Barcelona, Barcelona, Spain. [Crustacea: f-w. Entomostraca of w. Europe (Yes)]

MARGOLIS, Dr. L. Fisheries Research Board of Canada, Nanaimo, B. C., Canada. [Trematoda: Digenea, Nematoda, Acanthocephala, of marine fishes & marine mammals of n. e. Pacific (Yes); Crustacea: Amphipoda: Cyamidae of World (Yes)]

MARIANI, Prof. Mario. Via Sammartino 122, Palermo, Italy. [Lepidoptera of Italy (Yes); Diptera: Culicidae & Psychodidae of Italy (Yes)] [Istituto d'Igiene e Microbiologia dell'Università]

MARIANOS, Andrew W. P. O. Box 997, Chico, Calif., U. S. A. [Cretaceous Foraminifera of California (No)]

MARIE, Mr. P. Bureau de Recherches Géologiques, Géophysiques et Minières, 74 rue de la Federation, Paris (XV), France. [Cretaceous & Paleocene smaller Foraminifera, littoral, pelagic, & reef, of "Bassin de Paris" (Yes); Permo-Carboniferous of N. Africa (Yes); Recent of Indo-Pacific (No)]

MARIEN, Dr. Daniel. Department of Biology, Queens College, Flushing 67, N. Y., U. S. A. [Aves (No)]

* MARINOS, G. Institute of Geology & Subsurface Research, 29 Stadium Street, Athens, Greece. [Fossil Invertebrates]

MARION, H., Directeur de Minoterie, Moulin de la Fougère, par Decize (Nièvre), France. [Lepidoptera: Pyraloidaea of Palearctic & Paleotropical (Yes)]

MARK, Cand. Geol. E. ENSV Teaduste Akadeemia Geoloogia Instituut, Estonia pst 7, Tallinn, Estonian S. S. R. [Paleozoic Pisces: Heterostraci (Psammosteidae) & Arthrodira (g. Holonema, Homostius, Heterosteus) of Soviet Union (Yes)]

MARKELL, Dr. Edward K. Department of Infectious Diseases, UCLA Medical School, Los Angeles 24, Calif., U. S. A. [Trematoda: Gorgoderidae (Anaporrhutinae) from elasmobranchs (Yes)]

* MARKEVITCH, Akad. A. P. Zoological Institute, Academy of Sciences of Ukrainian SSR, Korolenko Street 55, Kiev, U. S. S. R. [Animal parasites]

MARKL, Dr. Walter. Naturhistorisches Museum, Augustinergasse 2, Basel, Switzerland. [Neuroptera: Myrmeleonidae of World (Yes); Hymenoptera: Formicidae of Europe (Yes); Coleoptera: Cerambycidae & Elateridae of Europe (Yes)]

MARKMAN, Dr. Borje. Lilljansplan 2, Stockholm II, Sweden. [Marine Rotifera of Swedish W. Cst. (No)] [Kristinebergs Zoological Station]

MARKOV, Dr. Georgi. Zoological Institute, Bulgarian Academy of Science, Sofia, Bulgaria. [Mammalia: Insectivora, Rodentia, Ungulata, of Europe & Asia (Yes)]

* MARKOV, Dr. Prof. G. S. Stalingrad Pedagogical Institute, Stalingrad, U. S. S. R. [Helminths of animals of U. S. S. R.]

* MARKS, Edward. 2713 Berger, Bakersfield, Calif., U. S. A. [Fossil Invertebrates]

MARKS, Dr. Elizabeth N. Department of Entomology, University of Queensland, Brisbane, Queensland, Australia. [Diptera: Culicidae of Australia (Yes); Marine Chironomidae of Australia (Yes)]

MARKS, Jay Glenn. P. O. Box 1131, Denver 1, Colo., U. S. A. [Tertiary Mollusca of New World (No)] [Carter Oil Company]

MARKS, Prof. Louis S. Department of Biology, Fordham University, New York 58, N. Y., U. S. A. [Lepidoptera: Papilionidae of World (Yes)]

van MARLE, J. G. Oud Crailoo, Museum laan 4, Bussum, Netherlands. [Aves of Palearctic & Indonesia (Yes)]

MARLER, Dr. P. Department of Zoology, University of California, Berkley 4, Calif., U. S. A. [Aves: Fringillidae of Europe, Asia, Africa, N. America (No)]

MARLIER, Dr. Georges. Laboratoire de Recherche Scientifique de l'Institut pour Recherche Scientifique en Afrique Centrale, Uvira, Belgian Congo. [Trichoptera; immature stages, of Europe & Africa (Yes); Pisces of C. Africa (Yes)]

MARLOW, Basil J. Australian Museum, College Street, Sydney, Australia. [Mammals: Marsupialia of Australia (Yes)]

MARPLE, Prof. Mildred F. Department of Geology, Ohio State University, Columbus 10, Ohio, U. S. A. [Pennsylvanian Ostracoda (Yes)]

MARPLES, Prof. B. J. Department of Zoology, University of Otago, Dunedin, New Zealand. [Araneida of Polynesia (Yes); Aves: Tertiary Penguins (Yes)]

MARQUARDT, William C. Veterinary Research Laboratory, Montana State College, Bozeman, Mont., U. S. A. [Protozoa: Sporozoa: Coccidia: Eimeria of cattle (Yes)]

MARQUARDT, W. Hengelolaan 486, Den Haag, Netherlands. [Arthropoda, incl. insects (No)] [Municipal Museum of Education]

MARQUES, Dr. Emerita. Junta das Missões Geográficas, e de Investigações do Ultramar, Centro de Zoologia, Rua da Junqueira No. 14, Lisboa, Portugal. [Free-swimming planktonic Copepoda of Guiné, Angola, S. Tomé (Yes)]

* MARQUEZ, Carlos M. Instituto de Biologia, Casa del Lago, Chapultepec, Mexico D. F., Mexico. [Orthoptera]

MARR, J. C. (La Jolla, Calif.; Pisces) Not now active in taxonomy.

MARRIAGE, Lowell D. Oregon Fish Commission, State Office Building, Portland 1, Ore.,
    U.S.A. [Marine Pelecypoda: Myacidae, Pholadidae, Ostreidae, Pectinidae, Mytilidae,
    Cardiidae, Veneridae, Solenidae (Yes); marine Crustacea: Decapoda: Cancridae & Pan-
    dalidae (No); all of n.w. cst. U.S. & Pacific Oc.]
MARS, Dr. Paul. Museum d'Histoire Naturelle, Palais Longchamp, Marseille, France.
    [Marine Mollusca of Mediterranean (Yes); Quaternary marine Mollusca of Mediterranean
    (Yes)]
MARSH, Gordon A. 207 Agriculture Hall, University of California, Berkeley 4, Calif., U.S.A.
    [Coleoptera: Pselaphidae of w.N.America (Yes); Curculionidae: g.Dyslobus of N.Ameri-
    ca (No)]
MARSHALL, G.A.K. (London, England; Coleoptera) Deceased.
* MARSHALL, J.F. British Mosquito Control Institute, Hayling Island, Hants, England. [Dip-
    tera]
MARSHALL, Dr. Joe T., Jr. Department of Zoology, University of Arizona, Tuscon, Ariz.,
    U.S.A. [Aves: g.Otus, fossil & recent, of N. & C.America (Yes); Melospiza melodia
    of Pacific Cst. of U.S. (Yes); Strigidae & Fringillidae of N. & C.America (Yes)]
MARSHALL, M.Y. (Murfreesboro, Tenn.; Coleoptera) Died 1958.
* MARSHALL, Mr. N.B. Department of Ichthyology, British Museum (Natural History), Crom-
    well Road, London, S.W.7, England. [Pisces]
MARSHALL, Dr. Sheina M. Marine Station, Millport, Isle of Cumbrae, Bute, Scotland. [Crus-
    tacea: Copepoda: Calanoida of Clyde Sea (No); Protozoa: planktonic Tintinnoinae & Sili-
    coflagellata of Clyde Sea (No); planktonic Dinoflagellata of temperate seas (No)]
* MARSHALL, T.C. Fisheries Department, Department of Harbours, Edward Street, Brisbane,
    Queensland, Australia. [Pisces]
MARSTON, Norman. Department of Entomolgoy, Kansas State College, Manhattan, Kans.,
    U.S.A. [Diptera: Bombyliidae: espec. G.Anthrax, of New World (Yes)]
MARTELLI, Prof. Dr. Minos, Direttore, Istituto di Entomologia Agraria, Universita degli
    Studi di Milano, Via Celoria 2, Milano, Italy. [Homoptera: Aphididae of Europe (Yes)]
MARTIN, Albert, Jr. (Pittsburgh, Penna.; Hymenoptera) Not now active in taxonomy.
MARTIN, Chas. H. Department of Entomology, Oregon State College, Corvallis, Ore., U.S.A.
    [Diptera: Asilidae of U.S. (Yes)]
MARTIN, Edward L. Geological Survey of Great Britain, Exhibition Road, London, S.W.7,
    England. [Lepidoptera: Pyralidae of World, espec. Africa (Yes)]
MARTIN S., Sr. F. Laboratorio de Biologia Pesqueras MAC, Caigüire, Cumaná, Venezuela.
    [F-w. & marine Pisces of Neotropics (Yes); "Paneidae" of Neotropics (No)]
MARTIN, Gene B. Gulf Oil Co., P.O.Box 1590, New Orleans, La., U.S.A. [Cretaceous to
    recent larger & smaller Foraminifera of G.cst. of N.America (Yes); Ordovician &
    Tertiary to Recent Bryozoa of N.America (Yes)]
MARTIN, G.C. 16 Wendy Drive, Belvedere, Salisbury, Southern Rhodesia. [Nematoda: Heter-
    oderidae: g.Meloidogyne of c.Africa (Yes)] [Department of Research & Specialist Ser-
    vices, Federal Department of Agriculture]
MARTIN, Dr. Gerald P.R. c/o Wintershall Aktiengesellschaft Mikropaläontologisches Labora-
    torium, Barnstorf, Bezirk Bremen, Germany. [Fossil Crustacea: Ostracoda: Cypridei-
    dae of Wealden-Portlandian (Yes); Malm Ostracoda of c.Europe (No); Miocene &
    Oligocene Foraminifera of c.Europe (No)]
MARTIN, John C. (Belleville, Canada; Hymenoptera, Odonata) Deceased.
* MARTIN, Mr. J.E.H. Insect Systematics & Biological Control Unit, Science Service Building,
    Carling Avenue, Ottawa, Ont., Canada. [Odonata]
MARTIN, Lewis. c/o Richmond Petroleum Co., Calle 34, No. 41-97, Barranquilla, Colombia.
    [Mesozoic-Tertiary smaller Foraminifera of California & Caribbean (No)]
MARTIN, Mr. Lloyd M. Los Angeles County Museum, Los Angeles 7, Calif., U.S.A. [Lepi-
    doptera: Heterocera of s.w.U.S., espec. Arizona (Yes)]
* MARTIN, Lois T. Department of Paleontology, Shell Oil Co., Sacramento, Calif., U.S.A.
    [Fossil Invertebrates]
MARTIN, P. Fish & Game Branch, 523 Columbia Street, Kamloops, B.C., Canada. [Mam-
    malia & Aves of British Columbia (Yes)]
MARTIN, P.S. Geochronology Laboratories, University of Arizona, Tuscon, Ariz., U.S.A.
    [Reptilia of Mexico (Yes)]
MARTIN, Prof. Walter E. Department of Biology, University of Southern California, Los
    Angeles 7, Calif., U.S.A. [Helminths of subtropics & tropics (Yes)]
MARTÍN del CAMPO, Rafael S. Instituto de Biologia, Ciudad Universitaria, Mexico 20, D.F.,
    Mexico. [Amphibia, Reptilia, Aves, of Mexico (No)]
MARTINEZ, Mr. A. Cuba California Oil Co., Apartado 3295, Habana, Cuba. [Fossil Fora-
    minifera, espec. pelagic, of n.S.America & Carribean (No)]
MARTINEZ, Antonio. Pte. J.Evaristo Uriburu 1015, d.2 (R-21), Buenos Aires, Argentina.
    [Diptera: Culicidae & Simuliidae of World (No), of Neotropical (Yes); Hemiptera: Tria-
    tomidae of Neotropical (Yes); Coleoptera: Staphylinidae of Neotropical (No); Meloidae of
    Neotropical (Yes); Lamellicornia of World, excl. Melolonthinae & Cetoniinae of Africa
    & Asia (Yes)]

MARTINEZ FONTES, Elena. Concepción Arenal 1996, Buenos Aires, Argentina. [Crustacea: Entomostraca of Antarctic & S. America]
MARTINEZ-PALACIOS, Prof. Amado. C. N. E. P., Lieja 8, Piso 11, Mexico 6, D. F., Mexico. [Diptera: Culicidae of America (Yes)]
MARTINEZ P., Prof. Ruben. Casilla 247, E. N. A. P., Punta Arenas, Chile. [Cretaceous-Recent smaller Foraminifera (Yes)] [Laboratorio Micropaleontologia, E. N. A. P.]
MARTIN S., Sr. F. Laboratorio de Biologia Pesqueras MAC, Caigüire, Cumaná, Venezuela. [F-w. & marine Pisces of Neotropica (Yes); "Paneidae" of Neotropics (No)]
MARTINSSON, Dr. Anders. Paleontologiska Institutionen, Uppsala, Sweden. [Paleozoic Crustacea: Ostracoda: Palaeocopa of Europe (Yes); Primitiopsidae & Beyrichiidae of all World (Yes)] [Institute of Palaeontology, University of Uppsala]
MARTOF, Dr. Bernard S. Department of Zoology, University of Georgia, Athens, Ga., U.S.A. [Amphibia: Ranidae, Hyalidae, g. Leurognathus of e. U.S. (Yes)]
MARTYNOVA, Mrs. Olga M. Paleontological Institute, Academy of Sciences, Lenin Avenue 33, Moscow V-71, U.S.S.R. [Fossil & Recent Mecoptera (No); fossil Neuroptera (No); Recent Neuroptera: Ascalaphidae & Nemopteridae of U.S.S.R. (No); fossil & Recent Raphidioptera of U.S.S.R (Yes); fossil Megaloptera (No); fossil Glosselytrodea (Orthopteroidea) (No); fossil Miomoptera (No)]
MARUMO, Nobukatsu. (Tagata-gun, Japan; Lepidoptera) Not now active in taxonomy.
MARUYAMA, Mr. Kiyoshi. Fisheries Research Laboratory, Same-Machi, Hachinohe City, Aomori Pref., Japan. [Pisces: Sternoptychidae of n. Japan (Yes); Ceratiidae of n. Japan (No)]
MARWICK, Dr. J. 70 Cambridge Terrace, Lower Hutt, Wellington, New Zealand. [Triassic to Recent marine Mollusca of New Zealand (Yes)]
MARX, Edward, J. F. 115 Plymouth Place, Merchantville, N. J., U.S.A. [Coleoptera: Donaciidae of New World (Yes)]
MARX, Mr. Hymen. Division of Reptiles, Chicago Natural History Museum, Roosevelt Road at Lake Shore Drive, Chicago 5, Ill., U.S.A. [Reptilia of n. Africa (Yes)]
* MARZORATTI, Ovidio. San Eduardo 1943, Buenos Aires, Argentina. [Hymenoptera: Apidae]
MASHIKO, Kikuya. Zoological Institute, University of Kanazawa, 37 Sengoku-Mati, Kanazawa, Japan. [Crustacea: Copepoda: f-w. Calanoida of Japan & China (Yes)]
* MASI, L. Dipartimento di Entomologia, Museo Civico di Storia Naturale, Via Brigata Liguria 9, Genova, Italy. [Hymenoptera]
MASLAKOVA, N. I. Department of Geology, Moscow State University, Moscow B-234, Lengory, U.S.S.R. [Up. Cretaceous Foraminifera: Globotruncanidae of s.w. U.S.S.R. (Yes)]
MASLIN, T. Paul. Department of Biology, University of Colorado, Boulder, Colo., U.S.A. [Amphibia & Reptilia of w. N. America (Yes)]
MASNER, Dr. Lubomir. U Letenského sadu 10, Praha 7, Czechoslovakia. [Hymenoptera: Proctotrupoidea of World (No); of Palearctic (Yes)] [Institute of Biology, Czechoslovakian Academy of Science]
MASON, Dr. James. Scottish Home Department Marine Laboratory, P.O.Box 101, Victoria Road, Torry, Aberdeen, Scotland. [Crustacea: Copepoda: g. Nicothoë of Scotland (Yes); Pelecypoda: Pectinidae, espec. g. Pecten of Europe, espec. Isle of Man (Yes)]
MASON, Dr. W. R. M. Insect Systematics & Biological Control Unit, Science Service Building, Carling Avenue, Ottawa, Ont., Canada. [Hymenoptera: Braconidae & Ichneumonidae of N. America (Yes); Ichneumonoidea of World (No)]
MASSEE, Dr. A. M., Head of Entomology Section, Research Station, East Malling, Kent, England. [Heteroptera & Coleoptera of Britain (Yes)]
* MASSERA, Dr. M. G. Dipartimento di Entomologia, Istituto di Zoologia, Universitá di Parma, Parma, Italy. [Collembola]
MASSMANN, Mr. W. H. Virginia Fisheries Laboratory, Gloucester Point, Va., U.S.A. [Pisces of Chesapeake Bay (Yes)]
MASSUTI, M. Laboratorio Oceanografico, S'Aigo Dolça, Palma de Mallorca, Spain. [Chaetognatha of Spain (Yes); Crustacea: Peneidae of Spain (No)]
* MASTERS, C. O. Address unknown. [Diptera]
MASUDA, Hisashi. Jyokoji, Makioka-machi, Higashiyamanashi-gun, Yamanashi-ken, Japan. [Hymenoptera: Cynipidae of Japan (Yes)]
MASUDA, Mr. Koichiro. Department of Geology, Faculty of Education, Tohoku University, Sendai, Japan. [Cenozoic Mollusca: Pectinidae of Japan, Korea, Formosa, Saghalien I. (Yes)]
MASUDA, Mr. Tatsuyoshi. Kominato Marine Biological Laboratory, Tokyo University of Fisheries, Amatsu-Kominato, Chiba, Japan. [Pisces: young stage of Teleostei of Pacific cst. of Japan (Yes)]
MATA, Oscar de. (Uruguay; Mollusca) Deceased.
* MATĚKIN, Mr. Peter Vladimirovič. Department of Zoology, Moscow State University, Leninskije gory, Moscow B-234, Lengora, U.S.S.R. [Land & f-w. Gastropoda]
MATESOVA, Mrs. G. Institute of Zoology, Academy of Science of Kazakh S.S.R., Alma-Ata, U.S.S.R. [Homoptera: Coccoidea of Kazakhstan & mid. Asia (Yes)]

* MATEU, J. Address unknown. [Coleoptera]

MATHER, Frank J., III. Woods Hole Oceanographic Institution, Woods Hole, Mass., U.S.A.
[Pisces: Scombridae, Carangidae, g. Coryphaena, of w. Atlantic (Yes)]

MATHER, Dr. W.B. Department of Zoology, University of Queensland, Brisbane, Queensland,
Australia. [Diptera: g. Drosophila of Australasia (Yes)]

MATHERS, Mr. Carol K. Department of Biology, Northern Illinois University, De Kalb, Ill.,
U.S.A. [Hirudinea of N. America (Yes)]

MATHESON, Mr. Colin, Keeper, Department of Zoology, National Museum of Wales, Cardiff,
Wales. [Mammalia & Pisces of Britain (Yes)]

MATHESON, Dr. Robert. (Ithaca, N.Y.; Diptera) Not now active in taxonomy.

* MATHEVOSSIAN, Dr. Vet. Sc. Prof. E.M. All-Union Skrjabin Institute of Helminthology,
Staropansky 3, Moscow K-12, U.S.S.R. [Cestoda of animals]

* MATHUR, Prof. P.N. Department of Zoology, Government College, Ajmer, India. [Reptilia]

MATHUR, Dr. R.N. 49 Lytton Road, Dehra Dun, U.P. India. [Hymenoptera: Braconidae &
Chalcidoidea of India (Yes); Homoptera: Psyllidae of India (Yes); Isoptera of India (Yes);
immature Coleoptera & Lepidoptera of India (Yes)] [Forest Research Institute]

MATIC, Mr. Zachiu. Catedra de Zoologia, Universitatea "Victor Babes", str. Miko 5-7, Cluj,
Rumania. [Chilopoda: of Rumania & s.e. Europe (Yes); Lithobiomorpha of Europe (Yes)]

* MATSUBARA, Prof. K. Department of Fisheries, Faculty of Agriculture, Kyoto University,
Maizuru, Japan. [Pisces: Scorpaenidae of Oriental]

* MATSUDA, Katsuki. 1-chome, Nishihachiman-Cho, Kokura Fukuoka Pref. Kyushu, Japan.
[Coleoptera: Cerambycidae]

MATSUDA, Ryuichi. c/o Department of Entomology, University of Kansas, Lawrence, Kans.,
U.S.A. [Heteroptera: Aradidae & Gerroidea]

MATSUI, Prof. Isao. Shimonoseki College of Fisheries, Yoshimi, Shimonoseki City, Yamaguchi Pref, Japan. [Pisces: Anguillidae of Indo-Pacific (Yes)]

MATSUMOTO, Prof. H. Medical College at Hukushima, Hukushima, Japan. [Ophiuroidea of
Pacific (Yes); Cenozoic Mammalia of Japan (Yes)]

MATSUMOTO, Kôichi. Tokyo-to Laboratories for Medical Science, 539 4-chome, Hyakunin-cho,
Shinjuku, Tokyo, Japan. [Crustacea: Isopoda: Asellidae of Japan (Yes); Amphipoda:
Gammaridae of Japan (No); Protozoa: Myxosporidia of Japan & w. Pacific Ocean (Yes)]

MATSUMOTO, Prof. T. Department of Geology, Kyushu University, Fukuoka, Japan. [Cepha-
lopoda: Up. Cretaceous Ammonoidea of Japan & California (Yes); of circum-Pacific area
(No)]

MATSUMURA, Shonen. 12 Oyama-chô, Shibuya-ku, Tokyo, Japan. [Hymenoptera; Homoptera:
Psyllidae; Lepidoptera; Coleoptera]

* MATSUNAGA, Takashi. Paleontological Laboratory, Sekiyu Shigen Kaihatsu KK, 952 Kichijoji,
Musashino-shi, Tokyo, Japan. [Fossil Foraminifera]

MATTESON, Prof. Max R. Department of Zoology, University of Illinois, Urbana, Ill., U.S.A.
[Gastropoda of Mississippi River Basin (Yes); Pelecypoda: Unionidae of Mississippi
River Basin (Yes)]

MATTHES, Dr. Dieter. Zoologisches Institut der Friedrich-Alexander-Universität, Erlangen,
Germany. [Protozoa: br.-water Suctoria of World (Yes); Peritricha: "Sessilia-Akoutrak-
tilia" of World (Yes)]

MATTHES, Prof. Dr. H.W. Geologisches Institut der Universität, Domstrasse 5, Halle (Saale),
German Democratic Republic. [Fossil Mammalia: Creodonta of "Rozan" (Yes)]

MATTHEWS, Mr. E.G. Department of Entomology, Cornell University, Ithaca, N.Y., U.S.A.
[Coleoptera: Scarabaeidae: Coprinae of New World (No); g. Copris (Yes)]

MATTHYSSE, John G. Department of Entomology, Cornell University, Ithaca, N.Y., U.S.A.
[Acarina of World (No); Tetranychidae, Phytoseiidae, Phytoptipalpidae, of n.e. U.S.
(No)]

MATTINGLY, Mr. P.F. Department of Entomology, British Museum (Natural History), Cromwell Road, London, S.W.7, England. [Diptera: Culicidae of World (Yes)]

MATTLIN, Robert H. 4000 Crandon Blvd., Key Biscayne, Miami 49, Fla., U.S.A. [Reptilia
of Ohio, Utah, Florida (Yes)][Crandon Park Zoo]

MATTONI, Rudolf H.T. Department of Botany, University of California, Los Angeles 24, Calif.,
U.S.A. [Lepidoptera: Rhopalocera of s. California (Yes); Lycaenidae: g. Philotes of
World (Yes)]

MATTOX, Dr. N.T. Hancock Foundation, University of Southern California, Los Angeles 7,
Calif., U.S.A. [Crustacea: Branchiopoda of New World (Yes); Gastropoda of N. America
(Yes)]

MATVEJEV, S.D. Institute of Biology, Poste Box 913, Beograd, Yugoslavia. [Aves of s.e.
Europe & Mediterranean (Yes); Orthoptera: Acrididae of Yugoslavia (No)]

MAUBEUGE, Dr. P.L. Les Rosiers, 141 Avenue Carnot, St. Max (M.&M.), France. [Juras-
sic Ammonites of Europe (Yes); Triassic Ammonites of "facies germaniques" of Europe
(Yes)]

MAUL, Mr. G.E. Museu Municipal do Funchal, Funchal, Madeira. [Pisces of Madeira (Yes);
of w. cst. of Africa (No)]

MAURIN, C. M. J. E, Chef de Laboratoire, Institut Scientifique des Pêches Maritimes, 6 rue Voltaire, Sète (Hérault), France. [Pisces: Gadidae of e. Atlantic & Mediterranean (Yes); Perciformes of trop. Atlantic (No); Crustacea: Decapoda of e. Atlantic & Mediterranean (Yes)]

MAVROMOUSTAKIS, G. A. 232 St. Andrew's St., Limassol, Cyprus. [Hymenoptera: Apoidea of Palearctic (Yes); Anthidiinae of World, excl. U. S. A. (Yes)]

MAWATARI, Dr. Shizuo. c/o Research Institute for Natural Resources, 4 Chome, Hyakunin-cho, Shinjuku-ku, Tokyo, Japan. [Marine Bryozoa of Japan & East Indies (Yes)]

MAWSON, Patricia. See THOMAS-MAWSON, Mrs. P. M.

MAXSON, Dr. John H. 5335 Montview Blvd., Denver 7, Colo., U. S. A. [Neogene Mammalia (No)]

MAXWELL, Dr. W. H. G. Department of Geology, University of Queensland, George Street, Brisbane, Australia. [Up. Paleozoic Brachiopoda: Spiriferida & Productacea of e. Australia (Yes)]

MAY, Mr. A. W. S. Department of Agriculture & Stock, P. O. Box 102, Toowoomba, Queensland, Australia. [Diptera: Trypetidae: Dacinae of Australia & New Guinea (Yes)]

MAY, Dr. Jan. (Praha, Czechoslovakia; Hymenoptera) Died February 18, 1959.

MAYAUD, N. 80 rue du Ranelagh, Paris (XVI), France. [Aves: of Palearctic; Procellarii of all oceans]

MAYER, Fritz. C/o Schümacher, Gryphinstrasse 10 III, Hamburg, Germany. [Hymenoptera of New World]

MAYER, Mr. Karl. Biologische Bundesanstalt für Land- und Forstwirtschaft, Institut für Physiologische Zoologie, Berlin-Dahlem, Germany. [Diptera: Heleidae of Europe (No); Larvae & Pupae of Heleidae of Europe & Africa (Yes)]

* MAYER, Rudolf. Muzeul National de Istorie Naturala, "Grigore Antipa", Sos. Kisselef 1, Bucureşti, Rumania. [Pisces]

MAYER, William V., Chairman. Department of Biology, Wayne State University, Detroit 2, Mich., U. S. A. [Hair of Mammals of World (Yes)]

MAYHEW, Dr. R. L. Box 8482, University Station, Baton Rouge 3, La., U. S. A. [Nematoda parasitic in bovine mammals (No)]

MAYHEW, Dr. Wilbur. University of California, Riverside, Calif., U. S. A. [Aves & Reptilia of Colorado & Mojave Deserts of California (Yes)]

MAYNARD, Prof. Elliott A. University of Rochester School of Medicine & Denistry, 260 Crittenden Boulevard, Rochester 20, N. Y., U. S. A. [Collembola of N. America (Yes)]

MAYNC, Dr. Wolf. Cons., Explor. Mgt. Compagnie d'Exploration Petrolière, 76 Grand Rue, Chambourcy (S. & O.), France. [Jurassic-Cretaceous Foraminifera: arenaceous Lituolidae & Orbitolinidae of World (Yes)]

* MAYO, V. K. Address unknown. [Odonata]

MAYR, Dr. Ernst. Museum of Comparative Zoology, Cambridge 38, Mass., U. S. A. [Aves of Oriental & Australian (No)]

* MAZEPOVA, Mrs. G. F. Baikalskaia Limnologicheskaia Stantsia, Listvenichnoe, Irkutsk, U. S. S. R. [Crustacea: Copepoda]

*MAZURMOVITCH, B. N. Kiev State University, Vladimirskaya Street 58, Kiev, U. S. S. R. [Helminths of Amphibia & Pisces of U. S. S. R.]

McALESTER, A. Lee. Peabody Museum, Yale University, New Haven, Conn., U. S. A. [Ordovician, Silurian, Devonian Pelecypoda (Yes)]

McALISTER, Mr. Wayne H. Route 4, Box 71, Cuero, Texas, U. S. A. [Amphibia: Anura of Texas (Yes); Reptilia: Squamata of Texas (Yes); Araneida: Pisauridae of c. Texas (Yes)]

McALPINE, Mr. D. K. Australian Museum, Hyde Park, Sydney, N. S. W., Australia. [Diptera: Acalyptrata of Australia (Yes)]

McALPINE, Mr. J. F. Systematic Entomology & Biological Control Unit, Entomology Division, Science Service Building, Ottawa, Ont., Canada. [Diptera: Tabanidae of N. America (No); Tachinidae of N. America (Yes); Lonchaeidae of New World, Africa, Australia, Micronesia (Yes)]

McALPINE, Wilbur S. 2501 Bogie Lake Road, Route 5, Milford, Mich., U. S. A. [Lepidoptera: Rhopalocera of New World (No); Riodinidae: g. Calephelis of New World (Yes)]

McAREAVEY, Rev. J. J., S. J. Xavier College, Kew, Vict., Australia. [Hymenoptera: Formicidae of Australia (Yes)]

McATEE, Mr. W. L. (Chapel Hill, N. C.; Hemiptera) Not now active in taxonomy.

McBEE, William, Jr. Standard Oil Co. of Texas, Box 2087, Amarillo, Texas, U. S. A. [Mississippian "micro" Crinoidea (No)]

McBETH, C. W. (Modesto, Calif.; Nematoda) Not now active in taxonomy.

McCARLEY, W. H. Department of Biology, Stephen F. Austin State College, Nacogdoches, Texas, U. S. A. [Mammalia: Rodentia & Carnivora of N. America (Yes); Aves & Amphibia of s. U. S. (Yes)]

McCAULEY, James E. Department of Zoology, Oregon State College, Corvallis, Ore., U. S. A. [Digenetic Trematoda: Hemiuridae of Pacific n. w. U. S. (Yes)]

273

McCAULEY, Dr. Robert H., Jr. 6405 Orchid Drive, Bethesda 14, Md., U.S.A. [Reptilia &
Amphibia of e.U.S. & Pacific n.w.U.S. (Yes)] [National Institutes of Health]
McCLAY, Mr. A.T. Department of Entomology, University of California, Davis, Calif.,
U.S.A. [Coleoptera: Chrysomelidae of N. America (Yes)]
McCOMB, Charles W. Department of Entomology, University of Maryland, College Park, Md.,
U.S.A. [Diptera: Simuliidae of Maryland (Yes); Hymenoptera: Braconidae: g. Chelonus
& Aphaereta of Nearctic (Yes)]
* McCONKEY, Edwin H. Address unknown. [Amphibia & Reptilia]
McCONNAUGHEY, Bayard H. Department of Biology, University of Oregon, Eugene, Ore.,
U.S.A. [Mesozoa of Pacific & Atlantic csts. of N. America (Yes); Cephalopoda of
Pacific cst. of N. America (Yes)]
McCONNELL, Harold S. (College Park, Md.; Homoptera) Deceased.
McCONNELL, Rosemary H. (nee LOWE). C/o Geological Survey, Box 754, Georgetown, Bri-
tish Guiana. [Pisces: Cichlidae of e. & c. Africa (Yes); of Guiana (No)]
McCOWAN, Vaughan F. Florida Forest Service, P.O. Box 1200, Tallahassee, Fla., U.S.A.
[Coleoptera: Curculionidae of N. America (No); Scolytidae & Tenebrionidae of N. America
(Yes)]
McCOY, Melville R. Sun Oil Co., Box 1732, Casper, Wyo., U.S.A. [Cambrian-Silurian Cono-
donts (Yes)]
McCRACKEN, Isabel. (Stanford, Calif.; Hemiptera) Deceased.
McCRAW, Bruce M. Division of Biology, Ontario Veterinary College, Guelph, Ont., Canada.
[Gastropoda; Pulmonata; Lymnaeidae: g. Lymnaea of Great Lakes of N. America (Yes)]
* McCUBBIN, Mr. C. 434 Punt Road, South Yarra, Vict., Australia. [Lepidoptera]
McCULLOCH, Irene. Allan Hancock Foundation, University of Southern California, Los Angeles
7, Calif., U.S.A. [Recent Foraminifera]
McDANIEL, Burruss, Jr. 808 Fairview, College Station, Texas, U.S.A. [Homoptera: Diaspi-
didae of N.America (Yes); Coccoidea of Micronesia: Heteroptera: Nabidae of World
(Yes)]
McDERMOTT, Bernard Thomas. (Detroit, Mich.; Acarina; Diptera) Not now active in taxonomy.
McDERMOTT, Frank A. 4664 Malden Drive, Liftwood, Wilmington 3, Del., U.S.A. [Coleoptera:
Lampyridae of New World (Yes)]
McDONALD, Mr. W.A. Dept. of Entomology, University of California, Los Angeles 24, Calif.,
U.S.A. [Diptera: Culicidae of Africa (Yes); Pedipalpi: g. Trithyreus & Schizomus of
World (Yes)]
McDOWELL, Mr. Samuel. Department of Reptiles & Amphibians, American Museum of Natural
History, New York 24, N.Y., U.S.A. [Pisces: Heteromi & Lyopomi of all oceans (Yes);
Reptilia: crocodilians & cryptodires of World (Yes); snakes of Africa, New Guinea, New
World (Yes)]
McDUNNOUGH, Dr. J.R.H. Nova Scotia Museum of Science, Halifax, Nova Scotia, Canada.
[Microlepidoptera: Eucosmidae & Coleophoridae of e.Canada & U.S. (No)]
McELVARE, Rowland R. P.O.Box 386, Southern Pines, N.C., U.S.A. [Lepidoptera: Noctuidae:
Heliothiinae of New World (Yes)]
McEVEY, Mr. A.R., Ornithologist, National Museum of Victoria, Russell Street, Melbourne,
Australia. [Aves of Australia (Yes)]
McEWEN, E.H. Canadian Wildlife Service, Box 117, Yellowknife, N.W.T., Canada. [Mamma-
lia: g. Vulpes of Arctic N. America (Yes)]
McFADDEN, Max W. Department of Entomology, University of Alberta, Edmonton, Alta.,
Canada. [Diptera: larvae of Stratiomyiidae of N.America (Yes)]
McFARLAND, W.N. Institute of Marine Science, The University of Texas, Port Aransas,
Texas, U.S.A. [Pisces of Texas cst. (Yes)]
McFARLANE, Mr. A.G. 69 Te Awakura Terrace, St. Andrew's Hill, Sumner, Christchurch,
S.E.3, New Zealand. [Trichoptera of New Zealand (Yes)]
McGILL, Mr. A.R. 119 Wollongong Road, Arncliffe, N.S.W., Australia. [Aves: Charadriidae
& Procellariidae of Australia (Yes)]
McGINTY, Thomas L. Box 765, Boynton Beach, Fla., U.S.A. [Marine Mollusca of Florida &
W. Indies (Yes)]
* McGREGOR, E.A. P.O.Box 70, Whittier, Calif., U.S.A. [Acarina: Tetranychidae]
McGREW, Dr. P.O. Department of Geology, University of Wyoming, Laramie, Wyo., U.S.A.
[Tertiary Mammalia of N. America (Yes)]
McGUFFIN, Dr. W.C. Forest Insect Laboratory, 402 Customs Building, Calgary, Alta.,
Canada. [Lepidoptera: Geometridae, immature stages, of Canada (Yes)]
McGUGAN, A. Department of Geology, Queen's University, Kingston, Ont., Canada. [Up.
Cretaceous Foraminifera of World (Yes)]
* McGUIRT, James H. 300 San Jacinto Building, Houston, Texas, U.S.A. [Fossil invertebrates]
McINTOSH, Allen. Animal Disease & Parasite Research Division, U.S. Department of Agricul-
ture, Agricultural Research Center, Beltsville, Md., U.S.A. [Nematoda of domestic
animals of N. America (No); Acarina: Ixodidae of N. America (Yes); Trematoda: g. Param-
phistomum of domestic animals (Yes)]

McKEE, Edwin Dinwiddie. U.S. Geological Survey, Federal Center, Denver, Colo., U.S.A. [Permian Brachiopoda (No)]

McKENNA, Malcolm Carnegie. 241 Los Altos Drive, Berkeley 8, Calif., U.S.A. [Late Mesozoic to early Cenozoic Mammalia (Yes)] [Museum of Paleontology, University of California]

McKENZIE, Howard L. Bureau of Entomology, State Department of Agriculture, Sacramento 14, Calif., U.S.A. [Homoptera: Coccoidea of N. America (Yes); Diaspididae of World (Yes)]

McKENZIE, Miss M.K. Fisheries Branch, Marine Department, Wellington, New Zealand. [Marine Pisces of New Zealand (No)]

McKENZIE, R.A. Atlantic Biological Station, Fisheries Research Board, St. Andrews, N.B., Canada. [Pisces of n.w. Atlantic]

McKENZIE, Mr. R.J. Department of Zoology, University of New England, Armidale 5N, N.S.W., Australia. [Araneida: Dipluridae of Australia (Yes)]

McKERROW, W.S. Department of Geology, University Museum, Oxford, England. [M. Jurassic Brachiopoda: Telotremata of England (Yes)]

McKEY-FENDER, Dorothy. (Mrs. K.M. Fender) Route 3, McMinnville, Ore., U.S.A. [Coleoptera: g. Cantharis of N. America (Yes); Gastropoda: g. Acmaea of Pacific cst. N. America (Yes); Oligochaeta: megadrilids & microdrilids, excl. Euchytraidae, of N. America (Yes)]

McKINNEY, Dr. D.F. Delta Waterfowl Research Station, Delta Station, Man., Canada. [Aves: Anatidae of N. America (Yes); of Britain (No)]

* McLACKLAN, Dr. G.F. Department of Ornithology, Port Elizabeth Museum, Port Elizabeth, Union of South Africa. [Aves]

McLANE, Dr. Wm. M. 1790 S.W. 37th Way, Ft. Lauderdale, Fla., U.S.A. [F-w. & br.-water Pisces of Florida (Yes)]

McLAREN, Dr. D.J. Department of Mines & Technical Surveys, Ottawa, Ont., Canada. [Devonian Brachiopoda & corals of w. & n. Canada (Yes)] [Geological Survey of Canada]

* McLAREN, I.A. Fisheries Research Board of Canada, 505 Pine Avenue West, Montreal, Que., Canada. [Mammalia]

McLAUGHLIN, Charles A. Los Angeles County Museum, Los Angeles 7, Calif., U.S.A. [Mammalia: of s. California (Yes); g. Geomys of c. U.S. (Yes)]

McLEAN, James D., Jr. P.O. Box 916, Alexandria, Va., U.S.A. [Cretaceous-Tertiary Foraminifera & Ostracoda of New World (Yes)]

* McLEARN, Dr. Frank H. Geological Survey of Canada, Ottawa, Ont., Canada. [Fossil invertebrates]

McLEOD, Dr. James A. University of Manitoba, Winnipeg, Man., Canada. [Cestoda & Trematoda of Canada (Yes)]

McMAHAN, Elizabeth A. Department of Zoology, University of Hawaii, Honolulu 14, Hawaii. [Odonata: g. Helocordulia of e. U.S. (No); Isoptera of Hawaii (No)]

* McMAHON, E. Department of Parasitology, Albert Agricultural College, Dublin, Glasnevin, Eire. [Nematoda]

McMICHAEL, Dr. Donald F. The Australian Museum, College Street, Sydney, N.S.W., Australia. [Terr. & f-w. Mollusca of Australia & New Guinea (Yes); marine Mollusca of Australia & S. Pacific (Yes)]

McMILLAN, Mr. R.P. 3 Saladin Street, Swanbourne, W. Australia. [Coleoptera of Australia, espec. Buprestidae & inguilines (Yes)] [Western Australian Museum]

* McMILLIN, Dr. Harvey C. Address unknown. [Pisces & Mollusca of Alaska, Puget Sound, Peru]

McMULLEN, Dr. Donald B. Army Medical Service Graduate School, Walter Reed Medical Center, Washington 12, D.C., U.S.A. [Trematoda, espec. Plagiorchiidae & Schistosomatidae, of World (Yes)]

* McNAIR, Mr. Andrew H. Department of Geology, Dartmouth College, Hanover, N.H., U.S.A. [Fossil invertebrates]

* McNEEL, Wakelin, Jr. Department of Zoology, Central Michigan College, Mt. Pleasant, Mich., U.S.A. [Coleoptera: Cerambycidae; Aves; Mammalia; all of Alaska]

McNEILL, Mr. Frank A. Australian Museum, College Street, Sydney, N.S.W., Australia. [Crustacea: Decapoda of Indo-Pacific (Yes)]

McNULTY, Prof. C.L., Jr. Department of Geology, Arlington State College, Arlington, Texas, U.S.A. [Cretaceous Foraminifera of New World (Yes); of Europe (No)]

McREYNOLDS, Prof. John W. 237 North Elm Street, Nevada, Mo., U.S.A. [Coleoptera of Atchison County, Kansas (No); Carabidae: g. Calosoma of World (Yes)]

McTAVISH, Mr. Robert. C/o Bureau of Mineral Resources, Geology & Geophysics, Turner, Canberra City, Australia. [Ordovician & Devonian Conodonts, espec. Australian (Yes); Tertiary Foraminifera of Indo-Pacific (Yes)]

McWHIRTER, Mr. Nolan. No Man's Land Historical Museum, Panhandle Agricultural & Mechanical College, Goodwell, Okla., U.S.A. [Tertiary Mammalia of Great Plains (Yes)]

* MEAD, Mr. A.P. Zoology Department, University College of Ghana, Achimota, Ghana. [Mammalia & Reptilia]

MEAD, Albert R., Head, Department of Zoology, University of Arizona, Tucson, Ariz., U.S.A. [Terr. Mollusca of N. America (No); Gastropoda: Limaiidae & Arionidae of N. America (Yes); Achatinidae of Africa (No)]

MEAD, Mr. Frank W. Department of Entomology, Box 5215, North Carolina State College, Raleigh, N.C., U.S.A. [Homoptera: Cicadellidae of s.e. U.S. (Yes); Heteroptera of Florida (Yes); Diptera: Culicidae of e. U.S. (Yes); Aves of e. U.S. (Yes)]

MEAD, Giles. W. 317 Queen Street, Alexandria, Va., U.S.A. [Pelagic & deep-sea Pisces of trop. America (No)] [U.S. Fish & Wildlife Service]

* MEADE, Dr. Grayson. 1403 Summit Street, Calgary, Alta., Canada. [Fossil Mammalia]

MEAGHER, J.W. Victoria Department of Agriculture, Plant Research Laboratory, Burnley Gardens, Burnley E.1, Vict., Australia. [Nematoda: g. Pratylenchus & Meloidogyne of Australia (Yes); g. Heterodera of Australia (No)]

MEANS, Mr. John A. Sun Oil Co., Paleontology Laboratory, 503 N. Central Expressway, Richardson, Texas, U.S.A. [Fossil Foraminifera of Gulf cst. of Texas & La. (Yes)]

MECHAM, John S. Department of Zoology, Alabama Polytechnic Institute, Auburn, Ala., U.S.A. [Reptila & Amphbia of s.w. & s.e. U.S.]

MEDEM, Prof. F. Universidad Nacional, Apartado Postal 25-35, Apartado Aereo 7495, Bogotá, Colombia. [Reptilia: Crocodylia of Africa, Asia, Australia, S. America, C. America (Yes); Testudinata of Colombia (Yes)] [Instituto de Ciencias Naturales, Universidad Nacional de Colombia]

MEDINA, Mr. Don. R. Museum of Vertebrate Zoology, University of California, Berkeley 4, Calif., U.S.A. [Terr. Aves of Mexico (Yes)]

* de MEDINA, Federico. Paysandu, Uruguay. [Diptera of S. America]

MEDINA P., Gonzalo. Estación Biologica Henri Pittier, Rancho Grande, Maracay, Est. Aragua, Venezuela. [Aves of Venezuela & nearby Caribbean islands (No)]

* de MEDINA, Prof. Nieves Pereira. Plaza Libertad 1175, Montevideo, Uruguay. [Mollusca & fossil Invertebrates]

MEDLER, Dr. John T. Department of Entomology, University of Wisconsin, Madison 6, Wis., U.S.A. [Hemiptera of m-w. U.S. (Yes); Homoptera of New World (Yes); Cicadellidae of U.S. (Yes)]

* MEDVEDEV, L.N. Address unknown. [Coleoptera: Chrysomelidae]

MEES, G.F., Curator, Western Australian Museum, Beaufort Street, Perth, W. Australia. [Aves of Europe, Indo-Australia, West Indies (Yes); Pisces of Indian Ocean (Yes)]

MEESTER, J. Transvaal Museum, P.O. Box 413, Pretoria, Union of South Africa. [Mammalia of s. Africa (Yes); Soricidae of Africa (No); of Angola, N. Rhodesia, s. Africa (Yes); Pleistocene Soricidae of Angola, N. Rhodesia, s. Africa (Yes)]

* MEEUSE, Dr. A.D.J. Mispelstraat 11, Den Haag, Netherlands. [Diptera: Syrphidae]

MEGGIOLARO, Giuseppe. S. Croce 121 A, Venezia, Italy. [Coleoptera: Carabidae of Europe (No), of Italy & Iberian Pen. (Yes); Pselaphidae of Palearctic & Africa (No), of w. Europe (Yes); Coleoptera cavernicola of Palearctic (Yes)]

MEGLITSCH, Dr. Paul A. Drake University, Des Moines 11, Iowa, U.S.A. [Sporozoa: Myxosporidia of World (Yes)]

MEGYERI, Dr. J. Állami Pedagógiai Föiskola, Aprilis 4, utja 6, Szeged, Hungary. [Rotatoria & Crustacea: Entomostraca of Hungary (Yes)]

MEHES, Dr. Gy. Magyar Nemzeti Museum, Döbrentei u. 8, Budapest I, Hungary. [Hymenoptera: gall wasps of Hungary (No)]

* MEHL, Prof. Maurice G. Swallow Hall, University of Missouri, Columbia, Mo., U.S.A. [Fossil invertebrates & conodonts]

* MEHRING, Albert G. (Harrisburg, Pa; Pisces) Not now active in taxonomy.

MEIER, Herbert. Schillerstrasse 29, Knittelfeld, Stm., Austria. [Lepidoptera: Psychidae of Palearctic (Yes); Zygaenidae: g. Zygaena of Europe (Yes)]

* MEIR, Maria. Zoologishces Institut, Universität Erlangen, Universitätstrasse 19, Erlangen, Germany. [Protozoa]

MEIER, Dr. W. Eidg. Landwirtschaftliche Versuchsanstalt, Zürich-Orlikon, Switzerland. [Homoptera: Aphididae: Dactinotini of Switzerland (Yes)]

de MEILLON, Dr. Botha. South African Institute for Medical Research, Johannesburg, Union of South Africa. [Diptera: Ceratopogonidae & Simuliidae of Ethiopian (Yes); Siphonaptera of Ethiopian (Yes)]

MEINERS, Dr. Edwin P. 6651 Enright Avenue, St. Louis 5, Mo., U.S.A. [Lepidoptera: butterflies of U.S. (Yes); Coleoptera of Missouri (Yes)]

MEINERTZ, Dr. Thydsen, Universitets Institut for Anatomi, Universitetsparken 3, København-ö, Denmark. [Crustacea: terr. Isopoda of Denmark (No); Arachnida: Pseudoscorpiones & Opiliones of Denmark (No)]

MEINERTZHAGEN, Col R. 17 Kensington Park Gardens, London, W.11, England. [Aves: all Palearctic genera of the World (Yes)]

MEINKEN, Hermann. Horner Strasse 100, Bremen, Germany. [Marine & f-w. Pisces of C. America, S. America, Africa, India, Indo-Malaya, Siam (Yes)]

MEINKOTH, N. A. Department of Biology, Swarthmore College, Swarthmore, Pa., U.S.A. [Cestoidea of N. America (No)]
* MEIRING, Dr. A. J. D. Department of Zoology, National Museum, Bloemfontein, Union of South Africa. [Worms & Fossil Mammalia]
* MEISE, Alfred. Engelbergstrasse 54, Essen, Germany. [Lepidoptera]
MEISE, Dr. Wilhelm, Kustos, Zoologisches Museum, Bornplatz 5, Hamburg 13, Germany. [Aves of World (Yes); terr. & f-w. Gastropoda of Germany (Yes); Arachnida: Scorpiones of Malaya & C. America (Yes)]
MELANDER, Dr. A. L. 4670 Ladera Lane, Riverside, Calif., U.S.A. [Diptera of World (No)] [University of California, Division of Biological Control]
MELENDEZ, Prof. Bermudo. Francisco Navacerrada 10, Madrid, Spain. [Paleozoic Echinodermata: Cistoidea & Carpoidea of Europe (Yes); Cambrian Archaeocyatha of Europe (No)] [Museo Nacional de Ciencias Naturales]
MELIS, Prof. Antonio, Direttore della Stazione di Entomologia Agraria, Via Romana 15-17, Firenze, Italy. [Thysanoptera of Italy (Yes)]
MELL, Dr. h. c. R. Hainbuchenstrasse 34, Berlin-Frohnau, Germany. [Lepidoptera of East Asia (No)]
MELLEN, F. F. P. O. Box 2584, West Jackson 7, Miss., U.S.A. [Paleozoic & Cretaceous index fossils of Mississippi (Yes)]
de MELLO-LEITAO, Prof. Aloysio. Rua 19 de Fevereiro 119, Botafogo, Rio de Janeiro, Brazil. [Pantopoda of Brazil; Porifera: Monaxonidae of Brazil] [Faculdade Nacional de Filosofia]
MELVILLE, R. V. International Commission on Zoological Nomenclature, 119 Parkway, Gloucester Gate, London, N. W. 1, England. [Fossil Echinoidea, espec. Mesozoic (Yes); Mesozoic invertebrate macrofossils, excl. Ammonitoidea (Yes)]
* MENDES, Dario. Instituto de Ecologia y Experimento Agricola, Caixa Postal 1620, Rio de Janeiro, Brazil. [Coleoptera]
* MENDES, Josue Camargo. Departamento de Geologia, Caixa Postal 105-B, Universidade, São Paulo, Brazil. [Fossil invertebrates]
MENDEZ, Dr. Eustorgio. Gorgas Memorial Laboratory, Apartado 1252, Panamá, Panama. [Siphonaptera of New World (Yes)]
* MENDIVIL-HERRERA, Javier. Museo de Historia Natural, Casilla de Correo 399, Montevideo, Uruguay. [Cestoda of World; Polychaeta of S. America]
de MENEZES, Dr. Rui Simões. Caixa Postal 1366, Bahia, Brazil. [Pisces of Brazil] [Secretaria da Agricultura, Serviço de Pesca]
MENGEL, Dr. Robert M. Museum of Natural History, University of Kansas, Lawrence, Kans., U.S.A. [Aves, espec. Passeriformes, of N. America (Yes); g. Empidonax of U.S. (Yes); Pleistocene Aves, excl. Passeriformes, of N. America (Yes)]
* MENGERT, Dr. H. Zoologisches Institut der Universität, Universtätsstrasse 19, Erlangen, Germany. [Nematoda]
MENHOFER, Herbert. Oberstudienrat, Apfelstrasse 10, Erlangen, Germany. [Lepidoptera of n. Bavaria (Yes)]
MENKE, Mr. Arnold. Department of Entomology, University of California, Davis, Calif., U.S.A. [Aquatic Heteroptera: Belostomatidae of World (Yes)]
MENON, Mr. A. G. K. Assistant Zoologist, Zoological Survey of India, 34 Chittaranjan Avenue, Calcutta 12, India. [Pisces: Cyprinoidea & Siluroidea of Indo-Australian Arch., e. & s. e. Asia (Yes)]
MENON, Mr. M. A. U. Department of Health Services, Trivandrum, Kerala State, India. [Diptera: Culicidae of India & S. Pacific (Yes)]
MENON, Dr. M. G. Ramdas. Systematic Entomologist, Indian Agricultural Research Institute, New Delhi-12, India. [Insecta of India: Hymenoptera, espec. Chalcididae of India (Yes); Embioptera of India (Yes); Psocoptera of India (Yes)]
MENZEL, Dr. Richard. Brandisstrasse 4, Chur, Switzerland. [Crustacea: Copepoda of Indonesia (No); Nematoda of Switzerland (No)]
MENZIES, Dr. Robert J. Lamont Geological Observatory, Columbia University, Palisades, N. Y., U.S.A. [Pleistocene Crustacea: Decapoda (No); Pleistocene-Recent Gastropoda: Pteropoda (No)]
* MEQUIGNON, A. 57 Avenue de Breteuil, Paris (VII), France. [Coleoptera]
MERCOVICH, Rev. T. C. Canisius College, 102 Mona Vale Road, Pymble, N. S. W., Australia. [Hymenoptera: Formicidae of Australia (Yes)]
MERE, R. M. Mill House, Chiddingfold, Surrey, England. [Lepidoptera, excl. g. Tineina & Nepticulina, of British Isles (Yes)]
MERINO, Dr. Gonzalo. 1207 Vito Cruz, Manila, Philippines. [Hymenoptera & Homoptera: Cicadellidae of Phillipines (No)] [Bureau of Plant Industry, Retired]
* MERISUO, Dr. A. K., Entomologist, Nummen koulu, Turku 3, Finland. [Hymenoptera]
* MERKLEY, Mr. Don R., Assistant Entomologist, Horticulture Branch Station, Corvallis, Mont., U.S.A. [Trichoptera]

277

MERKLIN, Prof. Roman L. Paleontological Institute, Academy of Sciences, Leninsky Prospect 33, Moscow B-71, U.S.S.R. [Oligocene-Recent marine Bivalvia of e.Mediterranean, Black, & Caspian Seas (Yes); Quaternary-Recent marine Bivalvia & Gastropoda of e. U.S.S.R. (No); Bivalvia: Taxodonta of N.Atlantic & N.Pacific (Yes)]

MERLA, Giovanni. (Firenze, Italy, Fossil Vertebrata) Not now active in taxonomy.

* MERMOD, Dr. G., Conservateur de Malacologie, Museum d'Histoire Naturelle, Genève, Switzerland. [Mollusca]

MERRIAM, Mr. C.W. 346 Felton Drive, Menlo Park, Calif., U.S.A. [Cretaceous-Cenozoic Gastropoda: g. Turritella of w.cst. N.America (Yes); Mid. Paleozoic rugose corals of w.N.America (Yes)] [U.S. Geological Survey]

* MERRILL, Arthur S. Box 473, Woods Hole, Mass., U.S.A. [Gastropoda of Florida]

* MERRILL, Mr. G.B., Entomologist, State Plant Board, Gainesville, Fla., U.S.A. [Homoptera: Coccidae]

MERRIMAN, Dr.Daniel, Director, Bingham Oceanographic Laboratory, Yale University, New Haven, Conn., U.S.A. [Pisces: Teleosti of w.Atlantic (Yes)]

MERTENS, Dr. Dipl. Geol. Erwin. Westenhellweg 26, Dortmund, Germany. [Mesozoic to Quaternary Ostracoda (Yes)] [Amt für Bodenforschung, Hannover]

MERTENS, Dr. Robert. Natur-Museum und Forschungsinstitut, Senckenberg-Anlage 25, Frankfurt a Main, Germany. [Reptilia & Amphibia of World]

* MESERVE, F.G. Department of Biology, Bowling Green State University, Bowling Green, Ohio, U.S.A. [Trematoda: Monogenea of World; Acarina: Tarsonemidae of World]

MESHKOVA, Dr. T. Hydrobiological Station of Sevan, Sevan, Armenian SSR, U.S.S.R. [F-w. Cladocera of Armenia (Yes)] [Armenian Academy of Sciences]

MESNIL, L.P. 36 Rue de Chêtre, Délémont, Switzerland. [Diptera: Tachinidae of Old World (Yes)] [Commonwealth Institute of Biological Control]

* MESSER, C.C.V. Department of Health, P.O.Box 8105, Causeway, Southern Rhodesia. [Diptera: Culicidae & Psychodidae: Phlebotominae] [Malaria & Bilharzia Research Laboratories]

* MESSGHALI, Dr. Ahmad. Institute of Malariology, Teheran University, Teheran, Iran. [Diptera: Psychodidae]

MESSIKOMMER, Dr. Edwin. Seegräben, Kt. Zürich, Switzerland. [Protozoa, Rotatoria, Crustacea: Cladocera & Entomostraca, of Switzerland & c.Europe (No)]

MESSINA, Angelina Rose. American Museum of Natural History, New York 24, N.Y., U.S.A. [Recent & Fossil Foraminifera (No)]

* MESTROV, Milan. Zoological Institute, University of Zagreb, Demetrova Nr. 1/III, Zagreb, Yugoslavia. [Crustacea]

METCALF, Z.P. (Raleigh N.C.; Homoptera) Died January 5, 1956.

* METSÄVAINIO, Dr. K. Director of Oulun Uhteislyseo, Suvantok 3A. 25, Oulu, Finland. [Aves, Mammalia, Coleoptera] [Biological Museum]

MEURER, J.J. Prinses Irenelaan 43, Hillegom, Netherlands. [Heteroptera of Netherlands]

MEYER, Prof. Marvin C. Department of Zoology, University of Maine, Orono, Maine, U.S.A. [Hirudinea of World (Yes)]

MEYER, Miss M.K.P. Institute for Zoological Research, Potchefstroom University, Potchefstroom, Union of South Africa. [Acarina: Trombidiformes of S.Africa (Yes)]

MEYERREICKS, Andrew J. Box 155, South Lincoln, Mass., U.S.A. [Aves: Ardeidae of N. America (Yes)]

MEYL, Dr. Arwed H. Rungsdorfer Strasse 1 A, Bad Godesberg, Bonn, Germany. [F-l. soil & f-w. Nematoda of World (Yes); plant parasitic Nematoda of World (No)]

* MICHAEL, Mr. Peter. 19 Green Lane, Shortheath, Farnham, Surrey, England. [Odonata]

* MICHAJŁOW, Dr. Włodzimierz. Zakład Parazytologii, Polska Akademia Nauk, ul. Pasteura 3, Warszawa, Poland. [Cestoda]

MICHALK, Otto. Kurt Eisnerstrasse 74, Leipzig S 3, German Democratic Republic. [Heteroptera larvae of c.Europe (Yes)]

MICHELBACHER, Prof. A.E. Department of Entomology, University of California, Berkeley 4, Calif., U.S.A. [Symphyla of World (Yes, to genus)]

MICHELSON, E.H. Harvard School of Public Health, 25 Shattuck Street. Boston 15, Mass., U.S.A. [F-w. Gastropoda of New World (Yes); Pulmonata: Stylommatophora of N.America (Yes)]

MICHENER, Dr. Charles D. Department of Entomology, University of Kansas, Lawrence, Kans., U.S.A. [Hymenoptera: Apoidea of New World (Yes)]

MICHERDZINSKI, Dr. W. Zoology Department, Jagiellonian University, SW. Anny 6, Kraków, Poland. [Acarina: Pterolichidae, Epidermoptidae, Laelaptidae, Haemogamasidae, Liponyssidae, of Europe & U.S.S.R (Yes); orchard mites of Europe (No)]

MICHIELI, Štefan. Biološki Institut, Slovenske Akademije Znanosti in Umetnosti, 13 Gosposka, Ljubljana, Yugoslavia. [Macrolepidoptera, espec. Rhopalocera & Noctuidae, of Europe (Yes); Neuroptera of Slovenia (No); Embioptera of Europe (Yes)]

MICKEL, Dr. Clarence E. Department of Entomology & Zoology, University of Minnesota, St. Paul 1, Minn., U.S.A. [Hymenoptera: Mutillidae of New World & Pacific Is. (Yes)]

MICKS, Dr. Don W. Department of Preventive Medicine & Public Health, University of Texas Medical Branch, Galveston, Texas, U.S.A. [Diptera: Culicidae, biochemical taxonomy, of World (Yes)]

MIDDLEKAUFF, Prof. Woodrow W. Department of Entomology, University of California, Berkeley 4, Calif., U.S.A. [Hymenoptera: Symphyta of N. America (Yes); Diptera: Tabanidae of California (Yes)]

MIDDLEMISS, Dr. F.A. Department of Geology, Queen Mary College, Mile End Road, London, E.1, England. [L. Cretaceous Brachiopoda: Terebratulacea of n.w. Europe (Yes)]

MIDDOUR, Eldridge S. Atlantic Refining Co., Drawer 1981, Corpus Christi, Texas, U.S.A. [Cretaceous-Recent Radiolaria of N. America (Yes); Cretaceous-Miocene Foraminifera of s.w. Texas & n.e. Mexico (Yes)]

MIHÁLYI, Dr. F. Magyar Nemzeti Muzeum, Baross u. 13, Budapest VIII, Hungary. [Diptera: Culicidae & Syrphidae of Europe (Yes); Trypetidae & Tachinidae of Europe (No)]

MIHARA, Minoru. Division of Medical Entomology, National Institute Health, Chojamaru 284, Kamiosaki, Shinagawa-ku, Tokyo, Japan. [Lepidoptera of Japan (No)]

MIHELČIČ, Dr. Franc. St. Johann i. Walde, Austria. [Acarina: Oribatei, Trombidiformes, Prostigmata of Europe (Yes); Tardigrada of Europe (Yes)]

MIKOŁAJCZYK, Mgr. Waldemar. Instytut Zoologiczny, Polska Akademia Nauk, ul. Wilcza 64, Warszawa, Poland. [Diptera: Mycetophilidae of c. Europe (Yes)]

MIKŠIČ, René. Institut za šumarstvo i Drvnu Industriju, ul. Maršala Tita 5 (Post. FAH 178), Sarajevo, Yugoslavia. [Coleoptera: Scarabaeidae of Europe, Asia Minor, n. Africa (Yes); Cetoniinae of Palearctic (Yes); Geotrupinae: g. Geotrupes of Europe, Asia, n. Africa, N. America (Yes)]

MIKULIN, M.A. Zavodskaya Street 14, Building 1, Apartment 1, Alma-Ata 22, Kazakh SSR, U.S.S.R. [Siphonaptera of Russia & c. Asia (Yes)]

MIKULSKA, Doc. Izabela. Zakład Zoologii Ogólnej, Uniwersytet Mikołaja Kopernika, ul. Sienkiewicza 30/32, Toruń, Poland. [Araneida of Holarctic (No)]

MIKULSKI, Prof. Dr. Józef. Zakład Ekologii, Uniwersytet Mikołaja Kopernika, ul. Sienkiewicza 30/32, Toruń, Poland. [Ephemeroptera of Holarctic (No); of Europe (Yes)]

MILBURN, William Patrick. 425 Iris Avenue, Corona del Mar, Calif., U.S.A. [Gastropoda: Opisthobranchiata of w. cst. N. America (No)]

* MILES, Dr. Cecil B. Address unknown. [Pisces]

MILES, Charles D. Room 125, Biological Sciences Bldg., University of Arizona, Tucson, Ariz., U.S.A. [Gastropoda: Succineidae of Kansas (Yes)]

* MILES, Lee O. P.O. Box 180, Bodega Bay, Calif., U.S.A. [Mollusca]

* MILES, Dr. Philip. "Sun Hill", High Street, Aberystwyth, Cardiganshire, Wales. [Collembola]

MILITANTE, Priscilla. Department of Geology & Geography, University of the Philippines, Diliman, Rizal, Philippines. [Fossil Foraminifera: Rissoinidae of Philippines (Yes)]

MILLAR, R.H. Marine Biology Station, Millport, Isle of Cumbrae, Scotland. [Ascidiacea of World (Yes)] [Scottish Marine Biological Association]

MILLARD, N.H. Department of Zoology, University of Cape Town, Cape Town, Union of South Africa. [Marine Hydrozoa of s. Africa]

MILLEMAN, Dr. Raymond E. University of Rochester, School of Medicine, Rochester 20, N.Y., U.S.A. [Nematoda: Spiruroidea of New World (Yes); Cestoda: Linstowiidae of New World & Europe (Yes); Trematoda: Monogenea: Hexostomatidae of New World & Europe (Yes)]

MILLER, Dr. Albert. Department of Tropical Medicine, Tulane University of Louisiana, 1430 Tulane Avenue, New Orleans 12, La., U.S.A. [Acarina: Ixodoidea & Diptera: Culicidae of N. America (Yes); Macrolepidoptera of N. America (No)]

MILLER, Prof. Alden H. Museum of Vertebrate Zoology, University of California, Berkeley 4, Calif., U.S.A. [Tertiary & Pleistocene Aves of N. America (Yes); Aves of New World (Yes)]

MILLER, Prof. A.K. Department of Geology, State University of Iowa, Iowa City, Iowa, U.S.A. [Paleozoic Cephalopoda: Ammonoidea (Yes); Cambrian-Recent Cephalopoda: Nautiloidea (Yes)]

MILLER, Mr. C.D.F. Insect Systematics & Biological Control Unit, Science Service Bldg., Carling Avenue, Ottawa, Ont., Canada. [Hymenoptera: Formicidae, of N. America, espec. Canada; Vespoidea of N. America, g. Vespula of World; Sphecoidea of N. America, espec. Canada; Encyrtidae: g. Copidosoma of N. America (all Yes)]

MILLER, Dr. David. Entomological Station, Cawthron Institute, Nelson, New Zealand. [Diptera of New Zealand]

MILLER, Dr. D.D. Department of Zoology, University of Nebraska, Lincoln 8, Neb., U.S.A. [Diptera: Drosophila affinis group of World (Yes, living specimens]

MILLER, Dr. E. Morton. Department of Zoology, University of Miami, Coral Gables 34, Fla., U.S.A. [Isoptera of s.e. U.S. (Yes)]

MILLER, Prof. Dr. Franz. Uvoz 17, Brno, Czechoslovakia. [Araneae of Europe (Yes)] [Vysoká škola zemědělská]

MILLER, Prof. Forrest W. Department of Biology, Hartwick College, Oneonta, N.Y., U.S.A. [Homoptera: Aphidae of N. America & World (Yes)]

MILLER, Prof. Halsey Wilkinson, Jr. Department of Geology, University of Arizona, Tucson, Ariz., U.S.A. [Cretaceous Macro Invertebrate Fossils of N. America (No); Cretaceous Pelecypoda of N. America (No)]

* MILLER, Dr. Joseph H. Louisiana State University School of Medicine, 1542 Tulane Ave., New Orleans 12, La., U.S.A. [Trematoda of n.e. U.S.]

MILLER, Lee D. 3331 Franklin Avenue, Des Moines 10, Iowa, U.S.A. [Lepidoptera: Lycaenidae, esp. Theclinae; Satyridae: Hesperiidae, excl. Amblyscirtes, Lerodea, & Erynnis; Megathymidae; of N. America (Yes)] [State University of Iowa]

MILLER, Prof., Loye Holmes. Museum of Vertebrate Zoology, University of California, Berkeley 4, Calif., U.S.A. [Tertiary-Recent fossil Aves of w.N. America (No)]

MILLER, Dr. Lawrence I. Virginia Agriculture Experiment Station, Holland, Va., U.S.A. [Nematoda: g. Belonolaimus, Meloidogyne (No)]

MILLER, Lowell S. (Davenport, Iowa; Mammalia) Died December 12, 1955.

MILLER, Prof. Milton A. Department of Zoology, University of California, Davis, Calif., U.S.A. [Crustacea: Isopoda & Tanaidacea of N. America, Hawaii, Micronesia, Bermuda, Caribbean (Yes)]

MILLER, N.C.E. Commonwealth Institute of Entomology, British Museum (Natural History), Cromwell Road, London, S.W.7, England. [Heteroptera: Reduviidae of Old World (No)]

MILLER, Dr. Richard B. Department of Zoology, University of Alberta, Edmonton, Alta., Canada. [Pisces (No); Platyhelminthes of fish (Yes); terr. & f-w. Gastropoda (Yes); all of Canadian Prairies & McKenzie Basin] See Addenda.

MILLER, Dr. Richard G. Department of Zoology, Long Beach State College, Long Beach 15, Calif., U.S.A. [Pisces of Antarctic & U.S. (Yes)]

* MILLER, Ross J. Department of Ornithology, Illinois Natural History Survey, Urbana, Ill., U.S.A. [Aves of N. America]

MILLER, Mr. Rudolph J. Conservation Department, Fernow Hall, Cornell University, Ithaca, N.Y., U.S.A. [Marine Pisces of Atlantic cst. U.S. (Yes); Serranidae g. Centropristes of N. America & C. America (Yes)]

MILLER, Dr. Robert R. Museum of Zoology, University of Michigan, Ann Arbor, Mich., U.S.A. [F-w. Pisces of w.N. America & C. America]

MILLER, W.V. 1909 Clifton Avenue, Chicago 14, Ill., U.S.A. [Coleoptera: Staphylinidae of N. & C. America (Yes); Heteroceridae of N. & S. America (Yes)]

MILLIDGE, Dr. A.F. 10 Wilheimina Avenue, Coulsdon, Surrey, England. [Araneida of British Isles & n.w. Europe (Yes)]

MILLIGAN, R.H. Forest Research Institute, P.B., Whaka, Rotorua, New Zealand. [Wood-boring Insects of New Zealand (Yes)]

MILLIRON, Dr. H.E. 911 Burley Avenue, Glen Dale, West Virginia, U.S.A. [Hymenoptera: Apidae: Bombini of New World (Yes); Torymidae: Megastigmini of Nearctic (Yes)]

MILLO, Bruno. Consorzio Agrario, 21 Via Fabio Filzi, Trieste, Italy. [Coleoptera: Coprophagous Scarabaeidae of Palearctic (Yes)]

MILLOT, Prof. J. Museum National d'Histoire Naturelle, Laboratoire d'Anatomie Comparée, 55 Rue de Buffon, Paris (V), France. [Arachnida of Indian Ocean (No)]

MILLOTT Prof. Norman. Department of Zoology, Bedford College, Regent's Park, London, N.W.8, England. [Echinodermata, espec. Echinoidea, of British Isles & Caribbean (No)] [University of London]

MILLS, Dr. Harlow B. State Natural History Survey, Urbana, Ill., U.S.A. [Collembola of N. & C. America (Yes)]

MILOW, E. Dean. Geology Department, San Diego State College, San Diego 15, Calif., U.S.A. [Cretaceous & early Tertiary Foraminifera of w.N. America (No); Recent Foraminifera of Gulf of Mexico (No)]

MILSTEAD, William W. Department of Biology, Sul Ross State College, Alpine, Texas, U.S.A. [Amphibia & Reptilia of s.w.U.S., n. Mexico, s.e. Brazil (Yes); Pleistocene Testudinata (No)]

MILWARD, Mr. Norman. Department of Zoology, University of Western Australia, Nedlands, W. Australia. [Pisces: Blennioidea of Australia (Yes)]

MINAMORI, Dr. Sumio. Zoological Laboratory, Faculty of Science, Hiroshima University, Hiroshima, Japan. [Pisces: Cobitidae of Japan (No)]

MINATO, Masau. Department of Geology & Mineralogy, Hokkaido University, Sapporo, Japan. [Up. Paleozoic Brachiopoda of e. Asia (Yes); fossil Tetracoralla of e. Asia (Yes)]

MINTON, Dr. Sherman A., Jr. Indiana University Medical Center, 1040 W. Michigan Street, Indianapolis, Ind., U.S.A. [Amphibia of e.N. America (Yes); Reptilia of N. America (Yes); poisonous snakes of World (Yes)]

de MIRANDA-RIBEIRO, Paulo, Naturalista do Museu Nacional, Quinta da Boa Vista, Rio de Janeiro, Brazil. [Pisces of S. America, espec. f-w. (Yes)]

de MIRE, P. Bruneau. See BRUNEAU de MIRE, P.

MIRIĆ, Djordje. Museum d'Histoire Naturelle, Njegoseva 51-Pošt, fah 401, Beograd, Yugo-
slavia. [Mammalia of Yugoslavia (Yes)]
* MIRSA, Dr. Artu. Institut Nacional de Hygiene, Ap. 4412, Oficina del Este, Ciudad Universi-
taria, Caracas, Venezuela. [Diptera: Ceratopogonidae: g. Phlebotomus]
MIRZA, Prof. M.B., Head, Department of Zoology, Muslim University, Aligarh, U.P., India.
[Nematoda (Yes)]
MISHCHENKO, Leo. Zoological Institute, Academy of Sciences of U.S.S.R, Leningrad V-164,
U.S.S.R. [Orthoptera of Europe, Asia, n. Africa (Yes)] See Addenda.
MISIK, Vitazoslav. Slowakishe Akademie der Wissenchaften, Laboratorium der Ichthyologie,
Bratislava, Czechoslovakia. [Recent Pisces of Europe & Asia (Yes)]
MISKIMEN, George W. V.I.Z.P., U.S. Department of Agriculture, Kingshill, St. Croix, U.S.
Virgin Islands. [Coleoptera: Cantharidae & Phenogodidae of New World (Yes)]
* MISLIN, Dr. H. Zoologische Anstalt der Universität, 9 Rheinsprung, Bale, Switzerland.
[Mammalia]
MISONNE, Dr. Xavier. Vertebrate Paleontology Department, Institut Royal des Sciences
Naturelles de Belgique, 31 rue Vautier, Bruxelles, Belgium. [Tertiary Mammalia: Ro-
dentia (Yes)] [Université Lovanium, Leopoldville, Congo]
MISRA, Prof. D.S., Head, Science Department, Kalicharan College, Lucknow, U.P., India.
[Reptilia: Ophidia, Elapidae & Viperidae of n. India (Yes)]
* MISRA, Dr. K.S. Assistant Superintendent, Zoological Survey of India, 34 Chittaranjan
Avenue, Calcutta 12, India. [Pisces]
MISTSHENKO, L.L. Zoological Institute, Academy of Sciences, Leningrad V-164, U.S.S.R.
[Orthoptera of Palearctic (Yes)] See Addenda.
* MITANI, Mr. Fumio. Department of Fisheries, Faculty of Agriculture, University of Kyoto,
Nagahama. Maizura City, Kyoto Pref., Japan. [Pisces]
MITCHELL, Mr. F.J. Department of Herpetology, South Australian Museum, Adelaide, S.
Australia. [Amphibia & Reptilia of Australasia (Yes); Lacertilia of Indo-Australian Arch.
(No)]
MITCHELL, Mr. M. Palaeontology Department, Geological Survey, Exhibition Road, London,
S.W.7, England. [L. Carboniferous corals of Britain (No)]
MITCHELL, Rodger. Department of Biology, University of Florida, Gainesville, Fla., U.S.A.
[Acarina; Water mites of World (Yes)]
MITCHELL, Robert T., Wildlife Biologist, Patuxent Research Refuge, Laurel, Md., U.S.A.
[Hymenoptera: Ichneumonidae of Nearctic (Yes)]
MITCHELL, T.B. Division of Biology & Entomology, Box 5215, State College Station, Raleigh,
N.C., U.S.A. [Hymenoptera: Apoidea of e. U.S. (Yes); g. Megachile & Lithurgus of
World (Yes)]
MITO, Mr. Satoshi. Department of Fisheries, Faculty of Agriculture, Kyushu University,
Hakozaki, Fukuoka City, Japan. [Pelagic eggs & larvae of marine Pisces of c. & s.
Japan (Yes)]
MITONO, Takeo. Division of Entomology, Shimane Agricultural Experiment Station, Izumo,
Shimane Pref., Japan. [Coleoptera: Cerambycidae of Japan, Formosa, Korea, Micro-
nesia (Yes)]
* MITSKEVITCH, V.Yu. Institute of Extending Veterinarian's Qualifications, Leningrad,
U.S.S.R. [Animal helminths]
* MITTLEMAN. M.B. Address unknown. [Reptilia &Amphibia]
MIWA, Yûshirô. Oshikabe 212, Tsu City, Mie Pref., Japan. [Coleoptera & Lepidoptera of
Palearctic & Oriental] [Mie Prefectural Museum]
MIYADI, Prof. Dr. Denzaburo. Department of Zoology, College of Science, Kyoto University,
Kyoto, Japan. [F-w. Pisces of Japan (Yes); of Manchuria (No)]
MIYAKE, Dr. Assist. Prof. Sadayoski. Zoological Laboratory, Faculty of Agriculture, Kyushu
University, Fukuoka, Japan. [Crustacea: Decapoda of Japan (Yes); Decapoda, Brachyura,
Anomura of Ryukyu Is., Formosa, Bonin Is., Sea of Japan, China, n. Japan, Aleutian Is.
(Yes)]
MIYAMOTO, Syôiti. Biological Laboratory, General Education Department, Kyushu University,
Fukuoka, Japan. [Heteroptera: Amphibiocorisae & Hydrocorisae of Japan (Yes)]
MIYATAKE, Mutsuo. Entomology Laboratory, College of Agriculture, Ehime University, Mat-
suyama City, Shikoku, Japan. [Coleoptera: Cocinellidae of e. Asia (Yes); fungivorous
groups, espec. Ciidae & Mycetophagidae of Japan (Yes)]
MIYAZAKI, Prof. Ichiro. Department of Parasitology, Faculty of Medicine, Kyushu University,
Fukuoka, Japan. [Nematoda: Gnathostomidae, g. Gnathostoma; Trematoda: Troglotrema-
tidae: g. Paragonimus; both of Asia & N. America (Yes); Insecta: Culicidae; Acarina:
Trombiculidae; both of Japan (Yes)]
MIYOSI, Yasunori. Matsuyama Kita High School, Teppocho, Matsuyama City, Shikoku, Japan.
[Diplopoda & Chilopoda of Japan & Ryuku Is. (Yes)]
* MIZELLE, Dr. John D. 908 South Vine, Urbana, Ill., U.S.A. [Trematoda: Monogenea]
* MIZOGUCHI, Osamu. 16 2-chome, Chibune-Higashi, Nishiyodogawa, Osaka, Japan. [Lepidop-
tera: Rhopalocera]

MIZUNO, Atsuyuki. Geological Survey of Japan, 135 Hisamoto-chô, Kawasaki, Japan. [Neo-gene & Paleogene marine & non-marine Mollusca of Japan (Yes)]

MŁYNARSKI, Dr. Marian. Instytut Zoologiczny, Polska Akademia Nauk, ul. Sławkowska 17, Kraków, Poland. [Tertiary fossil Reptiles of Eurasia (Yes); Recent Chelonia of World (Yes); Primitive snakes of Neotropics & Indo-Malaya (Yes)]

MOCKFORD, Edward L. Faunistic Section, Illinois Natural History Survey, Urbana, Ill., U.S.A. [Psocoptera of New World (Yes); of Old World (No)]

MÓCZÁR, Dr. L. Magyar Nemzeti Museum, Baross u. 13, Budapest VIII, Hungary. [Hymenoptera: Pompilidae, Sphecidae: Crabronini & Oxybelini, of Palearctic (No)]

MÓCZÁR, Dr. M. Magyar Nemzeti Museum, Baross u. 13, Budapest VIII, Hungary. [Hymenoptera: Apoidea: Apidae, Megachilidae, Melittidae, of Europe (No)]

MODELL, Hans. Brinzstrasse 130, (13b) Weiler (Allgäu), Germany. [Triassic-Recent f-w. Pelecypoda: Naiades of World (Yes)]

* MOGK, H. Address unknown. [Crustacea]

MÖHL, Ulrik. Zoologiske Museum, København Universitets, Krystalgade 27, København, Denmark. [Subfossil bones of Scandinavia & Greenland (No)]

MÖHN, Dr. Edwin. Staatliches Museum für Naturkunde, Entomologische Abteilung, Archivstrasse 4, Stuttgart-O, Germany. [Diptera: Cecidomyiidae, imagines, Larvae, & Galls of World (Yes)]

MOHR, Charles E. Swiss Pines Park, Route 1, Malvern, Penna., U.S.A. [Cave Vertebrates of e.N. America (Yes)]

MOHR, Dr. Erna, Kustos, Zoologisches Staatsinstitut und Zoologisches Museum, Bornplatz 5, Hamburg 13, Germany. [Mammalia: Pinnipedia of World (Yes)]

MOHR, J. L. Department of Biology, University of Southern California, Los Angeles 7, Calif., U.S.A. [Protozoa; Ciliata: Chonotrichida & Opalinida of World (Yes)]

MOHSENUL HAQUE, A. F. M. See HAGUE, A. F. M. Mohsenul.

* MOITRA, Mr. S.K. Department of Zoology, Lucknow University, Lucknow, India. [Pisces]

MOKIYEVSKY, O. B. Institute of Oceanology, Academy of Sciences of U.S.S.R., Luzhnikovskaya 8, Moscow, U.S.S.R. [Amphipoda: Gammaroidea: Talitridae of Far Eastern seas of U.S.S.R (Yes); Caprelloidea of same (No)]

MOLANDER, Dr. Arvid. Swedish Fisheries Laboratory, Lysekil, Sweden. [Pisces: Pleuronectidae & Clupeidae of n. Europe (Yes)] [Institute of Marine Research]

MOLANDER, Gene Emery. 15220 Alicante Road, La Mirada, Calif., U.S.A. [Cenozoic Foraminifera of w. cst. N. America (No)]

MOLINARI, Sr. Horacio. Calle 10, Trujui, B.A., Argentina. [Coleoptera: Tenebrionidae of World (No); of S. America (Yes)]

MOLTONI, Dr. E., Direttore, Museo Civico di Storia Naturale, Corso Venezia 55, Milano, Italy. [Aves of Europe & Africa (No)]

MOMENT, Dr. Gairdner B. Department of Biology, Goucher College, Baltimore 4, Md., U.S.A. [Oligochaeta of n.e. U.S. (Yes); Polychaeta: Maldanidae of e. cst. U.S. (Yes)]

MONACO, Dr. Lawrence H. 4217 Warwick Drive, Corpus Christi, Texas, U.S.A. [Trematoda: Monogenea: Dactylogyridae: g. Dactylogyrus & Rhamnocerus of N. America (Yes)] [Department of Biology, Del Mar College]

* MONARD, A. Musée d'Histoire Naturelle, La Chaux-defonds, Switzerland. [Crustacea: Copepoda]

* MONDOLFI, Edgardo. Museo de Biologia, Universidad Central de Venezuela, Caracas, Venezuela. [Mammalia]

MONGIN, Miss Denise. 9 rue de Mézières, Paris (VI), France. [Jurassic-Cretaceous marine Mollusca of w. Europe & n. Africa (No); Miocene marine Mollusca, espec. Pectinidae, of n. Africa & w. Europe (Yes); Chesapeake Bay, U.S. (No)] [Museum National d'Histoire Naturelle]

MONK, Prof. Cecil R. Department of Biology, Willamette University, Salem, Ore., U.S.A. [Crustacea: Copepoda: marine Harpacticoida of w. cst. N. America (No)]

MONK, Wilfred J. Ohio Oil Co., Box 39, Sidney, Neb., U.S.A. [Ordovician Brachiopoda, corals, Bryozoa, of Colorado & Oklahoma (Yes); Pennsylvanian corals, Bryozoa, Foraminifera of Nebraska, Kansas, Colorado (Yes)]

MOŃKO, Mgr. Agnieszka. Instytut Zoologiczny, Polska Akademia Nauk, ul. Wilcza 64, Warszawa, Poland. [Diptera: Larvaevoridae of Europe (Yes)]

MONOD, Th. Institut Français d'Afrique Noire, B. P. 206, Dakar, French West Africa. [Pisces (No); Crustacea: Brachyura of w. Africa (Yes); marine Isopoda of w. Africa (No)]

MONRÓS, Francisco de Asis. (Tucumán, Argentina: Coleoptera: Chrysomelidae) Deceased.

MONTANARO-GALLITELLI, Dr. Eugenia. Paleontological Institute, University of Modena, Modena, Italy. [Up. Cretaceous, Up. Tertiary, Quaternary Microforaminifera of Apennines (Yes); Up. Tertiary Anthozoa of Apennines (Yes); Permian Anthozoa of Sicily (Yes); Up. Tertiary & Quaternary Anthozoa of Red Sea; M. Miocene Mollusca of n. Apennines (Yes)]

MONTE, Oscar. (São Paulo, Brazil; Lepidoptera & Heteroptera) Deceased.

de MONTE, Dr. Med. Tiziano. Via S. Cilino 21, Trieste (221), Italy. [Coleoptera: Carabidae, g. Bembidion of Europe, Asia, Africa (Yes)] [Museo Civico di Storia Naturale]

MONTEIRO, R. P. Teodoro. Mosteiro de Singeverga, Negrelos, Portugal. [Lepidoptera, espec. Psychidae, of Portugal (Yes)]

* MONTÉN, Mr. E. Zoologiska Institution, Lunds Universitets, Lund, Sweden. [Gordiacea]

MONTEROSSO, Prof. Bruno. Istituto di Zoologia, Universitá di Catania, Via Androne 25, Catania, Italy. [Araneida: Dipneumonomorphae of Europe (No)]

MONTGOMERY, Prof. B. Elwood. Department of Entomology, School of Agriculture, Purdue University, Lafayette, Ind., U. S. A. [Odonata, adults, of World (Yes), naiads of N. America (Yes); Calopterygoidea, adults & naiads of New World (Yes)]

MONTGOMERY, Mr. David H. Department of Biological Sciences, California State Polytechnic College, San Luis Obispo, Calif., U. S. A. [Crustacea Copepoda: Enterocolidae & Notodelphyidae of Pacific cst. U. S. (Yes); Ascidicolidae, Doropygidae, Botryllophilidae, of Pacific cst. U. S. (No)]

* MONTGOMERY, J. C. P. O. Box 2279, Houston 1, Texas, U. S. A. [Fossil Invertebrates]

MONTREUIL, Paul, Director, Marine Biological Laboratory, Grindstone, Magdalen Is., Que., Canada. [Parasites of marine fish & invertebrates of n. w. Atlantic (No); Acanthocephala: Polymorphinae: g. Corynosoma of World (Yes)]

* MONTSHADSKIJ, Prof. Dr. Alexander S. Department of Entomology, Zoological Institute, Academy of Sciences, Leningrad, V-164, U. S. S. R. [Diptera]

MONZEN, Kota. Biological Laboratory, Iwate University, Morioka, Iwate-ken, Japan. [Hymenoptera: galls & gall insects of Oriental]

MOOJEN, Dr. Joao. Museu Nacional, Quinta da Boa Vista, Rio de Janeiro, Brazil. [Mammalia: Glires of S. America (Yes)]

* MOOK, Dr. C. C. 231 Chestnut Avenue, Metuchen, N. J., U. S. A. [Fossil Vertebrates]

MOORE, Dr. Barry Philip. Montrose, Stoneyfields, Farnham, Surrey, England. [Coleoptera: Carabidae of Europe & Australia (Yes); Odonata of Europe & Australia (Yes)]

MOORE, Mr. Donald. Gulf Coast Research Laboratory, Ocean Springs, Miss., U. S. A. [Minute marine Mollusca of Gulf of Mexico & Caribbean (Yes); Gastropoda: Vitrinellidae of same (Yes)]

MOORE, Donald V. Department of Microbiology, University of Texas-Southwestern Medical School, 5323 Harry Hines Blvd., Dallas, Texas, U. S. A. [Acanthocephala of New World (Yes); Trematoda: Schistosomatidae, of birds & mammals of N. America (Yes)]

MOORE, E. F. 205 Hillside Avenue, Chatham, N. J., U. S. A. [Amphibia: Salamanders of caves of e. U. S. (No)]

MOORE, Prof. G. A. Department of Zoology, Oklahoma State University, Stillwater, Okla., U. S. A. [F-w. Pisces of U. S. (Yes)]

MOORE, G. A. Lyman Entomological Collection, Redpath Museum, McGill University, Montreal, Que., Canada. [Hemiptera]

MOORE, Prof. George M. JUSMAG, Attn. U. S. Information Service, APO 74, Box B, San Francisco, Calif., U. S. A. [Gastropoda: Nudibranchiata of New England, U. S. (Yes)]

MOORE, Mr. Ian. 647 El Monte Road, El Cajon, Calif., U. S. A. [Coleoptera: Staphylinidae of World (No), of Nearctic & Neotropical (Yes)] [San Diego Natural History Museum]

MOORE, Prof. John A. Department of Zoology, Columbia University, New York 27, N. Y., U. S. A. [Amphibia of Australia (Yes); of N. America (No)]

MOORE, Dr. Joseph Curtis. Department of Mammals, American Museum of Natural History, New York 24, N. Y., U. S. A. [Mammalia: Sciuridae of Indomalayan (Yes); Cetacea of Atlantic Ocean (Yes); Sirenia of World (Yes)]

MOORE, Dr. J. Edward. Department of Zoology, University of Alberta, Edmonton, Alta., Canada. [Mammalia, Reptilia, Amphibia, of Alberta (Yes)]

MOORE, Prof. J. Percy. Highland Avenue, Media, Penna., U. S. A. [Annelida in general (No); Hirudinea of World (Yes)] [Department of Zoology, University of Pennsylvania]

* MOORE, Lucy B. 9 Hadfield Terrace, Wellington 1, New Zealand. [Crustacea]

MOORE, Dr. Norman W. The Nature Conservancy, Furzebrook Research Station, Wareham, Dorset, England. [Odonata, Aves, Reptilia, of British Isles (Yes)]

MOORE, Dr. Raymond C. Lindley Hall, University of Kansas, Lawrence, Kans., U. S. A. [Fossil Crinoidea of World; Up. Paleozoic Bryozoa & Anthozoa: Rugosa & Tabulata, of World]

MOORE, Mr. Reginald G. Museum of Paleontology, University of Michigan, Ann Arbor, Mich., U. S. A. [Mesozoic & Tertiary non-marine Gastropoda of N. America (Yes)]

MOORE, Robert T. (Los Angeles, Calif., U. S. A.; Aves) Died November, 1958.

MOORE, Dr. Thomas E. Museum of Zoology, University of Michigan, Ann Arbor, Mich., U. S. A. [Homoptera: Cicadidae of N. America & Mexico (Yes); Cercopidae & Cicadellidae of N. America (Yes); Heteroptera: Miridae of N. America (Yes)]

MOORE, Mr. Wayne E. Box 510, Pensacola, Fla., U. S. A. [Mesozoic & Tertiary large Foraminifera of Gulf Coast & Caribbean (Yes)]

MOORE, Dr. Walter G. Department of Biology, Loyola University, New Orleans 18, La., U. S. A. [Porifera: Spongillidae of U. S. (No); Crustacea: Branchiopoda: Anostraca of N. America & Mexico (Yes)]

283

* MOORE, Mr. W.W. The Texas Co., P.O. Box 252, New Orleans 9, La., U.S.A. [Fossil Invertebrates]
MOORTHY, V.N. (Bangalore, India; Nematoda) Deceased.
MOOS, Dr. Beata. Niedersächisches Landesamt für Bodenforschung, Wiesenstrasse 1, Hannover, Germany. [Jurassic-Recent marine Crustacea: Ostracoda of Germany (Yes)]
MOOSER-BARENDUN, Oswaldo. Avenido Madero 309, Aguascalientes, Mexico. [Lepidóptera: Sphingidae of Mexico (Yes); Pliocene & Pleistocene Mammalia: Equidae of Mexico (Yes)]
MORALES, Enrique. Instituto de Investigaciones Pesqueras, Blanes (Prov. de Gerona), Spain. [Cephalopoda of Mediterranean (Yes)]
MORALES AGACINO, E. Instituto Español de Entomologia, Gutierrez Abascal 2, Madrid, Spain. [Orthoptera of Europe & Africa (Yes)]
MOREAU, R.E. Edward Grey Institute, Oxford, England. [Aves of Ethiopian (Yes)]
MOREL, Pierre Claude. 28 rue Marsoulan, Paris (XII), France. [Acarina: Ixodidae & Argasidae of w. Europe, n. Africa, Ethiopian (Yes)] [Laboratoire Fédéral de l'Elevage, Dakar]
MORELAND, Mr. J. Dominion Museum, Buckle Street, Wellington C3, New Zealand. [Pisces: marine Teleosti of New Zealand, espec. Tripterygiidae, Uranoscopidae, Leptoscopidae (Yes)]
MOREMAN, W.L. Magnolia Petroleum Co., P.O. Box 900, Dallas 21, Texas, U.S.A. [Ordovican-Devonian arenaceous Foraminifera of Oklahoma (Yes); Ammonoidea of Texas (No)]
MORENO, Dr. Abelardo. Museo Poey, Cátedra U., University of Havana, Habana, Cuba. [Aves of Cuba (Yes); Scorpiones of Cuba & West Indies (Yes)]
MORENO, Dr. Amalia F. Instituto de Patologia Vegetal, Paseo Colon 922, 4º Piso, Buenos Aires, Argentina. [Plant parasitic Nematoda of Argentina (Yes)]
* MORERA, Antonio Benitez. C/o Instituto Español de Entomologia, Gutierrez Abascal 2, Madrid, Spain. [Odonata]
MORETON, B.D. Ministry of Agriculture, Fisheries & Food, Wye, Ashford, Kent, England. [Nematoda of economic importance (No)]
MORETTI, Prof. G.P. University of Perugia, Institut of Hydrobiology, Monte del Lago sul Trasimemo, Magione, Perugia, Italy. [Trichoptera, Larvae, Nymphae, Imagines, of Italy (Yes)]
MORGAN, Banner Bill. Died September 8, 1950.
MORGAN, Mr. C.V.G. Entomology Laboratory, Science Service, R.R. No. 1, Summerland, B.C., Canada. [Acarina: Tetranychidae: g. Bryobia of N. America (Yes)]
* MORGAN, Dr. D.O. Veterinary School, Cambridge, England. [Nematoda]
MORGAN, H.G. National Agricultural Advisory Service, Staplake Mount, Starcross, Exeter, Devon., England. [Heteroptera: Corixidae of Britain (Yes); Homoptera: Aphididae of Britain (No)]
MORGANTE, Gino Cadamuro. Calle Oslavia 10, S. Elena, Venezia, Italy. [Coleoptera: Carabidae of Palearctic (No); of Italy (Yes)]
MORGE, Günter, Diplom-Forstwirt, Walter-Rathenau-Strasse 3, Eberswalde bei Berlin, German Democratic Republic. [Diptera: Lonchaeidae, incl. larvae & Pupae, of Palearctic, Oriental, Africa (Yes); Pallopteridae, incl. larvae & pupae, of Palearctic (Yes)] [Institut für Forstzoologie, Humboldt, Universität, Eberswald]
* MORI, Prof. Tamezo. Zoological Department, Hyogo University of Agriculture, Sasayama, Hyogo-ken, Japan. [Pisces]
* MORICE, Mr. J., Chef du Laboratoire, Office Scientifique et Technique des Peches, 59 Avenue R. Poincaré, Paris (XVI), France. [Pisces]
MORIKAWA, Kuniyasu. Biological Institute, Ehime University, Matsuyama, Japan. [Acarina: Oribatid of Japan (Yes); Pseudoscorpiones of Japan (Yes); Tardigrada of Japan (Yes)]
MORIKAWA, Rokuro. Department of Earth Sciences, Saitama University, Urawa City, Saitama Pref., Japan. [Carboniferous & Permian Foraminifera: Fusulinidae of Japan (Yes)]
MORIMOTO, Katsura. Entomological Laboratory, Faculty of Agriculture, Kyushu University, Fukuoka, Kyushu, Japan. [Coleoptera; Curculionidae of Japan (Yes)]
MORISHIMA, Masao. Geological Institute, Faculty of Science, University of Kyoto, Kyoto, Japan. [Cenozoic & Recent Foraminifera of Japan & Pacific (Yes)]
* MORISHITA, Akiro. Geological Institute, University of Kyoto, Kyoto, Japan. [Echinodermata]
* MORISHITA, Mr. Kaoru. Department of Parasitology, Research Institute for Microbial Diseases, Osaka University, Osaka, Japan. [Nematoda]
MORISITA, Masaaki. Biological Institute, Faculty of Science, Kyushu University, Fukuoka, Japan. [Hymenoptera: Formicidae of Japan & e. Asia (Yes)]
MORISITA, Tetuo. Department of Parasitiology, Gifu Prefectural Medical School, Gifu, Japan. [Insects & Acarina of Japan (Yes)]
MORISON, Dr. Guy D. Entomological Department, North of Scotland College of Agriculture, Marischal College, Aberdeen, Scotland. [Thysanoptera of World (No); of Britain (Yes)]
* MORITSU, Magoshiro. Laboratory of Applied Entomology, Yamaguchi University, Chôfu, Shimonoseki City, Japan. [Homoptera: Aphididae]
van MORKHOVEN, F. Prinses Mariestraat 20, Den Haag, Netherlands. [Mesozoic-Recent Ostracoda, f-w., br-w., marine, (Yes); Paleozoic Ostracoda (No)]

MORLAN, Harvey B. 1941 Brogdon Street, Savannah, Ga., U.S.A. [Acarina: Gamasidae parasitic on vertebrates of N. America (Yes); Siphonaptera of N. America (Yes)] [U.S. Public Health Service]

MORO, Gio Batta. Corso Andrea Podestá 11/3, Genova, Italy. [Coleoptera: Histeridae of Europe (Yes)]

*MOROZOV, Dr. Prof. F.N. Pedagogical Institute, Ulyanova street 1, Gorky, U.S.S.R. [Helminthes of animals of U.S.S.R]

MOROZOVA, I.P. Paleontological Institute, Academy of Sciences of U.S.S.R, Avenue of Lenin 33, Moscow V-71, U.S.S.R. [Devonian & Carboniferous Bryozoa of U.S.S.R. (Yes)]

MORRIS, Charles B. American Overseas Petroleum Ltd., Posta Kutusu 1105, Ankara, Turkey. [Maestrichtian-Oligocene Foraminifera of s.e. Turkey (Yes)]

MORRIS, Dr. J.C.H. 10 College Street, Launceston, Tasmania. [Pseudoscorpiones: g. Neopsedogarypus, Synsphryronus of Tasmania (Yes)]

MORRIS, Robert Wynn. Arabian American Oil Co., Box 2576, Dhahran, Saudi Arabia. [Fossil Ostracoda: Paleocopa & Podocopa of Middle East (Yes); of N. America & Europe (No)]

MORRIS, Dr. W.J. Department of Geology, Occidental College, Los Angeles 34, Calif., U.S.A. [Eocene Mammalia of Rocky Mts. (Yes); Miocene g. Merychippus of Great Basin & Pacific U.S. (Yes); Cretaceous & Tertiary Foraminifera of California & Gulf Coast U.S. (Yes)]

MORRISON, Dr. Harold. Entomology Research Division, U.S. Department of Agriculture, Washington 25, D.C., U.S.A. [Hemiptera: Coccoidea of World (Yes)]

* MORRISON, J.P.E. Division of Mollusks, U.S. National Museum, Washington 25, D.C., U.S.A. [Mollusca]

* MORRISON, L. Gordon. Plant Quarantine Service, Department of Agriculture, Wellington, New Zealand. [Insecta]

MORRISON-SCOTT, Dr. T.C.S. Science Museum, London, S.W.7, England. [Mammalia of Palearctic & Ethiopian (No)]

MORROW, Dr. James E., Jr. Bingham Oceanographic Laboratory, Yale University, New Haven, Conn., U.S.A. [Pisces: Istiophoridae of World (Yes); Stomiatidae of Atlantic (Yes)]

MORSE, Mr. Wallace J. Department of Entomology, University of New Hampshire, Durham, N.H., U.S.A. [Odonata of e.N. America (Yes); Trichoptera of e.N. America (Yes)]

MORTON, Dr. J.E. Queen Mary College, Mile End Road, London, E.1, England. [Mollusca of Britain & New Zealand (No); Vermetidae, Siliguariidae, Strombidae, Ellobiidae & Pteropoda of World (No)]

MORTON, Wm. Markham. U.S. Fish & Wildlife Service, 6125 N. Mississippi, Portland 11, Ore., U.S.A. [Pisces: Salmonidae of Holarctic (Yes); Trematoda, Cestoda, Nematoda, Copepoda, Parasitic on Salmonidae (No)]

MÖRZER BRUIJNS, Dr. M.F. State Institute for Nature Conservation Research RIVON), Staatsbosbeheer, Soestdykseweg 33N, Bilthoven, Netherlands. [Aves of n.w. Europe (Yes)]

MOSCALEV, Mr. Lev I. Murman Marine Biological Institute, Academy of Sciences of U.S.S.R., Dalnie Zelentsy, Murman Region, U.S.S.R. [Gastropoda: Prosobranchia: Diotocardia; Docoglossa: Patellidae, Acmaeidae, Lepetidae; all of World (No); of n. Pacific Ocean (Yes)]

MOSCARDINI, Carlo. Istituto di Zoologia dell'Università, Modena, Italy. [Coleoptera of Europe (No); Cantharidae of Europe (Yes)]

MOSER, John C. Department of Entomology, Cornell University, Ithaca, N.Y., U.S.A. [Homoptera: g. Pachypsylla of World (Yes); Diptera: Cecidomyiidae, on Celtis of World (Yes); parasitic Hymenoptera of World (No)]

MOSHER, Dr Edna. (Newport, Nova Scotia; Immature stages of insects) Not now active in taxonomy.

MOSIMANN, Dr. James E. Institut de Biologie, Université de Montreal, Case Postal 6128, Montreal, Que., Canada. [Reptilia: Testudines of N. & C. America (Yes)]

* MOSKVIN, M.M. Department of Geology, Moscow State University, Moscow B-234, Lengory, U.S.S.R. [Fossil Echinoidea]

MOSSE-ROBINSON, Mr. I. (Gosford, Australia; Lepidoptera) Deceased.

MOSZYŃSKA, Mrs. Maria. ul. Grodziska 13/2, Poznan 26, Poland. [Oligochaeta: Lumbricidae of Poland (No)]

MOTAS, Prof. Dr. Constantin. Institut de Speologie "Emil Racovită", Raion Lenin, Str. Dr. Capsa 8, Bucureşti 15, Rumania. [Acarina: Hydracarina: Hydrachnellae & Halacaridae, of World (Yes)]

MOTODA, Dr. Sigeru. Faculty of Fisheries, Hokkaido University, Hakodate, Hokkaido, Japan. [Marine Crustacea: Copepoda of n. Pacific]

MOTTL, Dr. Maria, Custodian, Sectiongeologist o.d., Landesmuseum Joanneum, Raubergasse 10, Graz, Austria. [Miocene-Pleistocene Mammalia, espec. g. Hipparion, Mastodon, Dryopithecus, Ursus, Ibex, & Mustelidae of Austria & Hungary (Yes)]

MOUCHA, Josef. Entomologické Oddĕleni, Národni Museum, Václavské Námĕsti 1700, Praha II, Czechoslovakia. [Lepidoptera: of c. Europe (No); Pieridae of Palearctic (Yes); Diptera: Tabanidae of Palearctic (Yes)]

MOUCHAMPS, Dr. Raymond. Rue Paul Janson 29, Herstal (Liége), Belgium. [Coleoptera: Dytiscidae, Gyrinidae, Haliplidae & Hydrophilidae of World (Yes)] [Université de Liége]

* MOUCHET, J. Address unknown. [Coleoptera & Diptera]
* MOURA LIMA, N. See LIMA, M. M.
MOURE, Prof. Pe. J. S. Departamento de Zoologia, Universidade do Paraná - Caixa Postal 756, Curitiba, Paraná, Brazil. [Hymenoptera: Apoidea of Neotropics (Yeş); Meliponinae of World (Yes)]
MOUTERDE, Prof. l'Abbe R. Laboratoire de Géologie, Facultes Catholiques de Lyon, 25 rue de Plat, Lyon, France. [Mesozoic Ammonites (No)]
MOYES, Jean. Faculté des Sciences de Bordeaux, Centre de 30 Cycle de Géologie Approfondie, 351 Cours de la Libération, Talence (Gironde), France. [Miocene Ostracoda of Bassin d'Aguitaine (Yes)]
* MOYNIHAN, Martin H. Canal Zone Biological Area, Drawer C, Balboa, Panama Canal Zone. [Aves]
MOY-THOMAS, J. A. (Oxford, England; Pisces) Deceased.
*MOZGOVOY, Dr. A. A. Laboratory of Helminthology, Academy of Sciences of U. S. S. R., Lenin Highway 33, Moscow B-71, U. S. S. R. [Helminths of animals]
MOZLEY, Dr. Alan. C/o Barclay's Bank Foreign Branch, Pall Mall, London, S. W. 1, England. [F-w. Mollusca of sub-Arctic, Africa, Middle East (No)]
MRCIAK, Milan. Biological Institute, Czechoslovakian Academy of Sciences, Ņa Cvičišti 2, Praha XIX, Czechoslovakia. [Acarina: Laelaptidae, Haemogamasidae, Dermanyssidae, of Europe (Yes)]
MROCZKOWSKI, Dr. M. Instytut Zoologiczny, Polskiej Akademii Nauk, ul. Wilcza 64, Warsaw, Poland. [Coleoptera: Dermestidae of World (Yes)]
* MU, Mr. At. T. Institute of Paleontology, Academia Sinica, 1 Chimingssu Road, Nanking, People's Republic of China. [Echinodermata]
MUCHMORE, Dr. William B. Department of Biology, University of Rochester, Rochester 20, N. Y., U. S. A. [Arachnida: Pseudoscorpiones of e. N. America (Yes); Crustacea: Isopoda: Oniscoidea of e. N. America (Yes); Amphibia: Urodela: Plethodontidae of e. N. America (No)]
MUELLER, Joseph. R. D. 1, Lebanon, N. J., U. S. A. [Macrolepidoptera of New Jersey (Yes)]
MUELLER, Dr. J. F. Department of Microbiology, State University of N. Y., Upstate Medical Center, 766 Irving Avenue, Syracuse 10, N. Y., U. S. A. [Cestoda: g. Spirometra of World (Yes)]
MUELLER, Klaus J. See MÜLLER, K. J.
MUESEBECK, C. F. W. U. S. National Museum, Washington 25, D. C., U. S. A. [Hymenoptera: Braconidae of World (Yes)]
MÜHN, Juan B. Celegio Immaculada, Calle San Martin 1540, Santa Fe, Argentina. [Neuroptera: Embidae of S. America (No)]
MUIR-WOOD, Dr. Helen M. British Museum (Natural History), Cromwell Road, London, S. W. 7, England. [Fossil & Recent Brachiopoda of World (Yes)]
* de MUIZON, Mr. J. 33 Avenue Charles Floquet, Paris (VII), France. [Coleoptera]
* MUKERJI, Prof. D. Zoology Department, Calcutta University, 35 Ballygunj Circular Road, Calcutta 19, India. [Hymenoptera: Formicidae of w. Bengal, India (Yes)]
* MUKERJI, Prof. D. D. Zoological Survey of India, 34 Chittaranjan Avenue, Calcutta 12, India. [Pisces]
MULAIK, Stanley B. Division of Biology, University of Utah, Salt Lake City 12, Utah, U. S. A. [Acarina: Caeculidae of World (Yes); Crustacea: terrestial Isopoda of w. Hemisphere (Yes)]
MULDAL, Dr. S. Cytogenetics Department, Christi Hospital & Holt Radium Institute, Withington, Manchester 20, England. [Oligochaeta: Lumbricidae of n. w. Europe (Yes)]
MULDER, Mr. R. H. Box 31, Kogarah, Sydney, Australia. [Coleoptera: Scarabaeidae of Australia (No)]
MULES, Mr. M. W. Commonwealth Scientific & Industrial Research Organization, Animal Health Division, Park Street, Parkville, Vict., Australia. [Siphonaptera of Australia (Yes); Coleoptera: Buprestidae of Australia (Yes); Lepidoptera: Hepialidae of Australia (Yes)]
MULICKI, Dr. Zygmunt. Morski Instytut Rybacki, Al. Zjednoczenia 1, Gdynia, Poland. [Priapulidea, Polychaeta, Lamellibranchia, Crustacea, of sea bottom of Baltic Sea (Yes); Nemertini, Oligochaeta, Ascidiae, of same (No)]
MÜLLER, Prof. Dr. A. H. Geologisches Institut der Universität, Bergakademie Freiburg/Sachs., B. v. Cottastrasse, Jena, German Democratic Republic. [Up. Cretaceous Asteroidea & Ophiuroidea of n. & c. Europe (Yes); Triassic faunas of c. Europe (Yes); fossil Invertebrates in general]
MÜLLER, Prof. Dr. F. P. Institut für Phytopathologie & Pflanzenschutz, Universität Rostock, Satowerstrasse 48, Rostock, German Democratic Republic. [Homoptera: Aphididae of Africa & Europe (Yes); of New World (No)]
MULLER, Prof. Giuseppe. Museo Civico di Storia Naturale, 4 Piazza A. Hortis, Trieste, Italy. [Coleoptera of Adriatic Sea (No); Coleoptera cavernicola of Europe (No); Histeridae of Palearctic (No)]

MÜLLER, G.I. Cas Post. 53, Constanta, Rumania. [F-w. Pisces of Danube (Yes); Cyprinidae of Europe (Yes); marine Pisces of Black Sea (Yes); Crustacea: Anostraca of Europe (Yes); Nemertinea of Black Sea (Yes)]

MULLER, H.H. Landesmuseum für Vorgeschichte, Richard-Wagner-Strasse 9-10, Halle, Saale, German Democratic Republic. [Sub fossil domestic animals of Germany (Yes)]

MÜLLER, Prof. Dr. H.J. E. & I. Rosenberg Strasse 23, Quedlinburg, German Democratic Republic. [Homoptera: Auchenorrhyncha of Europe (Yes)] [Institut für Pflanzenzüctung]

* MÜLLER, Miss Ingeborg. Laboratorim für Korallenforschung, Hirschbergstrasse 27, Köln-Klettenberg, Germany. [Coelenterata: Zoantharia]

* MÜLLER, K., Assistant für Zoologie, Serpentarium, Brunnenstrasse 99, Berlin 31, Germany. [Reptilia & Amphibia]

MÜLLER, Dr. Klaus J. Department of Geology, Technische Universität, Charlottenburg 2, Berlin, Germany. [Paleozoic, espéc. Devonian, Ammonoidea (No); Conodonts of all ages of World (Yes)]

MÜLLER, Prof. Dr. L. (Munchen, Germany; Reptilia & Aves) Deceased.

* MÜLLER, Otto Herbert. Grenzstrasse 57 I, Offenbach (Main), Germany. [Odonata]

MÜLLER, Paul. (Germany; Coleoptera) Deceased.

MULLER, Prof. Siemon Wm. Box 655, Stanford University, Stanford, Calif., U.S.A. [Triassic & Jurassic Cephalopoda & Pelecypoda (Yes)]

MÜLLER-LIEBENAU, Dr. J. Limnologische Station Niederrhein, Krefeld-Hülserberg, Germany. [Ephemeroptera of Europe (No)]

MULVEY, Dr. Roland H. Nematology Section, Room 376, Science Service Building, Carling Avenue, Ottawa, Ont., Canada. [Nematoda: Mononchidae of Canada (Yes); Heteroderidae of N. America & Europe (Yes)]

MUMA, Dr. Martin H. Citrus Experiment Station, Lake Alfred, Fla., U.S.A. [Arachnida, Solpugidae of N. America (Yes); Araneida of e.U.S. (Yes); Acarina: Phytoseiidae of Florida (Yes)]

* MUMFORD, Mr. Russell E. Museum of Zoology, University of Michigan, Ann Arbor, Mich., U.S.A. [Aves]

MÜNCHBERG, Dr. Paul. Windmühlenweg 93, Soest (Westfalen), Germany. [Acarina: Hydrachnellae (g. Arrenurus) parasitic on Odonata, of Europe, Africa, New World, Australia (Yes)]

* MUNRO, Mr. G.C., Associate in Ornithology, Bernice P. Bishop Museum, 3029 Hibiscus Drive, Honolulu 15, Hawaii, U.S.A. [Aves]

* MUNRO, Dr. H.K. Division of Entomology, P.O.Box 513, Pretoria, Union of South Africa. [Diptera: Trypetidae]

MUNRO, I.S.R. Division of Fisheries & Oceanography, Commonwealth Scientific & Industrial Research Organization, Box 21, Cronulla, N.S.W., Australia. [Marine & f-w. Pisces of Australia, New Guinea, Indo-Pacific, Antarctic, including eggs & larval stages (Yes)]

MUNRO, J.A. Okanagan Landing, B.C., Canada. [Aves: Anatidae of N.America (Yes)]

MUNROE, Dr. Eugene G. Division of Entomology, Science Service Building, Central Experimental Farm, Ottawa, Ont., Canada. [Lepidoptera: Pyralidae & Pyraustidae of World (Yes)]

MUNSEY, Gordon C., Jr. C/o Atlantic Refining Company, P.O.Box 1346, Houston, Texas, U.S.A. [Mesozoic-Recent Ostracoda of N.America (Yes); fossil Foraminifera of N. America (No)]

MUNSTERMAN, Mr. H.E. Natural History Museum, Stanford University, Stanford, Calif., U.S.A. [Reptilia & Amphibia of e.Asia (Yes)]

MUNTANER, Sr. Andres. Sociedad de Historia Natural de Baleares (Estudio General Luliano), Calle de San Roque 8, Palma de Mallorca, Spain. [Mollusca of Balearic Is. & Mediterranean (Yes)]

MURAKAMI, Dr. Shiro. Seikai Regional Fisheries Research Laboratory, Maruo-machi 3-5, Nagasaki, Japan. [Ophiuroidea of n.w. Pacific (No)]

MURAKAMI, Yoshiteru. Oshima-chugakko, Niihama, Ehime-Ken, Japan. [Chilopoda: Anamorpha of Japan (No)]

MURATA, Assistant Prof. Shigeo. Kyushu Institute of Technology, Tobata City, Kyushu, Japan. [Tertiary & Recent Foraminifera of Kyushu, Japan (Yes)]

MURAYAMA, Prof. Dr. Jozo J. Faculty of Agriculture, Yamaguti University, Chofu-machi, Shomonoseki City, Japan. [Coleoptera: Scolytidae, Platypodidae, Scarabaeidae, of Japan, Korea, Manchuria, China (Yes)]

MURAYAMA, Prof. S. Shinjo-Cho 744, Ibaraki-shi, Osaka-fu, Japan. [Lepidoptera: Rhopalocera of Japan (Yes)]

MURCHIE, Dr. William R. Flint College, 1401 E. Court Street, Flint, Mich., U.S.A. [Oligochaeta: of N.America (Yes); Megascolecidae: g. Dichogaster of S. & C.America (Yes)] [University of Michigan]

* MURDOCH, G. National Agricultural Advisory Service, Entomology Department, Government Buildings, Lawnswood, Leeds 16, England. [Nematoda]

MURDOCH, Wallace P. 406th Medical General Laboratory (406), APO 343, San Francisco, Calif., U.S.A. [Diptera: Tabanidae & Culicidae of Far East (Yes)]

MURGOCI, Dr. Adriana, Maître de conferences, Facultatea de Stiinte Naturale, Splaiul Independentei Nr. 93-95, Bucuresti 35, Rumania. [Trichoptera of Europe (Yes); Pisces: Calliomymidae, Gobiesocidae, Mugilidae, Acipenseridae: Acipenserini, of Europe (Yes)]

MURIE, Dr. Olaus J. (Moose, Wyo., Aves & Mammalia) Not now active in taxonomy.

* MURILLO, Dr. Luis Maria. Instituto de Ciencias Naturales, Ciudad Universitaria, Carrera 5a No. 57-58, Bogotá, Colombia. [Homoptera; Coccidae]

MURINA, W.W. Institute of Oceanology, Academy of Sciences, Luzhnikovskaya 8, Moscow 127, U.S.S.R. [Sipunculoidea of Pacific (Yes); Priapuloidea of Pacific (Yes)]

MURPHY, Mr. Dennis H. Department of Zoology, Science Laboratory, Durham University, Durham, England. [Collembola of Britain & Gambia (w. Africa) (No)]

MURPHY, Michael A. Division of Physical Sciences, University of California, Riverside, Calif., U.S.A. [Lower Cretaceous Mollusca of California, incl. Ammonitoidea (Yes)]

MURPHY, Dr. Paul W. Zoology Section, School of Agriculture, University of Nottingham, Sutton Bonington, Loughborough, Leics., England. [Acarina: Oribatei of Europe (No)]

MURPHY, Dr. Robert Cushman. American Museum of Natural History, New York 24, N.Y., U.S.A. [Fossil & Recent Oceanic Aves of World (Yes)]

MURRAY, M.D. McMaster Animal Health Laboratory, Parramatta Road, Glebe, N.S.W., Australia. [Diptera: Calliphoridae, g. Calliphora of New Zealand (Yes); Anoplura: Echinophthiridae of Antarctic & Subantarctic (Yes)] [Commonwealth Scientific & Industrial Research Organization]

MURRAY, Rev. Desmond P. The Lodge, Stoke Golding, Leicester, England. [Lepidoptera: Lycaenidae of s. Africa (Yes)]

MURRAY, Grover E. Boyd Professor, School of Geology, Louisana State University, University Station, Baton Rouge 3, La., U.S.A. [Fossils of U.S. Coastal Province (No)]

MURRAY, Mr. Keith. Bureau of Vector Control 2151 Berkeley Way, Berkeley 4, Calif., U.S.A. [Reptilia & Amphibia of California (Yes); Mammalia: Rodentia, Lagomorpha, Chiroptera, Insectivora, of California (Yes)]

MURRAY, Dr. William D. Delta Mosquito Abatement District, 1621 W. Houston, Visalia, Calif., U.S.A. [Hymenoptera: Sphecinae of N. America (Yes)]

MURRAY, William S., Entomologist, District Public Works Office (Code D-111), Potomac River Naval Command, U.S. Naval Gun Factory, Washington 25, D.C., U.S.A. [Diptera: Culicidae of e.c.U.S. (Yes)]

MUSGRAVE, A., Curator of Insects, Australian Museum, Hyde Park, Sydney, N.S.W., Australia. [Heteroptera of Australia]

MUSIL, Dr. R. Bratislavská 4, Brno, Czechoslovakia. [Up. Pleistocene Mammalia of c. Europe (Yes); Pleistocene Elephantidae & Ursidae (Yes)] [Moravské Museum]

MUSPRATT, Mr. J. South African Institute for Medical Research, P.O. Box 1038, Johannesburg, Transvaal, Union of South Africa. [Diptera: Culicidae of Ethiopian (Yes)]

* MUTHUKRISHNA, T.S. Agricultural College & Research Institute, Coimbatore 3, India. |Hemiptera]

MUTUURA, Akira. Entomological Laboratory, University of Osaka Prefecture, Sakai City, Osaka-fu, Japan. [Lepidoptera: Pyralidae of Japan (Yes)]

MUUS, Mr. Bent. Danmarks Fiskeri og Havundersøgelser, Charlottenlund Slot, Charlottenlund, Denmark. [Cephalopoda of n. Atlantic (Yes); Teuthoidea of World (No)]

MYER, Donal G. Botany & Zoology Building, Ohio State University, Columbus 10, Ohio, U.S.A. [Terrestrial pulmonate Gastropoda of Ohio (Yes); Trematoda: Strigeata, Cyathocotylidae, cercariae & adults, of N. America (Yes)]

MYERS, Betty June. 131 High Street, Ashland, Ohio, U.S.A. [Nematoda of marine animals of World, incl. larvae (Yes); Cestoda & Trematoda of World (Yes)]

MYERS, Donald A. Room 1328, Building 25, Federal Center, Denver 2, Colo., U.S.A. [Up. Pennsylvanian & L. Permian Foraminifera: Fusulinidae of n.c. Texas (No)] [U.S. Geological Survey]

MYERS, Everett C., Curator of the Museum, Bowling Green State University, Bowling Green, Ohio, U.S.A. [Aves of n.e.U.S. (Yes); Pisces of n.e.U.S. (No)]

*-MYERS, Dr. Earl Hamlet. Department of Paleontology, University of California, Berkeley 4, Calif., U.S.A. [Fossil Foraminifera]

MYERS, Dr. George S. Natural History Museum, Stanford University, Stanford Calif., U.S.A. [Pisces, espec. Cyprinodontidae, Characidae, Zeidae, of World (Yes); Amphibia of World, espec. of Neotropics & Asia (Yes); Reptilia of World, espec. Neotropics & Asia (Yes)]

MYERS, Dr. R.J. Department of Zoology, Colgate University, Hamilton, N.Y., U.S.A. [Hirudinea of U.S. & Canada (Yes, excl. Piscicolidae)]

MYINT, Dr. Tha, Lecturer in Zoology, University of Rangoon, Rangoon, Burma. [Pisces: Ophiocephalidae, Anabantidae, Clariidae, Heteropneustidae, of Burma, India, Siam (Yes)]

* NABOKOV, Prof. Vladimir. Goldwin-Smith Hall, Cornell University, Ithaca, N.Y., U.S.A. [Lepidoptera: Lycaenidae of Holarctic]

NADIG, Dr. A. Lyceum Alpinum, Zuoz, Switzerland. [Orthoptera of Palearctic (No); of Europe (Yes)] [Zuoz College]

NADLER, Dr. A.M. 101 Ocean Parkway, Brooklyn 18, N.Y., U.S.A. [Corrodentia of Caribbean, Hawaii, Canal Zone (Yes)]

NAGABHUSHANAM, R. Department of Zoology, Andhra University, Waltair, S.India. [Pelecypoda: Teredinidae & Pholadidae of Bay of Bengal, Arabian Sea, Indian Ocean (Yes); Hydrozoa: Hydromedusae of same (Yes)]

NAGAHANA, Prof. M. Department of Medical Zoology, Kyoto Prefectural University of Medicine, Kyoto, Japan. [Siphonaptera of Korea (Yes)]

* NAGAO, T. Department of Paleontology, Imperial University, Sapporo, Hokkaido, Japan. [Fossil Vertebrata]

NAGAPPA, Mr. Yedatore. Assam Oil Company, Ltd., Digboi Post Office, Upper Assam, India. [Cretaceous & Tertiary Foraminifera of India, Burma, Pakistan (Yes); Recent Foraminifera of Indian coastal waters (No); Tertiary Ostracoda of India, Burma, Pakistan (No)]

NAGAPPAN, Mr. Nayar K. Research Unit, Central Marine Fisheries, Madras 5, India. [Amphipoda of India (Yes)]

* NAGASE, Mr. Hirohiko. 81 Nikaido, Kamakura City, Kanagawa Pref., Japan. [Hymenoptera]

NAGATOMI, Akira. Entomology Laboratory, Hyogo Agricultural University, Sasayama, Hyogo Pref., Japan. [Diptera: Rhagionidae of e. Asia (Yes)]

NAGY, B. Növenyvédelmi Kutató Intézet, Herman O. ut. 15, Budapest II, Hungary. [Orthoptera: Saltatoria of c. Europe, espec. Carpathian Basin (Yes)]

NAGY, Prof. Emer. Dr. E., Docent Ornithologiae, Mammalogia, Kelemen L.U. 14a, Budapest II, Hungary. [Aves & Mammalia of Eurasia (Yes)]

NAGY, István Z. Magyar Allami Földtani Intézet, Vorosilov-ut 14, Budapest XIV, Hungary. [Cretaceous Cephalopoda: Ammonoidea (Yes)]

NAIDU, Mr. K. Vanamala. Natural Science Department, Government Arts College, Cuddapah, India. [Oligochaeta: Aeolosomatidae, Naididae, Tubificidae, of Asia (Yes); Sporozoa: Actinomyxidia: Triactonomyxidae of Asia (Yes)]

NAIR, Dr. R.V. Central Marine Fisheries Research Station, Marine Fisheries P.O., Madras State, India. [Marine Pisces of India (Yes); Leptocephali of India (Yes)]

NAJARIAN Dr. Haig H. 81 Curve Street, Millis, Mass., U.S.A. [Digenetic Trematoda of N. America & Middle East (Yes); Gastropoda: Bulinidae of Middle East (Yes)]

NAJDIN, Prof. D.P. Department of Geology, Moscow State University, Moscow B-234, Lengora, U.S.S.R. [Cephalopoda: Cretaceous Ammonoidea & Belemnitellidae of Crimea, n. Caucasus, European Russia (Yes)]

NAKAGAWA, Dr. Hiroshi. Research Institute for Natural Resources, 4-400, Hyakunin-cho, Shinjuku, Tokyo, Japan. [Diptera: Culicidae of Japan (Yes); Siphonaptera of Japan (Yes); Mallophaga of Japan (Yes)]

NAKAHARA, Dr. Waro. 1141 Mejiro, Toshima-ku, Tokyo, Japan. [Neuroptera: Hemerobiidae & allies of World (Yes)]

NAKAMURA, Dr. Hiroshi. Nankai Regional Fisheries Research Laboratory, Sanbashi-Dori 6, Kochi City, Kochi Pref., Japan. [Pisces: Thunnidae & Istiophoridae of Indo-Pacific Ocean (No)]

NAKAMURA, Mr. Kazuo. Ueda Branch Station, Freshwater Fisheries Research Laboratory, Komaki, Ueda City, Nagano Pref., Japan. [Pisces: f-w. Cyprinidae of c. Japan (No)]

NAKAMURA, Masanao. Research Department of Saeki Mill. Kokoku Rayon & Pulp Company Ltd., Saeki, Oita-ken, Japan. [Lepidoptera: Notodontidae of Palearctic & Oriental (Yes)]

NAKAMURA, Dr. Morizumi. Research Institute of Natural Resources. 4-400 Hyakunin-cho, Shinjuku, Tokyo, Japan. [Pisces: f-w. Cyprinidae of Japan (Yes), of Asia (No); Salmonidae of Asia (No)]

NAKANE, Takehiko, Assistant Professor, Biological Laboratory, Saikyo University, Shimogamo, Kyoto City, Japan. [Coleoptera of Japan & Far East]

NAKANO, Mr. Mitsuo. Institute of Geology & Mineralogy, Faculty of Science, Hiroshima University, Hiroshima, Japan. [Mesozoic Pelecypoda: Trigoniidae of World (No), of Japan (Yes)]

NAKAO, Shunichi. Parasitological Laboratory, Kurume University, Fukuoka City, Kyushu, Japan. [Diptera: Conopidae of Japan (Yes)|

NAKAZAWA, Dr. Keiji. Geological & Mineralogical Institute, Faculty of Science, Kyoto University, Kyoto, Japan. [Triassic & Permian marine Pelecypoda of Japan (No), Bakevelliidae of Japan (Yes)]

NAKKADY, Prof. Saad E. Department of Geology, University of Assiut, Assiut, Egypt. [Cretaceous-Miocene Foraminifera (Yes)|

NALBANT, Teodor. Calea Dorobanti 40, Bucureşti, Rumania. [Pisces: Cobitidae & Cyprinidae of Europe & Asia (Yes)]

NAMBA, Dr. Ryoji. Department of Entomology, Hawaiian Agricultural Experiment Station, University of Hawaii, Honolulu 14, Hawaii. [Diptera: Otitidae: g. Rivellia of N. America (Yes); Homoptera: Cicadellidae of Hawaii (Yes)]

NANI, Alberto. Museo Argentino de Ciencias Naturales, Angel Gallardo 470, Buenos Aires, Argentina. [Pisces: f-w, marine, coastal Teleostomi of Argentina (Yes); Teleostomi of Antarctica (Yes)]

NAORA, Dr. Nubuo. Department of Mining, Waseda University, Tokyo, Japan. [Fossil & Recent Mammalia of Alaska, Siberia, Japan, China, (Yes)]

di NAPOLI, F. See DI NAPOLI, Enrico F. in Addenda.

* NARAIN, N. Shia College, Lucknow, India. [Protozoa]

NARAYAN, D. Shankar. Department of Entomology, University of Kansas, Lawrence, Kans., U.S.A. [Acarina: Penthaleidae of N. & S. America (Yes); Eupodidae of World (No)]

NARTSHUK, E.P. Zoological Institute, Academy of Sciences of U.S.S.R., Leningrad V-164, U.S.S.R. [Diptera: Chloropidae of Palearctic (Yes)]

* NASH, T.A. West Africa Institute for Trypanosomiasis Research, Kaduna, Nigeria. [Diptera]

* NAST, Prof. Dr. Janusz. Institut Zoologiczny, Polska Akademia Nauk, ul. Wilcza 64, Warszawa, Poland. [Homoptera]

NATH, Mr. B., Vertebrate Zoologist, Department of Anthropology, Indian Museum, 27 Chowringhee Road, Calcutta 13, India. [Fossil vertebrates of India (Yes); Mammalia of India (Yes)]

NATLAND, Mr. M.L. 18 E. Crest Road, Rolling Hills, Calif., U.S.A. [Tertiary Foraminifera of California (Yes)]

* NATVIG, Prof. Dr. L.R. Faculty of Medicine, University of Oslo, Oslo 45, Norway. [Diptera: Culicidae]

NAUMANN, Hans. Clara Zetkinstrasse 25, Döbeln (Sachsen), German Democratic Republic. [Coleoptera, Rhynchota, Odonata, of c. Europe (No)]

NAUMOV, Dr. Donat V. Zoological Institute, Academy of Sciences of U.S.S.R., Universitetskaia nab. no. 1, Leningrad B-164, U.S.S.R. [Hydrozoa: Hydroida & Hydromedusae of Arctic, Antarctic, Pacific (Yes); Scyphozoa of Arctic, Antarctic & N. Pacific (Yes)]

NAVAJAS, Eduardo. Instituto Biológico, Caixa Postal 7.119, São Paulo, Brazil. [Coleoptera: Elateridae of Brazil (Yes); Chrysomelidae: Chlamisinae of Brazil (No); Scarabaeidae: g. Eurysternus of Neotropics (Yes)]

* NAVANO, Leopoldo. Oficina Tecnica, Director General de Pesca, Secretaria de Marina, Mexico, D.F., Mexico. [Pisces]

NAVARRO-MARTIN, Sr. F. Instituto Oceanográfico, Alcala 27, Madrid, Spain. [Pisces: Clupeidae of e. N. Atlantic & Mediterranean (Yes)]

NAYAK, Miss P.D. Central Marine Fisheries Research Sub-Station, 3rd Floor, Botawalla Chambers, Sir P.M. Road, Bombay 1, India. [Marine Pisces of Bay of Bengal, Arabian Sea, Indian Ocean (Yes)]

NAYLOR, Dr. E. University College of Swansea, Singleton Park, Swansea, Glamorganshire, Wales. [Crustacea: Isopoda of n.w. Europe & Britain (Yes)]

NAYAR, Mr. K.K. Department of Zoology, Government Victoria College, Palghat, India. [Diptera: Itonididae of India & Ceylon (Yes)]

NEAL, Prof. G.M. Department of Zoology, University of Toronto, Toronto 5, Ont., Canada. [Rotifera: excl. Bdelloidea, of N. America (Yes); g. Hexarthra of World (Yes)]

NEAVE, Dr. Ferris. Biological Station, Fisheries Research Board, Nanaimo, B.C., Canada. [Pisces: Salmonidae of N. Pacific (Yes); Hymenoptera: Bombidae & Vespinae of Canada (Yes)]

NEBOISS, Mr. A. National Museum of Victoria, Russel Street, Melbourne, Vict., Australia. [Trichoptera of Australia & New Guinea (Yes); Plecoptera of Australia (No); Coleoptera: Elateridae & Cupedidae of Australia (Yes)]

NECTOUX, Mr. P. Ecole de Filles, Montcenis (S. & L.), France. [Sarcodina: Thecamoebae of Morvan, France (Yes)]

NEEDHAM, James G. (Ithaca, N.Y., Odonata) Deceased.

NEEDHAM, Dr. Paul R. Department of Zoology, University of California, Berkeley 4, Calif., U.S.A. [Pisces: Salmonidae of Pacific Cst. U.S. (Yes)]

NEELY, R.M. Magnolia Petroleum Company, 518 Pioneer Building, Lake Charles, La., U.S.A. [Miocene & Oligocene Crustacea: Ostracoda of Gulf Cst. U.S. (No); Sarcodina: Tertiary Foraminifera & Thecamoeba of Gulf Cst. U.S. (Yes); planktonic Foraminifera & Thecamoeba of Caribbean (Yes)]

NEFF, Mr. Stuart E. Department of Entomology, Cornell University, Ithaca, N.Y., U.S.A. [Diptera: Sciomyzidae of N. America (Yes); Tendipedidae of N. America (No); immature stages of both families]

* NEGHME-RODRIGUEZ, Dr. Amador, Professor de Biologia, Universidad de Chile, Casilla 9183, Santiago, Chile. [Diptera]

NEGRE, J. Museum National d'Histoire Naturelle, 9 Bd. de Lesseps, Versailles, France. [Coleoptera: Carabidae of Holarctic (No); of Neotropical (Yes)]

NEGRU, Ing. Stefan. Statiunea Zoologică Sinaia (reg. Ploeşti), Rumania. [Hymenoptera: Chrysididae of c. & e. Europe (Yes); Mallophaga of c. & e. Europe (Yes); Coleoptera: Ipidae of c. & e. Europe (Yes)]

NEGUS, Dr. Norman C. Department of Zoology, Tulane University, New Orleans 18, La., U. S. A. [Mammalia: Chiroptera of N. & C. America (Yes); Rodentia: Cricetidae of N. America (Yes)]

* NEILL, Mr. Wilfred T. Ross Allen's Reptile Institute, Silver Springs, Fla., U. S. A. [Reptilia & Amphibia]

* NEKHOROSHEV, V. P. Srdny prospect 72-C, W. S. E. G. E. Y., Leningrad W. O., U. S. S. R. [Bryozoa]

NELSON, Prof. C. A. Department of Geology, University of California, Los Angeles 24, Calif., U. S. A. [Cambrian Trilobita of N. America (Yes)]

NELSON, Donald O. Department of Paleontology, Mobil Oil Company of Canada, Box 690, Tripoli, Libya. [Paleozoic-Miocene Foraminifera of S. America & Middle East (No)]

* NELSON, Mr. Elmer R. Jr. Public Museum, Milwaukee, Wis., U. S. A. [Pleistocene Mammals of Wisconsin]

NELSON, Prof. Gid. E., Jr. Biology Department, Alabama College, Montevallo, Ala., U. S. A. [Aves: Fringillidae of N. America (Yes)]

NELSON, G. H. Department of Anatomy, College of Medical Evangelists, Loma Linda, Calif., U. S. A. [Coleoptera: of U. S. (No); Buprestidae of World (No), of U. S. (Yes)]

NELSON, Harry G. Biology Department Roosevelt University, 4305 Michigan Avenue, Chicago 5, Ill., U. S. A. [Coleoptera: Elmidae, Psephenidae, Limnichidae, Heteroceridae, Ptilodactylidae, Chelonariidae of World (Yes to genus); larvae of Elmidae & Psephenidae of New World (Yes); Dryopidae of World (Yes)]

NELSON, Prof. Lloyd A. Department of Geology, Texas Western College, El Paso, Texas, U. S. A. [Pennsylvanian marine Gastropoda of World (No), of s. w. U. S. (Yes)]

NELSON, Dr. Samuel J. Department of Geology, University of Alberta, Edmonton, Alta., Canada. [Up. Ordovician Brachiopoda, Corals, Cephalopoda, of w. & n. w. Arctic N. America (No); Carboniferous Brachiopoda & Corals of Canadian Rockies (Yes)]

NELSON, Thurlow C. 8 North Main Street, Cape May Court House, N. J., U. S. A. [Pelecypoda: oysters of N. America (Yes); of S. America & Europe (No)] [New Jersey Division of Shell Fisheries]

NEMENZ, Dr. Harald. Zoologisches Institut der Universitat, Wien I, Austria. [Arachnomorpha: halophile Araneae of Europe (No); Epeiridae, espec. g. Singa, of Europe (Yes); Acarina: Ixodidae of Europe & Near East (No)]

NEMENZO, Prof. Francisco. Department of Zoology, University of Philippines, Quezon City, Philippines. [Anthozoa: "Scleractinia (Madreporaria)" of Indo-Malaya (Yes)]

NEMOTO, Mr. Takahisa. 4, 12 Chome, Nishigashi-Dori, Tsukishima, Chuo-ku, Tokyo, Japan. [Crustacea: Copepoda of N. Pacific (Yes); Euphausiacea of N. Pacific (Yes); Mammalia: Cetacea: whales of N. Pacific & Antarctic (Yes)] [Whales Research Institute]

NERO, Dr. Robert W., Assistant Director, Saskatchewan Museum of Natural History, Regina, Sask., Canada. [Aves & Mammalia of Saskatchewan (Yes)]

NESBITT, Dr. Herbert H. J. Department of Biology, Carleton University, Ottawa, Ont., Canada. [Acarina: Acaridae & Phytoseiidae of N. America & Europe (Yes)]

NETTING, Dr. M. Graham, Director, Carnegie Museum, Pittsburgh 13, Penn., U. S. A. [Amphibia: Caudata of e. N. America; Reptilia: Serpentes of W. Indies; (Occasionally)]

NEUMAN, Teodor. Instytut Zoologiczny Uniwersytetu Warszawskeigo, Krakowskie Przedmiescie 26/28, Warszawa, Poland. [Acarina: Hydrachnellae of Palearctic]

* NEUMANN, Mme. M. Laboratoire de Géologie Appliqué, 191 rue St. Jacques, Paris (V), France. [Fossil Invertebrates]

de NÈVE, Prof. Dr. George A. Department of Geology, University of Northern Sumatra, Djalan Universitas no. 13, Medan, N. Sumatra, Indonesia. [Tertiary & Quaternary Foraminifera of Indonesia (Yes); Paleozoic Fusulinidae of Indonesia (Yes); Recent Foraminifera of Indonesia (Yes)]

NEVIN, Prof. F. Reese. State University Teachers College, Plattsburgh, N. Y., U. S. A. [Acarina: f-l. Oribatidae of n. e. U. S. (No)]

NEW, Prof. John G. Science Department, State University Teachers College, Oneonta, N. Y., U. S. A. [Mammalia & Pisces of n. e. U. S. (Yes); Aves, Reptilia, Amphibia, of n. e. U. S. (No)]

NEWELL, Dr. G. E. Department of Zoology, Queen Mary College, Mile End Road, London, E. 1, England. [Polychaeta of British muddy-sandy shores (Yes)]

NEWELL, Dr. Irwin M. Division of Life Sciences, University of California, Riverside, Calif., U. S. A. [Acarina of World (No); terrestrial Trombidiidae, Erythraeidae, Smarididae of World (Yes); Halacaridae of World (Yes)]

NEWELL, Prof. Norman D. American Museum of Natural History, New York 24, N. Y., U. S. A. [Paleozoic & Triassic Pelecypoda (Yes)]

NEWHOUSE, Mr. V. F. Box 539, Council, Idaho, U. S. A. [Diptera: Sarcophagidae of N. America (Yes)]

NEWMAN, John H. 9821 Peer Road, South Lyon, Mich., U.S.A. [Lepidoptera: Noctuidae of N. America, espec. Michigan (Yes); Macrolepidoptera of Michigan (Yes)]

NEWMAN, Murray. Vancouver Public Aquarium, Box 8, Stanley Park, Vancouver 5, B.C., Canada. [Marine Pisces of Pacific Cst. of Mexico & Canada (Yes)] [Institute of Fisheries]

NEWMAN, Mr. William A. Department of Zoology, University of California, Berkeley 4, Calif., U.S.A. [Cirripedia: Thoracica of World (No), of N. America & Micronesia (Yes)]

* NEWTH, Dr. D.R. Department of Zoology, University College, Gower Street, London, W.C. 1, England. [Amphibia]

* NIBLETT, Mr. M. 10 Greenway, Wallington, Surrey, England. [Diptera]

NICÉFORO MARIA, Hno., Director del Museo de La Salle, Instituto de La Salle, Apartado 473, Bogotá, Colombia. [Aves; Mammalia: Chiroptera; Reptilia; of Colombia (No)]

NICHOLAS, Brother G., F.S.C. La Salle College, 20th & Olney Avenues, Philadelphia 41, Penna., U.S.A. [Mammalia: Vespertilionidae: g. Myotis, Eptesicus, Pipistrel, Corynorhinus, Antrolous, of U.S.]

NICHOLS, Dr. David. Department of Zoology, University Museum, Oxford, England. [M. & Up. Cretaceous Echinoidea Micrasteridae (Yes); Recent Spatangoidea of British Seas (Yes)]

NICHOLLS, Dr. A.G. Commonwealth Scientific & Industrial Research Organization, Division of Fisheries & Oceanography, Stowell Avenue, Hobart, Tasmania. [Crustacea: Copepoda: Marine Calanoida, Cyclopoida, Harpacticoida (Yes)]

NICHOLS, J.T. (New York, N.Y.; Pisces & Birds) Died November 10, 1958.

NICHOLSON, H. Page. (Atlanta, Ga.; Diptera) Not now active in taxonomy.

NICKLES, M. 18bis rue Henri Barbusse, Paris (V), France. [Marine Mollusca of W. Africa (No)]

NICOL, Dr. David. Department of Geology, Southern Illinois University, Carbondale, Ill., U.S.A. [Fossil & Recent marine Pelecypoda (No); Glycymerididae, Cucullaeidae, Arcidae, Anadaridae, Parallelodontidae, Chamidae, Fimbriidae, Clossidae, g. Astartella (Yes)]

NICOLAI, Dr. J. Max-Planck-Institut, Seewiesen, Post Landsteeten über Starnberg, Oberbayern, Germany. [Aves: Passeres: Carduelidae of Palearctic & Africa (Yes)]

NICOLAUS, Dr. Hans. Amt für Bodenforschung, Wiesenstrasse 1, Hannover, Germany. [Carboniferous Goniatitaceae of Europe (Yes); L. Carboniferous Mollusca of Europe (Yes)]

NICOLAY, Lt. Col. S.S. 8349 Woody Drive, Norfolk, Va., U.S.A. [Lepidoptera: Hesperiidae & Lycaenidae: Theclinae, of New World (Yes)]

NICOLESCO, Dr. Eugen V. Str. Dr. Sion 6, Raionul Gheorghiu Dej, Bucureşti, Rumania. [Lepidoptera: Aegeriidae & Rholaplocera of Rumania (Yes); Macrolepidoptera of Rumania (No)]

van NIDEK, C.M.C. see BROUERIUS van NIDEK.

NIEDRACH, Robert J. Curator of Birds, Denver Museum of Natural History, Denver 6, Colo., U.S.A. [Aves of Colorado (No)]

NIELSEN, Dr. Anker. København Universitets, Zoologiske Museum, Krystalgade 27, København, Denmark. [Trichoptera of n. Europe (No)]

NIELSEN, Dr. Cesare. Via Letizia 6, Bologna, Italy. [Odonata of Palearctic & Ethiopian (Yes)] [Istituto di Entomologia, Universitá de Bologna]

NIELSEN, Dr. C. Overgaard. Molslaboratoriet, Femmøller, Denmark. [Non-parasitic soil Nematoda of Denmark (No); Enchytraeidae of Europe (Yes)]

NIELSON, Dr. Eigil. Mineralogisk Museum, Östervoldgade 7, København, Denmark. [Permian-Triassic Pisces of Greenland (Yes)]

* NIELSEN, Erik T. Address unknown. [Hymenoptera: Sphecidae]

NIELSEN, Mr. Peder. Frederiksberggade 44, Silkeborg, Denmark. [Diptera: Limoniidae of w. Palearctic (Yes)]

NIELSEN, Dr. Lewis T. Zoology Department, University of Utah, Salt Lake City 12, Utah, U.S.A. [Diptera: Culicidae of w. N. America (Yes)]

NIELSON, Dr. M.W. United States Department of Agriculture Laboratory, P.O. Box 857, Meza, Ariz., U.S.A. [Homoptera: Cicadellidae of N. America (No); g. Colladonus of New World (Yes)]

NIETHAMMER, Prof. Dr. G. Ornithology Department, Zoologisches Forschungsinstitut und Museum A. Koenig, Bonn, Germany. [Aves of s.w. Africa, Sahara, Europe, Canary Is., Asia Minor (Yes)]

NIEUWENHUIS, E.J. Bentincklaan 37A, Rotterdam, Netherlands. [Lepidoptera: Rhopalocera, excl. Hesperiidae, of Indonesia & New Guinea (Yes); Hesperiidae, of same (No); Heterocera, excl. Geometridae, of same (No)] [Natural History Museum, Rotterdam]

NIEVES, Mr. E.J. Dominion Oil, Limited, P.O. Box 199, Port-of-Spain, Trinidad. [Tertiary Foraminifera of s.e. Caribbean, n.S. America (Yes)]

NIEWIADOMSKA, K. Zakład Parazytologii, Polskiej Akademii Nauk, ul. Pasteura 3, Warszawa 22, Poland. [Trematoda: Strigeata of Europe (No)]

NIGON, Prof. V. Laboratoire de Zoologie Experimentale, Faculté des Sciences, 16 Quai Claude Bernard, Lyon, France. [Nematoda: g. Rhabditis of France (No)]

NIGRELLI, Dr. Ross F. New York Aquarium, Seaside Park, Coney Island, Brooklyn 24, N. Y., U. S. A. [Protozoa Parasitic in f-w. & marine Pisces of N. America (Yes); Helminth Parasites of same (No)]

NIKITIN, Dr. M. I. 84 Camden Street, Fairfield, Sydney, N. S. W., Australia. [Lepidoptera: Rhopalocera of Manchuria & China (Yes); of Australia (No); Diptera: Tabanidae of Manchuria & China (Yes); of Australia (No)]

* NIKOLAEVA, Dr. T. V. V. S. E. G. E. I., Sredny 72b, Leningrad, U. S. S. R. [Silurian Anthozoa: Rugosa]

NIKOLIĆ, Franjo, Assistent, Institut Biologique de l'Academie, P. p. 17, Dubrovnik, Yugoslavia. [Araneae of caves of Europe (Yes); Araneae of Yugoslavia & Balkan Pen. (Yes)]

NIKOLSKAYA, Dr. M. N. Zoological Institute, Academy of Sciences, Universitatskaja 1, Leningrad B-164, U. S. S. R. [Hymenoptera: Chalcidoidea & Chrysidoidea of Africa & s. Asia (No)]

NIKOLSKIJ, Prof. Dr. G. V. Zoological Museum, University of Moscow, Ul. Gerzena 6, Moscow K-9, U. S. S. R. [Recent, Quaternary, Up. Tertiary Pisces: "carpline & catfishes" of Palearctic (No)]

NILSSON, Arvid. Sparvägen 2, Landskrona, Sweden. [Terrestial & f-w. Mollusca of Scandinavia (No)]

NILSSON, Tage. (Lund, Sweden; fossil Mammalia) Not now active in taxonomy.

NINOMIJA, Prof. E. Biological Laboratory, Nagasaki Gakugei University, Nagasaki City, Japan. [Diptera: Syrphidae, incl. immature stages, of Kyushu & Honshu (Yes)]

NIPKOW, Fritz. (Zurich, Switzerland; Rotifera) Not now active in taxonomy.

NISHIJIMA, Yutaka. Entomological Institute, Hokkaido University, Sapporo City, Hokkaido, Japan. [Diptera: Chloropidae of Japan (Yes)]

NISHIO, Yoshiaki. Entomology Laboratory, Hokkaido Agricultural Experiment Station, Kotoni, Sapporo-gun, Hokkaido, Japan. [Coleoptera: Cerambycidae & Chrysomelidae of Asia, Europe, N. America (No); Acarina: Tetranychidae of Japan (No)]

NISHIWAKI, Dr. Masaharu. No. 17 Kowado-cho, Shinjuku-ku, Tokyo, Japan. [Mammalia: Cetacea: Balaenidae, Balaenopteridae, Physeteridae, Ziphiidae, Delphinidae of World (No), of Pacific Ocean (Yes)]

NISHIZAWA, Mr. T. Faculty of Agriculture, Nagoya University, Anjo, Aichi Pref., Japan. [Nematoda: Tylenchidae, Neotylenchidae, Heteroderidae, Criconematidae, Tylenchulidae, Aphelenchidae, of Japan (Yes)]

NISIYAMA, Prof. Syozo. Geology Department, Shimane University, Matsue City, Shimane Pref., Japan. [Paleozoic-Recent Echinoidea of Japan (Yes); Tertiary-Recent Echinoidea of Micronesia (Yes)]

NIWA, Mr. Hisashi. Shimono Fukokamura, Enagun, Gifu Pref., Japan. [Pauropoda of Japan (No); Pisces: Cobitidae of Japan (No)]

NIXON, Mr. G. E. J. Commonwealth Institute of Entomology, Department of Entomology, British Museum (Natural History), Cromwell Road, London, S. W. 7, England. [Hymenoptera: Braconidae: Microgasterinae of Old World, espec. Palearctic (Yes); of S. America (No)]

* NOAK, H., Entomologist, Elbchaussee 498, Hamburg-Blankenese, Germany. [Lepidoptera]

* NOBLE, Dr. Alden E. Department of Zoology, College of the Pacific, Stockton, Calif., U. S. A. [Protozoa, Nematoda] Died Feburary 19, 1960.

NOBLE, Elmer R. Santa Barbara College, University of California, Goleta, Calif., U. S. A. [Sporozoa: Myxosporidia of World (Yes)]

NOBLE, Dr. Glenn A. Department of Biology, California State Polytechnic College, San Luis Obispo, Calif., U. S. A. [Parasitic Amoebae & g. Entamoeba in vertebrates (Yes)]

NOBLE, James Eugene. (Oklahoma City, Okla., fossils) Not now active in taxonomy.

NOBUCHI, Mr. Akira. Laboratory of Forest Entomology, Government Forest Experiment Station, No. 770, 4-Chôme, Shimomeguro, Meguro-ku, Tokyo, Japan. [Coleoptera: Scolytidae, Ciidae, Erotylidae, of Japan (Yes)]

NOFFSINGER, E. M. Department of Plant Pathology, University of Wisconsin, Madison 6, Wis., U. S. A. [F-l. & plant parasitic Nematoda of N. America (Yes)]

NOIROT, Prof. C. Laboratoire d'Evolution des Etres Organizés, 105 Boulevard Raspail, Paris (VI), France. [Isoptera of World, espec. Africa (No)] [Faculté des Sciences, Paris]

NOIROT-TIMOTHÉE, C. Laboratoire d'Evolution des Etres Organisés, 105 Boulevard Raspail, Paris (VI), France. [Ciliata: Entodiniomorpha: Ophryoscolecidae & Cycloposthiidae of World (Yes)]

* NOLAND, George B. Biology Department, University of Dayton, Dayton, Ohio, U. S. A. [Araneida & Insecta of Michigan]

NOLAND, Prof. Lowell E. Birge Hall, University of Wisconsin, Madison 6, Wis., U. S. A. [F-w. Ciliata of U. S. (Yes)]

NOLTE, Dr. D. J. Department of Zoology, University of Witwatersrand, Johannesburg, Union of South Africa. [Diptera: Drosophilidae of s. Africa (Yes)]

NOMURA, Mr. Minoru. Tokyo University of Fisheries, Shiba Kaigandori 6, Minato-ku, Tokyo, Japan. [Pisces: Salmonidae of Japan & N. Pacific Ocean (Yes)]

NOMURA, Mr. Sizuma. 168 Nakaku, Kunitachi-machi, Kitatama-gun, Tokyo, Japan. [Coleoptera: Mordellidae & Serropalpidae of e. Asia (Yes); Lamellicornia of Japan (Yes)]

NONVEILLER, Guido. Entomologie Agricole, Faculté d'Agriculture, Université de Belgrade, Zemun, Yugoslavia. [Coeleoptera: Chrysomelidae: Halticinae; Rhizotrogini; Hymenoptera: Mutillidae all of Balkan Pen. (Yes)]

NOODT, Dr. Wolfram. Zoologisches Institut der Universität Kiel, Hegewischstrasse 3, Kiel, Germany. [Crustacea: Mystacocarida of World (Yes); Copepoda: Calanoida of World (No); Harpacticoida of World (Yes)]

* NORDMAN, A. Zoological Institute of the University, P. Rautatiek 13, Helsinki, Finland. [Lepidoptera]

NORDSTRÖM, Ph. D. Frithiof. Kungshomstorg 1, Stockholm, Sweden. [Macrolepidoptera of Scandinavia (No)]

* NORRIS, Dr. A. W. , Paleontologist, Geology Survey of Canada. Department of Mines, Ottawa, Ont. , Canada. [Fossil Invertebrates]

NORRIS, Mr. Kenneth S. , Curator, Marineland of the Pacific, Palos Verdes Drive South, Portuguese Bend, Calif. , U. S. A. [Reptilia: of Baja California (Yes); g. Uma of w. N. American deserts (Yes); Pisces: g. Girella of Atlantic & Pacific Oceans (Yes)]

NORRIS, Dr. Robert A. Dept. of Zoology, Physiology & Entomology, Louisiana State University, Baton Rouge 3, La. , U. S. A. [Aves, espec. Passeriformes, of s. e. U. S.

NORTHROP, Stuart A. Department of Geology, University of New Mexico, Albuquerque, N. Mex. , U. S. A. [Pennsylvanian & Silurian Brachiopods (No)]

* NORTON, Peter. Cuba California Company, Apartado Postal 3295, Habana, Cuba. [Fossil Invertebrates]

NOS, Sra. Pilar. Instituto Municipal de Ciencias Naturales, Museo de Zoologia, Apartado de Correos 593, Barcelona, Spain. [Mollusca of Mediterraean (Yes)]

NOSEK, Ing. J. , Candidate of Sciences Biol. , Patronka Mlynska dolina, Institute of Virology, Czechoslovak Academy of Sciences, Bratislava 9, Czechoslavakia. [Coleoptera: Scolytoidea of Czechoslovakia (Yes); Protura & Collembola of Czechoslovakia (Yes); Diplura & Thysanura of Czechoslovakia (No)]

NOSKIEWICZ, Dr. J. Instytut Zoologiczny, Sienkiewicza 21, Wrocław, Poland. [Hymenoptera: Apidae, Chrysididae of c. Europe (Yes); g. Colletes of Palearctic (Yes)]

NOSOW, Mr. Edmund. Box 282, Hopkinsville, Ky. , U. S. A. [Bryozoa: Trepostomata of Paleozoic (Yes)]

NOUVEL, Prof. Dr. H. Laboratoire de Biologie Générale, Faculté des Sciences, Université de Toulouse, Allées Jules-Guesde, Toulouse, France. [Crustacea: Mysidacea, Euphausiacea, Decapoda: Caridea, of World (Yes); Hymenoptera: Sphegidae, Pompilidae, Chrysididae, Scoliidae, Mutillidae, of France (Yes); Mesozoa: Dicyemida & Orthonectida of World (Yes)]

NOVAES, Fernando da Costa. Museu Paraense Emilio Goeldi, Caixa Postal 399, Belem, Pará, Brazil. [Aves of Neotropics (Yes)]

NOVAK, Petar. 28 Balkanska Ulica, Split (Dalmatie), Yugoslavia. [Coleoptera of Dalmatia & Montenegro]

NOVÁK, Dr. V. Na Folimance 9, Praha XII, Czechoslovakia. [Hymenoptera Formicidae of Palearctic (No); of c. Europe (Yes); Diptera: Simuliidae of c. Europe (Yes)] [Biological Institute]

* NOVATTI, Ricardo. Instituto Antarctico Argentino, Cerrito 1245, Buenos Aires, Argentina. [Aves]

NOVICKY, Svatoslav. Neulinggasse 42/26, Wien III, Austria. [Hymenoptera: Chalcidoidea, excl. Agaomidae, of w. Palearctic (No)]

NOWAKOWSKI, Mgr. J. T. Instytut Zoologiczny, Polskiej Akademii Nauk, Wilcza 64, Warszawa, Poland. [Diptera: Agromyzidae of Palearctic (Yes)]

NOZAWA, Christopher N. Department of Biology, Sophia University, Kioicho, Chiyoda-Ku, Tokyo, Japan. [Orthoptera: Acrididae, Tettigoniidae, Gryllidae of Far East (Yes)]

* NOZAWA, Dr. K. Laboratory of Animal Breeding, Nagoya University, Nagoya, Aichi-ken, Japan. [Diptera]

NUNBERG, Prof. Dr. Marian. Department of Entomology, Instytut Zoologiczny, Polska Akademia Nauk, ul. Wilcza 64, Warszawa, Poland. [Coleoptera: Scolytidae & Platypodidae of World (Yes)] [High School of Agriculture]

NUNES-RUIVO, Dr. Lidia. Museu Nacional de Historia Natural, Secçao de Zoologia, Faculdade de Ciencias, Lisboa, Portugal. [Crustacea: parasitic Copepoda of Atlantic & Mediterrean (Yes); Decapoda of cst. of Portugal]

* NÚÑEZ, René. Address unknown. [Decapoda: Penaeidae]

NUORTEVA, Dr. Pekka. Zoological Museum, Helsinki University, Helsinki, Finland. [Homoptera: Auchenorrhyncha; Diptera: Calliphorinae; of Finland (No)]

NURSE, Miss F. R. see ALLISON, Mrs. Frances.

NUTTALL, Mr. C. P. Department of Paleontology, British Museum (Natural History), Cromwell Road, London, S. W. 7, England. [Tertiary Gastropoda of British Empire (No)]
NUTTING, W. B. Zoology Department, University of Massachusetts, Amherst, Mass., U. S. A. [Acarina: g. Demodex of World (Yes)]
NUTTYCOMBE, Prof. John W. Baldwin Hall, University of Georgia, Athens, Ga., U. S. A. [Turbellaria: g. Catenula & Stenostomum of s. e. U. S. (Yes)]
NYBELIN, Prof. Orvar. Naturhistoriska Museet, Göteborg 11, Sweden. [Jurassic Pisces, espec. Leptolepidae; Recent Pisces & parasites of fishes]
NYBOM, Mr. O. Imatrankoski, Finland. [Trichoptera of n. Europe (Yes)]
* NYDEGGER, Prof. LeRoy. Department of Biology, Morningside College, Sioux City, Iowa, U. S. A. [Trematoda]
NYGREEN, Paul W. Standard Oil Company of Texas, P. O. Box 2087, Amarillo, Texas, U. S. A. [Fossil Foraminifera: Fusulinidae of U. S. (Yes)]
* NYHOLM, Dr. Karl-Georg. Zoological Institute, Uppsala Universitets, Uppsala, Sweden. [Coelenterata]
* NYHOLM, Tord. Naturhistoriska Riksmuseet, Stockholm 50, Sweden. [Coleoptera & Corrodentia]
NYI, Dr. Nyi. Department of Geology, University of Rangoon, Rangoon, Burma. [Neogene Micro-Foraminifera of Burma (Yes); Neogene Lamellibranchia & Gastropoda of Burma (No)]
NYVELDT, W. C. Diedenweg 89, Wageningen, Netherlands. [Diptera: Cecidomyidae of World (Yes)] [Instituut voor Plantenziektenkundig Onderzoek]

OAKESON, Dr. Barbara B. Department of Biological Science, Santa Barbara College, University of California, Goleta, Calif., U. S. A. [Aves: Zonotrichia leucophrys of Pacific cst. of N. America (Yes)]
* OAKLEY, Dr. K. P. Department of Paleontology, British Museum (Natural History), Cromwell Road, London, S. W. 7, England. [Fossil man]
OBATA, Yoshio. Department of Parasitology, Niigata University School of Medicine, No. 751, 1-Bancho, Asahimachi, Niigata, Japan. [Acarina: Trombiculidae of n. Japan (Yes), of s. Japan (No)]
OBENBERGER, Prof. Dr. Jan, Head, Entomological Laboratory, Academy of Sciences, Viničná 7, Praha II, Czechoslovakia. [Coleoptera: Buprestidae of World (Yes)]
OBERHAUSER, Dr. Rudolf. Geologische Bundesanstalt, Rasumovskygasse 23, Wien III/40, Austria. [Alpine Triassic & Up. Cretaceous Foraminifera, espec. g. Globotruncana & Trocholina of Turkey & Austria (Yes)]
* OBERHELOVÁ, N. Address unknown. [Fossil Pisces]
OBERHOLSER, Dr. Harry C. 2933 Berkshire Road, Cleveland Heights, Cleveland 18, Ohio, U. S. A. [Aves of Old World (No); of America (Yes)]
OBERTHÜR, Dr. K. Lauenauer Strasse 14, Hannover-Ricklingen, Germany. [Nematoda of Germany (No)]
OBR, Dr. S. Zoologický Ústav Masarykovy University, Kotlářská 2, Brno, Czechoslovakia. [Trichoptera & Psocoptera of c. Europe (Yes)]
OBRAZTSOV, Dr. Nicholas S. 68 Glenlawn Ave., Sea Cliff, N. Y., U. S. A. [Lepidoptera: Tortricidae of Holarctic (Yes); Ctenuchidae of Palearctic, Oriental, Australian (Yes)]
OBRECHT, Prof. Carl B. Department of Biology, Mercy College, 8200 W. Outer Drive, Detroit 19, Mich., U. S. A. [Diptera: Nematocera of e. N. America (Yes); cold blooded Vertebrates of Great Lakes (Yes)]
O'BRIEN, C. W. Department of Entomology, University of Arizona, Tuscon, Ariz., U. S. A. [Coleoptera: Curculionidae of North America (No); of e. U. S. (Yes)]
OBRTEL, Dr. R. 12 Tolstého, Brno XVI, Czechoslovakia. [Hymenoptera: Ichneumonidae of c. Europe (Yes)]
OBRUCHEV, Prof. Dr. Dmitri V. Paleontological Institute, Academy of Sciences, Lenin Prospect 33, Moscow 71, U. S. S. R. [Ordovican-Devonian Vertebrates (Yes); Carboniferous-Triassic Pisces: Edestidae & Helicoprionidae (Yes)]
OBRUCHEVA, Mme. O. P. Faculty of Geology, Department of Paleontology, Moscow University, Moscow V-234, U. S. S. R. [Devonian Pisces: Coccosteidae (Yes)]
OBST, Jürgen. Bünau Strasse 41, Dresden A 28, German Democratic Republic [Amphibia: Anura & Urodela of Europe (Yes); Salamandroidea & Cryptobranchoidea of Europe & Asia (No)]
OCHIAI, A. Department of Fisheries, Faculty of Agriculture, Kyoto University, Maizuru, Japan. [Pisces: Heterosomata: Cynoglossidae of Japan (Yes)]
OCHOTERENA, Dr. Hector. Instituto de Geologia, Ciudad Universitaria, Mexico 20, D. F., Mexico. [Fossil Brachiopoda: Terebratulidae of Mexico (Oxfordian) (No)]
* OCHS, Dr. George. Address unknown. [Coleoptera: Gyrinidae]
OCHS, J. 51 Avenue Vittone, St. Augustin, Nice (A. -M.), France. [Coleoptera "cavernicoles et endogés" of World (Yes); Staphylinidae & Pselaphidae of Europe (Yes)]

* O'CONNOR, Mr. B. A., Senior Entomologist, Department of Agriculture, Suva, Fiji. [Hemiptera: Coccidae]

O'CONNOR, F. B. Department of Zoology, Trinity College, University of Dublin, Dublin, Ireland. [Oligochaeta: Enchytraeidae of n. Wales (Yes), of Ireland (No)]

ODHIAMBO, Thomas R. Kawanda Research Station, P. O. Box 265, Kampala, Uganda. [Heteroptera: Miridae of Ethiopian (Yes); Anthocoridae & Pyrrhocoridae of Ethiopian (No)]

ODHNER, Dr. Nils H. Naturhistoriska Riksmuseet, Stockholm 50, Sweden. [Gastropoda: Opisthobranchia, Succineidae, g. Pisidia (No)]

*·ODLAUG, Dr. Theron O. Department of Zoology, University of Minnesota, Duluth 5, Minn., U.S.A. [Trematoda]

* O'DONOGHUE, C. H. Address unknown. [Bryozoa]

OELRICH, T., Assistant Professor, Department of Anatomy, University of Michigan, Ann Arbor, Mich., U.S.A. [Fossil Turtles of N. America (Yes)]

OERTLI, Dr. H. J. Compagnie d'Exploration Pétrolière, Chambourcy, (S.& O.), France. [Up. Devonian & L. Carboniferous Ostracoda of n. Africa (No); Mesozoic-Tertiary Ostracoda of w. Europe (Yes)]

von OETTINGEN, Keintach. (Lutherstadt Eisleben, German Democratic Republic; Embioptera) Deceased.

O'FARRELL, Prof. A. F. Department of Zoology, University of New England, Armidale 5N, N.S.W., Australia. [Odonata of e. Australia, Australasia, Britian (Yes)]

O'GARA, William Thomas. 2231 Hurley Avenue, Fort Worth 4, Texas, U.S.A. [Cretaceous Ammonoidea & Echinoidea: Irregularia, of Texas & Colombia (Yes)]

OGATA, Dr. Kazuki. Department of Medical Entomology, National Institute of Health, Kamiosaki, Shinagawa-ku, Tokyo, Japan. [Diptera: Simuliidae of Japan (Yes)]

OGATA, Dr. Masami. 18 Imabashi-3, Higashi-ku, Osaka, Japan. [Lepidoptera: Noctuidae, Agaristidae, Hesperiidae, of Japan (Yes)]

OGAWA, Prof. Dr. Teizo. Department of Anatomy, Medical Faculty, University of Tokyo, Tokyo, Japan. [Mammalia: Cetacea: Odontoceti of n. Pacific Ocean (Yes)]

OGLOBLIN, Dr. Alejandro A., Jefe del Instituto Acridiologia, Formosa 1275 Bella Vista, Argentina. [Hymenoptera; Myramaridae of Neotropics (Yes); Bethylidae & Proctotrupidae of Neotropics (No)]

* OGOSE, Sunao. Geological Institute, Tokyo University, Otsuka, Bunkyo-ku, Tokyo, Japan. [Fossil Invertebrates]

O'GOWER, A. K. School of Public Health & Tropical Medicine, University of Sydney, Sydney, N.S.W., Australia. [Diptera: Culicidae of Australasia (Yes)]

OGREN, Dr. Robert E. Dickinson College, Carlisle, Penn., U.S.A. [Cestoda of mammals of N. America (Yes); Nematoda of vertebrates of N. America (Yes); Turbellaria: g. Rhynchodemus of N. America (Yes)]

OHANDJANIAN, Anna. Zoological Institute, Academy of Sciences of Armenian S.S.R., Avanskoje shosse 20, Erevan, U.S.S.R. [Acarina: Ixodidae of Caucasus (Yes); Gamasoidea of Armenia (No)]

OHBAYASHI, Kazuo. Tsutsuiso Apartment No. 93, Higashi-ku, Nagoya, Japan. [Coleoptera: Cerambycidae & Lycidae of Japan (Yes)]

OHFUCHI, Prof. Dr. Shinryo. Zoology Laboratory, Tokyo Agriculture University, Setagaya, Tokyo, Japan. [Oligochaeta: g. Pheretima of Japan, Ryu Kyu Is., Micronesia (Yes)]

OHIRA, Hitoo. Aichi Gakugei University, Okazaki City, Aichi Pref., Japan. [Coleoptera: Elateridae, incl. Larvae, of Japan, Korea, Formosa (Yes)]

OHKURA, Masafumi. 46 Tenjinyama, Mikage, Higashinada-ku, Kobe, Japan. [Coleoptera: Cicindelidae, Carabidae, Haliplidae, Dytiscidae, Gyrinidae, of Japan (Yes); Scaritidae, Harpalidae, Brachinidae, of Japan (No)]

OHMACHI, Prof. Fumiye. Faculty of Agriculture, Mie University, Tsu City, Mie Pref., Japan. [Orthoptera: Gryllodea of Far East Asia (No), of Japan (Yes)]

OHSUMI, Mr. Seiji. 4, 12 chome, Nishigashi-Dori, Tsukishima, Chuo-ku, Tokyo, Japan. [Mammalia: Cetacea: whales of N. Pacific & Antarctic (Yes)] [Whales Research Institute]

OI, Assist. Prof. R. Department of Home Economics, Osaka City University, 5-chome, Nishinagabori-minami-dori, Nishi-ku, Osaka-shi. Japan. [Araneida of Japan (Yes)]

OINOMIKADO, Dr. Tsuneteru. C/o Taiwan Petroleum Exploration Office, Chinese Petroleum Corporation, Miaoli, Taiwan, Formosa. [Cenozoic smaller Foraminifera of Taiwan & Japan (Yes)]

OITICICA-FILHO, Dr. José. Museu Nacional, Quinta da Boa Vista, Rio de Janeiro, Brazil. [Lepidoptera: Saturnioidea & Sphingidae of New World (Yes)]

OKABE, Prof. K. Department of Parasitology, Faculty of Medicine, Kurume University, Kurume, Japan. [Trematoda of Japan (Yes)]

OKADA, Mr. Hihumi. Gonohe-tyugakko, Furudate, Gohohe-mati, Sannohe-gun, Aomori Pref., Japan. [Odonata of n. Honshu (Yes); Mammalia: Chiroptera of N. Honshu (No)]

OKADA, Prof. Ichiji. Laboratory of Entomology, Tamagawa University, Machida, Tokyo, Japan. [Diptera: Fungivoridae & Bibionidae of Japan (No)]

OKADA, Dr. Toyohi, Department of Biology, Tokyo Metropolitan University, Fukazawa-machi, Setagaya-ku, Tokyo, Japan. [Diptera: Drosophilidae of Japan (Yes)]

OKADA, Prof. Dr. Sci. Yaichiro. 131 Otanicho, Tsu City, Mie Pref., Japan. [F-w. & marine Pisces of Japan; marine Bryozoa of Indo-Pacific; Reptilia & Amphibia of Asiatic continent] [Dean of Faculty of Fisheries, Prefectural University of Mie]

* OKADA, Yasutoshi. 337-4, Hanaten-cho, Jyôto, Osaka, Japan. [Aves]

OKADA, Yô K., Director, National Science Museum, Ueno Park, Tokyo, Japan. [Coleoptera: Lampyridae of Japan (Yes); Crustacea: Cirripedia: Ascothoracida of World (Yes); Polychaeta: Syllidae of World (No)]

OKADA, Yoshio. (Kyoto City, Japan; Lepidoptera) Not now active in taxonomy.

OKAGAKI, Hiromu. 113 Higashihonzi-machi, Tottori-shi, Tottori Pref., Japan. [Lepidoptera: Rhopalocera: Notodontidae, Arctiidae of Japan (Yes); Geometridae of Holarctic (No)]

* OKANO, Kikumaro. Address unknown. [Hymenoptera: Formicidae]

OKANO, Mr. Masao. Biological Laboratory, Iwate University, Morioka, Iwate-ken, Japan. [Lepidoptera: Adelidae, Crambinae, Thyatiridae, Notodontidae, Arctiidae, Rhopalocera, of Japan & Formosa (Yes)]

* OKE, Mr. C.G. 34 Bourke Street, Melbourne, Vict., Australia. [Coleoptera]

OKLAND, Fridthjof. (Oslo, Norway; Mollusca) Deceased.

ØKLAND, Jan. Zoologisk Laboratorium, Universitetet, Blindern, Oslo, Norway. [F-w. Gastropoda of Scandinavia (Yes)]

* OKSALA, Dr. Tarvo. Institute of Genetics, P.Rautattekatu 13, Helsinki, Finland. [Odonata]

OKU, Toshio. Department of Pathology & Entomology, Prefectural Agricultural Experiment Station of Hokkaido, Kotoni, Sapporo, Japan. [Lepidoptera: Tortricidae of Japan (Yes)]

OKUGAWA, K.I. Zoological Laboratory, Kyoto Gakugei University, Fukakusa, Fujinomoricho, Fushimiku, Kyoto, Japan. [Turbellaria f-w. Tricladida: Probursalia of Japan, Kurile Is., RyuKyu Is., Saghalien I., Formosa (Yes)]

OKULITCH, Dr. Vladimir J. Division of Geology, University of British Columbia, Vancouver, B.C., Canada. [L. Cambrian Archaeocyatha (Yes): Ordovician Anthozoa: Tabulata & Tetracoralla of N. America (Yes)]

OKUMURA, Teiichi. 1271, 4-chome, Nakameguro, Meguro-Ku, Tokyo, Japan. [Odonata of Japan, Formosa, Korea (Yes)]

OKUTANI, Mr. T. Tokai Regional Fisheries Research Laboratory, Tsukishima, Tokyo, Japan. [Gastropoda: Heteropoda: Carinariidae & Pterotracheidae of Japan (No); Pelecypoda: g. Calyptogena & Halicardia of Japan (Yes); g. Pinctada of Indo-Pacific (No)]

OKUTANI, Prof. Teiichi. Hyogo University of Agriculture, Sasayama, Hyogo Pref., Japan. [Hymenoptera: Symphyta, espec. larvae, of Japan (Yes)|

OLD, Prof. Marcus C. Hofstra College, Hempstead, N.Y., U.S.A. [Marine Porifera of World (No); f-w. Spongillidae of World (Yes)]

OLD, William E., Jr. 728 Raleigh Avenue, Norfolk 7, Va., U.S.A. [Gastropoda: Patellidae of S. Africa (Yes); Acmaeidae & Cerithiidae of U.S. (Yes); Strombidae, Tonnidae, Thaisidae, of Indo-Pacific (Yes); Mammalia & Reptilia of World]

OLDHAM, Dr. J.N. Department of Pathology, Royal Veterinary College, Royal College Street, London, N.W.I., England. [Parasitic Nematoda of domesticated & wild animals of N. Temperate (No)]

OLDROYD, Mr. H. C/o Department of Entomology, British Museum (Natural History), Cromwell Road, London, S.W.7, England. [Diptera: Tabanidae of Africa & Palearctic (Yes); Brachycera of World (No)]

OLEKSYSHYN, Prof. John. Department of Geology, Boston University, 725 Commonwealth Avenue, Boston 15, Mass., U.S.A. [Cenozoic Invertebrates, espec. Mollusca, of N. America & Europe (Yes)]

* OLEXA, A. Lucemburské 43, Praha XI, Tirkov, Czechoslovakia. [Coleoptera: Elateridae & Melasidae]

OLIVA, Dr. O. Department of Systematic Zoology, Charles University, Viničná 7, Prague II, Czechoslovakia. [F-w. Pisces of Europe (Yes)]

OLIVE, A.T. Department of Entomology, North Carolina State College, Raleigh, N.C., U.S.A. [Homoptera: Aphidae of s.e. U.S. (Yes)]

de OLIVEIRA, Dr. Lejeune P.H. Estaçào de Hidrobiologia, Instituto Oswaldo Cruz, Caixa Postal 926, Rio de Janeiro, Brazil. [Crustacea: Copepoda & Harpacticoida of Rio de Janeiro State (No)]

de OLIVEIRA, Paulo Erichsen. Division de Geologia e Mineralogia, Departmento National da Producào Mineral, Avenida Pasteur 404, Praia Vermelha, Rio de Janeiro, Brazil. [Cretaceous marine Mollusca of Brazil (Yes)]

de OLIVEIRA, Dr. S.J. Instituto Oswaldo Cruz, Caixa Postal 926, Rio de Janeiro, Brazil. [Diptera: Culicidae, Chironomidae, Agromyzidae, Ephydridae: g. Dimecoenia, of Neotropics (Yes)]

OLIVER, Dr. James A. New York Zoological Society, New York 60, N.Y., U.S.A. [Reptilia: Serpentes of W. Hemisphere (No)]

* OLIVER, Mr. M. Laboratorio Oceanográfico, Calle Marques de la Cenia 119, Palma de Mallorca, Baleares, Spain. [Pisces & Mollusca]

OLIVER, William A., Jr. U.S. Geological Survey, Room 335, U.S. National Museum, Washington 25, D.C., U.S.A. [Pre-Mississipian Zoantharia: Rugosa of N. America (Yes)]

OLIVER, W.R.B. (Wellington, New Zealand; Aves) Died May 17, 1957.

OLIVIER, Georges. 6 rue Ch. Flavigny, Elbeuf (Seine Mar.), France. [Aves: g. Lanius of Euraisa & Africa (Yes); of N. America (No); g. Larus of World (No); Mammalia; Ungulata of Old World & N. America (No)]

* OLIVIER, Dr. L.J. Laboratory of Tropical Disease, National Institutes of Health, Bethesda 14, Md., U.S.A. [Trematoda]

OLROG, Prof. C.C. Instituto Miguel Lillo, Calle Miguel Lillo 205, Tucumán, Argentina. [Aves of s.S. America & Antarctic (Yes); Mammalia, excl. Cricetidae, of same (Yes); Reptilia: Serpentes, excl. Typhlidae & Hemityphlidae of same (Yes)]

OLSEN, A.M. Division of Fisheries & Oceanography, Commonwealth Scientific & Industrial Research Organization, Stowell Avenue, Hobart, Tasmania. [Pelecypoda: Pectinidae of Tasmania (Yes); Pisces: Galeidae of s. Australia (No); Crustacea: Panuliridae of s. Australia (No)]

OLSEN, Leland S. Department of Animal Pathology & Hygiene, University of Nebraska, Lincoln, Nebr., U.S.A. [Parasitic Nematoda of Vertebrates (No)]

OLSEN, Stanley. Box 631, Florida State Geological Survey, Tallahassee, Fla., U.S.A. [Miocene Carnivora of N. America (Yes); Pleistocene Mammalia of N. America (Yes)]

* OLSEN, Dr. O. Wilford. Department of Zoology, Colorado State University, Fort Collins, Colo., U.S.A. [Trematoda & Nematoda]

OLSEN, Yngve H. Bingham Oceanographic Laboratory, Box 2025, Yale Station, New Haven, Conn., U.S.A. [Marine Pisces: Blennioidei of N. & C. America (Yes)]

OLSON, Dr. Everett C. Department of Geology, Rosenwald Hall, University of Chicago, Chicago 37, Ill., U.S.A. [Permo-Carboniferous Reptilia & Amphibia (Yes)]

OLSON, Earl Parkinson. 2833 Marilyn Drive, Ogden, Utah, U.S.A. [Paleozoic Corals of N. America (Yes); Devonian-Permian Bryozoa, Brachiopoda, Ostracoda, of N. America (Yes)]

OLSON, Dr. Henry William. District of Columbia Teachers College, 11th and Harvard Streets, N.W., Washington D.C., U.S.A. [Oligochaeta: Lumbricidae of N. America (Yes)]

OLSON, Dr. J. Bennet. California Institute of Technology, Pasadena 4, Calif., U.S.A. [Crustacea: Copepoda: f-l. marine Cyclopoida of World (Yes)]

OLSON, Rex. Humble Oil & Refining Company, P.O. Box 999, Chico, Calif., U.S.A. [Cretaceous & Eocene Foraminifera (No); Cretaceous Mollusca (No)]

OLSON, Prof. Robert E. University of Maine, 313 Deering Hall, Orono, Maine, U.S.A. [Coleoptera: Cerambycidae: g. Monochamus of e. N. America (Yes)]

OLSSON, Axel A. 1906 Ferdinand Street, Coral Gables, Fla., U.S.A. [Tertiary Mollusca of e. cst. U.S., S. & C. America (Yes); Recent Mollusca of C. & C. America (No); Olividae of Panama (Yes)]

OMAN, Dr. P.W. Entomology Research Division, Beltsville, Md., U.S.A. [Homoptera: Cicadelloidea of World (No); of Nearctic (Yes)] [U.S. Department of Agriculture]

OMER-COOPER, Prof. Joseph. Department of Zoology & Entomology, Rhodes University, Grahamstown, Union of South Africa. [Crustacea: Isopoda of Africa (No); Coleoptera: Gyrinidae of Africa (Yes)]

OMER-COOPER, Dr. Joyce. Rhodes University, Grahamstown, Union of South Africa. [Coleoptera: Dytiscidae of Africa (Yes)]

OMODEO, P. Istituto di Zoologia, Piazza S. Agostino 4, Siena, Italy. [Oligochaeta of World (Yes)]

ÔMORI, Dr. Massao. Geological and Mineralogical Institute, Tokyo University of Education, Otuka-kubo-machi, Bunkyo-ku, Tokyo, Japan. [Cenozoic marine Mollusca, espec. Pectinidae, of Japan (Yes)]

OMORI, N. Department of Medical Zoology, Research Institute of Endemics, Nagasaki University, Nagasaki, Japan. [Diptera: Culicidae of Japan (Yes)]

OMURA, Dr. Hideo. Whales Research Institute, 4, 12 Chome, Nishigashi-Dori, Tsukishima, Chuo-Ku, Tokyo, Japan. [Mammalia: Cetacea of cst. of Japan (Yes); of Antarctic & Bering Sea (No)]

ONABAMAIRO, Dr. Sanya D. Parasitology Research Laboratory, University College, Ibadan, Nigeria. [Crustacea: Copepoda of Nigeria (Yes)]

ONDRIAS, Dr. John C. Department of Zoology, University of Athens, Athens, Greece. [Mammalia of Greece (Yes)]

O'NEILL, Miss Kellie. Entomology Research Division, Agricultural Research Service, U.S. Department of Agriculture, Washington 25, D.C., U.S.A. [Thysanoptera of World (No); economic species of U.S. (Yes)]

ONG, Mr. S.K., Naturalist, P.O. Box 1166, Taipei, Taiwan, Formosa. [Lepidoptera: Rhopalocera of Indo-Australian]

OOSTENBRINK, Dr. Ir M. Plantenziektenkundige Dienst, Landbouwhogeschool, Wageningen, Netherlands. [Nematoda: soil & f-w. Tylenchida (Yes)]
* van OOTSTROOM, Dr. S. J. Rijksherbarium Curator, Emmalaan 39, Oegstgeest, Netherlands. [Coleoptera]
* OPHEIM, Mr. Magne. Frognerveien 58, Oslo, Norway. [Lepidoptera]
* ÖPIK, A. Department of Paleontology, Bureau of Mineral Resources, 485 Bourne Street, Melbourne, C. 1. Vict., Australia. [Fossils]
* OPSAHL, James F. Winona State College, Winona, Minn., U.S.A. [Mammalia, Aves]
ORCES, V., Prof. G. Escuela Politécnica Nacional, Apartado 2759, Quito, Ecuador. [Reptilia: Teiidae & Elapidae of Ecuador (Yes); Pisces: Bunocephalidae, Doradidae, Loricariinae of Ecuador & Peru (No)]
ORCHARD, Mr. William R. Plant Pathology Laboratory, Saanichton, B. C., Canada. [Nematoda: g. Heterodera & Meloidogyne of Pacific n. w. N. America (Yes); g. Pratylenchus of B. C., Canada (Yes)] [Canada Department of Agriculture]
ORDWAY, Miss Ellen. Department of Entomology, University of Kansas, Lawrence, Kans., U.S.A. [Hymenoptera: Halictidae, espec. g. Augochlora, Augochloropsis, Agapostemon, of N. America (Yes)]
von ORELLI, Dr. M. Zoologische Anstalt, Universität, Basel, Switzerland. [Diplura (No)]
ORFILA, Dr. Ricardo N. Casilla Correo 2. -Suc. 28, Buenos Aires, Argentina. [Lepidoptera: Noctuoidea & Saturnioidea of Neotropics (Yes); Aves: Psittaciformes of Neotropics (Yes)]
* ORGHIDAN, T. Institutul de Speologie R. P. R. "Emil Racovita" Str. Dr. Capsa 8, Raion Lenin, Bucureşti 15, Rumania. [Acarina]
ORKIN, Dr. P. A. Natural History Department, Marischal College, Aberdeen, Scotland. [Pisces of Great Britain & n. w. Europe (No)]
*ORLOV, Dr. Prof. I. V. Technological Institute of Meat Industry, Talalichina Street 33, Moscow 29, U.S.S.R. [Helminths of animals]
ORLOV, Prof. J. A. Paleontological Institute, Academy of Sciences, 33 Lenin Prospectus, Moscow B-71, U.S.S.R. [Permian Reptilia: Theriodontia & Deinocephalia (Yes); Tertiary Mammalia: Carnivora (Yes)]
O'ROURKE, Prof. F. J. Department of Zoology, University College, National University of Ireland, Cork, Ireland. [Hymenoptera: Formicidae of World (No); of Palearctic (Yes)]
ORR, Phil C. Museum of Natural History, Santa Barbara, Calif., U.S.A. [Pleistocene Mammalia: Proboscidea: mammoths of w. N. America (Yes); Pleistocene Gravigrada of New World (Yes)]
ORR, Dr. Robert T. California Academy of Sciences, San Francisco 18, Calif., U.S.A. [Mammalia: espec. Chiroptera of N. America (Yes); Aves of N. America & Mexico (Yes)]
ORTENBURGER, Dr. A. I. Galiano I., B. C., Canada. [Reptilia: Serpentes of N. America (No)]
ORTIZ, Carlos S. See STUARDO ORTIZ, C.
* ORTIZ, Prof. Dr. E. Departmento de Zoologia, Universidad de Madrid, Madrid, Spain. [Crustacea]
ORTIZ de ZARATE, Adolfo. Nájera (Provincia de Logroño), Spain. [Terr. Mollusca of Spain & Portugal (Yes); of w. Equatorial Africa (No)]
ORTIZ CORDERO, Mr. Ignacio. Instituto de Higiene, Ciudad Universitaria, Apartado 4412, Oficina del Este, Caracas, Venezuela. [Diptera: Ceratopogonidae, Simuliidae, Psychodidae: g. Phlebotomus, of Neotropics (Yes); Acarina: Ixodiodea of Neotropics (Yes)]
ORTLEPP, Dr. R. J. Veterinary Laboratory, Onderstepoort, Transvaal, Union of South Africa. [Trematoda, Cestoda, Nematoda, of World, espec. s. Africa (Yes)]
* ORTON, Dr. Grace L. Scripps Institution of Oceanography, La Jolla, Calif., U.S.A. [Amphibia: frogs & tadpoles of World]
* ORTOYA ARBOLEDA, Francisco José. Instituto de Ciencias Naturales, Apartado Postal 2535, Apartado aereo 7495, Bogotá, Colombia. [Coleoptera: Scarabaeidae]
ØRVIG, Dr. Tor. Paleozoologiska Avdelningen, Naturhistoriska Riksmuseum, Stockholm 50, Sweden. [Silurian-Devonian Ostracodermi & Arthrodira (Yes); Ordovician-Carboniferous Vertebrate microfossils (Yes)]
* OSBORN, Dale J. Robert Colej, Bebek P. K. 8, Istanbul, Turkey. [Mammalia, espec. Rodentia, of Middle East & Arctic (Yes)]
OSCHE, Dr. Günther. Zoologisches Institut der Universität Erlangen, Universitätsstrasse 19, Erlangen, Germany. [Nematoda: Rhabditinae of World (Yes); Ascaridoidea (of Rodentia, Chiroptera, Insectivora) of Europe (Yes); Trichostrongyloidea (of Rodentia, Chiroptera, Insectivora) of Europe & N. America (Yes)]
* OSHIMA. Masamitsu. 180 Nakane-chô, Meguro-ku, Tokyo, Japan. [Pisces]
*OSHMARIN, P. G. Far-Eastern Branch, Academy of Sciences of U.S.S. R, Lenin Street 50, Vladivostok, U.S.S.R. [Helminths of animals]
OSMOLSKA, H. Zakład Paleontologii, Polska Akademia Nauk, Nowy -Swiat 67, Warszawa, Poland. [M. Devonian to L. Carboniferous Trilobita (Yes)]
OSSIANNILSSON, Dr. Frej. Lantbrukshögskolan, Uppsala 7, Sweden. [Heteroptera of n. Europe (Yes); Homoptera of n. Europe (Yes); Diptera: Simuliidae of n. Europe (No)] [Institute of Plant Pathology & Entomology]

von der OSTEN, Dr. Erimar. "Valhala", Avenida Avila, Altamira, Caracas, Venezuela. [Cretaceous Pelecypoda & Gastropoda (No); Pleistocene Edentata of S. America (No)]

OSTERGAARD, Jens M. 45 Laurel Avenue, Atherton, Calif., U.S.A. [Marine Gastropoda: Cypraeidae of Tropics (Yes)]

OSTROUMOVA, T.A. Institute of Oceanology, Academy of Sciences, Luzhnikovskaya 8, Moscow 127, U.S.S.R. [Pisces: Pleuronectidae, eggs & larvae, of Pacific Ocean (Yes)]

ØSTVEDT, O.J. Institute of Marine Research, Box 189, Bergen, Norway. [Crustacea: pelagic Copepoda of Norway & Arctic (Yes); Pisces: Clupeidae of Norway & North Sea (Yes)]

OTEIFA, Dr. B.A. Faculty of Agriculture, Cairo University, Giza, Egypt. [Plant parasitic & soil Nematoda of Egypt (No)]

OTSURU, Prof. Masamitsu. Department of Parasitology, Faculty of Medicine, Niigata University, Niigata, Japan. [Diptera: Culicidae: g. Anopheles of China, Japan, Formosa (Yes); Tabanidae of Japan (No)]

OTTERLIND, Fil. Lic. Gunnar. Havsfiskelaboratoriet, Lysekil, Sweden. [Cephalopoda of North Sea (Yes); races of herring in Baltic Sea (No)]

OTTO, Dr. G.F. Parasitology Department, Research Division, Abbott Laboratories, North Chicago, Ill., U.S.A. [Parasites of World (Yes)]

OUCHI, Prof. Y. Department of Biology, Aichi University, Toyohashi, Aichi Pref., Japan. [Diptera of E. Asia (Yes)]

den OUDEN, Mr. H. Instituut voor Plantenziektenkundig Onderzoek, Binnenhaven 4a, Wageningen, Netherlands. [Nematoda: Heterodera of w. Europe (Yes)]

OUELLET, Bro. Joseph. (Montreal, Canada; Diptera) Died January 9, 1952.

OUGHTON, Dr. John. Department of Entomology & Zoology, Ontario Agricultural College, Guelph, Ont., Canada. [Mollusca: land snails of n.e.N. America (Yes); Oligochaeta: Lumbricidae of n.e.N. America (Yes)]

* OUREISHI, Dr. M.R., Director, Central Fisheries, West Wharf, Karachi, West Pakistan. [Pisces]

OUTTEN, L.M. Mars Hill College, Box 722-C, Mars Hill, N.C., U.S.A. [Fresh-water Pisces: Osteichthyes of e. U.S. (No); g. Notropis of w. North Carolina (Yes)]

OVASSA, Dr. M. Section Onchocercose, Centre Muraz, Bobo Dioulasso, Upper Volta. [Diptera: Tabanidae of Ethiopian (Yes); Simuliidae of Ethiopian (No)] [Office de la Recherche Scientifique et Technique Outre-Mer]

OVERGAARD-NIELSEN, Dr. C. See NIELSEN, C.O.

* OVERLAET, F.G. (Belgium; Lepidoptera) Deceased.

OVEY, C.D. 111 Grantchester Meadows, Cambridge, England. [Protozoa: planktonic Foraminifera of deep-sea floor (Yes); Globigerinidae & Globorotalidae deep-sea cores] [St. John's College, Cambridge]

OWEN, E.F. British Museum (Natural History), Cromwell Road, London, S.W.7, England. [Cretaceous Brachiopoda of World (Yes)]

OWEN, Gareth. Department of Zoology, The University, Glasgow, Scotland. [Mollusca: Bivalvia of British Seas (Yes)]

OWEN, Prof. William B. Department of Zoology & Physiology, University of Wyoming, Laramie, Wyo., U.S.A. [Diptera: Culicidae of N. America (Yes)]

* OWEN-CAMPBELL, Mr. J. Clumps Point, Via El Arish, N. Queensland, Australia. [Coleoptera]

OWENS, Virgil H. 107 W. 7th Street, Kennett, Mo., U.S.A. [Coleoptera: Scarabaeidae of U.S. (Yes); Scorpiones of U.S. (Yes)] [Missouri Department of Agriculture]

OWRE, Dr. Harding B. (Mrs. Oscar T. Owre). University of Miami Marine Laboratory, 1 Rickenbacker Causeway, Miami 49, Fla., U.S.A. [Chaetognata of Atlantic & Gulf of Mexico (Yes); Crustacea: Copepoda: Calanoida of N. Atlantic (No)]

* OXFORD, A.E. Rowett Research Institute, Bucksburn, Aberdeenshire, Scotland. [Protozoa]

OYAMA, Dr. Katura. Geological Survey of Japan, 8 Kawada-cho, Shinjuku-ku, Tokyo, Japan. [Cenozoic & Recent Mollusca of Japan & Micronesia (Yes); of Philippines & Indonesia (No)]

van OYE, Prof. Dr. Paul. St. Lievenslaan 30, Gent, Belgium. [Rotatoria & Chaetognatha (No); Rhizopoda (Yes)]

OZAKI, Hiroshi. Department of Geology, National Science Museum, Ueno Park, Tokyo, Japan. [Pliocene Pelecypoda & Gastropoda of Japan (Yes)]

OZAKI, Prof. Y. Department of Zoology, Hiroshima University, Hiroshima, Japan. [Trematoda Monogenea: Polystomidae; Digenea: Allocreadiidae, Opecoeliidae, Schistosomatidae; all of Japan (No)]

*OZERSKAYA, V.N. All-Union Skrjabin Institute of Helminthology, Staropansky 3, Moscow K-12, U.S.S.R. [Helminths of animals of U.S.S.R.]

* OZOLS, Dr. Edgars. Baltijas Augu Aizsardzibas Instituts, Veidenbauma iels 4a/17, Riga, Latvia, U.S.S.R [Hymenoptera: Ichneumonidae]

PAAVER, K.L. Institute of Zoology & Botany, Academy of Sciences of Estonian S.S.R., Vanemuise 21, Tartu, Estonia, U.S.S.R. [Holocene & Recent Mammalia of n. Europe (Yes)]

PABST, Wolfgang. (Germany; Opiliones) Deceased.

PACKARD, Prof. Chas. E. 133 Richmond Ave., Morgantown, W.Va., U.S.A. [Gastrotricha of N.America (Yes); Protozoa: Flagellata of termites of N.America (Yes); Euglenoidina (Yes)]

PACKARD, Earl L. 235 Waverly Street, Palo Alto, Calif., U.S.A. [Cretaceous Ammonites of w.N.America]

PACKARD, Robert L. Museum of Natural History, University of Kansas, Lawrence, Kans., U.S.A. [Mammalia: Cricetinae, espec. g. Baiomys, of N.America (Yes)]

PACLT, Dr. Jiři. Department of Zoology, Slovak Academy of Sciences, Sienkiewiczova 1, Bratislava, Czechoslovakia. [Recent & Fossil Collembola, Diplura, Protura, Thysanura; Lepidoptera: Hepialidae of World (No)]

* PACOCK, A.F. Compania Petrolera California Limited, Apartado Postal 189, Guatemala City, Guatemala. [Fossil Invertebrates]

PÁDR, Dr. Z. 43 Legerova, Praha 2, Czechoslovakia. [Hymenoptera: Tenthredinoidea of Palearctic (Yes)]

* PADRON, Agustin Gonzalez. Primo Rivera 23, Santa Cruz de Tenerife, Canary Is., Spain. [Coleoptera]

PAESLER, Dr. Friedrich. Biologische Zentralanstalt, Weissenfelserstrasse 57a, Naumburg/Saale, German Democratic Republic. [Free-living plant-parasitic Nematoda of c. Germany (Yes)]

PAETZOLD, Dr. Dankwart. Zoologisches Institut, Martin-Luther-Universität, Domplatz 4, Halle/Salle, German Democratic Republic. [F-l. soil & f-w. Nematoda of Europe (Yes)]

PAGDEN, Dr. H.T. C/o Hongkong & Shanghai Bank, Penang, Malaya. [Hymenoptera: Methocidae, Mutillidae, Apidae: Meliponinae, of Malaysia (Yes); Vespidae: Stenogastrinae of Malaysia (No)]

PAGÉS, Jean. Laboratoire de Zoologie, Faculté des Sciences de Dijon, Bd. Gabriel, Dijon (C.d'O.) France. [Diplura, excl. Campodeidae, of World (Yes)]

PAGET, Dr. Oliver E. Naturhistorisches Museum, Burgring 7, Wien 1, Austria. [Gastropoda: Pulmonata of Austria (No)]

PAHL, Brother George, F.S.C. St.Marys College, Winona, Minn., U.S.A. [Amphibia of Great Lakes, U.S. (Yes); Gastropoda: Polygridae of m.w.N.America (Yes); Pelecypoda: Unionidae of Up.Mississippi Valley, U.S. (Yes)]

PAI, Mr. V.M. Central Marine Fisheries Research Centre, 40 Commercial Building, Vera Val (Sauriashtra), India. [Pisces: Percomorphi: Centropomidae: g. Psammoperca, Latis, & Ambassis, of India (Yes)]

PAIK, Prof. Kap Yong. Biological Institute, Teachers College, Kyungpook National University, Teagu, Korea. [Araneida of Korea (Yes); Diplopoda & Chilopoda of Korea (No)]

PAIN, Mr. T. 16 Landseer Buildings, Millbank, London, S.W.1, England. [Terr. & f-w. Mollusca of Neotropics & Ethiopian (Yes)]

PAINE, George H., Jr. 446 Ludlow Highway, Ludlow, Ky., U.S.A. [Diptera: fossil Chironomidae of N.America (Yes)]

PAINTER, Dr. Reginald H. Department of Entomology, Kansas State College, Manhattan, Kans., U.S.A. [Diptera: Bombyliidae & Apioceridae of New World (Yes)]

PAIRO, M. Crusafont. See CRUSAFONT PAIRO, M.

PALADE, X. See SCOBIOLA-PALADE, X.

PALAU CAMPS, J.M. Calle del Agua, 3 Pral., Palma de Majorca, Balearic Is., Spain. [Coleoptera: Curculionidae of Palearctic (Yes); Crustacea: Decapoda of Balearic Is. (Yes)]

PALISSA, Dr. A. Institut für Zoologie, Invalidenstrasse 42, Berlin N 4, German Democratic Republic. [Collembola of Europe (Yes)]

PALLISTER, John C. Department of Insects & Spiders, American Museum of Natural History, New York 24, N.Y., U.S.A. [Coleoptera: Chrysomelidae of New World (No); Cassidinae of New World (Yes); Erotylidae of C. & S.America (Yes); Elateridae: g.Semiotus of S. America (Yes), g. Chalcolepidius of C. & S.America (Yes)]

PALM, Dr. Nils-Bertil. Karl XI: sg. 5A, Lund, Sweden. [Lepidoptera: g. Tineina of Scandinavia (Yes)]

PALM, Phil. Dr. Thure. Idrottsgatan 65, Uppsala, Sweden. [Coleoptera: Anobiidae, Ptinidae, Lymexylonidae, of deciduous trees of Scandinavia (No)]

PALMÉN, Prof. Ernst. Zoological Institute, Helsinki University, P-Rautatiekatu 13, Helsinki, Finland. [Diplopoda & Chilopoda of n.Europe (Yes); Diptera: Chironomidae of n.Europe (No)]

PALMER, Allison R. U.S. Geological Survey, 333 U.S. National Museum, Washington 25, D.C., U.S.A. [Cambrian Trilobita of U.S. (Yes)]

* PALMER, Prof. E.L. 206 Oak Hill Road, Ithaca, N.Y., U.S.A. [Reptilia & Amphibia]

PALMER, Mr. G. Department of Zoology, British Museum (Natural History, Cromwell Road. London, S.W.7, England. [Pisces of Indo-Pacific (No); Trachypteridae of Mediterranean (Yes)]

PALMER, Mrs. Katherine Van Winkle. 206 Oak Hill Road, Ithaca, N.Y., U.S.A. [Cenozoic & Recent Gastropoda & Pelecypoda of New World (Yes)] [Paleontological Research Institution]

PALMER, Miss Miriam A. 621 South Howes Street, Fort Collins, Colo., U.S.A. [Homoptera: Aphidae of Rocky Mts., U.S. (Yes)]

PALMER, Dr. Ralph S. New York State Museum, Albany 1, N.Y., U.S.A. [Mammalia & Aves of N. America (Yes)]

PALMGREN, Prof. Dr. P. Department of Zoology, University of Helsinki, Helsinki, Finland. [Aves of n. Europe (No); Araneida of n. Europe (No)]

PALOMBI, Prof. Arturo. Stazione Zoologica, Villa Comunale, Napoli, Italy. [Turbellaria: Polycladida of Mediterranean & s. Africa (No); larval & adult Trematoda: Digenea & Monogenea of Mediterranean Sea (No)]

PALUDAN, Mr. Knud. Danish Game Biology Station, Rønde, Denmark. [Aves of Iran & Afghanistan (No)]

PANCHEN, Dr. A. L. Department of Zoology, King's College, Newcastle upon Tyne, England. [Permian & Triassic Amphibia: Brachyopidae: g. Plagiosaurus (Yes); Fossil Labyrinthodonts of British Coal Measures (Yes); Recent Amphibia & Reptilia of Britain (No); Carboniferous Amphibia: Labyrinthodontia of Britain (Yes)]

* PANFILOV, D. V. Institute of Geography, Academy of Sciences of U.S.S.R. [Staromonetnyi pereulok 29, Moskow B-17, U.S.S.R. [Hymenoptera]

PANIKKAR, Dr. N. Kesava. Fisheries Development Advisor, Ministry of Food & Agriculture, New Delhi, India. [Coelenterata: Actinaria & Ceriantharia of Indo-Pacific (No)]

PANIN, Sergiu. Facultatea de Biologie (Fauna R.P.R.), Splaiul Independentei nr. 93-95, Bucureşti, Rumania. [Coleoptera: Cicindelidae, Carabidae, Histeridae, Scarabaeidae, Cerambycidae, of e. Europe (No)]

PANNING, Dr. A. Zoologisches Museum, Bornplatz 5, Hamburg 13, Germany. [Holothurioidea: Aspidochirota & Dendrochirota of World (Yes)]

PANOUSE, Dr. J. B. Laboratoire de Zoologie, Institut Scientific Cherifien, Rabat, Morocco. [Solifuga of Mediterrean & n. & w. Africa (Yes), of Asia (No)]

* PAPADEPOL, A. Muzeul National de Istorie Naturala, "Grigore Antipa", Kisselef No. 1., Bucureşti III, Rumania.[Aves]

PAPANJAN, Seda. Institute of Zoology, Armenian Academy of Sciences, Awanskoe shosse 20, Erevan, U.S.S.R. [Amphibia of U.S.S.R (No), of Caucasus & Transcancasus (Yes)]

PAPI, Prof. Dr. Floriano. Istituto di Zoologia, Via Volta 4, Pisa, Italy. [Turbellaria: Tricladida & Polycladida of World (No); Turbellaria: Acoela, Rhabdocoela, Alloeocoela, of World (Yes); Gastrotricha of World (No)]

PAPP, Prof. Dr. Adolf. Palaeontologisches Institut, Universität Wien, Wien, Austria. [Up. Tertiary f-w. & br-w. Mollusca & terr. snails (Yes)]

PAPP, Charles S. Department of Entomology, University of California, Riverside, Calif., U.S.A. [Coleoptera: of s.w. U.S.; Chrysomelidae, Alleculidae, Heteroceridae, Scarabaeidae, of N. & C. America (Yes); Curculionidae: g. Conotrachelus of C. & S. America (Yes); Dermestidae & other stored products insects]

PAPP, Dr. Eugen. Bakonyi Museum, Postafiók 32, Veszprém, Hungary. [Hymenoptera: Braconidae & Tenthredinidae of Carpathian Basin (Yes)]

PAPPAS, George Demetrios. Department of Anatomy, Columbia University, College of Physicians & Surgeons, New York 32, N.Y., U.S.A. [F-w. & marine Protozoa: Sarcodina: f-l. amoebae (Yes)]

* PAPPENHEIM, P. Department of Ichthyology, Zoologisches Museum, Invalidenstrasse 43, Berlin, N. 4, German Democratic Republic. [Pisces]

PARAENSE, Dr. W. Lobato. Caixa Postal 2113, Belo Horizonte, Minas Gerais, Brazil. [Mollusca: Planorbidae of C. & S. America (Yes)]

*PARAMONOV, Dr. Prof. A. A. Laboratory of Helminthology, Academy of Science of U.S.S.R., Lenin Highway 33, Moscow B-71, U.S.S.R. [Parasitic, soil, plant Nematoda of World (Yes)]

PARAMONOV, Dr. S. J. Division of Entomology, Commonwealth Scientific & Industrial Research Organization, P.O. Box 109, Canberra, A.C.T., Australia. [Diptera: excl. Nematocera, of Australian (Yes); Bombyliidae of World (Yes)]

* PARASKIV, K.P. (Alma-Ata, U.S.S.R.; Reptilia) Died January 1959.

PARDO ALCAIDE, Anselmo. 2º Bloque Orgaz 7, 3º, dcha, Melilla, Spanish North Africa. [Coleoptera: Meloidae, Oedemeridae, Lagriidae, Malachiidae, of Mediterranean (Yes); Meloidae: g. Mylabris of World (Yes)]

* PARDUCZ, Dr. Bela, Magyar Nemzeti Museum, Baross. u. 13, Budapest VIII, Hungary. [Protozoa: f-l. Ciliata]

PARENTI, Dr. Umberto. Istituto di Zoologia, Universitá degli Studi di Modena, Modena, Italy. [Lepidoptera: Microlepidoptera of Italy (Yes)]

* PARFENTIJEV, V. J. Zoological Institute, Academy of Sciences of U.S.S.R., Leningrad B-164, U.S.S.R. [Hemiptera]

PARFIN, Miss Sophy. Division fof Insects, U.S. National Museum, Washington 25, D.C., U.S.A. [Mecoptera & Neuroptera of N. America (Yes); Neuroptera: Sisyridae of World (Yes)]

PARIN, N. V. Institute of Oceanology, Academy of Sciences of U. S. S. R., Luzhnikovskaya 8, Moscow 127, U. S. S. R. [Pisces: Exocoetidae of Pacific & Indian Ocean (Yes), of Atlantic Ocean (No)]

PARK, Prof. Orlando. Department of Zoology, Northwestern University, Evanston, Ill., U. S. A. [Coleoptera: Pselaphidae of New World (Yes)]

PARKE, Dr. M. The Laboratory, Citadel Hill, Plymouth, England. [Protozoa: marine Chrysomonadina of Europe (Yes)]

PARKER, Frank H. Route 1, Box 26A, Globe, Ariz., U. S. A. [Coleoptera, espec. Meloidae & Buprestidae, of N. America (No)]

PARKER, Francis L. Scripps Institution of Oceanography, La Jolla, Calif., U. S. A. [Tertiary-Recent Foraminifera of Atlantic, Gulf of Mexico, Mediterranean (Yes); Recent planktonic Foraminifera of World (Yes)]

* PARKER, Prof. G. H. (Cambridge, Mass.; Pisces) Deceased.

* PARKER, Dr. H. W. Address unknown. [Reptilia]

PARKER, Mr. Malcolm V. 3398 Seed Tick Road, Arlington, Tenn., U. S. A. [Amphibia & Reptilia of N. America & Mexico (Yes), of Australia (No); parasites of Amphibia & Reptilia of N. America (Yes)]

PARKER, Robert H. Scripps Institution of Oceanography, La Jolla, Calif., U. S. A. [Pleistocene Mollusca of Baja California & w. Atlantic (No); Recent of same (Yes); Crustacea: Decapoda of Gulf of Mexico (No); Echinodermata, Bryozoa, Coelenterata, of Gulf of Mexico (No)]

PARKER, William G. 4511 Banning Street, Houston 27, Texas, U. S. A. [Quaternary & Tertiary Foraminifera of Gulf Coast U. S. (Yes)]

PARKES, Dr. Kenneth C. Section of Birds, Carnegie Museum, Pittsburgh 13, Penna., U. S. A. [Aves of New World & Philippines (Yes)]

PARKINSON, Dr. D. 129 Monmouth Drive, Sutton Coldfield, Warwickshire, England. [L. Carboniferous Brachiopoda: Rhynchonellidae; g. Schizophoria, Brachythyris, Martinia, Dielasma, of England & Ireland (Yes)]

PARKS, Dr. James Marshall, Jr. Shell Development Company, 3737 Bellaire, Houston 25, Texas, U. S. A. [Up. Paleozoic Anthozoa: Rugosa (Yes); Up. Paleozoic Crinoidea (No)]

PARMALEE, Dr. Paul W., Curator of Zoology, Illinois State Museum, Springfield, Ill., U. S. A. [Pelecypoda: f-w. mussels of Illinois (Yes); Vertebrates from archaeological sites of m. w. US. (Yes)]

PARMELEE, David. Department of Biology, Kansas State Teachers College, Emporia, Kans., U. S. A. [Aves of Canadian Arctic Archipelago (Yes)]

PARMENTER, Mr. L. 94 Fairlands Avenue, Thornton Health, Surrey, England. [Diptera: Stratiomyidae, Rhagionidae, Tabanidae, Asilidae, Dolichopodidae, Syrphidae, Otitidae, Dryamyzidae, of British Isles (Yes)]

PARNES, A. Geology Department, Hebrew University, Jerusalem, Israel. [Mesozoic Ammonites of Israel (Yes)]

PARODIZ, Juan José. Section of Invertebrates, Carnegie Museum, Pittsburgh 13, Penna., U. S. A. [F-w. Gastropoda of e. U. S. (Yes); Pleistocene & Recent terr. & f-w. Gastropoda of S. America (Yes)]

PARRINGTON, Mr. F. R., Director, Univ. Museum of Zoology, Cambridge, England. [Mesozoic Mammalia of Africa (Yes); Reptilia: Permo-Triassic Theriodontia of Africa (Yes)]

PARROT, Dr. L. Institut Pasteur d'Algérie, Alger, Algeria. [Diptera: Psychodidae: g. Phlebotomus of Old World (Yes)]

PARROTT, Arthur W. "Lochiel", Wakapuaka Road, Hira, R. D., Nelson, New Zealand. [Hymenoptera: Braconidae & Ichneumonidae of Australia, New Zealand, Pacific Is. (Yes); Pisces of New Zealand (Yes); Araneida of New Zealand & Pacific Is. (Yes)]

* PARRY, Miss Gwyneth. Zoology Department, Bedford College, University of London, London, N. W. 1, England. [Coelenterata: Actiniaria]

PARSONS, Mr. Carl T. Dorset, Vermont, U. S. A. [Coleoptera: Simicripidae, Nitudulidae, Byturidae, Biphyllidae, Rhyzophagidae, Cucujidae, Silvanidae, Hypocopridae, Helotidae, Cryptophagidae, Erotylidae, Trogositidae, Mycetophagidae, Colydiidae, Lagriidae, Tenebrionidae, of Nearctic (Yes)]

PARTHASARATHY, Dr. M. D. Department of Zoology, Central College, Bangalore, India. [Scorpionida & Opiliones of India (Yes)]

PARTRIDGE, William H. Belgrano 363, Caseros, B. A., Argentina. [Aves of S. America, espec. Argentina (Yes)]

PARVIS, Adalberto, Direttore Sanatorio Aselli, Via Milano 24, Cremona, Italy. [Lepidoptera: Aegeriidae & Rhopalocera of Italy (No)]

* PASA, Prof. Angelo. Museo Civico di Storia Naturale, Lungadige Porta Vittoria, Verona, Italy. [Fossil Vertebrates]

* PASCENKO, Y. I. Zoological Museum, Kiev State University, Vladimirskaja 58, Kiev, Ukraine, U. S. S. R. [Amphibia]

PASPALEFF, Prof. Dr. G. W. Boulevard Anton Ivanoff, 12, Sofia 26, Bulgaria. [Mammalia: Rodentia of Bulgaria (Yes)] [Zoological Institute, University of Sofia]

dos PASSOS, Cyril F. Washington Corners, Mendham, N. J., U. S. A. [Lepidoptera: Rhopalo-
cera of Nearctic (Yes)]
PASTEELS, Prof. J. J. 97 rue aux Laines, Bruxelles, Belgium. [Hymenoptera: Tenthredinoi-
dea of Africa (Yes); Gasteruptionidae of World (Yes); Strepsiptera of Palearctic & Africa
(Yes)] [University of Brussels]
PASTRANA, José A. Solis 370, Buenos Aires, Argentina. [Lepidoptera: microlepidoptera of
Neotropics (Yes)]
PATALAS, Dr. K. Instytut Rybactwa Śródladowego, Olsztyn-Kortowo, Poland. [Crustacea:
f-w. Copepoda: Cyclopidae of Poland (Yes); Diaptomidae & Temoridae of Poland (No);
f-w. Cladocera of Poland (No)]
PATCH, C. L. (Ottawa, Canada: Reptilia & Amphibia) Died 1951.
* PATEL, G. A. Entomology Laboratory, College of Agriculture, Poona, India. [Exopterygota]
PATERSON, Mr. H. E. South African Institute for Medical Research, Box 1038, Johannesburg,
Transvaal, Union of South Africa. [Diptera: Muscidae of Ethiopian (Yes)]
PATERSON, Miss Mary. National Museum, P. O. Box 240, Bulawayo Southern Rhodesia. [Aves
of n. & s. Rhodesia & Bechuanaland (Yes)]
PATOCKA, Dr. J. Pobočka Československej, Akadémie, Vyskumný ustav lesného hospodárstva,
Banská Štiavnica, Czechoslovakia. [Larvae & pupae of forest Lepidoptera of c. Europe
(Yes)]
* PATRIZI, Saverio. Piazza Farnese 51, Roma, Italy. [Hymenoptera: Formicidae]
PATTEN, Dr. John A. Department of Biology, Middle Tennessee State College, Murfreesboro,
Tenn., U. S. A. [Trematodes & Aves of e. U. S. (No)]
* PATTERSON, Bryan. Museum of Comparative Zoology, Cambridge 38, Mass., U. S. A.
[Fossil Mammalia of New World]
* PATTERSON, P. M. Address unknown. [Acarina: Mesostigmata]
* PATTON, Mr. J. L. Department of Paleontology, Humble Oil & Refining Co., P. O. Box 2025,
Tyler, Texas, U. S. A. [Fossil Invertebrates]
* PATTON, Mr. Wendell K. 202 Winthrop Road, Columbus 14, Ohio, U. S. A. [Crustacea: Am-
phipoda]
* PAUL, Mr. F. S. Box 115, Grafton, N. S. W., Australia. [Coleoptera: Buprestidae; Lepidop-
tera]
de PAULA COUTO, Dr. Carlos, Museu National, Quinta da Boa Vista, Rio de Janeiro, Brazil.
[Cenozoic Mammalia of S. America & West Indies (Yes)]
* PAULIAN P. 9 rue Delabordère, Neuilly sur Seine, France. [Aves]
PAULIAN, Dr. R. M. A., Deputy Director, Institut de Recherche Scientific de Madagascar,
Tananarive, Tsimbazaza, Madagascar. [Coleoptera: Scarabaeidae, Corylophidae, Tri-
chopterygidae, Sphaeriidae, of Madagascar; Lepidoptera: Rhopalocera of Madagascar;
Zoraptera, Plecoptera, Anoplura, of Madagascar]
PAULSON, Mr. Edward. Department of Zoology, University of California, Berkeley 4, Calif.,
U. S. A. [Gastropoda: Ellobiidae of New World (Yes), of Micronesia (No); Helicidae of
California (No)]
PAVAN, Dr. Crodowaldo. Departmento de Biologia Geral, Universidad de São Paulo, Caixa
Postal 8105, São Paulo, Brazil. [Diptera: g. Drosophila of S. America (Yes)]
* PAVAN, Prof. Dr. Mario, Istituto d'Anatomia Comparata, Università, Pavia, Italy. [Coleop-
tera]
* PAVILLARD, Prof. J. Faculté des Sciences, Montpellier, Hérault, France. [Protozoa:
Flagellata & Sarcodina.]
PAVLOVSKAJA, Mrs. I. E. See BYCHOVSKAJA-PAVLOVSKAJA, Mrs. I. E.
* PAVLOVSKY, E. N. Zoological Institute, Academy of Sciences of U. S. S. R, Leningrad W-164,
U. S. S. R. [Acarina: Ixodidae]
PAWLOWSKI, Prof. L. K. Poludniowa 1 m 23, Pabianice, Poland. [Hirudinea of N. America,
Africa, Asia, Europe (Yes); Rotatoria of World (Yes)] [Universytet Lodzki]
PAWLOWSKY, Mr. E. N. See PAVLOVSKY, E. N.
PAX, Dr. Ferdinand. (Köln-Klettenberg, Germany; Anthozoa) Not now active in taxonomy.
PAYNE, Mr. K. Ellsworth. 1620 S. W. Park Avenue, Portland 1, Ore., U. S. A. [Amphibia of
Pacific N. W. U. S. (Yes)] [Portland State College]
PAYNE, Mrs. Mary Woods. Geological Department, Sun Oil Company, P. O. Box 2431, Corpus
Christi, Texas, U. S. A. [Mesozoic & Cenozoic Foraminifera (No)]
PAYNTER, Raymond A. Jr. Museum of Comparative Zoology, Cambridge 38, Mass., U. S. A.
[Aves of New World (Yes)]
PEABODY, Frank E. (Los Angeles, Calif.; Fossil Reptila) Deceased.
PEACHEY, J. E. Nematology Department, Rothamsted Experimental Station, Harpenden, Herts,
England. [Oligochaeta: Enchytraeidae of upland soils of Great Britain (No)]
PEARCE, Rev. E. J. Priory of St. Mary Magdalen, Codrington College, St. John, Barbados.
[Coleoptera: Haliplidae, Pselaphidae, Seydmaenidae, of Britain (Yes)]
PEARMAN, Mr. J. V. Beechcroft, Upper Icknield Way, Aston Clinton, Aylesbury, Bucks, Eng-
land. [Psocoptera of World (No); of Malaya, East Indies, Pacific Is. (Yes)] [The Zoo-
logical Museum, Tring]

PEARSE, A.S. (Durham, N.C.; Crustacea) Died December 11, 1956.
PEARSON, Henry R. Caixa Postal 5151, Rio de Janeiro, Brazil. [Lepidoptera: Mimallonidae (Lacosomidae & Perophoridae) of New World (Yes)]
PEARSON, Dr. J.C. University Veterinary School, University of Queensland, Brisbane, Australia. [Trematoda: Digenea: Strigeoidea of N. America & Australia (Yes)]
* PEARSON, Dr. Jay F.W. 2475 S. Bayshore Drive, Miami, Fla., U.S.A. [Hymenoptera & Echinodermata][University of Miami]
* PEARSON, N.E. (Indianapolis, Ind.; Pisces) Not now active in taxonomy.
PEARSON, Mr. Oliver P. Museum of Vertebrate Zoology, University of California, Berkeley 4, Calif., U.S.A. [Mammalia: Rodentia: g. Phyllotis of S. America (Yes); Mammalia of mountains of Peru (Yes)]
PEARSON, Dr. Paul G. Department of Zoology, Rutgers University, New Brunswick, N.J., U.S.A. [Mammalia of Florida & New Jersey (No)]
* PEASE, Roger W., Jr. 6 Trumbull Street, New Britain, Conn., U.S.A. [Lepidoptera]
PECHUMAN, Dr. L.L. 7 Davison Road, Lockport, N.Y., U.S.A. [Diptera: Tabanidae of World (Yes); Coenomyiidae of N. America (Yes); Pelecorhynchidae of New World (Yes)]
PECK, Joseph H., Jr. Museum of Paleontology, University of California, Berkeley 4, Calif., U.S.A. [Mesozoic & Tertiary marine Pelecypoda of w. U.S. (Yes); Mesozoic & Tertiary marine Gastropoda of w. U.S. (Yes); Fossil Cephalopoda of w. U.S. (Yes)]
PECK, Dr. Oswald. Division of Entomology, Science Service Building, Ottawa, Ont., Canada. [Hymenoptera: Chalcidoidea of Nearctic (Yes); Cynipoidea & Proctotrupoidea of Nearctic (No)] [Canadian Department of Agriculture]
PECK, Prof. R.E. 101 Swallow Hall, University of Missouri, Columbia, Mo., U.S.A. [Mesozoic non-marine Ostracoda of World (Yes); Mesozoic Crinoidea: Roveacrinidae of World (Yes)]
PEEBLES, C.R. Agricultural Experiment Station, Rio Piedras, Puerto Rico. [Nematoda of animals of New World (Yes)]
* PEETERS, E.M.E. S.E.R.A.M., B.P. 1190, Elisabethville, Belgian Congo. [Diptera: Culicidae]
von PEEZ, Ing. Alexander. Villa S. Francesco, Bressanone, Bolzano, Italy. [Coleoptera of s. Tyrol]
* PEI, Wen-Chung. Institute of Vertebrate Paleontology, Academia Sinica, P.O. Box 643, Peking, Peoples Republic of China. [Fossil Vertebrates]
PEJLER, Dr. Birger. Zoological Institute, Uppsala, Sweden. [Limnoplanktonic Rotatoria of Europe (Yes)]
PELÁEZ FERNÁNDEZ, Prof. Dionisio, Jefe del Laboratorio de Parasitologia, Escuela Nacional de Ciencias Biológicas, Instituto Politécnico Nacional, Apartado Postal 19186, Mexico 17, D.F., Mexico. [Homoptera: Membracidae of World, espec. African & Neotropical (Yes); Reptilia: Plasmodiidae of World (Yes); Scorpionida of New World espec. N. & C. America (No)]
PELHAM-CLINTON, Mr. E.C. Animal Diseases Research Assoc., Moredun Institute, Gilmerton, Edinburgh 9, Scotland. [Diptera: Ceratopogonidae, of Holarctic (No); g. Culicoides of Holarctic (Yes); Lepidoptera of Britain (Yes)]
PELIKAN, Dr. J. Zoological Laboratories, Czechoslovak Academy of Sciences, 25a Plotni, Brno, Czechoslovakia. [Thysanoptera of World.(No), of Palearctic (Yes); Mammalia of c. Europe (Yes)]
* PELLER, Walter. Address unknown. [Diptera]
PELLÉRDY, L. Állategészégügyi Kutató Intézet, Hungaria-korut 21, Budapest XIV, Hungary. [Protozoa: Sporozoa: Coccidiomorpha of Europe (Yes)] [Veterinary Research Institute]
PELTIER, Edward Joseph. Sohio Petroleum Company, P.O. Box 359, Casper, Wyo., U.S.A. [Pennsylvanian Foraminifera: Fusulinidae: g.Wedekindellina, Fusulinella, Fusulina, & Triticites of U.S. (Yes)]
* PELTON, Mr. John Z. 94 E. Tulane Road, Columbus 2, Ohio, U.S.A. [Odonata]
PENA, Sr. Luis E. Casilla 2974, Santiago, Chile. [Coleoptera: Tenebrionidae of Andes (Yes); of tropical S. America (No); of desert regions of Chile (Yes)] [Museo Nacional de Historia Natural]
PENDERGRAST, Dr. J.G. Zoology Department, Auckland University College, P.O. Box 2553, Auckland, New Zealand. [Heteroptera: Pentatomidae, Aradidae, Lygaeidae, of New Zealand (Yes); Cryptocerata of New Zealand (No)]
PENER, M.P. Department of Zoology, The Hebrew University, Jerusalem, Israel. [Orthoptera: Acrididae of Israel (No); g. Calliptamus of Middle East (Yes)]
* PENG, Dr. Oei Hong. Gereonshof 36, Köln, Germany. [Nematoda]
PENGELLY, David H. Department of Entomology, Ontario Agricultural College, Guelph, Ont., Canada. [Hymenoptera: Apoidea of e. Canada & n.e. U.S. (Yes)]
PENN, George H. Department of Zoology, Tulane University, New Orleans 18, La., U.S.A. [Diptera: Culicidae, larvae & pupae, of N. America (No); Crustacea: Astacidae of N. America (Yes)]

PENNAK, Robert W. Biology Department, University of Colorado, Boulder, Colo., U.S.A.
[F-w. Invertebrates of U.S. (No)]
PENNER, Lawrence R. Department of Zoology, University of Connecticut, Storrs, Conn.,
U.S.A. [Trematoda: Schistosomatidae of World (Yes); Diptera: Cuterebridae of World
(Yes)]
PENNEY, Dr. James T. Department of Biology, University of South Carolina, Columbia, S.C.,
U.S.A. [Porifera: Spongillidae of N. America (Yes)]
PEPPER, Prof. J. O. 413 Ridge Avenue, State College, Penna., U.S.A. [Homoptera: Aphi-
dae of U.S. (Yes)] [Pennsylvania State University]
* PERCIVAL, Prof. E. Department of Zoology, University of Canterbury, Christchurch, New
Zealand. [Brachiopoda & Crustacea: Copepoda]
PERCIVAL, Stephan F., Jr. Mobil Oil Co. de Venezuela, Apdo. del Este 5373, Caracas, Vene-
zuela. [Cretaceous-Recent pelagic Foraminifera: g. Globotruncana, Globigerina, Globig-
erinoides, Catapsydrax, Orbulina, Globorotalia, Globoquadrina, of Caribbean Area (No)]
PEREIRA, Prof. Francisco S. Departamento de Zoologia, Caixa Postal 7172, São Paulo, Brazil.
[Coleoptera: Scarabaeidae: Coprinae & Geotrupinae; Lucanidae; Passalidae; all of
World (Yes)]
* PEREIRA de CASTRO, Maria. Instituto Biologico, Secção de Parasitologia Animal, Caixa
Postal 119-A, São Paulo, Brazil. [Acarina]
* PEREIRA de Medina, N. See de MEDINA, N.P.
PERES, Prof. Dr. J.M., Directeur de la Station Marine d'Endoume, rue Batterie-des-Lions,
Marseille 7, France. [Ascidiacea of Atlantic, Mediterrean, Red Sea (No)]
* PÉREZ ALCALÁ, Raul, Jefe del Departmento de Sanidad Vegetal, Ministerio de Agricultura,
La Paz, Bolivia. [Coleoptera]
* PEREZ-CANTO, Jorge R. Echawuiran 241, Santiago, Chile. [Protozoa]
* PEREZ FARFANTE de CANET, Professora Isabel. Departmento de Malacologia, Museo Poey,
Universidad de la Habana, Habana, Cuba. [Crustacea: Decapoda & Mollusca]
PERIS, Dr. S.V. Laboratorio de Faunistica y Ecologia Animal, Instituto de Edafologia y Fisio-
logia Vegetal, Serrano 113, Madrid (6), Spain. [Diptera: Calliphoridae of Old World
(Yes); Rhiniini of World (Yes); Muscidae, excl. Anthomyiinae, of Old World (Yes)]
PERKINS, Bob F. Shell Development Company, 3737 Bellaire Boulevard, Houston 25, Texas,
U.S.A. [Cretaceous Anthozoa: Scleractina of W. Hemisphere (Yes); Cretaceous Crinoidea:
Comatulida of W. Hemisphere (Yes)]
PERKINS, Dr. E.J. Scottish Home Department, Marine Laboratory, Victoria Road, Torry,
Aberdeen, Scotland. [Crustacea: Copepoda: Harpacticoida; marine Nematoda; marine
Protozoa, excl. Foraminifera; all of British Isles (Yes)]
PERKINS, Mr. F.A. Department of Entomology, University of Queensland, Brisbane, Queens-
land, Australia. [Diptera: Trypetidae of s.e. Asia & Australasia (No); Plecoptera of
Australia & New Zealand (Yes)]
* PERKINS, Mr. J.F. Department of Entomology, British Museum (Natural History), Crom-
well Road, London, S.W.7, England. [Hymenoptera]
PERKINS, Mr. R. Marlin, Director, Lincoln Park Zoo, Chicago 14, Ill., U.S.A. [Amphibia &
Reptilia of U.S. (No)]
PERLMUTTER, Dr. Alfred. New York State Conservation Department, 65 West Sunrise High-
way, Freeport, N.Y., U.S.A. [Marine Pisces of W.N. Atlantic (Yes)]
PERRET, Prof. J.L. College de Foulassi, B. Postal 54, Sangmelima, Cameroun, French West
Africa. [Amphibia & Reptilia of Cameroun, (Yes)]
PERRY, Prof. T.G. Department of Geology, Indiana University, Bloomington, Ind., U.S.A.
[Ordovician, Silurian, Mississippian Bryozoa: Trepostomata, of N. America (Yes); Ordo-
vician-Permian Bryozoa: Cyclostomata: Fistuliporidae of N. American Species (Yes)]
PERRY, Mr. V.G. Department of Plant Pathology, University of Wisconsin, Madison 6, Wis.,
U.S.A. [Nematoda: Tylenchida of World (Yes); Dorylaimoidea of U.S. (Yes)]
* PERRY, Wm. J. 1607 Osage, Alexandria, Va., U.S.A. [Diptera]
* PERUTIK, Radomir. Kopernikova 1, Kroměříž, Czechoslovakia. [Odonata]
PESCHEV, Georgi Petrov. Zoologisches Institut, Bulgarischen Akademie der Wissenschaften,
Boulv. Ruski 1, Sofia, Bulgaria. [Orthoptera: Blattodea & Mantodea of Balkan Pen. (Yes)]
* PESCOTT, R.T.M., Director, National Museum of Victoria, Swanston Street, Melbourne,
Vict., Australia. [Lepidoptera]
PESSOA, Prof. Dr. Samuel B. (São Paulo, Brazil; Diptera) Not now active in taxonomy.
PESTA, Prof. Dr. Otto. Akademie der Wissenschaften, Dr. Ignaz Seipelplatz 2, Wien I, Austria.
[Crustacea: Copepoda, Cladocera, Decapoda, f-w. & marine]
* PETERFFI, Mr. Ferencs. Facultatea de Stiinte Naturale, Universitatea J. Bolyai, Str. Arany
11, Cluj, Rumania. [Diptera]
PETERS, Prof. Dr. B.G. Imperial College, Prince Consort Road, London, S.W.7, England.
[Parasitic & Soil Nematoda (No)]
PETERS, G. Zoologisches Museum, Humboldt Universität, Invalidenstrasse 43, Berlin N.4,
German Democratic Republic. [Reptilia: Lacertidae of Palearctic (Yes)]

PETERS, Prof. Dr. Hans M. Zoophysiologisches Institut der Universität, Hölderlinstrasse 12, (14 b), Tubingen, Germany. [Araneida: Argiopidae (No); Pisces: Cichlidae (No)]
PETERS, Mr. James A. Department of Biology, San Fernando Valley State College, Northridge, Calif., U.S.A. [Reptilia & Amphibia of C. & S. America (No); of Ecuador, (Yes)]
* PETERS, J. L. (Cambridge 38, Mass.; Aves) Died April 18, 1952.
PETERS, Dr. W. Malaria Control Pilot Project, Maprik, Sepik District, Papua, New Guinea. [Diptera: Culicidae of Macronesia (Yes); of Tropical Africa (No)]
PETERSEN, Cand. Mag. B. Zoologisk Museum, Krystalgade 27, København, Denmark. [Tardigrada of World (No); Hymenoptera of Greenland, Iceland, Spitzbergen (Yes)]
PETERSEN, Dr. B. Zoologiska Institutionen, Uppsala, Sweden. [Lepidoptera: Macrolepidoptera of Scandinavia (No); g. Pieris & Colias of Holarctic (No)]
PETERSEN, Dr. Günther. Deutsches Entomologisches Institut, Waldowstrasse 1, Berlin-Friedrichshagen, German Democratic Republic. [Lepidoptera: Tineidae of Palearctic (Yes)]
PETERSEN, Mr. J. A. Instituto de Ciencias Naturais, Departamento de Zoologia, Av. Paulo Gama, Porto Alegre, R. G. S., Brazil. [Diptera: g. Drosophila of s. Brazil (Yes)]
* PETERSEN, K. W. Zoologisk Museum, Krystalgade 27, København K, Denmark. [Coelenterata]
PETERSON, Dr. B. V. Canada Department of Agriculture, Entomology Laboratory, P. O. Box 248, Guelph, Ont., Canada. [Diptera: Simuliidae of N. America, espec. western (Yes)]
PETERSON, Clifford. Inter-American Tropical Tuna Commission, Scripps Institution of Oceanography, La Jolla, Calif., U.S.A. [Pisces: Engraulididae & Clupeidae of Pacific cst. of N. C. & S. America (Yes)]
PETERSON, Dr. James A. Department of Paleontology, Shell Oil Company, 705 W. Municipal Drive, Farmington, N. Mex., U.S.A. [Jurassic marine Ostracoda of w. U.S. (Yes); Tertiary non-marine Ostracoda of w. U.S. (No)]
PETERSON, Dr. Randolph L., Curator, Department of Mammalogy, Royal Ontario Museum, 100 Queens Park, Toronto 5, Ont., Canada. [Mammalia of Canada (Yes)]
PETERSON, Rex Marion. Apartment 1, 502 E. Kingsley, Ann Arbor, Mich., U.S.A. [M. Devonian Ostracoda (Yes)]
* PETIT, Dr. G. Department d'Ichthyologie, Museum d'Historie Naturelle, 57 rue Cuvier, Paris (V), France. [Pisces & Mollusca]
PETKOVSKI, Mr. Trajan K. Prirodonaučen Muzej, Orce Nikolov 11, Skopje, Yugoslavia. [Crustacea: Copepoda & Ostracoda of Mediterranean (Yes); Acarina: Hydracaridae of Mediterranean (Yes)]
PETRI, Prof. Leo H. (Waverly, Iowa; Trematoda) Not now active in taxonomy.
PETRI, Setembrino. Department of Geology, Universidad de São Paulo, Caixa Postal 8.105, São Paulo, Brazil. [Fossil & Recent Foraminifera of New World (Yes)]
*PETROTCHENKO, Dr. V. I. All-Union Institute Skrjabin of Helminthology, Staropansky 3, Moscow K-12, U.S.S.R. [Animal Helminths & Acanthocephala]
*PETROV, Dr. Prof. A. M. All-Union Skrjabin Institute of Helminthology, Staropansky 3, Moscow K-12, U.S.S.R. [Animal Helminths]
PETROVITZ, Rudolf. Natural History Museum, Burgring 7, Wien I, Austria. [Coleoptera: Scarabaeidae: Aphodiinae of World (Yes); Scarabaeidae of Palearctic (Yes)]
PETROWSKY, Basilio. Monasterio 829, Vicente Lopez, Argentina. [Lepidoptera: Noctuidae; Trifinae of c. & s. Argentina (No)]
* PETRUNKEVITCH, Alexander. Osborn Zoological Laboratory, Yale University, New Haven, Conn., U.S.A. [Paleozoic Arachnida; Tertiary-Recent Araneida]
PETRUSCHEWSKY, Mr. G. K. Zoological Institute, Academy of Sciences of U.S.S.R., Universitetskaja Naberežnaja I, Leningrad, U.S.S.R. [Trematoda of U.S.S.R.]
PETRUSEK, B. J. Department of Paleontology, Pan-American Petroleum Corporation, P. O. Box 14085, Houston 21, Texas, U.S.A. [Tertiary Foraminifera of Gulf Cst. U.S. (No)]
* PETRUSEWICZ, Prof. Dr. Kazimierz. Zakład Ekologii, ul. Nowy Świat 72, Warszawa, Poland. [Araneida]
PETTER, Dr. F. Laboratoire des Mammifères, Museum National d'Histoire Naturelle, 55 rue de Buffon, Paris (V), France. [Mammalia: Rodentia of Africa & Palearctic'(Yes)]
PETTER, Mr. J. J. Laboratoire d'Ecologie, Le Petit Chateau, Brunay (S. et O.), France. [Mammalia: Lemuridae, Indridae, Daubentoniidae, of Madagascar (Yes); Aves of Madagascar (Yes)] [Centre National de la Recherche Scientifique]
PETTER-ROUSSEAUX, Mme. A. Laboratoire de Physiologie, Faculté de Médecine, 45 rue des St. Péres, Paris, France. [Mammalia: Lemuridae, Indridae, Daubentoniidae, of Madagascar (Yes); Aves of Madagascar (Yes)] [Centre National de la Recherche Scientifique]
PETTERS, V. C/o International Petroleum (Colombia) Ltd., Bogota, Colombia. [Tertiary & Cretaceous smaller Foraminifera of C. & S. America & c. & s. Europe (No)]
PETTIBONE, Dr. Marian H. Zoology Department, University of New Hampshire, Durham, N. H., U.S.A. [Polychaeta of N. Atlantic & Arctic (Yes); Polynoidea of N. Pacific (Yes)]
PETTINGILL, Dr. O.S., Jr. Wayne, Maine, U.S.A. [Aves of N. America (Yes)]
PETTUS, David. Department of Zoology, Colorado State University, Fort Collins, Colo., U.S.A. [Amphibia of w. N. America (Yes)]

PEUS, Prof. Dr. Fritz, Kustos, Zoologisches Museum, Invalidenstrasse 43, Berlin N 4, German Democratic Republic. [Diptera: Culicidae, Dixidae, Liriopeidae, Tabanidae, Hippoboscidae, Muscidae: Stomoxyinae, of Europe (No); Siphonaptera of Europe (No)]

* PEYER, Dr. Bernhard. Zoologisches Museum der Universität, Kunstlergasse 16, Zürich, Switzerland. [Mesozoic Reptilia]

PFAFF, Dr. J.R., Mag. Scient. Universitetets Zoologiske Museum, Krystalgade København, Denmark. [Marine Mammalia & Aves of w. Africa (No); Pisces of Arctic, espec. Greenland (No)]

PFANNENSTIEL, Prof. Dr. Max. Geologisch-paläontologisches Institut der Universtität, Hebelstrasse 40, Freiburg, German Democratic Republic. [Triassic Stegocephalia of Germany (Yes)]

PFEFFER, Dr. Antonin. Lesnicka Fakulta, High School of Forestry, Dejvice, Studentska 14, Praha 6, Czechoslovakia. [Coleoptera: Scolytidae of Palearctic (Yes)]

PFEIFER, Dr. Heinrich. Hopfenversuchsgut Hüll, Post Wolnzach I (Obb), Germany. [Opiliones of Germany (Yes)]

* PFEIFFER, Rev. Roman, O. F. M. Siena College, Loudonville, N. Y., U. S. A. [Reptilia]

PFITZNER, Dr. Diplom-Biologe, Ingrid. Mergentheimer Strasse 12, Berlin-Südende, Germany. [Mollusca: Gastropoda: terr. Pulmonata of Germany (Yes); Ctenophora of Mediterrean (No); Turbellaria: f-l. & greenhouse Tricladida: Terricola of Germany (Yes)]

PHELPS, Mr. William H., Jr. Colleción Ornitológica Phelps, Apartado 2009, Caracas, Venezuela. [Aves of Venezuela (Yes)]

PHILIP, Dr. Cornelius Becker. Rocky Mountain Laboratory, U. S. Public Health Service, Hamilton, Mont., U. S. A. [Diptera: Tabanidae of World (Yes)]

PHILIP, Kenelm W. 224 Huntington Street, New Haven 11, Conn., U. S. A. [Lepidoptera: Theclinae of N. America (No)]

PHILIPPI, Dr. Rodolfo, Jefe de Seccion de Ornithologia, Museo Nacional de Historia Natural, Casilla 787, Santiago, Chile. [Aves of Chile (Yes)]

PHILIPPS, D. J. Address unknown. [Diptera: Culicidae]

PHILLIPPS, W. J. Dominion Museum, Wellington, New Zealand. [Pisces of New Zealand (No)]

PHILLIPS, Mr. Allan R. C/o L. L. Hargrave, P. O. Box 1979, Globe, Ariz., U. S. A. [Aves of Mexico & s. w. U. S. (Yes); Tryannidae of N. America (Yes)]

PHILLIPS, Henry H. Pan-American Petroleum Corporation, Box 3092, Houston, Texas, U. S. A. [Cretaceous-Miocene Foraminifera of Texas Gulf Cst. (No)]

PHILLIPS, Dr. John. Department of Bacteriology, University of California, Berkeley 4, Calif., U. S. A. [Coelenterata: Actiniaria: g. Anthopleura of California (No)]

PHILLIPS, Mr. J. B. California Department Fish & Game, Hopkins Marine Station, Pacific Grove, Calif., U. S. A. [Pisces: Scorpaenidae: g. Sebastodes of California (No)]

PHILLIPS, Dr. June R. P. Peabody Museum, Yale University, New Haven, Conn., U. S. A. [Paleozoic Bryozoa of Australia & N. America (Yes)]

PHLEGER, Prof. Fred B., Jr. Scripps Institution of Oceanography, La Jolla, Calif., U. S. A. [Recent Foraminifera (Yes)]

* PIATAKOV, M. L. Hydrobiologische Abteilung der Fischerei Station, Vladivostok, U. S. S. R. [Acarina]

* PIAZ, Dr. G. B. Dal. Istituto di Geologia, Universitá di Padova, Padova, Italy. [Fossil Mammalia]

* PIC, M. (St. Agnan, France; Coleoptera) Deceased.

PICARD, Dr. J. Station Marine d'Endoume, Chemin de la Batterie des Lions, Marseille VII, France. [Quaternary & Recent Invertebrates, espec. Hydroidea, of Mediterranean & e. Atlantic (Yes)]

PICCIOLO, Anthony R. Department of Zoology, University of Maryland, College Park, Md., U. S. A. [Pisces, espec. Anabantidae, of Malaysia (No)]

* PICKARD-CAMBRIDGE, Mr. David F. Box 53, Beaufort West, C. P., Union of South Africa. [Coleoptera]

PICKFORD, Grace E. Box 2025, Yale Station, New Haven, Conn., U. S. A. [Cephalopoda: Octopoda & Vampyromorpha of Indo-Malaya (Consultation); Oligochaeta (No)] [Bingham Oceanographic Laboratory]

* PIDOPLICHKO, I. G. Zoological Institute, Academy of Sciences, ul. Wladimirskaja 55, Kiev, Ukraine, U. S. S. R. [Fossil Mammalia]

PIERCE, Prof. E. L. Department of Biology, University of Florida, Gainesville, Fla., U. S. A. [Chaetognatha of Atlantic Ocean (Yes)]

PIERCE, Richard L. Department of Paleontology, Richfield Oil Corp., Box 147, Bakersfield, Calif., U. S. A. [Cenozoic Foraminifera of California (Yes)]

PIERCE, Dr. W. Dwight. Los Angeles County Museum, Los Angeles 7, Calif., U. S. A. [Coleoptera: Curculionidae: g. Trigonoscuta of Pacific Cst. U. S. (Yes); Pleistocene, Miocene, Oligocene, Insects of w. U. S. (Yes)]

PIERRE, F. Museum National d'Histoire Naturelle, Entomologie, 45bis rue de Buffon, Paris (V), France. [Coleoptera: Tenebrionidae of deserts of n. Africa (Yes), of s. e. Asia (No)]

PIETSCHKER, Harold. C/o Pure Oil Company, P. O. Box 239, Houston 1, Texas, U. S. A. [Cretaceous-Recent Foraminifera & Ostracoda of Gulf Coast U. S.]
* PIETSCHMANN, Viktor. (Wien, Austria; Pisces) Died November 1956.
PIFFL, Dr. Edward. Zoologisches Institut der Universität Wien, Dr. Karl Luegerring 1, Wien I, Austria. [Acarina: Oribatidae of Europe & Karakorum (Yes)]
PIKE, Gordon C. Fisheries Research Board of Canada, Biological Station, Nanaimo, B. C., Canada. [Mammalia: Cetacea of n. Pacific Ocean (Yes)]
PIKE, Dr. Richard B. Marine Station, Keppel Pier, Millport, Isle of Cumbrae, Scotland. [Crustacea: Isopoda Bopyridae of Europe (Yes); Decapoda, incl. larvae, of Europe (Yes)] [Scottish Marine Biological Association]
* de PIKELIN, Prof. Berta S. Gerschmán. Departamento de Entomologia, Museo Argentina de Ciencias Naturales, Avda Angel Gallardo 470, Casilla Correo 10, Sucursal 5, Buenos Aires, Argentina. [Araneida]
PILGRIM, Dr. R. Zoology Department, University of Cantebury, Box 1471, Christchurch, New Zealand. [Gastropoda: Opisthobranchia of New Zealand (Yes)]
PILLAY, N. K. Marine Biological Laboratory, Samkumughom, Trivandrum 7, South India. [Crustacea: Isopoda of Travancore Cst. (Yes); Amphipoda & Schizopoda of same (No)]
PILLERI, Dr. med. Georg. Hirnanatomisches Institut, Waldau bei Bern, Switzerland. [Coleoptera: Scarabaeidae: g. Anisoplia of Palearctic (Yes)]
* PILSBRY, H. A. (Philadelphia, Penna.; Mollusca; Cirripedia) Deceased.
PINHEY, Mr. E. C. G. National Museum, P. O. Box 240, Bulawayo, Southern Rhodesia. [Odonata of Ethiopian (Yes); Lepidoptera, excl. Tineidae, of c. & e. Africa (Yes); Homoptera of c. & e. Africa (No)]
PINKER, Dipl. Ing. Rudolf. Neugasse 12, Wien XXIII, Mauer, Austria. [Macrolepidoptera: Heterocera of Canary Is. & Balkans (Yes); Psychidae: g. Eupithecia of Europe (Yes); life history of Noctuidae & Geometridae of Palearctic (No)]
PINNIGER, E. B. 19 Endlebury Road, Chingford, London E 4, England. [Odonata of British Isles (Yes)]
* PINTEA, Miss Maria. Institutul de Speologie, Str. Miko 5, Cluj, Rumania. [Crustacea: Copepoda]
PINTERA, Dr. Albert. Biologický ústav, Československá Akadémie Věd, Na Karlovce 1, Praha-Dejvice, Czechoslovakia. [Homoptera: Aphidoidea of c. & e. Europe (Yes)]
* PINTO, Dr. Cesar. Departamento de Entomologia, Instituto Oswaldo Cruz, Caixa Postal 926, Rio de Janeiro, Brazil. [Diptera]
PINTO, Iraja Damiani. Instituto de Ciências Naturais, Av. Paulo Gama, Pôrto Alegre, Brazil. [Carboniferous-Cretaceous Ostracoda (No); Cretaceous f-w. Cytheriidae of World (Yes); Recent f-w. Ostracoda: g. Darwinula, Metacypris, Cytheridella, Gomphocythere (Yes); Pennsylvanian Corals (No)] [Universidade do Rio Grande do Sul]
PINTO, Dr. Oliverio M. O. Departamento de Zoologia da Secretaria da Agricultura, Caixa Postal 7172, São Paulo, Brazil. [Aves of Brazil (Yes)]
PINTO, Prof. Sérgio Y. Departamento de Vertebrados, Museu National, Quinta da Boa Vista, Rio de Janeiro, Brazil. [Marine Pisces of S. America (Yes); of N. & C. America (No); Cichlidae of World (Yes)]
PINTO da FONSECA, José. Instituto Biologico, Caixa Postal 7119, São Paulo, Brazil. [Homoptera: Membracidae of Neotropics (Yes)]
PIPIRINGOS, George Nicholas. U. S. Geological Survey, Federal Center, Denver 2, Colo., U. S. A. [M. & Up. Jurassic Pelecypoda & Gastropoda of Wyoming (No)]
PIPKIN, Dr. Sarah B. 801 East 23rd Street, Austin, Texas, U. S. A. [Diptera: Drosophilidae of Lebanon, Truk, Caroline Is., Trust Territory of Pacific (live specimens, Yes)]
PIRAN, Sr. Augusto A. Instituto de Patologia Vegetal, Ministerio de Agricultura, Paseo Colon 922, Buenos Aires, Argentina. [Heteroptera, excl. aquatics & Reduvioidea, of Neotropics (Yes)]
PIRLOT, Prof. P. L. Department of Biology, University of Montreal, C. P. 6128, Montreal, Canada. [Mammalia: Rodentia of trop. Africa (Yes); Mammalia of Tropics (No)]
* PISANO, R. G. Address unknown. [Odonata]
PISARSKI, B. Instytut Zoologiczny, Polska Akademia Nauk, ul. Wilcza 64, Warszawa, Poland. [Hymenoptera: Formicidae of Palearctic (Yes)]
* PISICA, Gh. C. Laboratorul de Zoologie, Universitatea "Al. I. Cuza", Strada Gh. Dimtrov nr. 72, Iaşi, Rumania. [Hymenoptera: Ichneumonidae: Pimplinae]
PITCHER, Dr. R. S. East Malling Research Station, Maidstone, Kent, England. [Nematoda: Tylenchida of Europe (No)]
* PITELKA, Prof. Frank A. Museum of Vertebrate Zoology, University of California, Berkely 4, Calif., U. S. A. [Aves of N. & C. America]
PITMAN, Capt. C. R. S. No. 12 Chelsea Embankment, Flat 9, London, S. W. 3, England. [Aves, bird eggs, Reptiles, Amphibians, of Africa (Yes); Mammalia of Africa (No)]
PITRAT, Prof. C. W. Department of Geology, University of Kansas, Lawrence, Kans., U. S. A. [Devonian to Mississippian Rugose Corals (Yes); Pennsylvanian to Permian Foraminifera: Fusulinidae (Yes)]

PITT, Mr. L. J. 1 Lancaster Road, North Harrow, Middlesex, England. [Jurassic-Cretaceous Bryozoa: Cyclostomata of Britain (Yes)]

PITTAM, Dr. M. J. Lister Institute of Preventive Medicine, Chelsea Bridge Road, London, S.W. 1, England. [Protozoa: Amoebina: g. Naegleri, Hartmannella, Acanthamoeba of Britain (Yes); Protomonadina: g. Bodo of Britain (Yes); Polymastigina: g. Tetramitus of Britain (Yes)]

* PITTIONI, Dr. Bruno (Wien, Austria; Hymenoptera) Died 1952.

* PIVETEAU, Prof. Jean. Laboratoire de Géologie, La Sorbonne, 1 rue Victor-Cousin, Paris (V), France. [Fossil Vertebrata]

PIZA, Prof. Dr. S. de T. Escola Superior de Agricultura, Universidade de São Paulo, Piracicaba (S. P,), Brazil. [Araneida, Scorpiones, Opiliones, Pedipalpi, of Neotropics (Yes); Orthoptera: Phaneropteridae, Copiphoridae, Conocephalidae, Mantida, & Blattariae of Neotropical (Yes)]

PLANT, Mr. J. 56 Jamieson Street, Red Cliffs, Vict., Australia. [Coleoptera & Hymenoptera of n. w. Victoria (Yes)]

PLATE, Dr. Hans-Peter, Schlüterstrasse 34/II, Berlin-Charlottenburg 4, Germany. [Terr. & f-w. Gastropoda of Europe (Yes)]

PLAVILSTSHIKOV, Prof. Dr. N. N. Zoological Museum, University of Moscow, Herzen street 6, Moscow K-9, U. S. S. R. [Coleoptera: Cerambycidae of Palearctic (Yes)]

de PLAZA, M. L. Fuster. Avenida Libertador Gral San Martin 5575, Buenos Aires, Argentina. [Pisces: Engraulidae of Neotropical (Yes)] [Departmento Investigaciones Pesqueras]

PLESA, Mr. Corneliu. Institutul de Speologie, Cas. Post 60, Cluj, Rumania. [Crustacea: Copepoda of Rumania (No); Cyclopoida: Poecilostoma of World (No); Gnathostoma of World (Yes)]

PLESKOT, Dr. Gertrud. Department of Zoology, University of Vienna, Wien 1, Austria. [Ephemeroptera of Europe (Yes)]

* PLJAKIC, Mrs. M. Prirodno-matematicki Fakultet, Zooloski zavod, Beograd, Yugoslavia. [Crustacea]

PLOMLEY, Mr. N. J. B. Medical School, University of Sydney, Sydney, N. S. W., Australia. [Diptera: Cyrtidae of Australia (No); Mallophaga from Marsupials of Australia (No); Marsupialia of Australia (No)]

*PLOTNIKOV, Dr. N. N. Institute of Malaria, Medical Parasitology & Helminthology, M. Pirogovskaya Street 20, Moscow, U. S. S. R. [Helminths of man]

PLOUGH, Prof. H. H. Biological Laboratory, Amherst College, Amherst, Mass., U. S. A. [Tunicata: Ascidiacea, Larvacea, Thaliacea, of World (Yes)]

POCOCK, Dr. M. A. 18 Milner Street, Grahamstown, Union of South Africa. [Protozoa: Mastigophora: g. Volvox of Europe, s. Africa, New World, Australia, Philippines (Yes)] [Botany Department, Rhodes University]

* PODTIAGUIN, B. Avenida España 505, Asunción, Paraguay. [Coleoptera]

*PODYAPOLSKAJA, Dr. Prof. V. P. Academy of Medical Sciences of U. S. S. R., Institute of Malaria, Medical Parasitology & Helminthology, Pirogovskaya Street 20, Moscow, U. S. S. R. [Helminths of man]

POGLAYEN, Dr. Ivo. Rio Grande Park Zoo, 903 Tenth Street, S. W., Albuquerque, N. M., U. S. A. [Reptilia: Chelonia. excl. sea turtles, of the World, excl. Africa (Yes)]

POGOSJAN, E. E. See BOGHOSSIAN, H. E.

POGUE, Jesse. Shell Development Company, 3737 Bellaire Boulevard, Houston 25, Texas, U. S. A. [Fossil & Recent Edrioasteroidea of World (Yes)]

* POHL, Bruno. Rua Pelotas 47, São Paulo, Brazil. [Lepidoptera]

POHL, Dr. Erwin R. Horse Cave, Ky., U. S. A. [Paleozoic Lamellibranchiata (No)]

* POHLE, Prof. Dr. H. E. Department of Vertebrates, Zoologisches Museum, Invalidenstrasse 43, Berlin N 4, German Democratic Republic. [Mammalia]

POISSON, Raymond. Department de Zoologie, Faculté des Sciences, Universite de Rennes, Rennes, France. [Aquatic Heteroptera of Europe & Ethiopian]

POKORNÝ, Dr. Vladimir. Geological Institute, Charles University, Albertov 6, Praha II, Czechoslovakia. [M. Devonian, Up. Cretaceous, Miocene Ostracoda of Europe (No)]

POLENEC, Dr. Anton. Musée d'Histoire Naturelle, Prešernova 20, Ljubljana, Yugoslavia. [Araneida of Slovenia (Yes)]

POLENTZ, Georg. Ernst-Thalmann-Strasse 10, Gernrode/Harz, German Democratic Republic. [Heteroptera of c. Europe (Yes)]

POLIVANOVA, E. N. Institute of Animal Morphology, Academy of Sciences of U. S. S. R., Leninskij Prospekt 33, Moscow, U. S. S. R. [Heteroptera: Pentatomoidea, imagines & larvae of U. S. S. R (No)]

* POLJANSKY, Prof. G. I. Zoological Laboratory, University of Leningrad, Leningrad W-164, U. S. S. R. [Protozoa: Infusoria]

POLK, Philip. Zeewetenschappelyk Instituut, Zeewezengebouw, Oostende, Belgium. [Crustacea: Isopoda: Oniscoidea of w. Europe (Yes); marine Isopoda of North sea (Yes)] [Universiteit Gent]

POLL, Prof. Dr. Max. Musée Royal du Congo Belge, Tervueren, Belgium. [F-w. Pisces of Congo Basin & L. Tanganika (Yes); marine Pisces of trop. Africa (No); f-w. & marine Pisces of Belgium (No)]

*POLOGENTSEV, Dr. Prof. P. A. Forestry Institute, Voroneg, U. S. S. R. [Soil Nematoda of World]

* POLUGAR, Morton. Dominion Oil Ltd., 29 St. Vincent Street, Port-of-Spain, Trinidad. [Fossil Invertebrates]

* POLUSZYŃSKI, Dr. Gustav. Address unknown. [Helminths]

POMEISL, E. Einwanggasse 23, Wien, Austria. [Plecoptera of Europe (Yes)]

PONOMAREVA, A. A. Zoological Institute, Academy of Sciences, Leningrad 164, U. S. S. R. [Hymenoptera: Apoidea of Palearctic (Yes)]

PONYI, Dr. E. Nagyar Tudomanyos Akademiz, Biologiai Kutatointezete, Tihany, Hungary. [Crustacea: Copepoda, Cladocera, Malacostraca: Bathynellidae, Amphipoda, of c. Europe (Yes)]

POOL, Dr. Georg. Nägelistrasse 3, Zürich 44, Switzerland. [Oligochaeta]

POOTS, Linda. Kooli 26-4, Tartu, Estonian S. S. R., U. S. S. R. [Mammalia: Vespertilionidae & Muridae of Baltic States (Yes)]

POP, Prof, Dr. V. Universitatea "Viktor Babes", Catedra de Zoologie, Str. Miko 5, Cluj 1, Rumania. [Oligochaeta: Lumbricidae of World (Yes); Branchiobdellidae of Europe (Yes)]

POPE, Mr. Clifford H. 389 Ridge Avenue, Winnetka, Ill., U. S. A. [Reptilia & Amphibia of China (Yes); Amphibia: Plethodontidae of e. U. S. (Yes)]

POPE, David E. Union Producing Company, P. O. Box 278, Kenner, La., U. S. A. [Tertiary Foraminifera of s. Louisiana (Yes)]

POPE, Miss Elizabeth. Australian Museum, College Street, Sydney N. S. W., Australia. [Crustacea: Cirripedia: Balanomorpha of Australasian (Yes)]

POPE, John Keyler. 7400 E. Galbraith Road. Cincinnati 43, Ohio, U. S. A. [Ordovician Brachiopoda, Trilobita, Echinodermata, Bryozoa, Gastropoda, Pelecypoda, of Kentucky (Yes); fossil Echinodermata: Ophiocistia & Cyclocystoidea (Yes)]

POPE, Mr. R. D. Commonwealth Institute of Entomology, c/o British Museum (Natural History), Cromwell Road, London, S. W. 7, England. [Coleoptera: Coccinellidae, excl. Epilachninae, of World (Yes); Colydiidae of African, Australian, Micronesia (Yes)]

POPENOE, Prof. W. P. Department of Geology, University of California, Los Angeles 24, Calif., U. S. A. [Up. Cretaceous Gastropoda & Pelecypoda of Pacific cst. U. S. (Yes)]

POPESCU-GORJ, Dr. Aurelian. Rue Poenaru Bordea 16, R. Nicolae Bălcescu, Bucureşti, Rumania. [Lepidoptera: of s. e. Europe (Yes); f-w. Pisces of s. e. Europe (Yes)]

POPHAM, Dr. E. J. Department of Zoology, The University, Manchester 3, England. [Heteroptera: Crybtocerata of Britain (Yes); Coleoptera: Hydradephaga of Britain (Yes)]

*POPOV, Dr. Prof. N. P. Kazan Veterinary Institute, Ershov field 26, Kazan, U. S. S. R. [Helminthes of animals]

POPOV, Prof. Dr. V. B. Zoological Institute, Academy of Sciences, Leningrad B-164, U. S. S. R. [Hymenoptera: Apoidea of Palearctic (No)]

* POPOVA, Mrs. Ariadna N. Zoological Institute, Academy of Science, Leningrad 164, U. S. S. R. [Odonata]

* POPOVA, Dr. Prof. T. I. Moscow State University, Moscow, U. S. S. R. [Helminths of animals]

POPOVICI BIZNOSANU, Andrei. Facultatea de Biologie, Splaiul Independentei nr. 93-95, Bucureşti, Rumania. [Orthoptera of Rumania (No)]

PÓR, F. Muzeul National de Istoria Naturala "Grigore Antipa", Sos. Kisselef No. 1, Bucureşti III, Rumania. [Crustacea: Copepoda: marine Harpacticoidea, Cyclopoida: Poecilostoma & Siphonostoma of Black Sea (Yes); f-w. Cyclopoida & Harpacticoidea of s. e. Europe (Yes); Odonata of s. e. Europe (No)]

* PORFIRIEV, Dr. G. S. W. N. I. G. R. I., Liteiny 39, Leningrad, U. S. S. R. [Carboniferous-Permian rugose corals] Died December 14, 1959.

PORTA, Prof. Antonio. Corso Garibaldi 120, San Remo, Italy. [Coleoptera]

PORTENKO, Prof. Dr. L. A. Zoological Institute, Academy of Sciences, Leningrad 164, U. S. S. R. [Aves of U. S. S. R. & c. Asia (Yes)]

PORTER, Dale A. Regional Animal Disease Research Laboratory, P. O. Drawer 952, Auburn, Ala., U. S. A. [Nematoda: Trichostronglyinae of domestic animals of U. S. (Yes); Cestoda: g. Moniezia of ruminants of U. S. (Yes)] [U. S. Department of Agriculture]

PORTER, Hugh J. Institute of Fisheries Research, University of North Carolina, Morehead City, N. C., U. S. A. [Crustacea: Portunidae: g. Callinectes of N. America (No); Mollusca: of Carolina coast U. S. (Yes)]

PORTER, Dr. T. Wayne. Department of Zoology, Michigan State University, East Lansing, Mich., U. S. A. [Heteroptera: Hebridae of World (Yes); aquatic & semiaquatic Heteroptera, excl. Corixidae, of N. America (Yes)]

PORTMANN, Prof. Adolf, Director, Zoologische Anstalt, Rheinsprung 9, Basel, Switzerland. [Gastropoda: Opisthobranchia of Mediterranean (Yes)]

* von POSCHINGER, Ferdinand. (Niederbayern, Germany; Coleoptera) Died January 7, 1958.

* POSNER, Gerald S. Institute of Fisheries Research, Morehead City, N.C., U.S.A. [Nemertinea]

POSPELOVA-SHTROM, Prof. M.V. Entomological Section, Institute of Malaria & Medical Parasitology, Varshavskoje shosse 5, Moscow 105, U.S.S.R. [Acarina: Ixodoidea; Argasidae of World (Yes); Ixodidae of U.S.S.R. (No)]

POST, Dr. Richard L. Department of Agricultural Entomology, North Dakota Agricultural College, Fargo, N.D., U.S.A. [Thysanoptera of Oregon & North Dakota (Yes)]

POSTEL, Dr. Emile. Office de la Recherche Scientifique et Technique Outre-Mer, 47 Boulevard des Invalides, Paris (VII), France. [Pisces of e. Atlantic (Yes)]

* POSTUMA, T.A. Box 5011 Karachi 2, Pakistan. [Protozoa: Flagellata]

*POTEMKINA, Dr. Prof. W.A. All-Union Skrjabin Institute of Helminthology, Staropansky 3, Moscow K-12, U.S.S.R. [Helminthes of animals]

POTTER, Mr. Floyd E., Jr. 1207 Richcreek Road, Austin 6, Texas, U.S.A. [Amphibia & Reptilia of Texas (Yes); Amphibia: Plethodontidae: g. Eurycea of Edwards Plateau, Texas]

POTTS, Mr. Robert W.L. Agriculture Building, Embarcadero at Mission, San Francisco 5, Calif., U.S.A. [Lepidoptera: Nymphalidae: Acraeinae of S. & C. America (Yes); Coleoptera: Scarabaeidae: Coprinae of N. America (Yes); Hymenoptera: Formicidae of America & the Pacific (No)] [California Bureau of Plant Quarantines]

POTTS, W.H. 45 Green Moor Link, Winchmere Hill, London N. 21, England. [Diptera: g. Glossina of Africa (Yes); Tabanidae of e. Africa (No)] [Commonwealth Institute of Entomology]

* POULSEN, Christian. Mineralogical Museum, Ostervolgade 7, København, Denmark. [Fossils]

POULSEN, Dr. Erik M. International Commission for the N.W. Atlantic Fisheries, Forrest Building, Carleton Street, Halifax, Nova Scotia, Canada. [Crustacea: f-w. Cladocera of n. Europe (Yes); Copepoda of n. Europe (No); Ostracoda: Halocypriformes of Oceans (Yes)]

POURRIOT, R. Centre de Recherches Hydrobiologiques Gif-Sur-Yvette (S. et O.), France. [Rotifera: f-w. planktonic Ploima of France (Yes); planktonic Floscularicacea & Collothecacea of France (No); Crustacea: f-w. planktonic Cladocera of France (Yes)]

POVOLNÝ, Ing. Dr. Dalibor. Czechoslovak Academy of Science, Department of Parasitology, 1 Zemědělská, Brno, Czechoslovakia. [Diptera: Nycteribiidae & Hippoboscidae of Europe (Yes); Calliphoridae, Muscidae, synanthropic flies, of Europe (Yes); Lepidoptera: Gracilariidae, Gelechiidae, Phalaenidae & Geometridae of Palearctic (Yes)]

POWELL, Dr. A.W.B., Assistant Director, Auckland Institute & Museum, P.O. Box 9027, Newmarket, Auckland, New Zealand. [Terr. & marine Mollusca of New Zealand (Yes); Mollusca of Antarctic & Subantarctic (Yes); Tertiary Mollusca of New Zealand (Yes)]

* POWELL, Dr. Eugene F. Department of Zoology, University of Nebraska, Lincoln 8, Nebr., U.S.A. [Crustacea & Hirudinea]

POWELL, Jerry A. Department of Entomology, University of California, Berkeley 4, Calif., U.S.A. [Microlepidoptera, espec. Tortricidae, of N. America (Yes)]

POWER, John H., Director, McGregor Museum, Kimberley, Union of South Africa. [Reptilia & Amphibia of Union of South Africa (Yes)]

* POWER, M.P. (Gambier, Ohio; Diptera) Deceased.

POYNTON, Mr. John C. Department of Zoology, University of Natal, Pietermaritzburg, Union of South Africa. [Amphibia: Anura of s. Africa (Yes)]

* POZARYSKI, Prof. Dr. Wladyslaw. Zakład Paleozoologii, Uniwersytetu Warszawskiego, ul. Nowy Swiat 67, Warszawa, Poland. [Fossil Foraminifera]

POZZI, Prof. Aurelio J.S. Diagonal 75, No. 271, La Plata, Argentina. [Pisces: Choracostei: Syngnathidae of S. Atlantic (Yes); Aulostomi: Macrorhamphosidae of S. Atlantic (Yes); Isospondyli: Clupeidae & Engraulidae of Argentina (Yes)]

PRABHU, M.S. Central Marine Fisheries Research Station, Mandapam Camp P.O., S. India. [Pisces: g. Trichiurus, Chirocentrus, Pampus, Parastromateus, Lethrinus & Pelates of India (Yes)]

de PRADA, Joaquin. Concejo n. 13, Salamanca, Spain. [Acarina: Ixodidae of Spain (Yes); Diptera: Culicidae of Spain (Yes)] [Sanidad Nacional]

PRADHAN, Mr. K.S. Invertebrate (Lower) Section, Zoological Survey of India, 34 Chittaranjan Avenue, Calcutta 12, India. [Aquatic Heteroptera of India (Yes); Porifera: Spongillidae of India (Yes)]

* PRADO BARRIENTOS, Dr. Luis. Escuela de Medicina, Universidad Mayor de San Andrés, La Paz, Bolivia. [Parasites]

* PRAKASH, Prof. Rair. Department of Zoology, Government Hanindia College, Bhopal, India. [Reptilia]

PRANTL, Ferdinand. National Museum, 1700 Václavské Námĕsti 68, Praha 2, Czechoslovakia. [Silurian-Devonian Bryozoa of Europe (Yes); Silurian-Devonian Rugosa & Tabulata of Europe (Yes); Silurian Devonian Trilobita of Europe (Yes)]

* PRASHAD, Dr. Baini. Department of Molluscs, Zoological Survey of India, 34 Chittaranjan Avenue, Calcutta 12, India. [Mollusca]

* PRASSE, Mr. J. Institut für Landwirtschaft Zoologie, Universität Halle, E. Abderhalden-strasse 20, Halle, German Democratic Republic. [Nematoda]
PRATT, Dr. Harry Davis. Communicable Disease Center, U.S. Public Health Service, 50 Seventh Street, Atlanta 23, Ga., U.S.A. [Diptera: Culicidae; Siphonaptera; Anoplura; all of N. America (Yes)]
PRATT, Dr. Ivan. Department of Zoology, Oregon State College, Corvallis, Ore., U.S.A. [Life cycles of Trematoda of Pacific cst. of N. America (Yes)]
PRATVIEL, Anne Marie. Attachée de Recherches, Centre de 3⁰ Cycle de Géologie Approfondie, 351 cours de la Libération, Talence (Gironde), France. [Oligocene Mollusca of Aquitaine Bassin (Yes)]
PRAVDIN, Prof. I. F. Canal Griboedov 74:41, Leningrad, U.S.S.R. [Pisces of Europe & Asia] [Zoological Institute, Academy of Sciences]
* PREBLE, Edward A. (Washington, D.C.; Mammalia) Deceased.
PRECHT, Dr. Herbert. Zoologisches Institut der Universität, Hegewischstrasse 3, Kiel, Germany. [Ciliata: Peritricha (No)]
PRECUPETU, Anna. Facultatea de Stiinte Naturale, Splaiul Independentei nr. 93-95, Bucureşti, Rumania. [Hymenoptera: Tenthredinoidea of Europe (Yes)]
* PRENANT, Marcel. Laboratoire d'Anatomie, Comparée et d'Histologie, Sorbonne, 1 rue Victor Cousin, Paris (V), France. [Bryozoa]
* PRENN, Prof. Fritz. Schillerstrasse 4, Kufstein (Tirol), Austria. [Odonata]
PRENTICE, J. E. Department of Geology, King's College, Strand, London, W.C.2, England. [Carboniferous Brachiopoda (Yes); Carboniferous Trilobita (Yes)]
PRESTON, Prof. Floyd W. Department of Petroleum Engineering, University of Kansas, Lawrence, Kans., U.S.A. [Lepidoptera: Rhopalocera of N. America]
PRETNER, Egon. Inštitut za raziskovanje Krasa Slovenske Akademije Znanosti in Umetnosti, Postojna, Ljubljana, Yugoslavia. [Cavernicolous Coleoptera of Balkans (Yes); Hydrophilidae of Palearctic (Yes); Coleoptera of Balkans (Yes)]
PREUSS, Dr. Günter. Pädagogische Akademie, Pfaffenbergstrasse 95, Kaiserslautern, Germany. [Hymenoptera: Sphecidae, Formicidae, Pompilidae, of c. Europe (Yes); Chrysididae of c. Europe (No)]
PŘIBYL, Dr. Alois. Podolská 761/112, Praha XV, Podoli, Czechoslovakia. [Paleozoic Ostracoda of Europe (Yes); Trilobita & Graptozoa of Europe & Asia (Yes); Paleozoic Eurypterida of Europe (Yes)] [Mining Institute]
PRICE, Dr. E.W. 1921 Lookout Street, Mitchell Park, Gadsden, Ala., U.S.A. [Trematoda: Digenetic & Monogenetic of World (Yes)]
PRICE, Mr. Homer F. Route 2, Payne, Ohio, U.S.A. [Aves, eggs, of Ohio (Yes); Lepidoptera: Butterflies & Skippers of Ohio (Yes); Odonata of Ohio (No)]
PRICE, Dr. John L. Maracas Valley c/o Curepe P.O., Trinidad. [Crustacea: Copepoda: Cyclopidae of e. Canada (Yes); of Trinidad (No)]
PRICE, L.I. Divisão de Geologia e Mineralogia, Avenida Pasteur 404, Praia Vermelha, Rio de Janeiro, Brazil. [Mesozoic Reptilia of S. America (Yes); Mesozoic & Cenozoic Crocodilia of S. America (Yes)]
PRIDDY, Dr. Ralph B., Associate Professor of Biology, Carthage College, Carthage, Ill., U.S.A. [Diptera: Bombyliidae of N. America (Yes)]
PRIESNER, Prof. Dr. Hermann, Rudolfstrasse 36, Linz, Austria. [Thysanoptera of World (Yes); Hymenoptera: Diapriidae of Europe (No)] [Landesmuseum]
PRIGOGINE, Dr. A. Kamituga, Belgian Congo. [Aves of highlands of e. Belg. Congo (Yes)]
PRINCE, Frank M. Department of Health, Education & Welfare, CDCA, San Francisco Field Station, 15th Avenue & Lake Street, Building 19, San Francisco 18, Calif., U.S.A. [Siphonaptera of U.S. (Yes)]
PRINCIPI, Prof. Maria M. Istituto di Entomologia della Universitá, Via Filippo Re N. 6, Bologna (117), Italy. [Neuroptera of Italy & Mediterranean (Yes)]
PRINCIS, Mr. K. Zoologiska Institution, Lunds Universitet, Lund, Sweden. [Blattariae of World (Yes)]
PRINGLE, Dr. J.A., Director, Natal Museum, Pietermaritzburg, Natal, Union of South Africa. [Reptilia, snakes of s. Africa (No); Mollusca: shells of s. Africa (No)]
PRIOLO, Dr. Prof. Ing. Ottavio. Via Gorizia 22, Catania, Italy. [Marine, terr., f-w. Mollusca of Mediterranean & Red Sea (Yes)]
* PRITCHARD, Dr. A.L. (Ottawa, Canada; Pisces) Not now active in taxonomy.
PRITCHARD, Dr. A. Earl. Division of Entomology, University of California, Berkeley 4, Calif., U.S.A. [Diptera: Asilidae & Cecidomyiidae of World (No); Acarina: Tetranychoidea of World (Yes); Odonata of N. America (No)]
PRITCHARD, Mrs. Claremont G. 6500 Knox Street, Lincoln 5, Nebr., U.S.A. [Digenetic Trematoda of marine fishes of Hawaii & Bermuda (No)]
PŘÍVORA, Dr. M. Institute of Epidemiology & Microbiology, Sŕobárova 48, Praha 12, Czechoslovakia. [Coleoptera: Carabidae of Europe (Yes); Carabini of Palearctic (Yes)]
* PROBST, Mr. Robert T. 4619 Manordene Rd., Baltimore 29, Md., U.S.A. [Aquatic Hemiptera & fish parasites]

PROLA, Sig. Carlo. Via Firenze 10, Roma, Italy. [Lepidoptera of Palearctic (No); of Italy
(Yes)]
PROSE, Herbert. Karolinenstrasse 5, Hof a. d. Saale, Germany. [Lepidoptera: Tortricidae of
Europe (No); Hesperiidae of Europe & Asia Minor (Yes); Odonata of c. Europe (Yes)]
PROSEN, Àlberto F. Virrey del Pino 2482, Buenos Aires, Argentina. [Coleoptera: Cerambyci-
dae of Neotropics (Yes)] [Instituto de Medicina Regional]
PROST, Dr. Maria. Zakład Parazytologii, Wyzszej Szkoły Rokniczej, ul. Akademicka 11,
Lublin, Poland. [Trematoda: Monogenoidea of fishes of Poland (Yes)]
* PROTIC, Milka. Prade Sur No. 225, Lomas de Chapultepec, Mexico, D. F., Mexico. [Fossil
Invertebrates]
* PROUTY, Dr. J. M. Address unknown. [Diptera: Pupipara]
PROVENZANO, Anthony J., Jr. Marine Laboratory, University of Miami, Rickenbacker Cause-
way, Miami 49, Fla., U. S. A. [Crustacea: Anomura: Paguridae & Coenobitidae of w. N.
America, circumtropical littoral (Yes)]
PRUDHOE, Stephen. British Museum (Natural History), Cromwell Road, London, S. W. 7,
England. [Turbellaria: Polycladida of World (Yes); Trematoda, Cestoda, Nemertinea,
of World (Yes)]
PRÜFFER, Prof. Dr. Jan. Zakład Zoologii Systemat., Uniwersytet Mikołaja Kopernika,
ul. Danielewskiego 6, Toruń, Poland. [Lepidoptera of n. Poland (Yes)]
PRUITT, Erna N. Box 282, College, Alaska. [Araneida of Arctic & Subarctic (No)]
PRUITT, William O., Jr. Box 282, College, Alaska. [Mammalia: Soricidae of Arctic & Sub-
arctic (Yes)]
PRUVOT-FOL, Mme. A. Rue de Fontenay 12, Sceaux, France. [Gastropoda: Opisthobranchia:
Nudibranchiata, Ascoglossa, Thecosomata, Gymnosomata]
PRYCHODKO, Dr. W. 4811 John R. Street, Detroit 1, Mich., U. S. A. [Mammalia: Rodentia:
Cricetidae & Gliridae of Europe (Yes)] [Detroit Institute of Cancer Research]
PSCHORN-WALCHER, Dr. H. European Laboratory, Commonwealth Institute of Biological
Control, Delémont, Switzerland. [Hymenoptera: Proctotrupidae & Heloridae of World,
espec. Holarctic (Yes)]
* PUCHOV, Dr. Prof. W. I. Stavropol Scientific Research Veterinary Station, Oktyabrskaya Street
38, Pyatigorsk, U. S. S. R. [Nematoda & Cestoda of animals of U. S. S. R.]
PUGACZEWSKA, H. Zakład Paleontologii, Uniwersytet Warszawski, Nowy-Swiat 67, Warszawa,
Poland. [M. & Up. Jurassic Belemnites of Poland (No)]
* PUGH, Mr. C. H. Wallace. Derwent Dene, Oswestry, Shropshire, England. [Diptera]
PUISSÉGUR, Prof. C. Lycée de Montpellier, Montpellier (Hérault), France. [Coleoptera:
Caraboidea of France (Yes); g. Carabus of World (Yes)]
PULAWSKI, W. J. Instytut Zoologiczny Universytetu, Sienkiewicza 21, Wrocław, Poland.
[Hymenoptera: Sphecidae of w. Palearctic (Yes)]
PULLEY Prof. T. E. Department of Biology, University of Houston, Houston 4, Texas, U. S. A.
[Pelecypoda of Gulf of Mexico (Yes)]
* PULS, Prof. Dr. J. J. Caixa Postal 989, Londrina, Parana, Brazil. [Insecta]
* PURASJOKI, Dr. K. J. Biological Laboratory, Institute of Marine Research, P. -Rautatiekatu
13, Helsinki, Finland. [Crustacea: f-l., f-w. & br-w. Copepoda, Ostracoda, Cladocera,
of Baltic Cst. of Finland (No)]
PURCHON, Prof. R. D. Department of Zoology, University of Malaya, Cluny Road, Singapore
10, Malaya. [Marine Mollusca of "British Waters" (No)]
PURI, Dr. H. S. State Geological Survey, Drawer 631, Tallahassee, Fla., U. S. A. [Mesozoic &
Cenozoic Foraminifera & Ostracoda of North America & Indo-Pacific (Yes); Pelecypoda:
Nuculanacea of World (Yes)]
* PURTOY, Maurice. 6 rue de Bordeaux, Aubière (Puy de Dome), France. [Coleoptera]
PUSCHNIG, Roman. (Klagenfurt, Austria; Orthoptera& Odonata) Not now active in taxonomy.
PUTSHKOW, W. J. Institute of Zoology, Academy of Sciences of U. S. S. R., ul. Wladimirskaja
55, Kiev, U. S. S. R. [Heteroptera of Palearctic (No); of European U. S. S. R. (Yes)]
de PUYTORAC, Dr. P. Laboratoire de Zoologie, Université de Clermont-Ferrand, 1 Avenue
Vercingetorix, Clermont-Ferrand, France. [Protozoa: Infusoria: Astomatida & Hystero-
cinetidae (Yes)]
PYBURN, W. F. Department of Biology, Arlington State College, Arlington, Texas, U. S. A.
[Amphibia & Reptilia of s. w. U. S. (Yes)]
PYEATT, Lloyd M. P. O. Box 624, Houston 1, Texas, U. S. A. [Eocene-Miocene Foraminifera
of Texas & Louisiana Gulf Coast (Yes)]

QASIM, Dr. S. Z. Department of Zoology, Aligarh University, Aligarh, U. P., India. [Pisces:
Blenniidae of Britain (Yes); Ophiocephalidae, Siluridae, Bagridae, of India (Yes)]
* QUADRI, Dr. M. A. H. Office of Forest Entomologist, Pakistan Forest Research Institute,
P. O. Upper Topa (Murree Hills), Pakistan. [Apterygota]
QUAST, Jay C. University of California Institute of Marine Resources, Box 109, La Jolla,
Calif., U. S. A. [Pisces: Hexagrammoidae of n. Pacific (Yes)]

QUATE, Dr. Larry W. Bishop Museum, 1355 Kalihi Street, Honolulu 17, Hawaii. [Diptera: Psychodidae, excl. Phlebotominae, of World (Yes); Coleoptera: Elateridae: g. Melanotus of N. America (Yes)]
QUAY, Dr. W. B. Department of Zoology, University of California, Berkeley 4, Calif., U.S.A. [Mammalia of N. America (No); Cricetidae: Microtinae of World (Yes); Anoplura of World (No)]
QUEDNAU, Dr. W. Biologische Bundesanstalt für Land- und Forstwirtschaft, Institute für Zoologie, Königin-Luise-Strasse 19, Berlin-Dahlem, Germany. [Homoptera: Aphidoidea: Lachnidae, Chaitophoridae, Callaphididae, of World (Yes); Hymenoptera: Trichogrammatidae: g. Trichogramma of World (Yes)]
* QUELLE, Dr. Ferdinand. Zoologisches Museum, Humboldt Universität, Invalidenstrasse 43, Berlin N 4, German Democratic Republic. [Coleoptera: Elateridae]
QUENTIN, R. M. I. D. E. R. T., 80 route d'Aulnay, Bondy, Seine, France. [Coleoptera: Cerambycinae: Prioninae of Africa (Yes); Clytini of World (No)]
QUICK, Mr. H. E. Craythorne, Shinfield Road, Reading, Berks, England. [Gastropoda: terr. & f-w. Pulmonata & Prosobranchiata of British Isles (Yes)]
QUICK, W. N. B. 5 Tintern Avenue, Toorak, Vict., Australia. [Lepidoptera: Hepialidae: g. Oxycanus of Victoria (Yes); Satyridae: g. Oreixenica of Victorian Alpine (No)]
QUIGLEY, Mr. C. M. C/o Standard Oil Company of Texas, P. O. Box 1249, Houston 1, Texas, U.S.A. [Tertiary-Cretaceous Foraminifera of Gulf Coast U.S. (Yes)]
QUINN, Dr. J. H. University of Arkansas, Fayetteville, Ark., U.S.A. [Miocene to Recent Mammalia: Equinae of N. America, Europe, Asia (Yes)]
QUIRSFELD, Edward D. 67 Patterson Street, Hillsdale, N. Y., U.S.A. [Coleoptera: Elateridae of World (Yes); Pselaphidae & Scydmaenidae of New World (No)]
* QUISENBERRY, B. F. California Spray Chemical Corporation, P. O. Box 6263, Memphis 11, Tenn., U.S.A. [Diptera]
QUIST, Prof. John A. Department of Entomology, Colorado State University, Fort Collins, Colo., U.S.A. [Diptera: Stratiomyidae & Coleoptera: Elateridae of Nearctic (Yes)]
QUTUBUDDIN, Mr. M. Gezina Research Farm, Wad Medani, Sudan. [Diptera: Culicidae: Megarhinini, Culicini & Anophelini of India (Yes); Psychodidae: Phlebotominae of Sudan (Yes)]

RAABE, Prof. Dr. Zdzislaw. Instytut Zoologiczny, Uniwersytetu Warszawskiego, Krakowskie Przedmieście 26/28, Warszawa 64, Poland. [Protozoa: Ciliata commensalia & parasitic of Palearctic (Yes)]
RABB, Dr. George B. Chicago Zoological Park, Brookfield, Ill., U.S.A. [Amphibia: Plethodontidae of Mexico (Yes); Reptilia: Iguanidae: g. Cyclura & Leiocephalus of West Indies (Yes)]
RABB, Robert L. (Raleigh, N. C.; Heteroptera) Not now active in taxonomy.
RABIEN, Dr. Arnold. Hessisches Landesamt für Bodenforschung, Wiesbaden, Germany. [Devonian Ostracoda: Entomozoacea (Yes)]
RABOR, Prof. D. S. Department of Biology, Silliman University, Dumaguete City, Negros Oriental, Philippines. [Mammalia, Aves, Reptilia, Amphibia, of Philippines (Yes)]
RACEK, Dr. A. A. New South Wales State Fisheries, G. P. O. Box 30, Sydney, N. S. W., Australia. [Crustacea: Decapoda, Penaeidae & Palinuridae of Indo-West-Pacific (Yes); Parastacidae & Atyidae of Australia & s. e. Asia (Yes); Porifera: Spongillidae of World (Yes)]
RACENIS, Dr. J. Apartado Este 4255, Caracas, Venezuela. [Odonata of World (No); Odonata: Coenagrioniidae of World (Yes); Odonata of Neotropics (Yes)] [Universidad Central de Venezueala, Escuela de Biologia]
* RACHOU, Dr. Rene. Departamento Nacional de Endemias Rurais, Avenida Rio Branco 80 (18), Rio de Janeiro, D. F., Brazil. [Diptera]
RADFORD, Dr. Charles D. 28 Kingsway, Manchester 19, England. [Parasitic Acarina: Trombiculidae, Laelaptidae, Entonyssidae, Macronyssidae, Myobiidae, Listrophoridae, of World (Yes)]
RADHAKRISHNAN, Mr. N. Central Marine Fisheries Research Unit, Karwar P. O., India. [Pisces: Sillaginidae & Scombridae of Indian Coasts (Yes)]
RADOVANOVIĆ, Prof. Dr. M. Department of Zoology, University of Belgrade, Beograd, Yugoslavia. [Amphibia & Reptilia of Europe (No); of Yugoslavia (Yes)]
RADU, Prof. Dr. V. Gh. Institutul de Zoologie, Str. Miko 5, Cluj, Rumania. [Crustacea: terr. Isopoda of Rumania (Yes)]
* RAEBEL, H. Park Hutniczy, Zabrze, Poland. [Lepidoptera]
RAFALSKI, Dr. Jan. Zakład Zoologii Ogólnej, Uniwersytetu A. Mickiewicza, ul. Fredry 10, Poznań, Poland. [Arachnida: Pseudoscorpiones of Europe & Caucasus (Yes); Opiliones of Europe & Caucasus (Yes); Cyphophthalmi of World, excl. Australia & New Zealand (Yes)]
RAFFI, Dr. Giorgio. Petrosud S. P. A., Via C. Colombo 15, Pescara, Italy. [Tertiary & Mesozoic pelagic Foraminifera of Mediterranean (No)]

RAGEAU, Mr. J. G. F. Office de la Recherche Scientifique Outre-Mer, Institute Français
    d'Océanie, B. P. 4, Nouméa, New Caledonia. [Medical & veterinary entomology of
    Fr. Pacific Is. (Yes); Diptera: Culicidae, Simuliidae, Tabanidae, of Fr. Pacific Is.
    (Yes); Acarina: Ixodidae of Fr. Pacific Is. (Yes); Diptera: Culicidae; Simuliidae;
    Psychodidae: g. Phlebotomus; Tabanidae; Anthomyidae: g. Glossina; of Fr. Camerouns
    (No); Acarina: Ixodidae of Fr. Camerouns (No)]
RAGGE, Dr. David R. Department of Entomology, British Museum (Natural History), Crom-
    well Road, London, S. W. 7, England. [Orthoptera: Tettigoniidae, espec. Phaneropteri-
    nae, of Africa (Yes)]
* RAHMAN-ANSARI, Dr. M. Atiqur. Institute of Hygiene & Preventive Medicine, 6 Birdwood
    Avenue, Lahore, Pakistan. [Diptera, Mallophaga]
* RAICA, Dr. V. J. See IUGA-RAICA, V.
RAIGNIER, Prof. R. P. Albert. Rue Des Recollets 11, Louvain, Belgium. [Hymenoptera:
    Formicidae of w. Europe & c. Africa (No)] [University of Louvain]
RAIKOW, I. B. Zoological Laboratory, University of Leningrad, Leningrad W-164, U. S. S. R.
    [Protozoa: Ciliata of Europe (Yes)]
* RAINEY, Dennis G. Department of Biology, Eastern Kentucky State College, Richmond, Ky.,
    U. S. A. [Mammalia]
RAINWATER, Mr. E. H. Technical Service Division, Shell Oil Company, 3737 Bellaire
    Boulevard, Houston 25, Texas, U. S. A. [Mesozoic-Recent Foraminifera of World (Yes)]
* RAITT, Ralph J. Department of Biology, New Mexico State University, State College, N. M.,
    U. S. A. [Mammalia, Aves, Reptilia, Amphibia]
RAJ, B. S. Park View, Miller Road, Madras 10, India. [Pisces of India, espec. s. India (Yes)]
    [Madras Fisheries Department]
RAJAGOPALAIENGAR, Mr. A. S. Mollusca Section, Zoological Survey of India, 34 Chittaranjan
    Avenue, Calcutta 12, India. [Pelecypoda: Teredinidae of India & Oriental (Yes)]
RAJSKI, Mgr. Aleksander. Instytut Zoologiczny, Oddział w Poznaniu, Polska Akademia Nauk,
    Ul. Świerczewskiego 19, Poznań, Poland. [Acarina: Oribatei of Poland (Yes)]
RAKOVEC, Dr. I. Geološko-paleontološki Institut, Univerza, Ljubljana, Yugoslavia. [Pleisto-
    cene Mammalia: Carnivora, Proboscidea, Perissodactyla, Artiodactyla of Yugoslavia
    (No)]
RAKSHPAL, Dr. R. Department of Zoology, Lucknow University, Lucknow, India. [Homoptera:
    Aleurodidae of n. India (Yes)]
RALPH, Miss Patricia M. Zoology Department, Victoria University of Wellington, P. O. Box
    196, Wellington, New Zealand.   [Coelenterata: Hydrozoa: Hydroida & Hydromedusae of
    Australia & New Zealand (Yes)]
* RAMADAN, Dr. M. M. Department of Zoology, Faculty of Science, University of Cairo,
    Abbassia, Cairo, Egypt. [Crustacea]
RAMAKRISHNA, Mr. G. Helminthology Section, Zoological Survey of India, 34 Chittaranjan
    Avenue, Calcutta 12, India. [Helminths & Crustacea: Decapoda & Copepoda of India (Yes)]
* RAMAKRISHNA-AYAYR, Prof. T. V. Address unknown. [Hymenoptera]
RAMASWAMI, Dr. L. S. Department of Zoology, Central College, University of Mysore,
    Bangalore, India. [Reptilia: Anura & Apoda of S. India]
RAMAZZOTTI, Giuseppe. Viale Vittorio Veneto 24, Milan, Italy. [Non-marine Tardigrada
    (Yes)]
RAMBLA, M. Instituto de Biologia Aplicada, Universidad de Barcelona, Barcelona, Spain.
    [Arachnida: Opiliones of Mediterranean (No); of Spain (Yes)]
* RAMONT, Dr. R. Address unknown. [Araneida]
RAMOS, Dr. Alberto. See da Silva Ramos, Alberto.
RAMOS, Dr. J. A. Biology Department, University of Puerto Rico, Mayaguez, Puerto Rico.
    [Homoptera: Auchenorhyncha of World (No); of Neotropics (Yes)]
RAMPI, Prof. Leopoldo. 17 Via Mentana, San Remo, Italy. [Marine planktonic Protozoa:
    Peridinina & Tintinnia of Mediterrean & Pacific (Yes)] [Centro Talassografico Ligure,
    Genova]
RAMSAY, Graeme W. 50 Rodrigo Road, Kilbirnie, Wellington E. 3, New Zealand. [Orthoptera
    of New Zealand (Yes); Acarina: Oribatei of New Zealand (No)] [Victoria University of
    Wellington]
RAMSDELL, Prof. Robert Cole. Geology Department, Williams College, Williamstown, Mass.,
    U. S. A. [Cretaceous Brachiopoda (No); Cretaceous Pelecypoda & Gastropoda (No)]
* RAMSDEN, Dr. Charles T. 18 y 19 Vista Alegre, Santiago de Cuba, Cuba. [Mollusca]
RAMSEY, Prof. L. W. Box 441, Texas Christian University, Fort Worth 29, Texas. [Amphibia
    & Reptilia (No)]
RANCUREL, M. Paul. Service Océanographique, B. P. 35, Abidjan, Ivory Coast. [Pelecypoda:
    Teredinidae of Europe & tropics of World (Yes)] [Office de la Recherche Scientifique et
    Technique Outre-Mer]
RAND, Dr. A. L. Chicago Natural History Museum, Chicago 5, Ill., U. S. A. [Aves of New
    Guinea & Madagascar (No); of Africa & Philippines (Yes)]

RAND, A. Stanley. Department of Zoology, Harvard University, Cambridge 38, Mass., U.S.A. [Reptilia: lizards of Puerto Rico & Hispaniola (Yes); chameleons of e. Africa (Yes)]

RAND, R.W. Division of Fisheries, Aquarium, Beach Road, Sea Point, Capetown, Union of South Africa. [Mammalia: southern fur seals of S. Africa (Yes); Aves: sea birds of s. Africa (Yes)]

RANDALL, Dr. John E., Jr. Marine Laboratory, University of Miami, Virginia Key, Miami 49, Fla., U.S.A. [Tropical marine Pisces, espec. Acanthuridae & Wrasses (Yes)]

RANEY, Prof. Edward C. Conservation Department, Fernow Hall, Cornell University, Ithaca, N.Y., U.S.A. [F-w. Pisces of e. N. America (Yes); euryhaline Pisces of e. N. America (Yes)]

RANGNEKAR, Prof. M.P. Zoology Department, D.G. Ruparel College, Tulsi Pipe Road, Matunga, Bombay 16, India. [Crustacea: parasitic Copepoda of Bombay, India (Yes)]

RANGNEKAR, Mr. P.G. Zoology Department, Ramnarain Ruia College, Matunga, Bombay 19, India. [Crustacea: parasitic Copepoda of Bombay, India (Yes)]

* RANISE, Dr. Stefania. Address unknown. [Crustacea: Copepoda]

RANKIN, Dr. John S., Jr. Marine Research Laboratory, University of Connecticut, Noank, Conn., U.S.A. [Polychaeta (Yes); marine Trematoda (Yes)]

RANKIN, Mr. Wilbur D. Room 104, 643 S. Flower Street, Los Angeles 17, Calif., U.S.A. [Fossil & Recent Foraminifera of World (Yes)]

RANSON, Mr. Gilbert. Laboratoire de Malacologie du Museum, 55 rue de Buffon, Paris (V), France. [Pelecypoda: Ostreidae of World (Yes); Coelenterata: Hydromedusae & Scyphomedusae & Corals of World (No)]

RAO, K. Pampapathi. Department of Zoology, S.V. University, Tirupati, Andhra, India. [Enteropneusta of World, espec. Indo-Pacific & w. cst. of Americas (Yes)]

RAO, Mr. K. Virabhadra. Central Marine Fisheries, Marine Fisheries P.O., S. India. [Bivalvia & Opisthobranchiata of India (Yes)] [Fisheries Extension Unit of Government of India]

* RAO, Dr. S.H., Chief Research Officer, Central Inland Fisheries Research Station, Ministry of Food & Agriculture, Barrackpore P.O., via Calcutta, India. [Mollusca, Porifera, Coelenterata]

RAO, Prof. S.N. College of·Science, Nagpur, India. [Hymenoptera: Ichneumonoidea; Diptera: Cecidomyiidae; of Oriental (Yes)]

* RAO, Prof. Dr. S.R.N. Department of Geology, Lucknow University, Lucknow, India. [Fossils]

RAO, T. Ramachandra. Malaria Organization, Public Health Department, Bombay State, Poona, India. [Diptera: Culicidae of Oriental (Yes); Acarina: Ixodidae of India (Yes); parasitic mites of India (No)]

RAO, Dr. T.S.S. Department of Zoology, Andhra University, Waltair, S. India. [Chaetognatha & parasitic Copepoda of Bay of Bengal, Arabian Sea, Equatorial Indian Ocean (Yes)]

RAO, Dr. V.P. Commonwealth Institute of Biological Control, Bangalore Station, Bellary Road, P.O. Box 112, Bangalore 1, India. [Homoptera: Coccidae of Oriental (Yes)]

* RAO, Dr. V.P. Directorate of Plant Production, Shah Jahan Road Hutments, New Delhi, India. [Hymenoptera]

RAPOPORT, Dr. E.H. Universidad Nacional del Sur, Av. Colon 80, Bahia Blanca, Argentina. [Collembola of S. America (Yes)]

RAPP, William F., Jr. 430 Ivy Avenue, Crete, Nebr., U.S.A. [Siphonaptera of World (Yes); Aves of N. America (Yes); Acarina: Mites & Ectoparasites of N. America (Yes)] [Division of Sanitation, Nebraska State Department of Health]

RAPSON, A.M. Division of Fisheries, Port Moresby, New Guinea. [Commercial Pisces of Melanesia (Yes)]

RASETTI, Dr. Franco. Department of Physics, Johns Hopkins University, Baltimore 18, Md., U.S.A. [Cambrian Trilobita of World (Yes)]

RASKI, Dr. Dewey J. Department of Plant Nematology, University of California, Davis, Calif., U.S.A. [Nematoda: Criconematidae & Tylenchulidae of World (Yes)]

RASMUSSEN, Dr. Birger. Institute of Marine Research, Directorate of Fisheries, Bergen, Norway. [Crustacea: shrimps; Pisces: Scorpaenidae: g. Sebastes; Mammalia: Phocidae; all of n. Atlantic]

RASMUSSEN, David I. Department of Zoology, University of Michigan, Ann Arbor, Mich., U.S.A. [Mammalia of w. U.S. (No)]

RASMUSSEN, Erik, Mag. Scient., Zoologisk Laboratorium, Den Kgl. Veterinaer- og Landbohøjskole, Bülowsvej 13, København V, Denmark. [Polychaeta, Crustacea, Mollusca, of N. Atlantic, espec. Danish waters (No)]

RASMUSSEN, Dr. H.W. Universitetets Mineralogisk-Geologiske Institut, Østervoldgade 7, København, Denmark. [Up. Cretaceous Asteroidea & Ophiuroidea of n. Europe (Yes); Cretaceous Crinoidea of World (Yes)]

RASS, Prof. T.S. Institute of Oceanology, Academy of Sciences of U.S.S.R., Lujnikovskaya 8, Moscow Y-127, U.S.S.R. [Pisces: eggs & larvae of marine Teleostei of Arctic, n. Atlantic & N. Pacific (Yes); deep-sea Pisces of n. Pacific (Yes)]

* RATCLIFFE, Mr. D.A. Nature Conservancy, 12 Hope Terrace, Edinburgh 9, Scotland. [Odonata]

* RATCLIFFE, Mr. F. N. (Canberra, Australia; Culicidae) Not now active in taxonomy.

RATHJEN, Warren F. U. S. Fish & Wildlife Service, Branch of Exploratory Fishing, Gloucester, Mass., U. S. A. [Pisces: Heterostomata of w. N. Atlantic (Yes)]

* RATTENBURY, Dr. Joan C. Department of Zoology, McGill University, Montreal, Que., Canada. [Phoronidea, Bryozoa, Entoprocta of Atlantic & Pacific N. America]

RAU, George J. Agricultural Research Service, U. S. Department of Agriculture, P. O. Box 327, Sanford, Fla., U. S. A. [Nematoda: Tylenchida & Dorylaimina of N. America (No)]

* RAU, Jon L. 1111 13th Avenue South, Grand Forks, N. D., U. S. A. [Fossil Invertebrates]

RAU, Dr. Weldon W. U. S. Geological Survey, 4 Homewood Place, Menlo Park, Calif., U. S. A. [Tertiary Foraminifera of w. cst. of U. S. & Alaska (Yes)]

RAUP, Dr. David Malcolm. Department of Geology, John Hopkins University, Baltimore 18, Md., U. S. A. [Tertiary Echinoidea of N. America (Yes)]

RAUSCH, Dr. Robert. U. S. Public Health Service, Box 960, Anchorage, Alaska. [Cestoda: Cyclophyllidea & Pseudophyllidea of arctic & boreal regions (Yes); Terr. Mammalia of arctic & boreal regions (Yes)] [Arctic Health Research Center]

RAUŠER, Dr. J. Šumavská 30, Brno, Czechoslovakia. [Plecoptera of Europe (Yes)] [Department of Geography, University of Brno]

RAUTHER, M. (Stuttgart, Germany; Pisces) Died in 1951.

RAVERA, Oscar. Istituto Italiano di Hidrobiologia, Pallanza, Italy. [Up. Miocene-Recent smaller Foraminifera (Yes)]

* RAVOUX, Ph. Laboratoire de Zoologie, Faculté des Sciences, Dijon, Cote d'Or, France. [Symphyla]

RAWLS, Prof. Hugh C. Department of Zoology, Eastern Illinois University, Charleston, Ill., U. S. A. [Terr. Gastropoda of N. America (Yes)]

RAWSON, Dr. George W. 603 Faulkner Street, New Smyrna Beach, Fla., U. S. A. [Macrolepidoptera of Nearctic (Yes)]

RAY, Mr. Clayton E. Museum of Comparative Zoology, Cambridge 38, Mass., U. S. A. [Cenozoic Mammalia of West Indies & Florida (Yes)]

RAY, Dr. Dixy Lee. Department of Zoology, University of Washington, Seattle 5, Wash., U. S. A. [Echiuroidea & Sipunculoidea of Pacific Ocean (Yes); Coelenterata: Zoanthidea; Ctenophora; Hemichordata; all (No); Protozoa: Soil Amebae: g. Hartmannella & Crustacea: g. Limnoria (Yes)]

* RAY, Eugene. Department of Insects, Chicago Natural History Museum, Chicago 5, Ill., U. S. A. [Coleoptera: Mordellidae]

* RAY, Dr. H. C. Department of Molluscs, Zoological Survey of India, 34 Chittaranjan Avenue, Calcutta 12, India. [Mollusca]

RAY, H. N., Professor of Protozoology, Calcutta School of Tropical Medicine, Central Avenue, Calcutta 12, India. [Sporozoa: Gregarina & Coccidia, parasitic Ciliata, of India (No)]

RAY, J. R., Hon. Secretary, Entomological Society of New South Wales, 5 Monterey Street, Ramsgate, N. S. W. Australia. [Hymenoptera: Formicidae: g. Myrmecia of Australia (No)]

RAYMENT, Mr. T. National Museum of Victoria, Melbourne C. 1., Victoria, Australia. [Hymenoptera of Australasia (Yes)]

RAYMONT, J. E. G. Department of Zoology, The University of Southhampton, Southhampton, England. [Crustacea: planktonic Copepoda of inshore waters of N. Atlantic]

RAZOWSKI, Ing. Mgr. Jozef. Instytut Zoologiczny, Polska Akademia Nauk, ul. Sławkowska 17, Kraków, Poland. [Lepidoptera of Poland (Yes); Tortricidae of Palearctic (Yes)]

RAZVIASKINA, G. M. Station of Plant Production, Moscow, U. S. S. R. [Homoptera: Cicadoidea of N. America & U. S. S. R. (Yes)]

READ, Dr. Clark R. School of Hygiene & Public Health, Johns Hopkins University, Baltimore 5, Md., U. S. A. [Nematoda of Reptilia & Rodentia of World (Yes); Cestoda of New World (No)]

READ, R. 43 Holly Terrace, Hensingham, Whitehaven, Cumberland, England. [Crustacea: Cirripedia of British Coast (No); Myriapoda of Britain (No)]

RÉAL, Mr. P. Ministère de la France d'Outre-Mer, 80 Route d'Aulnay, Bondy, (Seine), France. [Lepidoptera of France & Africa (Yes); g. Morpho & Prepona of New World (Yes); caterpillars of France & Africa (Yes); Trichoptera, Mecoptera, Planipennia, Ephemeroptera, Odonata, of France (No)]

* REBMANN, O. Address unknown. [Coleoptera]

* RECCHIA, Carlo. Viale Garibaldi N. 4. Verona, Italy. [Lepidoptera]

RECHNITZER, Mr. Andreas B. U. S. Navy Electronics Laboratory, San Diego 52, Calif., U. S. A. [Abyssal Pisces of World (Yes); littoral Pisces of N. America (Yes)]

RECK, Hans F. Institute of Zoology, Academy of Sciences of Georgian S. S. R., Dzerjinski Street 8, Tbilisi, (Tiflis) Georgia, U. S. S. R. [Acarina: Tetranychoidea of Georgian U. S. S. R. (Yes)]

REDICK, Dr. Thomas Ferguson. Department of Physiology & Pharmacy, School of Medicine, University of Pittsburgh, Pittsburgh 13, Penna., U. S. A. [Marine Pelecypoda of e. U. S. (No)]

* REDLINGER, L. M. 4531 Sunburst Street, Bellaire, Texas, U. S. A. [Diptera]
REED, Dr. C. A. College of Pharmacy, University of Illinois, 833 South Wood, Chicago 12, Ill., U. S. A. [Cenozoic Mammalia: Talpidae of World (Yes); Cenozoic g. Arctoryctes & Cryptoryctes of N. America (Yes)]
REED, Clyde T. 3202 North Rome, Tampa 7, Fla., U. S. A. [Marine Crustacea of Gulf of Mexico (Yes)] [University of Tampa]
REED, Mr. Edward B. Department of Biology, University of Saskatchewan, Saskatoon, Sask., Canada. [F-l., f-w. Copepoda, excl. Harpactoids, of N. America, Arctic, Subarctic, Alpine areas (Yes)]
* REED, John P. Department of Entomology, New Jersey Agricultural Experiment Station, New Brunswick, N. J., U. S. A. [Acarina: Tarsonemidae]
REEDY, Prof. John J. Department of Zoology, Stonehill College, North Easton, Mass., U. S. A. [Mammalia: Rodentia of n. e. U. S. (Yes); Amphibia: Anura of n. e. U. S. (Yes)]
REES, Dr. Bryant E. Fresno State College, Fresno 26, Calif., U. S. A. [Coleoptera, larvae, of N. America (No)]
REES, Prof. Don M. Department of Zoology, University of Utah, Salt Lake City 1, Utah. [Diptera: Culicidae (No)]
REES, Mr. William A. 934 South McDonnel Street, East Los Angeles 22, Calif., U. S. A. [Lepidoptera: Noctuidae of N. America (Yes)] [Los Angeles County Museum]
REES, Dr. W. J. British Museum (Natural History), Cromwell Road, London, S. W. 7, England. [Hydrozoa: Athecata of N. Atlantic (Yes); Anthomedusae of World (Yes)]
* REESIDE, John B., Jr. [Washington D. C.; Ammonites] Died July 2, 1958.
REGNELL, Prof. Dr. Gerhard. Paleontologiska Institutionen, Lund, Sweden. [Echinodermata: Paleozoic Pelmatozoa, excl. Crinoidea & Blastoidea (Yes)]
* do REGO-BARROS, Alfredo Rei. Departamento de Entomologia, Museu Nacional, Rio de Janiero, Brazil. [Lepidoptera]
* van REGTEREN ALTENA, C. O. See ALTENA, C. O. R.
ŘEHÁČEK, Josef. Sulekova 5, Bratislava, Czechoslovakia. [Homoptera: Coccidae of Europe (Yes)]
REHDER, Dr. Harald A. Division of Mollusks, National Museum, Washington 25, D. C., U. S. A. [Marine Mollusca of Indo-Pacific (Yes)]
REHN, James A. G. Academy of Natural Sciences, Philadelphia 3, Penna., U. S. A. [Orthoptera & Dermaptera of World (Yes)]
REHN, John W. H. District Public Works Office, Third Naval District, 90 Church Street, New York 7, N. Y., U. S. A. [Orthoptera, espec. Blattariae & Melanoplini, of World (Yes); fossil Blattaria of World (Yes); Grylloblattaria of N. America (Yes); Dermaptera of World (Yes); Neuroptera & Mecoptera of N. America (Yes)]
REICHART, Dr. Charles V., O. P. Providence College, Providence 8, R. I., U. S. A. [Heteroptera & immature aquatics of e. U. S. (Yes)]
REICHEL, Dr. Manfred, Professeur de Paleontologie, Institute de Géologie, Bernoullianum, Bâsel, Switzerland. [Cretaceous-Recent Foraminifera: Alveolinidae (Yes)]
REICHENBACH-KLINKE, Dr. H. Bayerische Biologische Versuchsanstalt, Veterinärstrasse 13, München, Germany. [Parasites of f-w. Pisces of c. Europe (Yes); parasites of marine Pisces of Mediterranean (Yes)]
REICHENOW, Prof. Dr. Eduard. Friedrich Bayer Strasse 10, Wuppertal-Vohwinkel, Germany. [Protozoa: Trypanosomidae: Sporozoa: Coccidia & Haemosporidia (Yes)]
REICHENSPERGER, Prof. Dr. A. Loewenburgstrasse 24, Bad Godesberg, Germany. [Coleoptera: Paussidae of Africa, India & S. America (Yes); ecitophilous Histeridae of S. American (Yes)]
REICHL, Dr. Ernst. Khevenhüllerstrasse 23/I, Linz a. d. Donau, Austria. [Lepidoptera: Zygaenidae of Palearctic (Yes)]
REID, Douglas M. Stoer, Lairg, Sutherland, Scotland. [Crustacea: Amphipoda of World (No)]
REID, Dr. George K. Department of Zoology, Rutgers University, New Brunswick, N. J., U. S. A. [Marine littoral Pisces of Atlantic & Gulf Coasts N. America (Yes); f-w. Pisces of e. & s. e. U. S. (Yes)]
REID, Dr. J. A. Institute for Medical Research, Kuala Lumpur, Malaya. [Diptera: Culicidae: Anophelinae of s. e. Asia (No)]
REID, R. E. H. Department of Geology, The Queen's University of Belfast, Belfast, Northern Ireland. [Mesozoic-Recent, espec. Cretaceous, Porifera: Hexactinellida: Hexactinosa & Lychniscosa (Yes)]
REID, Mr. Robert H. 4315 Russell Avenue, Los Angeles 27, Calif., U. S. A. [Lepidoptera: Noctuidae & Phalaenidae, espec. g. Oncocnemis of N. America (Yes)]
REID, Dr. W. Malcolm. Poultry Department, University of Georgia, Athens, Ga., U. S. A. [Cestoda of poultry (Yes)]
REIG, Prof. Osvaldo A. Instituto Miguel Lillo, Miguel Lillo 205, Tucumán, Argentina. [Fossil & Recent Amphibia: Anura of Neotropics (Yes); fossil & Recent Mammalia: espec. Marsupialia, Carnivora, Rodentia, of Neotropics (Yes)]

REILLY, Dr. E.M., Jr. New York State Museum, State Education Building, Albany 1, N.Y., U.S.A. [Aves, Mammalia, Reptilia: snakes of New York State (Yes)]

REIMANN, Irving G. University Museums, University of Michigan, Ann Arbor, Mich., U.S.A. [Devonian Echinodermata: Blastoidea (Yes)]

* REIMAN, Dr. V.M. Academy of Sciences of U.S.S.R., Stalinabad, Tadjik S.S.R., U.S.S.R. [Silurian Rugosa: Mesozoic Hexacoralla]

* REINHARD, Edward G. (Washington, D.C.; Cirrepedia & Isopoda) Died January 1958.

REINHARD, H.J. Department of Entomology, Agricultural & Mechanical College of Texas, College Station, Texas, U.S.A. [Diptera: Muscoidea of N. America (Yes), of S. America (No)]

REINHART, Phillip Wingate. (Denver, Colo.; fossils) Not now active in taxonomy.

REINHART, Dr. Roy H. Department of Geology, Miami University, Oxford, Ohio, U.S.A. [Mammalia: fossil Sirenia & Desmostylia of World (Yes); Devonian Pisces: Macropeta-lichthyida of N. America, Europe, Spitzbergen (Yes); Cretaceous Pisces: Ptychodontidae: g. Ptychodus of World (Yes)]

REINTHAL, Dr. W.J. Eastern State Hospital, Knoxville, Tenn., U.S.A. [Lepidoptera: Rhopa-locera of N. America (No), of c. Europe (Yes); Nymphalidae: g. Asterocampa of N. America (Yes)]

REINWALDT, Dr. E. Naturhistoriska Riksmuseum, Vertebratavdelingen, Stockholm 50, Swe-den. [Mammalia of Scandinavia (Yes)]

REISCHMAN, Rev. Placidus, O.S.B. Department of Biology, St. Martin's College, Olympia, Wash., U.S.A. [Crustacea: Cirripedia: Rhizocephala of New World (Yes)]

REISH, Dr. Donald J. Department of Biological Science, Long Beach State College, Long Beach 15, Calif., U.S.A. [Annelida: Polychaeta of e. & c. Pacific Ocean (Yes)]

REISINGER, Prof. Dr. Erich. Zoologisches Institut der Universität, Universitätplatz 2, Graz, Austria. [Small marine & f-w. Turbellaria (Yes); Tricladida & Polycladida (No)]

REISS, Hugo. Sapphirweg 6 III, (14a) Stuttgart N, Germany. [Lepidoptera: Zygaenidae: g. Zygaena of Palearctic (Yes); Zygaenidae of s. Africa & India (No)]

REISS, Mr. Z. Geological Survey of Israel, Hebron Road, Jerusalem, Israel. [Up. Cretaceous & L. Tertiary Foraminifera of e. Tethys (Yes)]

REISSER, Hans. Rathausstrasse 11, Wien 1, Austria. [Lepidoptera: Geometridae: Sterrhinae of Palearctic (No), of Europe & Mediterranean (Yes)]

* REITTER, Dr. Ewald. Waltherstrasse 27, München 15, Germany. [Coleoptera]

REJIC, Dr. Marjan. Institut za Zdravstveno Hidrotehniko, Univerze v Ljubljani, Hajdrihova ul. 28, Ljubljana, Yugoslavia. [Crustacea: f-w. Copepoda, excl Harpacticoida, of Slovenia (No); f-w. Amphipoda of Slovenia (No)]

* REMANE, Dr. A. Zoologisches Institut der Universität, Hegewischstrasse 3, (24b) Kiel, Germany. [Copepoda]

* REMANE, Dr. Reinhard. Zoologisches Institut u. Museum der Universität, Hegewischstrasse 3, Kiel, Germany. [Heteroptera]

REMAUDIERE, Dr. G. 28 rue du Dr. Roux, Paris (XV), France. [Homoptera: Aphidoidea of Europe & N. Africa (Yes); of Asia & America (No)] [Institut Pasteur]

REMINGTON, Charles L. Gibbs Research Laboratory, Yale University, New Haven 11, Conn., U.S.A. [Thysanura of World, espec. N. America (Yes); Lepidoptera of World (No); Entotrophi of World, espec. N. America (No)]

REMM, Mr. H. Tartu State University, Zoologia Kateeder, Vanemuise 46, Tartu, Estonia, U.S.S.R. [Diptera: Heleidae of Palearctic (Yes)]

REMMERT, Hermann. (Kiel, Germany; Diptera) Not now active in taxonomy.

REMPEL, Prof. J.G. Biology Department, University of Saskatchewan, Saskatoon, Sask., Canada. [Diptera: Culicidae & Chironomidae of Canadian Prairie (Yes)]

REMY, Jean-Marcel. Museum National d'Histoire Naturelle, Service de Museologie, 57 rue Cuvier, Paris (V), France. [Cretaceous-Tertiary Crustacea: Decapoda of World (Yes)]

REMY, Prof. Paul A. Faculté des Sciences, Universite de Nancy, Zoologie Général, 30 Rue Sainte-Catherine, Nancy, France. [Pauropoda & Palpigrada of World (Yes)]

RENDAHL, Prof. H. Naturhistoriska Riksmuseum, Stockholm 50, Sweden. [Tropical f-w. Pisces of China (Yes), of Oriental (No); Cobitidae of China & Oriental (Yes)]

* RENKONEN, Dr. O. Bredviksvagen 20 B 12, Helsinki, Finland. [Coleoptera: Staphlinidae: g. Stenus]

RENNGARTEN, Prof. V.P. Laboratory of Aero-methods, Academy of Sciences of U.S.S.R., Leningrad B-164, U.S.S.R. [Cretaceous Cephalopoda: Ammonoidea of Caucasus (Yes); Cretaceous Lammelibranchiata: Rudistae & Inoceramidae, of Caucasus (Yes)]

RENSCH, Prof. B. [Münster, Westfälen, Germany; Oriental land snails) Not now active in taxonomy.

RENZ, Dr. H.H. C/o Mene Grande Oil Company, Apartado 709, Caracas, Venezuela. [Cre-taceous & Tertiary Foraminifera of Caribbean (Yes)]

* RESVOY, Prof. P.D. Lwow State University, Lwow, Ukraine, U.S.S.R. See Addenda.

RETT, Egmont Z. Santa Barbara Museum of National History, Santa Barbara, Calif., U.S.A. [Aves of N. America (Yes)]

320

REUVER, Dr. Irma. (Leverkusen-Bayerwerk, Germany; Nematoda) Not now active in taxonomy.

REVILLIOD, Dr. P. E. (Genève, Switzerland; fossil Mammalia) Deceased.

REXROAD, Carl B. Address unknown. [Fossil Conodonts]

REYE, Dr. E. J. C/o N. B. A. Limited, Box 1418 T, G. P. O. , Brisbane, Queensland, Australia. [Diptera: Ceratopogonidae of Australia (Yes)]

REYMENT, Fil. Dr. Richard, Hägernäsvägen 8, Viggbyholm, Sweden. [Cretaceous & L. Liassic Ammonites (Yes); Paleozoic-Recent Cephalopoda; Up. Cretaceous to L. Eocene Ostracoda (Yes)] [Docent Geologiska Institute, University of Stockholm]

REYNE, Dr. A. Zoological Museum, Zeeburgerdijk 21, Amsterdam, Netherlands. [Homoptera: Coccidae of Holland & Indonesia (Yes); Pseudococcidae & Monophlebinae of Dutch New Guinea (Yes)]

REYNOLDS, Bruce D. (Charlottesville, Va.; Protozoa) Deceased.

* REYNOLDS, Father T. Emmett. Address unknown. [Fossil Mammalia]

REYNOLDSON, Dr. T. B. Zoology Department, University College, Bangor, Caerns, Wales. [Turbellaria: Triclada of n. w. Europe (Yes)]

RHOADES, Rendell. 1807 Northwest Boulevard, Columbus 12, Ohio, U. S. A. [Pleistocene & Recent f-w. Crayfishes (Yes)] [Ohio State University]

RHODES, Prof. Frank H. T. Geological Department, University College of Swansea, Swansea, Wales. [Conodonts of World (Yes)]

RIBAUT, Prof. Dr. Henri. 18 rue Lafayette, Toulouse (Hte. Garonne), France. [Homoptera of Palearctic (No); Hymenoptera: Vespiformes of France (Yes)]

* RICCI, Mario. Laboratorio di Parasitologia, Universitá di Roma, Viale Regina Margarita 299, Roma, Italy. [Lepidoptera & Helminths]

RICCIARDI, I. Organisation Panamericana de Salud, World Health Organization, Caixa Postal 2117, Lima, Peru. [Diptera: Culicidae: Anophelini of S. America (Yes)]

* RICCIO, Joseph Frank. (Whittier, Calif.; fossils) Not now active in taxonomy.

RICE, Elmer M. Trowbridge Sample Service, 515 Yazoo Street, Jackson, Miss. , U. S. A. [Paleozoic & Mesozoic Microfossils of s. e. & s. w. U. S. (Yes)]

RICHARDS, A. Glenn. (St. Paul, Minn.; Lepidoptera) Not now active in taxonomy.

RICHARDS, Dr. Aola M. Plant Diseases Division, Department of Scientific & Industrial Research, Private Bag, Auckland, New Zealand. [Orthoptera: Rhaphidophoridae & Henicidae of New Zealand (Yes); Coleoptera: Aphodiinae of New Zealand (Yes)]

RICHARDS, Edward F. Box 1945, University, Ala. , U. S. A. [Mollusca: Cretaceous Pelecypoda, Gastropoda, Echinoidea, of Gulf Coast U. S. (Yes)]

RICHARDS, Dr. Horace G. Academy of Natural Sciences, Philadelphia 3, Penn. , U. S. A. [Pleistocene marine Gastropoda & Pelecypoda of e. cst. N. America (Yes); Cretaceous & Tertiary marine Gastropoda & Pelecypoda of e. North America (No)]

RICHARDS, Prof. O. W. Department of Zoology, Imperial College, Prince Consort Street, London S. W. 7, England. [Diptera: Sphaeroceridae of World (Yes); Hymenoptera: Dryinidae of World (Yes); Aculeata of w. Europe]

RICHARDS, Mr. W. R. Insect Systematics & Biological Control Unit, Science Service Building, Carling Ave. , Ottawa, Ont. , Canada. [Homoptera: Aphididae & Coccoidea of Canada (Yes); Heteroptera, excl. Miridae, of N. America, espec. Canada (Yes); Collembola, espec. Sminthuridae, of World (Yes)]

RICHARDSON, Elwyn Stuart. 50 Lynwood Road, New Lynn, S. W. 4, Auckland, New Zealand. [Tertiary-Recent Mollusca of New Zealand (No)]

RICHARDSON, Dr. Eugene S. , Jr. Curator of Fossil Invertebrates, Chicago Natural History Museum, Chicago 5, Ill. , U. S. A. [Fossil Invertebrates of Pennsylvanian black shales (Yes); fossil Insecta of Pennsylvanian (Yes)]

RICHARDSON, Prof. L. R. Department of Zoology, Victoria University of Wellington, Box 196, Wellington, New Zealand. [Hirudinea: Piscicolidae of World (Yes)]

* RICHDALE, Dr. Launcelot Eric. 23 Skibo Street, Kew, Dunedin S. W. 1, New Zealand. [Aves]

RICHERT, Dr. T. H. 155 Dowsett Avenue, Honolulu, Hawaii. [Marine Mollusca shells of Hawaii (Yes)]

RICHMOND, Dr. Edward A. 14 Circle Drive, Moorestown, N. J. , U. S. A. [Coleoptera: Hydrophilidae of U. S. , incl. immature stages (Yes)]

RICHMOND, Mr. Neil D. Carnegie Museum, Pittsburgh 13, Penna. , U. S. A. [Amphibia of e. U. S. (Yes); Reptilia of N. America & West Indies (Yes)]

* RICHTER, Dr. A. A. Address unknown. [Coleoptera: Buprestidae]

RICHTER, Prof. Dr. Leopold. Apartado Aereo 7495, Bogotá, Columbia. [Homoptera: Membracidae of Colombia (Yes)] [Instituto de Ciencias Naturales]

RICHTER, Rudolf. (Frankfurt am Main, Germany; fossils) Deceased.

RICHTER, W. Staatliches Museum für Naturkunde, Entomologische Abteilung, Archivstrasse 4, Stuttgart O, Germany. [Orthoptera: Acridoidea of Palearctic (Yes)]

RICKENBACH, A. Office de la Recherche Scientifique et Technique Outre-Mer, 20 Rue Monsieur, Paris VII, France. [Diptera: Calliphoridae & Muscidae: g. Glossina of Ethiopian (Yes)]

RICKER, Dr. William E. Fisheries Research Board of Canada, Nanaimo, B. C., Canada.
[Plecoptera of N. America (Yes)]
* RICKETTS, H. O. Department of Molluscs, British Museum (Natural History), Cromwell
Road, London, S. W. 7, England. [Mollusca]
RIDE, Dr. W. L. D. Western Australian Museum, Beaufort Street, Perth, W. Australia. [Fossil
& recent Mammalia: Marsupialia of Australia (Yes); Muridae of Australia (No)]
RIEDÈL, Mag. Phil. A. Institute of Zoology, Polish Academy of Sciences, ul. Wilcza 64,
Warszawa, Poland. [Terr. Gastropoda of Palearctic (No); Zonitidae of Palearctic (Yes)]
RIEDEL, Dott Alfredo. Via dei Fabbri 11, Trieste, Italy. [Sub-fossil domestic Mammalia of
Stone, Bronze, Iron Ages, of n. Italy (Yes)]
RIEDEL, William R. Scripps Institution of Oceanography, La Jolla, Calif., U. S. A. [Radiolaria
of all ages of World, espec. Mesozoic to Recent (Yes); Tertiary & Quaternary Spumellina
& Nassellina of all oceans (Yes)]
RIEDL, Dr. R. Zoologisches Institut der Universität, Wien 1, Austria. [Turbellaria: Acoela of
World (Yes); Turbellaria, excl. Polycladida, of European Mediterrean (Yes)]
RIEGEL, Dr. Garland T. Department of Zoology, Eastern Illinois University, Charleston, Ill.,
U. S. A. [Hymenoptera: Braconidae: Alysiinae & Dacnusinae of N. America (No); g. Coeli-
nidea, Sarops, Chorebidella of N. America (Yes)]
RIEGEL, J. A. Department of Zoology, University of Cambridge, Downing Street, Cambridge,
England. [Crustacea: Decapoda: Astacidae: Astacinae of w. N. America (Yes)]
RIEK, Mr. E. F. Division of Entomology, Commonwealth Scientific & Industrial Research Or-
ganization, P. O. Box 109, Canberra, A. C. T., Australia. [Hymenoptera: Chalcidoidea,
Cynipoidea, Proctotrupidae, Heloridae, Cleptidae, Trigonalidae, Vespidae, Sphecoidea;
Mecoptera; Megaloptera; Neuroptera, excl. Myrmeleonidae & Hemerobiidae; Ephemer-
optera; Strepsiptera; Crustacea: f-w. Decapoda; Gordiacea; of Australia & Tasmania
(Yes); fossil Insects (Mecopteroid & Orthopteroid orders) of Australia]
RIEL, Arthur D. New Hampshire Fish & Game Department, Management & Research Division,
Concord, N. H., U. S. A. [F-w. Pisces of n. e. U. S. (Yes)]
RIEMANN, Mr. John. Department of Zoology, University of Texas, Austin, Texas, U. S. A.
[Homoptera: Psyllidae: g. Pachypsylla of N. America (Yes)]
REIMER, William J. University of Florida Collections, Flint Hall, Gainesville, Fla., U. S. A.
[Amphibia & Reptilia of N. America (Yes)] [Florida State Museum]
RIES, Dr. Donald T. Department of Biology, Illinois State Normal University, Normal, Ill.,
U. S. A. [Hymenoptera: Cephidae, Xiphydriidae, Siricidae (Yes)]
* RIES, Mary Davis. Normal, Ill., U. S. A. [Odonata]
RIEZLER, Dr. Hermann. Hauptschullehrer, Botanikerstrasse 11, Innsbruck, Austria. [Thy-
sanura: Machilidae of Austrian Tirol (Yes)]
RIGBY, Mr. J. K. Department of Geology, Brigham Young University, Provo, Utah, U. S. A.
[Paleozoic Porifera of N. America (Yes); Paleozoic Graptoloidea of w. U. S. (Yes);
Paleozoic Invertebrates of Utah (Yes)]
RIGGS, Dr. Carl D. Department of Zoology, University of Oklahoma, Norman, Okla., U. S. A.
[F-w. Pisces of Oklahoma (Yes)]
RIGGS, Elmer S. [Port Arthur; Texas; fossils) Not now active in taxonomy.
RIHA, Dr. P. Entomological Department, National Museum, Václavské Náměsti 1700, Praha
II, Czechoslovakia. [Coleoptera: Dytiscidae of Palearctic (Yes)]
RILEY, Mr. N. D. British Museum (Natural History), Cromwell Road, London, S. W. 7, Eng-
land. [Lepidoptera: Rhopalocera of World (Yes)]
RIMANDO, Mr. Leo C. Nagilian, La Union, Republic of the Philippines. [Acarina: Tetrany-
chidae of Philippines (Yes)]
RIND, Mrs. Shirley. (Christchurch, N. Z.; Porifera) Not now active in taxonomy.
RINDGE, Dr. Frederick H. Department of Insects & Spiders, American Museum of Natural
History, New York 24, N. Y., U. S. A. [Lepidoptera: Geometridae of N. America (Yes)]
* RINGDAHL, Dr. O. Gülichsgatan 9, Hälsingborg, Malmöhus, Sweden. [Diptera]
RINGDAL-GAARDER, Mrs. Karen. Institute for Marine Biology, University of Oslo, Blindern-
Oslo, Norway. [Protozoa: Dinoflagellates of northern waters; Coccolithophorids]
* de RINGUELET, Dra. Anderina B. Departamento de Paleontologia, Museo de La Plata, La
Plata, Argentina. [Fossil Vertebrates]
RINGUELET, Dr. Raul A. Museo de La Plata, La Plata, Argentina. [Hirudinea: of Neotropical
(Yes); Crustacea of S. America (Yes)]
* RIOJA, Dr. Enrique. Instituto de Biologia, Casa del Lago, Chapultepec, Mexico 18, D. F.,
Mexico. [Crustacea]
RIOS, Dr. E. de Carvalho. Museu Oceanographico de Rio Grande, Caixa Postal 379, Rio
Grande, Rio Grande do Sul, Brazil. [Marine Mollusca of Rio Grande do Sul (Yes)]
RIOS CASTANO, Danilo. Carrara 24, No 55-81, Manizales, Colombia. [Insecta of Caldas,
Colombia (No)] [Universidad de Caldas]
RIOUX, Prof. J. 18 rue Foch, Montpellier, France. [Diptera: Culicidae: Culicinae & Dixinae
of Mediterranean (Yes)] [Faculté de Medecine de Montpellier]

* von RIPER, Walker. Colorado Museum of Natural History, City Park, Denver, Colo., U.S.A
    [Araneida]
RIPLEY, S. Dillon. Peabody Museum of Natural History, Yale University, New Haven, Conn.,
    U.S.A. [Aves & Mammalia of s. & s.e. Asia (Yes)]
RISBEC, Dr. Jean J. (Paris, France; Hymenoptera) Not now active in taxonomy.
RISER, Nathan W. Biology Department, Northeastern University, Boston 15, Mass., U.S.A.
    [Cestoda: Tetraphyllidea of World (Yes); f-l. marine Nematoda (Yes); marine Nemerti-
    nea (Yes)]
RISHBETH, Mrs. Kathleen. 22 Sedley Taylor Road, (Cambridge, England; Copepoda) Not now
    active in taxonomy.
RISSO-DOMINGUEZ, Carlos Julio. Azcuenaga 1872, Buenos Aires, Argentina. [Mollusca:
    Gastropoda: Nudibranchiata of World (Yes); Fossil & Recent Gastropoda: Chilinidae of
    S. America (Yes)]
RISTO, Dr. Garevski. Department of Paleontology, Prirodonaučen Muzej, ul. Orce Nikolov II,
    Skopje, Yugoslavia. [Fossil Mammalia of Macedonia (No)]
RITCHER, Dr. Paul O. Department of Entomology, Oregon State College, Corvallis, Ore.,
    U.S.A. [Coleoptera: larvae of Scarabaeidae of N. America (Yes)]
* RITSEMA, L. Nieuwe Prinsengracht 130, Amsterdam, Netherlands. [Fossil Foraminifera]
* RITTER, Dr. Edward. Pace College, 41 Park Row, New York, N.Y., U.S.A. [Protozoa]
RITTER, Mr. M. Laboratoire de Nématologie, Boulevard du Cap, Antibes (A.M.), France.
    [Nematoda: Rhabditida & Tylenchida of Mediterranean (Yes)]
RIVALIER, Dr. E. 26 rue Alexandre-Guilmant, Meudon (S.et O.), France. [Coleoptera: Cicin-
    delidae, espec. Cicindelini, of World (Yes)]
RIVAS, Prof. Luis Rene. Box 488, University of Miami, Miami 46, Fla., U.S.A. [Marine Pis-
    ces of Gulf of Mexico, Caribbean, West Indies, American tropical Pacific (Yes); f-w.
    Pisces of s.U.S., Mexico, C. America, West Indies, S. America (Yes)]
* RIVERA GALLO, Dr. V. Instituto Oceanographico, Carretera de Sierra Nevada 8, Granada,
    Spain. [Echinodermata]
* RIVERO, Professora Frances C. Departamento de Geologia, Universidad Central de Venezuela,
    Avenida Blandin 12, Chacao, Miranda, Venezuela. [Fossil Invertebrates]
RIVERO, Dr. Juan A. Biology Department, University of Puerto Rico, College Station, Maya-
    quez, Puerto Rico. [Amphibia: Salientia of n. S. America (Yes)]
* RIVEROS ZUÑIGA, Prof. Francisco. Departamento de Invertebrados, Estacion de Biologia
    Marina, Universidad de Chile, Casilla 13 D, Viña del Mar, Chile. [Coelenterata &
    Mollusca]
RIVOSECCHI, Dr. Leo. Istituto Superiore di Sanità, Viale Regina Elena 299, Roma, Italy.
    [Diptera: Simuliidae & Ceratopogonidae of Italy (Yes)]
RJABOV, M.A. Ssiezdowsskaja Linja 29, Kw. 7, Leningrad, U.S.S.R. [Lepidoptera: Noctui-
    dae of Palearctic (Yes)]
ROARK, T.R. Box 74, Pickens, S.C., U.S.A. [F-w. Gastrotricha of U.S. (No)]
ROBACK, Selwyn S. Department of Limnology, Academy of Natural Sciences, Philadelphia 3,
    Penna., U.S.A. [Diptera: Sarcophagidae of World (No); Tendipedidae of New World;
    adults (No) & immatures (Yes)]
* RÖBER, Dr. H. Museum für Naturkunde, Himmelreichallee (Zoo), Münster (Westfälische,)
    Germany. [Orthoptera]
ROBERT, Rev. Frère Adrien, C.S.V. Institut de Biologie, Université de Montreal, Boite
    Postale 6128, Montréal, Que., Canada. [Odonata & Coleoptera of Quebec (Yes); Tri-
    choptera of Quebec (No)]
ROBERT, Paul A. Jorat sur Orvin, Pres Bienne, Switzerland. [Odonata of c. Europe (Yes)]
* ROBERTI, Dr. D. Istituto di Entomologia Agraria, Portici (Napoli), Italy. [Hemiptera]
ROBERTS, Mr. David. Cleveland Natural History Museum, 10600 East Boulevard, Cleveland 6,
    Ohio, U.S.A. [Eocene Reptilia: turtles of N. America (Yes)]
ROBERTS, Mr. F.H.S., Officer-in-Charge, Veterinary Parasite Laboratory, Yeerongpilly,
    Queensland, Australia. [Acarina: Ixodidae of Australasia (Yes)] [Commonwealth Scienti-
    fic & Industrial Research Organization.
ROBERTS, Mr. Henry B. Department of Geology, U.S.National Museum, Washington 25, D.C.,
    U.S.A. [Cretaceous-Pleistocene Crustacea: Decapoda of Atlantic, Gulf, & w.U.S. (Yes);
    Cretaceous-Oligocene Decapoda of West Indies & S. America (Yes)]
ROBERTS, H. Radclyffe. (Philadelphia, Penna.; Acrididae Culicidae) Not now active in
    taxonomy.
ROBERTS, Dr. Richard H. Insects Affecting Man & Animals Section, P.O.Box 232, Kerrville,
    Texas, U.S.A. [Diptera: Tabanidae of New World (Yes); Culicidae & Simuliidae of
    N. America (No)] [U.S. Department of Agriculture]
ROBERTS, Dr. Thomas G. Department of Geology, University of Kentucky, Lexington, Ky.,
    U.S.A. [Pennsylvanian & L. Permian Foraminifera: Fusulinidae (Yes)]
* ROBERTS, Travis S. 501 First National Bank Building, Vicksburg, Miss., U.S.A. [Diptera:
    Culicidae]

ROBERTSON, Dr. George M. Department of Biology, Brinnell College, Grinnell, Iowa, U.S.A. [Ordovician & Devonian Ostracodermi, espec. Osteostraci & Anaspida (Yes)]

* ROBERTSON, J.D. P.O.Box 116, Zanzibar, Zanzibar. [Mollusca]

ROBERTSON, Phyllis L. School of Public Health & Tropical Medicine, The University, Sydney, Australia. [Acarina: Tyroglyphoidea of World (Yes)]

ROBERTSON, Robert. Museum of Comparative Zoology, Cambridge 38, Mass., U.S.A. [Marine Mollusca: excl. Cephalopoda & Nudibrachiata, of w. Atlantic, espec. Bahamas & Caribbean (Yes); Aspidobranchia & Amphineura of same (Yes); marine Gastropoda of French Polynesia (No)]

* ROBERTSON, William B., Jr. Route 2, Box 83-C, Homestead, Fla., U.S.A. [Aves]

ROBIN, Dr. Maurice. 43 Boulevard Gambetta 4, Limoges, France. [Coleoptera: Cerambycidae, Buprestidae, Scarabaeidae, of France (No)]

ROBINS, Dr. C. Richard, Curator of Fishes, The Marine Laboratory, University of Miami, Coral Gables, Fla., U.S.A. [Pisces: f-w. Cottidae of World (Yes); Catostomidae; g. Moxostoma of World (Yes); Ophidiidae & Haemulidae of Atlantic (Yes); marine Pisces of Gulf of Mexico & Caribbean (Yes)]

ROBINSON, Dr. E.J. Department of Zoology, Kenyon College, Gambier, Ohio, U.S.A. [Trematoda: Brachylaimidae]

ROBINSON, Mr. G.G. (Livingstone, N. Rhodesia; Diptera) Not now active in taxonomy.

ROBINSON, Dr. J.E. Department of Geology, University College, Gower Street, London, W.C. 1, England. [Carboniferous Ostracoda & microfaunas of Britain (Yes)]

* ROBINSON, John H. Address unknown. [Coleoptera: Cicindelidae & Carabidae]

* ROBINSON, Mr. J.T. Department of Paleontology, Transvaal Museum, P.O.Box 413, Pretoria, Union of South Africa. [Fossil Vertebrates]

ROBINSON, Mark. 47 School Lane, Springfield, Penna., U.S.A. [Coleoptera: Scarabaeidae of New World (Yes)] [Academy of Natural Sciences]

* ROBINSON, Miss P. Department of Zoology, University College of London, Gower Street, London, W.C.1, England. [Reptilia]

ROBINSON, Mr. Peter. Peabody Museum, Yale University, New Haven, Conn., U.S.A. [Eocene Mammalia: Primates & Insectivora of N. America (Yes)]

ROBINSON, Perry E. Missouri Conservation Commission, 903A Elm Street, Columbia, Mo., U.S.A. [Warm-water Pisces of Missouri (Yes)]

* ROBLES-RAMOS, Mrs. Maria Luisa. Departamento de Paleontologia, Petroleos Mexicanos, Avenida Juarez 92, Mexico 1, D.F., Mexico. [Fossil Foraminifera]

ROCKER, Arthur W. Eastern Laboratory, E.I. Dupont de Nemours, Inc., 487 Rosenthal Avenue, Paulsboro, N.J., U.S.A. [Cretaceous Pelecypoda of New Jersey (Yes); Cretaceous Gastropoda of New Jersey (No)]

RODDA, Peter U. Bureau of Economic Geology, The University of Texas, Austin 12, Texas, U.S.A. [Cretaceous & Cenozoic Pelecypoda & Gastropoda of N. America & N. Pacific (Yes); Cretaceous & Cenozoic Ammonoidea of same (No)]

RODECK, Hugo G. University of Colorado Museum, Boulder, Colo., U.S.A. [Hymenoptera: Nomadidae: g. Nomada of World (No)]

* RODGERS, Mr. T.L. Department of Zoology, Chico State College, Chico, Calif., U.S.A. [Reptilia]

RODRIGUEZ-RODA, Dr. Julio, Director del Instituto de Investigaciones Pesqueras, Cadiz, Spain. [Tardigrada of Spain (Yes)]

ROE, Miss K. Zoology Department, University College, Upper Merriou Street, Dublin, Ireland. [Crustacea: Copepoda: Harpacticoida of Ireland & Britain (Yes)]

RØEN, Dr. Ulrik. Freshwater Biological Laboratory, Hillerød, Denmark. [Crustacea: f-w. Entomostraca of Greenland (Yes); f-w. Copepoda of Denmark (Yes); Euphyllopoda of Europe & Asia (Yes)]

ROEPKE, Prof. Dr. Walter C.J., Diedenweg 12, Wageningen, Netherlands. [Lepidoptera: Heterocera, excl. Geometridae & micros of Indo-Malayan & Papuan (No)]

ROESLER, Dr Rudolf. Gimmeldinger Strasse 228, 22 b. Neustadt, a.d. Weinstr., Germany. [Psocoptera of World (Yes)]

ROEWER, Prof. Dr. Carl-Friedrich, Direktor des Übersee-Museums, Bandelstrasse 14 (Horn), Bremen 23, Germany. [Arachnida: Araneae, Opiliones, Solifugae, of World (Yes)]

ROFEN, Dr. R.R. (Also as R.R. Harry & R.R. Harry-Rofen) George Vanderbilt Foundation, Natural History Museum, Stanford University, Stanford, Calif., U.S.A. [Pisces: Mesozoic-Recent deep-sea Iniomi (Yes); coral reef fishes of w. Pacific & Indian Ocean (Yes)]

ROGER, Dr. Jean. Service d'Information Géologique, Bureau de Recherche Géologiques Géophysiques et Minières, 74 rue de la Fédération, Paris (XV), France. [Neogene Lamellibranchiata of Europe (No)]

ROGERS, Andrew J. Entomological Research Center, Florida State Board of Health, Vero Beach, Fla., U.S.A. [Acarina: Ixodidae of s.e. U.S. (Yes)]

ROGERS, Mr. C.H., Curator, Princeton Museum of Zoology, Box 704, Princeton, N.J., U.S.A. [Aves, espec. Apodidae, of the World (Yes)]

* ROGERS, J. Speed. (Ann Arbor, Mich.; Diptera) Died May 17, 1955.

ROGERS, Kenneth J. Parkview Terrace, 148 Westchester Drive, Lafayette, La., U.S.A. [Miocene-Oligocene smaller Foraminifera of Gulf Coast U.S. (Yes)]

ROGERSON, J.P. National Agricultural Advisory Service. Elswick Hall, Elswick Park, Newcastle-on-Tyne 4, England. [Homoptera: Aphididae of Europe (Yes); Nematoda of Europe (No); Diptera: Syrphidae of Europe (No)]

ROGICK, Dr. Mary D. 25 Prospect Street, Apt. 1-K, New Rochelle, N.Y., U.S.A. [Marine Bryozoa: Entoprocta & Ectoprocta of Antarctic & e. cst. U.S. (Yes); f-w., of Lake Erie, e. & c. U.S. (Yes)] [College of New Rochelle]

ROHDE, Prof. Charles J., Jr. Biology Department, Northern Illinois University, DeKalb, Ill., U.S.A. [Acarina: Oribatei of c. U.S. (Yes)]

ROHDENDORF, Prof. B.B. Paleontological Institute, Academy of Sciences, B. Kaluzhskaja 33, Moscow V-71, U.S.S.R. [Diptera: Sarcophaginae of Europe, Asia, Africa (Yes); Tachinidae: Miltogrammatinae of World (Yes); Mesozoic Diptera (Yes)]

ROHDENDORF, Dr. Eugenia. Entomologická Laboratoř, Československá Akademie Věd, ul. Vinična 7, Praha II, Czechoslovakia. [Diptera: Agromyzidae & Calliphoridae: g. Protocalliphora of Europe & Asia (Yes)]

* ROHMER LINTZMANN, C.G. Sección de Entomologia, Instituto Miguel Lillo, Calle M. Lillo 205, Tucumán, Argentina. [Coleoptera: Curculionidae]

ROHRBACHER, Dr. G.H., Jr. Regional Laboratory, P.O. Drawer 952, Auburn, Ala., U.S.A. [Nematoda: Trichostrongylidae of N. America (Yes)] [U.S. Department of Agriculture]

ROHRS, Dr. Mandred. Institut für Haustierkunde, Hegewischstrasse 1, Kiel, Germany. [Mammalia: Canidae (Yes); Felidae (No)]

ROIVAINEN, Dr. H. Botanical Museum, University of Helsinki, Unioni 44, Helsinki, Finland. [Acarina: Eriophyidae of World (Yes)]

* ROJAS, Paulino. Instituto de Investigaciones Cientificas, Universidad de Nuevo Leon, Monterrey, N.L., Mexico. [Mammalia]

ROKITANSKY, DDr. Gerth. Naturhistorisches Museum, Burgring 7, Wien 1, Austria. [Aves of Europe (Yes)]

ROLFE, S.W.H. National Agricultural Advisory Service, Coley Park, Reading, Berks, England. [Diplopoda of Britain (Yes); of Europe (No); Nematoda: Tylenchidae of Europe (No)]

* ROLLEFSEN, G. Institute of Marine Research, Bergen, Norway. [Pisces]

ROLSHAUSEN, F.W. R.R. 4, Box 296B, Houston 27, Texas, U.S.A. [Fossil Foraminifera of Gulf of Mexico & Gulf Embayment (No)] [Humble Oil Co.]

ROMANISZYN, Doc. Dr. Włodzimierz. Instytut Zoologiczny, Polska Akademia Nauk, Oddział w Łodzi, Park Sienkiewicza, Łódź, Poland. [Diptera: Tendipedidae of Poland (Yes)]

ROMANOVSKY, Dr. A. Zoologicky ustav Biologické, Karlovy University Faculty, Viničná 7, Praha II, Czechoslovakia. [Crustacea: Branchiura: Argulidae of Europe (Yes)]

* ROMBOUTS, Mr. A. Transvaal Museum, P.O. Box 413, Pretoria, Union of South Africa. [Mollusca]

ROME, Dom Remacle, O.S.B. Musée de Paléontologie, Institut Geologique de l'Université de Louvain, 10 Rue Saint Michel, Louvain, Belgium. [Carboniferous Ostracoda of Belgium (No); Recent f-w. Ostracoda of Belgium & Belg. Congo (No)]

ROMER, Alfred S. Museum of Comparative Zoology, Harvard University, Cambridge 38, Mass., U.S.A. [Pre-Jurassic Reptilia & Amphibia (Yes)]

ROMER, Mr. J.D. C/o Urban Council Offices, Hong Kong. [Mammalia, Reptilia, Amphibia of Hong Kong (Yes)]

* RONAI, Lili. Department of Paleontology, Jersey Production Research Co., 1133 N. Lewis, Tulsa, Okla., U.S.A. [Fossil Foraminifera]

* RONAI, Peter H. Department of Paleontology, Barbados Gulf Oil Co. Ltd., P.O. Box 105, Bridgetown, Barbados. [Fossils]

RONALD, K. Department of Entomology & Zoology, Ontario Agricultural College, Guelph, Ont., Canada. [Trematoda: Monogenea parasitic of fishes of New World (No); ectoparasites of Pisces, espec. Copepoda, of World (Yes)]

ROONWAL, M.L., Director, Zoological Survey of India, 34 Chittaranjan Avenue, Calcutta 12, India. [Isoptera of Indo-Malaya (Yes)]

ROOTS, Dr. Betty I. Department of Biology, Royal Free Hospital School of Medicine, 8 Hunter Street, Brunswick Square, London, W.C.1, England. [Oligochaeta of Britain & Gough I. (Yes); Lumbricidae of World (Yes)]

* ROQUE, Dr. Madeleine. 2 Avenue Proudhon, Montpellier (Herault), France. [Ciliata: Holotricha]

ROSALES, Prof. Carlos Julio. Departamento de Entomologia, Facultad de Ingenieria Agronomica, Universidad Central, Apartado 4579, Maracay, Est. Aragua, Venezuela. [Coleoptera: Chrysomelidae of Venezuela (No); Cerambycidae: Prioninae of Venezuela (Yes); Homoptera: Fulgoridae of Venezuela (No)

da ROSA PINTO, Dr. A.A. C/o Museum Dr. Alvaro de Castro, Lourenço Marques, Moçambique, Portuguese East Africa. [Aves of s. Africa (Yes)]

ROSAS COSTA, Julio A. Lácar 3722, Buenos Aires 19, Argentina. [Acarina: Trombidiidae, Trombiculidae, Erythraeidae, Smarisidae, all of World (Yes); Sarcoptiformes: Acaridiae of World (No)]

ROSCOE, Ernest J. 1003 Elm Avenue, Salt Lake City, Utah, U.S.A. [Pleistocene-Reeent non-marine Mollusca of w.U.S. (Yes)]
* ROSE, Dr. Maurice. Department of Zoology, Faculty of Sciences, University of Algiers, Alger, Algeria. [Crustacea: Copepoda]
ROSE, Mr. Stanley. C/o The Shell Coy. of South Africa Ltd., P.O.Box 400, Durban, Natal, Union of South Africa. [Amphibia of South Africa (Yes)]
ROSE, Dr. Walter. "Oaknook", Protea Road, Newlands, Cape Province, Union of South Africa. [Reptilia & Amphibia of S. Africa (Yes)] [South African Museum]
ROSEN, Donn Eric. C/o Department of Icthyology, American Museum of Natural History, New York 24, N.Y., U.S.A. [Pisces: Cyprinodontiformes: Poeciliidae of New World (Yes)] [New York Zoological Society]
von ROSEN, Hans. Statens Växtskyddsanstalt, Stockholm 19, Sweden. [Hymenoptera: Pteromalidae: Eutelini of World (Yes)]
ROSENBLATT, Mr. Richard H. Department of Zoology, University of California, Los Angeles 24, Calif., U.S.A. [Pisces: Tripterygiidae of World (Yes); Anguilliformes of e. trop. Pacific (Yes); Haemulidae of New World (Yes)]
ROSENBOHM, Dr.Med. Axel. Cranachstrasse 32, Hamburg-Grossflottbek, Germany. [Odonata of c. Europe (Yes); Planipennia of c. Europe (No)]
ROSENDO, Pascual. Museo de La Plata, La Plata, Argentina. [Fossil Mammalia of S. America (Yes); Tertiary Notoungulata of Patagonia (Yes)]
ROSENKRANTZ, Prof. Alfred. Universitetets Mineralogisk-Geologiske Institut, Østervoldgade 7, København K, Denmark. [Mesozoic & Tertiary Mollusca of Denmark & Greenland (Yes); Cretaceous & Tertiary Tectibranchia (Yes)]
ROSEVEAR, D.R. British Museum (Natural History), London, S.W.7, England. [Mammalia of w.Africa (Yes)]
ROSEWALL, Prof. O.W. 8263 Jefferson Highway, Baton Rouge 8, La., U.S.A. [Hemiptera: Pentatomidae (No)]
ROSEWATER, Joseph. Department of Mollusks, Museum of Comparative Zoology, Cambridge 38, Mass., U.S.A. [Gastropoda: Lacunidae of w.Atlantic (No); Pleuroceridae of m. & e. U.S. (No); Bivalvia: Pinnidae of w.Atlantic (No)] [Harvard University]
* ROSICKÝ, Bohumir. Biologické Ústavy, Československá Akadémie Věd, Laboratoř, Na cvičišti 2, Praha XIX, Czechoslovakia. [Acarina: Ixodidae & Siphonaptera]
ROSINE, Dr. Willard N. Department of Biology, Augustana College, Sioux Falls, S.D., U.S.A. [Crustacea: f-w. Amphipoda of N.America (Yes)]
ROSKIN, G.J. Histology Department, Faculty of Biology, Moscow State University, Moscow, U.S.S.R. [Protozoa: Trypanosomidae]
ROSS, Mr. Charles A. Peabody Museum, Yale University, New Haven, Conn., U.S.A. [Pennsylvanian & Permian Foraminifera: Fusulinidae (Yes)]
ROSS, Dr. Edward S. Department of Entomology, California Academy of Sciences, San Francisco 18, Calif., U.S.A. [Embioptera of World (Yes); Coleoptera: Histeridae of U.S. (No)]
ROSS, Dr. Herbert H. 231 Natural Resources Building, Illinois Natural History Survey, Urbana, Ill., U.S.A. [Trichoptera, Fossil & Recent, of World (Yes); Hymenoptera: Tenthredinoidea of N.America (Yes): Neuroptera: Sialidae: Sialis of World (Yes); Homoptera: Cicadellidae: g.Empoasea & Erythroneura of World (Yes)]
ROSS, James B. Reinhold Book Division, 430 Park Avenue, New York 22, N.Y., U.S.A. [Aves of U.S. (No); Terrestrial Mammalia of e.U.S. (No)]
ROSS, Prof. Robert D. Biology Department, Virginia Polytechnic Institute, Blacksburg, Va., U.S.A. [Pisces of N.America (No), of e.U.S. (Yes)]
ROSS, Dr. Reuben James, Jr. Paleontology & Stratigraphy Branch, U.S. Geological Survey, Denver, Colo., U.S.A. [L. Paleozoic, espec. Ordovician, Trilobita & Brachiopoda of w.U.S. (Yes)]
ROSSI, Dr. Lucia. Istituto e Museo di Zoologia, Università di Torino, Via Accademia Albertina 17, Torion (204), Italy. [Coelenterata of Mediterranean (Yes); Madreporaria of Indo-Pacific & e. Atlantic (Yes)]
ROSSIGNOL, M. Laboratoire d'Oceanographie de l'Institut d'Etudes Centrafricaines, B. P. No. 322, Pointe-Noire, Moyen-Congo, French Equatorial Africa. [Pisces: Clupeidae: g.Sardinella of Gulf of Guinea (S. Atlantic) (Yes); Thonidae of e. S. Atlantic (Yes)] [Office de la Recherche Scientifique et Tecnhique Outre-Mer]
ROSSOUW, Mr. P.J. C/o Geological Survey, P. O. Box 401, Pretoria, Union of South Africa. [M. Devonian Gastropoda & Pelecypoda of s.Africa (Bokkeveld Series) (No)]
ROSTIGAYEV, B.A. Parasitological Laboratory, Sovietskaya 13-15, Stavropol, U.S.S.R. [Siphonaptera of U.S.S.R. (Yes); Hystricopsyllidae: g. Ctenophthalmus of Europe & Asia (Yes); of Africa & N.America (No)] [Research Anti-Plague Institute of the Caucasus & Transcaucasus, Ministry of Health of U.S.S.R.]
ROTH, Mr. Louis M. (Natick, Mass.; Diptera: Culicidae) Not now active in taxonomy.
ROTH, Mr. Maurice. 56 rue André Tessier, Fontenay Sous-Bois (Siene), France. [Homoptera: Auchenorrhyncha of France & Africa (No)]

ROTH, P. La Lézardière, Chemin Béziou, Pau, France. [Hymenoptera: Sphegidae of Palearctic (No); Sphecinae of Mediterranean (Yes)]

ROTH, Vincent D. Farm Advisor's Office, Court House, El Centro, Calif., U.S.A. [Araneida: Agelenidae of World (Yes)]

* ROTHPLETZ, Karl. Naturhistorisches Museum, Augustinergasse 2, Basel, Switzerland. [Fossils]

ROTHSCHILD, Hon. Miriam. C/o The Museum, Tring, Herts, England. [Siphonaptera of Europe (No); larval Trematoda of Europe (No)]

ROTHWELL, W. Thomas, Jr. Production Department, Richfield Oil Corporation, 5900 Cherry Avenue, Long Beach 5, Calif., U.S.A. [Miocene-Oligocene Foraminifera of Pacific cst. of N. America (No); shells of Recent marine Ostracoda of S. California & w. Gulf of Mexico (Yes); Cenozoic-Mesozoic shells of marine Teleostei (Yes)]

ROTTER, Jiři. Stalinova 14, Praha XII, Czechoslovakia. [Reptilia & Amphibia of Palearctic (No); of Europe & U.S.S.R. (Yes); Coleoptera: Histeridae of Palearctic (No)] [Zoo Prague]

ROUBAL, Prof. Jan. Ul. Baterie 6, Praha XVIII, Czechoslovakia. [Heteroptera of Europe & Mediterranean (No)] [Československá Entomologická Společnost]

* ROUBAUD, E. Institut Pasteur, 25 rue du Dr. Roux, Paris (XV), France. [Diptera]

ROUDABUSH, Robert L. Laboratory of Industrial Medicine, Eastman Kodak Company, Rochester 15, N.Y., U.S.A. [Protozoa & parasites]

ROUDIER, A.J. 6 Square Georges Lesage, Paris (XII), France. [Coleoptera: Curculionidae of World (No); of Africa & Palearctic (Yes)] [Museum d'Histoire Naturelle de Paris]

ROUSSET, André. Laboratoire de Zoologie, Faculté des Sciences, Dijon (Cote d'Or), France. [Neuroptera: Planipennia of France (No); Coniopterygidae of World (Yes)]

ROUSSOW, Dr. Georges. G3 Université de Montreal, Office de Biologie, 2900 Mt. Royal Boulevard, Montreal, P.Q., Canada. [Pisces: Acipenseridae of N. America & Europe (Yes)]

ROUX, Mr. Charles. Laboratoire des Pêches Outre-Mer, Museum National d'Histoire Naturelle, 57 rue Cuvier, Paris (V), France. [Marine Pisces of w. African coast (Yes); f-w. Pisces of c. Africa (Yes)]

ROUX-ESTEVE, Mme. Rolande. Museum National d'Histoire Naturelle, 57 rue Cuvier, Paris (V), France. [Pisces of Atlantic, Mediterranean, Red Sea]

* ROWAN, William. (Edmonton, Alta.; Mammalia) Deceased.

ROWELL, Dr. A.J. Department of Geology, The University, Nottingham, England. [Recent inarticulate Brachiopoda larval & adult (Yes); Ordovician-Recent Craniacea (Yes); Paleozoic Acrotretacea & Siphonotretacea (Yes)]

ROY, Mr. R. Institut Francais d'Afrique Noire, Université de Dakar, Dakar, Sénégal. [Orthoptera: Acridoidea of w. Africa (No); Mantodea of w. Africa (Yes)]

ROYO y GOMEZ, Prof. Dr. José. Apartado 4585-Este, Caracas, Venezuela. [Fossil Mammalia & Reptilia of S. America & Spain (Yes); Cretaceous & Tertiary Mollusca of S. America & Spain (Yes)] [Universidad Central de Venezuela]

ROZE, Prof. J.A. Escuela de Biologia, Universidad Central de Venezuela, Caracas, Venezuela. [Amphibia & Reptilia of Neotropics (Yes); Coleoptera: Passalidae of Neotropics (No)]

ROZEBOOM, Lloyd E. 615 N. Wolfe Street, Baltimore 5, Md., U.S.A. [Diptera: Culicidae of New World (No); g. Anopheles of World (No)] [School of Hygiene and Public Health, John Hopkins University]

ROZEN, Jerome G., Jr. Department of Insects & Spiders, American Museum of Natural History, New York 24, N.Y., U.S.A. [Immature Coleoptera, excl. Chrysomelidae, Scolytidae, Curculionidae, Tenebrionidae, Elateridae, Buprestidae, of World (Yes); Hymenoptera: Apoidea: g. Nomadopsis of World (Yes)]

ROZHDESTVENSKY, A.K. Paleontological Institute, Academy of Sciences of U.S.S.R., Lenin Prospectus 16, Moscow B-71, U.S.S.R. [Pisces: Tertiary Centriscidae of s. U.S.S.R. (No); Dinosauria; of c. Asia (Yes)]

ROZKOWSKA, Prof. Dr. Maria. Palaeozoological Institute, Polish Academy of Science, ul Swierczewskiego 19, Poznań, Poland. [Devonian Tetracoralla: Thamnophyllidae of Poland (Yes)]

RUBTZOW, Mr. I.A. Zoological Institute, Academy of Sciences of U.S.S.R., Leningrad 164, U.S.S.R. [Diptera: Simuliidae of Palearctic (Yes)]

* RUCHLYADEV, D.P. Cattle-Breeding Institute, M. Gadgieva Street 27, Makhatch-Kala, Daghestan, U.S.S.R. [Helminths of animals]

* RUCKER, L.M. Paleontology Laboratory, Sun Oil Company, Box 610, Lafayetta, La., U.S.A. [Fossil Invertebrates]

RUCKES, Prof. Herbert. 167-11 33rd Avenue, Flushing 58, N.Y., U.S.A. [Heteroptera: Pentatomidae of New World (Yes); Coreidae of New World (No)]

RUCKES, Dr. Herbert Jr. Department of Entomology, University of California, Berkeley 4, Calif., U.S.A. [Coleoptera: Anobiidae of N. America (No); g. Ernobius of N. America (Yes)]

RUCNER, Dra. R. See KRONEISL-RUCNER, Prof. Renata.

RUDD, Dr. Robert L. Department of Zoology, University of California, Davis, Calif., U.S.A. [Mammalia: Insectivora & Chiroptera of w. N. America (Yes)]

RUDEBECK, Dr. Gustaf E. Division of Vertebrates, Naturhistoriska Riksmuseum, Stockholm 50, Sweden. [Aves of Europe & Africa (Yes), of Asia (No); Falconiformes of World (Yes)]

* RUDESCU, Dr. Ludwig Rodewald. Section de l'Institut de Recherches Forestières, Str. Cpt. Preotescu 29, Bucureşti, Rumania. [Rotifera] See RODEWALD-RUDESCU in Addenda.

RUDICK, Walter. Paleontology Laboratory, Union Oil & Gas Corp. of Louisiana, 8th Floor Pioneer Building, Lake Charles, La., U.S.A. [Oligocene Foraminifera of Gulf Coast U.S. (Yes); Miocene-Eocene (No)]

* RUDLIN, Dr. C. "Owl Hoot", Queen Anne Road, West Mersea, nr. Colchester, Essex, England. [Rotifera]

RUDNICK, Albert. Department of Epidemiology & Microbiology, Graduate School of Public Health, University of Pittsburgh, Pittsburgh 13, Penna., U.S.A. [Acarina: Spinturnicidae of World (Yes)]

RUDWICK, Dr. M.J.S. Sedgwick Museum, Cambridge, England. [Fossil Brachiopoda of World (No)]

RUFFO, Prof. Dr. Sandro. Museo Civico di Storia Naturale, Lungadige Porta Vittoria 9, Verona, Italy. [Crustacea: Amphipoda of World (Yes); Coleoptera: Chrysomelidae of Mediterranean (No)]

RUGGIERI, Dr. Giuliano. Istituto di Geologia, Via Maqueda 172, Palermo, Italy. [Tertiary -Recent marine benthic Ostracoda of Mediterranean (Yes); Neogene-Recent marine Shells of Mediterranean (Yes)]

RÜHM, Dr. W. Bundes Forschungsanstalt für Forst-und Holzwirtschaft, Reinbek bei Hamburg, Scholss, Germany. [Insect & plant parasitic Nematoda (Yes); terrestrial & aquatic Nematoda (No)]

RÜHMANN, D. Pillauer strasse 4b, Hamburg-Wandsbek, Germany. [F-w. Rotatoria of n. Germany (No)]

RUIBAL, Rodolfo. Division of Life Sciences, University of California, Riverside, Calif., U.S.A. [Amphibia: Rana pipiens of N. & C. America (Yes); Reptilia & Amphibia of West Indies (Yes); Squamata: Teiidae of S. America (Yes)]

* RUIZ, Dr. Jose Manoel. Instituto Butantan, Caixa Postal 65, São Paulo, Brazil. [Trematoda]

* de RUIZ, Profesora Silvia Martini. Vidal 2362, Buenos Aires, Argentina. [Porifera]

RUIZ de GAONA, Dr. Máximo. Escuelas Pias, Pamplona (Navarra), Spain. [Fossil Foraminifera: g. Nummulites & Orbitoides of Europe (Yes)]

* RULLAN, Juan Bauza. Palma de Mallorca, Spain. See Addenda.

RULLIER, Prof. F. 20 rue des Ponts de Cé, Angers, France. [Annelida: Polychaeta of World (Yes)] [Université Catholic de l'Ouest]

RUNGS, Charles, Directeur, Laboratoire d'Entomologie, Service de la Recherche Agronomique, 95 Avenue de Temara, Rabat, Morocco. [Lepidoptera: Noctuidae of n. Africa & Sahara (Yes); Orthoptera of Morocco (No)]

RUPPEL, Dr. Robert F. Apartado Aereo 58-13, Bogotá, Colombia. [Homoptera: Cicadellidae of Neotropics (Yes)] [The Rockfeller Foundation]

RUSANOVA, Prof. V.N. Biological Faculty, S.M.Kirov Azerbaijan State University, Kommunischeskaya 8, Baku, U.S.S.R. [Homoptera: Aphidoidea of lowlands of Azerbaijan (Yes)]

* RUSCELLI, Dr. Maria A. Laboratoire Stratigrafico, Corso Vittorio Emanuele 21, Roma, Italy. [Fossil Foraminifera]

RUSCHI, Augusto. Museu de Biologia "Prof. Mello Leitão", Santa Tereza, Espirito Santo, Brazil. [Aves: Chiroptera: Microchiroptera of Brazil (Yes); Aves: Trochilidae of Brazil (Yes)]

RUSCONI, Carlos. Juan P. Morales 123, Las Heras, Mendoza, Argentina. [Paleozoic Invertebrates of S.America; Tertiary Vertebrates of S.America] [Museo de Historia Natural "Juan Cornelio Moyano"]

RUSSELL, Mr. C.R. Box 606, Christchurch, New Zealand. [Rotatoria of New Zealand & S. Pacific (Yes)] [Canterbury Museum]

RUSSELL, Donald E. Laboratoire de Paléontologie, Muséum National d'Histoire Naturelle, 3 Place Valhubert, Paris (V), France. [Paleocene Mammalia of World (Yes)]

RUSSELL, Dr. F.S., Director, The Plymouth Laboratory of the Marine Biological Association, Citadel Hill, Plymouth, England. [Coelenterata: Medusae of British Isles (Yes)]

RUSSELL, Dr. Henry D. Boston University, Boston 15, Mass., U.S.A. [Gastropoda: Nudibranchiata of New England, U.S. (No)]

RUSSELL, Harold G., Jr. 201 Bounty Road, Bayside, Va., U.S.A. [Acarina: Ixodidae & Siphonaptera of N. America (No)]

RUSSELL, Louise M. Entomology Research Division, U.S. Department of Agriculture, Washington 25, D.C., U.S.A. [Homoptera: Aleyrodidae, Aphidae, Coccoidea: g. Asterolecanium, Psyllidae, of World (Yes); Aetalionidae, Cercopidae, Cicadidae, Membracidae of New World & Europe (Yes)]

RUSSELL, Dr. L. S. National Museum of Canada, Ottawa, Ont., Canada. [Cretaceous &
L. Tertiary Vertebrates of Canada (No), Mammalia (Yes); Cretaceous & L. Tertiary
Mollusca, espec. non-marine, of N. America (Yes); Recent non-marine Mollusca of
Canada (Yes)]

RUSSELL, Robert J., Jr. Department of Biology, University of Kansas City, Kansas City 10,
Mo., U. S. A. [Mammalia of Mexico, espec. Morelos (Yes); Miocene-Recent Geomyidae
of Mexico (Yes); g. Dasypus of N. & C. America (Yes); Chiroptera of Mexico (No)]

RUSSELL, Richard W. Naturalist Section, Great Smoky Mountains National Park, Gatlinburg,
Tenn., U. S. A. [Reptilia & Amphibia of N. America (Yes)] [U. S. Department of Interior]

* RUSSO, Dr. Giuseppe, Director, Istituto di Entomologia, Portici, Napoli, Italy. [Homoptera:
Coccidae]

RUST, J. D. 5034 Bradley Boulevard, Apartment 22, Chevy Chase 15, Md., U. S. A. [Mollusca:
Pelecypoda: g. Macoma of Chesapeake Bay (No)]

RUTENBERG, E. P. Zoological Institute, Academy of Sciences of U. S. S. R., Leningrad 164,
U. S. S. R. [Marine Pisces of North Pacific, Baltic, Barentz Sea, White Sea (Yes)]

RUTER, G. 2 rue Emile Blemont, Paris (XVIII), France. [Coleoptera: Scarabaeidae: Cetoniinae of World (Yes)]

RUTH, John W. 529 Las Tunas Drive, Arcadia, Calif., U. S. A. [M. & Up. Tertiary Foraminifera of Los Angeles & Ventura basins of S. California (Yes)]

RUTHVEN, Alexander G. (Ann Arbor, Mich., Reptilia) Not now active in taxonomy.

RUTLLANT, Dr. J. Avenida Generalisimo 2, Pral. Izqda, Melilla, Spanish North Africa.
[Mollusca of World (No); of N. Africa (Yes)]

RUTSCH, Prof. Dr. Rolf F. Melchenbuhlweg 75, Bern, Switzerland. [Tertiary & Recent
marine Pelecypoda & Gastropoda of Europe & New World (No)] [Geological Institute,
University of Berne]

RUTTEN, M. G. Utrecht, Netherlands; Foraminifera) Not now active in taxonomy.

* RUTTNER-KOLISTO, Dr. Agnes. Biologische Station Lunz, Lunz am See, Nö, Austria.
[Rotifera]

RUUD, J. T. Oslo, Norway; Euphausiacea, Copepoda) Not now active in taxonomy.

RUŽIČKA, Prof. Dr. B. Zakrejsova 5, Ostrava 11, Czechoslovakia. [Paleozoic Pelecypoda of
c. Europe (Yes)] [High School of Mines]

RYAN, Mr. Edward P. Department of Zoology & Entomology, University of Hawaii, Honolulu 14,
Hawaii. [Crustacea: Brachyura: Portunidae & Xanthidae of Atlantic & Gulf cst. of U. S.,
Marshall & Hawaiian Islands (Yes)]

* RYBERG, Dr. Olof. Department of Entomology, State College of Agriculture, Åkarp, Malmöhus, Sweden. [Diptera & Mammalia]

RYCKMAN, Raymond E. Section of Entomology, School of Tropical Medicine, Loma Linda,
Calif., U. S. A. [Heteroptera: Reduviidae: Triatominae of World (Yes); hemophagus
Diptera of N. America (No); Culicidae (Yes); Siphonaptera of rodents of s. w. U. S. & n.
Mexico (Yes)] [College of Medical Evangelists]

RYDEN, Mr. Nils S. Skanegaten 41, Halsingborg, Sweden. [Diptera: Agromyzidae of Europe &
Greenland (Yes)]

*RYGIKOV, K. M. Laboratory of Helminthology, Academy of Sciences of U. S. S. R., Lenin High-
way 33, Moscow K-12, U. S. S. R. [Helminths of animals]

RYKE, Dr. P. A. J. Department of Zoology, Potchefstroom University, Potchefstroom, Union of
South Africa. [Acarina: Mesostigmata of s. Africa]

RYLAND, J. S. Marine Biological Station, Menai Bridge, Anglesey, Wales. [Marine Bryozoa,
espec. g. Bugula, of Europe (Yes); Kamtozoa of Europe (Yes)] [University College of
North Wales]

RYSZKA, Mr. Hans, Direktor, Oedenburgerstrasse 198, Wien XXI, Austria. [Lepidoptera:
Papilionidae of Palearctic (Yes); Parmassidae of Holarctic (Yes); Arctiidae of Palearctic
(Yes)]

RZOŚKA, Dr. J. 6 Blakesley Avenue, London, W. 5, England. [Crustacea: f-w. Cladocera &
Copepoda of Africa (No)]

* SABANEEF, P. Jahnstrasse 50, (16) Arolsen (Waldeck), Hesse, Germany. [Rotifera]

SABROSKY, Curtis W. Division of Insects, U. S. National Museum, Washington 25, D. C.,
U. S. A. [Diptera: Asteidae & Milichiidae of World (Yes); Chloropidae of World, excl.
Palearctic (Yes); Anthomyzidae of World (No)] [U. S. Department of Agriculture]

SACARRÃO, Prof. Dr. Germano da Fonseca. Museu Nacional de Historia Natural (Museu
Bocage), Faculdade de Ciências, Lisboa, Portugal. [Cephalopoda of Portuguese cst.
(Yes); Aves of Iberian Pen. (Yes)]

SACCÀ, Prof. Giuseppe. Istituto Superiore di Sanità, Viale Regina Elena 299, Roma, Italy.
[Diptera: Muscidae: g. Musca of World (Yes); Psychodidae: Phlebotominae: g. Phlebotomus
of Mediterranean (Yes); Sarcophagidae; g. Sarcophaga of Italy (Yes)]

SACCHI, Prof. Cesare. Stazione Zoologica, Napoli, Italy. [Mollusca: Gastropoda: Helicidae of
Mediterranean (Yes); br-w. fauna of Mediterranean (No)] [Centro di Studio per la Biologia
del C. N. R.]

329

SACHLAN, Mr. M.   Laboratory of Inland Fisheries, P. O. Box 51, Bogor, Indonesia. [Pisces:
    Cyprinidae of Indo-Australian Arch. (No)]
SACHS, Kelvin Norman, Jr. C/o Geology Department, Cornell University, Ithaca, N. Y. , U. S. A.
    [Tertiary Foraminifera: Camerinidae, Orbitoididae, Miogypsinidae, Discocyclinidae, of
    New World (Yes)]
SACHTLEBEN, Prof. Dr. Hans. Deutsches Entomologisches Institut, Josef-Nawrocki Strasse 10,
    Berlin, D. D. R. [Hymenoptera: Chalcidoidea & Ichneumonoidea of Palearctic (Yes)]
SACKS, Dr. Martin. 580 West 215th Street, New York 34, N. Y. , U. S. A. [Gastrotricha of
    World (Yes)] [Biology Department, City College of New York]
SADLICK, Walter. Department of Geology, Idaho State College, Pocatello, Idaho, U. S. A. [Car-
    boniferous marine Foraminifera: Fusulinidae; Anthozoa: Rugosa: Zaphrenthidae; Brachio-
    poda; Gastropoda: Pleurotomariacea; Cephalopoda: goniatites; Bryozoa: Fenestellidae;
    all of c. & w. U. S. (Yes)]
SADUN, Dr. E. H. 406th Medical General Laboratory, APO 343, San Francisco, Calif. , U. S. A.
    [Trematoda of man of Asia (Yes)]
* SAENZ SANGUINETTI, Abelardo. Colonia 1066, Montevideo, Uruguay. [Coleoptera]
SAEZ, Prof. Francisco A. , Head, Department of Cytogenetics, Instituto de Investigación de
    Ciencias Biologicas, Avenida Italia 3318, Montevideo, Uruguay. [Orthoptera of S. Ameri-
    ca (Yes)]
SAGE, Mr. Bryan L. "Caldey", 11 Deepdene, Potters Bar, Middlesex, England. [Odonata of
    w. Europe & Iraq (Yes); Coleoptera, excl. Staphylinidae, of w. Europe (No); Aves of
    Palearctic (Yes)]
SAHLI, F. Institut de Biologie Animale, Faculté des Sciences, Université de Dijon, Boulevard
    Gabriel, Dijon, France. [Diplopoda of Germany (No)]
* SAHNI, Dr. M. R. Geological Survey of India, 27 Chowringhee, Calcutta 13, India. [Fossil
    Brachiopoda]
SAID, Dr. Rushdi. 22 Road 6, Maadi, Cairo, Egypt. [Mesozoic & Cenozoic smaller Foramini-
    fera of Middle East (Yes)]
SAIDOVA, Mme. H. M. Institute of Oceanology, Academy of Sciences of U. S. S. R. , Luzhnikov-
    skaya 8, Moscow K-127, U. S. S. R. [Foraminifera of Pacific (Yes); of Antarctic (No)]
SAIGUSA, Toshiro. Yokohama Plant Protection Station, Ministry of Agriculture & Forestry,
    Shinyamashita, Naka-ku, Yokohama, Japan. [Nematoda: Tylenchida: g. Meloidogyne,
    Heterodera, Pratylenchus, of Japan & Okinawa (Yes)]
SAILER, Dr. R. I. Division of Insects, U. S. National Museum, Washington 25, D. C. , U. S. A.
    [Heteroptera of Alaska (Yes); Pentatomidae of World (Yes)] [U. S. Department of Agri-
    culture]
SAINT ----- . See also ST. ------.
* de SAINT-ALBIN, E. 23 Boulevard Latour-Maubourg, Paris (VII), France. [Coleoptera]
SAINT GIRONS, Mr. Hubert. Laboratoire d'Evolution des Etres Organisés, 105 Boulevard
    Raspail, Paris (VI), France. [Reptilia: Viperidae; g. Vipera of Palearctic (Yes)]
* SAINT-SEINE, Dr. Pierre. Laboratoire de Paléontologie, Muséum National d'Histoire Natur-
    elle, 3 Place Valhubert, Paris (V), France. [Fossil Vertebrates]
SAITO, Dr. Saburo. Faculty of Fisheries, Hokkaido University, Hakodate, Japan. [Araneida of
    Japan, Formosa, Korea, Saghalien (No)]
SAKAGAMI, Dr. Shôichi, Associate Professor, Zoological Institute, Faculty of Sciences, Hok-
    kaido University, Sapporo, Japan. [Hymenoptera: Apoidea: g. Bombus & Apis of Japan
    (No)]
SAKAGUTI, Kohei. 74 Hamawaki-cho, Nishinomiya City, Hyogo Pref. , Japan. [Siphonaptera of
    World (No); of Asia (Yes)]
SAKAI, Seiroku, Director of Laboratory, Institute for Agricultural Chemicals, Yashima Chemical
    Industry Co. Ltd. , 757 Futago, Kawasaki, Kanagawa, Japan. [Dermaptera: Eudermap-
    tera.& Protodermaptera of World, espec. Japan & Formosa (Yes)]
SAKAI, Dr. Tune. Faculty of Liberal Arts & Education, Yokohama National University, Kama-
    kura, Japan. [Crustacea: Brachyura of Japan, Far East, Melanesia, Micronesia (Yes)]
SAKIMURA, Mr. Kanjyo. Pineapple Research Institute, P. O. Box 3266, Honolulu, Hawaii.
    [Thysanoptera of Hawaii (Yes); Terebrantia of Indo-Malay & Oceania (No)]
SALA, Frank P, 1912 Hilton Drive, Burbank, Calif. , U. S. A. [Lepidoptera: Rhopalocera;
    Noctuidae, espec. g. Annaphilia; Geometridae, espec. g. Cochesia & Stamnoctenis; all of
    s. w. U. S. (Yes)] [Los Angeles State College]
SALEM, Dr. H. H. Professor of Tropical Medicine, Alexandria University, Alexandria, Egypt.
    [Diptera: Culicidae, Muscidae, Sarcophagidae: g. Sarcophaga & Wohlfahrtia of Palearctic
    (Yes)]
SALENTINY, Th. Services Agricoles, 16 route d'Esch, Luxembourg, Luxembourg. [Nematoda:
    Ditylenchus dipsaci (Yes)]
SALFI, Prof. Mario. Istituto di Zoologia, Universitá, Via Mezzocannone 8, Napoli, Italy.
    [Tunicata: Ascidiacea of World (No)]
SÁLIM, Ali. 114 Apollo Street, Bombay 1, India. [Aves of Pakistan & India (Yes)] [Bombay
    Natural History Society]

SALISBURY, A. E. Ormonde House, 51 Amersham Hill, High Wycombe, England. [Recent Mollusca of World (Yes)]

SALKILLD, Mr. B. W. 53 Wareemba Street, Abbotsford, N. S. W., Australia. [Coleoptera of World (Yes); Tenebrionidae, Carabidae, Lucanidae, Cerambycidae, of Australasia (Yes)]

SALMON, Dr. Eleanor S. 521 W. 112th Street, New York 25, N. Y., U. S. A. [Fossil & Recent Foraminifera (No); Fossil Ostracoda (No)] [American Museum of Natural History]

SALMON, Dr. J. T. Zoology Department, University of Wellington, P. O. Box 196, Wellington, New Zealand. [Collembola of World (Yes); Orthoptera & Lepidoptera of New Zealand (Yes)]

* SALMON, M. A. Address unknown. [Hemiptera]

SALOMONSEN, Dr. F., Curator of Birds, Zoologisk Museum, Krystalgade, København, Denmark. [Aves of Arctic, Europe, Philippines, Madagascar (Yes); Meliphagidae of World (Yes)]

SALT, Prof. W. Ray. Department of Anatomy, University of Alberta, Edmonton, Alta., Canada. [Aves of Alberta, Canada (Yes)]

SALTER, Mr. K. E. W. Department of Zoology, University of Sydney, Sydney, N. S. W., Australia. [Hymenoptera: Thynnidae of Australia, Austro-Malaya, & S. America (Yes); Coelenterata: Madreporaria of Great Barrier Reef (Yes)]

SALZANO, Dr. F. M. Instituto de Ciências Naturais, Av. Paulo Gama, Pôrto Alegre, R. G. S., Brazil. [Diptera: Drosophilidae: g. Drosophila of Brazil (No)]

SAMAAN, S. M. Paleontology Laboratory, Mobil Oil Egypt Inc., 35 Kasr Elali St., Garden City, Cairo, Egypt. [Miocene & Eocene Microforaminifera of Gulf of Suez (Yes)]

SAMBE GOWDA, Mr. S. Department of Geology, University of Malaya, Singapore 10, Malaya. [Cretaceous & Cenozoic Foraminifera & Holothurioidea of Indo-Pacific, Australia, India, Indonesia, Malaya, Siam, Burma (No)]

SAMPSON, Dr. W. W. 1473 Rancho View Drive, Lafayette, Calif., U. S. A. [Homoptera: Aleyrodidae of New World (Yes); Aphididae of California (No)] [Alameda County Health Department]

SAMŠIŇÁK, Dr. K. Biologické Ústavy, Československá Akademie Věd, Na Cvičišti 2, Praha 6, Czechoslovakia. [Acarina: Acaridae & Anoetidae of World (Yes); Acarina on insects of World (No); Hymenoptera: Formicidae of c. Europe (Yes)]

SAMSONOVNA-SENGELIA, Elena. Zoologiceskii Institut, Akademii Nauk Gruzinskoi S. S. R., ul. Dzerzinskogo 8, Tbilisi 4, U. S. S. R. [Odonata & Homoptera: Auchenorrhyncha]

* SANBORN, Colin Campbell. Department of Mammals, Chicago Natural History Museum, Chicago 5, Ill., U. S. A. [Mammalia Chiroptera]

* SANCHEZ, Antonio C. See COBOS-SANCHEZ, A.

SANCHEZ, Melle S. Laboratoire de Biologie Animale, Faculté des Sciences, Montpellier (Hérault), France. [Pycnogonida of cst. of France (Yes)]

SANCHEZ, Dr. Siro de Fez. Conde Salvatierra No. 21, Valencia, Spain. [Mollusca of World (No); Nudibranchiata of Spain (Yes)]

SANCHEZ REIG, Dr. Mario. Cerro 1962, Habana, Cuba. [Jurassic & Tertiary Fossils of West Indies (Yes)] [Instituto de Investigaciones Cientificas]

* SANCHEZ RUIZ, Dr. César. Medrano 852, 3 A, Buenos Aires, Argentina. [Coleoptera]

SANDARS, Dr. D. F. Queensland Institute for Medical Research, Herston Road, Valley, Brisbane, Australia. [Trematoda & Cestoda of Australia (Yes)]

SANDEMAN, Mr. I. Department of Zoology, The University, St. Andrews, Fife, Scotland. [Cestoda of Charadriiformes of Europe & Asia (Yes)]

SANDER, Nestor J. C/o Coronada Petroleum Corporation, Suite 3106, 630 Fifth Avenue, New York 20, N. Y., U. S. A. [Eocene & Paleocene larger Foraminifera of Persian Gulf (Yes)]

SANDERS, Dr. Howard L., Research Associate, Woods Hole Oceanographic Institution, Woods Hole, Mass., U. S. A. [Crustacea: Cephalocarida (Yes)]

SANDERS, John Essington. 2161 Yale Station, New Haven, Conn., U. S. A. [Mississippian Brachiopoda of e. N. America & n. w. Europe (Yes)]

SANDERS, Mr. Ottys. P. O. Box 4084, Sta A, Dallas 8, Texas, U. S. A. [Amphibia: Salientia: Bufonidae of N. America (Yes)] [Southwestern Biological Supply Company]

SANDERSON, Dr. George A. Shell Oil Company, P. O. Box 1509, Midland, Texas, U. S. A. [Pennsylvanian & Permian smaller Foraminifera of Texas & New Mexico (Yes); Pennsylvanian & Permian Fusulinidae of c. & s. w. U. S. (Yes)]

SANDERSON, Dr. Milton W. Illinois Natural History Survey, Urbana, Ill., U. S. A. [Coleoptera: Scarabaeidae: Phyllophaga of New World (Yes); Staphylinidae: g. Dianous & Stenus of Nearctic (Yes); Chrysomelidae: Cassidinae, Criocerinae, Hispinae, of Nearctic (Yes)]

* SANDGROUND, Dr. J. H. Department of Bacteriology, New York Medical College, New York 29, N. Y., U. S. A. [Parasites]

SANDIDGE, John R. Magnolia Petroleum Company, 1704 Alamo National Building, San Antonio 5, Texas, U. S. A. [Cretaceous & Tertiary Foraminifera of U. S. Gulf & Atlantic Coastal Plain (No)]

* SANDISON, Eyvor. Department of Zoology, University of Capetown, Rondebosch, C. P., Union of South Africa. [Crustacea]

SANDNER, Docent Dr. Henryk. Rynek Nowego Miasta 25, Warszawa, Poland. [Nematoda: Ty-lenchidae & Heteroderidae of Europe (No)] [Institute of Ecology, Laboratory of Applied Entomology]
SANDO, Mr. W. J. Room 325, U. S. National Museum, Washington 25, D. C., U. S. A. [Mississip-pian Corals of N. America (Yes); L. Ordovician Brachiopoda of Appalachian U. S. (Yes)] [U. S. Geological Survey]
* SANDON, Dr. M. Gordon Memorial College, Khartoum, Sudan. [Pisces]
SANDOSHAM, Prof. A. A. Department of Parasitology, University of Malaya, Singapore, Malaya. [Helminths (No); Diptera: Culicidae: Anophelinae of Malaysia (No)]
* SANDOVAL, José. Museo Geologico del Servicio Geologico Nacional, Bogotá, Colombia. [Fossil Invertebrates]
SANFILIPPO, Mr. Nino. Via Cesare Cobella 22D-14, Genova, Italy. [Coleoptera: Haliplidae, Dytiscidae, Gyrinidae, of Europe & n. Africa (Yes); Gyrinidae & Dytiscidae of World (No)]
SANJEAN, Prof. John. Department of Zoology, University of British Columbia, Vancouver 8, B. C., Canada. [Diptera: larvae of Sarcophagidae of N. America (No)]
SANJEEVA RAJ, Mr. P. J. Department of Zoology, Madras Christian College, Tambaram, (Madras), India. [Hirudinea: g. Ozobranchus & Branchellion of World (Yes)]
SANKEY, J. H. P. Juniper Hall Field Centre, Dorking, Surrey, England. [Opiliones of Britain (Yes)]
* SANNEMANN, Dietrich. Geology Department, University of Würzburg, Würzburg, Germany. [Fossil Conodonts]
SAN NICOLAS, Dra Emilia. Real Sociedad Española de Historia Natural, Paseo de la Castellana 84, Madrid (6), Spain. [Gastropoda of Spain (No)]
SANTMYER, Dr. Philip H. Research Department, Monsanto Chemical Corp., St. Louis 4, Mo., U. S. A. [Nematoda: Spirurida, Rhabditida, Tylenchida, of m. w. & s. N. America (Yes)]
SANTORO, Francisco H. Ingeniero Agrónomo Técnico de la Dirección de Investigaciones Fore-stales, Administración Nacional de Bosques, Azcuénaga 1344, Buenos Aires, Argentina. [Coleoptera: Lyctidae of World (No)]
SANTOS DIAS, J. T. See DIAS, J. T. Santos.
* SANTOS, Maria Eugenia. Division de Geologia e Mineralogia, Departamento Nacional da Produçao Mineral, Av. Pasteur 404, Praia Vermelha, Rio de Janeiro, Brazil. [Echinoi-dea]
dos SANTOS, Dr. Newton Dias. Departamento de Entomologia, Museu Nacional, Quinta da Boa Vista, Rio de Janeiro, Brazil. [Odonota of Neotropics (Yes)]
SANTUCCI, R. (Genova, Italy; Crustacea) Deceased.
SANWAL, Dr. K. C. Nematode Investigation, Science Service Laboratory, Carling Avenue, Ottawa, Ont., Canada. [Nematoda parasitic in Birds of India & Pakistan (Yes); soil & plant parasitic Nematoda of Canada (No)]
SAPORITI, Dr. Enrique J. Director (Interino), Jardin Zoológico, Buenos Aires, Argentina. [Reptilia of South America]
SARA, Mr. M. Istituto di Zoologia, Università, Via Mezzocannone 8, Napoli, Italy. [Diptera: Psychodidae: Psychodinae of Europe (Yes); Porifera of Mediterranean (Yes)]
SARAIVA, Dr. Laboratório Nacional de Engenharia Civil, Avenida do Brasil, Lisboa, Portugal. [Timber boring Coleoptera: Anobiidae, Bostrichidae, Lyctidae, Buprestidae, Cerambyci-dae, Curculionidae: Cossoninae, of Portugal & Spain (Yes)]
SÁRINGER, Gyula. Növényvédelemi Kutató Intézet, Herman O. u. 15, Budapest II, Hungary. [Homoptera: Auchenorrhyncha of Europe (No)] [Research Institute for Plant Protection]
SARKAR, Dr. Satya S. 33/4 Brindaban Mullick Lane, Howrah, India. [Uncoiled L. Cretaceous Ammonites of France (Yes); Up. Cretaceous Ammonites of India (Yes)] [Geological Sur-vey of India]
SARLET, M. Laurent. 47 rue Godin, Ensival-Verviers, Belgium. [Marcolepidoptera eggs of Belgium (Yes); Geometridae with wingless females of Europe (Yes)]
SARTENAER, Dr. Paul. Institut Royal des Sciences Naturelles de Belgique, Rue Vautier 31, Bruxelles, Belgium. [Brachiopoda: Devonian Rhynchonellidae of World (Yes); Devonian Spiriferidae of World (No); Devonian Pelecypoda & Gastropoda]
SARTONI, Dr. Samuele. Istituto di Geologia e Paleontologia dell'Università, Via Zamboni 63, Bologna, Italy. [Jurassic Foraminifera of Italy (Yes)]
SARWAR, Dr. M. M. Punjab College of Animal Husbandry, Chadda Building,. Dil Mohd Road, Lahore, Pakistan. [Nematoda of ruminants of World (Yes); Trichuridae of ruminants, carnivores, insectivores, primates, of World (Yes); Trematoda: Fasciolidae: g. Fasciola of World (Yes); Schistosomatidae of World (Yes)]
SARYTCHEVA, Prof. T. G. Paleontological Institute, Academy of Sciences, Leninsky Prospect 33, Moscow B-71, U. S. S. R. [Carboniferous-Permian Brachiopoda: Productida (Yes)]
SASA, Manabu. Institute for Infectious Diseases, Tokyo University, Shirokane-daimachi, Minato-ku, Tokyo, Japan. [Parasitic Acarina of Japan (Yes); Diptera: Culicidae & Simuliidae of Japan (Yes)]

SASAKAWA, Mitsuhiro, Assistant Professor, Entomological Laboratory, Saikyo University, Shimogamo, Kyoto, Japan. [Diptera: Agromyzidae of Japan, Oriental, Australasian (Yes); Clusiidae of Japan (Yes); Lonchaeidae of Japan (Yes)]

* SASAKI, Kota. Entomological Laboratory, Matsuyama Agricultural College, Matsuyama City, Ehime Pref., Japan. [Hemiptera]

SASS, Daniel B. Department of Geology, University of Cincinnati, Cincinnati, Ohio, U.S.A. [Fossil Brachiopoda: g. Syringothyris & Paraphorhynchus of Kinderhook of Pennsylvania (No)]

SASSER, Prof. J.N. Box 5397, North Carolina State College, Raleigh, N.C., U.S.A. [Nematoda: g. Meloidogyne of World (Yes)]

* SATCHELL, Mr. G.H. (Dunedin, New Zealand; Diptera) Not now active in taxonomy.

* SATO, Dr. Hayao. Miyagi Metropolitan Office, Sendai, Miyagi-ken, Japan. [Rotifera]

* SATO, Ikio. Zoological Laboratory, University of Hiroshima, Hiroshima, Japan. [Arthropoda]

* SATO, Osamu. 59 1-chome, Misaki-cho, Sumiyoshi, Osaka, Japan. [Hymenoptera: Aculeata of Japan (Yes)]

SATO, Dr. Shinichi. Faculty of Fisheries, Hokkaido University, Minato-Machi 253, Hokodate City, Hokkaido, Japan. [Pisces: Petromyzontidae of n. Japan (Yes); Hexagrammidae of n. Pacific (Yes)]

SATTLER, K. Schützenkuhle 23, Flensburg, Germany. [Lepidoptera: Gelechiidae of Palearctic (Yes)]

SATYAMURTI, Dr. S.T., Assistant Superintendent, Madras Government Museum, Egmore, Madras 8, India. [Marine Gastropoda & Pelecypoda of Krusadai Island, Gulf of Manaar, S. India (Yes); terr. & f-w. Mollusca of s. India (No)]

SAUER, Mr. M. C.S.I.R.O. Commonwealth Research Station, Merbein, Vict., Australia. [Nematoda: Tylenchida of Australia (Yes)] [Commonwealth Scientific & Industrial Research Organization]

SAUL, Mrs. LouElla Rankin. Geology Department, University of California, Los Angeles 24, Calif., U.S.A. [Up. Cretaceous & Recent marine Pelecypoda & Gastropoda of w. cst. N. America (Yes)]

* SAULGZ, Dr. P. Zoological Institute, Academy of Science of Ukranian U.S.S.R., ul. Wladimirskaja 55, Kiev, U.S.S.R. [Mollusca]

SAUNDERS, John Baverstock. Texaco Trinidad Inc., Point-a-Pierre, Trinidad. [Oligocene-Recent Foraminifera of Trinidad (Yes)]

SAUNDERS, Dr. L.G. University of Saskatchewan, Saskatoon, Sask., Canada. [Diptera: Heleidae: g. Forcipomyia, espec. early stages, of World (Yes)]

SAUSSEY, Michel. Laboratoire de Zoologie, Faculté des Sciences, Caen, France. [Oligochaeta: Lumbricidae of w. Europe (Yes)]

SAUTER, Dr. W. Entomologisches Institut der E.T.H., Universitätstrasse 2, Zürich, Switzerland. [Lepidoptera of Switzerland (Yes); Psychidae: g. Solenobia of World (Yes); Tortricidae: g. Cnephasia of Europe (Yes)] [Eidg. Technisches Hochschule]

SAVAGE, Dr. Donald E. 1205 Clover Court, Lafayette, Calif., U.S.A. [Cenozoic Mammalia (Yes) [Museum of Paleontology, University of California]

SAVAGE, Prof. Jay M. Department of Biology, University of Southern California, Los Angeles 7, Calif., U.S.A. [Fossil & Recent Reptilia: Squamata, espec. Iguanidae & Xantusiidae, of World (Yes); Fossil & Recent Salientia, espec. Leptodactylidae & Pelobatidae, of World (Yes); Recent Testudinata of World (Yes)]

SAVAGE, R.J.G. Geology Department, The University, Bristol 8, England. [Tertiary Mammalia: Carnivora of Old World (Yes)]

SAVARY, Dr. A. Station Fédérale d'Essais Agricoles, Nyon, Switzerland. [Plant parasitic Nematoda of Switzerland (No)]

SĂVESCU, Dr. Aurel. Institutul de Cercetări Horti-Viticole, Bd. N. Bălcescu Nr. 4-6, Bucuresti-Băneasa, Rumania. [Homoptera: Coccoidea of Rumania]

SAVOIE, Dr. A. 23 rue Guynemer, Busigny, Nord, France. [F-l. Infusoria of Nord, France (Yes)]

SAVORY, Mr. Theodore H. 9 Cornwall Gardens Court, London, S.W.7, England. [Araneida & Opiliones of Britain (Yes)]

SĂVULESCU, Dr. Nicolae. Str. Dianei Nr. 1, Et. II, Ap. 7, raion 1 Mai, Bucureşti, Rumania. [Coleoptera: Carabidae: g. Carabus; Cerambycidae; both of c. Europe (Yes)] [Centrul de Cercetări Biologice]

SAWADA, Prof. Hiromasa. Entomological Laboratory, Tokyo Agricultural University, Setagayu-Ku, Tokyo, Japan. [Coleoptera: Scarabaeidae: Pleurosticti of Japan, Korea, Loochoo Is., Formosa (Yes)]

SAWADA, Kohei. 18, 1-chome, Hamagichi-Higashi, Sumiyoshi, Osaka, Japan. [Coleoptera: Staphylinidae, Scydmaenidae, Pselaphidae, of Japan (Yes); Trichopterygidae of Japan (No)] [Biological Laboratory, Saikyo University]

* SAWAYA, Dr. Michel P. Departamento de Zoologia, Universidade de São Paulo, Caixa Postal 2926, São Paulo, Brazil. [Decapoda, Aves, Coleoptera, Pycnogonida, of S. America]

SAWAYA, Dr. Paulo. Departamento de Phisiologia, Universidade de São Paulo, Caixa Postal 2926, São Paulo, Brazil. [Amphibia, Turbellaria: Temnocephala, Enteropneusta, of S. America]
* SAWIN, Dr. Horace J. Department of Paleontology, University of Houston, Cullen Boulevard, Houston 4, Texas, U. S. A. [Fossil Vertebrates]
SAXE, Dr. L. H., Jr. Department of Pharmacology, West Virginia University Medical Center, Morgantown, W. Va., U. S. A. [Enteric Flagellata of laboratory rodents (Yes)]
SAXENA, Devendra B., Assistant Professor, Department of Zoology, D. A. V. College, Kanpur (U. P), India. [Pisces: Actinopterygii & Reptilia of India (Yes)]
* SAXENA, Ishwari Pol. 113 Newazganj, Lucknow, India. [Fossil Invertebrates]
* SAYED, Mohamed Taner. Entomological Department, Faculty of Science, Ibrahim University, Orman-Giza, Egypt. [Acarina: Tetranychidae]
SAYLOR, Mr. Lawrence W. 1232 Arguello Boulevard, San Francisco 22, Calif., U. S. A. [Coleoptera: Scarabeidae, espec. Melolonthinae of New World (No)]
* SCANLON, Lt. John E. 342 Cresham Drive, San Antonio, Texas, U. S. A. [Mallophaga & Anoplura]
SCARLATO, O. A. Zoological Institute, Academy of Sciences, Leningrad 164, U. S. S. R. [Mollusca marine Bivalvia of N. & Far East Seas of U. S. S. R. (Yes)]
SCARLETT, Mr. R. J., Recorder of Collections (Zoology), Canterbury Museum, Canterbury, New Zealand. [Sub-fossil Aves, espec. Dinornithiformes, of New Zealand (Yes)]
SCATTERGOOD, Mr. Leslie W., Director, Fishery Biological Station, Boothbay Harbor, Maine, U. S. A. [Pisces of N. Atlantic (Yes)] [U. S. Fish & Wildlife Service]
* SCHAAF, Ernst. Schenkendorfstrasse 2, Porz am Rhine, Germany. [Lepidoptera]
SCHAARSCHMIDT, Ludwig. Karl-Schurz-Strasse 43, Göppingen, Germany. [Acarina: Tarsonemidae of Europe, espec. Germany (Yes)]
* SCHACHTER, Mrs. 40 Boulevard Voltaire, Marseille, France. [Crustacea: Copepoda]
SCHAD, Dr. G. A. Institute of Parasitiology, Macdonald College, Macdonald College, P. O., Que., Canada. [Nematoda: Diaphanocephalidae of World (Yes); Nematoda of snakes of World (Yes); Linguatulida of reptiles of World (No)]
SCHAEFER, Hans. Naturhistorisches Museum, Augustinergasse 2, Basel, Switzerland. [Tertiary & Recent Mammalia of Europe (Yes)]
SCHAEFER, Dr. H. W. Transvaal Museum, P. O. Box 413, Pretoria, Union of South Africa. [Crustacea: f-w. Ostracoda of World (Yes); marine Ostracoda of World (No)]
SCHAEFER, Mr. L. 38 Chemin de Nazareth, Montpellier, Hérault, France. [Coleoptera: Buprestidae, Cerambycidae, Dytiscidae, Gyrinidae, of France (Yes)] [Service Protection des Végétaux]
SCHAEFFER, Prof. Asa A. Department of Biology, Temple University, Philadelphia 22, Penna., U. S. A. [Protozoa: f-w. & marine Amoebae (Yes)]
SCHAEFFER, Dr. Bobb. American Museum of Natural History, New York 24, N. Y., U. S. A. [Up. Paleozoic & Mesozoic Pisces (Yes); Cenozoic Pisces (No)]
SCHAFFNER, Mr. J. C. Department of Zoology & Entomology, Iowa State College, Ames, Iowa, U. S. A. [Heteroptera: Alydidae of World (Yes); Coreidae of World (No)]
SCHALDACH, Mr. William J., Jr. Department of Birds & Mammals, Los Angeles County Museum, Los Angeles 7, Calif., U. S. A. [Mammalia: Insectivora: Soricidae & Chiroptera of Mexico & C. America (Yes); Rodentia: Sciuridae & Cricetidae of U. S. (Yes); Pleistocene Rodentia of s. w. U. S. (No)]
van SCHALKWYK, Dr. H. A. D. Department of Agriculture, Division of Entomology, P. O. Box 513, Pretoria, Transvaal, Union of South Africa. [Coleoptera: Curculionidae: Brachyderinae: g. Protostrophus of s. Africa (Yes)]
SCHALLER, Prof. Dr. F. Zoologisches Institut der Technischen Hochschule, Pockels-Strasse 10, Braunschweig, Germany. [Scorpiones, Pseudoscorpiones, Pedipalpi, Acarina: Oribatei]
* von SCHANTZ, Max. Grudvagen 12, Munksnäs, Finland. [Lepidoptera]
SCHANTZ, Viola S. 2475 Virginia Avenue, N. W., Apt. 925, Washington 7, D. C., U. S. A. [Mammalia of N. America (Yes)] [U. S. Fish & Wildlife Service]
SCHAUB, Dr. Hans. Grenzacherstrasse 92, Basel, Switzerland. [Eocene Foraminifera: g. Nummulites & Assilina of Europe, Mediterranean, Africa, Asia (Yes)] [Geolog.-Palaeontolog. Institut der Universität Basel]
SCHAUB, Dr. Samuel. Rauracherstrasse 191, Riehen, Kanton Baselstadt, Switzerland. [Tertiary & Pleistocene Mammalia, espec. Rodentia] [Museum of Natural History]
SCHEDL, Professor Dr. Karl. Pfarrgasse 19, Lienz, Osttirol, Austria. [Coleoptera: Fossil & Recent Scolytidae & Platypodidae of World; Recent Brenthidae of World]
SCHEERPELTZ, Prof. Dr. Otto. Naturhistorisches Museum, Burgring 7, Wien 1, Austria. [Coleoptera: Staphylinidae of World (Yes)]
SCHEFFER, Dr. Victor B., Biologist, U. S. Fish & Wildlife Service, Sand Point N. A. S., Seattle 15, Wash., U. S. A. [Mammalia: Pinnipedia of World (No)]
SCHEIN, Hans, Stadtdirektor a. D. Implerstrasse 60/I, München 25, Germany. [Coleoptera: Scarabaeidae: Cetoniinae of World (Yes); Hopliini of s. Africa (Yes)]

SCHELL, Stewart C. (Moscow, Idaho; Helminths) Not now active in taxonomy.
SCHELL, W.W. Production Research Laboratory, Sun Oil Company, Richardson, Texas, U.S.A. [Mesozoic-Recent Foraminifera of U.S. (Yes)]
SCHELLENBERG, A. (Berlin, Germany; Copepoda) Died in 1954.
SCHELLER, Dr. Ulf. Lundsberg, Sweden. [Symphyla & Pauropoda (Yes)]
SCHENCK, Prof. Hubert G. Box 1528, Stanford, Calif., U.S.A. [Tertiary marine Pelecypoda & Gastropoda of Pacific Basin (No)] [Stanford University] Died June 19, 1960.
SCHEPENS, D. Maastrichtersteenweg 32, Tongeren, Belgium. [Rotatoria: Brachionidae of World (Yes)]
SCHERER, Dr. Gerhard. Entomologisches Institut, Museum G. Frey, Hofrat-Beisele Strasse 8, Tutzing b. München, Germany. [Coleoptera: Chrysomelidae of Africa & S. America (Yes); Alticinae of N. America (No)] [Museum G. Frey]
* SCHEVILL, Barbara Lawrence. See LAWRENCE, Barbara.
SCHEVILL, Mr. William E. Museum of Comparative Zoology, Cambridge 38, Mass., U.S.A. [Mammalia: Cetacea of World (Yes)]
SCHEYGROND, A. Van Itersonlaan 7, Gouda, Netherlands. [Mammalia of Europe (No)]
* SCHIAPELLI, Prof. Rita Delia E. Museo Argentina de Ciencias Naturales, Avda, Angel Gallardo 470, Casilla Correo 10, Sucursal 5, Buenos Aires, Argentina. [Araneida]
SCHICK, Robert X. Department of Entomology, University of California, Los Angeles 24, Calif., U.S.A. [Araneida: Thomisidae of w. U.S. (Yes)]
SCHIEMENZ, Dr. Hans. Institut für Landesforschung u. Naturschutz der Deutschen Akademie der Landwirtschaftswissenschaften, Stübelallee 2, Dresden A16, German Democratic Republic. [Odonata & Orthoptera of c. Europe (Yes)]
* SCHIKHOBALOVA, Dr. N.P. Skrjabin's Laboratory of Helminthology, Academy of Sciences of U.S.S.R., Lenin Highway 33, Moscow B-71, U.S.S.R. [Nematoda: Trichostrongyloidea, Trichocephaloidea, Cystoopsioidea]
SCHILDER, Prof. Dr. F.A. Schleiermacher Strasse 19, Halle (Saale), Democratic German Republic. [Gastropoda fossil & Recent Cypraeidae, Amphiperatidae, Eratoidae, of World (Yes)] [Zoologisches Institut, Universität Halle]
SCHILLER, Everett L. Department of Pathobiology, School of Hygiene & Public Health, 615 N. Wolfe Street, Baltimore 5, Md., U.S.A. [Cestoda: Hymenolepididae of N. America (Yes)] [The Johns Hopkins University]
SCHILLER, Joseph. (Wien, Austria; Protozoa) Not now active in taxonomy.
SCHINDEWOLF, Prof. Dr. O.H. Geologisch-Paläontologisches Institut, Universität Tübingen, Sigwartstrasse 10, Tübingen, Germany. [Paleozoic Ammonoidea (Yes); Paleozoic Madreporaria (No)]
SCHINDLER, Mr. A.F. Section of Nematology, Plant Industry Station, Beltsville, Maryland, U.S.A. [Plant parasitic & f-l. Nematoda, excl. marine forms, of World (Yes)] [U.S. Department of Agriculture]
SCHINDLER, Dr. Otto, Haupt-Konservator, Zoologische Staatssammlung, Menzingerstrasse 67, München 19, Germany. [F-w. Pisces of Europe, S. America, C. America (Yes)]
SCHIØTZ, Cand. Mag. Arne. Zoological Gardens, Roskildevej 32, København F, Denmark. [Amphibia of Nigeria (Yes); Sauria of trop. w. Africa (Yes); Amphibia & Reptilia of Scandinavia (Yes)]
* SCHJØTZ-CHRISTENSEN, K.B. Naturhistorisk Museum, Universitetsparken, Aarhus, Denmark. [Coleoptera]
SCHLESCH, Dr. H. Skansen, Sortsø Strand, Stubbekøbing, Denmark. [Non-marine Mollusca of Palearctic & Arctic (Yes)]
SCHLICKUM, Dr. W.R. Oberelfringhausen 63, über Hattingen/Ruhr, Germany. [Recent & fossil terr. & f-w. Mollusca of Europe (Yes)]
SCHLINGER, Dr. Evert I. Department of Biological Control, Citrus Experiment Station, Riverside, Calif., U.S.A. [Diptera: fossil Acroceridae of World (Yes); Therevidae of N. & C. America (Yes); Hymenoptera: Sphecidae: Oxybelinae of N. & C. America (Yes); Sclerogibbidae of World (Yes); Braconidae: Aphidiinae of California (Yes); Diptera: Bombyliidae of N. America (No); Araneae of N. America (No)] [University of California]
SCHLUGER, Mrs. E.G. Institute of Microbiology & Epidemiology, Academy of Medical Sciences, Baltijskyi Poselok 13, Moscow D-57, U.S.S.R. [Acarina: Trombiculidae & Erythraeidae]
SCHMASSMANN, Hansjorg. (Liestal, Switzerland; fossils) Not now active in taxonomy.
* SCHMID, Dr. Fernand. Department d'Entomologie, Musée Zoologique de Lausanne, Lausanne, Switzerland. [Diptera & Trichoptera]
SCHMID, Dr. Friedrich. Niedersächsisches Landesamt für Bodenforschung, Wiesenstrasse 1, Hannover, Germany. [Cretaceous Cephalopoda: Belemnitidae of n.w. Europe (Yes); Up. Cretaceous Scaphitaceae of Germany (Yes)]
* SCHMIDLIN, A. Engeriedwed 7, Berne, Switzerland. [Lepidoptera]
SCHMIDT, Dr. Erich. Mozartstrasse 22, (22) Bonn am Rhein, Germany. [Odonata of World (No); parasitic Hymenoptera of Old World (No)]
SCHMIDT, Fred H. Department of Entomology, University of Illinois, Urbana, Ill., U.S.A. [Collembola: Isotomidae of Illinois (No)]

335

SCHMIDT, Günter. Biologisches Forschungslaboratorium, Moislinger Allee 61 d, Lübeck, Germany. [Araneida of Europe, Africa, Atlantic Is. (Yes); immatures (No); Theraphosidae of S. America (No)]
SCHMIDT, Prof. Dr. Hermann. Planckstrasse 6, Göttingen, Germany. [Conodonts (No)]
SCHMIDT, Dr. Herta. Senckenberg Museum, Senckenberg Anlage 25, Frankfurt am Main, Germany. [Paleozoic Brachiopoda: Rhynchonellacea of Europe (Yes)] [Naturmuseum und Forschungsinstitut Senckenberg]
* SCHMIDT, J. Institut für Phytopathologie, Universität Rostock, Rostock, German Democratic Republic. [Nematoda]
SCHMIDT, Karl P. (Chicago, Ill., Amphibia & Reptilia) Died September 24, 1957.
* SCHMIDT, P. J. Mytninskaya Nab. 9/2, Leningrad 49, U. S. S. R. [Pisces] Deceased.
SCHMIDT, Dr. Robert. Department of Biological Science, Illinois State Normal University, Normal, Ill., U. S. A. [Isoptera: Apicotermes, Nests only, of trop. Africa (Yes)]
SCHMIDT, Dr. Walter J. Lustkandlgasse 44, Wien IX, Austria. [Fossil tubes of Polychaeta of World (Yes)]
SCHMITT, Dr. Waldo L., Honorary Research Associate, U. S. National Museum, Washington 25, D. C., U. S. A. [Crustacea: Decapoda (No)] [Smithsonian Institution]
* SCHMITZ, Mr. G. Institut National pour Etude Agronomique du Congo Belge, Bambesa, Uele, Belgian Congo. [Hymenoptera]
SCHMITZ, Dr. Herman S. J., Custos, Musei Wasmanniani, Elisabeth Strasse 18, Bad Godesberg, Germany. [Diptera: Phoridae of World] [Aloisius Kolleg] Deceased 1960.
SCHMÖLZER, Dr. Karl. Wiesbauerstrasse 4/1, Salzburg, Austria. [Terr. Acarina of c. Europe (No); terr. Isopoda of s. & c. Europe (Yes)]
SCHMUTTERER, Dr. Heinrich. Schulstrasse 11, Giessen, Germany. [Homoptera: Coccoidea of c. Europe (Yes); Hymenoptera: Chalcidoidea of c. Europe (No)] [Institut für Phytopathologie]
SCHNAIDER, Dr. Zbigniew. Instytut Badawczy Leśnictwa, ul. Nowoopaczewska 3, Warszawa 22, Poland. [Lepidoptera: Cossidae & Aegeriidae of c. Europe (Yes)]
SCHNAKENBECK, Dr. Bundesforschungsanstalt für Fischerei, Neuer Wall 72, Hamburg 36, Germany. [Marine Pisces of N. Atlantic (No); f-w. Pisces of n. Europe (No)]
* SCHNAPP, B. Muzeul National de Istorie Naturala "Grigore Antipa", Kisselef No. 1, Bucureşti III, Rumania. [Mammalia]
SCHNEIDER, Dr. Curt R. Department of Biology, Adelphi College, Garden City, N. Y., U. S. A. [Protozoa: Amoebida: Entamoebidae (Yes); Haemosporidia (No)]
SCHNEIDER, Dr. F. Eidg. Versuchsanstalt für Obst-, Wein- und Gartenbau, Wädenswil, Switzerland. [Diptera: Syrphidae of Europe (Yes)]
SCHNORF, Mme. Dr. A. Conservatrice de Paléontologie, Musée Géologique, Palais de Rumine, Lausanne, Switzerland. [Mesozoic Stromatoporoidea of Europe (Yes)]
SCHOFFENIELS, Dr. E. Institut Léon Fredericq, Université de Liège, Liège, Belgium. [Odonata of Palearctic (Yes)]
SCHÖNMANN, Dr. R. Entomologische Sammlung, Naturhistorisches Museum, Burgring 7, Wien 1, Austria. [Coleoptera: Carabidae: Trechinae of World (Yes)]
SCHOOF, Dr. Herbert F. Technical Development Laboratories, P. O. Box 769, Savannah, Ga., U. S. A. [Coleoptera: Curculionidae: Conotrachelus of New World (Yes)] [U. S. Public Health Service]
SCHOONOVER KENT, Lois. See KENT, Lois S.
SCHOPF, James M. Coal Geology Laboratory, Orton Hall, Ohio State University, Columbus, Ohio, U. S. A. [Paleozoic Hystrichosphaeridae & Peridinitidae (Yes)] [U. S. Geological Survey]
* SCHÖTTNER, Alfred. Katzenfurt 272, Kreis Wetzlar, Germany. [Odonata]
SCHOUTEDEN, Henri. Musée Royal du Congo Belge, Tervuren, Belgium. [Aves of trop. Africa; Heteroptera of trop. Africa]
* SCHOUTEN, Guillermo B. Instituto de Biologia, Ciudad Universitaria, Villa Obregón 20, Mexico, D. F., Mexico. [Fossil Invertebrates]
SCHRÖDER, Heinz. Senckenberg Museum, Senckenberg Anlage 25, Frankfort am Main, Germany. [Homoptera: Cicadellidae: Tettigellinae of America (Yes)]
* SCHRÖDER, J. Address unknown. [Fossil Vertebrates]
* SCHROEDER, N. 51 Avenue Berchem, Luxembourg-Howald, Luxembourg, [Mammalia]
SCHROEDER, Mr. William C. Museum of Comparative Zoology, Cambridge 38, Mass., U. S. A. [Pisces: Holocephali of Atlantic Ocean (Yes); Osteichthyes of n. w. Atlantic Ocean (Yes)]
SCHUBART, Dr. Otto. Estaçao Esperimental de Biologia, Pirassununga, S. P., Brazil. [Diplopoda of Europe, Africa, S. America]
SCHUBERT, F. Address unknown. [Coleoptera: Pselaphidae]
SCHUIERER, Mr. Frederick. Department of Biology, University of Southern California, Los Angeles 7, Calif., U. S. A. [Amphibia: Anura: g. Bufo (Yes)]
SCHUITEMA, A. K. Castorstraat 20, Delfzijl, Netherlands. [Marine, terr., & f-w. Mollusca of World (No); of Netherlands (Yes)] [Delfzijl Museum]

336

SCHULER, L. 29 Rue des Grandes Arcades, Strasbourg, France. [Coleoptera: Carabidae: Bembidiini of Europe, Asia, Africa (Yes)] [Musée Zoologique]

SCHULMANN, Dr. S. Litejni Prospect 61 Kv. 7, Leningrad, U. S. S. R. [Protozoa: Myxosporidia of World (Yes)] [Institute of Zoology, Academy of Science of U. S. S. R.]

SCHULMANN-ALBOVA, R. E. Laboratory of Zoology of Invertebrates, State University of Leningrad, Leningrad B-164, U. S. S. R. [Trematoda: g. Podocotyle of World (Yes)]

SCHULTE, Dr. Ad. Elsenborner Strasse 13, Hannover- Döhren, Germany. [Lepidoptera; Pieridae, espec. Colias, Lycaenidae; Argynnidae, espec. Melitaea & Brenthis; all of Palearctic (Yes)]

SCHULTZ, Dr. C. Bertrand, Director, University of Nebraska State Museum, Lincoln 8, Neb., U. S. A. [Pleistocene Mammalia of N. America (Yes); Oligocene-Pliocene Oreodontoidea of N. America (Yes)]

SCHULTZ, Dr. Leonard P., Curator of Fishes, U. S. National Museum, Washington 25, D. C., U. S. A. [Pisces of World (Yes)]

SCHULTZ, Dr. V. G. M. Müssen über Lage (Lippe), Germany. [Coleoptera: Carabidae & Staphylinidae of Germany (No); Lepidoptera: Agrotidae & Geometridae of Europe (No); Microlepidoptera of Germany (No)]

SCHULZ, Dr. Erich. Zoologisches Institut und Museum der Universität Kiel, Hegewischstrasse 3, (24b) Kiel, Germany. [Acarina: Halacarida of World (No); marine Tardigrada of World (Yes); Hydrozoa of World (No)]

SCHULZ, Prof. R. S. Institute of Veterinary Research, Kasakhstan Academy of Agricultural Sciences, Taschkentskaja 207, Alma-Ata 29, U. S. S. R. [Nematoda: Strongylata of ruminants & rodents (Yes)]

SCHUMANN, Hennig. Podbielskistrasse 26, II, Hannover, Germany. [Odonata of Germany (Yes); Neuroptera: Mecoptera, Megaloptera, of Germany (No)]

SCHUSTER, Dr. Reinhart. Zoologisches Institut der Universität Graz, Graz, Austria. [Acarina: espec. Oribatei, of World, espec. Europe (No)]

SCHUSTER, Mr. Robert O. Department of Entomology, University of California, Davis, Calif., U. S. A. [Coleoptera: Pselaphidae of Oregon & California (Yes)]

SCHUTTE, Mr. C. H. J. Council for Scientific & Industrial Research, Bilharzia Research Unit, Voortrekker Street, Nelspruit, Union of South Africa. [Gastropoda: Planorbidae of Africa (Yes)]

SCHÜTZE, Eduard. Landgraf-Karl-Strasse 31-3/4, Kassel, Germany. [Lepidoptera: Geometridae: g. Eupithecia of Palearctic (Yes)]

SCHUURMANS STEKHOVEN, J. H. (Utrecht, Netherlands; Nematoda, Crustacea, Diptera) Died 1959.

SCHÜZ, Prof. D. Ernst. (Stuttgart, Germany; Aves) Not now active in taxonomy.

SCHWABE, Andreas, Merchant, Hofgasse 15, Arlesheim, Switzerland. [Paleolithic & Mesolithic Aves of Switzerland, France, Germany (Yes); Felidae & Ursidae of same (No)]

SCHWARTZ, Dr. Albert. Albright College, Reading, Penna., U. S. A. [Amphibia, Reptilia, Mammalia of s. e. U. S. & Cuba (Yes)]

SCHWARTZ, Dr. Benjamin. Parasite Research Division, U. S. Department of Agriculture, Beltsville, Md., U. S. A. [Nematoda & Cestoda of World (No)]

SCHWARTZ, Dr. Frank J. Chesapeake Biological Laboratory, Department of Research & Education, Solomons, Md., U. S. A. [Pisces: Cyprinidae: Etheostomatinae of e. U. S. (Yes)]

SCHWARZ, Dr. Ernst. 107 Gladwyn Court, Bethesda 14, Md., U. S. A. [Pliocene & Pleistocene Mammalia of Europe, Africa, & Asia (Yes); Recent Mammalia of World (Yes); Reptilia: Viperidae of Europe, Africa, Asia]

SCHWARZ, Herbert F. Department of Insects & Spiders, American Museum of Natural History, New York 24, N. Y., U. S. A. [Hymenoptera: Meliponidae of W. Hemisphere & Indo-Malayan (No); Anthidiinae of N. America (No)] Died October 2, 1960.

SCHWARZ, Dr. Rudolf. U Studánky 32/II, Praha 7-Bubeneč, Czechoslovakia. [Lepidoptera: Pyralidae of c. Europe (No); Pterophoridae, Orneodidae, Psychidae, Sesiidae, of c. Europe (Yes)]

SCHWARZ, Dr. S. Vulkanstrasse 27, Greifswald, German Democratic Republic. [Protozoa: Ciliata: Tintinnoidea of Baltic, North Sea, N. Atlantic (Yes)]

SCHWEIGER, Dr. phil. Harald. Niederösterreichisches Landesmuseum, Herreng 9, Wein I, Austria. [Coleoptera of Antarctic, Subantarctic Is., S. Patagonia, Tristan da Cunha (Yes); Carabidae of Europe, incl. Ural Mts. (Yes); Carabidae: Trechinae, Catopidae, Scarabaeidae: Glaphirinae, of World (Yes); Coleoptera Fossil Tertiary & Quaternary Coleoptera of Europe (Yes)]

SCHWEIZER, J. Buchenstrasse 4, Birsfelden, Switzerland. [Acarina: Parasitiformes, Thrombidiformes, Sarcoptiformes, of Switzerland (No)]

SCHWENGEL, Dr. Jeanne S. Artillery Lane, Scarsdale, N. Y., U. S. A. [Marine Mollusca of w. Florida (Yes)]

SCHWOERBEL, Jürgen. Hydrobiologische Station für den Schwarzwald, Falkau (Schwarzwald), Germany. [Acarina: Hydrachnellae & Porohalacaridae of Europe (Yes)]

SCIACCHITANO, Prof. I. Istituto di Zoologia, Università, Firenze, Italy. [Hirudinea of Africa & Asia (No); Nematomorpha of Africa (No)]

SCOBIOLA-PALADE, Zenia. Sectia de Entomologie, Muzuel National de Istorie Naturala "Grigore Antipa", Sos. Kisselef No. 1, Bucureşti III, Rumania. [Hymenoptera: Sphecidae, Psammocharidae, Tenthredinidae, of c. Europe (Yes)]

SCORTECCI, Prof. Giuseppe. Istituto di Zoologia, Università di Genova, Via Balbi 5, Genova, Italy. [Reptilia & Amphibia of Europe & n. & e. Africa (Yes)]

SCORZA, Prof. J. V. Museo de Biologia, Universidad Central de Venezuela, Caracas, Venezuela. [Protozoa: Sporozoa & Mastigophora of S. America (Yes)]

* SCOSSIROLI, Dr. R. E. Universitá, Piazza Botta, Pavia, Italy. [Diptera]

SCOTT, David B. P. O. Box 727, Salinas, Calif., U. S. A. [Collembola of Pacific U. S. (Yes)]

SCOTT, Donald C. Department of Zoology, University of Georgia, Athens, Ga., U. S. A. [Recent f-w. Pisces of s. U. S. (No)]

SCOTT, Mr. E. O. G. "Plooranaloona", 82 Penquite Street, Launceston, Tasmania. [Pisces: Galaxiidae & Syngnathidae of Tasmania & s. Australia (Yes); Pisces, excl. Gobiidae, of Tasmania (Yes); Mammalia, excl. Chiroptera & Rodentia, of Tasmania (Yes); Fossil & Recent Marsupialia of Tasmania (No)]

SCOTT, Hugh. (London, England; Coleoptera) Not now active in taxonomy.

SCOTT, Dr. Harold George. 1245 McLynn Avenue, N. E., Atlanta 6, Ga., U. S. A. [Collembola: of World, espec. Nearctic & Oriental (Yes)] [Communicable Disease Center, U. S. Public Health Service]

SCOTT, Mr. H. W. 244 Natural History Building, University of Illinois, Urbana, Ill., U. S. A. [Fossil Ostracoda, Conodonts, Fusulinidae (Yes)]

SCOTT, Dr. K. M. F. Department of Zoology, University of Capetown, Capetown, Union of South Africa. [Trichoptera of South Africa (Yes)]

SCOTT, Peter. The Wildfowl Trust, Slimbridge, England. [Aves: Anatidae of World (Yes)]

SCOTT, Mr. T. D., Curator of Fishes, South Australian Museum, Adelaide, Australia. [Pisces: Percomorphi & Isospondyli of Australia & Indo Pacific (Yes)]

SCOTT, Dr. W. B. Royal Ontario Museum, 100 Queens Park, Toronto 5, Ont., Canada. [F-w. Pisces of Canada (Yes)]

SCOTT, Dr. W. Frank. Department of Geology, State College of Washington, Pullman, Wash., U. S. A. [Mississippian Brachiopoda of Rocky Mts. (No); L. Triassic Cephalopoda of N. America (Yes)]

SCUDDER, Mr. G. G. E. Department of Zoology, University of British Columbia, Vancouver 8, B. C., Canada. [Heteroptera of World (No); Lygaeidae of World (Yes); Heteroptera of Britain (Yes)]

SCULLEN, Dr. Herman A. Department of Entomology, Oregon State College, Corvallis, Ore., U. S. A. [Hymenoptera: Sphecidae: Cercerini: g. Cerceris & Eucerceris of New World (Yes)]

SDZUY, Dr. Klaus. Geologisch-Paläontologisches Institut, der Universität Würzburg, Pleichertorstrasse 34, Würzburg, Germany. [L. & M. Cambrian & L. Ordovician Trilobita (Yes)]

de SEABRA, A. F. (Lisboa, Portugal; Hemiptera) Deceased.

* SEABRA, Dr. Carlos A. Campos. Praia do Flamengo 340, Rio de Janeiro, Brazil. [Coleoptera & Hymenoptera]

SEALANDER, Dr. John A. Department of Zoology, 9 Chemistry Building, University of Arkansas, Fayetteville, Ark., U. S. A. [Mammalia of Arkansas (Yes)]

SEALE, Alvin. (Watsonville, Calif.; Pisces & Aves) Not now active in taxonomy.

SEAMSTER, Dr. Aaron Presley. Department of Science, Del Mar College, Corpus Christi, Texas, U. S. A. [F-w. & marine Trematoda: Monogenea of U. S. (Yes)]

SEARLE, Dr. Harriet Richardson. 3036 Klingle Road, Washington 8, D. C., U. S. A. [Isópoda (No)]

SEARLS, Ed M. (Madison, Wis.; Insect larvae) Not now active in taxonomy.

SEBESTYÉN, Dr. Olga. Magyar Tudományos Akademia, Biológiai Kutatóintézete, Tihany, Hungary. [F-w. Ciliata: Oligotricha, Porifera, Coelenterata, Bryozoa, of Hungary (No)]

ŠEDIVÝ, Dr. J. Československá Akademie Zemědělských věd Výzkumný ústav Rostlinné Výroby, Praha-Ruzyně 507, Czechoslovakia. [Hymenoptera: Ichneumonidae of Europe (No); of c. Europe (Yes); Gasteruptionidae of Europe·(Yes)]

SEDLACEK, J. 24201 Walnut Street, Lomita, Calif., U. S. A. [Coleoptera: Cleridae of Australia (No)]

SEDMAN, Y. Department of Biology, Western Illinois University, Macomb, Ill., U. S. A. [Diptera: Syrphidae of New World (Yes)]

SEEVERS, Dr. Charles H. Department of Biology, Roosevelt University, Chicago 5, Ill., U. S. A. [Coleoptera: Staphylinidae, termitophilous & myrmecophilous, of World (Yes); Aleocharinae of World (No)]

SEGERSTRÅLE, Dr. Sven G. Zoological Museum of the University, N. Jarnvagsgatan 13, Helsinki, Finland. [Marine Crustacea: Amphipoda: g. Gammarus of n. Europe, incl. Baltic (Yes)]

SEGUY, Eugene. (Paris, France; Diptera & Mallophaga) Not now active in taxonomy.

* SEIDEL, Prof. Dr. Friedrich. Max Planck Institut, Abt. Entwicklungsphysiologie, 20a Mariensee, Kr. Neustadt (Am Rüblenberge), Germany. [Odonata]
SEIDENSTÜCKER, Gustav. Römerstrasse 21 AOK, Eichstätt /Bayern, Germany. [Heteroptera of Palearctic (Yes)]
SEIGLIE, Ing. George A. Neptuno 908, Altos, Habana, Cuba. [Foraminifera: Globotruncanidae of Caribbean & Gulf Coast (Yes); Up. Cretaceous Heterohelicidae of Caribbean & Gulf Coast (Yes)]
SEILACHER, Adolf. Geologisches Institut der Universität, Senckenberg Anlage 32, Frankfurt am. Main, Germany. [Cambrian-Tertiary fossil tracks, trails, burrows of marine Invertebrates (Yes); Triassic Pisces: Selachii: Hybodontida of Europe (No); Mississippian-Cretaceous Calcispongea: Sphinctozoa (No)]
SEILER, Dr. Denis. 18 Promenade de la Seille, Metz-Queuleu (Moselle), France. [Lepidoptera: Nymphalidae: Apaturinae of New World, Africa, Asia (Yes); Papilionidae & Morphidae of New World, Africa, Asia (No); Coleoptera: Cerambycidae & Lucanidae of New World, Africa, Asia (No); Carabidae: g. Carabus of Palearctic (Yes)]
SEINHORST, Dr. J. W. Instituut voor Plantenziektenkundig Onderzoek, Binnenhaven 4, Wageningen, Netherlands. [Plant parasitic Nematoda of w. Europe (Yes)]
SEKHARAN, Mr. K. V. Central Marine Fisheries Research Sub-Station, Kozhikode-5, Westhill P. O., India. [Pisces: Clupeidae of India (Yes)]
SEKI, Kin-ichi. 1876 Tantakabayashi, Sumiyoshi-cho, Higashinada, Kobe, Japan. [Coleoptera: Cerambycidae of Japan (Yes); of Formosa (No)]
SEKIGUCHI, Dr. Koichi. Zoological Institute, Tokyo Kyoiku University, Otsuka, Bunkyo-ku, Tokyo, Japan. [Araneida: Argiopidae & Sparassidae of Japan (Yes)]
SELANDER, R. B. Department of Entomology, University of Illinois, Urbana, Ill., U. S. A. [Coleoptera: Meloidae of World (Yes); Rhipiphoridae of World (No); Lepidoptera: Blastobasidae of New World (Yes)]
SELANDER, Mr. Robert K. Department of Zoology, University of Texas, Austin 12, Texas, U. S. A. [Aves: Troglodytidae, Icteridae, Caprimulgidae, of U. S. & Mexico (Yes)]
SELF, Dr. J. Teague. Department of Zoology, University of Oklahoma, Norman, Okla., U. S. A. [Pentastomida of World (Yes)]
* SELGA, D. Instituto de Biologia Aplicada, Universidad de Barcelona, Barcelona, Spain. [Apterygota]
SELLARDS, E. H. (Austin, Texas; fossil Vertebrates) Not now active in taxonomy.
SELLERS, Mr. W. F. U. S. O. M., A. P. O. 146, San Francisco, Calif., U. S. A. [Diptera: Larvaevoridae of Nearctic & Palearctic (No)] [International Cooperation Administration]
SELLI, Prof. Raimondo. Istituto di Geologia e Paleontologia, Via Zamboni 63, Bologna, Italy. [Jurassic-Recent Foraminifera (Yes); Triassic-Liassic Mollusca & Brachiopoda (Yes)]
SELLIER de CIVRIEUX, Dr. J. M. Division Documentacion, Dirección de Geologia, Ministerio de Minas e Hidrocarburos, Caracas, Venezuela. [Microfossils of Venezuela (No)]
SELLNICK, Herr Max. Baggerkuhle 6, (24) Hoisdorf bei Gr. Hansdorf, Bez. Hamburg, Germany. [Acarina: Oribatei & Mesostigmata of World (Yes)]
SELTIN, Dr. Richard J. Museum, Michigan State University, East Lansing, Mich., U. S. A. [Permian primitive Reptilia (Yes); Permian Amphibia (Yes)]
SELWOOD, Dr. E. B. Geology Department, The University, Exeter, England. [Up. Devonian Ammonitoidea: g. Clymeniina (Yes); Up. Devonian Trilobita (No)]
* SEMENOV, Prof. V. D. Gorky Medical Institute, Minin & Pogarsky Street, 1/10, Gorky, U. S. S. R. [Platyhelminths of man of U. S. S. R.]
SEN, Prof. P. Entomology Department, School of Tropical Medicine, Calcutta 12, India. [Diptera: Ceratopogonidae: g. Culicoides of India (Yes); Culicidae of India (Yes)]
SENEŠ, Dr. J. Geolog. Ústav D. Štúra, Mlynská 1, Bratislava, Czechoslovakia. [Miocene-Oligocene Mollusca of c. Europe (Paratethys)]
SENEVET, Prof. Georges. Institut Pasteur d'Algérie, Université d'Alger, Alger, Algeria. [Diptera: Culicidae, espec. Anophelinae, of World, espec. Africa (Yes)]
SENGBUSCH, Dr. Howard G. State University of New York College for Teachers, Buffalo 22, N. Y., U. S. A. [Acarina: Oribatei of e. U. S. (Yes); Pyemotidae of e. U. S.]
SENGER, Dr. C. M. Department of Zoology, Montana State University, Missoula, Mont., U. S. A. [Protozoa: Coccidia from ruminants of N. America (Yes); Trematoda: Digenea from amphibians & mammals of N. America (Yes); Cestoda: Taeniidae from amphibians & mammals of N. America (Yes); Nematoda: Trichostrongyloidea of ruminants of N. America (No); Siphonaptera, Mallophaga, Anoplura, all of mammals of w. N. America (Yes)]
SENIOR-WHITE, R. A. (Port-of-Spain, Trinidad; Diptera) Deceased.
SERAFINSKI, Dr. W. Polska Akademia Nauk, Instytut Zoologiczny, Wilcza 64, Warszawa, Poland. [Small Mammalia of Palearctic (Yes)]
SERBAN, Ing. Mihai. Institutul de Speologie, Str. Miko 5, Cluj, Rumania. [Crustacea: Harpacticoida & Diaptomida of Rumania (Yes); Harpacticoida: Ameiridae: g. Nitocra of World (Yes); Laophontidae: g. Onychocamptus of World (Yes); Diaptomida: g. Hemidiaptomus, Acanthodiaptomus, Arctodiaptomus, of Palearctic (Yes)]

SERENE, Dr. R. Institut Oceanographique, Nhatrang, Viet-Nam. [Crustacea: Stomatopoda of
    Indo-Pacific (Yes); Decapoda: Brachyura of Indo-Pacific (No); Hapalocarcinidae of Indo-
    Pacific & Atlantic (Yes); Eumedoninae of Indo-Pacific (Yes)]
SERGEANT, David E. Fisheries Research Board of Canada, 505 Pine Avenue West, Montreal,
    P. Q., Canada. [Mammalia: Odontoceti of all seas (No); g. Globicephala (Yes)]
* SERRE, B. Institut Français du Petrole, 4 place Bir-Hackeim, Rueil (S. et O.), France.
    [Fossil Mammalia]
SERRE, Madame. Institut Français du Petrole, 4 place Bir-Hackeim, Rueil (S. et O.), France.
    [Conodonts & Paleozoic Foraminifera (No)]
* SERVAAS, M. Makassarstraat 116-3, Amsterdam Oost, Netherlands. [Coleoptera: Carabidae;
    Mollusca]
SERVADEI, Prof. Antonio. Direttore dell'Istituto di Entomologia, Via Grudenigo 6, Padova,
    Italy. [Hemiptera: Heteroptera & Homoptera: Auchenorrhyncha of Italy (Yes)]
SERVENTY, Dr. D. L. Commonwealth Scientific & Industrial Research Organization, University
    of Western Australia, Nedlands, W. Australia. [Aves of Australia (Yes); Aves: Tubinares
    of World (Yes); Pisces: Tunas of Australian (Yes)]
* SESHADRI, A. R. Agricultural College, Bapatla, Guntur District, S. India. [Embioptera]
* SETON, Mr. Henry. Fairhaven Hill, Concord, Mass., U. S. A. [Fossil Mammalia]
SETTEPASGI, Sig. F. Istituto Italiano di Paleontologia, Via Caccioni 1, Roma, Italy. [Pleis-
    tocene & Recent Mollusca of Meditteranean (Yes); g. Pomatias (Yes)]
SETZER. F. Marion. P. O. Box 3092, Houston, Texas, U. S. A. [Tertiary Microfossils of U. S.
    Gulf Coast (Yes)] [Pan American Petroleum Corp.]
SETZER, Dr. Henry W. Division of Mammals, U. S. National Museum, Washington 25, D. C.,
    U. S. A. [Mammalia of Middle East & N. Africa (Yes)]
SEVADJIAN, Dr. B. K. Zoological Institute, Academy of Sciences of Armenian S. S. R., Avan-
    skoe Shosse 20, Erevan, Armenia, U. S. S. R. [Trematoda: Digenea of Armenia (Yes);
    Dicrocoeliidae, larvae forms, of Transcaucasus (Yes)]
SEVASTOPULO, D. G. C/o Messrs. Ralli Bros. Ltd., Box 881, Mombasa, Kenya. [Lepidoptera
    of Brit. East Africa & India (Yes)]
SEVERAID, Dr. J. H. Life Science Department, Sacramento State College, 6000 J Street, Sacra-
    mento 19, Calif., U. S. A. [Mammalia: Lagomorpha: g. Lepus & Ochotona of N. America
    (No)]
SEYLER, Dr. Paul J. Department of Zoology, Marietta College, Marietta, Ohio, U. S. A. [Ara-
    neida of c. & e. U. S. (Yes)]
SEYMOUR SEWELL, Dr. R. B. Zoological Laboratory, Cambridge, England. [Crustacea:
    Copepoda of Indian Ocean (No)]
* SHACTACHTINSKAYA, Dr. Z. H. Baku Pedagogical Institute, Baku, U. S. S. R. [Platyhel-
    minthes of animals of World]
SHADIN, V. I. See ŽADIN, V. I.
* SHAFTESBURY, Prof. Archie D. Woman's College of the University of North Carolina,
    Greensboro, N. C., U. S. A. [Siphonaptera]
SHAHGUDIAN, Mr. Eugene R. Institute of Malariology, Teheran University, Teheran, Iran.
    [Diptera: Culicidae of Palearctic (Yes), of Oriental (No)]
* SHAJOVSKOY, Sergio S. Intendencia de Parques Nacionales, San Martin de los Andes, Argen-
    tina. [Lepidoptera]
SHANK, Dr. Max C. Biology Department, University of Illinois, Navy Pier, Chicago, Ill.,
    U. S. A. [Amphibia of e. N. America (Yes)]
SHANNON, Mrs. Ellen C. Box 276, Wickenburg, Ariz., U. S. A. [Up. Mesozoic Ammonoidea of
    Colombia & Peru (No)]
SHANNON, Dr. Frederick A. Box 276, Wickenburg, Ariz., U. S. A. [Reptilia & Amphibia of s. w.
    U. S., Mexico, China, Japan, Korea (Yes)]
* SHAPIRO, Dora S. Per Pokrowskii 8, kw. 50, Kharkov, U. S. S. R. [Coleoptera: Halticini]
SHAPIRO, Sidney. (Washington, D. C.; Pisces) Not now active in taxonomy.
* SHAPOSHNIKOV, Dr. G. Department of Entomology, Zoological Institute, Academy of Sciences
    of U. S. S. R., Leningrad-Centre, U. S. S. R. [Homoptera: Aphididae]
SHAPOVALOV, Leo. California Department of Fish & Game, 722 Capitol Avenue, Sacramento
    14, Calif., U. S. A. [F-w. & Anadromous Pisces of California (Yes)]
* SHARIF, Dr. M., Director, Zoological Laboratories, Government College, Lahore, Pakistan.
    [Siphonaptera]
SHAROV, Dr. A. G. Institute of Paleontology Academy of Sciences of U. S. S. R., Leninskij Pros-
    pect 33, Moscow V 71, U. S. S. R. [Thysanura of Palearctic (No); Paleozoic-Mesozoic
    Apterygota (Yes); Paleozoic-Mesozoic Orthopteroidea (Yes)]
SHAVER, Mr. R. H. Indiana Geological Survey, Indiana University, Bloomington, Ind., U. S. A.
    [Up. Paleozoic Ostracoda (Yes)]
SHAW, Dr. Alan B. Shell Oil Company, 1845 Sherman Street, Denver 3, Colo., U. S. A. [Cam-
    brian Trilobita (Yes); Mississippian-Permian Brachiopoda (Yes); Mississippian marine
    invertebrates (Yes)]
* SHAW, Mr. Charles E. 1025 Johnson Avenue, San Diego 3, Calif., U. S. A. [Reptilia]

SHAW, Dr. F. R. Fernald Hall, University of Massachusetts, Amherst, Mass., U.S.A.
    [Diptera: Mycetophilidae of New World (Yes); Sciaridae of Micronesia & New World
    (Yes)]
SHAW, S. Department of Natural History, Sheffield City Museum, Weston Park, Sheffield 10,
    England. [Coleoptera: Chrysomelidae: Cassidinae of World (Yes)]
SHAW, Prof. Tsen Hwang. Institute of Zoology, Academia Sinica, Peking (53), China. [Mam-
    malia of China (Yes); Aves of China (No)]
* SHAWHAN, Mrs. Fae M. Department of Biology, Drake University, Des Moines, Iowa,
    U.S.A. [Protozoa]
SHCHEDRINA, Z. G. Institute of Zoology, Academy of Sciences of U.S.S.R., Leningrad 164,
    U.S.S.R. [Recent Foraminifera of World (Yes)]
SHEALS, J. G. Ministry of Agriculture, Fisheries & Food, Woodthorne, Wolverhampton,
    Staffordshire, England. [Acarina: espec. soil species, of Europe (Yes)]
SHEARD, Dr. Keith. Division of Fisheries & Oceanography, Commonwealth Scientific & In-
    dustrial Research Organization, University Grounds, Nedlands, W. Australia. [Crustacea:
    Euphausiacea of all oceans (Yes); Amphipoda: Hyperiidea of Indo-Pacific (Yes); Gam-
    maridea of Indian Ocean (Yes); Decapoda: Palinuridae of all oceans (Yes)]
SHELJUZHKO, Leo. Zoologisches Sammlung der Bayerischen-Staates, München 38, Germany.
    [Macrolepidoptera of Palearctic]
* SHEN, Dr. C. J. Institute of Zoology, Academia Sinica, Haitien, Peking 53, China. [Crusta-
    cea: Decapoda]
SHENEFELT, Roy D. Department of Entomology, University of Wisconsin, Madison 6, Wis.,
    U.S.A. [Hymenoptera: Braconidae of World (No); of N. America (Yes)]
SHEPHERD, Dr. Audrey M. Rothamsted Experimental Station, Harpenden, Hertfordshire,
    England. [Nematoda: Heteroderidae: g. Heterodera of Britain (No)]
SHEPPARD, Arthur C. 5554 Coolbrook Avenue, Montreal 29, P.Q., Canada. [Lepidoptera:
    Macrolepidoptera of Quebec (Yes); Microlepidoptera of Quebec (No)]
SHEPPARD, Miss Edith. Department of Zoology, University College of South Wales, Cathays
    Park, Cardiff, Wales. [Marine Crustacea: Isopoda of Europe & Antarctic (Yes)]
SHEPPE, Walter, Jr. Department of Zoology, University of British Columbia, Vancouver,
    B.C., Canada. [Mammalia: Rodentia of w. N. America (No)]
SHER, Dr. S. A. Department of Plant Nematology, University of California, Riverside, Calif.,
    U.S.A. [Nematoda: Tylenchidae: Hoplolaiminae of World (Yes); Pratylenchinae of World
    (No)]
* SHERRIFFS, W. Rae. 27 Park Avenue, Portobello, Midlothian, Scotland. [Araneida]
SHEVTSHENKO, Valerij G.   Zoological Institute, Academy of Sciences of U.S.S.R., Lenin-
    grad 164, U.S.S.R. [Acarina: Acariformes: Tetrapodili of n. w. U.S.S.R. (Yes)]
SHEWELL, Mr. G. E. Insect Systematics & Biological Control Unit, Science Service Building,
    Ottawa, Ont., Canada. [Diptera Simuliidae of Holarctic (Yes); Lauxaniidae of World
    (Yes)]
* SHIBATA, Bunpei. Entomology Laboratory, University of Utsunomiya, Utsunomiya, Tochigi,
    Japan. [Homoptera: Aphididae]
SHIBATA, Yasuhiko. 1667 Higashi-Tarumi, Tarumi, Kobe, Japan. [Amphibia: Hynobiidae of
    Japan (Yes)]
* SHICHOBALOVA, Dr. N. P. Laboratory of Helminthology, Academy of Sciences of U.S.S.R.,
    Lenin Highway 33, Moscow B-71, U.S.S.R. [Platyhelminthes of animals of World]
SHIGEMATSU, A. Division of Health Care & Nursing, Faculty of Medicine, The University of
    Tokyo, 120 Zosigaya, Koisikawa, Tokyo, Japan. [Ciliata from intestine of Ophioplocus
    in Japan (Yes); Ciliata: marine Holotricha & Heterotricha of Setonaikai Bay of Tokyo,
    Japan (Yes)]
SHIINO, Prof. Dr. Sueo M. College of Fisheries, Mie Prefectural University, Otanicho 11, Tsu
    City, Mie Pref., Japan. [Crustacea: Copepoda: Caligoida, Lernaeopodoida, Ergasilioida,
    of Japan & Pacific (Yes); Isopoda: Epicaridea of Japan & Pacific (Yes); Cirripedia:
    Rhizocephala of Japan (Yes)]
SHIKAMA, Prof. Dr. Tokio. Geological Institute, Yokohama National University, Tateno 64,
    Naka-ku, Yokohama, Japan. [Fossil Mammalia: Proboscidea & Desmostylida of Japan
    (Yes); Pleistocene Carnivora & Ungulata of Japan (Yes)]
SHILLITO, Mr. James F. 48 Roebuck Lane, Buckhurst Hill, Essex, England. [Diptera: Diopsi-
    dae of World (Yes)] [National Leathersellers College]
* SHIMANSKY, V. N. Institute of Paleontology, Academy of Sciences of U.S.S.R., Leninskij
    Prospect 33, Moscow B-71, U.S.S.R. [Fossil Nautiloidea]
SHIMER, Hervey W. (Hingham, Mass.; fossils) Not now active in taxonomy.
SHINDO, Mr. Shigeaki. Seikai Regional Fisheries Research Laboratory, Maruo-mati 3-5,
    Nagasaki, Japan. [Pisces: g. Lepidotrigla of Yellow & E. China Seas (Yes)]
SHINJI, Orihei. (Tokyo, Japan; Aphidoidea) Deceased.
SHINN, A. F. Department of Entomology, University of Kansas, Lawrence, Kans., U.S.A.
    [Hymenoptera: Andrenidae: g. Calliopsis of N. & C. America (Yes)]

SHINNERS, Dr. Lloyd H. Herbarium, Southern Methodist University, Dallas 5, Texas, U.S.A. [Hymenoptera: Apoidea of Gulf s.w.U.S. (No)]

SHINODA, Prof. Osamu. Osaka University of Liberal Arts & Education, Ikeda City, Osaka, Japan. [Diptera: Phlebotominae of Japan (Yes) of Far East (No)]

SHINOHARA, K. Matsuyama Kôtô-Gakko, Higashi Matsuyama City, Saitama, Japan. [Chilopoda: Geophilomorpha & Scolopendromorpha of E. Asia & Micronesia (Yes); Lithobiomorpha: Lithobiidae & Henicopidae of E. Asia & Micronesia (Yes); Diplopoda: Polydesmidea of E. Asia & Micronesia (Yes)]

SHIPP, E. (Sydney, Australia: Diptera: Drosophila) Not now active in taxonomy.

SHIPWAY, Bruce. 8 Elizabeth Street, South Perth, Perth, Australia. [F-w. Pisces of W. Australia (Yes); f-w. Crustacea of W. Australia (Yes)]

SHIRAGA, Torao. Entomology Laboratory, (Okayama Agricultural Experiment Station), Okayama Kenitsu Nogyo Shikenjo, Okayama Pref., Japan. [Homoptera: Coccoidea of Japan (Yes)]

SHIRAISHI, Yoshikazu. Freshwater Fisheries Research Laboratory, Hino Machi, Minamitama Gun, Tokyo, Japan. [F-w. Pisces of Japan (Yes)]

SHIRAKI, Dr. Tokuichi. 20, 2 chome, Nagasaki, Toshima-ku, Tokyo, Japan. [Diptera: Syrphidae & Trypetidae of Asia, New Guinea, Philippines, Microneasia (Yes); Orthoptera of Japan, Ryukyu Is., Formosa (Yes); Dermaptera of Japan, Ryuku Is., Formosa (Yes)]

SHIRÔZU, Prof. Takashi. Biology Laboratory, Kyushu University, 1-chôme, Ôtsubo-machi, Fukuoka, Kyushu, Japan. [Lepidoptera: Rhopalocera of Japan, Korea, Manchuria, Loochoos, Formosa (Yes)]

SHISHOVA, N.A. Paleontological Institute, Academy of Sciences of U.S.S.R., Leninsky prospect 33, Moscow B-71, U.S.S.R. [Carboniferous & Permian Bryozoa of Moscow Basin & Ural Mts. (Yes)]

SHISHKIN, Dr. M.A. Paleontological Museum, Academy of Sciences of U.S.S.R, Leninsky Prospect 16, Moscow B-71, U.S.S.R. [Permian & Triassic Amphibia: Labyrinthodontia (Yes)]

* SHIVITSKIS, Akad. P.K. Veterinary and Cattle-Breeding Institute, Karolio-Pogelos Street 18, Vilnius, Lithuanian S.S.R. [Platyhelminths of animals of Lithuania]

* SHLUBSKY, Dr. Department of Fisheries, Jerusalem, Israel. [Pisces]

SHOEMAKER, Clarence R. U.S. National Museum, Washington 25, D.C., U.S.A. [Crustacea: Amphipoda of New World] Died December 28, 1958.

* SHOEMAKER, Ernest. (Brooklyn, N.Y.; Coleoptera) Died January 3, 1958.

SHOEMAKER, Prof. Hurst H. Vivarium Building, Wright & Healey Streets, Champaign, Ill., U.S.A. [Marine Pisces: Osteichthyes of Gulf of Mexico (Yes); f-w. Pisces of Illinois & Indiana (Yes)] [Natural History Museum, University of Illinois]

SHORT, Dr. J.R.T. Natural History Department, University of Aberdeen, Marischal College, Aberdeen, Scotland. [Hymenoptera: final instar larvae of Ichneumonidae of N. America & Europe (Yes); of Braconidae of Europe (Yes)]

SHORT, Lester L., Jr. Department of Conservation, Fernow Hall, Cornell University, Ithaca, N.Y., U.S.A. [Aves of World (Yes)]

SHORT, Dr. Robert B. Department of Biological Sciences, Florida State University, Tallahassee, Fla., U.S.A. [Trematoda: Schistosomatidae (No)]

SHOTWELL, Dr. J.A. Museum of Natural History, University of Oregon, Eugene, Ore., U.S.A. [Up. Tertiary Mammalia: Rodentia of N. America (Yes)]

SHOUMATOFF, Mr. Nicholas. Box 333, Bedford, N.Y., U.S.A. [Lepidoptera: Rhopalocera of Jamaica & Afghanistan (Yes)]

SHREVE, Benjamin. Museum of Comparative Zoology, Cambridge 38, Mass., U.S.A. [Amphibia & Reptilia of Neotropics (Yes)] [Harvard University]

SHROCK, Mr. R.R. (Cambridge, Mass.; fossils) Not now active in taxonomy.

SHUKLA, S.P. Zoological Survey of India, 34 Chittaranjan Avenue, Calcutta 12, India. [Coleoptera: Chrysomelidae of India, Burma, Ceylon (Yes)]

* SHULGA-NESTERENKO, M.I. Paleontological Institute, Academy of Sciences of U.S.S.R., Leninsky Prospect 33, Moscow W-71, U.S.S.R. [Fossil Invertebrates & Bryozoa]

* SHULMAN, S.S. Zoological Institute, Academy of Sciences of U.S.S.R., Leningrad B-164, U.S.S.R. [Platyhelminthes of man of U.S.S.R.]

SHULOV, Dr. Aharon. Department of Zoology, Hebrew University, Jerusalem, Israel. (Araneida: g. Entelegyne of Palestine (Yes); Scorpiones of Palestine (Yes)]

SHULZ, R.S. See Schulz, R.S.

* SHUMAKOVITCH, Dr. Prof. E.E. All-Union Skrjabin Institute of Helminthology, Staropansky 3, Moscow K-12, U.S.S.R. [Helminths of animals of World]

SHUSTER, Dr. Carl N., Jr. Department of Biological Science, University of Delaware, Newark, Del., U.S.A. [Fossil & Recent Xiphosura: Limulacea of N. America, Europe, Asia (Yes); Hirudinea of n.e.U.S. (Yes)]

* SHUTE, P.G. Malaria Reference Laboratory, Horton Hospital, Surrey, England. [Diptera]

SHUTO, Tsugio. Department of Geology, Kyushu University, Fukuoka, Japan. [Tertiary Pelecypoda & Gastropoda of w. Japan (Yes)]

SIBATANI, Prof. A. Cytochemistry Laboratory, Yamaguti Medical School, Nakaube, Ube, Yamaguti-ken, Japan. [Lepidoptera: Rhopalocera of e. & s.e. Asia (No)]
SIBLEY, Prof. Charles G. Fernow Hall, Cornell University, Ithaca, N.Y., U.S.A. [Aves of New World (Yes); bird hybrids of World (Yes)]
SIBSON, Mr. R.B. King's College, Otahuhu, Auckland, New Zealand. [Aves of New Zealand (Yes); Charadriiformes & Procellariiformes of s.w. Pacific (Yes)]
SICCARDI, Elvira. Museo Argentino de Ciencias Naturales, Angel Gallardo 470, Buenos Aires, Argentina. [Pisces: marine Elasmobranchii of Argentina (Yes)]
SICK, Dr. Helmut. Fundação Brasil Central, Av. Nilo Peçanha 23-III, Rio de Janeiro, Brazil. [Aves of s. America, espec. Brazil (Yes)]
SIDDIQUI, I.H. Pak Shell Oil Co. Ltd., Post Box 5011, Karachi 2, Pakistan. [Fossil Foraminifera of W. Pakistan (Yes)]
SIEBER, Prof. Dr. Rudolf. Paläontologisches Institute der Universität, Wien 1, Austria. [Paleozoic-Cenozoic Mollusca & Vertebrata of World (Yes); espec. Cenozoic of Europe]
SIEDER, Leo. St. Veiterring 35, Klagenfurt, Austria. [Lepidoptera: Psychidae of Europe (Yes)]
SIEGEL, Frederic. Department of Geology, University of Kansas, Lawrence, Kans., U.S.A. [Coelenterata: Anthozoa: Scleractinia: Recent Astrocoeniidae, Acroporidae, Agariciidae, Siderastreidae, Faviidae, Montastreidae, Meandrinidae, of Florida Reef Area (Yes)]
SIEKER, William E. 119 Monona Avenue, Madison 3, Wis., U.S.A. [Lepidoptera: Sphingidae, espec. g. Sphinx (Hyloicus), of World (Yes)]
SIENKIEWICZ, Ing. I. Muzeu de Istorie Naturală "Grigore Antipa", Sosea Kiselev 1, Bucureşti III, Rumania. [Heteroptera of Palearctic (No); Geocorisae of Central Europe (Yes); Hydrocorisae (No); eggs & larvae of Rumania (No)]
SIEVERTS-DORECK, Dr. Hertha. Reichenberger Strasse 12, Stuttgart-Möhringen, Germany. [Mesozoic & Tertiary Crinoidea Articulata of World (Yes)] [Staatliches Museum für Naturkunde, Stuttgart]
SIEWING, Dr. Rolf. Zoologisches Institut, Hegewischstrasse 3, Kiel, Germany. [Crustacea: Syncarida & Microcerberidae of World (Yes); Polychaeta: Pisionidae of World (Yes)]
SIGAL, Jacques. 33 rue de Montreuil, Vincennes (Seine), France. [Mesozoic & Cenozoic Foraminifera (Yes)] [Institute Français du Petrole]
SIIVONEN, Dr. Lauri. Finnish Game Foundation, Unionink. 45 B, Helsinki, Finland. [Mammalia of n.w. Europe (Yes); Oligochaeta: Lumbricidae of n.w. Europe (No)] [Game Research Institute]
SILAS, Dr. E.G. Central Marine Fisheries Research Station, Mandapam Camp, S. India. [Marine Pisces of Indian Ocean & Pacific Ocean (Yes); f-w. Pisces of s.e. Asia (Yes); marine Mammalia of Indian Ocean (Yes); Amphibia of India (Yes)]
SILBERLING, Dr. Norman J. U.S. Geological Survey, 4 Homewood Place, Menlo Park, Calif., U.S.A. [Triassic marine Invertebrates of World (Yes)]
SILÉN, Prof. Lars. Zootomiska Institutet, Stockholms Högskola Rådmansgatan 70 A, Stockholm, Sweden. [Marine Bryozoa of World (No); Phoronidea of World (Yes); Enteropneusta of Europe (No)]
ŠILHAVÝ, Dr. Vladimir. Stařeč u Třebiče, Czechoslovakia. [Opiliones of Europe (Yes); Araneida of c. Europe (Yes); Hymenoptera: Formicidae of c. Europe (Yes)]
SILLMAN, E.I. Department of Zoology, University of Manitoba, Winnipeg, Man., Canada. [Trematoda: Azygiidae & Opisthorchidae of World (Yes)]
de SILVA, Dr. P.H.D. Department of Zoology, Department of National Museums, P.O. Box 854, Colombo 7, Ceylon. [Polychaeta: Serpulidae: Spirorbinae of World (Yes); Hirudinea: marine Piscicolidae of World (Yes); Pisces, Amphibia, Reptilia, of Asia (Yes)]
da SILVA CRUZ, Maria Amelia. Quinta de S. João, Candal - V.N. de Gaia, Portugal. [Lepidoptera: Rhopalocera of Portugal; Heterocera of n. & c. Portugal (No)]
da SILVA RAMOS, Dr. Alberto. Servicio Profilaxia Malaria, Caixa Postal 2543, São Paulo, Brazil. [Diptera (No)]
da SILVA SANTOS, Dr. Rubens. Secção de Paleontologia, Divisão de Geologia e Mineralogia, Departamento Nacional da Produção Mineral, Avenida Pasteur 404, Praia Vermelha, Rio de Janeiro, Brazil. [Mesozoic & Cenozoic Pisces: Holostei & Teleostei: Isopondyli of Brazil (Yes)]
* SIMMONS, Mr. Ernest G. 4417 Ramsey, Corpus Christi, Texas, U.S.A. [Fossil fish otoliths]
SIMMONS, K.E.L. 50 Roslyn Road, Woodley, Reading, Berks, England. [Aves: Passeriformes of World, espec. Palearctic (Yes); Podicipitiformes of same (Yes)]
SIMON, Prof. A. 13 rue Arsene Meunier, Evreux (Eure), France. [Coleoptera: Cerambycidae of France, Britain, Italy, Spain, N. Africa (Yes); of Quebec, Canada (No)]
* SIMON, James R. 2352 Olympus Drive, Salt Lake City 7, Utah, U.S.A. [F-w. Pisces of Rocky Mts., U.S.A.]
SIMON, Dr. Ludwig K. Josef-Frankl-Strasse 58, München-Feldmoching, Germany. [Plant parasitic Nematoda of c. Europe (No); Porifera: Spongillidae of c. Europe (Yes)]
* SIMONET, Dr. Jean. Avenue Henri Golay 9, Chatelaine-Genève, Switzerland. [Hemiptera]
SIMONS, Dr. Elwyn L., Assistant Professor of Zoology, Division of Biology, University of Pennsylvania, Philadelphia 4, Penna., U.S.A. [Cenozoic Mammalia: Primates of World (Yes); Pantodonta of N. America, Europe, Asia (Yes)]

343

SIMONSON, Russell R. Paleontology Laboratory, The Ohio Oil Co., 550 South Flower Street, Los Angeles 17, Calif., U.S.A. [Fossil Invertebrates]
SIMPSON, Dr. G.G. Museum of Comparative Zoology, Cambridge 38, Mass., U.S.A. [Fossil Mammalia of World (No); Recent Mammalia chiefly genera of World (No)]
SIMPSON, James C. Idaho Fish & Game Department, 518 Front Street, Boise, Idaho, U.S.A. [Pisces of intermountain Pacific Northwest U.S. (Yes)]
SIMPSON, Prof. Scott. Geology Department, The University, Exeter, England. [L. Devonian Brachiopoda of Europe (Yes); fossil tracks, burrows, etc. (trace-fossils) of Europe (Yes)]
SIMS, Mr. R.W. British Museum (Natural History), Cromwell Road, London, S.W.7, England. [Aves of Oriental & Australasian (Yes)]
* SINCLAIR, Dr. G. Winston. Geological Survey of Canada, Ottawa, Ont., Canada. [Fossil Echinodermata]
* SINCLAIR, Mr. H., Curator, Southsea Aquarium, 174 Prince Albert Road, Milton, Southsea, Hants, England. [Amphibia, Reptilia, Pisces]
SINCLAIR, Ralph M. 4303 Dale Avenue, Nashville 4, Tenn., U.S.A. [Amphibia: Caudata of e.U.S. (Yes)]
SINGER, Dr. R. Anatomy Department, University of Cape Town Medical School, Mowbray, Union of South Africa. [Mammalia: Primates: Hominoidea of Africa (Yes); Quaternary Carnivora, Perissodactyla, Artiodactyla: Giraffidae, Bovidae, Elephantidae, of S. Africa (Yes)]
SINGH, S.N., Palaeontologist, Central Laboratories, Oil & Natural Gas Commission, 19 Rajpur Road, Dehra Dun, India. [Tertiary larger Foraminifera & Ostracoda of India (Yes); smaller Foraminifera: Planorbulinidae, Miliolidae, Lagenidae, Nonionidae, Rotalidae, Amphisteginidae, Calcarinidae, of India (Yes)]
* SINGLETON, O.P. Department of Geology, University of Melbourne, Melbourne, Vict., Australia. [Fossils]
SINHA, Dr. R.N. Entomology Section, Canada Agricultural Research Laboratory, Box 322, University of Manitoba, Winnipeg 9, Man., Canada. [Hymenoptera: Megachilidae, g. Osmia of World, espec. New World (No); Homoptera: Cicadellidae of N. America (No)]
SINHA, T.B. Zoology Department, T.D. College, Jaunpore, India. [Acarina: Trombiculidae & Laelaptidae of India (Yes)]
SISOJEVIČ, Ing. Pelagija. Biološki Institut, 29 Novembra 100, Beograd, Yugoslavia. [Diptera: Tachinidae of Europe (No)]
SIVERLY, Russell E. Science Department, Ball State Teachers College, Muncie, Ind., U.S.A. [Diptera: Muscidae & Calliphoridae of N. America (No)]
SIVERSTEN, Dr. E., Director, Museum det Kgl. Norske Videnskabers Selskab, Trondheim, Norway. [Crustacea: Decapoda & Isopoda of Arctic & Antarctic (No); f-w. Pisces of Norway (No); Mammalia: seals of Arctic & Antarctic (No)]
SIVIK, Frank P. Gamble Hall, Armstrong College, Savannah, Ga., U.S.A. [Hymenoptera: Apidae & Anthophoridae of Oriental, Ethiopian, Palearctic]
SJÖBERG, O. (Falun, Sweden; Coleoptera) Died June 15, 1959.
* SKALKIN, V.A. Marine Biological Station, South Sakhalin, U.S.S.R. [Echinodermata]
SKALON, O.I. Parasitological Laboratory, Sovietskaya 13-15, Stavropol, Caucasus, U.S.S.R. [Siphonaptera of U.S.S.R. & Mongolia (Yes); Thysanoptera of U.S.S.R. (No)]
SKARBILOVICH, Mrs. T.S. All-Union Institute of Helminthology, Staropansky 3, Moscow K-12, U.S.S.R. [Nematoda of plants of U.S.S.R. (Yes)]
SKEAD, C.J. Kaffrarian Museum, 3 Lower Albert Road, King Williams Town, Union of South Africa. [Aves of e. Cape Prov., S. Africa (Yes)]
SKINNER, Mr. Frank E. 1050 San Pablo Avenue, Albany 6, Calif., U.S.A. [Hymenoptera: Encyrtidae of World (No)] [University of California, Department of Biological Control]
SKINNER, Prof. Hubert C. 7307 St. Charles Avenue, New Orleans 18, La., U.S.A. [Up. Cretaceous & Miocene Foraminifera (Yes); Up. Cretaceous Ostracoda (Yes)] [Tulane University of Louisiana]
SKINNER, Mr. J.W. Humble Oil & Refining Co., Box 1600, Midland, Texas, U.S.A. [Pennsylvanian & Permian Foraminifera: Fusulinidae of N. America, Europe, Asia (Yes)]
SKINNER, Morris F. Frick Laboratory, American Museum of Natural History, New York 24, N.Y., U.S.A. [Pleistocene Mammalia: bison of World (Yes); Up. Tertiary Equidae of World (Yes)]
SKOLNICK, Dr. Herbert. Western Gulf Oil Co., 826 E. Main Street, Ventura, Calif., U.S.A. [Cretaceous Foraminifera: Lituolidae of Black Hills, Nebraska (Yes)]
SKOPIN, Docent N.G. Institut de Zoologie, Université d'Etat de Kazachstan, rue Kirova 136, Alma-Ata, Kazakh, S.S.R. [Coleoptera: Tenebrionidae, larvae of World (Yes), adults of c. Asia (No)]
SKREEN, Mr. E. P.O. Box 9, Bondi, N.S.W., Australia. [Lepidoptera: Rhopalocera of Australia (No)]
* SKRJABIN, Akad. Dr. K.I., Vice-President of the All-Union Lenin Academy of Agricultural .Sciences, B. Charitonjevsky 21, Moscow, U.S.S.R. [Platyhelminthes & Nematoda of animals & man of World]

SKUHRAVÁ, Mrs. Marcela. Entomolog. Laboratoř Československá Akademie Věd, Viničná 7, Praha II, Czechoslovakia. [Diptera: Itonididae of Europe (Yes)]

SKURATOWICZ, Dr. W. Zakład Zoologii Systematycznej, Uniwersytetu, A. Mickiewicza, ul. Fredry 10, Poznań, Poland. [Siphonaptera of c. & e. Europe (Yes); Mammalia of Poland (Yes)]

* SKVORTSOV, Dr. Prof. A. A. All-Union Helminthological Society, Academy of Sciences of U. S. S. R, Moscow, U. S. S. R. [Platyhelminthes of animals of U. S. S. R.]

* SLACK, Dr. H. D. Department of Zoology, The University, Glasgow W. 2, Scotland. [Pisces]

SLÁDEČEK, Dr. Vladimir, Lecturer in Hydrobiology, Department of Water Technology, Trojanova 13, Praha 2, Czechoslovakia. [Crustacea: f-l., f-w. Cladocera of Europe (Yes); f-l., f-w. Copepoda of Europe (No); f-l., f-w. Rotatoria of Europe (No)]

SLASTENENKO, Prof. Dr. E. P. 827 Manning Avenue, Toronto 4, Ont., Canada. [Pisces of Black Sea & Europe (Yes); Salmonidae: g. Salvelinus & Cristivomer of Canada (Yes)]

SLATER, Charles P. 7430 Village Drive, Prairie Village, Kans., U. S. A. [Lepidoptera Rhopalocera of c. & e. U. S. (Yes); Nymphalidae: g. Nymphalis & Vanessa of U. S. (Yes); Nymphalidae: g. Limenitis, Precis, Lethe, & Danaidae: g. Danaus, of Canada (Yes)]

SLATER, James A. Department of Zoology & Entomology, University of Connecticut, Storrs, Conn., U. S. A. [Heteroptera: Lygaeidae of World (No), of N. America & Africa (Yes); Miridae of e. N. America (No)]

SLATER, James R. 4801 N. 26th Street, Tacoma 7, Wash., U. S. A. [Amphibia & Reptilia of Pacific Northwest U. S. (Yes)] [College of Puget Sound]

SLEEPER, David A. Department of Entomology, Cornell University, Ithaca, N. Y., U. S. A. [Diptera: Simuliidae of Alaska & e. U. S. (No); Muscoidea of U. S. (No)]

SLEEPER, Elbert L. Department of Biological Sciences, Long Beach State College, Long Beach 15, Calif., U. S. A. [Coleoptera: Curculionoidea, excl. Scolytidae, of World (No); of New World, Philippines, Japan (Yes)]

* SLEVIN, J. R. (San Francisco, Calif.; Reptilia) Deceased.

SLIJPER, Prof. Dr. E. J. Zoological Laboratory, 44 Plantage Doklaan Amsterdam-C, Netherlands. [Mammalia: Cetacea of World (Yes)] [University of Amsterdam]

* van der SLIK, L. Berkendaal 56, Rotterdam, Netherlands. [Pliocene-Pleistocene marine Mollusca of Netherlands]

SLIPKA, Dr. J. Institute of Histology & Embryology, Faculty of Medicine, Charles University, Plzeň-Lochotin, Czechoslovakia. [Diptera: Tipulidae of c. Europe (Yes)]

SLOAN, Prof. Robert E. Department of Geology, University of Minnesota, Minneapolis 14, Minn., U. S. A. [Ordovician & Pennsylvanian Mollusca of c. U. S. (Yes)]

* SLOOTWEG, Dr. A. F. G. Address unknown. [Nematoda]

* SLUD, Mr. Paul. Museum of Zoology, University of Michigan, Ann Arbor, Mich., U. S. A. [Aves]

SLUITER, Dr. J. W. Zoological Laboratory, University of Utrecht, Janskerhof 3, Netherlands. [Mammalia: Chiroptera of w. Europe (Yes)]

ŚLUSARSKI, Dr. Wiesław. Zakład Parazytologii, Polska Akademia Nauk, ul. Pasteura 3, Warszawa 22, Poland. [Trematoda: Allocreadiidae of f-w. Pisces of Europe; Opecoelidae of f-w. Pisces of Europe; Fasciolidae of World]

SMALL, Eugene B. 1089 1/2 Strathmore Drive, Los Angeles 24, Calif., U. S. A. [Protozoa: Suctoria: Dendrocometidae of Holarctic (Yes); Discophryidae (Yes)] [University of California]

SMART, Dr. John. Department of Zoology, University of Cambridge, Downing Street, Cambridge, England. [Diptera: Simuliidae of World (No); of New Guinea region (Yes)]

* SMEDLEY, Derek N. 19 Neale Street, Ipswich, England. [Coleoptera]

* SMEDLEY, John Elwood. Room 332, U. S. National Museum, Washington 25, D. C. , U. S. A. [Fossils]

SMETANA, Dr. Aleš. Biologicky ústav Parasitologie, Československá Akademie Věd, Na cvičišti 21, Praha 6, Czechoslovakia. [Coleoptera: Staphylinidae of Palearctic (Yes)]

* SMIDT, Dr. E. Grøulands Fiskeriuwersøgelseg, Charlottenlund Slot, Denmark. [Crustacea: Copepoda]

* SMIRNOVA, M. A. Institute of Geology of Arctica, Moika 120, Leningrad, U. S. S. R. [Silurian & Devonian Anthozoa: Tabulata]

SMIT, Mr. F. G. A. M. The Zoological Museum, Tring, Herts, England. [Siphonaptera of World (Yes)]

SMITH, Mr. A. 10 Stanley Street, Pascoe Vale, Vict. , Australia. [Coleoptera of Australian (No); Lepidoptera of World (No)]

SMITH, A. B. Department of Geology, University of Washington, Seattle, Wash. , U. S. A. [Miocene-Recent marine Gastropoda & Pelecypoda of N. America (No)]

* SMITH, Albert G. Department of Zoology, Loyola University, 6526 Sheridan Road, Chicago 26, Ill. , U. S. A. [Reptilia]

SMITH, Mr. Allyn G. 722 Santa Barbara Road, Berkeley 7, Calif. , U. S. A. [Terr. , marine & f-w. Mollusca of Pacific Cst. U. S. (Yes); Recent & Fossil Polyplacophora (Yes)] [California Academy of Sciences, San Francisco]

SMITH, Mr. Baxter L. Sun Oil Company, Box 850, Jackson, Miss. , U. S. A. [Fossil Invertebrates & Foraminifera of Gulf Coast U. S. (No)]

SMITH, Dr. Clyde F. North Carolina State College, Raleigh, N. C. , U. S. A. [Homoptera: Aphidae of World (Yes); Aphidiinae of N. America (Yes)]

SMITH, Clarence Lavett, Jr. Fish Division, Museum of Zoology, University of Michigan, Ann Arbor, Mich. , U. S. A. [Shore Pisces, espec. Serranidae, of West Indies (Yes)]

SMITH, Dr. Carroll N. Entomology Research Division, U. S. Department of Agriculture, P. O. Box 3391, Orlando, Fla. , U. S. A. [Acarina: Ixodidae & Argasidae of N. America (No)]

SMITH, Mr. Denver Jeter. Gulf Oil Corporation, 5311 Kirby Drive, Houston 5, Texas, U. S. A. [Tertiary marine Foraminifera & Ostracoda, Eocene Anthozoa, Oligocene Coelenterata, Cretaceous & Tertiary Echinoidea, Tertiary Scaphopoda, Pelecypoda, Gastropoda; all of Gulf Coast U. S. (Yes)]

SMITH, D. S. Canada Agriculture Research Station, Lethbridge, Alta. , Canada. [Orthoptera: Acrididae of w. Canada (Yes)]

SMITH, Mrs. E. P. O. Box 74, Halfmoon Bay, Stewart Island, New Zealand. [Mollusca: g. Notosetia of Stewart Island, New Zealand (No)]

SMITH, Edgar A. USOM/Indonesia, c/o State Department Mail Room, Washington 25, D. C. , U. S. A. [Arthropoda of medical importance of Indonesia (No); Lepidoptera of World (No)] [U. S. P. H. S. , Malaria Institute, Djakarta]

SMITH, Mr. E. T. 22 Talmage Street, Sunshine, Vict. , Australia. [Coleoptera: Heteromera of Australia (No); Anthicidae of Australia (Yes)]

SMITH, F. G. Walton. (Miami, Fla. ; corals, insects) Not now active in taxonomy.

SMITH, Mrs. Hermon Dunlap. 121 Stone Gate Road, Lake Forest, Ill. , U. S. A. [Aves]. [Chicago Natural History Museum]

SMITH, Dr. Harry M. 215 S. White Street, Macomb, Ill. , U. S. A. [Aves of Burma, s. e. Asia, e. Mediterranean (Yes)]

SMITH, Dr. Hobart M. Department of Zoology, University of Illinois, Urbana, Ill. , U. S. A. [Amphibia & Reptilia of Mexico (Yes)]

SMITH, Hugh Preston. (Salt Lake City, Utah; fossils) Not now active in taxonomy.

SMITH, Dr. Howard W. Department of Entomology, University of Idaho, Moscow, Idaho, U. S. A. [Diptera: Sepsidae of World (Yes)]

SMITH, J. D. D. · Department of Paleontology, Geological Survey, Exhibition Road, London, S. W. 7, England. [L. Paleozoic Invertebrates of Britain (No)]

SMITH, Mrs. Jane E. Inch. Department of Geology, Michigan State University, East Lansing, Mich. , U. S. A. [Paleozoic Ostracoda (No)]

SMITH, Prof. J. L. B. Ichthyology Department, Rhodes University, Grahamstown, Union of South Africa. [Marine Pisces of Indian, w. & c. Pacific, s. e. Atlantic Oceans (Yes)]

SMITH, Mr. Kenneth G. V. Hope Department of Entomology, University Museum, Oxford, England. [Diptera: Brachycera & Acalypterae of Britain (Yes); Conopidae of World (Yes); Empididae of Europe, Australia, S. America (No)]

SMITH, Dr. Lois K. Division of Entomology, Canada Department of Agriculture, Science Service Building, Ottawa, Ont. , Canada. [Hymenoptera: Ichneumonidae of N. America (Yes)]

SMITH, Prof. Leslie M. Department of Entomology, University of California, Davis, Calif. , U. S. A. [Diplura: Japygidae & Projapygidae of New World (Yes)]

* SMITH, Dr. Maxwell. Box 8295, Asheville, N. C. , U. S. A. [Mollusca]

* SMITH, M. Eugene. Route 2, Newnan, Ga., U.S.A. [Odonata]
SMITH, Malcolm A. (London, England; Amphibia & Reptilia). Not now active in taxonomy.
SMITH, Dr. Marion E. Fernald Hall, University of Massachusetts, Amherst, Mass., U.S.A.
    [Diptera: Culicidae of N. America (No); Lepidoptera: Arctiidae, espec. g. Apantesis of
    N. America (Yes)]
SMITH, Marvin L. Shell Oil Company, 2005 Alamo National Building, San Antonio, Texas,
    U.S.A. [Devonian Ostracoda of New York (Yes)]
SMITH, Dr. M. R. Division of Insects, U.S. National Museum, Washington 25, D.C., U.S.A.
    [Hymenoptera: Formicidae of New World, espec. N. America (Yes)]
SMITH, Philip W. Illinois Natural History Survey, Urbana, Ill., U.S.A. [Reptilia & Amphibia
    of c. U.S. (Yes)]
SMITH, Prof. Ralph Albert. 2455 Westgate Avenue, San Jose 25, Calif., U.S.A. [Reptilia:
    Chelonia & Crocodilia of New World (Yes)] [San Jose State College]
SMITH, R. C. (Manhattan, Kans.; Neuroptera & Mecoptera) Not now active in taxonomy.
SMITH, Ronald E., Chairman, Biology Department, Buena Vista College, Storm Lake, Iowa,
    U.S.A. [Mammalia: Sciuridae: g. Cynomys of N. America (Yes)]
SMITH, Dr. Ray F. Department of Entomology, University of California, Berkeley 4, Calif.,
    U.S.A. [Coleoptera: Chrysomelidae: g. Diabrotica & Acalymma of C. & S. America (No);
    of Mexico & U.S. (Yes)]
SMITH, Roland F. (Milltown, N. J.; Copepoda) Not now active in taxonomy.
SMITH, Septima Cecilia. (University, Ala.; Invertebrates) Not now active in taxonomy.
SMITH, Vera Irwin. (Woolwich, Australia; Diptera) Not now active in taxonomy.
* SMITH, Mr. V. T. H. 20 Southway Street, Yallourn, Vict., Australia. [Lepidoptera]
SMITH, Mrs. Verna Z. (St. Andrews, Canada; Ostracoda) Died July 24, 1956.
SMITH, Mr. W. A. Department of Zoology, British Museum (Natural History), Cromwell Road,
    London, S.W.7, England. [Crustacea: Copepoda: Cyclopoida & Calanoida of Britain (Yes)]
* SMITH, Willard Newell. Address unknown. [Parasites of bats of e. U.S.]
SMITHERS, Courtenay N. The Australian Museum, College Street, Sydney, N.S.W., Australia.
    [Psocoptera & Neuroptera: Sisyridae of Africa (Yes)]
SMITHERS, R. H. N. National Museum of Southern Rhodesia, P.O. Box 240, Bulawayo, Southern
    Rhodesia. [Aves & Mammalia of c. Africa (Yes)]
SMITTER, Dr. Yvor H. 4 Retreat Avenue, Kingston 6, Jamaica. [Cretaceous, Tertiary,
    Recent smaller Foraminifera of s. Africa & Caribbean (Yes)]
SMOUT, Dr. A. H. Paleontology Laboratory, Iraq Petroleum Co. Ltd., 214 Oxford Street,
    London, W.1, England. [Fossil Foraminifera of Middle East (Yes); fossil Ostracoda of
    Middle East (No)]
SMRECZYNSKI, Prof. Dr. S. Institut de Zoologie, Sw. Anny 6, Krakow, Poland. [Recent &
    Pleistocene Coleoptera: Curculionidae of c. Europe (Yes)]
SMYTHIES, B. E. C/o Forest Department, Kuching, Sarawak, British North Borneo. [Aves of
    Borneo & Burma (No)]
ŠNAJDR, Dr. Milan. Ústřední geologický úrad, Lazarská 7, Praha II, Czechoslovakia. [Cam-
    brian-Carboniferous Trilobita of U.S.S.R. & Czechoslovakia (Yes); Ordovician-Devonian
    Ostracoda of Czechoslovakia (Yes); Paleozoic Polychaeta: Errantia of Czechoslovakia
    (Yes); Scolecodonta of Czechoslovakia & U.S.S.R. (Yes)]
SNELLING, R. R. Route 4, Box 430, Turlock, Calif., U.S.A. [Hymenoptera: social Vespidae,
    espec. g. Polistes, of N. & C. America (Yes); Anthophoridae: g. Centris of N. & C.
    America (Yes)]
SNOW, D. W. New York Zoological Society Field Station, Simla, Arima Valley, Trinidad. [Aves:
    Paridae of World, excl. Neotropics & Australasia (Yes); Pipridae of Neotropics (No)]
SNOW, Willis E. (Wilson Dam, Tenn.; Diptera & Coleoptera). Died June 12, 1959.
SNYDER, Charles Theodore. (Salt Lake City, Utah; fossil vertebrates) Not now active in
    taxonomy.
SNYDER, Dr. D. P. Department of Zoology, University of Massachusetts, Amherst, Mass.,
    U.S.A. [Mammalia: Sciuridae: g. Tamias of e. N. America (Yes)]
SNYDER, Dr. Fred M. 8405 Loch Raven Boulevard, Towson 4, Md., U.S.A. [Diptera: Musci-
    dae, Anthomyiidae, Scatophagidae, of World (Yes)]
SNYDER, Mr. L. L. Department of Ornithology, Royal Ontario Museum, 100 Queen's Park,
    Toronto 5, Ont., Canada. [Aves of Canada (Yes)]
SNYDER, Dr. Richard C. Department of Zoology, University of Washington, Seattle 5, Wash.,
    U.S.A. [Reptilia of w. cst. U.S. (No); Amphibia: salamanders of w. cst. U.S. (No)]
* SOAREC-TANASACHI, Jana. See TANASACHI, J.
* SOARES, Prof. Benedito. Escola Nacional de Agronomia, Caixa Postal 25, Rio de Janeiro,
    Brazil. [Araneida & Opiliones of Neotropics; Coleoptera: Cleridae & Brenthidae of
    Brazil]
SOBELS, Prof. Dr. F. H. Laboratorium voor Stralengenetica der Rijksuniversiteit te Leiden,
    Wassenaarseweg 60, Leiden, Netherlands. [Diptera: g. Drosophila of w. Europe (Yes)]
* SOBOLEV, Prof. A. A. Vladivostok State University, Vladivostok, U.S.S.R. [Nematoda of
    animals of World]

SOCHUREK, Erich. Hetzgasse 42/10, Wien III/40, Austria. [Amphibia & Reptilia of Europe, w. Asia, n. Africa, e. U. S. (Yes)]
SOCIN, Prof. C. Istituto Geologico, Palazzo Carignano, Torino (209), Italy. [Tertiary Mollusca & Up. Tertiary Foraminifera of n. Italy (Yes)]
SOEHARDJAN, - . Institute for Plant Diseases & Pests, Bogor, Indonesia. [Corrodentia of Indomalaya (No)]
* SOESER, F. Department of Vertebrate Zoology, University of Istanbul, Istanbul, Turkey. [Pisces]
* SOETERSDAL, G. Institute of Marine Research, Box 189, Bergen, Norway. [Pisces]
SOFFNER, J. Hohenerxlebener Strasse 31, (19b) Stassfurt, German Democratic Republic. [Lepidoptera: Pyralidae; Phycitinae of c. Europe (Yes)]
* SOGANDARES B., Franklin. 924 Lowerline Street, New Orleans 18, La., U. S. A. [Mammalia of C. America]
SOHL, Dr. Norman F. Room 331, U. S. National Museum, Washington 25, D. C., U. S. A. [Mesozoic Gastropoda of N. America (Yes)] [U. S. Geological Survey]
SOHN, Mr. I. G. U. S. Geological Survey, Washington 25, D. C., U. S. A. [Up. Paleozoic-Recent Ostracoda (Yes)]
SOIKA, A. Giordani. See GIORDANI-SOIKA, A.
SOKANOVSKY, B. V. Polevoj proezd 6, Moscov Gouvernem., Pushkino, U. S. S. R. [Coleoptera: Ipidae of Palearctic (Yes)]
SOKOL, Otto M. Zoologisches Institut der Universität, 1 Dr. Karl Lueger-Ring, Wien I, Austria. [Amphibia of World (No)]
* SOKOLOFF, Dr. Demetrio. Instituto de Biologia, Ciudad Universitaria, Villa Obregon 20, D. F., Mexico. [Nematoda, Trematoda]
SOKOLOV, Prof. B. S. Paleontological Laboratory, Wsesoyuzny Neftyanoy Nauchno-Issledovatelsky Geologo-Rasvedochny Institut (WNIGRI), Liteiny 39, Leningrad 104, U. S. S. R. [Paleozoic Anthozoa: Tabulata: Heliolitidae & Chaetetidae of U. S. S. R. (Yes)]
SOKOLOV, Dr. I. I. Institute of Cytology, Academy of Sciences of U. S. S. R., Prospect Maklina 52, Leningrad F 121, U. S. S. R. [Acarina: Hydracarina of U. S. S. R. (No)]
SOKOLOV, Dr. Ivan I. Zoological Institute, Academy of Sciences of U. S. S. R., Leningrad B-164, U. S. S. R. [Fossil Mammalia: Perissodactyla: Equidae of Europe & Asia (Yes); Artiodactyla: Bovidae of Europe & Asia (Yes); Cervidae of Europe & Asia (No)]
* SOKOLOWSKI, Kurt. Steenwisch 103 P, Hamburg-Stellingen, Germany. [Coleoptera]
SOKOŁOWSKI, Dr. Jan Bogumił. Zakład Zoologii, Wyzsza Szkoła Rolnicza, ul Wojska Polskiego 71c, Poznań, Poland. [Aves & Orthoptera of Poland (Yes)]
* SOKOLSKAJA, N. L. Zoological Museum, Moscow State University, Gertzena 6, Moscow K 9, U. S. S. R. [Oligochaeta]
SOKOLSKAYA, A. N. Paleontological Institute, Academy of Sciences, Leninskyi prospect 33, Moscow B-71, U. S. S. R. [Devonian-Permian Brachiopoda: Strophomenida, Chonetidae, Syringothyridae, of U. S. S. R. (Yes)]
SOLARI, Dr. Ferdinando. (Genova, Italy; Coleoptera) Died April, 1956.
SOLEM, Dr. G. Alan. Chicago Natural History Museum, Chicago 5, Ill., U. S. A. [Non-marine Mollusca of Pacific Ocean, Indonesia, New World (Yes)]
* SOLJAN, Univ. Prof. Dr. Tonko. Vase Miskina 16/III, Sarajevo, Yugoslavia. [Pisces]
SOLLAUD, Prof. Dr. E. Laboratoire de Zoologie de la Faculté des Sciences, 16, Quai Claude Bernard, Lyon, France. [Crustacea: Decapoda Natantia of North Sea, cst. of France, Spain, Portugal, Mediterranean (Yes)]
SOLLE, Prof. Dr. Gerhard. Institut für Geologie u. Technische Gesteinskunde, Technischen Hochschule, Alexanderstrasse 35, Darmstadt, Germany. [L. & M. Devonian Brachiopoda: Orthacea, Strophomenacea, Spiriferacea, of Germany & w. Europe (No)]
* SOLOMON, M. E., Officer in Charge, Biology Section, Department of Scientific & Industrial Research, Pest Infestation Laboratory, London Road, Slough, Bucks, England. [Acarina]
* SOŁTYS, Dr. Edward. Zakład Zoologie Systematycznej, Universytet Mikołaja Kopernika, ul. Danielewskiego 6, Toruń, Poland. [Lepidoptera]
van SOMEREN, Mrs. E. C. C. Medical Research Laboratory, P. O. Box 141, Nairobi, Kenya. [Diptera: Culicidae: Anophelini, Megarhinini: g. Toxorhynchites, Culicini, of trop. Africa (Yes)]
SØMME, Dr. Sven. Tøndergaard, Molde, Norway. [Odonata & f-w. Pisces of Scandinavia (No)]
SOMMERMAN, Dr. Kathryn M. Arctic Health Research Center, P. O. Box 960, Anchorage, Alaska, U. S. A. [Psocoptera of N. America (Yes); Diptera: Simuliidae of Alaska (Yes)]
van SON, Dr. G. Transvaal Museum, P. O. Box 413, Pretoria, Union of South Africa. [Lepidoptera: Rhopalocera of s. Africa (Yes)]
SONDERUP, H. P. S. (Lemvig, Denmark; Lepidoptera) Deceased.
SOÓS, Dr. Á. Magyar Nemzeti Muzeum Állattára, Baross-u. 13, Budapest VIII, Hungary. [Homoptera: Fulgoroidea of Europe (Yes)]
SOÓS, Dr. Lajos. Kanizsai utca 13, Budapest XI, Hungary. [Gastropoda: Pulmonata of Palearctic (No)] [Magyar Nemzeti Muzeum Allattára]

SOOTA, Mr. T. D. Invertebrate Section, Zoological Survey of India, 34 Chittaranjan Avenue, Calcutta 12, India. [Nematoda of India (Yes); Acanthocephala of India (Yes); f-w. Porifera of India (Yes)]

SOOT-RYEN, Helen (Rost). Zoological Museum, Sarsgatan 1, Oslo, Norway. [Pelecypoda: Arcidae of World (No); of America (Yes)]

SOOT-RYEN, T., Director, Zoological Museum, Sarsgatan 1, Oslo 47, Norway. [Pelecypoda: Mytilidae (No)]

* SORIANO-SEÑORANS, Juan. Departamento de Vertebrados, Museo de Historia Natural, Casilla de Correo 399, Montevideo, Uruguay. [Pisces of Atlantic Cst. of S. America]

SORNAY, Dr. J. Laboratoire de Paléontologie du Muséum, 13 Place Valhubert, Paris (V), France. [Cretaceous Ammonites of s.w. Europe & n. Africa (No); Up. Cretaceous Pelecypoda: g. Inoceramus of s.w. Europe & Madagascar (Yes)]

SOUAYA, Dr. Fernand J. Geological Department, Shell House, P. O. Box 228, Cairo, Egypt. [Miocene Foraminifera of Egypt (Yes); Miocene Bryozoa of Egypt (No); fossil smaller Foraminifera of Egypt (No)]

SOULE, John D. Hancock Foundation, University of Southern California, Los Angeles 7, Calif., U. S. A. [Marine Entoprocta & Bryozoa of Pacific Cst. of N. America (Yes)]

SOUSA DIAS, Vasco A. Laboratorio Central de Patologia Veterinaria, Caixa Postal 7, Nova Lisboa, Angola, Portuguese West Africa. [Acarina: Ixodoidea of c. Africa]

SOUTHCOTT, Dr. R. V. 13 Jasper Street, Hyde Park, Adelaide, Australia. [Acarina: Erythraeidae, Smarididae, Trombidiidae, of World (Yes); Trombiculidae of Australia (Yes); Scorpiones of Australia (Yes); Scyphozoa: Cubomedusae of World (Yes)]

SOUTHEY, Mr. J. F. Plant Pathology Laboratory, Milton Road, Harpenden, Herts, England. [Plant parasitic Nematoda of Britain (Yes)] [Ministry of Agriculture, Fisheries & Food]

SOUTHGATE, Mr. A. J. Teachers' College, Dunedin, New Zealand. [Terr. Nemertinea of S. Pacific (Yes); littoral Nemertinea of New Zealand (Yes)]

SOUTHGATE, B. J. Department of Science & Industrial Research, Pest Infestation Laboratory, London Road, Slough, Bucks, England. [Coleoptera: Bruchidae of World (Yes)]

SOUTHWARD, Dr. A. J. The Laboratory, Citadel Hill, Plymouth, England. [Sessile Cirripedia of World (No), of n.w. Europe (Yes)]

SOUTHWARD, Dr. E. C. Marine Biological Association, Citadel Hill, Plymouth, England. [Non-pelagic Polychaeta of n. Europe (No); Pogonophora of World (Yes)]

SOUTHWOOD, Dr. T. R. E. Department of Zoology & Applied Entomology, Imperial College Field Station, Silwood Park, Ascot, Berks, England. [Heteroptera of w. Europe (Yes); Miridae, espec. Orthotylinae, of World (Yes); Diptera: Chloropidae of Europe & N. America (No)]

de SOUZA LOPEZ, H. See LOPEZ, H. de Souza.

SOYER, Prof. B. Agrégé de l'Université, 12 Blvd. G., Crémieux, Marseille VIII, France. [Hymenoptera: Formicidae & Pompilidae, Orthoptera, Araneida, of Provence, France (No)]

SOYKA, Dr. Walter. Hundsheim 17, Post Bad Deutsch-Altenburg, Nieder-Österreich, Austria. [Hymenoptera: Mymaridae of Palearctic, Nearctic, Neotropical, India (Yes); Trichogrammatidae, Aphelinidae, Proctotrypoidea, of World (Yes)] [Naturhistorisches Museum]

SPAHNI, Jean-Christian. 9 rue Emile-Jung, Genève, Switzerland. [M. & Up. Paleozoic Mammalia of Europe (Yes)]

SPANGLER, Paul J. Division of Insects, U. S. National Museum, Washington 25, D. C., U. S. A. [Coleoptera: Hydrophilidae, espec. g. Tropisternus, of W. Hemisphere (Yes); Haliplidae, Dytiscidae, Gyrinidae of N. America (Yes); Acarina: Entonyssidae, Rhinonyssidae, Spinturnicidae, of N. America (No)]

* SPANOWSKAJA, V. D. Department of Ichthyology, Faculty of Biology, University Domonossov, Moscow, U. S. S. R. [Pisces]

SPARKS, Dr. Albert K. Texas A. & M. Research Foundation Marine Laboratory, Box 203, Thibodaux, La., U. S. A. [Digenetic Trematoda of marine animals (Yes)]

SPARKS, Mr. B. W. Department of Geography, University of Cambridge, Downing Place, Cambridge, England. [Recent & Pleistocene non-marine Gastropoda & Lamellibranchiata of British Isles (Yes)]

* SPARTA, Dr. A., Direttore dell'Istituto Talassografico, Universitá di Messina, Messina, Italy. [Pisces]

* SPASSKAJA, L. P. First Moscow Medical Institute, Moscow, U. S. S. R. [Cestoda of animals of U. S. S. R.]

SPASSKY, Dr. A. A. Laboratory of Helminthology, Academy of Sciences of U. S. S. R, Lenin Highway 33, Moscow, U. S. S. R. [Cestoda, Trematoda, Nematoda, of World (Yes)]

* SPASSKY, Mr. Boris. Department of Zoology, Columbia University, New York 27, N. Y., U. S. A. [Diptera]

SPASSKY, Dr. N. J. Mining Institute of Leningrad, Leningrad, U. S. S. R. [Devonian Anthozoa: Rugosa of Soviet Asia (Yes)]

SPASSKY, Prof. Dr. S. Komitetskaja 75, Novotcherkassk, U. S. S. R. [Araneida of s. U. S. S. R. (No)]

SPATH, L. F.   (London, England; Cephalopoda) Deceased.
* SPENCE, Mr. T. Veterinary Laboratory, Ministry of Agriculture, Weybridge, Surrey, England. [Diptera]
SPENCER, Prof. G. J. Department of Entomology, University of British Columbia, Vancouver, B. C., Canada. [Anoplura of N. America (Yes)]
SPENCER, Mr. H. E. P. 43 Benacre Road, Ipswich, Suffolk, England. [Pleistocene Mammalia of e. Anglian Crag & Interglacial deposits (Yes)] [Museum of Geology, Natural History and Archaeology]
SPENCER, Mr. K. A. 19 Redington Road, Hampstead, London, N. W. 3, England. [Diptera: Agromyzidae of World, excl. N. America (Yes)]
* SPENCER, Dr. Warren P. 702 North Beaver Street, Wooster, Ohio, U. S. A. [Diptera: Drosophilidae: g. Drosophila] [College of Wooster]
SPERBER, Dr. C. Luthagsesplanaden 15 D III, Uppsala, Sweden. [Oligochaeta: Naididae of World (No); of Europe (Yes)] [Zoologiska Institutionen]
SPEYER, Mr. E. R. Department of Entomology, British Museum (Natural History), Cromwell Road, London, S. W. 7, England. [Thysanoptera: Terebrantia of World (Yes)]
SPICER, V. D. P. 219 Downing Street, Centralia, Wash., U. S. A. [Mollusca of c. Pacific] [Washington State Capitol Museum]
SPIEGLER, Paul E. Department of Zoology, George Washington University, Washington, D. C., U. S. A. [Neuroptera of N. America (No); Coleoptera: Cicindelidae of N. America (Yes)]
* SPIEKER, Edmund M. (Columbus, Ohio; fossils) Not now active in taxonomy.
SPIETH, Dr. Herman T. (Riverside, Calif., Ephemeroptera & Drosophila) Not now active in taxonomy.
* SPILLER, Dr. Donald. Department of Scientific & Industrial Research, Plant Diseases Division, Auckland, New Zealand. [Exopterygota & Diptera]
SPILLMAN, Prof. Dr. Franz. Garcilazo de la Vega 2580, Lima, Peru. [Cretaceous & Tertiary Foraminifera of n. w. Peru (Yes); Fossil Mammalia of Peru, Ecuador, Bolivia (Yes)] [Universidad Nacional de Ingenieria]
SPILMAN, T. J. Division of Insects, U. S. National Museum, Washington 25, D. C., U. S. A. [Coleoptera: Tenebrionidae & Salpingidae of N. America (Yes)]
ŠPINAR, Doc. Dr. Zdeněk V. Geological-Geographical Faculty, Charles University, Albertov 6, Praha 2, Czechoslovakia. [Fossil Stegocephalla: Seymouriamorpha of Europe (Yes); Anura: Pelobatidae, Palaeobatrachidae of Europe (Yes); Stromatoporoidea of Europe (No)]
SPIVEY, Robert Charles. Shell Oil Company, 1008 W. 6th Street, Los Angeles, Calif., U. S. A. [Permian & Pennsylvanian Fusulinidae (No)]
SPJELDNAES, Dr. Nils. Institutt for Geologi, Adv. C, University of Oslo, Blindern, Oslo, Norway. [Ordovician & Silurian Bryozoa (Yes); Ordovician Brachiopoda: Strophomenida (No)]
SPOEK, G. L. Rijksmuseum van Natuurlijke Historie, Raamsteeg 2, Leiden, Netherlands. [Opiliones of World (Yes), excl. S. America & Africa (No); Araneida of Europe (No)]
SPOONER, Mr. G. M. Fiveoaks, Yelverton, Devon, England. [Crustacea: Amphipoda: Gammaridea of Europe (Yes); Hyperiidea of World (Yes); Hymenoptera: Aculeata of Britain (Yes); Diptera: Tachinidae of Britain (Yes)] [Marine Biological Laboratory, Plymouth]
SPREHN, Prof. Dr. C. Amelungstrasse 36A, Celle, Germany. [Parasitic Nematoda of Europe (Yes); Trematoda, Cestoda, Acanthocephala, of mammals & birds of Europe (Yes)]
SPRENG, Prof. A. C. Missouri School of Mines, Rolla, Mo., U. S. A. [Mississippian Brachiopoda of Missouri & Illinois (Yes)]
SPRENT, Prof. Dr. J. A. F. Veterinary School, University of Queensland, Yeerongpilly, Brisbane, Australia. [Nematoda: Ascaridoidea of mammals of World (Yes)]
* SPRINGER, Dr. Hans. Piazza Borsa 7, Trieste, Italy. [Coleoptera: Chrysomelidae: Halticini]
SPRINGER, Stewart. Branch of Commercial Fisheries, U. S. Fish & Wildlife Service, Washington 25, D. C., U. S. A. [Pisces: Selachii: sharks of World (Yes)]
SPRINGER, Dr. Victor G. Florida State Board of Conservation, Marine Laboratory, Maritime Base, Bayboro Harbor, St. Petersburg, Fla., U. S. A. [Marine Pisces of w. Atlantic (Yes); Clinidae of World (Yes)]
SPROSTON, Miss Nora G. Institute of Hydrobiology, Academia Sinica, 1100 Lo-Chia-Shan, Wuchang (Hupeh), People's Republic of Chica. [Crustacea: parasitic Copepoda of fishes of Asia (Yes); Trematoda: Monogenea of Asia & Europe (Yes); Digenea of fishes of Asia (No); Acanthocephala of fishes of Asia (Yes); Cestoda of fishes of Asia (No)]
SPURIS, Cand. Rer. Nat. Z. Biologijas Instituts, Kleisti, Riga 7, Latvia. [Odonota of Palearctic (Yes); Diptera: Syrphidae of Baltic Area (No)] [Biological Institute of Latvian Academy of Sciences]
SQUIRES, Dr. D. F. Department of Geology & Paleontology, American Museum of Natural History, New York 24, N. Y., U. S. A. [Triassic-Recent Anthozoa: Scleractinia of World, espec. deep-sea, (Yes)]
SQUIRES, H. J. Fisheries Research Station, Water Street East, St. John's, Newfoundland, Canada. [Crustacea: Decapoda of Arctic & n. w. Atlantic (Yes); Cephalopoda: Decapoda & Pisces of Newfoundland & Labrador (Yes)] [Fisheries Research Board of Canada]

SQUIRES, Mr. W. A., Curator, Natural Science Department, The New Brunswick Museum, 277 Douglas Avenue, St. John, New Brunswick, Canada. [Aves of n. e. N. America (Yes)]

ŠRÁMEK-HUŠEK, Doc. Dr. Rudolf. Biologický Ústav, Československá Akademie Věd, Dukelská 145, Třeboň I, Czechoslovakia. [Ciliata of Europe (Yes); Crustacea: Cladocera of Europe (Yes); Crustacea: Cyclopidae & Diaptomidae of c. Europe (No)]

SRINIVASACHAR, Dr. H. R. Department of Zoology, Central College, University of Mysore, Bangalore, India. [Pisces: Ostariophysi: Siluroidea of India (Yes)]

SRIVASTAVA, Dr. P. N. Department of Zoology, Allahabad University, Allahabad, India. [Fresh-water Pisces: Teleosti of Ganges Basin (Yes)]

STACH, Dr. Prof. Jan. Museum Przyrodnicze Polska Akademia Nauk, Sławkowska 17, Kraków, Poland. [Apterygota of World, espec. Poland (No)]

STACH, Leo W. 41 Herbert Street, Albert Park, S. C. 6, Victoria, Australia. [Marine Tertiary & Recent Bryozoa of Pacific (Yes); Tertiary & Recent Foraminifera of Pacific (Yes); ɾ   Recent Polychaeta: Arenicola of Pacific (Yes)]

STACKELBERG, Prof. A. A. Zoological Institute, Academy of Sciences of U. S. S. R., Leningrad V-164, U. S. S. R. [Diptera: Syrphidae & Dolichopodidae of World (No), Palearctic (Yes)]

STACY, Howard. Dominion Oil Ltd., P. O. Box 199, Port of Spain, Trinidad. [Mesozoic-Recent smaller Foraminifera of Gulf Coast & Caribbean (No); Mesozoic-Recent marine Ostracoda of Gulf Coast & Caribbean (No)]

STAESCHE, Dr. Karl. Staatliches Museum für Naturkunde, Archivstrasse 3, Stuttgart O, Germany. [Mesozoic & Cenozoic Reptilia: Testudinata of World (No); of Europe (Yes)]

STAFF, Prof. Dr. Franciszek. Zakład Ichtiobiologii, ul. Rakowiecka 8, Warszawa, Poland. [Pisces of c. Europe & Baltic Sea (No)] [College of Agriculture]

STAFFORD, Prof. E. W. Department of Entomology & Zoology, Mississippi State College, State College, Miss., U. S. A. [Mallophaga of N. America (Yes)]

STAGE, Mr. G. I. Route 4, Box 430, Turlock, Calif., U. S. A. [Hymenoptera: Mellitidae: g. Hesperapis of N. America (Yes)]

STAGER, Kenneth Earl, Curator of Birds & Mammals, Los Angeles County Museum, Los Angeles 7, Calif., U. S. A. [Aves of Neotropical & Oriental (Yes); Mammalia: Chiroptera of World (Yes)]

* STAHL, E. V. Route 1, Box 265, Fallbrook, Calif., U. S. A. [Diptera: Asilidae]

STAHNKE, Dr. H. L. 1400 Mill Avenue, Tempe, Ariz., U. S. A. [Scorpiones of World (No), of U. S. (Yes)] [Arizona State University]

STAINFORTH, Dr. R. M. Creole Petroleum Corporation, Jusepin, Monagas, Venezuela. [Tertiary planktonic Foraminifera (Yes)]

STALKER, Dr. Harrison. Department of Zoology, Washington University, St. Louis 5, Mo., U. S. A. [Diptera: Drosophilidae: g. Drosophila of n. e. & n. c. N. America (Yes)]

STALLINGS, Don B. 616 West Central, Caldwell, Kans., U. S. A. [Lepidoptera: Megathymidae, incl. all stages, of N. & C. America (Yes)]

STAMMER, Prof. Dr. Hans-Jürgen. Zoologisches Institut der Universitat Erlangen, Universitatsstrasse 19, Erlangen, Germany. [Acarina, Pyemotidae & Tarsonemidae of Europe (Yes); Mesostigmata of Europe; Podapolipodidae of World (Yes); Crustacea: f-w. Mysidacea of World (Yes); Insecta, larvae, of Europe (Yes)]

STAMPER, Prof. Maynard N. Department of Zoology, Colorado State College, Greeley, Colo., U. S. A. [Crustacea: Ostracoda of Colorado (Yes); g. Entocythere of U. S. (Yes)]

* STANCATI, Milton F. Address unknown. [Hymenoptera]

STANČIČ, Ing. Jovan. Institut za Zaštitu Bilja, T. Drajzera 7, Beograd, Yugoslavia. [Coleoptera: Curculionidae of c. & s. Europe (Yes); Coleoptera of sandy areas of Europe (Yes)]

STANGE, Mr. Lionel A. 843 West 99th Street, Los Angeles 44, Calif., U. S. A. [Neuroptera: Myrmeliontidae of N. America (Yes)]

* STANKOVIC, S. Address unknown. [Isopoda & Amphipoda]

STANLEY, Edward A. Department of Geology, Pennsylvania State University, University Park, Penna., U. S. A. [Up. Paleozoic Conodonts (No), Mississippian Conodonts (Yes)]

STANNARD, Dr. Lewis J., Jr. Illinois Natural History Survey, Urbana, Ill., U. S. A. [Thysanoptera of N. America (Yes); Acarina: ticks of Illinois (Yes)]

STANSBURY, Dr. David H. Botany & Zoology Building, Room 55, Ohio State University, Columbus 10, Ohio, U. S. A. [Crustacea: f-w. Decapoda of Great Lakes drainage (Yes); f-w. Pelecypoda, espec. Unionidae, of Great Lake drainage (Yes)]

* STANWORTH, Garn T. 1703 E. McDowell, Hemet, Calif., U. S. A. [Acarina: Oribatei]

STARCK, Prof. Dr. med. Dietrich. Anatomisches Institut der Universität, Ludwig Rehnstrasse 14, Frankfurt am Main, Germany. [Mammalia: Primates, espec. of Ethiopian (No); Accipitres & Striges of Palearctic & Ethiopian (No)]

* STARK, E. Zoological Institut, 14 Luisenstrasse, München 2, Germany. [Orthoptera]

STARK, Harold E. San Francisco Field Station, 14th Avenue & Lake Street, San Francisco 18, Calif., U. S. A. [Siphonaptera of N. America (Yes)] [U. S. Public Health Service]

* STARK, Dr. Vladimir N. Zoological Institute, Academy of Science of U. S. S. R., Leningrad 164, U. S. S. R. [Coleoptera: Ipidae]

* STARKOFF, Igor. Istituto di Parassitologia, Città Universitaria, Roma, Italy. [Acarina]

351

* STARLING, J. H. Department of Biology, Washington & Lee University, Lexington, Va.,
    U. S. A. [Pauropoda]
STARMÜHLNER, Dr. F. Zoologisches Institut der Universität, Dr. Karl Luegerring 1, Wien 1,
    Austria. [F-w. Gastropoda: Prosobranchiata & Opisthobranchiata of c. Europe, Persia,
    Madagascar (Yes); marine of Mediterranean (Yes)]
* STAROBOGATOV, Mr. Y. I. Invertebrate Zoology Chair, Moscow University, Moscow,
    U. S. S. R. [Gastropoda: Planorbidae of World]
STARQUIST, V. L. (Houston, Texas; fossils) Not now active in taxonomy.
STARRETT, Andrew. Department of Biology, University of Southern California, Los Angeles 7,
    Calif., U. S. A. [Quaternary Mammalia of N. America (Yes); Recent Cetacea of New
    World (Yes)]
STARRETT, Mrs. Priscilla. Department of Biology, University of Southern California, Los
    Angeles 7, Calif., U. S. A. [Amphibia: Anura: Centrolenidae of C. & S. America (Yes);
    Anura, tadpoles, of N. & C. America (Yes)]
STARÝ, Petr., Mg. Sc., Czechoslovak Academy of Science, Institute of Entomology, 7 Viničná,
    Praha 2, Czechoslovakia. [Hymenoptera: Braconidae of Europe (No); Aphidiinae of
    Palearctic (Yes)]
STASIŃSKA, Mgr. A. Zakład, Paleontologii, Polska Akademia Nauk, Nowy Swiat 67, Warszawa,
    Poland. [Fossil Anthozoa: Tabulata of Europe (No); Devonian Tabulata of Poland (Yes)]
* STAUBLE, A. Central Micropaleontological Laboratory of the N. V. Bataafsche Petroleum
    Maatschappy, Carel v. Bylandlaan 30, Den Haag, Netherlands. [Microfossils]
STEAD, D. G. (Watson's Bay, Australia: Pisces) Died "2. 8. 58."
STEADMAN, W. R. (St. Georges, Australia; Mollusca) Not now active in taxonomy.
STEARN, Colin W. Department of Geological Sciences, McGill University, Montreal, Que.,
    Canada. [Devonian Stromatoporoidea of N. America (Yes); Silurian Invertebrates of
    N. America (Yes)]
* STEARNS, Prof. Louis A. Department of Entomology, University of Delaware, Newark,
    Del., U. S. A. [Homoptera] Died March 5, 1960.
STEBBINS, Dr. Robert C. Department of Zoology, University of California, Berkeley 4, Calif.,
    U. S. A. [Amphibia & Reptilia of w. N. America (Yes)] [Museum of Vertebrate Zoology]
STECHOW, Prof. Dr. E. Zoologisches Staatssammlung, Menzingerstrasse 67, München 38,
    Germany. [Hydrozoa: Hydroida (No)]
STEEL, Mr. W. O. "Ken", Braywoodside, Maidenhead, Berkshire, England. [Coleoptera:
    Staphylinidae: Piestinae, Phloeocharinae, Pseudopsinae, Proteininae, Omaliinae, Oxyte-
    linae, Osoriinae, of World, espec. Australian & Oceania (Yes)]
STEELE, Mr. D. Department of Zoology, McGill University, Montreal, Que., Canada. [Crus-
    tacea: Amphipoda of Canada, e. Arctic & Subarctic (No)]
STEELE, Grant. Gulf Oil Corporation Laboratory, 6901 West Lakewood Place, Denver, Colo.,
    U. S. A. [Pennsylvanian & Permian Fusulinidae of w. U. S. (Yes)] [Gulf Oil Corporation]
STEEN, Dr. Edwin B. Department of Biology, Western Michigan University, Kalamazoo, Mich.,
    U. S. A. [Trematoda: Gorgoderidae of c. U. S. (Yes)]
STEFANI, Prof. Renzo. Istituto di Zoologia, Viale San Bartolomeo 1, Cagliari, Italy. [Embiop-
    tera of Mediterranean (Yes)]
STEFANSKI, Dr. Witold. Laboratoire de Parasitologie de la Faculté Veterinaire, Grochowska
    272, Warszawa-Praga, Poland. [Free-living & parasitic Nematoda of Vertebrates of
    Palearctic (Yes); plant parasitic Nematoda of Palearctic (No)]
STEFFAN, Mr. J. R. Museum d'Histoire Naturelle, Laboratoire d'Entomologie Tropicale, 57
    rue Cuvier, Paris (V), France. [Hymenoptera: Chalcididae of Europe, Asia, Africa,
    Oceania, N. America (Yes); of S. America & Australia (No); Perilampidae of World (No);
    of Europe (Yes); Torymidae, excl. Toryminae, of World (No); of Europe (Yes)]
* STEFFAN, Wilhelm. Zoologische Institut, Siesmeyerstrasse 70, Frankfurt, Germany. [Cole-
    optera: Dryopidae]
STEGMANN, D. O. Biological Division, Kruger National Park, P. O. Skukuza, Union of South
    Africa. [Reptilia: Snakes of s. Africa (Yes); Mammalia of s. Africa (No)]
STEHLI, Dr. F. G. 3553 South Urbana, Tulsa 5, Okla., U. S. A. [Upper Paleozoic, Mesozoic,
    Recent Brachiopoda (Yes)] [Pan American Petroleum Corporation Research Center]
STEHLIK, Dr. Jaroslav L. Entomological Department, Moravian Museum, Preslova 1, Brno II,
    Czechoslovakia. [Heteroptera: Pyrrhocoridae & Largidae of World (Yes)]
STEHR, Dr. William C. Department of Zoology, Ohio University, Athens, Ohio, U. S. A. [Cole-
    optera: Carabidae & Coccinellidae of Nearctic (Yes)]
* STEIN, Dr. Georg. Abteilung der Saugetiere, Zoologisches Museum, Invalidenstrasse 43,
    Berlin N. 4, German Democratic Republic. [Mammalia]
STEIN, Dr. Robert C. Department of Biology, Ursinus College, Collegeville, Penna., U. S. A.
    [Aves: Tyrannidae: g. Empidonax of e. N. America (No)]
* STEINBACH, Dr. Gerhard. Abteilung der Ichthyologie, Zoologisches Museum, Invaliden-
    strasse 43, Berlin N 4, German Democratic Republic. [Pisces]
STEINBACHER, Dr. F. Natur-Museum und Forschungsinstitut, Senckenberg-Anlage 25, Frank-
    fort, a. m., Germany. [Aves of Palearctic, Africa, S. America (Yes)]

STEINBERG, Prof. Dr. Dimitri M. Zoological Institute, Academy of Sciences of U. S. S. R.,
Leningrad B-164, U. S. S. R. [Hymenoptera: Scoliidae of Palearctic (No)]
STEINBERG, Miss Joan. 850 38th Avenue, San Francisco 21, Calif., U. S. A. [Crustacea: Am-
phipoda: Caprellidae of World (Yes); Gastropoda: Opisthobranchia of Pacific (No); Nudi-
branchia of w. cst. of N. America (Yes) [University of California]
STEINBÖCK, Univ. Prof. Dr. Otto. Zoologisches Institut, Universitität Innsbruck, Universi-
tätsstrasse 4, Innsbruck, Austria. [Marine Turbellaria (No); Acoela (Yes)]
STEINER, Dr. G. Experiment Station, Rio Piedras, Puerto Rico. [Marine & terr. Nematoda
(Yes)]
STEINER, Dr. W. Instituto de Edafologia, Consejo Superior de Investigaciones Cientificas,
Serrano 113, Madrid 6, Spain. [Collembola of Europe (No)]
STEINITZ, Dr. H. Department of Zoology, Hebrew University, Jerusalem, Israel. [Pisces:
Cyprinidae: g. Tylognathus, Garra, Acanthobrama, Phoxinellus; Cichlidae; Cyprinodon-
tidae; of Near East & Middle East (Yes); f-w. Blenniidae of Mediterranean (Yes); Pisces
of Red Sea (Yes); Amphibia of Near East (No); Urodela of Near East (Yes)]
STEINMANN, H. Magyar Nemzeti Museum, Természettudományi Múzeum Állattára, (Baross -
Utca 13, Budapest VIII, Hungary. [Orthoptera: Acridoidea of Palearctic (No), of Europe
(Yes); Odonata of Palearctic (Yes)]
STELCK, Mr. Charles R. Department of Geology, University of Alberta, Edmonton, Alta.,
Canada. [Cretaceous Foraminifera of w. Canada (Yes); M. Cretaceous Ammonites of w.
Canada (Yes); M. & Up. Devonian Brachiopoda & Corals of w. Canada (Yes)]
STELFOX, A. W. (Newcastle, England; Mollucsa & Hymenoptera) Not now active in taxonomy.
STELLA, Prof. Emilia. Istituto di Zoologia, Policlinico, 326 Viale Regina Elena, Roma, Italy.
[Crustacea: f-w. Planktonic Copepoda & Cladocera (No); Thermosbaenacea (Yes)]
STELTER, Mr. Helmut. Institut für Pflanzenzuchtung, Gross Lusewitz Krs., Rostock, German
Democratic Republic. [Diptera: Cecidomyidae of c. & n. Europe (Yes); Nematoda: Heter-
odera of Europe (Yes)]
STEMPFFER, Henri. 4 rue Saint Antoine, Paris, France. [Lepidoptera: Lycaenidae of Ethiop-
ian (Yes)]
* STENRAM, Hakan. Entomologiska Avdelningen, Zoologiska Institution, Lund Sweden. [Mal-
lophaga]
STENSIÖ, Prof. Dr. Erik A. Department of Paleontology, Naturhistoriska Riksmuseum, Stock-
holm 50, Sweden. [Ordovician-Cretaceous Pisces (No)]
STENUIT, D. F. E. Service Pedagologique de Belgique, Heverlee, Belgium. [Hemiptera: Heter-
odera of Belgium (Yes)]
STENZEL, H. B. 3726 Colquitt Street, Houston 6, Texas, U. S. A. [Mesozoic to Recent Mollusca:
Ostreidae (Yes); Mesozoic to Recent Crustacea: Decapoda (Yes)]
ŠTĚPÁNEK, Dr. M. Rosy Luxemburkové 20, Praha, Smichov, Czechoslovakia. [Protozoa:
terr., f-w. & parasitic Amoebina, Testacea, Heliozoa, Suctoria, of Europe, Africa,
Asia, Indonesia, espec. Belgium Kongo, Korea, Vietnam (Yes)]
ŠTĚPÁNEK, Dr. O. Národni Museum, Václavské Náměsti 1700, Praha II, Czechoslovakia.
[Reptilia & Amphibia of Europe (No); g. Gymnodactylus of trop. America (No)]
STEPANOV, E. M. Tsereteli Str. 18, Batumi (Adzharia), U. S. S. R. [Coleoptera: Elateridae of
Europe & Asia (Yes)] [Georgian Laboratory of Biological Control]
STEPHEN, Dr. A. C. Royal Scottish Museum, Edinburgh 1, Scotland. [Sipunculidae, Echiuridae,
Priapulidae, of World (Yes)]
STEPHEN, Dr. W. P. Department of Entomology, Oregon State College, Corvallis, Ore., U. S. A.
[Hymenoptera: Colletidae: g. Colletes of New World (Yes); Apidae: g. Bombus of World
(No), of America (Yes)]
STEPHENS, John S., Jr. Department of Biology, Occidental College, Los Angeles 41, Calif.,
U. S. A. [Pisces of e. Pacific (No); Emblemariidae of World (Yes)]
STEPHENSON, Lloyd W. (Dover, Ohio; fossils) Not now active in taxonomy.
STEPHENSON, Dr. N. G. Department of Zoology, University of Sydney, Sydney, Australia.
[Amphibia of Australia & New Zealand (Yes); Reptilia: Lacertilia of Australia & New Zea-
land (Yes); Ophidia of Australia (No)]
STEPHENSON, Prof. T. A. Zoology Department, University College, Cambrian Street, Abery-
stwyth, Wales. [Anthozoa: Actiniaria of World (No)]
STEPHENSON, Dr. W. Department of Zoology, University of Queensland, Brisbane, Australia.
[Crustacea: Stomatopoda & Decapoda: Portunidae of Indian & w. Pacific Oceans (Yes);
Anthozoa: Madreporaria]
ŠTĚRBA, Dr. Otakar. Zoologický Ústav, Masaryk University, Kotlářska 2, Brno, Czechoslovakia.
[Crustacea: Cyclopidae of Europe (Yes); Harpacticidae of Europe (Yes); Ephemeroptera
(No)]
* STERENS, Ray. Geology Department, Louisiana State University, Baton Rouge 3, La., U. S. A.
[Fossil Invertebrates].
STERNBERG, C. M. Department of Paleontology, National Museum of Canada, Ottawa, Ont.,
Canada. [Cretaceous Reptilia: dinosaurs of N. America (No)]

353

* STERNBERG, Mr. George F. Department of Geology & Paleontology, Fort Hays Kansas State College, Hays, Kan., U.S.A. [Fossil Mammalia]

STERNLICHT, M. 36 Shkedim Street, Tivon, Israel. [Orthoptera: Tettigoniidae & Gryllidae of Israel (Yes); Insects of oaks: Microlepidoptera, gall wasps, Coccoidea: Kermesidae of Israel (Yes)]

STETTENHEIM, Mr. Peter. U.S. Poultry Research Laboratory, 3606 East Mount Hope Road, East Lansing, Mich., U.S.A. [Aves: Charadriiformes of N. America (No); Alcidae of N. America (Yes)]

STEUSLOFF, U. Gelsenkirchen-Buer, Germany; Mollusca) Died 1953.

STEVEN, Dr. G.A. Marine Biological Laboratory, Citadel Hill, Plymouth, England. [Pisces: Scombridae & Raiidae of British seas (Yes)]

STEVENS, Dr. Belle A. 515 Harvard N, Seattle 5, Wash., U.S.A. [Crustacea: Callianasidae; Paguridae & shrimps of w. cst. N. America (Yes)] Deceased.

STEVENS, Mr. G.R. New Zealand Geological Survey, Department of Scientific & Industrial Research, Lower Hutt, New Zealand. [Jurassic-Cretaceous Cephalopoda: Belemnitidae of Indo-Pacific, N. & S. America, India, Africa (Yes)]

STEVENS, W.E. Canadian Wildlife Service, Ottawa, Ont., Canada. [Mammalia of Canadian N.W. Territories (Yes)]

* STEVENSON, A.G. C/o Bowers, 11 Swanson Street, Auckland C.1, New Zealand. [Mollusca]

STEWART, Dr. M.A., Dean, Graduate Division, Sproul Hall, University of California, Berkeley 4, Calif., U.S.A. [Siphonaptera of New World (Yes)]

STEWART, Dr. Margaret M. Department of Biology, New York State College for Teachers, Albany 3, N.Y., U.S.A. [Amphibia: Caudata of n.e. U.S. (Yes)]

* STEWART, Dr. Ralph B. Division of Mollusks, U.S. National Museum, Washington 25, D.C., U.S.A. [Fossil Pelecypoda] Died November 29, 1958.

* STEWART, Mr. Roscoe E. 4075 Castle Avenue, Portland 12, Oregon, U.S.A. [Fossil Invertebrates]

* STEWART, Mrs. Roscoe E. 4075 Castle Avenue, Portland 12, Oregon, U.S.A. [Fossil Invertebrates]

STEWART, Wendell J. The Texas Company, Box 1720, Fort Worth, Texas, U.S.A. [Fossil Foraminifera: Fusulinidae of N. America & Japan (Yes)]

STEYSKAL, George C. 27253 West River Road, Grosse Ile, Mich., U.S.A. [Diptera: Sciomyzidae & Otitidae of World (Yes)]

STICHEL, Dr. Wolfgang. Martin-Luther-Strasse 39, Berlin-Hermsdorf, Germany. [Heteroptera of Europe, n. Africa, w. Asia (No); Reduviidae, Coreidae, Pentatomidae, of S. America (No)]

STICKEL, Mr. William H. U.S. Fish & Wildlife Service, Patuxent Research Refuge, Laurel, Md., U.S.A. [Reptilia: Ophidia: g. Sonora (Yes)]

* STICKNEY, Mr. Alden P. Atlantic Salmon Investigations, U.S. Fish & Wildlife Service, Boothbay Harbor, Maine, U.S.A. [Mollusca, Arthropoda, Polychaeta]

van der STIGCHEL, Dr. J.W.B., Director, Gemeentelijk Museum voor het Onderwys, 's Gravenhage, Netherlands. [Pisces: Nematognathi of S. America (Yes)]

STILLE, Mr. W.T. Saunders Road, Lake Forest, Ill., U.S.A. [Amphibia & Reptilia of Chicago Area, U.S. (Yes)]

STILLER, Dr. J. Magyar Nemzeti Muzeum, Természettudományi Muzeum, Baross-u 13, Budapest VIII, Hungary. [F-w. & marine Protozoa: Peritricha of Europe (Yes)]

STINTON, Mr. F.C. 51 Craigmoor Avenue, Strouden Park, Bournemouth, England. [Tertiary & Quaternary Teleostean otoliths of World (Yes); Tertiary Mollusca of Britain (Yes)]

STIREWALT, Margaret A. Naval Medical Research Institute, Bethesda 14, Md., U.S.A. [Turbellaria: Acoela, Alloeocoela, Rhabdocoela, of N. America (Yes)]

* STIRRETT, Dr. George M. Department of Biology, Queen's University, Kingston, Ont., Canada. [Coleoptera: Chrysomelidae]

STIRTON, Dr. R.A. Department of Paleontology, University of California, Berkeley 4, Calif., U.S.A. [Fossil Mammalia of New World & Australia (Yes)]

ST. JEAN, Dr. J., Jr. Department of Geology & Geography, University of North Carolina, Chapel Hill, N.C., U.S.A. [Paleozoic Hydrozoa & Stromatoporoidea of World (Yes); Paleozoic Foraminifera of N. America (Yes)]

ST. JOHN, Prof. Philip A. Biology Department, Brandeis University, Waltham 54, Mass., U.S.A. [Crustacea: Copepoda: Calanoida of w. N. Atlantic (Yes)]

ST. JOSEPH, Dr. J.K.S. Selwyn College, University of Cambridge, Cambridge, England. [Ordovician-Silurian Brachiopoda, espec. Pentameracea (Yes)]

STOCK, Assoc. Prof. A. Department of Zoology, University of New England, Armidale, 5N., N.S.W., Australia. [Turbellaria of Australia (Yes)]

STOCK, Dr. J.H. Zoologisch Museum, Plantage Middenlaan 53, Amsterdam (C), Netherlands. [Crustacea: Copepoda parasitic on invertebrates of World (No); Isopoda: Epicaridea of World (No); Pycnogonida of World (Yes)]

STOCKMANN, Direktor Sten. Kaserngatan 20, Helsinki, Finland. [Coleoptera of n. Europe (No); Histeridae: g. Gnathoncus of Europe (Yes)]

STOCKTON, Prof. William D. Long Beach State College, Long Beach 4, Calif., U.S.A. [Coleoptera: Curculionidae: g. Hyperodes of Nearctic (Yes)]

STOECKHERT, Dr. F.K. Spardorferstrasse 35, Erlangen, Germany. [Hymenoptera: Apidae of Palearctic (No)]

STØEN, M. The Norwegian Plant Protection Institute, Vollebekk, Oslo, Norway. [Nematoda of Norway (No)]

STOHLER, Dr. Rudolf. Department of Zoology, University of California, Berkeley 4, Calif., U.S.A. [Gastropoda of California; Amphineura: chitons of world (No), of California (Yes)]

STOICA, Nicolae. Facultatea de Biologie, Splaiul Independentii 93, Bucureşti, Rumania. [Pisces of Rumania (Yes)]

STOJAŁOWSKA, Wanda. Zakład Biologii Akademii Medycznej, ul. Królewska 15, Lublin, Poland. [Diplopoda of Poland & Czechoslovakia (Yes)]

STOKELL, Mr. G. Springston, No. 4, R.D., Christchurch, New Zealand. [Pisces: Galaxiidae of New Zealand, Australia, S. America, s. Africa (Yes); Retropinnidae of New Zealand & Australia (Yes)]

STOKES, Prof. William Lee. Department of Geology, University of Utah, Salt Lake City, Utah, U.S.A. [Reptilia: Jurassic dinosaurs of w. N. America (Yes); fossil tracks of w. U.S. (Yes)]

* STOLK, A. Pr. Hendriklaan 27, Amsterdam (2), Netherlands. [Protozoa]

STOLL, Dr. Norman R. Rockefeller Institute, New York 21, N.Y., U.S.A. [Nematoda: Strongyloidea (No)]

* STOLTENBERG, Niels C. Amaliegade 35, København K, Denmark. [Mollusca]

STOMBAUGH, Prof. Tom A. Department of Biology, Southwest Missouri State College, Springfield, Mo., U.S.A. [Mammalia: g. Microtus of N. America (No)]

STONE, Dr. Alan. Division of Insects, U.S. National Museum, Washington 25, D.C., U.S.A. [Diptera: Culicidae, Simuliidae, Tabanidae of World (Yes)] [Entomology Research Division, U.S. Department of Agriculture]

STONE, Dr. Philip C. Department of Entomology, University of Missouri, Columbia, Mo., U.S.A. [Acarina: Ixodoidea of N. America (Yes)]

STONEHAM, Col. H.F., Director, Stoneham Museum & Research Centre, Kitale, Kenya. [Lepidoptera: Rhopalocera of Ethiopian (Yes); Heterocera of Ethiopian (No); Aves of Ethiopian (Yes)]

STØP-BOWITZ, C. University Zoological Museum, Sarsgatan 1, Oslo 45, Norway. [Polychaeta: Glyceridae, Opheliidae, Scalibregmidae, Flabelligeridae, of Arctic & n.e. Atlantic (Yes); pelagic Polychaeta of all Oceans (Yes); Oligochaeta: Lumbricidae of Scandinavia (Yes); Amphibia & Reptilia of Scandinavia (Yes)]

* STORÅ, Ragnar. Nykarleby, Finland. [Diptera: Chironomidae]

* STORACE, Luciano. Museo Civico di Storia Naturale, Via Brigata Liguria 9, Genova, Italy. [Lepidoptera]

STORER, Dr. Robert W. Museum of Zoology, University of Michigan, Ann Arbor, Mich., U.S.A. [Aves, skins & bones of N. & C. America (Yes); Alcidae, Podicipitidae, Thraupidae, of World (Yes)]

STORER, Tracy I. (Davis, Calif.; Amphibia) Not now active in taxonomy.

STOREY, Miss Margaret H. Natural History Museum, Stanford University, Stanford, Calif., U.S.A. [Pisces, Amphibia, Reptilia (No)] Deceased.

STORM, Dr. R.M. Department of Zoology, Oregon State College, Corvallis, Ore., U.S.A. [Amphibia & Reptilia of n. California, Oregon, Washington (Yes)]

STØRMER, Prof. Dr. Leif. Institutt for Geologi, Avd. C., Universitetet, Blindern, Oslo, Norway. [Paleozoic Merostomata of World (Yes); Cambrian-Silurian Trilobita of Scandinavia (No)]

STOUT, John D. 1 Katherine Avenue, Wellington, N.1, New Zealand. [Protozoa: non-parasitic Ciliophora of soil, moss, forest litter (Yes); Sarcodina: Testacea, of same (Yes)] [Soil Bureau, Department of Scientific & Industrial Research]

* STOUT, Dr. T.M. Address unknown. [Fossil Rodentia]

STOUT, Dr. V.M. Department of Zoology, University of Canterbury, Christchurch, New Zealand. [Acarina: Hydracarina of New Zealand (Yes)]

STOVER, Lewis E. Jersey Production Research Co., 1133 N. Lewis, Tulsa 10, Okla., U.S.A. [Paleozoic Ostracoda of U.S. (No)]

STOYANOW, Alexander. Department of Geology, University of California, Los Angeles 24, Calif., U.S.A. [M. & Up. Cambrian Trilobita; Up. Paleozoic Brachiopoda & Lamellibranchiata; Permo-Triassic & L. Cretaceous Ammonoidea & Lamellibranchiata; all of s.w. U.S., N. Mexico, Caucasus, Armenia, n. Iran (Yes)]

* STOYE, Mr. Frederick H. 4520 Kahala Avenue, Honolulu 15, Hawaii, U.S.A. [F-w. Pisces of World]

ST. QUENTIN, Dr. Douglas. Richard Kralikplatz 2, Wien 18, Austria. [Odonata of Palearctic & S. America (Yes)]

STRACHAN, Dr. I. Department of Geology, The University, Edgbaston, Birmingham 15, England. [Ordovician & Silurian Graptolithina of World (Yes)]

STRADNER, Dr. phil. H. Agnesstrasse 56, Klosterneuburg, Austria. [Fossil & Recent Proto-
zoa: Silicoflagellata (Yes); fossil & Recent Discoasterida (Yes)]
STRAIN, Mr. W. S. Department of Geology, Western College, El Paso, Texas, U. S. A. [Pleis-
tocene Vertebrates of s. w. U. S. (Yes)]
STRAND, Andreas. Melumveien 38, Röa, Oslo, Norway. [Coleoptera of Norway (Yes)]
STRAND, Embrik. (Riga, Latvia) Died in 1947.
STRANDTMANN, Russell. Department of Biology, Texas Technological College, Lubbock,
Texas, U. S. A. [Hymenoptera: Sphecidae of N. America (Yes); Acarina: parasitic Gama-
sidae of World (Yes)]
STRANEO, Prof. S. L. Istituto Professionale di Stato, Gallarate, Italy. [Coleoptera: Carabidae
of World (Yes)]
STRASBURG, Dr. Donald W. U. S. Fish & Wildlife Service, Box 3830, Honolulu, Hawaii, U. S. A.
[Pisces: Blenniidae of Indo-Pacific (Yes); Pisces of Hawaiian, Marshall, & Gilbert Is-
lands (No)]
STRAŠKRABA, Dr. Milan. Hydrobiologické a Ichthyologické Oddĕleni, Biologické Fakulty, Kar-
lova Universita, Viničná 7, Praha II, Czechoslovakia. [Crustacea: f-w. Amphipoda of
Palearctic (Yes); Copepoda: Cyclopidae of Europe (No); Cladocera of Europe (No)]
zur STRASSEN, Dr. Richard. Division of Entomology, Department of Agriculture, P. B. 134,
P. O. Vallis, Pretoria, Union of South Africa. [Thysanoptera of s. Africa (Yes), of Europe
(No)]
STRATTON, L. W. "Northcote", South Common, Redbourn, Herts, England. [Mollusca of Bri-
tain (Yes)]
STRAW, S. H. (Worthing, England; fossils) Not now active in taxonomy.
STRAWINSKI, Dr. Prof. Konstanty. Department of Zoology & Entomology, University Marie
Curie - Skłodowska, ul. Głowackiego 2, Lublin, Poland. [Heteroptera of Palearctic (Yes)]
STRAWN, Dr. Kirk. Department of Biological Sciences, Lamar State College of Technology,
Beaumont, Texas, U. S. A. [Pisces: Pigmy Seahorse of e. Atlantic (Yes); Percidae of
Edwards Plateau of Texas (Yes)]
* STREIFF-BECKER, Dr. Rudolf. Kantstrasse 11, Zürich, Switzerland. [Fossils]
STRELKOW, Prof. A. Zoological Institute, Academy of Sciences of U. S. S. R. , Leningrad W-164,
U. S. S. R. [Protozoa: Infusoria: Entodiniomorpha; Recent Radiolaria of Pacific Ocean]
STRENZKE, Dr. K. Max-Planck-Institut, Anton-Dohrn-Weg, Wilhelmshaven, Germany. [Aca-
rina: Oribatei of Palearctic (No); Diptera: Chironomidae with terrestial larvae, of World
(Yes); g. Chironomus of Holarctic (No); Collembola of seashores of Holarctic (No)]
STRESEMANN, Prof. Dr. Erwin. Zoologisches Museum, Invalidenstrasse 43, Berlin N. 4,
German Democratic Republic. [Aves of World (Yes)]
STRICKLAND, E. H. (Victoria, B. C. , Canada: Diptera & Hymenoptera) Not now active in
taxonomy.
STRIMPLE, Harrell L. 9821 E. Pine Street, Route 10, Tulsa 15, Okla. , U. S. A. [Pennsylvanian
Crinoidea of N. America (Yes); Mississippian (Chester) Crinoidea of Oklahoma (Yes);
Ordovician (Bromide), Devonian (Haragan), Silurian (Henryhouse) Echinodermata of Okla-
homa (Yes)]
STRINATI, Mr. P. Chemin des Còttages 9, Genève, Switzerland. [Chiroptera of Europe & n.
Africa (Yes)]
STRITT, Prof. Walter. Liebigstrasse 17, 17 a Karlsruhe, Germany. [Hymenoptera: Tenthredi-
noidea of Europe (Yes)]
STRNAD, Dr. Vladimir. Marxova 77, Olomouc, Czechoslovakia. [Devonian & L. Carboniferous
Trilobita (Yes)] [Museum SLUKO]
STROGANOV, Prof. Dr. S. U. Biological Institute, Siberian Branch of the Academy of Sciences,
Mitshurin Street 23, Novosibirsk, U. S. S. R. [Mammalia of Europe & Asia (Yes)]
STROHECKER, Dr. H. F. University of Miami, Box 8106, Coral Gables 46, Fla. , U. S. A.
[Orthoptera of N. America (Yes); Coleoptera: Endomychidae of World (Yes)]
* STRONG, Dr. Rudolph G. Department of Entomology, University of California, Riverside,
Calif. , U. S. A. [Coleoptera: Dermestidae]
STROUHAL, Prof. Dr. Hans, Director, Naturhistorisches Museum, Burgring 7, Wien 1, Austria.
[Crustacea: Terr. Isopoda of World (Yes); Asellota of Europe (Yes)]
STROYAN, Mr. H. L. G. 59 Milton Road, Harpenden, Herts, England. [Homoptera: Aphididae of
World (No); of w. Europe (Yes)] [Plant Pathology Laboratory]
* STRÜBING, Dr. Hildegard. Zoologisches Institut der Freien Universität, Königin-Luise-
Strasse 1-3, Berlin-Dahlem, Germany. [Hemiptera]
STRUVE, W. Geologische Abteilung, Forschungs-Institut und Natur-Museum, Senckenberg
Anlage 25, Frankfurt am Main, Germany. [Devonian Brachiopoda, espec. Atrypacea &
Spiriferacea, of c. Europe (Yes); Devonian & L. Carboniferous Trilobita: Proetidae of c.
Europe (Yes); Trilobita: Phacopacea, espec. Phacopidae, Dalmanitidae, Calmoniidae
(Yes)] [Forschungs-Institute und Natur-Museum Senckenberg, Geologische Abteilung]
STUARDO-ORTIZ, Prof. Carlos. Casilla 4019, Santiago, Chile. [Diptera: Nemestrinidae of S.
America (Yes)]

STUART, Dr. Laurence C. Department of Zoology, University of Michigan, Ann Arbor, Mich.,
U. S. A. [Reptilia & Amphibia of n. C. America & s. Mexico (Yes)]
STUBBLEFIELD, Dr. C. J. Geological Survey & Museum, Exhibition Road, London, S. W. 7,
England. [Trilobita of World (Yes)]
STUCKENBERG, Brian R. Natal Museum, Pietermaritzburg, Natal, Union of South Africa.
[Diptera: Rhagionidae, Sapromyzidae, Errinidae, Syrphidae: g. Paragus, of Ethiopian &
Madagascar (Yes); Blepharoceridae of World (No), of Ethiopian (Yes)]
STUCKEY, C. W. , Jr. Union Oil Co. of California, 800 Prudential Building, Houston 25, Texas,
U. S. A. [Tertiary Foraminifera of U. S. Gulf Coast (Yes)]
* STUDER, Mr. Floyd V. 435-439 Amarillo Building, Amarillo, Texas, U. S. A. [Fossil Mam-
malia]
STUGREN, Bogdan. Department of Reptiles, Institute of Zoology, University of Cluj, Str. Mikó
5-7, Cluj, Romania. [Amphibia & Reptilia of e. & s. e. Europe (Yes)]
* STULL, Prof. William D. R. D. 1, Delaware, Ohio, U. S. A. [Amphibia: salamanders]
STUMM, Prof. E. C. Museum of Paleontology, University of Michigan, Ann Arbor, Mich.,
U. S. A. [Paleozoic Corals of N. America (Yes); Devonian Trilobita of N. America (Yes)]
* STUMPER, Dr. Robert. 94 rue du Josse, Esch-sur-Alzette, Luxembourg. [Hymenoptera:
Formicidae]
STUNKARD, Prof. Horace W. American Museum of Natural History, New York 24, N. Y. ,
U. S. A. [Parasitic Platyhelminthes; Turbellaria, Trematoda, Cestoda (Yes)]
STURGEON, Dr. M. T. Department of Geography & Geology, Ohio University, Athens, Ohio,
U. S. A. [Pennsylvanian Invertebrates of e. N. America (No), Gastropoda & Cephalopoda
(Yes)]
* STURM, Dr. Catherine W. Department of Zoology, Ohio University, Athens, Ohio, U. S. A.
[Crustacea: f-w. Amphipoda]
STURTEVANT, Prof. Alfred H. Department of Genetics, California Institute of Technology,
Pasadena 4, Calif. , U. S. A. [Diptera: Acalyptrata of N. America (Yes)]
STURTEVANT, Dr. Frank M. , Jr. (Chicago, Ill. ; Diptera: Drosophilidae) Not now active in
taxonomy.
STURZ, Mr. C. E. Box 811, Ventura, Calif. , U. S. A. [Tertiary & Cretaceous Foraminifera of
California (Yes)] [Tidewater Oil Company]
STUSAK, RN. Dr. Josef M. Nevřeň 13, u Plzně, Czechoslovakia. [Heteroptera of c. Europe
(Yes); Tingidae, all stages, of Palearctic (Yes); Berytidae of World (No)] [Vysoka Skola
Zemedelska]
ŠTYS, P. Katedra Systematické Zoologie, Viničná 7, Praha II, Czechoslovakia. [Heteroptera of
w. Palearctic (Yes); Dipsocoridae, Anthocoridae, Microphysidae, of World (Yes); Dip-
tera: Syrphidae of w. Palearctic (No), Syrphinae (Yes)]
SUÁREZ, Francisco J. San Pedro 4, Almeria, Spain. [Hymenoptera: Mutillidae, Apterogynidae
& Myrmosidae of World (No), of Palearctic & Ethiopian (Yes)] [Instituto de Aclimatación
(C. S. I. C.)]
SUÁREZ-CAABRO, Dr. José A. , Director, Laboratorio de Biologia Marina, Universidad de
Villanueva, Apartado 6, Marianao, Habana, Cuba. [Chaetognatha of Cuba & West Indies
(Yes)]
* SUBBOTINA, Mme. Paleontogical Institute, Academy of Sciences of U. S. S. R. , 33 Lenin Pros-
pectus, Moscow B-71, U. S. S. R. [Fossil Invertebrates]
* SUBBOTINE, N. N. WNIGRI, W. O. Sjesdorskaja 27, Leningrad, U. S. S. R. [Protozoa]
SUBLETTE, Dr. James E. Dept. of Biological Sciences, Texas Western College of the Univ.
of Texas, El Paso, Texas, U. S. A. [Diptera: Tendipedidae of N. America (Yes)]
SUCIU, I. Laboratorul de Zoologie, Universitatea "Al. I. Cuza", Strada 23 August Nr. 11, Iasi,
Rumania. [Hymenoptera: Chalcidoidea of Rumania (Yes)]
* SUDARIKOV, E. Skrjabin Laboratory of Helminthology, Academy of Sciences of U. S. S. R. ,
Lenin Highway 33, Moscow, U. S. S. R. [Helminths of animals of World]
SUDZUKI, Mr. Minoru. Zoological Institute, Tokyo Kyoiku Daigaku, Bunkyo-ku, Tokyo, Japan.
[Rotatoria: Brachionidae, Notommatidae, Gastropodidae, Asplanchnidae, Synchaetidae,
Testudinellidae, of Japan (Yes); f-w. Nemertinea of Japan (No)]
SUEHIRO, Miss Amy. Bernice P. Bishop Museum, Honolulu 17, Hawaii, U. S. A. [Insects of
Hawaiian Is.]
SUEHIRO, Y. See SUYEHIRO, Y.
* SUENAGA, Hajime. Kyushu National Agricultural Experiment Station, Chikugo-kitayama,
Fukuoka-ken, Japan. [Homoptera: Aphidae]
SUFI, Mr. S. M. K. Zoological Survey of Pakistan, 183 McLeod Road, Karachi, Pakistan.
[Pisces: Mastacembebidae of Oriental (Yes); Sisoridae of Indo-Pakistan (Yes)]
SUGDEN, Dr. Brenda. Natural History Department, The University, Aberdeen, Scotland. [Pro-
tozoa: Ciliata of Rumens (Yes)]
* SUGDEN, L. Game Branch, Canada Department of Fish & Wildlife, Williams Lake, B. C. ,
Canada. [Mammalia]
SUGI, Shigero. 112, 4-chome, Iriarai, Otaku, Tokyo, Japan. [Lepidoptera: Noctuidae of Far
East (No); of Japan (Yes)]

357

* SUIRE, J. 12 Place de la Comedie, Montpellier (Herault), France. [Lepidoptera]
* SUKANOWA, K. M. Zoological Laboratory, Leningrad State University, Leningrad-Centre W-164, U. S. S. R. [Protozoa: Opalinata]
SUKHANOV, V. B. Paleontological Museum, Academy of Sciences of U. S. S. R. , Lenin Prospect 16, Moscow V-71, U. S. S. R. [Permian & Cretaceous Reptilia of e. Europe, n. & c. Asia (No)]
* SULEK, John A. Department of Paleontology, Creole Petroleum Corp. , Jusepin, Monagas, Venezuela. [Fossil Invertebrates]
SULLIVAN, Frank R. Scripps Institution of Oceanography, La Jolla, Calif. , U. S. A. [Up. Eocene to L. Miocene Foraminifera of California (Yes); L. Tertiary Coccolithophores & Discoasters of California (Yes)]
* SULTANOV, M. A. Institute of Zoology & Parasitology, Academy of Sciences of Uzbek S. S. R. , Lunacharsky, Tashkent, U. S. S. R. [Helminthes of animals of U. S. S. R.]
SUMMERS, Dr. Francis. Department of Entomology & Parasitology, University of California, Davis, Calif. , U. S. A. [Acarina: Stigmaeidae of America (Yes)]
SUMMERS, Ray. P. O. Box 124, Petaluma, Calif. , U. S. A. [Gastropoda: Cypraeidae shells of World (Yes)]
SUMMERS, Dr. William A. Indiana University School of Medicine, Indianapolis 7, Ind. , U. S. A. [Medical Helminths & Protozoa of World (Yes)]
SUMMERSON, Prof. Charles Henry. Department of Geology, Ohio State University, Columbus 10, Ohio, U. S. A. [Paleozoic arenaceous Foraminifera (Yes); Pennsylvanian Invertebrates, espec. microfossils but excl. Fusulinidae (Yes)]
* SUN, Ai-Ling. Institute of Vertebrate Paleontology, Academia Sinica, P. O. Box 643, Peking, People's Republic of China. [Fossil Vertebrates]
* SUNDBY, R. Zoologisk Laboratorium, Blindern, Oslo, Norway. [Lepidoptera]
* SUNDE, Leif A. Fisheries Branch, 200 Memorial Boulevard, Winnipeg 1, Man. , Canada. [Pisces]
SUNDHOLM, A. Landbrogatan 25, Karlskrona, Sweden. [Hymenoptera: Proctotrupoidea: Diapriidae & Platygasteridae of Palearctic (Yes)]
SUNDT, Eivind. Sondre Oppegard, Svartskog, Norway. [Coleoptera: Ptiliidae: g. Acrotrichis, of World (No), of Palearctic (Yes)]
SUNG, Mr. G. C. L. C/o Shell Trinidad Limited, Point Fortin, Trinidad. [Up. Jurassic & L. Cretaceous Ostracoda of Netherlands (Yes); Cretaceous Foraminifera of Netherlands (Yes); Up. Tertiary Foraminifera of Sumatra & Indonesia (No)]
SUOMALAINEN, Prof. Dr. Esko. Institute of Genetics, The University, P. Rautatiekatu 13, Helsinki, Finland. [Lepidoptera of n. Europe (Yes)]
SUOMALAINEN, Paavo. (Helsinki, Finland; Mammalia) Not now active in taxonomy.
SUPPERER, Dr. R. Parasitologisches Institut, Tierärztliche Hochschüle, III, Linke Bahngasse 11, Wien, Austria. [Parasitic Nematoda of birds & mammals of c. Europe (Yes)]
* SUSTERA, O. Entomology Department, Národni Museum, Václavské Námešti 1700, Praha 2, Czechoslovakia. [Hymenoptera]
SUSUKI, Takeo. Department of Geology, University of California, Los Angeles 24, Calif. , U. S. A. [Tertiary marine Gastropoda & Pelecypoda of Pacific Cst. U. S. (Yes); M. Cambrian Trilobita of California (No)]
SUTCLIFFE, Dr. A. J. Department of Paleontology, British Museum (Natural History), Cromwell Road, London, S. W. 7, England. [Pleistocene Mammalia of Britain (Yes)]
SUTCLIFFE, Dr. William H. , Jr. Bermuda Biological Station, St. George's West, Bermuda. [Crustacea: pelagic Copepoda of Atlantic (No)]
SUTHERLAND, Dr. Patrick K. Department of Geology, University of Oklahoma, Norman, Okla. , U. S. A. [Mississippian & Pennsylvanian Rugose Corals (Yes); Pennsylvanian Brachiopoda (Yes)]
SUTLIFFE, A. J. See SUTCLIFFE, A. J.
SUTTER, Dr. Ernst. Natural History Museum, Augustinergasse 2, Basel, Switzerland. [Aves of Indonesia & Europe (No)]
* SUTTER, Fritz. Zehntenstrasse 88, Pratteln, Switzerland. [Fossils]
SUTTKUS, Dr. Royal D. Zoology Department, Tulane University, New Orleans 18, La. , U. S. A. [Pisces: Cyprinidae of N. America (Yes); f-w. Pisces of N. America (No); marine Pisces of Gulf of Mexico (Yes)]
* SUTTON, Mr. E. Fletcher, Queensland, Australia. [Coleoptera]
SUTTON, Dr. George M. Department of Zoology, University of Oklahoma, Norman, Okla. , U. S. A. [Aves of Holarctic, Mexico, C. America (Yes)]
* SUVATTI, Chote. Department of Fisheries, Bangkok, Thailand. [Pisces]
SUYEHIRO, Prof. Yasuo. Chief, Department of Fisheries, Faculty of Agriculture, University of Tokyo, Bunkyo-ku, Tokyo, Japan. [Pisces: Teleostii blood sera]
* SUZUKI, --. 239 Bokke, Ichikawa-shi, Chiba-ken, Japan. [Lepidoptera]
SUZUKI, K. Faculty of Fisheries, Prefectural University of Mie, Tsu City, Mie Pref. , Japan. [Pisces: Carangidae of Japan (Yes)]

SUZUKI, Seisho. Zoological Laboratory, Faculty of Science, Hiroshima University, Hiroshima City, Japan. [Opiliones of Japan, Korea, Manchuria, China, Sakhalin, Formosa, Micronesia (Yes)]

ŠVAGROVSKÝ, J. Gotwaldovo 4, Bratislava, Czechoslovakia. [Tertiary-Neogene Gastropoda, Pelecypoda, Scaphopoda, of w. Karpaty, Czechoslovakia (Yes)] [Komensky University]

SVARDSON, Dr. Gunnar. Sötvattenslaboratoriet, Drottningholm, Sweden. [Pisces: Salmonidae of Palearctic (No)]

SVENDSEN, Dr. J. A. Department of Zoology, P. O. Box 656, Faculty of Science, University of Libya, Tripoli, Libya. [Oligochaeta: Lumbricidae of Britain (Yes)]

* SVENONIUS, Dr. B. Kungl. Fiskeriestyrelsen, Göteburg 2, Sweden. [Acarina: Hydrachnellae]

SVENSSON, Forester Ingvar. Box 47, Österslöv, Sweden. [Lepidoptera of n. w. Europe (Yes)]

SVESHNIKOV, V. A. Laboratory of Invertebrate Zoology, Biological Faculty, Moscow State University, Moscow W-234, U. S. S. R. [Annelida: Polychaeta of Arctic, N. America, S. America (Yes)]

* SVESHNIKOVA, Prof. Dr. N. M. Moscow Station of Plant Protection, Butirski hutor 2, Moscow W-234, U. S. S. R. [Nematoda]

SVETOVIDOV, Dr. A. N. Zoological Institute, Academy of Sciences of U. S. S. R., Leningrad B-164, U. S. S. R. [Pisces, espec. marine & f-w. Clupeiformes & Gadiformes, of U. S. S. R. (Yes)]

SVIHLA, Dr. Arthur. Department of Zoology, University of Washington, Seattle 5, Wash., U. S. A. [F-w. Porifera, Odonata, Amphibia, Reptilia, Mammalia, of World]

* SVIVASTAVA, V. K. Central Inland Fisheries Research Station, Cuttack, India. [Ostracoda]

SWAIN, Dr. F. M. Department of Geology, University of Minnesota, Minneapolis 14, Minn., U. S. A. [Crustacea: marine & f-w. Ostracoda of w. Hemisphere (Yes)]

SWAINE, Dr. J. M. (Ottawa, Canada; Coleoptera) Deceased.

SWAN, Mr. D. C., Head, Department of Entomology, Waite Agricultural Research Institute, University of Adelaide, Adelaide, Australia. [Acarina: Ixodoidea of Australia (Yes); Eriophyidae of Australia (No)]

SWAN, Dr. Emery F. Department of Zoology, University of New Hampshire, Durham, N. H., U. S. A. [Intertidal & shallow water Asteroidea, Ophiuroidea, Echinoidea, Pelecypoda, shelled Gastropoda, of n. e. & n. w. coasts of U. S. (Yes)]

SWANEPOEL, Mr. D. A. P. O. Box 413, Pretoria, Union of South Africa. [Lepidoptera: Rhopalocera of s. Africa (Yes)]

* SWANEVELD, C. "Woodlands", 41 Highstead Road, Rondebosch, Union of South Africa. [Mollusca]

SWANN, David Henry. Illinois State Geological Survey, Natural Resources Building, Urbana, Ill., U. S. A. [Silurian & Devonian Tabulata, espec. Favositidae (Yes)]

SWANSON, Paul L. R. F. D. 2, Polk, Penna., U. S. A. [Amphibia & Reptilia of Florida Keys & Pennsylvania (Yes)]

SWARTZ, Dr. Frank M. Department of Geology, Pennsylvania State University, University Park, Pa., U. S. A. [Ordovician, Silurian, Devonian Ostracoda (Yes)]

SWARTZWELDER, Dr. J. Clyde. School of Medicine, Louisiana State University, New Orleans 12, La., U. S. A. [Protozoa & Helminths parasitic in man of N. America (Yes)]

* SWATSCHEK, B. Pädagogium am Schlossberg, Baden/Baden, Germany. [Lepidoptera]

SWEDMARK, Bertil. Naturhistoriska Riksmuseum, Stockholm 50, Sweden. [Coelenterata: Halammohydridae; Gastrotricha: Macrodasyoidea: Archiannelida: Nerillidae; of European Atlantic Coast & Mediterranean (Yes)]

SWEENEY, R. C. H. Cotton Pest Research Scheme, c/o Department of Agriculture, P. O. Chiromo, Nyasaland. [Hymenoptera: Formicidae of Europe & c. Africa (No); Reptilia: Ophidia of trop. Africa (Yes)]

SWEET, Prof. Walter C. Department of Geology, Ohio State University, Columbus 10, Ohio, U. S. A. [Paleozoic Cephalopoda: Nautiloidea (Yes); Paleozoic Conodonts (Yes)]

SWINTON, Dr. W. E. British Museum (Natural History), Cromwell Road, London, S. W. 7, England. [Mesozoic Reptilia & Aves (Yes)]

SWIRSKI, Dr. E. Agricultural Research Station, Rehovot, Israel. [Homoptera: Aphidoidea of Middle East (Yes)]

SWYNNERTON, Mr. G. H. Game Department, P. O. Box 397, Arusha, Tanganyika. [Mammalia of Africa (No), of Tanganyika (Yes)]

SYKES, James E. U. S. Fish & Wildlife Service, Beaufort, N. C., U. S. A. [Pisces: Clupeidae & Serranidae of N. America (Yes)]

SÝKORA, Jan. Na Markvartce 14, Praha 6, Czechoslovakia. [Trichoptera Imagines, Larvae, & Nymphae, of Palearctic (Yes)]

SYLVESTER, Robert K. Geological Department, The Texas Company, P. O. Box 252, New Orleans 9, La., U. S. A. [Devonian & Mississippian Scolecodonts of N. America (Yes)]

SYLVESTER-BRADLEY, Mr. P. C. Department of Geology, The University, Leicester, England. [Ordovician-Recent Ostracoda (Yes); L. Jurassic Cephalopoda: Dactylioceratidae (Yes); Jurassic-Cretaceous Pelecypoda: Ostreidae (Yes); M. -Up. Jurassic Brachiopoda: g. Digonella & Obovothyris (Yes)]

SYME, Mr. Paul D. Department of Zoology, University of Toronto, Toronto 5, Ont., Canada. [Lepidoptera of N. America (No); Rhopalocera of Ontario (Yes)]
SYNAVE, Mr. H. 12, rue Jacques Manne, Anderlecht, Bruxelles, Belgium. [Homoptera: Fulgoroidea: Cixiidae, Flatidae, Tropiduchidae, Meenoplidae, Achilidae, Lophopidae, Dictyopharidae, of Africa (Yes)] [Institut Royal des Sciences Naturelles]
* SYTOVA, Dr. V. A. Moscow State University, Leninski Gory, Moscow B-234, U. S. S. R. [Silurian Rugosa]
SZABÓ, J. B. Országos Közegészségügyi Intézet, Gyáli-ut 2-6, Budapest IX, Hungary. [Hymenoptera: Proctotrupoidea of New Guinea, Africa, Palearctic, New World (Yes); Chalcidoidea of Palearctic & New World (Yes)]
SZALAY, Dr. L. Természettudományi Muzeum Állattár, Baross-utca 13, Budapest VIII, Hungary. [Arachnoidea of Hungary (No); Hydracarina of Europe & Asia (Yes)]
SZARSKI, Prof. Henryk. Universytet Mikołaja Kopernika, ul. Sienkiewicza 30/32, Torun, Poland. [Amphibia & Reptilia of Poland (Yes)]
SZCZEPANSKI, Mgr. Andrzej. Stacja Hydrobiologiczna, Mikolajki, Mragowa, Poland. [Oligochaeta: Limicola of Palearctic (No)]
SZCZEPSKI, Jan Bogusław. Ornithological Station, Górki Wschodnie, p. Sobieszewo, Gdańsk, Poland. [Aves: Charadriiformes, Anseriformes, Lariformes, of Palearctic (Yes)]
* SZÉKESSY, Dr. V. Magyar Nemzeti Múzeum, Természettudományi Múzeum Állattár, Baross-utca 13, Budapest VIII, Hungary. [Coleoptera: Staphylinidae]
SZELEGIEWICZ, Henryk. Institute of Zoology, Polska Akademia Nauk, Ul. Wilcza 64, Warszawa, Poland. [Homoptera: Aphididae of Palearctic (No); of Europe (Yes)]
SZELENYI, Dr. G. Novenyvedelmi Kutato Intezet, Hermann O u 15, Budapest II, Hungary. [Hymenoptera: Chalcidoidea & Proctotrupoidea of Europe (Yes); Homoptera: Coccidae of Europe (No)]
* SZENK, B. J. Department of Paleontology, Mene Grande Oil Co., Apartado Postal 709, Caracas, Venezuela. [Fossil Invertebrates]
SZENT-IVANY, J. J. H. (Port Moresby, New Guinea: Lepidoptera) Deceased.
SZIDAT, Prof. Dr. L. Navarro 2728, Buenos Aires, Argentina. [Trematoda of S. America (Yes); Crustacea: Isopoda: Cymothoidae of S. Atlantic (Yes)] [Instituto Nacional de Investigación de las Ciencias Naturales "Bernhardino Rivadavia"]
* SZIENKIEVICZ, Igor. Minist. Agriculturii, Serviciul de Protectia Plantelor, Bucureşti, Rumania. [Hemiptera]
SZIJJ, L. Department of Zoology, University of Toronto, Toronto, Ont., Canada. [Aves: Passeriformes of c. Europe (Yes); Coleoptera: Scarabaeidae of c. Europe (No)]
SZTANKAY-GULYÁS, Dr. M. State Hygienic Institute, Gyali-ut 2-4, Budapest IX, Hungary. [Diptera: Culicinae & Muscidae of Hungary (Yes)]
SZUJECKI, Mr. Andrzej. Zakład Ochrony Lasu i Entomologii, Szkoła Głowna Gospodarstwa Wiejskiego, ul. Rakowiecka 8, Warszawa, Poland. [Coleoptera: Staphylinidae, excl. Aleocharinae, of c. Europe (Yes); Steninae of Europe (Yes); of Asia (No)]
SZUNYOGHY, Dr. J. Magyar Nemzeti Muzeum, Baross-utca 13, Budapest VIII, Hungary. [Mammalia: Insectivora: Talpidae, Soricidae, Erinaceidae; Carnivora: Canidae; Lagomorpha: Leponidae; Artiodactyla: Cervidae; all of Europe (Yes); Rodentia: Spalacidae; of Europe & Asia (Yes)]
* SZMYT, A. M. Walki Młodych 9/4, Poznan, Poland. [Lepidoptera]
* SZTEJN, J. Instytut Geologiczny, Rakowiecka 4, Warszawa, Poland. [Fossil Foraminifera]
SZYMCZAKOWSKI, Dr. Wacław. Department of Entomology, Instytut Zoologiczny, Polska Akademia Nauk, ul. Sławkowska 17, Krakow, Poland. [Coleoptera: Catopidae, excl. Bathysciinae, of World (Yes)]

* TABACARU, Y. Institutul de Speologie, Str. Dr. Capsa, 8, Bucureşti 15, Rumania. [Odonata]
TABBERT, Robert L. Magnolia Petroleum Co., 518 Pioneer Building, Lake Charles, La., U. S. A. [Tertiary Foraminifera of U. S. Gulf Coast (Yes); Fusulinidae of New Mexico & Oklahoma (No)]
* TABERLY, Georges. Laboratoire de Biologie Général, Faculté des Sciences de Toulouse, Toulouse (H. G.), France. [Acarina]
TACHIKAWA, Mr. Tetsusaburo. Entomological Laboratory, College of Agriculture, Ehime University, Matsuyama City, Ehime, Shikoku, Japan. [Hymenoptera: Encyrtidae of Japan (Yes)]
* TACOLI, M. L. Istituto di Geologia, Universitá di Modena, Modena, Italy. [Fossil Foraminifera]
TAKAGI, Mr. Kazunori. Laboratory of Fishery Biology, Tokyo University of Fisheries, Shiba Kaigandori 6, Minato-ku, Tokyo, Japan. [Pisces: Gobiina of Japan (Yes); of Indo-Pacific (No)]
TAKAGI, S. Entomological Institute, Faculty of Agriculture, Hokkaido University, Sapporo, Japan. [Homoptera: Coccoidea of Japan (No); Diaspididae of Japan (Yes)]

360

TAKAHASHI, Prof. Keizo. Department of Zoology, Tokyo Kasei Daigaku, Itabashi 6-chome, Itabashi, Tokyo, Japan. [Polychaeta of Japan & Micronesia (Yes)]

TAKAHASHI, Dr. Ryoichi. Agricultural College, Osaku-fu University, Kuroyama, Osaka-fu, Japan. [Homoptera: Coccoidea of Japan & Formosa (Yes); Aleyrodidae of Asia & Micronesia (Yes); Aphidiidae of Japan & Formosa (Yes)]

TAKAHASI, Dr. Hirosi. 4495 Nakamachi 4-chome, Nerimaku, Tokyo, Japan. [Diptera: Tabanidae, Simuliidae, Heleidae, Culicidae, of Japan, Korea, Formosa, Manchuria, Saghalien (Yes); Conopidae, Leptidae, Bombyliidae, Hippoboscidae, Oestridae, of Japan, Korea, Formosa, Manchuria, & Saghalien (No)]

TAKAI, Prof. Dr. Fuyuji. Geological Institute, Tokyo University, Tokyo, Japan. [Fossil Mammalia of Japan (Yes)]

* TAKAI, Toru. Shimonoseki College of Fisheries, Shimonoseki City, Japan. [Pisces]

TAKAKUWA, Dr. Yosioki. 510, 3 chome, Asagaya, Suginami-ku, Tokyo, Japan. [Diplopoda & Chilopoda of Japan (Yes)]

TAKANO, Prof. Shuzo. Obihiro Zootechnical University, Obihiro, Hokkaido, Japan. [Diptera: Larvaevoridae of Japan (Yes)]

TAKASHIMA, Haruo. Biological Laboratory, Waseda University, Tokyo, Japan. [Scorpiones & Pedipalpi of Palearctic & Oriental (Yes); Symphyla & Diplopoda of Japan (No)]

TAKEUCHI, Kichizo. 6 Kumagayamachi, Shinomiya, Yamashina, Kyoto, Japan. [Hymenoptera: Symphyta of e. Asia (Yes)] [Takeuchi Entomological Laboratory]

* TAKEYA, Choku. Biological Laboratory, Faculty of Commerce, Kurume University, Kurume City, Kyushu, Japan. [Heteroptera: Tingidae]

TAKI, Dr. Isao. National Science Museum, Ueno Park, Tokyo, Japan. [Amphineura: Polyplacophora; Gastropoda: g. Titiscania & Calyptraeidae; all of Indo-Pacific (Yes)]

TAKI, Prof. Dr. Iwao. Department of Fisheries, Faculty of Fisheries & Animal Husbandry, Hiroshima University, Fukuyama, Japan. [Cephalopoda of Japan (Yes)]

TALBOT, F. South African Museum, P. O. Box 61, Capetown, Union of South Africa. [Pisces: Lutjanidae: g. Plectropomus of e. Africa cst. (Yes); marine Pisces, excl. abyssal, of s. Africa (Yes)]

TALENT, John Alfred. 114 The Boulevard, Essendon, W 5, Vict., Australia. [L. & M. Paleozoic Brachiopoda & Gastropoda (Yes); Paleozoic-Mesozoic Crustacea: Conchostraca (Yes)] [Geological Survey of Victoria]

* TALICE, Dr. Rodolfo V. Palmar 2415, Montevideo, Uruguay. [Parasites]

TALMADGE, Mr. Robert R. Box 71, Willow Creek, Calif., U.S.A. [Gastropoda: Haliotidae & Stimatellidae, of World (Yes)]

TAMAJO, Dr. Eleonora. Via Giusti 2, Palermo, Italy. [Fossil marine Foraminifera]

TAMANINI, Dr. L. Viale Trento 16, Rovereto (Trento), Italy. [Heteroptera of Europe (Yes)]

TAMBS-LYCHE, Dr. Hans. Biologisk Stasjon, Universitets Bergen, Espegrend, Bergen, Norway. [Araneida, Opiliones, Acarina: Ixodidae of n. Europe, Arctic, Antarctic (Yes); Pisces of Scandinavia (Yes)]

TAMS, Mr. W. H. T. Department of Entomology, British Museum (Natural History), Cromwell Road, London, S. W. 7, England. [Lepidoptera: Heterocera, espec. Noctuidae & Lasiocampidae, of World (Yes)]

* TANAKA, Azusa. 12 Sowa-machi 1, Nada-ku, Kobe, Japan. [Diptera: Conopidae]

TANAKA, Eiichi. Oba, Mashiko, Tochigiken, Japan. [Hymenoptera: Crabronidae of Chuzenki, Nikko, Japan.]

* TANAKA, Kazuo. 527 Kyodo-cho, Setagaya-ku, Tokyo, Japan. [Coleoptera: Carabidae]

TANAKA, Dr. Otohiko. Department of Fisheries, Faculty of Agriculture, Kyushu University, Tsuyazaki, Fukuoka, Japan. [Crustacea: free-swimming marine Copepoda of Japan (Yes)]

* TANAKA, Ryo. Zoology, Department, Women's College of Kochi, Kochi, Japan. [Fossil Mammalia]

TANAKA, Dr. Tadashi. Laboratory of Entomology, Faculty of Agriculture, Utsunomiya University, Utsunomiya, Tochigi Pref., Japan. [Homoptera: Aphididae of Asia & Japan (Yes)]

TANAKA, Yataroh. Hama Laboratory, Seikai Regional Fisheries Research Laboratory, Hama, Kashima, Saga Pref., Japan. [Pelecypoda of Japan (Yes); Oyster larvae of Japan (Yes)]

* TANASACHI, Jana. Institutul de Speologie al R. P. R., Str. Dr. Capsa 8, Raion Lenin, Bucureşti, Rumania. [Acarina: Hydrachnellae]

TANDAN, Dr. B. K. Department of Zoology, University of Lucknow, Lucknow, India. [Mallophaga of World (Yes)]

TANDON, Dr. R. S. Department of Zoology, Lucknow University, Lucknow, India. [Trematoda: Paramphistomatidae, Aspidogastridae, Fasciolidae, of World (Yes)]

TÅNING, Dr. Å. V., Director, Danmarks Fiskeri - og Havundersøgelser, Charlottenlund Slot, Charlottenlund, Denmark. [Pisces: Myctophidae of all Oceans (No); Pisces of N. Atlantic (No)]

* TANITA, Senji. Tohoku Regional Fisheries Research Laboratory, Shiogawa, Miyagi, Pref., Japan. [Porifera]

* TANNER, Vasco M. Department of Zoology, Brigham Young University, Provo, Utah, U.S.A. [Coleoptera; Pisces, Amphibia, Reptilia]

TANNER, Dr. W. W. Department of Zoology, Brigham Young University, Provo, Utah, U.S.A. [Amphibia & Reptilia of w.N.America (Yes); Plethodontidae of w.U.S., Mexico, C. America (Yes); Reptilia: Scincidae: g. Eumeces of w.U.S., Mexico, C.America (Yes)]

TAO, Charles Chiachu. Division of Applied Zoology, Taiwan Agricultural Research Institute, Taipeh, Taiwan, Formosa. [Homoptera: Aphididae of Asia & Pacific Islands (Yes)]

TAPIA, Profesora Esmenia A. Instituto de Sanidad Vegetal, Calle Araoz No. 2758, Ministerio de Agricultura, Buenos Aires, Argentina. [Homoptera: Coccoidea & Aphidoidea; Thysanoptera; of Neotropical (Yes)]

* TARASTSHUK, W.T. Department of Reptiles, Zoological Institute, Academy of Sciences, Kiev, U.S.S.R. [Reptilia, Amphibia]

TARCZYŃSKI, Dr. Stefan. Katedra Parazytologii, ul. Grochowska 272, Warszawa 26, Poland. [Helminthes: Helminths of Suidae of Europe (Yes); Nematoda: g. Wehrdickmansia of Europe (Yes)]

TARJAN, Dr. A.C. Citrus Experiment Station, Lake Alfred, Fla., U.S.A. [Nematoda: Rhabditidae, Diplogasterinae, Panagrolaiminae, Cephalobinae, Tylenchida, Dorylaimoidea, of World (Yes)]

TARLO, L.B. 34 Howard Walk, London, N.2, England. [Jurassic Sauropterygia: Pliosauridae (Yes); Devonian Heterostraci: Psammosteidae & Corvaspidae (Yes)] [Department of Palaeontology, British Museum (Natural History)]

TARRAS-WAHLBERG, Nils. Trägardsgatan 2, Kumla, Sweden. [Acarina: Oribatei of Europe (Yes)]

TARSHIS, Dr. I. Barry. Department of Entomology, University of California, Los Angeles 24, Calif., U.S.A. [Diptera: Hippoboscidae of World (No)]

TARTAMELLA, Natale J. (Corpus Christi, Texas; Fossils) Not now active in taxonomy.

TASCH, Dr. Paul. Department of Geology, University of Wichita, Wichita, Kans., U.S.A. [Fossil Branchiopoda, espec. Conchostraca, espec. Permian (Yes); Paleozoic faunas (No); Pennsylvanian & Permian microfaunas: Conodonts, Ostracoda, Foraminifera, (espec. Fusulinidae) (Yes); Cambrian & Carboniferous Trilobita (Yes)]

* TASHIAN, Richard E. Columbia University, 413 West 117th Street, New York 27, N.Y., U.S.A. [Aves of C. America]

* TASMAN, Mehlika I. Paleontology Laboratory, Esso Standard (Turkey) Inc., Bagindir Sokak 5/15, Yenisehir, Ankara, Turkey. [Cretaceous-Tertiary Foraminifera]

TATARINOV, Dr. L.P. Paleontological Museum, Academy of Sciences of U.S.S.R., Lenin Prospect 16, Moscow B-71, U.S.S.R. [Permian Triassic Reptilia: Anomodontia of U.S.S.R. (Yes); fossil Chelonia: Baenoidea (Yes); Cenozoic Amphibia of Palearctic (Yes)]

TATE, P. The Molteno Institute of Biology & Parasitology, Downing Street, Cambridge, England. [Diptera: larvae of Britain (Yes)]

TATGE, Ursula. See HOCH, Ursula.

TATTERSALL, Dr. Olive S. "Pendeen", Sinah Lane, Hayling Island, Hants, England. [Crustacea: Mysidacea of World (Yes)] [Department of Oceanography, "Discovery Investigations", British Museum (Natural History)]

TATUM, E.P. Paleontology Laboratory, Humble Oil & Refining Co., P.O.Box 2180, Houston 1, Texas, U.S.A. [Tertiary Foraminifera of Texas Gulf Coast (Yes)]

TAUFFLIEB, Dr. R. Institut Pasteur de l'Afrique Equatoriale Française, Brazzaville, French Equatorial Africa. [Acarina: larvae of Trombiculidae of Ethiopian (No); Laelaptidae ectoparasitic on vertebrates of Ethiopian (No)] [Office de la Recherche Scientific et Technique Outre-Mer]

* TAYLOR, A.G. West African Fisheries Research Institute, Freetown, Sierra Leone. [Pisces]

TAYLOR, Mr. Albert L. Section of Nematology, Plant Industry Station, Beltsville, Md., U.S.A. [Plant parasitic Nematoda (Yes)]

* TAYLOR, Mr. Beryl E. Frick Laboratory, American Museum of Natural History, New York 24, U.S.A. [Fossil Mammalia]

TAYLOR, Dr. Charles E. Scottish Horticultural Research Institute, Mylnefield, Invergowrie by Dundee, Scotland. [Homoptera: Aphididae of c. Africa (Yes), of Britain (No)]

TAYLOR, Mr. Donald P. Department of Plant Pathology & Botany, University of Minnesota, St. Paul 1, Minn., U.S.A. [Nematoda: plant parasitic Tylenchidae of U.S. (Yes)]

TAYLOR, Dwight W. 2425 Wyoming Avenue, N.W., Washington 8, D.C., U.S.A. [Tertiary non-marine Mollusca of N.America (Yes); Pleistocene non-marine Gastropoda of N. America (Yes); Recent f-w. Gastropoda of N.America (No)] [U.S. Geological Survey]

TAYLOR, Prof. Edward H. 118 Snow Hall, University of Kansas, Lawrence, Kans., U.S.A. [Amphibia & Reptilia of Mexico, Costa Rica, s.e.Asia, Siam, Malaya, Phillippines (Yes)]

TAYLOR, E.L. (Weybridge, England; Nematoda) Not now active in taxonomy.

TAYLOR, Dr. F.M. Department of Geology, The University, Nottingham, England. [Paleozoic Rugose Corals: Lithostrobiontidae, Lonsdaleiidae, Palaeosmiliidae, Acervulariidae, Phillipsastraeidae of Britain (Yes)]

TAYLOR, Mr. K.L. Division of Entomology, Commonwealth Scientific & Industrial Research Organization, P.O.Box 109, City, Canberra, Australia. [Homoptera: Psyllidae: Spondyliaspinae of Australia (Yes)]

* TAYLOR, Prof. Leland H. (Morgantown, W. Va.; Hymenoptera) Not now active in taxonomy.
TAYLOR, Dr. Peter Walter. Caracas Petroleum S. A., Apartado 89, Caracas, Venezuela.
[Devonian & Silurian Brachiopoda & Tetracoralla of World (Yes); Carboniferous Corals,
Brachiopoda, Goniatites, of Europe & N. America (Yes); Cambrian & Ordovician Trilo-
bita of N. America (Yes); Carboniferous Ostracoda of Europe & N. America (No)]
TAYLOR, R. W. Department of Zoology, University of Auckland, Auckland, New Zealand. [Hy-
menoptera: Formicidae of Australia & New Zealand (Yes); Hymenoptera of New Zealand
(Yes)]
TAYLOR, Walter P. (Claremont, Calif.; Mammalia) Not now active in taxonomy.
TAYLOR, William Ralph. Division of Fishes, U. S. National Museum, Washington 25, D. C.,
U. S. A. [Pisces of World (Yes)]
TCHINDONOVA, Mrs. Julia G. Institute of Oceanology, Academy of Sciences, Luznikovskaja 8,
Moscow, U. S. S. R. [Chaetognatha of Pacific & Indian Oceans (No); Gastropoda: Ptero-
poda of Pacific & Indian Oceans (No); Heteropoda of Pacific & Indian Oceans (Yes);
Mysidacea of Pacific, Indian, & Antarctic Oceans (No); Sergestidae of N. w. Pacific (No)]
TEBBLE, Mr. N. Spirit Building D. 7 (Annelids), British Museum (Natural History), Cromwell
Road, London, S. W. 7, England. [Polychaeta of World (No)]
TEDFORD, Mr. Richard H. Department of Paleontology, University of California, Berkeley 4,
Calif., U. S. A. [Mammalia: Tertiary & Quaternary Marsupsialia of Australasia (Yes);
Up. Tertiary Carnivora: Fissipedia of N. America (Yes); Up. Tertiary Equidae of N.
America (Yes)]
TEE-VAN, John. New York Zoological Park, New York 60, N. Y., U. S. A. [Tropical marine
Pisces of West Indies & trop. e. Pacific (Yes)] [New York Zoological Society]
TEICHERT, Mr. Curt. U. S. Geological Survey, Federal Center, Denver, Colo., U. S. A.
[Paleozoic Nautiloidea (Yes)]
* TEICHMANN, Harald. Zoologisches Institut der Universität, Luisenstrasse 14, München 2,
Germany. [Orthoptera]
* TEISSIER, Prof. G. Directeur, Station Biologique, Roscoff (Finistère), France. [Mollusca,
Coelenterata, marine Arthropoda]
TEIXEIRA, Prof. C. Museo e Laboratorio Mineralogico e Geologico, Faculdade de Ciencias,
Rua da Escola Politécnica, Lisboa, Portugal. [Permo-Carboniferous Insecta; Permo-
Carboniferous & Karroo Phyllopoda of Africa; Karroo Pisces of Africa]
* TEIXEIRA de FREITAS, J. F. See de FREITAS, J. F. Teixeira.
TELENGA, Prof. Dr. N. A. Institute of Plant Protection, Ukrainian Academy of Agricultural
Sciences, ul Repina 3, Kiev, U. S. S. R. [Hymenoptera: Braconidae of Palearctic (Yes)]
TELFORD, Dr. H. S. Department of Entomology, State College of Washington, Pullman, Wash.,
U. S. A. [Diptera: Syrphidae of U. S. (No)]
TELLER, Lt. Cmdr. Leslie W. Preventive Medicine Unit 2, Naval Base, Norfolk, Va., U. S. A.
[Acarina: Laelaptidae, Trombiculidae, Ixodoidea, of U. S. & Japan (Yes)]
* TELLEZ, Mrs. Clemencia. See ALVAREZ, Clemencia.
* TEMPÈRE, G. 106 rue de Pressensé, Le Bouscat (Gironde), France. [Coleoptera]
* TEMPLE, J. T. Department of Geology, Birkbeck College, Malet Street, London, W. C. 1,
England. [Fossil Invertebrates]
TEMPLEMAN, Dr. W. Biological Station, Fisheries Research Board of Canada, St. John's,
Newfoundland. [Marine Pisces of Newfoundland & Labrador]   •
TENDEIRO, Dr. João. Junta das Missões Geográficas e de Investigações do Ultramar, Centro
de Zoologia, Rua da Junqueira 14, Lisboa, Portugal. [Acarina: Ixodoidea of Europe &
Africa (Yes); Mallophaga of birds of Europe & Africa (Yes); Trematoda of fishes of
European & African Coasts (No)]
TENER, Mr. J. S. Canadian Wildlife Service, Department of Northern Affairs & National Re-
sources, Ottawa, Ont., Canada. [Mammalia: g. Ovibos of n. w. Territories (Yes)]
* TENISON, Lt. Col. W. P. C. Department of Fishes, British Museum (Natural History), Crom-
well Road, London, S. W. 7, England. [Pisces]
* TERÁN, A. Instituto Miguel Lillo, Miguel Lillo 205, Tucumán, Argentina. [Coleoptera]
* TERCIER, Prof. Dr. Jean. 73 Chemin Ritter, Fribourg, Switzerland. [Fossils]
* TÉRĚK, P. Address unknown. [Crustacea: Copepoda]
TERENTJEV, Dr. Paul V., Professor, Department of Vertebrate Zoology, Leningrad State
University, Leningrad-Centre 164, U. S. S. R. [Amphibia: espec. G. Rana of Palearctic
(Yes); Reptilia of Palearctic (Yes)]
* TERMIER, Mme. Genevieve. Faculté des Sciences, Université de Alger, Alger, Algeria.
[Fossil Invertebrates]
* TERMIER, Prof. Henri. Faculté des Sciences, Université de Alger, Alger, Algeria. [Fossil
Invertebrates]
TER-MINASIAN, Dr. Margarita E. Zoological Institute, Academy of Sciences, Leningrad B-164,
U. S. S. R. [Coleoptera: Attelabidae & Curculionidae of Palearctic (Yes)]
TERPSTRA, Dr. G. R. J. Bureau of Mineral Resources, Department of National Development,
Canberra, Australia. [Cretaceous-Recent Foraminifera (Yes)]

TESAŘ, Dr. Zdeněk. Department of Entomology, Slezské Museum, Opava, Czechoslovakia. [Coleoptera: Scarabaeidae of Palearctic (Yes); of Oriental (No)]

TESCHNER, Dr. Dietrich. Zoologisches Institut der Technischen Hochschule, Pockelsstrasse 10a, Braunschweig, Germany. [Diptera: Brachycera of Europe (Yes); Nematocera of Germany (No)]

TESMER, Dr. Irving H. Science Department, State University of New York College for Teachers, Buffalo 22, N. Y., U. S. A. [Up. Devonian Brachiopoda & Pelecypoda of s. w. New York & n. w. Pennsylvania (Yes)]

TESSAKOV, J. I. Wseoyuzny Neftyanoy Nauchnoissledovatelsky Geologo-Rasvedochny Institut (W. N. I. G. R. I.), Liteiny 39, Leningrad, U. S. S. R. [Ordovician & Silurian Tabulate Corals of Siberia (Yes)]

van TETS, Mr. G. F. Department of Zoology, University of British Columbia, Vancouver 8, B. C., Canada. [Aves: Phalacrocoracidae of World (Yes)]

TEUNISSEN, Dr. H. G. M. Zoologisch Museum, Plantage Middenlaan 53, Amsterdam C, Netherlands. [Hymenoptera: Icheumonidae, Sphegidae, Apidae, Vespidae, Chrysididae of Palearctic (No)]

* TEVES, Juan S. Bureau of Mines, Manila, Philippines. [Fossil Invertebrates]

TEWARI, Prof. B. S. Department of Geology, University of Lucknow, Lucknow, India. [Tertiary Foraminifera & Ostracoda of Indo-Pacific (Yes)]

TEYROVSKY, Dr. V. Vysoka Skola Pedagogicka, Zoologicky ustav, Krizkovskeho 10, Olomouc, Czechoslovakia. [Heteroptera: Corixidae of c. Europe (Yes); Odonata of c. Europe (Yes)]

* THAANUM, Ditlev. 43 Coelho Way, Honolulu, Hawaii. [Mollusca]

* THAKE, C. 292 Fleur de Lis Road, Birkirkara, Malta. [Mollusca]

THALMANN, Dr. Hans E. P. O. Box 1978, Stanford, Calif., U. S. A. [Mesozoic & Tertiary Foraminifera of World (Yes); Paleozoic to Tertiary Microfossils, excl. Foraminifera, of World (Yes)] [Stanford University]

THAMES, Walter H., Jr. Department of Soils, Agricultural Experiment Station, University of Florida, Gainesville, Fla., U. S. A. [Nematoda: Tylenchida of N. America (Yes)]

THAPAR, Dr. G. S. 14 Mahatma Ghandhi Road, Dilkusha, Lucknow, India. [Trematoda of India & Pakistan (Yes); Cestoda of India & Pakistan (No); Nematoda & Acanthocephala of India, Burma, Pakistan (Yes)] [Lucknow University]

THATCHER, Dr. T. O. Department of Entomology, Colorado State University, Fort Collins, Colo., U. S. A. [Coleoptera: Scolytidae, adults & larvae, of World (No), of N. & C. America & Europe (Yes)]

THEILER, Gertrud. Veterinary Research Laboratories, Onderstepoort, Union of South Africa. [Acarina: ticks of Africa (Yes)]

* THEMIDO, Antonio Armando. Museu Zoologico, Universidad de Coimbra, Coimbra, Portugal. [Reptilia]

THENIUS, Prof. Dr. Erich. Paläontologisches Institut der Universität, Wien (I), Austria. [Up. Tertiary & Pleistocene Mammalia: Theria of Europe (Yes)]

THEODOR, Prof. O. Department of Parasitology, The Hebrew University, Jerusalem, Israel. [Diptera: Nycteribiidae & Phlebotominae of Old World (Yes); Acarina: Argasidae of Old World (No)]

THÉODORIDÈS, Dr. J. 21 Boulevard de Grenelle, Paris (XV), France. [Protozoa: Eugregarina of insects of World (Yes); Nematoda of arthropods, excl. Mermithoidea, of World (No)] [Centre National de Recherche Scientifique]

THEOWALD, Dr. Br. (T. van Leeuwen) Kerkstraat 136, Amsterdam, Netherlands. [Diptera: Tipulidae, Larvae, pupae, imagines, of Palearctic (Yes); Calliphoridae of Indo-Australian (Yes)]

THEROND, Jean. 41 rue Seguier, Nimes (Gard.), France. [Coleoptera: Histeridae of Europe, Asia, Africa, Oceania (Yes); of America (No)]

THEW, Mr. Thomas B. 451 16th Avenue, East Moline, Ill., U. S. A. [Ephemeroptera of World (No), of New World (Yes); Leptophlebiidae & Caenidae of World (Yes); fossil Ephemeroptera of World (No)] [Davenport Public Museum, Iowa]

* THIENEMANN, Prof. Dr. August. Direktor, Hydrobiologische Anstalt, Max-Planck-Gesellschaft, Plön (Holstein), Germany. [Diptera] Died April 22, 1960.

* THINES, Georges. Address unknown. [Pisces]

* THOMANN, H. Address unknown. [Lepidoptera]

THOMAS, Dr. D. E. Laboratory of Paleontology, Department of Mines, Treasury Gardens, Melbourne C. 2, Australia. [Graptolithina of Australia, espec. e. Australia (Yes)]

THOMAS, Dr. Gwyn. Department of Geology, Imperial College of Science, London, S. W. 7, England. [Up. Devonian Pisces of Old Red Sandstone of Britain (Yes); Up. Devonian Brachiopoda: Spiriferidae of Britain (Yes)]

THOMAS, Dr. G. A. C/o Bureau of Mineral Resources, Geology & Geophysics, Department of Natural Development, Canberra, Australia. [Up. Paleozoic Brachiopoda of Australia (Yes)]

* THOMAS, Dr. G. E. States Experiment Station, Howard Davis Farm, Trinity, Jersey, C. I., England. [Nematoda]

THOMAS, George W. 106 Whitten Hall, University of Missouri, Columbia, Mo., U.S.A.
[Coleoptera: Mordellidae of c.U.S. (Yes); Chrysomelidae: Cryptocephalini of N.America
(Yes)]
THOMAS, Dr. H.D. British Museum (Natural History), Cromwell Road, London, S.W.7, Eng-
land. [Fossil Corals of World (Yes); Mesozoic & Tertiary Polyzoa of World (Yes)]
THOMAS, Dr. H.T. King's College Hospital Medical School, Denmark Hill, London, S.E.5,
England. [Diptera: g.Sarcophaga, Calliphora, Lucilia, Chrysomyia, Hemipyrellia, of
Oriental (Yes)]
* THOMAS, J.G. Department of Zoology, Royal Holloway College, Englefield Green, Surrey,
England. [Orthoptera]
* THOMAS, Dr. L.A. Department of Geology, Iowa State University, Ames, Iowa, U.S.A.
[Fossil Conodonts]
THOMAS, Dr. L.J. 103a Vivarium Building, Champaign, Ill., U.S.A. [Cestoda, Nematoda,
Acanthocephala, Trematoda, of N. & C.America (Yes)] [University of Illinois]
THOMAS, Mr. Lowell Phillip. 3421 S.W. 23rd Street, Miami 45, Fla., U.S.A. [Ophiuroidea:
Amphiuridae of e.cst. of N.America (Yes); Pisces: Opisthognathidae of Florida (Yes)]
[University of Miami Marine Laboratory]
THOMAS, Norman Louis. (Chicago 1, Ill.; Foraminifera) Not now active in taxonomy.
THOMAS, P.R. National Agricultural Advisory Service, Staplake Mount, Starcross, Exeter,
Devon, England. [Plant parasitic Nematoda of England & Wales (No)]
THOMAS, Mr. Raymond. 6 Place Louis Barthou, Bordeaux (Gironde), France. [Protozoa:
Thecamoebae of World (Yes)]
THOMAS-MAWSON, Mrs. P.M. Department of Zoology, University of Adelaide, Adelaide,
S.Australia. [Nematoda of Vertebrates of Australia (Yes); Free-living marine Nematoda
of Australia & Antarctic (Yes)]
THOMASSON, Kuno. Vaxtbiologiska Institutionen, Uppsala Universitet, Uppsala, Sweden. [Roti-
fera of S.America & Africa (Yes)]
THOMÉ, Prof. José W. Museu Rio-Grandense de Ciências Naturais, Rua Cel. Vincente 430,
Pôrto Alegre, Rio Grande Do Sul, Brazil. [Terr. Gastropoda of Rio Grande do Sul (No);
f-w. Pelecypoda of Rio Grande do Sul (No)]
THOMLINSON, Arnold G. A-4 Cañalta Apartments, 10905 17th Street, Dawson Creek, B.C.,
Canada. [Devonian Rugose & Tabulate Corals of Cordillera of Canada (Yes)]
THOMPSON, F.G. Museum of Zoology, University of Michigan, Ann Arbor, Mich., U.S.A.
[Terr. Gastropoda of C. & S.America (Yes); Reptilia & Amphibia of C. & S.America
(No)]
THOMPSON, Gordon B. 56 Beaumont Road, Cambridge, England. [Mallophaga of World (Yes)]
THOMPSON, H. (Melbourne, Australia; Tunicata) Died May 1957.
THOMPSON, Dr. Jesse C., Jr. Department of Biology, Hollins College, Va., U.S.A. [Pro-
tozoa: Holotricha of N. & S.America & Europe (Yes)]
THOMPSON, John R. P.O.Box 630, Pascagoula, Miss., U.S.A. [Pisces; Selachii of Gulf of
Mexico, Caribbean, w.Atlantic (No); Crustacea: Penaeidea, Caridea, Stenopodidea,
Eryonidae, Nephropsidae, Scyllaridae, Galatheidae, Chirostylidae, of Gulf of Mexico,
Caribbean, w.Atlantic (Yes)] [U.S. Fish & Wildlife Service]
THOMPSON, Mr. M.L. Illinois Geological Survey, Urbana, Ill., U.S.A. [Foraminifera: fossil
Fusulinidae of World (Yes)]
THOMPSON, Prof. R.H. Department of Botany, University of Kansas, Lawrence, Kans., U.S.A.
[Protozoa: f-w. Dinoflagellata & Chrysophyta of World (Yes)]
THOMPSON, Dr. T.E. Department of Zoology, University College, Cardiff, Wales. [Gastro-
poda: Nudibranchiata of w.Europe (Yes); Amphineura: Aplacophora of w.Europe (Yes)]
THOMPSON, Dr. W.R. Commonwealth Institute of Biological Control, Science Service Building,
Ottawa, Ont., Canada. [Diptera: Tachinidae of West Indies (Yes)]
* THOMSEN, Ricardo. Camino Tomkinson 6273, Paso de la Arena, Montevideo, Uruguay.
[Protozoa, Rotifera, Copepoda]
THOMSON, Dr. J.M. Marine Biological Laboratory, P.O.Box 21, Cronulla, N.S.W., Austra-
lia. [Pisces: Mugilidae of World (Yes); Chaetognatha of World (Yes); Pelecypoda:
Ostreidae of Australia (Yes)] [Commonwealth Scientific & Industrial Research Organiza-
tion, Division of Fisheries & Oceanography]
THORE, Dr. Sven. Nåsvägen 18, Bromma, Sweden. [Cephalopoda of World (Yes)]
THORMÄHLEN de GIL, Dra. Ana Luisa. (La Plata, Argentina; Pisces) Not now active in
taxonomy.
THORNE, Mr. Fred T. 1360 Merritt Drive, El Cajon, Calif., U.S.A. [Lepidoptera: Rhopalo-
cera of N.America (No); Lycaenidae: g.Mitoura of N.America (Yes)] [San Diego County
Department of Agriculture]
THORNE, Mr. Gerald. Department of Plant Pathology, University of Wisconsin, Madison,
Wisc., U.S.A. [Nematoda: Dorylaimoidea, Tylenchoidea, Cephalobidae, of World (Yes)]
THORNTON, Dr. Ian W.B. Department of Zoology, University of Hong Kong, Hong Kong. [Cor-
rodentia: espec. Psocoptera, of Hong Kong & S.China (Yes)]

THORNTON, Prof. W. A. Department of Biology, Sam Houston State Teachers College, Huntsville, Texas, U.S.A. [Amphibia: Anura: Bufonidae of N. America (Yes)]

THORSEN, Dr. Carl. The California Company, 800 The California Co. Building, New Orleans, La., U.S.A. [Cretaceous Ostracoda of U.S. Gulf Coast (No)]

* THORSLUND, Prof. P. Paleontological Institution, Uppsala, Sweden. [Fossil Invertebrates]

THORSON, Prof. Dr. Gunnar. Marine Biological Laboratory, Helsingoer, Denmark. [Gastropoda: marine Prosobranchia, developmental stages, of World (Yes)]

THORSTEINSSON, Dr. R. Geological Survey of Canada, Ottawa, Ont., Canada. [Cambrian-Silurian Graptolites (Yes); Pennsylvanian & Permian Fusulinidae (No)]

THRELKELD, Dr. W. L. Virginia Agricultural Experiment Station, Blacksburg, Va., U.S.A. [Parasitic Nematoda of s. e. U.S. (Yes)]

THUMANN, Dr. Marie-Elisabeth. Fürstenwalder Damm 381, Berlin-Friedrichshagen, German Democratic Republic. [F-w. Pisces of c. Europe (Yes)] [Institut für Fischerei, Deutsche Akademie der Landwirtschaftewissenschaften]

* THUNEBERG, Dr. E. Joutseno, Finland. [Diptera & Coleoptera]

THURLOW, Mrs. John. (Westbrook, Maine; Crustacea: Callianasidae) Not now active in taxonomy.

THURMAN, Ernestine B. 5617 Sonoma Road, Bethesda 14, Md., U.S.A. [Diptera: Culicidae of N. America & s. e. Asia (Yes); Streblidae of New World (No); Acarina: Laelaptidae of World (No)] [Division of Research Grants, National Institutes of Health]

THUROW, Dr. Gordon R. Newberry College, Newberry, S.C., U.S.A. [Amphibia: Plethodontidae of N. America (Yes)]

TIBBETTS, Ted. Box 967, Moab, Utah, U.S.A. [Acarina: Epidermoptidae, Ixodorhynchidae, Entonyssidae, of World (Yes); Myobiidae of World (No)]

TIDD, Dr. Wilbur M. Botany & Zoology Building, Ohio State University, Columbus 10, Ohio, U.S.A. [Crustacea: Parasitic Copepoda of New World (Yes)]

TIEDEMANN, Oswald. Ostpreussenplatz 16, (24a) Hamburg-Wandsbek, Germany. [Lepidoptera: Phycitidae: g. Ephestia of World (Yes)]

* TIEN, Prof. Dao Van. Laboratoire de Zoologie, Université de Hanoi, Hanoi, Vietnam. [Reptilia]

TIENSUU, L. Satamakatu 7. C. 10, Hamina, Finland. [Diptera: Muscidae of Europe (No); Tachinidae of Finland (No)]

TIFLOV, Dr. V. E. Parasitological Laboratory, Sovietskaya 13-15, Stavropol, Caucasus, U.S.S.R. [Siphonaptera of U.S.S.R. (Yes)]

TIHEN, Dr. Joseph A. 403 East Tenth Street, Harper, Kans., U.S.A. [Tertiary-Recent Amphibia of N. America (Yes); Tertiary-Recent Reptilia: Sauria of N. America (Yes)]

TILDEN, Dr. J. W. 125 Cedar Lane, San Jose, Calif., U.S.A. [Lepidoptera: Lycaenidae & Hesperiidae of N. America & Europe (Yes); Microlepidoptera of California (No); Coleoptera: Buprestidae, Meloidae, Cerambycidae, of U.S. (No); Diptera: Culicidae of California (Yes)] [San Jose State College]

TILL, W. M. The South African Institute for Medical Research, P.O. Box 1038, Johannesburg, Union of South Africa. [Acarina parasitic on Vertebrates of Ethiopian (Yes)]

TILLMAN, Prof. Chauncey G. Department of Geology, Virginia Polytechnic Institute, Blacksburg, Va., U.S.A. [Silurian Brachiopoda of c. & e. U.S. (Yes)]

* TILLMAN, John R. Museum of Paleontology, University of Michigan, Ann Arbor, Mich., U.S.A. [Fossil Invertebrates]

TIMBERLAKE, P. H. Citrus Experiment Station, Riverside, Calif., U.S.A. [Hymenoptera: Apoidea of N. America (Yes); Encyrtidae of N. America; Coleoptera: Coccinellidae of N. America]

TIMLIN, Dr. J. S. Entomology Division, Department of Scientific & Industrial Research, Box 223, Nelson, New Zealand. [Lepidoptera, larvae, of New Zealand (Yes)]

TIMM, Rev. Richard W., C.S.C. Notre Dame College, Dacca, East Pakistan. [Marine Nematoda of World (Yes); plant parasitic Nematoda of e. Pakistan (No)]

TIMM, Tarmo. Institute of Zoology & Botany, Academy of Sciences of Estonian S.S.R., Tartu, U.S.S.R. [Oligochaeta limicola of Baltic Area (Yes); Oligochaeta terricola of Estonia (No)]

TIMMERMANN, Dr. G. Alsterdorferstrasse 98, Hamburg 39, Germany. [Mallophaga & Cestoda of birds of World (Yes); Aves of World (No)]

TIMON-DAVID, Prof. Jean. Faculté des Sciences, Place Victor-Hugo, Marseille (3o), France. [Diptera: Asilidae of France (No); Trematoda: Digenea of France (No)]

* TINBERGEN, Dr. N. Department of Zoology, University Museum, Oxford, England. [Aves]

TINDALE, Mr. N. B. C/o South Australian Museum, Adelaide, S. Australia. [Lepidoptera: Rhopalocera of Australia & New Guinea (Yes); Hepialidae of World (Yes); Cossidae of Australia & New Guinea (Yes)]

TINER, Jack D. Department of Entomology, Rutgers University, New Brunswick, N.J., U.S.A. [Nematoda parasitic on mammals of N. America (No)]

* TING, Peter C. Bureau of Entomology, California Department of Agriculture, 1220 N Street, Sacramento 14, Calif., U.S.A. [Coleoptera & their larvae]

TINKER, Spencer. W. Waikiki Aquarium, 2777 Kalakaua Avenue, Honolulu 15, Hawaii. [Marine Pisces of Indo-Pacific (Yes); Gastropoda of Indo-Pacific (Yes)] [University of Hawaii]
TINKHAM, Dr. Ernest R. 81-441 Date Palm Avenue, Indio, Calif., U.S.A. [Orthoptera of N. American deserts (Yes); Acrididae & Tettigoniidae of China, Korea, Formosa (Yes)]
TINKLE, Dr. D.W. Department of Biology, Texas Technological College, Lubbock, Texas, U.S.A. [Reptilia of s. & s.w. U.S. (Yes); Chelonia of U.S. (Yes); Amphibia of s.w. U.S. (Yes)]
TINOCO, Prof. I.M. Curso de Geologia, Instituto de Geologia, Caixa Postal 2492, Recife-Pernambuco, Brazil. [Cretaceous & Paleocene Foraminifera of n.e. Brazil (Yes); Recent Foraminifera of S. Atlantic Ocean (Yes)]
TINTANT, Prof. Henri. Laboratoire de Géologie, Université de Dijon, Boulevard Gabriel, Dijon (Côte d'Or), France. [Jurassic (Bathonian to Oxfordian) Ammonoidea (Yes)]
TIPPMANN, Mr. F.F. Chiefengineer, Fasangasse 49/17, Wien III, Austria. [Coleoptera: Cerambycidae of World (Yes)]
TIPSWORD, Howard L. 506 Pioneer Building, Lake Charles, La., U.S.A. [Tertiary Foraminifera of New World (No)]
TIPTON, Captain Vernon J. Box 635, Fort Clayton, Panama Canal Zone. [Acarina: Laelaptidae of New World (Yes); Siphonaptera of New World (Yes)]
TISCHLER, Herbert. Department of Earth Science, Northern Illinois University, De Kalb, Ill., U.S.A. [Paleozoic Corals (No); fossil marine Invertebrates (No)]
TISSOT, Dr. A.N. Agricultural Experiment Station, University of Florida, Gainesville, Fla., U.S.A. [Homoptera: Aphidae of N. America (No), of e. U.S. (Yes)]
TITSCHACK, Prof. Dr. E. Jordanstrasse 13, Hamburg 26, Germany. [Thysanoptera of Palearctic (Yes)]
* TITTONI, Antonio. Via Panama 62, Roma, Italy. [Mollusca]
TIWARI, Dr. K.K. Zoological Survey of India, 34 Chittaranjan Avenue, Calcutta 12, India. [Crustacea: Decapoda, Isopoda, Stomatopoda, Branchiopoda, of Oriental (Yes)]
TIXIER-DURIVAULT, Mme. A. Chargée de Recherches, Laboratoire de Malacologie, Museum National d'Histoire Naturelle, 55 rue de Buffon, Paris (V), France. [Anthozoa: Alcyonaria (Yes)]
TJEDER, Dr. Bo. C.H. Nybrogatan 6, Falun, Sweden. [Neuroptera, incl. Megaloptera, of Europe, Asia, Africa (Yes); Diptera: Tipulidae of Scandinavia (Yes); Mecoptera of Asia, Europe, Africa (Yes)]
TJERNVIK, Dr. T.E. Åsgatan 17, Soderhamn, Sweden. [Ordovician Trilobita of Sweden (Yes)] [Paleontological Institution, Uppsala]
TOBIAS, Mr. V.I., Cand. Biol. Sc., Zoological Institute, Academy of Sciences of U.S.S.R., Vassilievsky Ostrov, Leningrad B-164, U.S.S.R. [Hymenoptera: Braconidae of Palearctic (No)]
TOBIEN, Prof. Dr. H. Hessisches Landesmuseum, Friedensplatz 1, Darmstadt, Germany. [Tertiary Mammalia of Europe (Yes)]
* TOBON, Yolanda Dumit. Museo Geologico Nacional, Carrera 15, No. 9-63, Bogotá, Colombia. [Fossil Foraminifera]
* TODD, Dr. A.C. Department of Veterinary Science, University of Wisconsin, Madison 6, Wisc., U.S.A. [Parasites of domestic animals]
TODD, Edward L. Division of Insects, U.S. National Museum, Washington 25, D.C., U.S.A. [Lepidoptera: Phalaenidae of w. Hemisphere (Yes); Hemiptera: Gelastocoridae of World (Yes)] [Division of Insect Identification, U.S. Department of Agriculture]
TODD, Miss Ruth. Room 303, U.S. National Museum, Washington 25, D.C., U.S.A. [Tertiary & Recent smaller Foraminifera (Yes)] [U.S. Geological Survey]
TODD, Dr. Valerie (Mrs. G.N. Davies). 29 Drivers Road, Dunedin, New Zealand. [Opiliones of Great Britain (No); Araneida: Mygalomorphae of New Zealand (Yes)] [Department of Zoology, University of Otago]
TODD, W.E. Clyde. Carnegie Museum, Pittsburg 13, Pa., U.S.A. [Aves of Labrador Peninsula & trop. America (Yes)]
TODOROVIC, Maksim. ul. 29 Novembra 100, Beograd, Yugoslavia. [Mammalia of Yugoslavia (Yes), of Balkans (No)] [Biološki Institut]
* TOEPELMANN, Walter C. Department of Geology, University of Colorado, Boulder, Colo., U.S.A. [Cretaceous microfossils of Colorado]
* TOERIEN, Dr. M.J. Department of Anatomy, University of the Witwatersrand, Johannesburg, Union of South Africa. [Fossils]
TOKEJI, Minoru. Shimorejaku 305, Mitaka-shi, Tokyo, Japan. [Coleoptera: Mordellidae of Japan & Micronesia (Yes), of s. e. Asia (No); Melandryidae of Japan (No)]
TOKIOKA, Dr. T. Seto Marine Biological Laboratory, Sirahama-tyo, Wakayama-Ken, Japan. [Pelagic Tunicata of World (Yes); Ascidiacea of n.w. Pacific (Yes); Chaetognatha of World (Yes); Recent Gastropoda: Pteropoda & Heteropoda (No); Crustacea: Copepoda: Branchiura of e. Asia (No)]
* TOKUDA, Mitoshi. Zoological Institute, Kyoto University, Kyoto, Japan. [Fossil Mammalia]

TOKUNAGA, Prof. Masaaki. Entomological Laboratory, Saikyo University, Shimogamo, Kyoto, Japan. [Diptera: Heleidae, Tendipedidae, Psychodidae, marine Tipulidae, of e. Asia & s. e. Asia & S. Pacific Islands (Yes)]

TOKUYAMA, Mr. Akira. Geological Institute, Faculty of Science, Tokyo University, Bunkyo-ku, Tokyo, Japan. [Triassic & Jurassic Brachiopoda of Japan (Yes); Triassic Pelecypoda of Japan (Yes)]

TOLL, Dr. Sergiusz. ul. Szafranka 1/3, Katowice, Poland. [Lepidoptera: Coleophoridae of Palearctic (Yes)] [Instytut Zoologiczny, Polska Akademia Nauk]

TOLLET, Mr. R. Institut Royal des Sciences Naturelles de Belgique, 31 rue Vautier, Brux-elles, Belgium. [Diptera: Mycetophilidae of World (Yes); Scatopsidae of Europe & Africa (Yes)]

TOMANTERÁ, Mr. E. A. Kemijärvi, Finland. [Odonata of n. Finland (No); Chilopoda of Finland (No)]

TOMILIN, Dr. A. G. Laboratory of Zoology, All-Union Agricultural Institute (WSHIZO), Korpus I, Kwartira 13, Balashika (Moscow), U. S. S. R. [Mammalia: Cetacea: Mystacoceti & Odontoceti of N. Hemisphere (Yes)]

TOMIYAMA, Dr. Itiro. Misaki Marine Biological Station, Misaki, Miura, Kanagawa-ken, Japan. [Pisces: Jugulares: Bleniidae & Pteropsaridae from Japan to E. Indies (Yes); Gobioidei of same (Yes)] [University of Tokyo]

TOMKINS, Mr. Ivan R. 1231 East 50th Street, Savannah, Ga., U. S. A. [Aves & Mammalia]

TOMLINSON, Dr. Jack. Natural Science Division, San Francisco State College, 1600 Holloway, San Francisco 27, Calif., U. S. A. [Fossil & Recent Crustacea: Cirripedia: Acrothoracica of World (Yes); Decapoda of w. cst. U. S. (No); Hirudinea of U. S. (No)]

* TOMSIK, Dr. Boleslav. Fakulta Lessnicka, Vysoká Skola Zemědělska, Brno, Czechoslovakia. [Hymenoptera]

TONGYAI, Mr. R. Chakratong. Entomology Section, Department of Agriculture, Bangkhen, Bangkok, Thailand. [Coleoptera: Buprestidae of World (No); Agrilini (Yes); Buprestidae of Thailand (Yes); Cicindelidae of Thailand (Yes); Lepidoptera: Rhopalocera of Thailand (Yes)]

TONOLLI, Prof. Livia. Istituto Italiano di Idrobiologia, Pallanza (Novara), Italy. [Crustacea: f-w. Copepoda & Cladocera of Europe (Yes)]

TONOLLI, Prof. Vittorio. Istituto Italiano di Idrobiologia, Pallanza (Novara), Italy. [Copepoda & Cladocera of Europe (No)]

* TOOMBS, Mr. H. A. Department of Palaeontology, British Museum (Natural History), Crom-well Road, London, S. W. 7, England. [Fossils]

TOOMEY, Donald P. Shell Development Co., 3737 Bellaire Boulevard, Houston 25, Texas, U. S. A. [Mississippian-Permian Foraminifera, excl. Fusulinidae, of World (Yes)]

TOOTS, Heinrich A. 705 W. 170th Street, New York 32, N. Y., U. S. A. [Paleozoic Bryozoa: Cryptostomata & Trepostomata (Yes)]

* TOPACHEVSKY, V. M. Zoological Institute, Academy of Science of the Ukranian S. S. R., ul. Wladimirskaja 55, Kiev, U. S. S. R. [Fossil Mammalia]

TOPÁL, G. Zoological Department, Hungarian National Museum, Magyar Nemzeti Muzeum, Allattár, Baross-utca 13, Budapest VIII, Hungary. [Pliocene to Recent Mammalia: Chiroptera of Palearctic (Yes)]

* TORDO, Dr. G. Missão Zoologica de Mocambique, c/o Almoxarifado da Fazenda, Lourenço Marques, Mozambique. [Coleoptera]

TORDOFF, Prof. Harrison B. Museum of Natural History, University of Kansas, Lawrence, Kans., U. S. A. [Recent & fossil Aves of N. America (Yes)]

TORIUMI, Dr. Makoto. Marine Biological Station, Tohoku University, Asmushi, Aomori Pref., Japan. [Bryozoa: Gymnolaemata: Victorellidae; Phylactolaemata: Fredericellidae, Plumatellidae, Lophopodidae, Cristatellidae; of World (Yes)]

TORIYAMA, Dr. Sci. Ryuzo. Department of Geology, Faculty of Science, Kyushu University, Fukuoka, Japan. [Permian & Pennsylvanian Foraminifera: Fusulinidae of Japan & e. Asia (Yes)]

von TÖRNE, Dr. E. Friedrich-Schelling Strasse 10, Jena, German Democratic Republic. [Collembola of Europe (Yes); Acarina: Oribatei of Europe (Yes)]

TORPY, Thomas F. 2240-1/2 Bentley Avenue, Los Angeles 25, Calif., U. S. A. [Larval Cestoda (No)]

de la TORRE, Dr. Alfredo. Museo Paleontologico, Linea 461, esq. a E, (Edif. Gari), Vedado, Habana, Cuba. [Marine Mollusca of Caribbean (Yes); fossils of Caribbean (Yes)]

de la TORRE, Mr. Luis. Museum of Natural History, University of Illinois, Urbana, Ill., U. S. A. [Mammalia: Chiroptera of Neotropical (Yes)]

TORRES, B. A. Facultad de Ciencias Naturales y Museo, La Plata, Argentina. [Homoptera: Cicadidae of S. America (Yes)]

de la TORRE y CALLEJAS, Dr. Salvador Luis. Departamento de Zoologia, Universidad de Oriente, Santiago de Cuba, Cuba. [Lepidoptera: Rhopalocera of Cuba (Yes); Heterocera of Cuba (No)]

TORSTENIUS, Stig. Celsiusgatan 7, Stockholm K, Sweden. [Lepidoptera: Macrolepidoptera of Sweden (Yes); Psychidae & Talaeporiidae of Sweden (Yes)]

TORTONESE, Prof. E. Museo Civico di Storia Naturale, Via Brigata Liguria 9, Genova, Italy. [Echinodermata, espec. Asteroidea of World (Yes); Pisces, espec. Selachii of Mediterranean, Atlantic, Red Sea (Yes)]

TOSCHI, Augusto. Laboratorio di Zoologia applicata all Caccia, Universitá di Bologna, Bologna, Italy. [Mammalia of Italy, Libia, n. e. Africa (Yes)]

TOSHIOKA, Seiichi. Laboratory of Parasitology, School of Medical Technology, Tokyo Bunka Women's College, 6-chôme, Honchôderi, Nakanoku, Tokyo, Japan. [Acarina: Ixodoidea & Trombiculidae of Japan, Korea, Ryukyu Is. (Yes)]

TOTTENHAM, C. E. University Museum of Zoology, Downing Street, Cambridge, England. [Coleoptera: Staphylinidae of Africa & Micronesia (Yes), Paederinae & Oxytelinae (No); g. Philonthus & Gabrius of World (Yes)]

TOTTON, Mr. A. Knyvett. British Museum (Natural History), Cromwell Road, London, S. W. 7, England. [Hydrozoa: Siphonophora of World (Yes)]

de TOULGOET, Vicomte H. 8 rue Rembrandt, Paris (VIII), France. [Lepidoptera: Arctiidae (Nolinae, Lithosiinae, Arctiinae, Rhodogastriinae) of Palearctic & Madagascar (Yes); of Africa (No)]

TOULMIN, Dr. Lyman D. Department of Geology, Florida State University, Tallahassee, Fla., U. S. A. [Paleocene & Eocene smaller Foraminifera of U. S. Coastal Plain (Yes)]

TOUMANOFF, Constantin, Chef du Service d'Entomologie Médical, Institut Pasteur, 25 rue du Docteur Roux, Paris, France. [Acarina: Ixodoidea of Far East (No); Diptera: Culicidae: Anophelinae of Far East (Yes)]

TOURING, R. M. Humble Oil & Refining Co., Room 206, Cloverleaf Annex, 6th & High Streets, Eugene, Ore., U. S. A. [Pliocene-Recent Mollusca of w. cst. of N. America]

TOWNES, Dr. Henry K. Museum of Zoology, University of Michigan, Ann Arbor, Mich., U. S. A. [Dermaptera of World (No); Hymenoptera: Ichneumonidae, Stephanidae, Trigonalidae, Evaniidae, Gasteruptiidae, Roproniidae, Psammocharidae of World (No); Diptera: Tendipedidae of Nearctic (No)]

TOWNSEND, A. L. H. (Nakuru, Kenya; Lepidoptera) Not now active in taxonomy.

TOWNSEND, Dr. J. Ives. Department of Zoology & Entomology, University of Tennessee, Knoxville, Tenn., U. S. A. [Diptera: Drosophilidae: g. Drosophila of West Indies (No)]

* TOWNSEND, Dr. Lee H. Department of Agricultural Entomology, University of Kentucky, Lexington 29, Ky., U. S. A. [Cyclorrhaphous Diptera]

TOWNSLEY, S. J. University of Hawaii, Honolulu, Hawaii. [Crustacea: Stomatopoda of World (Yes); Cephalopoda: Octopoda of Indo-Pacific (Yes)]

TOZER, Dr. E. T. Geological Survey of Canada, Department of Mines & Technical Surveys, Ottawa, Ont., Canada. [Triassic Ammonoidea & Pelecypoda (Yes)]

TRAPIDO, Harold. Virus Research Centre, P. O. Box 11, Poona 1, India. [Diptera: Culicidae: Culicini of s. Asia (No); Acarina: Ixodidae of s. Asia (No)]

TRASON, Mrs. Winona J. Bethune. Department of Zoology, University of California, Berkeley 4, Calif., U. S. A. [Tunicata: Ascidiacea of w. N. America (Yes)]

TRAUB, Lt. Col. Robert. U. S. Army Medical Research & Development, Main Navy Building, Washington 25, D. C., U. S. A. [Siphonaptera of World (Yes); Acarina: Trombiculidae of s. e. Asia & Korea (No)]

TRAUTMAN, Dr. Milton B. Ohio State Museum, Columbus 10, Ohio, U. S. A. [F-w. Pisces of e. N. America (No); Aves of e. N. America & Yucatan (No)] [Ohio State University]

TRAVASSOS, Dr. H. P. Museu Nacional, Quinta da Boa Vista, Rio de Janeiro, Brazil. [Pisces of S. America (Yes), of Africa (No)]

* TRAVASSOS, Dr. Lauro P., Filho. Departamento de Zoologia, Secretaria da Agricultura, Caixa Postal 7172, São Paulo, Brazil. [Lepidoptera, Diptera, Orthoptera]

TRAVÉ, J. Laboratoire Arago, Banyuls-sur-Mer (Pyrenées-Orientales), France. [Acarina: Oribatoidea of Pyrenées-Orientales & Mediterranée Occidentale (No)]

TRAVER, Dr. Jay R. Fernald Hall, University of Massachusetts, Amherst, Mass., U. S. A. [Ephemeroptera of New World (Yes)]

TRAYLOR, Melvin A. Chicago Natural History Museum, Chicago 5, Ill., U. S. A. [Aves of Old World, excl. Australasia (Yes)]

TREAT, Asher E. Department of Biology, The City College of New York, New York 31, N. Y., U. S. A. [Acarina: mites of tympanae of Moths of World (Yes)]

* TREBILCOCH, R. E. Wellington Street, Kerang, Vict., Australia. [Lepidoptera & Hymenoptera]

* TRECHMANN, Dr. C. T. Hudworth Tower, Castle Eden, County Durham, England. [Mollusca]

TREHAN, Dr. K. N. Zoology Department, Panjab University, Hoshiarpur, Punjab, India. [Homoptera: Aleurodidae of India & Britain (Yes)]

TREMEWAN, Mr. W. G. Department of Entomology, British Museum (Natural History), London, S. W. 7, England. [Lepidoptera: Zygaenidae of World (No)]

TREMLETT, Dr. W. E. Department of Geology, The University, Glasgow W. 2., Scotland. [Pelecypoda: Eocene & Oligocene Veneridae & Cardiidae of w. Europe (Yes)]

TRESSLER, Dr. Willis L. 4608 Amherst Road, College Park, Md., U.S.A. [F-w. & marine Quaternary & Recent Crustacea: Ostraçoda (No)] [U.S. Navy Hydrographic Office]

TRETZEL, Dr. Erwin. Zoologisches Institut der Universität, Universitatsstrasse 19, Erlangen, Germany. [Araneida of Europe (Yes)]

* TREVISAN, Dr. Livio. Istituto di Geologia dell'Università, Via S. Maria 31, Pisa, Italy. [Fossil Mammalia]

TREWAVAS, Dr. Ethelwynn. Department of Zoology (Fishes), British Museum (Natural History), Cromwell Road, London, S.W.7, England. [F-w. Pisces of World (Yes); espec. Cichlidae of Africa (Yes)]

TREXLER, David William. Department of Geology, Colorado School of Mines, Golden, Colo., U.S.A. [Cretaceous marine Pelecypoda of w.U.S. (Yes); Cretaceous Coccolithophoridae of w.U.S. (No)]

TRIANTAPHYLLOU, Anastasios Crist. Department of Plant Pathology, North Carolina State College, Raleigh, North Carolina, U.S.A. [Plant parasitic Nematoda of s. Europe (Yes)]

TRIEBEL, Dr. Erich. Department of Paleontology, Natur-Museum Senckenberg, Senckenberg-Anlage 25, Frankfort am Main, Germany. [Post-Palaezoic to Recent Crustacea: Ostracoda (No)]

* TRIKKALINOS, Prof. Dr. Johann. 4 rue Massalias, Athens, Greece. [Fossils]

TRIPATHI, Dr. Yogendra R. Central Inland Fisheries Research Station, P.O. Tungabhadra Dam, Mysore, India. [Crustacea: Copepoda of fish of India & s.e. Asia (Yes); Acanthocephala of fish of India (Yes); Trematoda: Monogenea of India & s.e. Asia (Yes)]

TRIPLEHORN, Charles A. Department of Entomology, Cornell University, Ithaca, N.Y., U.S.A. [Coleoptera: Tenebrionidae of New World (Yes); Reptilia & Amphibia of N. America (Yes)]

* TRIPP, Ronald P. 68 Lauderdale Gardens, Glasgow, W.2, Scotland. [Fossil Trilobita]

TRIVETTE, 1st Lt. Edward C. AO 3043597 5th Epidemiological Flight, APO 959, San Francisco, Calif., U.S.A. [Diptera: Calliphoridae of N. America (Yes); Culicidae of Japan, Korea, Okinawa (Yes)] [U.S. Air Force]

TRJAPITZIN, V.A. Zoological Institute, Academy of Sciences of U.S.S.R., Leningrad B-164, U.S.S.R. [Hymenoptera: Encyrtidae of Palearctic (Yes)]

* TROELSEN, Dr. J.C. Mineralogisk-Museum Østervoldgade 7, København K, Denmark. [Fossil Foraminifera]

TROFIMOV, Dr. B.A. Paleontological Museum, Academy of Sciences of U.S.S.R., Lenin Prospect 16, Moscow B-71, U.S.S.R. [Mammalia: Artiodactyla & Insectivora of U.S.S.R. & Mongolia (Yes)]

TROJAN, Mr. Przemysław. Polska Akademia Nauk, ul. Wilcza 64, Warszawa, Poland. [Diptera: Tabanidae of Palearctic (Yes)]

TROJANOWA-BAŃKOWSKA, Mrs. Regina. Polska Akademia Nauk, ul. Wilcza 64, Warszawa, Poland. [Diptera: Syrphidae & Conopidae of Europe (Yes)]

* TROOSTER, S.G. (Utrecht, Netherlands; Fossil Foraminifera) Deceased.

TROSSARELLI, Dr. F. Via di Porta Pinciana 1, Roma, Italy. [Arachnida: Opiliones of Italy]

* TROUGHTON, Ellis Le G. Australian Museum, Sydney, Australia. [Mammalia]

TRUEMAN, E.R. Department of Zoology, The University, Hull, England. [Mollusca of Europe (Yes)]

TRUMBULL, Mrs. Ellen J. Room 405, U.S. National Museum, Washington 25, D.C., U.S.A. [Oligocene-Pleistocene marine Mollusca of Pacific cst. of U.S. (Yes)] [U.S. Geological Survey]

TRÜMPY, Prof. Dr. Rudolf. Narzissenstrasse 5, Zürich 6, Switzerland. [Triassic Mollusca (Yes); Jurassic Ammonites of Europe (No)] [Swiss Federal Institute of Technology]

TRUXAL, Dr. Fred S. Los Angeles Museum, Exposition Park, Los Angeles 7, Calif., U.S.A. [Aquatic Hemiptera: Notonectidae of World (No), of New World (Yes)]

TRUYOLS-SANTONJA, Jaime. Calle Onésimo Redondo 148-6a, Sabadell, Spain. [Fossil Vertebrates]

TRYON, Dr. C.A., Jr. Department of Biological Sciences, University of Pittsburgh, Pittsburgh 13, Penna., U.S.A. [Mammalia: Rodentia of N. America (No); Pisces of Ohio River, U.S. (Yes)]

TSCHAPSKY, K.K. (or C.C.) See CHAPSKIY, K.K.

* TSCHERNOW. S.A. See CHERNOV, S.A.

TSCHUDINOV, Dr. P.K. Paleontological Museum, Lenin Prospect 16, Moscow, U.S.S.R. [Permian & Triassic Reptilia: Cotylosauria of U.S.S.R. (Yes)]

TSHEREPANOV, Dr. A.I. Biological Institute, Siberian Branch, Academy of Sciences of U.S.S.R., Mitshurin Street 23, Novosibirsk, U.S.S.R. [Coleoptera: Elateridae of Siberia (Yes); of Mongolia, north China, Canada, Alaska (No)]

* TSINOWSKII, Ya P. Institute of Biology, Academy of Sciences, Riga, Latvia, U.S.S.R. [Hymenoptera]

TSUDA, Prof. Matsunae. Zoological Laboratory, Nara Women's University, Nara-shi, Japan. [Trichoptera of Japan (No)]

* TSUKAHARA, Dr. Hiroshi. Department of Fisheries, Kyushu University, Hakozaki, Fukuoka City, Kyushu Prov., Japan. [Pisces]

* TSUKAMOTO, Keiichi. 13-1 Nakabayashi-chô, Shûgakuin, Sakyô-ku, Kyoto, Japan. [Coleoptera: Scarabaeidae]

TSUNEKI, Prof. K. Biological Laboratory, Fukui University, Makinoshima-cho, Fukui, Japan. [Hymenoptera: Sphecoidea, Formicidae, Chrysididae, of Palearctic (No)]

* TSURUTA, A. Shimonoseki College of Fisheries, Yoshimi, Shimonoseki City, Yamaguchi Pref., Japan. [Crustacea: Copepoda]

TSUTSUI, Yoshitaka. Osaka Museum of Natural History, Utsubo Park, Nishiku, Osaka, Japan. [Terr. Mammalia of Japan (No); Amphibia: Urodela of Japan (No)]

* TUBB, R. A. Department of Ichthyology, Rhodes University, Grahamstown, Union of South Africa. [Pisces]

TUCKER, Dr. Denys W. Department of Zoology (Fishes), British Museum (Natural History), Cromwell Road, London, S. W. 7, England. [Oceanic Pisces, espec. Trichiuridae & Gempylidae of World (Yes)]

TUFFRAU, Dr. Michel. Centre de Recherches Hydrobiologiques, Gif-sur-Yvette (Seine et Oise), France. [Protozoa: Ciliata, espec. Hypotrichida of f. w. & littoral of France (Yes)]

TULAGANOV, Prof. A. T. Tashkent State University, ul. Karla Marxa 35, Tashkent, U. S. S. R. [Soil & plant parasitic Nematoda of U. S. S. R. (Yes)]

TULESKOV, Dr. K. Zoological Garden, Boul. Tolbuchin 15, Sofia, Bulgaria. [Lepidoptera, Mallophaga, Anoplura, of Bulgaria (Yes)] [Zoological Garden of the Bulgarian Academy of Sciences]

TULLGREN, Dr. Albert. (Stockholm 50, Sweden; Araneida) Died in 1958.

TUOMIKOSKI, Dr. R. K. Temppelik 7, Helsinki, Finland. [Diptera: Sciaridae of World (Yes)] [Botanical Institute, University of Helsinki]

TURBOTT, Mr. E. G. Canterbury Museum, Christchurch C. 1, New Zealand. [Aves of New Zealand (Yes); Psittaciformes of New Zealand (Yes)]

TURCO, Caroline Ann. 799 Secaucus Road, Jersey City 7, N. J., U. S. A. [Up. Ordovician Conodonts of Eden Group of Ohio-Kentucky (Yes)] [Department of Micropaleontology, American Museum of Natural History]

TÜRK, Friedrich. A. Riemerschmidstrasse 25/II, Burghausen/(Oberbay), Germany. [Acarina: Tyroglyphidae of Europe (No); of c. Europe (Yes)]

TURK, Dr. Frank A. Shang-ri-la, Reskadinnick, Camborne, Cornwall, England. [Acarina: espec. soil, insecticolous, feather mites (Yes); Solifugida of Old World & Ethiopian (Yes); Chilopoda & Diplopoda of Palearctic, Neotropical, Ethiopian (Yes); Opiliones of Antilles, w. Europe, India, e. Mediterranean (No); Pseudoscorpiones: Antilles, w. Europe, India, e. Mediterranean (No)] [University of Exeter]

TURNBULL, Dr. A. L. Laboratory of Entomology, Box 179, Belleville, Ont., Canada. [Araneida of N. America (No)]

TURNBULL, Miss E. R. Department of Zoology, University of Glasgow, Glasgow W. 2, Scotland. [Trematoda: g. Gyrodactylus of World (Yes)]

* TURNBULL, Dr. William D. Department of Geology, Chicago Natural History Museum, Chicago 5, Ill., U. S. A. [Fossil Vertebrates]

* TURNER, C. Donnell. Address unknown. [Oligochaeta]

TURNER, Prof. C. L. Department of Biological Science, Northwestern University, Evanston, Ill., U. S. A. [Crustacea: Crayfishes of Ohio (Yes); Pisces: Goodeidae of Mexico (Yes)]

TURNER, Frederick B. Department of Biology, Wayne State University, Detroit 2, Mich., U. S. A. [Amphibia: Bufonidae & Ranidae of U. S. (No)]

* TURNER, J. R. Caldwell Kans., U. S. A. [Lepidoptera]

TURNER, J. S. Department of Geology, The University, Leeds 2, England. [Carboniferous Cephalopoda: Nautiloidea of Britain (Yes)]

TURNER, Ruth D. Museum of Comparative Zoology, Cambridge 38, Mass., U. S. A. [Marine Mollusca of w. Atlantic (Yes); boring Mollusca of World (Yes); terr. Mollusca of C. & S. America (Yes)]

TURNOVSKY, Dr. K. Zentralallabor der O. M. V., Reichsratstrasse 2, Wien 1, Austria. [Up. Cretaceous & Tertiary Foraminifera, excl. Fusulinidae (Yes); Tertiary Ostracoda (Yes)]

* TURPAEIA, Miss E. Moscow Institute of Oceanology, Academy of Sciences of U. S. S. R., Lujnikovaskaja 8, Moscow, U. S. S. R. [Arthropoda]

TUTHILL, Leonard D. Department of Zoology & Entomology, University of Hawaii, Honolulu 14, Hawaii. [Homoptera: Psyllidae of New World (Yes); of Pacific area (Yes)]

TUTMAN, Ivan. Institut Biologique, Dubrovnik, p. p. 17, Yugoslavia. [Aves of Yugoslavia (Yes); Fringillidae, Sylvidae, Turdidae, Motacillidae, Alaudidae, Paridae of Balcan Peninsula (Yes)]

TUTTLE, Donald M. University of Arizona Farm, Route 1, Box 587, Yuma, Ariz., U. S. A. [Coleoptera: Curculionidae of U. S. (Yes)]

TUXEN, Dr. S. L. Zoologisk Museum, Krystalgade, København, Denmark. [Protura of World (Yes); Apterygota of Northern Holarctic (No); Acarina: Trombiculidae & Oribatidae of Northern Holarctic (No)]

* TUZELAAT, Miss M. A. Zoology Department, University College of Ghana, Achimota, Ghana. [Oligochaeta]

TUZET, Prof. Odette. Faculté des Sciences, Université de Montpellier, Montpellier (Herault), France. [Sporozoa: Gregarinida & Coccidia of World (Yes)]

TWEEDIE, M. W. F. (Singapore, Malaya (now Rye, England); Decapoda & Reptilia) Not now active in taxonomy.

TWINN, C. R. (Ottawa, Canada; Diptera) Not now active in taxonomy.

TWINN, Mr. D. C. Horticultural Research Station, Fyfield Road, Ongar, Essex, England. [Terr., f-l., plant parasitic Nematoda of Europe (Yes); Coleoptera: wood borers of Britain (Yes)]

TWITTY, Prof. Victor C. Department of Zoology, Stanford University, Stanford, Calif., U. S. A. [Amphibia: Salamandridae: g. Taricha of Pacific Coast of U. S. (Yes)]

TWOMEY, Dr. Arthur C. Carnegie Institute, 4400 Forbes Street, Pittsburgh 13, Penna., U. S. A. [Aves of N. America (Yes); of C. & S. America (No)]

UBAGHS, Prof. G. Laboratoire de Paléontologie Animale, Université de Liège, 7 Place du Vingt-Août, Liège, Belgium. [Paleozoic Echinodermata: Pelmatozoa: espec. Crinoidea, of w. Europe & N. Africa (Yes)]

UCHIDA, Prof. Hajime. Faculty of Literature & Science, Hirosaki University, Hirosaki City, Aomori Pref., Japan. [Collembola: Sminthuridae & Entomobryidae; Thysanura: Lepismatidae; both of Japan, Korea, Formosa, Micronesia (Yes)]

* UCHIDA, Seinosuke. 8 Aobacho, Shibuya-ku, Tokyo, Japan. [Mallophaga]

UCHIDA, Prof. Tohru. Zoological Institute, Faculty of Science, Hokkaido University, Sapporo, Japan. [Hydrozoa: Scyphozoa, Actiniaria, of Pacific (Yes); Archiannelida of Pacific (Yes); Asteroidea of Pacific (Yes); Acarina: Hydracarina of Orient (Yes); Phoronidea of Pacific (Yes)]

UCHIDA, Prof. Toichi. Entomological Institute, Hokkaido University, Sapporo, Hokkaido, Japan. [Hymenoptera: Ichneumonidae of Japan (Yes)]

UCHIO, Dr. Takayasu. Department of Mining (Petroleum), University of Tokyo, Bunkyo-ku, Tokyo, Japan. [Cretaceous-Recent Foraminifera of Japan (Yes); Recent Foraminifera of California, Oregon, Washington (Yes)]

UDVARDY, Dr. M. D. F. Department of Zoology, University of British Columbia, Vancouver, B. C., Canada. [Tunicata: Appendicularia of N. & S. Atlantic & N. Pacific (Yes)]

UÉNO, Prof. Masuzo. Otsu Hydrobiological Station, Kyoto University, Otsu City, Shiga Pref., Japan. [Ephemeroptera of Asia (No); Crustacea: Cladocera of e. Asia (Yes); Phyllopoda of e. Asia (Yes); Syncarida of World (Yes)]

UÉNO, Shun-Ichi. Zoological Institute, College of Science, Kyoto University, Kyoto, Japan. [Cavernicolous Coleoptera of Far East (Yes); Caraboidea & Dytiscoidea of Japan (Yes); Catopidae, Liodidae, Pselaphidae, of Japan (No); Archiannelida: Nerillidae of Pacific (No)]

UENO, Mr. Tatsuji. Freshwater Fisheries Research Laboratory, Fisheries Agency, Hino Machi, Minamitama Gun, Tokyo, Japan. [Pisces: Cyclopteridae & Zoarcidae of n. Pacific & n. Japan (Yes); f-w. Salmonidae of Sea of Japan (Yes)]

UHMANN, Herr Erich, Studienrat i R., Lessingstrasse 15, Stollberg-Sachsen 10b, German Democratic Republic. [Coleoptera: Chrysomelidae: Hispinae of World (Yes)] [Zoologisches Museum der Humboldt Universtität, Berlin]

UICHANCO, Dean L. B. College of Agriculture (Entomology), University of the Philippines, Laguna, Philippines. [Homoptera: Aphididae, Chermidae, Cicadidae, of Oriental (No), of Malaysian (Yes)]

UJHELYI, Dr. S. Magyar Nemzeti Museum, Baross-u. 13, Budapest VIII, Hungary. [Odonata, Ephemeroptera, Plecoptera, Orthoptera, of Europe (No); Trichoptera of c. Europe (No)]

* ULMER, Frederick A., Jr. Zoological Society of Philadelphia, 34th Street & Girard Avenue, Philadelphia 4, Penna., U. S. A. [Mammalia: Insectivora & Cetacea of Pennsylvania, New Jersey, Delaware]

ULMER, Dr. G. Lohheide 28, Hamburg-Rahlstedt 24a, Germany. [Trichoptera & Ephemeroptera of World, excl. N. America (No)]

ULMER, Joseph W., Jr. 1808 Fulton Street, Apartment 2, San Francisco 17, Calif., U. S. A. [Devonian Brachiopoda of S. Africa (Yes)]

ULMER, Dr. Martin J. Department of Zoology & Entomology, Iowa State College, Ames, Iowa, U. S. A. [Trematoda: Digenea of N. America (Yes)]

ULOMSKY, S. N. Ul. Malysheva 58, Ural VNIORH, Sverdlovsk, U. S. S. R. [Crustacea: Copepoda: f-l. f-w. Calanoida of Palearctic (Yes); f-l. f-w. Cyclopoida: Cyclopidae of Palearctic (Yes); f-w. Cladocera of Palearctic (No)] [Institute of Fresh-water Fisheries, Leningrad]

ULRICH, Prof. Dr. W. Zoologisches Institut der Freien Universität, Königin Luise Strasse 1-3, Berlin-Dahlem, Germany. [Strepsiptera of World (Yes)]

UNDERHILL, Dr. James C. Zoology Department, University of South Dakota, Vermillion, S. D., U. S. A. [Pisces: Cyprinidae of n. c. U. S. (No)]

UNDERWOOD, Mr. Garth. University College of West Indies, Zoology Department, Mona, St. Andrew, Jamaica. [Reptilia: Sauria: geckos of World (No); Reptilia of Caribbean (No), of Jamaica (Yes)]

UNGUREANU, Prof. Ernest M. Faculté de Medicina, Universitatea Al. I. Cuza, Iasi, Rumania. [Diptera: Culicidae of Palearctic (Yes)]

UNKELSBAY, Prof. A. G. 210 Swallow Hall, University of Missouri, Columbia, Mo. , U.S.A. [Paleozoic Cephalopoda (Yes)]

UNO, Masayoshi. Agricultural Section, Gifu, City Office, Gifu City, Japan. [Coleoptera: Anthribidae of Japan (Yes)]

UNTERMANN, Billie R.   Utah Field House of Natural History, Box 141, Vernal, Utah, U.S.A. [Eocene-Pliocene Mammalia of Uinta Basin, U.S. (Yes); Cambrian-Recent Invertebrates of Uinta Basin (Yes)]

UNTERMANN, G. E. , Director, Utah Field House of Natural History, Box 141, Vernal, Utah, U.S.A. [Eocene-Pliocene Mammalia of Uinta Basin, U.S. (Yes); Cambrian-Recent Invertebrates of Uinta Basin (Yes)]

UOZUMI, Satoru. Department of Geology & Mineralogy, Hokkaido University, Sapporo, Japan. [Tertiary-Recent marine Pelecypoda & Gastropoda of n. Japan (Yes); Cretaceous marine Pelecypoda of Japan (Yes); Tertiary-Recent Brachiopoda of n. Japan (No)]

UPSHAW, Charles Francis. 216 Swallow Hall, University of Missouri, Columbia, Mo. , U.S.A. [M. Tertiary smaller Foraminifera of Gulf Coast U.S. (No)]

URBAHN, Dr. E. Poststrasse 15, Zehdenick (Havel), German Democratic Republic. [Lepidoptera: Macrolepidoptera of Europe (Yes); espec. Geometridae & Noctuidae of c. & n. Europe]

* URBANEK, A. Zakład Paleontologii Uniwersytet Warszawski, Nowy Świat 67, Warszawa, Poland. [Fossil Invertebrates]

* URBAŃSKI, Dr. Jarosław. Zakład Zoologii Ogólnej, Uniwersytet im Adama Mickiewicza, Ul. Fredry 10, Poznań, Poland. [Mollusca, Odonata]

* URETA, Dr. Elias. Rio Branco 1304, Apartamento 6, Montevideo, Uruguay. [Mollusca]

* URETA, Dr. Emilio Rojas. Departamento de Entomologia, Museo Nacional de Historia Natural, Santiago, Chile. [Lepidoptera]

URQUHART, Dr. F. A. Royal Ontario Museum of Zoology & Paleontology, 100 Queens Park, Toronto (5), Ont. , Canada. [Orthoptera of N. America (Yes)]

URSIN, Erik. (Charlottenlund, Denmark; Mammalia) Not now active in taxonomy.

* URSIN, Dr. T. 24 Agretevej, Lyngby, Denmark. [Mammalia]

USCHAKOV, Prof. P. V. Zoological Institute, Academy of Sciences of U.S.S.R. , Leningrad 164, U.S.S.R. [Polychaeta: espec. Phyllodocidae & Aphroditidae, of Arctic & Far Eastern Seas (Yes)]

USINGER, Dr. Robert L. Department of Entomology, 112 Agriculture Hall, University of California, Berkeley 4, Calif. , U.S.A. [Heteroptera of World (No)]

* USTINOV, Prof. Dr. A.A. Institute of Biology, State University, Danilevsky Street 5, Kharkov, U.S.S.R. [Plant parasitic Nematoda of U.S.S.R.]

UTHERBAKER, F. H. See BAKER, F. H. Uther. (Addenda)

UTINOMI, Prof. Dr. Huzio. Seto Marine Biological Laboratory, Sirahama, Wakayama, Pref. , Japan. [Anthozoa: Octocorallia of World (Yes); Crustacea: Cirripedia of World (Yes); Amphipoda: Caprellidea of w. Pacific (Yes); Pycnogonida of World (Yes); Echinoidea (Yes)]

* UTOTSCHKIN, - . Perm University, Perm, U.S.S.R. [Araneida]

UTTLEY, Dr. G. H. 292 Karori Road, Wellington, New Zealand. [Recent & Tertiary Bryozoa of New Zealand (Yes)]

UVAROV, Dr. B. P. Anti-Locust Research Centre, 1 Princes Gate, London, S.W.7, England. [Orthoptera: Acrididae of World (No)]

UYEMURA, Toshio. 23 Otsuka-nakamachi, Bunkyo-ku, Tokyo, Japan. [Araneida of Japan (Yes)]

UYENO, Teruya. Museum of Zoology, University of Michigan, Ann Arbor, Mich. , U.S.A. [Pisces: Cyprinidae of Japan & w. N. America (No)]

UZMANN, J. R. U.S. Fish & Wildlife Service, Western Fish Disease Laboratory, University of Washington, Seattle 5, Wash. , U.S.A. [Protozoan & Metazoan parasites of fishes & mollusks of N. America (Yes)]

UZZELL, Mr. Thomas M. , Jr. Museum of Zoology, University of Michigan, Ann Arbor, Mich. , U.S.A. [Cenozoic Amphibia & Reptilia of New World (Yes)]

* VAAS, Dr. K. F. Laboratory of Inland Fisheries, Tjikeumeuh 99, Bogor, Indonesia. [Crustacea]

VACELET, J. Station Marine d'Endoume, rue de la Batterie des Lions, Marseille (VII), France. [Porifera of Mediterranean (Yes)]

* VACHOLD, Dr. Julius. Faunisticke Laboratorium, Slovenská Akadémia Vied, Biologický Ustav, Oddelenie Zoólogie, Sienkiewiczova 1, Bratislava, Czechoslovakia. [Mammalia]

VACHON, Prof. Max. Museum National d'Histoire Naturelle, 61 Rue de Buffon, Paris (5), France. [Scorpiones of World (Yes); Pseudoscorpionida of Europe & Africa (No)]

VÁCLAV-HOUŠA, Dr. Paleontology Laboratory, Czechoslovakian Academy of Science, National Museum, Vaclavské Nam, 1.700, Praha II, Czechoslovakia. [Mesozoic & Tertiary Decapoda of Europe (Yes)]

VAILLANT, Mr. F. 26, Cours Berriat, Grenoble (Isère), France. [Diptera: Empididae: Atalantinae, all stages, of Europe, Africa, N. America (Yes); Psychodidae, Ceratopogonidae, Dolichopodidae, all stages, of w. Europe & n. Africa (No); Thaumaleidae of Europe, Africa, N. America (Yes)] [University of Grenoble]

VAISSIÈRE, Dr. Raymond. Faculté des Sciences d'Alger, Université d'Alger, Alger, Algeria. [Crustacea: marine Copepoda & free-living Caligoida of Mediterranean & w. Africa (Yes)]

VALENCIA, F. Carlos Lehmann. See LEHMANN VALENCIA, F. C.

VALENSI, L. 67 bis rue Aristide Briand, Fontainebleau, France. [Mesozoic Protozoa: Peridinea & Hystricospherida of France (Yes)]

* VALENTE, Domingos. Departamento de Zoologia, Universidad de São Paulo, São Paulo, Brazil. [Crustacea & Annelida of S. America]

VALENTINE, Barry D. Department of Entomology, Comstock Hall, Cornell University, Ithaca, N. Y., U. S. A. [Coleoptera: Anthribidae of World (Yes); Curculionidae of U. S. (Yes); Amphibia: Plethodontidae: g. Desmognathus & Gyrinophilus of U. S. (Yes)]

VALENTINE, Dr. J. Manson. 1260 S. W. First Street, Miami 35, Fla., U. S. A. [Coleoptera: cavernicolous Carabidae of World (No), of N. America (Yes)]

VALENTINE, James W., Assistant Professor, Department of Geology, University of Missouri, Columbia, Mo., U. S. A. [Pleistocene-Recent marine shelled Mollusca of w. N. America (Yes); Eocene marine Ostracoda of California (Yes)]

VALKANOV, Prof. A. Akvarium, Varna, Bulgaria. [Protozoa: f-w. Flagellata & Rhizopoda; Hydrozoa: Moerisiidae; Rotatoria; all of Bulgaria (Yes)]

VALKEILA, Mr. Erkki. Hämeentie 12, Hämeenlinna, Finland. [Hymenoptera: Sapygidae, Tiphiidae, Mutillidae, of Finland & Scandinavia (Yes); Chrysididae, Pompilidae, Sphecidae, Vespidae, Apidae, of Palearctic (No), of Finland & Scandinavia (Yes)]

VALLE, Antonio. Museo Civico di Storia Naturale, Piazza Vecchia 8, Bergamo, Italy. [Acarina: Uropodina of World (Yes)]

* VALLE, Prof. Dr. K. I. Zoological Laboratorium, University of Turku, Turku, Finland. [Odonata]

VALLETTA, Anthony. 257 Msida Street, B'Kara, Malta. [Lepidoptera & Odonata of Mediterranean (No)]

VAN --- See also van --- (under first capital letter)

* VANASIA, Santo. 71 via M. Macchi, Milano, Italy. [Fossil Invertebrates]

VANCEA, St. Universtitatea Al. I. Cuza, Laboratorul de Zoologie, Iasi, Rumania. [Amphibia & Reptilia of Rumania (Yes)]

VANDEL, Prof. A. Faculté des Sciences, Allées St. Michel, Toulouse, France. [Crustacea: Isopoda of Europe, n. Africa, U. S., S. America, Australia, New Zealand, Tasmania (Yes)]

VAN DEN --- . See van den --- (under first capital letter)

* VAN HOUTEN, Dr. Franklyn B. Department of Geology, Princeton University, Princeton, N. J., U. S. A. [Fossil Mammalia]

VAN DE POEL, Mr. L. Institut Royal des Sciences Naturelles de Belgique, rue Vautier 31, Bruxelles IV, Belgium. [Mesozoic marine Pelecypoda of World (Yes); Mesozoic marine Gastropoda of World (No)]

VAN DER ---. See also van der --- (under first capital letter)

VANDERCAMMEN, Dr. A. C. A. Department de Paleontologie, Institut Royal des Sciences Naturelles, 31 rue Vautier, Bruxelles, Belgium. [Cambrian-Jurassic Brachiopoda: Spiriferidae (Yes)]

VAN DER GOOT, V. S. Zoological Museum (Entomology), Municipal University, Zeeburgerdijk 21, Amsterdam O, Netherlands. [Diptera: Syrphidae of Europe (Yes)]

VANDERHOOF, Dr. V. L. Box 1411, Bakersfield, Calif., U. S. A. [Mammalia: Tertiary Sirenia & Up. Tertiary Canidae (Yes)] [INTEX Oil Company]

* VANDERPLANCK, Dr. F. L. West African Institute for Trypanosomiasis Research, Kadung, Nigeria. [Diptera]

VAN DER SCHALIE, Dr. Henry. Museum of Zoology, University of Michigan, Ann Arbor, Mich., U. S. A. [F-w. Mollusca, espec. Naiades, of N. America (Yes)]

VAN DER VLERK, Prof. I. M., Director, Rijksmuseum van Geologie & Mineralogie, Van der Werffpark 1, Leiden, Netherlands. [Tertiary larger Foraminifera (No); Lepidocyclinae (Yes)]

VAN DEUSEN, Mr. Hobart M. Department of Mammals, American Museum of Natural History, New York 24, N. Y., U. S. A. [Mammalia: Monotremata, Marsupialia, Rodentia, Chiroptera, of Australia, New Guinea, Indonesia (Yes); Chiroptera of w. Pacific (Yes); land Aves of New Guinea (No)]

VAN DORSSELAER, R. 111 Avenue Oscar de Burbure, Wezembeek-Oppem, Belgium. [Coleoptera: Carabidae: Calosoma, Cychrus, Carabus, of World (Yes); Cicindelidae of World (No)]

VAN EEDEN, Dr. J. A. Department of Zoology, Potchefstroom University, Potchefstroom, Union of South Africa. [F-w. Gastropoda: Basommatophora of s. Africa & s. w. Africa (Yes)]

* VANEK, Jaroslav. 19 Pristavni, Praha 7, Czechoslovakia. [Lepidoptera]

VANĚK, Mr. Jiři. Paleontological Laboratory, Czechoslovakian Academy of Sciences, National Museum, Václavske Námĕsti 1700, Praha II, Czechoslovakia. [Trilobita of Europe (Yes)]

VAN GELDER, Richard G. Department of Mammals, American Museum of Natural History, New York 24, N. Y., U. S. A. [Mammalia of World (Yes); Carnivora: Mustelidae of W. Hemisphere (Yes)]

VAN HILLE, Dr. J. C. Department of Entomology, Rhodes University, Grahamstown, Union of South Africa. [Coleoptera: Anthicidae of Africa (Yes)]

VAN HOEGARDEN, Albert. Rue G. van Laethem 5, Bruxelles, Evere, Belgium. [Coleoptera: Carabidae: g. Carabus & Cychrus of Europe, Asia, N. America (Yes); g. Calosoma of World (Yes)]

VAN NAME, Dr. Willard G. (New Haven, Conn,; Ascidiacea & Isopoda) Died April 25, 1959.

VANNUCCI, Dr. M. Instituto Oceanografico, Universidade de São Paulo, Caixa Postal 9075, São Paulo, Brazil. [Hydrozoa: Hydromedusae & Scyphozoa: Scyphomedusae of s. Atlantic (Yes); Chaetognatha of s. Atlantic (No)]

VAN PELT, Arnold F., Jr. Department of Biology, Tusculum College, Greeneville, Tenn., U. S. A. [Hymenoptera: Formicidae of s. Blue Ridge & Florida (Yes); g. Aphaenogster of U. S., Canada, Mexico (Yes)]

VAN PLETZEN, R. Department of Zoology, University of the Orange Free State, Bloemfontein, Union of South Africa. [Acarina: Oribatei & Collembola of s. Africa (No)]

VAN RAADSHOOVEN, Bertram. C/o Compania Shell de Venezuela, Apartado 809, Caracas, Venezuela. [Paleocene & Eocene larger Foraminifera of Caribbean (No)]

* VAN ROOYEN, R. J. Division of Mammalogy, Transvaal Museum, Box 413, Pretoria, Union of South Africa. [Mammalia]

VAN SANT, Jan F. Department of Geology, University of Kansas, Lawrence, Kans., U. S. A. [Pennsylvanian Foraminifera; Fusulinidae & arenaceous Foraminifera of c. N. America (No)]

VANSCHUYTBROECK, Mr. P. Institut des Parcs Nationaux du Congo Belge, 31 rue Vautier, Bruxelles, Belgium. [Diptera: Dolichopodidae, Sphaeroceridae, Celiphidae, of Africa (Yes)] [Institut Royal des Sciences Naturelles de Belgique]

VAN SOMEREN, Dr. V. G. L. P. O. Box 24947 Karen, Ngong, Kenya. [Lepidoptera: Rhopalocera of e. Africa (Yes)]

VAN STRAELEN, Dr. V. Institut Royal des Sciences Naturelles de Belgique, 31 rue Vautier, Bruxelles, Belgium. [Fossil Crustacea: Malacostraca & Merostomata (Yes)] [Institut Royal des Sciences Naturelles de Belgique]

VAN TYNE, Josselyn. (Ann Arbor, Michigan; Aves) Died January 30, 1957.

VAN WEERDT, Dr. L. G. P. O. Box 3777, University Station, Gainesville, Fla., U. S. A. [Nematoda: Tylenchida of s. e. U. S. (Yes)] [State Plant Board of Florida]

VANZOLINI, Dr. P. E. Departamento de Zoologia, Secretaria de Agricultura, Caixa Postal 7172, São Paulo, Brazil. [Reptilia of S. America (Yes)]

VAN ZWALUWENBURG, Mr. R. H. 2114 Spring Creek Drive, Santa Rosa, Calif., U. S. A. [Coleoptera: Elateridae of Oceania & New Guinea (Yes)]

VARDIKIAN, Seda Avacovna. Zoological Institut, Avanskoe Shosse 20, Erevan, Armenian S. S. R. [Lepidoptera: Geometridae of Caucasus (Yes)]

VARGA, Prof. Dr. L. Research Laboratory for Soilbiology, Hungarian Academy of Science, Sopron, Hungary. [Soil Protozoa, Rotatoria, Gastrotricha, of Europe (Yes)]

VARGAS, Dr. Luis. Laboratorio de Entomologia, Instituto de Salubridad, Apartado Postal 19205, Mexico 17, D. F., Mexico. [Diptera: Culicidae, Simuliidae, Psychodidae: g. Culicoides, of C. America (Yes)]

VÁRI, Dr. L. Transvaal Museum, P. O. Box 413, Pretoria, Union of South Africa. [Lepidoptera, espec. Tineina of s. Africa (Yes)]

VARIN, G. 4 Avenue de Joinville, Joinville-le-Pont (Seine), France. [Lepidoptera: Satyridae, excl. g. Erebia Europe & n. Africa (Yes)]

VARMA, Dr. M. G. R. Virus Research Centre, 20A Wellesley Road, Box 11, Poona 1, India. [Acarina: Ixodidae of s. e. Asia (Yes)]

* VASIČ, Dr. Konstantin. Šumarski Fakultet, Beograd, Yugoslavia. [Lepidoptera: Noctuidae & Hymenoptera: Ichneumonidae]

* VAŠÍČEK, M. Paleontology Laboratory, Václavské 68, Praha 2, Czechoslovakia. [Fossil Protozoa]

VASILIU, Dr. George D. Calea Vacaresti 176 A, Bucureşti 6, Rumania. [Pisces: Salmonidae & Cyprinidae of Palearctic (Yes)] [Institutul de Cercetari Piscicole]

VASILIU, Maria. Museul "Grigore Antipa", Sos. Kiseleff Nr. 1, Bucureşti, Rumania. [Orthoptera: Saltatoria of Rumania (Yes)]

VAUGHN, Dr. Peter P. U. S. National Museum, Washington 25, D. C., U. S. A. [Paleozoic Amphibia & Reptilia of N. America (Yes)]

VAURIE, Dr. Charles. Department of Ornithology, American Museum of Natural History, New York 24, N. Y., U. S. A. [Aves of Palearctic & Oriental]

VAURIE, Patricia. Department of Insects & Spiders, American Museum of Natural History, New York 24, N. Y. , U. S. A. [Coleoptera: Curculionidae, g. Calendra of N. America (Yes); Scarabaeidae: g. Trox & Diplotaxis of N. & C. America (Yes)]

VAVRA, J. Protozoology Laboratory, Czechoslovakian Academy of Science, Viničná 7, Praha II, Czechoslovakia. [Ciliata: sessile Peritricha epizoic on f-w. animals (Yes); Microsporidia of f. w. Crustacea (Yes)]

* VAYSSIÈRE, Prof. P. Museum National d'Histoire Naturelle, 57 Rue Cuvier, Paris (V), France. [Homoptera: Coccidae]

* VAZ-FERREIRA, Prof. Raúl. Departamento de Zoologia, Universidad de Montevideo, Caiguá 3610, Montevideo, Uruguay. [Pisces & Mammalia: Pinnipedia] [Servicio Oceanografico y de Pesca]

VAZQUEZ, Alberto. Biology Department, George Washington University, Washington, D. C. , U. S. A. [Coleoptera: Curculionidae: g. Curculio & Attelabus of N. America & Mexico (Yes)]

VAZQUEZ GARCIA, Dra. Leonila. Instituto de Biologia, Universidad Nacional de Mexico, Mexico 20, D. F. , Mexico. [Lepidoptera: Psychidae, Papilionidae, Pieridae, of Mexico (Yes)]

van der VECHT, J. Rijksmuseum van Natuurlijke Historie, Leiden, Netherlands. [Hymenoptera: Vespidae, Eumenidae, Sphecoidea, Pompilidae, of Oriental & Papuan (Yes)]

VEEVERS, Dr. J. J. Bureau of Mineral Resources, Canberra, Australia. [Devonian Brachiopoda of w. Australia (Yes); Carboniferous Brachiopoda: Camarotoechiidae of w. Australia (Yes)]

* da VEIGA FERREIRA, G. P. O. Box 1398, Lourenço Marques, Mozambique. [Coleoptera: Cerambycidae: Prioninae]

VEILLON, Mauricette Paule, Attachée de Recherches, Centre de 3º Cycle de Géologie Approfondie, 351 cours de la Libération, Talence (Gironde), France. [Eocene Foraminifera of n. Aquitania (Yes)] [Centre National de la Recherche Scientifique]

VELANKER, S. R. Vigyan Mandir Officer, Shapur, Dist. Sorath, Bombay State, India. [Diplopoda: Harpagophoridae of Mysore (No)] [Ministry of Education & Scientific Research]

* VELEZ, Manuel J. , Jr. P. O. Box 192, Isabela, Puerto Rico. [Rotifera]

VELLA, Paul. Geology Department, Victoria University of Wellington, P. O. Box 196, Wellington, New Zealand. [Up. Cretaceous-Recent Foraminifera of New Zealand (Yes); Miocene-Pliocene Gastropoda & Pelecypoda of New Zealand (No)]

VELLARD, Prof. J. Museo de Historia Natural "Javier Prado", Universidad San Marcos, Apartado 1109, Lima, Peru. [Amphibia: Salientia of S. America (Yes); Reptilia: Crotalinae of S. America (No); Arachnida: Araneae of S. America (Yes)]

VENARD, Dr. Carl. Department of Zoology, Ohio State University, Columbux 10, Ohio, U. S. A. [Helminths of f-w. fishes of e. N. America (Yes)]

VENMANS, Dr. L. A. W. C. Moergestel (N-B), Netherlands. [Terr. & f-w. Gastropoda of World (Yes)]

VENTURI, Prof. Dr. Filippo. Istituto di Entomologia Agraria, Università di Pisa, Via S. Michele 2, Pisa, Italy. [Diptera: Brachycera, excl. Phoridae, of Palearctic (Yes)]

VERBEKE, Dr. J. Institut Royal des Sciences Naturelles de Belgique, 31 Rue Vautier, Bruxelles, Belgium. [Diptera: Chaoboridae, Sciomyzidae, Micropezidae, Psilidae, Tachinidae of Africa (Yes)]

VERCAMMEN-GRANDJEAN, P. H. Laboratoire Médical Provincial du Kivu, B. P. 1156, Bukavu, Belgian Congo. [Acarina: Trombiculidae, Erythridae, Smaridae, Trombidiidae, of Africa (Yes); Trematoda & Insects of medical importance in Africa (No)]

VERDCOURT, Dr. Bernard. The East African Herbarium, P. O. Box 5166, Nairobi, Kenya. [Non-marine Mollusca of Kenya, Uganda, Tanganyika (Yes), of Britain (No); Cypraeidae of E. Africa (Yes)]

VERDIER, M. Faculté des Sciences, Université de Paris, 12 rue Cuvier, Paris (V), France. [Orthoptera: Phaneropteridae, g. Orphania & Barbitistes; Ephippigeridae: g. Ephippiger of Palearctic & Africa (No)]

VERESCHAGIN, Dr. H. K. Zoological Institute, Academy of Sciences of U. S. S. R. , Leningrad B-164, U. S. S. R. [Mammalia: Neogene & Recent Carnivora, Rodentia, Proboscidea, Perissodactyla, Artiodactyla, of Europe & Asia (Yes)]

* VERHAEGHE, Marcel A. P. Service Geologique, Bukavu, Belgian Congo. [Mollusca]

* VERHAEGHE, R. 84 rue de l'Eglise, Berchem, Bruxelles, Belgium. [Mollusca]

* VERHALHA, M. M. Instituto de Biologia, Caixa Postal 357, Curitiba, Brazil. [Coleoptera]

VERHEYEN, Rene K. Institut Royal des Sciences Naturelles de Belgique, Rue Vautier 31, Bruxelles 4, Belgium. [Aves of c. Africa (Yes); fossil birds of Old World (Yes)]

VERHEYEN, Dr. Walter. Section des Vertébrés, Musée Royal du Congo Belge, Tervuren, Belgium. [Mammalia of Belgium Congo (Yes)]

VERHOEFF, P. M. F. Dolderse Weg 42, Den Dolder, Netherlands. [Hymenoptera: Sphecidae of Europe & Mediterranean (No); Oxybelini of Palearctic (Yes)]

VERITY, Dr. Roger. Caldine, Firenze, Italy. [Lepidoptera: Hesperiidae & Zygaenidae of Palearctic (No)]

VERNBERG, F. J. Marine Laboratory, Duke University, Beaufort, N. C. , U. S. A. [Crustacea: Decapoda (Yes)]

VERNER, RNDr. Petr H. Bachmačská 8, Praha 6, Czechoslovakia. [Pseudoscorpiones of World (No), of Palearctic & Africa (Yes); Reptilia of c. & e. Europe (Yes)]
VERSCHUREN, Dr. J. Institut Royal des Sciences Naturelles de Belgique, 31 rue Vautier, Bruxelles 4, Belgium. [Mammalia of Belgium, w. Europe, trop. Africa]
VERSEVELDT, Dr. J. Wipstrikkerallee 126, Zwolle, Netherlands. [Coelenterata: Octocorallia: Stolonifera, Alcyonacea, Gorgonacea: Scleraxonia, of Indo-Pacific (Yes)]
* VERTSE, A., Directeur, Institute Ornithologie de Hongrie, Madártani Intézet, Mezögazdasági Museum, Budapest-Városliget, Hungary. [Aves]
VERVILLE, George J. Pan-American Oil Co., Tulsa, Okla., U.S.A. [Fossil Foraminifera: Fusulinidae of N. America (Yes)]
VERVOORT, Dr. W. Zoological Laboratory, University of Lieden, Leiden, Netherlands. [Crustacea: marine Copepoda: Calanoida of World (Yes)]
VESEY-FITZGERALD, L.D.E.F. P.O.Box 37, Abercorn, Northern Rhodesia. [Reptilia: snakes & Mammalia of c. Africa (Yes)] [International Red Locust Control Service]
VEVERS, Dr. H.G. Zoological Society of London, Regent's Park, London, N.W.1, England. [Echinodermata of n. e. Atlantic (No)]
* VEYRET, P. Rue Lavène, La Garde (Var), France. [Coleoptera]
VIA, Dr. Luis. Calle Iradier 27, Barcelona, Spain. [Eocene Crustacea: Decapoda of Spain (Yes)] [Facultad de Ciencias, Universidad de Barcelona]
* VIADO, Getulio B. Department of Entomology, University of the Philippines, College, Laguna, Philippines. [Larvae of Coleoptera]
VIALLI, Prof. Maffo, Direttore, Istituto di Anatomia Comparata, Universita di Pavia, Palazzo Botta, Piazza Botta 10, Pavia, Italy. [Turbellaria: Tricladida & Rhabdocoelida of Italy (No)]
VIALLI, Prof. Dr. V. Museo Civico di Storia Naturale, Corso Venezia 55, Milano, Italy. [Quaternary Mammalia of Italy (No); Foraminifera: Nummulitidae of Mediterranean (No)]
* VIANO, Manuel José. Avenida Luis Maria Campos 409, Buenos Aires, Argentina. [Coleoptera: Curculionidae]
VIBE, Dr..Christian. Universitetets Zoologiske Museum, Krystalgade 27, København, Denmark. [Terr. Mammalia of Greenland (Yes)]
VICHET, G. 5 rue du Grand, Saint Jean, Montpellier, France. [Orthoptera of Europe & Mediterranean (No); Phasmidae of Europe & Africa (No)]
VIDAL y LÓPEZ, Manuel. (Valencia, Spain; Mollusca & Coleoptera: Cicindelidae) Not now active in taxonomy.
* VIEIRA, Carlos O.C. Departamento de Zoologia, Secretaria de Agricultura, Caixa Postal 7172, São Paulo, Brazil. [Mammalia of S. America]
VIETS, Dr. Karl. Hastedter Osterdeich 183, (23) Bremen 11, Germany. [Acarina: Hydrachnellae of World (Yes); Halacaridae of World (No)]
VIETS, Dr. Kurt O. Friedenstrasse 4, Wilhelmshaven, Germany. [Acarina: Hydrachnellae of World (Yes); Porohalacaridae of World (Yes)]
VIETTE, Mr. Pierre. Department d'Entomologie, Muséum National d'Histoire Naturelle, 45 bis rue de Buffon, Paris (V), France. [Lepidoptera of Madagascar (Yes), of S. Pacific (No)]
VIGELAND, Dr. Immanuel. Zoologisk Museum, Sarsgatan 1, Oslo, Norway. [Bryozoa: Cheilostomata of Arctic Ocean, Antarctic, Chile (Yes)]
VIGNEAUX, Prof. Michel, Directeur du Centre de 3º Cycle de Géologie Approfondie, 351 Cours de la Libération, Talence (Gironde), France. [Tertiary Bryozoa (Yes)]
VIJAYARAGHAVAN, Dr. P. Research Centre of the Central Marine Fisheries, Annamalai University Field Biological Station, Porto Nova, S. India. [Marine Pisces, incl.eggs & larvae, of India (Yes)]
* VIKTOROV, G.A. Institut Morfologii Zivotnych, B. Kaluzskaya 33, Moskva V-70, U.S.S.R. [Hymenoptera]
VILBASTE, Juhan. ENSV Teaduste Akadeemia Zooloogia, ja Botaanika Instituut, Vanemuise 21, Tartu, Estonia, U.S.S.R. [Homoptera: Cicadina of U.S.S.R (Yes); Psyllina of Estonia (Yes); Heteroptera of Estonia (Yes)] [Academy of Sciences of the Estonian S.S.R., Institute of Botany & Zoology]
VILELA, Dr. H. Instituto de Biologia Maritima, Cais do Sodré, Lisboa 2, Portugal. [Pisces: Scombriformes of Portuguese West Africa & coast of Spain & Portugal (Yes)]
VILLADOLID, Dr. Deogracias. National Institute of Science & Technology, Herran & Taft Streets, Manila, Philippines. [F-w. Pisces of Philippines (Yes); f-w. Mollusca of Philippines (Yes)]
VILLALOBOS, Dr. Alejandro. Instituto de Biologia, U.N.A.M., Apartado Postal.29817, Mexico 18, D.F., Mexico. [Crustacea: Decapoda: Astacidae, Atyidae, Palaemonidae; Mysidacea; of New World (Yes)]
de VILLALTA COMELLA, Prof. Dr. J.F. Instituto Geologico, Universidad, Barcelona, Spain. [Neozoic & Quaternary Mammalia of Spain (Yes)]
VILLA RAMIREZ, Sr. B., Jefe de la Seccion de Mastozoologia, Instituto de Biologia, U.N.A.M., Ciudad Universitaria, Villa Obregón, Mexico, D.F., Mexico. [Mammalia of Mexico (Yes); Chiroptera of C. & S. America (Yes)]

377

VILLIERS, Dr. A. M., Sous-Directeur du Laboratoire d'Entomologie, Museum National d'Histoire Naturelle, 45 bis rue de Buffon, Paris (V), France. [Coleoptera: Languriidae of Old World (Yes); Cerambycidae of Madagascar & n. Africa (Yes); Hemiptera: Reduviidae of Africa (Yes)]

* VINCENT, André. Institut des Pêches, Casablanca, Morocco. [Pisces]

VINCENT, Lieut. Col. J. "Firle", P. O. Box 44, Mooi River, Natal, Union of South Africa. [Aves: espec. g. Cisticola, of Ethiopian, espec. s. Africa (Yes)]

* VINCKE, Dr. I. SERAM, B. P. 1190, Elisabethville, Belgian Congo. [Diptera]

VINOGRADOV, Dr. M. E. Institute of Oceanology, Academy of Sciences of U. S. S. R., Luzhnikovskaya 8, Moscow 127, U. S. S. R. [Crustacea: pelagic Amphipoda of Pacific, India, Antarctic (Yes)]

VINSON, Mr. J. L. J. The Mauritius Institute, Port Louis, Mauritius. [Coleoptera: espec. Carabidae, Scaphidiidae, Dasytidae, Elateridae, Eucnemidae, Cybocephalidae, Scarabaeidae, of Mascarene Islands (Yes)]

VIRET, Prof. Dr. Jean F. E., Directeur du Museum de Lyon, 28 Blvd., des Belges, Lyon (VI), France. [Fossil Mammalia of Europe (Yes)]

VISHNJAKOVA, V. N. Zoological Institute, Academy of Sciences of U. S. S. R., Leningrad 164, U. S. S. R. [Psocoptera of U. S. S. R. (Yes)]

VISSER, John D. "Mavis Bank", 7 Tamboerskloof Road, Tamboerskloof, Union of South Africa. [Reptilia: Sauria & Serpentes of Africa (Yes); Amphibia Salientia of Africa (Yes)] [Zoology Department, Stellenbosch University]

VJUSCHKOV, B. (Moscow, U. S. S. R.: Fossil Vertebrates) Died June 5, 1958.

VLADYKOV, Dr. V. D. Biological Laboratory, Department of Fisheries, Quebec, P. Q., Canada. [Pisces: Petromyzonidae, Acipenseridae, Salmonidae, of Holarctic (Yes)]

VLCEK, Dr. E. Quarter. Department of Archaeological Institut, Czechoslovak Academie of Sciences, Leteusvá 4, Praha 3, Czechoslovakia. [Mammalia: Primates: Cercopithecidae of Europe (Yes)]

VOCKEROTH, Dr. J. R. Entomology Division, Science Service Building, Ottawa, Ont., Canada. [Diptera: Muscidae: Scatomyzinae of World (Yes); Syrphidae of N. America (Yes); Culicidae of Canada (Yes)]

VOGE, Dr. Marietta. Department of Infectious Diseases, U. C. L. A. Medical School, Los Angeles 24, Calif., U. S. A. [Cestoda of New World (Yes)]

* VOGEL, Mr. W. C/o Eidg. Versuchsanstalt für Obst-, Wein- u. Gartenbau, Wädenswil/ZH, Switzerland. [Nematoda]

* VOGELSANG, Enrique G. Facultad de Medicina Veterinaria, Apartado 4563, Maracay, Venezuela. [Acarina: Ixodoidea]

* VOGLEV, Mr. E. A. Laboratory of Paleontology, Shell Oil Company, P. O. Box 1509, Midland, Texas, U. S. A. [Fossil Invertebrates]

VOGT, George B. Division of Insects, U. S. National Museum, Washington 25, D. C., U. S. A. [Coleoptera: Chrysomelidae of N. America (Yes); Buprestidae of New World & Malaysia (Yes); Cerambycidae of N. America (Yes)] [Insect Identification & Plant Parasite Introduction Laboratories, U. S. Department of Agriculture]

VOIGT, Prof. Dr. Ehrhard. Geologisches Staatsinstitut, Esplanade 1 B, Hamburg 36, Germany. [Up. Cretaceous Bryozoa (Yes)]

VOIGT, M. (Schleswig, Germany; Rotifera) Not now active in taxonomy.

VOIPIO, Dr. P. T., Professor of Zoology, Zoological Institute, University of Turku, Turku, Finland. [Aves of Palearctic (No); Mammalia of Europe (No)]

VOKES, Prof. Harold E. Department of Geology, Tulane University, New Orleans 18, La., U. S. A. [Mesozoic-Recent, espec. Cretaceous & Tertiary, Pelecypoda (Yes)]

VOLGIN, Mr. V. I. Zoological Institute, Academy of Sciences of U. S. S. R., Leningrad B-164, U. S. S. R. [Acarina: Tyroglyphoidea & Cheyletidae of Palearctic (Yes); Coleoptera: Chrysomelidae, Larvae & Imago, of Palearctic (No)]

VOLK, Dr. J. (Erlangen, Germany; Nematoda) Not now active in taxonomy.

* VOLKOVA, Dr. M. S. Kazakhstan Geological Survey, Alma-Ata, Kazakh S. S. R., U. S. S. R. [Carboniferous Anthozoa: Rugosa]

* VOLOGDIN, Prof. A. G. Paleontological Institute, Academy of Sciences of U. S. S. R., Leninsky Prospect 35, Moscow B-71, U. S. S. R. [Fossil Archaeocyatha]

* VOLOSCHINORA, N. A. W. N. I. G. R. I., Liteiny 39, Leningrad 104, U. S. S. R. [Protozoa]

VOLPE, Prof. E. Peter. Department of Zoology, Newcomb College, Tulane University, New Orleans 18, La., U. S. A. [Amphibia: Ranidae & Bufonidae of e. N. America (Yes)]

VOLSØE, Dr. Helge. Zoological Museum, Krystalgade 27, København K, Copenhagen, Denmark. [Insular Aves of Atlantic Islands (Yes)]

* VOLZ, Peter. Appenhofen bei Landau/Pfalz, Germany. [Nematoda]

VON BLOEKER, Prof. Jack C., Jr. Life Sciences Department, Los Angeles City College, Los Angeles 29, Calif., U. S. A. [Mammalia: Insectivora, Rodentia, Carnivora, of w. N. America, Africa, Philippines (Yes); Reptilia: Lizards & Snakes; Amphibia: Salamanders of California, Oregon, Arizona, Baja California (Yes); Coleoptera: Lamellicornia, espec. Scarabaeidae, of World (No); Aves: Picidae of w. N. America, Africa, Philippines (Yes)]

VONDRÁČEK, Dr. Karel, Prof. Assoc., University School of Agronomy & Silviculture, Institute of Zoology Brno, Zemědělská 1, Brno, Czechoslovakia. [Homoptera: Psylloidea of Palearctic, Africa, S. America (Yes); of India, Australia, Asia, Pacific, N. America (No)]

van VOORTHUYSEN, Dr. J. H. Service Géologique des Pays-Bas, Spaarne 17, Haarlem, Netherlands. [Tertiary-Recent Foraminifera of North Sea Basin (Yes)]

VOOUS, Prof. Dr. K. H. Curator, Zoologisch Museum, Plantage Middenlaan 53, Amsterdam, Netherlands. [Aves of Palearctic & Netherlands Antilles (Yes); of s. e. Asia (No)]

* VORNATCHSER, Dr. J. Landstr. Hauptstrasse 95/40, Wien, III, Austria. [Cave Mammalia]

VORONTSOV, N. N. Laboratory of Mammals, Zoological Institute, Academy of Sciences of U. S. S. R., University Embankment 1, Leningrad B-164, U. S. S. R. [Mammalia: Cricetidae: Cricetinae of Palearctic (Yes), of New World (No); Myospalacinae of World (Yes); Dipodidae, excl. g. Sicista, of World (Yes)]

* VORSTMAN, Dr. A. G. Zoological Laboratory of the University, Plantage Doklaan 44, Amsterdam-C, Netherlands. [Rotifera]

de VOS, Dr. A. P. C. Zoological Museum, Plantage Middenlaan 53, Amsterdam (C), Netherlands. [Marine & f-w. Crustacea: Ostracoda of Europe (No)]

VOSS, E. Hardenberg 115, über Osnabruck 5, Germany. [Coleoptera: Attelabidae of World (Yes); Curculionidae of Palearctic, Oriental, Ethiopian (Yes); fossil Coleoptera from amber (Yes)]

VOSS, Dr. Edward G. Museums Annex, University of Michigan, Ann Arbor, Mich., U. S. A. [Lepidoptera of Michigan (No)]

VOSS, Gilbert L. The Marine Laboratory, University of Miami, Coral Gables 34, Fla., U. S. A. [Recent Cephalopoda of World (Yes); marine Invertebrates, excl. Porifera & Annelida, of West Indies (Yes)]

VOSS, Mrs. Nancy A. Marine Laboratory, 1 Rickenbacker Causeway, Virginia Key, Miami 49, Fla., U. S. A. [Larval marine oceanic Pisces of West Indies (Yes)]

VRANOVSKÝ, M. Zoological Department, Slovak Academy of Sciences, Sienkiewiczova 1, Bratislava, Czechoslovakia. [Crustacea: Copepoda: Cyclopidae of c. Europe (Yes)]

VRYDAGH, Prof. Ing. J. M. Institute Royal des Sciences Naturelles de Belgique, Rue Vautier 31, Bruxelles 4, Belgium. [Coleoptera; Bostrychidae & Lyctidae of World (Yes)]

VULCANO, Maria Aparecida. See D'ANDRETTA, M. A. V.

VUXANOVICI, Inginer A. Raion 23 August, St. Popp de Bazesti 1, Bucureşti, Romania. [Ciliata: Infusoria Libera (No); f-l. Ciliata (No)]

WAAGE, Prof. Karl M. Peabody Museum of Natural History, Yale University, New Haven, Conn., U. S. A. [Cretaceous Cephalopoda: Ammonoidea of U. S. (Yes)]

* WADE, Charles B. Address unknown. [Pisces]

WADE, Jos. S. 1629 Columbia Road, N. W., Washington 9, D. C., U. S. A. [Coleoptera: Scarabaeidae & Tenebrionidae of U. S., Canada, Mexico (No)]

WADE, L. E. 3325 Copley Street, Vancouver 12, B. C., Canada. [Collembola of s. w. British Columbia (Yes)]

WADE, Dr. Mary. Department of Geology, University of Adelaide, Adelaide, South Australia. [Tertiary smaller Foraminifera (Yes)]

WADE, Otis. 1400 Madrid Street, Coral Gables 34, Fla., U. S. A. [Mammalia: Sciuridae of U. S. & Canada (No)]

WAERING, E. N. Kjellesvig. See KJELLESVIG-WAERING, E. N.

WAGENER, Rev. Fr. Dr. Sigbert, Ofm. Cap., Hemdenerstrasse 19, Bocholt in Westf., Germany. [Lepidoptera: Satyridae: g. Melanargia of Palearctic (No), of e. Asia Species (Yes)]

* WAGENKNECHT, Rodolfo. Casilla 206, Departamento de Caminos, La Serena, Chile. [Hymenoptera]

* WAGER, Dr. V. Botanic Station, Durban, Natal, Union of South Africa. [Amphibia]

WAGNER, C. W. Bataafse Internationale Petroleum Maatschappy, Carel van Bylandtlaan 30, Den Haag, Netherlands. [Quaternary Ostracoda of n. w. Europe (Yes)]

WAGNER, Dr. Eduard. Moorreye 103, Hamburg-Langenhorn, Germany. [Heteroptera of Palearctic (Yes); Miridae of Nearctic (No); g. Trigonotylus of World (Yes)]

WAGNER, Dr. Edward D. School of Tropical & Preventive Medicine, College of Medical Evangelists, Loma Linda, Calif., U. S. A. [Cestoda of U. S. (No)]

WAGNER, Dr. Frances Joan Estelle. Geological Survey of Canada, Ottawa, Ont., Canada. [Pleistocene marine Pelecypoda & Gastropoda of Canada (Yes)]

WAGNER, Dr. W. Farnstrasse 36, Hamburg-Fuhlsbüttel, Germany. [Homoptera: Auchenorrhyncha of Europe (Yes); Psyllidae of c. Europe (Yes)] [Zoologisches Museum]

WAHIS, Raymond. 141 rue Joseph Deflandre, Embourg (Liège), Belgium. [Hymenoptera: Pompilidae of World (No), of Europe (Yes); g. Hemipepsis of Indo-Oriental (Yes)]

von WAHLERT, Dr. Gerd. Überseemuseum, Bremen 1, Germany. [Amphibia: Urodela of World (Yes)]

* WAHLGREN, Dr. Einar. Föreningsgatan 30, Malmö, Sweden. [Diptera]
WAHRMAN, Dr. J. Department of Zoology, Hebrew University, Jerusalem, Israel. [Mammalia: Rodentia, espec. Gerbillinae, of Near East (Yes); Orthoptera: Mantodea of Near East (Yes)]
WAINSTEIN, B. A. Nekouzski r-n, Jaroslavskaja obC., Borok, U. S. S. R. [Acarina: Tetranychoidea, Phytoseiidae, Aceosejidae, of U. S. S. R. (Yes); Hydrachnellae of U. S. S. R. (No)] [Institute of the Biology of Reservoirs]
WAITE, Roy Harold. Shell Oil Company, 33 Richards Street, Salt Lake City, Utah. [Silurian Fossils of w. N. America (Yes); Foraminifera: Fusulinidae & Graptolitoidea of N. America (Yes)]
WAKELY, S. 26 Finsen Road, Ruskin Park, London, S. E. 5, England. [Microlepidoptera of Britain (Yes)]
WAKIYA, Y. (Kumamoto, Japan; Pisces) Deceased.
WALDEN, Dr. H. Zoological Institute, Radmansgatan 70A, Stockholm V, Sweden. [Terr. & limnic Gastropoda of Scandinavia, Baltic, Iceland, Greenland, Newfoundland (Yes); Terrestial Gastropoda, espec. Limacidae, of Holarctic, (No); fossil terr. Gastropoda of Scandinavia (Yes)]
* WALDRON, Kenneth D. Oregon Fish Commission, Newport Shellfish Studies Laboratory, 121 S. W. Bay Boulevard, Newport, Ore., U. S. A. [Crustacea: Decapoda]
* WALDRON, Robert P. Geology Department, Louisiana State University, Baton Rouge 3, La., U. S. A. [Fossil Invertebrates]
* WALES, J. H. California Department of Fish & Game, Mt. Shasta Hatchery, Mt. Shasta, Calif., U. S. A. [Pisces]
WALFORD, Dr. L. A. Atlantic Fishery Oceanographic Research Center, 734 Jackson Place, N. W., Washington, D. C., U. S. A. [Marine Pisces (No)]
WALKER, Dr. A. D. Department of Geology, King's College, Newcastle upon Tyne, England. [Triassic Reptilia: Pseudosuchia of n. Scotland (Yes); Triassic Rhynochosauridae of n. Scotland, (Yes); Permian Dicynodontia of n. Scotland (Yes)]
WALKER, Dr. Boyd W. Department of Zoology, University of California, Los Angeles 24, Calif., U. S. A. [Marine shore Pisces of e. tropical Pacific (Yes); Sciaenidae of World (No); shore Brotulidae of World (Yes)]
WALKER, Dr. Charles F. Museum of Zoology, University of Michigan, Ann Arbor, Mich., U. S. A. [Amphibia: Salientia & Urodela of New World (Yes)]
WALKER, Prof. Edmund M. Department of Zoology, University of Toronto, Toronto, Ont., Canada. [Odonata of n. N. America (Yes)]
* WALKER, Earl T. Maryland Department of Research & Education, Chesapeake Biological Laboratory, Solomons, Md., U. S. A. [Pisces]
WALKER, Miss Jane B. East African Veterinary Research Organization, P. O. Box 32, Kikuyu, Kenya. [Acarina: Argasidae & Ixodidae, espec. g. Rhipicephalus, of e. Africa (Yes)]
WALKER, Mr. Myrl V. Fort Hays Kansas State College, Hays, Kans., U. S. A. [Reptilia: Oligocene Amphisbaenidae: g. Rhineura (Yes); Cretaceous Pteranodontidae: g. Pteranodon & Nyctosaurus of Kansas Niobrara (Yes); Cretaceous Polycotylidae: g. Trinacromerum of Kansas Niobrara (Yes)]
WALKER, Neil A. Division of Biological Sciences, Fort Hays Kansas State College, Hays, Kans., U. S. A. [Acarina: Oribatei: g. Ptyctima of World (No); of N. America (Yes)]
WALKER, Dr. Thomas J. Department of Entomology, McCarty Hall, University of Florida, Gainesville, Fla., U. S. A. [Orthoptera: Gryllidae: Oecanthinae of N. America (Yes)]
WALKER, Dr. Warren F., Jr. Department of Zoology, Oberlin College, Oberlin, Ohio, U. S. A. [Amphibia & Reptilia of N. America (Yes); Reptilia: Serpentes of Peru (Yes)]
WALKINSHAW, Lawrence. 1703 Wolverine-Federal Tower, Battle Creek, Mich., U. S. A. [Aves: Gruidae of World (Yes)]
WALKLEY, Miss Luella M. Division of Insects, U. S. National Museum, Washington 25, D. C., U. S. A. [Hymenoptera: Ichneumonidae of New World (Yes); Coleoptera: Lathridiidae & Nitidulidae of N. America (Yes)]
WALL, Mr. John H. Box 1300, St. Stephen, N. B., Canada. [Jurassic & Cretaceous Foraminifera, espec. arenaceous, of w. Canada (Yes); Jurassic & Cretaceous marine & non-marine Ostracoda of w. interior of U. S. & Canada (Yes); Devonian & Mississippian Conodonts of w. Canada (Yes)]
WALL, Dr. William J., Jr. Department of Biology, State Teachers College, Bridgewater, Mass., U. S. A. [Thysanura of N. America (Yes)]
WALLACE, Dr. F. G. Department of Zoology, University of Minnesota, Minneapolis 14, Minn., U. S. A. [Protozoa: Trypanosomidae of Insects of World (Yes); Trematoda: Opisthorchiidae & Troglotrematidae of World (Yes)]
WALLACE, Dr. George E. Carnegie Museum, Pittsburgh 13, Penna., U. S. A. [Hymenoptera: Pteromalidae, Cleonymidae, incl. Miscogasteridae, of World (No); of N. America (Yes)]
WALLACE, Dr. George J. Department of Zoology, Michigan State University, East Lansing, Mich., U. S. A. [Aves of N. America (No); Turdidae of Neotropics (No)]

WALLACE, Prof. H. K. Department of Biology, University of Florida, Gainesville, Fla.,
U. S. A. [Araneida: Lycosidae & Salticidae of e. U. S. (No)]
WALLACE, Dr. H. R. Rothamsted Experiment Station, Harpenden, Herts, England. [Plant
parasitic Nematoda of Britain (No)]
WALLACE, Herbert S. Department of Biology, Northeast Louisiana State College, Monroe,
La., U. S. A. [Orthoptera of N. America (Yes); Acrididae of World (No)]
WALLACE, M. M. C. S. I. R. O. Laboratory, University Grounds, Nedlands, W. Australia. [Aca-
rina: Bdellidae of w. Australia (Yes)] [Commonwealth Scientific & Industrial Research
Organization]
WALLACE, Shelby L., Chairman, Science Division, Junior College of Augusta, Augusta, Ga.,
U. S. A. [Crustacea: Portunidae of s. e. U. S. (Yes)]
WALLEY, Mr. G. Stuart. Entomology Research Institute, Department of Agriculture, Ottawa,
Ont., Canada. [Hymenoptera: Ichneumonidae of Nearctic (Yes)]
WALLIS, J. B. 468 Niagara Street, Winnipeg, Man., Canada. [Coleoptera: Haliplidae, Dytisci-
dae, Gyrinidae & Scarabaeidae: g. Odontaeus, Cicindelidae: g. Cicindela, of N. America
(Yes)] [University of Manitoba]
WALLISER, Dr. O. H. Geologisch- Paleontologisches Institut der Universität, Deutschhaus-
strasse 10, Marburg / Lahn, Germany. [Paleozoic Conodonts of World (Yes); Devonian
Goniatitida of World (Yes)]
* WALLWORK, Dr. J. A. Zoology Department, University College of Ghana, Achimota, Ghana.
[Acarina]
WALMSLEY, Dr. V. G. Department of Geology, University College, Singleton Park, Swansea,
Wales. [Up. Silurian (Ludlovian) faunas of Britain (Yes); Upper Silurian Brachiopoda:
"dalmanellids" (Yes); Pelecypoda: Pteronitella (Yes)]
WALTER, Mr. Harold J. Museum of Zoology, University of Michigan, Ann Arbor, Mich.,
U. S. A. [Gastropoda: Lymnaeidae of World (No), of N. America (Yes)]
WALTER, Waldemar M. Department of Biology, Texas Woman's University, University Hill
Station, Denton, Texas, U. S. A. [F-w. Mollusca of s. e. & n. w. U. S. (Yes)]
* WALTERS, Dr. Vladimir. 116-03 128 Street, South Ozone Park, New York 20, N. Y., U. S. A.
[Pisces of Arctic Alaska]
WALTON, Prof. Arthur C. Division of Biology, Knox College, Galesburg, Ill., U. S. A. [Nema-
toda of Amphibia of World (Yes); Trematoda & Cestoda of Amphibia of World (No)]
WALTON, Capt. Bryce C. 406th Medical General Laboratory, APO 343, San Francisco, Calif.,
U. S. A. [Hirudinea: Arhynchobdellae of Oriental (Yes)]
WALTON, G. A. Department of Entomology, London School of Hygiene & Tropical Medicine,
Keppel Street (Gower Street), London, W. C. 1, England. [Aquatic Hemiptera of Britain
(Yes); Acarina: Argasidae: g. Ornithodoros (Yes)]
WALTON, M. L. 1108 N. Central Avenue, Glendale 2, Calif., U. S. A. [Mollusca: land shells of
U. S. (Yes)]
WANDSCHNEIDER, Willy Frühlingstrasse 13, Berlin-Wilhelmsruh, German Democratic Re-
public. [Lepidoptera: Saturniidae of World (No); Orthoptera: Mantidae & Phasmidae of
World (No)]
* WANG, C. C. Director, Institute of Hydrobiology, Academia Sinica, Wuchang, People's Re-
public of China. [Rotifera]
* WANG, Tze-Yi. Institute of Vertebrate Paleontology, Academia Sinica, P. O. Box 643, Pek-
ing, People's Republic of China. [Fossil Reptilia, Aves, Mammalia, of Shansi; Meso-
zoic & Pleistocene of n. China]
WANG, Dr. Yu-Hsi M. Department of Zoology, National Taiwan University, Taipeh, Taiwan,
Formosa. [Chilopoda & Diplopoda of Indo-Australian, Oriental, Pacific Is. (Yes)]
WANLESS, Harold R. 234 Natural History Building, University of Illinois, Urbana, Ill., U. S. A.
[Pennsylvanian-Permian Foraminifera: Fusulinidae (Yes); Pennsylvanian Invertebrates
(Yes)]
WARD, Helen L. Zoology Department, University of Tennessee, Knoxville, Tenn., U. S. A.
[Acanthocephala of World (Yes)]
WARD, John L. Room 701, Pacific Building, 327 N. E. 1st Avenue, Miami 32, Fla., U. S. A.
[Coleoptera: Chrysomelidae of Texas (Yes)] [Plant Quarantine Division, U. S. Depart-
ment of Agriculture]
WARD, Dr. Ronald A. Department of Biology, Gonzaga University, Spokane 2, Wash., U. S. A.
[Mallophaga of N. America, Pacific Islands, Micronesia (Yes); parasitic on tinamous
of New World (Yes); on g. Hohorstiella of World (Yes); g. Saemundssonia of World (Yes);
g. Geomydoecus of N. & C. America (Yes)]
* WARDLE, Dr. Robert A. Department of Parasitology, University of Manitoba, Winnipeg,
Man., Canada. [Cestoda]
* WARE, Mr. S. Department of Geology, British Museum (Natural History), Cromwell Road,
London, S. W. 7, England. [Paleozoic Mollusca, Polyzoa, Porifera, worms]
WARMKE, Germaine. Institute of Marine Biology, University of Puerto Rico, Mayaguez,
Puerto Rico. [Marine Mollusca of West Indies (Yes)]

381

WARNECKE, Mr. Georg. H. G. Hohenzollernring 32, Hamburg-Altona, Germany. [Lepidoptera: Nolidae of Palearctic (Yes); Noctuidae: Agrotinae & Caradrinidae of Europe (Yes)]

WARNER, Dr. Dwain W. Museum of Natural History, University of Minnesota, Minneapolis 14, Minn., U. S. A. [Aves of N. America & Mexico (Yes), of S. Pacific (No)]

WARNER, Dr. Edward N. Department of Biology, St. Lawrence University, Canton, N. Y., U. S. A. [F-w. Pisces of n. e. U. S. (Yes)]

WARNER, Miss Rose Ella. Room 394, U. S. National Museum, Washington 25, D. C., U. S. A. [Coleoptera: Curculionidae of N. & C. America (Yes)]

WARREN, A. D. Magnolia Petroleum Company, 518 Pioneer Building, Lake Charles, La., U. S. A. [Quaternary & Tertiary Protozoa: benthonic & planktonic Foraminifera of Gulf cst. of U. S. & Mexico (Yes); pelagic & planktonic Oligocene to Recent Foraminifera of Caribbean (Yes); Recent Thecamoebina of Gulf cst. of U. S. & Mexico & Caribbean (Yes); Cretaceous planktonic Foraminifera (No)]

WARREN, Mr. B. C. S. 3 Augusta Mansions, Folkestone, Kent, England. [Lepidoptera: Grypocera & Rhopalocera of Holarctic (No); Grypocera: g. Pyrgus of Palearctic (Yes); Nymphalidae: Argynninae of Holarctic (No); Satyridae: g. Erebia of Holarctic (Yes)]

WARREN, Percival S. (Edmonton, Canada; Fossils) Not now active in taxonomy.

* WARTHIN, Mr. Aldred S., Jr. Vassar College, Poughkeepsie, N. Y., U. S. A. [Fossil Invertebrates]

* WARWICK, T., Lecturer in Zoology, University of Edinburgh, Edinburgh, Scotland. [Mollusca]

WASEEM, Muhammed. Department of Plant Pathology, P. O. Box 7, Macdonald College, P. Q., Canada. [Nematoda: Tylenchidae: Hoplolaiminae of Quebec, s. e. U. S., e. Pakistan (No); g. Rotylenchus of Quebec, s. e. U. S., e. Pakistan (Yes)]

WASHBURN, R. H. Alaska Experiment Station, Palmer, Alaska. [Animals of Alaska (No)]

WASHBURN, Richard I. Forest Insect Laboratory, U. S. Forest Service Building, Ogden, Utah, U. S. A. [Coleoptera: Scolytidae of w. U. S. (No)] [U. S. Forest Service]

* WASHBUZKY, Mr. T. Staatliche Geologische Kommission des D. D. R., Invalidenstrasse 44, Berlin N 4, German Democratic Republic. [Protozoa: Flagellata]

WASS, Mr. Marvin L. Department of Biology, University of Florida, Gainesville, Fla., U. S. A. [Crustacea: Decapoda, espec. Paguridae, of Gulf & s. Atlantic coast of U. S. (Yes)]

WASSERMAN, Aaron. Department of Biology, City College, 139th Street & Convent Avenue, New York 31, N. Y., U. S. A. [Amphibia: Scaphiopodidae of U. S. (Yes)]

WASSERMAN, Dr. Marvin. Dept. of Zoology, Univ. of Melbourne, Parkville, N. 2, Victoria, Australia. [Diptera: Drosophilidae of Texas, C. America, n. S. America (Yes); Orthoptera of U. S. (No)]

WASSIF, Dr. K. Department of Zoology, Faculty of Science, Ain Shams University, Abbassia, Cairo, Egypt. [Mammalia: Insectivora, Chiroptera, Rodentia of Egypt (Yes)]

WATANABE, Prof. Chihisa. Entomological Institute, Hokkaido University, Sapporo, Hokkaido, Japan. [Hymenoptera: Braconidae of Japan (Yes)]

* WATANABE, Mr. Masao. Research Institute for Natural Resources, 4 Chôme, Hyakunin-cho, Shinjuku-ku, Tokyo, Japan. [Pisces]

WATANABE, Yasuaki. Ôi-Morishita-cho 3974, Shinagawa-ku, Tokyo, Japan. [Coleoptera: Staphylinidae of Japan (Yes)] [Entomological Laboratory, Tokyo Agricultural University]

WATERHOUSE, Mr. E. J. Wildlife Survey Section, Regional Pastoral Laboratory, Armidale 5 N, N. S. W., Australia. [Diptera: Culicidae of New England Tablelands, N. S. W. (Yes); Ceratopogonidae & Simuliidae of same (No)] [Commonwealth Scientific & Industrial Research Organization]

WATERHOUSE, Dr. J. B. New Zealand Geological Survey, P. O. Box 368, Lower Hutt, New Zealand. [Permian Brachiopoda, Gastropoda, Pelecypoda, of New Zealand & e. Australia (Yes); Triassic Pelecypoda of New Zealand (Yes)]

* WATERMAN, Talbot H. Josiah W. Gibbs Research Laboratories, Department of Zoology, Yale University, New Haven, Conn., U. S. A. [Xiphosura & Pisces]

* WATERS, Dr. James A. Paleontology Laboratory, Central Petroleum Company, Suite 201-7, 5531 Dyer Street, Dallas 6, Texas, U. S. A. [Fossil Invertebrates]

WATERSTON, Mr. A. R. Natural History Department, Royal Scottish Museum, Edinburgh 1, Scotland. [Heteroptera of Palearctic (Yes); Homoptera: Auchenorrhyncha of Palearctic (Yes); Gastropoda: Pulmonata of Britain & Near East (Yes)]

WATERSTON, Dr. Charles D. Department of Geology, Royal Scottish Museum, Edinburgh 1, Scotland. [Merostomata: fossil Eurypterida of Britain (Yes)]

WATKIN, Dr. E. E. Department of Zoology, University College of Wales, Cambrian Street, Aberystwyth, Wales. [Crustacea: Amphipoda; Haustoriidae of Europe (Yes)]

WATKINS, Mr. J. L. 1521 Pontiac Street, Ann Arbor, Mich., U. S. A. [Paleozoic Anthozoa: Tetracoralla & Tabulata (Yes)] [Museum of Paleontology, University of Michigan]

WATSON, Mr. A. Department of Entomology, British Museum (Natural History), Cromwell Road, London, S. W. 7, England. [Lepidoptera: Drepanidae of World (Yes)]

* WATSON, Mrs. Ben. Anatomy Department, Tulane University, New Orleans 18, La., U. S. A. [Odonata]

WATSON, Prof. D. M. S. Department of Zoology, University College, London, W. C. 1, England. [Fossil Pisces, Amphibia, Reptilia, excl. Tertiary, of World (Yes)]

WATSON, George E., 3rd. Peabody Museum, Yale University, New Haven, Conn., U. S. A. [Aves of Greece, Aegean, Cuba (No)]

WATSON, Mr. H. Hillscross, Hills Road, Cherryhinton, Cambridge, England. [Non-Marine Recent & Holocene Gastropoda of Britain (Yes), of Europe & Africa (No)]

* WATSON, Mrs. Margaret E. Department of Bacteriology, School of Agriculture, University of Wisconsin, Madison, Wis., U. S. A. [Trematoda]

WATSON, Dr. S. A., President, Penn College, Oskaloosa, Iowa, U. S. A. [Hemiptera: Miridae of c. U. S. (No)]

WATSON, Dr. W. Y. Forest Insect Laboratory, Box 490, Saulte Ste. Marie, Ont., Canada. [Coleoptera: Coccinellidae of N. America (Yes)]

* WATT, Morris N. Bacteriology Department, Medical School, Box 913, Dunedin, New Zealand. [Diptera]

WATTS, Dr. J. G. Department of Botany & Entomology, New Mexico State University, University Park, New Mexico. [Thysanoptera of s. e. & s. w. U. S. (No)]

* WAVLOFF, Dr. N. Department of Zoology, Imperial College of Sciences, Prince Consort Road, London, S. W. 7, England. [Orthoptera]

WAYNE, William J. Indiana Geological Survey, Bloomington, Ind., U. S. A. [Pleistocene & Recent terr. & f-w. Gastropoda of N. America (Yes)]

WEAVER, C. S. 1038 Mokulua Drive, Honolulu, Hawaii, U. S. A. [Marine Mollusca: bivalves & univalves of Hawaii (Yes)]

WEAVER, Donald W. Department of Physical Sciences, University of California, Santa Barbara Campus, Goleta, Calif., U. S. A. [Tertiary Mollusca & Foraminifera of w. cst. of N. America (Yes)]

* WEAVER, William Ray. Address unknown. [Fossil Invertebrates]

* WEBB, Mrs. Gwen C. Department of Zoology, University College, Ibadan, Nigeria. [Isoptera]

WEBB, Glenn R. R. R. 1, Box 256, Arkadelphia, Ark., U. S. A. [F-w. Mollusca of e. N. America (Yes); Pulmonata of N. America (Yes); Recent & fossil Polygyridae of N. America & Mexico (Yes)] [University of Oklahoma Museum]

WEBB, Prof. J. E. Department of Zoology, University College, Ibadan, Nigeria. [Anoplura of World (No); Cephalochordata of World (Yes)]

WEBB, J. H. 1 Edgemere Drive, Rochester 18, N. Y., U. S. A. [Pelecypoda: Pectinidae of World (Yes)]

* WEBB, R. Game Commission, Department of Lands & Forests, Edmonton, Alta., Canada. [Mammalia]

WEBB, Robert G. Museum of Natural History, University of Kansas, Lawrence, Kans., U. S. A. [Reptilia & Amphibia of c. U. S. & Durango, Mexico (Yes)]

WEBB, Walter Freeman. (Rochester, N. Y.; Mollusca) Died June 1957.

WEBER, H. (Tubingen, Germany; Heteroptera) Died November 1, 1956.

WEBER, Dr. Hans-Heinrich. Schülp über Nortorf (Holstein), Germany. [Heteroptera: espec. aquatic, of w. Palearctic (Yes)]

WEBER, Jay A. 10775 N. E. Bayshore Drive, Miami 38, Fla., U. S. A. [Marine Mollusca of w. Atlantic from Arctic Ocean to n. S. America, incl. Gulf of Mexico (Yes)]

WEBER, Dr. Neal A. Swarthmore College, Swarthmore, Pa., U. S. A. [Hymenoptera: Formicidae of World (No); Attini of New World (Yes); g. Acropyga (Rhizomyrma) of World (Yes)]

* WEBER, Mr. P. Steinhaldenstrasse 62, Zürich 2, Switzerland. [Lepidoptera]

* WEBSTER, Mr. G. A. (Macdonald College, Canada; Nematoda), Not now active in taxonomy.

WEBSTER, Dr. J. Dan. Hanover College, Hanover, Ind., U. S. A. [Aves of s. e. Alaska & w. Mexico (No); Cestoda of birds of New World (No); g. Aploparaksis of World (Yes)]

WEEMS, Dr. Howard V., Jr. Department of Entomology, State Plant Board of Florida, John F. Seagle Building, 408 W. University Avenue, Gainesville, Fla., U. S. A. [Diptera: Syrphidae of New World (Yes)]

WEGNER, A. M. R. Museum Zoologicum Bogoriense, Bogor, Java, Indonesia. [Lepidoptera: Rhopalocera of Indonesia (No); Reptilia: Serpentes of Indonesia (Yes)]

WĘGRZECKI, Mr. Mieczysław. Ul. Piwna 38/5, Warszawa, Poland. [Coleoptera: Chrysomelidae, espec. Halticinae & Galerucinae, of Palearctic (Yes)] [Institute of Zoology]

WEHR, E. E. Parasite Laboratory, Agricultural Research Center, Beltsville, Md., U. S. A. [Nematoda: Filarioidea of N. America (Yes)] [ADPD, ARS, USDA]

* WEHRLI, E. Address unknown. [Lepidoptera]

WEHRLI, Prof. Dr. H. Geologisch- Paläontologisches Institut, Universität Greifswald, Greifswald, German Democratic Republic. [Mammalia: Pleistocene "Marmotta" of Holarctic, (Yes); "Hipparionen" & "Anchitherium" of Europe (Yes)]

* WEHUNT, E. J. Tropical Research Department, United Fruit Company, La Lima, Honduras. [Nematoda]

WEIBEZAHN, Franz H. Departamento de Ictiologia, Museo de Ciencias Naturales, Parque Los Caobos, Caracas, D. F., Venezuela. [Pisces: Cichlidae, Cyprinodontidae, Poeciliidae, of S. America (Yes)]

WEIDHAAS, John A., Jr. Entomology Department, University of Massachusetts, Amherst, Mass., U.S.A. [Acarina: phytophagous mites of n. e. N. America (Yes); Coleoptera: Coccinellidae & Chrysomelidae: g. Haltica of n. e. N. America (No)]

WEIDNER, Prof. Dr. H. Zoologisches Staatsinstitut & Museum, Bornplatz 5, Hamburg 13, Germany. [Orthoptera & Dermaptera of c. Europe (Yes); Orthoptera: Locustidae: Hetrodinae of Africa (Yes); Fossil Orthoptera & Isoptera of Baltic Amber (Yes)]

WEIFFENBACH, Herbert. Friedrich-Wohler Strasse 32, Kassel, Germany. [Hymenoptera: Tenthredinoidea of Palearctic (No), of Europe (Yes)]

* WEIGEL, Ingria. Zoologische Sammlung des Bayerischen Staates, Menzingerstrasse 67, München 19, Germany. [Mammalia]

* WEILER, Dr. W. Lulingsland 22, Worms, Germany. [Fossil Vertebrates]

WEILL, Dr. Robert. Station Biologique d'Arcachon, Université de Bordeaux, Arcachon (Gironde), France. [Hydrozoa: Gymnoblastea & Actiniaria of s. w. France (Yes)]

WEINBERG, Medeea. Museul de Istorie Naturala "Gr. Antipa", Sos. Kiseleff Nr. 1, Bucureşti 3, Rumania. [Diptera: Asilidae of Rumania (Yes); Bombyliidae of Rumania (Yes); Cecidomyidae of Rumania (No)]

* WEINGÄRTNER, Dr. I. Von Hauck Platz 3, Bamberg, Germany. [Nematoda]

WEINREICH, Erich. Nelkenweg 9, (16) Wetzlar/Lahn, Germany. [Coleoptera: Lucanidae of World, espec. S. America (Yes)]

WEIR, Dr. J. Department of Geology, The University, Glasgow W2, Scotland. [Carboniferous non-marine Pelecypoda of Britain]

* WEIS, Dr. S. Wankmullerhofstrasse 66, Linz-Donau, Austria. [Hemiptera]

WEISBORD, Norman E. P. O. Box 1082, Tallahassee, Fla., U.S.A. [Cenozoic marine Mollusca of Caribbean (Yes)] [Department of Geology, Florida State University]

WEISCHER, B. Biologische Bundesanstalt, Institut für Hackfruchtkrankheiten und Nematodenforschung, Toppheideweg 88, Munster (Westf.), Germany. [Free-living & plant parasitic Nematoda of Europe (Yes)]

WEISE, Ernst. Saarbrücknerstrasse 268, Braunschweig, Germany. [Coleoptera: excl. Aleocharinae, Pselaphidae, Scydmaenidae, Orthoperidae, Ptiliidae, of Germany & Austria (Yes)]

WEISER, Jaroslav. Heralecka 964, Praha 14, Czechoslovakia. [Sporozoa Microsporidia, Myxosporidia, Schizogregarina, of World (Yes)] [Academy of Sciences, Institute of Biology]

WEISMAN, Donald M. Box 5215, State College Station, Raleigh, N. C., U.S.A. [Coleoptera: Chrysomelidae of s. e. U. S. (Yes)] [North Carolina State College]

WEISS, Lawrence. International Petroleum Company, Talara, Peru. [Tertiary Foraminifera of n. w. Peru (Yes)]

WEISS, Dr. M. P. Ohio State University, Columbus 10, Ohio, U.S.A. [Ordovician articulate Brachiopoda of Mississippi Valley (No)]

WEITMEIER, Dr. Herbert. Humboldstrasse 9, Bayreuth, Germany. [Thysanoptera of c. Europe, espec. n. Bavaria (Yes)] [Institut für Biologie, Universität Erlangen]

WEITZMAN, Stanley H. Natural History Museum, Stanford University, Stanford, Calif., U.S.A. [Pisces: Characidae of c. S. America & Africa (Yes); Siluroidea of S. America (No)]

WELANDER, Dr. Arthur D. Fisheries Center, University of Washington, Seattle 5, Wash., U.S.A. [Pisces: Elasmobranchii & Osteichthyes of n. w. U. S. & Marshall Islands (Yes); Scorpaenidae of n. w. U. S. & Alaska (Yes); Salmonidae of w. N. America (Yes)]

WELCH, Dr. d'Alte A. John Carroll University, Cleveland 18, Ohio, U.S.A. [Gastropoda: g. Achatinella of Hawaii (Yes)]

WELCH, Dr. Harold E. Entomology Laboratory, Box 179, Belleville, Ont., Canada. [Nematoda: Mermithidae of World (Yes)] [Science Service, Canadian Department of Agriculture]

WELD, Mr. L. H. 6613 N. Washington Boulevard, Arlington 13, Va., U.S.A. [Hymenoptera: Cynipoidea of N. America (Yes)]

WELFORD, N. D. N. Ministry of Agriculture, Fisheries & Food, "Woodthorne" Wolverhampton, Staffs., England. [Nematoda: Tylenchida: Tylenchoidea of World (Yes)]

WELLER, Mr. J. M. Walker Museum, University of Chicago, Chicago 37, Ill., U.S.A. [Carboniferous & Permian Trilobita of N. America (Yes)]

WELLES, Dr. Samuel P. Museum of Paleontology, University of California, Berkeley 4, Calif., U.S.A. [Mesozoic Plesiosauria (Yes); Triassic Labyrinthodontia (Yes)]

WELLS, Prof. G. P. Department of Zoology, University College, London, W. C. 1, England. [Polychaeta: Arenicolidae of World (Yes)]

WELLS, Prof. John W. Department of Geology, Cornell University, Ithaca, N. Y., U.S.A. [Mesozoic-Recent Anthozoa: Scleractinia of World (Yes)]

WELLS, Prof. L. H. Department of Anatomy, Medical School, University of Cape Town, Rondebosch, Union of South Africa. [Mammalia: Primates of s. Africa (Yes); Quaternary Bovidae]

WENDELER, Hans. Florastrasse 2, Berlin-Karow, German Democratic Republic. [Coleoptera: Staphylinidae, excl. Aleocharini, of World (Yes)]

WENGER, O. P. P. O. Box 1415, Bern 2, Switzerland. [Odonata of Europe (Yes)]

* WENHAM, H. T. Massey Agricultural College, University of New Zealand, Palmerston North, New Zealand. [Nematoda]
* WENRICH, Prof. David H. Department of Zoology, University of Pennsylvania, Philadelphia 4, Penna., U. S. A. [Protozoa: Ciliata]
WENZEL, Dr. Edgar. Zoologische Sammlung des Bayerischen Staates, Menzingerstrasse 67, München 19, Germany. [Mammalia: Viverridae of World (Yes)]
WENZEL, Dr. Fritz. Zoologisches Staatsinstitut, Bornplatz 5, Hamburg 13, Germany. [Ciliata: Holotricha, excl. Thigmotricha, Apostomea, Astomata, non-marine (Yes); Ciliata of soil, excl. Peritricha (Yes)]
WENZEL, Rupert L., Curator of Insects, Chicago Natural History Museum, Roosevelt Road & Lake Shore Drive, Chicago 5, Ill., U. S. A. [Coleoptera: Histeridae of World (Yes); Diptera: Streblidae & Nycteribiidae of World (Yes)]
WERBY, Helena J. (Seattle, Wash.; Acanthocephala) Deceased.
* WERLER, Dr. John E. Address unknown. [Amphibia & Reptilia]
WERMUTH, Dr. Heinz. Fritschestrasse 31, Berlin-Charlottenburg, Germany. [Reptilia: espec. crocidiles & turtles, of World (Yes)] [Zoologisches Museum]
WERNECK, Dr. Fabio L. Departmento de Entomologia, Instituto Oswaldo Cruz, Caixa Postal 926, Rio de Janeiro, Brazil. [Anoplura & Mallophaga of mammals of World (Yes)]
WERNER, Dr. Floyd G. Department of Entomology, University of Arizona, Tucson, Ariz., U. S. A. [Coleoptera: Meloidae of N. America (Yes), g. Epicauta of World (Yes); Aderidae of N. America (Yes); Anthicidae of Micronesia (No); Anthicidae, excl. g. Notoxus, of N. America (Yes)]
* WERNERT, Dr. P. 1 Rue Blessig, Strasbourg, France. [Fossil Mammalia]
WESENBERG-LUND, Elise. Zoological Museum, Krystalgade, København, Denmark. [Polychaeta: of n. Atlantic (No); Sipunculoidea of Antarctic & w. S. America (Yes); Echiuroidea of East Indies (No)]
WESENDUNK, Paul. P. O. Box 278, Oildale, Calif., U. S. A. [Eocene-Oligocene Foraminifera of Pacific N. America (Yes); Mollusca of California (No)]
WESSENBERG, Prof. Harry. Natural Science Division, San Francisco State College, San Francisco 27, Calif., U. S. A. [Protozoa: Opalinata: g. Opalina of w. U. S. (Yes)]
WESSING, Dr. A. Zoologisches Institut der Universität, Poppelsdorfer Schloss, Bonn, Germany. [Nematoda: Rhabditidae of Germany (No)]
WEST, David A. Department of Conservation, Fernow Hall, Cornell University, Ithaca, N. Y. [Aves]
WEST, Prof. Luther S. Department of Biology, Northern Michigan College, Marquette, Mich., U. S. A. [Diptera: Muscoidea of N. America (No)]
WESTBLAD, Dr. Einar. (Stockholm, Sweden; Turbellaria) Not now active in taxonomy.
WESTERGARD, A. H. (Stockholm Sweden; Trilobita) Not now active in taxonomy.
WESTERMANN, Dr. G. E. G. McMaster University, Hamilton, Ont., Canada. [Jurassic Ammonoidea of Germany (Yes); Jurassic Ammonoidea of World (Yes)]
WESTERSHEIM, Prof. Dr. Otto. See von WETTSTEIN, Prof. Dr. Otto.
WESTFALL, Dr. Minter J. Department of Biology, University of Florida, Gainesville, Fla., U. S. A. [Odonata, adults & nymphs, of New World (Yes)]
WESTLEY, Ronald E. Washington Department of Fisheries, State Shellfish Laboratory, Quilcene, Wash., U. S. A. [Pelecypoda: adults & juveniles of g. Crassostrea & Ostrea of Pacific U. S. (Yes)]
WESTMORELAND, F. S. Paleontology Laboratory, Atlantic Refining Company, Box 1346, Houston, Texas, U. S. A. [Tertiary Foraminifera of subsurface Texas Gulf Cst. (No)]
* WESTOLL, Dr. T. S. Department of Geology, Kings College, Newcastle-on-Tyne, England. [Paleozoic & Mesozoic Pisces]
WESTPHAL, Dr. Albert. Tropeninstitut, Hamburg 4, Germany. [Protozoa of medical importance (No)]
* WESTPHAL, Dr. F. Geologisch-Paläontologisches Institut, Sigwartstrasse 10, Tübingen, Germany. [Fossil Mammalia]
WESTRHEIM, Sigurd J. Oregon Fish Commission, Research Laboratory, Route 1, Box 31-A, Clackamas, Ore., U. S. A. [Pisces: Scorpaenidae of Pacific Ocean, Oregon & Alaska (No)]
WETMORE, Alexander. Smithsonian Institution, Washington 25, D. C., U. S. A. [Aves of New World; fossil birds of World]
von WETTSTEIN, Prof. Dr. Otto. Naturhistorisches Museum, Burgring 7, Wien I, Austria. [Reptilia: Lacertilia of Europe & w. Asia (Yes); Mammalia of Palearctic (No); Pleistocene & Recent Micromammalia of w. Europe (Yes)]
WETZEL, Prof. Dr. A. Talstrasse 33, Leipzig C 1, German Democratic Republic. [Ciliata (No)] [Zoologisches Institut, Leipzig]
WETZEL, Dr. Otto. L. Boldtstrasse, Eutin/Holstein, Germany. [Microfossils, espec. Peridinea & Hystricosphaeridea, of Kreide & Feuerstein (Yes)]
WETZEL, Prof. Dr. R. Institut für Vet. Med. Parasitologie, Justus Liebig Universität, Frankfurter Strasse 95, Giessen, Germany. [Nematoda: Ascaroidea & Strongyloidea of Europe & Africa (Yes); Trematoda & Cestoda of Africa & Europe (No)]

WETZEL, Dr. Ralph M. Department of Zoology, University of Connecticut, Storrs, Conn.,
U. S. A. [Mammalia of n. e. U. S. (Yes); Pleistocene Microtinae (Yes); Pleistocene-Recent
g. Synaptomys (Yes)]
WETZEL, Prof. Dr. W. Geologisches Institut der Universitat, Kiel, Germany. [Jurassic
marine Invertebrates (Yes); microfossils of World (Yes)]
WEYER, Fritz. (Hamburg, Germany; Diptera) Not now active in taxonomy.
WEYMOUTH, A. A. (Oakland, Calif.; Mollusca) Not now active in taxonomy.
WEYMOUTH, F. W. (Los Angeles, Calif.; Crustacea) Not now active in taxonomy.
WEYNSCHENK, Dr. R. Peter Mayrstrasse 7, Innsbruck, Austria. [Jurassic microfossils (Yes)]
WEYRAUCH, Prof. Dr. Wolfgang. Avenida Petit Thouars 1961, Lima, Peru. [Gastropoda:
Clausiliidae & Bulimulidae of S. America (Yes); Hymenoptera: social Vespidae of Pale-
arctic (Yes)] [Universidad de San Marcos]
WHARTON, Dr. G. W., Department of Zoology, University of Maryland, College Park, Md.,
U. S. A. [Families of Acarina of World (Yes); Trombiculidae of World (Yes)]
WHARTON, Mr. R. H. Institute for Medical Research, Branch Laboratory, Kuantan, Malaya.
[Diptera: Culicidae of Malaysia & Australasia (No)]
WHEATLAND, Sarah B. Bingham Oceanographic Laboratory, 2025 Yale Station, New Haven,
Conn., U. S. A. [Pisces, eggs, larvae, juveniles, adults, of temperate Atlantic (Yes)]
WHEDON, Arthur D. (New Haven, Conn.; Odonata) Not now active in taxonomy.
WHEELER, A. C. British Museum (Natural History), Cromwell Road, London, S. W. 7, England.
[Pisces: Solenichthyes of World (Yes)]
WHEELER, George C. Department of Biology, University of North Dakota, Grand Forks, N. D.,
U. S. A. [Hymenoptera: Formicidae of North Dakota (Yes); Formicidae larvae (Yes)]
WHEELER, Dr. Marshall R. Department of Zoology, University of Texas, Austin 12, Texas,
U. S. A. [Diptera: Drosophilidae of World (Yes); Diptera: Acalyptratae of U. S. (No)]
WHEELER, Prof. Walter H. Department of Geology & Geography, University of North Carolina,
Chapel Hill, N. C., U. S. A. [Paleocene & Eocene Dinocerata (Yes)]
WHELLAN, J. A. Entomology Branch, Ministry of Agriculture, P. O. Box 8100, Causeway,
Salisbury, Southern Rhodesia. [Orthoptera: Saltatoria, espec. Eumastacidae, of Rhodesia
& Nyasaland (Yes); Dermaptera of Rhodesia & Nyasaland (Yes); Odonata of Rhodesia &
Nyasaland (No)]
WHICHER, L. S. 6 Chisholm Road, Richmond, Surrey, England. [Coleoptera: Aphodiinae of
World (No); Aphodiinae of Britain (Yes)]
WHIPPLE, G. Leslie. (Houston, Texas; fossils) Deceased.
WHITCOMB, Lawrence. Department of Geology, Lehigh University, Bethlehem, Penna., U. S. A.
[Fossils]
* WHITE, Burdette E. P. O. Box 247, Perris, Calif., U. S. A. [Coleoptera: Chrysomelidae]
WHITE, C. M. N. C/o Secretariat, Lusaka, Northern Rhodesia. [Aves of Ethiopian (Yes)]
WHITE, Dr. E. Grace. 1312 Edgar Avenue, Chambersburg, Penna., U. S. A. [Pisces: Elasmo-
branchia: sharks of Oriental & Atlantic (Yes)] [Wilson College]
WHITE, Dr. E. I. British Museum (Natural History), Cromwell Road, London, S. W. 7, England.
[Fossil fishes of World (No); fossil Agnatha of World (Yes)]
WHITE, Jesse S. 118 West Sunflower Street, Cleveland, Miss., U. S. A. [Acarina: Spinturnici-
dae of e. U. S. (Yes)] [Delta State College]
WHITE, John A. Long Beach State College, 6101 East 7th Street, Long Beach 4, Calif., U. S. A.
[Mammalia: Sciuridae of N. America (No), g. Eutamias (Yes); Tertiary & Quaternary Ro-
dentia (No)]
WHITE, Mr. M. J. D. Department of Zoology, University of Missouri, Columbia, Mo., U. S. A.
[Orthoptera: Acridoidea of N. America & Australia (No)]
* WHITE, Miss Kathleen M. 5 Boyn Hill Avenue, Maidenhead, Berks, England. [Mollusca]
WHITE, Maynard P. (Queenstown, Md.; Fusulinidae) Not now active in taxonomy.
* WHITE, Mr. O. M. 78 Eastdale Road, Nottingham, England. [Diptera]
WHITEHEAD, Alan G. East African Agriculture & Forestry Research Organization, P. O. Box
21, Kikuyu, Kenya. [Nematoda: Tylenchida of World (Yes)]
WHITEHEAD, P. J. P. Ministry of Forest Development, Game & Fisheries, P. O. Box 30027,
Nairobi, Kenya. [F-w. Pisces: excl. Cichlidae, espec. Cyprinidae, of e. Africa (Yes)]
* WHITEHEAD, W. E. Entomology Department, MacDonald College, McGill University, Quebec,
Canada. [Ectoparasites of Vertebrates]
WHITLEY, Mr. G. P. Curator of Fishes, Australian Museum, College Street, Sydney, N. S. W.,
Australia. [Pisces & Elasmobranchii of Indo-Pacific, Australasia, Antarctic (No)]
WHITLOCK, Dr. J. H. New York State Veterinary College, Cornell University, Ithaca, N. Y.,
U. S. A. [Nematoda: Strongylata of mammals (Yes)]
WHITLOCK, L. S. Plant Pathology Department, Louisiana State University, Baton Rouge, La.,
U. S. A. [Soil & Plant parasitic Nematoda (Yes)] [U. S. Department of Agriculture]
WHITMORE, Dr. Frank C., Jr. U. S. Geological Survey, Washington 25, D. C., U. S. A. [Eocene
-Pleistocene Artiodactyla (Yes)]
* WHITSELL, Miss J. Sue. Department of Biology, Tulane University, New Orleans 15, U. S. A.
[Reptilia & Amphibia]

WHITTARD, Prof. W. F. Department of Geology, University Walk, The University, Bristol, England. [Ordovician & Silurian Trilobita & Brachiopoda of Britain (Yes); Fossil Reptilia of Karroo (S. Africa) (No)]

WHITTINGTON, Mr. H. B. Museum of Comparative Zoology, Harvard University, Cambridge 38, Mass., U. S. A. [Ordovician-Permian Trilobita (Yes); Ordovician Graptolithina (Yes)]

* WHITWORTH, Mrs. Phyllis. (Oklahoma City, Okla.; fossils) Not now active in taxonomy.

WIACKOWSKI, Dr. Stanislaw. Instytut Sadownictwa, Skierniewice, Poland. [Hymenoptera: Braconidae of Palearctic (Yes)]

WIBORG, Dr. K. F., Fiskeridirektoratets, Havforskningsinstitutt, Box 189, Bergen, Norway. [Crustacea: Copepoda of Norwegian & Barents Seas (No)]

* WICHMANN, H. E. Herbertshausen 38, München, Germany. [Coleoptera]

WICHTERMAN, Prof. Ralph. Biology Department, Temple University, Philadelphia 22, Penna., U. S. A. [Protozoa: Ciliata (Yes)]

WICKENDEN, Mr. R. T. D. Geological Survey of Canada, 406 Customs Building, Calgary, Alta., Canada. [Cretaceous Foraminifera of w. Canada (Yes)]

WIDDOWS, Mr. Richard E. Department of Zoology & Entomology, Iowa State College, Ames, Iowa, U. S. A. [Orthoptera: Tetrigidae of N. America (No)]

* WIDDOWSON, Mrs. Elizabeth. Nematology Department, Rothamsted Experimental Station, Harpenden, Herts, England. [Nematoda]

* WIDEN, C. J. Borgå, Finland. [Lepidoptera]

WIEBES, J. T. Rijksmuseum van Natuurlijke Historie, Leiden, Netherlands. [Araneae: Lycosidae of Netherlands (Yes); Hymenoptera of Netherlands (No); Agaoninae of Indo-Malayan (Yes)]

WIEHLE, Dr. Hermann. Wilhelm-Müller Strasse 18, Dessau-Anhalt, German Democratic Republic. [Araneae of Germany (Yes)]

van der WIEL, Mr. P. Zoologisch Museum, Plantage Middenlaan 53, Amsterdam-O, Netherlands. [Coleoptera: Silphidae of Palearctic (Yes)]

WIERING, Mr. H. Lorentzweg 183, Hilversum, Netherlands. [Hymenoptera: Apidae of w. Palearctic (Yes)] [Zoologisch Museum]

* WIERZBICKA, Maria. Instytut Biologii, ul. Pasteura 3, Warszawa 22, Poland. [Crustacea: Copepoda: Cyclopoidea]

WIESEND, Dr. Peter. Zoologisches Institut, Luisenstrasse 14, München 2, Germany. [Orthoptera: Acrididae, Tettigoniidae, Gryllidae, of s. Germany (Yes)]

WIESER, Dr. W. Schreiberweg 43, Vienna 19, Austria. [F-l. marine Nematoda of World (Yes); Gastrotricha & Archiannelida of all oceans (Yes)] [Zoologische Institut, Universität Wein]

* WIESMEIER, J. Zoologisches Institut, Luisenstrasse 14, München 2, Germany. [Orthoptera]

WIGGINS, G. B. Royal Ontario Museum, 100 Queen's Park, Toronto 5, Ont., Canada. [Trichoptera of N. America (Yes); Phryganeidae of World (Yes)]

WIGLEY, Dr. Roland L. U. S. Fish & Wildlife Service, Woods Hole, Mass., U. S. A. [Marine Pisces: demersal Teleostii of Gulf of Maine (Yes); Crustacea: marine Amphipoda: Stegocephalidae, Haustoriidae, Calliopidae, Pontogeneidae, Gammaridae, of Gulf of Marine (Yes)]

WIKGREN, Dr. Bo-Jungar. Biologiska Institutet, Åbo Akademi, Åbo, Finland. [Trematoda: larvae of Malacocotylea & Cestoda: larvae of g. Diphyllobothrium of Finland & Baltic (Yes)]

WIKTOR, Mgr. Andrzej. Zakład Biologii Ogólnej, Akademii Medycznej, Ul. Bujwida 9, Wrocław, Poland. [Mollusca of c. Europe (No); Limacidae & Arionidae of Europe (Yes)]

WILCKE, Dr. D. E. Institut für Pflanzenkrankheiten der Universität, Bonn, Germany. [Oligochaeta of c. Europe (No); Lumbricidae of Europe (Yes)]

* WILCKE, Dr. H. Address unknown. [Coleoptera]

WILCOX, Mr. John A. New York State Museum, Albany 1, N. Y., U. S. A. [Coleoptera: Chrysomelidae of U. S. & Canada (Yes); Chrysomelidae: Galerucinae of New World (Yes)]

WILCOX, Joseph. Box 70, Whittier, Calif., U. S. A. [Diptera: Asilidae of N. America (Yes)] [U. S. Department of Agriculture]

WILDE, Garner L. Box 1600, Midland, Texas, U. S. A. [Pennsylvanian-Permian Foraminifera: Fusulinidae of World (Yes)]

WILES, William W. 40 Rector Street, Newark 2, U. S. A. [Quaternary planktonic Foraminifera of Atlantic Ocean (Yes); Cenozoic planktonic Foraminifera of all oceans (Yes)] [Newark Colleges, Rutgers University]

WILEY, A. J. Veterinary Research Laboratories, Veterinary Department, Kabete, Kenya. [Acarina: Ixodidae of e. Africa (Yes)]

WILHOFT, D. C. Museum of Vertebrate Zoology, University of California, Berkeley 4, Calif., U. S. A. [Reptilia: Iguanidae of New World (Yes)]

WILIMOVSKY, Dr. Norman J. Institute of Fisheries, University of British Columbia, Vancouver 8, Canada. [Recent & Pleistocene Pisces of Alaska (Yes); Recent Pisces of n. Holarctic (Yes); Recent & fossil Cottoidea of World (Yes); Fossil & Recent Pisces Stichaeidae & Pholididae of World (Yes)]

WILKEY, R. F. Bureau of Entomology, California Department of Agriculture, 1220 N Street, Sacramento 14, Calif., U. S. A. [Collembola of N. America (Yes)]

WILKIE, Lorna Christine. 2516 E. 6th Street, Tulsa, Okla., U.S.A. [Paleozoic Conodonts (Yes); Ordovician Brachiopoda of c. U.S. (Yes)]

WILKINS, E.M. Shell Oil Company, P.O. Box 2099, Houston, Texas, U.S.A. [Subsurface Miocene-Eocene smaller Foraminifera of U.S. Gulf cst. (No)]

WILL, Dr. Homer C. Department of Biology, Juniata College, Huntington, Penna., U.S.A. [Hymenoptera: Tenthredinoidea of e.N. America (Yes)]

* WILLARD, Bradford. Department of Geology, Lehigh University, Bethlehem, Penna., U.S.A. [Paleozoic fossil Invertebrates]

WILLE, Dr. Hans Peter. Bienenabteilung der Eidg, Milchwirtsch, Versuchsanstalt, Liebefeld-Bern, Switzerland. [Homoptera: Psyllidae & Lachnidae of Switzerland (Yes)]

WILLE, Dr. Johanes E. Casilla 2791, Lima, Peru. [Diptera: Trypetidae of S. America (No)] [Estación Experimental Agricola La Molina]

WILLEMSE, C.J.M. Laurastraat 67, Eygelshoven (Z. L.), Netherlands. [Orthoptera, excl. Blattidae, of Indo-Malayan, Micronesia & Surinam (Yes)]

WILLEY, Prof. C.H. Department of Biology, New York University, New York 53, N.Y., U.S.A. [Trematoda: Paramphistomidae of N. America (Yes)]

* WILLEY, Dr. Ruth Lippitt. Biological Laboratories, Harvard University, Cambridge 38, Mass., U.S.A. [Odonata]

WILLGOHS, Johan Fr. Zoologisk Museum, University of Bergen, Bergen, Norway. [Aves of Norway (Yes)]

WILLIAMS, Prof. Alwyn. Queen's University of Belfast, Belfast, North Ireland. [Fossil & Recent Brachiopoda of World (No), L. Paleozoic (Yes)]

WILLIAMS, Dr. Austin B. University of North Carolina, Institute of Fisheries Research, Morehead City, N.C., U.S.A. [Decapoda: Astacidae: Cambarinae of Ozark & Ouachita Mountains & Great Plains, U.S. (Yes); Marine & estuarine Decapoda of s.e. U.S. (Yes)]

WILLIAMS, Mr. A.S. Department of Plant Pathology & Physiology, Virginia Agricultural Experiment Station, Blacksburg, Va., U.S.A. [Nematoda of Virginia (Yes)]

WILLIAMS, Dr. C.B. (Kincraig, Scotland; Thysanoptera) Not now active in taxonomy.

WILLIAMS, Dr. D.J. Commonwealth Institute of Entomology, c/o British Museum (Natural History), London, S.W. 7, England. [Homoptera: Coccoidea of World (Yes)]

WILLIAMS, D.W. Infestation Control, East Craigs, Edinburgh 12, Scotland. [Cyst-forming Nematoda (No); Insecta of stored products of World (No)] [Department of Agriculture for Scotland (Scientific Services)]

WILLIAMS, Dr. Eliot C., Jr. Department of Biology, Wabash College, Crawfordsville, Ind., U.S.A. [Symphyla of World (Yes)]

WILLIAMS, Dr. Ernest E. Museum of Comparative Zoology, Cambridge 38, Mass., U.S.A. [Reptilia of West Indies (Yes); Chelonia of World (Yes)] [Harvard University]

WILLIAMS, Dr. Francis X. 8908 Lemon Avenue, La Mesa, Calif., U.S.A. [Hymenoptera: Sphecidae: Larrinae: g. Pisonopsis, Plenoculus, Solierella, of U.S. & Mexico (Yes)] [San Diego Museum of Natural History]

WILLIAMS, George C. Department of Natural Science, Michigan State University, East Lansing, Mich., U.S.A. [Pisces of Great Lakes Region of N.A. (Yes); marine Pisces of n.e. U.S. (Yes); larvae of marine fishes]

* WILLIAMS, G.R. Department of Internal Affairs, Wellington, New Zealand. [Aves]

WILLIAMS, Mr. J.G. The Coryndon Museum, P.O. Box 658, Nairobi, Kenya. [Aves: Nectariniidae of Ethiopian (Yes)]

WILLIAMS, Dr. Joseph L. 5518 W. Girard Avenue, Philadelphia 31, Penna., U.S.A. [Lepidoptera of N. America & Europe (No)] [Mercy-Douglass Hospital]

WILLIAMS, James Steele. (Washington, D.C.; fossils) Died January 1957.

WILLIAMS, Merton Y. (Vancouver, B.C.; fossils) Not now active in taxonomy.

WILLIAMS, Norman E. Department of Zoology, State University of Iowa, Iowa City, Iowa, U.S.A. [Protozoa: Ciliata; Hymenostomatida: Frontoniidae & Tetrahymenidae (Yes)]

WILLIAMS, Dr. Roger W. School of Public Health & Administrative Medicine, Columbia University, 600 W. 168th Street, New York 32, N.Y., U.S.A. [Diptera: Culicidae & Heleidae: g. Culicoides of N. America (Yes)]

WILLIAMS, Thomas E. Peabody Museum, Yale University, New Haven, Conn., U.S.A. [Permian Foraminifera: Fusulinidae of w. Texas (Yes)]

WILLIAMSON, Dr. D.I. Marine Biological Station, Port Erin, Isle of Man, Great Britain. [Crustacea: larvae of Decapoda of World (No), of Europe (Yes)]

* WILLIAMSON, M.H. "Fairfield", Pollins Lane, Oxford, England. [Myriapoda]

WILLINER, R. Padre Gregorio J. Observatorio de Fisica Cósmica, San Miguel, Prov. Buenos Aires, Argentina. [Corrodentia of S. America (Yes); Neuroptera: Ascalaphidae & Mantispidae of S. America (Yes)]

WILLINK, Dr. A. Departamento de Zoologia, Instituto Miguel Lillo, Miguel Lillo 205, Tucumán, Argentina. [Hymenoptera: Vespidae, Masaridae, Eumenidae, Sphecidae, of Neotropical (Yes)]

WILLMANN, Dr. Carl. Basdahler Strasse 10, Bremen 13, Germany. [Acarina: terrestial & parasitic on small mammals]

388

* WILMOTH, George. R.D.2, Box 298, Kingston, N.Y., U.S.A. [Amphibia & Reptilia]
WILSON, Alice E. Geological Survey of Canada, Ottawa, Ont., Canada. [Paleozoic, espec.
    Ordovician, Invertebrates of Canada (Yes)]
WILSON, Prof. Clifton Arlie. Department of Zoology & Entomology, Mississippi State College,
    State College, Miss., U.S.A. [Aquatic & semiaquatic Hemiptera of U.S. (Yes)]
WILSON, Charles William, Jr. Department of Geology, P.O.Box 1591, Vanderbilt University,
    Nashville, Tenn., U.S.A. [Devonian & Pennsylvanian Ostracoda (No)]
* WILSON, Druid. Division of Paleontology, U.S. Geological Survey, Washington 25, D.C.,
    U.S.A. [Tertiary Mollusca]
WILSON, Dr. D.P. The Laboratory, Citadel Hill, Plymouth, Devon, England. [Polychaeta of
    Britain (No)]
WILSON, Mr. Edward O. Biological Laboratories, Harvard University, Cambridge 38, Mass.,
    U.S.A. [Hymenoptera: Formicidae of Pacific (Yes)]
WILSON, Prof. Francis H. Department of Biology, Lebanon Valley College, Annville, Penna.,
    U.S.A. [Mallophaga of N. America (No)]
WILSON, Dr. J.A. Department of Geology, University of Texas, Austin 12, Texas, U.S.A.
    [Miocene Mammalia & Permian-Triassic Reptilia & Amphibia (Yes)]
WILSON, Dr. James Lee. Shell Development Company, Exploration & Production Research,
    3737 Bellaire Boulevard, Houston 25, Texas, U.S.A. [Cambrian Trilobita of N. America
    (Yes)]
WILSON, Mr. J.O. 42 Wilson Terrace, Da Costa Park, Glenelg, S. Australia. [Microlepidop-
    tera, espec. Oecophoridae & Tortricina, of S. Australia (No)] [Commonwealth Scientific
    & Industrial Research Organization]
WILSON, Kent H. Department of Entomology, University of Kansas, Lawrence, Kans., U.S.A.
    [Lepidoptera: Papilionidae of World (Yes)]
* WILSON, Mr. Larry K. Address unknown. [Fossil Hystricospherida]
WILSON, Mrs. Mildred S. Box 960, Anchorage, Alaska. [Crustacea: Copepoda: f-w. & br-w.
    Calanoida & Harpacticoida of N. America, Greenland, West Indies (Yes)]
WILSON, Mr. Nixon. Department of Entomology, Purdue University, Lafayette, Ind., U.S.A.
    [Acarina parasitic on Vertebrates of N. America (Yes); Siphonaptera & Anoplura of N.
    America (Yes); Mallophaga of N. America (No); Mammalia: Chiroptera of N. America
    (Yes)]
WILSON, R.B. H. M. Geological Survey, 19 Grange Terrace, Edinburgh 9, Scotland. [Car-
    boniferous marine Lammellibranchia of Scotland (No)]
WILSON, Dr. Robert W. Department of Zoology, University of Kansas, Lawrence, Kans.,
    U.S.A. [Tertiary Mammalia: Rodentia of N. America (Yes); Paleocene Mammalia of
    N. America (Yes)]
WILTSHIRE, E.P. C/o Outward Bag Room, for bag to Bahrein, Foreign Office, London,
    S.W.2, England. [Lepidoptera: Noctuidae: Quadrifinae; Arctiidae: Lithosiinae & Nolinae;
    Lemoniidae, Lasiocampidae, Notodontidae, Sphingidae, Lymantriidae, Hesperiidae,
    Rhopalocera excl. Lycaenidae, Geometridae excl. Eupitheciinae; Zygaenidae: Procrinae,
    of Middle East, Balkans, Afghanistan, Arabia (Yes)]
* WIND, Jørgen. Lystrup St., Jylland (Jutland), Denmark. [Mollusca]
* WINDHAM, Steve. Geology Department, Louisiana State University, Baton Rouge 3, La.,
    U.S.A. [Fossil Invertebrates]
WING, Prof. Merle W. State University of New York, Cortland, N.Y., U.S.A. [Hymenoptera:
    Formicidae of World (No); of N. America (Yes); myrmecophilous insects of World
    (No)]
WINGO, Curtis. Department of Entomology, University of Missouri, Columbia, Mo., U.S.A.
    [Coleoptera: Coccinellidae of N. America (Yes)]
WINKLEMANN, John R. Museum of Zoology, University of Michigan, Ann Arbor, Mich., U.S.A.
    [Mammalia: Chiroptera of N. & C. America (Yes)]
WINKLER, Josef R. Bajkalská 14, Praha XIII, Czechoslovakia. [Acarina: Oribatoidea of World
    (Yes); Trombidiformes of c. Europe (No); Coleoptera: Cleridae of World (Yes); Lycidae
    of Palearctic (Yes)] [Zoology Department, Museum SLUKO]
WINKLER, Dr. Otto. Bajkalská 14, Praha XIII, Czechoslovakia. [Plecoptera of Europe, espec.
    c. Europe (Yes)]
WINKLER, Virgil. Geological Laboratory, Creole Petroleum Corporation, Apartado 889, Cara-
    cas, Venezuela. [Oligocene & Miocene Mollusca of Venezuela (No)]
WINN, Dr. Howard E. Zoology Department, University of Maryland, College Park, Md., U.S.A.
    [Marine shore Pisces of w. Atlantic (Yes); f-w. Pisces of N. America (Yes)]
* WINOGRADOV, K. Department of Zoology, Odessa University, Odessa, Ukraine, U.S.S.R.
    [Annelida: Polychaeta]
* WINOGRADOW, B. Zoological Institute, Academy of Sciences of U.S.S.R., University
    Embankment 1, Leningrad-Centre, U.S.S.R. [Mammalia]
* WINSLOW, Armour C. Humble Oil & Refining Company, P.O.Box 248, Anchorage, Alaska.
    [Fossil Invertebrates]

WINSLOW, Marcia Reid Ring. 603 North Fess Avenue, Bloomington, Ind., U.S.A. [Up. Devonian & L. Mississippian microfossils (No)]

WINSLOW, Dr. R.D. Nematology Department, Rothamsted Experimental Station, Harpenden, Herts, England. [Plant & soil Nematoda of Britain (No)]

* WINSNES, Th. Norsk Polarinstitutt, Observatoriegatan 1, Oslo, Norway. [Protozoa: Flagellata]

* WINSTON, Paul W. Department of Biology, University of Colorado, Boulder, Colo., U.S.A. [Coleoptera: Carabidae: Carabini of New World]

WINTER, Howard A. 2035 Ridgeview Avenue, Los Angeles 41, Calif., U.S.A. [Trematoda: Digenea & Monogenea of New World & e. Pacific Ocean (Yes)] [Instituto de Biologia, Universidad Nacional de Mexico]

WINTERBOTTOM, Dr. J.M. Box 61, Cape Town, Union of South Africa. [Aves of s. Africa (Yes)] [South African Museum]

WINTERMANN-KILIAN, Dr. G. Casilla 956, Valdivia, Chile. [Porifera of S. America (Yes)]

WINTERS, Mr. Herbert H. Museum of Paleontology, University of California, Berkeley 4, Calif., U.S.A. [Cenozoic Mammalia of N. America & n.S. America (Yes); fossil Reptilia: Trionychidae of World (Yes)]

WINTERS, Dr. Stephen S. Department of Geology, Florida State University, Tallahassee, Fla., U.S.A. [Pennsylvanian-Permian Gastropoda & Pelecypoda of w.U.S. (Yes)]

WINTON, Prof. W.M. Department of Biology & Geology, Texas Christian University, Fort Worth 9, Texas, U.S.A. [Comanchean fossils of n. Texas (No)]

WIRTH, Dr. Willis W. Division of Insects, U.S. National Museum, Washington 25, D.C., U.S.A. [Diptera: Heleidae & Ephydridae of World (Yes)]

WIRZ, Dr. Katherine. Laboratoire Arago, Université de Paris, Banyuls-sur-Mer (Pyr.-Orientales), France. [Cephalopoda of Mediterranean (Yes)]

WISE, John P. Box 364, Woods Hole, Mass., U.S.A. [Marine Pisces of n.w. Atlantic (Yes)] [U.S. Bureau of Commercial Fisheries]

WISE, Mr. K.A.J. Plant Diseases Division, Department of Scientific & Industrial Research, Private Bag, Auckland, New Zealand. [Trichoptera & Lepidoptera: Gracillariidae of New Zealand (Yes)]

WISELEY, Hunter B. (Cronulla, Australia; Plecoptera) Not now active in taxonomy.

WISNER, Robert L. Scripps Institution of Oceanography, La Jolla, Calif., U.S.A. [Pisces: Myctophidae of World (Yes)]

WISNIEWSKI, Wincenty Lesław. (Warszawa, Poland; Platyhelminthes) Died August 24, 1958.

WISSLER, Stanley G. Union Oil Center, Los Angeles 17, Calif., U.S.A. [Fossil Foraminifera of New World (Yes), of Micronesia (No)] [Union Oil Company of California]

* WISTAR, Miss Elizabeth M. 200 Montgomery Avenue, Chestnut Hill, Philadelphia 18, Penna., U.S.A. [Mollusca: Volutes]

WITENBERG, Prof. G. Department of Parasitology, Hebrew University, Jerusalem, Israel. [Trematoda, Nematoda, Acanthocephala, of World (No)]

WITHLER, Mr. F.C. Biological Station, Fisheries Research Board of Canada, Nanaimo, B.C., Canada. [Pisces: Salmonidae: g. Oncorhynchus of w. Canada (Yes)]

WITT, Dr. A., Jr. Stephens Hall, University of Missouri, Columbia, Mo., U.S.A. [Pisces of Missouri (Yes)]

de WITTE, G.F. Institut Royal des Sciences Naturelles, 31 rue Vautier, Bruxelles, Belgium. [Amphibia & Reptilia of Africa (Yes)]

WITTMER, Walter. Böhlstrasse 571, Herrliberg-Zürich, Switzerland. [Coleoptera: Malachiidae, Drilidae, Phengodidae, Cantharidae, of World (Yes)]

WLASTOV, Dr. B. Faculty of Biology, Moscow State University, Moscow B-234, U.S.S.R. [Rotatoria: Notommatidae of Palearctic (No)]

WODZICKI, Dr. Kazimierz. Animal Ecology Section, Department of Scientific & Industrial Research, Box 8018, Wellington, New Zealand. [Mammalia: Rodentia & Artiodactyla of New Zealand (Yes)]

WOJTUSIAK, Dr. Roman J. Polska Akademia Nauk, ul. Sławkowska 17, Krakow, Poland. [Lepidoptera: Pyralidae of Palearctic (No)]

WOKE, Dr. Paul A. Laboratory of Tropical Diseases, National Institutes of Health, Bethesda, Md., U.S.A. [Diptera: Culicidae (No)]

WOLBURG, Dr. J. Gewerschaft Elwerath, Geologische Abteilung, Wilhelmstrasse 31a, (23) Bentheim, Germany. [Jurassic to Cretaceous Ostracoda: Podocopa of Germany (No)]

WOLF, Dr. H., 2nd Director, Zoologisches Forschungsinstitut & Museum A. Koenig, Bonn, Germany. [Mammalia: Insectivora & Rodentia of Europe & n. Africa (Yes)]

WOLF, Dr. Heinrich. Studienassessor, im Erlenkamp 22, Plettenberg (Westfalen), Germany. [Hymenoptera: Formicidae, Apidae, Sphecidae, Pompilidae, Vespidae, of Palearctic (Yes)]

* WOLFE, Mr. L.S. Department of Zoology, Canterbury University College, Christchurch, New Zealand. [Odonata]

WOLFF, Niels L. Hellerupvej 12, Hellerup, Denmark. [Lepidoptera of Denmark (Yes)]

WOLFF, Dr. Torben. Universitetets Zoologisk Museum, Krystalgade 27, København K, Denmark. [Crustacea: Isopoda, abyssal & hadal (Yes); Brachyura of Europe & w. Africa (Yes); Decapoda, abyssal (Yes)]

WOLFGANG, Dr. Robert W. Hess & Clark Research Laboratory, Ashland, Ohio, U.S.A. [Parasitic Helminths of mammals of N. America & West Indies (Yes); Helminths of Chiroptera of New World (Yes)]

WOLFS, J. 23 Avenue de la Bergère, Beechem Ste. Agatha, Bruxelles, Belgium. [Diptera: Culicidae of Africa (Yes)]

WOLFSBERGER, Josef. Zoologische Sammlung des Bayerischen Staates, Menzingerstrasse 67, München 19, Germany. [Macrolepidoptera of Alps (Yes)]

WOLK, Mr. Robert G. Department of Biology, St. Lawrence University, Canton, N.Y., U.S.A. [Aves]

* WOLSKI, Prof. Dr. T. Zakład Zoologii Systematycznej, Uniwersytet Łódzki, Ul. Narutowicza 68, Łódz, Poland. [Pisces]

WOLTERS, H.E. Nikolaus Becker Strasse 28, Geilenkirchen, Bez. Aachen, Germany. [Aves: Passeriformes of Palearctic & Ethiopian (Yes); Estrildidae, incl. Viduinae, & Carduelinae of World (Yes)]

WOMERSLEY, Mr. H. South Australian Museum, Adelaide, S. Australia. [Apterygota & Acarina of Australia, New Zealand & Pacific (Yes)]

WONG, H.R. Forest Biology Laboratory, Box 2, University of Manitoba, Winnipeg 9, Man., Canada. [Hymenoptera: Symphyta of N. America (Yes), of Palearctic (No)]

WOO, Prof. Ju-Kang. Institute of Vertebrate Paleontology, Academia Sinica, Peking, People's Republic of China. [Mammalia: Hominidae & Pongidae of China (Yes)]

WOO, Bao-Ling. See WU, Bao-Ling.

WOOD, Prof. Alan. Department of Geology, University College, Aberystwyth, Wales. [Fossil Foraminifera (Yes)]

WOOD, Prof. Albert E. Department of Biology, Amherst College, Amherst, Mass., U.S.A. [Mammalia: Paleocene-Pliocene Rodentia & Lagomorpha (Yes)]

WOOD, Mr. D.M. 7 Dale Avenue, Toronto 5, Ont., Canada. [Diptera: Simuliidae of Canada (Yes); Coleoptera: Leptinidae of World (Yes)] [McMaster University]

* WOOD, Dr. G. Congdon. Birch Hill, Weston, Conn., U.S.A. [Coleoptera: Chrysomelidae]

WOOD, Dr. Horace E., 2nd. Rutgers University, 40 Rector Street, Newark 2, N.J., U.S.A. [Mammalia: Fossil & Recent Rhinoceratoidea of World (Yes); fossil Helaletidae of N. America (Yes)]

* WOOD, Dr. H.G. "Hawequa" St. Thomas Road, Newlands, Cape Province, Union of South Africa. [Diptera: Tipulidae]

WOOD, Dr. John Thornton. 1528 Greenview Dr., Ann Arbor, Mich., U.S.A. [Amphibia: Plethodontidae of e. U.S. (Yes)]

* WOOD, Leonard E. Address unknown. [Fossil Invertebrates]

WOOD, Dr. Raymond A. Orange County Community College, Middletown, N.Y., U.S.A. [Trematoda: Monogenea, f-w. & marine, of Atlantic & Gulf U.S. (Yes)]

WOOD, Dr. Richard L. Department of Anatomy, University of Washington, Seattle 5, Wash., U.S.A. [Anthozoa: Zoanthidea of Puget Sound & Washington (No)]

WOOD, Dr. S.L. Zoology Department, Brigham Young University, Provo, Utah, U.S.A. [Coleoptera: Scolytidae & Platypodidae of World (Yes); Bostrichidae of World (No)]

WOOD-BAKER, C.S. 77 Greenway, Chislehurst, Kent, England. [Homoptera: Aphididae of Britain & w. & s. Europe (Yes)] [The Woolwich Polytechnic]

WOODBURY, Angus M. (Salt Lake City, Utah; Reptilia) Not now active in taxonomy.

* WOODCOCK, A.T.A. 65 Rock Avenue, Gillingham, Kent, England. [Coleoptera]

* WOODFIELD, B.R.G. C/o Walter & Eliza Hall Institute, Royal Melbourne Hospital P.O., Parkville, Vict., Australia. [Diptera: Culicidae]

* WOODHEAD, Dr. Arthur E. Department of Zoology, University of Michigan, Ann Arbor, Mich., U.S.A. [Trematoda]

WOODHILL, A.R., Reader, Department of Zoology, University of Sydney, Chippendale, N.S.W., Australia. [Diptera: Culicidae of Australia & s.w. Pacific (No)]

WOODIN, William H. P.O. Box 5602, Tucson, Ariz., U.S.A. [Reptilia of Arizona (Yes)] [Arizona-Sonora Desert Museum]

WOODRING, Dr. W.P. Room 404, U.S. National Museum, Washington 25, D.C., U.S.A. [Tertiary marine Mollusca of Caribbean (Yes)] [U.S. Geological Survey]

WOODROFFE, G.E. Pest Infestation Laboratory, London Road, Slough, Bucks, England. [Coleoptera: Cryptophagidae: g. Cryptophagus of Holarctic (Yes); Heteroptera, excl. aquatics, of Europe (No); Acarina: Acaridae, Glycyphagidae, Cheyletidae, of stored products of World (No)]

WOODRUFF, Mr. Robert, Entomologist, Kentucky State Department of Health, 620 S. Third Street, Louisville, Ky., U.S.A. [Coleoptera: Scarabaeidae: Coprinae of World (Yes); Aphodiinae & Geotrupinae of World (No), of U.S. (Yes); Troginae & Acanthocerinae of World (Yes)]

WOODS, Loren P. Chicago Natural History Museum, Chicago 5, Ill., U.S.A. [Marine Pisces of Tropics & Subtropics (Yes)]

WOODWARD, Dr. T.E. Department of Entomology, University of Queensland, Brisbane, Queensland, Australia. [Hemiptera: Lygaeidae: Rhyparochrominae of Australian (Yes); Lygaeidae of New Zealand (Yes); Ericocephalidae of Australian (Yes); Miridae & Pentatomidae of New Zealand (Yes), g. Felisacus & Cyrtorhinus of Pacific (Yes); Homoptera: Meenoplidae & Peloridiidae of Australian (Yes)]

WOODWICK, Dr. Keith H. Biology Department, Fresno State College, Fresno, Calif., U.S.A. [Polychaeta: Spionidae of w. cst. of U.S. (Yes), g. Polydora of World (Yes); Enteropneusta of w. cst. of U.S. (Yes)]

WOOLCOTT, Prof. W.S. Box 296, University of Richmond, Richmond, Va., U.S.A. [Marine & f-w. Pisces of e. N. America (Yes)]

WOOLLATT, Mr. L.H. 123 Abbey Road, Torquay, S. Devon, England. [Hymenoptera: Symphyta of Britain (Yes)]

WOOLLEY, Dr. Tyler A. Department of Zoology, Colorado State University, Fort Collins, Colo., U.S.A. [Acarina: Oribatei of N. America (Yes); Mesostigmata, Trombidiiformes, Sarcoptiformes of N. America (No)]

WOOTTON, Mr. C.M. Union Producing Company, P.O. Box 711, Beeville, Texas, U.S.A. [Fossil Foraminifera of N. America (No)]

WOOTTON, Dr. Donald. 3520 LaEntrada, Santa Barbara, Calif., U.S.A. [Crustacea: Branchiopoda: Anostraca & Conchostraca of N. America (Yes); Holothurioidea of N. America (Yes); Trematoda: Digenea of N. America (Yes)]

de WORMS, Charles. Department of Entomology, British Museum (Natural History), Cromwell Road, London, S.W.7, England. [Lepidoptera of Palearctic & Africa (Yes)]

WORTHINGTON, Dr. E.B. The Nature Conservancy, 19 Belgrave Square, London, S.W.1, England. [F-w. Pisces of Africa & Europe (No)]

WRAY, Dr. David L., Jr. 510 Dixie Trail, Raleigh, N.C., U.S.A. [Collembola of New World (Yes)] [Division of Entomology, North Carolina Department of Agriculture]

WRIGHT, A.A. 113 E. Upland Road, Ithaca, N.Y., U.S.A. [Amphibia & Reptilia of N. America (Yes)]

WRIGHT, A. Gilbert. (Springfield, Ill., Araneida) Not now active in taxonomy.

WRIGHT, Prof. A.H. 113 E. Upland Road, Ithaca, N.Y., U.S.A. [Reptilia: frogs of U.S.] [Cornell University]

WRIGHT, Dr. C.A. British Museum (Natural History), Cromwell Road, London, S.W.7, England. [Gastropoda: Planorbidae of Africa (Yes); Trematoda: Renicolidae of World (Yes); Schistosomatidae of World (No)]

WRIGHT, Mr. C.W. 37 Phillimore Gardens, London, W.8, England. [Cretaceous Ammonoidea (Yes); Mesozoic Asteroidea (Yes); Cretaceous Echinoidea of Europe (Yes); Cretaceous Crustacea: Brachyura of Europe (Yes)]

WRIGHT, Edward Pulteney. 281 La Salle Place, Grosse Pointe Farms 36, Mich., U.S.A. [M. Devonian (Hamilton) Pelecypoda of s.w. Ontario (Yes)]

WRIGHT, Mr. H.G.S. Woodrow Bungalow, Holt Road, Cawston, near Norwich, Norfolk, England. [Rotifera: Sessile forms of Collothecacea & Flosculariacea of England (Yes)]

WRIGHT, Jean Davies (Mrs. E.P. Wright) 281 La Salle Place, Grosse Pointe Farms 36, Mich., U.S.A. [M. Devonian (Hamilton) Brachiopoda of s.w. Ontario (Yes)]

WRIGHT, Kenneth H. P.O. Box 4059, Portland 8, Ore., U.S.A. [Coleoptera: Scolytidae of N. America (No); Homoptera: Phylloxeridae: g. Adelges of w. N. America conifers (No)] [U.S. Forest Service]

WRIGHT, Dr. Philip L. Department of Zoology, Montana State University, Missoula, Mont., U.S.A. [Mammalia: Mustelidae of U.S. Rocky Mts. (Yes)]

WRIGHT, Mr. W.E. Entomological Branch, Department of Agriculture, Box 36, G.P.O., Sydney, N.S.W., Australia. [Lepidoptera: Rhopalocera of Australia (Yes)]

WRÓBLEWSKI, Dr. Aleksander. Instytut Zoologiczny, Polska Akademia Nauk, Oddział w Poznaniu, ul., Świerczewskiego 19, Poznań, Poland. [Heteroptera: Corixidae: Micronectinae of World (Yes); Aquatic Heteroptera of Palearctic (Yes); Saldidae of Poland (No)]

WU, Bao-Ling. Institute of Oceanology, Academia Sinica, Tsingtao, People's Republic of China. [Polychaeta of China coast (Yes)]

WU, Dr. Hsien-Wen. Institute of Hydrobiology, Academia Sinica, Wu-Chang, People's Republic of China. [F-w. Pisces of e. Asia (Yes)]

WU, Dr. L.Y. Nematology Section, Science Service Building, Carling, Avenue, Ottawa, Ont., Canada. [Plant Nematoda of N. America (Yes)]

WULFERT, K. Bad Lauchstädt, Kreis Merseburg, German Democratic Republic. [Rotatoria of World (Yes)]

WÜLKER, Dr. W. Hydrobiologische Station für den Schwarzwald Falkau, Schwarzwald, Germany. [Diptera: Chironomidae, imagines, pupae, larvae, of Europe (Yes)]

WURTZ, Dr. Charles B. 3247 Disston Street, Philadelphia 49, Penna., U.S.A. [F-w. Mollusca of N. America (Yes); terr. Gastropoda of New World (Yes); f-w. Porifera & Oligochaeta of e. N. America (No); f-w. Turbellaria, Amphipoda, Isopoda of e. cst. U.S. (No)]

WYATT, Alex K. C/o Insect Division, Chicago Natural History Museum, Chicago 5, Ill., U.S.A. [Lepidoptera: Noctuidae: Heliothiinae: g. Eubaphe & Papaipema of N. America (Yes)]

WYATT, Colin W. Cobbetts, Farnham, Surrey, England. [Lepidoptera: Papilionidae, Pieridae, Satyridae: g. Erebia, of Holarctic, espec. polar & alpine (Yes)]

WYGODZINSKY, Dr. Petr. Casilla 266, Tucumán, Argentina. [Thysanura: Machilidae & Lepismatidae of World (Yes); Heteroptera: Reduviidae of New World (No); Emesinae of World (Yes); Dipsocoridae of World (Yes)] [Instituto Miguel Lillo]

WYNNE, Colonel Owen Evelyn. Court Wood, Sandleheath, Fordingbridge, Hants, England. [Aves of Palearctic & Oriental (No)]

* XIMANEZ-TRIANON, I. Museo de Historia Natural, Casilla de Correo 399, Montevideo, Uruguay. [Pisces: Elasmobranchia & Mollusca: Cephalopoda]

* YABE, Dr. Hiroshi. Nankai Regional Fisheries Research Laboratory, Kochisanbashi, Kochi-Ken, Japan. [Pisces]

YAGINUMA, Mr. Takeo. Otemon Gakuin, 2 Kyobashi Mae-no-cho, Higashi-ku, Osaka, Japan. [Araneida of Japan (No)]

YAGIU, Ryôzô. Zoological Laboratory, Faculty of Sciences, Hiroshima University, Hiroshima, Japan. [Protozoa: Ciliata of Japan (Yes)]

YAJIMA, Dr. Asahiko. Department of Parasitology, Government Experiment Station for Animal Hygiene, Kodahira, Kitatama-gun, Tokyo, Japan. [Acarina: Ixodidae of Japan, Diptera: Tabanidae of Japan]

YAKHONTOV, V.V. Department of Entomology, Agricultural College, 32 Kirova Street, Taschkent, U.S.S.R. [Thysanoptera of c. Asia & U.S.S.R. (Yes)]

YAKOVLEV, Dr. N.N. Geological Institute, Srednij Prospekt 72b, Leningrad W.O., U.S.S.R. [Paleozoic Crinoidea of European & Asiatic U.S.S.R. (Yes)]

YAKOVLEVA, A.M. Medical Institute, Chernovtsy, Ukraine, U.S.S.R. [Amphineura: Loricata of seas of U.S.S.R. (Yes)]

YALDWYN, Mr. J.C. Zoology Department, Victoria University of Wellington, P.O. Box 196, Wellington, New Zealand. [Crustacea: Decapoda, espec. Natantia, of New Zealand (Yes); Decapoda of Indo-Pacific (No); Stomatopoda of New Zealand (Yes)]

YAMADA, Dr. Mayumi. Zoological Institute, Faculty of Science, Hokkaido University, Sapporo, Japan. [Marine Hydrozoa: Hydroida of Pacific & Mediterranean (Yes); Entoprocta of w. Pacific (Yes)]

YAMADA, Dr. Munesato. Department of Anatomy, School of Medicine, University of Okayama, 164 Oka, Okayama-shi, Japan. [Mammalia: Cetacea: Odontoceti of Japan (Yes)]

YAMAGUCHI, Prof. Hideji. Biological Laboratory, Hakodate Branch of Hokkaido Gakugei University, Hachiman-cho 153, Hakodate, Japan. [Oligochaeta: espec. Microdrili of Asia, espec. Japan (Yes)]

YAMAGUTI, Prof. Satyu, Department of Parasitology, Okayama University Medical School, Okayama, Japan. [Trematoda & Cestoda of Japan (Yes); parasitic Nematoda & Acanthocephala of Japan (Yes); parasitic Copepoda of Pisces of Japan (Yes); Diptera: Culicidae of Japan (Yes)]

YAMAMOTO, Mr. Hideho. Entomological Laboratory, Faculty of Agriculture, Kyushu University, Fukuoka, Japan. [Lepidoptera: Rhopalocera of Japan (No)]

YAMAMOTO, Ass't. Prof. K. Otsu Hydrobiological Station, Kyoto University, Kwannonji-manchi 109, Otsu-shi, Shiga-ken, Japan. [Rotatoria: Ploima of Japan (Yes)]

* YAMAMOTO, Yukio. No 5, 1 Chome Funabaracho, Mizuhoku, Nagoya, Japan. [Odonata]

* YAMASAKI, Mr. Kazuo. 327 Komachi, Kamakura, Kanagawa-ken, Japan. [Coleoptera]

YAMASHINA, Dr. Y. Yamashina Museum of Birds, 49 Nampeidai-Machi, Shibuya-Ku, Tokyo, Japan. [Aves of Japan, Manchuria, Korea, Micronesia, Formosa (Yes)]

YAMASHITA, Prof. J. Department of Parasitology, Faculty of Veterinary Medicine, Hokkaido University, Sapporo, Japan. [Trematoda & Nematoda of Japan (Yes)]

* YAMOTO, T. Zoological Institute, Nagoya University, Nagoya, Japan. [Pisces]

YANET, F.E. Vainera 55, Room III, Sverdlovsk, Ural, U.S.S.R. [Paleozoic Tabulata of the Urals (Yes)] [Geological Survey of the Urals]

* YANEZ ANDRADE, Dr. Parmenio, Director de la Estación Biológica de Montemar, Casilla 13-D, Viña del Mar, Chile. [Pisces]

* YANG, K.O. Institute of Paleontology, Academia Sinica, Chi-Ming-Szu, Nanking, People's Republic of China. [Fossils]

YANG, Mr. Won Tack. 827 Choryang Dong, Pusan, Korea. [Crustacea: Amphipoda: Hyperiidae, Dairellidae, Phrosinidae, Phronimidae, of Florida Current (Yes)]

YANKOWSKAJA, A.I. Zoological Institute, Academy of Sciences of U.S.S.R., Leningrad 164, U.S.S.R. [Acarina: Hydracarina of U.S.S.R. (No)]

* YANOVSKOYA, N.M. Paleontological Institute, Academy of Sciences of U.S.S.R., Lenin Prospectus 33, Moscow B-71, U.S.S.R. [Fossil Mammalia]

* YARROW, Dr. I.H.H. Department of Entomology, British Museum (Natural History), Cromwell Road, London, S.W.7, England. [Hymenoptera]

YASUDA, T. Entomological Laboratory, University of Osaka Prefecture, Sakai City, Osaka, Japan. [Lepidoptera: Tortricidae of Japan (Yes)]

YASUMATSU, Prof. Dr. Keizo. Entomological Laboratory, Faculty of Agriculture, Kyushu University, Fukuoka City, Kyushu, Japan. [Hymenoptera: Aculeata & Scelionidae of Asia & Micronesia (Yes); Cynipidae of Japan (Yes); Hymenoptera: Chalcidoidea of economic importance of World (No); Siphonaptera of Asia (No)]

YASUTOMI, Kazuo. Entomological Laboratory, Nacional Institute of Health, Shinagawa-ku, Tokyo, Japan. [Coleoptera: Chrysomelidae: Cassidinae of Japan & Far East (Yes)]

YAVORSKY, Prof. V.I. V.S.E.G.E.I., V.O. Sredny Prospect 72 b, Leningrad, U.S.S.R. ["Hydrozoa-Tabulata of U.S.S.R. (Yes, No)"]

YEATMAN, Dr. Henry C. Department of Biology, The University of the South, Sewanee, Tenn., U.S.A. [Crustacea: f-w. Copepoda: Cyclopoida & Harpacticoida of N. America (Yes)]

* YEDID, Henri. Rue Rafik Salloum, Beyrouth, Libya. [Mammalia]

YEH, Dr. Liang-Sheng. Department of Parasitology, London School of Hygiene & Tropical Medicine, Gower Street - Keppel Street, London, W.C.1, England. [Trematoda, Nematoda, Cestoda, (Yes); Acanthocephala & Nematomorpha (No)]

YEN, Dr. John T-C. 5031 Copley Road, Philadelphia 44, Penna., U.S.A. [Recent Mollusca of World (Yes); Mesozoic & Tertiary Gastropoda & Pelecypoda of N. America & Europe (Yes)] [Villanova University]

YERGER, Prof. Ralph W. Department of Biological Sciences, Florida State University, Tallahassee, Fla., U.S.A. [F-w. Pisces of U.S. (Yes); marine inshore Pisces of Gulf of Mexico (Yes); Mammalia of s.e.U.S. (Yes)]

* YIN, Dr. Wen-Ying. Department of Crustacea, Institute of Zoology, Academia Sinica, Hatien, Peking (53), People's Republic of China. [Crustacea: Copepoda]

YOCHELSON, Ellis. U.S. Geological Survey, Room 338, U.S. National Museum, Washington 25, D.C., U.S.A. [Paleozoic Gastropoda (Yes)]

YOKOO, Prof. Dr. Tamio. Faculty of Agriculture, Saga University, Akamatsu-cho 46, Saga, Japan. [Plant-parasitic Nematoda: Tylenchida of Japan (Yes)]

YOKOTA, E. (Niigata, Japan; Odonata) Not now active in taxonomy.

YONEDA, Mr. Hiromu. 177 Funato, Iwade-cho, Naga-gun, Wakayama Pref., Japan. [Araneida of Japan (No)]

YÔRÔ, Mr. Takeshi. 318 Komachi, Kamakura City, Japan. [Coleoptera: Erotylidae & Anisotomidae of Japan (No)]

* YOSHIDA, Akira. 139 Sanya-machi, Meguro-Ku, Tokyo, Japan. [Coleoptera: Carabidae]

YOSHIDA, Mr. Masahide. 406 Nishisue, Ohama, Amagasaki, Hyogo Pref., Japan. [Lepidoptera: Rhopalocera of Japan (Yes); of s.e. Asia (No)]

YOSHIKURA, Dr. Makoto. Department of Zoology, Faculty of Science, Kumamoto University, Kurokami-machi, Kumamoto-shi, Japan. [Araneida of Japan (No); Liphistiidae of "The East" (Yes)]

* YOSHIMOTO, Dr. Carl M. Apartado Postal 28970, Mexico 17, D.F., Mexico. [Diptera]

* YOSIFOV, Mikhail. Morska Biologicna Stancija, Varna, Bulgaria. [Hemiptera]

YOSII, Prof Narao. Biological Institute, General Education Department, Kyushu University, Fukuoka, Japan. [Cirripedia: Ascothoracica (Yes)]

YOSII, Riozo. Yoshida College of Kyoto University, Kyoto, Japan. [Collembola of World (No), of Australia & New World (Yes)]

YOUNG, Dr. Chung-Chien. Institute of Vertebrate Paleontology, Academia Sinica, 2 Ehr-Tao Chiao, Tianmen, Peking 9, People's Republic of China. [Mesozoic & Cenozoic Vertebrates of China]

YOUNG, Dr. David A., Jr. Department of Entomology, Box 5215, North Carolina State College, Raleigh, N.C., U.S.A. [Homoptera: Cicadellidae of World (No); of W. Hemisphere (Yes)]

YOUNG, Frank N., Jr. Department of Zoology, Indiana University, Bloomington, Ind., U.S.A. [Aquatic Coleoptera of e.U.S. (Yes); Dytiscidae of Antilles & Caribbean (Yes)]

YOUNG, Frederick Pentz, Jr. 21 Claremont Avenue, New York 27, N.Y., U.S.A. [Ordovician Trilobita, Brachiopoda, Cephalopoda, of N. America (Yes)] [Hunter College]

YOUNG, Gordon A. C/o Mene Grande Oil Company, Apartado 709, Caracas, Venezuela. [Cretaceous-Pliocene smaller Foraminifera of Venezuela (Yes)]

YOUNG, Prof. K.P. Department of Geology, University of Texas, Austin 12, Texas, U.S.A. [Cretaceous Ammonoidea (Yes)]

* YOUNG, Maxwell W. Fisheries Research Laboratory, Marine Department, Wingfield Street, Wellington, New Zealand. [Pisces]

YOUNG, Robert Spencer. 114 W. Park Drive, Charlottesville, Va., U.S.A. [Ordovician Brachiopoda: Orthacea: g. Finkelnburgia of Appalachian Mts. U.S. (No)]

YOUNGMAN, Phillip M. Museum of Natural History, University of Kansas, Lawrence, Kans., U.S.A. [Mammalia of N. America (Yes)]

YOUNGQUIST, Mr. Walter L. Department of Geology, University of Oregon, Eugene, Ore., U.S.A. [Fossil Conodonts & Devonian-Permian Cephalopoda (Yes)]

YOUNT, James L. Department of Biology, University of Florida, Gainesville, Fla., U.S.A. [Tunicata: Salpidae of World (Yes)]

YU, Feng-Ling. Taiwan Provincial College of Agriculture, 5 Ming-shan Road, Ping-tung, Tai-wan, Formosa. [Homoptera: Psyllidae of Oriental]
YUNKER, Conrad E. Middle American Res. Unit, Box 2011, Balboa Heights, Canal Zone. [Acarina of Egypt & n. Africa (Yes); Sarcoptiformes of World (No)]

ZACHER, Prof. Dr. Friedrich. Zimmermanstrasse 31, 1. Aufg. Berlin-Steglitz, Germany. [Coleoptera: Bruchidae of Europe (No); Acarina: Tetranychidae of Germany (No)]
ZACHVATKINA, Elizaveta Michailovna. Katedra Entomologii, Moskovskogo Universiteta, Lenin-skie Gory, Moscow W-234, U.S.S.R. [Acarina: Oribatei of U.S.S.R. (Yes)]
ŽADIN, Prof. V.I. Zoological Institute, Academy of Science, Leningrad 164, U.S.S.R. [F-w. Mollusca of U.S.S.R (Yes)]
ZAGULAJEV, A.K. Zoological Institute, Academy of Science, Leningrad 164, U.S.S.R. [Lepi-doptera: Tineidae, Incurvariidae, Adelidae, of Palearctic (Yes)]
* ZAHNER, Dr. Rudolf. Zoologisches Institut, München, Germany. [Odonata]
ZAHRADNÍK, Dr. Jiři. Národni Museum, Václavské námesti 68, Praha 2, Czechoslovakia. [Homoptera: Disaspididae of Palearctic (Yes); Pseudococcidae of c. & n. Europe (Yes); Aleyrodoidea of Palearctic (Yes)]
* ZAHVATKIN, A.A. C/o Zoological Institute, Academy of Science, Leningrad 164, U.S.S.R. [Homoptera]
ZAJONC, Ivo. Katedra zoológie, Vysoka škola polnohospodárska, Dobšinského 6, Nitra, Czecho-slovakia. [Oligochaeta: Lumbricidae of c. Europe (Yes)]
* ZALKIN, Prof. V.I. Societé des Naturalistes de Moscow, c/o Zoological Museum, Hertzen Street 6, Moscow K-9, U.S.S.R. [Mammalia]
ZAMITH, Dr. A.P.L. Escuela Superior de Agricultura "Luiz de Queiros", Piracicaba, S.P., Brazil. [Plant parasitic Nematoda of Brazil (Yes)]
ZANANDREA, Dr. Giuseppe. Istituto di Zoologia e Anatomia Comparata, Universitá Padova, Via Loredan 10, Padova, Italy. [Pisces: Cyclostomata: Petromyzontidae of Europe (Yes)]
ZANGERL, Dr. Rainer. Department of Paleontology, Chicago Natural History Museum, Chicago, Ill., U.S.A. [Fossil Reptilia: Nothosauria & Chelonia, excl. Testudinidae, of World (Yes)]
* ZANGHERI, Prof. Pietro. Corso Diaz 66, Forli, Italy. [Diptera]
ZANGHERI, Dr. S. Istituto di Entomologia Agraria, via Gradenigo 6, Padova, Italy. [Lepidop-tera of Italy (No), Geometridae (Yes)]
* ZANYIU, Gian H. Biological Laboratory, National Waban University, Kiating, Szechwan, People's Republic of China. [Protozoa]
ZAPFE, Dr. Helmuth. Naturhistorisches Museum, Burgring 7, Wien 1, Austria. [Tertiary & Pleistocene Mammalia, espec. Primates, of Old World (No)]
ZAPLETAL, Ing. Milan. Czechoslovak Academy of Science, Vertebratological Laboratories, Plotni 25a, Brno, Czechoslovakia. [Acarina: Parasitiformes, Gamasides, Listrophoridea, Analgesoidea & Ixodides of c. Europe (Yes)]
ZARIQUIEY ALVAREZ, Dr. Ricardo. Provenza 318, Barcelona, Spain. [Crustacea: Decapoda of Mediterranean (Yes)] [Instituto de Investigaciónes Pesqueras]
ZARNOWSKI, Dozent Dr. Eugeniusz. Veterinary Institute, Puławy, Poland. [Parasitic Nematoda: Trichostrongyloidea of c. Europe (Yes); Cestoda: Hymenolepididae of Mammals of Poland (Yes)]
* ZAVADIL, Vilem. (Brno, Czechoslovakia; Hymenoptera) Deceased.
ZAVATTARI, Edoardo. (Roma, Italy; Hymenoptera) Not now active in taxonomy.
ZAVODNIK, Mr. Dušan, Asistent, Institut za Biologiju Mora, Rovinj, Yugoslavia. [Crustacea: Copepoda: Corycaeidae of Adriatic (No); Echinodermata of Adriatic (No)]
de ZAYAS MUÑOS, Ing. Fernando. Departamento de Entomologia, Ministerio de Agricultura, Habana, Cuba. [Insects of Cuba: Coleoptera: Buprestidae & Cerambycidae of Cuba (Yes)] [Seccion de Sanidad Vegetal, Ministerio de Agricultura]
ZÁZVORKA, Vl. National Museum, Václavské námešti 68, Praha 2, Czechoslovakia. [Up. Creta-ceous Pelecypoda: Pectinidae of c. Europe (Yes); Up. Cretaceous Cephalopoda of c. Europe (No)]
* ZDUN, V.I. Institute of Agricultural Biology, Academy of Sciences of U.S.S.R., Dragomanova Street 17/16, Ljvov, U.S.S.R. [Trematoda of animals of U.S.S.R. (Yes)]
ZECCHINI, Renato. Cannaregio 425/A, Venezia, Italy. [Coleoptera of Italy (No); Hydrophilidae: Hydrophilinae, Hydrochinae, Sphaeridiinae, Limnebiinae, Spercheinae, Helophorinae, of Italy (Yes); Homoptera: Auchenorhyncha of Italy (Yes)]
* ZECK, Mr. E.H. 694 Victoria Road, Ryde, N.S.W. Australia. [Homoptera: Coccidae & Coleoptera: Dryopidae]
* ZEHLE, Edelgard. Biologische Zentralanstalt, Stahnsdorfer Damm 81, Berlin (Kleinmachnow), German Democratic Republic. [Nematoda]
ZEI, Prof. Dr. M. Zoological Laboratory, University, Ljubljana, Yugoslavia. [Pelagic Poly-chaeta of Adriatic & Mediterranean (Yes); Pisces of Adriatic (Yes)]
ZEIGLER, Dr. R. 307 W. Palmetto Street, Florence, S.C., U.S.A. [Gastropoda: g. Oliva of World (Yes)]

ZEISS, Dr. A. Geologisches Institut, Schlossgarten 5, Erlangen, Germany. [Jurassic (Callovian) Ammonitoidea of Europe & Asia (No); Hecticoceratinae of World (Yes); Up. Callovian to M. Oxfordian Cardioceratidae (No); Up. Jurassic (Kimmeridge) Ammonitoidea of s. Germany (Yes); M. Oxfordian g. Paraspidoceras & Extranodites (No)]
ZEISSLER, Miss Hildegard. Staatliches Museum für Tierkunde, Dresden A 1, German Democratic Republic. [Recent & Quaternary terr. & f-w. Mollusca of c. Europe (Yes)]
* ZELEDON, Dr. R. Facultad de Microbiologia, Universidad de Costa Rica, San José, Costa Rica. [Diptera]
ZELLER, Doris. Department of Geology, University of Kansas, Lawrence, Kans., U.S.A. [Mississippian & Pennsylvanian Foraminifera: Endothyroidea: g. Endothyra, Plectogyra, Granuliferella, Millerella, Paramillerella of New World, n. Africa, England, Russia (Yes)]
ZELNY, J. Marxova 5, Žilina, Czechoslovakia. [Lepidoptera: Pieridae: g. Pieris of w. Carpathian Mts. (Yes); Parnassiidae: g. Parnassius of c. Europe (Yes)]
ZENISEK, Cyril J. Science Department, Indiana State College, Indiana, Penn., U.S.A. [Amphibia: Caudata & Salientia of Ohio (Yes)]
ZENKEVITCH, L. A. Institute of Oceanology, Academy of Sciences of U.S.S.R., Moscow, U.S.S.R. [Marine Invertebrates, abyssal Invertebrates, Echiuroidea]
ZERECERO y DIAZ, Maria Cristina. Laboratorio de Helminthologia, Instituto de Biologia, de la Universidad Nacional Autónoma de Mexico, Ciudad Universitaria, Mexico 20, D. F., Mexico. [Trematoda of C. & S. America (Yes); Nematoda of Mexico (Yes)]
ZETEK, Dr. James. (Balboa, Canal Zone; Mollusca) Died June 2, 1959.
ZEUNER, Prof. F. E. Department of Environmental Archaeology, University of London, 31-34 Gordon Square, London, W. C. 1, England. [Recent & Fossil Orthoptera (Yes); Pleistocene Mammalia (No)]
ZHELOCHOVTSEV, Mr. A. N. Zoological Museum, Moscow State University, Hertzen Street 6, Moscow K-9, U.S.S.R. [Hymenoptera: Symphyta of Palearctic (Yes)]
ZHILTZOVA, Mrs. L. Zoological Institute, Academy of Sciences of U.S.S.R., Leningrad 164, U.S.S.R. [Plecoptera of U.S.S.R., Caucasus, Iran, Iraq, Turkey (Yes)]
* ZHIZHINA, Dr. M. S. Institute of Geology of Arctica, Moika 120, Leningrad, U.S.S.R. [Ordovician & Silurian Tabulata & Rugosa]
ZHOU, Dr. Ming-Zhen. Institute of Vertebrate Paleontology, Academia Sinica, P.O. Box 643, Peking, People's Republic of China. [Mesozoic & Cenozoic Reptilia: Dinosauria & Chelonia of e. Asia (Yes); Tertiary & L. Pleistocene Mammalia of e. Asia (Yes); Up. Mesozoic & Tertiary f-w. Mollusca of China]
ZHUKOV, Mr. E. V. Zoological Institute, Academy of Sciences of U.S.S.R., Leningrad Centre, U.S.S.R. [Trematoda of marine fishes of Atlantic, Pacific, Indian Oceans (Yes)]
ZHURAVLEVA, Dr. I. T. Siberian Department, Academy of Sciences of U.S.S.R., Sovetskaya 20, Novosibirsk, U.S.S.R. [Cambrian Archaeocyatha of U.S.S.R. (Yes); Porifera: Thalamida ("C + T") of U.S.S.R. (Yes); Porifera ("Cm + Pg") of U.S.S.R. (No)]
ZIARKIEWICZ, Dr. T. Katedra Ochrony Roślin, Wyzska Szkola Rolnicza, ul. Ractawickie 20, Lublin, Poland. [Heteroptera: Pentatomidae of Poland (No)]
ZICSÍ, András. Allatrendszertani Intézete, Pushkin u. 3, Budapest VIII, Hungary. [Oligochaeta: Lumbricidae of Europe (Yes)]
* ZIEGELMEIER, Dr. Erich. Biologische Anstalt, Forschungsinstitut der Bundesanstalt für Fischerei, List/Sylt, Germany. [Polychaeta]
ZIEGLER, Dr. B. Paläontologisches Institut und Museum der Universität, Künstlergasse 16, Zürich, Switzerland. [Jurassic Ammonitoidea: Haploceratacea (Yes); Up. Jurassic Perisphinctaceae (No)]
ZIEGLER, Dr. J. Benjamin. CIBA Pharmaceutical Products Inc., Summit, N. J., U.S.A. [Lepidoptera: Lycaenidae: Theclinae of N. America (Yes)]
ZIEGLER, Dr. Willi. Geologisch-Paläontologisches Institut, Deutschhausstrasse 10, Marburg a. d. Lahn, Germany. [Fossil Conodontida of Germany & e. Austria (Yes)]
* ZIELASKOWSKI, Dr. Hanns. Sanderweg 32, Bochum, Germany. [Lepidoptera]
ZIESENHENNE, Fred C. Hancock Foundation, Hancock Building Room 330, University of Southern California, Los Angeles 7, Calif., U.S.A. [Ophiuroidea of Pacific, Atlantic, Indian Oceans (Yes); Asteroidea & Echinoidea of Pacific (Yes)]
* ZILAHI-SEBESS, Dr. G. Kossuth Lajos Tudományegyetemi, Allattani Intézete, Debrecen 10, Hungary. [Diptera]
ZILCH, Dr. Adolf. Senckenberg-Museum, Senckenberg Anlage 25, Frankfurt am Main, Germany. [Gastropoda: land snails of World (Yes)]
* ZIMMER, John T. (New York, N. Y.; Aves) Died January 6, 1957.
ZIMMERMAN, Elwood C. Hunter House, MacDowell Road, Peterborough, N. H., U.S.A. [Coleoptera: Curculionidae of Pacific Islands (Yes)]
ZIMMERMAN, Dr. James Roscoe. Department of Zoology, University of Wichita, Wichita 14, Kans., U.S.A. [Coleoptera: Dytiscidae, Haliplidae, Hydrophilidae, of e. N. America (Yes)]
ZIMMERMANN, Donald A. 503 N. Central Expressway, Richardson, Texas, U.S.A. [Mississippian-Permian Foraminifera: Fusulinidae (Yes)]

ZIMMERMANN, Prof. Dr. Klaus. Zoologisches Museum der Humboldt Universität, Invalidenstrasse 43, Berlin N. 4, German Democratic Republic. [Mammalia: Cricetidae: g. Clethrionomys of Holarctic (Yes), g. Microtus of Palearctic (Yes); Muridae: g. Apodemus & Mus of Palearctic (Yes)]

ZIMMERMANN, Dr. Stephan. Josefstaedterstrasse 21, Wien VIII, Austria. [Hymenoptera: Chrysididae & Cleptidae of World (Yes)]

ZIMINA, Miss L. W. Zoological Museum, Moscow State University, Hertzen Street 6, Moscow K-9, U. S. S. R. [Diptera: Conopidae of Palearctic (Yes); Diptera: Syrphidae of U. S. S. R. (No)]

ZINGULA, Dr. Richard Paul. Humble Oil & Refining Company, P. O. Box 2180, Houston 1, Texas, U. S. A. [Jurassic & Cretaceous smaller Foraminifera, excl. Oribitoidea, of Cuba, w. N. America & Gulf Coast U. S. (Yes); Up. Cretaceous pseudorbitoid Foraminifera of Cuba (Yes)]

ZINN, Donald J. University of Rhode Island, Department of Zoology, Kingston, R. I., U. S. A. [Crustacea: marine Copepoda: Harpacticoida "of the Psammon" of coasts of U. S. (Yes); marine neritic Copepoda of Atlantic Ocean (Yes); f-w. pelagic Cladocera & Copepoda of New England (Yes); Ascidiacea of New World (Yes)]

ZINNA, Dr. Giulio. Laboratorio di Entomologia Agraria "Filippo Silvestri", Portici, Napoli, Italy. [Hymenoptera: Encyrtidae of Italy (Yes)] [Centro Nazionale di Lotta Biologica Portici]

* ZINOWIEW, Gleb Al. Zoological Institute, Academy of Sciences of U. S. S. R., Leningrad B-164, U. S. S. R. [Coleoptera: Ipidae]

ZIRNGIEBL, Fr. Dr. Irene. Bambergerstrasse 3, Leverküsen-Schlebüsch, Germany. [Acarina: Uropodina of Europe (Yes)]

ZIRNGIEBL, Lothar. Birkenheide-Pfalz, Germany. [Hymenoptera: Tenthredinoidea of Palearctic (No), of c. Europe (Yes); Chrysididae of Europe (Yes)]

ZIVKOVIC, Miss Vera. Veterinarski Fakultet (Parasitoloski Institut), Bulevar JNA 18, Beograd, Yugoslavia. [Diptera: Simuliidae & Phlebotominae of Yugoslavija (Yes); Acarina: Oribatei of Serbia (No)] [Institute of Medical Research of Serbian Academy of Sciences]

ŽIVOJINOVIĆ, Dr. Svetislav. Šumarski Fakultet, Kneza Višeslava 1, Beograd, Yugoslavia. [Coleoptera: Scolytidae of Yugoslavia (Yes)] [College of Forestry]

* ZŁOTORZYCKI, Mgr. J. Zakład Parazytologii, ul. Norwida 27, Wrocław, Poland. [Siphonaptera]

ZOCCHI, Prof. Rod. Stazione di Entomologia Agraria, Via Romana 15/17, Firenze, Italy. [Coleoptera: Scolytidae of Italy (Yes)]

ZOPP, Prof. J. Bahnhofstrasse 40/III/13, Tulln, Austria. [Lepidoptera: Sphingidae, espec. g. Celerio, of World (Yes)]

ŻUKOWSKI, Inz. Roman. Muzeum Parku Narodowego w Pieninach, Kroscienko n/Dunajcem, Poland. [Lepidoptera of s. Poland (No); Gelechiidae of Europe (Yes)]

ZUMPT, F. K. E. South African Institute for Medical Research, P. O. Box 1038, Johannesburg, Union of South Africa. [Diptera: Calliphoridae & Acarina parasitic on Vertebrates, of Ethiopian (Yes)]

* ZUSI, Mr. Richard. Museum of Zoology, University of Michigan, Ann Arbor, Mich., U. S. A. [Aves]

ZWEIFEL, Dr. Richard G. Department of Amphibians & Reptiles, American Museum of Natural History, New York 24, N. Y., U. S. A. [Amphibia & Reptilia of Mexico & w. U. S. (Yes); Amphibia of New Guinea (Yes); fossil frogs & toads of World (Yes)]

ZWÖLFER, Prof. Dr. Institut für Angewandte Zoologie, Amalienstrasse 52 GG, München 13, Germany. [Coleoptera: Scolytidae of c. Europe (Yes)]

ZWÖLFER, Dr. H. European Laboratory, Commonwealth Institute of Biological Control, Delémont, Switzerland. [Hymenoptera: Ichneumonidae: Pimplinae of Holarctic (Yes)]

ZŸLMANS, A. J. C. Burg. Elsenlaan 90, Rijswijk (Z. H.), Netherlands. [Cretaceous (Albian) to Recent pelagic Foraminifera (Yes)]

ZYROMSKA-RUDZKA, Mgr. Halina. Uniwersytet-Zaklad Ekologii, ul. Krakowskie Przedmiescie 26/28, Warszawa, Poland. [Acarina: Tyroglyphidae of Europe (Yes)]

ADDENDA

AFSHAR, Prof. Freydoun A. Box 1031, Teheran, Iran. [Tertiary Mollusca of Europe &
& Asia (Yes)] [University of Teheran]
* AGRAWAL, Dr. S. K. Department of Geology, Banaras Hindu University, Varanasi-5, U. P.,
India. [Fossil Pelecypoda]
AKRAMOWSKI, Nikolai N., Cand. Sci., Zoological Institute, Academy of Sciences of Armenian
S. S. R., Avan Road 20, Erevan, U. S. S. R. [Pliocene to Recent terr. & f-w. Mollusca
of Caucasus (Yes); Recent Odonata, adults & nymphs, of Caucasus (Yes)]
ANTOINE, Maurice. 6 rue du Roussillon, Casablanca, Morocco. [Coleoptera: Carabidae &
Tenebrionidae of Morocco (Yes)]
* APOSTOL, Prof. Leonid. Muzeul National de Istorie Naturala "Grigore Antipa", Soseaua
Kisselef No. 1, Bucureşti III, Rumania. [Fossil Mammalia]
ASHLOCK, Peter D. Division of Insects, U. S. National Museum, Washington 25, D. C.,
U. S. A. [Heteroptera, espec. terrestrial, of N. America (Yes); Lygaeidae of World
(Yes)] [U. S. Department of Agriculture]
* AUBERTIN, Daphne. See DINELEY, Daphne Aubertin.
AZZAROLI, Prof. Augusto. Istituto di Geologia dell'Universita, Via Lamarmora 4, Firenze,
Italy. [Tertiary larger Foraminifera of Italy & Somaliland (No); Up. Tertiary deer
(Yes)]
BAKER, Dr. F. H. Uther. Canning Highway & Allen Street, East Fremantle, W. Australia.
[Coleoptera: Curculionidae of Australia (No), of W. Australia (Yes)]
de BARROS, Rosina. Rua Veiga Filho, 61, (Higienopolis), São Paulo, Brazil. [Diptera:
Drosophilidae: g. Drosophila, gr. mercatorum of New World (No)]
* BENDUKIDSE, Dr. N. S. Academy of Sciences of Georgian S. S. R., Dzerjinski Street 8,
Tbilisi, U. S. S. R. [Mesozoic Anthozoa: Hexacoralla]
BENEWAY, Mr. David F. Department of Entomology, University of Kansas, Lawrence,
Kans., U. S. A. [Diptera: Tachinidae of N. America (No)]
BENOIT, Paul. Laboratoire de Biologie Forestière, Boite Postale 35, Sillery, Quebec,
Canada. [Coleoptera: Buprestidae of n. e. N. America (Yes)]
BENSON, W. Pedro. Casilla de Correo 100, Azul, Argentina. [Lepidoptera of Argentina
(La Pampa, Neuquen, Buenos Aires prov.) (Yes)]
van BENTHEM JUTTING, W. See van der FEEN, W. S. S.
van den BERGHE, Prof. L., Directeur de l'Institut pour la Recherche Scientifique en Afrique
Centrale, D. S., Bukavu, Belgian Congo. [Parasitic Protozoa of Africa, C. America,
S. America (Yes)]
* BESPROZVANNIKH, N. I. Siberian Department, Academy of Sciences, Sovetskaya 20,
Novosibirsk, U. S. S. R. [Devonian Anthozoa: Rugosa]
BIERNAT, Dr. G. Zakład Paleozoologii, Polskiej Akademii Nauk, ul. Nowy-Swiat 67,
Warszawa, Poland. [Devonian Brachiopoda: Orthoidea, Dalmanelloidea, Syntrophioi-
dea, of Poland & Germany (Yes); Cambrian-Devonian Syntrophioidea of U. S. A. (Yes)]
BLOK, Mr. A. "Downs Cot", Falmer Road, Rottingdean, Sussex, England. [Terr. f-w.,
marine Mollusca of World (no)]
BOLWIG, Dr. N. (Johannesburg, S. Africa; insects) Not now active in taxonomy.
BORGER, Harvey D. (Caracas, Venezuela; fossils) Not now active in taxonomy.
BORSETTI, Dott. Anna Maria. Istituto di Geologia e Paleontologia dell'Universita, Via
Zamboni 63, Bologna, Italy. [Fossil Foraminifera: Globotruncanidae of c. Appennines,
Italy (Yes)]
BOURGIN, P., Assistant au Museum National d'Histoire Naturelle, 55 rue de Buffon, Paris
(V), France. [Coleoptera: Carabidae: g. Carabus of France (No); Scarabaeidae:
Cetoniinae of Palearctic (No), of France (Yes); Dynastinae of World (No)]
BOWEN, Dr. R. N. C. Institute of Technology & Engineering, University of California, La
Jolla, Calif., U. S. A. [Eocene-Miocene Foraminifera of Europe (Yes); Eocene Crus-
tacea: Ostracoda of Europe (No)]
BRINCKMANN, Dr. Anita. Stazione Zoologica di Napoli, Villa Comunale, Napoli 101, Italy.
[Hydrozoa: Anthomedusae: Corymorphidae, Tubulariidae, Acaulidae, Corynidae,
Zankleidae, Cladonemidae, Eleutheridae, Cladocorynidae, Clavidae, Hydractinidae,
Rathkeidae, Pandeidae, Bougainvilliidae, Eudendridae; Leptomedusae: Halecidae,
Campanularidae, Sertularidae, Plumularidae, Laodiceidae, Mitrocomidae, Lovenelli-
dae, Eirenidae, Aequoridae, Eutimidae (all Yes)]
BUICK, W. G. 4 Devereux Road, Hazelwood Park, S. Australia. [Mollusca of S. Australia
(Yes); Pulmonata of Australia (No)]
* BULVANKER, Dr. E. Z. V. S. E. G. E. I., Sredny 72b, Leningrad, U. S. S. R. [Devonian
Anthozoa: Rugosa]

BURMEISTER, Dr. Fritz. Föhrenwald 25, Kleinmachnow-Berlin, Germany. [Coleoptera: Carabidae of c. Europe (Yes)]
CARBONELL, Carlos S. Casilla de Correo 490, Montevideo, Uruguay. [Orthoptera: Acridoidea of Uruguay (No)] [Universidad de la República Uruguay]
CÂRDEI, Prof. Filimon. Facultatea de Stiinte Naturale, Universitatea "Al. I. Cuza", Iasi, Rumania. [Odonata, Opiliones, Pseudoscorpionida, of Rumania (Yes)]
CATI, Dr. Franco. Istituto di Geologia e Paleontologia dell'Universita, Via Zamboni 63, Bologna, Italy. [Mesozoic Foraminifera: Lituolidae of n. Italy (Yes)]
* CHAI, Jen-Chieh. Institute of Vertebrate Paleontology, Academia Sinica, P. O. Box 643, Peking, People's Republic of China. [Fossil Vertebrata]
* CHEKHOVICH, Dr. V. D. V. S. E. G. E. I., Sredny 72b, Leningrad, U. S. S. R. [Silurian Anthozoa: Tabulata]
CHOPRA, Dr. B. N. 73 Ring Road, Lajpatnagar, New Delhi 14, India. [Ephemeroptera of India; Crustacea: Isopoda: Bopyridae of Indo-Pacific: Crustacea: Stomatopoda & Decapoda of Indo-Pacific (all No)] [National Council of Applied Eco. Research]
CHRISTODOULOU, Dr. G. Stadionstr. 29, Athens, Greece. [Neogene Foraminifera of Greece (No)] [Institute for Geology & Subsurface Research]
CORREIA DA COSTA, Dr. F. Rua Dr. António Candido, Lisboa, Portugal. [Marine Pisces, espec. Scombriformes, of w. Africa] [Centro de Biologia Piscatória]
* DAL PIAZ, Dr. G. B. Istituto di Geologia, Universitá di Padova, Padova, Italy. [Fossil Mammalia]
DI NAPOLI, Dr. Enrico F. Corso Vittorio Emanuele 21, Roma, Italy. [Fossil & Recent Foraminifera, espec. Nummulitidae & planktonic, of Mediterranean (Yes)]
DINNIK, Dr. Julius A. East African Veterinary Research Organization, Muguga, P. O. Box 32, Kikuyu, Kenya. [Trematoda: Paramphistomidae of Africa (Yes); Schistosoma of ruminants of Africa (No); parasitic worms of East African game mammals (Yes)]
* DUBATOLOV, Dr. V. N. Siberian Department, Academy of Sciences, Sovetskaya ul. 20, Novosibirsk, U. S. S. R. [Devonian Anthozoa: Tabulata]
* DZÜBO, P. S. S. N. I. I. G. G. I. M. S., Krasny Prospect, Novosibirsk, U. S. S. R. [Ordovician Anthozoa: Tabulata & Heliolitida]
ERMAKOVA, Dr. K. A. V. N. I. G. N. I., Shosse Entusiastov 124, Moscow, U. S. S. R. [Devonian Anthozoa: Tabulata & Rugosa of Russia (Yes)]
* EVANS, Dr. R. G. University College of North Staffordshire, Keele, England. [Gastropoda: Opisthobranchiata]
FIGG-HOBLYN, Dr. John P. Natural Mistory Museum, Stanford, Calif., U. S. A. [Coleoptera: Buprestidae: g. Acmaeodera & Acmaeoderides of w. U. S. & n. Mexico (Yes); Amphibia & Reptilia of Baja California (Yes)] [Stanford University]
FLEROVA, N. A. W. N. I. G. R. I., Liteiny 39, Leningrad, U. S. S. R. [Ordovician & Silurian Coelenterata of Siberia (Yes); Devonian & Ordovician Stromatoporoidea of Urals & c. Asia (No)]
* FOMICHEV, Prof. V. D. V. S. E. G. E. I., Sredny prospect 72b, Leningrad, U. S. S. R. [Carboniferous & Permian Anthozoa: Rugosa]
FORATTINI, Dr. O. P. Departamento de Parasitologia, Faculdade de Higiene e Saùde Pública, Universidade de São Paulo, Caixa Postal 8099, São Paulo, Brazil. [Insects of medical importance of Neotropics (Yes); Diptera; Psychodidae, Ceratopogonidae, Culicidae, of Neotropics (Yes)]
FORREST, J. E. Department of Zoology, Queen Mary College, Mile End Road, London, E. 1, England. [Gastropoda: Opisthobranchiata & Heteropoda of Europe, Atlantic Ocean, Azores, Antarctic (Yes)]
FORSTER, Dr. E. W. Same as FORSTER, Dr. Walter, in preceding section.
* FRAGOSO, Sergio S. Departamento de Entomologia, Instituto Oswaldo Cruz, Caixa Postal 926, Rio de Janeiro, Brazil. [Coleoptera]
GAHAN, A. B. (Washington, D. C., U. S. A.; Hymenoptera) Died May 23, 1960.
GHORAB, M. A. Geological Department, Shell House, P. O. Box 228, Cairo, Egypt. [Up. Cretaceous Foraminifera of Middle East (Yes); Tertiary Foraminifera of Egypt (No)] [The Anglo-Egyptian Oilfields, Ltd.]
* GONZALO, Perez H. Instituto de Biologia, Universidad Nacional de Mexico, Mexico 20, D. F., Mexico. [Lepidoptera]
GORSKY, Prof. I. I. Department of Geological & Geographical Sciences, Academy of Sciences of U. S. S. R., Leninsky Prospect 14, Moscow B-71, U. S. S. R. [Carboniferous & Permian Anthozoa: Rugosa of U. S. S. R. (Yes); fossil Enigmatica]
GRAHLE, Dr. Hans-Olaf. Niedersächsisches Landesamt für Bodenforschung, Wiesenstrasse 1, Hannover, Germany. [Quaternary & Recent Gastropoda: Viviparidae of c. Europe (Yes); Quaternary & Recent f-w. Mollusca of Germany (Yes)]
HAINES, Lauri Courtney. 25 Boomerang Street, Haberfield, Sydney, N. S. W., Australia. [Lepidoptera of N. S. W. (Yes)]
HALL, Mr. D. N. F. Marine Biological Laboratory, Citadel Hill, Plymouth, England. [Crustacea: Penaeidae of Indo-West-Pacific (Yes)]

HARMAN, Prof. Walter J. Louisiana Polytechnic Institute, Ruston, La., U.S.A. [Oligochaeta: Lumbricidae of N. America (Yes); Megascolecidae of N. America (No)]

HIGGINS, Mr. Robert P. Department of Zoology, Duke University, Durham, N.C., U.S.A. [Tardigrada & Kinorhyncha of N. America (Yes)]

HOFFMANN, Dr. Karl. Niedersächsisches Landesamt für Bodenforschung, Wiesenstrasse 1, Hannover, Germany. [L. & M. Jurassic Ammonoidea of World (Yes)]

HOUGH, Dr. Margaret Jean. Department of Vertebrate Paleontology, American Museum of Natural History, New York 24, N.Y., U.S.A. [Oligocene & Miocene Rodentia & Carnivora (Yes)]

* ICHOUDINOVA, Dr. I.I. Paleontological Institute, Academy of Sciences of U.S.S.R., Leninsky Prospect 33, Moscow B-71, U.S.S.R. [Devonian Anthozoa: Tabulata]

* IVANIA, Dr. V.A. Tomsk State University, Tomsk, U.S.S.R. [Devonian Anthozoa: Rugosa]

* IVANOVSKY, Dr. A.B. S.N.I.I.G.G.I.M.S., Krasny Prospect, Novosibirsk, U.S.S.R. [Silurian Anthozoa: Rugosa]

JOHANSEN, B.H. Biological Institute, Tomsk University, Tomsk, U.S.S.R. [Pisces of Siberia (No)]

JOHNSON, D.S. [Crustacea: marine Decapoda of Malaysia (No), Atyidae, Palaemonidae, Porcellanidae, of Malaysia (Yes); Cladocera of World (Yes)]

* KABAKOVICH, N.V. Paleontological Institute, Academy of Sciences of U.S.S.R., Leninsky Prospect 33, Moscow, U.S.S.R. [Carboniferous Anthozoa: Rugosa]

* KALJO, Dr. D.L. Academy of Sciences, Tallinn, Estonian S.S.R. [Ordovician & Silurian Anthozoa: Rugosa]

KARATAJŪTE-TALIMAA, V. Lietuvos T.S.R. Mokslu Akademija, Geologijos ir Geografijos Institutas, Tilto g. 4, Vilnius, Lietuvos T.S.R., U.S.S.R. [Pisces: fossil Antiarchi of Eurasia (Yes)]

* KHALFINA, V.K. Tomsk Politechnical Institute, Tomsk, U.S.S.R. [Ordovician-Devonian Stromatoporoidea]

* KOKSHARSKAYA, K.B. Yakutsk Department of Academy of Sciences of U.S.S.R., Yakutsk, U.S.S.R. [Silurian Anthozoa: Tabulata]

KUYTEN, Mr. P. Korreweg 328, Groningen, Netherlands. [Coleoptera: Lamellicornia of n.w. & c. Europe (Yes)]

LAMBERT, Dr. L. (Le Vésinet, France; Copepoda) Died July 27, 1957.

LANE, Frederico. Departamento de Zoologia, Secretaria da Agricultura, Caixa Postal 7172, São Paulo, Brazil. [Coleoptera: Cerambycidae of S. America (Yes); Lymexylonidae of Neotropics (Yes)]

LELESHUS, V.L. Academy of Sciences, Stalinabad, Tadjik S.S.R., U.S.S.R. [Fossil Anthozoa: Tabulata-Heliolitida of c. Asia (Yes)]

LÜLING, Dr. K.H. [Pisces, espec. Nematognathoidea & Characidae, of S. America, espec. Amazon Basin]

MATHIEU, Ing. Jean M. Instituto Tecnológico de Monterrey, Sucursal de Correos "J", Agricultura, Monterrey, N.L., Mexico. [Coleoptera: Elateridae & Scarabaeidae]

* MATTHEWS, G.V.T., Assistant Director, The Wildfowl Trust, Slimbridge, England. [Aves: Anatidae]

MILLER, Dr. Richard B. Died February 23, 1959.

* MIRONOVA, N.V. S.N.I.I.G.G.I.M.S., Krasny Prospect, Novosibirsk, U.S.S.R. [Devonian Anthozoa: Tabulata]

MISHCHENKO, Leo. (Same as Mistshenko, L.L.)

MISTSHENKO, L.L. (Same as Mishchenko, Leo.)

MOUTERDE, Prof. l'Abbé R. Laboratoire de Géologie, Faculté Catholic de Lyon, 25 rue de Plat, Lyon, France. [Mesozoic Ammonites (No)]

NOBLE, Alden E. Died February 19, 1960.

OCKELMANN, W.K. Marine Biological Laboratory, Grønnehave, Helsingør, Denmark. [Pelecypoda: Mytilacea, Pectinacea, Astartacea, Lucinacea, Pandoracea, Poromyacea, of e. N. Atlantic, North Sea, Iceland, Faroes, Greenland (Yes)]

* OW-YANG, Mr. C.K. Department of Zoology, University of Malaya in Singapore, Bukit Timah Road, Singapore 10. [Marine Crustacea: Brachyura of Malaya, espec. Portunidae & littoral forms]

PACHECO, Francisco. Departamento de Entomologia, Escuela de Postgraduados, Chapingo, Mexico. [Coleoptera: Heteroceridae of World (Yes)]

* REES, Dr. F.G. University College of Wales, Cambrian Street, Aberystwyth, Wales, Great Britain. [Parasites]

RESVOY, Prof. P.D. Department of Biology, Lwow State University, Lwow, U.S.S.R. [Porifera of Arctic Seas (No); f-w. Rotatoria & Crustacea: Copepoda & Cladocera of U.S.S.R. (No)]

RETTENMEYER, Carl W. Department of Entomology, Kansas State University, Manhattan, Kans., U.S.A. [Hymenoptera: Formicidae: Dorylinae of New World (Yes); Diptera: Tachinidae: g. Calodexia of Neotropical (Yes); Acarina: myrmecophilous Mesostigmata of New World (No)]

* RIGGIN, G. W. , Jr. Department of Biology, Furman University, Greenville, S. C. , U. S. A.
      [Tardigrada]
RODEWALD-RUDESCU, Dr. Ludwig. Str. Cpt. Preotescu 29, raion Nic. Balcescu, Bucureşti,
      Rumania. [Rotatoria, Gastrotricha, Tardigrada, Porifera: Spongillidae, of c. , s. , &
      e. Europe (Yes)]
* ROSS, Mary H. Airport Road, Blacksburg, Va. , U. S. A. [Devonian Anthozoa: Tabulata]
ROST, Helen. See SOOT-RYEN, Helen, in main list.
RULLAN, Juan Bauza. Ramon Berenguer III. n. 20, pral Palma de Mallorca, Spain. [Otoliths
      of Pisces]
SCALON, O. I. See SKALON, O. I. , in main list.
STARKOFF, Prof. Oleg. Istituto di Parassitologia, Città, Universitaria, Roma, Italy.
      [Ixodoidea of Italy & s. Europe (Yes); Sarcoptiformes & Prostigmata of Italy (No)]
STSCHEDRINA, Z. G. Zoological Institute, Academy of Sciences of U. S. S. R. , Leningrad
      W-164, U. S. S. R. [Recent Foraminifera of Arctic (Yes), of Antarctic (No)]
WICKSTEAD, J. H. Marine Biological Laboratory, Citadel Hill, Plymouth, England. [Marine
      Pelagic Copepoda of Indo-Malayan area, East African coastal area, Barbados (Yes)]